W9-BMQ-622

Marketing for Hospitality and Tourism

Third Edition

Philip Kotler
John Bowen
James Makens

Upper Saddle River, NJ 07458

Library of Congress Cataloging-in-Publication Data

Kotler, Philip.
Marketing for hospitality and tourism / Philip Kotler, John Bowen, James Makens.— 3rd ed.
p. cm.
Includes bibliographical references and index.
ISBN 0-13-099611-4
1. Hospitality industry—Marketing. 2. Tourism—Marketing. I. Bowen, John, (John T.), 1948- II. Makens, James C. III. Title.
TX911.3.M3 K68 2002
647.94'068'8—dc21

2002002217

Editor-in-Chief: Stephen Helba
Executive Assistant: Nancy Kesterson
Executive Acquisitions Editor: Vernon R. Anthony
Director of Manufacturing and Production: Bruce Johnson
Assistant Editor: Marion Gottlieb
Editorial Assistant: Ann Brunner
Managing Editor: Mary Carnis
Production Liaison: Adele M. Kupchik
Marketing Manager: Ryan DeGrote
Production Management: Pine Tree Composition, Inc.
Production Editor: Jessica Balch
Manufacturing Manager: Ilene Sanford
Manufacturing Buyer: Cathleen Petersen
Creative Director: Cheryl Asherman
Senior Design Coordinator: Miguel Ortiz
Design Coordinator: Christopher Weigand
Interior Design: Lorraine Mullaney/Miguel Ortiz
Formatting: Susan Rollock (Pine Tree Composition, Inc.)
Copy Editor: Diane Burke
Printer/Binder: Courier Kendallville
Cover Design: Anthony Inciong
Cover Illustration: Tim Grajek, SIS/Images.com
Cover Printer: Phoenix Color Corp.

Pearson Education Ltd.
Pearson Education Australia Pty, Limited
Pearson Education Singapore, Pte. Ltd.
Pearson Education North Asia Ltd.
Pearson Education North Asia Ltd.
Pearson Education Canada, Ltd.
Pearson Educación de Mexicao, S.A. de C.V.
Pearson Education—Japan
Pearson Education Malaysia, Pte. Ltd.

Chapter opening photo credits
Chapter 1: U.S. Franchise Systems, Inc.; Chapter 2: Victoria House; Chapter 3: Biltmore Estate; Chapter 4: Domino's; Chapter 5: Marriott International; Chapter 6: Hilton Hotels Corporation; Chapter 7: Jumeriah International; Chapter 8: Carnival Cruises; Chapter 9: Old San Francisco Steak House; Chapter 10: The Jamaica Tourist Board; Chapter 11: Promus Hotel Corporation; Chapter 12: Associated Press; Chapter 13: Associated Press; Chapter 14: Mirage Resorts, Inc.; Chapter 15: Associated Press; Chapter 16: Associated Press; Chapter 17: Ruth's Chris Steak House; Chapter 18: The Greater Milwaukee Convention and Tourist Bureau; Chapter 19: La Samanna-St. Martin

10 9 8 7 6 5 4 3 2 1
ISBN 0-13-099611-4

Contents

www.prenhall.com/kotler

9 Designing and Managing Products 299

10 Internal Marketing 349

11 Building Customer Loyalty through Quality 381

Preface

We would like to thank the students and instructors who have used this text in the past. Their support has enabled us to come out with our third edition in just seven years. This text is now available in five languages. Students have told us *Marketing for Hospitality and Tourism* is both readable and interesting. One student wrote, "I enjoyed reading this book—it didn't seem like I was reading a textbook." The third edition maintains that readability. We had a team of students read each of the chapters to make sure the concepts presented made sense to them. Additionally, students were involved in the final choice of illustrations for the text. We wanted to make certain the illustrations were both useful and interesting. For instructors, we made the text flow smoother from a teaching perspective. We have edited each chapter to keep the text current and relevant. For example, over the past four years the Internet has emerged as both a communication and distribution tool. In this edition, we incorporate discussions on the Internet throughout the text. We have also added a new chapter on electronic marketing. Other changes that were made in this edition are discussed later.

Persons employed in hospitality and travel-related businesses have to be customer oriented, as customers are part of the product their company is selling. How you answer the phone, greet customers, and solve customers' problems can make the difference between satisfied and dissatisfied customers. Marketing calls upon everyone in the company to "think customer" and do all that they can to help create and deliver superior customer value and satisfaction. As Professor Stephen Burnett of Northwestern puts it, "In a truly great marketing organization, you can't tell who's in the marketing department. Everyone in the organization has to make decisions based on the impact on the customer." Everyone has to embrace marketing as a business philosophy.

Each chapter in this book was carefully researched and constructed, using sound marketing concepts which are illustrated with examples from the hospitality and travel industry. The result is a book that provides a rich depth of practical examples and applications, showing the major decisions that hospitality and travel managers face in their efforts to balance the organization's objectives and resources against varying customer needs and opportunities in the global marketplace.

The book is written with the hospitality and travel student in mind. The solicited and unsolicited comments we received from both students and their instructors were incorporated. The authors have extensive experience working with hospitality and travel businesses around the globe. Our understanding of the hospitality and travel business ensured that the end result is a book that clearly explains marketing concepts and then shows how they apply to real-life situations.

Marketing for Hospitality and Tourism covers important principles and concepts that are supported by research and evidence from economics, the behavioral sciences, and modern management theory, yet it takes a practical, marketing-management approach. Concepts are applied through countless examples of situations in which well-known and little-known companies assess and solve their marketing problems. Color illustrations, "Marketing Highlight" exhibits, company cases, and video cases present further applications.

The book has an international focus. Domestic companies are expanding overseas, while their home markets are being invaded by international companies; business markets have become internationalized. We feel that students must be exposed to business and cultural examples from other parts of the world. Rather than have one chapter on international marketing, we have incorporated examples throughout the text.

In the Instructor's Manual, we have included a number of class outlines to show how this book can be used across a variety of different teaching formats: semesters or quarter-terms, universities or junior colleges, programs throughout.

New Features in this Edition

We have made a number of significant changes based on feedback from instructors and students.

New Chapter

This edition contains a new chapter on electronic marketing (Chapter 16). The Internet, databases, and direct marketing are discussed. The chapters in the promotion section were reorganized, and advertising is included in the opening chapter on promotion. This resulted in the number of chapters remaining constant at nineteen.

Internet Support

This edition features a Web site with support for both students and faculty (*www.prenhall.com/kotler*). The student site features Internet links that are relevant to each chapter. Included are test questions for students to try to get an idea of how well they understand the material. The student site also includes links to Web sites related to hospitality and tourism marketing. Finally, we have included current events for each chapter that relate to the concepts presented in the chapter.

The instructor's area includes PowerPoint slides and an electronic version of the Instructor's Manual. This will enable instructors to access these support materials at anytime and at locations around the world. Instructors will also want to check the current events section in the student section of the Web site. This feature will be updated throughout the year and can provide current examples for classroom presentations.

More Cases

We have added new cases, thereby increasing the total number to 31. Teaching notes for the cases can be found in the Instructor's Manual.

Video Cases

This edition features new video cases. We have found the use of video cases to provide an excellent bridge between marketing theory and reality. The video cases take only a few minutes of class time, but can lead into excellent discussions on the application of marketing concepts. Teaching notes for the videos are found in the Instructor's Manual. This is just another way *Marketing for Hospitality and Tourism* will increase classroom learning and interest.

End of Chapter Key Terms and a Complete Glossary

Reviewers told us that listing key terms at the end of the chapters would be useful. They also told us a complete glossary of hospitality and travel marketing terms at the end of the text is a benefit. This edition has both features.

Additional Marketing Highlights and Industry Examples

Reviewers told us they wanted more industry examples. We have expanded the number of Marketing Highlights.

Experiential Exercises and Internet Exercises

We have added experiential exercises at the end of each chapter. These exercises require the student to interact with the industry. They may involve a visit to a business or analyzing a specific aspect of a real business. The Internet exercises are relevant to the chapter and require the student to access the Internet.

The Following Features Continue in This Edition

Chapter Opening Cases and Boxed Marketing Highlights

Each chapter opens with a minicase describing a company situation. These cases show the students how the material in the chapter relates to actual business situations. Boxed Marketing Highlights, short examples, and color illustrations with high-interest stories, ideas, and marketing strategies make this an enjoyable and interesting book for the reader.

Chapter Objectives

Each chapter begins with a set of objectives.

Chapter Review

Each chapter ends with a review in outline form. This learning aid was suggested by a student and recommended by reviewers as the preferred way to summarize the chapter.

Review Questions

Each chapter contains a set of questions that cover the main points and can be used to develop classroom discussions.

Appendices

There were sections in a few chapters from the first edition that some instructors said were great and other instructors said they did not use. We incorporated these sections in the appendices. They are there for the instructors who want to use them, but they do not interrupt the flow of material.

Full Color

This is the first full-color hospitality and travel textbook. It was not done in full color to create a lively textbook, but rather to maintain the style of the book. *Marketing for Hospitality and Tourism* tells the stories that reveal the drama of modern marketing: Carnival Cruise Lines's rise to the largest cruise line company in the world; Domino's Pizza's initial positioning strategy against Pizza Hut; the failure of Wendy's breakfast in the 1980s; the success of Hampton Inns's service guarantee; Disney's marketing of positive customer attitudes to its employees; the brilliantly staged publicity stunt of the Mirage Corporation that reached an international audience of hundreds of millions; the building of Ruth Fertel's Ruth's Chris Steak House chain; and Marriott's use of corporate intelligence in building Fairfield Inns. These and hundreds of other examples and illustrations throughout the book reinforce key concepts and bring hospitality and travel marketing to life.

Class Outlines

The book contains some chapters and features not found in most hospitality and tourism marketing texts. For example, there is a complete chapter on internal marketing. Hospitality and tourism companies must get their employees enthused about their products if the employees, in turn, are going to get their customers enthused. This chapter discusses such topics as the establishment of a service culture, developing a marketing approach to human resource management, communicating with employees, and developing a reward and recognition system. The chapter titled "Building Customer Loyalty through Quality" focuses on how to use relationship marketing to improve customer satisfaction. This chapter includes a discussion of the popular service quality concepts and applies them to hospitality and travel marketing, as well as how capacity and demand management can impact quality. Finally, in the appendix to this chapter we include a section on forecasting. The text also includes a chapter on destination marketing intended for those programs that have a tourism option. We also added a full chapter on public relations that shows students how to use this powerful promotional tool.

We believe that these additional chapters cover important topics. And although most instructors welcome these new additions, some instructors may not have time to cover all the information presented in the book. Therefore, in the Instructor's Manual we have developed several course outlines, from a basic course using only fifteen chapters to an outline that incorporates all nineteen chapters. The Instructor's Manual also contains an overview of each chapter with teaching suggestions and chapter objectives.

Marketing for Hospitality and Tourism gives the marketing student a comprehensive and innovative, managerial and practical introduction to marketing. Its style and extensive use of examples and illustrations make the book straightforward, easy to read, and enjoyable.

Instructional Support

An Instructor's Manual, color PowerPoint slides, video cases, a computerized test bank, and Internet support are available to the instructors who adopt this book.

We Welcome Your Comments

We would like to hear your comments on this edition and your suggestions for future editions. Please address these comments to: John Bowen, Tourism and Convention Department, Mail Code 6023, UNLV, 4505 Maryland Parkway, Las Vegas, NV 89154-6023, USA, or by e-mail: *bowen@ccmail.nevada.edu*.

Acknowledgments

This book is the result of the efforts of many individuals. We owe special thanks to a number of people who helped make the first edition possible: Michael Gallo for his research efforts; Anna Graf Williams and Allen Reich of the University of Houston who served as early reviewers; Ming (Michael) Liang for suggesting the chapter review format; and Christa Myers for her help as project manager of the first edition. A special thanks to Carrie Tyler at UNLV for her research work and for serving as project manager for the second edition.

Many thanks to the many students and the following persons who reviewed the first edition of the text: Jennifer A. Aldrich, Johnson & Wales University, Providence, RI; James A. Bardi, Penn State Berks Campus, Reading, PA; Jonathan Barsky, McLaren School of Business, University of San Francisco; David C. Bojanic, University of Massachusetts; Tim H. Dodd, Texas Tech University, Lubbock, TX; Rich Howey, Northern Arizona University; C. Gus Katsigris, El Centro College, Dallas, TX; Ed Knudson, Linn-Benton Community College, Albany, OR; Allen Z. Reich, University of Houston; Howard E. Reichbart, Northern Virginia Community College; and Anna Graf Williams, Johnson & Wales University, Providence, RI.

The following reviewers were helpful in guiding us through the revisions in the second edition: Bonnie Canziani, San Jose State University, San Jose, CA; Andy Feinstein, Penn State University, University Park, PA; Marvel L. Maunder, Ph.D., Southwest Missouri State University, Springfield, MO; H. G. Parsa, Ph.D., SUNY College, Buffalo, NY; Edward B. Pomianoski, CFBE, County College of Morris, Randolph, NJ; Emily C. Richardson, CHA, Widener University, Chester, PA; Ralph Tellone, Middlesex County College, Edison, NJ; and Gregory R. Wood, Ph.D., Canisius College, Buffalo, NY.

The following reviewers were helpful in guiding us through the revisions in the third edition: Kimberly M. Anderson, University of Alabama; Mark Bonn, Florida State University; Harsha E. Chacko, University of New Orleans; Tim Dodd, Texas Tech University; Geralyn Farley, Purdue University Calumet; Richarde M. Howey, Northern Arizona University; Ken McCleary, Virginia Polytechnic Institute and State University; Joan Remington, Florida International University; John Salazar, Southern Illinois University.

The student team that worked on the third edition provided many useful comments. This team consisted of Walter Huertas, Kristine Miller, Michelle North, Tracee Nowlak, and Christine Smith. The authors would like to thank Shiang-Lih Chen McCain, Ph.D. for her help with the organization of the chapters.

We appreciate the support and enthusiasm of the companies that provided advertisements and illustrations for the book. These companies and organizations put forth a great deal of effort in finding and providing the materials we requested. Working with them was one of the most rewarding parts of producing the book.

We would also like to thank Vern Anthony, Marion Gottlieb, and Jessica Balch for their help and advice throughout the project.

Finally, we would like to thank our families for their support and encouragement.

Philip Kotler
John Bowen
James Makens

About the Authors

Philip Kotler is S. C. Johnson & Son Distinguished Professor of International Marketing at the Kellogg Graduate School of Management, Northwestern University. He received his master's degree at the University of Chicago and his Ph.D. at M.I.T., both in economics. Dr. Kotler is author of *Marketing Management: Analysis, Planning, Implementation, and Control* (Prentice Hall), now in its tenth edition and the most widely used marketing textbook in graduate schools of business. He has authored several other successful books, and he has written over ninety articles for leading journals. He is the only three-time winner of the coveted Alpha Kappa Psi award for the best annual article in the *Journal of Marketing.* Dr. Kotler's numerous major honors include the Paul D. Converse Award given by the American Marketing Association to honor "outstanding contributions to science in marketing" and the Stuart Henderson Britt Award as Marketer of the Year. He was named the first recipient of two major awards: the Distinguished Marketing Educator of the Year Award given by the American Marketing Association and the Philip Kotler Award for Excellence in Health Care Marketing presented by the Academy for Health Care Services Marketing. He has also received the Charles Coolidge Parlin Award, which each year honors an outstanding leader in the field of marketing. Dr. Kotler has served as chairman of the College on Marketing of the Institute of Management Sciences (TIMS) and a director of the American Marketing Association. He has consulted with many major U.S. and foreign companies on marketing strategy.

John Bowen is Professor and Director of Graduate Studies in the William F. Harrah College of Hotel Administration at the University of Nevada, Las Vegas. John has received wide recognition for his teaching and research in the area of hospitality marketing, marketing strategy, and services marketing. He has won awards for both his teaching and research. John has presented marketing courses and seminars in Asia, Australia, Central America, South America, and Europe and has published over eighty articles on marketing. John is the editor of UNLV *Gaming Research and Review Journal*, a regional editor for the Americas of *The International Journal of Contemporary Hospitality Management*, and the North American Research Director for Worldwide Hospitality and Tourist Trends (WHATT). John has managed hospitality businesses at both the unit and corporate level. He currently consults with hospitality businesses on customer loyalty, database marketing, and marketing strategy. John's formal education includes a B.S. in Hotel Administration from Cornell University, an MBA and M.S. from Corpus Christi State University, and a Ph.D. in marketing from Texas A&M University. John is a Fellow of HCIMA.

James C. Makens is actively involved with the travel industry. He has conducted executive training for the Sheraton Corporation, Regent International Hotels, The Taiwan Hotel Association, and Travelodge of Australia. He has also conducted marketing seminars for tourism ministries or travel associations in Australia, New Zealand, Canada, Indonesia, Singapore, Malaysia, and many nations of Latin America. Jim serves as a consultant and has written marketing plans for travel industry companies and tourism promotion boards. Other books he has authored or coauthored include *The Travel*

Industry and *Hotel Sales and Marketing Planbook*. His professional articles have appeared in *The Cornell Hotel and Restaurant Administration Quarterly*, *The Journal of Travel Research*, *The Journal of Marketing*, *The Journal of Marketing Research*, and *The Journal of Applied Psychology*. Dr. Makens earned an M.S., M.B.A., and Ph.D. from Michigan State University. He holds a B.S. from Colorado State University. He served as Associate Dean in the School of Travel Industry Management of the University of Hawaii. He was also an Associate Dean of INCAE, an affiliate of Harvard Business School in Central America. He is a faculty member of The Babcock Graduate School of Management at Wake Forest University.

1 Introduction: Marketing for Hospitality and Tourism

Marketing is so basic that it cannot be considered a separate function. It is the whole business seen from the point of view of its final result, that is, from the customer's point of view. . . . Business success is not determined by the producer but by the customer.
Peter Drucker

Michael Leven, one of the world's best hotel marketers, was hired from Americana Hotels to become the CEO of Days Inn.[1] During his tenure at Days Inn, the number of hotels and hotel rooms more than doubled. One of the keys to Leven's success was introducing a program showing Days Inn management and employees the importance of having a customer orientation. Under Leven's management, employees were rewarded, never penalized, for taking the initiative to help a customer. According to Leven, "Service falls short when employees are always trying to please their immediate boss. You end up putting layers between yourself and the customer."[2]

Leven's concern for the customer went back thirty years when he started as a sales rep at the Hotel Roosevelt in New York City. One day, he received a call from a meeting planner wishing to book a banquet for sixty people, requiring ten tables of six. After confirming the arrangements with the meeting planner, he proudly sent the function sheet to the banquet department. To his surprise, the function sheet was returned with a big red mark saying "No Way! We can't do tables of six." The banquet department went on to say that the union required banquet tables to be set for either eight or ten people. Leven then called the client. Years later he stated that the meeting planner's reply was never forgotten: "I don't care what the union contract says—I'm the customer. I'll go somewhere where my needs can be met," said the client before banging the phone down.

Instead of giving up, this future CEO returned to the banquet department and learned that waiters had to be paid a minimum of eight gratuities per table. This knowledge led to a creative solution. Leven phoned the meeting planner, explained the contract restrictions, and got the client to agree to pay for two extra gratuities at each table. Finding a way to meet the customer's needs salvaged the booking.[3]

Today Leven is CEO of US Franchise Systems, a new and rapidly growing hotel company franchising Microtel Inns, Best Inns, and Hawthorne Suites.

Chapter Objectives

After reading this chapter, you should be able to:

1. Understand the relationships between the hospitality and travel industry.
2. Define the role of marketing and discuss its core concepts.
3. Explain the relationships between customer value, satisfaction, and quality.
4. Discuss how marketing managers go about developing profitable customer relationships.
5. Understand how the marketing concept calls for a customer orientation.

As a manager, you will need to become familiar with marketing. Today, the customer is king. Satisfying the customer is a priority in most businesses. Managers must realize that they cannot satisfy all customers; they have to choose their customers carefully. They must select those customers who will enable the company to meet its objectives. To compete effectively for their chosen customers, companies must create a marketing mix that gives their target markets more value than their competitor's marketing mix.

1.1 Throughout the book, you will see this e indicating that the organizations mentioned are accessible through this book's Web site: *www.prenhall.com/kotler.*

Today's marketing isn't simply a business function: It's a philosophy, a way of thinking and a way of structuring your business and your mind. Marketing is more than a new ad campaign or this month's promotion; marketing is part of everyone's job, from the receptionist to the board of directors.[4] The task of marketing is never to fool the customer or endanger the company's image. Marketing's task is to design a product-service combination that provides real value to targeted customers, motivates purchase, and fulfills genuine consumer needs.

Marketing, more than any other business function, deals with customers. Creating customer value and satisfaction are at the heart of hospitality and travel industry marketing. Many factors contribute to making a business successful. However, today's successful companies at all levels have one thing in common—they are strongly customer focused and heavily committed to marketing. Accor has become one of the world's largest hotel chains by delivering L'espirit Accor, the ability to anticipate and meet the needs of their guests, with genuine attention to detail.[5] Ritz-Carlton promises and delivers truly "memorable experiences" for its hotel guests. McDonald's grew into the world's largest restaurant chain by providing its guests with QSC&V (quality, service, cleanliness, and value).

1.2 Accor
Ritz-Carlton
McDonald's

These and other successful hospitality companies know that if they take care of their customers, market share and profits will follow.

Whether you want to be a restaurant manager, executive housekeeper, or any other hospitality career choice, marketing will directly affect your personal and professional life. As a manager you will be motivating your employees to create superior value for your customers. You will want to make sure that you deliver customer satisfaction at a profit. This is the simplest definition of marketing. This book will start you on a journey that will cause your customers to embrace you and make marketing your management philosophy.

Customer Orientation

The purpose of a business is to **create and maintain** satisfied, profitable **customers.**[6] Customers are attracted and retained when their needs are met. Not only do they return to the same cruise line, hotel, rental car firm, and restaurant, but they also talk favorably to others about their satisfaction. Customer satisfaction leading to profit is the central goal of hospitality marketing.

"What about profits?" Hospitality managers sometimes act as if today's profits are primary and customer satisfaction is secondary. This attitude eventually sinks a firm as it finds fewer repeat customers and faces increasingly negative word of mouth. Successful managers understand that profits are best seen as the result of running a business well rather than as its sole purpose. When a business satisfies its customers, the customers will pay a fair price for the product. A fair price includes a profit for the firm.

Managers who forever try to maximize short-run profits are short-selling both the customer and the company. Consider the following episode:

> A customer arrived at a restaurant before closing time and was greeted with "What do you want?" Somewhat surprised, the customer replied that he would like to get a bite to eat. A surly voice informed the customer that the restaurant was closed. At this point, the customer pointed to a sign on the door stating that the restaurant was open until 9:00 P.M. "Yeah, but by the time I clean up and put the food away it'll be nine, so we're closed." The customer left and went to another restaurant a block away and never returned to the first restaurant.

Let's speculate for a moment. Why was the customer treated in such a shabby manner? Perhaps:

- The employee wanted to leave early.
- The employee suffered from a headache.
- The employee had personal or family problems.

What really happened in the restaurant episode is that this employee once served a customer right before closing time, resulting in the employee working until 10:30 P.M. Instead of the corporate office thanking her for serving the customer and staying late, it reprimanded her for putting in extra time. The corporate office wanted to keep down overtime

New cruise ships such as Royal Caribbean's Voyager of the Seas *create strong competition for resorts. Courtesy of Royal Caribbean International.*

expenses. The employee's response was to close the business by 9:00 P.M. whatever the cost. Now the corporate office is happy—they just don't realize they are losing customers and hundreds of dollars of future business. Much of the behavior of employees toward their customers is the result of management philosophy.

The alternative management approach is to put the customer first and reward employees for serving the customer well. Roger Dow, Marriott's vice president of sales and marketing services, remarks: "We used to reward restaurant managers for things that were important to us, such as food costs. When have you heard a customer ask for the restaurant's food costs? You have to reward for what customers want from your business."[7]

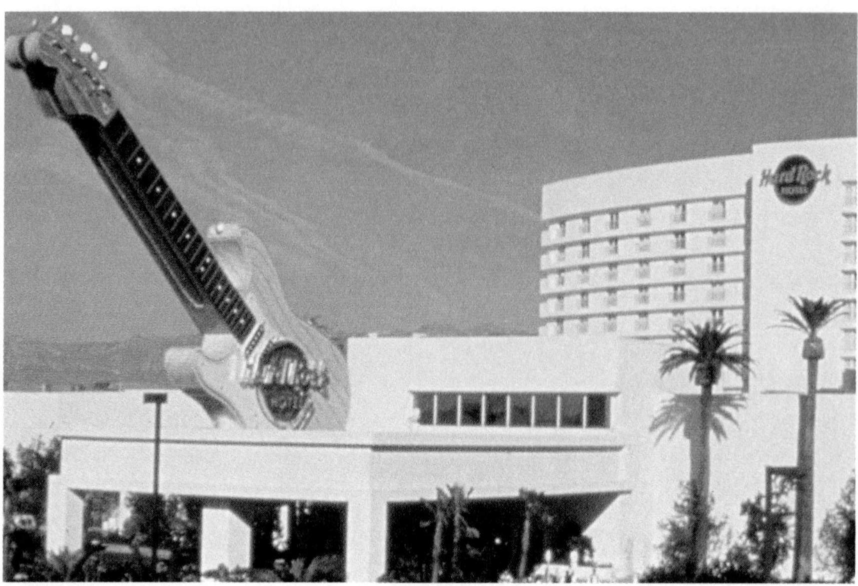

The Hard Rock Cafés throughout the world have acquired many loyal customers. This customer loyalty has helped extend the Hard Rock brand name into the resort business. Courtesy of The Hard Rock Hotel and Casino, Las Vegas.

1.3 Marriott
Scandinavian Airlines

It is wise to assess the customer's long-term value and take appropriate actions to ensure a customer's long-term support. Two recent studies document this. The Forum Company found that the cost of retaining a loyal customer is just 20 percent of the cost of attracting a new one.[8] Another study found that an increase of five percentage points in customer retention rates yielded a profit increase of 25 percent to 125 percent.[9] Accordingly, a hotel that can increase its repeat customers from 35 percent to 40 percent should gain at least an additional 25 percent in profits.[10] Jan Carlzon, president of Scandinavian Airlines, summed up the importance of a satisfied customer:

> Look at our balance sheet. On the asset side, you can still see so-and-so many aircraft worth so-and-so many billions. But it's wrong; we are fooling ourselves. What we should put on the asset side is that last year SAS carried so-and-so many happy passengers. Because that's the only asset we've got—people who are happy with our service and willing to come back and pay for it once again.[11]

Nothing validates Carlzon's point more than driving down Las Vegas Boulevard past McCarran International Airport. One can see rows of mothballed commercial aircraft that have been brought to the desert because the dry climate helps preserve the aircraft. These aircraft were once worth hundreds of millions of dollars and were listed on balance sheets for their full value less depreciation. Today they are worth a fraction of their former balance sheet value. Why? Because the airlines whose planes are sitting on the desert are either bankrupt or were forced to cut back on their schedules because of an insufficient customer base. Precisely the point that Carlzon was making! Without customers our assets have little value. Without customers a new multimillion-dollar restaurant will close,

Companies such as Pizza Hut have brought strong marketing skills to the restaurant industry. Courtesy of Pizza Hut.

and without customers a $20 million hotel will go into receivership, with the receivers selling the hotel at a fraction of its book value.

What Is Hospitality and Tourism Marketing?

In the hotel industry, marketing and sales are often thought to be the same, and no wonder. The sales department is one of the most visible in the hotel. Sales managers provide prospective clients with tours and entertain them in the hotel's food and beverage outlets. Thus the sales function is highly visible, whereas most of the nonpromotional areas of the marketing function take place behind closed doors. In the restaurant industry, many people confuse marketing with advertising and sales promotion. It is not uncommon to hear restaurant managers say that they "do not believe in marketing" when they actually mean that they are disappointed with the impact of their advertising. In reality, selling and advertising are only two marketing functions, and often not the most important. Advertising and sales are components of the promotional element of the **marketing mix.** Other marketing mix elements include product, price, and distribution. Marketing also includes research, information systems, and planning.

The four-P framework calls upon markets to decide on the product and its characteristics, set the price, decide how to distribute their product, and choose methods for promoting their product. For example, McDonald's has a fast-food product. It uses quality ingredients and developed products that it can sell at the prices people expect to pay for fast food. Most people will not spend more than fifteen minutes to travel to a McDonald's restaurant. As part of its distribution plan, McDonald's must have restaurants that are conveniently located to its target market. Finally, McDonald's appeals to different market segments and has many units throughout a city. This allows McDonald's to make effective use of mass media, such as television. The marketing mix must be just that—a mix of ingredients to create an effective marketing offer for the target market. Some critics feel the four Ps omit or underemphasize certain important activities. In chapter 2 we introduce three more Ps developed for services. The issue is not whether there should be four, seven, or ten Ps so much as what framework is most helpful in designing marketing strategy. The marketer sees the four Ps as a cabinet of tools that can guide market planning.

If marketers do a good job of identifying consumer needs, developing a good product, and pricing, distributing, and promoting it effectively, the result will be attractive products and satisfied customers. Marriott developed its Courtyard concept, General Mills designed its first Olive Garden, Mrs. Fields introduced her cookies, and they were swamped with customers. They designed differentiated products, offering new consumer benefits. Marketing means "hitting the mark." Peter Drucker, a leading management thinker, put it this way: "The aim of marketing is to make selling superfluous. The aim is to know and understand customers so well that the product or service fits them and sells itself."[12]

This does not mean that selling and promotion are unimportant, but rather, that they are part of a larger marketing mix, a set of marketing tools that work together to produce satisfied customers. The only way selling and promoting will be effective is if we first define customer targets and needs and then prepare an easily accessible and available value package.

Marketing in the Hospitality Industry

Importance of Marketing

The **hospitality industry** is one of the world's major industries. In the United States, it is the second largest employer. In more than half of the fifty states, it is the largest industry. In this book we focus on the hospitality and travel industries. These industries combine to form the foundation for tourism.

Marketing has assumed an increasingly important role in the restaurant sector of the hospitality industry. The entrance of corporate giants into the hospitality market transformed it from a mom-and-pop industry, where individually owned restaurants and hotels were the norm, into an industry dominated by chains. These chains operate in a highly competitive environment where aggressive marketing skills are needed to win customers. Twenty-four companies now account for over one-third of all restaurant sales. McDonald's leads the restaurant group with over 15,000 restaurants worldwide and sales of over $40 billion.[13]

The hotel industry is undergoing a consolidation with companies such as Accor, Cendant, Marriott, and Starwood buying hotel chains and operating different brands under one organization. The marketing expertise of these large firms has created a competitive marketing environment. In response to growing competitive pressures, hotel chains are relying more on the expertise of the marketing director. The position of food and beverage manager or rooms division manager is no longer the only career path leading to the general manager's position. In many chains, the position of marketing director is emerging as an alternative career path to general manager. Some hotel chains have created a structure in which the marketing director reports to a corporate manager, thus elevating the

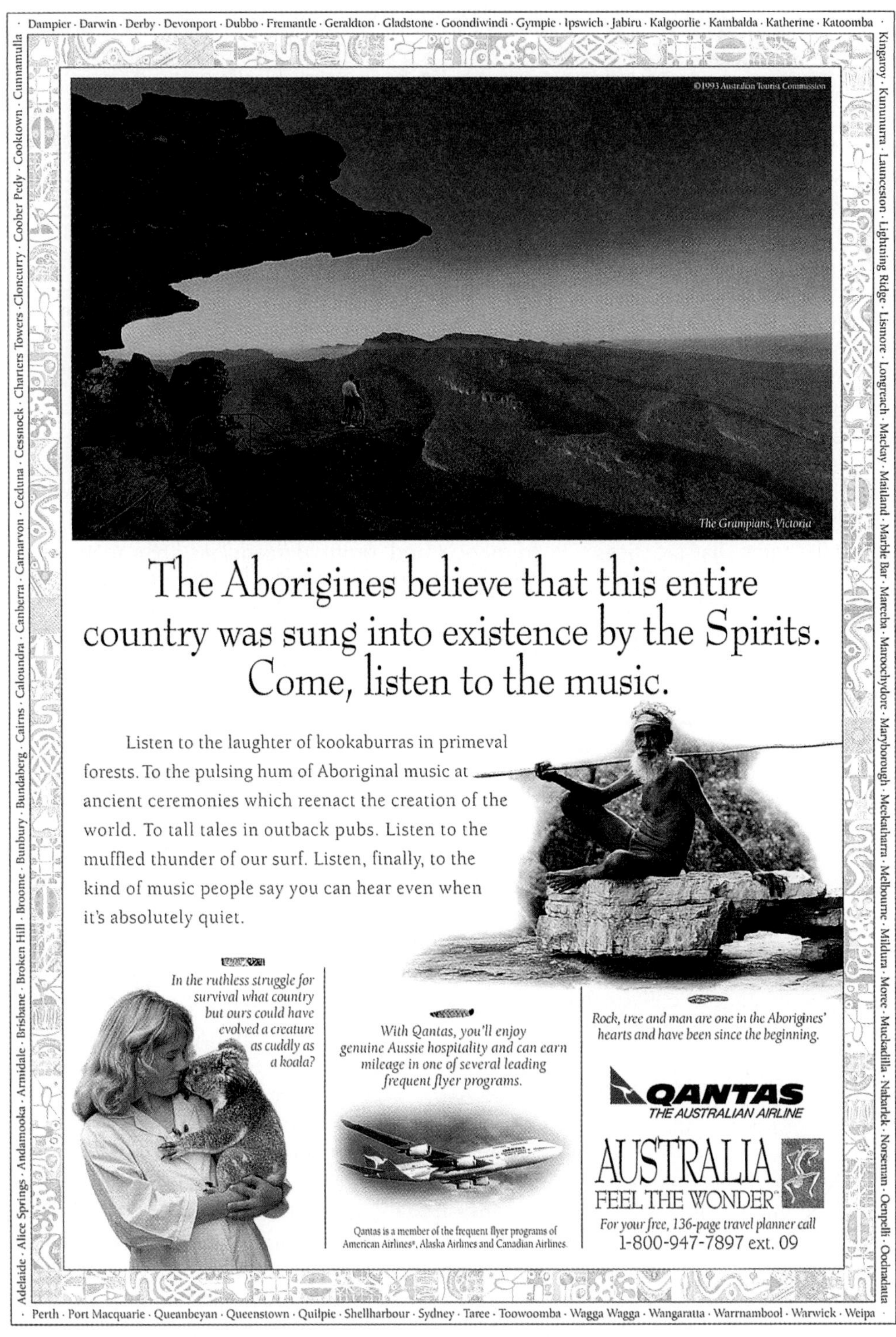

Few industries are as interdependent as travel–hospitality. This joint advertisement of the Australia Tourist Commission and Qantas will attract customers for hotels, restaurants, and tourist attractions. Courtesy of the Australian Tourist Commission.

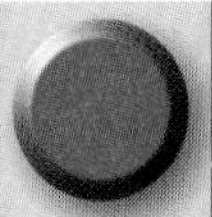

Marketing Highlight 1-1

As the guest's taxi pulled away, Roy Dyment, a doorman at Toronto's Four Seasons, noticed the guest's briefcase still sitting near the entrance to the hotel. Dyment phoned the guest in Washington, DC, to let him know that he had found the briefcase. He learned that the briefcase contained key documents for an important meeting in the morning. Dyment knew one sure way of getting the briefcase to Washington before the morning meeting—take it himself. He caught a plane and delivered the briefcase. His first concern was taking care of the guest. He didn't worry about getting his boss's approval. Upon his return, instead of getting reprimanded or terminated, he was made employee of the year. Four Seasons is one of the world's great hotel chains that practices the marketing concept. Isadore Sharp, CEO of Four Seasons, states that the company's top priority is a satisfied guest. Concern for the customer starts with top management and flows through the operation. Four Seasons's corporate culture encourages employees to go that extra mile and respond with concern and dedication to customer needs. Employees are never penalized for trying to serve the customer.

According to a study by Peat Marwick McClintock, Four Seasons is an oddity, because most hotel firms place profitability or growth as their number one goal. This, in part, explains why this small hotel company has won an international reputation for customer service. Four Seasons's exemplary customer service is highlighted in books such as *In Search of Excellence, The Service Edge, Service Breakthroughs,* and *Total Customer Service.* Four Seasons has also shown that putting the customer first leads to profits with above-average financial performance and profit percentages that many hotel chains only dream about.

Sources: Patricia Sellers, "Getting Customers to Love You," *Fortune* (March 3, 1989): 38–41; Isadore Sharp, "Quality for All Seasons," *Canadian Business Review* 17, no. 1 (spring 1990): 21–23.

hotel's chief marketer to the same level as the general manager. Marketing is a philosophy needed by all managers. While the marketing director is a full-time marketer, everyone else must be a part-time marketer.

Not many years ago, experience in food and beverage management was critical for the success of a hotel general manager. Today's general manager believes that training in marketing is one of the primary requirements for success.[14]

Tourism Marketing

The two main industries that comprise the activities we call tourism are the hospitality and travel industries. Thus, throughout this book we refer to the hospitality and travel industries. Successful hospitality marketing is highly dependent on the entire travel industry. For example, many resort or hotel guests purchase travel–hospitality packages assembled by wholesalers and offered through travel agents. By agreeing to participate in packages arranged by wholesalers, hotels effectively eliminate competitors. Similarly, hotels and rental car companies have developed cooperative relationships with airlines that offer frequent-flyer plans.

The success of cruise lines is really the result of coordinated marketing by many travel industry members. For example, the Port of Boston wanted to attract more cruise line business. Massport (the port authority) aggressively marketed Boston to cruise lines. Having convinced them to come, they then promoted Boston to key travel agents. This was critical because travel agents account for 95 percent of all cruise line business. The result was that Boston doubled the number of port calls by cruise lines and added $17.3 million to the local economy through this combined marketing effort.

That's only the beginning of travel industry marketing cooperation to promote cruise lines. Airlines, auto rental firms, and passenger railways cooperatively develop packages with cruise lines. This requires coordination in pricing, promotion, and delivery of those packages. Like Massport, government or quasi-government agencies play an important role through legislation aimed at enhancing the industry and through promotion of regions, states, and nations.[15]

Few industries are as interdependent as travel–hospitality. This interdependence will increase in complexity. The travel industry will require marketing professionals who understand the "Big Picture" and who can respond to changing consumer needs through creative strategies based on solid marketing knowledge.

Here is our definition of **marketing:** Marketing is a social and managerial process by which individuals and groups obtain what they need and want through creating and exchanging products and value with others. To explain this definition, we look at the following terms: needs, wants, and demands; products; exchange, transactions, and relationships; and markets (see Figure 1-1).

Needs, Wants, and Demands

Needs. The most basic concept underlying marketing is that of **human needs.** A human need is a state of felt deprivation. Included are the basic physical needs for food, clothing, warmth, and safety, as well as

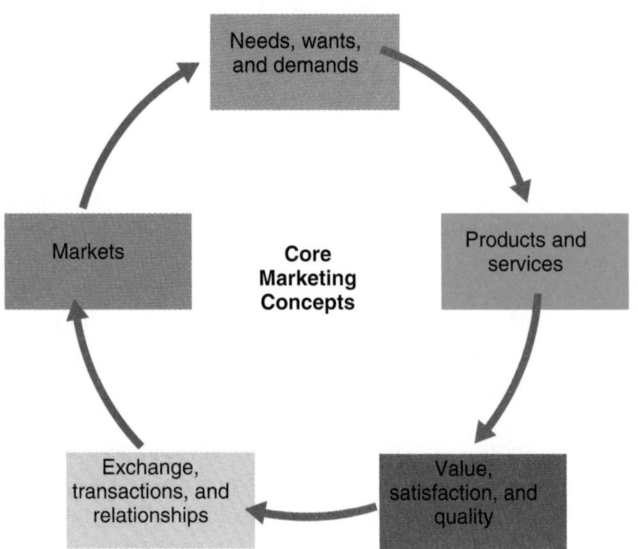

Figure 1-1
Core marketing concepts.

social needs for belonging, affection, fun, and relaxation. There are esteem needs for prestige, recognition, and fame, and individual needs for knowledge and self-expression. These needs were not invented by marketers but are part of the human makeup.

When a need is not satisfied, a void exists. An unsatisfied person will do one of two things: look for an object that will satisfy the need, or try to reduce the need. People in industrial societies try to find or develop objects that will satisfy their desires. People in poor societies try to reduce desires to what is available.

Some restaurants have built a business aimed at satisfying the esteem needs for prestige and recognition. Tony's is one of the finer and more expensive restaurants in Houston. Dining at Tony's, particularly on a regular basis, is a sign that one is financially successful. Some patrons ask to be seated at a center table where others will be sure to notice them and they can satisfy their need for recognition.

Other restaurants, such as Bennigan's, have built a business by satisfying social needs: the need to be with other people and the need to have fun and relax.[16] The restaurant chain creates a casual, relaxed atmosphere, and the open bar area encourages customers to use the restaurant as a neighborhood gathering place.

Wants. The second basic concept to marketing is that of **human wants,** the form human needs take as they are shaped by culture and individual personality. Wants are how people communicate their needs. A hungry aboriginal wants witchetty grubs, lizard eggs, and bush onions. A hungry person in the United States may want a hamburger, French fries, and a Coke. Wants are described in terms of objects that will satisfy needs. As a society evolves, the wants of its members expand. As people are exposed to more objects that arouse their interest and desire, producers try to provide more want-satisfying products and services. Restaurants were once able to serve generic white wine by the glass. Today, customers are more sophisticated; restaurants now serve Chardonnay, Sauvignon blanc, and Chenin Blanc by the glass. Today's restaurant customers want and expect good wine.

Many sellers often confuse wants with needs. A manufacturer of drill bits may think that customers need a drill bit, but what the customer really needs is a hole. These sellers suffer from "marketing myopia."[17] They are so taken with their products that they focus only on existing wants and lose sight of underlying customer needs. They forget that a physical product is only a tool to solve a consumer problem. These sellers get into trouble if a new product comes along that serves the need better or cheaper. The customer will then have the same need but want a new product.

Demands. People have almost unlimited wants, but limited resources. They choose products that produce the most satisfaction for their money. When backed by buying power, wants become **demands.**

1.4 Formule 1
Motel 6
Four Seasons
Kempinski
Marriott
Disney World

Consumers view products as bundles of benefits and choose those that give them the best bundle for their money. Thus Motel 6 and Formule 1 motels mean basic accommodations, a low price, and convenience. The Four Seasons and Kempinski Hotels mean comfort, luxury, and status. People choose the product whose benefits add up to the most satisfaction, given their wants and resources.

Outstanding marketing companies go to great lengths to learn about and understand their customer's needs, wants, and demands. They conduct consumer research about customer likes and dislikes. They observe customers using their own and competing products. For example, Bill Marriott personally reads 10 percent of the 8,000 letters and 2 percent of the 750,000 guest comment cards submitted by customers each year. All Disney World managers spend one week each year on the front line—taking tickets, selling popcorn, or loading and unloading rides. Understanding customer needs, wants, and demands in detail provides important input for designing marketing strategies.

Products

People satisfy their needs and wants with products. A **product** is anything that can be offered to satisfy a need or want. Suppose that an executive feels the need to reduce the stress of the job in a highly competitive industry. Products that may satisfy this need include a concert, dining at a restaurant, a four-day Caribbean vacation, and exercise classes. These products are not all equally desirable. The more available and less expensive products, such as a concert and dining at a restaurant, are likely to be purchased first and more often.

The concept of product is not limited to physical objects. Anything capable of satisfying a need can be called a product. More broadly defined, products also include such other entities as experiences, persons, places, organizations, information, and ideas. For example, by orchestrating several services and goods companies can create, stage, and market experiences. Disneyland is an experience. Starbuck's and Barnes and Noble have turned buying books into an experience. Starbuck's provides coffee, tea, and snacks, which allows book customers to relax and browse though books in the bookstore while enjoying a beverage and/or a snack. Border's bookstores have incorporated their own restaurant into their stores and provide musical groups as part of the entertainment. Marriott Vacation Club International, Marriott's time-share resort division, focuses on creating customer experiences. Customers remember vacation experiences. All resorts in the same class offer similar products; however, Marriott differentiates itself by creating guest experiences. An example might be a dolphin safari for its Newport Beach property or a water rafting trip for its Utah property. Marriott uses the resources of the destination to create guest experiences the guest remembers for a lifetime.

Thus, the term product includes much more than just physical goods or services. Consumers decide which events to experience, which tourist destinations to visit, which hotels to stay in, and which restaurants to patronize. To the consumer these are all products.

Value, Satisfaction, and Quality

Consumers usually face a broad array of products and services that might satisfy a given need. How do they choose among these many products and services? Consumers make buying choices based on their perception of value that various products and services deliver.

Customer Value

Customer value is the difference between the benefits that the customer gains from owning and/or using a product and the costs of obtaining the product. Costs can be both monetary and nonmonetary. One of the biggest nonmonetary costs for hospitality customers is time. In a survey done by one of the authors of this text, it was found that business travelers placed a value of $50 on one hour of their time. Ritz Carlton provides value to the business traveler by making their time as productive as possible. Domino's Pizza saves the customer time and provides convenience by delivering pizza to your home. Hampton Inn gives value to the overnight traveler by offering a free continental breakfast. One of the biggest challenges for management is to increase the value of their product for their target market. To do this, managers must know their customers and understand what creates value for them. This is an ongoing process as customers and competition change over time.

Customer Satisfaction

Customer satisfaction depends on a product's perceived performance in delivering value relative to a buyer's expectations. If the product's performance falls short of the customers' expectations, the buyer is dissatisfied. If performance matches expectations, the buyer is satisfied. If performance exceeds expectations, the buyer is delighted. Smart companies aim to delight customers by promising only what they can deliver, then delivering more than they promise.

Customer expectations are based on past buying experiences, the opinions of friends, and marketer and competitor information and promises. Marketers must be careful to set the right level of expectations. If they set expectations too low, they may satisfy those who buy, but fail to attract new customers. If they raise expectations too high, buyers will be disappointed.

Still, most of today's most successful companies are raising expectations—and delivering performance to match. These companies aim high because they know that customers who are merely satisfied will find it easy to switch suppliers when a better offer comes along. Thus, customer delight creates an emotional tie to a product or service, not just a rational preference, and this creates high customer loyalty. Highly satisfied customers make repeat purchases, are less price sensitive, remain customers longer, and talk favorably to others about the company and its products.

Managers must realize the importance of creating *highly satisfied* customers, rather than *just satisfied* customers. On a 7-point scale, with 1 being very satisfied and 7 being very dissatisfied, most managers are happy to receive a 2. However, from Figure 1-2, which shows the results of a guest survey at a Boston hotel,[18] one can see there is a huge gap between a guest who rates a hotel a 1, and one who rates it a 2. Think of the last time you went to a restaurant and were just satisfied—would you go back? Probably not. But when you walk out of a restaurant and say "WOW, that was great!" you will probably return and tell others about your discovery.

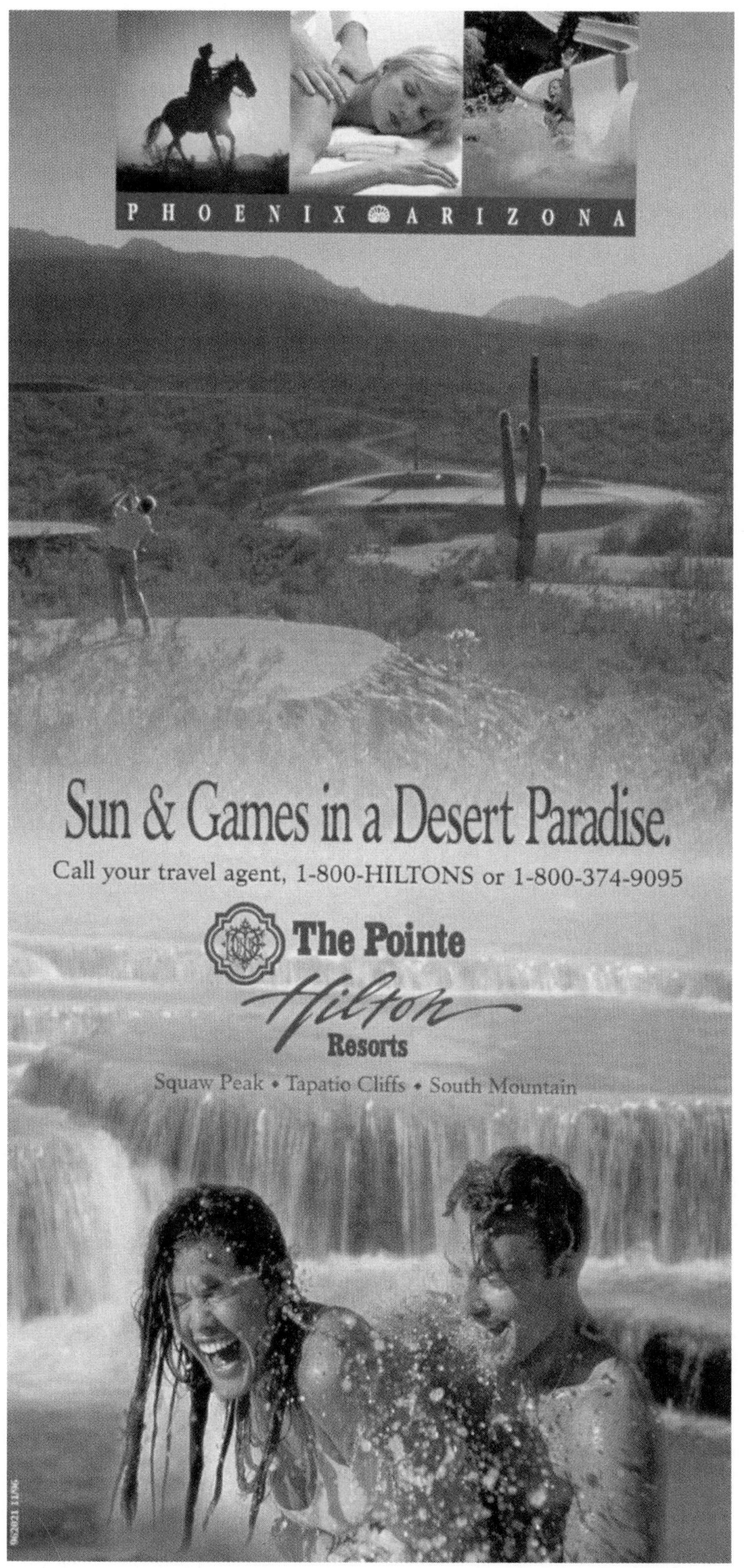

This advertisement for the Pointe Hilton Resorts communicates the variety of activities that the resorts offer. These activities will increase the value of the resort to those customers who perceive them as benefits. Courtesy of The Pointe Hilton Resorts, Phoenix, Arizona.

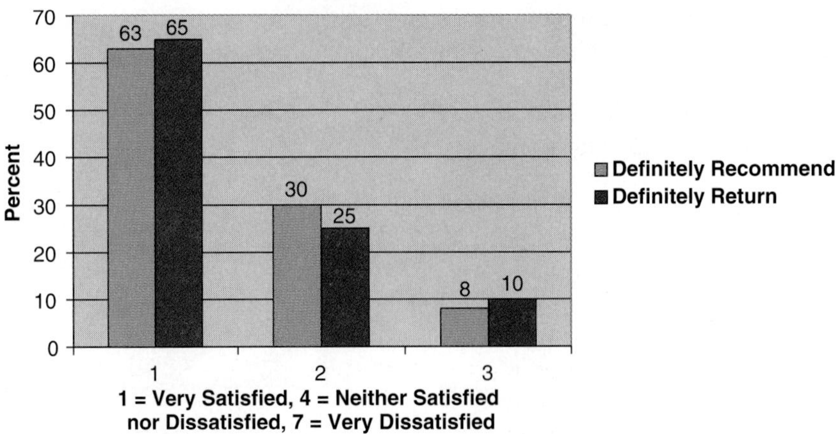

Figure 1-2 Satisfaction and customer behavior.

Although the customer-centered firm seeks to deliver high customer satisfaction relative to competitors, it does not try to maximize customer satisfaction. A company can always increase customer satisfaction by lowering its price or increasing its services, but this may result in lower profits. The purpose of marketing is to generate customer value profitably. This requires a very delicate balance: the marketer must continue to generate more customer value and satisfaction but not "give away the house."[19]

Quality

Quality has a direct impact on product or service performance. Thus, it is closely linked to customer value and satisfaction. In the narrowest sense, **quality** can be defined as "freedom from defects"; however, most customer-centered companies go beyond this narrow definition of quality. Instead, quality is defined in terms of customer satisfaction. For example, the vice president of quality at Motorola, a company that pioneered total quality efforts in the United States, says, "Quality has to do something for the customer. . . . Our definition of a defect is 'if the customer doesn't like it, it's a defect.'" Similarly, the American Society for Quality Control defines quality as the totality of features and characteristics of a product or service that bear on its ability to satisfy customer needs.

These customer-focused definitions suggest that quality begins with customer needs and ends with customer satisfaction. The fundamental aim of today's total quality movement (TQM) has become total customer satisfaction. The TQM is an approach in which all the company's personnel are involved in constantly improving the quality of products, services, and business processes. TQM swept the corporate boardrooms of the 1980s.

Many companies, however, adopted the language of TQM but not the substance, or viewed TQM as a cure-all for the company's problems. Still others became obsessed with narrowly defined TQM principles and lost sight of broader concerns for customer value and satisfaction. As a result, many TQM programs begun in the 1980s failed, causing a backlash.

When applied in the context of creating customer satisfaction, however, total quality principles remain a requirement for success. Although many firms don't use the TQM label anymore, for most top companies, customer-driven quality has become a way of doing business. Most customers no longer tolerate poor or average quality. Companies today have no choice but to adopt quality concepts if they want to stay in the race, let alone be profitable. Thus, the task of improving product and service quality should be a company's top priority. However, quality programs must be designed to produce measurable results. Many companies now apply the notion of return on quality (ROQ). They make certain that the quality they offer is the quality that customers want. This quality, in turn, yields returns in the form of improved sales and profits.

Marketers have two major responsibilities in a quality-centered company. First, they must participate in forming strategies that will help the company win through total quality excellence. They must be the customer's watchdog or guardian, complaining loudly for the customer when the product or the service is not right. Second, marketers must deliver marketing quality, as well as production quality. They must perform each marketing activity—marketing research, sales training, advertising, customer service, and others—to high standards.

These concepts are not restricted to North America or Europe, but are universal. An example is Hong Kong, in which the domestic restaurant market is saturated and mature. This has intensified the need for product differentiation through value, quality, and customer satisfaction. The real competition in Hong Kong is not just about price; it is also about the quality of the product, customer satisfaction, and value.[20]

1.5 Hong Kong

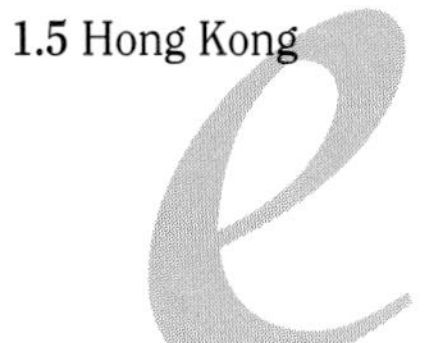

Exchange, Transactions, and Relationships

Exchange marketing occurs when people decide to satisfy needs and wants through exchange. **Exchange** is the act of obtaining a desired object from someone by offering something in return. Exchange is only one of several ways people can obtain a desired object. For example, hungry people can find food by hunting, fishing, or gathering fruit. They can also beg for food or take it from someone else, or they can resort to exchange. They can possibly offer money, another good, or a service in return for food.

As a means of satisfying needs, exchange has much in its favor. People do not have to prey on others or depend on charity. Nor do they need the skills to produce every necessity for themselves. They can concentrate on making the things that they are good at making and trade them for needed items made by others. Through a division of labor and specification, the people in a society produce much more than with any alternative system.

Whereas exchange is the core concept of marketing, a **transaction** is marketing's unit of measurement. A transaction consists of a trade of values between two parties. We must be able to say A gives X to B and gets Y in return at a certain time and place and with certain understood conditions. IBM gives $500 to Hilton and obtains the use of a meeting room. This is a classic monetary transaction. Not all transactions involve money. In a barter transaction, the Anchorage Restaurant might provide

1.6 Hilton Hotels

free meals to WBC radio station in return for free advertising on that station. A transaction involves at least two things of value, conditions that are agreed to, a time of agreement, and a place of agreement.

Transaction marketing is part of the larger idea of **relationship marketing.** Smart marketers work at building relationships with valued customers, distributors, dealers, and suppliers. They build strong economic relationships with social ties by promising and consistently delivering high-quality products, good service, and fair prices. Increasingly, marketing is shifting from trying to maximize the profit on each individual transaction to maximizing mutually beneficial relationships with consumers and other parties. The operating assumption is the following: build good relationships and profitable transactions will follow.

Relationship marketing is most appropriate with customers who can most affect the company's future. For many companies, a small proportion of customers account for a large share of the company's sales. Salespeople working with these key customers must do more than just call when they think a customer might be ready to place an order. They should monitor each key account, know its problems, and be ready to serve in a number of ways. They should call or visit frequently, make useful suggestions about how to improve the customer's business, take the customer out for a meal or entertainment event, and take an interest in the customer as a person.

The importance of relationship marketing will no doubt increase in the future. Most companies are finding that they earn a higher return from resources invested in getting repeat sales from current customers than from money spent to attract new customers. They realize the benefits gained from cross-selling opportunities with current customers. More companies are forming strategic partnerships, making skilled relationship marketing essential. For customers who buy large, complex products, such as facilities for conventions and large meetings, the sale is only the beginning of the relationship. Thus, although it is not appropriate in all situations, relationship marketing continues to grow in importance.

Relationship marketing within the hospitality industry is particularly important in the following areas:

- Between retailers of travel–hospitality services, such as hotels or airlines, and marketing intermediaries, such as tour wholesalers, incentive houses, and travel agency conglomerates
- Between retailers of travel–hospitality services and key customers, such as large corporations and government agencies

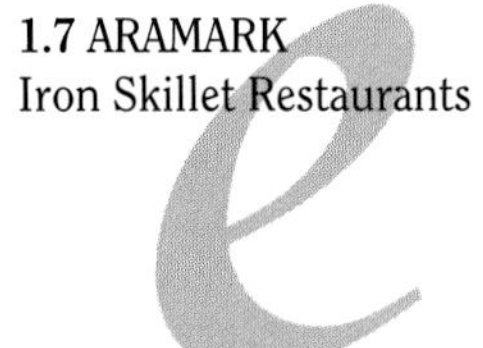
1.7 ARAMARK
Iron Skillet Restaurants

- Between retailers of food service, such as ARAMARK or McDonald's, and organizations such as universities, bus terminals, and large corporations in which this food chain is one of a handful of providers
- Between retailers of one type of travel–hospitality service, such as a motel chain and a restaurant chain. (Both are mutually interdependent. The Iron Skillet Restaurant chain is dependent on selected truck stops.)
- Between retailers of travel–hospitality services and key suppliers

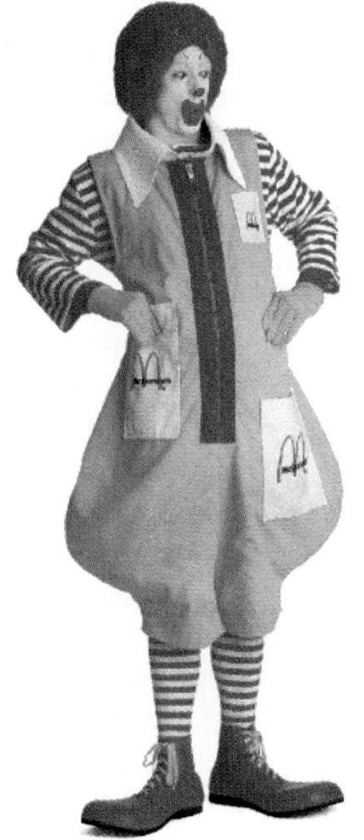

©1992, 2000 Southwest Airlines Co.

These Two Have More In Common
Than Just Their Keen Sense Of Style.
On October 8, 1999, Southwest Airlines and a bunch of guys in funny pants are teaming up to raise money for the Ronald McDonald House in our 14th annual LUV Classic and Party. Through the years, we've raised over 3 million dollars to help the Ronald McDonald House provide a home away from home for families with seriously ill children. And this year, we're going to do even better. At raising money, that is. As far as raising fashion standards, well, we'll hope for the best. For information, call 214-792-4LUV.

Southwest Airlines, through its relationships with associates in the travel industry and suppliers, is able get sponsors for the LUV Classic and Party. Courtesy of Southwest Airlines.

- Between hospitality organizations and their employees
- Between hospitality organizations and their marketing agencies, banks, and law firms

Markets

The concept of transactions leads to the concept of a **market.** A market is a set of actual and potential buyers who might transact with a seller. The size of a market depends on the number of persons who exhibit a common need, have the money or other resources that interest others, and are willing to offer these resources in exchange for what they want.

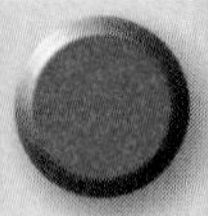

Marketing Highlight 1-2

Undesirable Customers

Today marketers want to build long-term relationships with customers. Like any relationship, we need to be selective regarding those we select for the relationship. Some customers are unprofitable, and some customers cause disruptions for other customers.

The actions of rude, boisterous, and boorish customers can negatively affect other customers and the image of the establishment. For this reason, country clubs and cruise ships "train" customers as to appropriate behavior such as dress codes, public drunkenness, loud talking, and other possible inappropriate behavior. Hospitality companies must be concerned with customer behavior, particularly when the actions of some customers affect the health and safety of other patrons and personnel. Carrying firearms, spitting on the floor, failure to wear shoes, and many other behaviors are legitimate concerns of hospitality managers.

Professors Borchgrevink, Knutson, and Woods developed this list of undesirable restaurant customers by interviewing servers in twenty-nine restaurants in midsize Michigan cities.

The Top 10 Undesirable Customers

Male	*Female*
10. Has been "in the business" and knows the right way of doing things (and will tell the server).	**10.** Throws a tantrum if anything goes wrong.
9. Screams loudly at servers.	**9.** Puts belongings on other seats.
8. Only wants to deal with the manager.	**8.** Thinks she is your only guest.
7. Acts worse with male servers than female servers.	**7.** Doesn't leave an appropriate tip.
6. Thinks he owns the place.	**6.** Wears too much perfume.
5. Sits far away from the table so servers have to work or walk around him.	**5.** Sits at the table long after finishing her meal.
4. Calls his server by a pet name.	**4.** Demands substitutions at no extra charge.
3. Makes inappropriate sexual remarks.	**3.** Changes her mind often.
2. Uses foul language.	**2.** Demands that the restaurant make special orders at no extra charge.
1. Has a big ego, which must be massaged constantly.	**1.** Sends items back to the kitchen.

Source: Knutson, Bonnie J., Robert S. Woods, & Carl P. Borchgrevink. "Examining the Characteristics of 'Customers from Hell' and Their Impact on the Service Encounter." *Journal of Hospitality and Tourism Education* 10, no. 4 (1999): p. 53.

Originally, the term market stood for a physical location where buyers and sellers gathered to exchange goods, such as a village square. In developing countries, this definition still applies. Sellers constitute the industry and buyers constitute the market. Sellers and buyers are connected by four flows. Sellers provide products for the market and also supply the market with information about these products. In return, the market provides sellers with money and information. The fact is that modern economies operate on the principle of the division of labor by which each person specializes in the production of something, receives payment, and buys needed things with money. Thus modern economies abound in markets.

Marketing

The concept of markets finally brings us full circle to the concept of marketing. Marketing means working with markets to bring about exchanges for satisfying human needs and wants. Thus we return to our definition of marketing as human activity directed at satisfying needs and wants through exchange processes.

Exchange processes involve work. Sellers have to search for buyers, identify their needs, design attractive products, promote them, deliver them, and set prices. Such activities as product development, research, communication, distribution, pricing, and service are core-marketing activities.

Although we normally think of marketing as being carried on by sellers, buyers also carry on marketing activities. Consumers do marketing when they search for the goods that they need at prices they can afford. Meeting planners do marketing when they track down hotel sales managers and bargain for good terms. A seller's market is one in which sellers have more power and buyers have to be the more active marketers. In a buyer's market, buyers have more power, and sellers have to be more active marketers.

During the early 1950s, the supply of goods began to grow faster than the demand. Marketing became identified with sellers trying to find buyers. This book primarily examines the marketing problems of sellers in a buyers' market.

Marketing Management

We define **marketing management** as the analysis, planning, implementation, and control of programs designed to create, build, and maintain beneficial exchanges with target buyers for the purpose of achieving organizational objectives.

Most people think of a **marketing manager** as someone who finds enough customers to buy the company's current output. But this is too limited a view. The marketing manager is interested in shaping the level, time, and composition of demand for the company's products and services. At any time, there may be no demand, adequate demand, irregular demand, or too much demand. For example, a hotel with a 75 percent occupancy rate would be considered to be doing reasonably well. However, the 75 percent occupancy may be achieved by running in the nineties during midweek and in the thirties on weekends. Many restaurants are empty at 11:30 A.M., have a waiting line at 12:30 P.M., and are empty again at 2:00 P.M. In the hospitality industry, there are incredible peaks and valleys. This is why we have devoted a section of Chapter 11 to managing capacity and demand.

Understanding demand is not always easy. One study found that in rapidly growing metropolitan areas there is a decline in the restaurant activity index, which measures preference for dining out.[21] Thus, a 10 percent growth in population may not translate into a 10 percent growth in restaurant activity. In their article "Restaurant Success and Population Growth," the authors look at the impact of population growth and restaurant activity. Using new mapping software programs and GIS (geographic information systems) programs, managers can predict growth trends for restaurant activity, enabling them to plan new restaurants effectively.

Marketing managers are concerned not only with finding and increasing demand, but also at times with changing or even reducing it.[22] Simply put, marketing management is demand management. By marketing managers, we mean company people who are involved in marketing analysis, planning, implementation, or control activities. They include general managers, sales managers and salespeople, advertising executives, sales promotion people, marketing researchers, public relations people, and consultants. We will say more about these marketing jobs in succeeding chapters.

Marketing Management Philosophies

We have described marketing management as carrying out tasks to achieve desired exchanges with target markets. What philosophy should guide these marketing efforts? What weight should be given to the varying and sometimes competing interests of the organization, customers, and society? Clearly, marketing activities should be carried out under some philosophy.

There are five concepts under which organizations conduct their marketing activity: manufacturing, product, selling, marketing, and societal marketing concepts.

Manufacturing Concept

The **manufacturing concept** (also called the production concept) is one of the oldest philosophies guiding sellers. The manufacturing concept holds that consumers will favor products that are available and highly affordable, and therefore management should focus on production and distribution efficiency. The problem with the manufacturing concept is that management may become so focused on manufacturing systems that they forget the customer.

1.8 Switzerland

A tourist was staying at a hotel in the Swiss Alps with a beautiful view of Lake Geneva. The dining room had an outdoor balcony that allowed one to experience fully the beauty of the surroundings. Enjoying breakfast on the balcony was a perfect way to start a summer day. To the guest, the balcony was a great benefit; to the hotel, it was a nuisance. The balcony was at the edge of the dining room and thus the farthest spot from the kitchen. There were no service stations near the balcony, so all supplies had to come from the dining room. There was only one entrance to the balcony, making access difficult. Simply put, serving customers on the balcony was not efficient.

The hotel discouraged customers from eating on the balcony by not setting up the tables. If one asked to eat on the balcony, they received a pained expression from the service person. Then they had to wait fifteen minutes for the table to be set. Once the food was served, the service person disappeared, never to be seen again. This was their way of reminding the guest that one should not eat on the balcony. Yet the hotel should have viewed the balcony as providing a competitive advantage. This point of difference creates customers and positive comments from those customers.

Every reader has surely experienced a common manufacturing-oriented restaurant after normal dining hours. The restaurant may be one-third filled, yet all customers are forced to cluster in one section of the restaurant, thus creating unnecessary density and customer dissatisfaction. This is usually done to facilitate cleaning or to enable the wait staff to provide service with a minimum of walking.

1.9 New Zealand

Unionization of service staff is another reason for a production mentality. As in many other nations, the passenger train crews in New Zealand are unionized. The train between the capital city Wellington and the largest city Auckland serves breakfast until 50 or 60 kilometers from Auckland. The kitchen then shuts down, and passengers are no longer able to acquire so much as a cup of coffee. For the next hour, the kitchen crew may be seen sitting together talking, smoking, and enjoying the train ride. A market- or customer-driven operation would keep the kitchen open until the train reaches Auckland. Crews would be expected to clean up and take inventory after the journey, not an hour before.

The New Zealand public is well aware of this unhelpful situation. The New Zealand travel industry realizes that it is a negative factor in attracting more travelers, but the unionized train crew is above reproach. A similar situation exists on many of the world's airlines and probably accounts for much of the decline in services and the inability of airlines to provide a truly differentiated product.

Product Concept

The **product concept,** like the manufacturing concept, has an inward focus. The product concept holds that consumers prefer existing products and product forms, and the job of management is to develop good versions of these products. This misses the point that consumers are trying to satisfy needs and might turn to entirely different products to better satisfy those needs, such as motels instead of hotels or fast-food outlets in student centers instead of cafeterias.

Victoria Station was a restaurant chain that specialized in excellent prime rib. They were very successful and expanded quickly into over fifty units. Management focused on how to make their product better and at a lower cost. They came up with the right number of days to age their beef. The rib roasts were slow cooked to maintain the juices and avoid shrinkage. They had an excellent product. Unfortunately, their customers no longer wanted red meat every time they went out. They wanted chicken, seafood, and pasta. Victoria Station had a product orientation when they should have had a marketing orientation.

Selling Concept

The **selling concept** holds that consumers will not buy enough of the organization's products unless the organization undertakes a large selling and promotion effort. The aim of a selling focus is to get every possible sale, not to worry about satisfaction after the sale or the revenue contribution of the sale.

The selling concept does not establish a long-term relationship with the customer, because the focus is on getting rid of what one has rather than creating a product to meet the needs of the market. Restaurants often advertise when sales start to drop, without first analyzing why sales are dropping. They do not try to change their product to fit the changing market. They sell harder, pushing their products on the customer through increased advertising and couponing. Eventually, they go out of business because their product no longer satisfies the needs of the marketplace.

The selling concept is endemic within the hospitality industry. A major contributing factor is chronic overcapacity. Virtually every major sector of this industry has suffered, is currently plagued by, or will soon experience overcapacity. When owners and top management face overcapacity, the tendency is to sell, sell, sell. Why do major sectors such as hotels, resorts, airlines, cruise lines, and even restaurants continuously face overcapacity?

- Pride in being the biggest, having the most capacity
- A false belief that economies of scale will occur as size increases
- Tax laws that encourage real estate developers to overbuild properties because of the generous tax write-offs
- New technology, such as new products from aircraft manufacturers that offer higher productivity through larger seating capacity despite adequate existing capacity
- Failure to merge revenue management with sales/marketing management
- Economic incentives by governments to build a larger tourism/hospitality infrastructure to create economic growth
- Poor or nonexistent forecasting and planning by owners, consultants, financial organizations, and governments
- A myth that the travel industry faces almost unlimited future demand
- The myth that a burgeoning population, a breakdown of international barriers, and increasing disposable income will correct temporary overcapacity problems

Marketing Concept

The **marketing concept** is a more recent business philosophy and one that is being rapidly adopted in the hospitality industry.[23] Many companies have adopted the marketing concept. We know that Four Seasons Hotels, Accor, and McDonald's follow this concept fully. The marketing concept holds that achieving organizational goals depends on determining the needs and wants of target markets and delivering the desired satisfaction more effectively and efficiently than competitors.

1.10 American Association of Retired Persons

Amazingly, niche opportunities sometimes remain available long after suppliers know the need. This is probably due to difficulties in changing behavior of those who supply the products, such as the wait staff in a restaurant. The American Association of Retired Persons conducted a survey of readers of its magazine, *Modern Maturity.* Fifty-nine percent replied that they frequently ate in a restaurant alone, and another 18 percent replied that they sometimes did. Eighty-four percent of those replied that the service they receive is worse than if they had company.

Some restaurants have established special seating areas for singles with round tables that encourage single diners to sit together. This provides an opportunity for the diners to engage in conversation with other diners and allows the restaurant to conserve seating space. Other restaurants have deuces that face each other, again encouraging conversation if it is desired. These restaurants value the single diner and have built up a profitable segment. But there are still many restaurants that continue to provide sub par service to people who dine alone.[24]

The marketing concept is frequently confused with the selling concept. Figure 1-3 compares the two. The selling concept takes an inside-out perspective. It starts with the company's existing products and calls for heavy selling and promoting to achieve profitable sales. The marketing concept starts with the needs and wants of the company's target customers. By contrast, the marketing concept takes an outside-in perspective. It starts with a well-defined market, focusing on customer needs. Second, marketing activities must be coordinated through the organization. Third, the marketing activities must work toward achieving the goals and objectives of the organization. The marketing concept is summarized in the following statement: the company coordinates all the activities that will affect customer satisfaction and makes its profits by creating and maintaining customer satisfaction.

Societal Marketing Concept

The **societal marketing concept** is the newest marketing concept. The societal marketing concept holds that the organization should determine the needs, wants, and interests of target markets and deliver the desired satisfactions more effectively and efficiently than competitors in a way that maintains or improves the consumer's and society's well-being. The societal marketing concept questions whether the marketing concept is adequate in an age of environmental problems, resource shortages, rapid population growth, worldwide inflation, and neglected social services.[25] It asks if the firm that senses, serves, and satisfies individual wants is always doing what's best for consumers and society in the long run. The pure

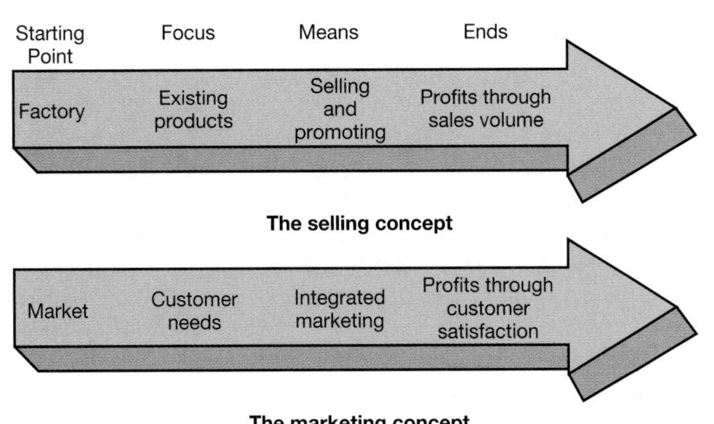

Figure 1-3
The selling and marketing concepts contrasted.

marketing concept ignores possible conflicts between short-run consumer wants and long-run societal needs.

Advocates of the societal marketing concept would like public-interest groups to guide corporations toward decisions that will benefit society over the long term. Societal pressures are already manifesting in the marketing of cigarettes and liquor. Hotel chains have established no-smoking floors and no-smoking sections in their restaurants. Mothers Against Drunk Driving (MADD) and other antidrunk–driving groups have brought about stiffer drunk-driving laws, laws against happy-hour promotions, and laws that increase restaurant liability for serving excessive alcoholic beverages to guests. Restaurants and their state associations have developed training programs on how to serve alcohol responsibly. The cocktail reception is a thing of the past; today at most receptions a variety of mineral waters, fruit juices, and soft drinks is served. Managers and employees must be aware of how to prevent customers from becoming intoxicated and how to handle customers who are intoxicated.

1.11 Mothers Against Drunk Driving (MADD)

Fast-food restaurants that practice the societal marketing concept will pursue more environmentally sound packaging and produce foods with more nutritional value. Smart restaurateurs will do this before public outcry or laws force them into it. Resort developers must consider the impact on the environment not only of their initial construction but also of the disposal of waste products and their use of water. The denigration of the earth's environment will make it necessary for marketers to become more socially responsible.

The hotel industry has been advised of many eco-friendly steps that can be taken. Among these are removing waste products such as plastics, glass, and metal from the trash; reducing chemical use; and extending the life of products and machinery—even linens, by using them as rags.[26] Energy conservation, landscaping, preventive maintenance, and water-saving plumbing fixtures are other popular recommendations. The area of green marketing has evolved from the public's concern about the environment. The Boston Park Plaza Hotel & Towers developed a total of sixty-five environmental initiatives, including everything from soap dispensers that reduced packaging and used less soap to a guideline for meeting planners on how to conduct "green" (environmentally conscious) meetings. The publicity received from these initiatives attracted additional convention business from groups sympathetic to the environmental movement.[27] Quaker Oats of Canada changed from polystyrene cups to reusable cups in its staff cafeteria for environmental reasons. At the end of the year, they were surprised to find that in addition to creating less solid waste, they had saved $6,000.[28] Thus, being environmentally conscious can produce positive publicity and reduce costs, in addition to helping the environment.

1.12 Boston Park Plaza Hotel & Towers

A broader issue facing the hospitality and travel industries is expansion that has a positive impact on local residents. Poorly planned tourism developments have the potential of creating great damage to an area. This damage can be caused by the disposal of solid waste, lack of proper sewage treatment facilities resulting in the contamination of groundwater, congested roads as the result of poor infrastructure support, increased

Responsible casinos ban players known to have compulsive gambling behavior. Courtesy of Hilton Hotels Corporation.

rents as the result of attracting employees to the area but not providing additional housing, and damage to the area's flora and fauna.

The hospitality and travel industries cannot insulate themselves from the continuing need for societal approval. Few industries have a greater need to recognize and proactively adopt the societal marketing concept.

MARKETING'S FUTURE

Marketing operates within a dynamic global environment. Every decade calls on marketing managers to think freshly about their marketing objectives and practices. Rapid changes can quickly make yesterday's winning strategies out of date. As management thought-leader Peter Drucker once observed, a company's winning formula for the last decade will probably be its undoing in the next decade.

As competition becomes more intense, companies will be forced to focus on satisfying their customers. The future will be short for those companies that do not. In his classic article, "The Marketing Revolutions," Robert Keith wrote about marketing's future forty years ago: "Soon it will be true that every activity of the corporation from finance to sales production is aimed at satisfying the needs and desires of the consumer. When that stage of development is reached, the marketing revolution will be complete."[29]

Today, for many successful firms, the marketing revolution is moving to completion. All departments are becoming involved in satisfying the customer. For example, accounting has to develop bills that the meeting planner can understand; maintenance people should be able to answer a guest's basic questions, such as where the hotel's restaurants are

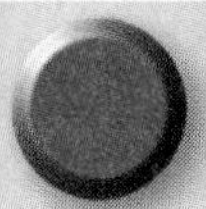

Marketing Highlight 1-3

The Internet Changes How We Market Hospitality Products

It costs Hyatt hotels $3 to book a reservation on its Web site compared with $9 through its call center. As a result of these cost savings, hotels and airlines promote their Web sites and selling billions of dollars of products over the Internet. The Best Western Rosedale on the Park in Hong Kong features HOTELINMYHAND, a file that can be downloaded into a handheld computer, such as a Palm Pilot. The file contains information about the hotel and the area around the hotel. The hotel also uses Kerbango Internet radio, giving guests access to over 5,000 radio stations, including ones from their own country. The Rosedale features wireless Internet access for its guests in some of its public spaces. The hotel will reserve a cell phone with a specific number for its frequent guests. This enables guests to have business cards printed with the address of the hotel and their "personalized" Hong Kong phone number. For these guests the Rosedale has become their Hong Kong business address, creating a bond with the hotel that will be difficult for competitors to break.

The Rosedale hotel has incorporated technology throughout the hotel to create a competitive advantage. Courtesy of The Best Western Rosedale on the Park.

FoodServiceSearch.com provides restaurants with recipes for new product ideas, food safety information, and equipment information. Web cams have become a popular promotion for resort restaurants. Sam's Café in Tiburon (near San Francisco) hooked up a Web camera, linked it to a number of Internet sites, and soon new customers were showing up, saying, "We saw you on the cam." CD-ROMs that are linked to a hotel's Web site are replacing expensive color brochures. We could go on and on with examples; in fact, we will throughout the book. We have also added a chapter on electronic marketing that features the Internet.

One of the support features of this book is a Web site to assist you in using this book, *www.prenhall.com/kotler.* The site serves as a portal to a wealth of information on marketing and travel and hospitality organizations. The site is designed to support each chapter, give you real world examples of how companies market, and provide information on the companies mentioned in the book. Look for the "*e*" in the margins of each chapter. This indicates the organization mentioned is linked under the chapter and the organization in the Web site. The site is organized into a general information section and a book section. The book section is organized by chapter and contains links to the companies mentioned in the chapter; these links will help with the chapter's Internet Exercise and links to hospitality and travel companies that provide supporting examples for the concepts presented in the chapter. The information section contains company information organized by industry type and by geographic region. The site also contains a resource guide where students can find information about marketing. The major association sites, job information, and research information can be found in this section.

This site is an exciting new resource. We hope you will use it and enjoy it. It is dynamic and will be updated on a regular basis; if you come across a site that should be included, including companies from your country, please e-mail the site's information to *bowen@ccmail.nevada.edu* and we will add it to our site.

See Destination Stations, *1 to 1 Magazine* (May–June 2001): 45+; Robert Klara, "Site Seeing," *Restaurant Business,* (January 2001): 33–38 and Terence Ronson, "Using Their Intelligence," *Hotel Asia Pacific,* (January/February 2001): 26–28.

located; and all employees should have a genuine concern about the customer's well-being.

Peter Drucker wrote: "It [marketing] encompasses the entire business. It is the whole business seen from the point of view of the final result, that is, from the customer's point of view."[30] This book is not just for students who desire a successful career in marketing; it is for students who desire a successful career. Marketing with its customer orientation has become the job of everyone.

1.13 Direct Marketing Association, Hospitality Sales and Marketing Association International, and the American Marketing Association are organizations that provide students with career information and job opportunities. They all provide student membership at greatly reduced prices.

Great Leaders

Although marketing is relatively new to the hospitality industry, a common characteristic among many of the great hospitality industry leaders is their successful application of basic marketing principles. These principles include focusing on guests to satisfy their wants (external marketing) and satisfying employees who serve the guests (internal marketing). On the book's Web site are sketches of four outstanding hospitality industry marketers. Early industry leaders of the past are all white males, but today's hospitality leaders are a diverse group, with representatives from different racial groups, ethnic backgrounds, and both genders. We can learn from these past leaders, but the future is yours.

1.14 Great Leaders
See this section on the Web site for brief notes on some of the great hospitality marketers.

Key Terms

Create and maintain customers The purpose of a business.

Demands Human wants that are backed by buying power.

Exchange The act of obtaining a desired object from someone by offering something in return.

Hospitality industry Made up of those businesses that do one or more of the following: provide accommodation, prepared food and beverage service, and/or entertainment for the traveler.

Human need A state of felt deprivation in a person.

Human want The form that a human need takes when shaped by culture and individual personality.

Manufacturing concept (production concept) Holds that customers will favor products that are available and highly affordable, and therefore management should focus on production and distribution efficiency.

Market The set of actual and potential buyers of a product.

Marketing A social and managerial process by which people and groups obtain what they need and want through creating and exchanging products and value with others.

Marketing concept The marketing management philosophy that holds that achieving organizational goals depends on determining the needs and wants of target markets and delivering desired satisfactions more effectively and efficiently than competitors.

Marketing management The analysis, planning, implementation, and control of programs designed to create, build, and maintain beneficial exchanges with target buyers for the purpose of achieving organizational objectives.

Marketing manager A person who is involved in marketing analysis, planning, implementation, and control activities.

Marketing mix Elements include product, price, promotion, and distribution. Sometimes distribution is called place and the marketing situation facing a company.

Product Anything that can be offered to a market for attention, acquisition, use, or consumption that might satisfy a want or need. It includes physical objects, services, persons, places, organizations, and ideas.

Product concept The idea that consumers will favor products that offer the most quality, performance, and features, and therefore the organization should devote its energy to making continuous product improvements.

Quality The totality of features and characteristics of a product that bear on its ability to meet customer needs (American Society for Quality Control).

Relationship marketing Relationship marketing involves creating, maintaining, and enhancing strong relationships with customers and other stakeholders.

Selling concept The idea that consumers will not buy enough of an organization's products unless the organization undertakes a large selling and promotion effort.

Societal marketing concept The idea that an organization should determine the needs, wants, and interests of target markets and deliver the desired satisfactions more effectively and efficiently than competitors in a way that maintains or improves the consumer's and society's well-being.

Transaction Consists of a trade of values between two parties; marketing's unit of measurement.

Chapter Review

I. Introduction: Marketing in the Hospitality Industry

1) Customer orientation. The purpose of a business is to create and maintain profitable customers. Customer satisfaction leading to profit is the central goal of hospitality marketing.

II. What Is Hospitality Marketing? Marketing is a social and managerial process by which individuals and groups obtain what they need and want through creating and exchanging products and value with others.

III. Importance of Marketing

1) The entrance of corporate giants into the hospitality market and the marketing skills these companies have brought to the industry have increased the importance of marketing within the industry.

2) Analysts predict that the hotel industry will consolidate in much the same way as the airline industry has, with five or six major chains dominating the market. Such consolidation will create a market that is highly competitive. The firms that survive this consolidation will be the ones that understand their customers.

3) In response to growing competitive pressures, hotel chains are relying on the expertise of the marketing director.

IV. Travel Industry Marketing

1) Successful hospitality marketing is highly dependent on the entire travel industry.

2) Government or quasi-government agencies play an important role in travel industry marketing through legislation aimed at enhancing the industry and through promotion of regions, states, and nations.

3) Few industries are as interdependent as the travel and hospitality industries.

V. Understanding Marketing. Marketing is a social and managerial process by which individuals and groups obtain what they need and want through creating and exchanging products and value with others. To understand the definition, we must understand the following terms: needs, wants, and demands; products; value, cost, and satisfaction; exchange, transactions, and relationships; and markets.

1) Needs, wants, and demands

a) Needs. Human beings have many complex needs. These include basic physical needs for food, clothing, warmth, and safety; social needs for belonging, affection, fun, and relaxation; esteem needs for prestige, recognition, and fame; and individual needs for knowledge and self-expression.

b) Wants. Wants are how people communicate their needs.

c) Demands. People have almost unlimited wants, but limited resources. They choose products that produce the most satisfaction for their money. When backed by buying power, wants become demand.

2) Products. A product is anything that can be offered to a market for attention, acquisition, use, or consumption and that might satisfy a need or want.

3) Value, satisfaction, and quality

a) Value. Value is the consumer's estimate of the product's overall capacity to satisfy his or her needs. Today's consumer behaviorists have gone beyond narrow economic assumptions of how consumers form value in their mind and make product choices. Modern theories of consumer-choice behavior are important to marketers because the entire marketing plan rests on assumptions about how consumers make choices. Therefore, concepts of value, quality, and satisfaction are crucial to the discipline of marketing.

b) Satisfaction. Satisfaction with a product is determined by how well the product meets the customer's expectations for that product.

c) **Quality.** The totality of features and characteristics of a product that bear on its ability to meet customer needs. The fundamental aim of today's total quality movements has become total customer satisfaction.

4) **Exchange, transactions, and relationships**

a) **Exchange.** Exchange is the act of obtaining a desired object from someone by offering something in return.

b) **Transactions.** A transaction is marketing's unit of measurement. A transaction consists of a trade of values between two parties.

c) **Relationship marketing.** Relationship marketing focuses on building a relationship with a company's profitable customers. Most companies are finding that they earn a higher return from resources invested in getting repeat sales from current customers than from money spent to attract new customers.

5) **Markets.** A market is a set of actual and potential buyers who might transact with a seller.

VI. Marketing Management. Marketing management is the analysis, planning, implementation, and control of programs designed to create, build, and maintain beneficial exchanges with target buyers for the purpose of achieving organizational objectives.

VII. Five Marketing Management Philosophies

1) **Manufacturing concept.** The manufacturing (or production) concept holds that customers will favor products that are available and highly affordable, and therefore management should focus on production and distribution efficiency.

2) **Product concept.** The product concept holds that customers prefer existing products and product forms, and the job of management is to develop good versions of these products.

3) **Selling concept.** The selling concept holds that consumers will not buy enough of the organization's products unless the organization undertakes a large selling and promotion effort.

4) **Marketing concept.** The marketing concept holds that achieving organizational goals depends on determining the needs and wants of target markets and delivering the desired satisfaction more effectively and efficiently than competitors.

5) **Societal marketing concept.** The societal marketing concept holds that the organization should determine the needs, wants, and interests of target markets and deliver the desired satisfactions more effectively and efficiently than competitors in a way that maintains or improves the consumer's and society's well-being.

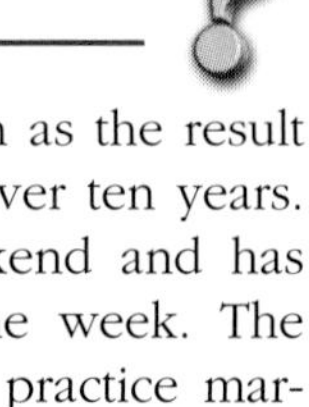

Discussion Questions

1. Discuss why you should study marketing.
2. Many managers view the purpose of business as making a profit, while some view the purpose as being able to create and maintain a customer. Explain how these alternative viewpoints could affect a company's interactions with its customers. If a manager views the purpose as being able to create and maintain a customer, does this mean that the manager is not concerned with profits?
3. A guest in your hotel complains that the air-conditioning in his room did not work and because of this he did not get a good night's sleep. What would you do?
4. Give a specific example of two firms in different areas of the travel and tourism industry joining forces to create a competitive advantage.
5. A restaurant has a great reputation as the result of providing consistent food for over ten years. The restaurant is full every weekend and has above-average business during the week. The manager claims that they do not practice marketing because they do not need marketing; they have more than enough business now. Is it true that this restaurant does not practice marketing?
6. Look at Figure 1-2. Why do you think persons who give you 2 (a relatively high score) out of 7 are not likely to return?
7. Give several examples you have found of hospitality companies being socially responsible. Include in your discussion how being socially responsible helps the company.

Experiential Exercises

Do one of the following:

Restaurant

Visit two restaurants in the same class, such as two fast-food restaurants or two casual restaurants. Observe the cleanliness of the restaurants, in-house signage, and other physical features. Then order a menu item and observe the service and the quality of the food. Write up your observations, and then state which restaurant you feel is more customer oriented. Explain why.

Hotel

Call the central reservation number of two hotels. Request information on room availability, different room types, and price for a date one month from now. (*Note:* Do not make a reservation). Write up your experience, including a description of how quickly the phone was answered, the customer orientation of information provided, and the friendliness of the employee. Based on your experiences, which hotel do you feel had the more customer-oriented reservation system?

Other Hospitality Companies

If you are interested in another area of the travel industry, you may compare two organizations in that area for their customer orientation using similar criteria, as mentioned earlier. For example, if you are interested in tourism you may contact two tourism organizations regarding their destinations. This could be a city convention and tourist bureau, or it could be a government tourist bureau.

INTERNET EXERCISES

Support for these exercises can be found on the Web site for *Marketing for Hospitality and Tourism*, www.prenhall.com/kotler.

Choose three restaurants or three hotels listed on the book's Web site under Internet Exercise Chapter 1. If you desire, you may use restaurant or hotel companies you have found on the Internet.

Based on information provided in each company's Web site:

A. Describe how each of these companies tries to satisfy a customer's wants.

B. How does each of these companies create value for the customer?

C. Do they segment the market by offering pages for a specific market segment? For example, a hotel may provide information for meeting planners, and a restaurant may provide information for customers who are concerned about nutrition or families.

D. Select the company you would purchase from and state why.

REFERENCES

1. Anthony E. Heffernan, "Franchises Are the Customers at Days Inn," *Franchising World* (January–February 1988), 52–54.
2. "Lodging Hospitality, Our People Our Strength," *Advertising Supplement II, Lodging Hospitality* 22, no. 1 (1988): 12–13.
3. Michael Leven, "What Does the H in Hospitality Mean?" in *The Practice of Hospitality Management II*, ed. Robert C. Lewis et al. (Westport, CT: AVI, 1986).
4. Regis McKenna, *Relationship Marketing* (Reading, MA: Addison-Wesley Publishing Co.)
5. Accor 2001–2002 *Asia Pacific Hotel Directory*, p. 1.
6. Theodore Levitt, *Marketing Imagination* (New York: Free Press, 1986).
7. Christian Gronroos, *Service Management and Marketing* (Lexington, MA: Lexington Books, 1990).
8. Patricia Sellers, "Getting Customers to Love You," *Fortune*, March 13, 1989, pp. 38–49.
9. Frederich Reichheld, *The Loyalty Effect* (Boston, MA: Harvard Business School Press, 1996).
10. James L. Heskett Jr., W. Earle Sasser, and W. L. Hart Christopher, *Service Breakthroughs* (New York: Free Press, 1990).
11. Karl Albrecht, *At America's Service* (Homewood, IL: Dow Jones Irwin, 1988), p. 23.
12. Peter F. Drucker, *Management: Tasks, Responsibility, Practices* (New York: Harper & Row, 1973), pp. 64–65.
13. *Restaurant Business*, November 1, 2000, pp. 35, 38.
14. Robert H. Woods, Denny G. Rutherford, Raymond Schmidgall, and Michael Sciarini, "Hotel General Managers," *Cornell Hotel and Restaurant Administration Quarterly 39*, no. 6 (December 1998): p. 44.
15. "Cruise Forum," *Travel Agent* (May 2, 1994), sec. B, p. 2.
16. Henry A. Murray, *Explorations in Personality* (New York: Oxford University Press, 1938).
17. Theodore Levitt, "Marketing Myopia," *Harvard Business Review* (July–August 1960): 45–56.
18. John T. Bowen and Shiang-Lih Chen, "The Relationship between Customer Loyalty and Customer Satisfaction," *International Journal of Contemporary Hotel Management, 13*(5) (2001): 13–17.
19. Leonard L. Berry, Valarie A. Zeithaml, and A. Parasuraman, "Quality Counts in Services, Too," *Business Horizons* 28 (May–June 1985): 44–52.
20. Li Lam and Mahmood A. Khan, "Hong Kong's Fast-Food Industry," *Cornell Hotel and Restaurant Administration Quarterly* 36, no. 3 (June 1995): 41.

21. Michael Shriber, Christopher Muller, and Christ Inman, "Population Changes and Restaurant Success," *Cornell Hotel and Restaurant Administration Quarterly* 36, no. 3 (June 1995): 48.

22. Philip Kotler, "The Major Tasks of Marketing Management," *Journal of Marketing* (October 1973): 41–49.

23. For more on the marketing concept, see Theodore Levitt, "Marketing and Its Discontents," *Across the Board* (February 1984): 42–48; and Franklin S. Houston, "The Marketing Concept: What It Is and What It Is Not," *Journal of Marketing* (April 1986): 81–87.

24. "Feedback," *Modern Maturity,* 40W, no. 4 (July–August 1997): 12. See also Dan Lago and James Kipp Poffley, "The Aging Population and the Hospitality Industry in 2010: Important Trends and Probable Services," *Hospitality Research Journal* 17, no. 1 (1993): 29–47.

25. Lawrence P. Fieldman, "Societal Adaptation: A New Challenge for Marketing," *Journal of Marketing* (July 1971): 54–60; Martin L. Bell and C. William Emery, "The Faltering Marketing Concept," *Journal of Marketing* (October 1971): 37–42.

26. Kirk Iwanowski and Cindy Rushmore, "Introducing the Eco-friendly Hotel," *Cornell Hotel and Restaurant Administration Quarterly* 35, no. 1 (February 1994): 34–38.

27. Leslee Jaquette, "Hoteliers Are Seeing Green with Ecology Efforts," *Hotel and Motel Management* 207, no. 13 (July 27, 1992): 19–20.

28. Patrick Carson and Julia Moulden, *Green Is Gold* (Toronto: Harper Collins Publishers, 1991), p. 58.

29. Robert J. Keith, "The Marketing Revolution," *Journal of Marketing* 20 (January 1960): 35–38.

30. *Business Week,* June 24, 1950, pp. 30–36.

2 Service Characteristics of Hospitality and Tourism Marketing

Managers do not control the quality of the product when the product is a service. . . . The quality of the service is in a precarious state—it is in the hands of the service workers who "produce" and deliver it.
Karl Albrecht

The Victoria House is a small Caribbean Island resort hotel located on an island off the shore of Belize. There is one phone, no television, and no newsstand. Looking at the ocean from the Victoria House's beach, guests can see waves breaking over the barrier reef renowned for its fishing and diving. Victoria House offers North American executives a chance to escape stress and relax in a tropical paradise. Victoria House's brochures communicate this message well, showing thatched villas, palm trees, and the Caribbean Sea.

But when guests arrived at the resort, the initial impression was much different than that created by the brochure. The resort consists of a main lodge (guest rooms upstairs and the reception, dining room, and bar downstairs), employee quarters, and twelve thatched roof guest cottages. The van delivering guests to the hotel dropped them off between the main lodge and the employee quarters. Instead of enjoying a beautiful ocean view, guests saw the kitchen, the employee quarters, their laundry hanging out to dry, and a car being repaired with its motor hanging from a tree.

Victoria House did not create a positive first impression. Guests stepping out of the van wondered if they had made a terrible mistake. The management of Victoria House grew up on the island and accept the breathtaking ocean views as common and uninspiring. The entrance was designed for efficiency to allow delivery trucks to drop their goods near storerooms and to drop the guests off at a convenient entrance to the lodge. The management of Victoria House failed to consider that many guests had never been to the island and were expecting a tropical paradise. The New York executive who purchased a Victoria House

vacation had only the promise of stress-free relaxation, an air ticket, and a hotel voucher before the trip. Management should have made certain that guests' impressions upon arriving at the resort matched those created by the brochure. In hospitality marketing, this is called managing the tangible evidence.

When management finally recognized this error, a separate driveway was built, allowing guests to be delivered to the front of the resort. The view now included beautifully landscaped grounds with native flowers, palm trees, and a breathtaking view of the ocean. This provided immediate positive guest reinforcement.

Chapter Objectives

After reading this chapter, you should be able to:

1. Describe a service culture.
2. Identify four service characteristics that affect the marketing of a hospitality or travel product.
3. Explain marketing strategies that are useful in the hospitality and travel industries.

Marketing initially developed in connection with selling physical products, such as toothpaste, cars, steel, and equipment. But today, one of the major trends in many parts of the world is the phenomenal growth of services, or products with little or no physical content. In many developed countries, services account for a majority of the gross domestic product. The following are some of the countries where 60 percent or more of the gross domestic product (GDP) comes from services: Australia (71%), Canada (66%), France (71%), Japan (63%), Norway (72%), the United Kingdom (73%), and the United States (80%).[1] Service economies are not limited to developed countries; in developing countries the majority of the workforce is often employed in the hospitality and travel industries. These industries are part of this growing service sector. Other service industries include banking, health care, entertainment, legal aid, and transportation. The growth of service industries has created a demand for research into their operation and marketing. Throughout the book we include the results of recent research into services and marketing issues. In this chapter, as well as in the remainder of the book, we examine the service characteristics of firms in the hospitality industry.

The Service Culture

Some managers think of their operations only in terms of tangible goods. Thus, managers of fast-food restaurants who think they sell only hamburgers often have "slow, surly service personnel, dirty unattractive facilities, and few return customers."[2] One of the most important tasks of a hospitality business is to develop the service side of the business, specifically, a strong service culture.

The **service culture** focuses on serving and satisfying the customer. The service culture has to start with top management and flow down.

2.1 Four Seasons Hotels

Isadore Sharp drives the service culture in Four Seasons Hotels through employee communications, company policies, and personal actions. This belief at Four Seasons is reinforced for all its employees when those employees who go to extraordinary efforts to satisfy the customer are made Employee of the Year.

A service culture empowers employees to solve customer problems. It is supported by a reward system based on customer satisfaction. Human beings generally do what is rewarded. If an organization wants to deliver a quality product, the organization's culture must support and reward customer need attention.[3] In Chapter 10 we discuss service culture in more detail.

Characteristics of Service Marketing

Service marketers must be concerned with four characteristics of services: intangibility, inseparability, variability, and perishability (see Figure 2-1).

Intangibility

Unlike physical products, services cannot be seen, tasted, felt, heard, or smelled before they are purchased. Prior to boarding an airplane, airline passengers have nothing but an airline ticket and the promise of safe delivery to their destination. Members of a hotel sales force cannot take a hotel room with them on a sales call. In fact, they do not sell a room; instead, they sell the right to use a room for a specific period of time. When hotel guests leave, they have nothing to show for the purchase but a receipt. Robert Lewis has observed that someone who purchases a service may go away empty-handed, but they do not go away empty-headed.[4] They have memories that can be shared with others. Marriott Vacation Club International realizes this, and they have made a deliberate effort to create memorable guest experiences. Marriott realizes that a white-water rafting trip can create memories a family visiting their Mountainside Resort in Utah will talk about for years. The fun the family had experiencing white-water rafting, along with their other experiences at the resort, will make them want to return. In the hospitality and travel industry, many of the products sold are intangible experiences.

If we are going to buy a car, we can take it for a test drive; if we are going to buy a meal at a restaurant, we do not know what we will receive

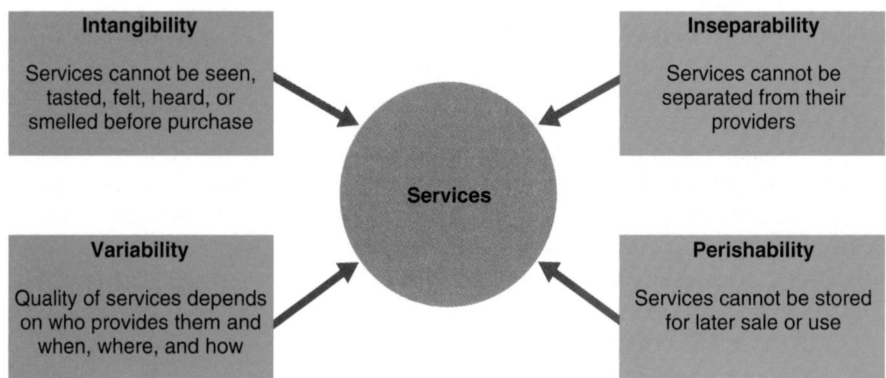

Figure 2-1
Four service characteristics.

until we have experienced the food and service. To reduce uncertainty caused by **service intangibility,** buyers look for tangible evidence that will provide information and confidence about the service. The exterior of a restaurant is the first thing that an arriving guest sees. The condition of the grounds and the overall cleanliness of the restaurant provide clues as to how well the restaurant is run. Tangibles provide signals as to the quality of the intangible service. The Regent Hotel in Hong Kong makes sure that all its uniformed and nonuniformed employees reinforce the hotel's image of elegance and professionalism. The appearance of the employees is part of the Regent's tangible evidence. This hotel also purposely parks luxury automobiles such as a Rolls-Royce in front to deliver an instant message of quality and upscale service.

As a niche segment of the hospitality–lodging industry, conference centers face a continuous need to make their products tangible. They must differentiate themselves from resorts and hotels. Product features that conference centers use to differentiate themselves include the following:

- Dedicated meeting rooms that cannot be used for other purposes as in most hotels
- Twenty-four-hour use, which offers security and personalization for clients (computers, briefcases, and the like can be left in the room)
- Continuous coffee, not just coffee breaks
- All-inclusive pricing, a set price per day, per meeting attendee

The International Association of Conference Centers offers an online database for travel planners. This important customer segment can access a great amount of information about conference centers, such as size of property, location, availability, and pricing. To help tangibilize the product, the system allows meeting planners to see a layout of a potential property's meeting space on the display screen. Clients can get a concrete idea of the mix of general session, breakout, boardroom, and amphitheater spaces to match their needs.[5]

2.2 International Association of Conference Centers
Marriott Vacation Clubs International
Regent Hong Kong

Inseparability

In most hospitality services, both the service provider and the customer must be present for the transaction to occur. Customer-contact employees are part of the product. The food in a restaurant may be outstanding, but if the service person has a poor attitude or provides inattentive service, customers will down-rate the overall restaurant experience. They will not be satisfied with their experience.

Service inseparability also means that customers are part of the product. A couple may have chosen a restaurant because it is quiet and romantic, but if a group of loud and boisterous conventioneers is seated in the same room, the couple will be disappointed. Managers must manage their customers so that they do not create dissatisfaction for other customers.

Another implication of inseparability is that customers and employees must understand the service delivery system, since they are both coproducing the service. Customers must understand the menu items in a restaurant so that they get the dish they expect. Hotel customers must know how to use the phone system and express checkout on the television. This means hospitality and travel organization have to train customers just as they train employees. The Holiday Inn Newark is popular with international tourists who have just arrived from overseas. Many of these guests pay in cash or with travelers' checks, as they do not use credit cards. On more than one occasion, the front-desk clerk has been observed answering the phone of an upset guest who claims that their movie system does not work. The clerk must explain that they did not establish credit, because they paid for the room only and therefore have to come to the front desk and pay for the movie before it can be activated. Guests obviously become upset upon receiving this information. The hotel could avoid this problem and improve customer relations by asking guests at arrival time if they would like to make a deposit for anything they might charge, such as in-room movies.

Finally, customer coproduction means organizations must select, hire, and train customers.[6] Fast-food restaurants train customers to get their own drinks. This gives the customer something to do while waiting and reduces the need for employees to fill drink orders themselves. Hotels, restaurants, airlines, and rental car companies train customers to use the Internet to get information and to make reservations. The customer using these services is performing the job of customer service agent *and* reservationist. The benefits provided to the guest by becoming an "employee" include reduced price, increased value (all you can eat or free drink refills), customization, and reduced waiting time. The characteristic of inseparability requires hospitality managers to manage both their employees and their customers.

Variability

Services are highly variable. Their quality depends on who provides them and when and where they are provided. There are several causes of **service variability.** Services are produced and consumed simultaneously, which limits quality control. Fluctuating demand makes it difficult to deliver consistent products during periods of peak demand. The high degree of contact between the service provider and the guest means that product consistency depends on the service provider's skills and performance at the time of the exchange. A guest can receive excellent service one day and mediocre service from the same person the next day. In the case of mediocre service, the service person may not have felt well or perhaps experienced an emotional problem. Lack of communication and heterogeneity of guest expectations is another source of variability. A restaurant customer ordering a medium steak may expect it to be cooked all the way through, whereas the person working on the broiler may define medium as having a warm, pink center. The guest will be disappointed when he or she cuts into the steak and sees pink meat. Restaurants have solved this cause of variability by developing common definitions of steak doneness and communicating them to the employees and customers. Sometimes the communication to the customer is verbal, and sometimes it is printed on the menu. Customers usually return to a restaurant because they enjoyed their last experience. When the product they receive is different and does not meet their expectations on the next visit, they often do not return. Variability or lack of consistency in the product is a major cause of customer disappointment in the hospitality industry.

Perishability

Services cannot be stored. A 100-room hotel that only sells 60 rooms on a particular night cannot inventory the 40 unsold rooms and then sell 140 rooms the next night. Revenue lost from not selling those 40 rooms is gone forever. Because of **service perishability,** some hotels charge guests holding guaranteed reservations even when they fail to check into the hotel. Restaurants are also starting to charge a fee to customers who do not show up for a reservation. They, too, realize that if someone does not show for a reservation, the opportunity to sell that seat may be lost. If services are to maximize revenue, they must manage capacity and demand because they cannot carry forward unsold inventory. The characteristic of perishability means that capacity and demand management are important to the success of a hospitality or travel company. In Chapter 11 we discuss capacity and demand in detail. This Club Med example is just one way companies can manage demand to reduce product loss:

2.3 Club Med

> Club Med operates hundreds of Club Med villages (resorts) around the world. If the company cannot sell its rooms and air packages, it loses out as the products are perishable. Club Med uses e-mail to pitch unsold, discounted packages to the 34,000 people in its database. These people are notified early to midweek on rooms and air seats available for travel that day. Discounts are typically 30 to 40 percent off the standard package. An average of 1.2 percent respond to the offers, and Club Med takes in anywhere from $25,000 to $40,000 every month from e-mail sales of distressed inventory.[7]

Before the program, Club Med's only alternative was to rely on travel agents to sell last-minute packages. Club Med's database includes such information as vacation preferences, preferred sports and activities, preferred time of year for travel and marital status, as well as geographic data. Although current e-mail offers aren't targeted, the company plans to create one-to-one marketing messages in the future.

Management Strategies for Service Businesses

Service marketers can do several things to increase service effectiveness in the face of intrinsic service characteristics.

Just like manufacturing businesses, good service firms use marketing to position themselves strongly in chosen target markets. Southwest Airlines positions itself as "Just Plane Smart" for commuter flyers—as a no-frills, short-haul airline charging very low fares. The Ritz-Carlton Hotel positions itself as offering a memorable experience that "enlivens the senses, instills well-being, and fulfills even the unexpressed wishes and needs of our guests." These and other service firms establish their positions through traditional marketing mix activities.

However, because services differ from tangible products, they often require additional marketing approaches. In a product business, products are fairly standardized and can sit on shelves waiting for customers. But in a service business, the customer and frontline service employee interact to create the service. Thus, service providers must work to interact effectively with customers to create superior value during service encounters. Effective interaction, in turn, depends on the skills of frontline service employees, and on the service production and support processes backing these employees.

Successful service companies focus their attention on both their employees and customers. They understand the **service-profit chain,** which links service firm profits with employee and customer satisfaction. This chain consists of five links:[8]

1. **Healthy service profits and growth**—superior service firm performance
2. **Satisfied and loyal customers**—satisfied customers who remain loyal, repeat purchase, and refer other customers
3. **Greater service value**—more effective and efficient customer value creation and service delivery
4. **Satisfied and productive service employees**—more satisfied, loyal, and hardworking employees
5. **Internal service quality**—superior employee selection and training, a high-quality work environment, and strong support for those dealing with customers

Therefore, reaching service profits and growth goals begins with taking care of those who take care of customers (see Marketing Highlight 2-1).

The concept of the service-profit chain is well illustrated by a story about how Bill Marriott Jr., chairman of Marriott Hotels, interviews prospective managers:

> Bill Marriott tells job candidates that the hotel chain wants to satisfy three groups: customers, employees, and stockholders. Although all of the groups are important, he asks in which order the groups should be satisfied. Most candidates say satisfy the customer first. Marriott, however, reasons differently. First, employees must be satisfied. If employees love their jobs and feel a sense of pride in the hotel, they will serve customers well. Satisfied customers will return frequently to the Marriott. Moreover, dealing with happy customers will make employees even more satisfied, resulting in better service and still greater repeat business, all of which will yield a level of profits that will satisfy Marriott stockholders.

All this suggests that service marketing requires more than just traditional external marketing using the four Ps. Figure 2-2 shows that service marketing also requires both internal marketing and interactive marketing.

Internal marketing means that the service firm must effectively train and motivate its customer-contact employees and all the supporting

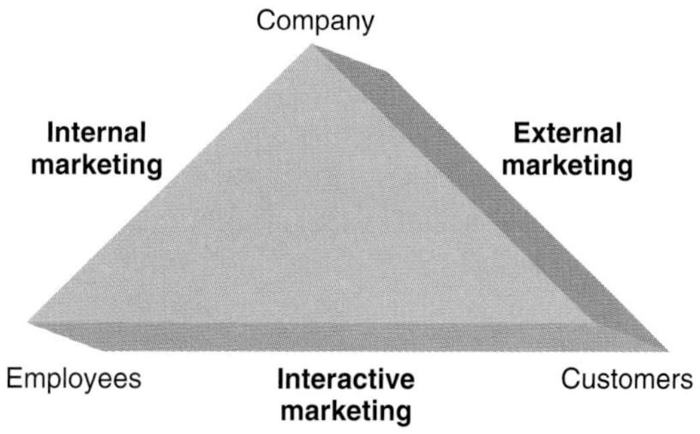

Figure 2-2
Three types of marketing in service industries.

service people to work as a team to provide customer satisfaction. For the firm to deliver consistently high service quality, everyone must practice a customer orientation. It is not enough to have a marketing department doing traditional marketing while the rest of the company goes its own way. Marketers also must get everyone else in the organization to practice marketing. In fact, internal marketing must precede external marketing. In Chapter 10 we discuss internal marketing.

Interactive marketing means that perceived service quality depends heavily on the quality of the buyer–seller interaction during the service encounter. In product marketing, product quality often depends little on how the product is obtained. But in services of marketing, service quality depends on both the service deliverer and the quality of the delivery. The customer judges service quality not just on technical quality (the quality of the food) but also on its functional quality (the service provided in the restaurant). Service employees have to master interactive marketing skills or functions as well.[9]

ARAMARK provides a good example of using technology to aid interactive marketing. ARAMARK decided to improve its food service to hospitals by creating a propriety database that tracks patient preferences individually, by hospital, regionally, and nationally. The accumulated information is immediately analyzed, and the database is updated. Future meal offerings are then based on the analysis. ARAMARK cannot rely on technology alone; the interaction of employees and customers is an important part of the hospitality businesses. ARAMARK cannot forget this high-touch component of the business. For the high-touch part of the equation, ARAMARK's kitchen staffers have been transformed into "hosts" through forty-hour training sessions that teach them to be courteous, efficient, and fast. ARAMARK combines high-tech and high-touch when the trained hosts deliver customized meals from carts preloaded according to database information on patient preferences. Using this system, ARAMARK slashed meal delivery time from twenty-four hours to two minutes. With better service, ARAMARK boosted patient satisfaction from 84 percent.[10]

2.4 ARAMARK
Marriott
Ritz-Carlton

Today, as competition and costs increase, and as productivity and quality decrease, more marketing sophistication is needed. Service companies face the task of increasing three major marketing areas: their competitive differentiation, service quality, and productivity.

Managing Differentiation

In these days of intense price competition, service marketers often complain about the difficulty of differentiating their services from those of competitors. To the extent that customers view the services of different providers as similar, they care less about the provider than the price.

The solution to price competition is to develop a differentiated offer, delivery, and image. The offer can include innovative features that set one company's offer apart from its competitors'. For example, airlines have introduced such innovations as in-flight movies, advance seating, air-to-ground telephone service, and frequent-flyer award programs to differentiate their offers. British Airways even offers international travelers a sleeping compartment, hot showers, and cooked-to-order breakfasts. Unfortunately, most service innovations are copied easily. Still, the service company that innovates regularly usually will gain a succession of temporary advantages and an innovative reputation that may help it keep customers who want to go with the best.

2.5 British Airways
Hyatt

Service companies can differentiate their service delivery in three ways: through people, physical environment, and process. The company can distinguish itself by having more able and reliable customer-contact people than its competitors, or it can develop a superior physical environment in which the service product is delivered. Finally, it can design a superior delivery process. For example, Hyatt offers its guest a computerized check-in option at some of its hotels. Finally, service companies can also differentiate their images through symbols and branding. For example, a familiar symbol would be McDonald's golden arches, and familiar brands include Hilton, Shangri-La, and Sofitel.

Managing Service Quality

One of the major ways that a service firm can differentiate itself is by delivering consistently higher quality than its competitors. Like manufacturers before them, many service industries have now joined the total quality movement. Many companies are finding that outstanding service quality can give them a potent competitive advantage that leads to superior sales and profit performance. Some firms have become almost legendary for their high-quality service.

The key is to exceed the customers' service-quality expectations. As the chief executive at American Express puts it, "Promise only what you can deliver and deliver more than you promise!" These expectations are based on past experiences, word of mouth, and service firm advertising. If perceived service of a given firm exceeds expected service, customers are apt to use the provider again. Customer retention is perhaps the best measure of quality—a service firm's ability to hang onto its customers depends on how consistently it delivers value to them. Thus, whereas the manufacturer's quality goal might be zero defects, the service provider's goal is zero customer defections.

The service provider needs to identify the expectations of target customers concerning service quality. Unfortunately, service quality is harder to define and judge than product quality. Moreover, although greater service quality results in greater customer satisfaction, it also results in higher costs. Still, investments in service usually pay off through increased customer retention and sales. Whatever the level of service provided, it is important that the service provider clearly define and communicate that level so that its employees know what they must deliver and customers know what they will get.

Many service companies have invested heavily to develop streamlined and efficient service-delivery systems. They want to ensure that customers will receive consistently high-quality service in every service encounter. Unlike product manufacturers who can adjust their machinery and inputs until everything is perfect, service quality will always vary, depending on the interactions between employees and customers. Problems inevitably will occur. As hard as they try, even the best companies will have an occasional late delivery, burned steak, or grumpy employee. However, although a company cannot always prevent service problems, it can learn to recover from them. Good service recovery can turn angry customers into loyal ones. In fact, good recovery can win more customer purchasing and loyalty than if things had gone well in the first place. Therefore, companies should take steps not only to provide good service every time but also to recover from service mistakes when they do occur.

The first step is to empower frontline service employees—to give them the authority, responsibility, and incentives they need to recognize, care about, and tend to customer needs. For example, Marriott has put some 70,000 employees through empowerment training which encourages them to go beyond their normal jobs to solve customer problems. Such empowered employees can act quickly and effectively to keep service problems from resulting in lost customers. The Marriott Desert Springs revised the job description for its customer-contact employees. The major goal of these positions now is to ensure that "our guests experience excellent service and hospitality while staying at our resort." Well-trained employees are given the authority to do whatever it takes, on the spot, to keep guests happy. They are also expected to help management ferret out the cause of guests' problems, and to inform managers of ways to improve overall hotel service and guests' comfort.

2.6 Marriott Desert Springs
MGM Grand Hotel and Casino
Outback Steakhouse
Disney
Swissair

Studies of well-managed service companies show that they share a number of common virtues regarding service quality. First, top service companies are "customer obsessed." They have a distinctive strategy for satisfying customer needs that wins enduring customer loyalty. Second, well-managed service companies have a history of top management commitment to quality. Management at companies such as Marriott, Disney, Delta Airlines, and McDonald's looks not only at financial performance but also at service performance. Third, the best service providers set high service–quality standards. Swissair, for example, aims to have 96 percent or more of its passengers rate its service as good or superior; otherwise, it takes action. The standards must be set appropriately high. A 98 percent accuracy standard may sound good, but using this standard, the MGM Grand Hotel would send fifty guests a day to rooms that are already occupied, the Outback Steak House chain would have hundreds of miscooked steaks, and Forte Hotels would make hundreds of errors in their central reservation office every week. This level of errors would be unacceptable for these companies. Top service companies do not settle merely for "good" service; they aim for 100 percent defect-free service.

Fourth, the top service firms watch service performance closely—both their own and that of competitors. They use methods such as comparison shopping, customer surveys, and suggestions and complaint forms. Good service companies also communicate their concerns about service quality to employees and provide performance feedback. Ritz-Carlton has daily meetings with its employees to go over customer feedback and to review the guest history of arriving guests.

With their costs rising rapidly, service firms are under great pressure to increase service productivity. They can do so in several ways. The service providers can train current employees better, or they can hire new employees who will work harder or more skillfully for the same pay. Or the service providers can increase the quantity of their service by giving up some quality. The provider can "industrialize the service" by adding equipment and standardizing production, as in McDonald's assembly-line approach to fast-food retailing. Commercial dishwashing, jumbo jets, and multiple-unit movie theaters all represent technological expansions of service.

Service providers also can increase productivity by designing more effective services. Many fast-food companies now have the customers get their own drinks. They hand the customer a cup, and the customer gets the ice and drink. Hotels, restaurants, and amusement parks are fitting employees with headsets so that they can maintain constant contact with other employees—increasing their productivity. However, companies must avoid pushing productivity so hard that doing so reduces perceived quality. Some productivity steps help standardize quality, increasing customer satisfaction; other productivity steps lead to too much standardization and can rob consumers of customized service. Attempts to industrialize a service or to cut costs can make a service company more

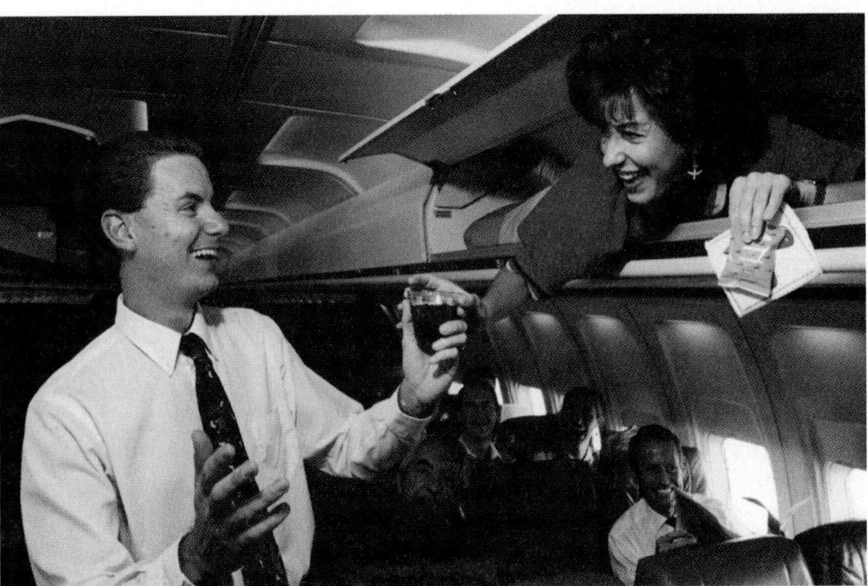

Southwest Airlines creates happy customers, which creates happy employees. Courtesy of David Woo.

efficient in the short run but reduce its longer-run ability to innovate, maintain service quality, or respond to consumer needs and desires. In some cases, service providers accept reduced productivity in order to create more service differentiation or quality.

Tangibilizing the Product

Service marketers should take steps to provide their prospective customers with evidence that will help tangibilize the service.[11] Promotional material, employees' appearance, and the service firm's physical environment all help tangibilize service. A hotel's promotional material might include a meeting planner's packet, containing photographs of the hotel's public area, guest rooms, and meeting space. The packet would also contain floor plans of the meeting space, including room capacities for the different types of setups, to help the meeting planner visualize the meeting space.

A banquet salesperson for a fine restaurant can make the product tangible by taking pastry samples on morning sales calls. This creates goodwill and provides the prospective client with some knowledge about the restaurant's food quality. The salesperson might also bring a photo album showing photographs of banquet setups, plate presentations for different entrees, and testimonial letters from past clients. For persons having a dinner as part of their wedding reception, some hotels will prepare the meal for the bride's family before the wedding day. Thus, the bride gets to actually experience the food before the reception, so there are no surprises.

The salesperson may be the prospective customer's first contact with that business. A salesperson who is well groomed and dressed appropriately and who answers questions in a prompt professional manner can do a great deal to help the customer develop a positive image of the hotel. Uniforms also provide tangible evidence of the experience. The uniforms

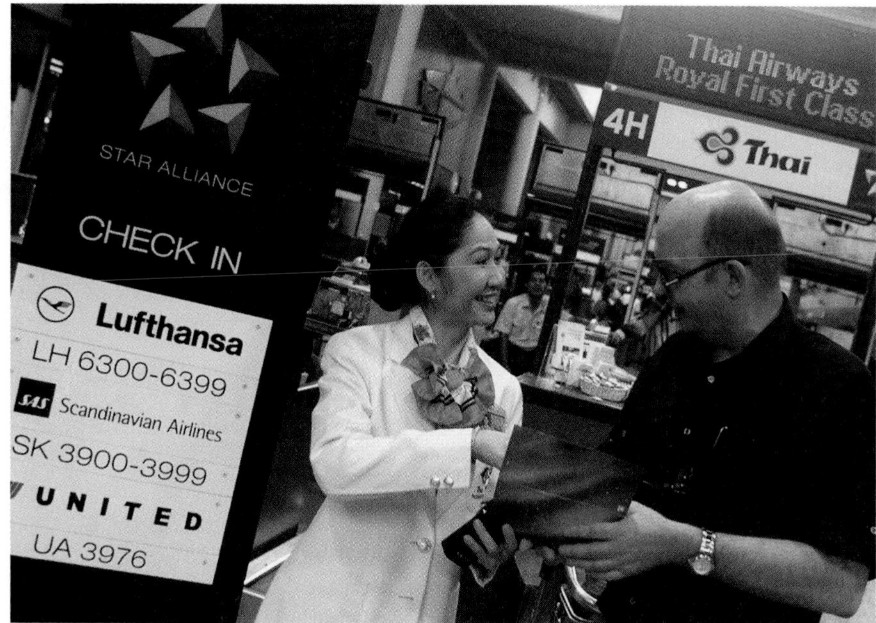

Uniforms provide tangible evidence that the persons delivering the experience are professional.

Marketing Highlight 2-1

Ritz-Carlton: Taking Care of Those Who Take Care of Customers

Ritz-Carlton, a chain of over fifty luxury hotels renowned for outstanding service, caters to the top 5 percent of corporate and leisure travelers. The company's credo sets lofty customer-service goals: "The Ritz-Carlton Hotel is a place where the genuine care and comfort of our guests is our highest mission. We pledge to provide the finest personal service and facilities for our guests, who will always enjoy a warm, relaxed, yet refined ambience. The Ritz-Carlton experience enlivens the senses, instills well-being, and fulfills even the unexpressed wishes and needs of our guests."

The credo is more than just words on paper—Ritz-Carlton delivers on its promises. In surveys of departing guests, some 95 percent report that they've had a truly memorable experience. In fact, at Ritz-Carlton, exceptional service encounters have become almost commonplace. Take the experiences of Nancy and Harvey Heffner of Manhattan, who stayed at the Ritz-Carlton in Naples, Florida. As reported in the *New York Times:* "The hotel is elegant and beautiful," Mrs. Heffner said, "but more important is the beauty expressed by the staff. They can't do enough to please you." When the couple's son became sick last year in Naples, the hotel staff brought him hot tea with honey at all hours of the night, she said. When Mr. Heffner had to fly home on business for a day and his return flight was delayed, a driver for the hotel waited in the lobby most of the night. Such personal, high-quality service has also made the Ritz-Carlton a favorite among conventioneers. Comments one convention planner, "They not only treat us like kings when we hold our top-level meetings in their hotels, but also we just never get any complaints."

In 1991, Ritz-Carlton received 121 quality-related awards, along with the industry-best rankings by all three hotel-rating organizations. In 1992, it became the first hotel company to win the Malcolm Baldrige National Quality Award. More important, service quality has resulted in high customer retention: more than 90 percent of Ritz-Carlton customers return. Despite its hefty $150 average room rate, the chain enjoys a 70 percent occupancy rate, almost nine points above the industry average. Most of the responsibility for keeping guests satisfied falls to Ritz-Carlton's customer-contact employees. Thus, the hotel chain takes great care in selecting its personnel. "We want only people who care about people," notes Patrick Mene, the company's vice president of quality. Once selected, employees are given intensive training in the art of coddling customers. New employees attend a two-day orientation in which top management drums into them the "20 Ritz-Carlton Basics." Basic number one: "The Credo will be known, owned, and energized by all employees."

Employees are taught to do everything they can never to lose a guest. "There's no negotiating at Ritz-Carlton when it comes to solving customer problems," says Mene. Staff learn that anyone who receives a customer complaint owns that complaint until it's resolved. They are trained to drop whatever they're doing to help a customer—no matter what they're doing or what their department. Ritz-Carlton

---

worn by stewards and stewardesses on BMI Midland Airlines are neat and professional looking.

Everything about a hospitality company communicates something. The wrappers put on drinking glasses in the guest rooms serve the purpose of letting the guest know that the glasses have been cleaned. The fold in the toilet paper in the bathroom lets the guest know that the bathroom has been tidied. The red and white awnings, the outside patio, and

employees are empowered to handle problems on the spot, without consulting higher-ups. Each employee can spend up to $2,000 to redress a guest grievance, and each is allowed to break from his or her routine for as long as needed to make a guest happy. "We master customer satisfaction at the individual level," adds Mene. "This is our most sensitive listening post . . . our early warning system." Thus, while competitors are still reading guest comment cards to learn about customer problems, Ritz-Carlton has already resolved them.

Ritz-Carlton instills a sense of pride in its employees. "You serve," they are told, "but you are not servants." The company motto states: "We are ladies and gentlemen serving ladies and gentlemen." Employees understand their role in Ritz-Carlton's success. "We might not be able to afford a hotel like this," says Tammy Patton, "but we can make it so people who can afford it want to keep coming here."

And so they do. When it comes to customer satisfaction, no detail is too small. Customer-contact people are taught to greet guests warmly and sincerely, using guests' names when possible. They learn to use proper language when speaking to guests—"Good morning," "Certainly," "I'll be happy to," and "My pleasure," never "Hi" or "How's it going?" The Ritz-Carlton Basics urge employees to escort the guest to another area of the hotel rather than pointing out directions, to answer the phone within three rings and with a "smile," and to take pride and care in personal appearance.

Ritz-Carlton recognizes and rewards employees who perform feats of outstanding service. Under its Five-Star Awards program, outstanding performers are nominated by peers and managers, and winners receive plaques at dinners celebrating their achievements. For on-the-spot recognition, managers award Gold Standard Coupons, redeemable for items in the gift shop and free weekend stays at the hotel. Ritz-Carlton further rewards and motivates its employees with events such as Super Sports Day, an employee talent show, luncheons celebrating employee anniversaries, a family picnic, and special themes in employee dining rooms. As a result, Ritz-Carlton's 25,000 employees appear to be just as satisfied as its customers. Employee turnover is less than 30 percent a year, compared with 45 percent at other luxury hotels. Ritz-Carlton's success is based on a simple philosophy: To take care of customers, you must first take care of those who take care of customers. Satisfied customers, in turn, create sales and profits for the company.

Sources: Quotes from Edwin McDowell, "Ritz-Carlton's Keys to Good Service," *New York Times,* March 31, 1993, p. D1; and Howard Schlossberg, "Measuring Customer Satisfaction Is Easy to Do—Until You Try," *Marketing News,* April 26, 1993, pp. 5, 8. See also Rahul Jacob, "Why Some Customers Are More Equal Than Others," *Fortune,* September 19, 1994, pp. 215–224; Don Peppers, "Digitizing Desire," *Forbes,* April 10, 1995, p. 76; "About Us, Fact Sheet," *http://www.ritzcarlton.com,* accessed November 7, 2001.

the blue-and-white striped building displaying the T.G.I. Friday's sign in large letters are signs to indicate that this restaurant offers informality and fun. A couple looking for an elegant, intimate restaurant would be disappointed at T.G.I. Friday's. T.G.I. Friday's uses their restaurant exterior to select customers that will enjoy the casual dining experience of a Friday's. Similarly, Hampton Inn's exterior appearance suggests to travelers that it will provide clean, comfortable, and safe lodging at a moderate price.

When guests arrive, they find no door or bell clerks, concierge desk, or other features of an upscale hotel. Instead, they find an attentive desk clerk in an appropriate uniform and a small lobby with comfortable but moderate furnishings.

Trade Dress

Hospitality companies have become very sensitive to protecting the distinctive nature of their total visual image and overall appearance; this is known as *trade dress*. McDonald's and Holiday Inn have brought lawsuits against competitors who dared to copy any form of the golden arches or Holiday Inn sign.

2.7 bmi British Midland Airlines
T.G.I. Fridays
Taco Cabana
Burger King

A U.S. court has found that the decor, menu, layout, and style of service of a restaurant was protectable trade dress.[12] The restaurant Taco Cabana sued Two Pesos, Inc., for trade dress infringement under the Lanham Act. Taco Cabana complained that the interior of Two Pesos was too similar to that of Taco Cabana. Similarly, Prufrock Ltd. sued Dixie House Restaurants, claiming that this competitor had copied its concept of a full-service restaurant serving down-home country cooking in a relaxed and informal atmosphere with a full-service bar, using booth seating, small-print wallpaper, antique drop-leaf tables, an exposed kitchen area, antique light fixtures, an antique bar, and country-style wall decor.[13]

Experts in this field have concluded: "It's not a simple matter to know when an operation's total visual image and overall product presentation can be considered exclusive to a particular chain or company." To compete effectively in today's marketplace, an entrepreneur, operator, or owner must design an effective trade dress while taking care not to imitate too closely that of a competitor.[14]

Members of the hospitality industry should not be misled by thinking that protection of trade dress is a worldwide concept. One only has to visit other nations, particularly those in the Third World, to observe that local entrepreneurs commonly copy successful trade dress from other nations. In some cases this makes it impossible for a company to use its own name or trade dress in a foreign nation. For a number of years, Burger King did not have the rights to use this name throughout Australia and instead called its restaurants Hungry Jack.

Managing the Physical Surroundings

Physical evidence that is not managed properly can hurt a business. Negative messages communicated by poorly managed physical evidence include signs that continue to advertise a holiday special two weeks after the holiday has passed, signs with missing letters or burned-out lights, parking lots and grounds that are unkempt and full of trash, and employees in dirty uniforms at messy workstations. Such signs send negative messages to customers. Restaurant managers are trained to do a preopening inspection of the restaurant. One of the things they look for is that all light bulbs are working. A little thing like a burned-out light bulb can give a guest sitting near it an impression that the restaurant does not pay attention to detail.

Physical surroundings should be designed to reinforce the product's position in the customer's mind. The front-desk staff in a luxury hotel should dress in professional apparel wool or wool-blend conservative

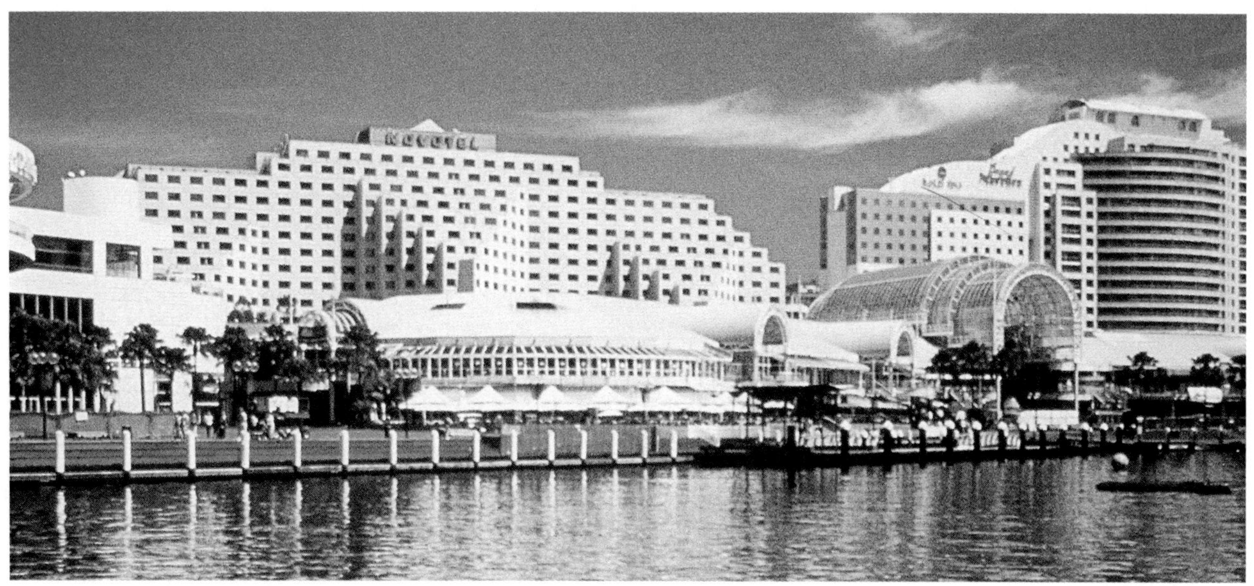

This publicity photo of Accor's ibis, Novotel, and Mercure hotels illustrates the excellent location of these hotels along Sydney's Darling Harbour.

clothes. The front-desk staff at a tropical resort might wear tropical, Hawaiian-style shirts. The counter staff at a fast-food restaurant might wear a simple polyester uniform.

A firm's communications should also reinforce their positioning. Ronald McDonald is great for McDonald's, but a clown would not be appropriate for a Four Seasons hotel. All said, a service organization should

Friday's exterior provides evidence that Friday's is a casual restaurant. Courtesy of T.G.I. Friday's, Inc.

review every piece of tangible evidence to make sure that each delivers the desired **organization image**—the way a person or group views an organization—to target customers.[15]

Stress Advantages of Nonownership

In a service the customer does not have ownership of the product. Lack of ownership, sometimes cited as a major characteristic of a service, can be stressed as a benefit.[16] For example, rather than own corporate lodging and provide a staff to maintain the lodging, corporations are usually better off negotiating a rate with a hotel. The advantages of nonownership in this case include only paying for the rooms when they are used, not having to maintain apartments, having access to capital that is not tied up in the ownership of the lodging facilities, and the extra services provided by the hotel (food and beverage, meeting rooms, and shops).

Managing Employees as Part of the Product

In the hospitality industry, employees are a critical part of the product and marketing mix. This means that the human resources and marketing departments must work closely together. In restaurants without a human resources department, the restaurant manager serves as the human resource manager. The manager must hire friendly and capable employees and formulate policies that support positive relations between employees and guests. Even minor details related to personnel policy can have a significant effect on the product's quality.[17] One fast-food restaurant had a policy that all employees must be off the clock by 10:15 P.M. To implement the policy, employees had to shut down the restaurant starting at 9:40 P.M., even though it advertised that it was open until 10 P.M.

In a well-run hospitality organization, there are two customers, the paying customers and the employees.[18] The task of training and motivating employees to provide good customer service is called internal marketing. In the hospitality industry, it is not enough to have a marketing department focused on traditional marketing to a targeted external market. The job of the marketing department includes encouraging everyone in the organization to practice customer-oriented thinking[19] (see Chapter 10). The following excerpt from *In Search of Excellence* illustrates the importance of well-trained employees in a hospitality operation:

> We had decided, after dinner, to spend a second night in Washington. Our business day had taken us beyond the last convenient flight out. We had no reservations but were near the new Four Seasons, had stayed there once before, and liked it. As we walked through the lobby wondering how best to plead our case for a room, we braced for the usual chilly shoulder accorded to latecomers. To our astonishment, the concierge looked up, smiled, called us by name, and asked how we were. She remembered our names! We knew in a flash why in the space of a brief year the Four Seasons had become the "place to stay" in the District and was a rare first-year holder of the venerated four-star rating.[20]

Points-of-Encounter

Efforts to control consistency in the hospitality industry are sometimes unsuccessful because concentration is not placed on the right areas. In the book *You Can't Lose If the Customer Wins,* Ron Nykiel, a former senior vice president of marketing for Stouffer Hotels, discusses the importance of points-of-encounter.[21]

A **point-of-encounter** is any point at which an employee encounters the customer. This seems simple enough, but let's take an imaginary journey in which we will be staying at the fictitious King's Crown Hotel.

Our flight has landed and we are now standing near the carousels waiting for our luggage. Suddenly, one of us gets the idea to call the hotel on those free phones you find in airports. The purpose of this call is to inform the hotel that we are here and arrange for a pickup in their free airport van.

Encounter Point 1: The Voice on the Phone. Unfortunately, the free phone must have been surplus World War II equipment, as a constant squeal resounds in one's ear. The phone is ringing and ringing and ringing. After what seems like a number of rings equal to the national debt, a voice answers, "Hello!" We wonder if this is the hotel or perhaps Tony's pool hall. Sure enough, after asking, the voice confirms it is the King's Crown Hotel. Before we can say more, the voice says, "Please hold," and bingo, the voice is gone. The squeal is now accompanied by elevator music.

When the voice returns, we state our name and ask if a van can be sent to pick us up. "Just a moment," says the voice and we now hear the phone ringing elsewhere. A voice from reservations now answers and asks why we called. We repeat our message and give our name. "We have you booked for tomorrow. Are you sure you're here?"

We reply we are very much here and in fact the only ones left at the carousel, as the baggage arrived sometime during the previous decade. After considerable discussion, we are told that we can have a room, but all the nonsmoking ones are gone. Fortunately, there is one available smoking room since the previous guest just died of emphysema, leaving available space.

We are then instructed to proceed to Section 32E across the street from Terminal 2 and through an unlit alley to the van loading area. Fortunately, no one is mugged as we backpack our way to this area and proceed to wait. By this time there is a constant cold drizzle, and the van waiting area is free of anything that resembles a roof.

Encounter Point 2: Our Delightful Driver. Twenty-nine-and-a-half minutes later the van arrives. A nonuniformed individual of questionable gender informs us that someone forgot to tell (him/her?) that passengers were waiting until just now so (he/she) cannot be blamed for being late. Mr. or Ms. driver threw a bad disc out of joint yesterday, so we place our own bags in the van. Upon arriving at the hotel, we also unload the bags, but find our driver waiting with palm up.

Encounter Point 3: The Invisible Bell Cap. Thirty centimeters before dragging ourselves to the front desk, a uniformed bell cap emerges from thin air and attempts to "debag" us. Having dragged tonnage this far, we

A well-trained employee with a positive attitude toward customers can be one of the company's most important product attributes. Courtesy of the Jamaica Tourist Board.

reject the offer only to be given that look of "miserable low-class skinflints."

Encounter Point 4: The Front Desk. The bell cap is not the only person to emerge suddenly, as now a Convention of Royal Muskrats of Muskeyon races in front of us to the only desk clerk on duty. Forty-seven-and-six-tenths minutes later, it is our turn.

You guessed it! Reservation somehow did not relay the message that we were coming and the body still has not been removed from that single remaining smoke-filled room. Suddenly, the desk clerk asks if we don't love the appearance of the lobby, which was just renovated with pure gold at a cost of $365 million. One or both of us is now being escorted to police headquarters for attempted strangulation of a desk clerk.

Contrast this to the experience Ron Nykiel claims is commonly accorded to top management and owners. "Picture the hotel executive being met at the airport and whisked off in the hotel's limo, bypassing vans and cabs. He then bypasses the front desk by being taken to his room by a member of the hotel's management team. I could go on to describe the prompt room service and the superb gourmet meal, all the way to bypassing the infamous check-out counter."[22]

Members of management do not purposely neglect points-of-encounter; they simply do not see them. Points-of-encounter are so familiar they become invisible. In far too many cases, management and owners are concerned with features such as the lobby. The owners of a Singapore hotel reportedly spent over $1 million on a staircase railing leading to the mezzanine.

Elegant features are nice, but do not rank in guest importance to encounter points. Encounter point service can be improved only if such points are recognized and experienced by management or their representatives, such as "mystery guests."

Managing Perceived Risk

Customers who buy hospitality products experience some anxiety because they cannot experience the product beforehand.[23] Consider a salesperson who is asked by her sales manager to set up a regional sales meeting. Suppose that the salesperson has never set up a meeting or worked with hotels. The salesperson is obviously nervous. If the meeting goes well, the sales manager will be favorably impressed; if it goes badly, the salesperson may be blamed.

In arranging for the meeting place, the salesperson has to trust the hotel's salesperson. Good hotel salespeople will alleviate client fears by letting them know that they have arranged hundreds of successful meetings. The salesperson's claims to professionalism can be affirmed through letters of praise from former clients and a tour of the hotel's facilities. A salesperson must reduce client fear and gain the client's confidence.

One way of combating concern is to encourage the client to try the hotel or restaurant in a low-risk situation. Hotels and resorts offer familiarization (or fam) trips to meeting planners and travel agents. Airlines often offer complimentary flight tickets because they are also interested in creating business. Hotels provide rooms, food, beverage, and entertainment at no cost to the prospective client in the hope that this exposure will encourage them to recommend the hotel. Fam trips reduce a product's intangibility by letting the intermediary customer experience the hotel beforehand.

The high risk that people perceive when purchasing hospitality products increases loyalty to companies that have provided them with a consistent product in the past. Crowne Plaza attracted their competitor's loyal customers by using the following tactic: Guests were billed at the regular room rate. However, they were free to pay less if they felt the accommodations and service were not worth the price. The promotion was highly successful, attracting a number of new guests, almost all of whom paid the full rate.

Managing Capacity and Demand

Because services are perishable, managing capacity and demand is a key function of hospitality marketing. For example, Mother's Day is traditionally a restaurant's busiest day of the year, with the peak time at brunch from 11 A.M. to 2 P.M. This three-hour period presents restaurateurs with one of the greatest sales opportunities during the year. To take full advantage of this opportunity, restaurant managers must accomplish two things: First, they must adjust their operating systems to enable the business to operate at maximum capacity. Second, they must remember that their goal is to create satisfied customers.

Many restaurants feature buffets on Mother's Day to increase capacity. An attractive buffet creates a festive atmosphere, provides an impression of variety and value, and expedites service by eliminating the need to prepare food to order. Customers provide their own service, with the service staff providing the beverage and check, which frees the staff to wait on more customers. Buffets eliminate the time required for order taking and preparing the order. Food is available when customers arrive,

BARBADOS
Making your vacation
the best it can be.

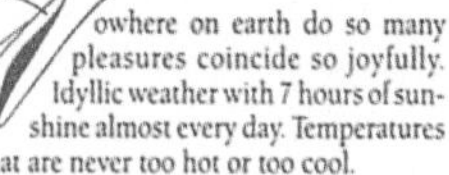

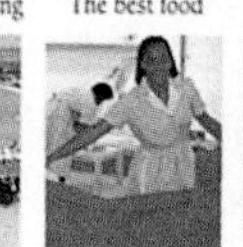

The best sailing
The best hotels
The best service
The best sports

Nowhere on earth do so many pleasures coincide so joyfully. Idyllic weather with 7 hours of sunshine almost every day. Temperatures that are never too hot or too cool.
Watersports on, in and under the sea. Beaches from the white sands on the Caribbean to the surf of the Atlantic.
Food from haute cuisine to local Barbadian. Shopping from the internationally sophisticated to local crafts.
Hotels from the luxurious to the simple. And everywhere our island's passion for friendly service.
Nothing has been left to chance in our quest to make your vacation the best it can be.
Call your travel agent today or for information and brochures,
call: U.S.A. 1-800-221-9831
Canada 1-800-268-9122

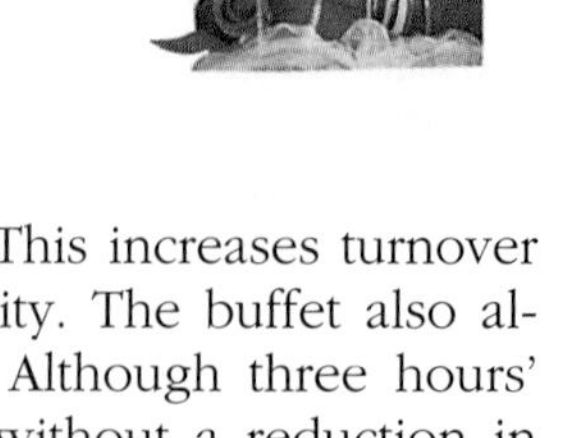

This advertisement for Barbados reduces a potential customer's perceived risk by stressing the consistency of its weather, the variety of activities available, good food, and the friendly characteristics of its people. Pictures in the advertisement provide tangible evidence of these features. Courtesy of Barbados Tourism Authority and D'Arcy, Masius, Benton, & Bowles.

allowing them to start eating almost immediately. This increases turnover of tables, further increasing the restaurant's capacity. The buffet also allows the restaurant to create a buffer inventory. Although three hours' worth of food cannot be kept on a steam table without a reduction in quality and attractiveness, the food can be cooked in batches that will last twenty to thirty minutes.

A few restaurants, such as Boomerangs of Steamboat Springs, expect guests to prepare their own entrees. Guests select a cut of meat and grill it over a charcoal grill. They also help themselves to the salad bar.

Good cafeterias such as K&W of North Carolina remain successful and popular because they manage inventory very well. Food is moderately priced, fresh, and selected to meet ordinary food preferences, such as roast beef and chicken pot pie, not specialty interests such as Indian curry.

How can a hotel prepare for an expected low-occupancy period? Suppose that the hotel projects a two-week period of low occupancy six months from now. One system is to reduce staff and other expenses when the period arrives, including arranging for the staff to take its holidays during the period. This, however, creates service problems. A more proactive move is to book extra corporate business during this period. Corporate group meetings are generally booked one to six months in advance, and national associations may book one to six years prior to the event. The sales manager may reassign a salesperson from association groups to corporate groups, thus putting more emphasis on a market with a high probability of producing business during the predicted soft spot. Hotels can also use this period for FAM trips and public relations in which members of the press, such as travel writers and food section reporters, can be invited to the hotel.

When hotels operate near capacity or restaurants are hit with a sudden influx of guests, problems are likely to occur. Research has shown that customer complaints increase when service firms operate above 80 percent of their capacity.[24] A restaurant may seat more customers than its service staff and kitchen can handle, which results in a negative guest experience. Guests may not return and may spread bad word of mouth to potential customers. Balancing demand and capacity is critical to success in the hospitality business (see Chapter 11).

Managing Consistency

Consistency is one of the key factors in the success of a service business.[25] Consistency means that customers will receive the expected product without unwanted surprises. In the hotel industry, this means that a wake-up call requested for 7 A.M. will occur as planned and that coffee ordered for a 3 P.M. meeting break will be ready and waiting. In the restaurant business, consistency means that the shrimp scampi will taste the same way it tasted two weeks ago, towels will always be available in the bathrooms, and the brand of vodka specified last week will be in stock next month.

Consistency seems like a logical and simple task to accomplish, but in reality it is elusive. Many factors work against consistency. The company's policy may not be clear. For example, one employee of an American plan hotel may credit a guest for a missed meal, while another refuses to do so on the grounds that the guest purchased a package and there are no refunds for unused parts of the package.

Company policies and procedures often unintentionally create service inconsistency. The purchasing manager may order a new brand of vodka or switch seafood suppliers to reduce costs. The effect of such a change on the shrimp scampi or guest satisfaction in the cocktail lounge may be immediate and negate the savings on the purchase order.

A corporate customer of a Sheraton Hotel in Dallas booked a successful conference for over 100 people, appreciated the hotel's service, and called two years later to rebook the same conference. The client had paid all bills promptly and expected the hotel's sales staff to respond accordingly. Instead, the client was told that a strict financial and room numbers guarantee was essential. The client explained that such a guarantee was not required two years ago and that conference participants always made their own room bookings, so the client could not assume responsibility for "no shows" but would assume responsibility as before for banquets and coffee breaks. In response, the client was told that a new sales manager was now in charge and required adherence to corporate policies. Sheraton lost that account! A competitive hotel was willing to bend corporate policy for the business after calling the Sheraton in Dallas to check on the credit worthiness of the client and being told that the client had an excellent rating.

Fluctuating demand can affect consistency. If a busload of high school students arrives at a fast-food restaurant two minutes before a family of three, no matter how well the restaurant is managed, employees will not be able to deliver good service to the family. Although it is impossible to eliminate variability completely, managers should strive to develop as consistent a product as possible. Today's customers are knowledgeable and have come to expect and demand consistency.

Overview of Service Characteristics: The Servuction Model

The term *servuction* was developed to describe a production system for services. The servuction model (see Figure 2-3) provides a good summary of the service characteristics mentioned in this chapter.

Interaction between Customer A and Customer B

Douglas Hoffman and John Bateson provide this story of how one customer cleared all the other customers out of a fast-food restaurant.[26]

> While eating at a fast-food restaurant, a customer was startled when his wife clutched her chest and exclaimed, "Don't look, don't look!" Believing that his wife was experiencing some sort of cardiac difficulty, the customer hastily inquired about the reason for the horrific expression now apparent on his wife's face. Still clutching her chest, she explained, "Somebody is getting sick over there. . . . " Upon hearing this unappetizing news, the husband's eyes fixated upon his wife's eyes as they both froze for an instant, deciding on their next course of action.

In this case, customer B had indeed made a significant impact on all the restaurant's customers. This particular customer B's actions cleared the entire restaurant in under sixty seconds. Particularly frustrating for the restaurant, it could not have foreseen the "upcoming event" and minimized its consequences. Even though the restaurant had no control over customer B's actions, the event profoundly influenced the husband and wife's future purchase intentions. The couple was unable to eat in any of the restaurant's franchises for more than a year and a half.

In some cases we can manage the interaction of customers. For example, exclusive restaurants may discourage children by not having children's menus. Restaurant managers sometimes have to contend with loud drunks who may ruin the dining experience for other customers. The

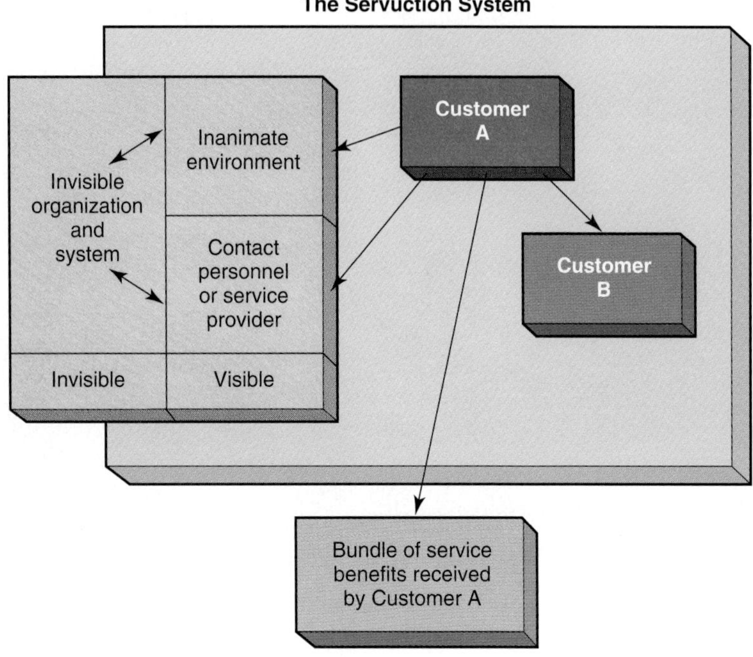

Figure 2-3
The servuction model.
Source: E. Langeard, J. Bateson, C. Lovelock, and P. Eiglier, *Marketing of Services: New Insights from Consumers and Managers,* Report No. 81-104, Cambridge, MA: Marketing Science Institute, 1981.

interaction of customers can also be positive. Guests at resorts often share information on things to do in the area with other guests. In these cases management wants to encourage interaction between the guests.

Contact Personnel

The model shows the inseparability of the employee and the customer from the service delivery system. The arrow from customer A to the contact personnel shows that the contact personnel will have a direct impact on the satisfaction of customer A. This could be positive if the employee performs well or it could be negative if the employee performs poorly. Chapter 10 is devoted to internal marketing, marketing directed toward employees, including contact personnel.

Inanimate Environment

The inanimate environment consists of all the physical elements other than employees and customers that are present during the service encounter. The inanimate environment provides tangible evidence and can be used to provide a point of differentiation. McDonald's makes sure that all of its restaurants are clean, which helps to tangibilize that it is a well-run restaurant chain. Ritz-Carlton hotels use original artwork to tangibilize that it is an upscale hotel chain. Entertainment-themed restaurants such as All Star Café, Hard Rock Café, and Planet Hollywood create a unique atmosphere that differentiates the restaurants from their competitors. The Hyatt Regency originally used atrium lobbies as a point of differentiation. This was later copied by other hotels.

2.8 All Star Café
Hard Rock Café
Planet Hollywood

Rainforest Cafe uses ambiance to create the sights, sounds, and aromas of a tropical rainforest. Courtesy of Rainforest Cafe, a wild place to shop and eat®.

The Invisible Organization and System

The physical environment, the customers, and the employees will be visible to customer A. In a restaurant the kitchen may not be visible unless the restaurant has an exhibition kitchen. If a restaurant decides to use an exhibition kitchen, it is critical that the kitchen and the employees be meticulously clean and professional in appearance. This is often very difficult to maintain continuously. Many chefs refuse to work in such an atmosphere. They view themselves as professionals, not actors on a stage. One of the choices in developing a service system is to decide what the customer should see. Some restaurants are designed so that the customer's first view upon entering is employees making fresh pasta or tortillas. Instead of hiding this food production in the kitchen, it is brought out front to help demonstrate the freshness of the restaurant's food. When planning, a service organization management must decide what they want the guest to see and what they what to keep out of the guest's vision. The servuction model shows that the service outcome is influenced by a host of highly variable elements.

Key Terms

Interactive marketing Marketing by a service firm that recognizes that perceived service quality depends heavily on the quality of buyer–seller interaction.

Internal marketing Marketing by a service form to train effectively and motivate its customer-contact employees and all the supporting service people to work as a team to provide customer satisfaction.

Organization image The way a person or group views an organization.

Physical evidence Tangible clues such as promotional material, employees of the firm, and the physical environment of the firm. Physical evidence is used by a service firm to make its product more tangible to customers.

Point-of-encounter Any point at which an employee encounters the customer.

Service culture A system of values and beliefs in an organization that reinforces the idea that providing the customer with quality service is the principal concern of the business.

Service intangibility A major characteristic of services; they cannot be seen, tasted, felt, heard, or smelled before they are bought.

Service inseparability A major characteristic of services; they are produced and consumed at the same time and cannot be separated from their providers, whether the providers are people or machines.

Service perishability A major characteristic of services; they cannot be stored for later use.

Service variability A major characteristic of services; their quality may vary greatly, depending on who provides them and when, where, and how they are provided.

Service-profit chain A model that shows the relationships between employee satisfaction, customer satisfaction, customer retention, value creation, and profitability.

Trade dress Hospitality companies total visual image and overall appearance.

Chapter Review

I. The Service Culture. The service culture focuses on serving and satisfying the customer. The service culture has to start with top management and flow down.

II. Four Characteristics of Services

1) Intangibility. Unlike physical products, services cannot be seen, tasted, felt, heard, or smelled before they are purchased. To reduce uncertainty caused by intangibility, buyers look for tangible evidence that will provide information and confidence about the service.

2) Inseparability. In most hospitality services, both the service provider and the customer must be present for the transaction to occur. Customer-contact employees are part of the product. Inseparability also means that customers are part of the product. The third implication of inseparability is that customers and employees must understand the service delivery system.

3) Variability. Service quality depends on who provides the services and when and where they are provided. Services are produced and consumed simultaneously. Fluctuating demand makes it difficult to deliver consistent products during periods of peak demand. The high degree of contact between the service provider and the guest means that product consistency depends on the service provider's skills and performance at the time of the exchange.

4) **Perishability.** Services cannot be stored. If service providers are to maximize revenue, they must manage capacity and demand because they cannot carry forward unsold inventory.

III. Management Strategies for Service Businesses

1) **Tangibilizing the service product.** Promotional material, employees' appearance, and the service firm's physical environment all help tangibilize service.

a) **Trade dress.** Trade dress is the distinctive nature of a hospitality industry's total visual image and overall appearance. To compete effectively, an entrepreneur, operator, or owner must design an effective trade dress while taking care not to imitate too closely that of a competitor.

b) **Employee uniform and costumes.** Uniforms and costumes are common to the hospitality industry. These have a legitimate and useful role in differentiating one hospitality firm from another and for instilling pride in the employees.

c) **Physical surroundings.** Physical surroundings should be designed to reinforce the product's position in the customer's mind. A firm's communications should also reinforce their positioning.

d) **"Greening" of the hospitality industry.** The use of outside natural landscaping and inside use of light and plants has become a popular method of creating differentiation and tangibilizing the product.

2) **Managing employees.** In the hospitality industry, employees are a critical part of the product and marketing mix. The human resource and marketing department must work closely together.

a) **Internal marketing.** The task of internal marketing to employees involves the effective training and motivation of customer-contact employees and supporting service personnel.

3) **Managing perceived risk.** The high risk that people perceive when purchasing hospitality products increases loyalty to companies that have provided them with a consistent product in the past.

4) **Managing capacity and demand.** Because services are perishable, managing capacity and demand is a key function of hospitality marketing. First, services must adjust their operating systems to enable the business to operate at maximum capacity. Second, they must remember that their goal is to create satisfied customers. Research has shown that customer complaints increase when service firms operate above 80 percent of their capacity.

5) **Managing consistency.** Consistency means that customers will receive the expected product without unwanted surprises.

Discussion Questions

1. Illustrate how a hotel, restaurant, or theater can deal with the intangibility, inseparability, variability, and perishability of the service it provides. Give specific examples.
2. Wendy's serves its hamburgers "fresh off the grill." This assures high quality but creates leftover burgers if the staff overestimates the demand. Wendy's solves this problem by using the meat in chili, tacos, and spaghetti sauce. Relate how airlines solve the perishability of unsold seats. Give additional examples of perishability and how service firms address it.
3. Discuss how the service person in a restaurant is part of the product the customer receives when purchasing a meal.
4. What are some common management practices that restaurants use to provide a consistent product?
5. What are internal and interactive marketing? Give an example of how a specific firm or organization might use these concepts to increase the effectiveness of its services. How might these concepts be linked to services differentiation?

Experiential Exercises

Do one of the following:

1. Perishability is very important in the airline industry; unsold seats are gone forever, and too many unsold seats mean large losses. With computerized ticketing, airlines can easily use pricing to deal with perishability and variations in demand.
   - **a.** Go to the Web site of an airline and get a fare for an eight-day stay between two cities they serve. Get prices on the same route for sixty days in advance, two weeks, one week, and tomorrow. Is there a clear pattern to the fares?
   - **b.** When a store is overstocked on ripe fruit, it may lower the price to sell out quickly. What are airlines doing to their prices as the seats get close to "perishing"? Why are tomorrow's fares often higher?
2. Visit a restaurant or a hotel. Observe and record how they manage their customers. This could include how they get them to move through the hotel, stand in line, or throw their trash away in a hotel. Write what you think the business does well and what it does poorly. Explain your answer.
3. Visit a restaurant or hotel and give an example of how they use tangible evidence to tell the customer what type of business they are and how they are run. Things to look at include the exterior of the business, the inside of the business, signage, and employee uniforms. Write what you think the business does well and what it does poorly. Explain your answer.

INTERNET EXERCISES

Support for this exercise can be found on the Web site for *Marketing for Hospitality and Tourism*, www.prenhall.com/kotler.

A. Visit the Web site of a hotel chain. What does the Web site do to make the product tangible for the customer? Is there anything in the site that deals with the characteristic of perishables, for example, specials at some of the properties?

B. Visit the Web site of a tourism destination; it can either be a city or a country. Explain how the site provides tangible evidence relating to the experiences a visitor to the destination can expect.

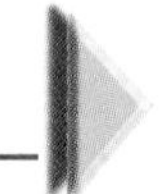

REFERENCES

1. See CIA (2000), *The World Factbook 2000*, GDP composition by sector, pp.1–24; *http://www.odci.gov/cia/publications/fa...fields/gdp_-_composition_by_sector/hmtl,* August 23, 2001; and Raymond Fisk, Stephen J. Grove, and Joby John, *Interactive Services Marketing* (Boston: Interactive Services Marketing, 2000).
2. Earl W. Sasser, R. Paul Olsen, and Daryl Wycoff, *Management of Service Operations* (Boston, MA: Allyn and Bacon, 1978).
3. See Karl Albrecht, *At America's Service* (Homewood, IL: Dow Jones Irwin, 1988). See also Karl Albrecht and Ron Zemke, *Service America!* (Homewood, IL: Dow Jones Irwin, 1985).
4. Robert C. Lewis and Richard E. Chambers, *Marketing Leadership in Hospitality* (New York: Van Nostrand Reinhold, 1989).
5. Bruce Serlen, "Call Conference Centers Up on Your Computer," *Business Travel Management* 5, no. 6 (June 1993): 42–44.
6. Robert C. Ford and Cherrill P. Heaton, "Managing Your Guest as a Quasi-Employee," *Cornell Hotel and Restaurant Administration Quarterly* 42, no. 2 (April 2001): 46–61.
7. Carol Krol: "Case Study: Club Med Uses E-Mail to Pitch Unsold, Discounted Packages," *Advertising Age* (December 14, 1998): 40.
8. See James L. Heskett, Thomas O. Jones, Gary W. Loveman, W. Earl Sasser, Jr., and Leonard A. Schlesinger, "Putting the Service-Profit Chain to Work," *Harvard Business Review* (March–April 1994): 164–174.
9. For more reading on internal and interactive marketing, see Christian Gronroos, "A Service Quality Model and Its Marketing Implications," *European Journal of Marketing* 18, no. 4 (1984): 36–44; and Leonard Berry, Edwin F. Lefkowith, and Terry Clark, "In Services, What's in a Name?" *Harvard Business Review* (September–October 1988): 28–30.
10. Marlene Piturro, "Getting a Charge Out of Service," *Sales & Marketing Management* (November 1998): 86–91.
11. G. Lynn Shostack, "Breaking Free from Product Marketing," *Journal of Marketing* (April 1977): 73–80.
12. Jeanna Abbott and Joseph Lanza, "Trade Dress: Legal Interpretations of What Constitutes Distinctive Appearance," *Cornell Hotel and Restaurant Administration Quarterly* 35, no. 1 (February 1994): 54.
13. Ibid., p. 56.
14. Ibid., p. 58.
15. Bernard H. Booms and Mary J. Bitner, "Marketing Services by Managing the Environment," *Cornell Hotel and Restaurant Administration Quarterly* 23, no. 1 (May 1982): 35–39.
16. Donald W. Cowell, *The Marketing of Services* (London: William Heinemann, 1984).
17. Richard Normann, *Service Management: Strategy and Leadership in Service Businesses* (New York: John Wiley & Sons, 1984).
18. See Karl Albrecht, *At America's Service* (Homewood, IL: Dow Jones Irwin, 1988).
19. See Leonard Berry, "Big Ideas in Services Marketing," in *Creativity in Services Marketing*, ed. M. Venkatesan et al. (Chicago: American Marketing Association, 1986), pp. 6–8.
20. Thomas J. Peters and Robert H. Waterman, Jr., *In Search of Excellence* (New York: Warner Books, 1922), p. xv.
21. Ronald A. Nykiel, *You Can't Lose If the Customer Wins* (Stanford, CT: Long Meadow Press, 1990).
22. Ibid., p. 19.
23. See Valarie A. Zeithaml, "How Consumer Evaluation Processes Differ between Goods and Services," in *Marketing of Services*, ed. James H. Donnelly and William George (Chicago: American Marketing Association, 1981), pp. 186–190.

24. Mary J. Bitner, Jody D. Nyquist, and Bernard H. Booms, "The Critical Incident as a Technique for Analyzing the Service Encounter," in *Services Marketing in a Changing Environment*, ed. Thomas M. Bloch et al. (Chicago: American Marketing Association, 1985), pp. 48–51; Robert C. Lewis and Susan V. Morris, "The Positive Side of Guest Complaints," *Cornell Hotel and Restaurant Quarterly* 27, no. 4 (February 1987): 13–15.

25. Diane Schanlensee, Kenneth L. Bernhardt, and Nancy Gust, "Keys to Successful Services Marketing: Customer Orientation, Creed, Consistency," in *Services Marketing in a Changing Environment*, ed. Thomas Bloch et al. (Chicago: American Marketing Association, 1985), pp. 15–18.

26. K. Douglas Hoffman and John E. G. Bateson, *Essentials of Services Marketing* (Fort Worth, TX: Dryden Press, 1997), p. 10.

3 The Role of Marketing in Strategic Planning

"Would you tell me, please, which way I ought to go from here?" said Alice.
"That depends a good deal on where you want to get to," said Cheshire Cat.
Lewis Carroll (*Alice in Wonderland*)

Inn on Biltmore Estate

The Inn on Biltmore Estate was designed to be a four-star hotel and one of the finest hotels in the southeastern United States. Competitors were The Greenbrier (West Virginia), Homestead (Virginia), Pinehurst (North Carolina), and Chateau Elan (Georgia). The opening date was set for March 2001. Stephanie Williams, director of Hotel Sales, and Randy Fluharty, senior vice president, had been planning the development and opening of the Inn for more than a year. Even the smallest of details were considered.

The Inn

The Inn would be the first and only lodging on the property of the Biltmore Estate. The magnificent French Renaissance Chateau mansion was advertised as "America's Largest Home." The Chateau serves as a museum with a curator. It is fully furnished and is viewed by hundreds of thousands of visitors each year, but it is not used for lodging or for the serving of food and beverage. Encompassing 8,000 acres in the Blue Ridge Mountains of North Carolina near Asheville, the estate consists of the Chateau, a vineyard, three restaurants, an ice cream parlor, a bake shop, and a spectacular flower garden; now it would have an inn with 222 guest rooms and suites to match its splendor. Stephanie and Randy believed that many transient visitors would come to the inn from the 900,000 annual paid visitors to the estate.

They expected to position the Inn as a weekend and holiday transient vacation property but with the added attraction of conference/seminar facilities designed with the midweek corporate guest in mind. The Inn's restaurant would feature classic cuisine: estate-raised beef, lamb, veal, and trout, as well as seasonal fruits, vegetables, and herbs.

The hotel site had been carefully selected to offer views of a meadow and mountain from one side and of downtown Asheville from the other. It was situated so as not to be seen from the Chateau. It was designed as a totally nonsmoking hotel with a covered area outside for smokers.

Nearby walking trails traverse woodland and ridges. A heated outdoor pool and optional sporting activities were planned to offer guests the ability to experience the mountain environment.

Corporate Business

Seminar and conference guests were expected to come from Charlotte, Raleigh, Greensboro, Atlanta, and Tennessee cities such as Knoxville. The Inn was planned to accommodate business meetings, corporate retreats, and small group functions. Two boardrooms, two banquet rooms, and a reception salon can comfortably accommodate groups of up to 144 people.

Planning

The hotel would not be affiliated with a chain such as Marriott or Hyatt so those responsible for planning did not have the benefit of a corporate planning department. Rooms were to be priced on a Modified American Plan (MAP) and would include afternoon tea, breakfast, parking, and gratuities. Prices were expected to range from \$300–\$500 per room per night. This placed the hotel at a premium position within the Asheville market. Stephanie said that the internal mission of the staff was to eventually position the hotel as a destination without overshadowing the Chateau, which would remain the principal feature of the estate.

Planning toward this goal meant that every detail had to be considered. Two test guest rooms had been built in a storage area in Asheville. Although the water was not connected, in all other respects the test rooms looked identical to future guest rooms. Details such as drapery, bed spreads, and the armoire were carefully studied in these test rooms. The designer and suppliers worked closely with the Inn's staff.

Stephanie had been working with travel media writers such as those from Southern Living Magazine *to create preopening knowledge and excitement among the travel-receptive public. She had also been working with staff members responsible for marketing the estate.*

The estate had a key customer pass holder program which allowed unlimited pass privileges to the property. This database contained over 49,000 pass holder names and addresses, 90 percent of whom lived outside the Asheville area. The reservation center for the estate reported that over 60 percent of those who called for information did not have lodging reservations. In fact, the Estate served as a broker for area hotels, but none of these approached the quality and price of the new Inn. Therefore, Stephanie did not see this as a problem. The reservations center agents could be trained to first attempt to sell the Inn and then offer a lesser-priced alternative if the caller showed heavy price resistance.

A problem that had to be reconciled was that of gate passes for friends and relatives of guests staying at the Inn. The estate had a strict policy that admittance to the property could be gained only through a paid ticket or pass. Obviously hotel guests would want to invite others to join them for dinner or cocktails, which was desirable for the hotel. At the same time, a mechanism had to be constructed to keep them from touring the Chateau, gardens, and winery without paying for the privilege.

As a graduate of the Cornell Hotel School and the recipient of an MBA from Wake Forest University, Stephanie felt that her education from both schools was being well used in the preplanning of the Inn on Biltmore Estate. One of the challenges facing her was a negative perception of the area by those in Atlanta—an issue discovered through focus group interviews. In addition to the estate, the area offered hiking, white-water rafting, sightseeing from the Blue Ridge Parkway, and a Native American casino about one hour away. Asheville is only three and one-half hours from Atlanta, but the focus groups revealed that many Atlantians believed it was a greater distance and was located in the middle of nowhere with nothing to do.

The importance of yield management was recognized by Stephanie. A corporate planner had recently called and wanted to book future business with a discount. Unfortunately, this booking called for a spillover into the weekend. It was turned down in expectation of higher yield due to weekend occupancy by transient customers. Without a history of bookings for the hotel, this was a bold decision. Stephanie was looking for a yield management specialist to join her staff, but had discovered that such individuals were in short supply.

Stephanie identified market segments that she felt offered opportunities for the Inn. One of these was the wedding market, which could be very important for the Inn. The call center received five to ten calls per day about holding weddings on the estate, and 80 percent of these calls were from out of state. Stephanie felt that planning and developing this market offered great potential.

Other market segments that needed to be developed included international visitors who seemed attracted by the Vanderbilt name. Europeans have many castles and large estates, so a large home might not be an attraction, but they do seem to be attracted by the historical family name.

Another possible segment was the Butterfield Robinson walking tour. These are top-of-the-market mountain tours in the area that cater to affluent individuals. These and many other considerations kept Stephanie and Randy constantly occupied in both planning and development at strategic and tactical levels. They put to use many of the concepts discussed in this chapter on strategic planning.

Chapter Objectives

After reading this chapter, you should be able to:

1. Explain companywide strategic planning.
2. Understand the concepts of stakeholders, processes, resources, and organization as they relate to a high-performing business.
3. Explain the four planning activities of corporate strategic planning.
4. Understand the processes involved in defining a company mission and setting goals and objectives.
5. Discuss how to design business portfolios and growth strategies.
6. Explain the steps involved in the business strategy planning process.

In previous chapters we discussed the need to satisfy changing consumer needs continuously. Companies that view this as fundamental to success practice the art of market-oriented strategic planning.

Market-oriented strategic planning is the managerial process of developing and maintaining a feasible fit between the organization's objectives, skills, and resources and its changing market opportunities. The aim of strategic planning is to help a company select and organize its businesses in a way that keeps the company healthy despite unexpected upsets occurring in any of its specific businesses or product lines. In this chapter we discuss strategic planning, whereas in Chapter 19 we apply the concepts to the development of a marketing plan. When managers develop a good marketing plan or business plan, the principles of strategic planning must be clearly understood.

Three key ideas define strategic planning. The first calls for managing a company's businesses as an investment portfolio, for which it will be decided whether the business entities deserve to be built, maintained, phased down (harvested, milked), or terminated.

The second key idea is to assess accurately the future profit potential of each business by considering the market's growth rate and the company's position and fit. It is not sufficient to use current sales or profits as a guide. For example, if Hyatt, Marriott, and Holiday Inns had used only current profits as a guide to investment opportunities, they would have continued to invest primarily or solely in commercial hotels in downtown and airport locations and, in the case of Holiday Inns, solely in family motels. Instead, Marriott offers a diverse portfolio of brand-name lodging, such as Marriott Marquis, Courtyard, Fairfield Inn, and Residence Inn, for different market segments. Hyatt has been very active in resort development and is a recognized leader in programs for children and teenagers with Camp Hyatt and Rock Hyatt. Holiday Inn has a diversified portfolio of hospitality products, including casino hotels and Holiday Inn Express.

The third key idea underlying strategic planning is that of strategy.[1] For each business, the company must develop a game plan for achieving its long-run objectives. Furthermore, no one strategy is optimal for all competitors in that business. Each company must determine what makes the most sense in the light of its industry position and its objectives, opportunities, skills, and resources. Thus, in the airline industry American Airlines is pressing for cost reduction as a full-service airline and a strong global market share. Southwest continues to strive for low-cost, limited domestic service while acquiring other carriers, such as Mark Air, with similar strategies. The future of the airline industry remains uncertain, but it is possible that the strategies of both carriers could prove to be correct.

Marketing and strategic planning should be viewed as partnerships contributing to the long-run success of a hospitality firm. Prior to 1986, Motel 6 did virtually no consumer research or planning. The chain was then purchased by Kohlberg Kravis Roberts & Company (KKR), leveraged buyout specialists. The new owner, wanting to expand the chain and enhance its investment value, initiated a process of strategic planning.

As those responsible for marketing planning at Motel 6 knew, "Even a brilliant marketing plan or creative concept will misfire if it is lost in competitive advertising clutter. Likewise, a highly visible effort will be ineffective if it is not based on a sound, relevant strategy."[2]

The Tom Bodett Motel 6 advertising campaign proved to be a winner. This advertising was not a random, chance occurrence but was instead the result of carefully studying the needs of target consumers and responding to them. For instance, the choice of radio as the medium was based on the listening habits of this group, not simply media cost. "The lesson of the Motel 6 campaign is not necessarily to use radio, a witty spokesperson, or even to appeal to consumers' desire to make a smart choice. The lesson of this campaign is to use a disciplined process that begins with research to learn about consumers' behavior, responds unwaveringly to those insights, and then follows through with consistent creativity and measurement."[3]

To understand strategic planning, we need to recognize that most large companies consist of four organizational levels: corporate, division, business, and product. In recent years, hospitality companies such as Marriott or Disney have taken on the organizational appearance of multilevels. Corporate headquarters is responsible for designing a corporate strategic plan to guide the whole enterprise into a profitable future; it makes decisions on how much resource support to allocate to each division, as well as which businesses to start or eliminate. Each division establishes a division plan covering the allocation of funds to each business unit within that division. Each business unit in turn develops a business unit strategic plan to carry that business unit into a profitable future. Finally, each product level (product line, brand) within a business unit develops a marketing plan for achieving its objectives in its product market. These plans are then implemented at the various levels of the organization, results are monitored and evaluated, and corrective actions are

3.1 Marriott
Hyatt
Motel 6

taken. The whole planning, implementation, and control cycle is shown in Figure 3-1.

In this chapter, we first examine three questions:

1. What are the characteristics of a high-performance business?
2. How is strategic planning carried out at the corporate level?
3. How do individual business units carry out strategic planning?

Nature of High-Performance Business

The major challenge facing today's hospitality companies is how to build and maintain healthy businesses in the face of the rapidly changing marketplace and environment. The consulting firm of Arthur D. Little proposed a model of the characteristics of a high-performance business.[4] They pointed to the four factors shown in Figure 3-2. We review these factors here.

Stakeholders

The starting point for any business is to define the stakeholders and their needs. Traditionally, most businesses primarily nourished their stockholders. Today's businesses increasingly recognize that unless other stakeholders, customers, employees, suppliers, and distributors are nourished, the business may never earn sufficient profits for the stockholders. Thus, if British Airways employees, customers, dealers, and suppliers are unhappy, profits will not be achieved. This leads to the principle that a business must at least strive to satisfy the minimum expectations of each stakeholder group.

It has been suggested that an employee stakeholder group, which may be of increased importance to hospitality firms, is that of women with small children who do not wish to work full time. Many do not want to leave the workplace entirely but are forced to do so as their employers do not permit flexible scheduling and reduced work hours. Many of these

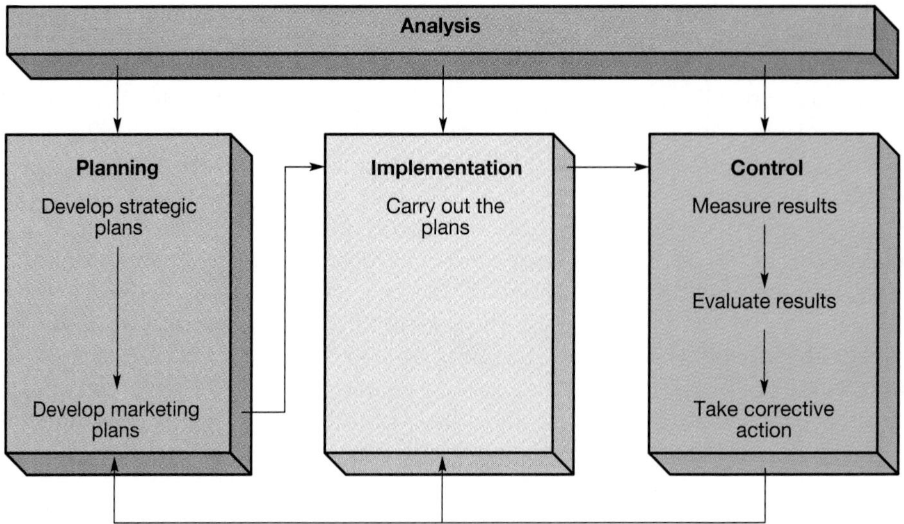

Figure 3-1
The relationship between analysis, planning, implementation, and control.

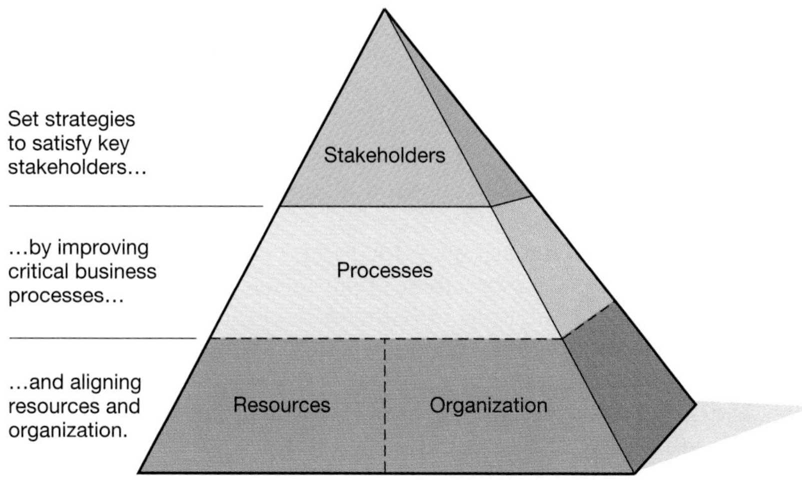

Figure 3-2
The high-performance business. Excerpted from the first quarter 1992 issue of *Prism,* the quarterly journal for senior managers, published by Arthur D. Little, Inc.

individuals could provide valuable contributions but find it impossible to do so under the current organizational structure and policy.[5]

As shown in Figure 3-3, a dynamic relationship connects the stakeholder groups. The progressive company creates a high level of employee satisfaction, which leads employees to work on continuous improvements, as well as breakthrough innovations. The result is higher-quality products and services, which create high customer and stakeholder satisfaction.

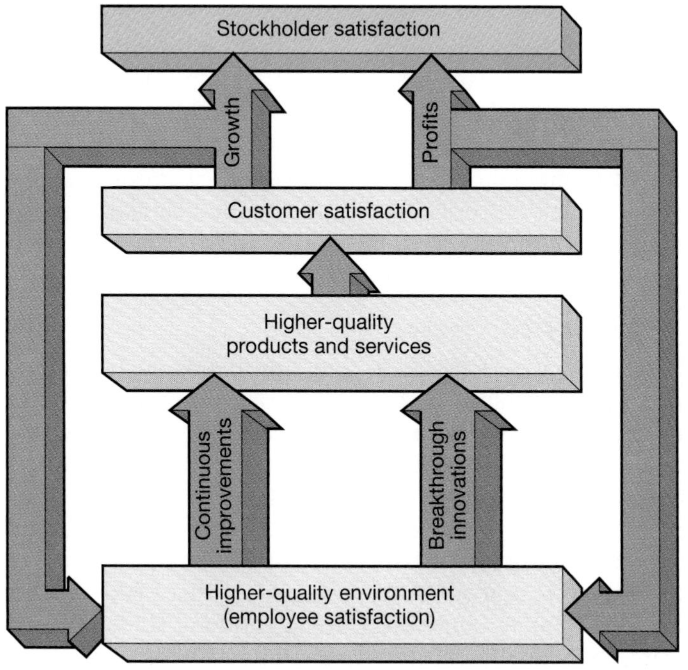

Figure 3-3
Dynamic relationships among stakeholder groups in a high-performance business. Excerpted from the fourth quarter 1992 issue of *Prism,* the quarterly journal for senior managers, published by Arthur D. Little, Inc.

Processes

Company work is traditionally carried on by departments. However, departmental organization poses some problems. Departments typically operate to maximize their own objectives, not necessarily the company's. Walls come up between departments, and there is usually less than ideal cooperation. Work is slowed down and plans often are altered as they pass through departments.

Companies are increasingly refocusing their attention on the need to manage processes even more than departments. They are studying how tasks pass from department to department and the impediments to effective output. They are now building cross-functional teams that manage core business processes.

3.2 Las Vegas Hilton

The Las Vegas Hilton was concerned with the profit contribution from various market segments and how to deal with this issue. The result was a radically different approach to hotel accounting called market segment accounting. This new approach incorporated marketing and strategic planning into accounting rather than viewing them as separate, stand-alone areas and philosophies.[6]

The Las Vegas Hilton decided that "it is important to determine the optimal mix of the major market segments before deciding the strategic direction of the property." This demanded an interdepartmental analysis, as different guests may have widely varying impacts on the profit implications for various departments.

This hotel wanted answers to the following questions:

1. What is the relative profitability of the gaming guest? The premium-gaming guest? The tour and travel guest?
2. How many room nights can each segment fill a year?
3. How much money should be spent to attract each segment?
4. How should rooms be priced for each segment?
5. How should these rooms be allocated to the segments during critical periods of the year?

Interdepartmental teams were formed representing finance, marketing, and information services. Eventually, the heads of all the hotel's major departments contributed to the new market segment accounting model.

Resources

To carry out processes, a company needs such resources as personnel, materials, machines, and information. Traditionally, companies sought to own and control most of the resources that entered the business. Now that is changing. Companies are finding that some resources under their control are not performing as well as those that they could obtain from outside. More companies today have decided to outsource less critical resources. On the other hand, they appreciate the need to own and nurture those core resources and competencies that make up the essence of their business. Smart companies are identifying their core competencies and using them as the basis for their strategic planning.

Organization

The organizational side of a company consists of its structure, policies, and culture, all of which tends to become dysfunctional in a rapidly changing company. Although structure and policies can be changed, the company's culture is the hardest to change. Companies must work hard to align their organization's structure, policies, and culture to the changing requirements of business strategy.

The corporate culture at Rockresorts worked for thirty years, but in the late 1980s, it became an obstacle to meeting customer needs. Rockresorts was founded by Laurence A. Rockefeller in the 1950s. The original market for Rockresorts was the CEO who could delegate business so that his vacation wouldn't be disturbed. At that time, decisions could wait until the CEO returned.

3.3 Rockresorts

Policies at Rockresorts were sacrosanct and involved no phones in the guest rooms, no television, adherence to a mandatory meal plan (the modified American plan), and small, nonostentatious guest rooms. The corporate culture had been product driven. A change in corporate culture is now occurring at Rockresorts. Michael Glennie, president and CEO, said, "We have to listen to what the customer wants and cater to that without compromising the philosophy and ideals of our founder."

This meant, among other changes, pampering guests with more amenities, larger bathrooms, and placing telephones in the room. "I believe that the mission for Rockresorts is to take a company with a wonderful tradition and build on that to meet the expectations of today's guests" said Glennie.[7] The management of stakeholders, processes, resources and a company's organization are critical to strategic planning.

Corporate Strategic Planning

Corporate headquarters has the responsibility for setting into motion the whole planning process. Some corporations give a lot of freedom to their business units but let them develop their own strategies; others set the goals and get heavily involved in the individual strategies.

The hospitality industry faces the need for greater empowerment of employees, particularly at middle-management levels. It has been suggested that many of the traditions within the hospitality industry have experienced little change. "Most of its managers, for instance, were trained in the classical management style." That system ensured that "formal rules and regulations guide decision making and ensure organizational stability. Work is done by the book . . . one's rank in the hierarchical structure determines authority and decision making tends to be centralized, coming primarily from the top."[8] Increasingly, hospitality industry executives and researchers view this traditional approach as needing change.

Next we examine four planning activities that all corporate headquarters must undertake:

- Defining the corporate mission
- Establishing strategic business units (SBUs)
- Assigning resources to each SBU
- Planning new businesses

Defining the Corporate Mission

A hospitality organization exists to accomplish something: to entertain, provide a night's lodging, and so on. Its specific mission or purpose is usually clear at the beginning. Over time some managers may lose interest in the mission, or the mission may lose its relevance in light of changed market conditions.

When management senses that the organization is drifting, it must renew its search for purpose. According to Peter Drucker, it is time to ask some fundamental questions.[9] What is our business? Who is the customer? What is value to the customer? What will our business be? What should our business be? These simple-sounding questions are among the most difficult the company will ever have to answer. Successful companies raise these questions continuously and answer them thoughtfully and thoroughly.

The company's mission is shaped by history. Every company has a history of aims, policies, and achievements. The organization must not depart too radically from its past history. It would not make sense for Denny's Restaurant to begin to manufacture glass bottles. Current preferences of the owners and management also affect a company's mission. Laurence Rockefeller clearly had a preference for his Rockresorts, but several years later Glennie set a new vision.

The organization's resources determine which missions are possible. Singapore Airlines would be deluding itself if it adopted the mission to become the world's largest airline.

Finally, the organization should base its mission on its distinctive competencies. McDonald's could probably enter the solar energy business, but that would not use its core competence, that is, providing low-cost food and fast service to large groups of customers.

Organizations develop **corporate mission statements** in order to share them with their managers, employees, and, in many cases, customers and other publics. A well worked-out mission statement provides company employees with a shared sense of purpose, direction, and opportunity. Writing a formal mission statement is not easy. Some organizations spend a year or two trying to prepare a satisfactory statement about their company's purpose.

Good mission statements embody a number of characteristics. They should focus on a limited number of goals. The mission statement should define the major competitive scopes within which the company will operate.

- **Industry scope.** The range of industries that the company will consider. Some companies will operate in only one industry, some in only a set of related industries, some in only hotels, some in airlines, and some in any industry.
- **Products and applications scope.** The range of products and applications in which the company will participate. American Airlines has demonstrated a willingness to diversify into technology that drives the airline industry, such as Sabre Reservations Systems and Yield Management Systems, but has indicated no desire to construct airports and runways.

- **Competencies scope.** The range of technological and other core competencies that the company will master and leverage.
- **Market-segment scope.** The type of market or customers the company will serve. Some companies will serve only the upscale market. For example, Four Seasons Hotels and Resorts have shown no inclination to enter the budget roadside motel sector.
- **Vertical scope.** The number of channel levels from raw materials to final product and distribution in which the company will engage. At one extreme are companies with a large vertical scope. Many individuals have dreamed of a huge travel corporation that vertically ties together an airline, a hotel chain, and a chain of travel agents. Thus far, attempts in this area in the United States have been unsuccessful. At the other extreme are corporations with low or no vertical integration, such as the "hollow corporation" or "pure marketing company," which consists of a person with a phone, fax, computer, and desk who contracts outside for every service, including design, manufacture, marketing, and physical distribution.[10] Some tour operators may be viewed as hollow corporations. They tie together airline travel, ground transportation, sightseeing, restaurant meals, club entertainment, hotel lodging, and even travel gifts to send home without owning any of the enterprises. Eventually, many tour operators begin to acquire one or more of these enterprises and may eventually become a vertically integrated company.
- **Geographic scope.** The range of regions, countries, or country groups where the corporation will operate. At one extreme are companies that operate in a specific city or state, such as the fast-food chain Biscuitville in North Carolina. At the other extreme are large multinationals such as Sheraton or Hilton Hotels and smaller multinationals that may operate in only a few countries, such as Canada's Delta Hotels, which operates in Canada, the United States, and Thailand, or the Camino Real Hotel chain in Latin America. Choice Hotels International clearly has decided to become a major multinational chain. Currently Choice Hotels International has over 350 hotels in Europe.[11]

The company's mission statement should be motivating. Employees need to feel that their work is significant and contributes to people's lives. Missions are at their best when they are guided by a vision, an almost "impossible dream." Thomas Monaghan wanted to deliver hot pizza to any home within thirty minutes, and he created Domino's Pizza. Bob Burns wanted to develop world-class luxury hotels throughout Asia, and he created Regent International Hotels. Ruth Fertel wanted to provide customers with the finest steak dinners available, and she created Ruth's Chris Steak Houses. Phil Roberts wanted to bring back the warmth and passion of the immigrant southern Italian family-style neighborhood restaurant so he created Bucca di Beppo.[12] The corporate mission statement should stress major policies that the company wants to honor. Policies define how employees should deal with customers, suppliers, distributors, competitors, and other important groups.

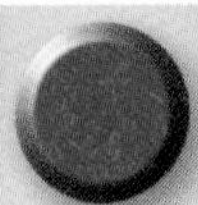

Marketing Highlight 3-1

Pubs represent a way of life for Britons and are an important tourist attraction. The results of a 1989 investigation by the Monopolies and Mergers Commission found that British pubs were a complex monopoly operating in favor of big brewers who controlled pubs through a "tiered-house" system in which the pub was obligated to buy beer and related products from a single brewery. Parliament passed the "Supply & Beer Order," requiring major breweries to release 50 percent of their pubs.

Brewers were forced to think strategically, which resulted in (a) closure of marginal pubs, (b) formation of independent chains of pubs released by brewers such as Inntrapreneurs Estates with over 6,500 pubs, and (c) an influx of new operators who develop "green field" (new sites) pubs.

New thinking by innovative pub managers recognized market segments among Britons, such as those who want a family friendly place or pubs for the growing 55+ age segment, such as the White Horse Pubs with a Golden Club membership card.

Social attitudes in England are becoming intolerant of beer swilling. Britons want to drink less and eat more in pubs. "Pub grub" is now one of the fastest-growing sectors in the British restaurant industry, leading to such branded food concepts as Big Steak and Toby Grills.

Innovative thinking led to the development of branded pubs overseas, such as the John Bull chain in Bangkok, with plans for expansion in Asia and Europe. Theme pubs are also growing in popularity: Irish and sports pubs with names such as Scruffy Murphy's and Football offer an ambience and product line different from traditional pubs.

"The traditional pub is being replaced by multifaceted leisure outlets." The CEO of Whitehead, a leading pub chain operator and retailer, was not the least embarrassed to say that one of his chain's new pubs is more like Disney World than a place for boozers.

Source: Care Eldwood Williams, "The British Pub," *Cornell Hotel and Restaurant Quarterly* 37, no. 6 (December 1996): 62.

The company's mission statement should provide a vision and direction for the company for the next ten to twenty years. Missions are not revised every few years in response to every new turn in the economy. On the other hand, a company must redefine its mission if that mission no longer defines an optimal course.[13]

The Ruby Tuesday group of restaurants was developed as being fully consistent with the mission statement of its parent, Morrison Hospitality Group, the oldest food-service company on the New York Stock Exchange. This mission statement is that "our mission is to be a great restaurant company that provides the highest quality and greatest value to every guest, every team member, and every shareholder we serve."[14] Michael Jordan's Restaurant in Chicago has the following mission statement: "Through consistency, integrity and world-class staff, we will create a unique, high profile atmosphere in an establishment that provides excellent service and . . . The Michael Jordan Experience!"[15]

Establishing Strategic Business Units

Most companies operate several businesses. However, they often fail to define them carefully. Businesses are too often defined in terms of products. Companies are in the "hotel business" or the "cruise line business." However, market definitions of a business are superior to product definitions.[16] A business must be viewed as a customer-satisfying process, not a

Radisson has defined its business broadly enough to include cruise ships as well as hotels. This ad positions the cruise ship against upscale resorts in the incentive travel market. Courtesy of Radisson Hospitality Worldwide.

goods-producing process. Companies should define their business in terms of customer needs, not products.

Las Vegas has changed dramatically from a city based primarily on adult casinos to an entertainment complex for the entire family. Contrast Las Vegas to Reno, where the emphasis is still basically on casinos, lodging, food and beverage, and adult entertainment, with the exception of Circus Circus Hotel. Ski resorts are no longer content to sell only ski tickets. Today major ski resorts offer children's programs, summer mountain biking, and rock concerts.

Management, of course, should avoid a market definition that is too narrow or too broad. Holiday Inns, Inc., the world's largest hotel chain, with over 300,000 rooms, fell into this trap. Some years ago it broadened its business definition from the "hotel business" to the "travel industry." It acquired Trailways, Inc., then the nation's second-largest bus company, and Delta Steamship Lines, Inc., but did not manage these companies well and later divested the properties. Holiday Inns decided to "stick close to its knitting" and concentrate on the "hospitality industry."[17]

Companies have to identify those of its businesses that they must manage strategically. These businesses are called **strategic business units** (SBUs). An SBU has three characteristics:

1. It is a single business or a collection of related businesses that can be planned for separately from the rest of the company.
2. It has its own set of competitors.
3. It has a manager who is responsible for strategic planning and profit performance and who controls most of the factors affecting profits.

Assigning Resources to Each SBU

The purpose of identifying the company's strategic business units is to assign to these units strategic-planning goals and appropriate funding. These units send their plans to company headquarters, which approves them or sends them back for revision. Headquarters reviews these plans to decide which of its SBUs to build, maintain, harvest, and divest. Management cannot rely just on impressions. Analytical tools are needed for classifying businesses by profit potential. One of the best-known business portfolio evaluation models is the Boston Consulting Group model.[18]

Boston Consulting Group Approach

The Boston Consulting Group (BCG), a leading management consulting firm, developed the growth–share matrix shown in Figure 3-4. The ten circles represent the current sizes and positions of businesses making up a hypothetical company. The dollar-volume size of each business is proportional to the circle's area. The location of each business indicates its market growth rate and relative market share.

Specifically, the market growth rate on the vertical axis indicates the annual growth rate of the market in which the business operates. In Figure 3-4, it ranges from zero to 20 percent, although a larger range could be shown. A market growth rate above 10 percent is considered high.

The horizontal axis, relative market share, refers to the SBU's market share relative to that of the largest competitor. It serves as a measure of the company's strength in the relevant market. A relative market share of 0.1 means that the company's sales volume is only 10 percent of the leader's sales volume, and 10 means that the company's SBU is the leader and has ten times the sales of the next-strongest company in that market. Relative market share is divided into high and low share, using 1.0 as the dividing line.

The **growth–share matrix** is divided into four cells, each indicating a different type of business.

- **Question marks.** Question marks are company businesses that operate in high-growth markets but have low relative market shares. Most businesses start off as a question mark. A question mark requires a lot of cash. The term question mark is well chosen because the company has to think hard about whether to keep pouring money into this business. The company in Figure 3-4 operates three question-mark businesses, and this may be too many.
- **Stars.** If the question-mark business is successful, it becomes a star. A star is the market leader in a high-growth market. This does not necessarily mean that the star produces a positive cash flow for the company. The company must spend substantial funds to keep up with the high market growth and fight off competitors' attacks. Stars are usually profitable and become the company's future cash cows. In the illustration, the company has two stars.
- **Cash cows.** When a market's annual growth rate falls to less than 10 percent, the star becomes a cash cow if it still has the largest relative market share. A cash cow produces a lot of cash for the company. Because the business is the market leader, it enjoys

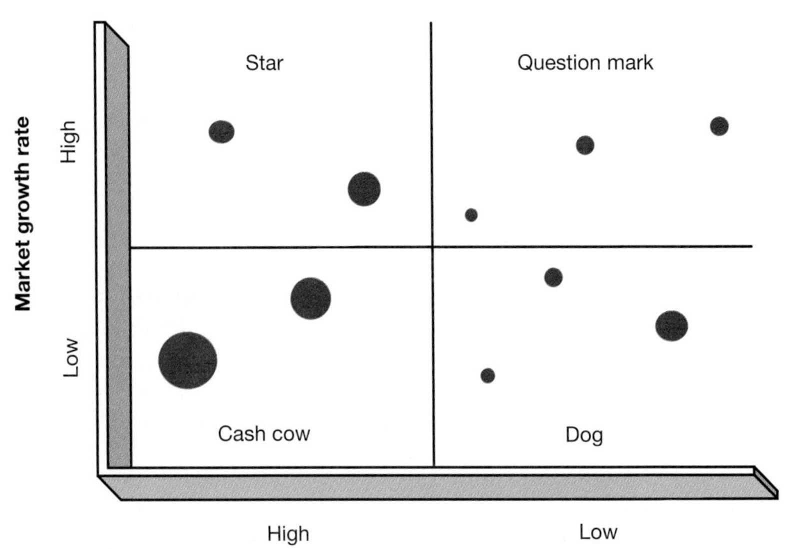

Figure 3-4
The BCG growth–share matrix.

economies of scale and higher profit margins. The company uses its cash-cow businesses to pay its bills and support the stars, question marks, and dogs, which tend to be cash hungry. In the illustration, the company has two cash-cow businesses.

- **Dogs.** Dogs describe company businesses that have weak market shares in low-growth markets. They typically generate low profits or losses, although they may throw off some cash. The company in the illustration manages three dog businesses. Dog businesses often consume more management time than they are worth.

Having plotted its various businesses in the growth–share matrix, the company then determines whether its business portfolio is healthy. An unbalanced portfolio would have too many dogs or question marks and/or too few stars and cash cows.

The company's next task is to determine what objective, strategy, and budget to assign to each SBU. Four alternative objectives can be pursued.

- **Build.** Here the objective is to increase the SBU's market share, even foregoing short-term earnings to achieve this objective. Building is appropriate for question marks whose shares have to grow to become stars.
- **Hold.** Here the objective is to preserve the SBU's market share. This objective is appropriate for strong cash cows if they are to continue to yield a large positive cash flow.
- **Harvest.** Here the objective is to increase the SBU's short-term cash flow regardless of the long-term effect. This strategy is appropriate for weak cash cows whose future is dim and from whom more cash flow is needed. Harvesting can also be used with question marks and dogs.
- **Divest.** Here the objective is to sell or liquidate the business because resources can be better used elsewhere.

As time passes, SBUs change their position in the growth–share matrix. Successful SBUs have a life cycle. They start as question marks, become stars, then cash cows, and, finally, dogs. For this reason, companies should examine not only the current positions of their businesses in the growth–share matrix but also their moving positions.

Although the portfolio in Figure 3-4 is basically healthy, wrong objectives or strategies could be assigned. The worst mistake would be to require all the SBUs to aim for the same growth rate or return level. The very point of SBU analysis is that each business has a different potential and requires its own objective. Additional mistakes would include the following:

1. Leaving cash-cow businesses with too little in retained funds, in which case they grow weak, or leaving them with too much in retained funds, in which case the company fails to invest enough in new growth businesses.
2. Making major investments in dogs hoping to turn them around, but failing each time.

3. Maintaining too many question marks and underinvesting in each. Question marks should either receive enough support to achieve segment dominance or be dropped.

Just as a corporation uses the BCG grid to manage its businesses, a restaurant manger can apply the concepts of the BCG grids to manage individual menu items. Kasavana and Smith used a similar matrix for menu planning. Their menu-engineering matrix has plow horses: high-volume, low-contribution items; stars: high-volume, high-contribution items; puzzles: high-contribution, low-volume items; and dogs: low-volume, low-contribution items.[19] The models used for strategic analysis can often be adapted and used at the business, division, and product level.

Critique of Portfolio Models

The use of portfolio models has produced a number of benefits. The models have helped managers to think more strategically and to better understand the economics of their businesses. On the other hand, portfolio models must be used cautiously. They may lead the company to place too much emphasis on market-share growth and entry into high-growth businesses to the neglect of managing the current businesses well. The results are sensitive to the ratings and weights and can be manipulated to produce a desired location in the matrix. A lot of businesses will end up in the middle of the matrix owing to compromises in ratings, and this makes it hard to know what the appropriate strategy should be. Finally, the models fail to delineate the synergies between two or more businesses, which means that making decisions for one business at a time might be risky. There is a danger of terminating a losing business unit that actually provides an essential core competence needed by several other business units.

Developing Growth Strategies

Beyond evaluating current businesses, designing the business portfolio involves finding businesses and products the company should consider in the future. Companies need growth if they are to compete more effectively, satisfy their stakeholders, and attract top talent. "Growth is pure oxygen," states one executive. "It creates a vital, enthusiastic corporation where people see genuine opportunity. . . . In that way growth is more than our single most important financial driver; it's an essential part of our corporate culture." At the same time, a firm must be careful not to make growth itself an objective. The company's objective must be "profitable growth."

Marketing has the main responsibility for achieving profitable growth for the company. Marketing must identify, evaluate, and select market opportunities and lay down strategies for capturing them. Ansoff has proposed a useful framework for detecting new intensive growth opportunities. Called the **Ansoff product–market expansion grid,** it is shown in Figure 3-5.[20] Management first considers whether it could gain more market share with its current products in their current markets (market penetration strategy). Next it considers whether it can find or develop new markets for its current products (market development strategy). Then

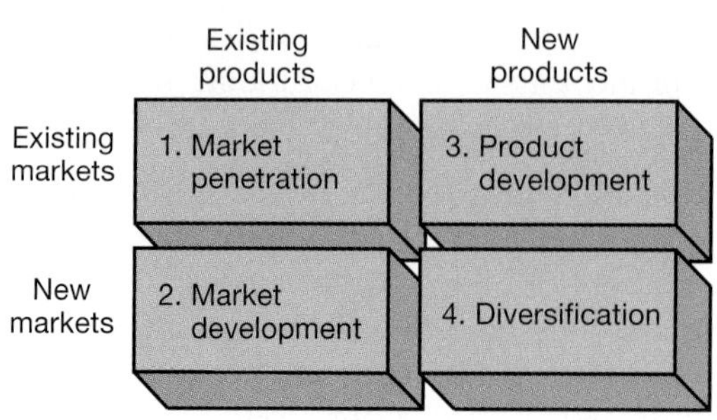

Figure 3-5 Market opportunity identification through the product–market expansion grid.

it considers whether it can develop new products of potential interest to its current markets (product development strategy). We apply it here to Starbucks.

Intensive Growth

Market Penetration. First, Starbucks management might consider whether the company can achieve deeper market penetration—making more sales to current customers without changing its products. It might add new stores in current market areas to make it easier for more customers to visit. Improvements in advertising, prices, service, menu selection, or store design might encourage customers to stop by more often or to buy more during each visit. For example, Starbucks recently began adapting its menu to local tastes around the country.

3.4 Starbucks

> In the South, where customers tend to come later in the day and linger for a bit, this meant adding more appealing dessert offerings, as well as designing larger, more comfortable locations. In Atlanta, Starbucks opened bigger stores with such amenities as couches and outdoor tables, so that people would feel comfortable hanging out, especially in the evening. . . . Building on its Atlanta experience, Starbucks is tailoring its stores to local tastes around the country. That's why you find café-au-lait as well as toasted items in New Orleans, neither of which is available elsewhere in the country. Bagel sales in New Orleans tripled once Starbucks began toasting them. Or why coffee cake is featured in the Northeast, where it's more popular. Basically, Starbucks would like to increase patronage by current customers and attract competitors' customers to Starbucks shops.

Market Development Strategy. Starbucks management might consider possibilities for market development—identifying and developing new markets for its current products. For instance, managers could review new demographic markets—such as senior consumers or ethnic groups—to see if new groups could be encouraged to visit Starbucks coffee shops for the first time or to buy more from them. Managers also could review new geographic markets. Starbucks is now expanding swiftly into new U.S. markets, especially in the southeast and southwest. It is also developing its international markets, with stores popping up rapidly in Asia, Europe, and Australia.

Product Development Strategy. Next, management should consider product development—offering modified or new products to current markets. By examining these three intensive growth strategies, management will hopefully discover several ways to grow. Still, that may not be enough, in which case management must also examine diversification and integrative growth opportunities. For example, Starbucks is increasing its food offerings in an effort to bring customers into its stores during the lunch and dinner hours and to increase the amount of the average customer's sales ticket. The company is also partnering with other firms to sell coffee in supermarkets and to extend its brand to new products, such as coffee ice cream (with Breyer's) and bottled Frappuccino drinks (with PepsiCo).

Diversification Growth

Diversification growth makes sense when good opportunities can be found outside the present businesses. A good opportunity is one where the industry is highly attractive and the company has the mix of business strengths to be successful. Three types of diversification can be considered. First, the company could seek new products that have technological and/or marketing synergies with existing product lines, even though the products may appeal to a new class of customers (**concentric diversification strategy**). Second, the company might search for new products that could appeal to its current customers, although technologically unrelated to its current product line (**horizontal diversification strategy**). Hotels, restaurants, cruise lines, and airlines all pursue this strategy when

Grand Lux was developed as an upscale product to attract Cheesecake Factory customers and new customers. Courtesy of The Cheesecake Factory, Inc.

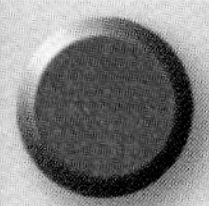

Marketing Highlight 3-2

A Strategic Look at Starbucks Coffee

Back in 1983, Howard Schultz hit on the idea of bringing a European-style coffeehouse to America. He believed people needed to slow down, to "smell the coffee," and to enjoy life a little more. The result was Starbucks, the coffeehouse chain that started the trend in America of enjoying coffee to its fullest. Starbucks doesn't sell just coffee, it sells an experience. Howard Behar, Starbucks's international president, says, "We're not in the business of filling bellies, we're in the business of filling souls."

Starbucks is now a powerhouse premium brand in a category where only cheaper commodity products existed just a decade ago. As the brand has percolated, Starbucks's sales and profits have risen like steam off a mug of hot java. Nine million customers visit the company's more than 2,100 stores each week—10 percent of them drop by twice a day. During the past five years, Starbucks's total sales have grown at an average of over 34 percent annually, and profits have grown at an incredible 68 percent. Starbucks's success, however, has drawn a full litter of copycats, ranging from direct competitors such as Caribou Coffee to fast-food merchants. These days it seems that everyone is peddling its own brand of premium coffee. "Pull up to a Mobil gas station and the convenience store has certified organic coffee supplied by Green Mountain Coffee Co.," observes one analyst. "In the Pacific Northwest, McDonald's pours a blend from Seattle Coffee Co." To maintain its phenomenal growth in an increasingly overcaffeinated marketplace, Starbucks has brewed up an ambitious, multipronged growth strategy. Let's examine the key elements of this strategy.

More store growth. Over 85 percent of Starbucks's sales come from its stores. So, not surprisingly, Starbucks is in the thick of its biggest wave of store openings ever. It plans to open one new store a day, every day, for the next two years. Although it may seem that there aren't many places left without a Starbucks, there's still plenty of room to expand. For example, Kansas City has only two Starbucks; the entire state of Indiana has only one; and the states of Alabama, Arkansas, Mississippi, and Tennessee have none. Even in crowded markets, such as New York City or San Francisco, the company seems unconcerned about store saturation. "Three years ago, when I said we were going to have 100 stores in New York, people thought it was crazy," says Schultz. "Well, now we have 70, and we're going to 200." He points to Vancouver, Canada, where competing Starbucks stores are located directly across the street from one another. Both stores generate more than $1 million in annual sales, each well above the sales of a typical Starbucks. One three-block stretch in Chicago contains six of the trendy coffee bars.

Beyond opening new shops, Starbucks is expanding each store's food offerings, testing everything from Krispy Kreme doughnuts in New York City to Fresh Fields gourmet sandwiches in Washington, DC. Currently, beverages account for 80 percent of Starbucks's sales. By offering more food, the company hopes to increase the average customer sales ticket while also boosting new retail channels.

New retail channels. The vast majority of coffee in America is bought in stores and sipped at home. To capture this demand, Starbucks is also pushing into America's supermarket aisles. However, rather than going head-to-head with giants such as Procter & Gamble (Folgers) and Kraft (Maxwell House, Sanka), Starbucks struck a cobranding deal with Kraft. Under this deal, Starbucks will continue to roast and package its coffee, and Kraft will market and distribute it. Both companies benefit: Starbucks gains quick entry into 25,000 U.S. supermarkets, supported by the marketing muscle of 3,500 Kraft salespeople. Kraft tops off its coffee line with the best-known premium brand and gains quick entry into the fast-growing premium coffee segment.

Beyond supermarkets, Starbucks has forged an impressive set of new ways to bring its brand to market. For example, Host Marriott operates Starbucks kiosks in more than 30 U.S. airports and several airlines serve Starbucks coffee to their passengers; Westin and Sheraton hotels offer packets of Starbucks brew in their rooms; and Barnes & Noble serves Starbucks coffee in all of the 375 cafés in its bookstores, making it one of the nation's largest retailers of both books and specialty coffees. Starbucks also sells gourmet coffee, tea, gifts, and related goods through business and consumer catalogs. It recently opened its own Web site, *www.starbucks.com,* where it sells coffee, tea, coffee-making equipment, compact discs, gifts, and collectibles. Starbucks customers' demographics are ideal for e-commerce—about 70 percent of customers are already on the Web and their typical household income approaches $75,000.

New products and store concepts. Starbucks has partnered with several firms to extend its brand into new categories. For example, it joined with PepsiCo to sump the Starbucks brand on bottled Frappuccino drinks. Marketed in a joint venture with Breyer's, Starbucks ice cream is now the leading brand of coffee ice cream. Moreover, at the same time it is trying to squeeze more business out of its regular coffee shops, Starbucks is also examining new store concepts. In Seattle, it is testing Café Starbucks, a European-style family bistro with a menu featuring everything from huckleberry pancakes to oven-roasted seared sirloin and Mediterranean chicken breast on focaccia. Whereas Starbucks's traditional coffeehouses ring up about half their sales before 11 A.M., Café Starbucks is designed to generate sales evenly throughout the day. Starbucks is also testing Circadia in San Francisco—a kind of bohemian coffeehouse concept with tattered rugs, high-speed Internet access, and live music, as well as coffee specialties.

International growth. Finally, Starbucks is taking its American-brewed concept global, especially in Asia. Long lines are common at the more than fifty Japanese Starbucks stores, and the company plans to have at least 250 stores in Japan by the end of 2003. It is expanding rapidly in Taiwan, Malaysia, Singapore, and the Philippines, and this year the company opened its first three locations in China. Starbucks also operates eighty stores in the United Kingdom and is currently expanding into western Europe.

Although Starbucks's growth strategy so far has met with great success, some analysts express strong concerns. What's wrong with Starbucks's rapid expansion? Some critics worry that the company may be overextending the brand name. "People pay up to $3.15 for a cafe latte because it's supposed to be a premium product," asserts one such critic. "When you see the Starbucks name on what an airline is pouring, you wonder." Others fear that, by pursuing such a broad-based growth strategy, Starbucks will stretch its resources too thin or lose its focus. According to one account, "All this sounds properly ambitious and aggressive, but to some . . . it has an ominous ring. The late 1990s are littered with the wreckage of restaurant chains that expanded too fast for their market and eventually collapsed. Two years ago, Planet Hollywood, with high-profile backers like Bruce Willis and Arnold Schwarzenegger, was an investor darling. The stock hit $25 a share; today it trades for just over $1." Then there's Boston Market, the once high-flying chain that ended up declaring bankruptcy in 1998.

Others, however, remain true believers. Some even see similarities between Starbucks and a young McDonald's, which rode the humble hamburger to such incredible success. "The similar focus on one product, the overseas opportunities, the rapid emergence as the dominant player in a new niche," says Goldman Sachs analyst Steve Kent, "all applies to Starbucks, too." Only time will tell whether Starbucks turns out to be the next McDonald's or the next Boston Market. It all depends how well the company manages growth. For now, things are really perking, but Starbucks has to be careful that it doesn't boil over.

Sources: Quotes from Nelson D. Schwartz, "Still Perking after All These Years: *Fortune,* Nov 24, 1999, pp. 203–10; Janice Matsumoto, "More than Mocha-Cafe Starbucks," *Restaurants and Institutions,* October 1, 1998, p. 21; and Kelly Barron, "The Cappuccino Conundrum," *Forbes,* February 22, 1999, pp. 54–55. Also see Mark Harnstra, "Starbucks' Pasqua Purchase Dovetails with Food-Cafe Tests," *Nation's Restaurant News,* January 4, 1999, pp. 3, 104; Richard Gibson, "Starbucks Plans a New Category in Cybercommerce," *Wall Street Journal,* April 26, 1999, p. B10; Eli Lehrer, "When Starbucks Takes over the World," *Insight on the News,* July 19, 1999, p. 4; information accessed on-line at www.starbucks.com, September 1999; and Louise Lee, "Now Starbucks Uses Its Bean," *Business Week,* February 14, 2000, pp. 92–94.

they sell gift items such as T-shirts, perfume, and luggage. Many restaurants, such as the Hard Rock Café franchise, have found that the sale of restaurant-logo clothing in their restaurants is highly profitable and that clothing serves as an excellent advertising medium.

Finally, the company might seek new businesses that have no relationship to the company's current technology, products, or markets (**conglomerate diversification strategy**). Some hotel chains have entered markets such as retirement homes. Hyatt operates a retirement division known as Classic Residence: Senior Living by Hyatt.

The company Sodexho of Marseille, France, was experienced and successful in providing hospitality services on ocean liners and cruise ships.[21] The company's founder, Pierre Bellon, decided to expand into other industries with similar needs, such as healthcare facilities and schools, and to seek international expansion. Within five years the company was successful in Belgium, then expanded to North and South America and went public on the Paris Bourse.

Starbucks is considering diversification as it is testing two restaurant concepts outside of its current products and markets. These new restaurant concepts are Café Starbucks and Circadia. Starbucks hopes to offer new formats to related but new markets. In a more extreme diversification, Starbucks might consider leveraging its strong brand name by making and marketing a line of branded casual clothing consistent with the "Starbucks experience." However, this would probably be unwise. Companies that diversify too broadly into unfamiliar products or industries can lose their market focus, something that some critics are already concerned about with Starbucks. Thus we see that a company can systematically identify new business opportunities by using a marketing systems framework, first looking at ways to intensify its position in current product markets, then considering ways to integrate backward, forward, or horizontally in relation to its current businesses, and, finally, searching for profitable opportunities outside its current businesses.

Integrative Growth

Opportunities in diversification, market development, and product development can be seized through integrating backward, forward, or horizontally within that business's industry. A hotel company could select **backward integration** by acquiring one of its suppliers, such as a food distributor, or it could acquire tour wholesalers or travel agents (**forward integration**). Finally, the hotel company might acquire one or more competitors, provided that the government does not bar the move (**horizontal integration**).

Marriott developed a restaurant supply distribution system known as Marriott Distribution Systems. This grew out of Marriott's Fairfield Farms Commissary operation. The commissary operation was shut down, and the business was refocused on distribution. Marriott opened six of these distribution centers to service concentrations of Marriott Hotels. With this guaranteed core business, each distribution center then aggressively markets to other restaurants in the area.[22]

Through investigating possible integration moves such as those by Marriott, a company may discover additional sources of sales volume increase over the next ten years. These new sources may still not deliver the desired sales volume. In that case, the company may consider diversification moves. Integrative growth offers opportunities in related businesses, but a company must have the expertise to succeed in the new business.

Thus we see that a company can systematically identify new business opportunities by using a marketing systems framework, looking at ways to intensify its position in current product markets, searching for profitable opportunities outside its current businesses, and considering ways to integrate backward, forward, or horizontally in relation to its current businesses.

Business Strategy Planning

Having examined the strategic planning tasks of company management, we can now examine the strategic planning tasks facing business unit managers. The business unit strategic planning process consists of eight steps. We shall examine these steps.

Business Mission

Each business unit needs to define its specific mission within the broader company mission. Thus an SBU must define its various scopes more specifically, that is, its products and applications, competence, market segments, vertical positioning, and geography. It must also define its specific goals and policies as a separate business.

SWOT Analysis

The overall evaluation of a company's strengths, weaknesses, opportunities, and threats is called SWOT analysis. The external analysis looks at opportunities and threats created by the environment. The internal analysis looks at the strengths and weakness of the company. In strategic planning the company matches its capabilities with the opportunities created by the environment and takes action to minimize the environmental threats.

External Environmental Analysis (Opportunity and Threat Analysis)

The business manager now knows the parts of the environment to monitor if the business is to achieve its goals. In general, a business unit has to monitor key **macroenvironmental forces** (demographic-economic, technological, political-legal, and social-cultural) and significant **microenvironmental forces** (customers, competitors, distribution channels, suppliers) which will affect its ability to earn profits in this marketplace. The business unit should set up a marketing intelligence system to track trends and important developments. For each trend or development, management needs to identify the implied opportunities and threats.

3.5 Loews Hotels

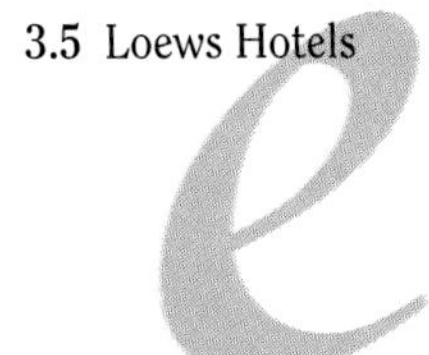

Jonathan Tisch, president and CEO of Loews Hotels, predicted that the resort industry would see a decline in megaresorts due to intense competition. Tisch believed that midsized resorts capable of handling a group of 250 would be well positioned to meet current and future market needs.[23]

The trend to bring one's spouse on a business trip was observed at many golf resorts, particularly those in Seattle, San Francisco, San Diego, Chicago, and Washington, DC. Golf resort developers and managers need to assess whether this is a trend that might offer opportunities to position one's resort competitively in an increasingly crowded market.[24]

Opportunities

A major purpose of environmental scanning is to discern new opportunities. We define a **marketing opportunity** as follows: an area of need in which a company can perform profitably.

Opportunities can be listed and classified according to their attractiveness and the success probability. The company's success probability depends on whether its business strengths not only match the key success requirements for operating in the target market but also exceed those of its competitors. The best performing company will be the one that can generate the greatest customer value and sustain it over time.

The concept of incorporating recreation clubs into resorts might be an opportunity for some resorts. Such programs are aimed at local markets, allowing members to enjoy the resort facilities and sometimes even stay in the rooms. Membership programs offer opportunities for increased revenue, but there is a negative side if they are not well managed. Resort guests who pay full rack rates may not appreciate the competition for tennis or golf times from local residents.[25]

The franchising of B&Bs (bed and breakfasts) offer a tremendous opportunity for a franchise company that is able to overcome considerable obstacles. The B&B industry in the 1990s is comparable to the hotel–motel industry in the 1950s. B&B owners do not view franchising favorably, yet have specific needs that could be met through franchising under a well-planned strategic franchise program.[26]

Threats

Some developments in the external environment represent marketing threats. We define an *environmental threat* as follows: A challenge posed by unfavorable trends or developments that would lead, in the absence of defensive marketing action, to sales or profit deterioration. Threats should be classified according to their seriousness and probability of occurrence.

By assembling a picture of the major threats and opportunities facing a specific business unit, it is possible to characterize its overall attractiveness. Four outcomes are possible. An ideal business is high in major opportunities and low in major threats. A speculative business is high in both major opportunities and threats. A major business is low in major opportunities and threats. Finally, a troubled business is low in opportunities and high in threats.

3.6 Pizza Hut
Dunkin Donuts
Burger King

Traditional institutional food-service providers to hospitals, schools, government offices, and office buildings face the threat of competition from quick-service restaurants (QSR). Many QSRs, such as Pizza Hut, Dunkin Donuts, Burger King, and others, have entered this market. Traditional institutional food-service firms such as ARAMARK cannot ignore this threat.[29]

Internal Environmental Analysis (Strengths–Weaknesses Analysis)

It is one thing to discern attractive opportunities in the environment; it is another to have the necessary competencies to succeed in these opportunities. Each business needs to evaluate its strengths and weaknesses periodically. This internal environmental analysis can be done by using a form such as shown in Figure 3-6. Management or an outside consultant reviews the business's marketing, financial, manufacturing, and organizational competencies. Each factor is rated as to whether it is a major strength, minor strength, neutral factor, minor weakness, or major weakness. A company with strong marketing capability would show up with the ten marketing factors all rated as major strengths.

Figure 3–6
Strengths–weaknesses analysis.

	Performance					Importance		
	Major Strength	Minor Strength	Neutral	Minor Weakness	Major Weakness	Hi	Med	Low
Marketing								
1. Company reputation	___	___	___	___	___	___	___	___
2. Market share	___	___	___	___	___	___	___	___
3. Product quality	___	___	___	___	___	___	___	___
4. Service quality	___	___	___	___	___	___	___	___
5. Pricing effectiveness	___	___	___	___	___	___	___	___
6. Distribution effectiveness	___	___	___	___	___	___	___	___
7. Promotion effectiveness	___	___	___	___	___	___	___	___
8. Salesforce effectiveness	___	___	___	___	___	___	___	___
9. Innovation effectiveness	___	___	___	___	___	___	___	___
10. Geographical coverage	___	___	___	___	___	___	___	___
Finance								
11. Cost/availability of capital	___	___	___	___	___	___	___	___
12. Cash flow	___	___	___	___	___	___	___	___
13. Financial stability	___	___	___	___	___	___	___	___
Manufacturing								
14. Facilities	___	___	___	___	___	___	___	___
15. Economies of scale	___	___	___	___	___	___	___	___
16. Capacity	___	___	___	___	___	___	___	___
17. Able dedicated workforce	___	___	___	___	___	___	___	___
18. Ability to produce on time	___	___	___	___	___	___	___	___
19. Technical manufacturing skill	___	___	___	___	___	___	___	___
Organization								
20. Visionary capable leadership	___	___	___	___	___	___	___	___
21. Dedicated employees	___	___	___	___	___	___	___	___
22. Entrepreneurial orientation	___	___	___	___	___	___	___	___
23. Flexible/responsive	___	___	___	___	___	___	___	___

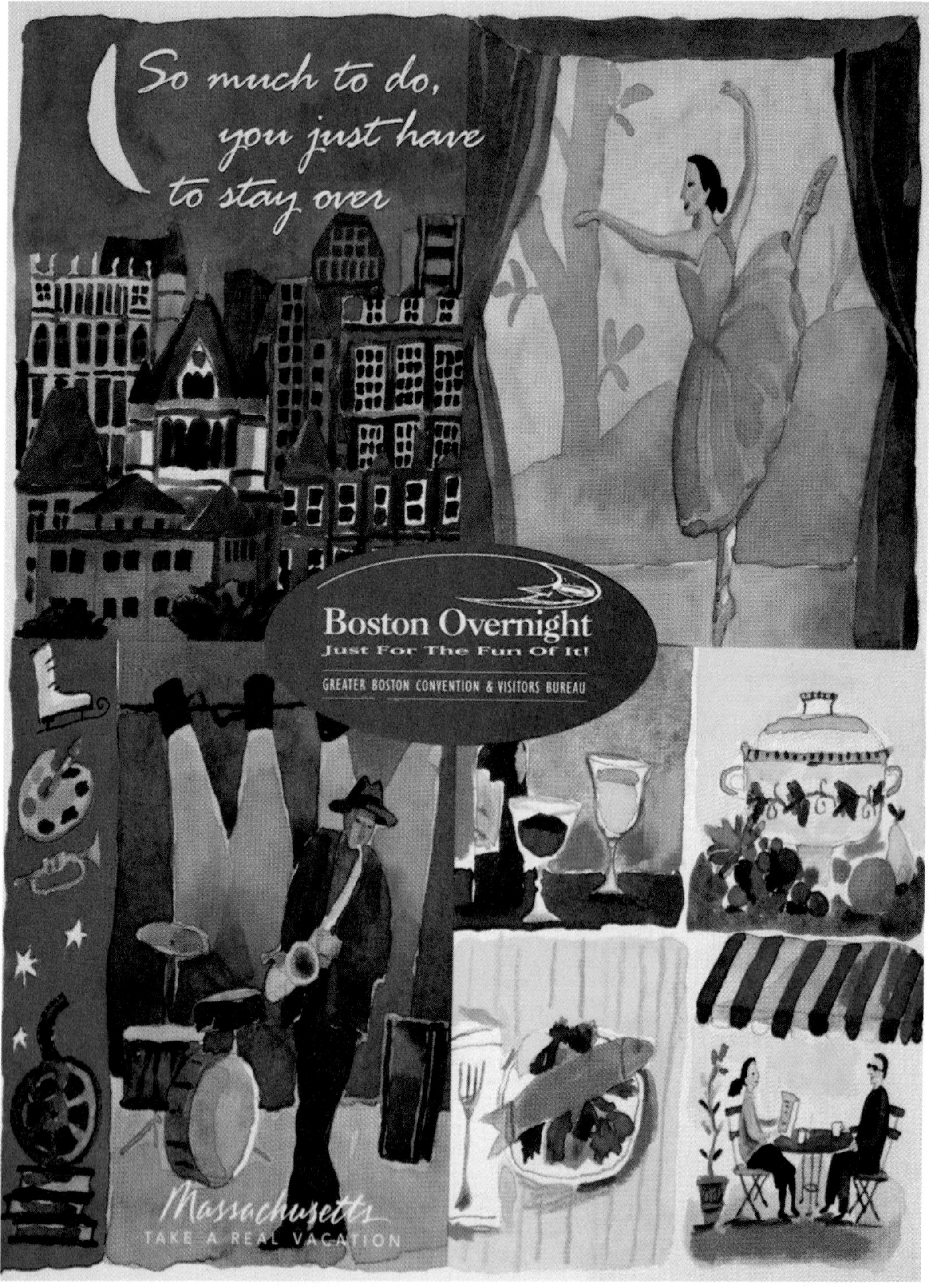

One of the strengths of Boston is the incredible variety of activities the city offers. These include a variety of live musical performances, theater, professional spots, museums, great restaurants, and special events such the Boston Wine Expo and Disney on Ice. The Boston Greater Convention and Visitors Bureau developed this promotional piece to encourage people living in the region to come to Boston, enjoy the activities the city offers, and spend the night in one of Boston's hotels. Courtesy of The Boston Greater Convention and Visitors Bureau.

In examining its pattern of strengths and weaknesses, clearly the business does not have to correct all its weaknesses or gloat about all its strengths. The big question is whether the business should limit itself to those opportunities for which it now possesses the required strengths or should consider better opportunities.

Many hospitality industry specialists believe that to compete effectively, companies such as hotels, resorts, and cruise lines will need seamless connectivity within their computer reservation systems (CRS), including a global distribution system (GDS). If a hotel company wishes to increase its international business and its reservations through travel agents, the existence or development of such a system would surely be viewed as a strength.[30]

Sometimes a business does poorly not because its department lacks the required strengths, but because they do not work together as a team. In some hospitality companies, salespeople are viewed as overpaid, good-time playboys and playgirls who produce business by practically giving it away to customers. In turn, salespeople often view those in operations as incompetent dolts who consistently foul up their orders and provide poor customer service. It is therefore critically important to assess interdepartmental working relationships as part of the internal environmental audit.

Every company must manage some basic processes, such as new-product development, raw materials to finished products, sales leads to orders, customer orders to cash payment, and so on. Each process creates value, and each process requires interdepartmental teamwork. Although each department may possess a core competence, the challenge is to develop superior competitive capability in managing these processes.

3.7 The Boston Greater Convention and Visitors Bureau

Goal Formulation

After the business unit has defined its mission and examined its Strengths/Weaknesses/Opportunities/Threats (called SWOT analysis), it can proceed to develop specific objectives and goals for the planning period. This stage is called goal formulation.

Very few businesses pursue only one objective. Most business units pursue a mix of objectives, including profitability, sales growth, market-share improvement, risk containment, innovativeness, reputation, and so on. The business unit sets these objectives and manages by objectives.

The business unit should strive to arrange its objectives hierarchically, from most to least important. Where possible, objectives should be stated quantitatively. The objective "increase the return on investment (ROI)" is not as satisfactory as "increase ROI to 15 percent" or, even better, "increase ROI to 15 percent within two years." Managers use the term goals to describe objectives that are specific with respect to magnitude and time. Turning objectives into measurable goals facilitates management planning, implementation, and control. A business should set realistic goals. The levels should arise from an analysis of the business unit's opportunities and strengths, not from wishful thinking.

Finally, the company's objectives need to be consistent. Objectives are sometimes in a trade-off relationship. Here are some important trade-offs:

- High profit margins versus high market share
- Deep penetration of existing markets versus developing new markets
- Profit goals versus nonprofit goals
- High growth versus low risk

The hotel industry is faced with unique challenges concerning goal formulation and performance measurement due to management agreements between hotel owners and hotel operating companies. Most industries, such as manufacturing, construction, or retailing, hire their own management staff rather than contracting with an independent operations management company. "Of all the issues addressed in the negotiation of a hotel management agreement, among the most difficult to resolve is establishing an appropriate performance test that is acceptable to both parties."[29]

Performance measures with management contracts usually encompass three areas:[30]

1. **A hotel's return.** Returns-based performance tests measure income before fixed costs (IBFC) or net operating income (NOI). Owners and management companies can usually find agreement in the use of these measures.
2. **Operating margins.** Owners also often insist on performance measures based on increases in operating margins, such as increasing IBFC from 20 percent of revenue to 28 percent. Operating margin tests focus management's attention on an initial area but sometimes cause managers to think and act "short term," which may discourage management from using revenue management programs that accept some low-margin business during periods of weak occupancy.
3. **Revenue per available room (REVPAR).** REVPAR tests assume that room revenue is a good indicator of a hotel's overall performance. These performance tests do not measure other revenue, such as laundry, food and beverage, rents, and telephone. As a result, some hotel managers pay little attention to the marketing of these product lines. REVPAR tests also ignore the expense side. A hotel may achieve a high REVPAR through exceptional service by overstaffing but be less profitable than hotels with lower REVPAR and lower expenses. Those who use REVPAR often compare their results with other hotels, but the accuracy of comparative data may be questioned.

Strategy Formulation

Goals indicate what a business unit wants to achieve; strategy answers how to get there. Every business must tailor a strategy for achieving its goals. Although we can list many types of strategies, Michael Porter has condensed them into three generic types that provide a good starting point for strategic thinking.[31]

1. **Overall cost leadership.** Here the business works hard to achieve the lowest costs. The problem with this strategy is that

other firms will usually emerge with still lower costs. The real key is for the firm to achieve the lowest costs among those competitors adopting a similar differentiation or focus strategy.

2. **Differentiation.** Here the business concentrates on achieving superior performance in an important customer benefit area valued by a large part of the market. The relative importance of customer benefit areas shift as demographic and psychographic characteristics of market populations change. Younger, active hotel guests may value the existence of a swimming pool, a sauna, or exercise room, whereas older guests have been shown to place high value in reliability and assurance of consistent hotel service.[32]
3. **Focus.** Here the business focuses on one or more narrow market segments rather than going after a large market. The firm gets to know the needs of these segments and pursues either cost leadership or a form of differentiation within the target segments.

According to Porter, those firms pursuing the same strategy directed to the same market or market segment constitute a strategic group. Porter suggests that firms that do not pursue a clear strategy—middle-of-the-roaders—do the worst. Middle-of-the-roaders try to be good on all strategic dimensions, but these firms end up being not particularly excellent at anything.

Strategic Alliances

Companies are also discovering that they need strategic partners if they hope to be effective. Even giant companies—Accor, Hyatt, and McDonald's—often cannot achieve leadership, either nationally or globally, without forming strategic alliances with domestic or multinational companies that complement or leverage their capabilities and resources.

The Star Alliance allows the customers of its partners to have seamless international travel. Photo courtesy of Star Alliance.

3.8 Star Alliance
Accor

Strategic alliances are cooperative agreements between organizations that allow them to benefit from each other's strengths. The Star Alliance, for example, brings together Air Canada, Air New Zealand, ANA, Ansett Australia, Austrian Airlines, bmi, Lauda, Lufthansa, Mexicana, SAS, Singapore Airlines, Thai Airways, Tyrolean, United Airlines, and Varig in a huge global partnership that allows over 300 million travelers a year to make nearly seamless connections to about 900 destinations.[33]

The Star Alliance makes it *impossible* for any of the airlines to expand the scope of their operations, thereby making it *possible* for their customers to have access to a worldwide system. Technology standards are creating partnerships. For example, in the casino industry gaming equipment manufacturers are working together so that player tracking systems can easily integrate with different machines. The strength of the brand name also leads to alliances: Starbucks has replaced the existing coffee kiosks in some Hyatt hotels. The global expansion of business has also created the need for alliances.

Just doing business in another country may require the firm to license its product, form a joint venture with a local firm, or buy from local suppliers to meet domestic content requirements. As a result, many firms are rapidly developing global strategic networks. And victory is going to those who build the better global network.

Program Formulation

Once the business unit has developed its principal strategies, it must work out supporting programs. Thus, if an upscale hotel has decided to attain service leadership, it must run recruiting programs to attract the right employees, conduct training programs, develop leading-edge products and amenities, motivate the sales force, develop ads to communicate its service leadership, and so on.

The Hilton Group PLC, formally Ladbroke Group PLC of the United Kingdom, owns the largest chain of betting shops in that nation and also operates 217 Hilton International properties.[34] Additionally, the Group owns two racetracks in the United States and a card club in northern California; it decided it wanted a much larger presence in the U.S. wagering market. Instead of developing new casinos, which involve time and considerable risk, or purchasing an expensive casino in Las Vegas, the Group decided to purchase proven smaller casinos in Colorado and acquired two Bullwhacker casinos and the Silver Hawk casino for $85 million. This provided them with a U.S. casino base from which it could build.[35]

Implementation

Even a clear strategy and well-thought-out supporting programs may not be enough. The firm may fail at implementation. Employees in a company share a common way of behaving and thinking. They must understand and believe in the company's strategy. The company must communicate its strategy to the employees and make them understand their part in carrying it out. To implement a strategy, the firm must have the required resources, including employees with the necessary skills to carry out that strategy.

Feedback and Control

As it implements its strategy, the firm needs to track results and monitor new developments in the environment. Some environments are fairly stable from year to year. Others evolve slowly in a fairly predictable way. Still other environments change rapidly. The company can count on one thing: The environment will change. And when it does, the company will need to review and revise its implementation, programs, strategies, or even objectives. Peter Drucker pointed out that it is more important to do the right thing (being effective) than to do things right (being efficient). Excellent companies excel at both.

Once an organization starts losing its market position through failure to respond to a changed environment, it becomes increasingly harder to retrieve leadership. Organizations, especially large ones, have much inertia. Yet organizations can be changed through leadership, hopefully in advance of a crisis but certainly in the middle of one. The key to organizational health is the organization's willingness to examine the changing environment and to adopt appropriate new goals and behaviors. Adaptable organizations monitor the environment continuously and attempt through flexible strategic planning to maintain a fit with the evolving environment.

The Emperor Hotel, a three-star property in Singapore, caters primarily to independent and corporate travelers, many in the oil industry. Due to a recession in Singapore, corporate income fell from $2.2 million to $1.9 million, a loss of $300,000.

Problem areas were the following:

- A 45 percent drop in food and beverage revenue
- Declining hotel occupancy from 92 percent to 57 percent
- Intensive competition
- Rising fixed costs
- Shrinking market niche (fewer people in the oil industry)
- Autocratic management style

The owner conducted a strategic analysis of the hotel and determined critical strengths and weaknesses.

STRENGTHS	WEAKNESSES
Image	Need for a face lift
Location	Slow management response
Financial support	Weak market niche
Service orientation	Poor cultural orientation
	Intensified competition

As a result of the strategic analysis, the Emperor Hotel decided to "shrink selectively," particularly in the food and beverage area. Food and beverage operations were contracted out. This strategy was selected because it was felt that if a hotel boom occurred, the hotel would be in a good position to take advantage of the good times. If not, the hotel would be attractive to a prospective buyer and could be sold on short notice.[36]

The hotel-resort industry faces unique challenges in strategic planning. Most other members of the hospitality industry, such as airlines, cruise lines, and major restaurant chains, may approach strategic planning in much the same manner as a manufacturing company. These organizations have highly centralized management operations in which major strategic decisions are made.

Unique Challenges of the Hotel Industry

The hotel-resort industry is characterized by a unique management and ownership structure that complicates the process of strategic planning.

- Major chains commonly do not own all the properties that they manage. Some hotel chains may, in fact, own no individual properties.
- Owners of hotels-resorts often show surprisingly little interest or knowledge of their properties. Hotels throughout the world have commonly been acquired because of tax benefits, perceived real estate appreciation, or as an ego-fulfilling device, particularly in the case of upscale showcase properties. A study of hotel investment returns in Southeast Asia demonstrated that "ego capital" or prestige associated with hotels was a dominant reason for ownership. "Such non-economic benefits may drive up prices for hotels and make it possible to accept relatively low yields in comparison to other real-estate opportunities or investments in other global markets."[37]
- Occasionally, owners complain that hotel management companies are nonresponsive, have little expertise in planning, and do not work closely with owners or their representatives. In Asia, there reportedly exists an association of hotel owners who have grouped together in an effort to place pressure on hotel management companies.
- Hotel management companies that are generally unknown or invisible to the general public may own or manage many diverse properties, such as Ramada, Holiday Inn, and Days Inn hotels.
- Professional managers of individual properties have commonly been educated and trained to manage properties with concern for areas such as maintenance and front-desk operations but with little or no training in strategic planning. Many feel that this is the responsibility of the owner, yet if the owner has little interest in this function, strategic planning at the property level is overlooked.
- Hotel management companies often have little real power to force owners to make necessary investments or the strategic changes deemed essential. In many cases, the only alternative has been to drop the property from the chain.
- Hotels may or may not own or manage secondary properties within the hotel, such as restaurants, retail stores, health and fit-

ness centers, and nightclubs. This creates added complexity in strategic planning.

- Strategic alliances between hotel chains on a global basis may further complicate the planning process.

Marketing has a definite role to play in strategic planning. This department must maintain close and continuous ties with customers. Marketing is responsible for identifying and studying consumer needs and, as such, has a level of expertise in this area that is invaluable in strategic planning.

KEY TERMS

Ansoff product–market expansion grid A matrix developed by cell, plotting new products and existing products with new products and existing products. The grid provides strategic insights into growth opportunities.

Backward integration A growth strategy by which companies acquire businesses supplying them with products or services, for example, a restaurant chain purchasing a bakery.

Competencies scope The range of technological and other core competencies that the company will master and leverage.

Concentric diversification strategy A growth strategy whereby a company seeks new products that have technological or marketing synergies with existing product lines.

Conglomerate diversification strategy A product growth strategy in which a company seeks new businesses that have no relationship to the company's current product line or markets.

Corporate mission statement A guide to provide all the publics of a company with a shared sense of purpose, direction, and opportunity, allowing all to work independently, yet collectively, toward the organization's goals.

Forward integration A growth strategy by which companies acquire businesses that are closer to the ultimate consumer, such as a hotel acquiring a chain of travel agents.

Geographic scope The range of regions, countries, or country groups where the corporation will operate.

Growth–share matrix A model developed by the Boston Consulting Group to assist managers to plan business portfolios.

Horizontal diversification strategy A product growth strategy whereby a company looks for new products that could appeal to current customers, which are technologically unrelated to its current line.

Horizontal integration A growth strategy by which companies acquire competitors.

Industry scope The range of industries that a company will operate in.

Macroenvironmental forces Demographic, economic, technological, political, legal, social, and cultural factors.

Microenvironmental forces Customers, competitors, distribution channels, suppliers.

Marketing opportunity An area of need in which a company can perform profitably.

Market-oriented strategic planning The managerial process of developing and maintaining a viable fit between the organization's objectives, skills, and resources and its changing market opportunities.

Market-segment scope The type of market or customers a company will serve.

Products and applications scope The range of products and applications in which the company will participate.

Strategic alliances Relationships between independent parties that agree to cooperate but still retain separate identities.

Strategic business units (SBUs) A single business or collection of related businesses that can be planned separately from the rest of the company.

Vertical scope The number of channel levels (from raw materials to final product and distribution) in which the company will engage.

Chapter Review

I. The Aim of Strategic Planning. Strategic planning helps a company select and organize its business in a manner that keeps the company healthy despite unexpected upsets in any of its specific business or product lines.

II. Three Ideas that Define Strategic Planning

1) Managing a company's business as an investment portfolio to determine which business entities deserve to be built, maintained, phased down, or terminated.

2) Assessing accurately the future profit potential of each business by considering the market's growth rate and the company's position and fit.

3) Underlying strategic planning is that of strategy and developing a game plan for achieving long-run objectives.

III. Four Major Organizational Levels

1) Corporate level. The corporate level is responsible for designing a corporate strategic plan to guide the entire enterprise. It makes decisions on how much resource support to allocate to each division, as well as which businesses to start or eliminate.

2) Division level. Each division establishes a plan covering the allocation of funds to support that business unit within that division.

3) **Business level.** Each business unit in turn develops its business unit's strategic plan to carry that business unit into a profitable future.

4) **Product level.** Each product level within a business unit develops a marketing plan for achieving its objectives in its product market.

IV. Four Natures of High-Performance Business

1) **Stakeholder.** The principle that a business must at least strive to satisfy the minimum expectations of each stakeholder group.

2) **Processes.** Companies build cross-functional teams that manage core business processes in order to be superior competitors.

3) **Resources.** Companies decide to outsource less critical resources. They identify their core competencies and use them as the basis for their strategic planning.

4) **Organization.** Companies align their organization's structure, policies, and culture to the changing requirements of business strategy.

V. Four Elements of Defining the Corporate Mission. A mission statement provides company employees with a shared sense of purpose, direction, and opportunity. The company mission statement guides geographically dispersed employees to work independently and collectively toward realizing the organization's goal.

1) **History.** Every company has a history of aims, policies, and achievements, and the organization must not depart too radically from its past history.

2) **Preferences.** Consideration of the current preferences of the owner and management.

3) **Resources.** The organization's resources determine which missions are possible.

4) **Competencies.** The organization should base its mission on its distinctive competencies.

VI. Mission Statement's Characteristic and Focused Goals

1) **Industry scope.** The range of industries that the company will consider.

2) **Products and application scope.** The range of products and applications in which the company will participate.

3) **Competencies scope.** The range of technological and other core competencies that the company will master and leverage.

4) **Market-segment scope.** The types of market or customers that the company will serve.

5) **Vertical scope.** The number of channel levels from raw materials to final products and distribution in which the company will engage.

6) **Geographic scope.** The range of regions or countries where the corporation will operate.

VII. Establishing Strategic Business Units. Three dimensions in defining a business: customer groups, customer needs, and technology.

VIII. Strategic Business Units (SBUs). An SBU is a single business or collection of related businesses that can be planned for separately from the rest of the company. It has its own set of competitors and a manager who is responsible for strategic planning and profit performance.

IX. Boston Consulting Group Model

1) **Question marks.** Company businesses that operate in high-growth markets but have relatively low market shares.
2) **Stars.** The market leader in a high-growth market. This does not necessarily mean that the star produces a positive cash flow for the company.
3) **Cash cows.** When a star's annual growth rate falls to less than 10 percent, it becomes a cash cow. A cash cow produces a lot of cash for the company and enjoys economies of scale and higher profit margins.
4) **Dogs.** Dogs describe company businesses that have weak market shares in low-growth markets. They typically generate low profits or losses.

X. **Planning New Businesses.** The strategic planning gap is the gap between future desired sales and projected sales. There are three ways to fill the gap:
1) **Intensive growth opportunities.** To identify further opportunities to achieve growth within the company's current business.
2) **Integrative growth opportunities.** To identify opportunities to build or acquire businesses that are related to the company's current business.
a) **Backward integration.** A hotel company acquires one of its suppliers.
b) **Forward integration.** A hotel company acquires a tour wholesaler or travel agents.
c) **Horizontal integration.** A hotel company acquires one or more competitors, provided that the government does not bar the move.
3) **Diversification growth opportunities.** To identify opportunities to add attractive businesses that are unrelated to the company's current businesses.
a) **Concentric diversification strategy.** Company seeks new products that have technological and/or marketing synergies with the existing product line, even though the product may appeal to a new class of customers.
b) **Horizontal diversification strategy.** Company searches for new products that could appeal to its current customers though technologically unrelated to its current product line.
c) **Conglomerate diversification strategy.** Company seeks new businesses that have no relationship to the company's current technology, product, or market.

XI. **Business Strategy Planning**
1) **Business mission.** SBU defines its various scopes: its products and applications, competence, market segments, vertical positioning, and geography. It must also define its specific goals and policies as a separate business.
2) **External environment analysis**
a) **Macroenvironment forces.** Demographic, economic, technological, political, legal, competition, and social-cultural.
b) **Microenvironment factors.** Customers, competitors, distribution channels, suppliers.

c) **Opportunities.** A marketing opportunity is an area of need in which a company can perform profitably. Opportunities can be listed and classified according to their attractiveness and the success probability.

d) **Threats.** An environmental threat is a challenge posed by unfavorable trends or developments that would lead, in the absence of defensive marketing action, to sales or profit deterioration. Threats can be classified according to their seriousness and probability of occurrence.

3) **Internal environment analysis (strengths analysis and weaknesses analysis).** Company reviews the business' marketing, financial, manufacturing, and organizational competencies. Each factor is rated as to whether it is a major strength, minor strength, neutral factor, major weakness, or minor weakness.

4) **Goal formulation (What do we want?)** Four characteristics of an SBU's objectives:

a) **Hierarchical.** The business unit should strive to arrange its objectives hierarchically, from the most to the least important.

b) **Quantitative.** Managers use the term goals to describe objectives that are specific with respect to magnitude and time.

c) **Realistic.** The levels should arise from an analysis of the business unit's opportunities and strengths, not from wishful thinking.

d) **Consistent.** Long-run market-share growth and high current profits, for example.

5) **Strategy formulation (How do we get there?)** Michael Porter's three generic types of strategy:

a) **Overall cost leadership.** The real key is for a firm to achieve the lowest costs among those competitors adopting a similar differentiation or focus strategy.

b) **Differentiation.** The firm cultivates strengths that will give it a competitive advantage in one or more benefits.

c) **Focus.** The firm gets to know the needs of these segments and pursues either cost leadership or a form of differentiation within the target segments.

6) **Program formulation.** Supporting programs, such as running recruiting programs to attract the right employee, conducting training programs, developing leading-edge products and amenities, motivating the sales force, and developing advertisements to communicate its service leadership.

7) **Implementation.** To implement a strategy, the firm must have the required resources, including employees with the skills needed to carry out the company's strategy.

8) **Feedback and control.** The firm needs to track results and monitor new developments in the environment. The company will need to review and revise its implementation, programs, strategies, or even objectives.

Discussion Questions

1. Look at an annual report of a hospitality company and give an example of their strategic planning. Annual reports are available on-line through the text's Web site.
2. Is strategic planning the same thing as marketing planning, sales planning, and restructuring?
3. In a series of job interviews, you ask three recruiters to describe the missions of their companies. One says, "To make profits." Another says, "To create customers." The third says, "To fight world hunger." Analyze and discuss what these mission statements tell you about each of the companies.
4. What is the significance of an SBU?
5. What forms of vertical integration do you feel are likely to occur in the travel industry during the next ten years?
6. Think about the shopping area near your campus. Assume that you wish to start a business here and are looking for a promising opportunity for a restaurant.
   - **a.** Is there an opportunity to open a distinctive and promising business? Describe your target market, and how you would serve it differently than current businesses do.
   - **b.** What sort of marketing mix would you use for your business?

Experiential Exercises

Do one of the following:

1. Visit two hotels, restaurants, or other hospitality businesses. From your observations write down what you think are the strengths and weaknesses of the businesses. You will be able to observe elements such as location, physical facilities, employee attitude, quality of products, reputation of the brand (if it is a brand), and other factors.
2. Find a strategic alliance between a hotel company and another company (this can be for another hospitality organization or a company outside the hospitality industry). State what you think the benefits of the alliance are for each partner.

Internet Exercises

WWW

Support for these exercises can be found on the Web site for *Marketing for Hospitality and Tourism*, www.prenhall.com/kotler.

A. Find the mission statement of a hospitality or travel company on the Internet. Critique the mission statement against the guidelines for a mission statement, as stated in the text. If you have difficulty finding a mission statement, you can check the Web site under this exercise, and you will find the URL to some mission statements.

B. Visit the annual report of a hospitality organization (these can usually be accessed through the company's home page). What does the annual report tell you about their strategy?

References

1. See Francis Buttle, "The Marketing Strategy Worksheet: A Practical Tool," *Cornell Hotel and Restaurant Administration Quarterly* 33, no. 3 (June 1992): 55–67.
2. Mark W. Cunningham and Dev S. Chekitan, "Strategic Marketing: A Lodging End Run," *Cornell Hotel and Restaurant Administration Quarterly* 33, no. 4 (August 1992): 43.

3. Ibid.
4. See Tamara J. Erickson and C. Everett Shorey, "Business Strategy: New Thinking for the 90's," *Prism* (Fourth Quarter 1992): 19–35.
5. Cathy A. Enz, "Organizational Architectures for the 21st Century: The Redesign for Hospitality Firms," *Hospitality Research Journal* 17, no. 1 (1993), p. 108.
6. Christopher W. Nordling and Sharon K. Wheeler, "Building a Market-Segment Accounting Model to Improve Profits," *Cornell Hotel and Restaurant Administration Quarterly* 33, no. 3 (June 1992): 29–36.
7. Al Glanzberg and Glenn Withiam, "Culture at the Crossroads: Boca Raton and Rockresort," *Cornell Hotel and Restaurant Administration Quarterly* 32, no. 1 (May 1991): 39.
8. Bruce J. Tracey and Timothy R. Hinkin, "Transformational Leaders in the Hospitality Industry," *Cornell Hotel and Restaurant Administration Quarterly* 35, no. 2 (April 1994): 18.
9. See Peter Drucker, *Management: Tasks, Responsibilities, and Practices* (New York: Harper & Row, 1973), Chapter 7.
10. See "The Hollow Corporation," *Business Week*, March 3, 1986, pp. 57–59.
11. Choice Hotels International. Retrieved February 5, 2001 from the World Wide Web: *http://www.choicehotels.com/cgi-bin/res/webres?europe.html.*
12. "Mission Statements for the Next Millennium," *Restaurant Hospitality* (December 1998): 46.
13. For more discussion, see Laura Nash, "Mission Statements, Mirrors and Windows," *Harvard Business Review* (March–April 1988): 155–156. See also Tom Feltenstein, "Strategic Planning for the 1990's: Exploiting the Inevitable," *Cornell Hotel and Restaurant Administration Quarterly* 33, no. 3 (June 1992): 50–54.
14. Robert H. Woods, "Strategic Planning: A Look at Ruby Tuesday," *Cornell Hotel and Restaurant Administration Quarterly* 35, no. 3 (June 1994): 45.
15. "Mission Statements for the Next Millennium," *Restaurant Hospitality* (December 1998), 46.
16. Theodore Levitt, "Marketing Myopia," *Harvard Business Review* (July–August 1960): 45–56.
17. See "Holiday Inns: Refining Its Focus to Food, Lodging, and More Casinos," *Business Week*, July 21, 1980, pp. 100–104.
18. See Roger A. Kerin, Vijay Mahajan, and P. Rajan Varadarajan, *Contemporary Perspectives on Strategic Planning* (Boston: Allyn and Bacon, 1990).
19. Michael L. Kasavana and Donald I. Smith, *Menu Engineering* (Lansing, MI: Hospitality Publishers, 1982).
20. Igor H. Ansoff, "Strategies for Diversification," *Harvard Business Review* (September–October 1957): 113–124.
21. Dennis Reynolds, "Managed-Services Companies," *Cornell Hotel and Restaurant Administration Quarterly* 38, no. 3 (June 1997): 90.
22. Gregory X. Norkus and Elliott Merberg, "Food Distribution in the 1990's," *Cornell Hotel and Restaurant Administration Quarterly* 35, no. 3 (June 1994): 60–61.
23. Sarah Morse and Pamela Lanier, "Golf Resorts: Driving into the 90's," *Cornell Hotel and Restaurant Administration Quarterly* 33, no. 4 (August 1992): 45.
24. Ibid.
25. Michael P. Sim and Chase M. Burritt, "Enhancing Resort Profitability with Membership Programs," *Cornell Hotel and Restaurant Administration Quarterly* 34, no. 4 (August 1993): 59–63.
26. Ali A. Poorani and David R. Smith, "Franchising as a Business Expansion Strategy in the Bed & Breakfast Industry: Creating a Marketing and Development Advantage," *Hospitality Research Journal* 18, no. 2 (1994): 32–33.
27. H. G. Parsa and Mahmood A. Khan, "Quick Service Restaurants of the 21st Century: An Analytical Review of Macro Factors," *Hospitality Research Journal* 17, no. 1 (1993): 164.
28. Rita M. Emmer, Chuck Tauck, Scott Wilkinson, and Richard G. Moore, "Marketing Hotels Using Global Distribution Systems," *Cornell Hotel and Restaurant Administration Quarterly* 34, no. 6 (December 1993): 80–89.
29. Jonathan Berger, "Applying Performance Tests in Hotel Management Agreements," *Cornell Hotel and Restaurant Administration Quarterly* 38, no. 2 (April 1997): 25.
30. Ibid.
31. See Michael E. Porter, *Competitive Strategy: Techniques for Analyzing Industries and Competitors* (New York: Free Press, 1980), Chapter 2.
32. Beth E. A. Wuest, Richard F. Tax, and Daniel A. Emenheiser, "What Do Mature Travelers Perceive an Important Hotel/Motel Customer Service?" *Hospitality Research Journal* 20, no. 2 (1996): 90.
33. Fact Sheet, Press Room, Retrieved September 21, 2001 from *http://www.star-pr.com.*
34. The Hilton Group Retrieved February 26, 2000 From the World Wide Web: *http://hiltongroup.com/company00.html.*
35. Steve Raabe, "Top Casino Operator Sold," *Denver Post*, July 22, 1997, p. 1C.
36. Kee Lee Weng and B. C. Ghosh, "Strategies for Hotels in Singapore," *Cornell Hotel and Restaurant Administration Quarterly,* 31, no. 1 (May 1990): 78–79.
37. Anna Mattila, "Investment Returns and Opportunities for Hotels in Asia," *Cornell Hotel and Restaurant Administration Quarterly* 38, no. 1 (February 1997): 78.

Domino's
Domino's Pizza
DRIVERS DO NOT LEAVE
STORE WITH OVER $20
Domino's Pizza
Domino's
The Pizza Delivery Experts

4 The Marketing Environment

It is useless to tell a river to stop running; the best thing is to learn how to swim in the direction it is flowing.
Anonymous

Domino's is the leader today in the home-delivery pizza business and the number two pizza maker in the country. Tom Monaghan started the chain with his brother in 1960 in Ypsilanti, Michigan; it was based on the concept of delivering pizzas to homes within thirty minutes. The first week's sales averaged less than $15 a day. After eight months, Tom's brother decided to leave the pizza business. Monaghan's ambitious expansion program brought with it a large debt that the company could not support. After working with Domino's for nearly a decade, Monaghan was forced to give the chain up to his creditors. The creditors soon discovered that managing a restaurant chain was a difficult task. They brought Monaghan back to manage the company in exchange for equity. Tom Monaghan managed to revive the chain and expand it to 290 restaurants by 1980. Domino's sales skyrocketed in the 1980s.

Several environmental factors during the 1980s propelled Domino's growth. An increase in the number of two-income families caused Americans to place increasing value on their time. Growth in the number of one- and two-person households with high discretionary incomes led people to buy prepared food more often. Childless, middle-aged, singles and couples are responsible for the highest consumption of restaurant-prepared meals eaten at home. Domino's success can be attributed to sound management and its development of a marketing mix aimed at the rapidly growing home-delivery segment of the market.

Domino's maintained its competitive lead with the use of technology. It was the first pizza maker to use a VCM (vertical chopper mixer) and the first to deliver the product in a specially designed corrugated box, which helped keep

moisture from weakening the box, while preventing cheese from sticking to the top during delivery. Another Domino's innovation was airtight fiberglass boxes to hold dough, which eliminated the need to brush dough balls with oil. Domino's was also one of the first chains to use Ferris wheel–type ovens. Today they use an even more advanced technology, conveyor ovens.

Success does not go unnoticed. Arthur Gunther, chairman of Pizza Hut, announced in 1985 that they would aggressively pursue the delivery market. Yet Monaghan welcomes competition. As he states in his book Pizza Tiger, *"Competition makes us sharper, keeps us looking for answers, and prevents us from getting complacent and thinking we know it all."*

Every business is bound to face some environmental backlashes. Domino's delivery of more than a million pizzas by 80,000 drivers inevitably resulted in accidents. In 1988 alone, Domino's drivers were involved in accidents that resulted in twenty fatalities. This fact was publicized on NBC's First Edition *news magazine, on* CBS News, *in the* New York Times, *and in local papers. Some groups claimed that the accidents were a direct result of Domino's promise of delivery in thirty minutes or less. Domino's responded with a campaign stating that safety had always been a major company concern. A toll-free number was instituted that people can call if they witness traffic violations by Domino's drivers.*

In 1989, Monaghan announced that he was considering selling the chain to devote more time to religious and philanthropic concerns. This made the franchises, suppliers, and competitors wonder who would purchase the chain and how the new owner might change the organization. Pizza Hut began to eat into Domino's share of the home-delivery market. Domino's, which at one time owned the home-delivery market with a 90 percent market share, was down to 46 percent in 1991, whereas Pizza Hut was up to 24 percent. Little Caesar's also started to erode Domino's sales and is currently battling with Domino's for the number two spot. As a result of these setbacks, Monaghan turned his attention back to Domino's.

Domino's focus on speed was no longer a competitive advantage—other chains had matched that speed. The baby boomers who were Domino's original customers had grown up and had families; their needs had changed. Monaghan sold off assets that were not directly related to the pizza business and started listening to his customers. In 1993, Domino's came out with its first new product in over thirty years, a thin-crust pizza. This resulted in the first positive sales growth in two and one-half years. Dominos then added breadsticks and Buffalo wings. Later they added a deep-dish pizza and expanded their variety of soft drinks. The product variety increased their delivery time from twenty-four to twenty-eight minutes, but the customers didn't care—they were getting what they wanted. Domino's was back in touch with its customers, and its customers were coming back.

Domino's provides an excellent example of how a business interacts with external forces. The pizza home-delivery concept grew because it was presented at a time when the entire home-delivered food concept was growing. The company used technology to gain a competitive advantage. As Domino's became more successful, other pizza chains entered the home-delivery market more aggressively. When Domino's drivers had accidents, it suffered adverse publicity from those who claimed the accidents resulted from company pressure on drivers to deliver within thirty minutes. Social groups who opposed Monaghan's beliefs demonstrated against the chain. When Monaghan turned his attention away from the company, it began to suffer. However, when Domino's turned its focus back to its customers, the customers came back.

Tom Monaghan retired and sold Domino's Pizza in December 1998 to Bain Capital, Inc., resulting in Bain's acquiring 93 percent of the company. Bain Capital, Inc., of Boston, is one of the nation's leading private equity investment firms.

Advantages in electronic communication brought new challenges and opportunities for Domino's. In the fall of 1999, Domino's became the first pizza company to use television as a distribution channel. The company placed interactive TV ads on SkyDigital in Europe, allowing customers to order their pizza live from the interactive ad. The viewers used an interactive button on their SkyDigital remote that took them to the Domino's Pizza site. Once they selected their products, the order was sent to Domino's server and then dispatched to the nearest Domino's. If the viewer did not have a Domino's Pizza nearby, the order was not accepted. The majority of the orders Domino's received using this channel were from new customers, with an average check that was 20 percent higher than telephone orders.

In the U.S. market in 1999, Domino's was starting to falter because of increased discounting and lack of new product introductions. To offset this, in January 2001 Domino's came out with its CinnaStix, a bread product sprinkled in sugar and cinnamon and served with a creamy vanilla icing.

Domino's provides an example of an externally oriented company that took advantage of new opportunities created by the environment. In 2001 they dropped their "Bad Andy" ads, which featured a mischievous monkeylike puppet and the slogan, "bad Andy, good pizza." Ken Calwell, the new vice president of marketing at Domino's, stated he felt positioning based on Domino's delivery would be more effective in an economy where consumers were stressed and in need of convenience. Calwell also stated he would focus on customer research to develop new products and also to evaluate Domino's existing product line. He felt some products might not create value for the customer in 2001. Like all companies, Domino's must maintain alertness in a rapidly changing environment.[1] Today Domino's Pizza operates 7,112 stores throughout the United States and sixty-five international markets. Domino's is the recognized world leader in pizza delivery with 2000 worldwide sales topping $3.54 billion. Headquartered in Ann Arbor, Michigan, Domino's is the largest privately held restaurant chain in the world, and the eighth largest of all restaurant chains.

Chapter Objectives

After reading this chapter, you should be able to:

1. List and discuss the importance of the elements of the company's microenvironment, including the company, suppliers, marketing intermediaries, customers, and public.
2. Describe the macroenvironmental forces that affect the company's ability to serve its customers.
3. Explain how changes in the demographic and economic environments affect marketing, and describe the levels of competition.
4. Identify the major trends in the firm's natural and technological environments.
5. Explain the key changes that occur in the political and cultural environments.
6. Discuss how companies can be proactive rather than reactive when responding to environmental trends.

A company's marketing environment consists of the outside actors and forces that affect a company's ability to develop and maintain successful transactions with its target customers. The marketing environment is made up of a microenvironment and a macroenvironment. The **microenvironment** consists of actors and forces close to the company that can affect its ability to serve its customers, the company itself, marketing channel firms, customer markets, and a broad range of publics. The **macroenvironment** consists of the larger societal forces that affect the entire microenvironment, that is, demographic, economic, natural, technological, political, competitor, and cultural forces. We first examine the company's microenvironment and then its macroenvironment.

The Company's Micro-environment

Marketing management's task is to create attractive offers for target markets. Various actors in its microenvironment will affect its degree of success. These actors are shown in Figure 4-1. They include the company, suppliers, market intermediaries, customers, and publics.

The Company

Marketing managers don't operate in a vacuum. They must work closely with top management and the various company departments. The finance department is concerned with finding and using the funds required to carry out the marketing plan. The accounting department has to measure revenues and costs to help marketing know how well it is achieving its objectives. Product development is responsible for creating new products to fit the needs of the changing marketplace. Housekeeping is responsible for delivering clean rooms sold by the sales department. All company departments will have some impact on the success of marketing plans.

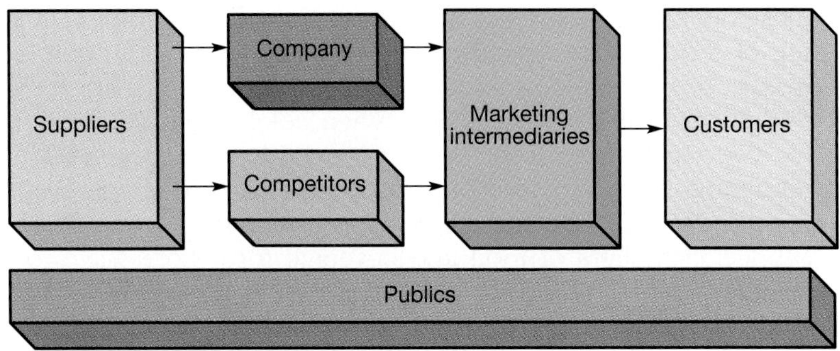

Figure 4-1
Major actors in the company's microenvironment.

Suppliers

Suppliers are firms and individuals that provide the resources needed by the company to produce its goods and services. Trends and developments affecting suppliers can, in turn, seriously affect a company's marketing plan. Suppose that a restaurant manager decides to run a live lobster special for the weekend. The seafood supplier is called, who promises to supply 200 lobsters for the weekend promotion. Friday morning the supplier calls and reports that lobsters were shorted on the shipment from Boston, and they will not be delivered until Saturday morning. The manager must now find an alternative source or disappoint guests who have reservations for Friday night.

In another case, Steak and Ale wanted to add a new scallop seafood dish to its menu. The corporate offices spent six months perfecting the scallop dish. During the development period, the price of scallops doubled. The restaurant would now have to charge a price higher than customers would pay. The project was scrapped. Marketing management must pay attention to changes in supply availability (as affected by shortages and strikes) and supply costs.

Some hotels have contracted with restaurant companies to supply their food and beverage services. The Lenox Hotel in Boston made an arrangement with the management of Anago, a well-known Boston restaurant, to move their restaurant to The Lenox. The New York Palace got Le Cirque, one of New York's most popular restaurants, to move to the Palace. New York, New York in Las Vegas has contracted with ARC restaurants to manage its restaurants. These and other hotels are bringing branded restaurants to their hotels to create value for their guests and expose restaurant guests to the hotel. The outsourcing of food and beverage operations allows the hotel to concentrate on lodging, while letting a food and beverage specialist handle this area within the hotel. On paper this sounds like a great arrangement, and in real life it often works out well. However, the outsourcing is not as simple as it may seem. Coffee shop operations are important to business customers. In fact, in focus groups business people have told us that a coffee shop suitable for a business meeting is sometimes the deciding factor in the choice of a hotel. A problem for some hotels that have leased out their operations to upscale operators is that upscale restaurant operators often are not interested in the coffee shop and room service operations, and

4.1 The Lenox
The New York Palace
Le Cirque
New York, New York Hotel and Casino, Las Vegas

these operations often suffer as a result. Another problem is that the leasing of food service operations ties up hotel space through lease agreements. This can be a problem if the hotel decides to renovate and change the design of the public spaces. When hotel guests complain about poor food service at the front desk, saying the hotel does not operate the restaurants is *not* an acceptable answer. Thus, service recovery programs need to be worked out between the restaurant and the hotel. Like any supplier, suppliers of food and beverage for a hotel have to be chosen carefully.

On a macrobasis, tourist destinations need suppliers. Airline service, hotel, restaurants, ground operations, meeting facilities, and entertainment are some of the components of a tourist destination. One of the roles of a regional convention and visitors bureaus (CVB) is to make sure that there is a good selection of suppliers of tourist products in their area. They must recruit organizations to provide visitors with a variety of tourist activities and options. CVBs must also work to represent the interests of these suppliers to make sure they do well after they are recruited.

Marketing Intermediaries

Marketing intermediaries are a specialized group of suppliers that help the company promote, sell, and distribute its goods to the final buyers. Intermediaries are business firms that help hospitality companies find customers or make sales. They include travel agents, wholesale tour operators, and hotel representatives. For example, a wholesaler creates leisure packages that include air transportation, ground transportation, and hotel accommodations. These packages are promoted through newspaper advertising and travel agents. Through volume purchasing, the wholesaler receives reduced prices, which enable the wholesaler to pay the travel agent a commission for selling the product, give the customer a good price, and produce a profit. In choosing wholesalers, hotels must select reputable firms that will deliver the promised product to the customer and pay the hotel for their services.

4.2 Red Lobster
Sheraton

In manufacturing industries, transportation systems move the product from the factory to the customer. The firm makes contractual arrangements with transportation companies to perform this service for them or has their own transportation system. Like manufacturing firms, some hospitality firms have central commissaries and depend on transportation systems to move the product to their restaurants. Red Lobster, for example, has a large food-processing plant in Orlando, Florida. The majority of Sheraton's guests arrive by airline (60%), whereas 70 percent of car rental customers arrive by air; both industries will be adversely affected by a rise in airfares.[2] Many resort destinations, especially islands, depend on air transportation. After terrorist attacks on the United States in September 2001, hotel occupancy rates dropped drastically as business people and tourists stopped traveling by air. Particularly hard hit were tourist and convention destinations such as Las Vegas, Orlando, and Hawaii. Las Vegas occupancy rates dropped from above 90 percent to below 50 percent, showing how dependent tourist destinations are on airlines. Tourist retail shops, rental car companies, resorts, and convention centers are dependent on air travel to bring their guests. These organizations must work with local and state tourist bureaus to ensure that there are enough airline flights serving their region.

Marketing services agencies are suppliers that help the firm formulate and implement its marketing strategy and tactics. These suppliers include public relations agencies, advertising agencies, and direct mail houses. They work directly with the company's marketing program and also include marketing research firms, media firms, and marketing consulting firms which help companies target and promote their products to the right markets. These firms can vary in creativity, quality, service, and price. The company should regularly review their performance and replace those that no longer perform well.

Financial intermediaries include banks, credit companies, insurance companies, and other firms that help hospitality companies finance their transactions or insure the risks associated with the buying and selling of goods and services. Rising insurance costs, in particular liquor liability insurance, has forced some hospitality firms out of business. Because rising credit costs, limited credit, or both can seriously affect a company's marketing performance, the company has to develop strong relationships with important financial institutions. Small multiunit chains often feel the pressure to grow to keep their stock price up and their stockholders happy. This is what happened to Boston Market, Fuddrucker's, and Del Taco. These companies have all reorganized and recovered, but they went through some hard times. Companies must be careful that they do not succumb to the unmanageable growth expectations of their financial intermediaries.

The Company's Macroenvironment

The company and its suppliers, marketing intermediaries, customers, and publics all operate in a larger macroenvironment that shapes opportunities and poses threats. The company must watch and respond to these uncontrollable forces. The macroenvironment consists of the seven major forces shown in Figure 4-2. In the remaining sections of this chapter, we examine these forces and show how they can affect marketing plans.

Competitors

Every company faces a broad range of competitors. The marketing concept states that to be successful a company must satisfy the needs and wants of consumers better than its competitors. Marketers must do more

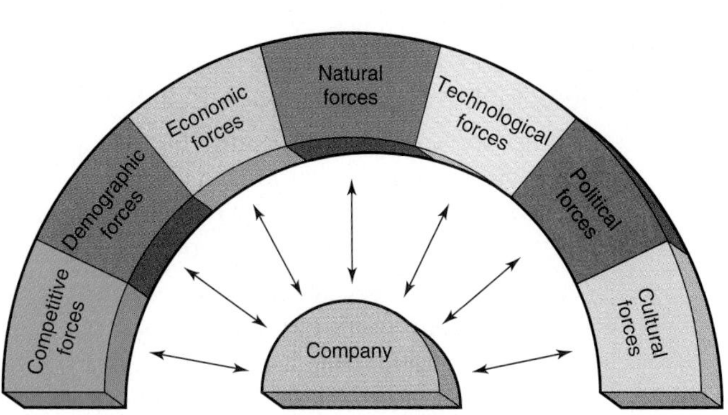

Figure 4-2
Major forces in the company's macroenvironment.

than adapt to the needs of target customers. They must also adapt to the strategies of other companies serving the same target markets. Companies must gain strategic advantage by strongly positioning their product in the minds of consumers.

No single competitive marketing strategy is best for all companies. Each firm must consider its size and industry position in relation to that of its competitors. Large firms with dominant positions in an industry can use certain strategies that smaller firms cannot afford. Small firms can also choose strategies that give them certain advantages. For example, a large restaurant chain can use its buying power to purchase national advertising, spreading the cost among hundreds or thousands of operations. But small, individually owned restaurants are able to adjust quickly to local trends and can offer more menu variety because they do not have to worry about standardizing menu items across thousands of restaurants. Both large and small firms must find marketing strategies that give them specific advantages over competitors operating in their markets. In general a company should monitor three variables when analyzing each of its competitors:

1. *Share of market:* the competitor's share of the target market
2. *Share of mind:* the percentage of customers who named the competitor in responding to the statement, "Name the first company that comes to mind in this industry."
3. *Share of heart:* the percentage of customers who named the competitor in responding to the statement, "Name the company from whom you would prefer to buy the product."

Managers often fail to identify their competitors correctly. The manager of a Houston seafood restaurant said that his restaurant had no competition because there were no other seafood restaurants within several miles. Several months later the restaurant was out of business. Customers decided to spend their money at competitors, either by driving farther to other seafood restaurants or by dining at nearby nonseafood restaurants.

Every company faces four levels of competitors (see Figure 4-3):

4.3 McDonald's
Boston Market
Kentucky Fried Chicken
Taco Bell
Arby's

1. A company can view its competitors as other companies that offer similar products and services to the same customers at a similar price. At this level, McDonald's will view its competition as Burger King, Wendy's, and Hardee's.
2. A company can see its competitors as all companies making the same product or class of products. Here McDonald's may see its competition as all fast-food restaurants, including Boston Market, Kentucky Fried Chicken, Taco Bell, and Arby's.
3. A company can see its competitors more broadly as all companies supplying the same service. Here McDonald's would see itself competing with all restaurants and other suppliers of prepared food, such as the deli section of a supermarket.
4. A company can see its competition even more broadly as all companies that compete for the same consumer dollars. Here McDonald's would see itself competing with grocery stores and the self-provision of the meal by the consumer.[3]

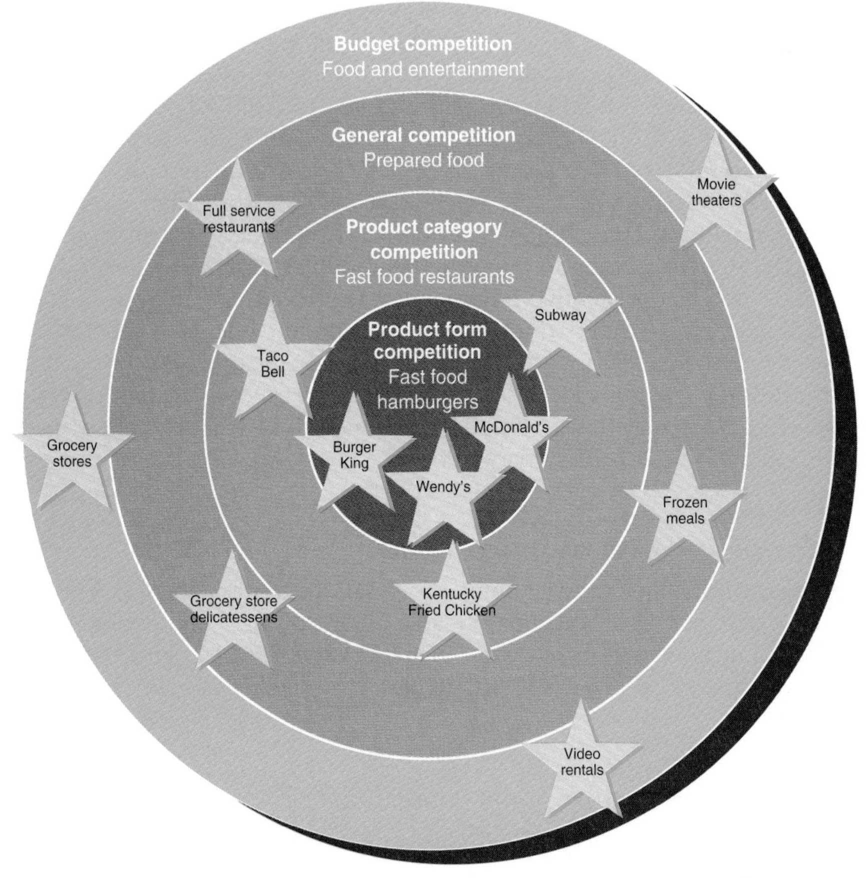

Figure 4-3
Levels of competition. Adapted from *Analysis for Market Planning,* Donald R. Lehmann and Russell S. Winer, p. 22, © 1994 by Richard D. Irwin.

McDonald's "You deserve a break today" advertising campaign was aimed at the fourth level of competition, telling the homemaker to give herself a break from cooking. Carnival Cruise Lines viewed its competition at the third level, that is, as other vacation destinations, such as Hawaii. Subway sandwich shops came out with advertising targeting second-level competition. The ads stressed the nutritional value of their sandwiches compared with other types of fast food, such as hamburgers.

Barriers to Entry, Exit, and Competition

Two forces that affect the competition are the ability of companies to enter and exit markets.[4] Entry barriers prevent firms from getting into a business, and barriers to exit prevent them from getting out. Low barriers to entry characterize the restaurant industry. It takes a relatively small amount of capital to get started in the restaurant business. Some restaurant managers who open without direct competition soon find themselves with four or five competitors in a year's time. This points out the importance of anticipating competition and operating on the premise that one always has competition. Always assume that customer satisfaction is important, because the customer can always go somewhere else.

4.4 Renaissance Hotels
Emerald Hotel
Courtyard by Marriott
Marquis Hotel
Crown Plaza Hotel
Embassy Suites
Residence Inns
Park Suites
Quality Inn

Hotels have moderately high barriers of entry, due to the costs of building a hotel and the scarcity of good locations. However, hotels find themselves with a different problem, that is, high barriers to exit from the industry. The large capital investment required to build a hotel becomes a sunk cost. As a result, hotels that cannot meet all their debt payments, taxes, and other fixed costs, but can produce enough gross profit to offset their fixed costs partially, may operate at a loss rather than close their doors completely. Thus, when hotel demand plummets, room supply remains the same, resulting in intensified competition for customers.

The hotel's competitive environment is affected by another factor—most hotels are planned during upswings in the business cycle when there is not enough supply to meet demand. But it can take four years or more from the planning stages to the opening of a hotel. By that time the economic cycle may have turned down. Sadly, new hotels often open their doors during a recessionary period.[5]

Demographic Environment

Demography is the study of human populations in terms of size, density, location, age, sex, race, occupation, and other statistics. The demographic environment is of major interest to marketers because markets are made up of people. The most important demographic trends are described here.

Changing Age Structure of the Population

The U.S. population stood at 278 million in 2001 and is expected to reach 300 million by the year 2010.[6] The single most important demographic trend in the United States is the changing age structure of the population. The age distribution of the U.S. population is rapidly assuming an "hourglass" shape. Two very large age groups, the baby boomer generation and the echo boomer generation, surround the smaller Generation X.

The Baby Boomers. The post–World War II baby boom produced 78 million baby boomers born between 1946 and 1964. Since then, the baby boomers have become one of the most powerful forces shaping the marketing environment. The boomers have presented a moving target, creating new markets as they grew from infancy to preadolescent, teenage, young adult, and now middle age to mature years. Today's baby boomers account for about 30 percent of the population but earn more than half of all personal income.

Baby boomers do not feel old. They will spend billions of dollars on travel, looking for active vacations, where they can have adventure or explore, such as a polar bear sighting expedition in northern Canada or historical tours of Europe. Through their continuing education departments universities have developed educational tours which target the baby boomers. Butterfield and Robinson, agents for upscale biking tours, market two-week bike tours with overnight stays in luxury accommodations to the boomers. They look for value and research their vacations. One of the reasons cruises are popular with boomers is because of the value of the all-inclusive vacation.

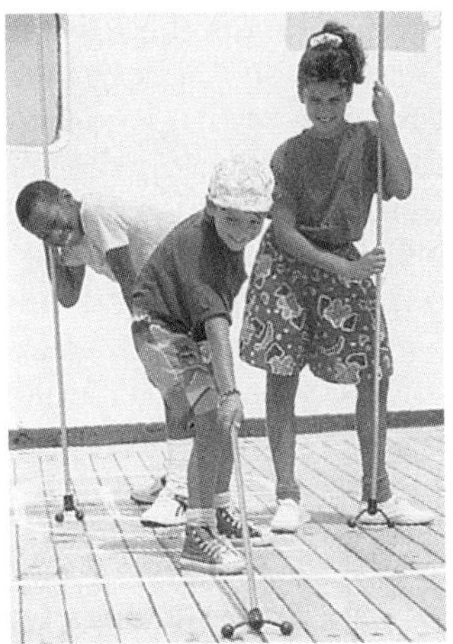

The average age when someone gets married for the first time is increasing. As a result many couples are well into their careers when they have their first child. These couples are used to traveling and eating out. When their children arrive they continue this pattern of traveling and dining out, creating a need for restaurants, hotels, and resorts to provide activities for their children. Courtesy of Carnival Cruise Lines.

Baby boomers cut across all walks of life. However, marketers typically have paid the most attention to the smaller upper crust of the boomer generation—its more educated, mobile, and wealthy segments. These segments have gone by many names. In the 1990s, they were called "yuppies" (young urban professionals), "bumpies" (black upwardly mobile professionals), "yummies" (young upwardly mobile mommies), and "DINKs" (dual-income, no-kids). In the 1990s, however, yuppies and DINKs gave way to a new breed, with names such as "DEWKs" (dual earners with kids) and "MOBYs" (mother older, baby younger). Now, to the chagrin of many in this generation, they are acquiring such titles as "WOOFs" (well-off older folks) or even "GRUMPIES" (just what the name suggests).

The oldest boomers are now in their mid-fifties; the youngest are in their mid-to-late thirties. Thus, the boomers have evolved from the "youthquake generation" to the "backache generation." They are also reaching their peak earning and spending years. Thus, they constitute a lucrative market for travel, resorts, and restaurants.

The maturing boomers are experiencing the pangs of midlife and rethinking the purpose and value of their work, responsibilities, and relationships. They are approaching life with a new stability and reasonableness in the way they live, think, eat, and spend. As they continue to age, they will create a large and important seniors' market. By 2025, there will be 64 million baby boomers aged 61 to 79, a 90 percent increase in the size of this population from today.[7]

Generation X. The baby boom was followed by a "birth dearth," creating a generation of 45 million people born between 1965 and 1976. Author Douglas Coupland calls them "Generation X," because they lie in the shadow of the boomers and lack obvious distinguishing characteristics. Others call them the "baby busters," "shadow generation," or "yiffies"—young, individualistic, freedom-minded few.

The GenXers are defined as much by their shared experiences as by their age. Increasing divorce rates and higher employment for their mothers made them the first generation of latchkey kids. Whereas the boomers created a sexual revolution, the GenXers have lived in the age of AIDS. Having grown up during times of recession and corporate downsizing, they have developed a more cautious economic outlook. As a result, the GenXers are a more skeptical bunch, cynical of frivolous marketing pitches that promise easy success. They buy lots of products—fast food, beer, computers, and mountain bikes. However, their cynicism makes them more savvy shoppers, and their financial pressures make them more value conscious. They like lower prices and a more functional look. The GenXers respond to honesty in advertising; they like irreverence and sass and ads that mock the traditional advertising approach. For example, recent Miller Brewing Company ads appealing to this group advised, "It's time to embrace your inner idiot" and one features images of a frenetic, sloppy hot dog–eating contest.

GenXers share new cultural concerns. They care about the environment and respond favorably to socially responsible companies. Although they seek success, they are less materialistic; they prize experience, not acquisition. They are cautious romantics who want a better quality of life and are more interested in job satisfaction than in sacrificing personal happiness and growth for promotion.

Once labeled as "The MTV generation: Net surfing, nihilistic [body piercing slackers] whining about McJobs," the GenXers are now growing up and beginning to take over. They do surf the Internet more than other groups, but with serious intent. The GenXers are poised to displace the lifestyle, culture, and materialistic values of the baby boomers. They represent $125 billion in annual purchasing power. By the year 2010, they will have overtaken the baby boomers as a primary market for almost every product category.

Several restaurant chains have developed products or modified products to appeal to Generation X. The Kimpton Group, in San Francisco, developed a restaurant named Ponzu for Generation Xers. The

The echo boomers spend over $130 billion of their own money, and will become the most important generation from an economic standpoint.

restaurant features a loungelike atmosphere and features a feng shui hour, which has gone over well because this crowd wants something different. Another concept that is catching on with this age group is the Indo-French concept of a "hookah den," a lounge for after dinner drinks and smoking. Tom Walters, the president of Chart House Restaurants, says they have added bright and airy space, lots of music, and more seafood and vegetarian specials to try to attract generation Xers.[8]

The Echo Boomers. Both the baby boomers and GenXers will one day be passing the reins to the latest demographic group, the **echo boomers** (or baby boomlet generation). Born between 1977 and 1994, these children of the baby boomers now number 72 million, dwarfing the GenXers and almost equal in size to the baby boomer segment. Ranging from preteens to mid-twenties, the echo boomer generation is still forming its buying preferences and behaviors.

The baby boomlet has created large and growing kids' and teens' markets. Teens and preteens spend $130 billion on their own and influence $500 billion and upward of their parents' spending.[9]

Like the trailing edge of the Generation Xers ahead of them, one distinguishing characteristic of the echo boomers is their utter fluency and comfort with computer, digital, and Internet technology. For this reason, one analyst has christened them the NetGens (or N-Gens). He observes:

> What makes this generation different . . . is not just its demographic muscle, but it is the first to grow up surrounded by digital media. Computers and other digital technologies, such as digital cameras, are commonplace to N-Gen members. They work with them at home, in school, and they use them for entertainment. Increasingly these technologies are connected to the Internet. Constantly surrounded by technology, today's kids are accustomed to its strong presence in their lives. And it is through their use of the digital media that N-Gen will develop and superimpose its culture on the rest of society. Already these kids are learning, playing, communicating, working, and creating communities very differently than did their parents. They are a force for social transformation.[10]

Generational Marketing. Do marketers have to create separate products and marketing programs for each generation? Some experts caution that each generation spans decades of time and many socioeconomic levels. "These segments are so large they're meaningless as marketing targets," notes one such expert. "'Matures' age range fits all 54 to 91; that isn't a target, it's a happening." Similarly, boomers span almost twenty years: He suggests that marketers should form more precise age-specific segments within each group.[11]

Others warn that marketers have to be careful about turning off one generation each time they craft a product or message that appeals collectively to another.[12]

The Changing American Family

The "traditional household" consists of a husband, wife, and children (and sometimes grandparents). Yet, the once American ideal of the two-child, two-car suburban family has lately been losing some of its luster. In fact, couples with children under eighteen now make up only about 35 percent of all U.S. families.[13] In the United States today, one in eight households is "diverse" or "nontraditional" and includes single live-alones, adult live-togethers of one or both sexes, single-parent families, childless married couples, or empty nesters. More people are divorcing or separating, choosing not to marry, marrying later, or marrying without time intention to have children. Marketers must increasingly consider tile special needs of nontraditional households, because they are now growing more rapidly than traditional households. Each group has a distinctive set of needs and buying habits. For example, people in the SSWD group (single, separated, widowed, divorced) need smaller apartments, inexpensive and smaller appliances, furniture and furnishings, and food packaged in smaller sizes.

The number of working women has also increased greatly. This trend has spawned the child day care business and increased consumption of convenience foods and services, career-oriented women's clothing, financial services, and many other business opportunities.

Geographic Shifts in Population

This is a period of great migratory movements between and within countries. Americans, for example, are a mobile people with about 12 million U.S. households (more than one out of every ten) moving each year.[14] Over the past two decades, the U.S. population has shifted toward the sunbelt states. The west and south have grown while the midwest and northeast states have lost population. Such population shifts interest marketers because people in different regions buy differently.

Also, for more than a century Americans have been moving from rural to metropolitan areas. In the 1950s, they made a massive exit from the cities to the suburbs. Today, the migration to the suburbs continues, and demographers are noting another shift that they call "the rural rebound." Nonmetropolitan counties that lost population to cities for most of this century are now attracting large numbers of urban refugees. More and more Americans are moving to "micropolitan areas," small cities located beyond congested metropolitan areas. These smaller micros offer many of the advantages of metro areas—jobs, restaurants, diversions, community organizations—but without the population crush, traffic jams, high crime rates, and high property taxes often associated with heavily urbanized areas.[15]

A Better-Educated and More White-Collar Population

The U.S. population is becoming better educated. For example, in 1996, 82 percent of the U.S. population over age twenty-five had completed high school and 24 percent had completed college, compared with 69 percent and 17 percent in 1980. The rising number of educated people will increase the demand for quality products, books, magazines, travel, personal computers, and Internet services. It suggests a decline in television viewing because college-educated consumers watch less TV than the population at large. The workforce also is becoming more white collar. Between 1950 and 1985, the proportion of white-collar workers rose from 41 percent to 54 percent, that of blue-collar workers declined from 47 percent to 33 percent, and that of service workers increased from 12 percent to 14 percent. These trends have continued into the new millennium.[16]

Increasing Diversity

Countries vary in their ethnic and racial makeup. At one extreme is Japan, where almost everyone is Japanese. At the other extreme is the United States, with people from virtually all nations. The United States has often been called a melting pot in which diverse groups from many nations and cultures have melted into a single more homogenous whole. Instead, the United States seems to have become a "salad bowl" in which various groups have mixed together but have maintained their diversity by retaining and valuing important ethnic and cultural differences.

Marketers are facing increasingly diverse markets, both at home and abroad, as their operations become more international in scope. In the United States alone, ethnic population growth is six times greater than the Caucasian growth rate, and ethnic consumers buy more than $600 billion of goods and services each year. The U.S. population is 72 percent white, with African Americans making up another 13 percent. The Hispanic population has grown rapidly and now stands at about 11 percent. The U.S.-Asian population also has grown rapidly in recent years and now totals about 3 percent. The remaining 1 percent of the population is made up of Native Americans, Eskimos, and Aleuts. During the next half-century, the proportions of both Hispanics and Asians will more than double. Moreover, there are nearly 25 million people living in the United States—over 9 percent of the population—who were born in another country. Many hospitality companies develop products for one or more of these groups.

Diversity goes beyond ethnic heritage. For example, there are more than 52 million disabled people in the United States—a market larger than African Americans or Hispanics—representing almost $1 trillion in annual spending power. This spending power is likely to increase even more in the years ahead, as the wealthier, freer-spending baby boomers enter the "age of disabilities." Julie Perez sees the difference when she goes to the Divi Hotels resort at Flamingo Beach on the Caribbean island of Bonaire. "It is famous for being totally accessible," she says. "The hotel brochures show the wheelchair access. The dive staff are trained and aware, and they really want to take disabled people diving. They're not afraid." Perez, 35, of Ventura, California, is an experienced scuba diver, a travel agent, and a quadriplegic. Before she had children, she made five trips a year to the Caribbean; these days, she gets there only once or twice a year.[17]

Economic Environment

Markets require buying power as well as people. The **economic environment** consists of factors that affect consumer purchasing power and spending patterns. Nations vary greatly in their levels and distribution of income. Some countries have subsistence economies—they consume most of their own agricultural and industrial output. These countries offer few market opportunities. At the other extreme are industrial economies, which constitute rich markets for many different kinds of goods. Marketers must pay close attention to major trends and consumer spending patterns both across and within their world markets. Following are some of the major economic trends in the United States.

Changes in Income

During the 1980s—tabbed the "roaring eighties" by some—American consumers fell into consumption frenzy, fueled by income growth, federal tax reductions, rapid increases in housing values, and a boom in borrowing. They bought and bought, seemingly without caution, amassing record levels of debt. "It was fashionable to describe yourself as 'born to shop.' When the going gets tough, it was said, the tough go shopping."[18]

During the 1990s the baby boom generation moved into its prime wage-earning years, and the number of small families headed by dual-career couples continued to increase. Thus, many consumers continued to demand quality products and better service, and they were able to pay for them. However, the free spending and high expectations of the 1980s were dashed by the recession in the early 1990s. In fact, the 1990s became the decade of the "squeezed consumer." Along with rising incomes in some segments came increased financial burdens—repaying debts acquired during earlier spending splurges, facing increased household and family expenses, and saving for college tuition payments and retirement. These financially squeezed consumers sobered up, pulled back, and adjusted to their changing financial situations. They spent more carefully and sought greater value in the products and services they bought. Value marketing became the watchword for many marketers.

As we move into the twenty-first century, despite several years of strong economic performance, consumers continue to spend carefully. Hence, the trend toward value marketing continues. Rather than offering high quality at a high price, or lesser quality at very low prices, marketers are looking for ways to offer today's more financially cautious buyers greater value—just the right combination of product quality and good service at a fair price.

Marketers should pay attention to income distribution as well as average income. Income distribution in the United States is still very skewed. At the top are upper-class consumers, whose spending patterns are not affected by current economic events and who are a major market for luxury goods. There is a comfortable middle class that is somewhat careful about its spending but can still afford the good life of the time. The working class must stick close to the basics of food, clothing, and shelter and must try hard to save. Finally, the underclass (persons on welfare and many retirees) must count their pennies when making even the most basic purchases.

Over the past three decades, the rich have grown richer, the middle class has shrunk, and the poor have remained poor. In 1994, the top 5 percent of income-earning households in the United States captured over 21 percent of aggregate income, up from 16.6 percent in 1970. Meanwhile, the share of income captured by the bottom 20 percent of income-earning households decreased from 4.1 percent to 3.6 percent. This distribution of income has created a two-tiered market.

Changing Consumer Spending Patterns. Changes in major economic variables such as income, cost of living, interest rates, and savings and borrowing patterns have a large impact on the marketplace. Companies use economic forecasting to anticipate changes in these variables. With

FantastiQue, EconomiQue.*
U.S.-CAN
38%*
Save thanks to the exchange rate!
* Exchange rate quoted as of June 3, 1994 Subject to change. Call for current rate.

"The hills, the snow, the thrills, the view, the people...that's the MagiQue of skiing in Québec, your ski heaven right next door!"

Ski conditions available toll free at 1 800 463-9777 from mid-November 1994 to mid-March 1995.
For your free brochure and Winter Holiday Guide, call the number below.

For information
Call toll free
1 800 363-7777
Ask for operator 226
(9 am to 5 pm, 7 days a week)
or call your travel agent.

Québec
It Feels So Different.

One aspect of the economic environment that is increasing in importance with the growth of international travel is the currency exchange rate. Quebec uses Canada's favorable exchange rate to attract skiers from the United States. Courtesy of Tourisme Quebec and Cossette Communication–Marketing.

adequate warning, businesses can reduce their costs and adjust their marketing mix to ride out the economic storm. Restaurants, for example, can vary their menus and offer a number of lower-priced entrees during a recession.

People have different spending patterns as their income increases. For example, people earning $20,000 to $30,000 spend 15.8 percent of their income on food, whereas people making $50,000 and over only spend 12.8 percent of their income on food. The amount spent on entertainment jumps from 4.7 percent for the $20,000 to $30,000 group to 6.1 percent for the $50,000 and over group.[19] Ernst Engel found that as family income increases, the percentage spent on food declines, the percentage spent on housing remains almost constant, and the percentage spent on other categories increases. Studies have generally supported Engel's laws.

Global Economic Patterns. With many markets in Europe and North America saturated with hotels, companies are looking to other global markets. As a region's economy develops, demand is created for lodging and food facilities. Some companies look for areas where their product is already well known. For example, Roy Murray, vice president, International Division of Choice Hotels International, states, "We look to markets where our product is known or where we have the largest demand for our U.S. domestic product. In other words, where there's a knowledge of our products." Other companies look for a demand for their product. Mike Leven of U.S. Franchise Systems, decided to go overseas after having only forty-two hotels open in the United States. He feels his product will sell overseas.[20]

4.5 McDonald's Choice Hotels

McDonald's turned to overseas expansion after the market in the United States became saturated. Today more than half (15,000) of McDonald's 28,000 restaurants are located outside the United States in 119 countries. Companies such as McDonald's collect money in local currencies, thus exchange rates can affect their profitability. If prices are not able to keep up with decreases in local currency, McDonald's profits erode. Conversely, if the U.S. dollar weakens, McDonald's overseas will increase. McDonald's has become a symbol of American capitalism. With 15,000 stores around the world, it can become a target of anti-American sentiment.[21] For example, in France the farmer's union called for demonstrations outside of McDonald's restaurants to protest U.S. trade sanctions against French food products, including Roquefort cheese, foie gras, and truffles. In Aveyron, the region that produces Roquefort cheese, framers ransacked a building site for a new McDonald's restaurant. The U.S. sanctions were retaliation for a European Union ban on North American hormone-treated beef. The global growth creates many opportunities; however it also greatly increases the complexity of the macroenvironmental forces.[22]

Natural Environment

The natural environment consists of natural resources required by marketers or affected by marketing activities. During the 1960s, the public grew concerned that the natural environment was being damaged by modern industrial activities. Popular books warned about shortages of natural resources and about the damage to water, earth, and air caused by industrial activity. Watchdog groups such as the Sierra Club and Friends of the Earth sprang up, and legislators proposed measures to protect the environment.

Communities are finding that preserving the natural environment can be good for tourism. Hong Kong saw the coming of Disneyland as a chance to improve its natural environment. Forums were held to gain community support for improving the green space in Hong Kong. Edward Stokes stated Hong Kong lavishes thoughtful design and care on its environs, and as a result people praise it for its green environs. He states that even though Hong Kong is blessed with a superb natural setting it has not maintained this asset.[23]

A 1994–1995 recreation survey found that 55 million Americans watched birds, up 155 percent from 1982. The interest in bird watching has been further evidenced by the tripling of the membership in the American Birding Association between 1990 and 1996. Jan Erik Pierson, cofounder of Field Guides, charges tourists $1,500 each for an eight-day bird-watching trip through Maine. He also conducts tours in Canada, Brazil, and Australia.[24] The expansion of bird watching in South Nebraska, associated with the migration of the Sandhill Crane, currently brings up to $60 million to the area every spring.[25] Bird watching and ecotourism activities are a growing source of visitors.

4.6 Ventana Canyon Resort
Hyatt Regency Waikloloa
Inter-Continental Hotels
Disney
The International Ecotourism Society
The Ecotourism Society

One way of protecting the environment is to recyle and reduce waste. Disney has an aggressive program to reduce waste. For example, purchasing tomato paste in fifty-five-gallon drums instead of number 10 cans saves 100,000 cans a year. Disney shreds its paper products and sends the shredded paper to the gift shops to use as packing material, and torn linens are made into rags, reducing the need for paper towels. A 25 percent reduction in the size of its napkins reduced paper waste by over 150 tons. Disney World uses gray water (treated wastewater) to water its golf courses, lawns, and gardens. Robert Penn, director of environmental affairs of Disney's municipal arm, Ready Creek improvement district, states that using gray water can help operators of many lodging facilities. Gray water is not only less expensive than municipal water, but it is also an environmentally sound method of watering large gardens and golf courses.

Disney's waste management has eliminated tons of waste, and its recycling program handles 40 tons of waste a day. Disney receives anywhere from $10 a ton for newspaper to $650 a ton for aluminum cans. Even with this income, Disney's waste reduction is not a moneymaker. The efforts continue because management feels it's the right thing to do, and they are following the wishes of the company's founder. Walt Disney said, "Our forests, waters, grasslands, and wildlife must be wisely protected and used. I urge all citizens to join the effort to save America's natural beauty."[26]

Technological Environment

The most dramatic force shaping our destiny is technology. Technology has given us wireless access to the Internet, the ability to send documents around the globe electronically, and relatively inexpensive transportation

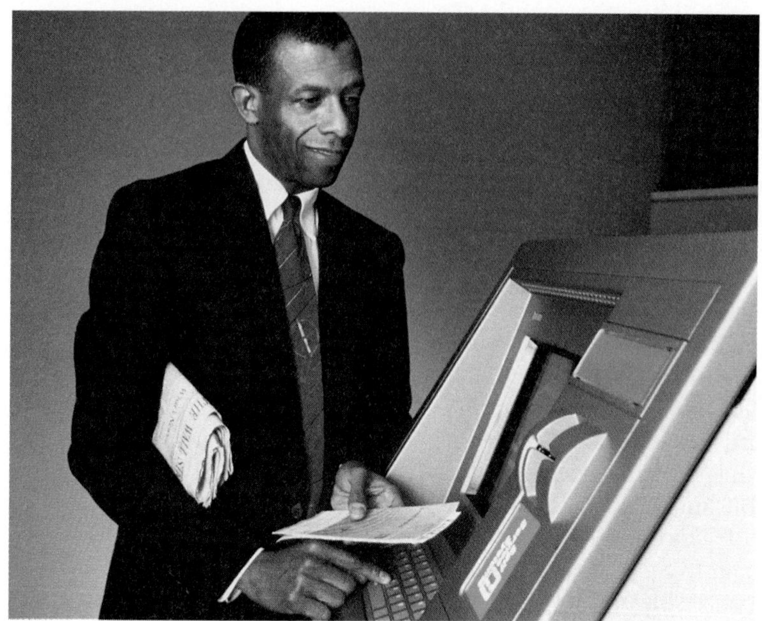

System One was the first computer reservation system to have electronic ticket delivery through an electronic ticket delivery network. Hyatt Hotels has used similar technology to develop a computerized check-in system. Courtesy of System One Corporation.

to other parts of the world. It has also released such horrors as the hydrogen bomb, nerve gas, and chemical warfare, and produced products with mixed blessings, such as television and the automobile.

Technological change is occurring at an ever-increasing rate.[27] Many products that are taken for granted today either were uncommon or did not exist 30 years ago: cell phones, copier machines, fast-food chains, personal computers, jet airplanes, all-suite hotels, fax machines, and VCRs, to name a few. Scientists are now speculating on products for the future, such as flying cars, personal rocket belts, and voyages to space that include a stay at a space hotel. In fact, we have already had our first space tourist.

Technology has affected the hospitality industry in many ways: Robots are used to deliver hospital food trays to stations throughout a hospital. Machines cook food automatically, eliminating human error. Computerized video checkout services are now common in many hotels. Electronic guest room locking systems tell housekeepers which rooms are occupied; the minibar lock tells which guests accessed their minibar, making restocking easier. Locking fax machines now receive orders at restaurants. Taco Bell is working with robotics to develop production processes for its food products. It has a Taco Flex-Station that can produce 900 tacos per hour. Computerized yield management systems are helping hotels to optimize their profits through pricing to demand. These and other technological advances will help companies to be more effective in the marketplace. Firms that adopt useful technological advances will gain a competitive advantage.[28]

Technology has also made communication easier. The city of Boston posted restaurant inspection scores on a Web site. Some customers said they would check out the site before going out to eat. The Massachusetts

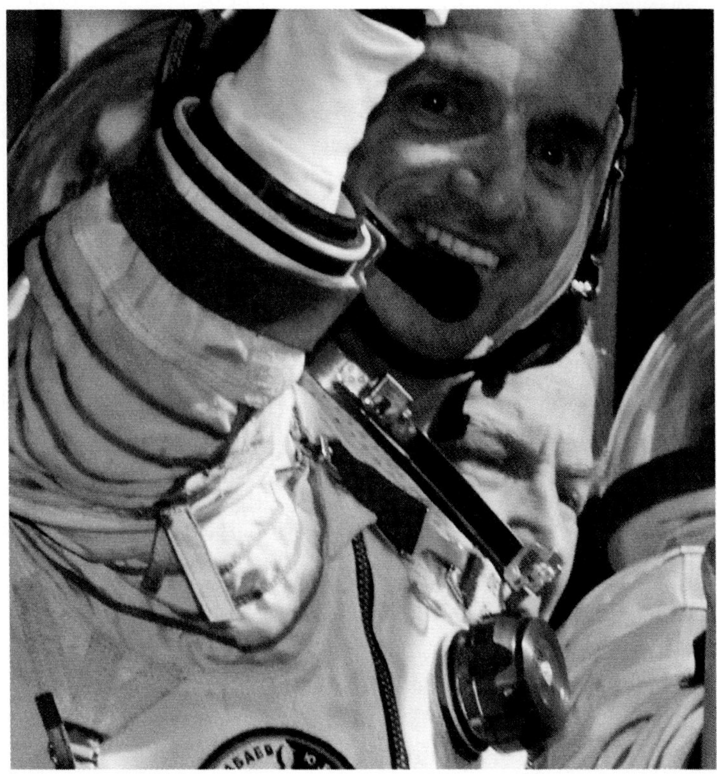

Dennis Tito was the first person to pay for a trip into space, thus becoming the world's first space tourist. He is seen here just before the launch of the Russian Soyuz spaceship. Advances in technology will make space travel a viable form of tourism in the future. (AP photo/Mikhial Metzel)

Restaurant Association and some state food safety officials raised concerns that the generic explanations of the violation may be misconstrued. For example, a portable rack on wheels placed in front of a hand-washing sink would be listed as a major violation. A major violation is described as one that has the potential for danger to public health.[29] Boston no longer posts the scores, but the Internet needs to be monitored to see what others are saying about your business. Word of mouth is no longer spread to people we know, but it can be spread to large numbers of people over the Internet. The Web site for this chapter contains a list of several of the sites used by consumers to spread word of mouth.

4.7 Qantas Airlines
Continental Airlines

Qantas was one of the first airlines to add a power source for notebook computers for their first-class passengers. This concept has been followed by other airlines, including Continental, which also provides the service on selected rows in economy. The internal power source on notebook computers is about three hours. This is adequate for most domestic flights, but hardly adequate for a thirteen-hour flight over the Pacific or a fifteen-hour flight from Hong Kong to New York.[30] With 50 percent of business travelers carrying a notebook computer, business hotels are providing an in-room combination fax machine and printer.[31] They are also providing ISDN lines so the guest can have high-speed access to the Internet.

The Internet has had a profound effect on the hospitality and travel industries. The Internet has created a new distribution channel for hospitality and travel products. In the first three months of 2001, Expedia

Marketing Highlight 4-1

Managing in Uncertain Times

On September 11, 2001, terrorists hijacked four planes in the United States and crashed two of the planes into the World Trade Center Towers, the largest buildings in the United States, bringing these buildings down. Another plane crashed into the Pentagon. The fourth plane crashed in a field in Pennsylvania when the passengers attempted to regain control from the hijackers. These events had a profound psychological effect on Americans and changed travel plans of people throughout the world. Terrorist events of this magnitude had not happened in the United States before, changing the environment for travel organizations to an uncertain one. No one was able to predict the depth and length of the downturn in travel created by the attacks. Airline travel was suspended for several days immediately following the events. When it did resume, most airlines were operating only 80 percent of their flights, and equivalent staff reductions were made. In the week following the attacks, airline traffic in the United States dropped by over 50 percent from the equivalent period in 2000. By November airline traffic seemed to stabilize at a level 20 to 25 percent below the previous year's rate.

The decrease in travel illustrated how the different facets of the travel industry are interdependent. Taxis drivers and persons checking baggage at airports lost their jobs. Small event management companies, which put together events for conferences, found themselves struggling to survive after conferences canceled. In Las Vegas, 249 business groups cancelled their meetings. Occupancy rates in hotels dropped, and the resorts in Las Vegas made thousands of employees redundant. Tourist-oriented retailing suffered, resulting in the closure of DFS, a duty-free shop in Las Vegas. The Hansa House restaurant near Disneyland lost 700 meals after several Japanese tourist buses canceled. In some Hawaiian tourist shows, the performers outnumbered the audience. Travel agents lost their jobs and owners of small agencies went out of business. The loss of jobs in the travel industry could be felt throughout the economy, as those who lost their jobs cut back on spending. The travel industry was faced with rebuilding itself.

Some companies immediately reacted by cutting staff to preserve their capital. Southwest Airlines was one of the companies that did not lay off employees, reestablishing its commitment to its workforce. Destination promotion agencies revaluated their marketing expenditures. Hotels and tourist-oriented attractions developed local and regional promotions. Some companies acted on instinct; others acted on research. The New Orleans Tourism and Marketing Association, working with sixty hotels, launched a $250,000 campaign focused on regional tourists. The promotion offered travelers one hotel night free when they purchased two. The campaign featured newspaper, radio and e-mail advertisements in markets stretching from Houston, Texas, to Pensacola, Florida. The Las Vegas Convention and Visitors Authority conducted a telephone survey of 1,800 consumers. One of the findings of their study was that travelers wanted a reassurance that it was okay to come to Las Vegas. The ad campaign featured ads that provided this reassurance, and the communication itself was another form of reassurance. The $13 million campaign was focused on visitors that could drive to Las Vegas. It was effective in filling the hotels on the weekends. Meanwhile the Authority also focused on rebuilding the convention business. One of the tactics they used was to provide

sold more than one million hotel room nights. Most hotel, rental car companies, and hotel chains have set up their own on-line reservation systems, allowing the guest to book directly on line.

The Internet also is a great source of information for travelers. Smart CVBs provide detailed information on their destination for potential visitors. Business-card size CD-ROMs provide a brief overview of a destina-

over a million free postcards to organizations holding conventions to reassure their members that the convention was going on as scheduled.

The terrorist attacks had a worldwide impact. Travel agencies in Europe reported a drop of 20 percent in their bookings. Tourism agencies in Mexico and Argentina declared a state of emergency. Mexico announced a $35 million investment in tourism promotion and infrastructure to work on rebuilding its tourism industry. In Peru, visitors to tourist attractions dropped by 50 percent, prompting the government to cut rates of tourists' services in an effort to attract visitors from Argentina and Chile. Venezuela announced a $4 million campaign targeted at Canada and the United States. Australia received a double blow as Ansett, one of the nation's domestic airlines, shut down on September 14. The Australian states quickly developed marketing campaigns aimed at regional markets. Australia and New Zealand also positioned themselves as safe destinations, hoping to attract Asians who were anxious about traveling to the United States.

At a meeting of hospitality consultants, one of the topics was that most organizations did not have a plan in place to deal with major environmental impacts, such as the terrorist attacks. There were no plans on how to manage the organization under such extreme circumstances. Some hotels did a great job of keeping guests informed of the latest developments, others did a terrible job. Some organizations did an excellent job working with customers, others did not. Some companies evaluated the situation using customer research, while others acted on gut feelings. Some companies, such as Southwest Airlines, used their culture to tell them how they ought to act. Organizations need to develop plans for dealing with rapid and major changes in the environment. These plans should allow them to move swiftly, but thoughtfully. The plans should also set up both internal and external communication channels.

Sources: Laura Claverie, "'New Orleans for a Song' Campaign Targets Regional Visitors with Hotel Deals," New Orleans Online, retrieved 11/05/01, *http://www.hospitality1st.com/PressNews/NOTMC-pr.html;* Bruce Dunford, "Terrorist Attacks Land Indirect Hit on Tourist Spots," *Nando Times,* retrieved 11/06/01, *http://www.nandotimes.com;* Leslie Earnest and Bonnie Harris, "Foreign Visitors Stay Away in Droves," Latimes.com, retrieved 11/05/01, *http://www.latimes.com/news/nationworld/nation/la-092001tour.story;* Ivor Hayman, "South Seen as a Safe Haven," *Southland Times,* retrieved 11/05/01, *http://www.stuff.co.nz/in1/index/0,1008,961329a1940,FF.html;* Richard H. Levey, "Sin City Hedges Its Bets," *Direct Magazine, retrieved, http://www.directmag.com;* Online Pioneer, "Tourism Industry Feels Impact of Terror Attacks," retrieved 11/05/01, *http://www.thepioneer.com/international/oct06_impact.htm;* Spiros Papadopoulos and Kris J. Bernie, "Australian Markets Outlook—Tourism and Terrorism," National Australian Bank, retrieved from the World Wide Web, *http://www.nabmarkets.com;* J. Reuters, "Terrorist Attacks a Huge Blow to Global Tourism," *Economic Times Online,* retrieved 11/05/01, *http://www.economictimes.com/;* Knight Ridder, "Many in Tourism Industry Feel Effects of Attacks, but Business Rebounds Slowly," Hotel Online: New for the Hospitality Executive, retrieved 11/05/01, *http://www.hotel-online.com/Neo/News/2001_Oct_05/k.HOT.102319338.html;* Ellen Schroeder, "Passanger Traffic Drops 26.1 Percent in October at Dallas/Fort Worth Airport," Hotel Online: New for the Hospitality Executive, retrived 11/05/01 from World Wide Web *http://www.hotel-online.com/Neo/News/2001_Nov_02/k.FTA.1004979095.html;* David Smith, "Queenslanders Urged to Make Time and Spend It There," Tourism Queensland, retrieved 11/05/01, *http://www.qttc.com.au/media/information/new/release.asp?id=256&typeID=1.*

tion with links to the CVB's Web site. Hotels are also using this type of promotion, which is less expensive than producing a color brochure.

Starbuck's coffee shops announced an agreement with Microsoft to provide wireless Internet connection at selected company stores. This will allow customers the capability to access the Internet while they are enjoying their coffee. Darren Houston, the senior vice president of Starbucks,

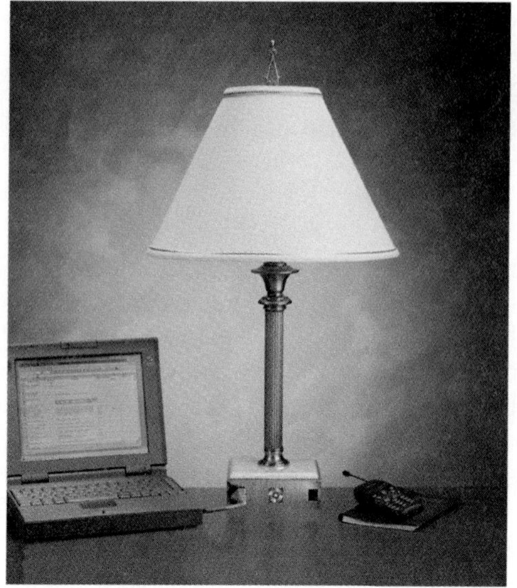

Technology is having an impact on hotel room amenities. Many business class hotels have a combination fax machine, printer, and copier in each room. This hotel lamp provides business travelers with a plug and data line for their computers. Courtesy of MICROSUN An Advanced Technology Company.

stated, "We want this service to add to the Starbucks experience. . . . We think the opportunity to access corporate Internet and get your email on the road will be of great value."[32] Those companies that effectively use the Internet can create a competitive advantage over companies who are not utilizing it. The ways to effectively use the Internet as a marketing tool are discussed later in the book in Chapter 16.

Technological change faces opposition from those who see it as threatening nature, privacy, simplicity, and even the human race. Various groups have opposed the construction of restaurants in suburban and historical areas and high-rise hotels, airports, and recreational facilities in national parks. Marketers must understand and anticipate changes in the technological environment and utilize technologies that serve human needs. They must be sensitive to aspects of any innovation that might harm users and bring about opposition.

Political Environment

Marketing decisions are strongly affected by developments in the political environment. The **political environment** is made up of laws, government agencies, and pressure groups that influence and limit the activities of various organizations and individuals in society. We will cite some current political trends and their implications for marketing management.

Increased Legislation and Regulation Affecting Business

As products become more complex, public concern about their safety increases. Governmental agencies have become involved in the investigation and regulation of everything from fire codes to food-handling practices. Employment and employee practices fall under government regulation, as do sales of liquor, which vary from state to state and sometimes from precinct to precinct in the same county. Politicians also see travelers as good sources of revenue, because non-residents spend money but cannot vote against them. Hotel taxes and restaurant taxes have become popular sources of revenue for local governments. In many cases, hotel taxes are supposed to be used to support tourism; however, the spending of this money has been subject to liberal interpretation, such as for statues for suburban parks. Hotel managers must make sure that those taxes designated to promote tourism are used effectively. Managers must also work with hotel and restaurant associations to make sure that the taxes do not become oppressive. New York City hiked its hotel tax to over 21.25 percent for rooms over $100 in 1990. Many meeting and convention planners avoided New York because of the unfriendly tax; they simply took their business elsewhere. Convention business plunged by 37 percent during the next three years, and overall tax revenue declined despite the increase in the tax. The real loser was New York City's hospitality industry. New York has since reduced its hotel tax in line with other cities.[33]

Legislation and regulation affecting business have been enacted for three reasons. First, it protects companies from each other. Although most businesses praise competition, they try to neutralize it when it affects them. In the United States, it is the job of the Federal Trade Commission and the Antitrust Division of the Justice Department to define and prevent unfair competition. Cases often emerge in which one company lodges a complaint that another is guilty of an unfair practice, such as deceptive pricing or deceptive advertising, thereby injuring its business.

Second, government legislation and regulation also aim at protecting consumers from unfair business practices. If unregulated, firms might make unsafe or low-quality products, be untruthful in their advertising, or deceive through packaging and pricing. Various government units define unfair consumer practices and offer remedies. Businesses, of course, can minimize government intervention through active self-regulation. Such associations as the American Hotel and Motel Association and the National Restaurant Association define and encourage good trade practices. These associations have developed guidelines for truth in menu presentation, alcoholic beverage service, and sanitation.

Third, government regulation also aims to protect society's interests against unrestrained business behavior. Profitable business activity does not always improve the quality of life. Thus regulations are passed to discourage smoking, littering, polluting, overcongestion of facilities, and the like, all in the name of protecting society's interests. Regulation aims to make firms responsible for the social as well as private costs of their production and distribution activities.

Government regulation and enforcement are likely to increase in the future. Business executives must know the major laws protecting competition, consumers, and society when planning their products and marketing programs.

International Legislation

Legislation affecting business around the world has increased steadily over the years. The United States has many laws on its books covering such issues as competition, fair trade practices, environmental protection, product safety, truth in advertising, packaging and labeling, pricing, and other important areas. The European Commission has been active in establishing a new framework of laws covering competitive behavior, product standards, product liability, and commercial transactions for the twelve member nations of the European Community. Several countries have gone farther than the United States in passing strong consumerism legislation. For example, Norway bans several forms of sales promotion—trading stamps, contests, premiums—as being inappropriate or unfair ways of promoting products. Thailand requires food processors selling national brands to market low-price brands also, so that lower-income consumers can find economy brands on the shelves. In India, food companies must obtain special approval to launch brands that duplicate those already existing on the market, such as additional cola drinks or new brands of rice.

Understanding the public policy implications of a particular marketing activity is not a simple matter. Moreover, regulations are constantly changing—what was allowed last year may now be prohibited, and what was prohibited may now be allowed. For example, with the demise of the Soviet bloc, ex-Soviet nations are rapidly passing laws to both regulate and promote an open-market economy. Marketers must work hard to keep up with the changes in regulations and their interpretations.

Government Intervention in Natural Resource Management

The governments of different countries vary in their concern and efforts to promote a clean environment. For example, the German government vigorously pursues environmental quality, partly because of the strong public green movement and partly because of the ecological devastation in former East Germany. In contrast, many poor nations do little about pollution, largely because they lack the needed funds or political will. It is in the interests of richer nations to subsidize poorer ones to control pollution, but today even the richer nations lack the vast funds and political accord required to mount a worldwide environmental effort. The major hope is that companies around the world accept more social responsibility and that less expensive devices can be found to control and reduce pollution.

In the United States, the Environmental Protection Agency (EPA) was created in 1970 to set and enforce pollution standards and to conduct research on the causes and effects of pollution. In the future, companies doing business in the United States can expect strong controls from government and pressure groups. Instead of opposing regulation, marketers should help develop solutions to the material and energy problems facing the world.

Changing Government Agency Enforcement

To enforce laws, Congress has established several federal regulatory agencies: the Federal Trade Commission, the Food and Drug Administration, the Interstate Commerce Commission, the Federal Communications Commission, the Federal Power Commission, the Civil Aeronautics Board, the Consumer Products Safety Commission, the Environmental Protection

Agency, and the Office of Consumer Affairs. These agencies can have a major impact on a company's marketing performance. Government agencies have some discretion in enforcing the laws, and from time to time, they appear to be overly eager. Lawyers and economists, who often lack a practical sense of marketing and other business principles, frequently dominate the agencies. In recent years, the Federal Trade Commission has added marketing experts to its staff to gain a better understanding of these complex issues.

4.8 American Airlines

The power of government is so great that government can often dramatically affect a hospitality business without ever enforcing a law. An example is the case of a strike by American Airlines flight attendants in 1993. President Clinton intervened by calling Robert Crandal, CEO of American Airlines, and urging him to resolve the problem. The power and prestige of a head of state is so large that American Airlines settled in favor of the flight attendants. An airline is subject to many federal agencies, and the management at American Airlines obviously was intimidated.

Another example is offered by the proposed sale of the Tarrytown Hilton in Westchester County, New York. The property's owners, Prudential Insurance and Hilton, put the hotel up for sale. Normally, hotel sales are concluded in private and without publicity. In this case, the chairman of Westchester's County Board publicly announced that the county was considering purchasing the hotel as a temporary shelter for the homeless. This caused public outcry and forced the owner to cancel the sale of the hotel. The public thought the property was going to become a homeless shelter and canceled reservations for parties, meetings, and banquets. Management of the Tarrytown Hilton estimated the loss of revenue at $800,000 and a 45 percent reduction in market share for some of its services.[34]

Growth of Public-Interest Groups

The number of public-interest groups has increased during the past two decades, as has their clout in the political arena. MADD (Mothers Against Drunk Driving) has had a major impact on the hospitality industry by demanding that restaurants be more responsible in their serving of alcohol. Hundreds of consumer, environmental, minority, and other interest groups, both private and governmental, operate at the national, state, and local levels. Alert members of the hospitality industry have recognized that many of these groups represent excellent marketing opportunities for seminars, conferences, meetings, and social gatherings; for instance, there is a National Association of Black Skiers that is aggressively courted by ski resorts.

Increased Emphasis on Ethics and Socially Responsible Actions

Written regulations cannot possibly cover all potential marketing abuses, and existing laws are often difficult to enforce. However, beyond written laws and regulations, business is also governed by social codes and rules of professional ethics. Enlightened companies encourage their managers to look beyond what the regulatory system allows and simply "do the right thing." These socially responsible firms actively seek out ways to protect the long-run interests of their consumers and the environment.

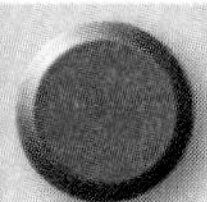

Marketing Highlight 4-2

Popcorn's Cultural Trends

Futurist Faith Popcorn runs BrainReserve, a marketing consulting firm that monitors cultural trends and advises companies such as AT&T, Citibank, Black & Decker, Hoffman–La Roche, Nissan, Rubbermaid, and many others on how these trends will affect their marketing and other business decisions. Using its trend predictions, BrainReserve offers several services: BrainJam generates new product ideas for clients, and BrainRenewal attempts to breathe new life into fading brands. FutureFocus develops marketing strategies and concepts that create long-term competitive advantage. Another service, TrendBank, is a database containing culture-monitoring and consumer interview information. Popcorn and her associates have identified the following major cultural trends affecting U.S. consumers.

1. Cashing out: the urge to change one's life to a slower but more rewarding pace. An executive suddenly quits his or her career, escapes the hassles of big city life, and turns up in Vermont or Montana running a small newspaper, managing a bed-and-breakfast establishment, or starting a band. People cash out because they don't think the stress is worth it. They try nostalgically to return to small town values, seeking clean air, safe schools, and plain-speaking neighbors.
2. Cocooning: the impulse to stay inside when the outside gets too tough and scary. Many people are turning their homes into nests by redecorating their houses, becoming "couch potatoes," watching TV movies, ordering from catalogs, and using answering machines to filter out the outside world. In reaction to increases in crime and other social problems, cocooners are burrowing in and building bunkers. A recent survey said that 33 percent of consumers have changed their shopping habits because of crime. Of these, 43 percent no longer shop after dark. Even on college campuses, the days of Animal House are over. Fraternities and sororities are getting stricter about whom they let roam into their parties. At Penn State there are no more "open house" parties; guest lists are now the norm on Fraternity Row.
3. Clanning: linking up with people who have common interests, ideas, aspirations, and addictions. It's easy to find people of similar leisure activities amid the sudden upsurge in memberships at private clubs in every city and state, from Princeton Club to the Maidstone to the Bel-Air Country Club. There's a smugness and an aura of safety when you belong to a bastion of sameness—whether it's based on a shared interest in golf, tennis, or squash; on being college alumni; or simply on keeping the rest of the world out. In Beverly Hills, a clan of cigar aficionados has emerged at Havana, a nightspot where people get together to light up stogies. On Christmas Eve, Jewish Americans, who possibly feel left out of the Santa loop, can attend one of nine "Matzoh Balls" across the country.
4. Down-aging: the tendency to act and feel younger than one's age. Today's sex symbols include Cher (over fifty) and Paul Newman (over seventy). Older people spend more on youthful clothes, hair coloring, and facial plastic surgery. They engage in more playful behavior and act in ways previously thought not to be appropriate for their age group. They buy adult toys, attend adult camps, and sign up for adventure vacations.
5. Egonomics: the desire to develop individuality in order to be seen and treated as different from others. This is not an ego trip, simply the wish to individualize oneself through possessions and experiences. People increasingly subscribe to narrow-interest magazines, join small groups with narrow missions, and buy customized clothing, cars, and cosmetics. Egonomics gives marketers an opportunity to succeed by offering customized goods, services, and experiences. If you click into the trend of egonomics, it's one of the most effective ways to reach customers, by

appealing to their individuality, the singular part of them that says, "There is no one out there quite like me."

6. Fantasy adventure: the need to find emotional escapes to offset one's daily routines. People might seek vacations, eat exotic foods, go to Disneyland and other fantasy parks, or redecorate their homes with a Santa Fe look. For marketers, this is an opportunity to create new fantasy products and services or to add fantasy touches to their current products and services. For example, Atlanta-based Sky Warriors enables everyday-citizens (no flying experience necessary) to participate in real air-to-air dog fighting. You go up with a former fighter pilot in a military T-34A (or T6) aircraft and fly combat maneuvers against a real opponent. The fantasy part is that the "machine gun" you fire is a laser "gun," so that any direct hits are simulated by billowing smoke from the other plane's exhaust. A subcategory of the fantasy adventure trend is called *wildering.* It's about modern man and woman breaking out of the monotony and pitting their cityselves against the wild. Wildering is the reason why 275,000 people per year have decided to raft down the river in the Arkansas headwaters. Many travelers are spending many thousands of dollars to trek in New Guinea with local tribesmen, walk with the elephants in India, or hike to an outback bush camp in Australia.
7. Pleasure revenge: characterized by many people saying a sporadic good-bye to dieting, smoking, and watching how they drink. Layoffs by large corporations, increasing crime rates, and salaries that don't keep up with the cost of living have made people realize that things still happen, so why not enjoy life? The number of Americans who say they're trying to avoid fats is slipping down to about 50 percent. Sales of Hebrew National hot dogs are up. Butter sales have bounced to levels of thirty years ago. Nondiet sodas are increasing in sales while diet sodas are declining. In the Los Angeles–area McDonald's, one McLean was sold for every 60 Big Macs. McDonald's finally dropped its McLean. People are moving back to eating things that taste good.
8. Small indulgences: a softer trend than pleasure revenge. It is thinking highly enough about yourself to treat yourself well. Sometimes when one is feeling shaky or stressed out, a short stint of travel can qualify as a small indulgence, such as a three-day trip to unwind at Canyon Ranch in the Berkshires. Or a theater/museum fix in any major metropolis can feel like a "reward-thyself" happening. If you go to a place for an overnight stay, the small indulgence hotel should be someplace small. Nothing with elevator banks or long hallways. Small chic hotels are finally coming into American cities and coming up to the standards of London's The Draycott or Paris's L'Hotel.
9. Ninety-nine lives: the desperate state of people who must juggle many roles and responsibilities. An example is the "Supermom," who must handle a full-time career while also managing her home and children. People today feel time-poor. They attempt to relieve time pressures by using fax machines and car phones, eating at fast-food restaurants, and through other means.
10. S.O.S. (save our society): the drive on the part of a growing number of people to make society more socially responsible with respect to education, ethics, and the environment. People join groups to promote more social responsibility on the part of companies and other citizens. The best response for marketers is to urge their own companies to practice more socially responsible marketing.
11. Being alive: enhancing the current quality of our lives—adding to the present value of our lives, right now. Staying alive was a trend that was part of the Popcorn Report published in 1991; it is the drive to live longer and better lives. The staying-alive trend is giving way to being alive—

quality of life and being healthy are more important than longevity. In many parts of Asia, the Chinese communities go to health restaurants where certain foods are consumed for wellness. *Wall Street Journal* reporter M. Brauchli described one such establishment in Hong Kong, the always-crowded Yat Chau Health Restaurant. There "the restaurant's thoughtful host listens sympathetically and jots things down on an order pad. But unlike your conventional maitre d', Mr. Wong doesn't recommend dishes, he prescribes them. Have swollen glands? Try chicken and sea-horse stew. Feeling dizzy? Perhaps some fried rice with wolfberries?"

12. The vigilante consumer: a person who will no longer tolerate shoddy products and poor service. Such consumers want companies to be more aware and responsive. They want auto companies to take back "lemons" and fully refund their money. They subscribe to the National Boycott News and Consumer Reports, join MADD (Mothers Against Drunk Driving), buy "green products," and look for lists of good companies and bad companies. Marketers must serve as the consciences of their companies to bring these consumers better, more responsible products and services. The underlying theme here is a lack of trust. Vigilante consumers are suspicious of corporate motives, corporate sales pitches, and corporate bigwigs.

13. FemaleThink: those who focus on women being different from men—not inferior, not superior—just different. Although it's been politically incorrect to say this over the past decade or so, men and women don't think the same way, don't communicate the same way, don't buy for the same reasons. That's the sum and substance of this trend. If you can click into the new female-oriented positioning for products and services, you can click into FemaleThink.

OldThink	***FemaleThink***
Works through hierarchy	Uses teamwork (familial)
Needs to know answers	Wants to ask the right question
Role identity	Identity is divided in many roles
Singleminded	Multiminded
Resists change	Seeks change
Goal-driven	Process-aware
Moving toward a destination	On a journey
Transaction-oriented: thinks in terms of getting from A to B to C in a direct line	Relationship-oriented: sees how A relates to C, how B relates to F, what B and D share in common

Source: Clicking by Faith Popcorn and Lys Marigold, New York: HarperCollins, 1996. Used by permission of HarperCollins.

The recent rash of business scandals and increased concerns about the environment have created fresh interest in the issues of ethics and social responsibility. Almost every aspect of marketing involves such issues. Unfortunately, because these issues usually involve conflicting interests, well-meaning people can disagree honestly about the right course of action in a particular situation. Many industrial and professional trade associations have suggested codes of ethics, and many companies are now developing policies and guidelines to deal with complex social responsibility issues.

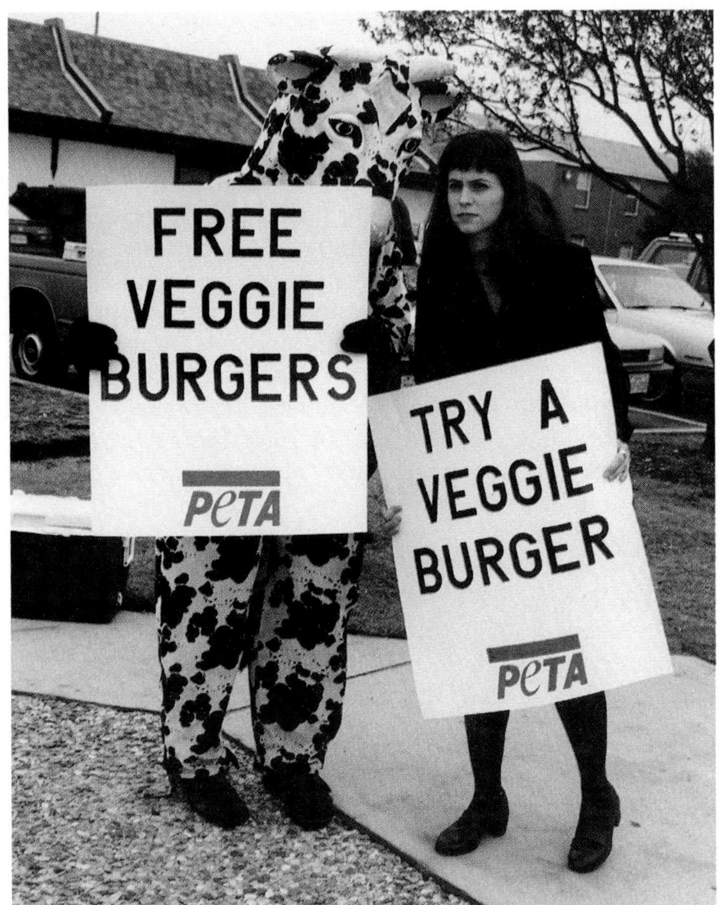

People for Ethical Treatment of Animals (PETA) is the world's largest animal rights group. "The food industry kills nine billion animals a year," says Lisa Lange, pictured here. One of PETA's tactics is to picket restaurants and let people know what the animals go through to become food. They would like to see everyone become vegetarians and all restaurants serve only vegetarian meals. Courtesy of PETA.

Cultural Environment

The cultural environment includes institutions and other forces that affect society's basic values, perceptions, preferences, and behaviors. As a collective entity, a society shapes the basic beliefs and values of its members. They absorb a worldview that defines their relationship with themselves and others. The following cultural characteristics can affect marketing decision making.

Persistence of Cultural Values

People in any society hold certain persisting core beliefs and values. For example, most Americans believe in working, getting married, giving to charity, and being honest; these beliefs shape the more specific attitudes and behaviors found in everyday life. Core beliefs and values are passed on from parents to children and are reinforced by schools, churches, business, and government. Secondary beliefs and values, however, are more open to change. Believing in marriage is a core belief; believing that people should get married early is a secondary belief. Family planning marketers, for instance, could argue more effectively that people should get married later rather than not getting married at all. Marketers have some chance of changing secondary values, but little chance of changing core values.

Throughout much of the Western world, cultural values concerning certain personal habits such as drinking and smoking have changed. The United States has witnessed wide swings in cultural values concerning the drinking of alcoholic beverages. During the days of the frontier, the attitude toward the use of alcohol was relatively relaxed. Prohibition attempted to eliminate alcoholic beverages completely. Today, society approves the use of alcohol but has called for increased responsibility on the part of those who drink and those who sell and serve alcoholic beverages. The alcoholic beverage industry has responded with its leading companies encouraging responsible drinking. The hospitality industry has responded with employee training and rules regulating the sale of alcohol. The industry has also been urged to assume proactive marketing. In place of pushing alcoholic beverages, the operator can stress the social side of the tavern experience, or offer food as a happy-hour business stimulant. The current popularity of menu items designed for "grazing" can be the basis for promotions. For example, the Westwater Inn in Olympia, Washington, uses table tents to sell absorbers: meatballs, chicken wings, stuffed mushrooms, and deep-fried snacks.[35]

The hospitality industry is worldwide. Chances are very good that many readers of this book will find themselves serving in a foreign setting sometime during their careers. Cultural norms and cultural prohibitions may affect their managerial roles in ways quite different from in the United States and Canada. For example, hoteliers in Israel are expected to understand and observe the rules of kashruth, or keeping kosher. These are complicated and require constant supervision. Hotels in Israel must have two kitchen setups, one for meat and one for dairy products. Because kosher meat is expensive in Israel, hotel food costs are higher.[36]

A practice widely followed in China, Hong Kong, and Singapore (and which has also spread to Japan, Vietnam, and Korea), *feng shui* means wind and water. Practitioners of feng shui, or geomancers, will recommend the most favorable conditions for any venture, particularly the placement of office buildings and the arrangement of desk, doors, and other items within. To have good feng shui, a building should face the water and be flanked by the mountains. It should also not block the view of the mountain spirits. The Hyatt Hotel in Singapore was designed without feng shui in mind, and, as a result, had to be redesigned to boost business. Originally, the front desk was parallel to the doors and road, and this was thought to lead to wealth flowing out. Furthermore, the doors were facing northwest, which easily let undesirable spirits in. The geomancer recommended designed alterations so that wealth could be retained and undesirable spirits kept out.[37]

Subcultures

Each society contains subcultures, groups of people with shared value systems based on common life experiences or situations. Episcopalians, teenagers, and working women all represent separate subcultures whose members share common beliefs, preferences, and behaviors. To the extent that subcultural groups have specific wants and buying behavior, marketers can choose subcultures as their target markets.

Linked Environmental Factors

In 1992, the total expenditures on food in restaurants and food-service operations exceeded food expenditures in grocery stores for the first time, and in 1996, people in the United States ate more meals prepared outside the home than they ate home-prepared meals. One of the forces behind this change is both heads of the household are working in many families. The average time spent on preparing meals is currently fifteen minutes and dropping. No longer is the woman expected to prepare home-cooked meals for the man. Families are purchasing meals at restaurants or taking prepared food home. Many people still prefer to eat at home; they just do not have time to cook. The "home-meal replacement" restaurant has developed as a result of these trends. Robert Del Grande's Café Express restaurants in Texas and Arizona and the Brennan family's Foodies Kitchen in New Orleans are examples of restaurant concepts creating quality meals with the convenience of self-service. Patrons can eat the meals on premise or take them home. Foodies Kitchen in New Orleans was developed to take advantage of this trend.

4.9 Hy-Vee
Foodies Kitchen
Café Express

Grocery stores are starting to provide competition for restaurants. According to David Audrian, vice president of the Texas Restaurant Association, the number one trend in the food service industry today is the growth of food service in supermarkets and convenience stores.[38] Most grocery stores have a food display near the deli counter of microwavable freshly prepared meals. These entrees include pot roast, teriyaki chicken, and pasta dishes that range in price from $2.50 to $7. The Hy-Vee grocery store at 14th and Park Avenue in Des Moines, Iowa, even has a drive-through window. People on their way home from work can order prepared meals from the store's deli to take home.[39]

The example above shows how the elements of the environment are linked. Economic forces result in families with both heads of the household working. This is a demographic statistic that can be tracked over time. Women are also able to build careers and take management positions once reserved for men. The working heads of the household no longer have time to cook. Culturally, thirty to forty years ago women were expected to stay home and cook. That is no longer the case. Thus we have seen a cultural change where men now participate in home duties and no one member of the household is expected to prepare all meals. Technology has also made it easier to reconstitute food and to warm prepared meals at home. Finally, the competitive environment between grocery stores and quick-service restaurants is expected to heat up. Grocery stores are building more elaborate delicatessens with a variety of prepared meals; they have fresh microwavable meals to go, and the drive-through window on the Hy-Vee store may become commonplace in the future. The change in food consumption patterns relates to economic, demographic, technological, cultural, and competitive trends.

Responding to the Marketing Environment

Many companies view the marketing environment as an "uncontrollable" element to which they must adapt. They passively accept the marketing environment and do not try to change it. They analyze environmental forces and design strategies that will help the company avoid the threats and take advantage of the opportunities that the environment provides.

Other companies take an **environmental management perspective.**[40] Rather than simply watching and reacting, these firms take aggressive action to affect the publics and forces in their marketing environment. Lobbyists are hired to influence legislation affecting their industries and to stage media events to gain favorable press coverage. They run advertorials (ads expressing editorial points of view) to shape public opinion. They press lawsuits and file complaints with regulators to keep competitors in line. They form contractual agreements to control their distribution channels better.

One of the elements of the macroenvironment that can be influenced is the political environment. Large companies will hire lobbyists to present their interests at the local, state and federal levels of government. These companies, along with smaller companies, join trade organizations such as the American Hotel and Lodging Association (AH&LA), the American Society of Travel Agents (ASTA) and Catering International Management Association (HCIMA), and the National Restaurant Association (NRA). The trade associations also hire lobbyists and form Political Action Committees (PACs) to represent and communicate their industry's concerns to government officials. By communicating the possible effects of proposed legislation on the industry and the community, PACs can sometimes influence pending legislation.

Marketing management cannot always affect environmental forces; in many cases, it must settle for simply watching and reacting to the environment. For example, a company would have little success trying to influence geographic population shifts, the economic environment, or major cultural values. But whenever possible, smart marketing managers take a proactive rather than a reactive approach to the publics and forces in their marketing environment.

Environmental Scanning

Use of an environmental scanning plan has proved beneficial to many hospitality companies. The following steps are involved: (1) determine the environmental areas that need to be monitored; (2) determine how the information will be collected, including information sources, the information frequency, and who will be responsible; (3) implement the data collection plan; and (4) analyze the data and use them in the market planning process. Part of the analysis is weighing the importance of the trends so the organization can keep the trends in proper perspective.

One of the most important tasks, especially in a small business such as a restaurant, is to assign responsibilities for the collection of data. Bob Southwell, former manager of the Houston Country Club, urged his secretarial staff to scan magazines for new menu ideas. Bar managers can look for lounge promotions. Dining room managers can study serving and promotional ideas. The staff then feeds ideas to the manager. Table 4-1 is an example of an environmental scanning plan. The details would differ for each restaurant or hotel.

Table 4-1
Example of an Environmental Scanning System for a Restaurant

ENVIRONMENTAL FACTOR	SOURCE OF INFORMATION	PERSON RESPONSIBLE	FREQUENCY
Customers	Customers	Service staff	Daily
	Employees	Management	Daily
	Customer counts	Accountant	Daily
	Tourist/convention bureau	Management	Monthly
	Internet	Management/staff	Weekly
Social/cultural	Trade magazines	Management Bartender Service staff Secretarial staff Accounting	Weekly or monthly
	Consumer magazines	Management Host/hostess Secretarial staff	Weekly or monthly
	Newspaper	Management	Daily
	Internet	Management/staff	Weekly or monthly
Competition	Customers	Management Service staff	Daily
	Newspaper	Management	Daily
	Visits	Management, chef	Weekly
	Internet	Management/staff	Weekly
Economic	Newspaper	Management	Daily
	Average check	Accountant Sales	Daily
	Economic newsletters	Management	Weekly or monthly
	Chamber of commerce	Management	Monthly
	Internet	Management	Monthly
Legal	Trade magazines	Management association	Monthly
	Newsletters		
	Trade magazines	Management	Weekly or monthly
	Internet	Management	Monthly
Technology	Trade magazines	Management Chef Accountant	Weekly or monthly
	Trade shows	Management Chef Accountant	Yearly
	Internet	Management	Monthly

Using Information about the Marketing Environment

It is never sufficient simply to collect data about the environment. Information must be reliable, timely, and used in decision making. William S. Watson, senior vice president of Best Western Worldwide Marketing, offered advice on this subject:

> As marketers, we are willing to make some intuitive leaps because of the creative aspects of our characters. Nevertheless, we need enough information to make reasonable decisions, enough good data so that we can let our judgment move beyond the obvious, traditional interpretations we have learned as professionals. Researchers must put less emphasis on data and more on the interpretation of those data. They must work toward turning data into useful information. Collecting data for its own value is like collecting stamps. It is a nice hobby but it does not deliver the mail.[41]

Key Terms

Demography The study of human populations in terms of size, density, location, age, sex, race, occupation, and other statistics.

Echo boomers (baby boomlet generation) Born between 1977 and 1994, these children of the baby boomers now number 72 million, dwarfing the Gen-Xers and almost equal in size to the baby boomer segment.

Economic environment The economic environment consists of factors that affect consumer purchasing power and spending patterns. Markets require both power and people. Purchasing power depends on current income, price, saving, and credit; marketers must be aware of major economic trends in income and changing consumer spending patterns.

Environmental management perspective A management perspective in which a firm takes aggressive actions to affect the publics and forces in its marketing environment rather than simply watching and reacting to it.

Financial intermediaries Banks, credit companies, insurance companies, and other businesses that help finance transactions or insure against the risks associated with the buying and selling of goods.

Generation X A generation of 45 million people born between 1965 and 1976; named Generation X because they lie in the shadow of the boomers and lack obvious distinguishing characteristics; others names include "baby busters," "shadow generation," or "yiffies"—young, individualistic, freedom-minded few.

Macroenvironment The larger societal forces that affect the whole microenvironment: competitive, demographic, economic, natural, technological, political, and cultural forces.

Marketing environment The actors and forces outside marketing that affect marketing management's ability to develop and maintain successful transactions with its target customers.

Marketing intermediaries Firms that help the company to promote, sell, and distribute its goods to final buyers; they include middlemen, physical distribution firms, marketing-service agencies, and financial intermediaries.

Marketing services agencies Marketing research firms, advertising agencies, media firms, marketing consulting firms, and other service providers that help a company to target and promote its products to the right markets.

Microenvironment The forces close to a company that affect its ability to serve its customers: the company, market channel firms, customer markets, competitors, and the public.

Political environment Laws, government agencies, and pressure groups that influence and limit the activities of various organizations and individuals in society.

Suppliers Firms and individuals that provide the resources needed by a company and its competitors to produce goods and services.

Chapter Review

I. Microenvironment. The microenvironment consists of actors and forces close to the company that can affect its ability to serve its customers. The actors in the microenvironment include the company, suppliers, market intermediaries, customers, and publics.

1) **The company.** Marketing managers work closely with top management and the various company departments.
2) **Suppliers.** Firms and individuals that provide the resources needed by the company to produce its goods and services.
3) **Marketing intermediaries.** Firms that help the company promote, sell, and distribute its goods to the final buyers.
4) **Transportation system.** The system moves the product from the factory to the customer. The hospitality industry depends on transportation systems to move supplies and customers to their businesses.
5) **Marketing services agencies.** Marketing research firms, advertising agencies, media firms, and marketing consulting firms help companies to target and promote their products to the right market.
6) **Financial intermediaries.** Includes banks, credit companies, insurance companies, and other firms that help hospitality companies to finance their transactions or insure risks associated with the buying and selling of goods and services.

II. Macroenvironment. The macroenvironment consists of the larger societal forces that affect the whole microenvironment demographic, economic, natural, technological, political, competitor, and cultural forces. Following are the seven major forces in a company's macroenvironment.

1) **Competitive environment.** Each firm must consider its size and industry position in relation to its competitors. A company must satisfy the needs and wants of consumers better than its competitors do in order to survive.

2) **Demographic environment.** Demography is the study of human populations in terms of size, density, location, age, sex, race, occupation, and other statistics. The demographic environment is of major interest to marketers because markets are made up of people.

3) **Economic environment.** The economic environment consists of factors that affect consumer purchasing power and spending patterns. Markets require both power as well as people. Purchasing power depends on current income, price, saving, and credit; marketers must be aware of major economic trends in income and changing consumer spending patterns.

4) **Natural environment.** The natural environment consists of natural resources required by marketers or affected by marketing activities.

5) **Technological environment.** The most dramatic force shaping our destiny today is technology.

6) **Political environment.** The political environment is made up of laws, government agencies, and pressure groups that influence and limit various organizations and individuals in society.

7) **Cultural environment.** The cultural environment includes institutions and other forces that affect society's basic values, perceptions, preferences, and behaviors.

III. Responding to the Marketing Environment. Many companies view the marketing environment as an "uncontrollable" element to which they must adapt. Other companies take an environmental management perspective. Rather than simply watching and reacting, these firms take aggressive actions to affect the publics and forces in their marketing environment. These companies use environmental scanning to monitor the environment.

Discussion Questions

1. How has the McDonald's concept changed since the 1960s? What environmental forces were behind these changes? How will the McDonald's concept change in the next decade, given the new forces operating in the environment?
2. What environmental trends will affect the success of a first-class hotel chain, such as Hyatt or Sofitel, over the next ten years? If you were corporate director of marketing for this type of hotel, what plans would you make to deal with these trends?
3. The 75 million members of the baby boom generation are aging, with the oldest members in their mid-fifties. List some marketing opportunities and threats associated with this demographic trend for the hospitality and travel industry.
4. How have environmental trends affected the design of hotels?
5. Explain how environmental trends have affected the food and beverage offerings of a business-class hotel such as Sheraton, Hilton, or Sofitel.

6. If we have little control over the macroenvironment, why should we be concerned with it?
7. What environmental trends will affect the success of The Walt Disney Company in the first decade of the 21st century? If you were in charge of marketing at Disney, what plans would you make to deal with these trends?

Experiential Exercises

Do one of the following:

1. View the annual reports of several hospitality companies. How did you find out about how they might be changing their business to fit the environment from their annual report? If you do not have access to an annual report, visit the book's Web site for electronic access to annual reports.
2. Choose and visit a restaurant, club, or a hotel you feel is designed for one of the generations discussed in the book (baby boomers, Generation X, echo boomers). After doing some research on the generation, state what the business you chose has done to cater to its target generation.

Internet Exercises

Support for this exercise can be found on the Web site for *Marketing for Hospitality and Tourism*, www.prenhall.com/kotler.

A. On the Internet, find how ecotourism is being used to attract tourists by different organizations.

B. From information you can find on the Internet, when do you think space tourism will be a viable form of tourism? What organizations are working to develop space tourism?

References

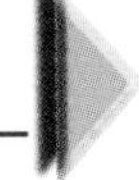

1. Tom Monaghan, *Pizza Tiger* (New York: Random House, 1986); "Domino's Launches Safety Ads," *Nation's Restaurant News,* August 14, 1986, p. 11; "Domino's Truck Kills 2 en Route to Delivery," *Nation's Restaurant News,* August 29, 1988, p. 4; "Domino's May Go to the Block," *Houston Chronicle,* September 12, 1989, p. 46; "Fight on Quick Pizza Delivery Grows," *New York Times,* August 29, 1989, sec. D, p. 11; "Policy on Drivers at Domino's Pizza," *The New York Times* (June 23, 1989), sec. D, p. 4; "Domino's Pizza: How It Became the No. 2 Chain," *Business Week,* August 15, 1983, p. 114; "Tom Monaghan: The Fun-Loving Prince of Pizza," *Business Week,* February 8, 1988, pp. 90, 93; Ron Simpson, "Can Monaghan Deliver," *Restaurant Business,* April 10, 1992, pp. 78–88; "Domino's Pizza Fails to Deliver: Some Lessons on 'Laser-Beam Focus,' " *International Journal of Retail and Distribution Management,* April 14, 1997, pp. 17–41; Puppy Brech, "Domino's Trails First Live Order TV Ad," *Marketing,* September 14, 2000, p. 4+; "Best Use of New Channel to Market," *Marketing,* June 6, 2000, p. 16+; Kathleen Sampey, "Domino's New Marketing Chief Talks Priorities, *Adweek,* July 2, 2001, p. 6+.
2. Jonathan Dahl, "Car-Rental Firms and Hotels Hit Hard by High Air Fares," *Wall Street Journal,* May 16, 1989, sec. B, p. 1.
3. Philip Kotler, *Marketing Management* (Upper Saddle River, NJ: Prentice Hall, 1988); Donald R. Lehmann and Russel S. Winer, *Analysis for Marketing Planning* (Plano, TX: Business Publications, 1988).
4. Michael Porter, *Competitive Strategy* (New York: Free Press, 1980).
5. Melinda Bush, "The Critical Need to Know," *Cornell Hotel and Restaurant Administration Quarterly* 26, no. 3 (November 1985): 1.

6. See Population estimates Program, Population Division, U.S. Census Bureau, Washington, DC 20233, retrieved March 5, 2001, from the World Wide Web: *http://www.census.gov/population/estimates/nation/intfile1-1.txt*.
7. Jennifer Lach, "Dateline America: May 1, 2025," *American Demographics* (May 1999): 19–20.
8. Margot Hornblower, "Great X," *Time*, June 9, 1997, pp. 58–69. Janus Dietz, "When Gen X Meets Aging Baby Boomers," *Marketing News*, May 10, 1999, p. 17; Ben Van Houten, "The X factor, *Restaurant Business*, October 1, 2000, p. 13+.
9. Phillip Kotler, *Marketing Management: Analysis, Planning, Implementation, and Control*, 10th ed. (Upper Saddle River, NJ: Prentice Hall, 2000), p. 142.
10. Accessed on-line from *www.growingupdigital.com/Flecho.html*, October 1999. Also see Douglas Tapscott, *Growing Up Digital: The Rise of the Net Generation* (New York: McGraw-Hill, 1999).
11. Philip Kotler and Gary Armstrong, *Principles of Marketing*, 9th edition. (Upper Saddle River, NJ: Prentice Hall, 2001), p. 97.
12. J. Walker Smith and Adam Clurman, *Rocking the Ages* (New York: Harper Business, 1998).
13. Diane Crispell, "Married Couples Endure," *American Demographics* (January 1998): 39; and *www.census.gov/population/projections/nation/hh-fam/table/table5n.txt*, accessed June 1999.
14. Dan Fost, "Americans on the Move," *American Demographics* (January-February 1997): 10–13.
15. Kevin Heubusch, "Small Is Beautiful," *American Demographics* (January 1998): 43–49; Brad Edmundson, "A New Era for Rural Americans," *American Demographics* (September 1997): 30–31; and Kenneth M. Johnson and Calvin Blake, "The Rural Rebound," *Wilson Quarterly* (Spring 1998): 50–56.
16. Fabian Linden, "In the Review Mirror," *American Demographics* (April 1984): 5; Peter Francese, "America at Mid-Decade," *American Demographics* (February 1995): 23–29; Rebecca Piirto Heath, "The New Working Class," *American Demographics* (January 1998): 51–55; and "Digest of Education Statistics 1997," *National Center for Education Statistics*, January 1998, at *http://nces01.ed.gov/pubs/digest97*.
17. Marydee Ojala, "The Daze of Future Business Research," *Online* (January–February 1998): 77; and Guy Kawasaki, "Get Your Facts Here," *Forbes*, March 23, 1998, p. 156.
18. James W. Hughes, "Understanding the Squeezed Consumer," *American Demographics* (July 1991): 44–50; for more on consumer spending trends, see Cheryl Russell, "The Consumer Paradigm," *American Demographics* (April 1999): 50–58.
19. Thomas Exter, "Where the Money Is," *American Demographics* (March 1987): 26–32; William Lazer, "How Rising Affluence Will Reshape Markets," *American Demographics* (February 1984): 17–20; Kern, "USA 2000," *Sales and Marketing Management* (October 27, 1986): 19; Bickley Townsend, "Dollars and Dreams," *American Demographics* (December 1987): 10, 55.
20. Frank H. Andorka Jr., "Hot Global Markets," *Hotel and Motel Management* 87.
21. McDonald's Corporate Fact Sheet, accessed August 6, 2001, *http://www.mcdonalds.com/corporate/investor/about/fact.../factsheet.htm*.
22. "McDonald's Protests Urged in France," *Financial Times*, August 20, 1999, World Trade Section, p. 5.
23. Edward Stokes, "Greening Hong Kong: Imagining Environmental Renewal," Hong Kong Conservation Photography Foundation, 2000.
24. Shoshana Hoose and Lida Madsen, "Field Day, The Birding Business Is Looking Up," *Portland Press Herald*, September 21, 1997: p. 1F.
25. The Ecotourism Society.
26. Philip Hayward, "Disney Does the Environment," *Lodging* 19, no. 7 (March 1994): 46–51.
27. Leonard D. Goodstein, Timothy M. Nolan, and J. William Pfeiffer, *Shaping Strategic Planning* (Glenview, IL: Scott, Foresman, 1989), pp. 3–4.
28. Don Nichols, "Taco Machine Proves a Big Hit in Its Test Run," *Restaurant Business* 92, no. 4 (March 1, 1993): 16.
29. Bruce Mohl, "Public Digests Restaurants' Low Scores," *Boston Globe*, March 17, 2000, p. A1+.
30. Ibid.
31. "Survey Reveals a Growing Usage of Technology among Business Travelers," *Hotel Business*, November 7–20, 2000, p. 52.
32. John Gaffney, "Starbucks and Microsoft Go for That Wireless Buzz," *Revolution* (February 2001): 9.
33. Gene Sloan, "Restaurant Taxes Gain Weight in Cash-Strapped Cities," *USA Today*, International Edition (Asia), September 28, 1994, sec. B, p. 7.
34. Glenn Withiam, "The Strange Death and Energetic Rebirth of the Tarrytown Hilton Inn," *Cornell Hotel and Restaurant Administration Quarterly* 30, no. 3 (November 1989): 46.
35. Denney G. Rutherford, "Managing Guest Intoxication: A Policy to Limit Third-Party Liability," *Cornell Hotel and Restaurant Administration Quarterly* 26, no. 3 (1985): 67.
36. Kenneth J. Gruber, "The Hotels of Israel: Pressure and Promise," *Cornell Hotel and Restaurant Administration Quarterly* 28, no. 4 (February 1988): 42.
37. J. S. Perry Hobson, "Feng Shui: Its Impacts on the Asian Hospitality Industry," *International Journal of Contemporary Hospitality Management* 6, no. 6 (1994): 21–26; Bernd H. Schmitt and Yigang Pan, "In Asia, the Supernatural Means Sales," *New York Times* February 19, 1995, sec. 3, p. 11.

38. Richard L. Papiernik, "Foodservice–Food-Market Lines Blur, but Focus Is on the Big $650 Billion Pie," *Nation's Restaurant News,* September 1, 1997, p. 57.

39. Matthew Schifrin and Bruce Upton, "Crab Rangoon to Go," *Forbes,* March 24, 1997, pp. 124–128.

40. Carl P. Zeithaml and Valarie Zeithaml, "Environmental Management: Revising the Marketing Perspective," *Journal of Marketing* (spring 1984): 46–53.

41. William S. Watson, "Letters, The New Research Responsibility," *Cornell Hotel and Restaurant Administration Quarterly* 34, no. 5, (October 1993): 7.

FAIRFIELD INN
Marriott

5 Marketing Information Systems and Marketing Research

Know your enemy and know yourself, and in a hundred battles you will never be in peril.
Sun-Tzu

One Sunday morning in the summer of 1986, six Marriott employees checked into an inexpensive hotel outside the Atlanta airport. Once they were inside their $30-a-night room, decorated with red shag rugs and purple velour curtains, the team went into their routine. One called from the front desk saying that his shoelace had broken—could someone get him a new one? Another carefully noted the brands of soap, shampoo, and towels. A third took off his suit jacket, laid it down on the bed, and began moaning and writhing and knocking the headboard against the wall, while a colleague in the next room listened for the muffled cries of feigned ecstasy and noted calmly that the room wasn't soundproof.

For six months, Marriott's intelligence team traveled the country gathering information on the players in the economy hotel business, a market Marriott strongly wished to enter. Armed with detailed data about potential rivals' strengths and weaknesses, Marriott budgeted $500 million for a new hotel chain that would beat the competition in every respect, from soap to service to soundproof rooms.

Marriott also hired an executive placement firm to interview fifteen regional managers of the five leading economy chains. From these managers they learned about the needs and expectations of the unit managers they were supervising. They gained knowledge on the managers' career expectations, training, and salary ranges. They gained insights into the cultures of each chain—their values, beliefs, and ideals. Lee Pillsbury, formerly a Marriott executive, defended the ethics of this competitive intelligence campaign by stating that the Marriott

employees identified themselves as Marriott employees upon checking into the hotels. The recruitment firm told the regional managers that there were no immediate openings, but there may be some positions in the future. In fact, Marriott hired five of the regional managers from among the interviewees.[1]

Marriott named its entry into the economy hotel business Fairfield Inns. Inspecting competitors' products was just one way Marriott gained information that aided in the development of its new chain. They also hired a headhunting team to interview their competitors' district and regional managers. Through talking with employees and making their own observations, Marriott discovered their competitors' weaknesses and developed a superior product. Marriott continues to collect marketing information after opening each Fairfield Inn hotel. The company conducts extensive marketing research, including phone and mail surveys, to track its standing in the marketplace and investigate client perceptions of its services.[2] *Marriott managers understand the value of marketing information, both for special projects such as developing its Fairfield Inn concept and for introducing further improvements. The attention Marriott's managers pay to collecting, interpreting, and using information has contributed greatly to the company's growth. Today there are more than 450 Fairfield Inn hotels and in 2000 Marriott launched its new brand extension Fairfield Inn and Suites.*

Chapter Objectives

After reading this chapter, you should be able to:

1. Explain the concept of the marketing information system.
2. Identify the different kinds of information the company might use.
3. Outline the marketing research process, including defining the problem and research objectives, developing the research plan, implementing the research plan, and interpreting and reporting the findings.

In carrying out marketing analysis, planning, implementation, and control, marketing managers need information at almost every turn. They need information about customers, competitors, suppliers, and other forces in the marketplace. One marketing executive put it this way: "To manage a business well is to manage its future; and to manage the future is to manage information."[3]

During the past century, most hotels and restaurants were independently owned or part of a small regional chain. Managers obtained information by being around people, observing them, and asking questions. During this century, many factors have increased the need for more and better information. As companies become national or international in scope, they need information on larger, more distant markets. As companies become more selective, they need better information about how buyers respond to different products and appeals. As companies use more complex marketing approaches and face intensified competition, they need information on the effectiveness of their marketing tools. Finally, in today's rapidly changing environments, managers need up-to-date information to make timely decisions.

The supply of information has also increased greatly. John Naisbitt suggests that the United States is undergoing a "megashift" from an industrial to an information-based economy.[4] He found that more than 65 percent of the U.S. workforce is now employed in producing or processing information, compared with only 17 percent in 1950. Using improved computer systems and other technologies, companies can provide information in great quantities. In fact, today's managers sometimes receive too much information. For example, one study found that with many companies offering data and information available through supermarket scanners, a packaged-goods brand manager is bombarded with one million to one billion new numbers each week.[5] As Naisbitt points out: "Running out of information is not a problem, but drowning in it is."[6]

Yet managers frequently complain that they lack enough information of the right kind and accumulate too much of the wrong kind. They also complain that marketing information is so widely spread throughout the company that it takes great effort to locate even simple facts. Subordinates may withhold information that they believe will reflect badly on their performance. Important information often arrives too late to be useful or is not accurate. Marketing managers need precise and timely information. Many companies are now studying their managers' information needs and designing systems to meet those needs.

The Marketing Information System

A **marketing information system (MIS)** consists of people, equipment, and procedures to gather, sort, analyze, evaluate, and distribute needed, timely, and accurate information to marketing decision makers. The marketing information system concept is illustrated in Figure 5-1. The MIS begins and ends with marketing managers, but managers throughout the organization should be involved in the MIS. First, it interacts with managers to assess their information needs. Next, it develops needed information from internal company records, marketing intelligence activities, and the marketing research process. Information analysts process information to make it more useful. Finally, the MIS distributes information to managers in the right form and at the right time to help in marketing planning, implementation, and control.

Figure 5-1
Marketing information system.

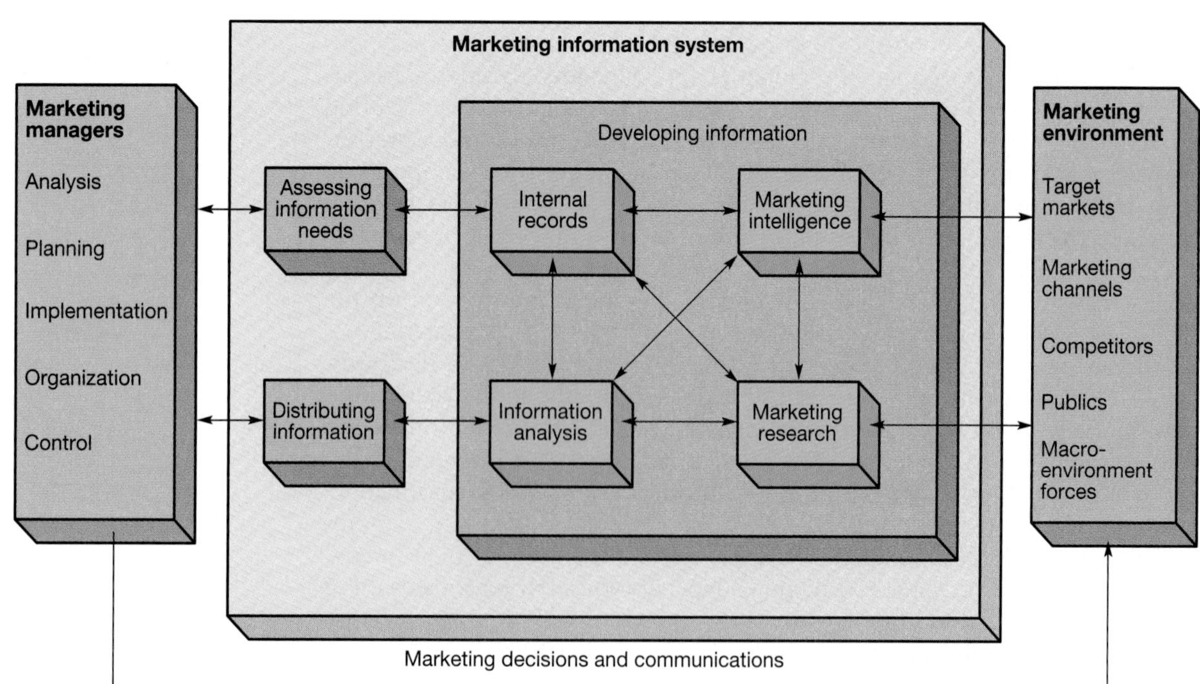

We now take a closer look at the functions of a company's marketing information system.

Assessing Information Needs

A good marketing information system balances information that managers would like to have against that which they really need and is feasible to obtain. A company begins by interviewing managers to determine their information needs. For example, Mrs. Field's Cookies provides their managers with sales forecasts with updates each hour. When sales are falling behind, the computer suggests merchandising techniques such as sampling in the mall to pick up sales.[7]

Some managers will ask for whatever information they can get without thinking carefully about its cost or usefulness. Too much information can be as harmful as too little. Other busy managers may fail to ask for things they need to know, or managers may not ask for some types of information that they should have.

For example, managers need to anticipate new competitive product offerings. However, competitors withhold information to prevent their competition from knowing about the product. During KFC's development of their "Chicken Little" sandwich, only a few corporate managers knew of the project. KFC had developed ingredient specifications for the making of the sandwich, and its suppliers had to sign secrecy agreements. KFC did not want competitors to learn about the new product offering before its test marketing. Yet a competitor with a good MIS system might have picked up clues in advance about KFC's plans. They may have heard a bread supplier commenting about KFC's orders for small hamburger-style buns. They may have heard an executive stating how KFC would be strengthening its lunch business. Even with secret agreements, news inadvertently leaks out. Managers who keep their eyes and ears open can pick up on competitive moves using legal and ethical sources of information such as speeches by company executives and trade publications.

5.1 Kentucky Fried Chicken

The company must estimate the value of having an item of information against the costs of obtaining it. The value depends on how it will be used, and this judgment is highly subjective. Similarly, estimating the cost of obtaining a specific item of information may be difficult.

The costs of obtaining, processing, storing, and delivering information can add up quickly. Sometimes additional information will contribute little to improving a manager's decision. Its cost may exceed its benefit. Suppose that a restaurant manager estimates that launching a new menu item without further information will yield a lifetime profit of $500,000. The manager believes that additional information will improve the marketing mix and increase the company's profit to $525,000. It would be foolish to pay $30,000 or more to obtain the additional information.

Developing Information

Information needed by marketing managers can be obtained from internal company records, marketing intelligence, and marketing research. The information analysis system processes this information and presents it in a form that is useful to managers.

Internal Records

Most marketing managers use internal records and reports regularly for making day-to-day planning, implementation, and control decisions. **Internal records information** consists of information gathered from sources within the company to evaluate marketing performance and to detect marketing problems and opportunities. The company's accounting department develops financial statements and keeps detailed records of sales, costs, and cash flows. Daily reports from restaurants can include total sales, sales by service person, sales by menu item, guest counts, and average check. Hotel daily reports can include occupancy, number of guests, total revenue, average daily rate, no-shows, and groups in the house. The answers to the questions in Table 5-1 will help managers assess their marketing information needs.

Many companies use internal records to build extensive internal databases, computerized collections of information obtained from data sources within the company. Marketing managers can readily access and work with information in the database to identify marketing opportunities and problems, plan programs, and evaluate performance.

Internal databases usually can be accessed more quickly and cheaply than other information sources, but they also present some problems. Because internal information was collected for other purposes, it may be incomplete or in the wrong form for making marketing decisions. For example, point of purchase sales in a restaurant software system used for ordering from the kitchen and the development of guest checks can be used for server evaluation, product evaluation, and to collect conformation on individual customers. Data ages quickly; keeping the database current requires a major effort. In addition, a large company produces mountains of information, and keeping track of it all is difficult. The database information must be well integrated and readily accessible through user-friendly interfaces so that managers can find it easily and use it effectively

Table 5-1

Questions for Assessing Marketing Information Needs

1. What types of decisions do you make regularly?
2. What types of information do you need to make these decisions?
3. What types of useful information do you get regularly?
4. What types of information would you like to get that you are not getting now?
5. What types of information do you get now that you don't really need?
6. What information would you want daily? weekly? monthly? yearly?
7. What topics would you like to be kept informed about?
8. What databases would be useful to you?
9. What types of information analysis programs would you like to have?
10. What would be the four most helpful improvements that could be made in the present information system?

Every company contains more information than any manager can possibly know or analyze. The information is scattered in countless databases, plans, and records, and in the heads of many longtime managers. The company must somehow bring order to its information gold mine, so that its managers can more easily find answers to questions and make informed decisions. Increasingly, companies are creating **data warehouses** to house their customer data in a single, more accessible location. Then, using powerful data mining techniques, they search for meaningful patterns in the data and communicate them to managers.

Useful marketing information is contained in kitchen production schedules and sales reports, front-desk reports, sales call reports, and functions. Managers can use information gathered from these and other sources to evaluate performance and detect problems and opportunities. Here are some examples of how companies use internal records to make marketing decisions:[8]

- Hotel managers use reservations records and registration information to aid in timing their advertising and sales calls. If most vacationers book February reservations in November, advertising in December will be too late.
- Reservation records also provide information concerning the hotel's top-producing travel agents. Hotel representatives can phone, fax, or visit travel agents to inform them of hotel-sponsored promotional activities in an effort to generate a higher volume of room sales.
- Louisiana found through visitors studies that most families plan for their summer vacations in the spring. They now advertise to the family market January through May, so their message will be in front of prospective visitors while they are making the vacation decision.

Guest History Information. The single most important element in any hospitality marketing information system is to have a process for capturing and using information concerning guests. Guest information is vital to improving service, creating effective advertising and sales promotion programs, developing new products, improving existing products, and developing marketing and sales plans and to the development and use of an effective revenue management program. Unfortunately, far too many hospitality firms have only a vague idea of who their guests are.

Specific guest information needs may include any or all of the information shown in Table 5-2. At first appearance this list undoubtedly seems overbearing and unduly inquisitive. The fact is that hospitality companies increasingly collect and use this type of information. Obviously, a hotel, resort, cruise line, or other hospitality company must be very careful not to infringe on the privacy rights of guests or to disturb them. An amazing amount of this information is available from internal records. This requires interfacing with other departments, such as reservations and accounting.

Guest Information Trends. Information concerning guest trends is vital to planning and revenue/yield management. Types of guest trend

Table 5-2
Specific Guest Information That Might Be Collected

Personal guest information
- Name
- Address
- Postal code
- Fax numbers
  - Home
  - Business
- Phone numbers
  - Home
  - Work
  - Auto
- E-mail
- Number in party
- Reason for trip
  - Business
  - Pleasure
  - Emergency
- Person who made reservation
  - Self-days stayed
  - Employer
  - Travel agent
- Name of employer
- Address of employer
- Title/position
- Method of payment
  - Credit card
    - Which?
  - Cash
  - Check
  - Bill to company

Type of primary product/service purchased
- Examples for a hotel:
  - Regular sleeping room
  - Suite
  - Deluxe suite

Other purchases (cross purchases)
- Examples for a hotel:
  - Long-distance phone
  - Laundry
  - Room service
  - Minibar
  - Other food and beverage
  - Health club
  - Recreational facilities
  - Retail products charged to bill

Length of stay

Specific dates as guest

Method of arrival
- Personal auto
- Rental auto
- Tour bus
- Train
- Taxi or limo

Member of frequent guest programs
- This hotel (number)
- Others presented for credit
  - Airline (number)
  - Company (number)

information used by hotels, airlines, cruise lines, and auto rental companies include the following:

- Booking patterns
- Cancellations
- Conversion percentages (percent of inquiries to reservations)
- Overbooking patterns
- Historical trends on occupancy for prime, shoulder, and low seasons
- Yield patterns by season

Gathering this vital information requires careful planning by a management information system. It is seldom, if ever, sufficient to try to retrieve and use data from a company's files if prior consideration was not given to the form in which it would be needed.

Guest history records enable hotel marketers to identify repeat guests and their individual needs and preferences. If a guest requests a particular newspaper delivered during one stay, a notation entered into the guest's file will ensure that the newspaper is received during all future visits. If a luxury hotel upgrades its guests to a better room on their fifth visit, its managers are increasing guest satisfaction. Frequent guests appreciate the free upgrade, and many request the higher-priced room on the next visit.

Guest Information Management

Acquisition of this critical information cannot be left to chance or the whims of department managers. A system for obtaining guest information may include any or all of the techniques discussed below.

Handwritten Journals and Card Files from Guest Registrations and Personal Observations. This system has disappeared from use except for B&Bs, fishing lodges, small hotels, country inns, and farm/ranch guest homes. Despite its apparent nineteenth-century style, this technique is often adequate for small hospitality enterprises.

Guest Comment Cards. Guest comment cards are often found on dining room tables and in guest rooms or are handed to departing customers. They provide useful information and can provide insights into problem areas. For example, several negative comments on food would indicate a potential problem for a restaurant. If corrective action is taken and fewer negative comments are registered, the correction has been successful.[9] A problem with guest comment cards is that they may not reflect the opinions of the majority of guests. Commonly, only people who are very angry or well pleased take the time to complete a card. Thus comment cards can be useful in spotting problem areas, but they are not a good indication of overall guest satisfaction. Also, if the distribution and control of comment cards is not well thought out, employees may selectively distribute comment cards to guests they feel will give a positive response. Employees may also discard negative comment cards if they have the opportunity to do so. Many companies have the card mailed to a corporate office to avoid this problem.

Listening to and Speaking with Guests. Many organizations have developed formal ways of interacting with guests. Hotels will offer free receptions in the afternoon for their frequent guests. This not only is a way of saying thank you to the guests, but it also provides an opportunity for managers to speak with guests. Sea World in Australia requires managers take several customer surveys every week. This is an excellent way to find out what guests think, and let management hear it firsthand. Wyndham hotels now call all guests five minutes before their room service order will arrive. This procedure was developed as a result of a guest's comment. The female business traveler said she often orders room service, takes a shower, gets dressed, and then eats breakfast. The call lets her know when the service person will arrive so she does not get caught in the shower. Wydham found that all business travelers appreciated this thoughtfulness and they were able to create a better service based on talking with their customers.[10]

If employees are trained to listen to guest comments and feed them back to management, this can be a powerful source of information. Your employees can be like microphones recording guest comments. For this listening to work, management has to feedback to the employees how they are using the information and there must be trust between the employees and management. Ritz Carlton makes excellent use of the "listening posts" concept. Horst Schulze, former president of Ritz Carlton said, "Keep on listening to customers because they change. And if you want to have 100% satisfied customers then you have to make sure that you listen and change—just in case they change their expectations that you change with them."[11]

Automated Systems. The decreasing cost and increasing capacity of automated guest history systems will allow hotels to create close relationships with their customers once again.[12]

Obviously, any hotel property or hospitality company, such as a large cruise line, must utilize an automated system. A variety of systems are available and should be examined carefully and tested before purchasing. Remember that an automated guest information system is part of broader systems such as database marketing and yield/revenue management.

An automated guest history system can be of great benefit to the sales force. Salespeople can pull guest histories by a specific geographic area, such as a city. This information can greatly assist in a sales blitz by identifying frequent guests who can receive top priority in the blitz. The guest history can also identify former frequent guests who are no longer using the hotel. Salespeople will want to call on these former clients to see if they can regain their business.

An automated guest history system offers a real competitive advantage to a chain, particularly a smaller chain. "By means of a centralized system or network, a group of hotels could share guest information. Imagine how impressed a guest would be if he or she requested a suite, champagne, and a hypoallergenic pillow when staying at a hotel in Boston, then received the same services at a chain affiliate in Maui without even having to ask."[13]

Disguised Shoppers. Hospitality companies often hire disguised or mystery shoppers to pose as customers and report back on their experience. The managers of Ruby's, a chain of restaurants based in California, uses shoppers to alert managers and employees to pay attention to important areas of the operation. Employees realize that they may be "shopped." The management of Ruby's hopes to catch employees doing the right things and doing them well. When employees score well on the shopper's report, Ruby's scores well.[14]

A mystery shopper works best if there is a possibility for recognition and reward for good job performance. This is the concept of positive reinforcement. If employees feel that the only purpose of a disguised shopper program is to report poor service and reprimand them, the program will not fulfill its full potential.

Company Records. One of the most misused sources of information is company records. Marketing managers should take advantage of the information that is currently being generated by various departments. Guest history and client history on potential corporate clients is also useful information.

Point-of-Sale Information. For restaurants, the point-of-sale (POS) register will undoubtedly offer opportunities to compile and distribute, through a computer, information that is currently entered into reports manually. A POS system could collect information about individual restaurant patrons where credit cards are used.

Some observers of the fast-food industry believe that future POS systems will use expert systems that employ computers using artificial intelligence. One possible scenario is the "computaburger." Data concerning customer preference, order size, and volume will be taken from a POS machine and provided to an expert system. The expert system will then predict and possibly even order a volume of hamburger and the accompanying condiments for specific times in each day.[15]

The casino industry has displayed a high interest in POS systems and their increasing sophistication. Some slot machines are now capable of recording the numbers of play and the win/loss record of frequent players who activate the machines through use of a magnetic card. The player receives points based on the amount of play, and the casino is able to track the playing habits of players using the slot club cards.

Systems are also in place in most casinos to track players who are brought to the casino by junket reps. Tracking of these players is the responsibility of the pit boss in each gaming area, such as blackjack.

The Las Vegas Hilton provides an example of an internal system that can provide needed marketing information,[16] which includes the following:

- A front-desk tracking system that can classify each room night sold into the proper market segment
- A casino player tracking system that can identify players by market segments, that is, gaming rate versus slot tournament
- A database of all customers staying at the Hilton to identify their spending patterns by market segment
- Market research detailing guests' demographic characteristics, visitor frequency, and spending habits by customer segment

The need to develop and use reliable guest information, particularly guest satisfaction data, has been examined by researchers within the restaurant industry, who observed that "restaurant failures are partly a result of management's lack of strategic orientation in measuring and focusing on customer satisfaction."[17]

Corporate Customer and Marketing Intermediary Information

A database of customers/prospects is of great value to a professional sales force. The sales force of Benchmark Hospitality Conference Resorts is trained to go beyond demographic studies and to target prospects by geography and industry segment. Benchmark's salespeople monitor the health of specific industries and qualify prospects. Before arranging a sales meeting with any corporate meeting planner, the salesperson obtains marketing information concerning the prospect, such as the following:

- The industry standing and strategic outlook for growth
- Profit and loss statements from annual reports

- Debt to equity ratios
- Corporate culture information
- Data concerning how this company uses meetings

5.2 Ritz Carlton
Ruby's
Las Vegas Hilton
Benchmark
Wall Street Journal

This information can be obtained from annual reports, financial analyses of public companies, and articles on the company, and by talking with company employees. In addition to detailed information concerning prospects, Benchmark expects sales force members to be regular readers of the business press, such as the *Wall Street Journal* and the *New York Times*.[18]

Marketing Intelligence

Marketing intelligence includes everyday information about developments in the marketing environment that helps managers prepare and adjust marketing plans and short-run tactics. Marketing intelligence systems determine the needed intelligence, and collect and deliver it in a useful format to marketing managers.

Internal Sources of Marketing Intelligence

Marketing intelligence can be gathered by a company's executives, front-desk staff, service staff, purchasing agents, and sales force. Employees, unfortunately, are often too busy to pass on important information. The company must sell them on their role as intelligence gatherers and train them to spot and report new developments. Managers should debrief contact personnel on a regular basis.

Hotel owners and managers are essential parts of a marketing intelligence system. John F. Power, the general manager of the New York Hilton and Towers, served in this role on a trip to Japan. "I realized how different a Japanese breakfast is from our own," said Power, "and while most people like to sample the cuisine of the country they are visiting, everyone prefers to eat familiar food for breakfast."

As a result of marketing intelligence gathered on Power's trip, the New York Hilton now serves miso soup, nori (dried seaweed), yakizanaka (grilled fish), raw eggs, natto (fermented beans), oshiako (pickled vegetables), and rice as an authentic Japanese breakfast buffet.[19]

External Sources of Marketing Intelligence

A hospitality company must encourage suppliers, convention and tourist bureaus, and travel agencies to pass along important intelligence. There are three types of external marketing information: (1) macromarket information, (2) competitive information, and (3) new innovation and trends. The three types and their sources are shown in Table 5-3. It is worthwhile for a hospitality company to encourage the gathering of this information by treating vendors, salespeople, and potential employees in a friendly and receptive manner. Members of management should be encouraged to join community and professional organizations where they are likely to obtain essential marketing information.

Hotel and restaurant managers are in a particularly good position to acquire excellent information by entertaining key information sources in

Table 5-3
External Marketing Information Needs and Concerns for the Hospitality Industry

TYPES OF INFORMATION	EXTERNAL SOURCES OF INFORMATION
Visitor Marketing Information	
Profile of visitors to area	Visitors bureau (local, state, federal)
Visitor trends	Chambers of commerce
Visitor expenditures	Colleges/universities
Visitation days	Public utility companies
Purpose of visit	Ski resorts
Recreational facilities desired/used	Publications (newspapers, magazines)
Lodging accommodation desired/used	Public parks, national forests, Bureau of Land Management
Food and beverage accommodation desired/used	
Retail shopping desired/used	Airlines, cruise lines
	Associations (hotel, restaurant, airline, cruise line, casinos)
	Environmental groups
	Historic restorations and museums
	Private companies offering plant tours
	Banks and other financial institutions
Competitive Information	
Pricing strategy	Suppliers/vendors
Product mix	Consultants
Planned expansion, renovation	Travel agencies
Product line extensions	Tour operators
Customer mix	Airlines, cruise lines, bus and rail companies
Strategic direction	Publications of competitors
Advertising/promotional thrust	Trade publications
Employee dissatisfaction/satisfaction	Association publications
Occupancy rates, discounts	Meetings/conventions
	Employees of competitors
	Trade association representatives
New Innovations and Trends	
Technological improvements in products/services	Same list as those who provide competitive information
Pricing technology, such as yield management	
Technological advances in equipment	

their properties. Sales force members are excellent conduits of information.

Sources of Competitive Information

Competitive intelligence is available from competitors' annual reports, trade magazine articles, speeches, press releases, brochures, and advertisements. Hotel and restaurant managers should also visit their competitors' premises periodically. As mentioned in Chapter 4, a major consideration in any competitive information system is clearly defining the competition.

Commercial Sources of Marketing Information

Companies can also purchase information from outside suppliers. One such source of information is a system called Dialogue that provides access to over 350 databases. While sitting at a computer, managers can retrieve information on new products and locations, industry trends and projections, press releases, and the detailed finances of public and privately held businesses.[20] Today there are thousands of on-line databases of information services. For example, Adtrack on-line database tracks all the advertisements of a quarter-page or larger from 150 major consumer and business publications. Companies can use these data to assess advertising strategies and styles, shares of advertising space, media use, and ad budgets. The Donnelly Demographics database provides demographic data from the U.S. census plus demographic projections by state, city, or zip code. Companies can use it to measure markets and develop segmentation strategies. The Electronic Yellow Pages, containing listings from nearly all the nation's 4,800 phone books, is the largest directory of American companies available. A firm such as Burger King might use this database to count McDonald's restaurants in different geographic locations. A readily available on-line database exists to fill almost any marketing information need.[21]

Associations sometimes collect data from member companies, compile it, and make it available to members for a reasonable fee. Information of this nature can often be misleading, because member companies frequently provide incorrect data or may refuse to contribute any statistics if they have a dominant market share.

Marketing Research

Managers cannot always wait for information to arrive in bits and pieces from the marketing intelligence system. They often require formal studies of specific situations. When McDonald's decided to add salads to its menu, its planners needed to research customers' preferences for types of vegetables and dressings.

Ben's Steakhouse in Palm Beach, Florida, would like to know what percentage of its target market has heard of Ben's, how they heard about Ben's, what they know, and how they feel about the steak house. This would enable Ben's Steakhouse to know how effective their marketing communications have been. Casual marketing intelligence cannot answer these questions. Managers sometimes need to commission formal marketing research.

Marketing research is a process that identifies and defines marketing opportunities and problems, monitors and evaluates marketing actions and performance, and communicates the findings and implications to management.[22] Marketing researchers engage in a wide variety of activities. Their ten most common activities are measurement of market potentials, market-share analysis, the determination of market characteristics, sales analysis, studies of business trends, short-range forecasting, competitive product studies, long-range forecasting, marketing information systems studies, and testing of existing products.

A company can conduct marketing research by employing its own researchers or hiring outside researchers. Most large companies—in fact, more than 73 percent—have their own marketing research departments.

But even companies with their own departments hire outside firms to do fieldwork and special tasks.

Frank Camacho, a former vice president of corporate marketing services for Marriott, listed Marriott's research priorities as follows:[23]

5.3 Marriott

- Market segmentation and sizing
- Concept development and product testing
- Price-sensitivity assessment
- Advertising and promotions assessment
- Market tracking
- Customer satisfaction

Small hotels or restaurants can obtain research help from nearby universities or colleges with business or hospitality programs. College marketing classes can be used to do exploratory research, find information about prospective customers, and conduct customer surveys. Instructors often arrange for their classes to gain marketing research experience in this way.

Marketing Research Process

The marketing research process consists of four steps (see Figure 5-2): defining the problem and research objectives, developing the research plan, implementing the research plan, and interpreting and reporting the findings.

The Cantonese Opera is a tourist attraction of Hong Kong. Tourist authorities such as the Hong Kong Tourist Association use research to determine who comes to their cities and what tourist attractions create value for them. Courtesy of the Hong Kong Tourist Association.

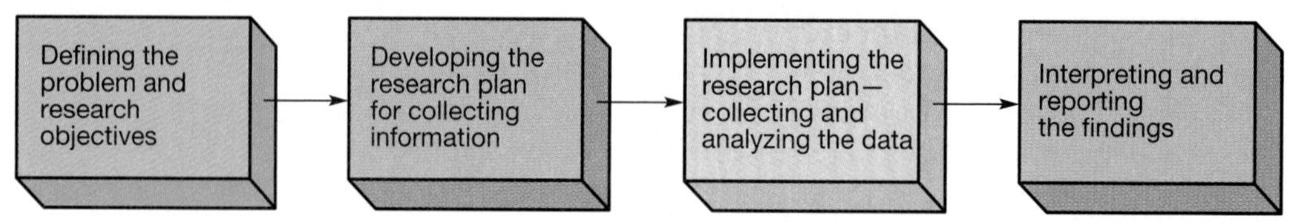

Figure 5-2
Marketing research process.

Defining the Problem and Research Objectives

Managers must work closely with marketing researchers to define the problem and the research objectives. The manager best understands the problem or decision for which information is needed, and the researcher best understands marketing research and how to obtain information.

Managers must know enough about marketing research to interpret the findings carefully. If they know little about marketing research, they may accept the wrong information, draw the wrong conclusions, or request much more information than they need. Marketing researchers can help the manager define the problem and use the findings correctly.

In one case a restaurant manager hired a researcher to determine the restaurant's level of awareness among the target market. The manager felt that lack of awareness explained low patronage. The researcher found, to the contrary, that many people were aware of the restaurant but thought of it as a special-occasion rather than an everyday restaurant. The manager had misdefined the problem and the research objective.

Assuming that the problem is well defined, the manager and researcher must set research objectives. A marketing research project can have one of three types of objectives: **exploratory research,** to gather preliminary information that will help define the problem and suggest hypotheses; **descriptive research,** to describe the size and composition of the market; and **causal research,** to test hypotheses about cause-and-effect relationships. Managers often start with exploratory research and later follow with descriptive and/or causal research.

A sad example of the need for marketing research was a self-help project initiated on U.S. Indian reservations. A total of fifty-two hotels were built as a result of promoting and anticipating tourism. Only two survived due to poorly conceived plans. In several cases, hotels were built in seldom-visited remote areas. Marketing research could have provided valuable information such as visitor trends to the areas, identification of possible market segments, plus their size and travel preferences.[24]

Developing the Research Plan

The second marketing research step calls for determining the needed information and developing a data collection plan.

Determining Specific Information Needs. Research objectives must be translated into specific information needs. When Marriott decided to research a new, lower-priced hotel system, it had two goals: to pull travelers away from competitors and to minimize cannibalization of its own existing hotels. This research might call for the following specific information:[25]

- What features should the hotel offer?
- How should the new hotels be priced?
- Where should the hotels be located? Can they safely be located near existing Marriott hotels without incurring cannibalization?
- What are the probable sales and profits?

Gathering Secondary Information. To meet a manager's information needs, researchers can gather secondary data, primary data, or both. **Secondary data** consist of information already in existence somewhere, having been collected for another purpose. **Primary data** consist of information collected for the specific purpose at hand.

Researchers usually start by gathering secondary data. Secondary data are usually obtained more quickly and at a lower cost than primary data. Table 5-4 shows many secondary sources, both internal and external.

For example, *Restaurants USA,* published by the National Restaurant Association, provides a yearly projection of sales for food-service establishments, presenting the projections by state and by industry segment. A company has the options of paying a research firm to develop this information or of joining the National Restaurant Association and receiving this information through its publication. The latter is more cost-effective.

5.4 National Restaurant Association

Basing decisions on secondary data, however, can also present problems. The required information may not exist. Even when it exists, it might not be very relevant, accurate, current, and impartial. For example, a trade magazine wanted to identify the best hotel chains in the minds of corporate travel managers and travel agents. It distributed its survey as inserts in its magazine. The response rate was less than 0.05 percent. Yet the magazine issued a ranking based on this unreliable response rate.[26] Additionally, if research of this type is not properly designed, it can favor the companies with the most hotels or restaurants, because they will be more familiar to the respondent.

Secondary data provide a good starting point for marketing research. However, when secondary sources cannot provide all the needed information, the company must collect primary data.

Planning Primary Data Collection. Some managers collect primary data by developing a few questions and finding people to interview. But data collected casually can be useless or, even worse, misleading. Table 5-5 shows that designing a plan for primary data collection calls for decisions about research approaches, contact methods, a sampling plan, and research instruments.

Research Approaches. Three basic research approaches are observations, surveys, and experiments. **Observational research** is the gathering of primary data by observing relevant people, actions, and situations. For example, a multiunit food-service operator sends researchers into competing restaurants to learn menu item prices, check portion sizes and consistency, and observe point-of-purchase merchandising. Another restaurant evaluates possible new locations by checking the locations of competing restaurants, traffic patterns, and neighborhood conditions. A

Table 5-4
Sources of Secondary Data

A. Internal Sources

Internal sources include company profit and loss statements, balance sheets, guest checks, sales figures, sales call reports, invoices, inventory records, daily reports, prior research reports, registration cards, and reservation information.

B. Government Publications

- *Statistical Abstract of the United States,* updated annually, provides summary data on demographic, economic, social, and other aspects of the U.S. economy and society.
- *County and City Data Book,* updated every three years, presents statistical information for counties, cities, and other geographical units on population, education, employment, aggregate and median income, housing, bank deposits, retail sales, and so on.
- *U.S. Industrial Outlook* provides projections of industrial activity by industry and includes data on production, sales, shipments, employment, and the like. *Marketing Information Guide* provides a monthly annotated bibliography of marketing information. Other government publications include the *Annual Survey of Manufacturers; Business Statistics; Census of Manufacturers; Census of Population; Census of Retail Trade, Wholesale Trade, and Selected Service Industries; Census of Transportation; Federal Reserve Bulletin; Monthly Labor Review; Survey of Current Business;* and *Vital Statistics Report.*

C. Periodicals and Books

- *Business Periodicals Index,* a monthly, lists business articles appearing in a wide variety of business publications.
- *Standard and Poor's Industry Surveys* provide updated statistics and analyses of industries.
- *Moody's Manuals* provide financial data and names of executives in major companies.
- *Encyclopedia of Associations* provides information on every major U.S. trade and professional association.
- Marketing journals include the *Journal of Marketing, Journal of Restaurant and Foodservice Marketing, Journal of Services Marketing,* and *HSMAI Marketing Review.*
- Useful trade magazines include *Advertising Age, Business Travel News, The Consultant, Food Management, Lodging, Lodging Hospitality, Nation's Restaurant News, Restaurant Business, Restaurant Hospitality, Restaurants and Institutions, Restaurants USA,* and *Travel Weekly.*
- Useful general business magazines include *Business Week, Cornell Hotel and Restaurant Administration Quarterly, Fortune, Forbes,* and *Harvard Business Review.*

D. Commercial Data

- A.C. Nielsen Company provides data on products and brands sold through retail outlets (Retail Index Services), data on television audiences (Media Research Services), magazine circulation data (Neodata Services, Inc.), and more.
- Market Research Corporation of America provides data on weekly family purchases of consumer products (National Consumer Panel), data on home food consumption (National Menu Census), and data on 6000 retail, drug, and discount retailers in various geographical areas (Metro Trade Audits).
- Selling Areas–Marketing, Inc., provides reports on warehouse withdrawals to food stores in selected market areas (SAMI reports).

Table 5-4
Sources of Secondary Data (*continued*)

D. Commercial Data—*continued*

- Simmons Market Research Bureau provides annual reports covering television markets, sporting goods, proprietary drugs, and others, giving demographic data by sex, income, age, and brand preferences (selective markets and the media reaching them).
- Other commercial research houses selling data to subscribers include the Audit Bureau of Circulation, Audits and Surveys, Dun and Bradstreet, National Family Opinion, Standard Rate and Data Service, and Starch.

E. Electronic Databases

See book's Web site (*www.prenhall.com/kotler*) for list of current databases.

hotel chain sends observers posing as guests into its coffee shops to check on cleanliness and customer service.

Observational research can yield information that people are normally unwilling or unable to provide. Observing numerous plates containing uneaten portions of the same menu item indicates that the food is not satisfactory. On the other hand, feelings, beliefs, and attitudes that motivate buying behavior cannot be observed. Long-run or infrequent behavior is also difficult to observe. Because of these limitations, researchers often supplement observation with survey research.

Survey research is the approach best suited to gathering descriptive information. Survey research can be structured or unstructured. Structured surveys use formal lists of questions asked of all respondents in the same way. Unstructured surveys let the interviewer probe respondents and guide the interview according to their answers.

Survey research may be direct or indirect. In the direct approach, the researcher asks direct questions about behavior or thoughts; for example, "Why don't you eat at Arby's?" Using the indirect approach, the researcher might ask: "What kinds of people eat at Arby's?" From the response, the researcher may be able to discover why the consumer avoids Arby's. In fact, it may suggest factors of which the consumer is not consciously aware.

Table 5-5
Planning Primary Data Collection

RESEARCH APPROACHES	CONTACT METHODS	SAMPLING PLAN	RESEARCH INSTRUMENTS
Observation	Mail	Sampling unit	Questionnaire
Survey	Telephone	Sample size	Mechanical instruments
Experiment	Personal	Sampling procedure	
	Internet		

The major advantage of survey research is its flexibility. It can be used to obtain many different kinds of information in many different marketing situations. Depending on the survey design, it may also provide information more quickly and at lower cost than can be obtained by observational or experimental research.

Survey research also has some limitations. Sometimes people are unable to answer survey questions because they cannot remember or never thought about what they do and why. Or they may be reluctant to answer questions asked by unknown interviewers about things that they consider private. Busy people may not want to take the time. Respondents may answer survey questions even when they do not know the answer in order to appear smart or well informed. Or they may try to help the interviewer by giving pleasing answers. Careful survey design can help minimize these problems.

In the early 1980s, Hardee's fast-food restaurant chain knew it was not responding effectively to consumer needs. Extensive consumer perception surveys were conducted. The results showed that consumers were confused about what kind of chain Hardee's was. Research results also showed that the chain needed to improve its service and ambience. Hardee's responded with a new positioning statement, upgraded equipment, improved decor, and committed the company to a total redesign of the hamburger manufacturing process.

Although observation is best suited for exploratory research and surveys for descriptive research, **experimental research** is best suited for gathering causal information. Experiments involve selecting matched groups of subjects, giving them different treatments, controlling unrelated factors, and checking for differences in group responses.

Researchers at Arby's might use experiments before adding a new sandwich to the menu to answer such questions as the following:

- By how much will the new sandwich increase Arby's sales?
- How will the new sandwich affect the sales of other menu items?
- Which advertising approach would have the greatest effect on sales of the sandwich?
- How would different prices affect the sales of the product?
- Should the new item be targeted toward adults, children, or both?

5.5 Arby's

For example, to test the effects of two different prices, Arby's might set up the following simple experiment. The company could introduce the new sandwich at one price in its restaurants in one city and at another price in restaurants in a similar city. If the cities are very similar and if all other marketing efforts for the sandwich are identical, differences in sales volume between the two cities should be related to the price charged. More complex experiments can be designed to include other variables and other locations.

Contact Methods. Information can be collected by mail, telephone, or personal interview. Table 5-6 shows the strengths and weaknesses of each contact method.

Mail questionnaires have many advantages. They can be used to collect large amounts of information at a low cost per respondent. Respon-

Table 5-6
Strengths and Weaknesses of the Three Contact Methods

	MAIL	TELEPHONE	PERSONAL	INTERNET
Flexibility	Poor	Good	Excellent	Fair
Quantity of data that can be collected	Good	Fair	Excellent	Good
Control of interviewer effects	Excellent	Fair	Poor	Excellent
Control of sample	Fair	Excellent	Fair	Fair
Speed of data collection	Poor	Excellent	Good	Excellent
Response rate	Poor	Good	Good	Fair
Cost	Good	Fair	Poor	Excellent

Source: Adapted with permission of Macmillan Publishing Company from *Marketing Research Measurement and Method,* 6th ed., by Donald S. Tull and Del I. Hawkins, © 1993 by Macmillan Publishing Company.

dents may give more honest answers to personal questions on a mail questionnaire than they would to an unknown interviewer in person or over the phone. No interviewer is involved to bias the respondent's answers. Mail questionnaires are convenient for respondents, who can answer the survey when they have time. It is also a good way to reach people who often travel, such as meeting planners.

Mail questionnaires also have some disadvantages. They are not very flexible, they require simple and clearly worded questions, all respondents answer the same questions in a fixed order, and the researcher cannot adapt the questionnaire based on earlier answers. Mail surveys usually take longer to complete than telephone or personal surveys, and the response rate (the number of people returning completed questionnaires) is often very low. When the response rate is low, respondents may not be typical of the population being sampled. Also, the researcher has little control over who answers the questionnaire in the household or office.

Telephone interviewing provides a method for gathering information quickly. It also offers greater flexibility than mail questionnaires. Interviewers can explain questions that are not understood; they can skip some questions and probe more on others, depending on the respondent's answers. Telephone interviewing allows greater sample control. Interviewers can ask to speak to respondents who have the desired characteristics or can even request someone by name, and response rates tend to be higher than with mail questionnaires.

Telephone interviewing also has drawbacks. The cost per respondent is higher than with mail questionnaires, and some people may not want to discuss personal questions with an interviewer. Using an interviewer increases flexibility but also introduces interviewer bias. The interviewer's manner of speaking, small differences in the way interviewers ask questions, and other personal factors may affect respondents' answers. Different interviewers may interpret and record responses in a variety of ways, and under time pressures, there is the possibility that some interviewers may record answers without actually asking the questions.

Unfortunately, the general public has become increasingly reluctant to participate in telephone surveys. Many unethical companies have misled respondents into believing that legitimate research is being conducted when in fact this was a ruse for a sales call. Thieves have also used this approach to find out when homeowners are likely to be away and even to determine the contents of the house.

Personal interviewing takes two forms: individual (intercept) and group. Intercept interviewing involves talking with people in their homes, offices, on the street, or in shopping malls. The interviewer must gain the interviewee's cooperation, and the time involved can range from a few minutes to several hours. For longer surveys, a small payment is sometimes offered to respondents in return for their time.

Intercept interviews are widely used in tourism research. For instance, Steamboat Springs, Colorado, used this technique to interview 600 summer visitors to the city. Intercept interviews allow the research sponsor to reach known visitors in a short period of time. There may be few or no alternative methods of reaching visitors whose names and addresses are unknown. Intercept interviews generally involve the use of judgmental sampling. The interviewer may be given guidelines as to whom to "intercept," such as 20 percent under age 20 and 40 percent over age 60. This always leaves room for error and bias on the part of the interviewer, who may not be able to correctly judge age, race, and even sex from appearances. Interviewers may also be uncomfortable talking to certain ethnic or age groups.

Internet surveying is a relatively new contact method. It has a number of advantages. The survey can be available to a global sample without having to worry about international postal rates. Another advantage is there are software packages available that enable the survey responses to be tabulated as the respondent is entering them. As in any form of computer-aided interviewing, the next question automatically comes up in branching questions or skip sequences. For example, if a business traveler is to answer one set of questions and a pleasure traveler another set, when asked if you were traveling for business or pleasure the proper set will come up.

A drawback to Internet surveying is that it is not accessible to everyone. Some people do not access the Internet on a regular basis. Although people over sixty-five are one of the fastest growing segments of Internet users, they have been light users. Thus, one could expect to get a younger sample through an Internet survey. Tourism research has found significant differences in responses received from pen and paper surveys and Internet surveys, including demographic differences.[27] If interviewing is being done on a particular Internet site, the researcher must make sure those going to the site are representative of the population of interest. To increase the response rate, some researchers will send a letter to the respondent giving the location of the survey. Other researchers will send an e-mail with the Internet's URL. Some researchers give respondents a choice of a paper survey or using an Internet-based survey to avoid sample bias. Although only about 5 percent of the surveys use the Internet as a contact method, speed and the potential for low cost will increase the popularity of Internet surveying. If you use the Internet for surveying, you must make sure you have access to a sample that is representative of the population of interest.

Focus group interviewing is usually conducted by inviting six to ten people to gather for a few hours with a trained moderator to talk about a product, service, or organization. The moderator needs objectivity, knowledge of the subject and industry, and some understanding of group and consumer behavior. Participants normally receive a small sum or gift certificates for attending. The meeting is held in a pleasant place, and refreshments are served to create a relaxed environment. The moderator starts with broad questions before moving to more specific issues, encouraging open and easy discussion to foster group dynamics that will bring out true feelings and thoughts. At the same time, the interviewer focuses the discussion: hence the name focus group interviewing. Comments are recorded through note taking or on videotape and studied later to understand the consumers' buying process. In many cases a two-way mirror separates respondents from observers, who commonly include personnel from the ad agency and the client.

Focus group interviewing is rapidly becoming one of the major marketing research tools for gaining insight into consumers' thoughts and feelings. This method is especially suited for use by managers of hotels and restaurants, who have easy access to their customers. For example, some hotel managers often invite a group of hotel guests from a particular market segment to have a free breakfast with them. During the breakfast the manager gets a chance to meet the guests and discuss what they like about the hotel and what the hotel could do to make their stay more enjoyable and comfortable. The guests appreciate this recognition, and the manager gains valuable information. Restaurant managers use the same approach by holding discussion meetings with guests at lunch or dinner.

Here are examples of how restaurants have used group interviews:

- A steak house suffering from declining sales went to its customers to gain insight into the causes of its problem. Two focus groups were conducted, one composed of customers who indicated they would return and another composed of those who said they would not. From these sessions the owners learned that patrons considered the restaurant a fun place but thought the food was boring. The problem was solved by expanding and upgrading the menu.[28]
- Focus groups provided critical information to Andy Reis of Café Provincial in Evanston, Illinois. He found that his clientele wanted valet parking. Reis had assumed, because there was on street parking and a nearby parking garage, that parking was not a problem. He also found that his diners felt uncomfortable in the restaurant's Terrace Room. This was a casual dining room with glass tables and porch furniture. Apparently, it was too casual for his diners. The Terrace room was remodeled, and valet parking was added. Now people request to sit in the Terrace Room. Reis states that focus groups are worthwhile if you listen carefully.[29]

5.6 Café Provincial

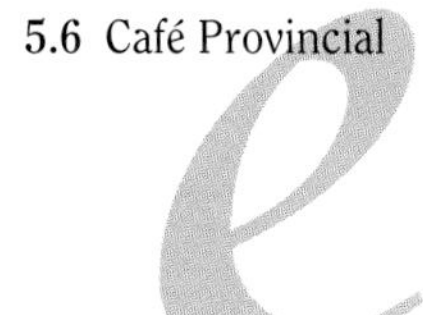

Personal interviewing is very flexible and can be used to collect large amounts of information. Trained interviewers can hold the

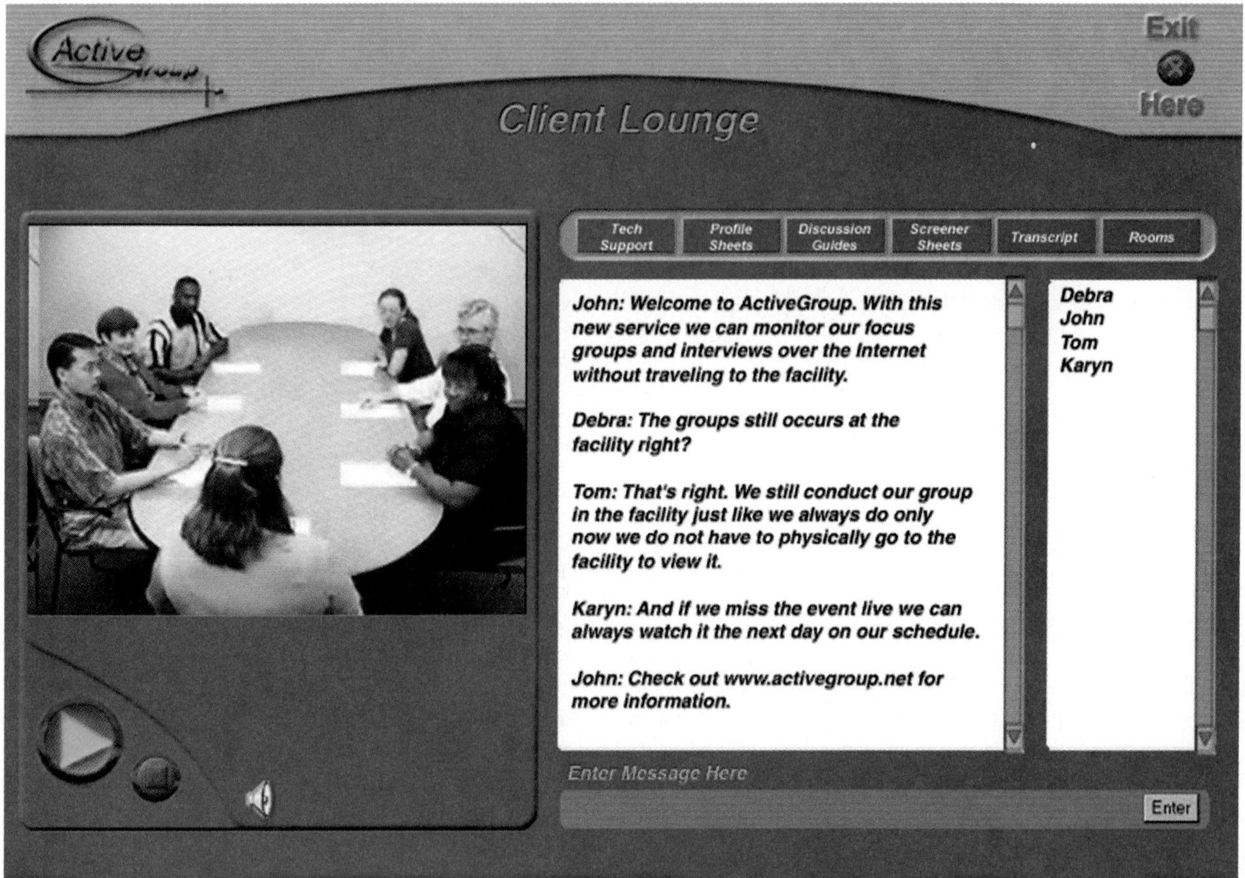

Active Group has a feature called Client Lounge that allows members of the organization conducting the focus group. Managers can view the focus group live on the Internet and discuss the event just as if they were physically present at the event. Courtesy of Active Group.

respondent's attention for long periods of time and are available to clarify difficult questions. They can guide interviews, explore issues, and probe as the situation requires. Personal interviews can be used with any type of questionnaire. Interviewers can show subjects actual products, advertisements, or packages and observe and record their reactions and behavior. Personal interviews usually can be conducted fairly quickly.

The main drawbacks to personal interviews are cost and sampling. Personal interviews may cost three to four times as much as telephone interviews. Because group interview studies generally utilize small sample sizes to keep time and costs down, it may be difficult to generalize from the results. In addition, because interviewers have more freedom in personal interviews, however, interview bias is a greater problem.

The contact method that is most effective depends on the information the researcher wants and on the number and types of respondents to be contacted. Advances in computers and communications have had an impact on methods of obtaining information. Some research firms now use computer-aided interviewing (CAI). The interviewer reads a set of questions from a video screen and types the respondent's answers directly into the computer, eliminating data editing and coding, reducing errors, and saving time. This type of interview is particularly useful for guests checking into or out of a hotel. The computer can be placed in the lobby, making it easily accessible to the hotel's guests. The high visibility of the computer also promotes an image that the hotel is concerned about their guests' opinions.

Sampling Plan. Marketing researchers usually draw conclusions about large consumer groups by taking a sample. A **sample** is a segment of the population selected to represent the population as a whole. Ideally, the sample should be representative and allow the researcher to make accurate estimates of the thoughts and behaviors of the larger population.

Designing the sample calls for four decisions. First, *who will be surveyed?* This is not always obvious. For example, to study the decision-making process for a family vacation, should the researcher interview the husband, wife, other family members, the travel agent, or all of these? The researcher must determine what type of information is needed and who is most likely to have it.

Second, *how many people should be surveyed?* Large samples give more reliable results than small samples. However, it is not necessary to sample the entire target market or even a large portion to obtain reliable results. If well chosen, samples of less than 1 percent of a population can give good reliability.

Third, *how should the sample be chosen?* Sample members might be chosen at random from the entire population (a probability sample), or the researcher might select people who are easiest to obtain information from (a convenience sample). The researcher might also choose a specified number of participants from each of several demographic groups (a quota sample). These and other ways of drawing samples have different costs and time limitations and varying accuracy and statistical properties. The needs of the research project will determine which method is most effective. Table 5-7 lists the various kinds of samples.

A fourth decision—*when will the survey be given?*—is important in personal surveys. The days and hours should be representative of the flow of traffic. For example if 70 percent of the customers come after 7 P.M., then the data collection needs to be heavier in the evening. The type of guest may change depending on the day or time. People working in the area may visit a restaurant at lunch whereas people living in the area visit the restaurant for dinner. Businesspersons stay at a hotel Sunday through Thursday, and pleasure travelers are heavier users on weekends. Thus, if the population of interest is business travelers, there should be heavier sampling during the week. Failure to match the time the data is collected with business patterns can result in invalid survey results.

Research Instruments. In collecting primary data, marketing researchers have a choice of primary research instruments: the interview (structured and unstructured), mechanical devices, and structured models such as a test market. Structured interviews employ the use of a questionnaire.

The questionnaire is by far the most common survey instrument. A questionnaire consists of a set of questions presented to a respondent for

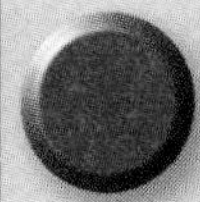

Marketing Highlight 5-1

A "Questionable" Questionnaire

Suppose that the following questionnaire has been prepared by a restaurant manager to build a profile of his potential market. How do you as a consumer feel about each question?

1. What is your income to the nearest hundred dollars?

   People don't necessarily know their income to the nearest hundred dollars, nor do they want to reveal their income that closely. Furthermore, a questionnaire should never open with such a personal question.
2. How often do you go out to eat?

   The question is very ambiguous. It does not specify the meal or the type of restaurant. For a descriptive survey, it would be useful to add appropriate response categories.
3. During the business week, how often do you eat breakfast?

   1 _____ 2 _____ 3 _____ 4 _____ 5 _____

   The responses are not collectively exhaustive. That is, they do not provide all responses possible. What if a person never eats breakfast? The addition of a sixth response, 0 ____, would solve the problem.
4. On average, how much do you spend for lunch?

   _____ 0 to $2 _____ $2 to 4

   _____ $4 to $6 _____ $6 to 8

   The choices are overlapping. If someone spent $2, $4, or $6, they could mark their response in one of two spots. Also, the response choices are not collectively exhaustive. If someone spends more than $8, there is nowhere to mark this response.
5. Would you like (name of restaurant) to have live bands on Friday and Saturday night?

   Yes ( ) No ( )

   The word "like" does not indicate purchase behavior. Many respondents would answer yes, because it offers them an entertainment option, but they would not come out on a regular basis. Also, many times there is a cost to adding an extra feature. If the respondent is going to pay for the cost through a cover charge or higher drink prices, it should be addressed. Finally, the question does not specify the type of band. Someone who wants a country and western band may answer yes and then be disappointed when the manager puts in a heavy metal band.
6. Did you receive more restaurant coupons this April or last April?

   Who can remember this?
7. What are the most salient and determinant attributes in your evaluation of restaurants?

   What are "salient and determinant attributes"? Don't use big words that the respondent may not understand.

answers. Because there are many ways to ask questions, the questionnaire is very flexible. Questionnaires should be developed and tested carefully before being used on a large scale. You can usually spot several errors in a carelessly prepared questionnaire (see Marketing Highlight 5-1).

In preparing a questionnaire, the marketing researcher must decide what questions to ask, what form the questions should take, and how to word and sequence the questions. Questionnaires too often omit questions that should be answered and include questions that cannot, will not, or need not be answered. Each question should be examined to ensure that it contributes to the research objectives. Questions that are merely interesting should be dropped.

The form of the question can influence the response. Marketing researchers distinguish between closed-end and open-end questions. Closed-end questions include all possible answers, and subjects are asked to choose among them. Examples include multiple-choice and scale questions. Open-end questions allow respondents to answer in their own words. In a survey of airline users, Delta might ask: "What is your opinion of Delta Airlines?" Or it might ask people to complete this sentence: "When I choose an airline, the most important consideration is. . . ." These and other kinds of open-end questions often reveal more because respondents are not limited in their answers. Open-end questions are especially useful in exploratory research where the researcher is trying to find out how people think rather than measuring how many people think in a certain way. Closed-end questions, on the other hand, provide answers that are easier to interpret and tabulate.

Care should be taken in the phrasing of questions. The researcher should use simple, direct, unbiased wording. The questions should be pretested before they are widely used, and care should also be taken in the ordering of questions. The first question should create interest. Questions should follow in a logical order, with difficult or personal questions asked last so that respondents do not become defensive. Table 5-8 provides an overview of common formats for closed- and open-end questions.

Researchers in the hospitality industry must be extremely careful in developing questions and selecting the sample not to offend respondents unwittingly. This problem is less pervasive with many products, such as building tile or brass fittings. A classic example of a marketing research mistake was made by a U.S. airline. This company offered a special companion price for business travelers with the idea that the companion

Table 5-7
Types of Samples

Probability samples	
Simple random sample	Every member of the population has a known and equal chance of selection.
Stratified random sample	The population is divided into mutually exclusive groups (such as age groups), and random samples are drawn from each group.
Cluster (area) sample	The population is divided into mutually exclusive groups (such as blocks), and the researcher draws a sample of the groups to interview.
Nonprobability samples	
Convenience sample	The researcher selects the easiest population members from which to obtain information.
Judgment sample	The researcher uses his or her judgment to select population members who are good prospects for accurate information.
Quota sample	The researcher finds and interviews a prescribed number of people in each of several categories.

Table 5-8
Types of Questions

A. CLOSED-END QUESTIONS

NAME	DESCRIPTION	EXAMPLE
Dichotomous	A question offering two answer choices.	"In arranging this trip, did you personally phone Delta?" Yes ☐ No ☐
Multiple choice	A question offering three or more answer choices.	"With whom are you traveling on this flight?" No one ☐ Children only ☐ Spouse ☐ Business associates/friends/relatives ☐ Spouse and children ☐ An organized tour group ☐
Likert scale	A statement with which the respondent shows the amount of agreement or disagreement.	"Small airlines generally give better service than large ones." Strongly disagree 1 ☐ · Disagree 2 ☐ · Neither agree nor disagree 3 ☐ · Agree 4 ☐ · Strongly agree 5 ☐
Semantic differential	A scale is inscribed between two bipolar words, and the respondent selects the point that represents the direction and intensity of his or her feelings.	*Delta Airlines* Large _X_ : ___ : ___ : ___ : ___ : ___ : Small Experienced ___ : ___ : ___ : ___ : _X_ : ___ : Inexperienced Modern ___ : ___ : ___ : _X_ : ___ : ___ : Old-fashioned
Importance scale	A scale that rates the importance of some attribute from "not at all important" to "extremely important"	"Airline food service to me is" Extremely Important 1 ___ · Very important 2 ___ · Somewhat important 3 ___ · Not very important 4 ___ · Not at all important 5 ___
Rating scale	A scale that rates some attribute from "poor" to "excellent."	"Delta's food service is" Excellent 1 ___ · Very good 2 ___ · Good 3 ___ · Fair 4 ___ · Poor 5 ___
Intention-to-buy scale	A scale that describes the respondent's intentions to buy.	"If in-flight telephone service were available on a long flight, I would" Definitely buy 1 ___ · Probably buy 2 ___ · Not certain 3 ___ · Probably not buy 4 ___ · Definitely not buy 5 ___

B. OPEN-END QUESTIONS

Completely unstructured	A question that respondents can answer in an almost unlimited number of ways.	"What is your opinion of Delta Airlines?"
Word association	Words are presented, one at a time, and respondents mention the first word that comes to mind.	"What is the first word that comes to your mind when you hear the following?" Airline ________ Delta ________ Travel ________
Sentence completion	Incomplete sentences are presented, one at a time, and respondents complete the sentence.	"When I choose an airline, the most important consideration in my decision is ________
Story completion	An incomplete story is presented, and respondents are asked to complete it.	"I flew Delta a few days ago. I noticed that the exterior and interior of the plane had very bright colors. This aroused in me the following thoughts and feelings." *Now complete the story.*
Picture completion	A picture of two characters is presented, with one making a statement. Respondents are asked to identify with the other and fill in the empty balloon.	WELL HERE'S THE FOOD. Fill in the empty balloon.
Thematic apperception tests (TATs)	A picture is presented, and respondents are asked to make up a story about what they think is happening or may happen in the picture.	Make up a story about what you see.

would be the executive's spouse. Following the promotion, questionnaires were sent to the spouse, not the executive. These innocently asked, "How did you like the recent companion trip?" In several cases the answer was, "What trip? I didn't go!" The airline received angry calls and threats of suits for invasion of privacy or contribution to the breakup of a marriage.

The Observation City Resort Hotel in Perth, Australia, offers an example of a hotel that used marketing information and research to produce enviable results.[30] This hotel had reached a plateau and wished to emerge from this static position into one of greater success. The hotel's manager collected government statistical abstracts to establish a profile of guests to the area. From this they realized that the hotel needed more than leisure travelers to be more successful. Managers also analyzed competition in Perth. From this, occupancy-trend differences were discovered between hotels.

Competitive analysis convinced management that the hotel needed and could attract away from competitors a piece of the weekday corporate market. Management of the Observation City Resort knew that the hotel would have to develop a plan to obtain corporate business and that the staff would have to be heavily involved.

A marketing research study was conducted to provide information essential to developing a marketing plan.

- A business-consumer survey was conducted at Perth's central business district and the airport.
- Questionnaires were given to travel managers and executives in charge of travel.
- Observations were made of high-profile properties known for their corporate-client service.
- The hotel's human resources department trained hotel staff members to collect primary data. Survey teams were then placed in Perth and its suburbs to administer questionnaires.

The results were excellent. The program produced a percentage increase in corporate room-nights from 8 percent before the research to 40 percent four years later. A further advantage was that the management and staff of the hotel learned the market, became close to the customer, and found ways to satisfy their needs.

Presenting the Research Plan. At this stage, the marketing researcher should summarize the plan in a written proposal. A written proposal is especially important when the research project will be large and complex or when an outside firm will be engaged to carry out the research. The proposal should cover the management problems addressed, as well as research objectives, information to be obtained, sources of secondary information or methods for collecting primary data, and how the results will aid in management decision making. The proposal should also include research costs. A written research plan or proposal ensures that the marketing manager and researchers have considered all the important aspects of the research and that they agree on why and how the research will be done. The manager should review the proposal carefully before approving the project.

Implementing the Research Plan

The researcher puts the marketing research plan into action by collecting, processing, and analyzing the information. Data collection can be done by the company's marketing research staff, which affords the company greater control of the collection process and data quality or by outside firms. Outside firms that specialize in data collection can often do the job more quickly at lower cost.

The data-collection phase of the marketing research process is generally the most expensive and the most subject to error. The researcher should watch the fieldwork closely to ensure that the plan is implemented correctly and to guard against problems with contacting respondents who refuse to cooperate or who give biased or dishonest answers, and interviewers who make mistakes or take shortcuts.

The collected data must be processed and analyzed to pull out important information and findings. Data from questionnaires are checked for accuracy and completeness and coded for computer analysis. The researcher applies standard computer programs to prepare tabulations of results and to compute averages and other measures for the major variables.

Interpreting and Reporting the Findings

The researcher must now interpret the findings, draw conclusions, and report the conclusions to management. The researcher should avoid overwhelming managers with numbers, complex statistical techniques, and focus. Instead, management desires major findings that will be useful in decision making.

Interpretation should not be left entirely to the researcher. Findings can be interpreted in different ways, and discussions between researchers and managers will help point to the best interpretations. The manager should also confirm that the research project was executed properly. After reviewing the findings, the manager may raise additional questions that can be answered with research data. Researchers should make the data available to marketing managers, so that they can perform new analyses and test relationships on their own.

Interpretation is an important phase of the marketing process. The best research is meaningless if a manager blindly accepts wrong interpretations. Similarly, managers may have biased interpretations. They sometimes accept research results that show what they expected and reject those that did not provide expected or hoped for answers. Thus, managers and researchers must work closely together when interpreting research results. Both share responsibility for the research process and resulting decisions.

Interpreting and reporting findings is the last step of the four-step research process. It is important for managers to remember that research is a process and that the researcher must proceed through all steps of the process. Marketing Highlight 5-2 explains some of the problems that can occur during a research project.

Companies conduct research to help direct and test their advertising. Courtesy of Pizza Hut, Inc.

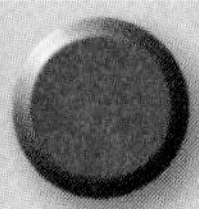

Marketing Highlight 5-2

Research Problem Areas

1. *Making assumptions. A restaurant was considering* adding a piano bar. Researchers developed a customer survey. One question asked customers if they would like entertainment in the lounge, without mentioning the type of entertainment. The customers could answer this question positively, thinking of a dance band. The manager, seeing the positive responses, would put in the piano bar and then wonder why so many customers did not respond to the piano bar. Luckily, this question was modified during a pretest of the survey.

   A country club asked its members if they felt the club needed a renovation. Most members said "yes." The club then paid consultants to draw up designs for the renovations. When these, along with the proposed dues increase, were presented, the members expressed outrage at the higher dues. If the original survey had addressed the costs associated with the renovation, it could have saved thousands of dollars in consulting fees.
2. *Lack of qualitative information.* Most surveys reported in trade magazines provide descriptive information. For example, a study done by Procter & Gamble found that the most important attribute in the frequent travelers decision to return to a hotel was a clean appearance. To use this information, management needs to know how their guests judge clean appearance. Through focus groups, managers can learn what guests look for to determine whether the room is clean, what irritants there are concerning cleanliness, and other more specific information.
3. *Failing to look at segments within a sample.* Survey results should be analyzed to determine differences between customer groups. Often, the arithmetic means (averages) for each question are calculated, and the survey is analyzed based on this information, which can mask important differences between segments. For example, a club surveyed its membership on how satisfied they were with the lunches purchased in the dining room. The average of all responses was 2, with 1 being very satisfied, 3 being satisfied, and 5 being not satisfied. However, when the total sample was divided into membership classes, it was found that one class had a high level of satisfaction, 1.5, while another class gave an average rating of 2.7. This information is more useful

Information Analysis

Information gathered by the company's marketing intelligence and marketing research systems can often benefit from additional analysis. This might include advanced statistical analysis to learn more about the relationships within a set of data. Such analysis allows managers to go beyond means and standard deviations in the data and answer such questions as the following:

- What are the major variables affecting sales, and how important is each?
- If the price is raised 10 percent and advertising is increased 20 percent, what will happen to sales?
- What are the best predictors of who are likely to come to my hotel versus my competitor's hotel?
- What are the best variables for segmenting my market, and how many segments exist?

to management than the overall mean of 2. Management now had to decide whether to build satisfaction for the members who gave the room a lower rating or promote its food and beverage room to the satisfied segment.

4. *Improper use of sophisticated statistical analysis.* One researcher reported that faculty size explained a remarkable 96 percent of the enrollment in hospitality management programs housed in business schools. He then presented a formula for projecting student enrollment based on the number of faculty, implying that if a school had three faculty members they would have 251 students, but if two more faculty were hired, they would have 426 students. Schools that base decisions on this formula might be disappointed.

   The factors can contribute to disappointment with survey research results. It may appear that customers fail to act as they indicated they would in the survey, when in fact research results were skewed or misinterpreted because of mistakes made in these problem areas.

5. *Failure to have the sample representative of the population.* A sample is a segment of the population selected to represent the population as a whole. Ideally, the sample should be representative so that the researcher can make accurate estimates of the thoughts and behaviors of the larger population. It is common for hotel managers to receive a bonus based on a customer satisfaction score. Sometimes segments of the population will give ratings that are lower than other segments, even though they seem satisfied with the service. For example, in one customer satisfaction survey, respondents aged between twenty-six and thirty-five years rated the service attributes of the company lower than other segments. However, they also rated the competition lower, making the company's relative satisfaction compared with the competition the same as other segments. This segment did not appear to be displeased with the service; they just tended to rate lower on the scale. When segments like this are present in the population, they can skew the results of the survey if they are over- or underrepresented. If they are underrepresented, the overall satisfaction will increase; if they are overrepresented, the overall satisfaction score will decrease.

Mathematical models might also help marketers to make better decisions. Each model represents a real system, process, or outcome. These models can help answer the questions "what if" and "which is best." In the past twenty years, marketing scientists have developed a great number of models to help marketing managers make better marketing-mix decisions, design sales territories and sales call plans, select sites for retail outlets, develop optimal advertising mixes, and forecast new-product sales.[31]

Distributing Information

Marketing information has no value until managers use it to make better decisions. The information gathered must reach the appropriate marketing managers at the right time. Large companies have centralized marketing information systems that provide managers with regular performance reports, intelligence updates, and reports on the results of studies.

Marriott's MountainSide, A Marriott Vacation Club Resort. Marriott uses marketing research to make certain they provide maximum value for their guests. This is one of the reasons for Marriott's success.

Managers need these routine reports for making regular planning, implementation, and control decisions. But marketing managers also need nonroutine information for special situations and on-the-spot decisions. For example, a sales manager having trouble with an important customer needs a summary of the account's sales during the past year. Or a restaurant manager whose restaurant has stocked-out of a best-selling menu item needs to know the current inventory levels in the chain's other restaurants. In companies with centralized information systems, these managers must request the information from the MIS staff and wait. Often, the information arrives too late to be useful.

Recent developments in information handling have led to a revolution in information distribution. With recent advances in microcomputers, software, and communications, many companies are decentralizing their marketing information systems and giving managers direct access to information stored in the systems. In some companies, marketing managers can use a desk terminal to tie into the company's information network. Without leaving their desks, they can obtain information from internal records or outside information services, analyze the information, prepare

Marketing Highlight 5-3

The Internet: A Great Source of Marketing Information

The Internet allows access to commercial services such as Dialog, CompuServe, Lexis/Nexis, and Research Library Information Network. One of the most useful sites for researchers in the hospitality and travel industries is *http://www.nscee.edu/unlv/Tourism/*. This site was developed by Professor Patti Shock, chair of the Department of Tourism and Convention Administration at UNLV. Professor Shock is an expert on sources of hospitality and tourism information on the Internet. She is the editor of the Internet section of the *Journal of Restaurant and Foodservice Marketing*. This section features examples of marketing excellence on the Internet. Her Web site includes direct links to hospitality associations as well as individual companies. The site is divided into key areas, such as associations, catering, clubs, restaurants, hotel chains, and hospitality marketing. The company sites provide a good overview of the company and often include a copy of the latest annual report. Individual hotels and restaurants are also linked to the site. The restaurants often include a copy of their menus, providing menu ideas, as well as competitive pricing information. Some sites, such as Holiday Inns, provide special rates for properties that have excess capacity. The Internet has chat groups on a wide variety of topics. For example, there are chat groups on resort destinations. Discussants on these sites tell others what they liked and disliked about the destination. Hotels or restaurants, as well as members of the convention and tourist bureau, can find useful information by "listening" in on these chat groups. The Internet is a rich source of information for both environmental scanning and marketing research projects.

reports on a word processor, and communicate with others in the network through telecommunications. The Internet is an excellent source of marketing information (see Marketing Highlight 5-3).

Such systems offer exciting prospects. They allow managers to obtain needed information directly and quickly, and tailor it to their needs. As more managers become skilled in using these systems and as improvements in technology make them more economical, hospitality companies will increasingly use decentralized marketing information systems.

International Marketing Research

International marketing researchers follow the same steps as domestic researchers, from defining the research problem and developing a research plan to interpreting and reporting the results. However, these researchers often face more and different problems. Whereas domestic researchers deal with fairly homogeneous markets within a single country, international researchers deal with markets in many different countries. These different markets often vary dramatically in their levels of economic development, cultures and customs, and buying patterns.

In many foreign markets, the international researcher has a difficult time finding good secondary data. Whereas U.S. marketing researchers can obtain reliable secondary data from any of dozens of domestic research services, many countries have almost no research services at all. Even the largest international research services operate in only a relative handful of countries. For example, A. C. Nielsen, the world's largest marketing research company, has offices in many countries outside the United States.[32] Thus, even when secondary information is available, it usually must be obtained from many different sources on a country-by-country basis, making the information difficult to combine or compare.

Because of the scarcity of good secondary data, international researchers often must collect their own primary data. Here researchers face problems not encountered domestically. For example, they may find it difficult simply to develop appropriate samples. Whereas U.S. researchers can use current telephone directories, census tract data, and any of several sources of socioeconomic data to construct samples, such information is largely lacking in many countries. Once the sample is drawn, the U.S. researcher usually can reach most respondents easily by telephone or mail or in person. Reaching respondents is often not so easy in other parts of the world. In some countries, few people have phones—there are only four phones per 1,000 people in Egypt, six in Turkey, and thirty-two in Argentina. In other countries, the postal system is notoriously unreliable. In Brazil, for instance, an estimated 30 percent of the mail is never delivered. In many developing countries, poor roads and transportation systems make certain areas hard to reach, making personal interviews difficult and expensive.[33]

Differences in cultures from country to country cause additional problems for international researchers. Language is the most obvious culprit. For example, questionnaires must be prepared in one language and then translated into the languages of each country researched. Responses then must be translated back into the original language for analysis and interpretation. This adds to research costs and increases the risks of error.

Translating a questionnaire from one language to another is far from easy. Many points are "lost," because many idioms, phrases, and statements mean different things in different cultures. A Danish executive observed, "Check this out by having a different translator put back into English what you've translated from the English. You'll get the shock of your life. I remember [an example in which] 'out of sight, out of mind' had become 'invisible things are insane.'"[34]

Buying roles and consumer decision processes vary greatly from country to country, further complicating international marketing research. Consumers in different countries also vary in their attitudes toward marketing research. People in one country may be very willing to respond; in other countries, nonresponse can be a major problem. For example, customs in some Islamic countries prohibit people from talking with strangers—a researcher simply may not be allowed to speak by phone with women about brand attitudes or buying behavior. High functional illiteracy rates in many countries make it impossible to use a written survey for some segments. In addition, middle-class people in developing countries often make false claims in order to appear well off. For example, in a study of tea consumption in India, over 70 percent of middle-income respondents claimed that they used one of several national brands. How-

Marketing Highlight 5-4

Marketing Research in Small Business

Managers of small businesses often believe that marketing research can be done only by experts in large companies with large research budgets. But many marketing research techniques can be used by smaller organizations and at little or no expense.

Managers of small businesses can obtain good marketing information by observing what occurs around them. Thus restaurateurs can evaluate their customer mix by recording the number and type of customers in the restaurant at different times during the day. Competitor advertising can be monitored by collecting advertisements from local media.

Managers can conduct informal surveys using small convenience samples. The manager of a travel agency can learn what customers like and dislike about travel agencies by conducting informal focus groups, such as inviting small groups to lunch. Restaurant managers can talk with customers; hospital food service managers can interview patients. Restaurant managers can make random phone calls during slack hours to interview consumers about where they eat out and what they think of various restaurants in the area. Managers can also conduct simple experiments. By changing the design in regular direct mailings and watching results, a manager can learn which marketing tactics work best. By varying newspaper advertisements, a manager can observe the effects of ad size and position, price coupons, and media used.

Small organizations can obtain secondary data. Many associations, local media, chambers of commerce, and government agencies provide special help to small organizations. The U.S. Small Business Administration offers dozens of free publications giving advice on topics ranging from planning advertising to ordering business signs. Local newspapers often provide information on local shoppers and their buying patterns.

Sometimes volunteers and colleges will carry out research. Many colleges are seeking small businesses to serve as cases for projects in marketing research classes. Sales management classes are eager to do sales blitzes for hotels.

Thus, secondary data collection, observation, surveys, and experiments can be used effectively by small organizations with small budgets. Although informal research is less complex and costly, it must still be done carefully. Managers must carefully think through the objectives of the research, formulate questions in advance, and recognize the biases systematically. If carefully planned and implemented, low-cost research can provide reliable information for improving marketing decision making.

---

ever, the researchers had good reason to doubt these results; more than 60 percent of the tea sold in India is unbranded, generic tea.

Despite these problems, the recent growth of international marketing has resulted in a rapid increase in the use of international marketing research. Global companies have little choice but to conduct such research. Although the costs and problems associated with international research may be high, the costs of not doing it—in terms of missed opportunities and mistakes—might be even higher. Once recognized, many of the problems associated with international marketing research can be overcome or avoided.

Marketing Research in Smaller Organizations

So far in this section, we have looked at the marketing research process—from defining research objectives to interpreting and reporting results—as a lengthy, formal process carried out by large marketing companies. But many small businesses and nonprofit organizations also use marketing research.

Almost any organization can find informal, low-cost alternatives to the formal and complex marketing research techniques used by research experts in large firms (see Marketing Highlight 5-4).

KEY TERMS

Causal research Marketing research to test hypotheses about cause-and-effect relationships.

Descriptive research Marketing research to better describe marketing problems, situations, or markets, such as the market potential for a product or the demographics and attitudes of consumers.

Experimental research The gathering of primary data by selecting matched groups of subjects, giving them different treatments, controlling related factors, and checking for differences in group responses.

Exploratory research Marketing research to gather preliminary information that will help to better define problems and suggest hypotheses.

Internal records information The product life-cycle stage when a new product is first distributed and made available for purchase.

Marketing information system (MIS) A structure of people, equipment, and procedures to gather, sort, analyze, evaluate, and distribute needed, timely, and accurate information to marketing decision makers.

Marketing intelligence Everyday information about developments in the marketing environment that help managers to prepare and adjust marketing plans.

Marketing research The systematic design, collection, analysis, and reporting of data and findings relevant to a specific marketing situation facing a company.

Observational research The gathering of primary data by observing relevant people, actions, and situations.

Primary data Information collected for the specific purpose at hand.

Sample (1) A segment of a population selected for marketing research to represent the population as a whole; (2) Offer of a trial amount of a product to consumers.

Secondary data Information that already exists somewhere, having been collected for another purpose.

Survey research The gathering of primary data by asking people questions about their knowledge, attitudes, preferences, and buying behavior.

Chapter Review

The Marketing Information System (MIS). An MIS consists of people, equipment, and procedures to gather, sort, analyze, evaluate, and distribute needed, timely, and accurate information to marketing decision makers. The MIS begins and ends with marketing managers, but managers throughout the organization should be involved in the MIS. First, the MIS interacts with managers to assess their information needs. Next, it develops needed information from internal company records, marketing intelligence activities, and the marketing research process. Information analysts process information to make it more useful. Finally, the MIS distributes information to managers in the right form and at the right time to help in marketing planning, implementation, and control.

I. Assessing Information Needs. A good marketing information system balances information that managers would like to have against that which they really need and is feasible to obtain.

II. Developing Information. Information needed by marketing managers can be obtained from internal company records, marketing intelligence, and marketing research. The information analysis system processes this information and presents it in a form that is useful to managers.

1) **Internal records.** Internal records information consists of information gathered from sources within the company to evaluate marketing performance and to detect marketing problems and opportunities.

2) **Marketing intelligence.** Marketing intelligence includes everyday information about developments in the marketing environment that help managers to prepare and adjust marketing plans and short-run tactics. Marketing intelligence can come from internal sources or external sources.

a) **Internal sources.** Internal sources include the company's executives, owners, and employees.

b) **External sources.** External sources include competitors, government agencies, suppliers, trade magazines, newspapers, business magazines, trade association newsletters and meetings, and databases available on the Internet.

c) **Marketing research.** Marketing research is a process that identifies and defines marketing opportunities and problems, monitors and evaluates marketing actions and performance, and communicates the findings and implication to management. Marketing research is project oriented and has a beginning and an ending. It feeds information into the marketing information system that is ongoing. The marketing research process consists of four steps: defining the problem and research objectives, developing the research plan, implementing the research plan, and interpreting and presenting the findings.

i) **Defining the problem and research objectives.** There are three types of objectives for a marketing research project:

a) **Exploratory.** To gather preliminary information that will help define the problem and suggest hypotheses.

b) **Descriptive.** To describe the size and composition of the market.

***c)* Causal.** To test hypotheses about cause-and-effect relationships.

ii) Developing the research plan for collecting information

***a)* Determining specific information needs.** Research objectives must be translated into specific information needs. To meet a manager's information needs, researchers can gather secondary data, primary data, or both. Secondary data consist of information already in existence somewhere, having been collected for another purpose. Primary data consist of information collected for the specific purpose at hand.

***b)* Research approaches.** Three basic research approaches are observations, surveys, and experiments.

***i)* Observational research.** Gathering of primary data by observing relevant people, action, and situations.

***ii)* Survey research** (structured/unstructured, direct/indirect). Best suited to gathering descriptive information.

***iii)* Experimental research.** Best suited to gathering causal information.

***c)* Contact methods.** Information can be collected by mail, telephone, or personal interview.

***d)* Sampling plan.** Marketing researchers usually draw conclusions about large consumer groups by taking a sample. A sample is a segment of the population selected to represent the population as a whole. Designing the sample calls for four decisions.

i) Who will be surveyed?
ii) How many people should be surveyed?
iii) How should the sample be chosen?
iv) When will the survey be given?

***e)* Research instruments.** In collecting primary data, marketing researchers have a choice of primary research instruments: the interview (structured and unstructured), mechanical devices, and structured models such as a test market. Structured interviews employ the use of a questionnaire.

***f)* Presenting the research plan.** At this stage the marketing researcher should summarize the plan in a written proposal.

iii) Implementing the research plan. The researcher puts the marketing research plan into action by collecting, processing, and analyzing the information.

iv) Interpreting and reporting the findings. The researcher must now interpret the findings, draw conclusions, and report them to management.

d) Information analysis. Information gathered by the company's marketing intelligence and marketing research systems can often benefit from additional analysis. This analysis helps to answer the questions related to "what if" and "which is best."

III. Distributing Information. Marketing information has no value until managers use it to make better decisions. The information that is gathered must reach the appropriate marketing managers at the right time.

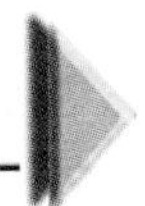

DISCUSSION QUESTIONS

1. What role should marketing research play in helping a firm to implement the marketing concept?
2. How does a marketing information system differ from a marketing intelligence system?
3. You own an elegant, high-priced restaurant in your area and want to improve the level of service offered by your thirty-person staff. How could observational research help you accomplish this goal?
4. List some research tasks for the following areas: distribution decisions, product decisions, advertising decisions, personal selling decisions, and pricing decisions.
5. Explain why defining the problem and research objectives is often the most difficult step in the research process.
6. Researchers usually start the data-gathering process by examining secondary data. What secondary data sources would be available to the manager of a full-service restaurant that wanted to research consumer trends?
7. Discuss the advantages and disadvantages of using guest comment cards in a restaurant.
8. Which type of research would be most appropriate in the following situations, and why?
   a. A fast-food restaurant wants to investigate the effect that children have on the purchase of its products.
   b. A business hotel wants to gather some preliminary information on how business travelers feel about the menu variety, food, and service in its restaurants.
   c. A casual restaurant is considering locating a new outlet in a fast-growing suburb.
   d. A fast-food restaurant wants to test the effect of two new advertising themes for its roast beef sandwich sales in two cities.
   e. The director of tourism for your state wants to know how to use her promotion dollars effectively.
9. Focus group interviewing is both a widely used and widely criticized research technique in marketing. What are the advantages and disadvantages of focus groups? What are some kinds of questions that are appropriate for focus groups to investigate?

EXPERIENTIAL EXERCISES

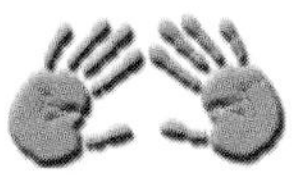

Do one of the following:

1. You have been asked to find out how the campus community feels about the food service on campus.
   a. Who is the population for this study?
   b. Develop a sampling plan, including times and places that will provide you with a sample that is representative of the population of interest.
2. Get a customer comment from a local hospitality company. What, if any, design changes would you make to the form? If you were the manager, how would you use the information collected from the comment cards?

INTERNET EXERCISES

Support for these exercises can be found on the Web site for *Marketing for Hospitality and Tourism,* www.prenhall.com/kotler.

A. You are asked to develop a loyalty program for a hotel or restaurant. Go on the Internet and find out what information you can find out about loyalty programs, including existing hotel or restaurant loyalty programs. Write up a summary of your findings. The book's Web site has some suggestions on how to set up your search.

B. You are asked to survey visitors to the area where you live or go to school. In developing the survey, you need to find out what is important to visitors when they visit a destination. The book's Web site has some suggestions on how to set up your search.

i. Use the Internet to see if you can access previous research to find out what is important to visitors. Summarize your findings.

ii. Did any of the studies find differences amongst different segments, such as older visitors or families?

REFERENCES

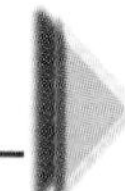

1. Brian Dumaine, "Corporate Spies Snoop to Conquer," *Fortune* (November 1988): 68–76.
2. Kate Bertrand, "With Customers, the Closer the Better," *Business Marketing* (July 1989): 68–69.
3. Marion Harper Jr., "A New Profession to Aid Management," *Journal of Marketing* (January 1961): 1.
4. John Naisbitt, *Megatrends: Ten New Directions Transforming Our Lives* (New York: Warner Books, 1984).
5. "Harnessing the Data Explosion," *Sales and Marketing Management* (January 1987): 31.
6. Naisbitt, *Megatrends*, p. 16.
7. Tom Richman, "Mrs. Field's Secret Ingredient" (October 1987) as cited in *Managing Services* by Christopher Lovelock (Upper Saddle River, NJ: Prentice Hall, 1992), pp. 365–372.
8. John Bowen, "Computerized Guest History: A Valuable Marketing Tool," in *The Practice of Hospitality Management II,* ed. Robert C. Lewis et al. (Westport, CT: AVI, 1990).
9. David Menzies, "Comment Cards," *Foodservice and Hospitality* 21, no. 5 (July/August 1988): 14; Robert C. Lewis and Abraham Pizam, "Guest Surveys: A Missed Opportunity," in *Strategic Marketing and Planning in the Hospitality Industry*, ed. Robert L. Bloomstrom (East Lansing, MI: Educational Institute of the AH&MA, 1988).
10. Cary Jehl Broussard, "Inside the Customer-Focused Company, *Harvard Business Review* (May 2000): S20.
11. James L. Heskett, W. Earl Sasser Jr., and Leonard A. Schlesinger, *The Service Profit Chain* (New York: Free Press, 1997, p. 67.
12. Chekitan S. Dev and Bernard O. Ellis, "Guest Histories: An Untapped Service Resource," *Cornell Hotel and Restaurant Administration Quarterly* 32, no. 2 (August 1991): 31.
13. Tammy P. Bieber, "Guest History Systems: Maximizing the Benefits," *Cornell Hotel and Restaurant Administration Quarterly* 30, no. 3 (November 1989): 22.
14. Paul B. Brown, "Who Was That Masked Shopper," *Inc.* 11, no. 10 (October 1989): 135–136.
15. Joseph F. Durocher and Neil B. Neiman, "Technology: Antidote to the Shakeout," *Cornell Hotel and Restaurant Administration Quarterly* 31, no. 1 (May 1990): 35.
16. Christopher W. Nordling and Sharon K. Wheeler, "Building a Market-Segment Accounting Model to Improve Profits," *Cornell Hotel and Restaurant Administration Quarterly* 33, no. 3 (June 1992): 32.
17. Laurette Dubé, Leo M. Renaghan, and Jane M. Miller, "Measuring Customer Satisfaction for Strategic Management," *Cornell Hotel and Restaurant Administration Quarterly* 35, no. 1 (February 1994): 39.
18. Burt Cabanas, "A Marketing Strategy for Resort Conference Centers," *Cornell Hotel and Restaurant Administration Quarterly* 33, no. 3 (June 1992): 47.

19. "Making Them Feel at Home," *Cornell Hotel and Restaurant Administration Quarterly* 30, no. 3 (November 1989): 4.
20. John Bowen, "Scanning the Environment: Electronically," *Hospitality Education and Research Journal* 14, no. 2 (1991): 95–102; "Business Is Turning Data into a Potent Strategic Weapon," *Business Week,* August 22, 1987, p. 92.
21. Tim Miller, "Focus: Competitive Intelligence," *Online Access Guide* (March–April 1987): 43–57.
22. *American Marketing Association*, officially adopted definition (1987).
23. Frank E. Camacho and D. Matthew Knain, "Listening to Customers: The Market Research Function at Marriott Corporation," *Marketing Research* (March 1989): 5–14.
24. "The Entrepreneurial Approach to Indian Affairs," *Cornell Hotel and Restaurant Administration Quarterly* 29, no. 2 (August 1988): 5.
25. Jerry Wind, Paul E. Green, Douglas Shifflet, and Marsha Scarbrough, "Courtyard by Marriott: Designing a Hotel Facility with Consumer-Based Marketing," *Interfaces* 19, no. 1 (January–February 1989): 25–47.
26. Robert C. Lewis and Richard E. Chambers, *Marketing Leadership in Hospitality: Foundations and Practices* (New York: Van Nostrand Reinhold, 1989), p. 518.
27. Stephen W. Litvin and Goh Hwai Kar, "E-surveying for tourism research: Legitimate tool or a researcher's fantasy?," *Journal of Travel Research* (February 2001): 308–314.
28. Joe L. Welch, "Focus Groups for Restaurant Research," *Cornell Hotel and Restaurant Administration Quarterly* 26, no. 2 (August 1985): 78–85.
29. Dorothy Dee, "Focus Groups," *Restaurants USA* 10, no. 7 (August 1990): 30–34.
30. David H. Sogar and Michael H. Jones, "Attracting Business Travelers to a Resort," *Cornell Hotel and Restaurant Administration Quarterly* 34, no. 5 (October 1993): 43–47.
31. For further reading, see Gary L. Lilien, Philip Kotler, and K. Sridhar Moorthy, *Marketing Models* (Upper Saddle River, NJ: Prentice Hall, 1992).
32. Jack Honomichl, "Top Marketing/Ad/Opinion Research Firms Profiled," *Marketing News,* June 2, 1992, p. H2.
33. Many of the examples in this section, along with others, are found in Subhash C. Jain, *International Marketing Management*, 3rd ed. (Boston: PWS-Kent, 1990), pp. 334–339. See also Vern Terpstra and Ravi Sarathy, *International Marketing* (Chicago: Dryden Press, 1991), pp. 208–213.
34. Jain, *International Marketing Management*, p. 338.

6 Consumer Markets and Consumer Buying Behavior

To be a bullfighter, you must first learn to be a bull.
Anonymous

A look at how the hotel industry reacted to the growing number of women business travelers provides some insight into why it is important to understand behavior. It also illustrates that understanding consumers is not easy. In 1970, women accounted for less than 1 percent of all business travelers. They currently account for almost half of all business trips, and by the year 2005, they will account for 50 percent of all business travelers. In the late 1970s, hotel managers started to realize the importance of this new group of consumers. But they were not sure how they should attract them. Should they develop special floors for women only? Should they designate certain rooms for women travelers, placing extra lights around the mirrors, hair dryers, and skirt hangers in these rooms? Should they develop a special program for women travelers and put "Lady" in front of their brand name as the name for this program? Hotel chains did all this and more. Some conducted research asking women how they wanted to be treated differently from their male counterparts. This provided little insight, as most women had not traveled as males, so they did not know how their male counterparts were treated. Second, they wanted to be treated as business travelers; they didn't want to be differentiated as a unique type of business traveler.

Many of the early programs aimed at the woman business traveler were unsuccessful. The male management of hotel chains did not understand the behavior of this new segment. Women did not want to be patronized, or singled out as a special group, but they did have special needs. James Evans, a senior vice president with Hyatt, pointed out some of these needs. He stated that

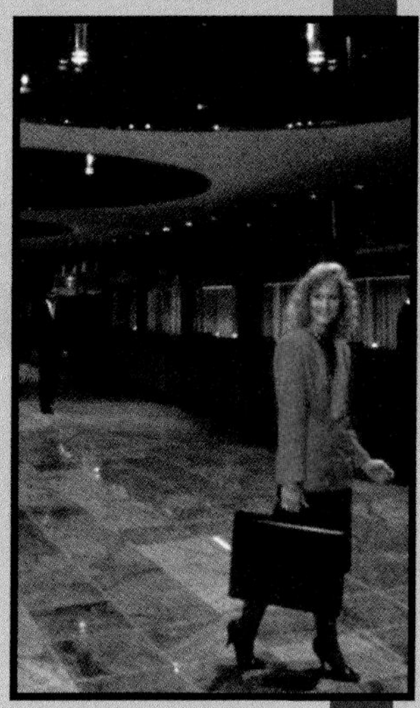

security is more important for the female traveler. Extended room service hours, makeup mirrors, well-lit bathrooms, light food entrees, and open-air lounges were other features mentioned by Evans.

Hotels reacted by lighting parking lots, changing menus, adding full-length mirrors in rooms, decorating rooms in lighter colors, increasing the selection of bathroom amenities, providing hair dryers in rooms, and putting skirt hangers in the closets. With the exception of skirt hangers, the male business traveler would view most of these changes positively. In the security area, training at the front desk was increased so that room numbers of guests were not announced to bellmen, allowing them to be overheard by others. New hotels installed electronic locking devices and lowered the height of peepholes in doors so that women would not have to stand on stools to see who was at the door. As a result of comments from women, concierges now find out what type of attire the guest would like to wear (i.e., casual, dressy) before suggesting restaurants. The other major change that can be attributed to women is the increased construction of concierge and club floors. These floors require a key to gain access. They have a special lounge area where cocktails and continental breakfasts are served. Women prefer these floors because they can meet clients in the lounge area rather than their room, and they can relax in the concierge floor lounge instead of going to the hotel's public lounge.

Below are some specific amenities that were developed based on researching the women's market. The Luxury Collection in Houston provides a running escort, others such as the Omni in Detroit provide this service for a fee. The Pebble Beach Resorts, known for their golf, have developed golf lessons for businesswomen because many business deals are developed while executives play golf. The Nob Hill Lambourne, a small boutique hotel in San Francisco, has developed an amenity for working mothers. The package includes a free fifteen-minute phone call home to talk to their kids, a free gift to take back for each child, and a framed photo of the guest's children is placed in the room.

Hotels spent a great deal of effort and resources to please the female business traveler, a segment for which they projected rapid growth but that they did not understand. Hotels that gained an understanding of this segment were able to attract more than their fair share of the market. Women business travelers responded. A recent study by Total Research found 81 percent of the women interviewed said they would be more loyal to companies that address their needs. As marketers it is important that we gain an understanding of how our consumers behave. Wyndham Hotels & Resorts has gained an understanding of women through its "Women on Their Way" program. This program includes a women's advisory board, an Internet site, and research on women business travelers conducted with New York University. Wyndham's desire to understand and meet the wants of women business travelers has resulted in a fifty percent increase in business from this segment since 1997. [1]

Chapter Objectives

After reading this chapter, you should be able to:

1. Name the elements of the stimulus–response model of consumer behavior.
2. Outline the major characteristics affecting consumer behavior, and list some of the specific cultural, social, personal, and psychological factors that influence consumers.
3. Explain the buyer decision process and discuss need recognition, information search, evaluation of alternatives, the purchase decision, and postpurchase behavior.

6.1 Wyndham Hotels and Resorts

Marketers must exercise care in analyzing consumer behavior. Consumers often turn down what appears to be a winning offer. As soon as managers believe that they understand their customers, buyer decisions are made that appear to be irrational. But what looks like irrational behavior to a manager is completely rational to the consumer. Buying behavior is never simple. It is affected by many different factors, yet understanding it is the essential task of marketing management.

Chambers, Chacko, and Lewis have summarized the basic beliefs about consumer behavior into five premises. These premises provide a good basis on which to start a discussion of consumer behavior.[2]

- **Premise 1:** Consumer behavior is purposeful and goal oriented. As we mentioned in the introduction, what looks like irrational behavior to a manager is completely rational to a consumer.
- **Premise 2:** The consumer has free choice. Consumers do not have to pay attention to your marketing communications. Messages are processed selectively. In most cases the consumer has several products from which to choose.
- **Premise 3:** Consumer behavior is a process. Marketers need to understand the process.
- **Premise 4:** Consumer behavior can be influenced. By understanding the purchase decision process and the influences on this process, marketers can influence how consumers behave.
- **Premise 5:** There is a need for consumer education. Consumers may act against their own interests because of a lack of knowledge. For example, some people think they can handle their alcohol

and drive safely after excessive drinking. Marketers have a social responsibility to educate consumers.

In this chapter we explore the dynamics of consumer buying behavior and the consumer market. Consumer buying behavior refers to the buying behavior of final customers—individuals and households who buy goods and services for personal consumption. The consumer market consists of all these individuals and households. The U.S. consumer market includes over 280 million persons who consume more than $2.5 trillion of goods and services, almost $10,000 worth for every man, woman, and child. Each year this market grows by several million persons and by more than $100 billion, making it one of the most attractive consumer markets in the world.

Consumers vary tremendously in age, income, education level, and tastes, and they buy an incredible variety of goods and services. We now look at how consumers make their choices among these products.

A Model of Consumer Behavior

Today's marketplace has become very competitive. During the last thirty years, hundreds of multiunit restaurant and hotel companies have been formed, resulting in the development of thousands of hotels and restaurants. In addition, during recent years the hospitality and travel industries have undergone globalization. Hotel companies headquartered in nations as diverse as Germany, the United States, and Hong Kong compete aggressively in markets such as Singapore and Japan. The result is a fiercely competitive international market with companies fighting for their share of consumers. To win this battle, they invest in research that will reveal what customers want to buy, which locations they prefer, which amenities are important to them, how they buy, and why they buy.

The central question is: How do consumers respond to the various marketing stimuli that a company might use? The company that really understands how consumers will respond to different product features, prices, and advertising appeals has a great advantage over its competitors. As a result, researchers from companies and universities have heavily studied the relationship between marketing stimuli and consumer response. Their starting point is the model of buyer behavior shown in Figure 6-1. This figure shows that marketing and other stimuli enter the consumer's "black box" and produce certain responses. Marketers must determine what is in the buyer's black box.

On the left side of Figure 6-1, the marketing stimuli consist of the four Ps: product, price, place, and promotion. Other stimuli include major forces and events in the buyer's environment: economic, technological, political, and cultural. All these stimuli enter the buyer's black box, where they are turned into the set of observable buyer responses shown on the right: product choice, brand choice, dealer choice, purchase timing, and purchase amount.

Marketers must understand how the stimuli are changed into responses inside the consumer's black box. The black box has two parts. First, a buyer's characteristics influence how he or she perceives and reacts to the stimuli. Second, the buyer's decision process itself affects out-

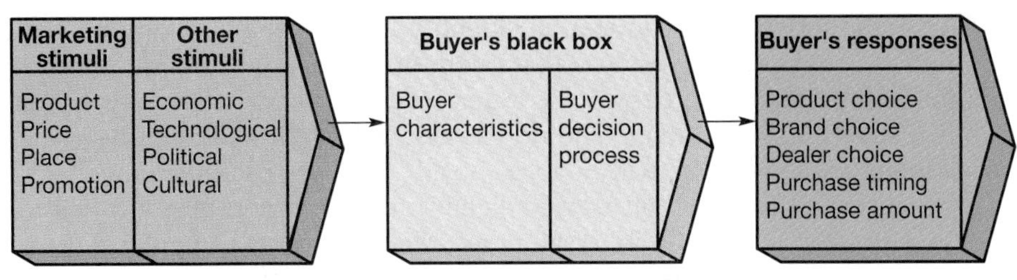

Figure 6-1
Model of buyer behavior.

comes. In this chapter we look first at buyer characteristics that affect buying behavior and then examine the buyer decision process.

Personal Characteristics Affecting Consumer Behavior

Consumer purchases are strongly influenced by cultural, social, personal, and psychological characteristics. These factors are shown in Figure 6-2. For the most part, they cannot be controlled by the marketer, but they must be taken into account.

Cultural Factors

Cultural factors exert the broadest and deepest influence on consumer behavior. We examine the role played by the buyer's culture, subculture, and social class.

Culture

Culture is the most basic determinant of a person's wants and behavior. It comprises the basic values, perceptions, wants, and behaviors that a person learns continuously in a society. Today, most societies are in a state of flux. Determinants of culture learned as a child are changing in societies from Chile to California. Culture is expressed through tangible items such as food, buildings, clothing, and art. Culture is an integral part of the hospitality and travel business. It determines what we eat, how we travel, where we travel, and where we stay. Culture is dynamic, adapting to the environment.

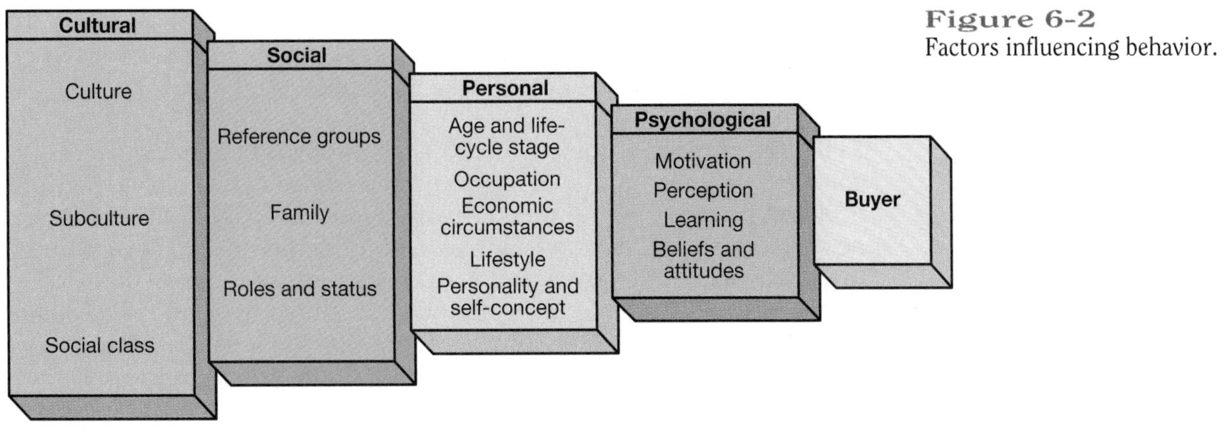

Figure 6-2
Factors influencing behavior.

Marketers try continuously to identify cultural shifts in order to devise new products and services that might find a receptive market. For example, the cultural shift toward greater concern about health and fitness has resulted in many hotels adding exercise rooms or health clubs or developing an agreement with a local health club so that their guests can have access to it. The shift toward lighter and more natural food has resulted in menu changes in restaurants. The shift toward lighter-colored and simpler home furnishings is reflected in new restaurant designs.

At the same time, a significant number of consumers seem to be rebelling against foods that are good for them, preferring good taste. Restaurants face a consumer who orders broiled flounder and a light salad only to top it off with high-butterfat ice cream for dessert.

Consumer Behavior across International Cultures

Understanding consumer behavior is difficult enough for companies marketing within the borders of a single country. For companies operating in many countries, however, understanding and serving the needs of consumers can be daunting. Although consumers in different countries may have some things in common, their values, attitudes, and behaviors often vary dramatically. International marketers must understand such differences and adjust their products and marketing programs accordingly. Consider the following examples:[3]

- *Germany*. Be especially punctual. A U.S. businessperson invited to someone's home should present flowers, preferably unwrapped, to the hostess. During introductions, greet women first and wait until, or if, they extend their hands before extending yours.
- *United Kingdom*. Toasts are often given at formal dinners. If the host honors you with a toast, be prepared to reciprocate. Business entertaining is done more often at lunch than at dinner.
- *Saudi Arabia*. Although men will kiss each other in greeting, they will never kiss a woman in public. An American woman should wait for a man to extend his hand before offering hers. If a Saudi offers refreshment, accept—it is an insult to decline it.
- *Japan*. Friendliness from service providers is viewed as being disrespectful and formality is unequally preferred. Japanese expect promptness and prefer quick unfriendly service over having a conversation with the service provider.

Failing to understand such differences in customs and behaviors from one country to another can spell disaster for a company's international products and programs. On the other hand, those companies who adapt can be winners. Restaurants in Israel learned to modify their products during the seven days of Passover. Many restaurants close during Passover, a time when many people travel and there is a high demand for restaurant products. KFC, Pizza Hut, Burger King, and McDonald's adapted their menus to make them kosher for Passover. Burger King made rolls from corn flour and soy flour, McDonald's rolled its chicken McNuggets in matzo meal, Pizza Hut used unleavened dough for its pizza crusts, and KFC replaced its breaded fried chicken with barbecued chicken.[4]

Marketers must decide on the degree to which they will adapt their products and marketing programs to meet the unique needs of consumers in various markets. They want to standardize their offerings in order to simplify operations and take advantage of cost economies. On the other hand, adapting marketing efforts within each country results in products and programs that better satisfy the needs of local consumers. The question of whether to adapt or standardize the marketing mix across international markets has created a lively debate in recent years.

Social Class

Almost every society has some form of social class structure. **Social classes** are relatively permanent and ordered divisions in a society whose members share similar values, interests, and behaviors. Social scientists have identified the seven American social classes: upper uppers (less than 1%), lower uppers (2%), upper middles (12%), middle (32%), working (38%), upper lowers (9%), and lower lowers (7%).[5]

Social class in newer nations such as the United States, Canada, Australia, and New Zealand is not indicated by a single factor such as income but is measured as a combination of occupation, source of income, education, wealth, and other variables. In many older nations, social class is something into which one is born. Bloodlines often mean more than income or education in such societies. Marketers are interested in social class because people within a given class tend to exhibit similar behavior, including buying behavior. Social classes show distinct product and brand preferences in such areas as food, travel, and leisure activity. Some marketers focus on only one social class. The Four Seasons restaurant in upper Manhattan targets upper-class patrons; Joe's Coffee Shop in lower Manhattan focuses on lower-class patrons. Social classes differ in media preferences, with upper-class consumers preferring magazines and books and lower-class consumers preferring television. Even within media category such as television, upper-class consumers prefer news and drama whereas lower-class consumers prefer soap operas and sports programs. There are also language differences between social classes, which means advertisers must compose copy and dialogue that ring true to the social class being targeted.

Social Factors

Consumer behavior is also influenced by social factors, including the consumers' groups, family, social roles, and status. Because social factors can strongly affect consumer responses, companies must take them into account when designing marketing strategies.

Groups

An individual's attitudes and behavior are influenced by many small groups. Those to which the person belongs that have a direct influence are called membership groups. They include primary groups, such as family, friends, neighbors, and coworkers—specifically, those with whom there is regular but informal interaction. Secondary groups are more formal and have less regular interaction; they include religious groups, professional associations, and trade unions. In some societies, secondary groups may be **membership groups.** Members of the Mormon faith, for example, are greatly influenced by their religious affiliation. Mormons do not drink alcoholic beverages; therefore, they are a less attractive group for fine restaurants serving wine and other alcoholic beverages.

Reference groups serve as direct (face-to-face) or indirect points of comparison or reference in the forming of a person's attitudes and behavior. People can also be influenced by **aspirational groups** to which they do not belong but would like to. For example, a college freshman may aspire to be part of Hyatt's management team and may identify with this group even though not a member.

Marketers try to identify the reference groups of their target market. Reference groups influence consumers in at least three ways: (1) they expose the person to new behaviors and lifestyles; (2) they influence the person's attitudes and self-concept; and (3) they create pressures to conform that may affect the person's product, brand, and vendor choices.

The importance of group influence varies by product and brand. It tends to be strongest when the product is visible to others whom the buyer respects. Purchases of products that are used privately are not greatly affected by group influence. Certain nightclubs can be associated with reference groups attracting people who belong or wish to belong to the groups who frequent the nightclubs. Country clubs and city clubs tend to attract members who want to affiliate with their type of members.

Groups commonly have **opinion leaders.** These are people within a reference group who, because of special skills, knowledge, personality, or other characteristics, exert influences over others. Opinion leaders are found in all strata of society, and one person may be an opinion leader in one product area and a follower in another. A business should identify the opinion leaders in their community and make sure that they are invited to important events. For example, the guest list for the grand opening of a restaurant or the first anniversary of a hotel should include opinion leaders.

Family

Family members have a strong influence on buyer behavior. The family remains the most important consumer buying organization in American society and has been researched extensively. Marketers have examined the role and influence of the husband, wife, and children on the purchase of different products and services. Children, for instance, exert a large influence on decisions involving fast-food restaurants. McDonald's aims fast-food advertising directly at children. The chain's advertisements appear during Saturday morning cartoon shows and regularly offer new toys with its Happy Meals.

Roles and Status

A person belongs to many groups: family, clubs, and organizations. An individual's position in each group can be defined in terms of role and status. A **role** consists of the activities that a person is expected to perform according to the persons around him or her. Common roles include son or daughter, wife or husband, and manager or worker.

Each role influences buying behavior. For example, college students dining with their parents may act differently than when they are dining with peers. A person purchasing a banquet for his church's men's club may be more price conscious than usual if he believes church activities call for frugality. The same person might be more interested in detail and quality than in price when purchasing a banquet for his company. Thus a person's role at that time significantly affects his or her purchasing behavior.

Our roles are also influenced by our surroundings. People dining at an elegant restaurant behave differently than when they dine at a fast-food restaurant. They also have expectations about the roles that employees in different establishments should play. Failure to meet these role expectations creates dissatisfaction.[6] For example, diners at an elegant restaurant might expect waiters to hold their chairs during seating. The same diners would be surprised and possibly offended if a person cleaning tables at a White Castle hamburger restaurant assisted with seating.

Each role carries a status reflecting the general esteem given to it by society. People often choose products that show their status in society. For example, a business traveler became upset when all first-class seats were sold on a desired flight. The traveler was forced to fly economy class. When questioned about his concern over flying economy class, the traveler's main concern was what someone he knew might think if they saw him sitting in the economy section. He did not seem to be concerned over the lower level of service or the smaller seating space provided by the economy section. These illustrations show that role and status are not constant social variables. Many marketing and sales professionals have made serious judgmental errors relative to the role and status of prospective customers.

Personal Factors

A buyer's decisions are also influenced by personal characteristics such as age and life-cycle stage, occupation, economic situation, lifestyle, personality, and self-concept.

Age and Life-Cycle Stage

The types of goods and services people buy change during their lifetimes. Preferences for leisure activities, travel destinations, food and entertainment are often age related. Important age-related factors are often overlooked by marketers. This is probably due to wide differences in age between those who determine marketing strategies and those who purchase the product/service. A study of mature travelers showed that this segment places great importance on grab bars in bathrooms, night-lights, legible, visible signs in hallways, extra blankets, and large printing on menus. Despite the logical importance of the factors, researchers found that this information "is not usually included in advertising and information listings."[7]

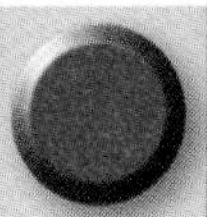

Marketing Highlight 6-1

Senior Consumers

As the U.S. population ages, seniors (people fifty-five and older) are becoming a very attractive market. They currently make up a market of over 55 million people. There were 4 million baby boomers that turned fifty-five in 2001. Similar numbers will turn fifty-five each year until 2019. Those fifty-five and over control almost half of the discretionary income in the United States—$600 billion dollars. Those in the fifty-five to sixty-four age group have the highest discretionary income of any group. These seniors will create excellent opportunities for hospitality and travel companies.

This group is different from other senior groups before them, because they feel young, not old. Phil Goodman, president of Western Media, said hospitality organizations should advertise to the fifty-five year olds the same way they advertised to them when they were thirty-five years old. Pete Favat, Arnold Communications, does the creative advertising for Royal Caribbean cruises. He agrees with Goodman, stating this age group is seeking more adventure and experiences than their demographics a decade earlier. His ads will feature moped riders in Rome and rock climbers in Corsica. Arnold states, "They are going to be much younger—in their minds—than the elderly population has ever been. This generation is trying to stay as young as possible as long as they can."

American Resort and Development Association (ARDA), the professional association for the timeshare industry, see the baby boomers as a market group that has vacation and travel written all over them. One of the distinguishing factors of this group and the seniors before them is the current seniors are confident and independent travelers seeking new experiences. They are also more traveled than any other group of seniors. Thus, a new experience is not going to Rome, Paris or New York. It is a bike trip through Europe, or a wine and culinary tour of Australia, or a white-water rafting trip in British Columbia.

Today's seniors will reward those hospitality and travel organizations that understand their wants. The losers will be those organizations that treat them as they have treated seniors in the past. Understanding consumer behavior is critical to a business's success.

Sources: Tobi Elkin, "Enlightened age: 50+," *Brandweek; New York;* May 10, 1999, pp. 20–26; Mike Malley, "Baby Boomers Fuel Growth of Timeshare Opportunities," *Hotel and Motel Management,* November 16, 1998, p. 4; and "Boomers Loyal to Brands," *Hotel and Motel Management,* Duluth; January 12, 1998, p. 15; Thomas T. Semon and Leslie M. Harris, "The Baby Boomers: A Maturing Market," *Marketing News,* Chicago; January 3, 2000, p. 20.

Successful marketing to various age segments may require specialized and targeted strategies. This will almost certainly require segmented target publications and database marketing. It may also require a marketing staff and advertising agency with people of varying ages and cultural backgrounds.

Buying behavior is also shaped by the **family life cycle** stages. Young unmarried persons usually have few financial burdens, and spend a good portion of their discretionary income on entertainment. Young married people without children have high discretionary incomes and dine out frequently. Once they have children, their purchases from restaurants can change to more delivery and carry out. When the children leave home, the discretionary income can jump, and expenses on dining out can increase. Marketers often define their target markets in life-cycle terms and develop appropriate products and marketing plans.

El Questro is a unique tourist destination in Western Australia. The Homestead provides 6 luxurious rooms for those who want to visit a remote destination, but enjoy the amenities of a world-class resort. The Homestead appeals to baby boomers who want to enjoy unique destinations and who have the discretionary income and desire to stay at luxurious facilities. Courtesy of Accor Asia Pacific.

6.2 Steak and Ale Restaurant

Bill Watson, vice president of marketing of Steak and Ale Restaurants, states that empty-nesters (couples without children) are fewer than 20 percent of Steak and Ales business, but they make up a far greater share of sales than 20 percent. A National Restaurant Association study found that empty-nesters spend 65 percent more on dining than couples with children at home. Watson and his company are now shaping new offerings to satisfy the wants of the baby boomers that are fast becoming empty nesters. One of these products is a "nine-pepper filet," to pique the taste buds of the 50-plus diner.[8]

Occupation

A person's occupation affects the goods and services bought. For example, construction workers often buy their lunches from industrial catering trucks that come out to the job site. Business executives purchase meals from a full-service restaurant, whereas clerical employees may bring their lunch or purchase lunch from a nearby quick-service restaurant. Employees of some consulting firms are not allowed to eat in fast-food restaurants. The managers of these companies do not think it creates a proper image to have their clients see consultants they have just been billed $200 an hour for eating in a fast-food restaurant. Marketers try to identify occupational groups that have above-average interest in their products.

Economic Situation

A person's economic situation greatly affects product choice and the decision to purchase a particular product. Consumers cut back on restaurant meals, entertainment, and vacations during recessions. They trade down in their choice of restaurants and/or menu items and eat out less frequently, looking for a coupon or deal when they do go out. Marketers need to watch trends in personal income, savings, and interest rates. If economic indicators point to a recession, they can redesign, reposition, and reprice their products. Restaurants may need to add lower-priced menu items that will still appeal to their target markets.

Conversely, periods of economic prosperity create opportunities. Consumers are more inclined to buy expensive wines and imported beers, menus can be upgraded, and air travel and leisure expenditures can be increased. Companies must take advantage of opportunities caused by economic upturns and take defensive steps when facing an economic downturn. Managers sometimes react too slowly to changing economic conditions. It pays to remain continuously aware of the macroenvironment facing customers. Regular reading of publications such as the *Wall Street Journal,* the business section of the local press, and regional economic reports by local and regional banks help to keep managers informed.

Lifestyle

People coming from the same subculture, social class, and occupation may have quite different lifestyles. A **lifestyle** is a person's pattern of living as expressed in his or her activities, interests, and opinions (Table 6-1). Lifestyle portrays the "whole person" interacting with his or her environment. Marketers search for relationships between their products and people who are achievement oriented. A chef may then target his restaurants more clearly at the achiever lifestyle. A study of tourists who purchase all-inclusive travel packages versus those who make travel arrangements independently revealed that lifestyle characteristics varied. All-inclusive travel purchasers were "more socially interactive, solicitous, and take their vacations mainly to relax." Tourists who preferred independent travel arrangements were more self-confident and often sought solitude.[9]

Table 6-1
Lifestyle Dimensions

ACTIVITIES	INTERESTS	OPINIONS	DEMOGRAPHICS
Work	Family	Themselves	Age
Hobbies	Home	Social issues	Education
Social events	Job	Politics	Income
Vacation	Community	Business	Occupation
Entertainment	Recreation	Economics	Family size
Club membership	Fashion	Education	Dwelling
Community	Food	Products	Geography
Shopping	Media	Future	City size
Sports	Achievements	Culture	Stage in life cycle

Source: Joseph T. Plummer, "The Concept and Application of Life-Style Segmentation," *Journal of Marketing* (January 1974), p. 34.

One of the most popular classifications based on psychographic measurements is the VALS 2 framework. SRI International's Values and Lifestyles (VALS) framework has been the only commercially available psychographic segmentation system to gain widespread acceptance. The VALS 2 classifies all U.S. adults into eight groups based on psychological attributes. The segmentation system is based on responses to a questionnaire featuring five demographics and forty-two attitudinal questions, as well as questions about use of on-line services and Web sites.

The VALS 2 questionnaire asks respondents to agree or disagree with statements such as, "I like my life to be pretty much the same from week to week," "I often crave excitement," and "I would rather make something than buy it."[10]

Two of the eight American lifestyles are:

Believers: principle-oriented consumers with more modest incomes. They are conservative and predictable consumers who favor American products and established brands. Their lives are centered on family, church, community, and nation.

Achievers: successful, work-oriented people who get their satisfaction from their jobs and their families. They are politically conservative and respect authority and the status quo. They favor established products and services that show off their success.

Prizm, developed by Jonathan Robbin, is another commonly used lifestyle classification scheme. Prizm is a geodemographic system that allows researchers to know the mix or density of lifestyle groups in each of the nation's 36,000 zip code areas. A profile of one of these Prizm clusters is provided below. Blue-Chip Blues comprise about 6 percent of the U.S. population and are one of the largest users of fast food restaurants.

> **Blue-Chip Blues** (2% of U.S. households): The nation's most affluent blue-collar households are concentrated in Blue-Chip Blues, composed of postwar suburban subdivisions in major metropolitan areas. Here lives a blue-collar version of the American dream: the majority of adults have high-school educations and own comfortable, middle-class homes. Boasting one of the highest concentrations of married couples with children, Blue-Chip Blues is the type of neighborhood with fast-food restaurants attached to every shopping center, baseball diamonds in the parks, and motorboats in the driveways.[11]

One of the criticisms of geodemographic systems is they assume everyone is like their neighbors. Although certain neighborhoods may contain more of a certain profile of person, not everyone in the neighborhood is the same. For example, most neighborhoods contain families and people without children. Jock Bickert developed a classification called Cohorts. Cohorts is built from a wealth of actual, self-reported household level data, rather than the inferred or geographic level data used in other segmentation systems. The Cohorts are identified by twenty-seven highly cohesive groups of households. Cohorts results in a classification that is unique to the household. Marketing Highlight 6-2 provides an example of a successful application of Cohorts.

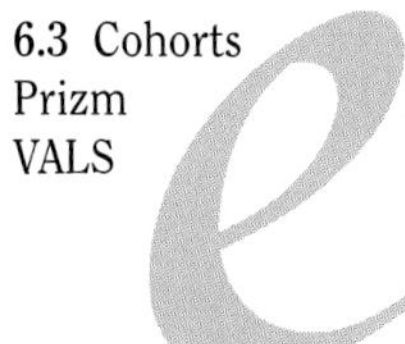
6.3 Cohorts
Prizm
VALS

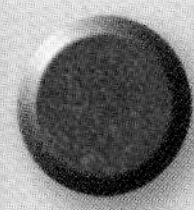

Marketing Highlight 6-2

The San Diego Padres Baseball Club

The San Diego Padres had experienced a steady decline in attendance over a three-year period, culminating in the second lowest average attendance in the major leagues in 1995.

Fan disenchantment could be traced to a number of factors: a former owner who had stripped the team of superstars in an attempt to drastically reduce the payroll; a resulting decline of on-field performance; and the baseball strike that aborted the 1994 season and the beginning of the 1995 season.

Specifically, the San Diego Padres wanted to:

- Increase attendance
- Understand distinct baseball behavior
- Increase fan loyalty
- Build a fan database
- Identify multiticket package marketing opportunities
- Identify a support base for a new baseball-only stadium

The San Diego Padres selected Looking Glass to help them achieve their objectives. As the first step in the database-building process, the Padres ran a questionnaire in the *San Diego Union-Tribune* the last week of the 1995 season. That questionnaire carried a number of questions regarding baseball behavior, as well as the demographics and lifestyle questions needed to Cohort-encode the respondents. Nearly 6,500 individuals responded. A similar questionnaire was also sent to season ticket holders. Looking Glass identified eleven Cohort segments that made up the baseball fan base in San Diego. Three segments accounted for more than half of the season ticket holders. Each segment had distinctive baseball behavior, whether it be price sensitivity or participation in numerous other sporting events. The Jules & Roz Cohort group, for example, displayed no price sensitivity—despite the presence of hot dog-snarfing teenagers—but their attendance at Padres games was attenuated by their attendance at competing sports events.

The ability to marry actual baseball behavior with Cohort segment membership has given the Padres unusual sales and promotional insights, translatable into finely targeted promotions, both for single game and season tickets. For example, the Padres learned that a major fan segment of retirees—the Elwood & Willamae Cohort group—was intensely loyal to the team, regardless of win-loss record. However, they shunned night games. Knowing this gave the Padres the opportunity to package day games with less attractive opponents and target the 62,000 Elwood & Willamaes in the San Diego area. Also, at the beginning of the 1996 season, the Padres initiated a membership program called the Compadres Club. Fans attending home games were encouraged to complete an application form that asked for name, address, and the demographic and lifestyle questions necessary to Cohort encode each member. On completion of the application, fans were given a bar-coded membership card. By "swiping" that card at any game attended, the member earned points, redeemable for team merchandise and privileges in the ballpark.

The Compadres Club continues today, with over 100,000 members. During the 1996–1997 season, the Padres estimate they increased ticket sales by over $2.5 million, and nearly that same amount in additional concessions and merchandise sales, solely attributable to the Compadres Club.

Cohort Descriptions

Elwood & Willamae

Retired couples with modest incomes that dote on their grandchildren and, when not touring the United States, engage primarily in domestic pursuits. Median Age = 63; Median Income = $23,336.

Jules & Roz

Urban families who, despite having children at home, have sufficient financial resources to own the latest high-tech products and lead very active recreational and cultural lifestyles. Median Age = 43; Median Income > $100,000.

®Cohorts is a registered trademark of Looking Glass, Inc.

Elwood & Willamae

®Cohorts is a registered trademark of Looking Glass, Inc.

Jules & Roz

Note: Cohorts were named based on first names of members that were much more common in the cohort than in the general population.

Lifestyle classifications are by no means universal. Advertising agency McCann-Erikson London, for example, found the following British lifestyles: Avant Guardians (interested in change); Pontificators (traditionalists, very British); Chameleons (follow the crowd); and Sleepwalkers (contented underachievers). The D'Arcy, Masius, Benton, & Bowles agency identified five categories of Russian consumers: Kuptsi (merchants), Cossacks, Students, Business Executives, and Russian Souls. Cossacks are characterized as ambitious, independent, and status seeking; Russian Souls as passive, fearful of choices, and hopeful.[12]

Personality and Self-Concept

Each person's personality influences his or her buying behavior. By **personality** we mean distinguishing psychological characteristics that lead to relatively consistent and enduring responses to the environment.

Personality can be useful in analyzing consumer behavior for some product or brand choices. For example, a beer company may discover that heavy beer drinkers tend to rank high in sociability and aggressiveness. This information can be used to establish a brand image for the beer and to suggest the type of people to show in an advertisement.

6.4 Drake Hotel

Stanley Paskie, the seventy-two-year-old head bartender at the Drake Hotel in Chicago's Gold Coast, said, "It's imperative that a bartender possess the human touch. Unfortunately, human relations isn't a required course at the nation's bartending schools where most bartenders now learn the craft. I've had conversations with customers in which I never said a word. I remember one customer who, as he was leaving, said 'thanks for listening to me, fella.'"[13] Paskie believed that a good bartender is part father, part philosopher, part confessor, and part devil's advocate. These traits are undoubtedly important in many areas of hospitality and travel marketing.

Many marketers use a concept related to personality: a person's **self-concept** (also called self-image). Each of us has a complex mental self-picture, and our behavior tends to be consistent with that self-image.[14] People who perceive themselves as outgoing and active will be unlikely to purchase a cruise vacation if their perception of cruises is one of elderly persons lying on lounge chairs. They would be more likely to select a scuba-diving or skiing vacation. The cruise line industry has been quite successful in changing its "geriatric" image and now attracts outgoing and active consumers.

The role of self-concept obviously has a strong bearing on the selection of recreational pursuits, including golf, sailing, dirt bike riding, fishing, and hunting. Anyone who enjoys boating will testify to the difference between boaters who use sails and those who use engines. Yachters/sail boaters refer to those who use engines as "stink potters." Stink potters think of the sailing crowd as stuffy, pretentious, and generally not much fun.

Psychological Factors

A person's buying choices are also influenced by four major psychological factors: motivation, perception, learning, and beliefs and attitudes.

Here's where you send them to play, play, play.
Your #1 salesman. Makes 25 calls before most people get out of bed. Relentlessly cheerful. Never relaxes.
Your best manager. Saves your company thousands whenever she touches a calculator. Meticulous. A gourmet cook. Also plays killer ragtime piano.
All year long they work, work, work.
Your most talented designer. Dreams in color. Improves the wheel daily. Up on all the latest fashion trends.
Your best team player. Ex-varsity everything. Salt of the earth. Sends his friends postcards from every vacation. Mr. Handshake.
He'll serve his way through our 13 Har-Tru and 5 clay tennis courts. On our 7,040-yard Robert Trent Jones-designed championship golf course, he'll challenge other A+ types from around the world, and probably win a hole or two.
PLAY THE PALACE
Your best people all have different personalities. So make sure the trip they earn gives them plenty to do. Send them to play, play, Play The Palace.
It's Workplay at the Palace, where you'll find great recreation combined with an attentive staff, up to 45,000 square feet of flexible meeting and banquet space, including two elegant ballrooms, and 20 versatile breakout rooms. Plus a level of service you don't usually expect in the islands.
There's a new attitude in The Bahamas since the elections. Smiles are wider. Service is friendlier. And faster. When Vernal Sands, our Ambassador of Goodwill, bellows "Top of the morning!" to the breakfast crowd, his good humor echoes throughout the day. So come, Play The Palace.
For information and reservations call 1-800-222-7466.
Carnival's
CRYSTAL PALACE
RESORT & CASINO, NASSAU, THE BAHAMAS

Robinson, Yesawich, and Pepperdine created this advertisement to position Crystal Palace as the best vacation destination for high-energy "achievers." Courtesy of Robinson, Yesawich, and Pepperdine.

Motivation

A person has many needs at any given time. Some are biological, arising from hunger, thirst, and discomfort. Others are psychological, arising from states of tension, such as the need for recognition, esteem, or belonging. Most of these needs are not strong enough to motivate a person to act at a given point in time. A need becomes a **motive** when it is aroused to a sufficient level of intensity. Creating a tension state causes the person to act to release the tension. Psychologists have developed theories of human motivation. Two of the most popular, the theories of Abraham Maslow and Herzberg's Theory, have quite different meanings for consumer analysis and marketing.

Maslow's Theory of Motivation. Abraham Maslow sought to explain why people are driven by particular needs at particular times.[15] Why does one person spend much time and energy on personal safety and another on gaining the esteem of others? Maslow's answer is that human needs are arranged in a hierarchy, from the most pressing to the least pressing. Maslow's hierarchy of needs in order of importance are physiological needs, safety needs, social needs, esteem needs, and self-actualization needs. A person tries to satisfy the most important need first. When that important need is satisfied, it will stop being a motivator, and the person will then try to satisfy the next most important need. For example, a starving man (need 1) will not take an interest in the latest happenings in the art world (need 5), or in how he is seen or esteemed by others (need 3 or 4), or even in whether he is breathing clean air (need 2). But as each important need is satisfied, the next most important need will come into play.

Normally, needs are prioritized. For example, a college student with $500 to pay for incidental and recreational expenses during the term is unlikely to spend $400 on a trip to Florida over spring break. Instead, the money will probably be spent on smaller purchases of entertainment throughout the semester. If the student unexpectedly receives $2,000, there might be a strong temptation to satisfy a higher-order need.

Herzberg's Theory. Frederick Herzberg developed a *two-factor theory* that distinguishes dissatisfiers (factors that cause dissatisfaction) and satisfiers (factors that cause satisfaction). The absence of dissatisfiers is not enough; satisfiers must be actively present to motivate a purchase. For example, a computer that does not come with a warranty would be a dissatisfier. Yet the presence of a product warranty would not act as a satisfier or motivator of a purchase, because it is not a source of intrinsic satisfaction with the computer. Ease of use would be a satisfier.

Herzberg's theory has two implications. First, sellers should do their best to avoid dissatisfiers (for example, a poor training manual or a poor service policy). Although these things will not sell a product, they might easily unsell it. Second, the manufacturer should identify the major satisfiers or motivators of purchase in the market and then supply them. These satisfiers will make the major difference as to which brand the customer buys.

Perception

A motivated person is ready to act. How that person acts is influenced by his or her perception of the situation. In the same situation, two people with the same motivation may act quite differently based on how they perceive conditions. One person may perceive the waiters at T.G.I. Friday's as casual and unsophisticated, while another person may view them as spontaneous with cheerful personalities. Friday's is targeting those in the second group.

Why do people have different perceptions of the same situation? All of us experience a stimulus by the flow of information through our five senses: sight, hearing, smell, touch, and taste. However, each of us receives, organizes, and interprets this sensory information in an individual way. Perception is the process by which an individual selects, organizes, and interprets information to create a meaningful picture of the world.[16]

The key word in the definition of perception is *individual*. One person might perceive a fast-talking salesperson as aggressive and insincere; another, as intelligent and helpful. People can emerge with different perceptions of the same object because of three perceptual processes: selective attention, selective distortion, and selective retention.

Selective Attention. People are exposed to a tremendous amount of daily stimuli: the average person may be exposed to over 1,500 ads a day. Because a person cannot possibly attend to all of these, most stimuli will be screened out—a process called selective attention. Selective attention means that marketers have to work hard to attract consumers' notice. The real challenge is to explain which stimuli people will notice. Here are some findings:

- *People are more likely to notice stimuli that relate to a current need.* A person who is motivated to buy a computer will notice computer ads; he or she will probably not notice stereo-equipment ads.
- *People are more likely to notice stimuli that they anticipate.* You are more likely to notice computers than radios in a computer store because you do not expect the store to carry radios.
- *People are more likely to notice stimuli whose deviations are large in relation to the normal size of the stimuli.* You are more likely to notice an ad offering $100 off the list price of a computer than one offering $5 off.

Selective Distortion. Even notice stimuli do not always come across in the way the senders intended. Selective distortion is the tendency to twist information into personal meanings and interpret information in a way that will fit our preconceptions. Unfortunately, there is not much that marketers can do about selective distortion.

Selective Retention. People will forget much that they learn but will tend to retain information that supports their attitudes and beliefs. Because of selective retention, we are likely to remember good points mentioned about competing products. Selective retention explains why marketers use drama and repetition in sending messages to their target market.

Learning

When people act, they learn. **Learning** describes changes in an individual's behavior arising from experience. Most human behavior is learned. Learning theorists say that learning occurs through the interplay of drives, stimuli, cues, responses, and reinforcement.

When consumers experience a product, they learn about it. Members of the site-selection committee for a convention often sample the services of competing hotels. They eat in the restaurants, note the friendliness and professionalism of the staff, and examine the hotel's features. Based on what they have learned, a hotel is selected to host the convention. During the convention, they experience the hotel once again. Based on their experience and those of the attending conventioneers, they will either be satisfied or dissatisfied.

Hotels should help guests to learn about the quality of their facilities and services. Luxury hotels give tours to first-time guests and inform them of the services offered. Repeat guests should be updated on the hotel's services by employees and by letters and literature.

Beliefs and Attitudes

Through acting and learning, people acquire beliefs and attitudes, which, in turn, influence their buying behavior. A **belief** is a descriptive thought that a person holds about something. A customer may believe that Adam's Mark Hotels have the best facilities and most professional staff of any hotel in the price range. These beliefs may be based on real knowledge, opinion, or faith. They may or may not carry an emotional charge.

Marketers are interested in the beliefs that people have about specific products and services. Beliefs reinforce product and brand images. People act on beliefs. If unfounded consumer beliefs deter purchases, marketers will want to launch a campaign to change them.

Unfounded consumer beliefs can severely affect the revenue and even the life of hospitality and travel companies. Among these beliefs might be the following:

- A particular hamburger chain served ground kangaroo meat.
- A particular hotel served as Mafia headquarters.
- A particular airline has poor maintenance.
- A particular country has unhealthy food-handling standards.

People have attitudes about almost everything: religion, politics, clothes, music, and food. An **attitude** describes a person's relatively consistent evaluations, feelings, and tendencies toward an object or an idea. Attitudes put people into a frame of mind for liking or disliking things and moving toward or away from them. For example, many people who have developed the attitude that eating healthy food is important perceive chicken as a healthy alternative to beef and pork. As a result, the per capita consumption of chicken has increased during recent years, leading the American Beef Council and National Pork Producers Council to try to change consumer attitudes that beef and pork are unhealthy. The National Pork Producers Council promotes pork as "the other white meat," trying to associate pork with chicken. Companies can benefit by researching attitudes toward their products. Understanding attitudes and beliefs is the first step toward changing or reinforcing them.

Attitudes are very difficult to change. A person's attitudes fit into a pattern, and changing one attitude may require making many difficult adjustments. It is easier for a company to create products that are compati-

THE NEXT PARTY

Pork Satay Appetizers
Slice 2 pounds boneless **pork loin** into thin strips. Stir together 4 minced **garlic cloves**, 1 cup **soy sauce**, 12 ounces **Dijon style mustard** and 1/2 cup **honey**. Save half the sauce for dipping; marinate pork in other half for 30 minutes. Remove strips from marinade, discarding marinade and weave on bamboo skewers. Grill or broil 3-4 minutes. Serve with reserved sauce. Preparation Time: 20 minutes. Makes 16 servings.

Nutrient Information, Approximately, per Serving: Calories: 94, Protein: 13 gm., Fat: 3 gm., Sodium: 354 mg., Cholesterol: 33 mg.

Nutrient analysis done by The Food Processor II Diet Analysis Software. Pork data from USDA Handbook 8-10 (1991).

A great party has two main ingredients. Interesting guests and interesting food. Assuming you've taken care of the former, allow us to give you a delicious idea for the latter -- The Other White Meat®

Pork's a natural for dipping. Try bottled or homemade sauces (think salsa, sweet & sour, honey mustard) and don't forget the peanut sauce!

TASTE WHAT'S NEXT™

Pork. The Other White Meat.

Try tying bunches of herbs with ribbons for a refreshing, charming centerpiece. Or, light candles around the house for an instantly elegant look.

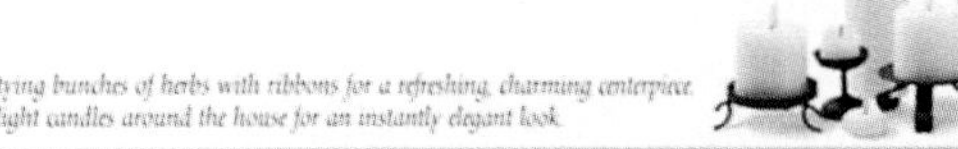

For the Lick Your Chops Cookbook, send $5.95 (includes shipping & handling) to Lick Your Chops Cookbook Ad, Box 10383, Des Moines, IA 50306.
America's Pork Producers.

The National Pork Producers Council is trying to direct people's attitudes toward pork, a healthier and more versatile meat, and away from fatty, unhealthy meats. Courtesy of the National Pork Producers Council.

ble with existing attitudes than to change the attitudes toward their products. There are exceptions, of course, where the high cost of trying to change attitudes may pay off.

There is a saying among restaurateurs that a restaurant is only as good as the last meal served. Attitudes explain in part why this is true. A customer who has returned to a restaurant several times and on one visit receives a bad meal may begin to believe that it is impossible to count on having a good meal at that restaurant. The customer's attitudes toward the restaurant begin to change. If this customer again receives a bad meal, negative attitudes may be permanently fixed and prevent a future return. Serving a poor meal to first-time customers can be disastrous. Customers develop an immediate negative attitude that prevents them from returning.

Attitudes developed as children often influence purchases as adults. Children may retain negative attitudes toward certain vegetables, people, and possibly places. Chances are equally good that they may retain very positive images toward McDonald's and Disneyland. Hospitality and travel companies are particularly subject to lifelong consumer attitudes that result from positive or negative childhood experiences. Harsh words from the manager of a miniature golf course or air sickness on a commercial flight in which the flight attendant showed little sympathy are negative attitude-building experiences.

Disney and McDonald's both view children as lifelong customers. They want children to return as teenagers, parents, and grandparents and treat them in a manner to ensure future business. Many hospitality and travel companies have still not learned from McDonald's and Disney.

6.5 Adam's Mark Hotels
Camp Hyatt
National Pork Producers
Omni Sagamore
Smuggler's Notch

Ski, golf, and ocean resorts have taken heed and have developed special programs, menus, and activities for kids. In many cases, hospitality and travel companies have discovered that there is good profit potential in kids' programs, as well as future patron building potential. Steamboat Springs Ski Resort offers a professionally run children's program for kids from six months to fifteen years of age. Emphasis is on safety and fun at Steamboat. Other examples of top-notch kids' programs may be found at Smuggler's Notch in Vermont and the Omni Sagamore in New York. Hyatt Hotels is a leader in the field with its Camp Hyatt. Hyatt has proved that a hotel can be upscale and child directed.

Once negative attitudes are developed, they are hard to change. New restaurant owners often want quick cash flow and sometimes start without excellent quality. A new restaurateur complained that customers are fickle. When his restaurant first opened, there were lines of people waiting for a seat. A few months later, he had plenty of empty seats every night. Obviously, he had not satisfied his first guests. Even though he may have subsequently corrected his early mistakes, his original customers had been disappointed, were not returning, and probably were reporting negative comments to their friends.

We can now appreciate the many individual characteristics and forces influencing consumer behavior. Consumer choice is the result of a complex interplay of cultural, social, personal, and psychological factors. Many of these cannot be influenced by the marketer; however, they help the marketer to better understand customers' reactions and behavior.

The Buyer Decision Process

We are now ready to look at how consumers make buying decisions. Figure 6-3 shows that the buyer decision process consists of five stages: need recognition, information search, evaluation of alternatives, purchase decision, and postpurchase behavior. This model emphasizes that the buying process starts long before and continues long after the actual purchase. It encourages the marketer to focus on the entire buying process rather than just the purchase decision.

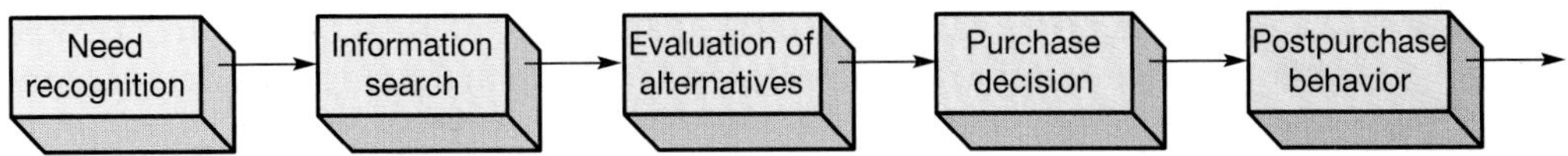

Figure 6-3
Buyer decision process.

The model appears to imply that consumers pass through all five stages with every purchase they make. But in more routine purchases, consumers skip or reverse some of these stages. A customer in a bar purchasing a glass of beer may go right to the purchase decision, skipping information search and evaluation. This is referred to as an *automatic response loop*.[17] The dream of every marketer is to have customers develop an automatic response to purchase their products. However, this does not typically happen. The model in Figure 6-4 shows the considerations that arise when a consumer faces a new and complex purchase situation.

To illustrate this model, we will follow Rosemary Martinez, a college student. She has just remembered that next Saturday is her boyfriend's birthday.

Need Recognition

The buying process starts when the buyer recognizes a problem or need. The buyer senses a difference between his or her actual state and a desired state. The need can be triggered by internal stimuli. From previous experience, the person has learned how to cope with this need and is motivated toward objects that he or she knows will satisfy it.

Needs can also be triggered by external stimuli. Rosemary passes a restaurant, and the aroma of freshly baked bread stimulates her hunger; she has lunch with a friend who just came back from Bali and raves about her trip; or she watches a television commercial for a Hyatt resort. All these stimuli can lead her to recognize a problem or need.

At this stage, marketers must determine the factors and situations that trigger consumer problem recognition. They should research consumers to find out what kinds of needs or problems led them to purchase an item, what brought these needs about, and how they led consumers to choose this particular product.

Rosemary might have mentioned that she passed a card shop and noticed birthday cards, which reminded her that her boyfriend's birthday was approaching. She knew he liked German food, so she decided to take him to a German restaurant.

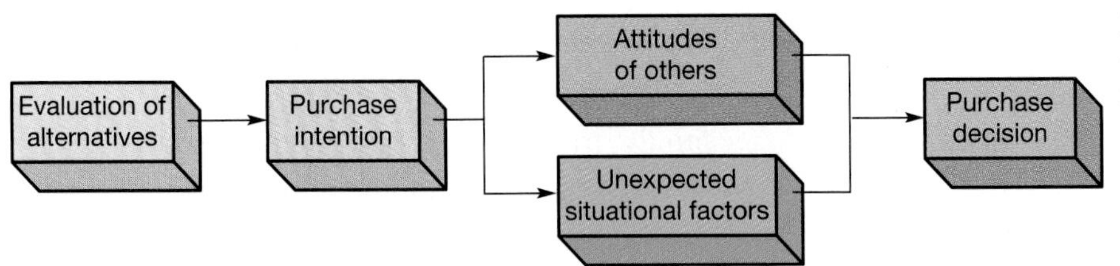

Figure 6-4
Steps between evaluation of alternatives and a purchase decision.

6.6 T.G.I.Friday's
Travel Industry Association

By gathering such information, marketers can identify stimuli that most often trigger interest in the product and develop marketing programs that involve these stimuli. Marketers can also show how their product is a solution to a problem. For example, T.G.I. Friday's advertised its gift certificates as a solution to Christmas shopping. Friday's food and atmosphere attracts a broad range of people; the gift certificates are easy to buy, avoiding the need to go to crowded shopping centers; and they can be bought in denominations that fit with planned expenditures. Friday's promoted gift certificates as a solution to a common problem experienced before Christmas.

When looking for a hotel, "business travelers want a hotel to give them the tools to get their work done efficiently, which includes having competent staff members on duty, more than they want personalized services and fancy surroundings." Unfortunately, some hotels seem to confuse product opulence with providing features that will be benefits for the business market because they meet the needs of the business traveler. They provide great lobbies and restaurants, but give businesspersons rooms that are not equipped as an office away from home, failing to meet the needs of this important market.[18]

The Travel Industry Association of America found that families with both heads of the household employed were finding it difficult to find a week when everyone was free. As a result this segment needed three- and four-day getaways that could be booked at the last minute, because 42 percent of this group makes plans within two weeks of the actual vacation.[19] These examples show that businesses must understand the needs of their customers and how these needs are translated into wants.

Information Search

An aroused consumer may or may not search for more information. If the consumer's drive is strong and a satisfying product is near at hand, the consumer is likely to buy it at that moment. If not, the consumer may simply store the need in memory and search for relevant information.

How much searching a consumer does will depend on the strength of the drive, the amount of initial information, the ease of obtaining more information, the value placed on additional information, and the satisfaction one gets from searching.

Rosemary asked several of her friends if they knew of a good German restaurant. Then she scanned a city magazine's restaurant listings. Finally, she looked in the Yellow Pages to see if she could find additional German restaurants. As a result of her search, Rosemary identified three German restaurants. She then tried to find friends and acquaintances who had been to one or more of the restaurants to get their impressions. She also looked in the *Zagat Restaurant Guide* for her city to see how the restaurants were rated.

The consumer can obtain information from several sources. These include:

- *Personal sources:* family, friends, neighbors, acquaintances
- *Commercial sources:* advertising, salespeople, dealers, packaging, displays
- *Public sources:* restaurant reviews, editorials in the travel section, consumer-rating organizations

With hospitality and travel products, personal and public sources of information are more important that advertisements. This is because a customer does not know what they are going to receive until they have received it. A customer cannot try out an intangible product before they purchase it. For example, people may hear of a restaurant through advertising but ask their friends about the restaurant before they try it. Responses from personal sources have more impact than advertising because they are perceived to be more credible. Christopher Lovelock lists these sources of information as ways customers can reduce the risk of purchasing a service:

- Seeking information from respected personal sources (family, friends, peers)
- Relying on a firm that has a good reputation
- Looking for guarantees and warranties
- Visiting service facilities or trying aspects of the service before purchasing
- Asking knowledge employees about competing services
- Examining tangible cues or other physical evidence
- Using the Internet to compare service offerings

By gathering information, consumers increase their awareness and knowledge of available choices and product features. A company must design its marketing mix to make prospects aware of and knowledgeable about the features and benefits of its products or brands. If it fails to do this, it has lost its opportunity to sell the customer. A company must also gather information about competitors and plan a differentiated appeal.

Marketers should carefully identify consumers' sources of information and the importance of each source. Consumers should be asked how they first heard about the brand, what information they received, and the importance they place on different information sources. This information is helpful in preparing effective communication.

Evaluation of Alternatives

We have seen how the consumer uses information to arrive at a set of final brand choices. But how does the consumer choose among the alternatives? How does the consumer mentally sort and process information to arrive at brand choices? Unfortunately, there is no simple and single evaluation process used by all consumers or even by one consumer in all buying situations. There are several evaluation processes.

Rosemary Martinez preferred a restaurant with good food and service. However, she believed that all the restaurants under consideration offered these attributes. She also wanted to patronize a restaurant with entertainment and a romantic atmosphere. Finally, she had a limited amount of money, so price was important. If several restaurants met her criteria, she would choose the one with the most convenient location.

Certain basic concepts will help explain consumer evaluation processes. First, we assume that each consumer sees a product as a bundle of product attributes. For restaurants, these attributes include food quality, menu selection, quality of service, atmosphere, location, and price. Consumers vary as to which of these attributes they consider relevant. The most attention is paid to attributes connected with their needs.

Second, the consumer attaches different degrees of importance to each attribute. That is, each consumer attaches importance to each attribute according to his or her unique needs and wants. Third, the consumer is likely to develop a set of beliefs about where each brand stands on each attribute. The set of beliefs held about a particular brand is known as the **brand image.** The consumer's beliefs may vary from true attributes because of the consumer's experience and the effects of selective perception, selective distortion, and selective retention. Fourth, the consumer is assumed to have a utility function for each attribute. A utility function shows how the consumer expects total product satisfaction to vary with different levels of different attributes. Fifth, the consumer arrives at attitudes toward the different brands through some evaluation procedure. One or more of several evaluation procedures are used, depending on the consumer and the buying decision.

Purchase Decision

In the evaluation stage, the consumer ranks brands in the choice set and forms purchase intentions. Generally, the consumer will buy the most preferred brand, but two factors can come between the purchase intention and the purchase decision. These factors are shown in Figure 6-4.

Attitudes of others represent the first. Rosemary Martinez selected a German restaurant because her boyfriend likes German food. Rosemary's choice depended on the strength of another person's attitudes toward her buying decision and on her motivation to comply with those wishes. The more intense the other person's attitude and the closer that person is to the decision maker, the more influence the other person will have. Nowhere is this better identified than in the case of children. Children do not hide their desires and parents and grandparents are affected intensely.

Purchase intention is also influenced by unexpected situations. The consumer forms a purchase intention based on factors such as expected family income, expected price, and expected benefits from the product. When the consumer is about to act, unexpected situations may arise to change the purchase intention. Rosemary Martinez may have an unexpected car problem that will cost $200 for repairs. This may cause her to cancel dinner reservations and select a less expensive gift.

Because the customer does not know what the experience will be until after the purchase, managers must remember that first-time customers are not really customers, they are only trying the product. While the customer is in the purchase act, employees must do everything possible to ensure they will have a good experience and the postpurchase evaluation will be favorable.

Postpurchase Behavior

The marketer's job does not end when the customer buys a product. Following a purchase, the consumer will be satisfied or dissatisfied and will engage in postpurchase actions of significant interest to the marketer. What determines postpurchase satisfaction or dissatisfaction with a purchase? The answer lies in the relationship between consumer expectations and perceived product performance.[20] If the product matches expectations, the consumer will be satisfied. If it falls short, the consumer will experience dissatisfaction.

Consumers base expectations on past experiences and on messages they receive from sellers, friends, and other information sources. If a seller exaggerates the product's likely performance, the consumer will be disappointed. The larger the gap between expectations and performance, the greater the consumer's dissatisfaction. This suggests that sellers must faithfully represent the product's performance so that buyers are satisfied. For example, Bermuda enticed tourists to enjoy the island during the off season at a lower price. They called this period "Rendezvous Time" and advertised that all the island's amenities would be available. When tourists arrived, they found that many facilities and attractions were closed. Hotels had shut down many of their food and beverage facilities, leaving tourists disappointed. Advertising claims initially brought tourists, but the truth got out and hotel occupancy dropped by almost 50 percent over a period of six years.[21]

6.7 Continental Airlines

In May 1994, Continental Airlines announced a "save now, eat later" program. The purpose was to save money by eliminating food service in coach class. Unfortunately, many passengers were not notified of this change until they reached the airport and even then were notified only through a few signs on seats in the waiting area or in the seat pockets on the plane. Passengers who had paid full coach fare and had expected a light meal were furious. Many read the notice and then immediately complained to the flight attendant. Continental failed to meet postpurchase expectations and compounded the problem by communication that was perceived as haughty and noncustomer oriented. The message was perceived as completely in favor of the airline. Harassed flight attendants, who had not participated in the decision, were left to accept blame. In some cases they responded by saying, "Your travel agent should have notified you of the change," thus attempting to shift blame and only making matters worse.

Almost all major purchases result in **cognitive dissonance,** or discomfort caused by postpurchase conflict. Every purchase involves compromise. Consumers feel uneasy about acquiring the drawbacks of the chosen brand and losing the benefits of the rejected brands. Thus consumers feel some postpurchase dissonance with many purchases, and they often take steps after the purchase to reduce dissonance.[22]

Dissatisfied consumers may take any of several actions. They may return the product or complain to the company and ask for a refund or exchange. They may initiate a lawsuit or complain to an organization or group that can help them get satisfaction. Buyers may also simply stop purchasing the product and discourage purchases by family and friends. In each of these cases, the seller loses.

Marketers can take steps to reduce consumer postpurchase dissatisfaction and help customers to feel good about their purchases. Hotels can send a letter to meeting planners congratulating them on having selected their hotel for their next meeting. They can place adds featuring testimonials of satisfied meeting planners in trade magazines. They can encourage customers to suggest improvements.

Understanding the consumer's needs and buying process is the foundation of successful marketing. By understanding how buyers proceed through problem recognition, information search, evaluation of alternatives, the purchase decision, and postpurchase behavior, marketers can acquire many clues as to how to better meet buyer needs. By understanding the various participants in the buying process and major influences on buying behavior, marketers can develop a more effective marketing program.

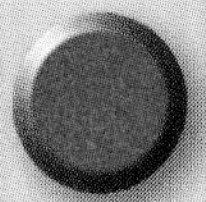

Marketing Highlight 6-3

Unique Aspects of Hospitality and Travel Consumers

Valarie Zeithaml, a marketing consultant, published a classic article describing how the consumer evaluation process differs between goods and services. Persons purchasing hospitality and travel services rely more on information from personal sources. When looking for a good restaurant, people will ask friends or people familiar with the town, such as front-desk employees or the concierge. Restaurants should attempt to affect positively those persons who potential customers may contact. In larger cities there is a concierge association. Smart restaurateurs seek to host this club, letting their members experience the restaurants.

Postpurchase evaluation of services is important. The intangibility of services makes it difficult to judge the service beforehand. Consumers may seek advice from friends but will use the information they receive from actually purchasing service to evaluate it. The first-time customer is on a trial basis. If the hotel or restaurant satisfies the customers, they will come back.

When purchasing hospitality and travel products, customers often use price as an indication of quality. A business executive who has been under a lot of pressure decides to take a three-day vacation now that the project is complete. She wants luxury accommodations and good food service. She is prepared to pay $175 a night for the room. She calls a hotel that offers a special rate of $85. This hotel may be able to satisfy her needs and has simply dropped its rate to encourage business. In this case, the hotel has dropped its rate too low to attract this customer. Because she has never visited the hotel, she will perceive that the hotel is below her standard. Similarly, a person who enjoys fresh seafood and sees grilled red snapper on the menu for $7.99 will assume that it must be a low-quality frozen product, because fresh domestic fish usually costs at least twice as much. When using price to create demand, care must be taken to ensure that one does not create the wrong consumer perceptions about the product's quality.

When customers purchase hospitality and travel products, they often perceive some risk in the purchase. If customers want to impress friends or business associates, they will usually take them to a restaurant they have visited previously. Customers tend to be loyal to restaurants and hotels that have met their needs. A meeting planner is reluctant to change hotels if the hotel has been doing a good job.

Customers of hospitality and travel products often blame themselves when dissatisfied. A man who orders scampi may be disappointed with the dish but not complain because he blames himself for the bad choice. He loves the way his favorite restaurant fixes scampi, but he should have known that this restaurant would not be able to prepare it the same way. When the waiter asks how everything is, he replies that it was okay. Employees must be aware that dissatisfied customers may not complain. They should try to seek out sources of guest dissatisfaction and resolve them. A waiter noticing someone not eating their food may ask if they could replace it with an alternative dish and suggest some items that could be brought out very quickly.

Source: Valarie Zeithaml, "How Consumer Evaluation Processes Differ between Goods and Services," in *Marketing of Services*, ed. James Donnelly and William R. George (Chicago: American Marketing Association, 1981), pp. 186–190.

Key Terms

Aspirational group A group to which a person wishes to belong.

Attitude A person's enduring favorable or unfavorable cognitive evaluations, emotional feelings, and action tendencies toward some object or idea.

Belief A descriptive thought that a person holds about something.

Brand image The set of beliefs consumers hold about a particular brand.

Cognitive dissonance Buyer discomfort caused by postpurchase conflict.

Culture The set of basic values, perceptions, wants, and behaviors learned by a member of society from family and other important institutions.

Family life cycle The stages through which families might pass as they mature.

Learning Changes in a person's behavior arising from experience.

Lifestyle A person's pattern of living as expressed in his or her activities, interests, and opinions.

Membership groups Groups that have a direct influence on a person's behavior and to which a person belongs.

Motive (or drive) A need that is sufficiently pressing to direct a person to seek satisfaction of that need.

Opinion leaders People within a reference group who, because of special skills, knowledge, personality, or other characteristics, exert influence on others.

Personality A person's distinguishing psychological characteristics that lead to relatively consistent and lasting responses to his or her environment.

Reference groups Groups that have a direct (face to face) or indirect influence on a person's attitude or behavior.

Role The activities that a person is expected to perform according to the persons around him or her.

Self-concept Self-image, the complex mental pictures people have of themselves.

Social classes Relatively permanent and ordered divisions in a society whose members share similar values, interests, and behaviors.

Chapter Review

I. Model of Consumer Behavior. The company that really understands how consumers will respond to different product features, prices, and advertising appeals has a great advantage over its competitors. As a result, researchers from companies and universities have heavily studied the relationship between marketing stimuli and consumer response. The marketing stimuli consist of the four Ps: product, price, place, and promotion. Other stimuli include major forces and events in the buyer's environment: economic, technological, political, and cultural. All these stimuli enter the buyer's black box, where they are turned into a set of observable buyer responses: product choice, brand choice, dealer choice, purchase timing, and purchase amount.

II. Personal Characteristics Affecting Consumer Behavior

1) Cultural factors

a) Culture. Culture is the most basic determinant of a person's wants and behavior. It compromises the basic values, perceptions, wants, and behaviors that a person learns continuously in a society.

b) Subculture. Each culture contains smaller subcultures, groups of people with shared value systems based on common experiences and situations.

c) Social classes. These are relatively permanent and ordered divisions in a society whose members share similar values, interests, and behaviors. Social class in newer nations such as the United States, Canada, Australia, and New Zealand is not indicated by a single factor such as income, but is measured as a combination of occupation, source of income, education, wealth, and other variables.

2) Social factors

a) Reference groups. These groups serve as direct (face-to-face) or direct point of comparison or reference in the forming of a person's attitude and behavior.

b) Family. Family members have a strong influence on buyer behavior. The family remains the most important consumer-buying organization in American society.

c) Role and status. A role consists of the activities that a person is expected to perform according to the persons around him or her. Each role carries a status reflecting the general esteem given to it by society. People often choose products that show their status in society.

3) Personal factors

a) Age and life-cycle stage. The types of goods and services people buy change during their lifetimes. As people grow older and mature, the products they desire change. The makeup of the family also affects purchasing behavior. For example, families with young children dine out at fast-food restaurants.

b) Occupation. A person's occupation affects the goods and services bought.

c) Economic situation. A person's economic situation greatly affects product choice and the decision to purchase a particular product.

d) **Lifestyle.** Lifestyles profile a person's whole pattern of acting and interacting in the world. When used carefully, the lifestyle concept can help the marketer understand changing consumer values and how they affect buying behavior.

e) **Personality and self-concept.** Each person's personality influences his or her buying behavior. By personality we mean distinguishing psychological characteristics that disclose a person's relatively individualized, consistent, and enduring responses to the environment. Many marketers use a concept related to personality: a person's self-concept (also called self-image). Each of us has a complex mental self-picture, and our behavior tends to be consistent with that self-image.

4) **Psychological factors**

a) **Motivation.** A need becomes a motive when it is aroused to a sufficient level of intensity. Creating a tension state causes a person to act to release the tension.

b) **Perception.** Perception is the process by which a person selects, organizes, and interprets information to create a meaningful picture of the world.

c) **Learning.** Learning describes changes in a person's behavior arising from experience.

d) **Beliefs and attitudes.** A belief is a descriptive thought that a person holds about something. An attitude describes a person's relatively consistent evaluations, feelings, and tendencies toward an object or an idea.

III. Buyer Decision Process

1) **Problem recognition.** The buying process starts when the buyer recognizes a problem or need.

2) **Information search.** An aroused consumer may or may not search for more information. How much searching a consumer does will depend on the strength of the drive, the amount of initial information, the ease of obtaining more information, the value placed on additional information, and the satisfaction one gets from searching.

3) **Evaluation of alternatives.** Unfortunately, there is no simple and single evaluation process used by all consumers or even by one consumer in all buying situations. There are several evaluation processes.

4) **Purchase decision.** In the evaluation stage, the consumer ranks brands in the choice set and forms purchase intentions. Generally, the consumer will buy the most preferred brand.

5) **Postpurchase behavior.** The marketer's job does not end when the customer buys a product. Following a purchase, the consumer will be satisfied or dissatisfied and will engage in postpurchase actions of significant interest to the marketer.

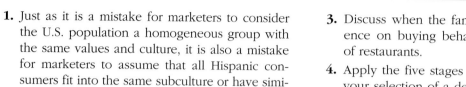

Discussion Questions

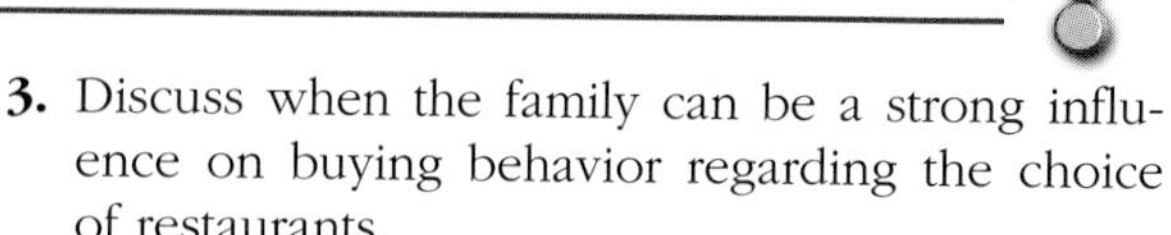

1. Just as it is a mistake for marketers to consider the U.S. population a homogeneous group with the same values and culture, it is also a mistake for marketers to assume that all Hispanic consumers fit into the same subculture or have similar buying habits. Comment on this statement.
2. Choose a restaurant concept that you would like to take overseas. How will the factors shown in Figure 6-2 work for or against the success of this restaurant?
3. Discuss when the family can be a strong influence on buying behavior regarding the choice of restaurants.
4. Apply the five stages in the decision process to your selection of a destination for your next vacation.
5. An advertising agency president says, "Perception is reality." What does he mean by this? How is perception important to marketers?

Experiential Exercises

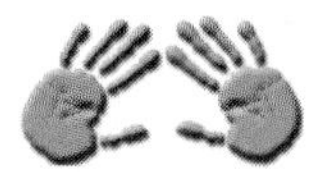

Do one of the following:

1. Choose a hospitality or travel organization. You are in charge of designing a consumer advertisement for that organization. How would you determine the message of the advertisement?
2. Talk to several people about how they would choose a hotel in a city they have never been to before, a restaurant for a special occasion, or a place to vacation. What did you learn about the buyer decision process from these discussions?

Internet Exercise

Support for these exercises can be found on the Web site for *Marketing for Hospitality and Tourism,* www.prenhall.com/kotler.

Go to the sites for VALS (Values and Lifestyles Program) and Cohorts. Both sites have a link under this chapter in the text's companion Web site. Do you feel this lifestyle information is more helpful in explaining consumer behavior than demographics? Please explain why or why not.

References

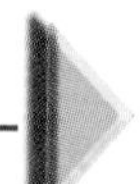

1. See Molly Cahill (February 2000), "Expecting Nearly Half of Business Travelers to Be Women, the Pan Pacific San Francisco Is Fine Tuning Amenities," retrieved on October 1, 2001, from the World Wide Web: *http://www.hotel-online.com/Neo/News/Pressreleases2000_1st/feb00_womensurvey.html;* Christine Calloway-Holt (2001), "The Nob Hill Lambourne Creates 'Rebalancing Services' for Professsional Women Travelers," retrieved on October 1, 2001, from the World Wide Web: *http://www.hotel-online.com/Neo/News/PR2001_2nd/Jun01_Lambourne.html;* Suzanne Crampton and Jitendra Mishra, Women in Management. *Public Personnel Management* 28, 87–106, retrieved April 6, 2000, from the World Wide Web: *http://proquest.umi.com/pqdweb?TS=...=1&Did=000000039998327 &Mtd=1&Fmt=4;* Ruth Hill, "Women Road Warriors," *HSMAI Marketing Review* (Winter 2000/2001); Salina Khan, "Aiming to Please Women Business Travel Industry Introduces More Services for Female Customers," retrieved on October 24, 2001, from World Wide Web:

http://www.usatoday.com; Regina McGee, "What Do Women Travelers Really Want?" *Successful Meetings* 37, no. 9 (August 1988): 54–56; "The Woman Traveler, A Special Report," *Lodging Hospitality* (December 1985): 32–48; Michele Manges, "Hotels Change Pitch to Businesswomen," *Wall Street Journal,* October 14, 1988, sec. B, p. 1; John Naisbitt and Patricia Aburdene, *Megatrends 2000* (New York: William Morrow, 1990); Harry Nobles and Cheryl Thompson, "Female Business Travelers' Expectations," retrieved on October 24, 2001, from the World Wide Web: *http://www.hotel-online.com/Neo/News/PR2001/Jun01_femaletravelers.html.*

2. Richard Chambers, Harsha Chacko, and Robert Lewis, *Marketing Leadership in Hospitality* (New York: Van Nostrand Reinhold, 1995), p. 199.
3. Susan Harte, "When in Rome, You Should Learn to Do What the Romans Do," *Atlanta Journal-Constitution,* January 22, 1990, pp. D1, D6. See also Lufthansa's *Business Travel Guide/Europe;* Sergey Frank, "Global Negotiating," *Sales and Marketing Management* (May 1992): 64–69. Valarie Zeithmal and Mary Jo Bitner, *Services Marketing* (New York: McGraw-Hill, 2000); Kathryn Frazer Winsted, "The Service Experience in Two Cultures," *Journal of Retailing,* 73 no. 3 (1997): 337–360.
4. "Briefcase—It's Fast and It's Kosher," *Houston Chronicle,* April 25, 1997, p. 4c.
5. See Richard P. Coleman, "The Continuing Significance of Social Class to Marketing," *Journal of Consumer Research,* December 1983, pp. 264–80; Leon G. Shiffman and Leslie Lazar Kanuk, Consumer Behavior, 6th ed. (Upper Saddle River, NJ: Prentice Hall, 1997), p. 388.
6. John E. G. Bateson, ***Managing Services Marketing*** (New York: Dryden, 1989), pp. 291–300.
7. Richard M. Howey, Ananth Mangala, Frederick J. De Micco, and Patrick J. Moreo, "Marketplace Needs of Mature Travelers," *Cornell Hotel and Restaurant Administration Quarterly* 33, no. 4 (August 1992): 19–20.
8. Joan Raymond, "The Joy of Empty Nesting," *American Demographics,* (May 2000).
9. Jihwan Yoon and Elwood L. Shafer, "An Analysis of Sun-Spot Destination Resort Market Segments: All Inclusive Package versus Independent Travel Arrangements," *Journal of Hospitality and Tourism Research* 21, no. 1 (1997): 157–158.
10. Arnold Mitchell, *The Nine American Lifestyles* (New York: Warner Books), pp. viii–x, 25–31; Personal communication from the VALS™ Program, Business Intelligence Center, SRI Consulting, Menlo Park, CA, February 1, 1996. See also Wagner A. Kamakura and Michel Wedel, "Lifestyle Segmentation with Tailored Interviewing," *Journal of Marketing Research* 32, no. 3 (August 1995): 308–317.
11. Source: © 1988 by Michael J. Weiss. *The Clustering of America* (New York: Harper & Row). Reprinted by permission of HarperCollins Publishers, Inc.
12. Stuart Elliot, "Sampling Tastes of a Changing Russia," *New York Times,* April 1, 1992, pp. D1, D19; and Miller, "Global Segments from 'Strivers' to 'Creatives,' p. 11. For an excellent disscussion of cross-cultural lifestyle systems, see Phillip Kotler, Gary Armstrong, John Saunders, and Veronica Wong, *Principles of Marketing,* 2nd ed. (London: Prentice Hall Europe, 1999), pp. 240–242.
13. Edmund O. Lawler, "50 Years behind the Bar," *F&B Magazine* 2, no. 1 (March–April 1994): 44.
14. James U. McNeal, *Consumer Behavior: An Integrative Approach* (Boston: Little, Brown, 1982), pp. 83–90.
15. Abraham H. Maslow, *Motivation and Personality,* 2nd ed. (New York: Harper & Row, 1970), pp. 80–106.
16. M. Joseph Sirgy, "Self-Concept in Consumer Behavior: A Critical Review," *Journal of Consumer Research* (December 1982): pp. 287–300.
17. McNeal, *Consumer Behavior,* p. 77.
18. Anna Mattila, "Consumers' Value Judgments," *Cornell Hotel & Restaurant Administration Quarterly* 40, no 1 (February 1999): 40.
19. "TIA Study: Weekend Trips Increasing in Popularity," *Travel Weekly,* July 2, 2001, p. 4.
20. Priscilla A. LaBarbara and David Mazursky, "A Longitudinal Assessment of Consumer Satisfaction/Dissatisfaction: The Dynamic Aspect of the Cognitive Process," *Journal of Marketing Research* (November 1983): 393–404.
21. Thomas Beggs and Robert C. Lewis, "Selling Bermuda in the Off Season," in *The Complete Travel Marketing Handbook* (Lincolnwood, IL: NTC Business Books, 1988).
22. Leon Festinger, *A Theory of Cognitive Dissonance* (Stanford, CA: Stanford University Press, 1957); Leon G. Schiffman and Leslie Lazar Kanuk, *Consumer Behavior* (Upper Saddle River, NJ: Prentice Hall, 1991), pp. 304–305.

7 Organizational Buyer Behavior of Group Market

The ideal salesperson in the company meetings segment isn't a salesperson in the traditional sense, but rather the problem-solver.
Robert C. Mackey

Don Walter is a member of the Convention Liaison Council's Hall of Leaders. He received this honor because of his contribution to the meetings and convention business over the last thirty years. During his career, Don Walter has purchased or influenced the purchase of close to a $100 million worth of hospitality and travel products. When asked what is the important factor in negotiating with a hotel, he replied, "Honest, straightforward negotiations." He states that "if both the meeting planner and the hotel sales manager are up front with each other, it saves hours of unnecessary negotiation for each party."

Walter does not buy on price alone and avoids properties that appear desperate for his business. He claims that often these hotels have financial problems, which result in staff turnover and understaffing. In this type of hotel, you may have to deal with several people because of the turnover problem. When the meeting is held, the service is poor, meals that should take an hour end up taking an hour and a half because of understaffing, and changes in setups are difficult to accomplish. When people do show up to change the meeting room for you, they are often irritated and let the meeting planner know it. Walter goes on to say that this type of poor service can ruin a meeting. If the meeting does not go off well, the savings in cost seems trivial in comparison to the damage done to the sponsoring association's reputation.

Thus, when negotiating, Walter looks for a fair deal. He expects the hotel to make money, but he also expects good service and overall value. He observes the employees during a site visit to get a good idea of the type of service he can

expect for his meeting. When he sees an employee bend over and pick up a gum wrapper, this is an indication to him that the employees have pride in their hotel. He likes to go back to a hotel where he sees the same faces he saw last year. Low turnover and promotion from within give him a good feeling about a hotel. Similarly, when an employee greets him by name as he enters the hotel, this shows that the hotel has gone to the effort of getting the employees to recognize him—a sign of attention to detail and caring.

After signing a contract with a hotel, he likes to deal with one person. By the way, Walter brings his own contract; he does not use the hotel's contract. Sometimes it is necessary to make changes to the room layouts he provides to the hotel. When he needs to make changes, he expects them to be done promptly and cheerfully.

When discussing things that have affected the meeting business, Walter said that requirements because of the Americans with Disabilities Act (ADA) should be a concern to both hotels and meeting planners. First, compliance ensures that everyone wanting to attend the meeting has access to the meeting. Second, failure to comply could result in lawsuits from attendees against both the meeting sponsor and hotel.

Don Walter provides an example of the tremendous purchasing power of an organizational buyer. He also provides some insights into what is important to meeting planners and association executives. They want good service at a fair price. They do not want any surprises, and when they need to make some changes during the event, they expect the hotel or convention hall to be supportive.

In most hotels and many food-service operations, organizations account for a large percentage of sales. In some ways, business markets are similar to consumer markets. For example, both involve people who assume buying roles and make purchase decisions to satisfy needs. However, business markets differ in many ways from consumer markets.[1] *The differences are in market structure and demand, the nature of the buying unit, the types of decisions, and the decision process involved.*

Chapter Objectives

After reading this chapter, you should be able to:

1. Understand the organizational buying process.
2. Identify and discuss the importance of the participants in the organizational buying process.
3. Identify the major influences on organizational buyers.
4. List the eight stages of the organizational buying process.
5. Identify and describe the group markets in the hospitality industry.

The Organizational Buying Process

Market Structure and Demand

The American Marketing Association holds more than twenty conferences annually. Hyatt and Marriott share the majority of the AMA's conference business, with Marriott's share close to 3,000 room-nights a year. When food and beverage sales are included, the value of this account approaches $1,000,000. In addition to expenditures in the hotel a delegate also spends about $850 on transportation and $425 entertainment, plus expenditures in local restaurants.[2] Each organizational customer can deliver tens of thousands of dollars worth of business to the hotel, airlines, and the destination's economy.

Organizational demand is **derived demand;** it comes ultimately from the demand for consumer goods or services. It is derived or a function of the businesses that supply the hospitality and travel industry with the meetings, special events, and other functions. The American Marketing Association plans and hosts conferences because its members, who are marketing managers, suppliers, and educators, have attended past conferences on these topics. If a particular conference receives poor attendance, the AMA drops it from future schedules. Ultimately, the demand for the AMA member's products determines the demand for AMA products. For example, if class enrollments are low, universities typically cut travel budgets. If car sales fall, GM will cut its travel budget for its marketing department. Both events will cause attendance at AMA conferences to fall, resulting in less revenue for the hotels and cities that host these events. Through good environmental scanning, marketers can identify emerging industries, companies, and associations. They screen these organizations to find good business partners.

Compared with consumer purchases, a business purchase usually involves more buyers and a more professional purchasing effort. Corporations that frequently use hotels for meetings may hire their own meeting planners. Professional meeting planners receive training in negotiating skills. They belong to associations such as Meeting Planners International, which educates its members in the latest negotiating techniques. A corporate travel agent's job is to find the best airfares, rental car rates, and hotel rates. Therefore, hotels must have well-trained salespeople to deal with well-trained buyers, creating thousands of jobs for salespeople. Additionally, once the meeting is sold the account is turned over to a convention service manager who works with the meeting planner to make sure the event is produced according to the meeting planner's expectations. Outside the hotel jobs relating to meetings include corporate meeting planners, association meeting planners, independent meeting planners, and convention and visitor bureau salespersons.

Types of Decisions and the Decision Process

Organizational buyers usually face more complex buying decisions than consumer buyers. Their purchases often involve large sums of money, complex technical features (room sizes, room setups, breakout rooms, audiovisual equipment, and the like), economic considerations, and interactions among many people at all levels of the organization. The **organizational buying process** tends to be more formalized than the consumer process and a more professional purchasing effort. The more complex the purchase, the more likely it is that several people will participate in the decision-making process. The total bill for a one-day sales meeting for twenty people can be several thousands of dollars. If IBM is having a series of sales meetings around the country, it will be worthwhile for the company to get quotations from several hotel chains and spend time analyzing the bids.

Finally, in the organizational buying process, buyer and seller are often very dependent on each other. Sales has become a consultative process. The hotel staff develops interesting and creative menus, theme parties, and coffee breaks. The hotel's convention service staff works with meeting planners to solve problems. In short, the hotel's staff members roll up their sleeves and work closely with their corporate and association customers to find customized solutions to customer needs. When management at the Sands Exposition Center in Las Vegas discovered that there was insufficient floor space to accommodate a major automobile parts trade show, the Sands rented a temporary 40,000-square-foot pavilion. To help attract attendees to the pavilion, the Sands positioned a restaurant at the back of the facility. In the end, hotels and catering firms retain customers by meeting their current needs and thinking ahead to meet the customer's future needs.

e 7.1 Sands Exposition Center

Participants in the Organizational Buying Process

The decision-making unit of a buying organization, sometimes called the buying center, is defined as "all those individuals and groups who participate in the purchasing decision-making process, who share common goals and the risks arising from the decisions."[3]

The *buying center* includes all members of the organization who play any of six roles in the purchase-decision process:[4]

1. **Users.** Users are those who will use the product or service. They often initiate the buying proposal and help define product specifications. If attendees of a sales meeting have a poor experience, they will usually be able to influence the company against using that hotel in the future.
2. **Influencers.** Influencers directly influence the buying decision but do not themselves make the final decision. They often help define specifications and provide information for evaluating alternatives. Past presidents of trade associations may exert influence in the choice of a meeting location. Executive secretaries, a spouse, regional managers, and many others can and do exert considerable influence in the selection of sites for meetings, seminars, conferences, and other group gatherings.
3. **Deciders.** Deciders select product requirements and suppliers. For example, a company's sales manager for the Denver area will select the hotel and negotiate the arrangements when the regional sales meeting is held in that area.
4. **Approvers.** Approvers authorize the proposed actions of deciders or buyers. Although the Denver sales manager arranges the meeting, the contracts may need to be submitted to the corporate vice president of marketing for formal approval.
5. **Buyers.** Buyers have formal authority for selecting suppliers and arranging the terms of purchase. Buyers may help shape product specifications and play a major role in selecting vendors and negotiating.
6. **Gatekeepers.** Gatekeepers have the power to prevent sellers or information from reaching members of the buying center. For example, a hotel salesperson calling on a meeting planner may have to go through a secretary. This secretary can easily block the salesperson from seeing the meeting planner. This can be accomplished by failing to forward messages, telling the salesperson the meeting planner is not available, or simply telling the meeting planner not to deal with the salesperson.

Buying centers vary by number and type of participants. Salespersons calling on organizational customers must determine the following:

- Who are the major decision participants?
- What decisions do they influence?
- What is their level of influence?
- What evaluation criteria does each participant use?

When a buying center includes multiple participants, the seller may not have the time or resources to reach all of them. Smaller sellers concentrate on reaching the key buying influencers and deciders. It is important not to go over the decider's head. Most deciders like to feel in control of the purchasing decision; going over a decider's head and working with the boss will be resented. In most cases the boss will leave the decision up to the decider, and the ill-will created by not dealing with the decider directly will result in him or her choosing another company. Larger sellers utilize multilevel, in-depth selling to reach as many buying participants as possible. Their salespeople virtually "live" with their high-volume customers.

Major Influences on Organizational Buyers

Organizational buyers are subject to many influences as they make their buying decisions. Some vendors assume that the most important influences are economic. They see buyers as favoring the supplier who offers the lowest price, best product, or most service. This view suggests that hospitality marketers should concentrate on price and cost variables.

Others believe that buyers respond to personal factors such as favors, attention, or risk avoidance. A study of buyers in ten large companies concluded that emotions and feelings play a part in the decision process of corporate decision makers. They respond to "image," buy from known companies, and favor suppliers who show them respect and personal consideration. They "overreact" to real or imagined slights, tending to reject companies that fail to respond or delay in submitting bids.[5]

In reality, organizational buyers commonly respond to both economic and personal factors. Where there is substantial similarity in supplier offers, price becomes an important determinant. When competing products differ substantially, buyers are faced with many decision variables other than price comparisons.

The various influences on organizational buyers may be classified into four main groups: environmental, organizational, interpersonal, and individual.[6] Figure 7-1 illustrates these groups.

Environmental Factors

Organizational buyers are heavily influenced by the current and expected economic environment. Factors such as the level of primary demand, the economic outlook, and the cost of money are important. In a recession,

Figure 7-1
Major influences on business buying behavior.

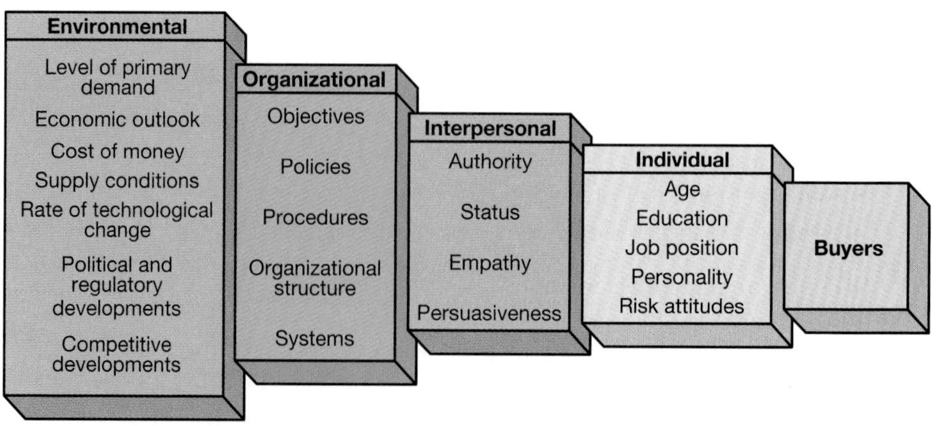

companies cut their travel budgets, whereas in good times, travel budgets are usually increased.

Organizational Factors

Each organization has specific objectives, policies, procedures, organizational structures, and systems related to buying. The hospitality marketer has to be as familiar with them as possible and will want to know the following: How many people are involved in the buying decision? Who are they? What are the evaluation criteria? What are the company's policies and constraints on the buyers?

Interpersonal Factors

The buying center usually includes several participants, with differing levels of interest, authority, and persuasiveness. Hospitality marketers are unlikely to know the group dynamics that take place during the buying decision process. However, salespeople commonly learn the personalities and interpersonal factors that shape the organizational environment and provide useful insight into group dynamics.

Individual Factors

Each participant in the buying decision process has personal motivations, perceptions, and preferences. The participant's age, income, education, professional identification, personality, and attitudes toward risk all influence the participant in the buying process. Buyers definitely exhibit different buying styles. Hospitality marketers must know their customers and adapt their tactics to known environmental, organizational, interpersonal, and individual influences.

Organizational Buying Decisions

Organizational buyers do not buy goods and services for personal consumption. They buy hospitality products to provide training, to reward employees and distributors, and to provide lodging for their employees. Eight stages of the organizational buying process have been identified and are called *buyphases*.[7] This model is called the *buygrid framework*. The eight steps for the typical new-task buying situation follow.

1. Problem Recognition

The buying process begins when someone in the company recognizes a problem or need that can be met by acquiring a good or a service. **Problem recognition** can occur because of internal or external stimuli. Internally, a new product may create the need for a series of meetings to explain the product to the sales force. A human resource manager may notice a need for employee training and set up a training meeting. A CEO may feel that the executive team would benefit from a weekend retreat to reformulate the firm's strategy. Externally, the buyer sees an ad or receives a call from a hotel sales representative who offers a favorable corporate program. Marketers can stimulate problem recognition by developing ads and calling on prospects.

2. General Need Description

Having recognized a need, the buyer goes on to determine the requirements of the product and to formulate a **general need description.** For a training meeting, this would include food and beverage, meeting space, audiovisual equipment, coffee break, and sleeping room requirements. The corporate meeting planner will work with others—the director of human resources, the training manager, and potential participants to gain insight into the requirements of the meeting. Together, they determine the importance of the price, meeting space, sleeping rooms, food and beverage, and other factors.

The hotel marketer can render assistance to the buyer in this phase. Often, the buyer is unaware of the benefits of various product features. Alert marketers can help buyers define their companies' needs and show how their hotel can satisfy them.

3. Product Specification

Once the general requirements have been determined, the specific requirements for the meeting can be developed. For example, a meeting might require twenty sleeping rooms, a meeting room for twenty-five set up classroom style with a whiteboard and overhead projector, and a separate room for lunch. For larger meetings with an exhibit area, the information need becomes more complex. Information often requested includes availability of water, ceiling heights, door widths, security, and procedures for receiving and storing materials prior to the event. A salesperson must be prepared to answer their prospective client's questions about their hotel's capabilities to fulfill the **product specification.**

4. Supplier Search

The buyer now conducts a **supplier search** to identify the most appropriate hotels. The buyer can examine trade directories, do a computer search, or phone familiar hotels. Hotels that qualify may receive a site visit from the meeting planner, who eventually will develop a short list of qualified suppliers.

5. Proposal Solution

Once the meeting planner has drawn up a short list of suppliers, qualified hotels will be invited to submit proposals. Thus hotel marketers must be skilled in researching, writing, and presenting proposals. These should be marketing oriented, not simply technical documents. They should position their company's capabilities and resources so that they stand out from the competition. Many hotels have developed videos for this purpose.

6. Supplier Selection

In this stage, members of the buying center review the proposals and move toward **supplier selection.** They conduct an analysis of the hotel, considering physical facilities, the hotel's ability to deliver service, and the professionalism of its employees. Frequently, the buying center specifies desired supplier attributes and suggests their relative importance. In general, meeting planners consider the following attributes in making their selection of a location:

- Sleeping rooms
- Meeting rooms
- Food and beverage
- Billing procedures
- Check-in/checkout
- Staff

The buying center may attempt to negotiate with preferred suppliers for better prices and terms before making the final selection. There are several ways the hotel marketer can counter the request for a lower price. For example, the dates can be moved from a high demand period to a need period for the hotel, or menus can be changed. The marketer can cite the value of the services the buyer now receives, especially where services are superior to competitors.

7. Order-Routine Specification

The buyer now writes the final order with the chosen hotels, listing the technical **order-routine specifications** of the meeting. The hotel will respond by offering the buyer a formal contract. The contract will specify cutoff dates for room blocks, the date when the hotel will release the room block for sale to other guests, and minimum guarantees for food and beverage functions. Many hotels and restaurants have turned what should have been a profitable banquet into a loss by not having or enforcing minimum guarantees.

8. Performance Review

The buyer does post purchase **performance review** of the product. During this phase the buyer will determine if the product meets the buyer's specifications and if the buyer will purchase from the company again. It is important for hotels to have at least daily meetings with a meeting planner to make sure everything is going well and to correct those things that did not go well. This manages the buyer's perceived service and helps to avoid a negative postpurchase evaluation by the buyer.

Group Business Markets

One of the most important types of organizational business is group business. It is important for marketing managers to understand the differences between a group market and a consumer market. The group business market is often more sophisticated and requires more technical information than the consumer market. Many group markets book more than a year in advance. During this time, cognitive dissonance can develop; thus marketers must keep in contact with the buyer to assure them that they made the right decision in choosing the seller's hotel.

There are four main categories of group business: conventions, association meetings, corporate meetings, and the SMERF (social, military, educational, religious, and fraternal organizations) groups. Figure 7-2 shows

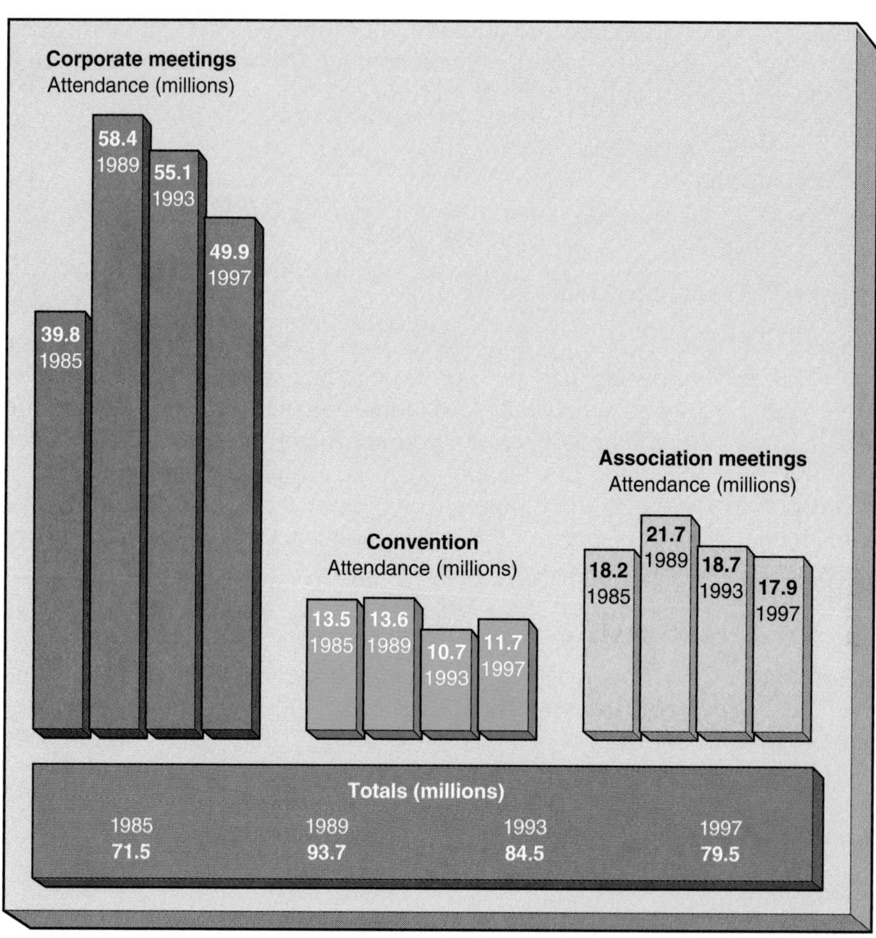

Figure 7-2
Meeting attendance. From *Meetings and Convention Magazine,* March 1994, October 1998.

the attendance at three types of functions, and Figure 7-3 gives the number of functions held. From these figures we can see that conventions attract large numbers but that meetings occur much more frequently than conventions. There are about ninety meetings held for each convention. A thousand people attend the average convention, sixty-five people attend the average corporate meeting, and ninety-five people attend the average association meeting. When choosing a hotel, an important consideration for a meeting planner is whether the hotel can house the participants. Most hotels have the potential of attracting hundreds of small meetings, whereas larger hotels can attract conventions. Group business is a very important segment for most hotels. Successful hotels know which groups to attract, how to use group business to fill need dates, and how to sell groups on the hotel's benefits rather than just price.

Conventions

Conventions are a specialty market requiring extensive meeting facilities. They are usually the annual meeting of an association and include general sessions, committee meetings, and special-interest sessions. Hotels

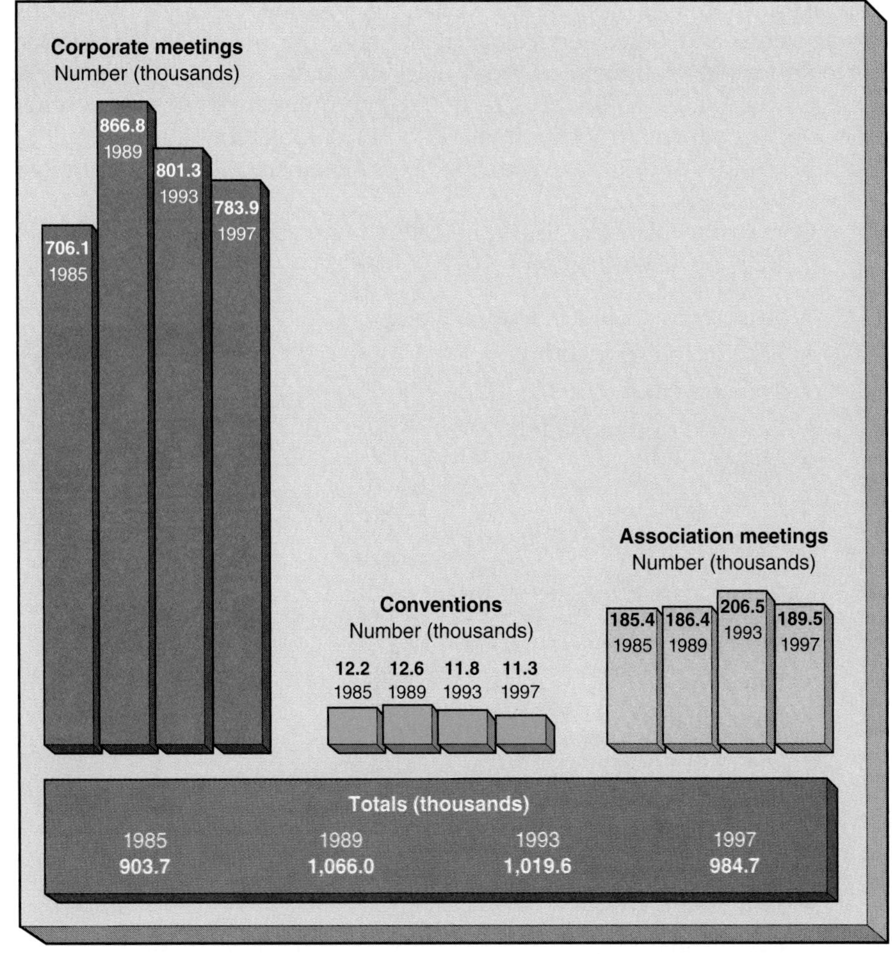

Figure 7-3
Number of meetings. From *Meetings and Convention Magazine,* March 1994, October 1998.

with convention facilities, such as the Chicago Hyatt or the Atlanta Marriott Marquis, can house small and midsized conventions. Conventions that use a major facility, such as the Jacob Javitts Convention Center in New York, often have tens of thousands of delegates. They are called *citywide conventions,* because hotels throughout the city house their delegates. There are over 12,000 conventions held each year in the United States.

Associations usually select convention sites two to five years in advance, with some large conventions planned ten to fifteen years before the event. October is the most popular month for conventions, followed by November, September, and June.[8] Some associations prefer to have their conventions in the same city year after year, whereas others prefer to move to a different area of the country each year.

A convention can be a major source of income for the sponsoring organization. Registration fees from attendees and sales of exhibition space in the trade show are major sources of revenue. A trade show gives suppliers to the association's member a chance to show and sell their products. Companies such as Greyhound Exposition Services work with the association and conference center to provide electrical hook-ups, booth setup and other services to make sure the trade show exhibitors have the resources they need to set up their exhibit. The price that can be charged for exhibition space is related to the number of attendees. When choosing a convention location, an association looks for sites that will be both accessible and attractive to members. Balancing the annual budget depends on a good turnout.

Convention planners listed the following as the most important factors in choosing a destination:

- Availability of hotels and facilities
- Ease of transportation
- Transportation costs
- Distance from attendees
- Climate
- Recreation
- Sights and cultural activities

The most important attributes of the hotel are:[9]

- Meeting rooms
- Rates
- Food quality
- Sleeping rooms
- Support services
- Billing procedures
- Check-in/checkout
- Staff assignment
- Exhibit space
- Previous experience

Note that food quality is very important to the convention planner. Exceptional banquets, out-of-the-ordinary receptions, and unique coffee breaks can be a point of differentiation at a convention, something the attendees will discuss with colleagues. On the other hand, poor food and poor service can generate negative feelings about the convention among the participants. Support services must be available when needed. A nonfunctioning VCR must be repaired or replaced quickly to ensure that the presenter's flow is not interrupted. The author once attended a convention at which two advertising executives had been flown in to give a presentation. When they turned on the slide projector, it would not work. The hotel was unable to resolve the problem, and after about twenty minutes the presentation was canceled.

Many hotels now contract with independent audiovisual (AV) companies to supply and maintain this equipment. In large hotels, AV companies will have an office in the hotel to store equipment and house technicians. For large meetings, AV companies will have on-site technicians to remain with the group during the meeting to correct problems as they occur, thus ensuring that speaker presentations proceed as planned.

Billing procedures are also important to convention planners. Billing can create problems for hotels who take it for granted and do not have a customer-oriented accounting department. Professional meeting planners want a bill that is understandable, accurate, and delivered in a timely manner. Without these characteristics, the bill can be a nightmare. Important attributes for a convention planner other than facilities and rates are food quality, billing procedures, and the professionalism and attention of the hotel's staff.

Convention Bureaus. Convention bureaus are nonprofit marketing organizations that help hotels sign conventions and meetings. These organizations are often supported by a hotel or sales tax and are run by chambers of commerce, visitor bureaus, or city and county governments. They are often one of the first sources of information for a convention or meeting planner. A hotel relying on meeting business for a significant portion of its occupancy should have a good working relationship with the convention bureau, which includes active membership in the organization.

Association Meetings

Associations sponsor many types of meetings, including regional, special interest, educational, and board meetings. There are about 200,000 association meetings annually, creating revenues of over $65 billion.[10] For example, the American Marketing Association (AMA) has chapters in many large cities. These chapters gather once a month, usually at a luncheon or dinner meeting. The AMA sponsors or cosponsors educational meetings. It also has special-interest meetings, such as the marketing educators meeting held every August and February. Every major association schedules scores of meetings held throughout the year in various locations.

The most important attributes of a destination for an association meeting planner are availability of hotel and facilities, ease of transportation, distance from attendees, and transportation costs. Climate, recreation, and cultural activities are not as important as they are to the convention market, because the meeting itself is the major draw. In selecting a hotel, the association meeting planner looks for food quality, rates, meeting rooms, billing procedures, and attributes similar to the convention planner except for exhibition space.[11] Notice that for the association meeting planner, food and beverage are the most important attributes.

Membership in the American Society of Association Executives (ASAE) is beneficial for hotels actively pursuing association business. It provides an opportunity to network with association executives and is a source of information on national and local associations. Many of the hotel's corporate clients are also members of trade associations. These customers can become ambassadors for the hotel at their trade association meetings.

7.2 American Society of Association Executives

Members attend association meetings voluntarily. The hotel should work with meeting planners to make the destination seem as attractive as possible. Making sure that the meeting planner is aware of local attractions, offering suggestions for spousal activities, and assisting in the development of after-convention activities can be useful to the hotel and the

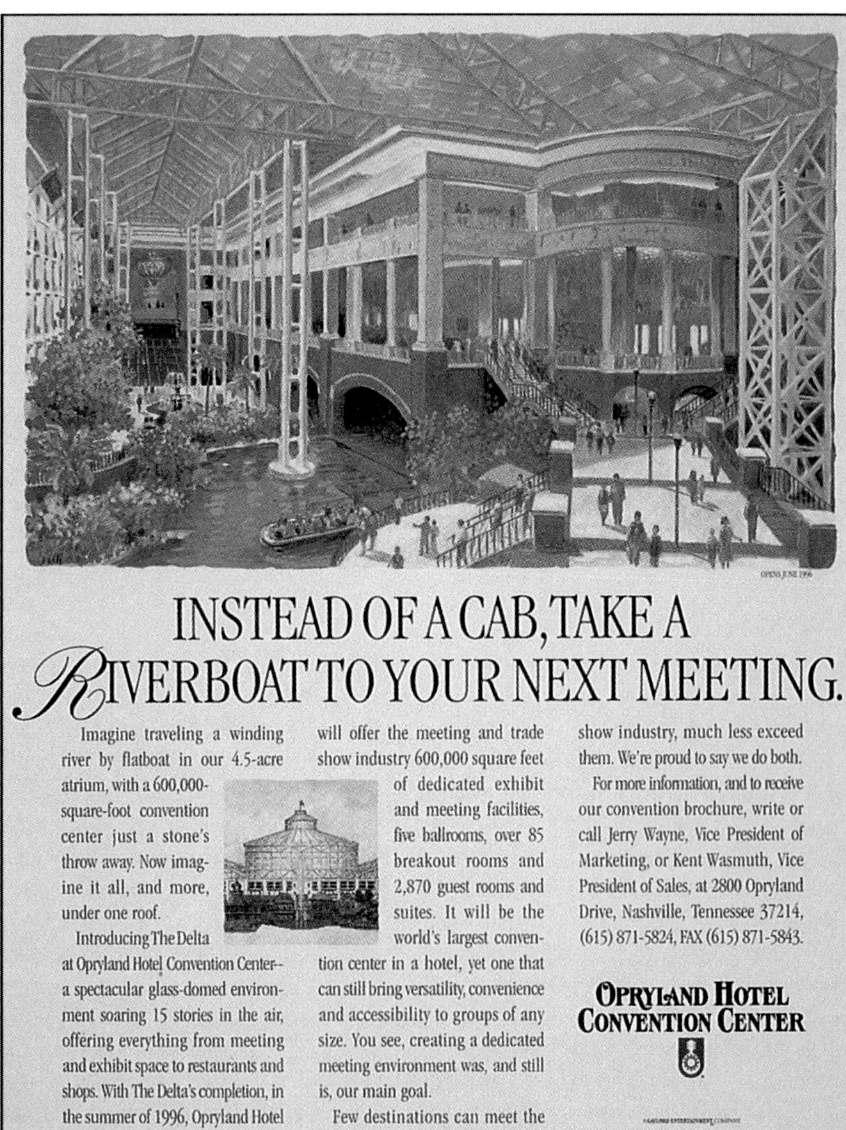

The most important attribute of a hotel for a convention planner is meeting space. This advertisement introduces planners to Opryland's new addition. The copy focuses on meeting space. Courtesy of Opryland Hotel Convention Center, A Gaylord Entertainment Company.

meeting planner. It is important to market both the destination and the hotel.

Corporate Meetings

For employees of a company, a **corporate meeting** is a command performance. They are directed to attend the meeting without choice. One implication of required attendance is a short lead time. Because corporations do not have to develop and implement a marketing plan to gain attendees, they often plan meetings with a few weeks' lead time. Today, there are about 800,000 corporate meetings with an average expenditure exceeding $36,000 per meeting, creating a $45 billion market. Corporate meetings are smaller than association meetings, and there are about four times as many corporate meetings as there are association meetings.[12]

The corporation's major concern is that the meeting be productive and accomplish the company's objectives. Types of corporate meetings include training, management, and planning. Another type of corporate meeting is the incentive meeting, which is discussed later.

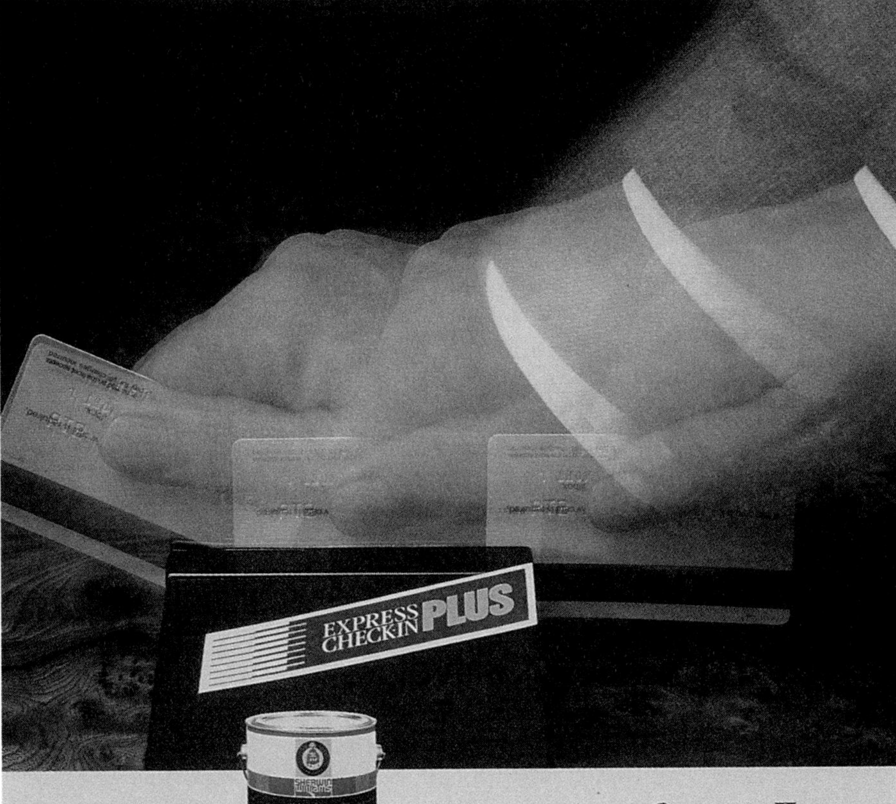

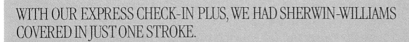

Opryland developed a system to avoid the long check-in lines often associated with meetings. Courtesy of Opryland Hotel Convention Center, A Gaylord Entertainment Company.

To a corporate meeting planner, the most important attributes in the choice of a destination are the availability of hotels, ease of transportation, transportation costs, and distance from the attendees. The most important factors in the choice of a hotel are:

- Food quality
- Meeting rooms
- Rates
- Sleeping rooms
- Support service
- Billing procedures

Corporate meeting planners want to ensure that meetings are productive and that the corporation gets good value for the money it spends. Their success depends on planning smooth-running meetings. Hotels interested in capturing and retaining corporate meeting business must make sure that meeting rooms are adequate and set up properly. Because meeting planners want attendees to be comfortable, sleeping rooms are important to them. They are also concerned about the quality of food. Recreation facilities may also be important. In a multiday technical meeting, the interaction of the participants outside the formal meetings is valuable. Golf or tennis can be used to encourage participants to interact on a social basis and break up the monotony of the classroom sessions. Similarly, an evening outing to an area restaurant, sporting, or cultural event can serve as an enjoyable break for participants.

7.3 Meeting Planners International

Corporate culture also plays an important part in the choice of a hotel. Hotel salespeople must develop an understanding of the client's corporate culture to gain insight into benefits the hotel can offer. Some companies feel meetings should be austere, rather than lavish. Such companies may feel that they are setting an example for their employees, encouraging them by example to spend money wisely. Others view meetings as a time for employees to relax and enjoy themselves, a well-deserved break. Companies that believe meetings should both educate and rejuvenate employees and build their enthusiasm toward the company are willing to spend more money on food and beverage, entertainment, and deluxe hotel facilities.

Small Groups

The small corporate meeting, less than fifty rooms, is gaining the attention of hotel chains. Although small in terms of number of participants, there are thousands of small meetings held every month. Hotels and hotel chains have developed special packages for small meetings, a segment often overlooked by large hotels. Upscale hotels such as the L'Ermitage and The Peninsula, both in Beverly Hills, go after executive meetings where expense is not a problem.[13]

Sheraton has also developed executive conference centers. These centers are designed for board meetings, strategic planning sessions, and training sessions. The amenities in the centers were developed as the result of focus groups with clients to find out what they wanted in small meetings; these amenities were included in the executive conference centers and their smart meeting rooms. Select Sheraton hotels in Europe offer "Sheraton Smart Meetings." Smart meetings is a program designed to provide small meeting planners with the technology needed for today's meeting. The smart meeting offers rooms equipped with ISDN lines, data port entries in the floor, built-in projection, and landline videoconferencing. Small meetings often have a thirty-day or less lead-time, thus Sheraton has also expedited the reservation process by targeting meetings of fifteen to forty people that book on short notice.[14]

The Holiday Inn Oceanfront in Ocean City, Maryland, near Washington, DC, has developed a small meeting plan targeted at the many government agencies located in the area. Their "government package" provides a double occupancy room, continental breakfast, meeting room with audiovisual equipment, and morning and afternoon beverage breaks for $79 per person. The set price makes it easy for meeting planners to understand their costs. Simplifying small meeting arrangements is critical because those who plan small meetings are often not meeting planners. The meeting package is available Sunday through Thursday, reserving the weekends for leisure travelers who want to come to the beach.[15]

7.4 Holiday Inn Oceanfront
Sheraton Hotels

Incentive Travel

Incentive travel, a unique subset of corporate group business, is a reward participants receive for achieving or exceeding a goal. Companies give awards for both individual and team performance. For instance, the employees of the best-performing region might be recognized. Because travel serves as the reward, participants must perceive the destination and the hotel as something special. Climate, recreational facilities, and sightseeing opportunities are high on an incentive meeting planners list of attributes looked for in a site.[16] The Caribbean, Hawaii, Europe, and resort destinations within the continental United States are common incentive travel destinations. Incentive trips used to last from three to seven days; however, the current trend is to keep the trips short and get the participants back to their jobs. Most incentive trips last from three to five days. The average expenditure is over $3,000 per person.[17] Winners of incentive trips sometimes receive a cash deposit to their account that can be used for charges to their account or services provided through the hotel, such as rental cars. For example, participants in an incentive trip sponsored by Revlon for the best regional sales performance received a $500 credit on their hotel bill that could be spent as they wished. In such cases the participants spend freely in the hotel's restaurants and bars, often supplementing the credit with their own money. Thus, incentive travel can be very profitable for a hotel.

Incentive travel planners usually determine the budget on a per person basis. It is important for hotel salespeople to recognize that incentive meeting planners work on a per person cost, because certain costs may not be proportional. For example, a meeting room may cost $8 per person for fifty people, but the cost can be reduced to $4 per person for 100 people. Similarly, the entertainment for a gala banquet may cost $2,000—if 100 people attend, this is $20 per person; if 200 attend, the cost is reduced to $10 per person. When the meeting planner is thinking in per person costs, the hotel salesperson must also think in per person costs.[18]

7.5 Society of Incentive Travel Executives

Incentive travel is handled in house or by incentive houses, travel agencies, consultants, and travel fulfillment firms that handle only the travel arrangements. The trend is moving away from in-house planners to incentive houses, fulfillment houses, and travel agencies.[19] One reason for the shift is that outside organizations specializing in incentive travel often buy blocks of airline seats and hotel rooms. As a result, they can put together packages more efficiently than in-house planners. Incentive houses usually provide a choice of several locations to the company, so the ultimate choice of location is made by the company, even when it uses an incentive house. The hotel must work with both the incentive house and the decision makers within the company.

SMERFs

SMERF stands for social, military, educational, religious, and fraternal organizations. On a broader scale, this meeting classification includes smaller specialty organizations that are price sensitive. The majority of the functions sponsored by these organizations are paid for by the individual, and sometimes the fees are not tax deductible. As a result, participants are usually price conscious. They want a low room rate and often find the food and beverage within the hotel too expensive, preferring to eat elsewhere or purchase food and eat in their rooms. Many groups within this category do not make use of the hotel beverage outlets.

On the positive side, SMERFs are willing to be flexible to ensure a lower room rate. They are willing to meet during the off-season or on

The Lygon Arms, part of The Savoy Group, is a distinguished hotel that dates back to 1532. The reputation and prestige of the hotel enable it to attract small incentive groups. Courtesy of The Savoy Group.

weekends. Weekends are often preferred, because most participants attend meetings during their free time. Thus SMERFs provide good filler business during off-peak times.

Segmentation of Group Markets by Purpose of the Meeting

Besides dividing group markets into convention, association, corporate, and SMERF, they also can be broken into the purpose of the meeting. Four major purposes are conventions, conferences, seminars, and meetings. A matrix describing some of the critical sales decision variables for these types of gatherings is given in Table 7-1. This matrix reflects the general nature of sales decision variables within the group market. Exceptions can and do exist. A discussion of major sale segments of the group market follows.

Table 7-1
Decision Variable Matrix—Group Markets

SALES DECISION VARIABLES	CONVENTIONS	CONFERENCES	SEMINARS	MEETINGS
Decision makers	Many: committees, chapter presidents, high-ranking officers	Conference organizer, meeting planner	Seminar organizer, boss, secretary	Boss, secretary, regional manager, meeting planner
Decision influencers	Many	Limited	Limited	Few
Degree of politicalization	Highly political	Somewhat political	Personal	Highly personal
Decision time	Years	One year or less	Months	Short time, sometimes one day
Customer price sensitivity	Very	Somewhat	Somewhat	Not highly sensitive
Personal service sensitivity	Low	Moderate	High	Extreme
Opportunity for upsell	Low	Moderate	Moderate	High
Team selling opportunity	Definitely	Sometimes	Probably not	No
Special advertising promotion	Definitely	Usually no	No	No
International	Definitely	Possible	Probably not	Usually not, but opportunities exist (board of directors)
Repeat sales opportunity	Long time, poor	Moderate time	Yes	Definitely
Need for personal sales call (travel)	Probably yes	Probably no	Probably no	Depends on the situation

Dealing with Meeting Planners

When negotiating with meeting planners, it is important to try to develop a win-win relationship. Meeting planners like to return to the same property. Jim Jones, president of James E. Jones Associates, states, "For me, prior successful experience is the number one factor in choosing a site.

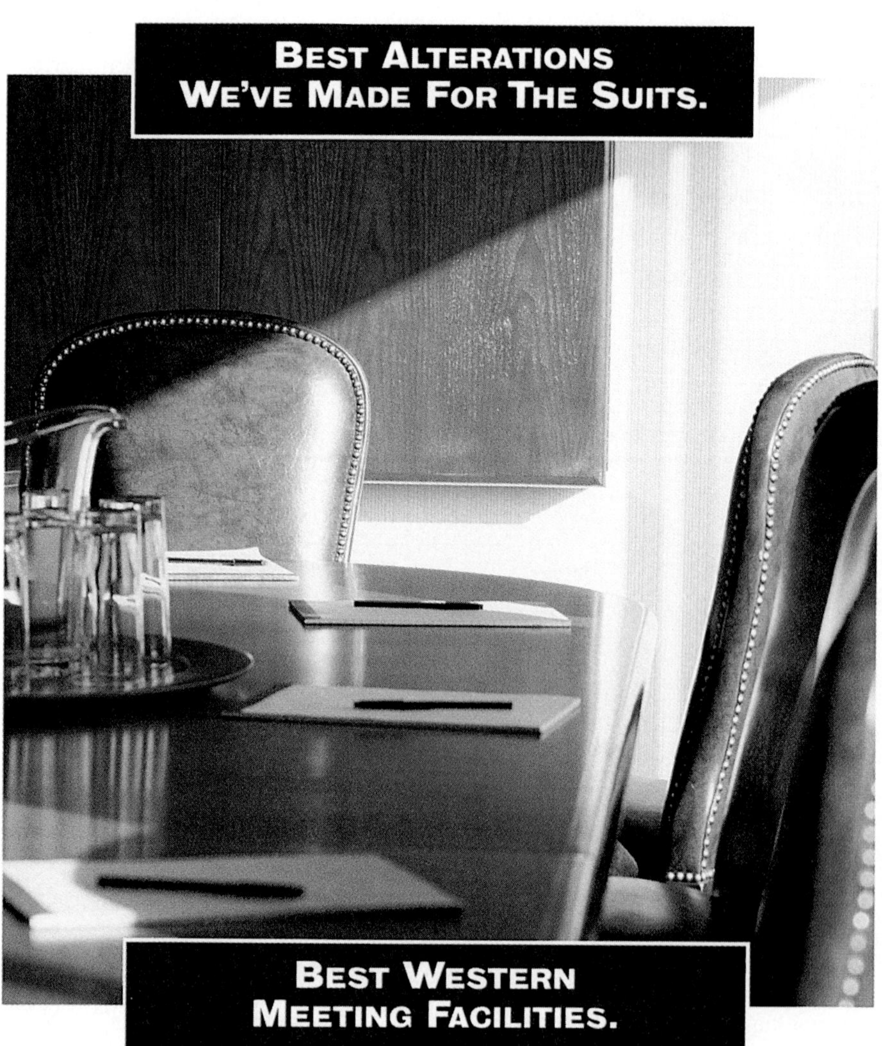

BEST ALTERATIONS
WE'VE MADE FOR THE SUITS.
BEST WESTERN
MEETING FACILITIES.
Best Western is now tailor-made for the business traveler. For starters, we've invested close to a billion and a half dollars upgrading hotels. And we've enacted tougher inspection standards to keep them that way.
There's more that's new too. We've introduced new frequent traveler clubs, a corporate rate program and group rates for meetings and conventions.
And with 3,400 locations in more than 50 countries, you will find we do business wherever your clients do business. Just tell them to look for our brand new sign. It's dark blue with red pinstripes. For more information, call Best Western's First Place Meetings and Conventions Hotline at 1-800-541-8657. For reservations call, 1-800-528-1234.
Best Western
YOUR BEST BET IS A BEST WESTERN.

Not all meetings are large. There are thousands of meetings held with less than 20 attendees. Courtesy of Best Western International, Inc.

Knowing the property takes away most of the anxiety. I know what the hotel can and cannot do, and I know that they're familiar with the idiosyncrasies of my client. I never book a hotel if I plan to use it once."[20]

Discussions over price can drive the meeting planner and the hotel sales executive apart, or they can bring them together. One successful technique for negotiating with a meeting planner is to determine the group's requirements in detail and work out a package based on needs and budget. Some meeting planners try to negotiate every item separately, starting with the room rate. Then they choose a $35 banquet and try to negotiate the price to $25. In this scenario, every line item becomes a point of contention between the meeting planner and the hotel salesperson.

Taking a consultative approach is much more effective. If the hotel knows that the meeting planner wants to spend $25 for dinner, the chef can develop alternatives within this price range, suggesting something the attendees will enjoy, and the hotel can produce at a profit and sell for $25. The hotel gains a profitable meeting, and the meeting stays within the planner's budget. Debra Kaufman, an association meeting planner, states if attendees are able to get work done while they are at the conference they will stay longer.[21] If space is available, the hotel can offer a small meeting room set up with business services, including Internet access, computers, and printers. Given the space is available, this can be a low-cost item to the hotel that has a high value to the meeting planner.

The hotel salesperson must remember that most group rates are noncommissionable. Meeting planners sometimes turn meetings over to travel agents, who book about 5 percent of all corporate meetings. If the meeting planner does so without understanding that the rate is noncommissionable, problems can arise when the travel agent tries to collect a commission. If the rates are to be commissionable, it should be determined during the negotiation process. It is also common for hotels to give one complimentary room-night for every fifty room-nights that the group produces—another point of negotiation. Suites are usually counted as two rooms. Thus a suite for three nights would be the equivalent of six room-nights. When a hotel has a smaller meeting room that it will not be able to sell during a proposed meeting, it can be used in the negotiation process as a boardroom or a space for the meeting manager to work. The hotel salesperson must look for items that will create value for the meeting planner without creating costs or sacrificing revenue for the hotel.

Many associations have a president, elected from the membership, and a professional executive, often called the executive vice president. In such case, the executive vice president usually sets up the meeting or supervises a meeting planner. In larger associations there may be a paid executive director, a convention manager, and one or more meeting managers who handle the association's meetings. In some associations the elected officers also like to get involved in the selection of sites and hotels for meetings or conventions. To further complicate matters, last year's president usually becomes the chairman of the association's board of directors and as such, can hold great power in the association, as can other past presidents. It is important for the salesperson to find out who is involved in the decision-making process, both officially and unofficially. Gatekeepers can give useful insights into the decision-making process within the organization.

A major shift in food and beverage is toward lighter, healthier meals, particularly at lunch. Salad and cold-cut buffets make a nice lunch break. Pasta was once an indicator of a low budget. Today, it is considered a healthy and enjoyable meal. Breaks now include flavored mineral water, yogurt, and fruit, instead of (or in addition to) cookies and brownies. Health clubs have become more important as meeting attendees become more health conscious.

Meeting planners may be divided into three levels of professionalism.[22] The *facilitator* makes up 50 percent to 60 percent of meeting planners. This category includes the secretary who calls the hotel to reserve rooms and the salesperson that is given responsibility for setting up the regional sales meeting. The facilitator usually has other responsibilities in addition to setting meetings. The *meeting manager* is a professional meeting planner. Meeting managers make up about 25 percent of the meeting planners. The *meeting administrator* is a highly qualified meeting planner. Most have advanced degrees and years of experience. Meeting administrators often earn more than $100,000 per year. As you can see, there is a great deal of difference in the level of expertise of those who plan meetings.

When the vice president of sales asks a junior salesperson to organize a sales meeting, the salesperson is usually unsure of how to proceed with newly assigned and unfamiliar tasks. On the other hand, meeting administrators often know the business as well as the hotel salesperson. Salespeople should listen to the meeting administrator to understand their requirements. Sometimes they will know exactly what they want and simply desire a quote for the meeting according to their specifications. If this is the case, a salesperson trying to alter their specifications arbitrarily can appear unprofessional and lose the meeting administrator's business. For example, a hotel salesperson altered the meeting administrator's menu and developed a quotation based on the altered menus. The meeting administrator was planning a series of training sessions to be presented at various locations throughout the United States and had developed menus to meet group needs. This uninvited intrusion by the hotel salesperson infuriated the meeting administrator, who then proceeded to a competitive hotel.

Most meeting planners maintain a history of the group for the purpose of planning future meetings. This includes past dates, locations, and attendance figures. They also have evaluations of past meetings. A salesperson can gain valuable information by asking questions about past conferences. These questions can provide insight into room pickups, attendance at banquets, past problems with a hotel, and what their members have enjoyed. In addition to information volunteered by the meeting planner, the salesperson should interview hotels that hosted the conference in past years.

Consider the following expectations of meeting planners.[23] Meeting planners want their calls returned the same day they are received. When they ask about the availability of meeting space, they expect a response the same day and a complete proposal in five days. They want check-in and checkout to last no more than four minutes. Most meeting planners want their bill within one week of the event, and 25 percent want it within two days. Planners feel that hotel management should empower the convention service manager to solve their problems. They do not want to wait while the convention service manager checks with a superior. The top four amenities desired by meeting planners are nonsmoking rooms, twenty-hour room service, a gift shop, and a fitness center.

7.7 Loews Hotels

Ultimately, when dealing with group business, the hotel has to please both the meeting planner and the meeting planner's clients. These clients include those attending the conference, association executives, and the president or senior officer of a corporation. Jonathan Tisch, president and CEO of Loews Hotel, states, "What we're looking to do is to create a win-win situation. If the senior officer is happy, then the planner's happy, and if the planner's happy, we've done our job."[24]

The Corporate Account and Corporate Travel Manager

A nongroup form of organizational business is the individual business traveler. Most hotels offer a corporate rate, which is intended to provide an incentive for corporations to use the hotel. Because of competitive pressures, most hotels have dropped the qualification requirements for their basic corporate rate, offering it now to any businessperson who requests the corporate rate. To provide an incentive system for heavy users, hotels developed a second set of corporate rates. The basic corporate rate is about 10 percent to 15 percent below the hotel's rack rate;[25] the contract rate is a negotiated rate, usually 10 percent to 40 percent below the hotel's rack rate. It often includes other benefits besides a discounted rate. Common benefits include morning newspapers, upgrades when available, use of the hotel's fitness center, early check-ins, and late checkouts.[26] When negotiating a corporate contract, it is important to understand what creates value for the company.

The corporate business traveler is a sought-after segment. Although the corporate contract rate is a discounted rate, it is higher than the group rate. In addition to paying a good rate, the business traveler is also on an expense account and makes use of the hotel's restaurants, health club, laundry, and business center facilities.

The competition for business travelers, once limited to midclass and luxury hotels, has spread to limited-service hotels. Budget and economy hotels now have a 34.5 percent market share of rooms generated by the business traveler. The strong showing of economy hotels in this segment can be attributed to the upgrading of amenities found in economy hotels and businesses needing to cut costs to remain competitive. Companies that would have not thought of putting their people in an economy brand (two star hotels) a few years ago are now using economy brand hotels. These companies realize that they can save thousands of dollars by purchasing less expensive accommodations.

Larger companies have corporate traveler management programs run by the company or in-house branches of a travel agency. These managers negotiate the corporate hotel contracts. The most important attributes to the travel managers when negotiating a hotel contract are:

- A favorable image of the hotel's brand by the company's travelers
- Guaranteed availability of negotiated rate (Focus groups have told us that a quick way to lose their business is to charge them a higher rate during citywide conventions, or tell them rooms are not available during these conventions.)
- Location
- Reputation of the hotel's brand
- Negotiated rate
- Flexibility on charges for late cancellation of room reservations[27]

In addition to developing corporate hotel contracts, the travel managers set per diem rates, specifying the amount a company traveler can spend on food and beverage. Often, these rates are set at different levels, with the per diem amount increasing as one moves up in the corporation. It is important to find out what a company's per diem rates are to determine whether the hotel is in the company's price range and what level of manager the hotel can expect to attract. The hotel can use this information to determine the volume the company will give them. For example, if the per diem for a company's salespeople is in the hotel's rate range, the hotel can expect more volume than it could expect if only the executive management falls within the price range.

Some corporations use in-house travel agencies, or in-plants, that also represent other corporations, providing the advantage of negotiating leverage. A business represented through an in-plant may have only 100 room-nights a year in New York, but the travel agency represented by the in-plant may service ten companies with a total of 1,500 room-nights in New York. The travel agency can negotiate a rate based on the 1,500 room-nights and pass this rate along to the individual companies. The hotel compensates in-plants by straight commissions, monthly fees, or a combination of a fee and commission.[28]

Key Terms

Buying center All those individuals and groups who participate in the purchasing and decision-making process and who share common goals and the risks arising from the decisions.

Convention A specialty market requiring extensive meeting facilities. It is usually the annual meeting of an association and includes general sessions, committee meetings, and special-interest sessions.

Corporate meeting A meeting held by a corporation for its employees.

Derived demand Organizational demand that ultimately comes from (derives from) the demand for consumer goods.

General need description The stage in the industrial buying process in which a company describes the general characteristics and quantity of a needed item.

Incentive travel A reward participants receive for achieving or exceeding a goal.

Order-routine specification The stage of the industrial buying process in which a buyer writes the final order with the chosen supplier(s), listing the technical specifications, quantity needed, expected time of delivery, return policies, warranties, and so on.

Organizational buying process The decision-making process by which formal organizations establish the need for purchased products and services and identify, evaluate, and choose among alternative brands and suppliers.

Performance review The stage of an industrial buying process in which a buyer rates its satisfaction with suppliers, deciding whether to continue, modify, or drop the relationship.

Problem recognition The stage of the industrial buying process in which someone in a company recognizes a problem or need that can be met by acquiring a good or a service.

Product specification The stage of an industrial buying process in which the buying organization decides on and specifies the best technical product characteristics for a needed item.

SMERF SMERF stands for social, military, educational, religious, and fraternal organizations. This group of specialty markets has a common price-sensitive thread.

Supplier search The stage of the industrial buying process in which a buyer tries to find the best vendor.

Supplier selection The stage of the industrial buying process in which a buyer receives proposals and selects a supplier or suppliers.

Chapter Review

I. **The Nature of Organizational Buyers.** Their purchases often involve large sums of money, complex technical, economic considerations, and interactions among many people at all levels of the organization. Buyer and seller are often very dependent on each other.

II. Participants in the Organizational Buying Process

1) **Users.** Users are those who will use the product or service.

2) **Influencers.** Influencers directly influence the buying decision but do not themselves make the final decision.

3) **Deciders.** Deciders select product requirements and suppliers.

4) **Approvers.** Approvers authorize the proposed actions of deciders or buyers.

5) **Buyers.** Buyers have formal authority for selecting suppliers and arranging the terms of purchase.

6) **Gatekeepers.** Gatekeepers have the power to prevent sellers or information from reaching members of the buying center.

III. Major Influences on Organizational Buyers

1) **Environmental factors.** Organizational buyers are heavily influenced by the current and expected economic environment.

2) **Organizational factors.** Each organization has specific objectives, policies, procedures, organizational structures, and systems related to buying.

3) **Interpersonal factors.** The buying center usually includes several participants with differing levels of interest, authority, and persuasiveness.

4) **Individual factors.** Each participant in the buying decision process has personal motivations, perceptions, and preferences. The participant's age, income, education, professional identification, personality, and attitudes toward risk all influence the participants in the buying process.

IV. The Organizational Buying Process

1) **Problem recognition.** The buying process begins when someone in the company recognizes a problem or need that can be met by acquiring a good or a service.

2) **General need description.** The buyer goes on to determine the requirements of the product.

3) **Product specifications.** Once the general requirements have been determined, the specific requirements for the product can be developed.

4) **Supplier search.** The buyer now tries to identify the most appropriate suppliers.

5) **Proposal solicitation.** Qualified suppliers will be invited to submit proposals. Skilled research, writing, and presentation are required.

6) **Supplier selection.** Once the meeting planner has drawn up a short list of suppliers, qualified hotels will be invited to submit proposals.

7) **Order-routine specification.** The buyer writes the final order, listing the technical specification. The supplier responds by offering the buyer a formal contract.

8) **Performance review.** The buyer does post purchase evaluation of the product. During this phase the buyer will determine if the product meets the buyer's specifications and if the buyer will purchase from the company again.

V. The Group Business Markets

1) **Conventions**. Conventions are usually the annual meeting of an association and include general sessions, committee meetings, and

special-interest sessions. A trade show is often an important part of an annual convention.

2) Association meetings. Associations sponsor many types of meetings, including regional, special-interest, educational, and board meetings.

3) Corporate meetings. A corporate meeting is a command performance for employees of a company. The corporation's major concern is that the meeting be productive and accomplish the company's objectives.

4) Small groups. Meetings of less than fifty rooms are gaining the attention of hotels and hotel chains.

5) Incentive travel. Incentive travel, a unique subset of corporate group business, is a reward participants receive for achieving or exceeding a goal.

6) SMERF groups. SMERF stands for social, military, educational, religious, and fraternal organizations. This group of specialty markets has a common price-sensitive thread.

VI. Dealing with Meeting Planners. When negotiating with meeting planners, it is important to try to develop a win-win relationship. Meeting planners like to return to the same property.

VII. The Corporate Account and Travel Manager. A nongroup form of organizational business is the individual business traveler. Most hotels offer a corporate rate, which is intended to provide an incentive for corporations to use the hotel.

Discussion Questions

1. What is derived demand? Give an example of derived demand for a hotel in your town.
2. The buying center consists of six roles. Why is it important for marketers to understand these roles?
3. Discuss the major environmental influences that affect the purchase meeting space by IBM for its sales meetings.
4. How would a catering sales manager handle a mother and daughter making arrangements for the daughter's wedding differently from a meeting planner from a major corporation wishing to get a quote on a regional sales meeting which she has already done in five other cities?
5. How can a hotel sales representative identify who is responsible for purchasing meeting space, banquets, and rooms for corporate travelers in the corporate headquarters of an insurance company?

Experiential Exercise

Do the following:

Talk with someone who travels for business. Ask them if they can choose their own hotel and airline when they travel for their company. If they can choose their own hotels and airline, ask if they have any restrictions or guidelines. If they are not able to choose their own hotels and airlines, ask if they have any input into where they stay. How would this information help you market travel products to their organization?

Internet Exercise

Support for this exercise can be found on the Web site for *Marketing for Hospitality and Tourism*, www.prenhall.com/kotler.

Go to the Internet site of a travel organization. Do they have a separate section for group or organizational purchases? If so, how does the information in this section differ from their consumer site? If they do not have a separate site, go to another organization until you find one that has a separate site for group or organizational purchases.

References

1. For discussions of similarities and differences in consumer and business marketing, see Edward F. Fern and James R. Brown, "The Industrial/Consumer Marketing Dichotomy: A Case of Insufficient Justification," *Journal of Marketing* (Fall 1984): 68–77; Ron J. Kornakovich, "Consumer Methods Work for Business Marketing: Yes; No," *Marketing News,* November 21, 1988, pp. 4, 13–14.
2. Julie Barker, "The State of the Industry Report." *Successful Meetings* (January 1999): 35–47.
3. Federick E. Webster Jr. and Yoram Wind, *Organizational Buying Behavior* (Upper Saddle River, NJ: Prentice Hall, 1972), pp. 33–37.
4. Ibid., pp. 78–80.
5. See Murray Harding, "Who Really Makes the Purchasing Decision?" *Industrial Marketing* (September 1966): 76. This point of view is further developed in Ernest Dichter, "Industrial Buying Is Based on Same 'Only Human' Emotional Factors That Motivate Consumer Market's Housewife," *Industrial Marketing* (February 1973): 14–16.
6. Webster and Wind, *Organizational Buying Behavior.*
7. Patrick J. Robinson, Charles W. Faris, and Yoram Wind, *Industrial Buying Behavior and Creative Marketing* (Needham Heights, MA: Allyn and Bacon, 1967), p. 14.
8. Sarah J. F. Braley, "The Big Picture," *Meetings & Conventions* (October 1998): 2–35.
9. Larry Letich, "Let's Make a Deal," *Meeting and Conventions Meeting Market Report,* March 1, 1992, p. 123.
10. Barker, "The State of the Industry Report," pp. 35–47.
11. Ibid.
12. Ibid; See also Braley, "The Big Picture," pp. 2–35.
13. Amy Drew Teitler, "Getting Personal," retrieved from the World Wide Web on November 12, 2001, *http://www.meetings-conventions.com/issues/0100/features/feature3.html.*
14. The World of Sheraton, "Meeting Services, Smart Meetings," retrieved from the World Wide Web on November 12, 2001, *http://www.starwood.com/sheraton/meetings/smart_meetings.html;* See also Braley, "The Big Picture," pp. 2–35.
15. Holiday Inn, "Government Package," retrieved from the World Wide Web on November 12, 2001, *http://www.ocmdhotels.com/holidayinn/meetings.html.*
16. Braley, "The Big Picture," pp. 2–35.
17. "Corporate Meetings and Incentives," *Annual Incentive Trends* (January 1997): 26–30. See also Barker, "The State of the Industry Report," pp. 35–47.
18. Margaret Shaw, *The Group Market: What It Is and How to Sell It* (Washington, DC: Foundation of the Hotel Sales and Marketing Association, 1986), pp. 45–49.
19. Penny C. Dotson, *Introduction to Meeting Management* (Birmingham, AL: Professional Convention Management Association), p. 17.

20. Letich, "Let's Make a Deal," p. 127.
21. Barker, "The State of the Industry Report," pp. 35–47
22. Richard A. Hildreth, *The Essentials of Meeting Management* (Upper Saddle River, NJ: Prentice Hall, 1990).
23. Howard Feiertag, "New Survey Reveals Meeting Planners' Priorities," *Hotel and Motel Management,* November 23, 1992, p. 11.
24. James P. Abbey, *Hospitality Sales and Advertising* (East Lansing, MI: Educational Institute of the American Hotel and Motel Association, 1993), p. 569.
25. Lisa Casey Weiss, "How Different Hotel Rate Programs Stack Up," *Business Travel News,* July 26, 1993, pp. 9–16.
26. Days Inn, retrieved April 20, 2000 from the World Wide Web: *http://www.daysins.com/ctg/cgi-bin/DaysInn/inncentives/AAAksrACwAAAANxAAO.*
27. Weiss, "How Different Hotel Rate Programs Stack Up," pp. 9–16.
28. Robert Lewis and Richard E. Chambers, *Marketing Leadership in Hospitality; Foundations and Practices* (New York: John Wiley and Sons, Inc., 2000).

8 Market Segmentation, Targeting, and Positioning

The mythological homogeneous America is gone.
We are a mosaic of minorities.
Joel Weiner

In 1972, the Mardi Gras, *an old transatlantic cruise ship, went on its maiden voyage for Carnival Cruise Lines. Carnival was hosting 300 travel agents on the* Mardi Gras, *hoping to set up a distribution network that would fill up its cruises in the coming years. The* Mardi Gras *ran aground, sinking the hopes of its owners. It was not until 1975 that the ship sailed again. Ted Arison, a founder of Norwegian Cruise Lines, purchased Carnival for $1, assumed the company's debt, and quickly turned it into a profitable venture.*

The tired Mardi Gras *could not compete directly with the luxury cruise liners of Royal Viking, Holland America, Princess, Sitmar, Royal Caribbean, and Norwegian Caribbean Lines. The* Mardi Gras *was older and less efficient than its competition. To reduce fuel consumption, the ship had to operate at slower speeds, making fewer port calls than liners owned by competitors. Arison was able to convert this obstacle into a new approach for marketing cruises. Instead of promoting exotic ports of call, his company created the idea of the "fun ship" and promoted it. The fun ship had nightclubs, a casino, shows, twenty-four-hour room service, and enough activities to keep passengers busy. The ship itself became the destination. Carnival also went after less sophisticated first-time cruise passengers, forging a new market segment that included families with household incomes of $25,000 to $35,000. While other cruise lines competed for the older, more sophisticated market, with incomes of $50,000 plus, Carnival brought cruising to the blue-collar market. Its three- and four-day cruises allowed the first-time passenger to try cruising without spending a great deal of time or money.*

Carnival had identified a new market for cruises. Recognizing that only 5 percent of the population had at that time taken a cruise, Carnival went after the segment that the other cruise lines were ignoring—the middle and lower-middle class. Carnival positioned itself as a destination vacation, competing against other vacation spots, such as Disneyland or Hawaii, rather than other cruise lines. Carnival defined its market as the 150 million people who take vacations, rather than the 10 million people who take cruises. Today, Carnival's biggest competitors are Las Vegas and Disney World.

Once Carnival dominated the younger age market segment, they realized that as their customers grew older and wanted a different style of cruise they had nothing to offer them. Carnival Corporation, the parent company of Carnival Cruise Lines, has purchased other cruise lines to expand its market base. They have elected to operate the cruise lines as independent brands, with each brand being strong in a particular target market. Their latest acquisition was Costa Cruises in 1997. Costa is Europe's number one cruise line and is renowned for its excellent food and service provided by its Italian crews. Another acquisition was Holland American, a deluxe cruise line with an excellent reputation for food and service that has a clientele with an average age of 55. In the luxury end, Carnival purchased Seabourn, a cruise line of three 200-passenger ships featuring a yacht-like experience and personal service. For the more adventurous, Carnival formed Windstar Cruises by acquiring a 148-passenger sail-cruise ship that visits exotic ports such as Tahiti, Costa Rica, and the yacht harbors of the Caribbean.

The Carnival brand is undergoing rapid expansion. Carnival has added at least one new ship since 1998, with three ships added in 2002. Carnival is also changing with the times. As more families travel, they are expanding their Camp Carnival program and providing alternative dining such a pizza restaurant aimed at families and children. Earlier in the book, we mentioned that families are taking shorter vacations; Carnival has responded by adding more under-seven-day cruises. Today about half of Carnival's 2 million-plus passengers opt for a cruise of five days or less. Along with shorter cruises, Carnival is now sailing from sixteen ports in the United States, making it easier for vacationers to get to their cruise ships.

Bob Dickinson, president of Carnival Cruises, states most vacation products use demographic segmentation, while Carnival uses psychographic segmentation. Passengers that fit Carnival's psychographic profile are vacationers that travel to Orlando, Las Vegas, and all-inclusive resorts. It is an excellent example of a hospitality company that understands and uses market segmentation. By identifying a market opportunity and targeting a segment that the competition had neglected, Carnival was able to grow into the largest cruise line in the world. Carnival used the profits and expertise gained from serving this segment to acquire other cruise lines that serve different segments. Carnival continues to refine its segmentation strategy and is now using one of the most sophisticated types of segmentation, psychographics. Carnival has a good understanding of who its customers are and what they want. It is continually refining its product to provide the activities and amenities its passengers want.[1]

Chapter Objectives

After reading this chapter, you should be able to:

1. Explain market segmentation, and identify several possible bases for segmenting consumer markets, business markets, and international markets.
2. List and distinguish among the requirements for effective segmentation: measurability, accessibility, substantiality, and actionability.
3. Outline the process of evaluating market segments, and suggest some methods for selecting market segments.
4. Illustrate the concept of positioning for competitive advantage by offering specific examples.
5. Discuss choosing and implementing a positioning strategy, and contrast positioning based on product, service, personnel, and image differentiation.

8.1 Carnival Cruises

MARKETS

8.2 McDonald's
Burger King
Kentucky Fried Chicken

The term *market* has acquired many meanings over the years. In its original meaning, a market was a physical place where buyers and sellers gathered to exchange goods and services. To an economist, a market is all the buyers and sellers who transact for a good or service. Thus the fast-food market consists of many sellers, such as Burger King, McDonald's, and Kentucky Fried Chicken, and all the consumers who buy fast-food meals. To a marketer, a market is the set of all actual and potential buyers of a product.

Organizations that sell to consumers and industrial markets recognize that they cannot appeal to all buyers in those markets or at least not to all buyers in the same way. Buyers are too numerous, widely scattered, and varied in their needs and buying practices.

Sellers have not always practiced this philosophy. Their thinking passed through three stages:

1. **Mass marketing.** In mass marketing, the seller mass produces, mass distributes, and mass promotes one product to all buyers. At one time McDonald's produced only one size of hamburger for the entire market, hoping it would appeal to everyone. The argument for mass marketing is that it should lead to the lowest costs and prices and create the largest potential market.
2. **Product-variety marketing.** Here the seller produces two or more products that have different features, styles, quality, sizes, and so on. Today, McDonald's offers regular hamburgers, Big Macs, and quarter pounders. The product line is designed to offer variety to buyers rather than to appeal to different market segments. The argument for product-variety marketing is that consumers have different tastes that vary over time. Consumers seek variety and change.

3. **Target marketing.** Here the seller identifies market segments, selects one or more, and develops products and marketing mixes tailored to each selected segment. For example, McDonald's developed its salad line to meet the needs of diet-conscious diners.

Today, many companies are moving away from mass marketing and product-variety marketing toward target marketing. Target marketing helps sellers to find better marketing opportunities and allows companies to develop the right product for each target market. Companies can adjust their process, distribution channels, and advertising to reach each market efficiently. Instead of scattering their marketing efforts (the "shotgun" approach), they can focus on buyers who have the greatest purchase interest (the "rifle" approach).

As a result of increasing fragmentation of U.S. mass markets into hundreds of micromarkets, each with different needs and lifestyles, target marketing is increasingly taking the form of **micromarketing.** Using micromarketing, companies tailor their marketing programs to the needs and wants of narrowly defined geographic, demographic, psychographic, or behavior segments. The ultimate form of target marketing is **customized marketing,** in which the company adapts its offers to the needs of specific customers or buying organizations.

Figure 8-1 shows the three major steps in target marketing. The first is **market segmentation,** dividing a market into distinct groups of buyers who might require separate products and/or marketing mixes. The company identifies different ways to segment the market and develops profiles of the resulting market segments. The second step is **market targeting,** evaluating each segment's attractiveness and selecting one or more of the market segments. The third step is **market positioning,** developing a competitive positioning for the product and an appropriate marketing mix. We also describe the principles of market segmentation, market targeting, and market positioning.

Market Segmentation

Markets consist of buyers, and buyers differ in one or more ways. They may differ in their wants, resources, locations, buying attitudes, and buying practices. Because buyers have unique needs and wants, each buyer is potentially a separate market. Ideally, then, a seller might design a separate marketing program for each buyer. For example, a caterer can customize the menu, entertainment, and the setting to meet the needs of a

Figure 8-1
Steps in segmentation, targeting, and positioning.

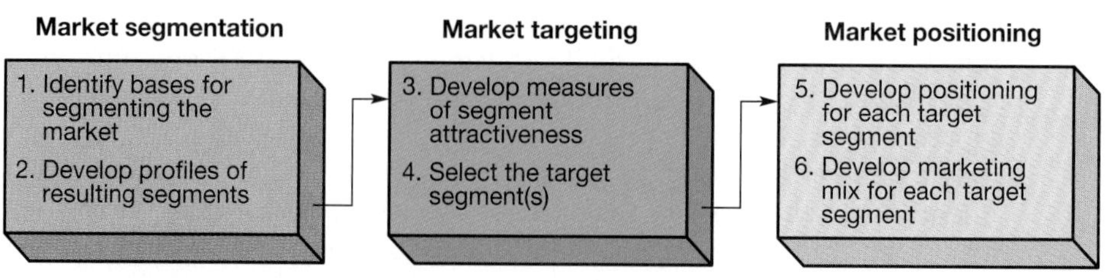

specific client. However, most companies are unable to offer complete segmentation. The cost of complete segmentation is high, and most customers cannot afford completely customized products. Companies therefore look for broad classes of buyers who differ in their product needs or buying responses. For example, married adults who vacation with small children have different needs and wants than vacationing young single adults. Thus, Club Med has developed resorts for families and resorts for couples without children.

The restaurant industry offers many examples of segmentation by a variety of variables.

> Because each customer group in an eating-out market will want a different product, a restaurant cannot reach out to all customers with equal effectiveness. The restaurant must distinguish the easily accessible consumer groups from those that are hard to reach and the responsive segments from the unresponsive ones. To gain an edge over its competition, a restaurant must examine market segments by identifying one or more subsets of customers within the total market and concentrating its efforts on meeting their needs.[2]

There is no single way to segment a market. A marketer has to try different segmentation variables, alone and in combination, hoping to find the best way to view the market structure. Table 8-1 outlines major variables that might be used in segmenting consumer markets. Here we look at the major geographic, demographic, psychographic, and behavioristic variables used in segmenting consumer markets.

Geographic Segmentation

Geographic segmentation calls for dividing the market into different geographic units, such as nations, states, regions, counties, cities, or neighborhoods. A company decides to operate in one or a few geographic areas or to operate in all, paying attention to geographic differences in needs and wants. For example, General Foods's Maxwell House ground coffee is sold nationally but is flavored regionally. People in the west want stronger coffee than people in the east. Fast-food companies often vary their menus to take regional tastes into account. For example, McDonald's introduced a Texas Burger, a large burger with lettuce, tomato, and the condiments of choice for many Texans: pickles and mustard. One local Texas chain, Whataburger, had been providing Texans successfully with a good pickle and mustard burger. Recognizing the importance of this regional variation, McDonald's developed and introduced a new product for this market.

Within the United States, national fast-food chains such as Burger King, Taco Bell, Wendy's, and McDonald's exist. Despite this powerful competition, a rich variety of regional or local chains continues to thrive, such as Biscuitville, Bojangles, Uncle John Tacos, and the Waffle House. Some may have the potential for national expansion, but others serving regional tastes may find it difficult to reach a national market.

8.3 Wendy's
Taco Bell
Waffle House
Holiday Inn
Motel 8

Lodging companies also begin as local or regional firms but seem to have greater flexibility in national expansion. Holiday Inn began as a

Table 8-1
Major Segmentation Variables for Consumer Markets

VARIABLE	TYPICAL BREAKDOWN
Geographic	
Region	Pacific, Mountain, West North Central, West South Central, East North Central, East South Central, South Atlantic, Middle Atlantic, New England
City or metro size	Under 5,000; 5,000–20,000; 20,000–50,000; 50,000–100,000; 100,000–250,000; 250,000–500,000; 500,000–1,000,000; 1,000,000–4,000,000; 4,000,000 or over
Density	Urban, suburban, rural
Climate	Northern, southern
Demographic	
Age	Under 6, 6–11, 12–19, 20–34, 35–49, 50–64, 65 or over
Gender	Male, female
Family size	1–2, 3–4, 5 or more
Family life cycle	Young, single; young, married, no children; young, married, youngest child under 6; young, married, youngest child 6 or over; older, married, with children; older, married, no children under 18; older, single; other
Income	Under $10,000; $10,000–$15,000; $15,000–$20,000; $20,000–$30,000; $30,000–$50,000; $50,000–$100,000; $100,000 and over
Occupation	Professional and technical; managers, officials, and proprietors; clerical, sales; craftspeople, foremen; operatives; farmers; retired; students; housewives; unemployed
Education	Grade school or less; some high school; high school graduate; some college; college graduate
Religion	Catholic, Protestant, Jewish, Muslim, Hindu, other
Race	White, Black, Asian, other
Nationality	American, British, French, German, Italian, Japanese
Psychographic	
Social class	Lower-lower class, upper-lower class, working class, middle class, upper-middle class, lower-upper class, upper-upper class
Lifestyle	Straights, swingers, longhairs
Personality	Compulsive, gregarious, authoritarian, ambitious

Table 8-1
Major Segmentation Variables for Consumer Markets (*cont'd*)

VARIABLE	TYPICAL BREAKDOWN
Behavioral	
Occasions	Regular occasion, special occasion
Benefits	Quality, service, economy, speed
User status	Nonuser, ex-user, potential user, first-time user, regular user
Usage rate	Light user, medium user, heavy user
Loyalty status	None, medium, strong, absolute
Readiness stage	Unaware, aware, informed, interested, desirous, intending to buy
Attitude toward product	Enthusiastic, positive, indifferent, negative, hostile

regional motel company out of Memphis, Tennessee. Motel 8 began in Aberdeen, South Dakota, with original appeal to the midwestern and western market, but expanded well beyond regional boundaries.

Hyatt Hotels recognized the need to modify its product line to meet regional needs. Hyatt initiated a program to offer regional dishes on its menus. The Four Seasons Hotel in Washington, DC, became so concerned about offering local cuisine that it contracted with nearby farmers to ensure a supply of local products that were not always available from traditional wholesale vendors.[3]

Demographic Segmentation

Demographic segmentation consists of dividing the market into groups based on demographic variables such as age and life cycle, gender, income, occupation, education, religion, race, and nationality. Demographic factors are the most popular bases for segmenting customer groups. One reason is that consumer needs, wants, and use rates often vary closely with demographic variables. Another is that demographic variables are easier to measure than most other types of variables. Even when market segments are first defined using other bases, such as personality or behavior, demographic characteristics must be known to assess the size of the target market and to reach it efficiently. Now we show you how certain demographic factors have been used in market segmentation.

Age and Life-Cycle Stage

Consumer needs and wants change with age. Some companies offer different products or marketing strategies to penetrate various age and life-cycle segments. For example, McDonald's offers Happy Meals that include toys, aimed at young children. These toys are often part of a series, encouraging children to return until they have collected the entire set. The chain has added salads to attract the health-conscious adult market. Appeals to the senior-citizen market have employed advertisements with elderly actors.[4]

Marketing Highlight 8-1

Jollibee: A Regional Fast Food Chain

When someone says "fast-food restaurant," what's the first name that comes to mind? Chances are good that it's McDonald's, the world's largest food service organization. McDonald's holds a more than 40 percent share of the U.S. fast-food burger market, many times the share of its nearest competitor, Burger King, and is rapidly expanding its worldwide presence. Ask the question in the Philippines, however, and the first name uttered likely will be Jollibee. That's right, Jollibee. In the grand scheme of global commerce, Jollibee Foods Corporation isn't exactly a household name. But by focusing on its region, the Philippines, Jollibee has been able to become the king of the burger market.

At first glance, the rivalry between Jollibee and McDonald's looks like no contest. McDonald's has more than 24,500 outlets in 116 countries, 2,735 of them in Asia alone, and nearly $36 billion in annual systemwide sales. By comparison, Jollibee has fewer than 250 restaurants, contributing about $350 million in annual revenues. Its sales equal only a fraction of the $1 billion or more that McDonald's spends annually just on U.S. advertising. Despite these lopsided numbers, in the Philippines, small Jollibee is giving giant McDonald's more competition than it can handle. Jollibee captured a 75 percent share of the Philippines's hamburger chain market and 53 percent of the fast-food market as a whole. Its sales are growing rapidly and profitably. "Jollibee is one of only two or three examples in the world of a fast-food company that is able to compete with McDonald's," comments an industry analyst.

What's Jollibee's secret? Smart niching. Whereas McDonald's exports largely standardized fare to consumers around the world, Jollibee is relentlessly local—it concentrates on serving the unique tastes of Filipino consumers. In many ways Jollibee's operations mirror those of McDonald's. Both offer cleanliness. fast service, and convenient locations. Jollibee's Champ burger competes with the Big Mac and its peach-mango pie replicates McDonald's apple version. However, in contrast to the fairly bland fare that McDonald's serves so successfully worldwide, Jollibee's menu and flavors are specially suited to Filipino tastes. The local chain cooks up sweet, spicy burgers and serves seasoned chicken and spaghetti with sweet sauce, the way Filipinos like it. It serves these meals with rice or noodles, not French fries. "We've designed these products, which are really all-American delights, to suit the Filipino palate," says Jollibee's marketing vice president. Some items, however, are uniquely Filipino. For example, Jollibee's Palabok Fiesta meal, featuring noodles with fish and shrimp, is very popular in the Philippines, but probably would not fare as well with American consumers.

8.4 Marriott
Hyatt
Southwest

American Express focuses much of its marketing attention on the "mature" market as individuals in this age segment account for 70 percent of the tour industry's bookings. Historic restorations such as Williamsburg and Old Salem receive a large percentage of elderly bus tours. The entire museum and historic sites industry depends heavily on this market segment.

Although most older adults will never enter a nursing home, Deborah Fine Freundlich reports in *Retirement Living Communities* that 12 percent of people over sixty-five, 37 percent of people over seventy-five, and 70 percent of people over eighty-five will need assistance with transportation, shopping, housekeeping, meal preparation, and medications. Companies such as Marriott and Hyatt have developed senior living centers to meet the needs of this market segment. In their communities people can purchase homes, or they can have assisted-living facilities that offer daily assistance but not continuous nursing care. One of the popular

Beyond its special understanding of the Filipino palate, Jollibee has also mastered the country's culture and lifestyle. "What happens in the normal Filipino family is that weekends are especially for children," notes a Philippines business analyst, "and parents try to ask their children where they want to eat." Jollibee lures kids with in-store play activities and a cast of captivating characters. Its hamburger-headed Champ, complete with boxing gloves, goes head-to-head with McDonald's Hamburger. Its massive orange-jacketed bee and a blond spaghetti-haired girl named Hetti are better known and loved in the Philippines than Ronald McDonald.

Jollibee has some additional advantages in this seemingly unfair rivalry. Although much smaller in global terms than McDonald's, Jollibee concentrates most of its limited resources within the Philippines, where its restaurants outnumber McDonald's two to one. It also receives a measure of protection through government regulations that limit McDonald's and other foreign competitors. But its primary advantage comes from simply doing a better job of giving Filipino consumers what they want. Small can be beautiful, and Jollibee has shown that through smart niching small players can compete effectively against industry giants.

In an effort to conquer Jollibee's niche, McDonald's is launching a comeback. It's rapidly adding new locations and introducing its own Filipino-style dishes—spicy fried chicken with rice, sweet-tasting spaghetti, and a heavily seasoned burger called the McDo. However, Jollibee managers don't seem overly worried about their rival's new moves. McDonald's may have greater universal appeal, but Jollibee knows its niche. "Maybe they'll gain market share," says Jollibee's chief executive, "but I don't think anybody can beat us out because, in the final analysis, the customer is the one deciding." For most Filipinos, the choice is clear. Notes the business analyst, "The Jollibee burger is similar to what a Filipino mother would cook at home."

Sources: Quotes from Hugh Filman, "Happy Meals for McDonald's Rival," *Business Week,* July 29, 1996, p. 77; Cris Prystay and Sanjay Kumar, "Asia Bites Back," *Asian Business* (January 1997): 58–60; and Dominic Jones and Nicholas Bradbury, "Blue Chips of the Future," *Euromoney* (December 1998): 99–102. Also see Andrew Tanzer, "Bee Bites Clown," *Forbes,* October 20, 1997, pp. 182–183; David Leonhardt, "McDonald's: Can It Regain Its Golden Touch?" *Business Week,* March 9, 1998, pp. 70–77; Rogoberto Tiglao, "Hamburger Heaven," *Far Eastern Economic Review,* December 31, 1999, pp. 76–78; and James Leung and Tony Jordan, "AMAC: Asia's Most Admired Companies," *Asian Business* (May 1999): 24–32.

amenities of these communities is the dining hall. Food sales alone in the life-care segment amount over $2.5 billion.[5]

Age and life-cycle variables can be misleading. For example, the Ford Motor Company used buyers' age in developing the target market for its initial Mustang automobile. But when Ford found that the car was being purchased by all age groups, it realized that its target market was not the physiologically young but the *psychologically* young. Similarly, Southwest Airlines realized that many senior citizens are psychologically young. Their advertisements for senior fares show active older people enjoying themselves.

Gender

Gender segmentation has long been used in marketing clothing, hairdressing, cosmetics, and magazines. It is just beginning to be used in the

Marketing Highlight 8-2

Targeting Families by Targeting Kids

Friendly's is a casual restaurant originally known for its ice cream. Scott Colwell, Friendly's vice president of marketing, said, "We were known for sandwiches and ice cream, but not somewhere where a family would go for dinner." He wanted to reposition the restaurant as a place where customers would go for lunch and dinner. Research had shown that when determining where a family will eat, kids have a major influence. In fact children influenced over $110 billion in restaurant spending last year. Families with children account for 56 percent of all dollars spent on food away from home. Colwell also realized that parents were pressed for time, and often felt guilty about not spending more time with their children. If he could make a dining experience that the children would enjoy, the family would have fun together, and everyone would be a winner.

To find out what would make a good dining experience, Colwell held focus groups with children. One of the things that came out of the focus groups was that children wanted "real" menus, like their parents' menus. They didn't want placemat menus. The kids also told them what kind of food they wanted, and how they wanted it presented. Besides talking to kids it is also useful to talk to their parents. At the Kids' Marketing Conference, parents told restaurant managers that comfortable seating was important, because kids squirm in hard seats. They also said they did not like play areas in sit-down service restaurants; they want to be with their kids. They also expect more nutritious meals in a sit-down service restaurant than they do in a fast-food restaurant.

Friendly's put a kids coordinator on each shift, to make sure the wants of the children were met. Parents mentioned having servers that can deal with kids as being important. According to image research done before and after the program, Friendly's effort to reposition as a family restaurant was successful, as their image as a good place for kids jumped 50 percent. Notice how Friendly's used marketing research to find out about the market it wanted to target. The marketing information it gathered helped it understand the consumer behavior of the family market, namely, kids played a major role in where the family dined. Knowing this, Friendly's created a program to become a place where children would want to come.

Sources: "Family Friendly," *Restaurant Hospitality* (June 1998): 48; Katie Smith, "Kiddin' Around," *Restaurant Hospitality* (April 2001): 52–64.

hotel industry. In 1970, women accounted for less than 1 percent of all business travelers. Currently, that figure stands at about 40 percent.[6] Hotel corporations are now taking women into consideration in designing their hotel rooms. Design changes include lobby bars, fitness facilities, hair dryers, and rooms decorated in lighter colors. Although these changes are attractive to women, many are also attractive to men. Hotel corporations are also subtly including more women executives in their advertisements.[7]

Researchers at the University of Guelph reported another difference in consumer behavior based on gender. They discovered single women living in the city are more likely than single males or married couples to increase their spending on restaurants when they received a salary increase.[8]

Income

Income segmentation has long been used by marketers of products and services such as automobiles, boats, clothing, cosmetics, and travel. Other industries have also recognized its possibilities. For example, Suntory, a Japanese liquor company, introduced a scotch selling for $75 to attract high-income drinkers who want the very best. Country clubs often use income to identify potential members for their direct-mail campaigns.

Income does not always predict which customers will buy a given product or service. Some upscale urban restaurateurs opened branches in upper-middle-class suburbs. They were attracted by high suburban household incomes. But many had to close their doors. Why? Urban dwellers tend to be singles and couples without children. A large portion of their income is discretionary, and their lifestyle includes frequent dining out. According to the National Restaurant Association, singles spend more than half of their food budget dining out, whereas married couples spend only 37% of their food budget eating out.[9] Suburbanites spend their money on housing, automobiles, and children. Dining out is reserved for weekends and special occasions. Thus, income alone can be misleading as a segmentation variable.

8.5 St. Moritz On-the-Park Hotel

Income segmentation is commonly believed to be one of the primary variables affecting pricing strategies. Price is not solely determined by income, but there is often a close correlation. The St. Moritz On-the-Park Hotel in New York City has combined income and geographic segmentation variables. This hotel charges rates at least half those charged by competitors and appeals heavily to middle-income international travelers.[10]

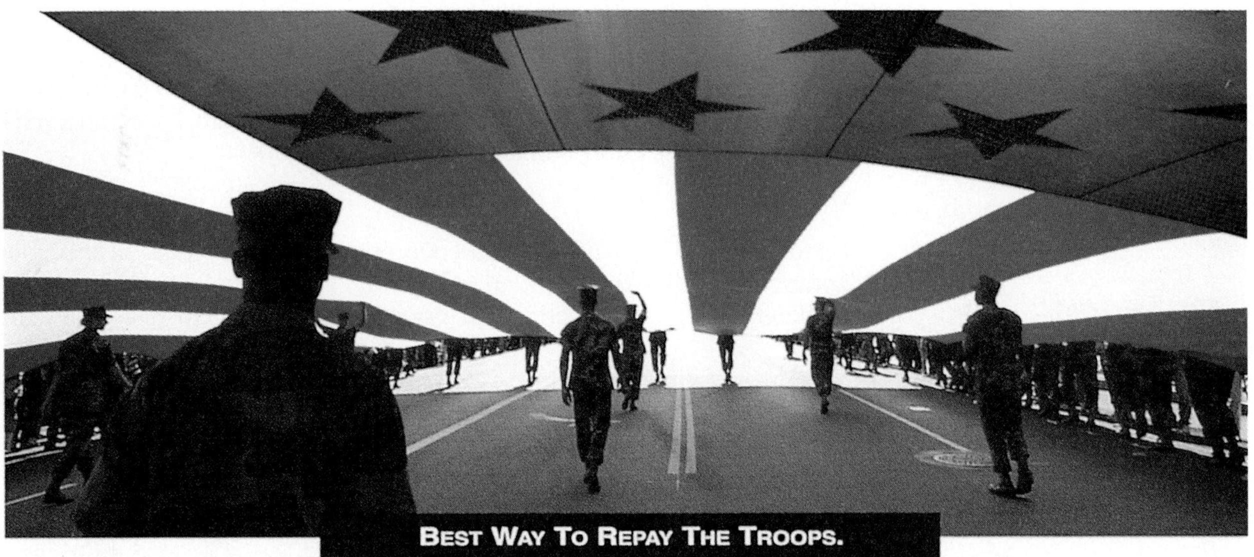

BEST WAY TO REPAY THE TROOPS.
Here's a benefit your recruiter didn't tell you about. Best Western gives special rates and packages to military personnel. That means you can get a great night's sleep without surrendering your entire per diem. And you'll find all our locations will pass your inspection. We've spent more than a billion dollars upgrading properties and our tough new standards keep them shipshape.
There are more than 3,400 Best Westerns from the halls of Montezuma to just outside the base. YOUR BEST BET IS A BEST WESTERN.
Best Western
CALL 1-800-528-1234 FOR RESERVATIONS OR A FREE BEST WESTERN GOVERNMENT RATE DIRECTORY.
© 1994 Best Western International, Inc.

The U.S. military gets a daily travel allowance called a per diem. The amount of the per diem not spent on lodging can be spent on food and entertainment or saved. Hotels targeting this market offer special military rates. Courtesy of Best Western International.

A study of Singapore hotels showed that income was not as strong a segmentation variable as purpose of the visit.[11] This demonstrates the importance of studying and clearly understanding the relative importance of segmentation variables on a market-by-market approach. It is very dangerous to assume that income or any other segmentation variable will be of equal importance in all markets.

Psychographic Segmentation

Psychographic segmentation divides buyers into different groups based on social class, lifestyle, and personality characteristics. People in the same demographic group can have very different psychographic profiles.

The Claire Tappan Lodge near the Sugar Bowl ski area on the northern shore of Donner Lake was built by the Sierra Club in the 1930s. This lodge appeals to individuals within a common psychographic segment. Guests represent varying ages and income brackets, but all have a common interest in seminars hosted by this cozy lodge, on topics such as outdoor photography, orienteering, and nature.

Social Class

8.6 Ritz Carlton

In Chapter 6 we described the six American social classes and explained that social class has a strong effect on preferences for cars, clothes, home furnishings, leisure activities, reading habits, and retailers. Afternoon tea at the Ritz-Carlton is aimed at the upper-middle and upper classes. A neighborhood pub near a factory targets the working class. The customers of each of these establishments would probably feel uncomfortable in the other establishment.

Lifestyle

Chapter 6 also showed the influence of people's lifestyles on the goods and services that they buy. Marketers are increasingly segmenting their markets by consumer lifestyles. For example, nightclubs are designed

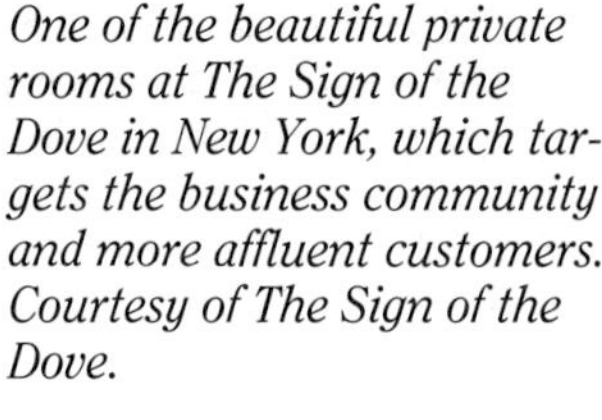

One of the beautiful private rooms at The Sign of the Dove in New York, which targets the business community and more affluent customers. Courtesy of The Sign of the Dove.

with certain clientele in mind: young singles wanting to meet the opposite sex, singles wanting to meet the same sex, and couples wanting to avoid singles bars and enjoy each other's company.

Personality

Marketers also use personality variables to segment markets, endowing their products with personalities that correspond with those of consumers. For example, Southwest Airlines developed a promotion showing seniors having fun scooting around on snowmobiles. The setting of the ad would have been just as appropriate for 20-year-olds. Southwest was appealing to active seniors, who still viewed themselves as young. The airline was appealing to the kid inside all adults.

Behavioral Segmentation

In **behavioral segmentation,** buyers are divided into groups based on their knowledge, attitude, use, or response to a product. Many marketers believe that behavior variables are the best starting point for building market segments.

Occasions

Buyers can be grouped according to occasions when they get the idea, make the purchase, or use a product. Occasion segmentation helps firms to build product use. For example, air travel is triggered by occasions related to business, vacation, or family. Airline advertisements aimed at the business traveler often incorporate service, convenience, and on-time-departure benefits in the offer. Airline marketing aimed at the vacation traveler utilizes price, interesting destinations, and prepackaged vacations. Airline marketing aimed at the family market often shows children traveling alone to visit a relative, under the watchful eye of an airline employee. A message of this nature is particularly relevant to the single-parent segment.

Occasion segmentation can help firms to build product use. For example, Mother's Day has been promoted as a time to take your mother or wife out to eat. St. Patrick's Day has been promoted as a night of celebration. Monday holidays, such as Labor Day and Memorial Day, have been promoted as times to enjoy a minivacation. These are examples of occasion marketing.

The honeymoon market represents an occasion with excellent potential for the hospitality industry. In many cultures, the honeymoon trip is paid for by parents or other family members. As a gift, the honeymoon package may contain upscale products and services such as a hotel suite and first-class airfare.

Some hotels, such as those in the Pocono Mountains of Pennsylvania, specialize in the honeymoon market. In some cases, rooms are equipped with heart-shaped beds and champagne glass–shaped spas. The Japanese honeymoon market is particularly important to the hospitality industry of Guam, Hawaii, New Zealand, and Australia. Group honeymoon tours have proved to be successful, in which several Japanese newlyweds participate in a tour of one or more destinations.

8.7 Double Tree Hotel

One of the most unusual examples of occasion segmentation is the "Room at the Inn" program offered by Doubletree Hotels of Canadian Pacific Hotels and Resorts. Doubletree offers free short-term lodging for travelers needing emergency lodging between Thanksgiving and Christmas. These are persons who travel to visit loved ones undergoing emergency medical treatment. Local hospitals, the Red Cross, and United Way provide referrals of eligible guests.

Benefits Sought

Buyers can also be grouped according to the product benefits they seek. After studying patrons and nonpatrons of three types of restaurants—family popular, atmosphere, and gourmet—one researcher concluded that there are five major appeal categories for restaurant customers.[12] The relative importance of food quality, menu variety, price, atmosphere, and convenience factors across each group was studied. It was found that patrons of family service restaurants sought convenience and menu. Variety patrons of atmosphere restaurants ranked food quality and atmosphere as the top attributes. Patrons of gourmet restaurants valued quality.

Knowing the benefits sought by customers is useful in two ways. First, managers can develop products with features that provide the benefits their customers are seeking. Second, managers communicate more effectively with their customers if they know what benefits they seek. For example, some hotel customers like the benefit of feeling refreshed after exercising in a health club. Thus, they will seek out hotels that have health clubs. Other guests do not value exercising. To these guests the health club will not add value to their hotel stay. Thus, a benefit is a positive outcome received from a product feature. Those product features that create positive outcomes for guests create value. Those features that create no positive outcomes for the guest will have no value. By understanding what benefits a customer is seeking marketers can communicate to the guest about features that will create the desired benefits. They can also develop product that will create benefits customers are seeking.

User Status

Many markets can be segmented into nonusers, former users, potential users, first-time users, and regular users of a product. High-market-share companies such as major airlines are particularly interested in keeping regular users and attracting potential users. Potential users and regular users often require different marketing appeals.

Usage Rate

Markets can also be segmented into light-, medium-, and heavy-user groups. Heavy users are often a small percentage of the market but account for a high percentage of total buying. A study of seven key international markets found heavy users of fast-food restaurants account for only 20 percent of the customers but 60 percent of fast-food transactions. Heavy users have been known to purchase $40 per day in fast food restaurants and visit these restaurants twenty times per month. Barry Schwartz, Burger King's director of brand research and analysis, stated heavy users come in more often, spend more money, and are familiar with the restaurant. Researchers have discovered that 4.1 percent of airline travelers account for 70.4 percent of total airline trips, whereas 7.9 percent of pleasure trip users of hotels and motels account for 59.4 percent of room nights.[13]

One of the most controversial programs ever employed by the hospitality and travel industries to ensure heavy patronage by key customers is the frequent flyer or frequent guest program. Many professors, consultants, and industry executives seriously question the long-run value of these programs. However, the results of one study of frequent guest programs concluded: "While it is expensive to maintain frequent guest programs, they seem to be effective in keeping a large lucrative portion of the business travel market coming back to those hotels that offer such programs. Therefore, unless the industry as a whole drops these programs, it appears that individual chains will be forced to maintain them as a means of encouraging and maintaining customer loyalty."[14] Clearly, marketers are eager to identify heavy users and build a marketing mix to attract them. Too many firms spread their marketing resources evenly across all potential customers. Seasoned marketers identify heavy users and focus marketing strategies toward them.

Loyalty Status

A market can also be segmented on the basis of consumer loyalty. Consumers of hospitality products can be loyal to brands, such as Courtyard by Marriott, or to companies such as American Airlines. Others are only somewhat loyal. They may be loyal to two or three brands or favor one brand but buy others. Still other buyers show no brand loyalty at all. They want variety or simply buy whichever brand is cheapest or most convenient. These people will stop at a Ramada Inn or Holiday Inn, depending on which they see first when looking for a motel.

8.8 American Airlines

In the hospitality and travel industries, marketers attempt to build brand loyalty through relationship marketing. Whereas manufacturing companies often lack direct contact with their customers, most hospitality and travel marketers do have direct contact. They can develop a guest history database and use this information to customize offers and customer communications.

One restaurant keeps a file on its frequent customers, detailing their preferred captain, wines, table choice, last visit, and even their appearance (making it easier for restaurant employees to recognize them). VIP customers are given a special reservation phone number by this restaurant. People who call that number are immediately identified as key customers and treated accordingly.

A review of marketing strategies for resorts suggested that the first and most basic strategy was "to keep and expand the current market base. To encourage vital repeat business, resorts should stay in contact with their former guests through direct mail that lets them know of special events, discount offers, and new programs and facilities."[15]

Buyer Readiness Stage

At any given time, people are in different stages of readiness to buy a product. Some are unaware of the product; some are aware; some are informed; some want the product; and some intend to buy. The relative number in each stage makes a big difference in designing a marketing program.

A group travel operator wanted to sell long-haul destinations to incentive travel planners who normally purchased close-by destinations. Travel planners were aware of the long-haul product but were uninterested. The group travel operator implemented a direct marketing campaign in an attempt to change short-haul into long-haul buyers. The objective of the campaign was to convince incentive travel planners to visit the travel operator's booth at an upcoming travel show. As a result of the mail campaign, personal contact at the booth, and follow-up sales calls, a significant number of travel planners became convinced that long-haul incentive trips to exotic destinations were appropriate for some of their customers. The group travel operator attributed nearly $400,000 in sales increases to the campaign.[16]

Requirements for Effective Segmentation

Although there are many ways to segment a market, all are not equally effective. For example, buyers of restaurant meals could be divided into blond and brunette customers. But hair color does not affect the purchase of restaurant meals. Furthermore, if all restaurant customers buy the same number of meals each month, believe all restaurant meals are of equal quality, and are willing to pay the same price, the company would not benefit from segmenting this market.

To be useful, market segments must have the following characteristics:

- **Measurability:** the degree to which the segment's size and purchasing power can be measured. Certain segmentation variables are difficult to measure, such as the size of the segment of teenagers who drink primarily to rebel against their parents.
- **Accessibility:** the degree to which segments can be accessed and served. One of the authors found that 20 percent of a college restaurant's customers were frequent patrons. However, frequent patrons lacked any common characteristics. They included faculty, staff, and students. There was no usage difference among part-time, full-time, or class year of the students. Although the market segment had been identified, there was no way to access the heavy-user segment.
- **Substantiality:** the degree to which segments are large or profitable enough to serve as markets. A segment should be the largest possible homogeneous group economically feasible to support a tailored marketing program. For example, large metropolitan areas can support many different ethnic restaurants, but in a smaller town, Thai, Vietnamese, and Moroccan food restaurants would not survive.
- **Actionability:** the degree to which effective programs can be designed for attracting and serving segments. A small airline, for example, identified seven market segments, but its staff and budget were too small to develop separate marketing programs for each segment.

MARKET TARGETING

Marketing segmentation reveals the firm's market-segment opportunities. The firm now has to evaluate the various segments and decide how many and which ones to target. We now look at how companies evaluate and select target markets.

Evaluating Market Segments

When evaluating different market segments, a firm must look at three factors: segment size and growth, segment structural attractiveness, and company objectives and resources.

Segment Size and Growth

The company must first collect and analyze data on current segment sales, growth rates, and expected profitability for various segments. It will be interested in segments that have the right size and growth characteristics. But "right size and growth" is a relative matter. Some companies will want to target segments with large current sales, a high growth rate, and a high profit margin. However, the largest, fastest-growing segments are not always the most attractive ones for every company. Smaller companies may find they lack the skills and resources needed to serve the larger segments, or that these segments are too competitive. Such companies may select segments that are smaller and less attractive, in an absolute sense, but that are potentially more profitable for them.

Segment Structural Attractiveness

A segment might have desirable size and growth and still not offer attractive profits. The company must examine several major structural factors that affect long-run segment attractiveness. For example, a segment is less attractive if it already contains many strong and aggressive competitors. The existence of many actual or potential substitute products may limit prices and the profits that can be earned in a segment. For example, grocery stores are getting into the home-meal replacement market. As they become more competitive in this market, they will have an impact on the restaurant market. The relative power of buyers also affects segment attractiveness. If the buyers in a segment possess strong bargaining power relative to sellers, they will try to force prices down, demand more quality or services, and set competitors against one another, all at the expense of seller profitability. Large buyers, such as an airline that has a hub in Dallas that needs fifty rooms a night, will be able to negotiate a low price. Finally, a segment may be less attractive if it contains powerful suppliers who can control prices or reduce the quality of or quantity of ordered goods and services. Suppliers tend to be powerful when they are large and concentrated, when few substitutes exist, or when the supplied product is an important input. In certain areas, restaurants specializing in fresh seafood may be limited to a few suppliers. When seafood becomes scarce they have little control over the price they will charge.

Company Objectives and Resources

Even if a segment has the right size and growth and is structurally attractive, the company must consider its own objectives and resources in relation to that segment. Some attractive segments could be dismissed quickly because they do not mesh with the company's long-run objectives. Although such segments might be tempting in themselves, they might divert the company's attention and energies away from its main goal. Or they might be a poor choice from an environmental, political, or social

Marketing Highlight 8-3

"Elite-Napping" the Frequent Business Traveler

The business traveler is the hotel industry's largest segment, accounting for over half of all hotel room revenues. Starwood hotels estimates that a frequent business traveler is worth over $10,000 in lifetime value. Hilton estimates it captures six of the twenty nights their frequent business travelers spend in hotels. If Hilton could move that up to seven nights, it would mean an additional $500 million dollars in sales! But if Hilton is to get their extra night of the frequent stayers' twenty stays, another hotel is going to lose that night. Jennifer Taylor, manager of frequent traveler programs for Bass Hotels and Resorts, calls this stealing of frequent hotel guests "elite-napping."

This frequent business traveler is better educated, more affluent, and employed in sales, managerial, or professional positions. The business traveler reads more and watches less television than the average American. The number one reason for making a business trip is for sales.

In selecting a hotel, business travelers give attention to a convenient location, cleanliness and service, the room rate, and reputation. Desirable room amenities include good-quality mattresses, heavy bath towels, a desk, and a telephone with no charge for local calls and no surcharges for long-distance calls. The no charge for local calls is an important factor for the salesperson. The number one benefit sought by the business traveler is a speedy check-in. There is also a trend toward requesting no-smoking rooms. Howard Feiertag of VPI states, "Initially, hotels allocated 10% of their rooms as non-smoking rooms. Today most hotels allocate 50% of their rooms as non-smoking and I would not be surprised if at some point 90% of the rooms are allocated toward non-smokers."

For the upscale business traveler, the most crucial elements of the business-class room are an enhanced work area with an oversized desk, data ports for a modem connection, multiple phones, easy-to-reach electrical outlets, a comfortable chair, and bright lighting. Frank Camacho, vice president and director of sales and marketing, North American Division of Sheraton, explains that a room cannot compete in the business class market without these amenities. Research conducted at Sheraton found that the combination printer/fax/copier creates a lot more value for the business traveler than the single-purpose fax machine.

A surprising finding is that over 60 percent of business travelers make their own reservations. Toll-

responsibility viewpoint. For example, in recent years, some hotel chains have decided not to get involved in the gaming business. Disney has avoided this segment of the hospitality industry. If a segment fits the company's objectives, the company then must decide whether it possesses the skills and resources needed to succeed in that segment. If the company lacks the strengths needed to compete successfully in a segment and cannot readily obtain them, it should not enter the segment. Even if the company possesses the required strengths, it needs to employ skills and resources superior to those of the competition in order to really win in a market segment. The company should enter segments only where it can offer superior value and gain advantages over competitors.

Selecting Market Segments

After evaluating different segments, the company must now decide which and how many segments to serve. This is the problem of target-market selection. A target market consists of a set of buyers who share common needs

free numbers are very important to business travelers. Those not booking reservations themselves use travel agents or secretaries. Information on the business traveler helps hotels to develop a marketing offer to attract this segment.

One way of subsegmenting this large segment is through prices that travelers are willing to pay. Those seeking economy lodging are usually traveling salesmen, self-employed, or government workers. This group's daily expenditures are limited by their organization, or in the case of the self-employed, it comes directly out of their income. This group will trade-off other features, such as a hotel restaurant, to get a clean comfortable room for under $70. La Quinta, Red Roof Inns, Hampton Inns, and Fairfield Inns have targeted this segment.

The next segment is the midpriced business traveler. A broad range of full-service hotels pursue this segment. They include Courtyard by Marriott, Hilton, Holiday Inns, Marriott, and Ramada. Notice that Marriott has two products going after this market. Courtyard is at the lower end of the range, whereas Marriott hotels are at the upper end of the range. Marriott felt it could not cover this segment adequately with just one product.

The upscale business traveler would be attracted to Four Seasons, Ritz-Carlton, Stouffers, and Westin. These hotels offer extra services and amenities that the upscale business traveler wants. They are able to cover the costs generated by these extra features by charging more for their rooms. As the hotel market becomes more competitive, chains will develop further brands and variations aimed at well-defined market segments.

Sources: Howard Feiertag, "Corporate Travelers Rate Some Special Considerations, *Hotel and Motel Management,* April 21, 1997, p. 13; Glenn Haussman, "Heightened Emphasis Is Placed on Business Amenities as Hotels Vie for Market Share," *Hotel Business,* June 7–20, 1997, p. 34; Toni Giovanetti, "Hyatt Studies Travelers' Habits on Road," *Hotel Business,* September 21–October 7, 1997, p. 3; George Taininecz, "1990 Business Traveler Survey," *Hotel and Motel Management* 205, no. 1, (June 1990): 29; Kenneth Ray and James L. Haskett, "Fairfield Inn," *Harvard Case Study 9-689-092* (October 1989); James R. Abbey, *Hospitality Sales and Advertising* (East Lansing, MI: Educational Institute of the AH&MA, 1989), pp. 389–402; and Arch Woodside, Victor J. Cook Jr., and William Mindale, "Profiling the Heavy Traveler Segment," *Journal of Travel Research* 25, no. 4 (April 1987): 9–14.

or characteristics that the company decides to serve. Figure 8-2 shows that the firm can adopt one of three market-coverage strategies: undifferentiated marketing, differentiated marketing, and concentrated marketing.

Undifferentiated Marketing

Using an undifferentiated marketing strategy, a firm ignores market segmentation differences and goes after the entire market with one market offer. It focuses on what is common in the needs of consumers rather than on differences. It designs a marketing plan that will reach the greatest number of buyers. Mass distribution and mass advertising serve as the basic tools to create a superior image in consumers' minds.

Undifferentiated marketing provides cost economies. The narrow product line keeps down production, inventory, and transportation costs. The undifferentiated advertising program holds down advertising costs. The neglect of segmentation holds down marketing research costs and product development costs.

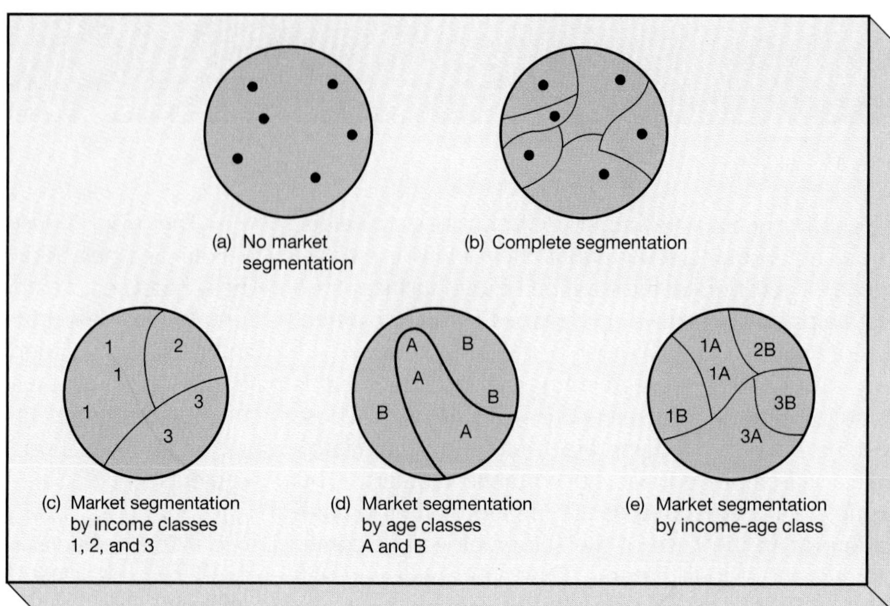

Figure 8-2
Three alternative market-coverage strategies.

Most modern marketers have strong doubts about this strategy in today's competitive environment. It is difficult to develop a product or brand that will satisfy all or even most consumers. When several firms aim at the largest segments, the inevitable result is heavy competition. Small firms generally find it impossible to compete directly against giants and are forced to adopt market-niche strategies. Larger segments may become less profitable due to heavy marketing costs, including the possibility of price cutting and price wars. In recognition of this problem, many firms target smaller segments or niches where product differentiation is appreciated.

The U.S. beer industry is an example. Smaller breweries cannot directly compete with Budweiser, Miller, and Coors. Smaller firms cannot achieve the distribution of the Big 3, nor can they match advertising and sales promotion budgets. Instead, a proliferation of microbreweries has occurred. Each microbrewery serves a limited market area, and many depend on a company-owned pub or restaurant as the primary distribution center.

A similar situation exists within the world's commercial aviation industry. This is an oligopolistic industry with a few giant carriers. Many smaller "flag" carriers exist only because some nations feel they must have a national airline and are willing to subsidize it.

8.9 Spirit Airlines
US Air

Within the North American market, several new niche market airlines have emerged, such as Casino Express, which flies between Denver, Colorado, and Elko, Nevada, and Spirit Airlines, based in Atlantic City. These airlines are unlikely to pose a direct threat to American, Delta, United, or US Air. One of the last startup airlines to pose such a threat was People's Express, which was unable to withstand the intense competition from major carriers when it expanded from a regional to a national carrier.

Differentiated Marketing

Using a differentiated marketing strategy, the firm targets several market segments and designs separate offers for each. Accor Hotels, a French company, operates under twelve trade names and manages several brands and types of hotels. Included in its brands are international luxury hotels (Sofitel), three-star hotels (Novotel), two-star hotels (ibis), limited-service hotels (Formula One and Motel 6), and extended-stay hotels aimed at the elderly (Hotelia). This segmentation has allowed Accor to become one the world's foremost hotel groups.

8.10 Accor

Differentiated marketing typically produces more total sales than undifferentiated marketing. Accor gets a higher hotel room market share with three different brands in one city than if it only had one brand in that city. Sofitel attracts the upscale business traveler, Novotel attracts the midscale traveler, whereas Formula One attracts the families and the budget traveler. Accor offers a different marketing mix to each target market. At the same time, its costs are higher. It has to have marketing plans, marketing research, forecasting, sales analysis, promotion planning, and advertising for each brand. Thus, companies must weigh increased sales against increased costs in considering a differentiated marketing strategy.

Concentrated Marketing

A third market-coverage strategy, concentrated marketing, is especially appealing to companies with limited resources. Instead of going for a small share of a large market, the firm pursues a large share of one or more small markets.

There are many examples of concentrated marketing. Four Seasons Hotels and Rosewood Hotels concentrate on the high-priced hotel room market. Through concentrated marketing, firms achieve a strong market position in the segments that they serve, thanks to their greater knowledge of those segments' needs and the special reputation the firm acquires. The firm also enjoys many operative economies because of specialization in production, distribution, and promotion. If the segment is well chosen, the firm can earn a high rate of return on investment.

At the same time, concentrated marketing involves higher than normal risks. The particular market segment can turn sour. For example, Victoria Station's menus were heavily concentrated on red meat items. When consumers started eating less red meat, Victoria Station's customer count plummeted. Additionally, meat prices jumped. Victoria Station's most profitable product, alcoholic beverages, also began a sales decline as a result of antidrunk driving campaigns. Thus, it experienced declining and less profitable sales and eventually went out of business. For these reasons, many companies prefer to operate in two or more markets.

Choosing a Market-Coverage Strategy

Companies need to consider several factors in choosing a market-coverage strategy. One factor is the **company's resources.** When the company's resources are limited, concentrated marketing makes the most sense. Another factor is the **degree of product homogeneity.** Undifferentiated marketing is more suited for homogeneous products. Products that can vary in design, such as restaurants and hotels, are more suited to differentiation or concentration. The product's life-cycle stage must also be considered. When a firm introduces a new product, it is practical to launch only one version, and undifferentiated or concentrated marketing makes the most sense. For example, the early McDonald's restaurants had a very limited selection, compared with their present menu selection. In the mature stage of the product life cycle, differentiated marketing becomes more feasible. Another factor is **market homogeneity.** If buyers have the same tastes, buy a product in the same amounts, and react the same way to marketing efforts, undifferentiated marketing is appropriate. Finally, **competitors strategies** are important. When competitors use segmentation, undifferentiated marketing can be suicidal. Conversely, when competitors use undifferentiated marketing, a firm can gain an advantage by using differentiated or concentrated marketing.

Market Positioning

Once a company has chosen its target market segments, it must decide what positions to occupy in those segments. A product's position is the way the product is defined by consumers on important attributes—the place the product occupies in consumers' minds relative to competing products. Consumers are overloaded with information about products and services. They cannot reevaluate products every time they make a buying decision. To simplify buying decision making, consumers organize products into categories—they "position" products and companies in their minds.

Marketers do not want to leave their products' positions to chance. They plan positions that will give their products the greatest advantage in selected target markets and then design marketing mixes to create the planned positions. In the fast-food hamburger business, Wendy's promotes never-frozen meat, hot off the grill; Burger King is known for its flame-broiled food, and Rally's double drive-through uses low prices to position itself in the marketplace.[17]

> A hotel brand's position can be viewed from two perspectives—that of the brand's management and that of the guests. The brand's management must have a firm's concept of the hotel's intended position, and its promotional efforts must articulate not only what the brand offers, but how its offerings are different from those of other brands. In the final analysis, however, a brand's position is determined by its customers.[18]

Positioning Strategies

Marketers can follow several positioning strategies. They can position their products based on **specific product attributes.** Motel 6 advertises its low price; Hilton advertises its locations. Products can also be positioned on the *needs they fill* or the *benefits they offer*. Bennigans advertises itself as a fun place, while many bars promote their image as a meeting place for singles. Marketers can also position for certain classes of users, such as a hotel advertising itself as a women's hotel.

A product can be positioned against an **existing competitor.** In the "Burger Wars," Wendy's ran its "Where's the beef?" campaign against McDonald's and Burger King, and Burger King used its flame-broiled

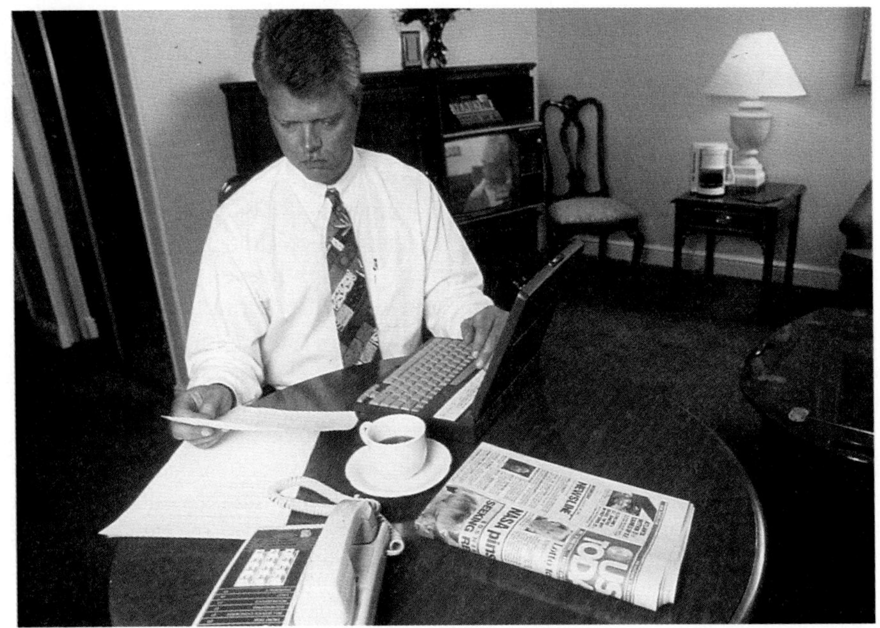

Radisson created the Radisson Business Class, a bundle of products to attract the corporate customer. Their business class includes a full breakfast, daily newspaper, free movies, complimentary coffee, data port for computers, free telephone access, and immediate-priority fax. Courtesy of Radisson Hospitality Worldwide.

campaign against McDonald's. Taco Bell positioned itself as an alternative to typical fast-food meals. 7-Up successfully positioned itself as the "uncola" at a time when cola beverages were engaged in a fierce battle for market-share dominance. The strategy of Taco Bell and 7-Up has many applications in the hospitality industry.

Finally, products can be positioned against another product class. Cruise ships have positioned themselves against other vacation alternatives, such as destination resorts, and customers have positioned B&Bs as an alternative to all other forms of lodging. Conference centers have consistently positioned their product against hotels with conference facilities. B&Bs position their comfortable home atmosphere against hotels.

The hotel industry should take warning from the plight of mighty IBM. Few competitors found it possible to attack IBM directly for market share. IBM was dominant in mainframe computers, in its sales/distribution force, and in the position it held in the minds of the business community. Competitors attacked IBM with flanking or guerrilla attacks rather than a frontal assault. Little by little, niche competitors began to chew at the computer market through specialized software, PCs, specialty computers, and specialty service. IBM suddenly found it was surrounded by competitors who had captured niche markets at the same time that the demand for its traditional products was softening.

Traditional hotels with a ballroom, conference seminar rooms, full-service restaurant, a bar, an exercise room, and other product offerings are experiencing the IBM phenomenon. Market-niche players in the hospitality industry continue to attack full-service hotels with specialized products such as conference centers, specialized food and beverage (F&B) outlets, fitness centers, B&Bs, all-suite lodging, condo hotels, meeting/seminar rooms within convention centers, and even athletic arenas.

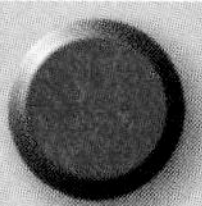

Marketing Highlight 8-4

Airline Positioning: Southwest Airlines

Southwest Airlines knows its niche. From the start, it has positioned itself firmly as the short-haul, no-frills, low-price airline. Its average flight time is just one hour; its average one-way fare just $76. Southwest's passengers have learned to fly without the amenities. For example, the airline provides no meals—just peanuts. It also offers no first-class section, only three-across seating in all of its planes. There's no such thing as a reserved seat on a Southwest flight. Passengers receive numbered boarding passes—first come, first served—and are herded onto the plane in groups of thirty.

"Southwest will get you and your luggage where you're going," comments an industry analyst, "but we don't call their planes cattle cars for nothing. It's a mercy that Southwest is a short-haul airline, because you can get pretzeled on their planes p.d.q." Why, then, do so many passengers love Southwest? Perhaps, most important, Southwest excels at the basics of getting passengers where they want to go and on time. In 1992, Southwest received the U.S. Department of Transportation's first-ever Triple Crown Award for best on-time service, best baggage handling, and best customer service, a feat it repeated for the next five straight years. For more than a decade, Southwest has been an industry leader in on-time performance.

Beyond these basics, however, there are two key elements to Southwest's strong positioning. The analyst sums up Southwest's positioning this way: "It is not luxurious. . . . but it's cheap and it's fun." Southwest is a model of efficiency and low-cost operations. As a result, its prices are shockingly low. In fact, prices are so low that when Southwest enters a new market, it actually increases total air traffic by attracting customers who might otherwise travel by car or bus. For example, when Southwest began its Louisville-Chicago flight at a one-way rate of $49 versus competitors' $250, total weekly air passenger traffic between the two cities increased from 8,000 to 26,000.

No frills and low prices, however, don't mean drudgery. To lighten things up, Southwest adds another key positioning ingredient: lots of good, clean fun. With its happy-go-lucky CEO, Herb Kelleher, leading the charge, Southwest refuses to take itself seriously. Cheerful employees go out of their way to amuse, surprise, or somehow entertain passengers. According to one account:

8.11 Motel 6
IBM
Regent Hyatt

The Asian market such as Hong Kong or Singapore has consisted largely of deluxe five-star full-service hotels with world-class competitors such as the Peninsula, Mandarin, Shangrila, Regent, Hilton International, and Hyatt Hotels. Less expensive hotel properties existed, but these appealed predominantly to nearby markets and to GIT (group inclusive tour) segments. As rack rates increased in these markets and as customer familiarization with these destinations grew, niche products have begun to emerge.

The YMCA is a surprising niche competitor in Hong Kong. The YMCA enjoys a good location near the harbor and has been remodeled to meet the needs of American, European, and Australian guests. Occupancy and guest satisfaction in the YMCA remain high and serve as a warning to traditional five-star luxury properties that guests are willing to accept alternative lodging products.

When two or more firms pursue the same position, each must seek further differentiation, such as "a business hotel for a lower cost" or "a business hotel with a great location." Each firm must build a unique

Southwest employees are apt to dress as leprechauns on St. Patrick's Day, rabbits on Easter, and almost anything on Halloween. I have heard flight attendants sing the safety lecture as country music, blues, and rap; I have heard them compare the pilot to Rocky Raccoon and insist that passengers introduce themselves to one another, then hug, then kiss, then propose marriage.

Kelleher himself has been known to dress up as Elvis Presley to greet passengers.

During delays at the gate, ticket agents will award prizes to the passenger with the largest hole in his or her sock. Flight attendants have been known to hide in overhead luggage bins and then pop out when passengers start filing on board. Veteran Southwest fliers have learned to listen up to announcements over the intercom. On a recent flight, the pilot suggested, "Flight attendants will please prepare their hair for departure." Later in the flight, he announced, "Good morning, ladies and gentlemen. Those of you who wish to smoke will please file out to our lounge on the wing, where you can enjoy our feature film, *Gone with the Wind.*" Safety instructions from the flight attendant included the advice, "In the event of a water landing, please remember to paddle, kick, kick, paddle, kick, kick, all the way back."

As a result of its strong positioning, Southwest has grown to become the nation's fourth-largest domestic carrier. The company has successfully beaten off determined challenges from several major competitors who have tried to copy its winning formula, including Continental Lite, Delta Express, and Shuttle by United. Over the past ten years, Southwest's revenues have grown 388 percent; its net earnings have soared 1,490 percent; and its stock has yielded an average annual return to investors of 29 percent.

Sources: Quotes from Molly Ivins, "From Texas, with Love and Peanuts," *New York Times*, March 14, 1999, p. 11; and Dani Pedersen, "Cookies and Champagne," *Newsweek* April 27, 1998, p. 60. Also see "One Midwest Carrier Proves That Smaller Can Be Better," *Money* (November 1997): 123; Ellen Jovin, "Buckling Up the Business Traveler," *American Demographics* (December 1998): 48–51; Thomas A. Stewart, "America's Most Admired Companies," *Fortune*, March 2, 1998, pp. 70–73; Stephanie Gruner, "Have Fun, Make Money," *Inc.* (May 1998): 123; Chad Kayclo, "Riding High," *Sales & Marketing Management* (July 1998): 64–69; "How Herb Keeps Southwest Hopping," *Money* (June 1999): 61–62; and *Southwest Airlines Fact Sheet—November 1999* at *www.southwest.com.*

bundle of competitive advantages that appeals to a substantial group within the segment. This subpositioning is often called *niche marketing*.

Most cruise lines offer a multiday cruise experience with stops at several ports. A few niche cruise lines have found it profitable to offer a one-day cruise with no ports of call. On the other hand the *QE-2* (*Queen Elizabeth 2*) has successfully developed a market niche as the Rolls-Royce of cruise ships, with costs of several thousand dollars and lengthy cruise times.

Choosing and Implementing a Positioning Strategy

The positioning task consists of three steps: identifying a set of possible competitive advantages upon which to build a position, selecting the right competitive advantages, and effectively communicating and delivering the chosen position to a carefully selected target market.

A company can differentiate itself from competitors by bundling competitive advantages. It gains **competitive advantage** by offering consumers lower prices than competitors for similar products or by providing more benefits that justify higher prices.[19] Thus a company must compare its prices and products to those of competitors and continuously look for possible improvements. To the extent that it can do better than its competitors, the company has achieved a competitive advantage.

8.12 Club Med

Club Med used a successful bundling strategy of offering all services other than retail purchases to a young market segment that was unfamiliar with tipping, ordering from a menu, selecting wines, and asking a concierge for help in acquiring a tennis lesson. Club Med bundled all these products/services and eliminated the use of money at their resorts. Instead of dollars, pesos, or francs, Club Med's international guests could buy a round of drinks with beads given to them at check-in.

In some cases, unbundling of products has also worked as a positioning tactic. Until the early 1970s, many destination resorts sold only a bundled product known as the American plan (AP), in which all or most of the resort's services such as F&B were included. Consumer preferences changed as many guests no longer wanted three daily meals and a Friday evening formal dance included in a package. Resort managers who observed this behavior change began to differentiate their properties by offering a modified American plan (MAP), in which lunch was not included, or a European plan, which did not include meals.

Not every company faces an abundance of opportunities for gaining a competitive advantage. Some companies can identify only minor advantages, which are often easily copied and therefore highly perishable. These companies must continue to identify new potential advantages and introduce them one by one to keep competitors off balance. Few or perhaps no companies can achieve a major permanent advantage, but instead, gain smaller advantages that help them build their market share over time. Hotels, resorts, and restaurants sometimes believe that their locations on a beach, near an airport, next to a ski hill, or in the central business district provide them with a permanent advantage. History clearly depicts a different scenario. Beaches erode or become polluted, ski hills lose their popularity, airports move, and central business districts lose their appeal. In many cases the management of hospitality companies with perceived permanent advantages lose interest in customers and employees, thus further contributing to their inevitable demise.

Product Differentiation

A company can differentiate its product or offer products similar to competitors. Today, most products try to differentiate themselves from their competitors. In what ways can a company differentiate its offer from those of competitors? A company can differentiate along the lines of physical attributes, service, personnel, location, or image.

Physical Attribute Differentiation

Classic hotels that have been renovated, such as the Sheraton Place in San Francisco, Palmer House in Chicago, Waldorf-Astoria in New York, and Raffles in Singapore, differentiate themselves on the grandeur of the past. Their physical environment offers something a newly constructed hotel cannot match. Planet Hollywood, with its memorabilia from the motion picture industry, and Hard Rock Café, with its music memorabilia, offer an environment that competitors will have a hard time duplicating. MGM airlines offered a plane that was designed to serve first-class passengers only. The plane had a stand-up bar, couches, and other physical features that were not found in the first-class sections of major domestic carriers.

8.13 Hard Rock Café
Palmer House
Planet Hollywood
Raffles
Waldorf-Astoria

Service Differentiation

Some companies differentiate themselves on service. For example, Sheraton provides an in-room check-in service. Red Lobster allows its customers to call from home and put their name on the waiting list, reducing the amount of time that they have to wait at the restaurant. Some restaurants offer home delivery as a point of differentiation. By providing services that will benefit its target market, a company can achieve differentiation.

Personnel Differentiation

Companies can gain a strong competitive advantage through hiring and training better people than their competitors. Thus, Singapore Airlines enjoys an excellent reputation largely because of the grace of its flight attendants. Herb Kelleher of Southwest Airlines claims that a competitor possibly could replicate their low-cost system, but a competitor will never be able to create a spirit similar to the spirit of Southwest's employees.[20]

Personnel differentiation requires that a company select its customer-contact people carefully and train them well. These personnel must be competent and must possess the required skills and knowledge. They need to be courteous, friendly, and respectful. They must serve customers with consistency and accuracy, and they must make an effort to understand customers, to communicate clearly with them, and to respond quickly to customer requests and problems.

Location Differentiation

In the hospitality and travel industries, location can provide a strong competitive advantage. For example, hotels facing Central Park in New York City have a competitive advantage over those hotels a block away with no view of the park. Motels that are located right off a freeway exit can have double-digit advantages in percentage of occupancy over hotels a block away. Restaurants on the top of a mountain advertise their views as a competitive advantage, and restaurants with an ocean view do the same. International airlines often use their location as a point of differentiation in their home markets. For example, Qantas promotes itself as Australia's airline and has a strong following in its home market. Hospitality and travel firms should look for benefits created by their location and use these benefits to differentiate themselves from their market.

Image Differentiation

Even when competing offers look the same, buyers may perceive a difference based on company or brand images. Thus, companies need to work to establish images that differentiate them from competitors. A company

8.14 Chili's

or brand image should convey a singular or distinctive message that communicates the product's major benefits and positioning. Developing a strong and distinctive image calls for creativity and hard work. A company cannot implant an image in the public's mind overnight using a few advertisements. Chili's has developed an image as a casual and fun neighborhood restaurant. This message is conveyed by their advertising, menu, the physical atmosphere, and the employees. The image must be supported by everything that the company says and does. Studebaker's positioned itself as a singles nightclub for adults over twenty-five (product class and user), naming itself after a car. The name Studebaker and the use of a Studebaker auto in the facility had no meaning to a younger market segment, which had very possibly never seen this automobile on the streets and highways. Thus the word *Studebaker* meant something to their target market but held little meaning for younger markets.

Selecting the Right Competitive Advantages

Suppose that a company is fortunate enough to discover several potential competitive advantages. It now must choose the ones on which it will build its positioning strategy. It must decide how many differences to promote and which ones.

How Many Differences

Many marketers think that companies should aggressively promote only one benefit to the target market. Ad-man Rosser Reeves, for example, said a company should develop a *unique selling proposition* (USP) for each brand and stick to it. Each brand should pick an attribute and tout itself as number one on that attribute. Buyers tend to remember number one better, especially in an over-communicated society. Thus Motel 6 consistently promotes itself as the lowest-priced national chain, and Ritz-Carlton promotes itself as a value leader. What are some number one positions to promote? The major ones are best quality, best service, lowest price, best value, and best location. A company that hammers away at a position that is important to its target market and consistently delivers on it probably will become the best known and remembered.

Other marketers think that companies should position themselves on more than one differentiating factor. A restaurant may claim that it has the best steaks and service. A hotel may claim that it offers the best value and location. Today, in a time when the mass market is fragmenting into many small market segments, companies are trying to broaden their positioning strategies to appeal to more segments. For example, the Boulders in Arizona promotes itself as a top golf resort and as a luxury resort, giving guests a chance to experience the flora and fauna of the Sonora Desert. By doing this, the Boulders can attract both golfers and non-golfers.

However, as companies increase the number of claims for their brands, they risk disbelief and a loss of clear positioning. In general, a company needs to avoid three major positioning errors. The first is **underpositioning,** or failing ever to position the company at all. Some companies discover that buyers have only a vague idea of the company or that they do not really know anything special about it. Many independent hotels trying to capture an international market are underpositioned. The Seoul Plaza Hotel, a luxury hotel in Seoul, is not well known in Europe or North America. To establish positions in distant markets, hotels like the Seoul Plaza are affiliating with marketing groups such as "Leading Hotels of the World" and "Preferred Hotels." The second positioning error is **overpositioning,** or giving buyers a too narrow picture of the company. Finally, companies must avoid **confused positioning,** leaving buyers with a confused image of a company. For example, Burger King has struggled for years to establish a profitable and consistent position. Since 1986 it has fielded eight separate advertising campaigns, with themes ranging from "Herb the nerd doesn't eat here" and "This is a Burger King town" to "The right food for the right times" and "Sometimes you've gotta break the rules." Its last three campaigns have been "Get Your Burger's Worth," followed by "It Just Tastes Better," in 1998 and "Got the Urge," in 2001. In late 2001, the president of Burger King was thinking of replacing their advertising agency, which Burger King had used for the last eight years. He stated, "We don't have an advertising campaign that resonates with the customer as strongly as we would like." This barrage of positioning statements created by their advertising campaigns has left consumers confused and Burger King franchises with lower than expected sales.[21]

8.15 Seoul Plaza Hotel

Which Differences

Not all brand differences are meaningful or worthwhile. Not every difference makes a good differentiator. Each difference has the potential to create company costs as well as customer benefits. Therefore, the company must carefully select the ways in which it will distinguish itself from competitors. A difference is worth establishing to the extent that it satisfies the following criteria:

- *Important.* The difference delivers a highly valued benefit to target buyers.
- *Distinctive.* Competitors do not offer the difference, or the company can offer it in a more distinctive way.
- *Superior.* The difference is superior to other ways that customers might obtain the same benefit.
- *Communicable.* The difference is communicable and visible to buyers.
- *Preemptive.* Competitors cannot easily copy the difference.
- *Affordable.* Buyers can afford to pay for the difference.
- *Profitable.* The company can introduce the difference profitably.

Many companies have introduced differentiations that failed one or more of these tests. The Westin Stamford Hotel in Singapore advertises that it is the world's tallest hotel, a distinction that is not important to many tourists; in fact, it turns many off.

Some competitive advantages may quickly be ruled out because they are too slight, too costly to develop, or too inconsistent with the company's profile. Suppose that a company is designing its positioning strategy and has narrowed its list of possible competitive advantages to four. The company needs a framework for selecting the one advantage that makes the most sense to develop.

Communicating and Delivering the Chosen Position

Once having chosen positioning characteristics and a positioning statement, a company must communicate their position to targeted customers. All of a company's marketing mix efforts must support its positioning strategy. If a company decides to build service superiority, for example, it must hire service-oriented employees, provide training programs, reward employees for providing good service, and develop sales and advertising messages to broadcast its service superiority.

Building and maintaining a consistent positioning strategy is not easy. Many counterforces are at work continuously. Advertising agencies hired by the company may not like a selected position and may overtly or covertly work against it. New management may not understand the positioning strategy. Budgets may be cut for critical support programs such as employee training or sales promotion. The development of an effective position requires a consistent, long-run program with continuous support by management, employees, and vendors.

Companies normally develop a memorable statement to communicate their desired position. Burger King's "Have it your way" lets customers know that they can get their choice of condiments. La Quinta's "Just right overnight" catches the attention of travelers coming in by car and needing overnight accommodation but not needing a full-service hotel. Avis Auto Rental originally positioned itself with a statement and strong supportive program to convince the customer, "We're only No. 2, so we try harder." This also positioned Avis with the number one company, Hertz, and away from Budget, Dollar, National, and Thrifty. These statements aim to create a positive image in the target customer's mind.

8.16 Budget
Dollar
Hertz
National Car Rental
Olive Garden

Olive Garden opened a restaurant in Tuscany, Olive Garden Riserva di Fizzano, and developed the Culinary Institute of Tuscany. They have added Tuscan dishes to their menu, are sending their chefs to the Culinary Institute of Tuscany, and have developed a Tuscan farmhouse design for their new restaurants. They have also included recipes and cooking tips on their Web site. The restaurant and Culinary Institute in Italy help communicate Olive Garden's position as an authentic Italian restaurant. Their advertisements reinforce this by featuring Italian families dining at Olive Garden.[22]

A company's positioning decisions determine who its competitors will be. When setting its positioning strategy, the company should review its competitive strengths and weaknesses and select a position that places it in a superior position vis-à-vis its chosen competitors.

Positioning Measurement: Perceptual Mapping

Perceptual mapping, a research tool, is sometimes used to measure a brand's position. Figure 8-3 is an example of hotels plotted on the attributes of price and perceived service. On this map we see that there is a

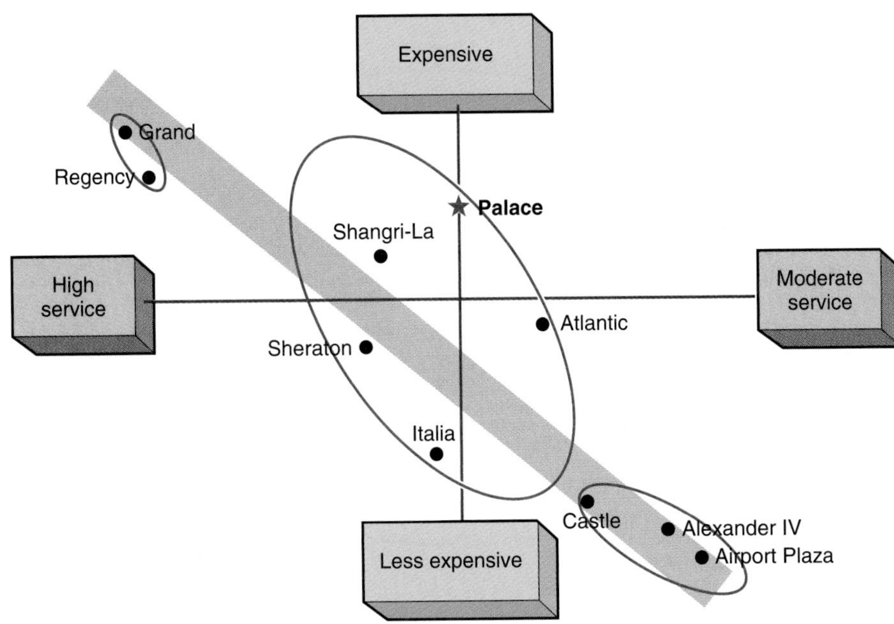

Figure 8-3
Positioning map of service level versus price. From Christopher Lovelock, *Services Marketing* (Upper Saddle River, NJ: Prentice Hall, 1996), p. 178, used with permission.

correlation between service and price; as price goes up, so does service. However, some hotels appear to offer a better value than others. For example, Italia offers a little higher level of service than the Palace, but is less expensive. Two-by-two perceptual maps provide an easy-to-read picture, but one often has to study multiple maps plotting different attributes to get a good feel of the marketplace. Perceptual maps can also be developed using consumers' perceptions of a number of product attributes. Dev, Morgan, and Shoemaker developed a perceptual map based on the ratings of eight attributes using a technique known as *probabilistic multidimensional* scaling to derive the coordinates for the perceptual map shown in Figure 8-4.

This technique is useful for identifying one's competitive set and also open spaces that can represent an opportunity for repositioning away from the competition. The circles are drawn around clusters of points that are not statistically significant distances from each other. Thus the hotels in the circles can be viewed by the consumer as being similar. The authors note that in this type of map the positions are essentially value neutral; that is, one spot on the map does not inherently have to be better or worse than another.[23] Increased competition or an ineffective positioning strategy can make repositioning necessary. Perceptual maps can provide data supporting the need for repositioning.

8.17 Fairfield Inn

In 2000, Marriott International announced a plan for the repositioning of Fairfield Inn. Fairfield had expanded into urban markets with an upgraded product. The existing Fairfield Inns will receive upgraded furniture. Marriott will try to sell its new Fairfield Inn and Suites concept to franchisees building new hotels. The Fairfield Inn and Suites costs $3,000 more to build than a regular Fairfield Inn; it has an average rate of $70, compared with $60 for a Fairfield Inn. Joe Lavin, senior vice president of

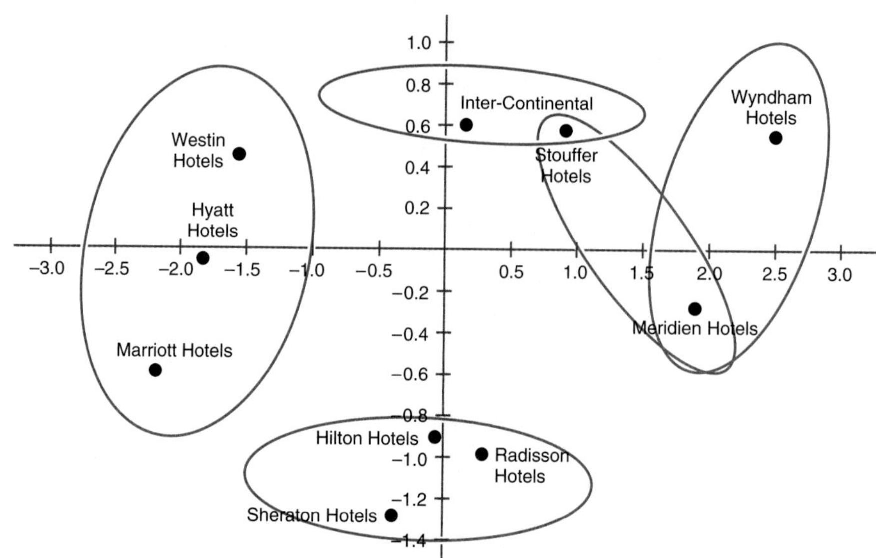

Figure 8-4
Positioning map using multiple attributes to position hotels. From Chekitan S. Dev, Michael S. Morgan, and Stowe Shoemaker, "A Positioning Analysis of Hotel Brands," *Cornell Hotel and Restaurant Administration Quarterly,* 36 (December 1995), pp. 48–55. Courtesy of Cornell Hotel and Restaurant Administration Quarterly. Copyright Cornell University. Used by permission.

franchising for Marriott International, said Fairfield's customers were changing; they were becoming savvier. Thus, the upgrade will allow Fairfield to keep up with its customers and also position itself apart from other limited service competitors.[24]

KEY TERMS

Behavioral segmentation Dividing a market into groups based on consumers' knowledge, attitude, use, or response to a product.

Benefit segmentation Dividing the market into groups according to the different benefits that consumers seek from the product.

Competitive advantage An advantage over competitors gained by offering consumers greater value either through lower prices or by providing more benefits that justify higher prices.

Competitors' strategies When competitors use segmentation, undifferentiated marketing can be suicidal. Conversely, when competitors use undifferentiated marketing, a firm can gain an advantage by using differentiated or concentrated marketing.

Confused positioning Leaving buyers with a confused image of a company.

Customized marketing Marketing in which the company adapts its offers to the needs of specific customers or buying organizations.

Degree of product homogeneity Undifferentiated marketing is more suited for homogeneous products. Products that can vary in design, such as restaurants and hotels, are more suited to differentiation or concentration.

Demographic segmentation Dividing the market into groups based on demographic variables such as age, gender, family size, family life cycle, income, occupation, education, religion, race, and nationality.

Existing competitor Companies can position themselves against current competitors.

Gender segmentation Dividing a market on the basis of gender.

Geographic segmentation Dividing a market into different geographic units such as nations, states, regions, counties, cities, or neighborhoods.

Income segmentation Dividing a market into different income groups.

Market The set of actual and potential buyers of a product.

Market homogeneity If buyers have the same tastes, buy a product in the same amounts, and react the same way to marketing efforts, undifferentiated marketing is appropriate.

Market positioning Formulating competitive positioning for a product and a detailed marketing mix.

Market segmentation Dividing a market into direct groups of buyers who might require separate products or marketing mixes.

Market targeting Evaluating each market segment's attractiveness and selecting one or more segments to enter.

Micromarketing A form of target marketing in which companies tailor their marketing programs to the needs and wants of narrowly defined geographic, demographic, psychographic, or benefit segments.

Overpositioning Giving buyers a too-narrow picture of the company.

Psychographic segmentation Dividing a market into different groups based on social class, lifestyle, or personality characteristics.

Specific product attributes Price and product features can be used to position a product.

Underpositioning Failing ever to position the company at all.

Chapter Review

I. Market. A market is the set of all actual and potential buyers of a product.

II. Three Steps of the Target Marketing Process

1) **Market segmentation** is the process of dividing a market into distinct groups of buyers who might require separate products and/or marketing mixes.

2) **Market targeting** is the process of evaluating each segment's attractiveness and selecting one or more of the market segments.

3) **Positioning** is the process of developing a competitive positioning for the product and an appropriate marketing mix.

III. Market Segmentation

1) **Bases for segmenting a market.** There is no single way to segment a market. A marketer has to try different segmentation variables, alone and in combination, hoping to find the best way to view the market structure.

a) **Geographic segmentation** calls for dividing the market into different geographic units, such as nations, states, regions, counties, cities, or neighborhoods.

b) **Demographic segmentation** consists of dividing the market into groups based on demographic variables such as age, gender, family life cycle, income, occupation, education, religion, race, and nationality.

c) **Psychographic segmentation** divides buyers into different groups based on social class, lifestyle, and personality characteristics.

d) **Behavior segmentation** divides buyers into groups based on their knowledge, attitude, use, or response to a product.

2) **Requirements for Effective Segmentation**

a) **Measurability.** The degree to which the segment's size and purchasing power can be measured.

b) **Accessibility.** The degree to which segments can be accessed and served.

c) **Substantiality.** The degree to which segments are large or profitable enough to serve as markets.

d) **Actionability.** The degree to which effective programs can be designed for attracting and serving segments.

IV. Evaluating Market Segments

1) **Segment size and growth.** Companies will analyze the segment size and growth and choose the segment that provides the best opportunity.

2) **Segment structural attractiveness.** A company must examine major structural factors that affect long-run segment attractiveness.

3) **Company objectives and resources.** The company must consider its own objectives and resources in relation to a market segment.

V. Selecting Market Segments. Segmentation reveals market opportunities available to a firm. The company then selects the most attractive segment or segments to serve as targets for marketing strategies to achieve desired objectives.

1) **Market-coverage alternatives**

a) **Undifferentiated marketing strategy.** An undifferentiated marketing strategy ignores market segmentation differences and goes after the whole market with one market offer.

b) **Differentiated marketing strategy.** The firm targets several market segments and designs separate offers for each.

c) **Concentrated marketing strategy.** Concentrated marketing strategy is especially appealing to companies with limited resources. Instead of going for a small share of a large market, the firm pursues a large share of one or more small markets.

2) **Choosing a market-coverage strategy.** Companies need to consider several factors in choosing a market-coverage strategy.

a) **Company resources.** When the company's resources are limited, concentrated marketing makes the most sense.

b) **Degree of product homogeneity.** Undifferentiated marketing is more suited for homogeneous products. Products that can vary in design, such as restaurants and hotels, are more suited to differentiation or concentration.

c) **Market homogeneity.** If buyers have the same tastes, buy a product in the same amounts, and react the same way to marketing efforts, undifferentiated marketing is appropriate.

d) **Competitors' strategies.** When competitors use segmentation, undifferentiated marketing can be suicidal. Conversely, when competitors use undifferentiated marketing, a firm can gain an advantage by using differentiated or concentrated marketing.

VI. Market positioning. A product's position is the way the product is defined by consumers on important attributes—the place the product occupies in consumers' minds relative to competing products.

1) **Positioning strategies**

a) **Specific product attributes.** Price and product features can be used to position a product.

b) **Needs products fill or benefits products offer.** Marketers can position products by the needs that they fill or the benefits that they offer. For example, a restaurant can be positioned as a fun place.

c) **Certain classes of users.** Marketers can also position for certain classes of users, such as a hotel advertising itself as a women's hotel.

d) **Against an existing competitor.** A product can be positioned against an existing competitor. In the "Burger Wars," Burger King used its flame-broiled campaign against McDonald's, claiming that people prefer flame-broiled over fried burgers.

2) **Choosing and implementing a positioning strategy.** The positioning task consists of three steps: identifying a set of possible competitive advantages upon which to build a position, selecting the right competitive advantages, and effectively communicating and delivering the chosen position to a carefully selected target market.

3) **Communicating and delivering the chosen position.** Once having chosen positioning characteristics and a positioning statement, a company must communicate their position to targeted customers. All of a company's marketing mix efforts must support its positioning strategy.

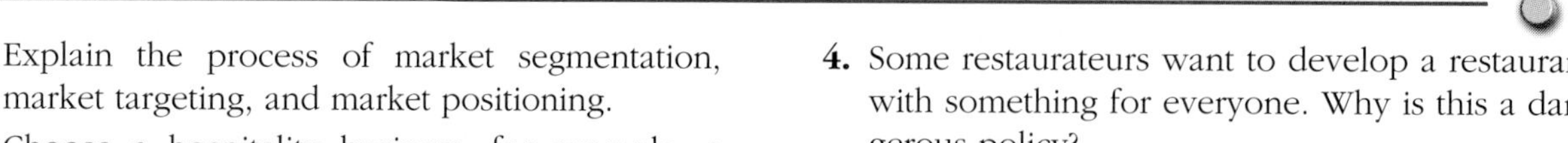

Discussion Questions

1. Explain the process of market segmentation, market targeting, and market positioning.
2. Choose a hospitality business, for example, a Comfort Inn or McDonald's. Explain some of the segments in their overall market (in this case the hotel market or restaurant market), one of these markets that they targeted, and how they differentiated themselves from their competitors in this market to position themselves in the market.
3. Identify a restaurant or hotel market segment in your community that you feel would be a good market segment to target. Explain the marketing mix you would put together to go after this market segment.
4. Some restaurateurs want to develop a restaurant with something for everyone. Why is this a dangerous policy?
5. Think about your classmates in this course. Can you classify them into different segments with specific names? What is your major segmentation variable? Could you effectively market products to these segments?
6. What roles do product attributes and perceptions of attributes play in the positioning of a product? Can an attribute common to several competing brands contribute to a successful positioning strategy?

Experiential Exercise

Find an advertisement from a hospitality or travel company that targets a specific segment, such as children, young adults, seniors, upper-income customer, and so on. Then visit a location of that company. What does the company do at the location with its marketing mix to attract the segment that it targeted in the advertisement? This can include sales promotions, signage, product mix, location of the company, and pricing of products.

Internet Exercise

Support for this exercise can be found on the Web site for *Marketing for Hospitality and Tourism*, www.prenhall.com/kotler.

Go to the Web site of a major brand of a hospitality or travel company. Explain how they use appeal to different segments through the Web site. Give specific examples.

References

1. Faye Rice, "How Carnival Stacks the Decks," *Fortune* 11, no. 21 (January 1989): 108–116; Paula Schnorbus, "Liner Notes," *Marketing and Media Decisions* 22, no. 1 (January 1987), pp. 63–72.
2. William R. Swinyard and Kenneth D. Struman, "Market Segmentation: Finding the Heart of Your Restaurant's Market," *Cornell Hotel and Restaurant Administration Quarterly* 27, no. 1 (May 1986): 96.
3. John Jesitus, "The Regional Page: Diners Search for That Down-Home Flavor," *Hotel and Motel Management* 207, no. 1 (January 1992): 25–26.
4. David Kalish, "McTargeting," *Marketing and Media Decisions* 24, no. 4 (April 1989): 28–29.
5. "Senior Living: Dining in Community," *Restaurants and Institutions* 106, no. 9 (April 1996): 32.
6. Regina McGee, "What Do Women Business Travelers Really Want?" *Successful Meetings* 37, no. 9 (August 1988): 55–57.
7. Lisa Wells, "Hotels Warily Woo Women Travelers," *Advertising Age* 56, no. 59 (August 1985): 4.
8. "Who's Dining Out?" *Cornell Hotel and Restaurant Administration Quarterly* 26, no. 3 (November 1985): 4.

9. Gary M. Stern, "Solo Diners," *Restaurants USA* 10, no. 3 (March 1990): 15–16.
10. Robert Selwitz, "St. Moritz Drops Rates to Hit Niche," *Hotel and Motel Management* 207, no. 3 (February 1992): 2+.
11. Subhash C. Mehta and Vera Ariel, "Segmentation in Singapore," *Cornell Hotel and Restaurant Administration Quarterly* 31, no. 1 (May 1990): 83.
12. Robert C. Lewis, "Restaurant Advertising: Appeals and Consumers' Intentions," *Journal of Advertising Research* 21, no. 5 (October 1981): 69–75.
13. Victor J. Cook Jr., William Mindak, and Arch Woodside, "Profiling the Heavy Traveler Segment," *Journal of Travel Research* 25, no. 4 (April 1987): 9–14; Jennifer Ordonez, "Cash Cows—Hamburger Joints Call Them 'Heavy Users' but Not to Their Faces," *Wall Street Journal*, January 12, 2000, p. A1; Annette M. Budzisz, "QSR Foodservice: The International Market," Press Release from Euromonitor International, received on August 1, 2000.
14. Ken W. McCleary and Pamela A. Weaver, "Are Frequent-Guest Programs Effective?" *Cornell Hotel and Restaurant Administration Quarterly* 32, no. 2 (August 1991): 45.
15. William P. Whelihan III and Kye-Sung Chon, "Resort Marketing Trends in the 90's," *Cornell Hotel and Restaurant Administration Quarterly* 32, no. 2 (August 1991): 58.
16. David Tonnison, "Marketing to Marketers," *Industrial Marketing Digest* 12, no. 2 (1987): 67–72.
17. For more reading on positioning, see Yoram Wind, "New Twists for Some Old Tricks," *Wharton Magazine* (spring 1980): 34–39; David A. Aaker and J. Gary Stansby, "Positioning Your Product," *Business Horizons* (May–June 1982): 56–62; Regis McKenna, "Playing for Position," *Inc.* (April 1985): 92–97.
18. C. S. Dev, M. S. Morgan, and S. Shoemaker, "A Positioning Analysis of Hotel Brands Based on Travel-Manager Perceptions." *Cornell Hotel and Restaurant Administration Quarterly* 36, no. 6 (December 1995): 49.
19. See Michael Porter, *Competitive Advantage* (New York: Free Press, 1980), Chapter. 2. For a good discussion of the concept of competitive advantage and methods for assessing it, see George S. Day and Robin Wensley, "Assessing Advantage: A Framework for Diagnosing Competitive Superiority," *Journal of Marketing* (April 1988): 1–20.
20. *Mobilizing People for Breakthrough Service* (video) (Boston: Harvard Business School Management Productions, 1993).
21. Gail DeGeorge and Mark Landler, "Tempers Are Sizzling over Burger King's New Ads," *Business Week*, February 2, 1990, p. 33; Philip Stelly Jr., "Burger King Rule Breaker," *Adweek*, November 9, 1990, pp. 24, 26.
22. Nancy Brumback, "Room at the Table," *Restaurant Business* (March 15, 2001), pp. 71–82.
23. Dev, Morgan, and Shoemaker, "A Positioning Analysis of Hotel Brands," pp. 48–55.
24. Shannon McMullen, "Marriott International Repositions Fairfield Inn," *Hotel Business News*, February 21–March 6, 2000, p. 3.

SHAVE
SINCLAIR HC GASOLINE
PURE
TRINITY
KALEM
THE SACRIFICE AT THE SPILLWAY
OLD SAN FRANCISCO

9 Designing and Managing Products

Profit is payment you get when you take advantage of change.
Joseph Schumpeter

Being fed a decent meal in a casual environment is a commodity in far more supply than demand.
Barry M. Cohen

Entertain Me!

Do customers today want to be "entertained?" No—they demand it. Being fed a decent meal in a casual environment is a commodity in far more supply than demand. The same can be said for receiving a hamburger and fries in a brown paper bag or a clean room with a coffeemaker and a color television reasonably close to the airport. Trouble is, as most of us know, commodities go to the lowest bidder, and the lowest bidders in our business find it very difficult indeed to make money. In order to create a profit, hospitality providers have been forced to escape this commodity trip by adding value to their product. This added value is what may generally be called "entertainment."

Let's take a brief look at how entertainment is forcing the restaurant industry to add value. No longer can Bennigan's sell itself as a neighborhood watering hole with a grilled chicken Caesar salad and nightly drink specials. The casual dining innovator has had to re-create itself in the image of an Irish pub.

The trend has affected upscale restaurants as well. In our latest steak house (located just north of Atlanta, in Roswell), we've evolved the Old San Francisco concept to include day care and an authentic, late nineteenth-century sports bar. Attaching these elements to an upscale steak house such as ours would have been unthinkable ten years ago. Now we understand them to be not only desirable, but also essential. There are a dozen other steak houses vying for our business.

Before we go any further, let me make a critical distinction between endogenous and exogenous entertainment. Endogenous elements are incorporated into the dining experience itself and, therefore, redefine both the concept and the customer's perception of who we are. On the other hand, exogenous elements are those outside of the actual hospitality experience, that is, advertising and media relations. Exogenous entertainment is often called "hype" or "buzz." There is a good deal to suggest that exogenous entertainment matters far less than endogenous entertainment. A few examples are Cheesecake Factory, Rainforest Café, and The Cracker Barrel. Each spends 2 percent of revenues or less on advertising, yet each boasts the highest average unit volumes in its category. The reason is unparalleled endogenous entertainment—that is, unique atmospheres, high-quality signature products, and very large portions. (Yes, guests do eat with their eyes much of the time.)

Now consider a few celebrated examples of exogenous entertainment over the last couple of years: the product launches of Bigfoot Pizza (Pizza Hut), Arch Deluxe (McDonald's), and most recently Gorditas (Taco Bell). All created swarms of publicity and excitement outside of the restaurants, and each resulted in average unit sales declines. In the casual dining arena, the Rainforest Café achieves average unit volumes roughly 33 percent higher than those at Planet Hollywood. The latter churns out a near-constant flow of exogenous entertainment due to its celebrity investors and public relations spending. But Rainforest Café focuses far more on the dining experience itself. At the end of the day, more customers flock to Rainforest Café than Planet Hollywood.

Forget Me Not!

The secret to success in the hospitality industry is repeat business. A growing stream of loyal customers ensures success. Therefore, dining experiences must be both positive and memorable. A positive dining experience is largely a function of operations—great service, terrific food, and so on—while a memorable dining experience goes one step further. A memorable experience plants a seed in the guest's head to return in the near future. Just as the promise of another teenie beanie baby will lurk in a child's mind and create a reason to return to McDonald's, the memory of a unique experience plants the urge in most adults' minds to return at some point in the future. At Old San Francisco, our memorable experience includes huge portions, a gigantic block of Swiss Cheese on every table, dueling grand pianos, and regular performances by the "girl on the red velvet swing," who literally flies over the dining room. Believe me, people remember us! And when they want to treat friends to a really unique experience—when they want to be entertained—they come to Old San Francisco Steak House. A memorable experience is sometimes our only competitive advantage.

Our concept of entertainment is still evolving. In the past couple of years, we've worked on making our special events days even more entertaining. Last

Father's Day, for example, all our restaurants in Texas sponsored antique car auctions. The result? Same-store sales were up more than 30 percent, and we received television coverage in three markets. When you create interesting entertainment inside your four walls, the excitement outside follows. In other words, endogenous entertainment leads directly to exogenous entertainment and not vice versa. Don't expect great advertisements or a great "buzz" to fuel your success; expect great experiences to create an ever-widening reputation.

Respect Me!

Our guests have become more sophisticated than ever. Why? They dine out more than ever. In fact, more meals are now prepared away from home than at home. Where Americans used to be experts in the kitchen and at the grocery store, they are now experts in our dining rooms and at our drive-through windows.

Most of us are struggling to meet our newly sophisticated guests' demands in a variety of ways. Some programs can be quite expensive, for example, day care, live music, and complimentary valet parking. Others are far less costly, but even more creative. For example, we will publish To Kiss the Rain, *a fictionalized romance based on the history of our steak house. We plan to sell the books at a profit and generate quite a bit of revenue and media coverage in the process. More important is that we will add one more dimension to the Old San Francisco experience—memorable and, of course, unique.*[1]

Chapter Objectives

After reading this chapter, you should be able to:

1. Define the term product, including the core, facilitating, supporting, and augmented product.
2. Explain how atmosphere, customer interaction with the service delivery system, customer interaction with other customers, and customer coproduction are all elements with which one needs to be concerned when designing a product.
3. Understand branding and the conditions that support branding.
4. Explain the new product development process.
5. Understand how the product life cycle can be applied to the hospitality industry.

What Is a Product?

A room at the Four Seasons in Toronto, a Hawaiian vacation, McDonald's French fries, a vacation package in Bali, a catered luncheon, a bus tour of historic sites, and a convention in a modern convention center with group rates in a nearby hotel are all products. Consider the variety of products in a typical casino hotel.

We define the term *product* as follows:

> A product is anything that can be offered to a market for attention, acquisition, use, or consumption that might satisfy a want or need. It includes physical objects, services, places, organizations, and ideas.

This definition refers to the planned component of the product that the firm offers. Besides the planned component, the product also includes an unplanned component. This is particularly true in hospitality and travel products, which are often heterogeneous. For example, a consumer entered a restaurant in Dallas and was greeted by the hostess, who presented him with a menu. When he opened his menu, he saw a dead roach stuck to the inside. After receiving this unexpected bonus, the consumer decided to leave the restaurant. The restaurant certainly did not plan on having a dead roach in the menu. The product the customer receives is not always as management plans. Managers of service organizations need to work hard to eliminate unexpected surprises and make sure the guests get what they expected.

Product Levels

Hospitality managers need to think about the product on four levels: the core product, the facilitating product, the supporting product, and the augmented product.

Core Product

The most basic level is the **core product,** which answers the following question: What is the buyer really buying? Every product is a package of problem-solving services. Theodore Levitt pointed out that buyers "do not buy quarter-inch drills; they buy quarter-inch holes." As all good steak houses have learned, "Don't sell the steak, sell the sizzle." Marketers must uncover the core benefit to the consumer of every product and sell these benefits rather than merely selling features.

9.1 Old San Francisco Steak House

Facilitating Products

Facilitating products are those services or goods that must be present for the guest to use the core product. A first-class corporate hotel must have check-in and checkout services, telephones, a restaurant, and valet service, for instance. In a limited-service economy hotel, facilitating services might be no more than check-in and checkout service and public phones on the property. One important aspect of facilitating products is **accessibility.** Resort condominiums often close the office and registration desk in the evenings. They can get by with this if they notify guests and make arrangements for late-arriving guests to pick up the keys. A business hotel could never get by with closing the front desk. Guests expect it to be accessible. Likewise, if guests expect a hotel to have a business center, it must be accessible when the guests want to uses its services. Product design requires an understanding of the target market and the facilitating services that they require.

Supporting Products

Core products require facilitating products but do not require supporting products. **Supporting products** are extra products offered to add value to the core product and help to differentiate it from the competition. In a corporate hotel, a business center or a full-service health spa are supporting products that may help to draw customers to the hotel. The distinction between facilitating and supporting products is not always clear. Facilitating products for one market segment may be supporting products for another. For example, although families may not require restaurants and valet service when staying at a hotel, business travelers depend on them. Hyatt was among the first chains to offer a broad line of bathroom amenities, including shampoo, conditioners, and several choices of soap. When it introduced these amenities, they were supporting the core product rooms. Today, in Hyatt and similar hotels, amenities have become facilitating products. Other hotels began to match Hyatt's amenity packages, and soon travelers began to expect them in this class of hotel. Hilton spent two years analyzing consumer trends before developing its amenity package, which costs the company $225,000 on an average night.[2]

Bob Burns, the founder of Regent International Hotels, personally selected products that would enhance the chain's luxury image and provide differentiation. Guests staying at the Regent of Hong Kong find full-size bottles of high-quality shampoo in the bathroom. Orange juice is a common menu item in hotels and restaurants throughout the world, but Bob Burns insisted that Regent Hotels serve fresh-squeezed orange juice, in keeping

9.2 Hyatt
Hilton
Regent

with his concept of luxury service. Burns had studied and worked in the hotel industry for years, including a position as general manager of the upscale Kahala Hilton Resort in Hawaii. He had talked with thousands of guests over the years and felt that he knew what they wanted.

Ideally, firms should choose supporting products that are not easily matched by the competition. They should also be able to deliver supporting services in a professional manner. For example, some midscale hotels offer room service because they see it as a competitive advantage in attracting the business traveler. However, the unprofessional delivery of supporting products can do more harm than good. Many midpriced hotels offering room service lack a designated area in the kitchen for room-service carts, a room-service coordinator to answer the phone and write up the tickets, and designated room-service waiters. Necessary equipment and personnel are assembled at the time of the order, and as one might imagine, the results are sometimes disastrous. The person answering the phone lacks the proper training needed to ask the right questions: for example, how the steak is to be cooked, the type of salad dressing the customer would like, and the type of potatoes desired. After taking the order, the next step is to find someone to set up the cart and take the order up to the room. Likely candidates are the bell person, bus person, or a service person from the dining room. Personnel in the first two categories are not properly trained but may jump at the opportunity to gain a tip. Because they are not trained, the bell person and bus person may forget such essential items as salt and pepper, sugar, forks, and napkins when setting up the cart. To damage the hotel's image further, the guest puts the tray in the hallway after finishing the meal. The tray will sit in the hallway until housekeeping picks it up the next morning.

A supporting product offered in some hotels is the technology butler at Ritz-Carlton hotels. The position is described as a person who provides "on-the-road-office support." The technology butler helps people sort out problems with printers, laptops, handhelds, and scanners. The butlers, who have been known to help a businessperson create a sharp-looking presentation for a meeting the next day, also provide software advice. The W hotel in New York has a tech concierge, and Inter-Continental Hotel & Resorts has designated employees as "CyberAssist Coordinators." Certainly the services provided by a technology butler can be invaluable for the anxious businessperson trying to get the printer to print reports for tomorrow's meeting.[3]

Accessibility is also important in supporting services. A hotel health club or a swimming pool that opens at 7:00 A.M. does not help the businessperson who wants to work out at 6:00 A.M., eat breakfast, and go to an 8:00 A.M. business appointment. Including supporting services is not enough; they must be accessible when the guest wants to use them. In summary, supporting products do not offer a competitive advantage if they are not properly planned and implemented. They must meet or exceed customer expectations to have a positive effect.

Augmented Product

The **augmented product** includes accessibility, atmosphere, customer interaction with the service organization, customer participation, and customers' interaction with each other. These elements combine with the core, facilitating, and supporting products to provide the augmented product (Figure 9-1).

From a managerial standpoint, the core product provides a focus for the business; it is the reason for being. Facilitating products are those that are essential for providing the core product to the target market. Supporting products can help position a product. According to Christian Gronroos, a services marketing expert, the core, facilitating, and supporting products determine what the customer receives but not how they receive it.[4] The delivery of the service affects the customer's perception of the service, illustrated by the room service example earlier. The augmented service offering combines what is offered with how it is delivered.

The augmented product is an important concept because hospitality and travel services require customer coproduction of the service. For most products we sell the customer comes to the service delivery system. The customer has to interact with the service delivery system. For example, guests have to check in at the front desk, get to the room, and understand how to use the television and phone systems. They also have to interact with other customers and employees. Because guests come to the service,

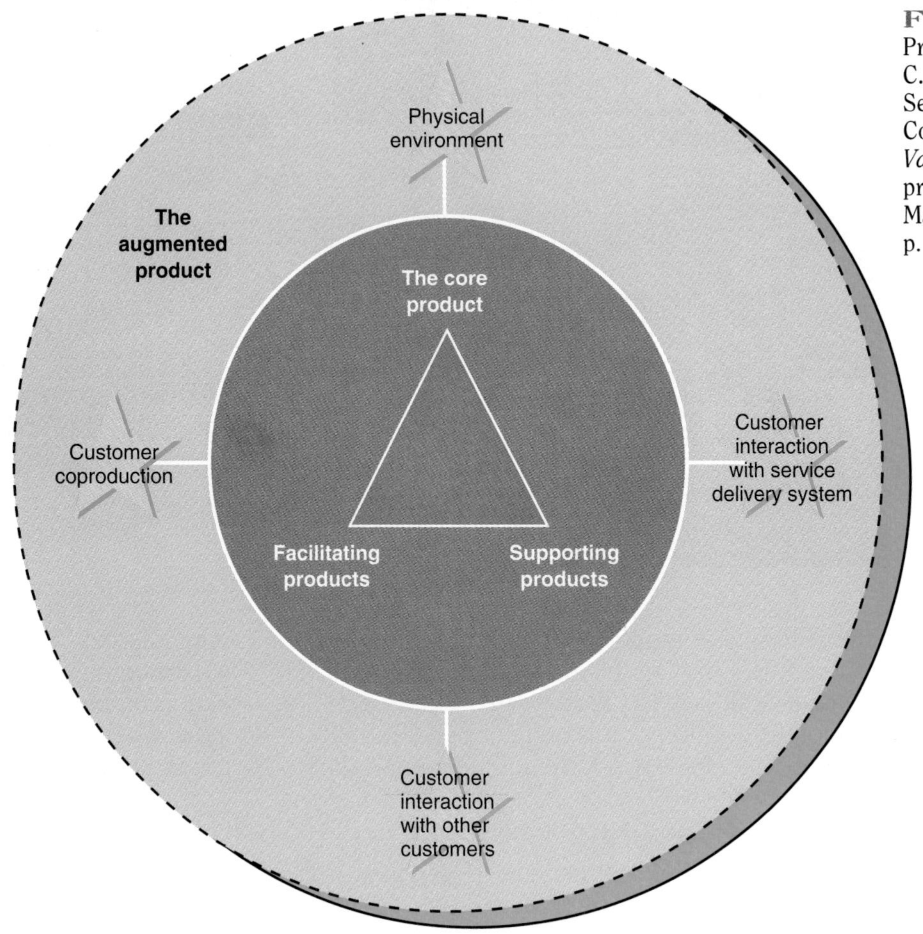

Figure 9-1
Product levels. Adapted from C. Gonroos, "Developing the Service Offering—A Source of Competitive Advantage," in *Add Value to Your Service,* C. Surprenant, ed., (Chicago: American Marketing Association, 1987), p. 83.

The Aureole Restaurant features a four-story tall wine tower, housing almost 10,000 bottles of wine. The enclosed structure holds the wine at 55°F and 70 percent humidity, an ideal climate for wine. The wine stewards fetch the wine by going up and down the sides of the tower on mechanical hoists. The wine tower and the wine stewards create a "wow" effect for the Aureole restaurant. Courtesy of Aureole Las Vegas.

the atmosphere is an important part of the product. The augmented product captures the key elements that must be managed when the customer comes to the service factory; that is, the hotel, restaurant, country club, conference center, or amusement park, and so on. We now take a look at some of the elements of the augmented product.

Atmosphere: The Physical Environment

Atmosphere is a critical element in services. It can be the customer's reason for choosing to do business with an establishment. Burgundy's, a restaurant in Houston, lacked street appeal and went out of business. The restaurant was located in a strip shopping center with a glass panel exterior wall, common in many strip centers. The owners carpeted the concrete floor, put in booths, installed a sign over the door, and opened the restaurant. Perhaps they felt that their food quality and service would attract customers. But few customers ever reached the restaurant. The restaurant's exterior lacked identity or character and was not inviting to potential customers. People who saw Burgundy's simply did not come into the restaurant. Conversely, T.G.I. Friday's has used atmosphere effectively. Their brightly painted buildings with red-and-white awnings suggest a restaurant with a friendly atmosphere. The interior, with its wall decorations and the uniforms of the employees, reinforces the initial perception that T.G.I. Friday's is a casual restaurant.

9.3 Casa Bonita
El Torito
Las Vegas Flamingo
T.G.I. Friday's

Atmosphere is appreciated through the senses. Sensory terms provide descriptions for the atmosphere of a particular set of surroundings. The main sensory channels for atmosphere are sight, sound, scent, and touch. Specifically:

- The main **visual** dimensions of atmosphere are color, brightness, size, and shape.
- The main **aural** dimensions of atmosphere are volume and pitch.
- The main **olfactory** dimensions of atmosphere are scent and freshness.
- The main **tactile** dimensions of atmosphere are softness, smoothness, and temperature.

The following examples illustrate how sensory terms are used to describe particular surroundings. The typical atmosphere of an upscale French restaurant is subdued, quiet, and orderly. The typical atmosphere of a discotheque is bright, noisy, loud, and dynamic.

Atmosphere can affect purchase behavior in at least four ways. First, atmosphere may serve as an attention-creating medium. For example, El Torito uses a Mexican-style building to attract attention. The Casa Bonita Mexican Restaurant in Denver, Colorado, expanded the Mexican theme to include artificial volcanoes and a replica of the diving cliffs of Acapulco from which divers perform for dinner patrons.

Second, atmosphere may serve as a message-creating medium to the potential customer. The tile roof and stucco Spanish exterior architecture lets the prospective customer know that El Torito is a Mexican restaurant. The cheerful, informal appearance suggests a restaurant that is casual without being fast food.

Third, atmosphere may serve as an effect-creating medium. Colors, sounds, and textures directly arouse visceral reactions that stimulate the purchase of a product. At El Torito and Casa Bonita, bright colors and music create a festive atmosphere conducive to selling margaritas.

Finally, environment can be a mood-creating medium. An environmental psychologist has described environments as high load and low load.[5] High and low refer to the information that one receives from the environment. Bright colors, bright lights, loud noises, crowds, and movement are typical elements of a high-load environment, whereas their opposites are characteristic of a low-load environment.[6] A high-load environment creates a playful, adventurous mood, whereas low-load environments create a relaxing mood. Vacationers going to Las Vegas are likely to react positively to a high-load environment which offers the excitement that they were expecting to find. The front desk of the Flamingo Hilton is adjacent to the hotel's casino. While waiting to check in, guests hear the sounds of the casino, watch the players, and feel the excitement. On the other hand, business travelers, who often wish to relax in a homelike setting after a busy day, tend to prefer low-load environments. From the lobby of the Luxeford in Houston, guests can view the club area, with its comfortable stuffed chairs, end tables, and reading materials, a relaxing refuge for the tired executive.

The environments of cities such as New York, Hong Kong, Tokyo, and Mexico City are by nature high load. Many of the successful hotels and restaurants in these cities purposely create a low-load atmosphere as a refuge. Conversely, many cities and towns exude low-load atmospheres, otherwise referred to as dull and boring. Visitors to these towns are often surprised to find a successful restaurant or nightclub in which the level of excitement, color, and movement seem completely out of character. Managers of a company in Florence, South Carolina, were worried when they learned that an important buyer from London had unexpectedly arrived on a Saturday and would spend the weekend alone in their town. They need not have been concerned; the Englishman discovered several country/western dance halls and pronounced that he had never before enjoyed such a great weekend.

Atmosphere must be considered when creating hospitality products. As marketers we should understand what the customer wants from the buying experience and what atmospheric variables will fortify the beliefs and emotional reaction that the buyers are seeking or, in some cases, escaping. Will the proposed atmosphere compete effectively in a crowded market?[7]

Customer Interaction with the Service Delivery System

9.4 Wyatts Cafeterias
Inter-Continental Hotel

The customer participates in the delivery of most hospitality and travel products. There are three phases to this involvement: joining, consumption, and detachment.[8] In the **joining stage,** the customer makes the initial inquiry contact. When designing products we must make it easy for people to learn about the new product. This information must be delivered in a professional way. Wyatts Cafeterias provide an example of a well-planned joining phase. When Wyatts decided to expand their product line by offering takeout meals, a special takeout counter that allowed customers to bypass the cafeteria queue was developed.

The joining phase is often enhanced through sampling. Visitors to foreign countries are often reluctant to order a full meal of native foods. The Inter-Continental Hotel of Jakarta, Indonesia, took steps to introduce visitors to the local cuisine by selling sample plates of selected native foods from a typical native pushcart in the afternoon cocktail area of the hotel adjacent to the lobby. This innovation created excitement, enhanced the atmosphere, introduced guests to native foods served in the hotel's restaurant, and served as a profit-making product line.

The **consumption phase** takes place when the service is consumed. In a restaurant it occurs when the customer is dining; in a hotel,

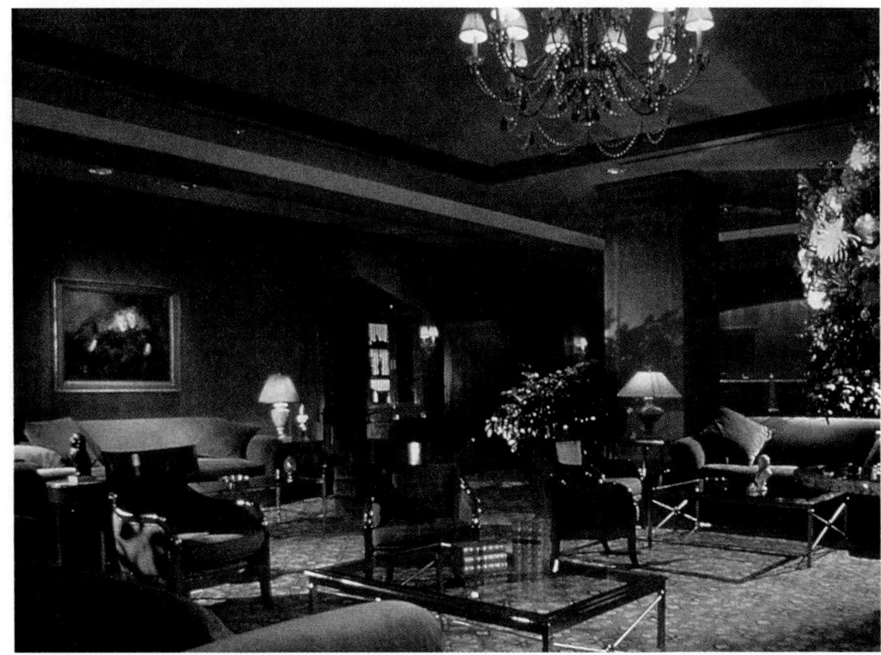

Corporate hotels such as the Hilton at Short Hills use a low-load environment. Courtesy of Hilton Hotels Corporation.

when an individual is a guest. Designers of hospitality products must understand how guests will interact with the product. The employees, customers, and physical facilities are all part of the product. A business hotel that opens a concierge floor aimed at the luxury market must train its employees to meet the expectations of this new class of traveler. In addition to employee customer interaction, hospitality firms also have to consider how customers will interact with each other during the consumption stage. A business hotel in Houston located near Astroworld, a large amusement park, developed a package for the summer family market. The package proved to be so popular that some of the hotel's main market, business travelers, was driven away. The noise of the children in the hallways and the lobby changed the atmosphere. Gone was the comfortable atmosphere desired by the business traveler.

Physical features, layout, and signage can also be used to help customers interact with the product. In many hotels, finding your way to a meeting can be frustrating. This problem can be overcome by proper attention to directional signage. Signage can also be used to make customers aware of the existence of supporting products. Guests may leave a hotel not realizing that it had a health club or a business center. It does no good to invest in supporting products if guests aren't aware of their existence.

Occasionally, even the best designed signage is not observed or understood. Guests who appear lost in the Orlando Peabody Hotel are very apt to discover that an employee, including the general manager, will personally escort them to their destination. This does not occur by accident. Training and positive reinforcement in hotels such as the Peabody ensure that this type of service is an integral part of the hotel's product.

The **detachment phase** is when the customer is through using the product and departs. For example, in a hotel guests may need a bell person to help with the bags. They will need to settle their account and require transportation to the airport. International travelers may need an airport departure tax stamp.

Thinking through these three stages helps management to understand how the customer will interact with the service delivery system, resulting in a product designed to fit the needs of the customer. For example, where it is legal, some hotels purchase and resell airport departure tax stamps. The guest does not have to wait in line at the airport, and the hotel has eliminated one concern for the guest. Although the hotel does not receive income from reselling departure stamps, the guest leaves with a good impression. Similarly, well-managed international hotels will ask guests if they have their passports and airline tickets and if they have cleared their safety deposit box when they are checking out. Managers should think through and then experience the joining, consumption, and detachment phases of their guests.

Customer Interaction with Other Customers

An area that is drawing the interest of hospitality researchers is the interaction of customers with each other. An airline flight on Friday afternoon from Dallas to Houston was sold out with a number of people on standby. Some on standby were construction workers returning home. They worked on jobs in Dallas during the week and had come straight from their job sites. The airline's ground crew, in an effort to maximize revenue, put a construction worker in an empty first-class seat. The passenger paying a premium to sit in first class did not appreciate a worker in dirty construction clothes in the next seat. Hospitality organizations must manage the interaction of customers to ensure that some customers do not negatively affect the experience of others.

The issue of customer interaction is a serious problem for hotels and resorts. The independent, nontour guest consistently objects to the presence of large group-inclusive tours (GIT). This problem is magnified if the GIT guests represent a different culture, speak a foreign language, or are from an age group years different from that of independent, nontour guests.

The Shangrila Hotel of Singapore dealt successfully with this problem by constructing three different hotel properties on the same ground. The tower hotel serves GIT and lesser-revenue, independent, nontour guests. The Bougainvillea section serves a more upscale guest, and a third executive property is for the exclusive use of very upscale guests. Interaction among the three groups is limited to the common outdoor swimming pool.

Ski resorts are facing a serious problem of guest interaction. Traditionally, skiers have been a fairly homogeneous group with common cultural norms, even though they arrive from widely separated geographic areas. German, French, Japanese, American, and Mexican skiers tended to have societal commonalities, despite differences in language.

The arrival of the snowboard changed this congenial mix of guests. Skiers began to complain that they must share the slopes with people dressed in baggy counterculture clothing who often show blatant disregard

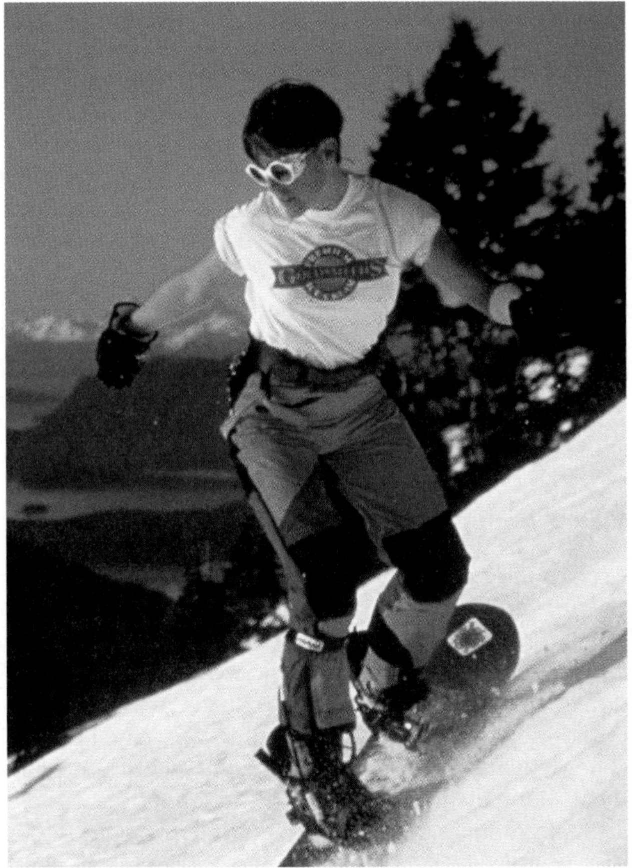

Ski resorts are now faced with how to manage the interaction of skiers and snowboarders. Courtesy of Juneau Conventions and Visitors Bureau.

for slope-side courtesy. The management of ski resorts was suddenly faced with a serious problem. Resorts such as Aspen responded by refusing entry to snowboarders; others, such as Heavenly Valley in California/Nevada, refused entrance to part of the terrain.

The problem for management is compounded by the fact that a ski family often has a preteen or teenage member who wants to snowboard while other members wish to ski. The resort feels that if snowboarders are denied admittance, the family will go elsewhere. This problem is certain to grow as the percentage of snowboarders increases. Some observers feel that the ultimate answer will be to develop separate snowboard resorts, but others feel that this is unrealistic because snowboarders tend not to have the disposable income or spending habits of skiers.

9.5 Hampton Inn

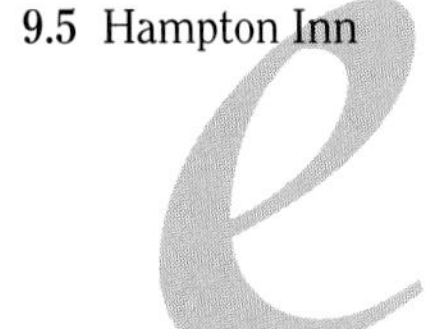

Customer Coproduction

Involving the guest in service delivery can increase capacity, improve customer satisfaction, and reduce costs. Hampton Inn serves a cold breakfast buffet. The combination of cold food and self-service means that breakfast can be served with little labor cost. The Las Vegas Sports Club used to have an attendant handing out keys and towels to members. The attendants would have to ask each member which locker they would like, negotiate alternatives when the member's favorite locker was unavailable, collect the member's card, issue the key, and return their card when the member was finished with the locker. The club installed a device that releases the locker key when the membership card is placed in a slot. When this occurred the towel attendant simply gave out towels. The members are happy because they can pick out a locker in an uncrowded area, and the club's management is pleased because they were able to reduce the number of attendants at the towel counter. Then someone figured out that members could get their own towels if they were neatly stacked on shelves. Now there was no need for the towel and key attendants or counter. The club saved over 100 hours of labor costs per week and incorporated the space into its massage and spa service. Processes like this that can be given to the customer to perform are a win-win for the customer and the business.

Brand Decisions

Branding has long been popular in consumer goods. Some brands have become so powerful that they are used as generic terms for the product itself. Aspirin, shredded wheat, and cellophane were all brand names at one time. The real growth of branding came after the Civil War, with the growth of national firms and national advertising media. Some of the early brands survive, notably Borden's, Quaker Oats, Vaseline, and Ivory Soap. Most national brands in the hospitality industry are less than thirty years old. Today, branding has become a powerful force in the hospitality industry.[9]

9.6 Burger King
Disney
Hilton
McDonald's
Starbucks
Virgin Airlines

A **brand** is a name, term, sign, symbol, design, or a combination of these elements that is intended to identify the goods or services of a seller and differentiate them from those of competitors. A brand name is the part of a brand that can be vocalized. Examples are Disneyland, Hilton, Club Med, and Sizzler. A brand mark is the part of a brand that can be recognized but is not utterable, such as a symbol, design, or distinctive coloring or lettering. Examples are McDonald's golden arches and Hilton's H. A trademark is a brand or part of a brand that is given legal protection; it protects the seller's exclusive rights to use the brand name or brand mark.

It's what the brand stands for in the customer's mind that is important to the company. Scott Davis, author of *Brand Asset Management,* states,

> Brands are among a company's most valuable assets and smart companies today realize that capitalizing on their brands is important. . . . These companies know that brands are more than just products and services. They know that brands are also what the company does and more importantly, what the company is. . . . A brand is a critical component of what a company stands for. It implies trust, consistency, and a defined set of expectations. The strongest brands in the world own a place in the customer's mind, and when they are mentioned almost everyone thinks of the same things. (p. 3)

If we look at the value of a brand as a percentage of market capitalization, we can see that some brands are very valuable. The following are some brand values of companies in the hospitality business: Disney, $32.6 billion; McDonald's, $25.3 billion; Starbucks, $41.8 billion; Burger King, $2.4 billion; and Hilton, $1.2 billion.[10] Thus, by properly managing the brand a company can create a lot of equity.

Richard Branson of Virgin Airlines states, "It is my conviction that what we call shareholder value is best defined by how strongly employees and customers feel about your brand. Nothing seems more obvious to me than that a product or service only becomes a brand when it is imbued with profound values that translate into fact and feelings that employees can project and customers embrace."[11]

If we review the concept of branding, it's really about communicating values, mission, and vision of the company to the employees and customer. If we do a good job at branding, all employees know what the values of the company are, and both employees and customers also know who we are and what we stand for.

Conditions That Support Branding

The following five conditions contribute to the branding decision:[12]

1. The product is easy to identify by brand or trademark.
2. The product is perceived as the best value for the price.
3. Quality and standards are easy to maintain.
4. The demand for the general product class is large enough to support a regional, national, or international chain. Developing a critical mass to support advertising and administrative overhead is important.
5. There are economies of scale.

We review these next.

The Product Is Easy to Identify by Brand or Trademark

Hotel and restaurant chains provide many examples of easily identifiable features. The red-and-white awnings and distinctive painting of T.G.I. Friday's and Holiday Inn's green sign are recognizable to customers. Most freeway billboards are directional signs relying on brand identification. They simply display the brand name and/or the brand mark and directions to the outlet.

The development of a brand name is a key element in developing the identity of the brand. Among the desirable characteristics of a brand name are these:

1. It should suggest something about the product's benefits and qualities. *Examples:* Dairy Queen, Comfort Inns, Pizza Hut, Burger King, American Airlines.
2. It should be easy to pronounce, recognize, and remember. Short names help. *Examples:* Wendy's, Hilton, the Shuttle (United's limited-service airline).
3. It should be distinctive. *Examples:* El Torito, Avis, Bennigan's.

4. For larger firms looking at future expansion into foreign markets, the name should translate easily into foreign languages. Some firms have found that their names have a negative meaning when translated into the language of the countries into which they want to expand.
5. It should be capable of registration and legal protection.

9.7 Accor

Accor Asia Pacific offers ten different brands to differentiate the products that it offers. These range from its travel agency, Carlson Wagonlit Travel, to its catering company Eurest Australia, to its seven lodging brands. The different brands allow each of the products to establish their own position within the market. Sofitel is an upscale hotel, Novotel is a business-class hotel, ibis is a limited-service hotel that offers simplicity, quality, and value for money, and Formule 1 provides consistent motel-style service at budget rates.

Sometimes a company will outgrow its original name.[13] Name changes by major chains include Western International to Westin and Hilton Hotels to Hilton Hotels and Resorts. Companies may wish to change their image through their logos without changing their name. Hyatt recently changed its logo. The new logo matches the company's leading-edge image and capitalizes on its strongest symbol, the Hyatt name. Darryl Hartley-Leonard, president of Hyatt International at the time of the change, explained that there was a gap between consumer perception of their logo and the hotel chain. Research showed that consumers perceived Hyatt to be stylish, contemporary, innovative, and high quality. Conversely, they perceived their logo to be dull and old-fashioned. The new logo was created to fit the chain's consumer image. In major chains such as Hyatt, a logo change that will affect all signage on all hotels, supplies, and merchandise costs millions of dollars.[14] Hyatt invested over $8 million in this change.

Once a name has been chosen, it must be protected. Quality International (now Choice Hotels International) once chose the name McSleep for its line of budget hotels. Quality changed the name to Sleep Inns as a result of legal action by McDonald's.[15] Companies realize that they must protect their trade names or risk losing exclusive use.

The Product Is Perceived as the Best Value for the Price

A brand name derives its value from consumer perceptions. Brands attract consumers by developing a perception of good quality and value. La Quinta developed a good image with the overnight business traveler, whereas Embassy Suites developed an image of good value for those wanting an all-suites hotel. In Chapter 5 we provided an example of how Marriott carried out extensive research to ensure that Fairfield Inns would be perceived as giving good value. Customers must perceive the brand as a better value than other existing choices.

The concept of a brand name extends to tourist destinations. Vail, Aspen, Acapulco, Palm Springs, and the French Riviera have developed strong reputations, consumer perceptions, and expectations. People who promote and develop tourist destinations must assume responsibility for enhancing and ensuring favorable brand images.

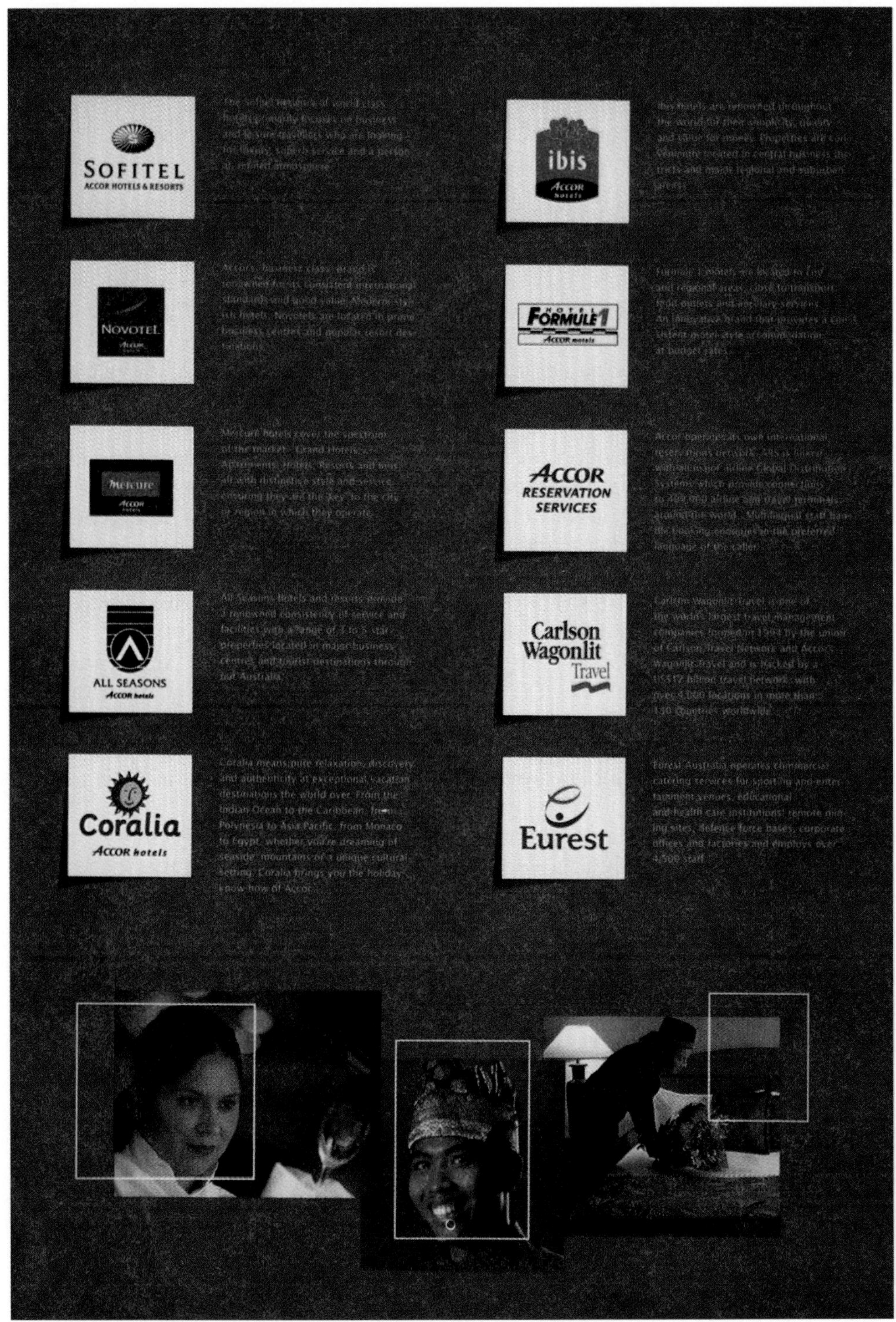

Accor has developed logos for each of its brands so they can be easily identified. Courtesy of Accor Asia Pacific.

Strict building codes, promotional coordination, presentation of historic sites, and protection against environmental degradation are essential to the success of tourist destinations. Chambers of commerce, visitor promotion associations, town councils, county commissioners, environmental groups, and historical societies play a vital role in protecting and enhancing the brand image of a destination.

Quality and Standards Are Easy to Maintain

To be successful, a large multiunit brand such as Pizza Hut, Holiday Inn, Chili's, or Nathan's Hot Dogs must develop systemwide standards to meet the expectations of the customer. If the brand is successful in developing an image of quality, customers will expect quality in all outlets carrying the same brand name. Inconsistent standards and policies will detract from the value of the brand. Consistency and standardization are critical factors.

Consumers often become brand loyal. The major benefit of branding comes from the development of loyal customers. They purchase the brand whenever it is available; the greater the availability, the greater the power of the brand name. Most major hotel chains try to have locations at major destinations in their market areas. Some chains in the United States have opened hotels that they knew would not be profitable for years in order to provide a hotel for their customers in a major city.

McDonald's in Paris attracts Parisians, Germans, Americans, and other nationalities from around the world that are familiar with the McDonald's name. The golden arches have become one of the most powerful brand marks in the world. McDonald's created a demand for its product and then developed more than 15,000 restaurants to meet this demand.

Not all brands are as successful as McDonald's. Peter Yesawich, president of Yesawich, Pepperdine, & Brown, claims that the success of a brand depends on creating a clear differentiation in the customer's mind. Yesawich states that advertising must communicate the perception of a new product. The new brand must communicate benefits to the customer.[16] Robert Hazzard, CEO of Choice Hotels International, says that "people will go for a good deal. The problem is you've got to tell them what a good deal is." Hazzard claims that other hotel brands fail to differentiate themselves by telling why they offer a better deal than their competition in their advertising. He states that "Holiday Inns had Bugs Bunny jumping across a swimming pool; likewise, other major chains had television spots that failed to say here is the benefit, to you the consumer. In our ads we had Vanna White, hostess of *Wheel of Fortune,* coming out of a suitcase saying, 'Stay with us; not only do you get a comfortable room, but you get a thousand dollars in free discount coupons.'"[17]

The Demand for the General Product Class Is Large Enough to Support a Regional, National, or International Chain

New products are generally developed to serve a particular market niche. Later, the product may be expanded to encompass multiniches, or the original niche may grow in market size until it is a huge market-share product such as McDonald's.

The product class of limited-service hotels developed as a small niche within the hotel market but grew until it encompassed many brand names, including limited-service brands of hotel chain companies, such as Hampton Inn (Promus), Ramada Express, and Fairfield Inn (Marriott).

Some hospitality products are strictly regional in nature. Biscuitville, the Waffle House, and Bo Jangles are restaurant chains that have enjoyed considerable success in southern states but have not expanded nationally. In a nation as large as the United States, a strong regional brand is worth multimillions of dollars in sales. As regional tastes cross boundaries, firms that were once considered to be geographically limited have expanded nationwide and even internationally.

9.8 Biscuitville
Bo Jangles
Hampton Inn
Waffle House

La Quinta Inns of San Antonio, Texas, has entered Mexico with a strategy of bypassing large cities such as Monterrey and instead concentrating on smaller cities, such as Leon and Aguascalientes. Because La Quinta is based near the Mexican border and has many Spanish-speaking employees, the company believed that starting a Mexican operation made good sense. "We're pretty well geared up for this kind of thing," stated Gary L. Mead, president and CEO.[18]

Demand estimation for a general product class such as all-suite hotels, roasted chicken, or Mexican foods is not a precise science, but examples abound of entrepreneurs who successfully envisioned a growing demand for a product class. For example, those who built Boston Market saw the need for what is now termed home-meal replacement (HMR). The demographic and lifestyle trends driving the growth of HMR have been evident for some years now and show no signs of letting up. These include DINK households where neither partner feels like cooking, families where both heads of the household are working and both are too

Best Western has developed a name and logo that are recognized internationally. This is a photo of the Best Western in Winsford, England. Courtesy of Best Western International, Inc.

tired to cook or do not have the time to cook but want to provide their children with nutritious meals, young singles who do not know how to cook, and sole survivors who do not want to cook for one person. Many of these restaurant customers prefer to eat in the comforts of their own home. Thus, picking up HMRs at Boston Market, Kenny Roger's Roasters, and similar restaurants is a growing trend. The NPD Group, a research firm, reported that for the first time in 1996, American restaurants sold more takeout meals than meals to be eaten on the premises.[19]

There Are Economies of Scale

Branding costs money. The company promoting a brand name has to develop standards, systems, and quality assurance programs. The brand name must be promoted. To justify expenditures for administration and advertising, the brand should provide economies of scale. Typical economies of scale include reduced promotional costs, because all brand units in the area of influence of the advertising benefit from the promotion. Management information systems, reservation systems, national purchasing contracts, and common architectural designs are ways in which brands can provide economies of scale. Quincy's Steak House and Red Roof Inns appear to follow a strategy of developing multiple units within an area within a short period of time. The number of units within an area serves as a promotional tactic because the public suddenly sees several. Word-of-mouth promotion is a direct result. The cost of advertising in local or regional media such as newspaper, television, and radio broadcast can be allocated among several units. A single stand-alone restaurant or hotel lacks the mass impact of multiunits and does not have the advertising budget to make an impact in a regional or national market.

Leveraging Brand Equity

Brand equity can be leveraged through cobranding and partnerships. In some cases companies that have common ownership offer their brands under one roof. For example, Tricon Global, which owns Taco Bell, KFC, and Pizza Hut, will feature these brands under one roof. Another strategy Tricon uses is to have the brands in separate units but right next to each other. This creates cross promotion of the brands, as well as satisfies the family where the kids want chicken and mom wants Mexican food. Tim Horton's donut shops and Wendy's also have common ownership and are commonly found under one roof in Canada.[20]

9.9 Green Burrito

Sometimes companies will create their own brand in order to cobrand. Carl's Jrs. has the Green Burrito, a Mexican fast-food restaurant in the same space with some of its hamburger restaurants. Blimpie created Pasta Central to partner with its sandwich shoppes, but it also went outside the company to partner with an existing fast-food company, Winner's Chicken and Biscuits. In addition to the drawing power of two brands, cobranding also provides efficiency of scale. Joseph Morgan, group president of Blimpie, points out that cobranding under one roof provides more revenue, allowing the restaurant operation to hire more qualified management. Hannibal Myers, vice president of new business development for Church's, states that using a common back-of-the-house also saves money.[21]

In addition to similar businesses, business partners can provide synergy by each providing a different but complimentary product. A franchisor of Comfort Inn has also made an agreement with Huddle House to franchise a restaurant next to its hotel. Marriott signed a long-term licensing agreement with Starbucks for both Starbucks shops, kiosks, and shops to be placed in its hotels. A year later in 2001 Hyatt signed a similar agreement with Starbucks. Damon's restaurants of Columbus, Ohio, used Oreo cookies brand name to help promote its Damon's Oreo Pie. Michael Branigan, vice president of marketing, states that the Oreo name gives customers a level of credit. In one study 51 percent of restaurant customers agreed that brand names provide more consistent quality, and 50 percent of those surveyed were willing to pay a little more for brand-name products.[22]

New Product Development

A company has to be good at developing new products. It also has to be good at managing them in the face of changing tastes, technologies, and competition. Every product seems to go through a life cycle: it is born, passes through several phases, and eventually dies as younger products come along that better serve consumer needs.

The product life cycle presents two major challenges. First, because all products eventually decline, a firm must find new products to replace aging ones (the problem of new product development). Second, the firm must understand how its products age and change marketing strategies as products pass through life-cycle stages. We look first at the problem of finding and developing new products and then at the problem of managing them successfully during their life cycles.

All hospitality companies must continuously be alert to trends and ready to try new products. Every company needs a new product development program. One expert estimates that half of the profits of all U.S. companies come from products that didn't exist ten years ago.

A company can obtain new products in two ways. One is through acquisition—buying a whole company, a patent, or a license to produce someone else's product. As the cost of developing and introducing major new products climbs, many companies decide to acquire existing brands rather than create new ones. Thus Accor acquired Motel 6; McDonald's acquired Boston Market; Choice acquired Rodeway, Econo Lodge, and Friendship Inns; and Carnival acquired Holland American, Windstar, Costa, and Seabourn.

A company can also obtain new products through new product development by setting up its own research and development department. By new products we mean original products, product improvements, product modifications, and new brands that the firm develops through its own research and development (R&D) efforts. In this chapter we concentrate on new product development.

In a two-year period, 1,000 hotels and motels in the United States failed according to one estimate.[23] Max Schnallinger has been involved in the development of 200 restaurants; one of his latest restaurants is China Max in Hong Kong. He claims that nine of ten restaurants in the United States fail. Why do so many new products fail? There are several reasons.

A high-level executive might push a favorite idea despite poor marketing research findings. Or if the idea is good, the market size may have been overestimated. Or the actual product was not designed as well as it should have been. Or it has been incorrectly positioned in the market, priced too high, or advertised poorly. Sometimes the costs of product development are higher than expected, or competitors fight back harder than expected.

Thus companies face a problem: they must develop new products, but the risk of failure is high. The solution lies in strong new product planning and in setting up a systematic new product development process for finding and nurturing new products. The major steps in this process are shown in Figure 9-2.

Idea Generation

New product development starts with idea generation, the systematic search for new ideas. A company typically has to generate many ideas to find a few good ones. The search for new product ideas should be systematic rather than haphazard. Otherwise, the company risks finding new ideas that will not be compatible with its type of business.

The company should carefully define the new product development strategy. The strategy should state what products and markets to emphasize. It should also state what the company wants from its new products, whether it is high cash flow, market share, or some other objective. For example, McDonald's added salads to defend against the threat of market share loss from Wendy's salad bar, and Pizza Hut added individual pizzas to attract lunch customers. Finally, the strategy should state the amount of effort that is to be devoted to developing original products, changing existing products, and imitating competitors' products.

To obtain a flow of new product ideas, the company must tap several idea sources. Major sources of new product ideas are discussed next.

Internal Sources

One study found that more than 55 percent of all new product ideas come from within the company. Companies can find new ideas through formal research and development, or company executives can brainstorm new product ideas. The company's salespeople are another good source, because they are in daily contact with customers. Guest-contact employees, who are in a position to get feedback from customers, are another excellent source of product ideas. Just as managers look for new ideas

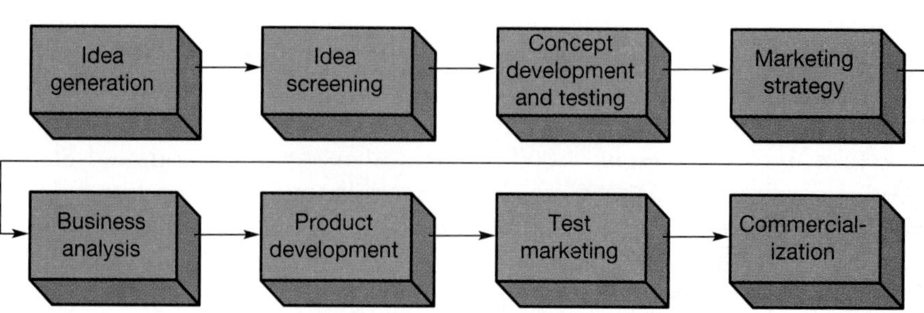

Figure 9-2
Major stages in new product development.

when they visit other restaurants or hotels, employees who care about their jobs do the same thing. Often management never takes advantage of this resource by asking the employees to share their observations.

Within the hotel industry, new product decisions are made at both the corporate and the property levels. New product decision makers at the corporate level include midlevel to top management. In some cases, people not employed directly by the company but closely affiliated with it, such as bankers, lawyers, and consultants, become involved in this process.

Decision makers at the property level often include the owner if the hotel is not owned by a chain. In some cases, the owner is represented by someone, such as a president. Others involved in the process are the general manager, department managers, and directors of various areas. Often, a corporate vice president from the chain may participate in the process.

Customers

Almost 28 percent of all new product ideas come from watching and listening to customers. Consumer needs and wants can be examined through consumer surveys. The company can analyze customer questions and complaints to find new products that better solve consumer problems. Company management or salespeople can meet with customers to obtain suggestions. Managers gain insight into guest needs by walking around the hotel or restaurant and talking with customers. Finally, consumers often create new products on their own. Companies can benefit by finding these products and putting them on the market. Pillsbury gets promising new recipes through its annual Bake-Off. One of Pillsbury's four cake-mix lines and several variations of another came directly from Bake-Off winners' recipes. The owner of a country inn held a dinner party for her friends. She asked guests to bring their favorite dishes and enough copies of the recipes so that all the guests could have a copy. This provided an interesting evening, as well as several menu ideas for the country inn.

Many upscale hotels hold a weekly cocktail reception for special guests. The general manager and managers of various departments serve as hosts. This provides management with an opportunity to ask these guests informally for suggestions as to how the hotel can continue to provide outstanding service. Because these guests visit hotels throughout the world and are often innovators in their respective fields, their opinions and ideas are valuable and respected.

Competitors

About 27 percent of new product ideas come from analyzing competitors' products. Many companies buy competing new products, see how they are made, analyze their sales, and decide whether they should bring out new products of their own. A company can also watch competitors' ads and other communications to obtain clues about new products. When taking a competitor's idea, one should be able to do it as least as well as the originator. Customers will compare the copy with the original; if that comparison is negative, the product will suffer.

One can appear to be innovative by picking up ideas from other markets. Michael Turback, formerly of Turback's Inn in Ithaca, New York, made it a point to go to the restaurant show in Chicago and to visit restaurants in New York City to gather ideas for his restaurant. His customers viewed him as an innovator.

Many successful hospitality products have been copied by international entrepreneurs. Often, the copy product is of inferior quality and may create a poor reputation for the product class, so when the original company enters the market it must overcome a negative image. In other cases, the foreign company may develop a product that is so successful that it sets the standard for its product class. The restaurant chain Pollo Campero of Central America has become the standard against which competitors such as KFC are compared.

When companies transplant ideas from other areas of the country, they must be careful to take regional cultural and social differences into consideration. A former chef of a restaurant on the California coast, specializing in excellent cuisine served in a casual atmosphere, transported the restaurant's concept to Bryan, Texas. The California restaurant offered fine cuisine at a moderate price. Unfortunately, tastes and spending habits were not the same in the small Texas town. Rather than elegantly prepared seafood, the people of Bryan preferred fried seafood or a steak and potato. What was moderately priced in California was high priced in Bryan. The chef's elegant seafood restaurant has closed, and the location now houses a steak house.

Hotel executives can pick up competitive information by staying at a competitor's hotel. Excellent competitive information is available from the annual reports of publicly traded hotel companies. The hotel industry is relatively small. Executives and owners tend to know and associate with their peers from competitive hotels. This is true for most communities. Internationally, general managers of different chains tend to know each other and to swap information. The hotel industry is one of the least secretive industries. Managers can easily obtain competitive information.

Distributors and Suppliers

Distributors are close to the market and can pass along information about consumer problems and new product possibilities. Suppliers can tell the company about new concepts, techniques, and materials that can be used to develop new products. They can also tell which food products are moving in competitive restaurants and new products ordered by hotels.

Hospitality suites are often sponsored by distributors and suppliers at industry trade shows, seminars, and conferences. It is usually a good idea to visit these suites for purposes of picking up information about trends and competitive strategies, as well as to meet important contacts.

Other Sources

Other idea sources include trade magazines, shows, and seminars; government agencies; new product consultants; advertising agencies; marketing research firms; university and commercial laboratories; and inventors.

Idea Screening

The purpose of idea generation is to create a large number of ideas. The purpose of the succeeding stages is to reduce the number of ideas. The first such stage is idea screening. The purpose of screening is to spot good ideas and drop poor ones as quickly as possible. Product development costs rise greatly in later stages, so the company wants to proceed only with ideas that will turn into profitable products. Most companies require their executives to write up new product ideas on a standard form that can be reviewed by a new product committee. The executives describe the product, the target market, and the competition. They make some rough estimates of market size, product price, development time and costs, manufacturing costs, and rate of return. They also answer the following questions: Is this idea good for our particular company? Does it mesh well with the company's objectives and strategies? Do we have the people, skills, equipment, and resources to make it succeed? Many companies have well-designed systems for rating and screening new product ideas. Figure 9-3 is a qualitative and quantitative screening work sheet developed by Tom Feltenstein of the American Restaurant Marketing Group.

The idea or concept screening stage is the appropriate time to review carefully the question of product line compatibility. A common error in new product development is to introduce products that are incompatible with the company. The following describes major compatibility issues. How will the product assist us to:

- Fulfill our mission?
- Meet corporate objectives?
- Meet property objectives?
- Protect and promote our core business?
- Protect and please our key customers?
- Better utilize existing resources?
- Support and enhance existing product lines?

Concept Development and Testing

Surviving ideas must now be developed into product concepts. It is important to distinguish between a product idea, a product concept, and a product image. A **product idea** envisions a possible product that company managers might offer to the market. A **product concept** is a detailed version of the idea stated in meaningful consumer terms. A **product image** is the way that consumers picture an actual or potential product.

Major restaurant chains cannot afford to place an untested menu in all their restaurants. Burger King, like others, uses test market restaurants in selected cities. The Piedmont area of North Carolina was used as a test market for American fries. Apparently, the product performed poorly, because it disappeared from the menus. Hotels commonly introduce new product ideas to selected floors and to selected properties.

Concept Development

In the late 1970s, Marriott recognized that the urban market for its current hotel products was becoming saturated. They needed a hotel concept that would work in secondary sites and suburban locations. Marriott decided

Qualitative screening worksheet

1. Proposed new product ____________________
2. General description ____________________
3. Company objectives it will meet ____________________
4. Role it will play: new entree side dish new product category
5. Key strengths or opportunities ____________________
6. Key weaknesses or threats ____________________
7. Expected impact on sales: increase traffic increase frequency trade up draw new customer group(s) increase average check
8. Yearly sales goal ________ Profit-impact goal ____________________
9. Items it will cannibalize ________ To what degree ____________________
10. Target customers ____________________
11. Day part(s) affected ____________________
12. Target price ________ Target portion size ____________________
13. Key ingredients ____________________
14. Estimated food costs ____________________
15. Expected production required ____________________
16. Current equipment required ____________________
17. New equipment required ____________________
18. Space required ____________________
19. Labor required ____________________
20. Additional employees required ____________________
21. Special training required ____________________
22. Negative effects on current production ____________________
23. Negative effects on staff ____________________
24. Similar competitive items ____________________
25. Likely competitive response ____________________
26. Key benefits ____________________
27. Key disadvantages ____________________
28. Required for development:
    a. facilities ____________________
    b. budget ____________________
    c. personnel ____________________
    d. special expertise ____________________
    e. time ____________________

Quantitative screening worksheet

CRITERIA	RATING (A)	WEIGHT (B)	TOTAL (A x B)
Image			
Menu approach			
Overall company goals			
Company strengths			
Company opportunities			
Desired role			
Level of quality			
Pricing			
Current customers			
Targeted customers			
Services			
Specialties			
Menu voids			
Day-part voids			
Production procedures			
Labor content			
Equipment			
Space availability			
Suppliers			
Developmental capabilities			
TOTAL			

Each new product idea is rated on a scale of 1 (low) to 5 (high) on each of the criteria. Then a weight of 1 to 5 is assigned to each criterion. The product of the rating and the weight gives a total score for the product on each criterion. The sum of these scores gives a final grand total for comparison with other proposed products.

Figure 9-3
Qualitative and quantitative screening worksheets. Reprinted by permission of Elsevier Science, Inc., from "New Product Development in Food Service: A Structural Approach," by Tom Feltenstein, *Cornell Hotel and Restaurant Administration Quarterly,* 27, no. 3, pp. 66–67. © 1996 by Cornell University.

to focus its assets on the company's core business, lodging, through the development of a new product.

This was a product idea. Customers, however, do not buy a product idea; they buy a product. The marketer's task is to develop this idea into alternative product concepts, determine how attractive each is to customers, and choose the best one.

The concept for the new product was called Courtyard by Marriott. Marriott selected persons from different areas of the company to manage the development of this new product. The company conducted extensive competitor and market analysis and, as a result of this research, developed the following conceptual framework for the project:[24]

1. It would be tightly focused for the transient market.
2. It would house fewer than 150 rooms.
3. It would project a residential image. (Through their research Marriott identified a major segment of hotel users who did not like hotels! These consumers preferred homelike settings.)
4. It would not have significant cannibalization of Marriott's other hotels.
5. It would have a limited-menu restaurant.
6. Public and meeting spaces would be limited.
7. It would be a standardized product with five to eight in a region.
8. The Marriott name would be attached for recognition and a halo effect. (Halo or umbrella effect refers to the carryover of a corporate or brand name to other products. The name Nabisco has a halo effect for many products, from Oreo cookies to shredded wheat.)

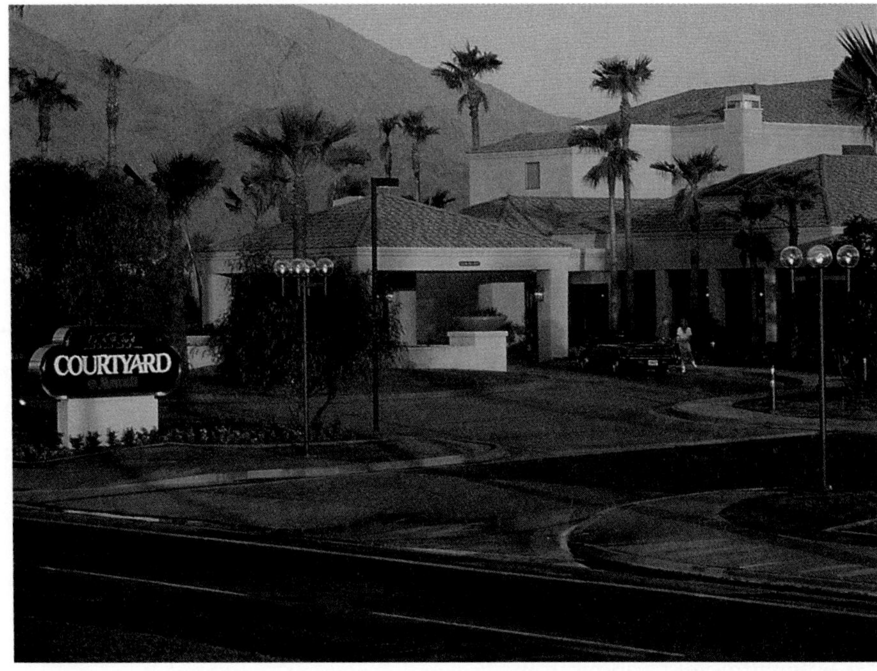

Courtyard by Marriott went through extensive concept testing before it was introduced to the market. Courtesy of Marriott International; Jim Burnett, photographer.

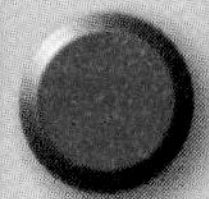

Marketing Highlight 9-1

In the early 1980s, Wendy's spent more than three years testing a concept for breakfast. Wendy's vice president of research and development at the time, Jim Stubblefield, stated that Wendy's previous failure at breakfast made them "extra cautious." He felt the reason for the previous failure was that Wendy's was offering a "me too" breakfast. The objectives for the new breakfast menu were quality and uniqueness.

Wendy's chose three items: an omelet made to order with a choice of fillings, French toast, and a breakfast sandwich. The products were taste-tested at Wendy's headquarters. The R&D equipment testing lab chose the equipment to produce the new products. Next, Wendy's tested the products in a few stores and gave free samples to customers to get their reactions. At the same time, Wendy's tested the production capability of an actual Wendy's unit by producing the items in a store during the night. As a result of these tests, Wendy's made some refinements and test marketed the breakfasts in a few stores. Revisions were made based on these tests. For example, premade omelet shells were filled to order. Wendy's decided to cook the omelets to order so that customers could see their omelet cooking on the grill. They revised the menu to include a scrambled egg platter and changed the format of the breakfast sandwich. The revised menu was tested in Columbus, Ohio, getting customer input on the new variations. Finally, Wendy's introduced the breakfast on a store-by-store basis. By January 1983, it had been introduced in seventy units. The company planned the first television advertisement for the spring of 1983.

Wendy's continued to move cautiously with its breakfast menu for the next two years. Finally, in the summer of 1985 it rolled out a multimillion dollar advertising campaign for its breakfast. Despite research and cautious entry, the breakfast failed. Wendy's developed a system to produce made-to-order omelets in ninety seconds. Yet they failed to consider what would happen when a group of customers came in at the same time. When omelets were cooked to order, the wait could exceed several minutes. As one analyst put it, this was no longer a fast-food business. Dave Thomas, the founder of Wendy's, said, "We made every omelet to order. Our competitors make things up and put them under a heat lamp. We just could not compete with that." He added, "I think we made a mistake. I don't think our testing was as accurate as it should have been."

During the development of its breakfast, Wendy's put its new breakfast program through seemingly exhaustive testing. It had developed a unique and quality product. The delivery time was fast compared with a family restaurant such as Denny's, but not fast enough for a fast-food restaurant. Also, cooking the items to order made it difficult, if not impossible, to purchase the items through the drive-through window. Thus sales were also lost from this growing segment of the business. Even with significant research efforts and test marketing, products fail.

Introducing a new product is a complex process. It is difficult to consider all the variables. In research and test marketing, you want to answer as many questions as possible, to increase a product's chances of success or remove a product failure before it moves to the commercialization stage.

Source: Julie Liesco, "The Taste of Time," *Restaurants and Institutions* (February 1, 1983): 79–84.

Concept Testing

Concept testing occurs within a group of target consumers. New product concepts may be presented through word or picture descriptions. Marriott tested their concept for the Courtyard Motel using a statistical technique called *conjoint analysis*. This involved showing potential target guests different motel configurations and having them rank them from the most to the least desirable. The rankings were statistically analyzed to determine the optimal motel configuration.[25]

In most cases, however, simpler consumer attitude surveys are used. Suppose that 10 percent of the consumers said they "definitely" would buy and another 5 percent said "probably." The company would project these figures to the population size of this target group to estimate sales volume. But the estimate would be uncertain, because people do not always carry out their stated intentions.

Unfortunately, the Marriott example is far too rare within the hospitality industry. The corporate headquarters of major hotel, resort, and restaurant chains do engage in professional concept testing, but smaller chains and individual properties often pass over this critical stage. They often move directly from product idea to full implementation.

In some cases, intuition or luck proves to be correct, and the new product is a winner, thus placing the company well ahead of competition. However, the history of the hospitality industry has proved that in many cases the idea needed the evidence of concept testing, because the product proved to be a disastrous mistake. In the case of a tactical product decision, such as a hotel room amenity or a new room service beverage, there may be relatively little damage from an incorrect new product decision. This is not true of new product decisions involving heavy capital expenditures, such as a new ship for a cruise line or a new destination resort. These decisions involve multimillions of dollars and have sometimes proved so disastrous that hospitality companies have been forced into bankruptcy. The expenditure of a few thousand dollars and a few extra months for concept testing might prove invaluable in the long run.

Marketing Strategy

The next step is marketing strategy development—designing an initial marketing strategy for introducing the product into the market. The marketing strategy statement consists of three parts. The first part describes the target market, the planned product positioning, and the sales, market share, and profit goals for the first few years. The target markets for Courtyard by Marriott were business travelers who wanted moderately priced, high-quality rooms and pleasure travelers who wanted a safe, comfortable room.

The second part of the marketing strategy statement outlines the product's planned price, distribution, and marketing budget for the first year. Statistical software enabled Marriott to build sophisticated models. These models provided information on pricing and expected market share based on these prices. The segmentation information gave Marriott the information it needed for marketing the hotels.

The third part of the marketing strategy statement describes the planned long-run sale, profit goals, and marketing-mix strategy over time.

Business Analysis

Once management decides on the product concept and marketing strategy, it can evaluate the business attractiveness of the proposal. Business analysis involves a review of the sales, costs, and profit projections to determine whether they satisfy the company's objectives. If they do, the product can move to the product-development stage.

To estimate sales, the company should look at the sales history of similar products and should survey market opinion. It should estimate minimum and maximum sales to learn the range of risk.

After preparing the sales forecast, management can estimate the expected costs and profits for the product. The costs are estimated by the R&D, operations, accounting, and finance departments. The analysis includes the estimated marketing costs. The company then uses the sales and costs figures to analyze the new product's financial attractiveness.

The tools in Figure 9-4 can assist managers in their business analysis.

Product Development

If the product concept passes the business test, it moves into product development. Here the product concept develops into a prototype of the product. Up to now it existed only as a word description, a drawing, or a mock-up. This step, which calls for a large increase in investment, will show whether the product idea can be turned into a workable product. The company will develop one or more physical versions of the product concept. It hopes to find a prototype that meets the following criteria:

1. Consumers perceive it as having the key features described in the product concept statement.
2. It performs safely under normal use.
3. It can be produced for the budgeted costs.

Developing a successful prototype can take days, weeks, months, or even years. Marriott built a Courtyard room prototype with portable walls. They developed three room types: a standard, a short, and a narrow configuration. The consumers liked the overall concept. They rejected the narrow version but did not object to the short version, which Marriott estimated would save close to $100,000 per hotel.

One problem with developing a prototype is that the prototype is often limited to the core product. Many of the intangible aspects of the product, such as the performance of the employees, cannot be included. Marketers have to remember that they must try to give the prospective customer an idea of the intangible aspects of the product, including the supporting and facilitating goods and services.

Test Marketing

If the product passes functional and consumer tests, the next step is market testing. Market testing is the stage in which the product and marketing program are introduced into more realistic market settings.

Market testing allows the marketer to gain experience in marketing the product, to find potential problems, and to learn where more information is needed before the company goes to the great expense of full introduction. Market testing evaluates the product and the entire marketing program in real market situations. The product, its positioning strategy, advertising, distribution, pricing, branding, packaging, and budget levels are evaluated during market testing. The company uses market testing to learn how consumers and dealers will react to handling, using, and repur-

CORPORATE	Effect on Corporate Image Long Run Compatibility/Cannibalism Finance—Millions Corporate Form—Ownership, Franchise, Contracts Marketing—Compatibility w/other Company Products Human Resources Others
PROPERTY	Effect on Property's Image Effect on Corporate Image Compatibility w/Existing Product Line Financing—"0" to over $1,000,000 Cash Flow/Profits Compatibility—Operations—w/Various Departments (particularly Human Resources) Timing—Product Life Cycle Customer/Guest—Reaction

PROPERTY—NEW PRODUCT EVALUATION

Objectives		*Expected Resources Required*	
$	________	$ Capital Investment	________
Volume	________	Personnel	
Expected Effect on:	________	Existing—Full Time	Days ________ $
Margins	________	New—Full Time	Days ________ $
Occupancy	________	Existing—Part Time	Day + $
Yield	________	New—Part Time	Day + $
Average Daily Rates	________	Materials—Not Covered in Capital Investment	
Other Cash Flow	________	$	
Etc.	________	Units	
Other—Qualitative Objectives		Support	
________________		Promotional	$ ________
________________		Administrative	$ ________
________________		Other	$ ________

Figure 9-4
New product decision factors.

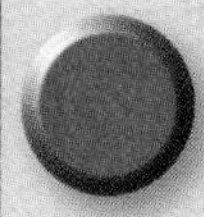

Marketing Highlight 9-2

The National Food Laboratory Helps Restaurants Develop New Products and Improve Existing Products

Consider for a moment the enormous effort and expense it takes to put a new or improved restaurant item on the menu, or when producing and marketing a restaurant-branded product: R&D, purchasing, ramp up, packaging, transport, advertising, even store product-slotting fees. After spending tens of thousands to millions, possibly, to develop and promote a new item, a restaurant chain cannot afford to have a product that is off-taste, off-color, off-odor, or worse, with features no one's willing to pay for.

Targeting Consumer Tastes with Accuracy. In a food service environment, where even large restaurants and companies no longer have full-size R&D staffs, getting the product right the first time is more critical than ever. Often this means teaming up with the right partner, who can help ensure a product rollout is worth the effort. For decades, marketing professionals have turned to the National Food Laboratory (NFL), a leader in food and beverage-related consumer research, descriptive analysis, testing, and product development.

"The NFL understands our needs, our business, and is excellent at follow through, which is what relationship building is all about," said Ed Yuhas, vice president of marketing for Aurora Food's breakfast division. "We look at them as a partner in bringing the right product to market in the right time frame." With the NFL as a partner, clients decide how wide or narrow the research focus is, and often receive integrated advice that can solve small problems before they become big ones. Typically, the NFL custom matches its research methods and protocol to suit each client's goals. For example, a custom roll-in, roll-out kitchen allows restaurant clients to test products on their own equipment, such as stoves and fryers, for practical, reality-based results.

"From no prep to high prep, The NFL can prepare and serve food the way our clients would in their own restaurants," says Kevin Buck, the NFL president. "Whether you're testing desserts or specialty pastas, we ensure product consistency and keep chefs on staff so we can start with raw ingredients."

The NFL can help guide marketing efforts with greatest accuracy in concept stage using focus groups. In fact, consumer panels, which marketers often rely on to differentiate products from competitors and verify need, are one of The NFL's specialties. Because knowing what consumers want can make the difference between promoting a successful product or one that fails, savvy marketers follow the adage, "It's better to measure twice and cut once."

Riding a Consumer Trend through Product Development and Scale-Up. For smaller restaurant chains that do not have their own product develop-

chasing the product. Market testing results can be used to make better sales and profit forecasts.

The amount of market testing needed varies with each new product. Market testing costs can be enormous, and market testing takes time, during which competitors may gain an advantage. When the costs of developing and introducing the product are low or when management is already confident that the new product will succeed, the company may do little or no product testing. Minor modifications of current products or

ment kitchen and chefs, the NFL provides trained chefs. Their chefs are cross-trained in food technology, and work hand-in-hand with food scientists. This can be key in creating a hit that brings restaurant trends to the consumer level, and can speed product development as well. Chefs are particularly good at brainstorming viable concepts at the early stages of product development in a short amount of time. Perhaps, more important, with a wide knowledge of food trends and ethnic dishes, chefs can help clients spot emerging consumer trends before spending further resources. Blending art and science, restaurants and food-service companies can develop better food and beverage products in less time, with more consumer panache.

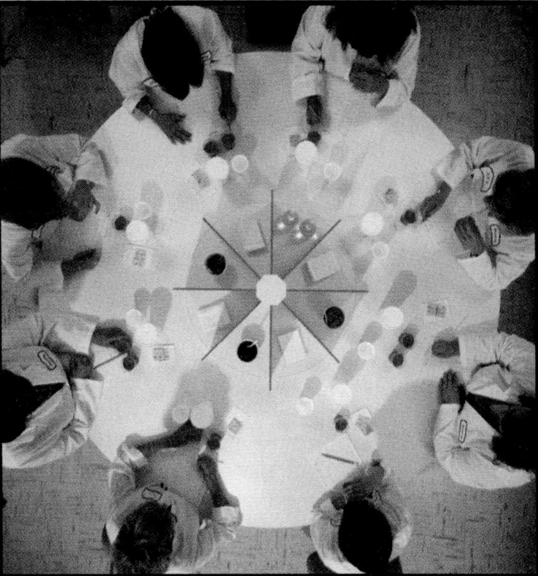

"The NFL chef, working with food scientists, can help marketing departments zero in on the next consumer hot button," says Lohmeyer. "Our chef can immediately pull grocery store ingredients and put together a variety of concepts to jump start product development." Because chefs draw on a broad knowledge of food techniques and styles, they can think up exciting new uses for existing products. For example, using a salad dressing as a marinade may significantly expand product use while opening new markets. From a chef's new product or line extension ideas, clients can quickly pick the most promising variations for further development.

An effective product development team requires a balance of skills and resources. The NFL has provided product development expertise for restaurant and food service companies. They provide chefs to help develop new products and panelists to test the finished products. Developing new products is a process gaining expert help during this process can increase the chances for success.

Source: Press release for NFL by Del Williams.

copies of successful competitor products might not need testing. The company may do considerable market testing if one of these conditions is present: The introduction of a new product requires a large investment, or management is not sure of the product or the marketing program. Some products and marketing programs are tested, then withdrawn, changed, and retested many times over a period of several years before they are finally introduced. The costs of market tests are high but are often small compared with the costs of making a major mistake.

Marketing Highlight 9-3

Restaurants and Hotels Develop New Product Ideas

This marketing highlight looks at some examples of creative hospitality products. The companies identified a target market and created successful products for that target market.

Airport Hotel Develops "Flite Bite." A number of hotels are taking advantage of the poor image airline food has received over the years by providing their guests with takeout meals designed for the air traveler. The Ritz-Carlton Marina Del Ray, located less than ten minutes away from the Los Angeles International Airport, developed a snack for travelers called Flight Bite, consisting of a granola bar, fresh fruit, a brownie, and sparkling water. Other Flight Bites include a continental breakfast, a light lunch, and a dinner. The Four Seasons Hotel in Houston offers "Fly-Away Gourmet" meals for $14.50 each. The airport Hiltons in Atlanta, Miami, Newark, and Chicago (O'Hare) have also developed takeout meals aimed at the air traveler.

Arizona Biltmore Promotes "Ladies Choice" Package. "Ladies Choice" is a package designed by the Arizona Biltmore hotel in Phoenix. This package is targeted at women needing time out from the rigors of daily life: job, husband, children. They also want social interaction with friends and other women. The program features a massage or facial, afternoon teas, and a chocolate workshop. The women can also choose from an assortment of extra activities, including wine tastings, cooking classes (see photo), a personal trainer in the health club, and golf lessons.

McDonald's and Ukrop's Supermarkets Joint Venture at Virginia Commonwealth University. The two McDonald's on campus are now offering students a choice between fast food and home-meal replacement products. McDonald's was able to expand its product line by joint venturing with Ukrop's supermarket. The supermarket provides it "Fresh Express," a series of home replacement meal products, ranging from macaroni and cheese to grilled dijon chicken. Under the arrangement, Ukrop's supplies the meals to McDonald's for resale. The meals are displayed in a refrigerated case set off by an awning. The home replace-

Marriott chose Atlanta as a test market for its first Courtyard by Marriott, which opened in 1983. The test market model contained different-sized rooms to gain consumer perceptions. Marriott discovered that the rooms could be smaller than they had originally planned. Also, the guests said that they wanted doors on the closets. The test model had doorless closets, which was common in that category.

Commercialization

Market testing gives management the information it needs to make a final decision about whether to launch the new product. If the company goes ahead with commercialization, it will face high costs. It may have to spend between $10 million and $100 million for advertising and sales promotion alone in the first year. For example, McDonald's Corporation, best known for its Big Mac and Golden Arches, opened two 4-star hotels as a test market in Switzerland. If successful, McDonald's would extend its product offering through Golden Arch Hotels in Europe. McDonald's believes that European customers will appreciate the same qualities in homent meals have accounted for up to one-third of McDonald's sales. Through the joint venture, McDonald's was able to acquire a new product line and increase its sales. By partnering with the developer of the product, McDonald's avoided the cost of new product development.

Problem of Foreign Exchange Solved by Technology. The Milford Plaza Hotel in New York City has an equal number of international and domestic guests. The hotel did not want to get into the foreign exchange business. Doing so would have meant training employees, setting up controls, and tying up the front desk staff during peak check-in and checkout times. So it sent the twenty to thirty guests a day requesting foreign exchange down the street to exchange their money. Then the hotel's management came across a machine that exchanges ten different currencies. The rates are easily changed each day, and the commission fees are built into the exchange rate. Anthony Bergamo, managing director, says the machines make the stay more enjoyable for the guests. Through this self-service machine, the hotel can now offer guests a currency exchange service without burdening its front desk staff with this duty. The product creates customer satisfaction and provides additional income for the hotel.

Source: Glenn Haussman, "How Hotels Use Amenities, Services to Attract New Business," *Hotel Business,* March 21–April 6, 1997, pp. 23–26; Heather Vogel Frederick, "Student Union," *Restaurant Business,* December 1, 1997, p. 16; Carl Corry, "Airport Hotels Cater to Travelers by Offering a Selection of Take-out Items," *Hotel Business,* September 21–October 6, 1997, p. 9.

tels that they expect of hamburgers: quality, service, cleanliness, and value. In launching a new product, the company must make four decisions: when, where, to whom, and how.[26]

When?

The first decision is whether it is the right time to introduce the new product. In Marriott's case the test market hotel experienced an occupancy of 90 percent.

Where?

The company must decide whether to launch the new product in a single location, a region, several regions, the national market, or the international market. Few companies have the confidence, capital, and capacity to launch new products into full national distribution. Instead, they develop a planned market rollout over time. Small companies in particular tend to select an attractive city and put on a blitz campaign to enter the market. They may enter other cities one at a time. Large companies may decide to introduce their product into one region and then move to the next. Companies with national distribution networks, such as auto companies, often launch their new models in the national market. Marriott decided to introduce the Courtyard in regional markets of five to eight. By January 1986, they had 300 sites open, under contract, or under construction.

To Whom?

Within the rollout markets, the company must target its distribution and promotion to the best prospect groups. Management should have determined profiles of prime prospects during earlier market testing. It must now fine-tune its market identification, looking for early adopters, heavy users, and opinion leaders.

How?

The company must develop an action plan for introducing the new product into the selected markets and spend the marketing budget on the marketing mix.

Product Development through Acquisition

9.9 Chevy's
PepsiCo
Romano's Macaroni Grill

Large companies will sometimes buy a small restaurant chain rather than develop their own new concepts. They are able to watch the fledgling chain grow. They sit back and observe its customer base, volume of sales per unit, and how easy or difficult it is to open new stores. When they are convinced that the new chain looks like a winner and makes a good strategic fit with their organization, the large company simply buys the chain. This is what Brinker International did when they purchased Romano's Macaroni Grill, and PepsiCo purchased Chevy's and California Pizza Kitchen. This method of product development reduces the risk considerably for large companies that have the assets to purchase and then develop the chain. This acquisition strategy has a new class of restaurant entrepreneurs, those who try to develop a chain with the specific purpose of getting it going and selling it to a large chain.

Another technique is to purchase distressed chains. The mismanagement of a chain and resulting poor performance can drive the market value of the chain down. These chains become attractive targets for companies who feel they can turn them around. This is what PepsiCo did when they purchased KFC and Taco Bell.[27] Thus, rather than develop your own products, an option is to purchase new products.

Product Life-Cycle Strategies

After launching a new product, management wants the product to enjoy a long and lucrative life. Although the product is not expected to sell forever, managers want to earn enough profit to compensate for the effort and risk. To maximize profits, a product's marketing strategy is normally reformulated several times. Strategy changes are often the result of changing market and environmental conditions as the product moves through the product life cycle (PLC).

The product life cycle is marked by five distinct stages (Figure 9-5):

1. **Product development** begins when the company finds and develops a new product idea. During product development, sales are zero and the company's investment costs add up.

2. **Introduction** is a period of slow sales growth as the product is being introduced into the market. Profits are nonexistent at this stage because of the heavy expenses of product introduction.
3. **Growth** is a period of rapid market acceptance and increasing profits.
4. **Maturity** is a period of slowdown in sales growth because the product has achieved acceptance by most of its potential buyers. Profits level off or decline because of increased marketing outlays to defend the product against competition.
5. **Decline** is the period when sales fall off quickly and profits drop.

Not all products follow this S-shaped product life cycle. Some products are introduced and die quickly. For example, trendy nightclubs will often have a short life cycle with a steeper curve. Fried vegetables are an example of a menu product that had a short life and a steep curve. They were very popular in the early 1980s but by the end of the decade had lost their popularity. Hotels often start into decline and then through a major renovation regain their popularity and a new growth stage. Diners popular in the 1950s and then replaced by fast-food chains became a popular style of restaurant again in the 1980s. Other products may stay in the mature stage for a very long time.

The PLC concept can describe a product class (fast-food restaurants), a product form (fast-food hamburgers), or a brand (Wendy's). The PLC applies differently in each case. Product classes have the longest life cycles. The sales of many product classes stay in the mature stage for a long time. Product forms, on the other hand, tend to have the standard PLC shape. Product forms such as the drive-in restaurant and roadside tourist court pass through a regular history of introduction, rapid growth, maturity, and decline. A specific brand's life cycle can change quickly because of changing competitive attacks and responses.

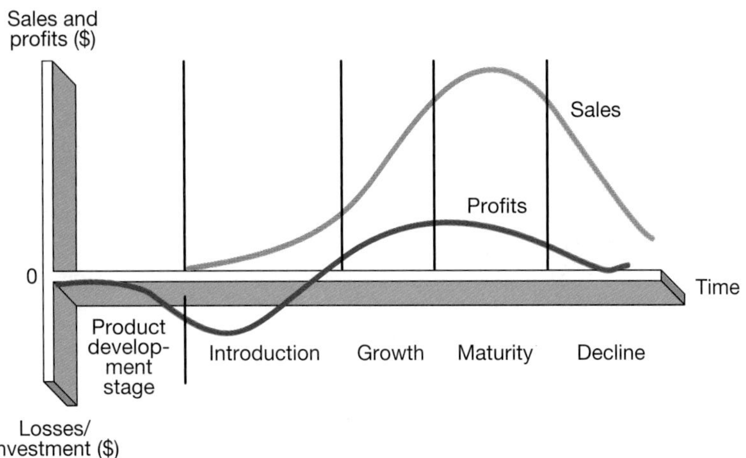

Figure 9-5
Sales and profits over the product's line from inception to demise.

The PLC concept is a useful framework for describing how products and markets work. But using the PLC concept for forecasting product performance or for developing marketing strategies presents some practical problems. For example, managers may have trouble identifying a product's current life-cycle stage, determining when it has moved into the next stage, and enumerating the factors that affect how it will move through the stages. In practice, it is very hard to forecast the sales level at each PLC stage, the length of each stage, and the shape of the PLC curve.

Most marketing texts feature the PLC, yet very few managers claim that they use it in the development of marketing strategy.[28] There are two explanations for this. First, managers make strategic decisions based on the characteristics of each stage of the product life cycle, without using the product life cycle itself as a tool. The second reason is that accurate prediction of the shape of the product life cycle is impossible. Many products do not follow the typical curve.

The product life cycle is not a predictive tool to determine the length of a product's useful life. It is, instead, a means of conceptualizing the effect of the market, the environment, and competition and understanding how that product may react to various stimuli.[29] Recognizing that products have life cycles with identifiable stages can provide insights into how to manage the cycle to extend its life. Unmanaged products travel along the life cycle with little resistance. Environmental and competitive changes move a product through its life cycle, and companies must react to keep their products salable. Victoria Station moved quickly through its product life cycle, but McDonald's has been able to extend by modifying the product concept. The McDonald's of today is a different concept than the McDonald's of the 1960s. The menu and the store design are different. McDonald's has evolved from stands with no seating into fast-food restaurants with attractive indoor seating areas and playgrounds for children. The company also changed its distribution strategy. In addition to its traditional suburban locations, McDonald's has developed international, urban, and institutional locations such as hospitals and colleges.

Many observers thought McDonald's would peak in the mid-1970s.[30] Often, when a product begins to peak in sales, management assumes that it has started its decline stage. The downturn could be attributable to many factors: ineffective marketing support, competition, economic conditions, or lack of market development. If managers wearing "product life-cycle blinders" do not investigate these reasons, they risk seeing the product life cycle as the cause of the slowdown.[31] The management of McDonald's was not wearing life-cycle blinders; they kept growth going.

Using the PLC concept to develop marketing strategy can be difficult. Strategy is both a cause and a result of the product's life cycle: The product's current PLC position suggests the best marketing strategies, and the resulting marketing strategies affect product performance in later life-cycle stages. Yet when used carefully, the PLC concept can help in developing good marketing strategies for different stages of the product life cycle.

We looked at the product development stage of the product life cycle earlier. We now examine strategies for each of the other life-cycle stages.

Introduction Stage

The introduction stage starts when the new product is first made available for purchase. Introduction takes time, and sales growth is apt to be slow. Some products may linger in the introduction stage for many years before they enter a stage of rapid growth; suite hotels followed this pattern. Many companies take what Theodore Levitt calls the "used apple policy." They watch others go into the market first as pioneers. When suite hotels were introduced, many players sat on the sidelines until the product proved itself in the marketplace. Being a pioneer involves risk, but those who sit on the sidelines may watch others build market share quickly if the product is hot. The pioneers are then in an excellent position to defend their market share against attacks by late arrivals. In the introductory stage, profits are negative or low because of the low sales and high distribution and promotion expenses. A company needs capital to attract distributors and "fill the pipelines." Promotion spending is high to inform consumers of the new product and encourage them to try it.

In the introductory stage, there are only a few competitors who produce basic versions of the product, because the market is not ready for product refinements. The firms focus on selling to buyers who are ready to buy, usually the higher-income groups. Prices tend to be on the high side because of low output, production problems, and high promotion and other expenses.

Growth Stage

If the new product satisfies the market, it will enter the growth stage, and sales will start climbing quickly. The early adopters will continue to buy, and later buyers will start following their lead, especially if they hear favorable word of mouth. Competitors will enter the market, attracted by the opportunity for profit. They will introduce new product features, which will expand the market. The increase in competitors leads to an increase in the number of outlets, and sales jump.

Prices remain where they are or fall only slightly. Companies keep their promotion spending at the same or at a slightly higher level to meet competition and continue educating the market. Profits increase during this growth stage as promotion costs are spread over a large volume, more efficient systems are developed, and corporate management costs are spread over a larger number of units.

The firm uses several strategies to sustain rapid market growth as long as possible:

1. The firm improves product quality and adds new product features and models.
2. It enters new market segments.
3. It enters new distribution channels.
4. It shifts some advertising from building product awareness to building product conviction and purchase.
5. It lowers prices at the right time to attract more buyers.

In the growth stage, the firm faces a trade-off between high market share and high current profit. By investing heavily in product improvement, promotion, and distribution, it can capture a dominant position. But it sacrifices maximum current profit in the hope of making this up in the next stage.

Maturity Stage

At some point a product's sales growth slows down, and the product enters the maturity stage. This stage normally lasts longer than the preceding two stages, and it poses strong challenges to marketing management. Most products are in the maturity stage of the life cycle, and therefore most of marketing management deals with the mature product.

The slowdown in sales growth causes supply to exceed demand. This overcapacity leads to greater competition. Competitors begin lowering prices, and they increase their advertising and sales promotions. "Burger wars" and "pizza wars" are the result of these products being in the mature stage. In the mature stage, real sales growth for a product form is about the same as population growth. The only way to increase sales significantly is to steal customers from the competition. Thus, price battles and heavy advertising are often the means used to do this, both of which result in a drop in profit. Weaker competitors start dropping out. The industry eventually contains only well-established competitors in the main market segments, with smaller competitors pursuing the niche markets.

A good offense is the best defense. The product manager should not simply defend the product but should consider modifying target markets, the product, and the marketing mix.

Market Modification

At this point the aggressive product manager tries to increase consumption of the product. The manager looks for new users and market segments and ways to increase use among present customers. McDonald's added breakfast, salads, desserts, and chicken sandwiches in its effort to attract new users and increase use. Product managers may also reposition the brand to appeal to a larger or faster-growing segment. When antidrunk-driving campaigns reduced alcoholic beverage consumption, Bennigan's emphasized its food, changing the image from a fun place to drink to a fun place to dine.

Product Modification

The product manager can also change product characteristics, product quality, features, or style to attract new users and stimulate more usage. A strategy of quality improvement aims at increasing the performance of the product—its durability, reliability, speed, or taste. This strategy is effective when quality can be improved, when buyers believe the claim of improved quality, and when enough buyers want higher quality.

Marketing-Mix Modification

The product manager can also try to improve sales by changing one or more marketing-mix elements. Prices can be cut to attract new users and competitors' customers. A better advertising campaign can be developed.

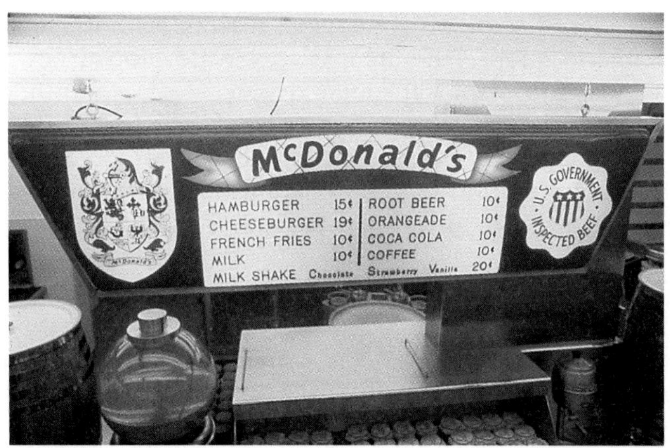

This is McDonald's original menu. One of the ways McDonald's has avoided going into decline is through the development of new products. Courtesy of McDonald's Corporation.

Aggressive sales, promotion trade deals, cents-off, gifts, and contests can be used. The company can move into larger market channels, using mass merchandisers, if these channels are growing. The company can also offer new or improved services to buyers.

Decline Stage

Sales of most product forms and brands eventually decline. The decline may be slow, as in the case of Steak and Ale, or rapid, as in the case of Victoria Station. Sales may plunge to zero, or they may drop to a low level and continue there for many years.

Sales decline for many reasons, including technological advances, shifts in consumer tastes, and increased competition. As sales and profits decline, some firms withdraw from the market. Those remaining may reduce the number of their product offerings. They may drop smaller market segments and marginal trade channels. They may cut the promotion budget and reduce their prices further.

Carrying a weak product can be very costly to the firm, and not just in terms of reduced profit. There are also hidden costs. A weak product may take up too much of management's time. It often requires frequent price and inventory adjustments. The advertising and sales force attention consumed by the weak product could be used to make the healthy products more profitable. Its failing reputation can shake customer confidence in the company and its other products. But the biggest cost may well lie in the future. Keeping weak products delays the search for replacements, creates a lopsided product mix, hurts current profits, and weakens the company's foothold on the future.

For these reasons, companies must pay more attention to their aging products. Regularly reviewing sales, market shares, costs, and profit trends for each of its products will help to identify products in the decline stage.

For each declining product, management has to decide whether to maintain, harvest, or drop it. Management may decide to harvest the product, which means reducing various costs. For example, as restaurants featuring red meat products fell out of favor with customers, Steak and

Ale closed some of its marginal restaurants but maintained its more profitable locations. The company even developed new restaurants in areas where customers still sought a good steak when they went out to eat. If successful, harvesting will increase the company's profits in the short run. Or management may decide to drop the product from the line. It can sell it to another firm or simply liquidate it at salvage value. If the company plans to find a buyer, it will not want to run down the product through harvesting.

Product Deletion

As we have seen, the product life cycle illustrates that most products will become obsolete, lose their attractiveness in the marketplace, and have to be replaced. One danger of the product life cycle is that a product may be replaced prematurely. Products take time, effort, and money to introduce. Only about half of all new products become profitable. When a company has a winner, it wants to receive the maximum benefit from this product. Management will not want to delete it while profit potential exists. If a product is no longer sellable, it is important to terminate that product rather than continue to pour time and resources into reviving it.

Thus, understanding the product deletion process is just as important as understanding product development. The Strawberry Patch, a successful restaurant in Houston, served a chicken breast topped with sautéed mushrooms. This dish enjoyed success for more than ten years. When sales started to drop and the decline continued, it appeared that the product was no longer in favor with the restaurant's customers. Management asked customers about the dish, and they responded that it was too greasy. When the sautéed mushrooms were poured over the chicken breast, the butter collected at the bottom of the plate. In the 1970s, this was viewed as a nice sauce, but by the 1980s, the butter was viewed as excess fat. As the restaurant's customers became more health conscious, the dish became less popular. The restaurant revitalized the dish by removing the sautéed mushrooms and garnishing the chicken with fresh sliced mushrooms. If management of the Strawberry Patch had been wearing life-cycle blinders, they would have deleted the product.

The deletion analysis is a systematic review of a product's projected sales and estimated costs associated with those sales (Figure 9-6). If a product no longer appears to be profitable, the analysis looks at possible ways to make modifications and return it to profitability. If the analysis indicates that the product should be deleted, there are three choices: phase-out, run-out, or drop it immediately.[32]

Sometimes a product line becomes so entrenched in our culture and in business practices that its existence and future are taken for granted. Cocktails, cocktail hours, and cocktail parties represent such a product. In some areas and among some segments, the traditional Manhattan or Martini cocktail has been replaced by wine and soft drinks. All members of the hospitality industry who serve alcoholic beverages should seriously examine the importance and future of cocktails as a product line.[33]

Phase-out is the ideal method; it enables a product to be removed in an orderly fashion. For example, a menu item would be replaced on

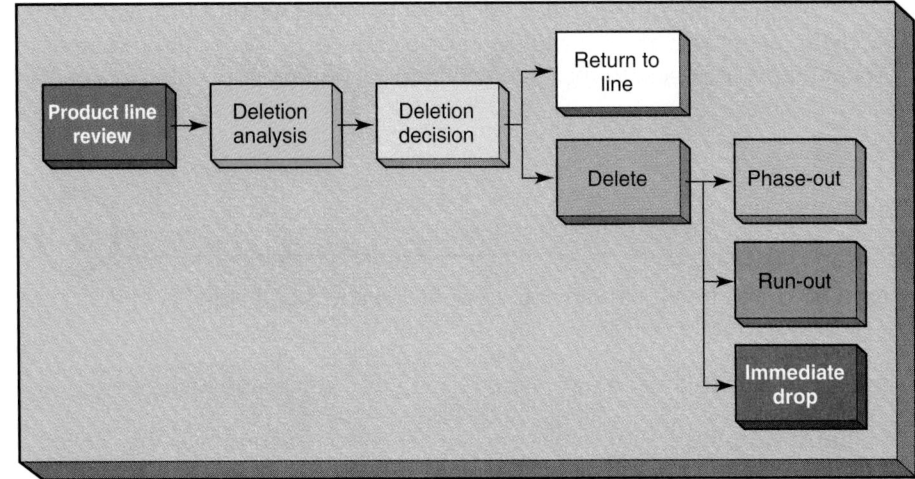

Figure 9-6
Product deletion process. From Martin J. Bell, *Marketing: Concepts and Strategy,* 3rd ed., p. 267; © 1979, Houghton Mifflin Company; used by permission, Mrs. Marcellette (Bell) Chapman.

the next revision of the menu. A **run-out** would be used when sales for an item are low and costs exceed revenues, such as the case of a restaurant serving a crabmeat cocktail with sales of only one or two items per week. If the restaurant decides to delete the product, it may choose to deplete its existing stock of crabmeat rather than reorder. The last option is an immediate **drop.** This option is usually chosen when the product may cause harm or customer dissatisfaction. When a menu item draws a large number of complaints, it is best to drop the item rather than continuing to create unhappy customers.

The political aspects of dropping a product often lead to a product being left on the menu longer than it should be. For example, if the bouillabaisse is the general manager's own recipe, the food and beverage manager may be reluctant to remove the dish from the menu. Deletion of a menu item can also be viewed as a failure. If the resident manager of a hotel fought to include an item on the menu, strong arguments may be made against its deletion. Politics must be addressed when conducting a deletion analysis.

The issue of dropping a product is particularly complex in the case of the properties of a hotel chain. Management is usually quite aware of individual properties that should be dropped from the chain affiliation due to deterioration of the property or the neighborhood in which the property is located. In many cases it is impossible or impractical to close the hotel quickly or drop it from chain affiliation:

- Contracts may prohibit a quick close.
- The hotel may be an historical property or have sentimental attachments to the community and to management.
- Closure might have a negative effect on the community.
- The hotel may be owned by the chain, and a buyer may not be readily available.
- Special relationships may exist between the franchisee and the franchisor.

Despite difficulties in closing hotels or disassociating properties from a chain, eventually the inevitable must occur. As in the earlier example of menu items, it is best to make this difficult decision as quickly as possible.

KEY TERMS

Augmented products Additional consumer services and benefits built around the core and actual products.

Aural The dimension of atmosphere relating to volume and pitch.

Consumption phase Takes place when the customer consumes the service.

Core product Answers the question of what the buyer is really buying. Every product is a package of problem-solving services.

Customization A product designed to meet the specific needs of customers.

Decline The period when sales fall off quickly and profits drop.

Detachment phase When the customer is through using the product and departs.

Drop The action taken towards a product that may cause harm or customer dissatisfaction.

Facilitating products Those services or goods that must be present for the guest to use the core product.

Growth The product life-cycle stage when a new product's sales start climbing quickly.

Introduction The product life-cycle stage when a new product is first distributed and made available for purchase.

Joining The product life-cycle stage when the customer makes the initial inquiry contact.

Maturity The stage in a product life cycle when sales growth slows or levels off.

Olfactory The dimension of atmosphere relating to scent and freshness.

Phase-out The ideal method of removing an unpopular or unprofitable product; it enables a product to be removed in an orderly fashion.

Product development Developing the product concept into a physical product to assure that the product idea can be turned into a workable product.

Run-out Removing a product after existing stock has been depleted; used when sales for an item are low and costs exceed revenues, such as the case of a restaurant serving a crabmeat cocktail with sales of only one or two items per week.

Standardization Creating a standard of quality for customers within the product and maintaining it.

Supporting products Extra products offered to add value to the core product and to help to differentiate it from the competition.

Tactile The dimension of atmosphere relating to softness, smoothness, and temperature.

Visual The dimension of atmosphere relating to color, brightness, size, and shape.

Chapter Review

I. Product. A product is anything that can be offered to a market for attention, acquisition, use, or consumption that might satisfy a want or need. It includes physical objects, service, places, organizations, and ideas.

II. Product Levels

1) **Core product** answers the question of what the buyer is really buying. Every product is a package of problem-solving services.
2) **Facilitating products** are those services or goods that must be present for the guest to use the core product.
3) **Supporting products** are extra products offered to add value to the core product and to help to differentiate it from the competition.
4) **Augmented products** include accessibility (geographic location and hours of operation), atmosphere (visual, aural, olfactory, and tactile dimensions), customer interaction with the service organization (joining, consumption, and detachment), customer participation, and customers' interactions with each other.

III. Product Considerations

1) **Accessibility.** This refers to how accessible the product is in terms of location and hours of operation.
2) **Atmosphere.** Atmosphere is a critical element in services. It is appreciated through the senses. Sensory terms provide descriptions for the atmosphere as a particular set of surroundings. The main sensory channels for atmosphere are sight, sound, scent, and touch.
3) **Customer interactions with the service system.** Managers must think about how the customers use the product in the three phases of involvement: joining, consumption, and detachment.
4) **Customer interactions with other customers.** Customers become part of the product you are offering.
5) **Coproduction.** Involving the guest in service delivery can increase capacity, improve customer satisfaction, and reduce costs.

IV. Reasons Companies Use Brands and Identify the Major Branding Decisions. Brand is a name, term, sign, symbol, design, or a combination of these elements that is intended to identify the goods or services of a seller and differentiate them from those of competitors.

1) **Conditions that support branding**
   a) The product is easy to identify by brand or trademark.
      i) It should suggest something about the product's benefits and qualities.
      ii) It should be easy to pronounce, recognize, and remember.
      iii) It should be distinctive.
      iv) For larger firms looking at future expansion into foreign markets, the name should translate easily into foreign languages.
      v) It should be capable of registration and legal protection.
   b) The product is perceived as the best value for the price. A brand name derives its value from consumer perceptions. Brands attract consumers by developing a perception of good quality and value.
   c) Quality and standards are easy to maintain. If the brand is successful in developing an image of quality, customers will expect quality in all outlets carrying the same brand name. Consistency and standardization are critical factors for a multiunit brand.
   d) The demand for the general product class is large enough to support a regional or national chain. New products are generally developed to serve a particular market niche. Later the product may be expanded to encompass multiniches, or the original niche may grow in market size until it is a huge market share product.
   e) There are economies of scale. The brand should provide economies of scale to justify expenditures for administration and advertising.

V. **New Product Development**

1) **Product life cycle.** The product life cycle presents two challenges:
   a) All products eventually decline.
   b) The firm must understand how its products age and change marketing strategies as products pass through life-cycle stages.
2) **New product development strategy**
   a) A company has to develop new products to survive. New products can be obtained through acquisition or through new product development.
3) **New product development process**
   a) **Idea generation.** Ideas are gained from internal sources, customers, competitors, distributors, and suppliers.
   b) **Idea screening.** The purpose of screening is to spot good ideas and drop poor ones as soon as possible.
   c) **Concept development and testing.** Surviving ideas must now be developed into product concepts. These concepts are tested with target customers.
   d) **Marketing strategy development.** There are three parts to the marketing strategy statement. The first part describes the target market, the planned product positioning, and the sales, market share, and profit goals for the first two years. The second part outlines the product's planned price, distribution, and marketing budget for the first year. The third part describes the planned long-run sales, profit, and the market-mix strategy over time.

e) **Business analysis.** Business analysis involves a review of the sales, costs, and profit projections to determine whether they satisfy the company's objectives.
f) **Product development.** Product development turns the concept into a prototype of the product.
g) **Market testing.** Market testing is the stage in which the product and marketing program are introduced into more realistic market settings.
h) **Commercialization.** The product is brought into the marketplace.

VI. **Product Life-Cycle Stages**
1) **Product development** begins when the company finds and develops a new product idea.
2) **Introduction** is a period of slow sales growth as the product is being introduced into the market. Profits are nonexistent at this stage.
3) **Growth** is a period of rapid market acceptance and increasing profits.
4) **Maturity** is a period of slowdown in sales growth because the product has achieved acceptance by most of its potential buyers.
5) **Decline** is the period when sales fall off quickly and profits drop.

Discussion Questions

1. A "hot" concept in fast-food marketing is home delivery of everything from pizza to hamburgers to fried chicken. Why do you think the demand for this service is growing? How can marketers gain a competitive advantage by satisfying the growing demand for increased services?
2. Use a product from the hospitality or travel industries to explain the following terms (provide an example in your explanation): (a) facilitating product; (b) supporting product; (c) augmented product.
3. ARAMARK, a large contract food-service company, is introducing branded food as part of its campus feeding. Why would ARAMARK pay a royalty to Burger King when it is capable of making its own hamburgers very efficiently?
4. As a hotel or restaurant manager, how would you gain new product ideas?
5. Less than one-third of new product ideas come from the customer. Does this percentage conflict with the marketing concept's philosophy of "find a need and fill it"? Why or why not?
6. If you were the director of new product development for a national fast-food chain, what factors would you consider in choosing cities for test marketing a new sandwich? Would the place where you live be a good test market? Why or why not?
7. Explain why many people are willing to pay more for branded products than for unbranded products. What does this tell you about the value of branding?
8. ITT Sheraton recently changed the name of its eighty-eight Sheraton Inns located throughout the country. The new chain is known as Four Points Hotels. What were the possible risks and rewards of this strategy? Link your answer to brand strategy.
9. Apply the concept of the product life cycle to a hotel. How does a company keep its products from going into the decline stage?

Experiental Exercises

Do one of the following:

1. Visit a hospitality or travel company. Look around at the physical facilities and the atmosphere of the company. Things you should look at include the exterior appearance, cleanliness, employees, atmosphere, and signage. Does the physical atmosphere support the image the company is or should be trying to communicate to prospective customers and customers? Explain your answer.

2. Visit two locations of the same brand, such as two restaurants or two hotels. Does each location portray the same brand image? Explain your answer. If the images are inconsistent, how could this affect prospective customers?

Internet Exercise

Support for these exercises can be found on the Web site for *Marketing for Hospitality and Tourism*, www.prenhall.com/kotler.

Go to the Internet site of a hospitality or travel company. Think about the company's target market and the brand image they should portray. Does the company's Web site reinforce this brand image? Why or why not? What suggestions do you have for enhancing the image that the site portrays?

References

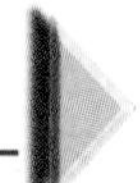

1. From Barry M. Cohen, "The Truth about Entertainment," *Hospitality Business Review,* Spring 1999, vol. 2(2). Reprinted with permission.
2. Karl Albrecht and Lawrence J. Bradford, *The Service Advantage* (Homewood, IL: Dow Jones–Irwin, 1990), p. 69.
3. Neal Templin, "For Hotel Guests With Glitches, High-Tech Room Service," *Wall Street Journal,* August 30, 1999, p. B1+.
4. Christian Gronroos, *Service Management and Marketing* (Lexington, MA.: Lexington Books, 1990).
5. Albert Mehrabian, *Public Places and Private Spaces* (New York: Basic Books, 1976).
6. Bernard Booms and Mary J. Bitner, "Marketing Services by Managing the Environment," *Cornell Restaurant and Hotel Administration Quarterly* (May 1992): 35–39.
7. See Philip Kotler, "Atmospherics as a Marketing Tool," *Journal of Retailing* 49, no. 4 (Winter 1973–1974): 48–64.
8. Gronroos, *Service Management and Marketing.*
9. Paul Slattery, "Hotel Branding in the 1990's," *EIU Travel and Tourism Analyst* 1 (1991): 23–35: Neil Gross, "Best Global Brands," *Business Week:* Special Report, August 6, 2001, pp. 50–60.
10. "Interactive Global Brands Scoreboard," Business Week Online, *http://bwnt.businessweek.com/brand/,* retrieved 3/22/02.
11. Richard Branson, "Foreword" in Daryl Travis, *Emotional Branding* (Roseville, CA: Prima Venture, 2000).
12. E. Jerome McCarthy and William D. Perreault Jr., *Basic Marketing* (Homewood, IL: Irwin, 1990), p. 236.
13. Robert Selwitz, "Quality Takes on 'Choice Name,'" *Hotel and Motel Management* 205, no. 14 (August 20, 1990), pp. 1+.
14. Susan M. Bard, "New Logo Rises at Hyatt," *Hotel and Motel Management* 205, no. 15 (September 10, 1990): 1, 117.
15. Tom Ichniowski, "Hey, Little Spender, Have These Motels Got a Deal for You," *Business Week* 3024 (November 2, 1987): 63.
16. Glenn Withiam, "Hotel Companies Aim for Multiple Markets," *Cornell Hotel and Restaurant Administration Quarterly* 26, no. 3 (November 1985): 39–51.
17. Edward C. Achorn, "The Game of Choice," *Lodging* 15, no. 2 (October 1990): 26–30.
18. Laura E. Keeton, "La Quinta Plans Mexican Venture with 22 Hotels," *Wall Street Journal,* September 23, 1994, p. B3.

19. Carol Cooper, "Some Place Like Home," *Restaurant Business,* August 1, 1997, pp. 63–78; Mary Ann Tasoulas, "Grab Your Partner," *Restaurant Business,* May 1, 2000, pp. 79–88.
20. Tasoulas, "Grab Your Partner."
21. Mary Ann Tasoulas, "Brand Power: The Building Blocks of Profit," *1998 Supplement to Restaurant Business* (Fall 1998); Cathy Urell, "Comfort Inn Has Teamed Up with Huddle House Restaurant in Virginia," *Hotel Business News,* February 21–March 6, 2000, p. 53; Kelly Wayne, "Hyatt Signs with Coffee Giant Starbucks to Further Its F&B Branding Initiatives," *Hotel Business,* April 7–20, 2001, p. 13; see also Rebecca Ordon, "Marriott Properties to Feature Starbucks Stores, Kiosks," *Hotel Business,* June 7–20, 2000, p. 28.
22. Shelia M. Poole, "Huddle House, Hotel Firm Reach Agreement," *The Atlanta Constitution,* November 3, 1999, p. E3; "Wake Up and Smell The Coffee: Starbucks Checks Into Hyatt," *The Standard* (Hyatt Newsletter), *http://www.netletter.net/hyatt/standard/spring2001/,* retrieved 3/22/02; Mari Snyder, "Licensing Agreement Brings Starbucks Coffee to Marriott International, Inc. Properties, *Hospitalitynet, http://www.hospitalitynet.org/ihra/news/4004536.htm;* and James Scarpa, Editor, *Brand Power,* New York: Restaurant Business, 1998.
23. Morris E. Lasky, "Hotel/Motel Workouts: Ask Fundamental Questions to Uncover Problems," *Commercial Lending Review* 5, no. 2 (Spring 1990): 44–48.
24. The Marriott example and this list were drawn from Christopher W. L. Hart, "Product Development: How Marriott Created Courtyard," *Cornell Hotel and Restaurant Administration Quarterly,* 27, no. 3 (November 1986): 68–69; and Jerry Wind, Paul E. Green, Douglas Shifflet, and Marsha Scarbrough, "Courtyard by Marriott: Designing a Hotel Facility with Consumer-Based Marketing," *Interfaces* 19, no. 1 (January–February): 25–47.
25. J. L. Heskett and R. Hallowell, Courtyard by Marriott, *Harvard Case* 9-693-036 (Boston, MA: Harvard Business School Publishing, 1993).
26. Margaret Studer and Jennifer Ordonez, "The Golden Arches: Burgers, Fries & 4-Star Rooms," *Wall Street Journal* (Eastern Edition), November 17, 2000, p. B1+.
27. Bradford T. Hudson, "Innovation through Acquisition," *Cornell Hotel and Restaurant Administration Quarterly* 35, no. 2 (June 1994): 82–87.
28. Theodore Levitt, *The Marketing Imagination* (New York: Free Press, 1986), p. 173.
29. See John E. Smallwood, "The Product Life Cycle: A Key to Strategic Marketing Planning," in *Strategic Marketing*, ed. Barton A. Weitz and Robin Wensley (Boston, MA: Kent Publishing, 1984), pp. 184–192; Nariman K. Dhalla and Sonia Yuspeh, "Forget the Product Life Cycle Concept," *Harvard Business Review* (January–February 1976): 102–112; and Christopher W. Hart, Greg Casserly, and Mark J. Lawless, "The Product Life Cycle: How Useful?" *Cornell Hotel and Restaurant Quarterly* 25, no. 3 (November 1984): 54–63.
30. Robert C. Lewis and Richard E. Chambers, *Marketing Leadership in Hospitality* (New York: Van Nostrand Reinhold), p. 314.
31. Dhalla and Yuspeh, "Forget the Product Life Cycle Concept," pp. 102–112.
32. William Pride and O. C. Ferrell, *Marketing* (Boston, MA: Houghton Mifflin, 1995), pp. 312–313.
33. Anthony V. Seaton, "Cocktail Culture in the 1920's and 1930's: Prefiguring the Postmodern," *Hospitality Research Journal* 18, no. 2 (1994): 35–51.

10 Internal Marketing

In a service organization if you are not serving the customer, you had better be serving someone who is.
Jan Carlzon

Dear Mr. Marriott,

I'd like to tell you about my recent experience in your Anaheim Marriot Hotel. After checking in, I ordered room service. A young man named Charles came up with my order. As I signed the check, he asked, "Ma'am, do you have allergies or have you been crying?"

"I've been crying," I replied. "My sister has been terminally ill and my brother just called to tell me she died while I was on the flight here. I need to go home right away, but the first flight isn't until eight A.M. *So you see, I don't want to be in your hotel tonight, but I have no choice. There's really nothing you can do."*

Charles paused. "Well, I want you to know that you have my sympathy. If there's anything you need tonight, please don't hesitate to call me. It would be my pleasure."

Somehow, knowing that Charles the room-service waiter cared made me feel a little bit better. About forty-five minutes later Charles knocked at my door. I assumed he had returned for my tray, but he was holding another tray with a pot of coffee and a piece of warm apple pie.

"Our chef makes the best apple pie in the entire company. We heated up a piece for you—it's on us," he said. Then he reached into his pocket and pulled out a sympathy card.

I opened the card to find seven signatures. Charles told me who each person was and what they did at the hotel. He explained that these were his friends, and they kind of ran the place at night.

"We got you this card to let you know you're not alone tonight—lots of us care."

Mr. Marriott, I'll never meet you. And I don't need to meet you because I met Charles. I know what you stand for. I know what your values are. I want to assure you that as long as I live, I will stay at your hotels and tell my friends to stay at your hotels. That night I realized you care more about me as a person than you do about the few dollars I spent at your hotel.

Reprinted with permission from: Roger Dow and Susan Cook, Turned On: Eight Vital Insights to Energize Your People, Customers and Profits, *pp. 41–43. Reprinted with permission of HarperCollins Publishers Inc.*

Chapter Objectives

After reading this chapter, you should be able to:

1. Understand why internal marketing is an important part of a marketing program.
2. Explain what a service culture is and why it is important to have a company where everyone is focused on serving the customer.
3. Describe the four-step process involved in implementing an internal marketing program.
4. Explain why the management of nonroutine transactions can create the image of being an excellent service provider.

INTERNAL MARKETING

Everyone has a story to tell about the time he or she received poor service at a hotel or restaurant. Customer service expert John Tscholl tells about the one and only time he stayed in one of Marriott's Courtyard Inns.[1] He was never given an emergency message that his father-in-law had suffered a heart attack, nor did he receive his wake-up call the next morning. He said that he will never return to a Courtyard Inn and has told this story to thousands of Marriott's customers and potential customers. Marriott spent much time and effort developing the Courtyard concept, but a well-designed concept and good physical facilities are not enough. If the hotel's employees do not perform to expectations, guests will not return.

10.1 Marriott

Stories are not always negative. Most travelers have stories to tell about employees who gave them excellent service. These two examples show how hotels can retain customers by solving their needs and recognizing employees who do something extra for the hotel. Barry Urquhart tells of the time he went back to his room and walked out on the balcony to get a breath of fresh air, only to hear cries for help coming from several stories up. The balcony door had shut, locking the guest out of the room. Urquhart called the front desk, and in a few minutes the guest was let back in the room. The next day the hotel delivered a bottle of champagne to Urquhart's room to thank him for making them aware of the problem.[2] This unexpected gift increased positive feelings about the hotel.

Karl Albrecht, coauthor of *Service America,* was staying in a hotel in Sydney. He requested a late checkout so he could hold a business meeting in his room. Unfortunately, the hotel was fully booked, and the room was needed for guests arriving that afternoon. The manager made provisions for him to use a conference room free of charge. Albrecht offered to pay, but the hotel refused. The future business the hotel received from Karl Albrecht and the positive word of mouth more than equaled the lost revenue.[3]

Marketing in the hospitality and travel industries must be embraced by all employees; it cannot be left up to the marketing or sales department. Marketing should be part of the philosophy of the organization, and the marketing function should be carried out by all line employees. In manufacturing firms the marketing function is often carried out by a marketing department, because many employees do not interact with the customers. In service industries the line employees carry out a majority of the marketing function (see Figure 10-1). Internal marketing involves marketing to the firm's internal customers, its employees.

Managers must understand that bad service encounters receive more attention than good ones. When guests have been treated badly, they respond by talking about the incident. A study done by the Technical Assistance Research Program found that when people have a good experience, they tell five people. If they have a bad experience, they tell ten.[4] Spreading positive word of mouth is difficult. A few negative stories can offset many good stories. The goal is to have every guest's expectations met or exceeded.

The front-desk clerk, dining room service person, door attendant, and concierge all influence whether the guest departs satisfied. Their attitude, appearance, and willingness to handle the guest's requests help form an impression of the hotel. Employees deliver the products of hospitality organizations, and through their delivery they become part of the product. It is often hard to differentiate the tangible part of the product of competing companies. Steak dinners and hotel rooms in the same price range tend to be similar. Product differentiation often derives from the people who deliver the service. In the hospitality industry, most marketing activity is carried out by employees outside the marketing department, not the marketing staff. The hotel's marketing program brings guests to the hotel. The hotel's staff must turn the first-time guest into a repeat customer. There is a positive relationship between the number of repeat

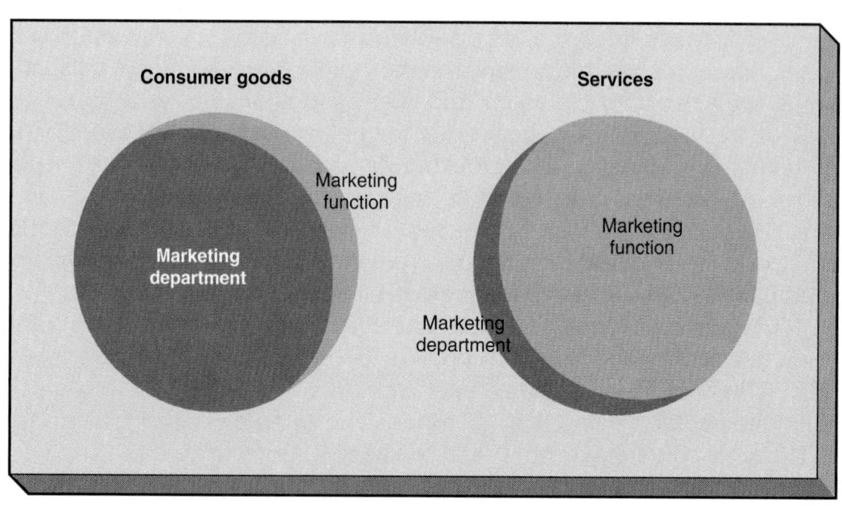

Figure 10-1
The relationship between the marketing function and the marketing department. From Christian Gronroos, "Designing a Long Range Marketing Strategy for Services," *Long Range Planning* (April 1980), p. 40.

guests and profit. Research has shown that a 5 percent increase in retention can lead to 25 percent to 125 percent increases in the bottom line.[5]

Richard Normann of the Service Management Group says that a key ingredient in almost all service companies is some innovative arrangement or formula for mobilizing and focusing human energy.[6] Normann developed the term moments of truth, which Jan Carlzon of SAS later popularized. A **moment of truth** occurs when employee and customer have contact. Normann states that when this occurs, what happens is no longer directly influenced by the company. It is the skill, motivation, and tools employed by the firm's representative and the expectations and behavior of the client together that create the service delivery process.[7] Norman borrowed the idea from bullfighters, who used the term to describe the moment when the bullfighter faces the bull in the ring. Despite all his training and preparation, a wrong move by the bullfighter or an unanticipated move by the bull can result in disaster. Similarly, when employees and customers interact, a careless mistake by an employee or an unanticipated request by a guest can result in a dissatisfied guest.

The hospitality industry is unique in that *employees are part of the product.* The hotel must have a staff that will perform well during moments of truth. When people think of marketing, they usually think of efforts directed externally toward the marketplace, but a hotel or restaurant's first marketing efforts should be directed internally to employees. Managers must make sure that employees know their products and believe that they are a good value. The employees must be excited about the company that they work for and the products they sell. Otherwise, it will be impossible for the guests to become excited. External marketing brings customers into the hotel but does little good if the employees do not perform to the guest's expectations.

Employee Satisfaction and Customer Satisfaction Are Linked

Good internal programs create employee satisfaction, which in turn creates customer satisfaction. Thus, internal marketing has two benefits: customer satisfaction and employee satisfaction. They later add to the bottom line by reducing employee turnover. Citing a 1995 study by Forte Hotels in London, two U.K. researchers (Owen and Teare) state, "Clearly, if staff is happy about what they and the company need to do in order to satisfy customers and are well trained and supported, they will, on average, remain with their employer three to four times longer than employees who feel less secure."[8] Berry and Parasuraman state that interacting with frustrated and dissatisfied customers can deflate employee's enthusiasm for the job, decrease their commitment, and result in increased employee turnover.[9] These studies found there is a link between customer satisfaction and employee satisfaction. Good employees do not like dealing with dissatisfied customers. There is a two-way relationship between customer satisfaction and employee satisfaction. When customer satisfaction decreases, employee satisfaction decreases; however, when customer satisfaction increases, employee satisfaction increases. Reichheld, a well-known service consultant and author of *The Loyalty Effect,* states that employee retention has a direct link to

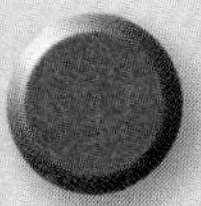

Marketing Highlight 10-1

When Employee Communications Go against Customer Expectations

The Sheraton Perth is one of Perth, Australia's, finest hotels. Barry Urquhart, a services management consultant, was looking forward to celebrating his niece's wedding at the hotel. Urquhart does not drink beverages containing caffeine, except on special occasions when he enjoys a cappuccino. Relaxing after the wedding dinner, Urquhart decided to forget his diet. When the banquet staff was serving the after-dinner tea and coffee, he asked the server for a cappuccino. He realized it was not part of the set menu and said he would be happy to pay for it. The server replied that the rest of the guests would first have to be served. Urquhart felt that this was reasonable, as it would take time to prepare his special order. Later he noticed that all the guests were served, and he was without a cappuccino. When the server was reminded of the order, a reply was given that the supervisor had refused the order. Urquhart became irritated and asked to speak to this person. The supervisor then appeared and explained that the reception dinner was a set menu, and cappuccino was not on the menu. Urquhart again explained that he was willing to pay for the cappuccino and wait for it to be prepared. The supervisor replied that cappuccino was available only from the restaurant downstairs, and company policy did not allow it to be brought upstairs. When Urquhart asked the banquet supervisor if he knew the slogan placed next to every Sheraton bed, the supervisor said that he didn't. "At the Sheraton, little things mean a lot" was the slogan.

Urquhart now says that his image of the entire Sheraton network has been altered. He had been a guest in Sheraton Hotels throughout the world. When he had asked for similar service in the past, he had received it. The sign by the bed meant something to him as a guest. It reinforced his belief that Sheraton delivered good service. On his niece's wedding day, he understood that sometimes little things really do not mean a lot to some of the hotel's staff. In the future, he wondered, how would he identify those Sheratons where little things do mean a lot? Sheraton has an excellent reputation as a five-star hotel chain in the Asia Pacific region, but all it took was one banquet supervisor to put uncertainty about Sheraton in Urquhart's mind. The supervisor thought he was carrying out company policy by preventing an employee from fulfilling a guest's request. This example shows how employees can influence guest satisfaction. When a company's external guest communications conflict with its employee communications, problems are inevitable.

Source: Barry Urquhart, *Serves You Right* (Kalamunda, Western Australia: Marketing Focus, 1991), pp. 83–85.

10.2 Forte Hotels

customer retention and acquisition. David Owen of Forte Hotels cites a study done in the United Kingdom by Posthouse that revealed a close correlation between employee satisfaction and guest satisfaction. He states, "In essence, the hotels achieving consistently high levels of guest satisfaction were also achieving high employee morale ratings and low turnover ratings."[10] There is considerable evidence that employee retention and customer retention are related.

There is also a relationship between quality and employee satisfaction. John Tschohl (a customer service consultant) states that "increased turnover should be considered a warning that a company may not be customer focused." Tschohl cites a worldwide study by The Forum Corporation which found that turnover is associated with employee opinion of service quality. Some employees who leave companies do so because of the poor level of service being given to customers and the overall negative attitude of the organization.[11] Joseph Benoy (1996) cites a study by the American Society for Quality Control which found that when consumers were asked what quality in services meant, the largest group of responses cited employee contact skills such as courtesy, attitude, and helpfulness.[12] The research cited above supports the development of an internal marketing program. We must first market to employees. Satisfied employees create satisfied customers. Employees enjoy working with satisfied customers; thus higher levels of customer satisfaction create higher levels of employee satisfaction. The human resource function and marketing are inseparable in hospitality and travel organizations. They must work together to create both satisfied employees and satisfied customers.

The Internal Marketing Process

Marketers must develop techniques and procedures to ensure that employees are able and willing to deliver high-quality service. The internal marketing concept evolved as marketers formalized procedures for marketing to employees. Internal marketing ensures that employees at all levels of the organization experience the business and understand its various activities and campaigns in an environment that supports customer consciousness.[13] The objective of internal marketing is to enable employees to deliver satisfying products to the guest. As Christian Gronroos notes, "The internal marketing concept states that the internal market of employees is best motivated for service-mindedness and customer-oriented performance by an active, marketing-like approach, where a variety of activities are used internally in an active, marketing-like and coordinated way."[14] Internal marketing uses a marketing perspective to manage the firm's employees.[15]

Internal marketing is marketing aimed internally at the firm's employees. Internal marketing is a process that involves the following steps:

1. Establishment of a service culture
2. Development of a marketing approach to human resource management
3. Dissemination of marketing information to employees
4. Implementation of a reward and recognition system

Establishment of a Service Culture

An internal marketing program flows out of a service culture. A service marketing program is doomed to failure if its organizational culture does not support serving the customer. An article in a recent issue of *The Australian,* a national newspaper, reported that four firms had pumped $2 million into customer service programs with little result.[16] One reason these customer service efforts failed was that the companies' culture was not service oriented. The companies carried out the customer service programs because they thought that they would produce satisfied customers and make the firm more money. These firms soon discovered that a good customer-service program involves much more than working with line employees. *An internal marketing program requires a strong commitment from management.*

A major barrier to most internal marketing programs is middle management. Managers have been trained to watch costs and increase profits. Their reward systems are usually based on achieving certain cost levels. Imagine a hotel's front-desk clerks returning from a training session, eager to help the guests. They may take a little extra time with the customers or perhaps give away a health club visit to help a dissatisfied guest recover from an unsatisfactory experience at the hotel. The front-office manager, who has not been through similar training, may see the extra time spent as unproductive and the services given away as wasteful.

If management expects employees' attitudes to be positive toward the customer, management must have a positive attitude toward the customer and the employees. Too often, organizations hire trainers to come in for a day to get their customer-contact employees excited about providing high-quality customer service. The effect of these sessions is usually short-lived because the organizations do little to support the customer-contact employees. Managers tell receptionists to be helpful and friendly, yet often the receptionists are understaffed. The greeting developed to make receptionists sound sincere and helpful—"Good morning, Plaza Hotel, Elizabeth speaking, how may I help you?"—becomes hollow when it is compressed into three seconds with a "Can you please hold?" added to the end. The net result from the guest's perspective is to wait fourteen rings for the phone to be answered and then receive a cold, rushed greeting. Management must develop a **service culture:** a culture that supports customer service through policies, procedures, reward systems, and actions.

An **organizational culture** is the pattern of shared values and beliefs that gives members of an organization meaning, providing them with the rules for behavior in the organization.[17] In well-managed companies, everyone in the organization embraces the culture. A strong culture helps organizations in two ways. First, it directs behavior. Culture is important to service organizations because every customer and each experience is different. The employee must have some degree of discretion over the creation and delivery of the experience to ensure that the customer's differing needs and expectations are met.[18] Second, a strong culture gives employees a sense of purpose and makes them feel good about their company.[19] They know what their company is trying to achieve and how they are helping the company achieve that goal.

Culture serves as the glue that holds an organization together. When an organization has a strong culture, the organization and its employees act as one. But a company that has a strong culture may not necessarily have a service culture. A strong service culture influences employees to act in customer-oriented ways and is the first step toward developing a customer-oriented organization.

Developing a customer-oriented organization requires a commitment from management of both time and financial resources. The change to a customer-oriented system may require changes in hiring, training, reward systems, and customer complaint resolution, as well as empowerment of employees. It requires that managers spend time talking to both customers and customer-contact employees. Management must be committed to these changes. A service culture does not result from a memorandum

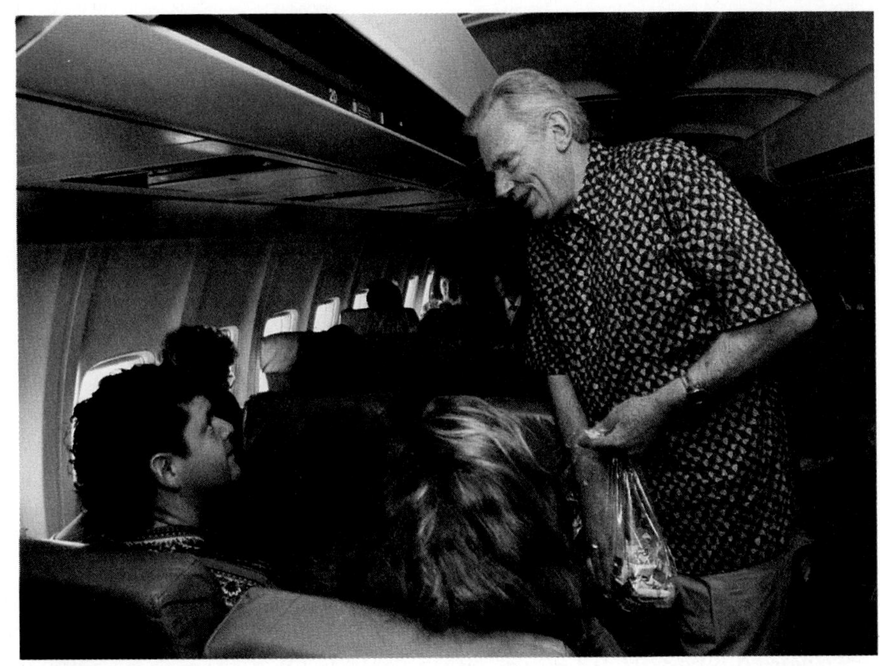

Herb Kelleher, the CEO of Southwest Airlines, spends time on Southwest's planes with employees and customers. Courtesy of Southwest Airlines.

sent by the CEO. It is developed over time through the actions of management. For example, a hotel manager who spends time greeting guests and inquiring about their welfare during morning checkout and afternoon check-in demonstrates caring about guests.[20]

In some companies, including Hyatt, McDonald's, and Hertz, management spends time working alongside customer-contact employees serving customers. This action makes it clear to employees that management does not want to lose touch with operations and that managers care about both employees and customers. An internal marketing program that is developed without the support of management will be unproductive. Organizations cannot expect their employees to develop a customer-oriented attitude if it is not visibly supported by company management.

10.3 Hertz
Hyatt
McDonald's

Weak Culture

In firms that have weak corporate cultures, there are few or no common values and norms. Employees are often bound by policies and regulations, although these policies may make no sense from a customer-service perspective. As a result, employees become insecure about making decisions outside the rules and regulations.[21] Because there are no established values, employees do not know how the company wants them to act, and they spend time trying to figure out how to behave. When they do come up with a solution, they must get their supervisor's permission before applying it to the problem. Supervisors, in turn, may feel the need to pass the responsibility upward. During the decision process, the guest is kept waiting minutes, hours, days, or even months to receive a reply. In a company with a strong service culture, employees know what to do, and they do it. Customers receive a quick response to their questions and quick solutions to their problems.

La Quinta Motor Inns brings employees from each of its eighteen regions to corporate headquarters for brainstorming sessions. The purpose of these sessions is to (1) demonstrate appreciation for employees, and (2) emphasize that all employees are empowered to do what is necessary to meet guest expectations.[22] When a firm **empowers** employees, it moves the authority and responsibility to make decisions from the supervisor to the line employees.

Professor Peter Ricci said one of his goals as general manager of the Crowne Plaza Resort in Orlando was to win the coveted "Newcomer" Award, which Bass Hotels & Resorts (now 6 Continents) gives to its highest-achieving new properties:

> Not only did we win the award, we were #1 of all Crowne Plaza properties in North America. To obtain the results needed to win the award, we had to get everyone from part-time bellman to controller in the mindset that we were casual, elegant, and outstanding. We had to get the employees to really believe we were the best. But we also had to support this by showing the employees we thought they were the best. The staff was empowered to allow them to be all they could be. The results of these efforts enabled us to win the prestigious "Torchbearer" Award in our 2nd year of operation by again being #1 in guest satisfaction and excelling on a number of other variables.

The hotel achieved these results by creating a service-oriented culture and empowering the employees so they could best serve the guest.

A fast-food restaurant had a policy of not letting the public use its business phone, although there were no public phones on the premises. One evening a man who had been assaulted several blocks from the restaurant asked if he could use the phone. The employees refused and turned the man away. The policy manual said that guests were not to use the phone. Their corporate culture had trained them to act by the book. They were incapable of making a decision that went against the company's written policies. The press featured this as a great story about the insensitivity of a business toward a member of the community. The restaurant received negative publicity because of its employee's action. It was fortunate to avoid a suit.

When you come into contact with an organization that has a strong service culture, you recognize it right away. In the Marriott culture, there is an instinctive and automatic impulse to turn toward the customer in making decisions about how to run the organization. Chairman J. Willard "Bill" Marriott, Jr. is consistent in preaching, teaching, and reminding people about the customer and about service.[23] Four Seasons Hotels had two hotels in Houston, the Four Seasons and the Inn on the Park. When guests enter either of these hotels, they received a genuinely warm reception from the employees, who sincerely want to make their guests comfortable. There is a difference in the feeling a guest receives from an employee who is required to memorize a greeting and recite it back to the guests and an employee who has a genuine interest in guests and communicates this personally. The employees at the Four Seasons' hotels were genuine; they reaffirmed the guest's decision to stay at the hotels.

Turning the Organizational Structure Upside Down

The conventional organizational structure is a triangular structure. For example, in a hotel the CEO (chief executive officer) and COO (chief operating officer) are at the peak of the triangle. The general manager is on the next level, followed by department heads, supervisors, line employees, and the customers (Figure 10-2). Ken Blanchard, author of *One Minute Manager,* states that the problem with a conventional organizational structure is that everyone is working for their boss. Employees want to do well in the organization. Thus, line employees are concerned with what their supervisors think of their performance, department heads are concerned with how the general manager views them, and the general managers want the corporate office to think highly of them. The problem with this type of organization is that everyone is concerned with satisfying people above them in the organization, and very little attention is paid to the customer.[24]

When a company has a service culture, the organizational chart is turned upside down. The customers are now at the top of the organization, and corporate management is at the bottom of the structure. In this

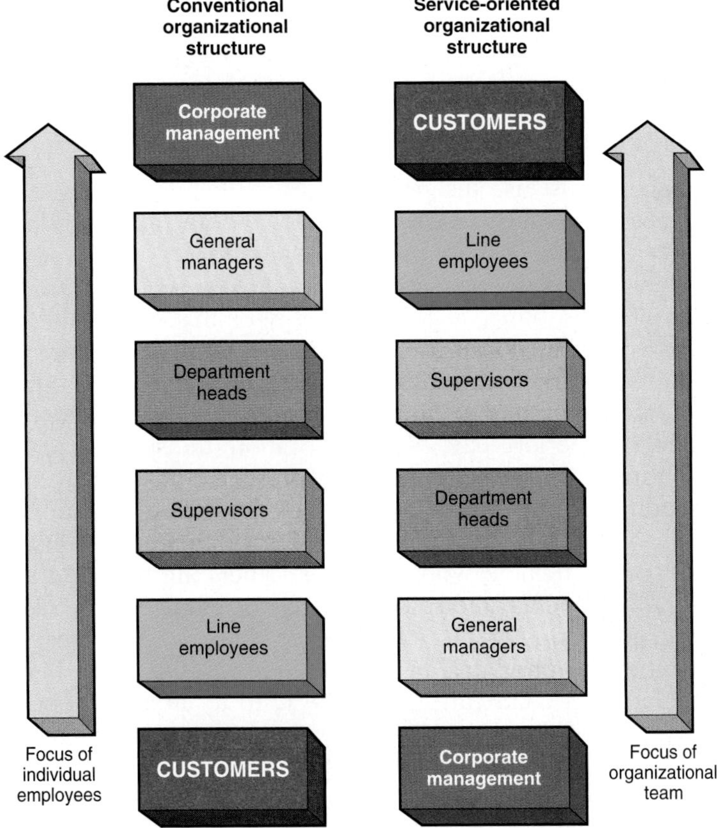

Figure 10-2
Turning the organizational structure upside down.

type of organization, everyone is working to serve the customer. Corporate management is helping their general managers to serve the customer, general managers are supporting their departments in serving the customer, department heads are developing systems that will allow their supervisors to better serve the customer, and supervisors are helping line employees serve the customer.

10.4 La Quinta Motor Inn
Ritz Carlton

A bell person at a Ritz-Carlton hotel delivered baggage to a guest about an hour after he had checked in due to an error. After he had delivered the luggage, he told his supervisor. The supervisor apologized to the guest and noted in the hotel's computer that this guest had experienced a problem and should receive exceptional service during the rest of his stay.[25] This seems like a rational way to handle the problem, but it is really an extraordinary event. In a hotel with a conventional organizational structure, if any employee makes a mistake, they hope their supervisor never finds out about it; they may even try to cover it up. They know that if their supervisor does find out about a mistake, they may be reprimanded. The Ritz-Carlton has a service culture; they have turned the organizational structure upside down. The bell person was concerned about the guest and knew his supervisor would take action that would enable the hotel to recover from his mistake. The supervisor was not afraid to communicate the department's mistake to other departments. When you turn the organization upside down, everyone works to serve the guest. When you have a conventional organizational structure, everyone works to please the boss.

Development of a Marketing Approach to Human Resources Management

Creating Jobs that Attract Good People

Managers must use the principles of marketing to attract and retain employees. They must research and develop an understanding of their employees' needs, just as they examine the needs of customers. Not all employees are the same. Some employees seek money to supplement their incomes; others are looking for work that will be their sole source of income. Marketers can use marketing research techniques to segment the employee market, choosing the best segments for the firm and developing a marketing mix to attract those segments. For employees, the marketing mix is the job, pay, benefits, location, transportation, parking, hours, and intangible rewards, such as prestige and perceived advancement opportunities. Just as customers look for different attributes when they purchase a product, employees look for different benefits. Some may be attracted by flexible working hours, others are attracted by good health insurance benefits, and still others may be attracted by child-care facilities. Flexible working hours for office or housekeeping positions, cafeteria-style benefit programs in which employees design their own benefit package, and child care can all be used to attract a certain type of employee. Advertising should be developed with prospective employees in mind, building a positive image of the firm for present and future employees and customers. Employees choose employers and leave them the same way that guests select certain hotels and then decide to switch. It is expensive to lose both guests and employees.[26] Using a marketing approach to develop positions and company benefits helps to attract and maintain good employees.

The cost of employee turnover was estimated in the late 1980s to average $2,100 for an hourly position. This means that turnover would cost over $400,000 for a hotel with a 100 percent turnover and 200 employees. This cost is undoubtedly higher today.[27] A reduction in turnover can result in hundreds of thousands of dollars in savings.

La Quinta Motor Inns examined the problem of burnout at management levels and reduced this problem from 36 percent to 21 percent annually. The company identified four principal factors as critical in helping to reduce the problem:[28]

1. *Selection.* La Quinta maintains strict standards and has a policy of hiring couples. Prospective couples go through an extensive interview process.
2. *Orientation.* Each selected couple must complete an intensive thirteen-week training program plus on-the-job training as fill-in managers.
3. *Stability.* The management team (couples) cannot request a transfer before completion of two years at a property. La Quinta discovered that frequent transfer contributes to high turnover.
4. *Training.* La Quinta's executive vice president for development, Anne Binns Bliss, stated, "You have to select and keep people that you want to be part of your team." La Quinta believes strongly in ongoing training for employees.

The problem of burnout was studied in the restaurant industry, with the following conclusions:[29]

1. More chain restaurant managers than hotel food and beverage managers suffered from burnout.
2. Assistant managers were more prone than general managers.
3. General managers were more likely to suffer from depersonalization than assistant managers.
4. Burnout was higher among singles than among married people.
5. Men were less likely to experience burnout than women.
6. Good communication on the part of general managers seems to reduce burnout among assistant managers.

These conclusions seem to indicate that burnout is not consistent among groups and different types of restaurants. Training programs and employee motivational programs obviously must be customized to meet the needs of different employee groups. Just as a single marketing strategy is unlikely to attract all market segments, a single approach to dealing with employees is equally likely to fail.

Students enrolled in college/university hospitality programs clearly demonstrate that many factors in addition to salary and benefits are important to them when selecting an employer. Nonmonetary variables of interest to hospitality students when selecting an employer are (by rank order) as follows:[30]

1. Chance for promotion and growth
2. Work that keeps me interested
3. A chance for increasing responsibility
4. Good working conditions
5. Feeling in on things, being a part
6. Full appreciation of work done
7. Job security
8. Good training program
9. Personal loyalty to worker by company
10. Good salary
11. Nice people to work with
12. Good fringe benefits
13. Access to superior
14. Geographic location
15. Reasonable hours
16. Sympathetic help with personal problems

The Hiring Process

The service product is, at least in part, the attitude the employee displays as he or she delivers the service experience. It is unlikely that the service provider can teach the service attitude that all their customer contact employees need. Service organizations need to hire for attitude and train for skills.[31] "Service characteristics like intangibility and customer contact require service employees to display more initiative, to cope more effectively with stress, to be more interpersonally flexible and sensitive, and to be more cooperative than their colleagues who work in manufacturing."[32] This idea means that service firms place more emphasis on personality, energy, and attitude than on education, training, and experience in their recruitment, selection, and training strategies. Finding employees who are good at creating a service experience is a vital goal and major hiring criterion of service organizations.

> Selecting people for customer service roles is similar to casting people for roles in a movie. First, both require artful performances aligned with the audience expectations. Creating an interpersonal experience that customers remember as satisfactory, pleasant, or dazzling is like an actor's mission of having audiences so caught up in the play or movie that they start believing the performer is the person portrayed. Second, both requirements need a casting choice based on personality.[33]

This discussion supports the need for careful selection processes in hospitality and travel businesses. Yet, employee turnover rates of 100 percent or more are common in the hospitality industry. For example, limited-service restaurants have a turnover rate of 123 percent, whereas full-service restaurants have a turnover rate of 88 percent for hourly employees.[34] In companies with high turnover, managers tend to put very little effort into hiring; they simply fill gaps in the schedule.

If you want friendly, courteous service, you must hire friendly, courteous people. Hospitality firms that deliver good service seem to follow this advice. These firms understand that it is difficult to train people to be friendly. It is possible to provide employees with the technical skills needed for the job, but difficult to train them to be friendly and caring.

Swissair carefully screens its applicants, selects candidates for personal interviews, and puts them through a five- to six-hour selection process. The airline then puts successful applicants on probation for a three-month period. They invest a great deal in each candidate because they realize that it is better to spend money choosing the right employee than trying to repair mistakes caused by poor employees. Swissair understands the importance of hiring the right employees.[35]

Southwest strongly believes inherent attitudes cannot be changed in people. To test for behaviors such as a sense of humor, ability to work with others, and friendliness, Southwest's interview process includes group interviews where applicants tell jokes and role-play a variety of situations to demonstrate team work and the capacity to act spontaneously. Southwest can afford to be very selective because it receives an extremely large number of job applications with little active advertising thanks to its reputation for being a unique and excellent place to work.

Southwest places special emphasis on preparing its people to perform and on teamwork. It considers employee training to be a continuous process rather than a single event. Throughout their careers, employees are cross-trained on multiple jobs to enrich every employee's work experience and to prepare them to perform flexibly in different positions as needed. In addition, employees are specifically assigned to work with a senior employee who serves as a mentor to provide a clear demonstration of Southwest's service quality and to be available to answer questions.[36]

Disney World allows its best employees, its star "cast members," to pick future employees. Disney gives cast members who will be used in the selection process three weeks of training. They are then turned loose in a forty-five-minute interview session to select potential new employees. James Poisant, a former manager at Disney World, explains that employees choose employees who mirror their own values. "In 45 minutes the cast members pick up on who's fooling and who's genuine."[37]

10.5 Disney

In times of low unemployment, companies may need to look at nontraditional labor sources to find employees with a good attitude. Days Inns initiated a program to hire greater numbers of older workers for its reservation center in Atlanta. Older workers designed and distributed flyers and worked at a job fair where they registered participants, conducted tours, answered questions about their jobs, and acted as enthusiastic recruiters for Days Inns.[38]

An effective internal marketing program demands close cooperation between marketing and human resources management. Hiring and training, traditionally the responsibility of human resources management, are key areas in any internal marketing program. A marketing-like approach to human resources management starts with hiring the right employees. Selection methods that identify customer-oriented candidates are used as part of the hiring process.

Teamwork

Employees who are not customer oriented often try to pass the responsibility for serving employees to others. They are not team players. In companies that practice internal marketing, if one employee makes an error, other employees try to cover it before the guest notices. In these organizations, guests do not have to understand the hotel's organization and business to ensure that their needs are met. The front desk handles most requests, relaying the guest's desire to the appropriate department. In restaurants that have used internal marketing to create a service culture, staff members cover for each other. Employees who see that a guest needs something will serve the guest, even though it may not be their table.

Organizations that lack teamwork create an uncomfortable environment for the guest. For example, a guest called the front desk of Las Hadas, a five-star resort in Mexico, and asked for extra towels. The front-desk clerk answering the telephone acted puzzled. Surely a guest would know to call housekeeping for towels. The operator stated that this was the front desk, not housekeeping, told the guest to call housekeeping, and hung up. Many restaurant guests have asked for a drink while they are sitting at their tables looking over the dinner menu. The response to some of these guests is that they have mistaken the food-service person for a cocktail-service person. Food service then tells the customer to redirect their request to cocktail service and departs, leaving the guest's needs unfilled. In both of these incidents, the first employee contacted should have taken care of the customer's request and passed it along to the appropriate person. This is referred to as *ownership of the problem*. In Ritz-Carlton, the first employee to receive a guest request or complaint "owns" it. The employee is responsible for making sure that guests receive what they need by following up with the other departments involved and then contacting the guest to make sure that everything was satisfactory. Customers should not have to learn the hotel or restaurant's organizational chart. They should not have to redirect their request for service to another employee. Hiring procedures need to identify these employees who are team players.

Older employees were one group that surprised some managers by their willingness to support other employees. Some managers believed that the elderly might not be willing to cooperate with much younger workers or to accept direction from a youthful supervisor. Kentucky Fried Chicken and McDonald's were among the first hospitality firms to prove the invalidity of these assumptions. A survey of National Restaurant Association members demonstrated that older workers were regarded to have better relations with guests and fellow employees than the "average employees."[39]

The Importance of Initial Training

While staying at a franchised Holiday Inn, a guest asked the desk clerk about the management company: How many hotels did they manage? Where were they located? The employee was unable to answer either question. On another occasion a conversation was overheard between a guest and the dining-room hostess of a Ramada Inn. The guest asked for a recommendation concerning a good place to eat in the area. Managers would hope that the hostess first would suggest the hotel's restaurant and then mention other restaurants in the area. Instead, the hostess said she had just moved to the area and had not yet found a good place to eat. Too often, employees know nothing about the hotel they work for or its products and other items of interest to guests. If employees are not enthusiastic about the company they work for and the products they sell, it will be difficult to create enthusiastic customers.

To be effective, employees must receive information regularly about their company. The company's history, current businesses, and its mission statement and vision are important for employees to know. They must be encouraged to feel proud of their new employer. Desire to contribute to the company's success must be instilled in them. At Disney all new employees take a course called "Traditions," in which they learn about the company, its founder, and its values and beliefs. Employees then receive specific training for their particular assignments. Disney trains its ticket takers for four days, because the company wants them to be more than ticket takers; they want them to be cast members. The term cast members implies that they are members of a team. Like other Disney cast members, they are putting on a performance. While they work in the ticket booths, guests will ask many questions. They must know the answers to these questions or be able to find them quickly. Disney understands the importance of these moments of truth. They provide their staff with extensive training before the first moment of truth is faced.[40] Disney has become so well known for its training and human resources management that it now conducts courses for other companies.

10.6 Delta Airlines
Homestead
Opryland Hotel

Opryland Hotel has developed a training program that begins with an orientation, for new employees, designed to instill pride in the history, culture, and stature of the hotel. The purpose of the orientation process is to create an inspiring atmosphere and build a solid work commitment that helps reduce turnover. According to Marc Clark, the director of training at Opryland, "the new employee orientation program and all employee policies are built on a foundation of a sincere service attitude. If employees, particularly managers, are not serving guests directly, then they should be serving those who are."[41]

The Homestead in Virginia's Allegheny Mountain region is a resort heavy with tradition. Guests feel the nearly 100 years of tradition through the architecture and the customs such as "gentlemanly sports" and afternoon tea, but principally through the employees. The vision of H. H. Ingalls, Jr., president, is "to preserve what is wonderful about this place and to communicate and serve it effectively to guests." Ingalls credits the Homestead employees for earning a five-star designation for the hotel. In praise, he stated, "The support of our employees is like the support of a large family. They deliver the kind of service people expect." This feeling of being a member of a family is precisely the effect that successful companies such as Disney World, Opryland Hotel, and the Homestead have created and that all members of the hospitality industry must strive to attain.

Continuous Training

Two principal characteristics have been identified in companies that lead their industries in customer service: They emphasize **cross-training,** and they insist that everybody share certain training experiences. Delta Airlines flight attendants must learn several back-office jobs before they start their careers as attendants.[42] Most hotel training programs for college graduates rotate new employees through all departments in the hotel. This gives the trainees an insight into the importance of each department and how they work together to provide customer service. James' Coney Island, a fast-food restaurant chain, cross-trains its employees so that they understand all the positions in the restaurant. Embassy Suites Hotels goes a step further, providing employees an opportunity to increase their wages based on the number of positions they have mastered.

Companies must make sure that their employees are familiar with all the products the organization sells. For example, all restaurant employees should be prepared to tell guests about the restaurant's Sunday brunch, even those who do not work on Sundays. A restaurant service person in a hotel should be able to give directions to the hotel's health club. Often, employees do not have knowledge of products in their own areas because they have never been given the opportunity to sample them. When a service person does not know how an item tastes, it promotes the perception that the employee or management does not care about the customer.

A front-desk clerk said that she felt uneasy when guests asked her about the show in the hotel's nightclub. The hotel had stressed the importance of promoting it favorably but did not give the front-desk employees an opportunity to see the show. As a result, the front-desk clerk would tell the guest that it was a great show. Sometimes, the guest would start asking specific questions about the show. When this happened, her answers usually reflected her lack of firsthand knowledge about the show and made her feel foolish. It would have been wise for the hotel to provide an opportunity for front-desk employees to see the show. They could have enthusiastically promoted the show with firsthand knowledge instead of cringing when someone asked about the show. They may even have promoted the show on their own rather than waiting for a guest to ask about it.

In well-managed restaurants, employees know the menu. They are trained to direct guests to the menu selections that will best suit their taste and instructed in how to sell the choices on the menu. Every restaurant should have tastings where employees sample the products that they are selling. Product training is a continuous learning process; it should be part of every company's employee training.

Product training sometimes must extend into the visual arts. The Grand Hyatt of Hong Kong is a magnificent hotel with caring and well-trained personnel. Yet even here there is room for additional training. The Grand Hyatt is truly an art museum within a hotel, as the decor features sculpture, paintings, and other fine works of visual art. Unfortunately, none of the employees seems to have sufficient knowledge of these expensive and carefully selected art pieces to discuss them with inquiring guests. If exquisite art is part of the product, it should be part of the training. Guests will be impressed, and employees will gain pride in the hotel.

This results in the circular effect of creating satisfied and proud employees who in turn create satisfied guests. The results of a study of this circular effect clearly demonstrated that "as employee's job satisfaction, job involvement, and job security improve, their customer focus also improves."[43]

Insurance executives checking out of the Sheraton Boca Raton locked their keys in the car. The car was blocking traffic, and the executives had a plane to catch. The bellman telephoned the car's make and serial number to a nearby locksmith, and the hotel staff rolled the car out of traffic. Fifteen minutes after the bellman's call, the locksmith arrived with replacement keys.[44] The employees were successful in handling the problem because they were prepared for such an incident. They knew that a car blocking the entrance could cause problems, so they stored a car jack attached to a dolly nearby. The bell staff knew the phone numbers of nearby locksmiths. They also understood the importance of keeping guests informed to relieve anxiety. Throughout this event, they kept the insurance executives informed of what was going on. Leaving the Sheraton Boca Raton could have been a disaster; instead, it provided an exciting incident that enabled the staff to show their professionalism and to convince the guests further that they had indeed chosen the right hotel.

The Hyatt Sanctuary Cove in Australia has adjusted its training programs. Training is now conducted by each department instead of by a trainer from the human resources department. Departments decide what their training needs are and develop programs to fill those needs. The hotel also allows any employee to attend any training session and posts all training sessions on the employee bulletin board so that every employee can review the hotel's training program for the coming month. During a visit to the Hyatt, an accounting department employee was observed training a food-service waiter on the hotel's computerized food and beverage accounting system. It became obvious from their

The Hyatt Sanctuary Cove develops its employees through training programs that are open to all employees, allowing employees from one department to learn about other departments. Courtesy of Sanctuary Cove, Queensland, Australia.

conversation that each was learning about the other's department and how the departments could better support each other.

The development of a good training program can start organizations on an upward spiral. A research study found that service quality is related inversely to staff turnover. Properly trained employees can deliver quality service, which helps the image of the firm, attracting more guests and employees to the organization. Some firms ask why they should spend money training employees if they are just going to leave. This can turn into a self-fulfilling prophecy for firms that have this attitude. The employees are not properly trained and thus are not capable of delivering quality service. Not being able to deliver good service, they will feel uncomfortable in their jobs and quit. Unfortunately, this reinforces employers' beliefs that they should not spend money training their employees, but not investing in employee training programs leads to a cycle of high employee turnover and guest dissatisfaction.

Hospitality companies with a strong commitment to employee training are well advised to make this philosophy well known to all employees in action and in word. The Centennial Hotel Management Company of Canada has a written statement of human resources philosophy that includes orientation and training. This statement is an excellent internal marketing tool:

> *Orientation*
>
> - The purpose of Centennial Hotel orientation is to assure the new employee that he or she has made the right decision and to build a strong sense of belonging to the company, the team, and the industry.
> - Orientation assures the employees that the company provides the support that they require to be successful. It is also a time to share the values of Centennial Hotel and to introduce the facilities of the hotel.
>
> *Training*
>
> - Centennial Hotel is committed to providing consistent basic training throughout the company, as well as continuous upgrading. Training is for everyone and must be planned, systematic, and comprehensive. The success of training must be measurable.[45]

Employee Involvement in Uniform Selection

The selection of uniforms is often left to designers and managers with little input from the service worker. Uniforms are important because employee dress contributes greatly to the guest's encounter with customer contact employees. Uniforms also become part of the atmospherics of a hospitality operation or travel operation; they have the ability to create aesthetic, stylish, and colorful impressions of the property.[46] They distinguish employees from the general public, making employees accessible and easily identified. In cases where uniforms are lacking, guests may become frustrated because they have difficulty identifying employees when they need help. Uniforms have the ability to create attitudes about an employee's job. Employees dressing in formal wear state that they feel and behave differently once they put on their uniform. This anecdotal evidence has been supported by research. Clothing has been found to be a contributing factor in role-playing, acting as a vivid cue that can encourage employees to engage in the behaviors associated with the role of the employee.[47] Putting on the costume can mean putting on a role and shedding other roles. Employees' dress can direct employees' behavior to be more consistent with the goals and standards of behavior established by the organization. A recent study of resort employees found a significant relationship between employees' perceptions of their uniforms and their overall job attitude. The higher the employee's perception of the uniform, the more positive was their rating of their overall attitude toward their job.[48]

Uniforms should be functional and accepted by the employees. Management often looks for uniforms that represent the property, acting as a marketing tool—enhancing the image of the organization. It is paramount to allow employees to be involved in uniform choices regarding both function and projected image. For example, food servers at a pirate-themed restaurant complained about the loose-fitting sleeves on their shirts and blouses. The uniforms looked great until the servers began working. The sleeves dragged across plates when they were being cleared or when trays were being unloaded at the dishwasher. In a few hours the sleeves were stained with food. The employees stated that this made them embarrassed when they approached a guest, and they became less outgoing in their dealings with guests. Other problems with functionality include uniforms that are designed without pockets and uniforms that are uncomfortable. The selection of uniforms can have an impact on both the employees' attitude and their ability to serve the customer well. Managers need to consider the employees and involve them in uniform decisions.

Managing Emotional Labor

In the hospitality industry, managers require employees to display friendliness and courtesy toward guests. According to Zeithaml and Bitner, two services marketing experts, friendliness, courtesy, empathy, and responsiveness directed toward customers all require huge amounts of emotional labor from front-line employees who shoulder this responsibility.[49] The term emotional labor was first used by Hochschild and has been defined as the necessary involvement of the service provider's emotions in the delivery of the service.[50] The display of emotions can strongly influence the customer's perception of service quality. To manage emotional labor, managers must hire employees who can cope with the stress caused by dealing with customers. Then emotional labor must be managed on a day-to-day basis. Some common techniques used to manage emotional labor include monitoring overtime and avoiding double shifts, work breaks, and support from fellow workers and managers. Managers are sometimes the cause of emotional stress, for example, by chewing an employee out before a shift, then sending the employee out to work with customers.

One of the biggest causes of emotional stress is long hours. Employees often find it hard to manage their emotions after working for ten hours straight. At this point the employees are tired and often care little about the customer. We have all been in that position or observed service providers who were rude or uncaring after working a long shift. The cause of such behavior is that the employee is emotionally drained. Bernard Booms likes to tell the story of the stewardess who was having a particularly hard flight when a customer complained about the food. The customer shouted that his baked potato was bad. The stewardess picked up the potato, slapped it a couple of times, yelling "bad potato, bad potato," put the potato back on the customer's tray, and walked away. Although this is a humorous story, the customer was not amused. When employees are overworked emotionally, service suffers.

Dissemination of Marketing Information to Employees

Often, the most effective way of communicating with customers is through customer-contact employees. They can suggest additional products, such as the hotel's health club or business center, and they can upsell when it is to the guest's benefit. Employees often have opportunities to solve guest problems before these problems become irritants. To do this, they need information. Unfortunately, many companies leave customer-contact employees out of the communication cycle. The director of marketing may tell managers and supervisors about upcoming events, ad campaigns, and new promotions, but some managers may feel employees do not need to know this information.

Beth Lorenzini of *Restaurants and Institutions* states, "Promotions designed to generate excitement and sales can do just the opposite if employees aren't involved in planning and execution." Monica Kass, sales and marketing coordinator for Lawry's the Prime Rib, Chicago, says that employees and marketing people who develop promotions must communicate. Lawry's increased its Thanksgiving Day sales by 48 percent through employee involvement. Lawry's invited all the "wait staff" to a Thanksgiving dinner a week before Thanksgiving. This was the same meal that it was serving to guests on Thanksgiving Day. The dinner not only served as a festive affair to get everybody into the Thanksgiving holiday mood, but also served as a training tool. Employees knew exactly what was going to be served on Thanksgiving Day, including wines that went well with the meal. The management of Lawry's also asked the staff for their input as to how to make the promotion run smoothly. On Thanksgiving Day, each wait person was given a corsage or a boutonniere. Like the employees at Lawry's, all staff should be informed about promotions. They should hear about promotions and new products from management, not from advertisements meant for external customers.[51]

The actions of management are one way that an organization communicates with its employees. Management at all levels must understand that employees are watching them for cues about expected behavior. If the general manager picks a piece of paper up off the floor, other employees will start doing the same. A manager who talks about the importance of employees working together as a team can reinforce the desire for teamwork through personal actions. Taking an interest in employees' work, lending a hand, knowing employees by name, and eating in the employee cafeteria are actions that will give credibility to the manager's words.

Hospitality organizations should use printed publications as part of their internal communication. Most multiunit companies have an employee newsletter, and larger hotels usually have their own in-house newsletters. Besides mass communication, personal communication is important to the effective communication of new products and promotional campaigns. Leonard Berry suggests having two annual reports, one for stockholders and one for employees. His suggestion is now being implemented by many firms.[52]

McDonald's initiated a "talking" annual report on videotape complete with commercials. This unusual and creative approach to presenting the required annual report proved to be an excellent means for reaching stockholders and employees. When introduced, it also produced a wealth of free publicity in major news media.

Ongoing communication between management and employees is essential—not just group meetings but regular individual meetings between the employee and management. Every customer-contact employee communicates with hundreds of customers. Managers should meet with these employees to gain customer need insights and determine how the company can make it easier for the employee to serve the customer.

Ansett Airlines in Australia provides an example of what can happen when employees are not informed of changes in the company's marketing plans. A traveler called Ansett to ask the airline about a promotion that they had just read about in a newspaper advertisement. The airline representative did not know anything about the promotion and asked the caller how he found out about it. When the caller stated that he had read it in today's newspaper, the airline representative explained that that was why she had not heard about it. She said it would be several days before she would get a copy of the details of the promotion. Hospitality organizations often spend time and effort developing campaigns for specific markets, which are effective in enticing customers. But if customers must deal with employees who are uninformed and cannot provide them with information, they may walk away dissatisfied.

Front-desk clerks are the communication center of the hotel, yet they frequently do not know the names of entertainers or the type of entertainment featured in the hotel's lounges. They may also be unaware of special marketing promotions. The roof-top lounge of the Westin Oaks Hotel in Houston was known for having good entertainment. When the hotel was called to find out who was playing in the lounge, the front-desk clerk gave the name of an unfamiliar group. When asked what type of music they played, the clerk had no idea.

10.7 Westin Oaks Hotel

Hotels can use technology and training to provide employees with product knowledge. Technology can be used to develop a database. Information can be readily accessible to employees, who should then be trained in the hotel's products and services. Finally, employees can be encouraged to try the company's products. They can eat in the restaurants, stay overnight in the hotel, and receive special previews of lounge entertainment. It is much more convincing if the front-desk employee can give a potential guest firsthand information rather than reading a description.

Employees should receive information on new products and product changes, marketing campaigns, and changes in the service delivery process. All action steps in the marketing plan should include internal marketing. For example, when a company introduces a new mass media campaign, the implementation plan should include actions to inform employees about the campaign. The first time that most employees see company advertisements is in the media in which the advertisement is placed. Before the advertisements appear in the media, the company should share the ad with its employees. Managers should also explain the objective of the campaign and the implications.

One of the authors once worked in a restaurant whose owner decided to install a computer system without discussion with the staff. The system was first used during a busy lunch period, and the restaurant had given the staff almost no prior training. The system did not perform well, and the staff grew determined to get rid of it. They found that the system was sensitive to grease spots on the check. If a service person got butter on a check, the guest would be charged for all sorts of extra items. Some staff would deliberately put grease spots on their checks to develop false charges for the customer. When the customer complained about the bill, the server would explain to the guest the problems that they were having with the new system. Customers quickly sided with the service personnel, and within three months the owner was forced to eliminate the new system. If management has consulted employees before installation, the employees might have supported the computer. Management could have shown the employees how the system would help them better serve the guest by adding their tickets automatically and keeping them current. This would have created employee support. Instead, without the proper information and training, employees were determined from the beginning to get rid of the computer.

Implementation of a Reward and Recognition System

Employees must know how they are doing to perform effectively. Communication must be designed to give them feedback on their performance. An internal marketing program includes service standards and methods of measuring how well the organization is meeting these standards. The results of any service measurement should be communicated to employees. Sheraton, Marriott, and other major hotel companies survey their guests to determine their satisfaction level with individual attributes of the hotel. One researcher found that simply communicating information collected from customers changed employee attitudes and performance.[53] Customer-service measurements have a positive effect on employee attitudes if results are communicated and recognition is given to those who serve the customer well. If you want customer-oriented employees, seek out ways to catch them serving the customer and reward and recognize them for making the effort.[54]

10.8 Sheraton

Most reward systems in the hospitality and travel industry are based on meeting cost objectives such as achieving a certain labor cost or food cost. They are also based on achieving sales objectives. A few companies are now starting to give rewards based on customer satisfaction, but these companies are the exception, not the rule. If companies want to have customer-oriented employees, they must reward them for servicing the customer. Reward systems and bonuses based on customer satisfaction scores are one method of rewarding employees based on serving the customer.

Nonroutine Transactions

A good internal marketing program should result in employees who can handle non-routine transactions, such as Barry Urquhart's request for a cappuccino. Training programs and manuals can prepare employees to handle normal or routine transactions with customers. Internal marketing programs will help them deal with guests in a positive and friendly manner. But not all transactions are routine. In this chapter we discussed Barry Urquhart's request for a cappuccino, Karl Albrecht's request for a late checkout when the hotel was full, and the hotel guest who locked his keys in his car. One benefit of an internal marketing program is that it provides employees with the right attitude, knowledge, communication skills, and authority to deal with nonroutine transactions. The ability to handle nonroutine transactions separates excellent hospitality companies from mediocre ones. A nonroutine transaction is a guest transaction that is unique and usually experienced for the first time by the employees. The number of possible nonroutine transactions is so great that they cannot be covered in a training manual.

Management must be willing to give employees the authority to make decisions that will solve guests' problems. Management should exhibit confidence in their ability to hire and train employees by trusting the employees' ability to make decisions. Simon Cooper, president of Delta Hotels and Resorts, a twenty-five-location chain headquartered in Toronto, believes that having staff do nothing but control other staff reflects poorly on the organization. He states that the job of an assistant housekeeper is to go around and check that the maids are doing their job. Having that position is an admission that we can't hire the right people. Cooper says that Delta has successfully eliminated that position. They have a few assistant housekeepers, who are now in training positions. When their housekeepers finish a room, they know that the next person in it will be a guest. Cooper states that the degree of trust makes them far better workers.[55] When we trust employees, they solve guest problems more effectively and create fewer causes for the guest to complain.

Hospitality companies that rely on rigid policies and procedures rather than motivated, well-trained, and empowered employees have little hope of achieving maximum guest satisfaction. This sentiment was expressed very well by Robert C. Lewis:

> The success of the internal-marketing concept ultimately lies with management. Lower-level employees cannot be expected to be customer-conscious if the management above them does not display the same focus. Operations-oriented managers who concern themselves primarily with policies and procedures, often instituted without regard to the customer, undermine the firm's internal-marketing effort, reducing employee's jobs to mechanical functions that offer little in the way of challenge, self-esteem or personal gratification.

> Moreover, by requiring employees to adhere rigidly to specific procedures, the operations-oriented manager ties their hands and restricts their ability to satisfy the customer.[56]

The issue of nonroutine transactions will become increasingly important in the future. Hospitality firms are now using technology to serve routine customer transactions. This use of technology will become even more pervasive. Computerized check-in, video checkout, and robotics will be adapted to the hospitality industry, so employees will find themselves dealing more frequently with nonroutine tasks. Self-confident guests will take advantage of technology designed to enhance and hasten guest service. The uncertain guest or guests with problems will wish to deal with an employee. As the workplace becomes more automated, employees will take a greater role in answering questions and solving guests' problems. They must also be prepared to handle nonroutine transactions.

As Parasuraman says, "Customer service earned through several satisfactorily performed routine transactions can be badly damaged by just one botched attempt at processing a non-routine transaction. No amount of written procedures, guidelines, or specifications can prevent the occurrence of such botched attempts; only true organizational dedication to customer satisfaction can."[57] A strong service culture enables employees to make decisions required to handle non-routine transactions.

KEY TERMS

Cast members A term used for employees. It implies that employees are part of a team that is performing for their guests.

Cross-training Training employees to do two or more jobs within the organization.

Empowerment When a firm empowers employees, it moves the authority and responsibility to make decisions to the line employees from the supervisor.

Internal marketing Marketing by a service firm to train effectively and motivate its customer-contact employees and all the supporting service people to work as a team to provide customer satisfaction.

Moment of truth Occurs when an employee and a customer have contact.

Organizational culture The pattern of shared values and beliefs that gives members of an organization meaning and provides them with the rules for behavior in that organization.

Service culture A system of values and beliefs in an organization that reinforces the idea that providing the customer with quality service is the principal concern of the business.

Chapter Review

I. Internal Marketing

1) The hospitality industry is unique in that employees are part of the product.

2) Marketers must develop techniques and procedures to ensure that employees are able and willing to deliver quality service.

3) Internal marketing is marketing aimed internally at the firm's employees.

4) Employee satisfaction and customer satisfaction are correlated.

II. The Internal Marketing Process

1) Establishment of a service culture

a) A **service culture** is an organizational cultural that supports customer service through policies, procedures, reward systems, and actions.

b) An **organizational culture** is a pattern of shared values and beliefs that gives members of an organization meaning, providing them with the rules for behavior in the organization.

c) Turning the organizational chart upside down. Service organizations should create an organization that supports those employees who serve the customers.

2) Development of a marketing approach to human resources management

a) Create positions that attract good employees.

b) Use a hiring process that identifies and results in hiring service-oriented employees.

c) Provide initial employee training designed to share the company's vision with the employee and supply the employee with product knowledge.

d) Provide continuous employee training programs.

e) Uniforms can affect an employee's attitude. Employees should be involved in the selection of uniforms.

f) Employees must be able to maintain a positive attitude. Managing emotional labor helps maintain a good attitude.

III. Dissemination of Marketing Information to Employees

1) Often, the most effective way of communicating with customers is through customer-contact employees.

2) Employees should hear about promotions and new products from management, not from advertisements meant for external customers.

3) Management at all levels must understand that employees are watching them for cues about expected behavior.

4) Hospitality organizations should use printed publications as part of their internal communication.

5) Hotels can use technology and training to provide employees with product knowledge.

6) Employees should receive information on new products and product changes, marketing campaigns, and changes in the service delivery process.

IV. Implementation of a Reward and Recognition System

1) Employees must know how they are doing to perform effectively. Communication must be designed to give them feedback on their performance.

2) An internal marketing program includes service standards and methods of measuring how well the organization is meeting these standards.

3) If you want customer-oriented employees, seek out ways to catch them serving the customer, and reward and recognize them for making the effort.

V. Nonroutine Transactions

1) A good internal marketing program should result in employees who can handle nonroutine transactions.

2) One benefit of an internal marketing program is that it provides employees with the right attitude, knowledge, communication skills, and authority to deal with nonroutine transactions.

3) A nonroutine transaction is a guest transaction that is unique and usually experienced for the first time by the employees.

4) Management must be willing to give employees the authority to make decisions that will solve guests' problems.

DISCUSSION QUESTIONS

1. Why are employees called internal customers?
2. What is a service culture? Why is it a requirement for an internal marketing program?
3. Discuss the possible ways that marketing techniques can be used by human resources managers.
4. What are the benefits of explaining advertising campaigns to employees before they appear in the media?
5. The handling of nonroutine transactions will separate excellent hospitality companies from mediocre ones. Discuss this statement.

EXPERIENTIAL EXERCISE

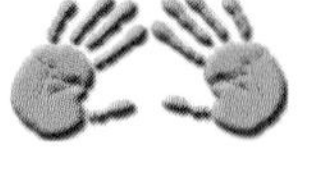

Do the following;

Visit a hospitality or travel company. Ask some questions about their products. For example, at a restaurant you many ask about the hours they are open and about menu items. You may state you are looking for a good steak restaurant and ask them about their steaks. At a hotel you may ask about their rooms or restaurants. The idea is to have enough dialogue with their employees to be able to judge the customer orientation of the employees. Write your findings supporting how the employees demonstrated they had a customer orientation and ideas you have on how they could have been more customer oriented.

INTERNET EXERCISE

Support for these exercises can be found on the Web site for *Marketing for Hospitality and Tourism*, www.prenhall.com/kotler.

Explain the advantages and disadvantages of having a "live chat" option or other option to have a live dialogue with an employee on a Web site.

REFERENCES

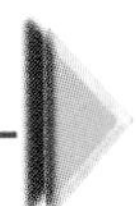

1. John Tschohl, *Achieving Excellence through Customer Service* (Upper Saddle River, NJ: Prentice Hall, 1991).
2. Barry Urquhart, *Serves You Right* (Kalamunda, Western Australia: Marketing Focus, 1991), p. 86.
3. Karl Albrecht and Ron Zemke, *Service America!: Doing Business in the New Economy* (Homewood, IL: Dow Jones-Irwin, 1985), pp. 127–128.
4. Tschohl, *Achieving Excellence*, p. 3.
5. Frederick F. Reichheld and W. Earl Sasser, Jr., "Zero Defections: Quality Comes to Services," *Harvard Business Review*, Sep/Oct 1990, pp. 105–111.
6. Richard Normann, *Service Management: Strategy and Leadership in Service Businesses* (New York: Wiley, 1984), p. 33.
7. Ibid., p. 9.
8. David Owen and Richard Teare, "Driving Top-Line Profitability through the Management of Human Resources," in *The International Hospitality Business*, ed. Richard Kotas, Richard Teare, Jeremy Logie, Chandana Jaywardena, and John Bowen (London: Cassel, 1996), pp. 186–190.
9. Leonard L. Berry and A. Parasuraman, *Marketing Services: Competing through Time* (New York: Free Press, 1991), pp. 18–19.
10. Owen and Teare, "Driving Top-Line Profitability."
11. Tschohl, *Achieving Excellence*, pp. 160–162.
12. Joseph W. Benoy, "Internal Marketing Builds Service Quality," *Journal of Health Care Marketing* 16, no. 1 (1996): 54–64.
13. William R. George and Christian Gronroos, "Developing Customer-Conscious Employees at Every Level: Internal Marketing," in *The Handbook of Marketing for the Service Industries,* ed. Carole A. Congram (New York: American Management Association), pp. 85–100.
14. Christian Gronroos, *Strategic Management and Marketing in the Service Sector* (Cambridge, MA: Marketing Science Institute, 1983), as cited in C. Gronroos, *Service Management and Marketing* (Lexington, MA: Lexington Books, 1990), p. 223.
15. Ibid., p. 85.
16. *The Australian,* October 10, 1990.
17. S. M. Davis, *Managing Corporate Culture* (Cambridge, MA: Ballinger, 1985).
18. John Bowen and Robert Ford, "Service Organizations—'Does Having a Thing Make a Difference,'" *Journal of Management,* forthcoming.
19. Terrence E. Deal and Allan A. Kennedy, *Corporate Cultures* (Reading, MA.: Addison-Wesley, 1982), pp. 15–16.
20. A. Parasuraman, "Customer-Oriented Corporate Cultures Are Crucial to Services Marketing Success," *Journal of Services Marketing* 1, no. 1 (Summer 1987): 39–46.
21. Ibid.
22. John J. Hogan, "Turnover and What to Do about It," *Cornell Hotel and Restaurant Administration Quarterly* 33, no. 1 (February 1992): 41.
23. Karl Albrecht, *At America's Service* (Homewood, IL: Dow Jones–Irwin, 1988), p. 130.
24. Ibid., p. 107; Nathan Tyler, *Service Excellence,* Tape 2 (videotape) (Boston, MA: *Harvard Business School Management Productions*, 1987).
25. James L. Heskett, W. Earl Sasser, and Leonard A. Schlesinger, *Saving Customers with Service Recovery* (videotape) (Boston, MA: Harvard Business School Management Productions, 1994).
26. Leonard L. Berry, "The Employee as Customer," *Journal of Retail Banking* 3, no. 1 (1981): 33–40.
27. Hogan, "Turnover," p. 40.
28. Ibid., p. 41.
29. Dennis Reynolds and Mary Tabacchi, "Burnout in Full Service Chain Restaurant," *Cornell Hotel and Restaurant Administration Quarterly* 34, no. 2 (April 1993): 68.
30. Ken W. McClearly and Pamela A. Weaver, "The Job Offer: What Today's Graduates Want," *Cornell Hotel and Restaurant Administration Quarterly* 28, no. 4 (February 1988): 31.
31. Bowen and Ford, "Service Organizations."
32. B. Schneider and D. Bowen, *Winning the Service Game* (Boston, MA: HBS Press, 1995).
33. C. R. Bell and K. Anderson, "Selecting Super Service People," *HR Magazine* 37, no. 2 (1992): 52-54.
34. Bruce Grindy, "The Restaurant Industry: An Economic Powerhouse," *Restaurants USA* (June/July 2000): 40–45.
35. Miliand Lele, *The Customer Is Key* (New York: Wiley, 1987), p. 252.
36. Andrew J. Czaplewski, Jeffery M. Ferguson, and John F. Milliman, "Southwest Airlines: How Internal Marketing Pilots Success," *Marketing Management* (Chicago: September/October 2001), pp. 14–17.
37. Tschohl, *Achieving Excellence*, p. 113.
38. Frederick J. De Micco and Robert D. Reid, "Older Worker: A Hiring Resource for the Hospitality Industry," *Cornell Hotel and Restaurant Administration Quarterly* 29, no. 1 (May 1988): 56.
39. Ibid., p. 58.
40. N. W. Pope, "Mickey Mouse Marketing," *American Banker* (July 25, 1979), as included in W. Earl Sasser, Jr., Christopher W. L. Hart, and James L. Heskett, *The Service Management Course: Cases and Reading* (New York: Free Press, 1991), pp. 649–654.

41. Marc Clark, "Training for Tradition," *Cornell Hotel and Restaurant Administration Quarterly* 31, no. 4 (February 1991): 51; Robert C. Rod and Cherrill P. Heaton, *Managing the Guest Experience in Hospitality* (Albany, NY: Thomson Learning, 2000).
42. William H. Davidow and Bro Utall, *Total Customer Service: The Ultimate Weapon* (New York: Harpertrade, 1990), p. 128.
43. John R. Dienhart and Mary B. Gregoire, "Job Satisfaction, Job Involvement, Job Security and Customer Focus of Quick Service Restaurant Employees," *Hospitality Research Journal* 16, no. 2 (1993): 41.
44. Christopher W. L. Hart, James L. Heskett, and W. Earl Sasser, Jr., *Service Breakthroughs* (New York: Free Press, 1990), p. 109.
45. Michael K. Haywood, "Effective Training: Toward a Strategic Approach," *Cornell Hotel and Restaurant Administration Quarterly* 33, no. 6 (December 1992): 46.
46. M. R. Solomon, "Dress for Effect," *Psychology Today* 20, no. 4 (1986): 20–28.
47. A. Rafaeli and M. G. Pratt, "Tailored Meanings: On the Meaning and Impact of Organizational Dress," *Academy of Management Review* 18, no. 1 (1993): 32–55.
48. Kathy Nelson and John Bowen, "The Effect of Employee Uniforms on Employee Satisfaction," *Cornell Hotel and Restaurant Administration Quarterly,* Vol. 41 (2), 2000, pp. 86–95.
49. Valarie A. Zeithaml and Mary Jo Bitner, *Services Marketing* (New York: McGraw-Hill, 1996).
50. A. R. Hochschild, *The Managed Heart* (Berkeley: University of California Press, 1983); definition from Gunther Berghofer, "Emotional Labor," *Working Paper* (Bond University, Robina, Queensland, Australia, 1993).
51. Beth Lorenzini, "Promotion Success Depends on Employee's Enthusiasm," *Restaurants and Institutions,* February 12, 1992, p. 591.
52. Berry, "Employee as Customer," pp. 33–40.
53. Albrecht and Zemke, *Service America.*
54. Chip R. Bell and Ron Zemke, *Managing Knock Your Socks Off Service* (New York: American Management Association, 1992), p. 169.
55. Carla B. Furlong, *Marketing for Keeps* (New York: Wiley, 1993), pp. 79–80.
56. Robert C. Lewis, "Hospitality Marketing: The Internal Approach," *Cornell Hotel and Restaurant Administration Quarterly* 30, no. 3 (November 1989): 43.
57. A. Parasuraman, "Customer-Oriented Corporate Cultures," pp. 33–40.

Hampton Inn
San Diego
mazda

11 Building Customer Loyalty through Quality

To understand service quality and make quality management effective, we need profound knowledge about the details and activities connected with the emergence of a service. This presupposes interest in service design and service production.
Evert Gummesson

In January, 1990, Hampton Inns began advertising a service guarantee. The guarantee offered a free night's stay if the guest was dissatisfied. Most hotel managers are strongly opposed to offering such guarantees; they feel the hotel will end up giving away rooms to dishonest customers who claim that they were not satisfied just to get their money back. Because of this attitude among hotel managers, the move by Hampton Inns was a bold one. The company had faith in their guests' honesty and in their employees' ability to deliver a quality product. This trust in their guests and employees gave them a competitive advantage over hotel companies without a service guarantee.

A survey of Hampton Inns' customers found that more than 85 percent of the guests viewed the guarantee as appealing: The guests ranked it as one of the ten most important attributes of the hotel. Ninety-nine percent of the guests who invoked the guarantee said that they would give the chain another chance, and a tracking study revealed that almost 40 percent of those guests returned to the Hampton Inns within a relatively short period. When management feels that the guest is taking advantage of the guarantee without a valid reason, a note is made in Hampton Inns' database. When these guests call to make a reservation, the operator tells the guest that they will be happy to take their reservation; however, the guarantee will not be valid. Thus a few guests may take advantage of the system one or two times and then they are eliminated from the system.

Hampton Inns tracked the costs of its guarantee. They found that about 2 percent of their guests, representing 157,000 room-nights, came to the hotel in 1990 because of the guarantee. These guests generated $7 million in sales, and guests who returned after invoking the guarantee represented another $1 million

in sales. During the year, Hampton Inns paid out $350,000 to customers who invoked the guarantee. In 1991, Hampton Inns put its sales generated by the guarantee at $18 million, while compensation paid to customers invoking the guarantee remained constant.[1]

One reason for the success of Hampton Inns' guarantee is that the company regularly performs quality audits. Hampton Inns realized that its guarantee could be a financial disaster if it did not provide a product that would satisfy its guests. Their audit includes a corporate employee posing as a guest invoking the guarantee. The employee tracks how the Inn resolves the problem and if they follow up with the guest to make sure that everything is satisfactory.[2]

The guarantee also had an effect on the hotel's employees. When asked to make comments about their job, almost 50 percent suggested (unaided) that the guarantee made them work harder. The employees also stated that it gave them the confidence to solve guest problems on their own without waiting for a manager's approval. Management claimed that the guarantee made Hampton Inns a better place to work and improved employee morale. The service guarantee provides an example of how hospitality firms are focusing on improving the quality of the services they offer.[3] It also provides evidence that employees prefer working for a company that helps them deliver a quality product and satisfy their customers.

Some managers are afraid of a guarantee because they expect customers will unfairly take advantage of the guarantee to get a free meal or a free room. This will happen, but researchers estimate that there will be nineteen legitimate complaints for every cheater.[4] Hampton Inns controls cheating by advising guests who are suspected of cheating and have invoked the guarantee on more than one occasion that they are welcome as guests, but they will no longer be offered the guarantee. The real danger with guarantees is from businesses who offer a guarantee but do not provide a satisfactory product.

The use of service guarantees is increasing. Three types of service guarantees exist within the hospitality industry: unconditional, specific, and implicit.

Unconditional guarantees such as that by Hampton Inns promises 100 percent money back guarantee. Hampton Inns advertises, "We guarantee high quality accommodations, friendly and efficient service, and clean comfortable surroundings. If you're not completely satisfied, we don't expect you to pay."

Specific guarantees are oriented around particular departments within the company such as food and beverage, AV equipment, or room service. These guarantees are especially used for conferences, meetings and for the business traveler.

Implicit guarantees are not stipulated but customers are made aware that the organization stands solidly behind its products/service. The Four Seasons hotel prides itself on high-operating standards. If a service failure occurs, Four Seasons offers compensation far exceeding the norm. An implicit guarantee is viewed by many in the hospitality industry as a "classier way" to guarantee reliability than a written guarantee.

Service guarantees perform two primary functions (1) to help establish service standards, and (2) to help ensure customer loyalty and positive word-of-mouth by saying "we are sorry" in a very positive way when guests receive an unacceptable product/service.[5]

Chapter Objectives

After reading this chapter, you should be able to:

1. Define customer value and customer satisfaction.
2. Understand the difference between customer satisfaction and customer loyalty.
3. Discuss attracting new users and retaining current customers by developing relationship marketing.
4. Know tactics for resolving customer complaints and understand the importance of resolving complaints.
5. Define quality and discuss the importance of the benefits of quality.
6. Implement capacity and demand management tactics.

11.1 Hampton Inn

Today's companies face their toughest competition in decades, and things will only get worse in years to come. In earlier chapters we have argued that to succeed in today's fiercely competitive marketplace, companies will have to adopt a marketing philosophy. In this chapter we spell out in more detail how companies can go about winning customers and outperforming competitors. The answer lies in doing a better job of meeting and satisfying customer needs.

To succeed, or simply to survive, companies need a new philosophy. To win in today's marketplace, companies must be **customer centered;** they must deliver superior value to their target customers. They must become adept in building customers, not just building products. They must be skillful in market engineering, not just product engineering.

Too many companies think that obtaining customers is the job of the marketing or sales department. But winning companies have come to realize that marketing cannot do this job alone. In fact, although it plays a leading role, marketing can be only a partner in attracting and keeping customers. The world's best marketing department cannot successfully sell poorly made products that fail to meet consumer needs. The marketing department can be effective only in companies in which all departments and employees have teamed up to form a competitively superior customer value delivery system.

Consider McDonald's. People do not swarm to the world's 28,000 McDonald's restaurants only because they love the chain's hamburgers.[6] Consumers flock to the McDonald's system, not just to its food products. Throughout the world, McDonald's finely tuned system delivers a high standard of what the company calls QSCV: quality, service, cleanliness, and value. The system consists of many components, both internal and external.

11.2 McDonald's

McDonald's is effective only to the extent that it successfully partners with its employees, franchisees, suppliers, and others to deliver exceptionally high customer value.

In this chapter we discuss the philosophy of customer-value-creating marketing and the customer-focused firm. It addresses several important questions: What are customer value and customer satisfaction? How do leading companies organize to create and deliver high value and satisfaction? How can companies keep current customers as well as get new ones? How can companies practice total quality marketing?

Defining Customer Value and Satisfaction

More than thirty-five years ago, Peter Drucker insightfully observed that a company's first task is "to create customers." However, creating customers can be a difficult task. Today's customers face a vast array of product and brand choices, prices, and suppliers. The company must answer a key question: How do customers make their choices?

The answer is that customers choose the marketing offer that gives them the most value. Customers are value-maximizers, within the bounds of search costs and limited knowledge, mobility, and income. They form expectations of value and act upon them. Then they compare the actual value they receive in consuming the product to the value expected, and this affects their satisfaction and repurchase behavior. Managers need to remember that consumer expectations vary by type of business. For example, travelers to Hong Kong had different service expectations for four types of Hong Kong airport restaurants. Expectations were highest for full-service restaurants. Unfortunately, actual service levels fell short for each of the restaurant types.[7] Managers of each hospitality firm should be aware of service expectations for that enterprise and continuously strive to equal and surpass those expectations.

We now examine the concepts of customer value and customer satisfaction more carefully.

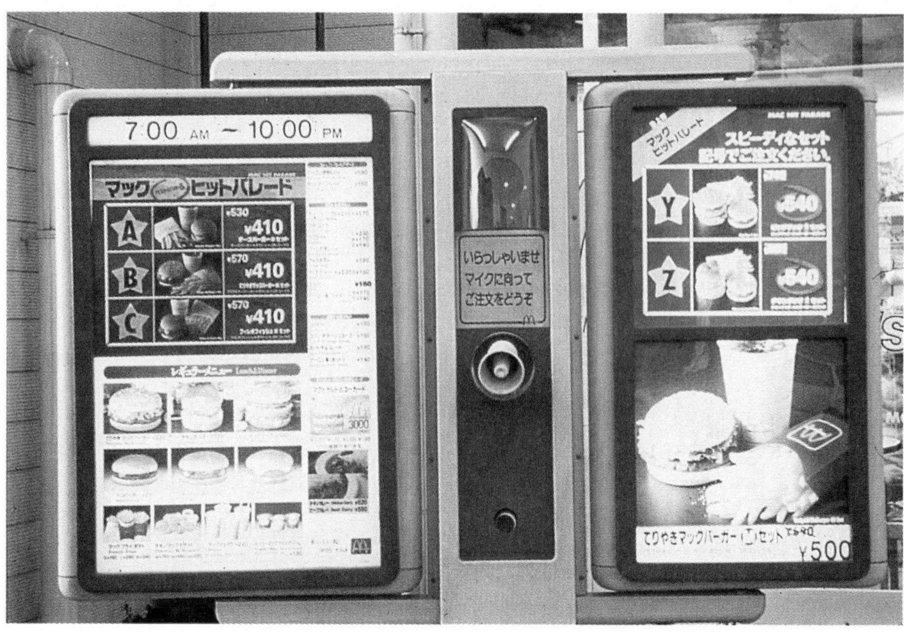

McDonald's consistency is one of the main reasons for its global acceptance. There is little variation in its products within a region, its restaurants are clean, and its service is quick. Courtesy of McDonald's.

Customer-Delivered Value

The consumers' assessment of the product's overall capacity to satisfy his or her needs determines customer value. The difference between total customer value and total customer cost of a marketing offer is "profit" to the customer or customer-delivered value. *Total customer value* is the total of all the product, services, personnel, and image values that a buyer receives from a marketing offer. *Total customer cost* is the total of all the monetary, time, energy, and psychic costs associated with a marketing offer (Figure 11-1). For example, a business traveler will value a nonstop flight over a direct flight that makes a stop because of the reduced travel time. They may avoid certain airports as connecting points because they are large and require a lot of walking. Going from the East Coast of the United States to the West Coast, they may prefer to change planes in Memphis rather than Dallas. Finally, they prefer an airline that has a good on-time record and customer service record. This can reduce the mental cost of worrying if the plane and baggage will arrive on time. These attributes create value for the customer. Suppose that an airline offers a nonstop for $25 more than a competitor's flight stopping in Dallas. The flight stopping in Dallas will take two hours longer and require changing planes. The hassle of walking through the airport and the two hours of extra time will increase the total customer cost of this flight even though it is monetarily less than the nonstop. The business traveler will prefer the nonstop because it has a higher customer-delivered value.

Luxury hotel guests were asked which hotel features would cause them to be more loyal to a hotel. A total of eighteen possible benefits developed from in-depth interviews were listed. The hotel customers were asked to rate each feature on a scale from 1, "would have no impact on loyalty," to 7, "would have a great impact on loyalty." In a separate area of the questionnaire, they were asked which of these features were offered currently at hotels to which they were loyal. If one considers what hotels are actually doing and compares this information with what customers would like hotels to do, one is easily able to see where hotels are either meeting the needs of guests or falling short. This is denoted as a gap (performance–importance). The gap for loyalty features is shown in Table 11-1.

Table 11-1 shows that there is tremendous opportunity to increase loyalty further. Of the eleven features tested, only one has a positive gap. Interestingly, the top two features where the largest gaps occur should be very easy and inexpensive for luxury hotels to implement. This type of analysis helps managers identify areas of opportunity for creating more customer-delivered value. In this case they see those attributes that create loyalty or value. They also see those areas that most hotels do not offer, giving them a chance to create a competitive advantage. Finally, they can cost out the

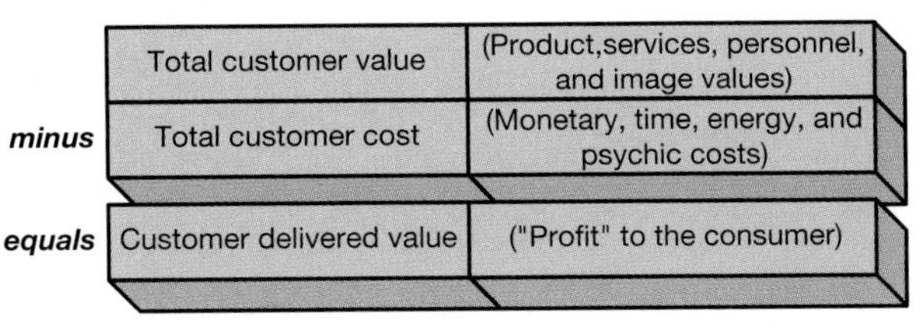

Figure 11-1
Customer delivered value.

Table 11-1
Gap Analysis of Loyalty Features

FEATURE	PERFORMANCE (%)	IMPORTANCE (%)	GAP
The hotel provides upgrades when available.	18.7	69.4	−50.7
You can request a specific room.	4.9	44.7	−39.8
If the hotel is likely to be sold out at a time you normally visit, someone from the hotel will call you to ask if you would like to make a reservation.	3.0	37.7	−34.7
The hotel uses information from your prior stays to customize services for you.	24.3	57.7	−33.4
The staff recognizes you when you arrive.	15.1	38.3	−23.2
Employees communicate the attitude that your problems are important to them.	24.0	42.6	−18.6
The hotel has a frequent stayer program that allows you to earn points toward free accommodations.	9.6	27.8	−18.2
The hotel has a credit card that allows you to accumulate points toward the hotel's frequent stayer program each time you use it.	5.1	19.6	−14.5
When you return to this hotel, your registration process is expedited.	31.2	41.1	−9.9
The hotel provides you with occasional gifts.	18.7	23.7	−5
This hotel has connections with individuals or organizations that help you enjoy your stay or be more productive.	19.5	13.4	6.1

Source: John Bowen and Stowe Shoemaker, University of Nevada/Las Vegas, Las Vegas, NV, 89154-6023.

price of providing the features. For example, giving guests unexpected periodic upgrades can be inexpensive if you are using unsold suites for this program.[8]

If a seller finds that competitors deliver greater value, it has two alternatives. It can try to increase total customer value by strengthening or augmenting the product, services, personnel, or image benefits of the offer. Or it can decrease total customer cost by reducing its price and simplifying the ordering and delivery process.[9]

Customer Satisfaction

Thus, consumers form judgments about the value of marketing offers and make their buying decisions based on these judgments. Customer satisfaction with a purchase depends on the product's performance relative to a buyer's expectations. A customer might experience various degrees of satisfaction. If the product's performance falls short of expectations, the customer is dissatisfied. If performance matches expectations, the customer is satisfied. If performance exceeds expectations, the customer is highly satisfied or delighted.

But how do buyers form their expectations? Expectations are based on the customer's past buying experiences, the opinions of friends and associates, and marketer and competitor information and promises. Marketers must be careful to set the right level of expectations. If they set expectations too low, they may satisfy those who buy but fail to attract enough buyers. In contrast, if they raise expectations too high, buyers are likely to be disappointed. For example, Holiday Inn ran a campaign a few years ago called "No surprises," which promised consistently trouble-free accommodations and service. However, Holiday Inn guests still encountered a host of problems, and the expectations created by the campaign only made customers more dissatisfied. Holiday Inn had to withdraw the campaign.

11.3 Holiday Inn
Ritz Carlton
Southwest Airlines

Still, some of today's most successful companies are raising expectations and delivering performance to match. These companies embrace total customer satisfaction. For example, Ritz-Carlton views the Baldrige

SHERATON "9 TO 5" PLAN

YOU'VE ALWAYS WANTED TO COME AND GO AS YOU PLEASE.

NOW YOU CAN.

From now on, everything around here will run according to a very strict schedule.

Yours.

That's the whole idea behind the new Sheraton "9 to 5"℠ plan. The only plan that lets you check in as early as 9 a.m. on arrival, and check out as late as 5 p.m. when you leave. It gives you more time to get things done. (And more time to fix things back at the office that have become undone.)

The Sheraton "9 to 5" plan is available to all guests paying corporate rates who are members of SCI, our frequent guest program. If you're not currently a member of SCI, simply inquire while making reservations or upon arrival.

And don't forget to use your Visa® card when calling your travel planner or **1-800-325-3535** to request the "9 to 5" plan. For reservations on-line, visit www.sheraton.com. Advance reservations required.

The Sheraton "9 to 5" plan is available to all SCI members and Visa cardholders paying business rates (RAC, COR or any SET rate) at participating properties in the United States and Canada, and is not valid with group or discounted rates. *Member of The Luxury Collection.℠ © 1997 ITT Sheraton Corporation.

Sheraton realizes allowing business travelers to check in early and check out late creates value. Courtesy of ITT Sheraton North American division.

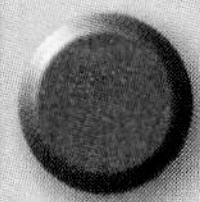

Marketing Highlight 11-1

Tracking Customer Satisfaction

Tools for tracking and measuring customer satisfaction range from the primitive to the sophisticated. Companies use the following methods to measure how much customer satisfaction they are creating.

1. **Complaint and suggestion systems.** A customer centered organization makes it easy for customers to make suggestions or complaints. Restaurants and hotels provide forms on which guests can check off their likes and dislikes. Such systems not only help companies to act more quickly to resolve problems, they also provide companies with many good ideas for improved products and service.
2. **Customer satisfaction surveys.** Simply running complaint and suggestion systems may not give the company a full picture of customer satisfaction and dissatisfaction. Studies show that one of every four purchases results in consumer dissatisfaction, but that less than 5% of dissatisfied customers bother to complain—most customers simply switch suppliers. As a result, the company loses customers needlessly.

   Responsive companies take direct measures of customer satisfaction by conducting regular surveys. They send questionnaires or make telephone calls to a sample of recent customers to find out how they feel about various aspects of the company's performance. They also survey buyers' views on competitor performance.

   A company can measure customer satisfaction in a number of ways. It can measure satisfaction directly by asking: "How satisfied are you with this product? Are you highly dissatisfied, somewhat dissatisfied, neither satisfied or dissatisfied, somewhat satisfied, or highly satisfied?" Or it can ask respondents to rate how much they expected of certain attributes and how much they actually experienced. Finally, the company can ask respondents to list any problems they have had with the offer and to suggest improvements.

   While collecting customer satisfaction data, companies often ask additional useful questions. They often measure the customer's repurchase intention; this will usually be high if customer satisfaction is high. Companies also might ask about the customer's likelihood or willingness to recommend the company and brand to other people. A strongly positive word-of-mouth rating suggests high customer satisfaction.

Award as a milestone in its quality journey, not the finish line. Hampton Inns offers a guarantee, and Southwest Airlines consistently has one of the highest on-time arrival rates in the industry. At the Salish Lodge in Snoqualmie, Washington, if a waiter notices a left-handed guest, they automatically reverse the table setting for that person. Michael McPhie, the Lodge's manager, said, "We've had people from all over the world say that it was the most amazing thing they've ever seen in a restaurant."[10] These companies aim high because they know that customers who are only satisfied will still find it easy to switch suppliers when a better offer comes along.

Although the customer-centered firm seeks to deliver high customer satisfaction relative to competitors, it does not attempt to maximize customer satisfaction. A company can always increase customer satisfaction by lowering profits. In addition to customers, the company has many stakeholders, including employees, dealers, suppliers, and stockholders. Spending more to increase customer satisfaction might divert funds from increasing the satisfaction of these other "partners." Thus, the purpose of marketing is to generate customer value profitably. Ultimately, the company must deliver a high level of customer satisfaction while delivering at least acceptable levels of satisfaction to the firm's other stakeholders. This requires a very delicate balance. The marketer must continue to generate more customer value and satisfaction but not "give away the house."[11]

Today's winning companies track their customers' expectations, perceived company performance, and customer satisfaction. However, customer satisfaction measures are meaningful only in a competitive context. For example, a company might be pleased to find that 80 percent of its customers say they are satisfied with its products. However, if a competitor is attaining 90 percent customer satisfaction and aiming for 100 percent, the company may find that it is losing customers to the competitor. Thus companies must monitor both their own and their competitors' customer satisfaction performance. Marketing Highlight 11-1 describes the ways in which companies can track customer satisfaction.

For example, McDonald's found that customers were more satisfied with Wendy's and Burger King's made-to-order sandwiches. For years McDonald's had made prewrapped sandwiches and stored them in a heated rack. When a customer ordered the sandwich was removed from the rack. McDonald's built an efficient delivery system by building a buffer inventory of sandwiches. The other chains built the sandwiches to order for the customer, which customers seemed to prefer. To compete, McDonald's reengineered its delivery system, producing a system where sandwiches could be built to order in thirty seconds.

This was not an easy task. Bob Marshall, who oversaw the system's development, stated, "We needed to understand the optimum temperature and humidity components of the holding cabinet. This enabled us to keep cooked patties fresh for twenty minutes." Now McDonald's holds the patties in inventory and builds the sandwich to order, creating a better product. A product that resulted in increased customer satisfaction.[12]

For customer-centered companies, customer satisfaction is both a goal and a major factor in company success. These and other companies realize that highly satisfied customers produce several benefits for the company. They are less price sensitive, and they remain customers for a longer period. They buy additional products over time as the company introduces related products or improvements, and they talk favorably to others about the company and its products.

Customer Satisfaction versus Customer Loyalty

Customer satisfaction measures how well a customer's expectations are met. If customers received what they expected, they are satisfied. If their expectations were exceeded, they are extremely satisfied. Customer loyalty, on the other hand, measures how likely customers are to return and their willingness to perform partner shipping activities for the organization.

Customer satisfaction is a requisite for loyalty. The customer's expectations must be met or exceeded in order to build loyalty. However, there are several reasons why satisfied customers may not become loyal customers. First, some travelers do not return to an area on a regular basis. Thus, a customer may think a hotel is great, but they never return to the hotel because they never return to the area. Second, some customers like to experience different hotels and restaurants when they return to an area. These customers may be satisfied with each hotel or restaurant, but they keep changing to gain a new experience. Third, some guests are price sensitive and will shop for the best deal. Even though they were satisfied with the last hotel, they will try out another hotel because of the deal they were offered. Finally, customers expect to be satisfied with their purchase; if not, they would not have made the purchase. Thus, satisfaction ratings tend to be inflated. To develop loyal customers, managers must have extremely satisfied customers.

For example, two researchers found that 90 percent of customers who change suppliers were satisfied with their previous supplier.[13] In addition, Heskett, Sasser, and Schlesinger, developers of the service profit chain model, found that the link between customer satisfaction and customer loyalty was the weakest relationship in their model.[14] Thus, although customer satisfaction is a requisite for customer loyalty customer satisfaction does not mean your customers will return.

The important point to this discussion of satisfaction versus loyalty is that loyal customers are more valuable than satisfied customers. A satisfied customer who does not return and does not spread positive word of mouth has no value to the company. On the other hand, a loyal customer who returns and spreads positive word of mouth has a net present value of more than $100,000 to a luxury hotel. Managers must identify those patrons who are likely to become loyal customers and create more customer-delivered value than the competition for these customers.

Relationship Marketing

Once a manager has identified patrons who are likely to become loyal customers, the manager must identify ways of creating a relationship with these customers—a relationship that leads to customer loyalty. Relationship marketing involves creating, maintaining, and enhancing strong relationships with customers. The concept of relationship has expanded to include developing a relationship with all stakeholders who can help the company serve its customers. For example, employees and marketing intermediaries would fall into this group. Table 11-2 shows the differences between traditional marketing and relationship marketing.

Increasingly, marketing is moving away from a focus on individual transactions and toward a focus on building value-laden relationships and marketing networks. Relationship marketing is oriented more toward the long term. The goal is to deliver long-term value to customers, and the measure of success is long-term customer satisfaction. Relationship marketing requires that all the company's departments work together with marketing as a team to serve the customer. It involves building relationships at many levels: economic, social, technical, and legal, resulting in high customer loyalty.

We can distinguish five different levels of relationships that can be formed with customers who have purchased a company's product, such as a meeting or a banquet:

Table 11-2
Relationship Marketing Compared with Traditional Marketing

RELATIONSHIP MARKETING	TRADITIONAL MARKETING
Orientation to customer retention	Orientation to single sales
Continual customer contact	Episodic customer contact
Focus on customer value	Focus on product features
Long-term horizon	Short-term horizon
High customer-service emphasis	Little emphasis on customer service
High commitment to meeting customer expectations	Limited commitment to meeting customer expectations
Quality concerns all staff members	Quality concerns only production staff

Traditional marketing can also be considered transactional marketing, in which each sale is considered to be a discrete event.
This table is based on ideas from F. Robert Dwyer, Paul Schurr, and Sejo Oh, "Developing Buyer-Seller Relationships," *Journal of Marketing*, 51 (April 1987): 11–27; and Adrian Payne, Martin Christopher, Helen Peck, and Moira Clark, *Relationship Marketing* (Oxford: Butterworth-Heinemann, 1995).

1. **Basic.** The company sells the product but does not follow up in any way.
2. **Reactive.** The company sells the product and encourages the customer to call whenever he or she has any questions or problems.
3. **Accountable.** The company's representative phones the customer a short time after the booking to check with the customer and answer questions. During and after the event, the salesperson solicits from the customer any product improvement suggestions and any specific disappointments. This information helps the company to improve its offering continuously.
4. **Proactive.** The salesperson or others in the company phone the customer from time to time with suggestions about improvements that have been made or creative suggestions for future events.
5. **Partnership.** The company works continuously with the customer and with other customers to discover ways to deliver better value.

What specific marketing tools can a company use to develop stronger customer bonding and satisfaction? It can adopt any of three customer value-binding approaches.[15] The first relies primarily on adding financial benefits to the customer relationship. For example, airlines offer frequent-flyer programs, hotels give room upgrades to their frequent guests, and restaurants have frequent diner programs. Although these reward programs and other financial incentives build customer preference, they can be imitated easily by competition and thus may fail to differentiate the company's offer permanently. Frequency programs often used tiered programs to encourage guests' preference for one hotel brand. For example, Marriott has gold (15 nights), black (50 nights), and platinum (75 nights). Hilton has silver (10 nights), gold (36 nights), and diamond (60 nights). As guests move up in into higher tiers, they gain more benefits.[16]

The second approach is to add social benefits, as well as financial benefits. Here company personnel work to increase their social bonds with customers by learning individual customers' needs and wants and then individualizing and personalizing their products and services. They turn their customers into clients: Customers may be nameless to the institution; clients cannot be nameless. Customers are served as part of the mass or as part of larger segments; clients are served on an individual basis. Customers are served by anyone who happens to be available; clients are served by the professional assigned to them.[17] For example, a server recognizes repeat guests and greets them by name. A salesperson develops a good relationship with his or her clients. Both these people have developed social bonds with their clients. This keeps the client coming back, but also often means clients will follow that person when he or she changes jobs. Managers of hospitality and travel organizations want to make sure that their key clients have social bonds with multiple people in the organization. The general manager, front desk manager, food and beverage manager, convention services manager, banquet manager, and restaurant mangers should all know key clients. In fact, general managers should go on sales calls to key clients. If this is done, when the salesperson leaves the client feels like they still know key people in the hotel and are not dependent on the salesperson.

The third approach to building strong customer relationships is to add structural ties, as well as financial and social benefits. For example, airlines developed reservation systems for travel agents. Frequent guests have special phone lines that they can call. Airlines have developed lounges for their first-class customers, and some will send a limousine to deliver them to the airport. Sheraton developed flexible check-in and checkout time for their best customers. Hilton is using technology to provide a personalized welcome message on the guest's television. Hilton is also experimenting with a personalized tracking system that provides a proximity card to guests expecting a package, visitor, or a fax. This allows staff to track guests no matter where they are on property. Hilton is also developing "Wireless Anticipated Information," which allows messages from the hotel to be forwarded to a wireless personal digital assistant (PDA). Thus, if a guest receives a telephone message at the hotel, the message could be forwarded to their PDA.[18] Structural changes are difficult to implement, but are harder for competitors to match and they create a competitive advantage until they are matched. Here are the main steps in establishing a relationship marketing program in a company:

- *Identify the key customers meriting relationship management.* Choose the largest or best customers and designate them for relationship management. Other customers can be added who show exceptional growth or who pioneer new industry developments.
- *Assign a skilled relationship manager to each key customer.* The salesperson currently servicing the customer should receive train-

ing in relationship management or be replaced by someone more skilled in relationship management. The relationship manager should have characteristics that match those of, or appeal to, the customer.

- *Develop a clear job description for relationship managers.* Describe their reporting relationships, objectives, responsibilities, and evaluation criteria. Make the relationship manager the focal point for all dealings with and about the client. Give each relationship manager only one or a few relationships to manage.
- *Have each relationship manager develop annual and long-range customer relationship plans.* These plans should state objectives, strategies, specific actions, and required resources.
- *Appoint an overall manager to supervise the relationship managers.* This person will develop job descriptions, evaluation criteria, and resource support to increase relationship manager effectiveness.

When it has properly implemented relationship management, the organization begins to focus on managing its customers, as well as its products. At the same time, although many companies are moving strongly toward relationship marketing, it is not effective in all situations:

> When it comes to relationship marketing you don't want a relationship with every customer. In fact, there are some bad customers. A company should develop customer relationships selectively: Figure out which customers are worth cultivating because you can meet their needs more effectively than anyone else.[19]

One of the purposes of customer frequency is to help companies track purchases so they know the characteristics of their customers and can classify them by their purchasing characteristics. Table 11-3 breaks customers into categories based on their frequency of purchase and their profitability. Those customers who are high on profitability and frequency deserve management attention. These are Marriott's Platinum members and Hyatt's Diamond members. The customers high on profitability but low on frequency sometimes can be developed in higher frequency customers. Some of these customers are spreading their business across several different providers of the same service. If we can make our company the preferred provider for this type of customer, then we can turn them to our best customers. For some of the high-frequency, low-profitability customers, there is a chance to motivate them to purchasing by showing the value of additional purchases. For example, hotels can show a business traveler the advantage of staying on the concierge floor where there is a lounge with beverages to work in when they want to take a break from working in their office. The concierge lounge also provides a quick and accessible breakfast, saving the guest time. Those guests who see the value in concierge floors are willing to pay the extra $20 a room. The guests who are in the low-frequency, low-profitability quadrant are often bargain hunters. They come when there is a promotion and avoid paying full price at all costs. It is important to build promotions so this type of

Table 11-3
Types of Customers

	LOW FREQUENCY	HIGH FREQUENCY
HIGH PROFITABILITY	Try to get these customers to come more often.	These are your best customers, reward them.
LOW PROFITABILITY	These customers will follow promotions. Make sure your promotions make money.	Some of these guests have the potential to become more profitable.

customer does not take advantage of the business. For example, if the hotel is full on a holiday, promotions should not be done or not be valid during this period. Knowing customers helps to develop a relationship with them and to strengthen the relationship over time.

Retaining Customers

The benefits of relationship marketing come from continued patronage of loyal customers, reduced marketing costs, decreased price sensitivity of loyal customers, and partnership activities of loyal customers. Reduced marketing costs are the result of requiring fewer marketing dollars to maintain a customer than to create one and the creation of new customers through the positive word of mouth of loyal customers. Loyal customers are less likely to switch because of price, and loyal customers make more purchases than do similar, nonloyal customers.[20] Partnership activities of hotel customers include strong word of mouth, business referrals, providing references, publicity, and serving on advisory boards. The combination of these attributes of loyal customers means that a small increase in loyal customers can result in a major increase in profitability. Riechheld and Sasser found that a 5 percent increase in customer retention resulted in a 25 percent to 125 percent increase in profits in nine service industry groups they studied.[21] As a result, the researchers claim that building a relationship with customers should be a strategic focus of most service firms.

Many products have reached the mature stage of the product life cycle. Competition is strong and often there is little differentiation between products in the same product class. For example, general managers from Sheraton in Asia were shown pictures of hotel rooms from both their own chain and those of three competitors. Most managers could not give the brand identity of one room, even though they were given a list of eight brands from which to choose.[22] This exercise illustrates that it is very difficult to distinguish among competing hotel brands based on the physical attributes of a hotel's core product. Increased competition with little differentiation between core products is one of the factors that led to the development of relationship marketing in the 1990s. Relationship marketing enables companies to build loyalty with their customers.[23] Developing customers as partners is different from traditional marketing, which is more transaction based.

Beyond building a stronger relation with their partners in the supply chain, companies today must work to develop stronger bonds and loyalty with their ultimate customers. In the past, many companies took their customers for granted. Customers often did not have many alternative suppliers, or the other suppliers were just as poor in quality and service, or the market was growing so fast that the company did not worry about fully satisfying its customers. A company could lose 100 customers a week but gain another 100 customers and consider its sales to be satisfactory. Such a company, operating on a "leaky bucket" theory of business, believes that there will always be enough customers to replace the defecting ones. However, this high customer churn involves higher costs than if a company retained all 100 customers and acquired no new ones. Another problem is that the dissatisfied customers are spreading negative word of mouth. This makes it increasingly difficult to gain the 100 new customers per week. In businesses that depend on local customers, such as a neighborhood restaurant, it soon becomes impossible to gain an equal amount of replacement customers.

Cost of Lost Customers

Companies must pay close attention to their customer defection rate and undertake steps to reduce it. First, the company must define and measure its retention rate. Next, the company must identify the causes of customer defection and determine which of these can be reduced or eliminated. Not much can be done about customers who leave the region or about business customers who go out of business. But much can be done about customers who leave because of poor service, poor-quality food, or prices that are too high. The company needs to prepare a frequency distribution showing the percentage of customers who defect for different reasons.

Companies can estimate how much profit they lose when customers defect unnecessarily. For an individual customer, this is the same as the customer's lifetime value. Ritz-Carlton knows that its repeat customers are worth over $100,000 over their lifetime. A restaurant customer can be worth several thousand dollars' worth of business, and a travel agency customer can generate over $50,000 during his or her lifetime by utilizing the agency. The lifetime value is calculated by measuring how much a member of a market segment produces per year, on average, and multiplying this amount by the average life of a member of that segment. The average life is determined through surveys or guest history. People move, get transferred, change companies, and become dissatisfied; thus the average life for an individual business traveler might be four years. The average life of a restaurant customer might be only three years in a transient community. Hotel chains with a guest history system can track the lifetime value of guests to the chain, not just an individual hotel. The lifetime varies by location and market segment; it is unique to an individual business.

The company needs to figure out how much it would cost to reduce the defection rate. If the cost is less than the lost profits, the company should spend that amount to reduce customer defections. Today, outstanding companies go all out to retain their customers. Many markets have settled into maturity, and there are not too many new customers entering most categories. Competition is increasing, and the costs of attracting new customers are rising. In these markets, it might cost five times as much to attract a new customer as to keep a current customer happy. Offensive marketing typically costs more than defensive marketing, because it takes a great deal of effort and spending to coax satisfied customers away from competitors.

Unfortunately, classic marketing theory and practice centers on the art of attracting new customers rather than retaining existing ones. The emphasis has been on creating transactions rather than relationships. Discussion has focused on presale activity and sale activity rather than on postsale activity. Today, however, more companies recognize the importance of retaining current customers. According to one report, by reducing customer defections by only 5 percent, companies can improve profits from 25 percent to 85 percent.[24] Unfortunately, however, most company accounting systems fail to show the value of loyal customers.

Thus, although much current marketing focuses on formulating marketing mixes that will create sales and new customers, the firm's first line of defense lies in customer retention. The best approach to customer retention is to deliver high customer satisfaction, resulting in strong customer loyalty.

Resolving Customer Complaints

11.6 Savoy Hotels

According to Michael Shepard, general manager of the Savoy Hotel, London, "Guests are less forgiving. Competition allows guests to expect seamless delivery with no tolerance of shortfall. If something goes wrong and we fix it they might return, if we do not fix it, they will not return."[25]

Resolving customer complaints is a critical component of customer retention. One study by the Technical Research Programs Institute found that if a customer has a major complaint, 91 percent will not buy from you again, but if it was resolved quickly, 82 percent of those customers will return. The complaint resolution drops the customer defection from 91 out of 100 to 18 out of 100. With resolution of minor complaints, the defection rate can be reduced to less than 5 out of 100.[26] In complaint resolution there are two important factors. First, if you resolve a complaint, do it quickly—the longer it takes to resolve, the higher the defection rate—and second, seek out customer complaints.

For example, a businesswoman had just returned from an overseas trip. After a good night's sleep in a New York hotel, she was ready for an American breakfast. She dialed room service, and her breakfast was delivered promptly. A cheerful waiter wheeled the table into the room and positioned it so that the woman could look out the window. He opened the heating compartment and pulled out the breakfast that the woman had been waiting for: a full, hot American breakfast. The waiter handed the woman the bill, and she promptly signed the bill and added a handsome tip. Now she was ready to start her breakfast.

The waiter said, "I'm sorry, you will have to pay cash." She explained that she did not have any money with her and pulled out her credit cards, getting the American Express gold card she had used to check into the hotel. The waiter called on the phone and after 5 minutes it was resolved that the woman could use her credit card. The woman, now upset, sat down to a cold breakfast.[27]

A meeting planner ordered a bus to take a group of club managers on a tour of a country club. The bus was ordered for a 9:30 A.M. departure on Saturday morning. The bus company usually scheduled the buses to arrive at least fifteen minutes before the departure time. The meeting planner became concerned when the bus had not arrived by 9:20. He called the dispatcher at the bus company. The dispatcher told him in a matter-of-fact way that the bus drivers were still sleeping and that they would not be there until 11 A.M. It seems they were working with a tour that did not get through until 2:30 A.M. the previous night and federal regulations called for at least eight hours off between trips. The dispatcher hung up after explaining the reason for the delay. The meeting planner called a fleet of taxi cabs to transport his group so that they would make the 10 A.M. appointment. He then called back to cancel the bus. On Monday he called the bus company to get his money back. The bus company required payment in full when the bus was reserved. He was told he would not be entitled to a refund, as the bus was canceled with less than twenty-four hours' notice. After several weeks of phone calls and a letter, the bus company agreed to refund the money. Six months later the meeting planner received another check for $125 and an apology from the national sales manager.

The bus company had refunded the cost of the bus rental and an additional $125, but still lost the customer. After six months, the meeting planner had found another bus company and was satisfied with their service. He was not about to change. If the bus company had refunded the money promptly and offered $125 toward the meeting planner's next trip, they might have been able to salvage the customer. The waiter at the New York hotel could have told the businesswoman he was sure her signature would be fine and left, telling her to enjoy her meal. He then could have resolved the problem outside her room. This would have resulted in the woman enjoying the meal she was looking forward to. In both these cases, the customer received a resolution to the problem, but it came too late.

Savvy leaders pounce on complaints because they know that each customer is conveying three things:

- My business and I can still be wooed if you personally show that you care about me and fix the mess. You don't have to lose my repeat business and my word-of-mouth marketing. And even though I'm threatening that you've lost me, if I really didn't care I'd just walk away without a word to you.
- I represent others. You be sure that if I'm unhappy, others are too. You really ought to thank me on this one, for quieter customers who are just as disgruntled have silently moved on or will do so at the first opportunity.
- I am pointing out the adverse results of glitches in your systems and business philosophy. Consider me a fire alarm. I'm warning

> you that something bad is happening which needs immediate attention. So whatever it is you're doing, you had better change—fast.

Don't you pay consultants big bucks to tell you how to grow your customer base and fix certain parts of your business to prevent that base from deteriorating (along with your revenues and margins)? Well, folks, I offer you an alternative: advice that's specific, readily available, generously given if asked for, and emotionally targeted, rather than analytically detached in a mind-numbing report. And best of all: IT'S FREE!

Another critical area in complaint resolution is that most customers do not complain. They do not give managers a chance to resolve their problem. They just leave and never come back. Managers must develop ways to encourage customers to complain. Methods to seek complaints include customer hotlines that encourage customers to call about problems that they are having. Customer comment cards encourage customers to discuss problems that they had with the product. Managers can train employees to look out for guests who look dissatisfied and try to determine their problems. A service guarantee is another way of getting customers to complain; to invoke the guarantee, they have to complain.

When a customer does complain, management should be grateful. Janelle Barlow and Claus Moller write in *Complaint Is a Gift:*

> When customers feel dissatisfied with products and services, they have two options: They can say something or they can walk away. If they walk away, they give organizations virtually no opportunity to fix their dissatisfaction. Complaining customers are still talking with us, giving us the opportunity to return to a state of satisfaction so they will be more likely to buy from us again. So as much as we might not like to receive negative feedback, customers who complain are giving us a gift.
>
> If we shift our perspective in this way to see complaints as gifts, we can more readily use the information the complaints generate to grow our own business. Customer complaints are one of the most available yet underutilized sources of customer and market information.[28]

Complaints that come in by letter should be responded to quickly by a letter or phone call. If you respond by letter, customize part of the letter acknowledging the customer's specific complaint and what will be done to prevent it from happening again. A resolution to the complaint should be offered to the guest. A more effective way of resolving the complaint can be through the use of the telephone. Today it often costs less to make a telephone call than it does to send out a letter. The telephone call allows personal contact with the guest and allows the manager to probe, finding out exactly what happened to the guest. The worst thing a company can do is send out a form letter that shows no empathy to the guest's problem or not respond at all. *Restaurant Business* had an employee contact twenty-five customer service representatives of restaurant chains, stating she had received poor service. Of the twenty-five companies contacted, only fifteen responded to her complaint. One customer-service representative told her, "I'm busy right now, can you call back in a half an hour?" When she called back, the customer service rep said, "Okay, I have a minute now. What's your problem—slow service, is that all? Okay, I can write up a report if you want. On second thought, no one's going to bother to call you." Of those restaurants that did respond, ten did a good or excellent job of resolving the complaint. The customer service representatives at these restaurants did a nice job of showing concern on the initial phone call and followed up with a letter and coupons. In one case, a regional vice president called the customer back to find out what went wrong.[29]

When customers fill out a comment card, managers should respond. There should be a personalized section to the response, to let the customer know you understand their concerns. This is an example of a customized response to a guest, awaiting the general manager's review and signature.

ROYAL CARIBBEAN

March 2, 1995

Mr. & Mrs. C. Wirt
200 Apple Lane
Schaumburg,
Illinois 60193
U.S.A.

Dear Mr. & Mrs. Wirt:

Thank you for taking the time to complete our Guest Questionnaire upon check-out recently. We trust that you had a wonderful time and that we will have the opportunity of welcoming you back to Sandals Royal Caribbean - **the # 1 Fully Ultra All Inclusive in the Caribbean** in the not too distant future.

We have noted the areas with which you expressed concern, i.e. "some food colder than it should, main hot tub should be 104 degrees, include more vegetarian options" and assure you that we are investigating these with a view to taking prompt remedial action. It is through comments like yours that we are able to improve our facilities and keep our "extended family" (you, our guests), happy and satisfied.

We ask that you advise us when you will be returning to Sandals Royal Caribbean to experience firsthand, our improved product.

Yours sincerely,

EARL R. FOSTER
GENERAL MANAGER

P.O. Box 167, Mahoe Bay, Montego Bay, Jamaica, W.I.
Telephone: (809)953-2231, 953-2232 Fax: (809)953-2788

THE CARIBBEAN'S #1 ULTRA ALL-INCLUSIVE℠ LUXURY RESORTS FOR COUPLES ONLY
SANDALS MONTEGO BAY • SANDALS ROYAL CARIBBEAN • SANDALS NEGRIL • SANDALS OCHO RIOS • SANDALS DUNN'S RIVER • SANDALS INN / JAMAICA • SANDALS ANTIGUA • SANDALS ST. LUCIA • SANDALS INN / ST. LUCIA • SANDALS BARBADOS
Unique Vacations is the Worldwide Representative for Sandals Resorts, 1-800-SANDALS

Bob Martin, a former professor at the University of Nevada at Las Vegas, was spending a summer as an administrative assistant at a resort. One day while he was in the general manager's office, the manager began complaining about a stack of customer complaint letters he had to answer. The manager stated further that he hated to answer complaint letters. The manager also indicated that it was a waste of time as he would be lucky if 5 percent returned to the hotel. Bob picked up the stack of letters and said, "I will take care of this." As he left, he said, "I will get all of them back."

Bob Martin developed a letter that acknowledged receipt of a complaint and thanked the guest for taking the time to write. He apologized for the problem and mentioned what the resort was doing to correct the problem. He offered the guest a complimentary room and asked them to call the executive secretary to make their reservation. This made the guest feel important and allowed the resort to track returning guests. He closed by saying that he hoped other guests would not be the only ones to benefit from the corrections made as a result of the complaint letter, but that they would return again as a valued guest. By the end of the summer, 90 percent of the writers had returned or made reservations to return. The lifetime value of these guests was over $100,000 in revenues. The complaint resolution also turned a lot of negative word-of-mouth advertising into positive word-of-mouth advertising. In fact, some of the returning guests had talked another couple into coming with them. Resolving complaints is one of the easiest ways to plug up a hole in a "leaky bucket." It is an effective way of preventing customer defection. Managers should seek complaints and resolve them quickly.

The Link between Marketing and Quality

On June 24, 1980, NBC aired the television program "If Japan Can, Why Can't We?" This program introduced W. Edwards Deming to the American public. Deming is credited as the man responsible for leading the Japanese on their successful quest for quality. Japanese automakers invaded the American markets in the 1970s and gained a significant market share, in part because of the superior quality of Japanese cars. During that time, Sony became known for its superior quality in television sets, and Japanese cameras took over the 35mm market, again based on their quality. This invasion by the Japanese started a quality revolution in the United States and elsewhere.

11.7 Pricewaterhouse Coopers

A study of fifty of America's largest firms by Pricewaterhouse Coopers found that quality and customer service were top priorities for these firms.[30] Quality service has emerged as an important area in hospitality management. The number of articles on quality in the hospitality industry dramatically increased in the late 1980s. In 1992, Ritz-Carlton became the first hospitality company to win the Malcolm Baldrige National Quality Award. This award was established by the U.S. Congress in 1987 and is awarded annually to recognize companies that have achieved excellence through adherence to quality improvement programs.[31] Ritz-Carlton's success in the Baldrige Award competition helped to accelerate the growing interest of hospitality firms in service quality.

Philip Crosby states in *Quality Is Free* that quality is conformance to specifications, an act controlled by the firm.[32] Other researchers claim that customers determine quality. These researchers define quality as meeting or exceeding the guest's expectations. Still others view moving from the standards of a two-star hotel to a four-star hotel as improving quality. But is this really quality improvement? And is quality free as Philip Crosby claims, or does it cost money? Initial discussions of quality often raise more questions than they answer. We will now define quality, look at quality models, provide a link between quality and marketing, explain why quality is important, and discuss how hospitality firms can improve the quality of their products.

The hospitality industry involves a high degree of contact and coordination between employees and guests. Total quality can never be achieved. Employees will make mistakes, and systems will fail. The pursuit of quality is a never-ending journey, but today it is a journey that every hospitality organization must take. Through total quality programs, managers strive to eliminate failures and increase the guests' perception of product quality. Companies that fail to provide quality products can incur significant costs.

After finishing college, a new food and beverage manager arrived at the University Center at Ohio University. Shortly thereafter, the university's food-service workers went on strike. This meant management had to train unskilled students to fill all the positions in the operation. The center had been trying for some time to sell the Rotary Club on using its facilities for their evening dinner meeting, and when they finally decided to try out the center, the event fell in the middle of the strike.

Recognizing the importance of the event, the new food and beverage manager developed a special menu of beef stroganoff made with beef tenderloin. In college the young manager watched a famous chef give a demonstration in the foods class, after which students commented to the professor in charge of the course that the beef stroganoff was wonderful. The instructor, unimpressed with the chef's talents, replied that anyone could make good beef stroganoff if they used tenderloin. The manager, remembering this, decided he could make good beef stroganoff if he used beef tenderloin.

The sauce was excellent. The salads were well presented, and the manager looked forward to converting the Rotary Club to a regular customer. As the event unfolded, the manager observed that most guests were leaving a large portion of the beef stroganoff on their plates. Suddenly the manager realized that in haste a bag of stew meat cubes had been grabbed instead of the beef tenderloin cubes. The university center lost the group due to poor quality and lack of quality control. That group would have been worth $10,000 a year, or $50,000 over a five-year period, an expensive mistake that illustrates the importance of quality.

What Is Quality?

A distinction can be made between two types of quality: **product features,** which enhance customer satisfaction, and **freedom from deficiencies,** which increases customer satisfaction.[33] The first type of quality, product features, adds to the cost of the product. Customers must either be willing to pay for the added costs of additional product features, or these features must make them more loyal. For example, lettuce and tomato are found only on McDonald's more expensive hamburgers. Hotel rooms on concierge floors have more features than standard rooms and command a higher price. La Quinta Inns offers free local telephone calls to encourage loyalty among salespeople.

The expectations of guests are formed by company image, word of mouth, the company's promotional efforts, and price. A guest paying $45 for a room at a Motel 6 will have different expectations than a guest paying $300 for a room at the Four Seasons Hotel in Washington, DC. The person staying at the Motel 6 could be perfectly satisfied. The room features meet their expectations. The first type of quality, product features, relates to guest expectations. People staying in a Motel 6 may perceive it as the best quality motel for under $50. They are not comparing it with a Four Seasons Hotel. Both the guests of a Motel 6 and a Four Seasons Hotel will expect the room to be free from deficiencies. For example, guests at the Four Seasons and those at a Motel 6 are both likely to get upset if they return in the evening to rooms that have not been made up.

11.8 Four Seasons

There is another way to view quality. A distinction can be made between technical and functional quality. **Technical quality** refers to what the customer is left with after the customer–employee interactions have been completed. For example, technical quality relates to the guest room in the hotel, the meal in the restaurant, and the car from the rental agency. **Functional quality** is the process of delivering the service or product. While the service is being delivered, customers go through many interactions with the firm's employees. A guest makes a reservation, is greeted by the door attendant, is escorted to the front desk by a bell person, checks in with the desk clerk, and is escorted to the room. The experience of checking into a hotel is an example of functional quality. Excellent functional quality may make up for a room that is not quite up to expectations. If functional quality is unpleasant, a high-quality room might not overcome the guests' previous dissatisfaction.

Earlier in the chapter we mentioned that it is hard to differentiate among hotel rooms in the same class. The differentiating factor is not technical quality, it is functional quality. How hotels deliver the product (functional quality) or their customer service becomes the point of differentiation. A model of service quality using technical and functional quality as determinants of total quality is shown in Figure 11-2.

In addition to technical quality and functional quality, we feel there is a third element of quality, **societal (ethical) quality.** Societal quality is a credence quality; it cannot be evaluated by the consumer before purchase and is often impossible to evaluate after purchase.

Some products can provide satisfaction in the short term, but may have long-term adverse effects for their users. For example, McDonald's French fries were proclaimed as the best in the world. One reason they were so popular was that they were fried in beef fat, which added flavor. When the public became aware that animal fats were not desirable, McDonald's changed the ingredients of their frying oil. In the 1970s chemical antioxidants were commonly used by restaurants to keep salads crisp and potatoes white. Antioxidants allowed restaurants to produce products that were more acceptable to the consumer, but the product could have long-term adverse health effects. In these examples, the product component that increased satisfaction in the short term could create problems for the customer in the long term.

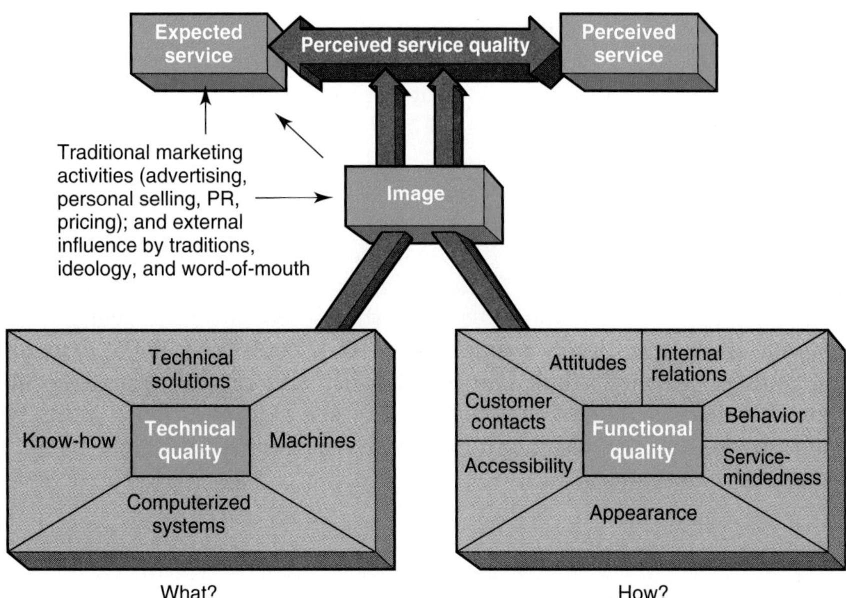

Figure 11-2
Managing the perceived service quality. From Christian Gronroos, *Strategic Management and Marketing in the Service Sector* (Helsingfors, Finland: Swedish School of Economics and Business Administration, 1982), p. 79.

Some hotel managers do not know the location of their fire plans. Other managers know where the plans are but do not train employees to carry out the fire plan. This lack of life safety management will have no impact on the guests unless a fire occurs. The guest can leave the hotel feeling perfectly satisfied, ready to return, and may recommend the hotel to others. An airline may skimp on maintenance to save costs, a fact that will never be noticed by the customer unless there is a crash and the resulting investigation uncovers poor maintenance standards. Airlines and hotels that do a good job in preventive maintenance and safety training usually do not advertise the fact, because it relates to a negative aspect of their products.

Firms must consider ethical responsibilities when developing products and services, avoiding product features that can cause harm and adding those that eliminate potential safety hazards. Often, these features may not affect customer satisfaction immediately, but in the long term they can prevent undesirable situations. Restaurant owners have learned this the hard way, watching negative publicity destroy their businesses after cases of food poisoning or hepatitis were traced to their restaurants.

Third World hospitality enterprises that maintain strict safety and health regulations usually find that the market responds in a very positive manner, particularly if they serve guests from industrialized nations. Surveys among residents of Third World nations often show that safety is a primary reason for selecting an airline. Safety is seldom listed as a primary decision factor by passengers of industrialized nations.

A company's corporate image affects how customers perceive quality. Customers of a firm that has a good image may overlook minor mistakes as being atypical. The perceived quality of the service will be enhanced for firms that have a good corporate image and diminished for firms with a poor one. Societal quality relates design and delivery of safe products for the guest and society. A firm has a responsibility to its publics to provide societal quality. This makes good ethical sense and in the long run is good for the business.

A widely used model of service quality is the five-gap model. This model is explained in Appendix A at the end of this chapter.

Benefits of Service Quality

Earlier in the chapter we discussed some of the benefits of customer loyalty. In this section we expand on these benefits by showing the benefits that come from customer loyalty created by quality. Firms that have a higher market share and better perceived quality than competitors can earn returns dramatically higher than those of firms with smaller market share and inferior quality. In the book *The PIMS Principles,* the authors identify a link between quality and profitability. They illustrate this through Figure 11-3. As we can see from the figure, firms with high market share and high quality have the greatest return on investment.

Customer Retention

High quality builds loyal customers and creates positive word of mouth. It is an important factor in the purchase decision. It determines customer satisfaction, which affects repeat business and word of mouth. Studies have shown that it costs four to six times as much to create a customer as it does to maintain an existing one. Bill Marriott is credited with saying that it costs $10 to get a Marriott hotel a guest the first time, but only $1 in special effort to get this guest to return. If a potential client is happy with an existing hotel, it is difficult to convince him to use another. Often, a substantial reduction in price by a competitor will not be enough to encourage a client to switch. Hotel salespeople may have to wait until a

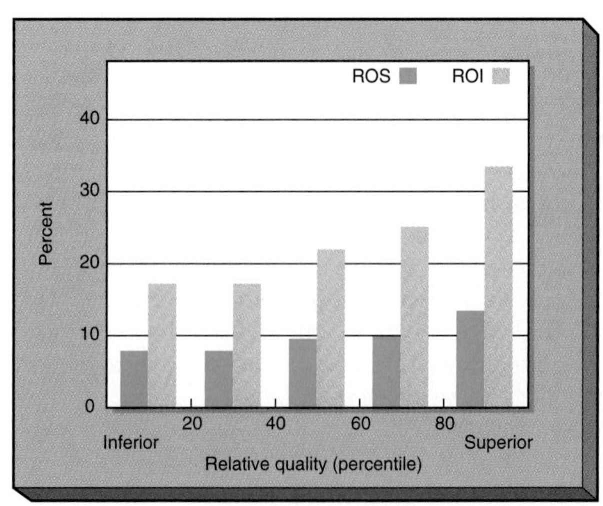

Figure 11-3
Relative quality boosts rates of return. *Source:* Robert D. Buzzell and Bradly T. Gale, *The PIMS Principle,* New York: The Free Press, 1987, p. 107.

competitive hotel makes a mistake before they can convince a client to try their hotel. This may take months or even years. During this time the salesperson is making calls, leaving specialty advertising materials, and inviting the potential client to breakfast or lunch at the hotel. The hotel is spending money on advertising and public relations and sending potential clients direct-mail pieces. The hotel may spend several thousands of dollars trying to obtain a client to use their products. If a major client decides to use the hotel, the money spent on marketing is well invested. However, if a potential client tries the hotel and perceives the quality of service to be inferior, he or she will leave. When this happens, all marketing efforts that went into getting this customer have been wasted.

A satisfied customer will also spread a recommendation by word of mouth. On average, one satisfied guest will tell five others, while a dissatisfied guest will tell ten or more people. Just to balance positive word of mouth with negative word of mouth, two or more customers must leave feeling good about the service for every person who feels the quality of service is poor. The market perceives a hotel or restaurant that receives mixed reviews as mediocre. The hotel striving to build an excellent reputation must do much better.

Hospitality firms that seek excellent quality set a goal of zero errors. A 200-room hotel can have more than 50,000 guests during the year. Most hoteliers feel that 90 percent conformance to standards is satisfactory.[34] If housekeepers clean the rooms according to the hotel's specifications 90 percent of the time in a 200-room hotel, 5,000 guests a year may receive rooms that were not cleaned to specifications. Perhaps half the guests will never notice the nonconformance. If 2,500 noticed the errors and half of those guests do not return, the hotel has lost 1,250 customers. If each of these customers has a potential lifetime revenue stream to the hotel of $1,000, the hotel lost $125,000 in future revenue because of housekeeping errors. Repeating the exercise with food and beverage, front desk, and reservations, it is easy to see that dollars lost from poor quality can be significant.

Avoidance of Price Competition

Frank Perdue, a well-known chicken producer, once said, "Customers go out of their way to buy superior products, and you can charge them a toll for the trip."[35] The PIMS data showed that firms in the top third in quality could charge 5 percent to 6 percent higher than those in the bottom third. High quality can help to avoid price competition and help to maximize potential revenue.

A restaurant with a reputation for good-quality food and service is in a much stronger competitive position than one with a reputation for inconsistent or poor quality. The restaurant with the good image can count on positive word of mouth and repeat customers to bring in new business. The restaurant with a poor reputation will not get its fair share of repeat customers and will receive more negative word of mouth than positive. Restaurants in this situation often revert to price discounting through two-for-one coupons and other means.

Hospitality companies sometimes fail to concentrate on what the customer really wants. Having newspapers delivered to one's hotel door appeals to more guests than a health club costing thousands of dollars to build and maintain. Differentiating products in the hospitality industry is sometimes as easy as simply asking guests what they really want.

Retention of Good Employees

Employees appreciate working in operations that are well run and produce high-quality products. Front-desk clerks do not enjoy receiving guest complaints. Absenteeism, turnover, and loss of employee morale are listed as costs of poor quality.[36] Two researchers developed a list of reasons that recent graduates of hotel and restaurant management schools gave for quitting their jobs. One reason cited by the graduates was the lack of quality in the organization.[37] When an operation has good quality, it can retain good employees. Recruiting is easier, and training costs are reduced.

Reduction of Costs

Costs associated with quality include internal and external costs and quality system costs. *Internal costs* are those associated with correcting problems discovered by the firm before the product reaches the customer. The following are examples of internal costs: An air conditioner breaks down because of improper maintenance, and the guest room is placed out of order until it is repaired. A cook prepares fried grouper instead of the grilled grouper ordered by the guest. The server discovers the mistake when he picks up the food in the kitchen and has the cook grill a new piece of fish.

External costs are associated with errors that the customer experiences. They can be very expensive when the customer decides not to return because of a service problem. Here are some examples of external costs: A restaurant manager gives guests a free bottle of wine because they complained about slow service. A guest receives a complimentary breakfast because it took room service an hour to deliver the meal. A guest receives a complimentary fruit basket because the front-desk clerk assigned a dirty room. A group has problems with the hotel's audiovisual service and cancels future bookings. Unfortunately, it is more difficult to detect errors before they reach the customer because of simultaneous production and consumption in the hospitality industry.

A high-quality service system does not come without costs. However, these are usually less than those associated with the internal and external costs resulting from poor-quality service. Some examples of the costs of a quality system are customer service audits, training, management meetings with employees and customers, and the introduction of new technology. These costs can be viewed as investments in the future of the company. They help to ensure that customers return. Internal costs, on the other hand, neither add to nor detract from customer satisfaction. They are simply money down the drain. External costs associated with errors are often high. A firm may go to great expense to maintain the goodwill of a customer who has received a poor-quality product. Sometimes these efforts are not successful, and the firm loses the customer's business forever.

Developing a Service Quality Program

A service quality program involves a cooperative effort between marketing and operations. To develop high-quality service, a firm must follow certain principles. It is not in the scope of this book to provide a detailed procedure for developing total quality management. However, these ten principles of quality service offer a framework for a quality service program.[38]

1. Supply Strong Leadership

The CEO of the organization must have a clear vision for the company, but it is not enough to have a vision. The CEO must also communicate that vision and convince employees to believe in and follow it. Domino's Pizza was almost destroyed because Monaghan and his partner had disparate visions for the company. Monaghan envisioned a company based on the delivery concept, whereas his partner insisted on a sit-down service concept. Finally, Monaghan took over the company and united it under his vision.[39] Good leaders communicate their dedication to service quality through actions visible to both employees and customers. When one thinks of good quality, several names come to mind: Bill Marriott, Isadore Sharp of Four Seasons, Horst Schulze of Ritz-Carlton, Doug Roth of Bistro 110 in Chicago, Robert Del Grande of Cafe Annie in Houston, Joseph Baum of the Rainbow Room in New York, and Norm Brinker of Brinker International. These leaders pay attention to detail, spend time in their hotels and restaurants, talk to employees and customers, and do not accept compromises on service quality. They are committed to service quality, and they show it through their actions.

2. Integrate Marketing throughout the Organization

The marketing concept states that marketing should be integrated throughout the organization. Tom Fitzgerald, vice president of corporate marketing for ARAMARK Services, believes that marketing functions in a hospitality organization are the responsibility of people outside the marketing department. He challenges marketing executives to recognize this and avoid creating a large, separate marketing department. Marketing must be integrated into operations.[40]

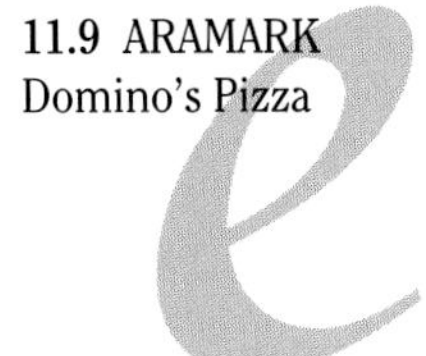
11.9 ARAMARK
Domino's Pizza

3. Understand the Customer

Customers perceive quality. Companies with quality products know what the market wants. The product must be designed for and aimed at a target market. Firms must understand the needs of target markets.

Mr. Steak restaurants conducted marketing research to determine the needs of their "empty nester" customer segment. The results showed that this important customer group resented standing in line to pay. For years, the standard operating procedure at Mr. Steak had been to present guests with the check and expect them to take it to the cash register. In response to the research information, Mr. Steak changed its procedures by giving guests their choice of taking the check to the register or having the server take it for them.[41]

The worldwide hospitality industry has much to gain by expanding its breadth of customer understanding of international visitors. Although it is impossible to understand the customs and language of all international visitors, visitor destinations commonly attract the majority of these guests from relatively few nations.

A survey of the top thirty-eight lodging chains showed that nearly two-thirds of the respondents indicated that management personnel were expected to communicate in a language other than English.[42] The top three languages were Spanish, French, and Japanese. However, only eight of the chains required competency in a foreign language for front-of-the-house personnel, and only six offered in-house foreign language programs. The authors concluded that a gap exists in the ability of the U.S. hotel industry to serve international guests effectively and proposed a program of multicultural training in hotels committed to serving the guest.

4. Understand the Business

Delivering good quality service takes teamwork. Employees must realize how their job affects the rest of the team. Many firms that deliver quality service use cross-training. Cross-training exposes employees to different perspectives and encourages them to view the operation from other perspectives. They see how their jobs affect those of other employees and how they affect the customer. They begin to understand the business.

5. Apply Operational Fundamentals

The organization has to be well planned and managed. This starts with the design of the concept. Earlier in the book we discussed Marriott's planning process for Courtyard Inns. Courtyard Inns were designed so that their features provided benefits for a selected market segment. Systems are required to provide management information and to enable the hotel to operate. Examples of these systems include hiring and training procedures, purchasing procedures, management information systems, property information systems, reservation and front-office systems, equipment maintenance systems, quality control systems, and production procedures for the kitchen. Companies that deliver high-quality service have good operational procedures.

11.10 Courtyard Inns

6. Leverage the Freedom Factor

In first-class restaurants and four- and five-star hotels, guests expect more customized service. The service delivery system has to be flexible. Employees must have the freedom to shape the delivery of the service to fit the needs of their guests. They should not be bound to strict procedures and inflexible rules. Managers should support and guide the staff rather than provide barriers with rules and regulations that prevent the employees from serving the customer.

7. Use Appropriate Technology

Technology should be used to monitor the environment, help operational systems, develop customer databases, and provide methods for communi-

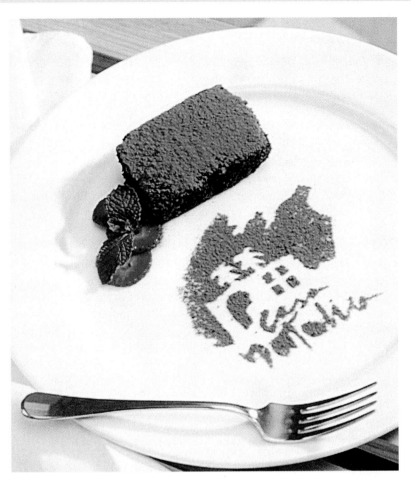

Mi Cocina Restaurant at Casa Natalia in San Jose del Cabo, Mexico, provides tangible evidence of its service quality program through its attention to detail. The restaurant is known for its Nouvelle Mexican-Euro cuisine and the creation of memorable meals. Courtesy of Casa Natalia and ProHotel International.

cation with customers. The Ritz-Carlton Hotel Company, winner of the Malcom Baldrige award for service excellence, has developed a computerized guest history profile that provides information on 240,000 repeat guests. The Ritz-Carlton collects daily production reports from 720 work areas in the hotel. These reports serve as an early warning system to identify problems that might impede customer service. Other information used by Ritz-Carlton includes annual guest room preventive maintenance cycles and percentage of check-ins with no queuing. This hotel company effectively utilizes advanced technology, including an automated building and safety system and a computerized reservation system, for the purpose of ensuring a continuously high level of guest satisfaction.[43]

Dave Johnson, executive vice president of Wyndham hotels, said, "We collect data on all customers through a central database and single of out members of our frequency program to understand them more fully. At Wyndham it is not about earning free stuff. We want to know more about our guests so we can treat them better and offer them better choices."[44] Ritz-Carlton and Wydham use technology to provide better service quality.

8. Practice Good Human Resources Management

In the section on internal marketing, we discussed the need to hire the right people. Employees must be capable of delivering the services promised to the customer.

9. Set Standards, Measure Performance, and Establish Incentives

The most important way to improve service quality is to set service standards and goals and then teach them to employees and management. These standards must be improved continuously. Employees who deliver good service should be rewarded.

10. Feed Back the Results to the Employees

The results of your measurements should be communicated to all employees. This should be done through communications from top management and as a part of departmental meetings. Employees should know what guests like and what they do not like. They should also know the areas that are and are not improving. A study of quality assurance programs in hotels showed that "the rewards of quality assurance were worth the initial investment." Nevertheless, some hotels reported that such programs did not work. Three basic reasons existed for these failures: (1) a lack of top-middle management commitment, (2) departure of the person responsible for quality assurance, and (3) a change in the hotel's ownership.[45]

Capacity and Demand Management

Quality in the hospitality industry requires a different focus from quality in manufacturing firms. Hospitality products are produced and consumed simultaneously, whereas production and consumption in manufacturing firms are separated by time and distance. This gives manufacturing firms time to inspect and discard defective products before customers receive them. Defective products cost a firm money, but not as much as the customer who defects. In the hospitality industry during periods of peak demand, quality controls become difficult to carry out. We feel managing demand to a level that can be properly serviced by a hospitality or travel organization is part of quality management.

The following example illustrates how mistakes can occur during busy periods. A guest made a reservation for a room at the Marriott Hotel in Surfers Paradise, Australia. The new hotel offered a special promotional rate to people who lived in the area to familiarize them with its services, creating positive word of mouth. The guest was informed by the hotel that check-in could occur after 2:00 P.M. When the guest arrived at 2:30, the front-desk clerk stated that there were no rooms available and asked the guest to check back in a little while. After waiting an hour, the desk clerk said that the room was ready. The guest proceeded to the room, opened the door, saw a group of people in the room, and returned to the front desk, where the clerk was informed of the situation. Puzzled, the clerk checked the computer again, and then made a few phone calls.

The clerk found that a salesperson had been showing the room to potential guests and had not bothered taking it out of order. Normally, this would not have created a problem, but on the day of the incident, there was a backlog of guests waiting for rooms. As the rooms were released by the housekeeping department, they were assigned to guests. The front-desk clerk explained what had happened and asked the guest to return to the room. Later, champagne and strawberries arrived with an apologetic note from the manager.

The guest ended up leaving satisfied—the Marriott had recovered successfully from their mistake. When demand exceeds capacity and customers receive a poor quality product, some will go away unhappy. They will not become loyal customers. For example, a 100-seat restaurant may normally serve 30 customers on a Monday night. One cook and two service persons should be able to handle this demand. If 65 customers show up on Monday, the restaurant will not be able to service them well when it is staffed for 30. The dinning room manager can turn some customers away. These customers will go away unhappy and not understand why they were turned away if there are empty seats in the restaurant. The manager can sit people as they come, providing them with poor service. The manager can tell the customer there will be a wait and space the flow of customers into the restaurants. Many customers may not understand the reason for the wait when many tables are empty. Finally, the manager can call in extra help or shift cross-trained employees from other areas of the hotel to the dining room and kitchen to help meet demand. The last solution is obviously the best solution. This manager had made contingency plans for increasing capacity during periods of unusually heavy demand. It is important for managers to understand the importance of managing demand and capacity if they want to have a consistently high level of quality and customer satisfaction.

We close the chapter on customer loyalty and quality with a discussion of capacity and demand management. A key element of managing capacity and demand is forecasting. We have included a section on forecasting in Appendix B at the end of this chapter. Students interested in forecasting are encouraged to read Appendix B before starting this section.

Managing Capacity

Managers have two major options for matching capacity with demand: change capacity or change demand. For example, an airline can change capacity on a heavily traveled route by assigning a larger plane to the route. If a larger plane is not available, they can reduce demand by eliminating discounted fares. In this section we discuss capacity management, and in the next section we focus on demand management.

Corporate management is responsible for matching capacity with demand on a long-term basis; unit managers are responsible for matching capacity with fluctuations in short-term demand. The techniques presented in this section assist in managing short-term demand. The actions managers can take to adjust to short-term capacity include the following:

1. Involve the customer in the service delivery system.
2. Cross-train employees.
3. Use part-time employees.
4. Rent or share extra facilities and equipment.
5. Schedule downtime during periods of low capacity.
6. Extend service hours.
7. Use technology.[46]

Involve the Customer in the Service Delivery System

Getting the customer involved in service operations expands the number of people that one employee can serve, thus increasing the capacity of the operation. The concept has wide acceptance in food and beverage operations, but modern technology is responsible for its increasing use in the accommodation sector.

Food and beverage operations can develop systems that permanently involve customers in service delivery or use customer involvement as a way to increase capacity during extremely busy periods. Many convention hotels have self-service food and beverage operations. Examples of kiosks or self-service coffee shops can be found in the Lowe's Anatole in Dallas, the Wyndham Greenspoint in Dallas, and Stouffer's Hotel in Orlando. These operations can serve many people in a short time. They feature premade sandwiches and salads, enabling the operator to build a buffer inventory. When a meeting breaks and a number of the participants want a meal or snack, these operations have the capacity to serve many people quickly.

On the rooms side, hotels have taken advantage of technology that enables the customer to check in through a computer. Guests who choose to use the computer avoid standing in line at the front desk, which takes pressure off the lines. These examples illustrate how managers can use customers to increase the capacity of service delivery systems.

Some fast-food operations have customers get their own drinks, making it possible for employees to handle more customers. It is particularly effective for a restaurant when the food is customized for the guest and the guest has to wait for the food. Examples of this type of restaurant are Burger King, Subway, and Taco Bell. The task occupies customers during their wait, reducing the perceived wait.

Besides permanent service delivery systems, hotels and restaurants can develop temporary systems for periods of unusually high demand. Some hotels also serve breakfast buffets when they know that the house will be full and that there are large meetings booked without a breakfast function. The breakfast buffet allows them to move people in and out of the restaurant. Using customers as self-servers is one way that hospitality firms can increase their capacity.

11.11 Burger King
Subway
Taco Bell

Cross-Train Employees

In a hotel, the demand for all services does not rise and fall in unison. One outlet may experience sudden strong demand while other areas enjoy normal levels. When managers cross-train their employees, they can shift employees to increase the capacity. A hotel restaurant that does only 30 to 40 covers a night cannot justify more than two service people, even though it may have 80 seats. However, such low staffing levels mean that the restaurant may have a difficult time serving more than 60 guests, especially if they arrive at about the same time. Having front-desk staff and banquet staff that are trained in à la carte service means that the restaurant manager has a group of employees that can be called on if demand for the restaurant on any particular night exceeds the capacity of two service people. It also provides the manager with a group of substitute service people who can fill in should a regularly scheduled employee call in sick. Cross-training employees gives the operation flexibility by allowing the business to increase capacity by shifting employees and can help to prevent the organization from reducing capacity when an employee calls in sick.

Use Part-time Employees

Managers can use part-time employees to expand capacity during an unusually busy day or meal period or during the busy months of the year for seasonal businesses. Summer resorts hire part-time staff to work during the summer period. They reduce their staff during the slower seasons and either reduce staff further or close during the low season. Part-time employees allow a hotel or restaurant to increase or decrease its capacity efficiently. Part-time employees can also be used on an on-call basis. Hotels usually have a list of banquet waiters to call for large events. Part-time employees give an organization the flexibility to adjust the number of employees to the level required to meet demand.

Rent or Share Extra Facilities and Equipment

Businesses do not have to be constrained by space limitations or equipment limitations. A hotel with an opportunity to book a three-day meeting from Tuesday to Thursday may have to turn down the business because all the function space is booked Wednesday evening, and there is no space for the group's Wednesday evening dinner. Rather than lose the group, a creative solution would be to suggest that the group go outside the hotel for a unique dinner experience. In Paris, the alternative might be a dinner cruise on the Seine. In Arizona it might be an outdoor steak fry, and in Hong Kong it could be a dinner at Jumbo, the famous floating restaurant.

Hotels and restaurants can also work with sister properties. In Fiji, the Regent and Sheraton are within walking distance of each other on Denru Island, and EIE owns both hotels. Although different companies manage the hotels, they work together if it means getting a piece of business for the island. Omni has three hotels on Canton Road in Hong Kong. These hotels refer business to each other. When a property is capacity constrained, alliances with other businesses can be beneficial to both.

Catering firms often purchase only the amount of equipment that they will regularly use. When they have a busy period, they rent equipment. Renting, sharing, or moving groups to outside facilities can increase capacity to accommodate short-term demand.

The Clock Tower in Bermuda doubles as a meeting room. Hotels can expand their meeting space by use of off-premise locations for functions. Courtesy of the Bermuda Department of Tourism.

Schedule Downtime during Periods of Low Capacity

Businesses in seasonal resorts have periods of high and low demand. The actions we have discussed so far enable a business to increase capacity to meet peak demand. There are also cases when a business needs to handle low demand periods as efficiently as possible by decreasing capacity. One way to decrease capacity is to schedule repairs and maintenance during the low season. Employees can take vacations during periods of low demand or be utilized for other activities. Wet-n-Wild, a water park in Las Vegas, uses employees to print and collate its marketing material during the off season. As a result, several key employees can be kept on the payroll year round. The employees develop and build marketing kits to be used in the coming season. Shifting activities is one way of reducing the negative effects of slow periods and ensuring maximum capacity during busy periods. Training can also be scheduled for slow periods.

Extend Service Hours

Restaurants and entertainment facilities can increase capacity by extending their hours. A hotel coffee shop that is full by 7:30 A.M. may find it useful to open at 6:30 A.M. instead of 7:00 A.M. If five tables arrive in the first half-hour, these should be free in about a half-hour, allowing the restaurant to have more tables available during the peak period. Leaps and Bounds, a children's entertainment center that is normally closed at night, offers all-night parties for groups of twenty or more. When the demand exists, they supply the capacity by opening at night. Fast-food operations have expanded their capacity by opening for breakfast. Many businesses can increase their capacity by expanding their hours of operation.

Use Technology

Phone systems with automatic wake-up capability allow many guests to receive wake-up calls simultaneously. Although a wake-up call from a computer is impersonal, it ensures that guests in large hotels receive their wake-up calls in a timely and accurate manner. Technology will become increasingly important as advances are made in robotics. Technology also makes it easier to involve the customer in the service delivery system.

Use Price

As discussed previously, there is a relationship between pricing strategy and capacity management. Car rental firms attempt to manage capacity through the use of one-way drop fees. A spokesperson for Avis said, "You lose too much business if your cars are in another part of the country and everyone wants to rent from you."

Alamo Rent-A-Car offered daily rates in Houston as low as $18, but if the car was driven into Louisiana and dropped at New Orleans, the cost would be an additional $600.[47] Conversely, rent-a-car companies may offer low or no drop-off rates to areas where they need cars.

Managing Demand

In an ideal situation, managers simply expand capacity to meet demand. However, during a citywide convention, a hotel may receive requests for rooms that exceed its capacity. The Saturday before Christmas, a restaurant could book more banquets if it had space, and during a summer holiday a resort could sell more rooms, if it had them. All successful hospitality businesses become capacity constrained. Capacity management allows a business to increase its capacity, but it will not prevent situations where demand exceeds capacity. Besides managing capacity, managers must manage demand. The following strategies for managing demand are discussed:

11.12 Alamo Rent-A-Car

1. Use price to create or reduce demand.
2. Use reservations.
3. Overbook.
4. Use queuing.
5. Shift demand.
6. Change the salesperson's assignment.
7. Create promotional events.

Use Price to Create or Reduce Demand

Pricing is one method used to manage demand. Price is inversely related to demand for most products. Managers can create more demand for a product by lowering its price. To create demand, restaurants offer specials on slow days. For example, some Subway restaurants, a submarine sandwich shop, offer two-for-one specials on Tuesdays. Port of Subs (a competitor) offers special discounts after 5:00 P.M., because most people do not eat sandwiches for the evening meal. Resorts lower prices during the off-season, and city hotels offer weekend specials. Managers must make sure that the market segments attracted by the lower price are their desired targets.

When demand exceeds capacity, managers raise prices to lower demand. On New Year's Eve, many restaurants and nightclubs offer set menus and packages that exceed the normal average check. They realize that even with higher prices, demand remains sufficient to fill to capacity.

Club Med uses e-mail to pitch unsold, discounted packages to the 34,000 people in its database. These people are notified early to midweek

Airlines have many different fare classes. Lower fare classes are closed when demand is high and opened when demand is low. Courtesy of Southwest Airlines.

THE LOW

Unrestricted Fare, One-Way
$69
Sacramento to LAX

LOWER

14-Day Advance Purchase Fare, One-Way
$59
Sacramento to LAX

LOWEST

Friends Fly Free
FREE
Sacramento to LAX

FARES IN THE AIR.

As the airline that invented low fares, it's only natural that we offer you a choice of low fares. So here goes: First, there's our low everyday, unrestricted fare—good on every seat, every flight, every day. Next, our lower 14-day advance purchase, no stayover fare—the fare that doesn't penalize you if your plans change because it's fully refundable. And finally, our Friends Fly Free fare. The only fare that lets you bring along a friend, absolutely free, with the purchase of a roundtrip unrestricted-fare ticket. (Tickets are fully refundable and reservations are required.) So fly Southwest Airlines. And pick your favorite low.

Call your travel agent or 1-800-I-FLY-SWA.

Seats are limited and some restrictions apply on 14-day fare and Friends Fly Free. Does not include Passenger Facility Charge of $6 roundtrip. ©1994 Southwest Airlines

on rooms and air seats available for travel that weekend. Discounts are typically 30 percent to 40 percent off the standard package. An average of 1.2 percent respond to the offers, and Club Med takes in anywhere from $25,000 to $40,000 every month from e-mail sales of distressed inventory. Before the program, Club Med's only alternative was to rely on travel agents to sell last-minute packages. Club Med's database includes such information as vacation preferences, preferred sports and activities, preferred time of year for travel and marital status, as well as geographic data. Although current e-mail offers aren't targeted, the company plans to create one-to-one marketing messages in the future.[48]

Use Reservations

Hotels and restaurants often use reservations to monitor demand. When it appears that they will have more demand than capacity, managers can save capacity for the more profitable segments. Reservations can also limit demand by allowing managers to refuse any further reservations when capacity meets demand.

Although reservations in restaurants can help manage demand, they can also decrease capacity. This is the reason that high-volume midpriced restaurants do not usually take reservations. A group may arrive ten minutes late, or one couple of a two-couple party may arrive on time and wait twenty minutes at the table until the other shows up. The estimated times of customer arrival and departure may not fit precisely, resulting in tables remaining empty for twenty minutes or more. In high-priced restaurants, guests expect to reserve a table and have it ready when they arrive. Customers of midpriced restaurants have different expectations, allowing popular restaurants to increase their capacity by having customers queue and wait for the next available table. Queues allow managers to inventory demand for short periods of time and fill every table immediately when it becomes available, eliminating dead time.

A few restaurants serve patrons on long picnic-style tables similar to those in German beer halls. Customers are mixed together even though they may not know one another. This system helps with the issue of capacity but has definite restrictions for use in the marketplace.

To maximize capacity, some restaurants accept reservations for seating at designated times. For example, they may have six o'clock, eight o'clock, and ten o'clock seatings. When customers call to make a reservation, the receptionist makes them aware of the seating times and lets them know that the table is theirs for up to two hours. After two hours, another party will be waiting to use the table. The use of seatings increases capacity by ensuring that the restaurant will have three turns and by shifting demand. As the eight o'clock seating fills, managers can shift demand to either six or ten o'clock, depending on the customer's preference.

In cases where demand is greater than capacity, guests can be asked to prepay or make a deposit. For example, some New Year's Eve parties at hotels and restaurants require that guests purchase their tickets in advance. Resorts often require a nonrefundable deposit with a reservation. By requiring an advance payment, managers help to ensure that revenue matches capacity. If a customer fails to arrive, the resort does not lose revenue.

Disney Land has come up with its own form of reservations, Fastpass. Guests may go up to one of the rides offering the Fastpass service and obtain a reservation to come at a certain time. When the guests come back, they bypass the waiting line and move to the Fastpass line, often saving an hour or more in waiting. Guests are limited to one Fastpass every four hours to ensure that the rides are able to accommodate both Fastpass and regular guests. The beauty of Fastpass is that rather than waiting in line guests can now spend money in the restaurants and shops. By handling demand with Fastpass, Disney has created a more satisfying customer experience and also created the opportunity for more sales.

Reservation systems can be very complex. It is not within the scope of this book to explore the variations of reservations for hotels, restaurants, and other hospitality organizations.

Overbook

Not everyone who reserves a table or books a room shows up. Plans change and people with reservations become no shows. Overbooking is another method that hotels, restaurants, trains, and airlines use to match demand with capacity. Hotel managers who limit reservations to the number of available rooms frequently find themselves with empty rooms. For example, at one hotel 20 percent of guests holding nonguaranteed reservations and 5 percent of those holding guaranteed reservations typically do not honor those reservations. If this hotel has 80 guaranteed reservations and 40 nonguaranteed reservations, it will, on average, be left with 12 empty rooms. For a hotel with an average room rate of $75, this can mean a potential annual loss of more than $500,000 in room, food, and beverage revenue.

Overbooking must be managed carefully. When a hotel fails to honor its reservations, it risks losing the future business of guests whose reservations are not honored and possibly the business of their companies and travel agents. Usually, it is better to leave a room unoccupied than to fail to honor a reservation.

Developing a good overbooking policy minimizes the chance of walking a guest. This requires knowing the no-show rate of different types of reservations. Groups who reserve rooms should be investigated to see what percent of their room block they have filled in the past. One study found that reservations made one day before arrival and on the day of arrival had a higher no-show rate than reservations made much earlier.[49] Through an analysis of the types of reservations, the time when the reservation is made, and the segment making the reservation, a model can be built to develop an overbooking policy.

Some hotels do nothing for the traveler whose reservation is not honored. However, many hotels find alternative accommodations, pay for one night's stay at the new hotel, and provide transportation to the hotel. They may also give the guest a free phone to inform those back home of the new arrangements and keep the guest's name on their information rack so that they can refer any phone calls the guest may receive to the hotel where the guest is staying. Smart managers try to get turned-away guests back by offering a free night's stay at their hotel the next day. Hotels that are careless in handling their reservations can be held liable. In one case a travel agent, Rainbow Travel Service, reserved forty-five rooms with the Fontainebleau Hilton for clients going to a Miami-Oklahoma football game. The Fontainebleau walked a number of Rainbow's clients and Rainbow sued for damage to its reputation. A jury awarded the travel agency $250,000. The jury believed that the Fontainebleau should have altered their policy of overbooking by 15 percent because of the demand created by the football weekend.[50]

Overbooking is one method of managing demand. It can increase demand by compensating for no shows, but managers should use it judiciously. Turning away guests who have reservations destroys long-term relationships with customers, their companies, and their travel agents.

11.13 Fontainebleau Hilton

Amtrak faces a particularly difficult management problem regarding no shows. Amtrak overbooks only 5 percent to 10 percent of seats because its trains leave once a day, and too much overbooking would strand passengers. Airlines can place an overbooked passenger on the next flight, so the reservations systems of airlines don't declare a flight oversold until it has been overbooked by 20 percent.[51]

Booking Curve Analysis. Yield management professionals include booking curve analysis in the decision-making process. An awareness of booking curves is important to sales and marketing managers throughout the hospitality industry. Convention and conference planners witness a pattern in which reservations occur. Assume that a conference is announced and promoted ninety days prior to the conference date. A certain percentage of reservations will occur in stages during the ninety days. In recent years, planners complain that the booking curve has shortened, with most reservations occurring near the conference date. Organizers of a conference on yield management noticed that 80 percent of the reservations were made ten days or less prior to the conference. This is a nightmare situation for a conference organizer and the hotel, because attendance predictions must be delayed.

Information regarding when reservations or orders occur should be documented and stored routinely by hospitality marketers. An analysis of booking curves provides valuable information for use in forecasting and better managing capacity. Figure 11-4 shows how booking curve analysis is used in the hotel industry.

Use Queuing

Earlier in this chapter, the taking of reservations was mentioned as a method of inventorying demand. When capacity exceeds demand and guests are willing to wait, queues will form. Sometimes guests make the decision to wait; in other cases they have no choice. For example, when the host tells a restaurant guest that there will be a forty-minute wait, the guest can either go somewhere else or accept the wait. At check-in, hotel guests may not have a choice. A taxi has dropped them at the hotel where they have made a reservation. They have told their business associates where they will be staying. As a result, they will endure the twenty-minute wait at check-in.

Voluntary queues, such as waits at restaurants, are a common and effective way of managing demand. Good management of the queue can

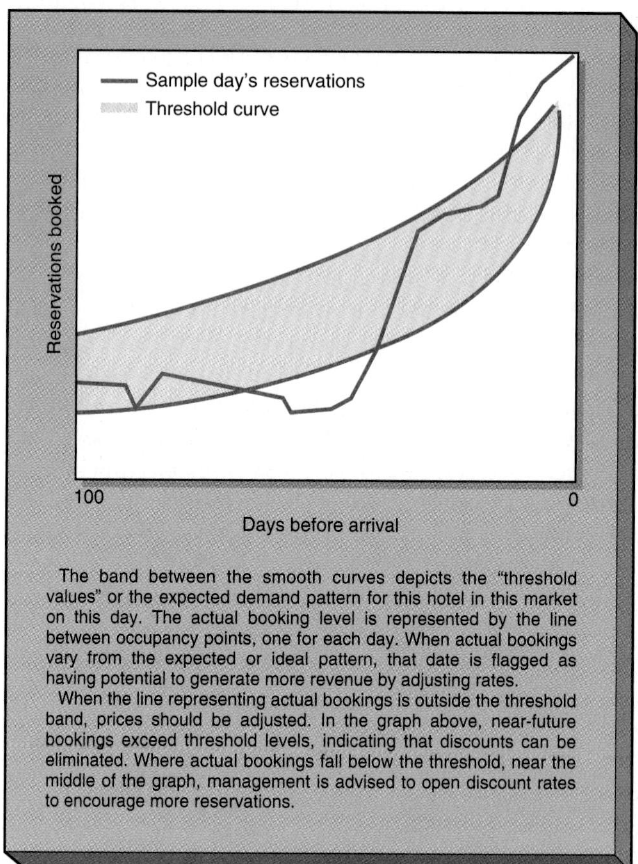

Sample day's reservations
Threshold curve
Reservations booked
100
0
Days before arrival
The band between the smooth curves depicts the "threshold values" or the expected demand pattern for this hotel in this market on this day. The actual booking level is represented by the line between occupancy points, one for each day. When actual bookings vary from the expected or ideal pattern, that date is flagged as having potential to generate more revenue by adjusting rates.
When the line representing actual bookings is outside the threshold band, prices should be adjusted. In the graph above, near-future bookings exceed threshold levels, indicating that discounts can be eliminated. Where actual bookings fall below the threshold, near the middle of the graph, management is advised to open discount rates to encourage more reservations.

Figure 11-4
Booking curve analysis. Reprinted by permission of Elsevier Science, Inc., from "The Yield Management Approach to Hotel Room Pricing," by Walter J. Relihan III, *Cornell Hotel and Restaurant Administration Quarterly,* 30, no. 1, p. 43, copyright 1989 by Cornell University.

make the wait more tolerable for the guest. Always overestimate the wait. When the estimated wait is thirty minutes, it is better to tell guests that it will be a thirty-five-minute wait than to tell them they will have a twenty-minute wait. Some managers fear that if the wait is too long they will lose guests, so they "shorten" the wait time. Once customers have accepted the wait time, they may sit down and have a drink, but they tend to keep their eyes on their watches. When their names have not been called after the allotted time, they run up to the host and ask where they are on the list. When guests wait longer than they were told they would, they go to their dining table upset and in a mood that makes them tend to look for other service failures. It can be difficult for the restaurant to recover from this initial failure, and many guests leave with memories of an unsatisfactory experience.

If the host tells guests it will be a thirty-five-minute wait and then seats them in thirty minutes, the guests will be delighted. If a guest decides not to accept the wait, the host can suggest a time when the wait will be shorter.

In general, the higher the level of service, the longer the guest is willing to wait. Twenty minutes for sit-down service might be acceptable, whereas a five-minute wait at a fast-food restaurant will be unacceptable. Fast-food restaurants must raise their capacity to meet demand or lose customers.[52]

David Maister, a service expert, provides the following tips for the management of a waiting line:[53]

1. *Unoccupied time feels longer than occupied time.* The Showboat Hotel has a magician who entertains guests waiting to check in at the front desk. The entertainment makes a ten-minute wait pass very quickly. Entertainment parks have characters who talk to kids in waiting lines, occupying time and making the wait pass faster. Restaurants send customers waiting for a dinner table into their cocktail lounge, where a cocktail and conversation make the time pass more quickly. The Rio Hotel places television monitors over the line for their buffet. The monitors promote different products that the resort has to offer, such as their entertainment and other food and beverage outlets. These are a few examples of how managers can occupy guests' time and make their wait more enjoyable.
2. *Unfair waits are longer than equitable waits.* Guests can become upset and preoccupied with a wait if they feel that they are being treated unfairly. Restaurants with a limited number of large tables try to maximize the capacity of these tables. For example, rather than put a party of four at a table for six, the restaurant will seat a party of six at the table, even if there are several parties of four in front of them. This sometimes leads to anger on the part of the guests in the passed-over party of four. Because they were next, they feel that the host should seat them next. In such cases the host should explain what is going on to the next party in line. Another example of an unfair wait is when a guest who has been waiting for twenty minutes to check in finally reaches the front of the line. Just as he is starting to give the details of his reservation to the front desk clerk, the phone rings. The phone is answered promptly by the clerk, who gets involved in a ten-minute conversation with the caller. Marriott has started a policy of removing phones from the front desk to avoid this distraction and eliminate unfair waits.

Maister states that the customer's sense of equity is not always obvious and needs to be managed. Whatever priority rules apply, the service provider must make vigorous efforts to ensure that these rules match with the customer's sense of equity, either by adjusting the rules or by convincing the client that the rules are appropriate.

Shift Demand

It is often possible to shift the demand for banquets and meetings. A sales manager may want to set up a sales meeting for the end of October or the beginning of November and knows that when the hotel is called to check availability, a date must be given. Suppose that October 31 is picked, although it could have been October 24 or November 7 just as easily. Twenty rooms will be needed the night before and a meeting room the day of the event. The hotel is forecast to sell out on October 31, but presently has rooms available. The smart manager asks whether October 31 is a firm date. If the date is flexible, the manager will shift the date to a period when the hotel is not projected to sell out.

Change the Salesperson's Assignment

In hotels, the director of sales assigns salespeople to specific segments. If a soft spot is forecast for two months in the future, the director of sales can focus more effort on short-term business in an attempt to fill the soft period. This can be accomplished by shifting a salesperson from the association market, which books a year or more out, to the corporate market, which can produce bookings in a month or less.

Create Promotional Events

An object of promotion is to shift the demand curve to the left. Casinos have slot tournaments and table game tournaments during their slow periods as a way of building up business. The Sheraton Inn in Steamboat Springs, Colorado, developed "The Way It Wuz Days" to promote summer business. This campaign brought local businesses together to develop summer business for this seasonal ski resort. During slow periods, creative promotions can be an effective way of building business.

KEY TERMS

Customer centered Companies that deliver superior value to their target customers.

Customer-delivered value The difference between total customer value and total customer cost.

Expected service The service that the customer feels he will receive from a service provider.

Freedom from deficiencies A type of service quality that focuses on conformance to specifications.

Functional quality The quality of the process of delivering a service.

Product features Product features that enhance customer satisfaction is one type of service quality.

Societal (ethical) quality Delivering products that will not cause harm to a customer or society as a whole. It is a type of quality that often goes unobserved by the guest.

Technical quality The quality of the core product that a guest receives in a transaction. It is the quality of the guest room in a hotel, the meal in a restaurant, and the car from a rental agency.

Chapter Review

I. To win in today's marketplace, companies must be customer-centered: they must deliver superior value to their target customers.

II. Consumers buy from the firm that they believe offers the highest customer-delivered value, the difference between *total customer value* and *total customer cost.*

1) The customer derives **value** from the core products, the service delivery system, and the company's image.

2) **Costs** to the customer include money, time, energy, and physic costs.

3) **Customer satisfaction** with a purchase depends on the product's performance relative to a buyer's expectations.

4) **Customer loyalty,** on the other hand, measures how likely a customer is to return, and their willingness to perform partner shipping activities for the organization.

III. Relationship marketing involves creating, maintaining, and enhancing strong relationships with customers.

IV. Retaining Customers

1) **The cost of lost customers.** Companies should know how much it costs when a customer defects; this is the same as the customer's lifetime value.

2) **Resolving customer complaints.** Resolving customer complaints is a critical component of customer retention.

V. The Link between Marketing and Quality. The pursuit of high quality is the never-ending journey that hospitality organizations must take in order to achieve a link between the product and their customers.

VI. What Is Quality? There are several views of product quality. One is based on product features, another is based on freedom from deficiencies, and a third is based on categories.

1) **Product features.** Some view product features that enhance customer satisfaction as a way of measuring quality. According to this, a luxury hotel has a higher level of quality than that of a limited-service hotel.

2) **Freedom from deficiencies.** Freedom from deficiencies is another way of viewing quality. According to this view, a limited-service hotel and a luxury hotel could both be quality products if the product they offered was free of deficiencies.

3) **Three categories of service quality.** A third view divides quality into three categories:

a) **Technical quality** refers to what the customer is left with after the customer-employee interactions have been completed.

b) **Functional quality** is the process of delivering the service or product.

c) **Societal quality** is a credence quality; it cannot be evaluated by the consumer before purchase and is often impossible to evaluate after purchase.

VII. Benefits of Service Quality

1) **Retaining customers.** High quality builds loyal customers and creates positive word of mouth.

2) **Avoidance of price competition.** The PIMS data show that firms in the top third in quality could charge 5 percent to 6 percent higher than those in the bottom third. High quality can help to avoid price competition and help to maximize potential revenue.

3) **Retention of good employees.** Employees appreciate working in operations that are well run and produce high-quality products. When an operation has good quality, it can retain good employees. Recruiting is easier and training costs are reduced.

4) **Reduction of costs**

a) **Internal costs** are those associated with correcting problems discovered by the firm before the product reaches the customers.

b) **External costs** are associated with errors that the customers experience.

c) **Quality system costs** are costs viewed as investment in the future of the company to ensure that customers return.

VIII. Developing a Service Quality Program

1) **Supply strong leadership.** The CEO of the organization must have a clear vision for the company, but it is not enough just to have a vision. The CEO must also communicate that vision and convince employees to believe in it and follow it.

2) **Integrate marketing throughout the organization.** The marketing concept states that marketing should be integrated throughout the organization.

3) **Understand the customer.** Companies with high-quality products know what the market wants.

4) **Understand the business.** Delivering high-quality service takes teamwork. Employees must realize how their jobs affect the rest of the team.

5) **Apply operational fundamentals.** The organization has to be well planned and managed.

6) **Leverage the freedom factor.** Employees must have the freedom to shape the delivery of the service to fit the needs of their guests.

7) **Use appropriate technology.** Technology should be used to monitor the environment, help operational systems, develop customer databases, and provide methods for communication with customers.

8) **Practice good human resources management.** Employees must be capable of delivering the services promised to the customer.

9) **Set standards, measure performance, and establish incentives.** The most important way to improve service quality is to set service standards and goals and then teach them to employees and management. Employees who deliver good service should be rewarded.

10) **Feed back the results to the employees.** The results of measurement should be communicated to all employees.

IX. Managing Capacity. Corporate management is responsible for matching capacity with demand on a long-term basis, whereas unit managers are responsible for matching capacity with fluctuations in short-term demand.

1) **Involve the customer in the service delivery system.** Getting the customer involved in service operations expands the number of

people that one employee can serve, thus expanding the capacity of the operation.

2) Cross-train employees. Cross-training employees gives the operation flexibility, allowing the business to increase capacity by shifting employees, and can help to prevent the organization from reducing capacity when an employee calls in sick.

3) Use part-time employees. Managers can use part-time employees to expand capacity during an unusually busy day or meal period or during the busy months of the year for seasonal businesses.

4) Rent or share extra facilities and equipment. Businesses do not have to be constrained by space limitations or equipment limitations.

5) Schedule downtime during periods of low capacity. One way to decrease capacity is to schedule repairs and maintenance during the low season.

6) Extend service hours. Businesses can increase capacity by extending their hours.

7) Use technology. Technology can be used to increase the capacity of systems. One example is the automatic wake-up call system in hotels that can make hundreds of wake-up calls in an hour.

8) Use price. Price can be used to adjust capacity in companies using mobile products such as rental car companies.

X. Managing Demand

1) Use price to create or reduce demand. In most cases price and demand are inversely related.

2) Use reservations. Hotels and restaurants often use reservations to monitor demand. When it appears that they will have more demand than capacity, managers can save capacity for the more profitable segments. Reservations can also limit demand by allowing managers to refuse any further reservations when capacity meets demand.

3) Overbook. Not everyone who reserves a table or books a room shows up. Plans change and people with reservations become no shows. Overbooking is another method that hotels, restaurants, trains, and airlines use to match demand with capacity.

4) Use booking curve analysis. An analysis of booking curves provides valuable information for use in forecasting and better managing capacity.

5) Use queuing. Voluntary queues, such as waits at restaurants, are a common and effective way of managing demand. Good management of the queue can make the wait more tolerable for the guest.

6) Shift demand. It is often possible to shift the demand for banquets and meetings.

7) Change the salesperson's assignment. If a soft spot is forecast two months in the future, the director of sales can focus more effort on short-term business in an attempt to fill the soft period.

8) Create promotional events. An object of promotion is to shift the demand curve to the left.

DISCUSSION QUESTIONS

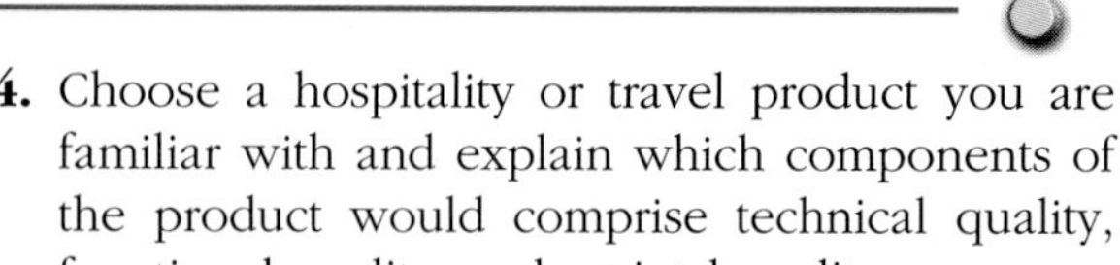

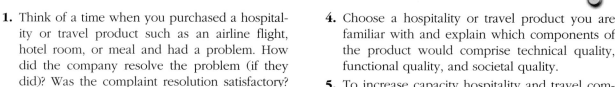

1. Think of a time when you purchased a hospitality or travel product such as an airline flight, hotel room, or meal and had a problem. How did the company resolve the problem (if they did)? Was the complaint resolution satisfactory? Why or why not?
2. Describe a situation in which you became a "lost customer." Did you leave because of poor product quality, poor service quality, or both?
3. Does McDonald's have a high-quality product? Explain your answer and include the criteria you used to evaluate quality.
4. Choose a hospitality or travel product you are familiar with and explain which components of the product would comprise technical quality, functional quality, and societal quality.
5. To increase capacity hospitality and travel companies involve the customer in the delivery of the service. Give some examples of this from your own experiences. Did this involvement increase or decrease your satisfaction with the product being purchased?
6. How does good quality increase employee satisfaction?

EXPERIENTIAL EXERCISE

Do the following:

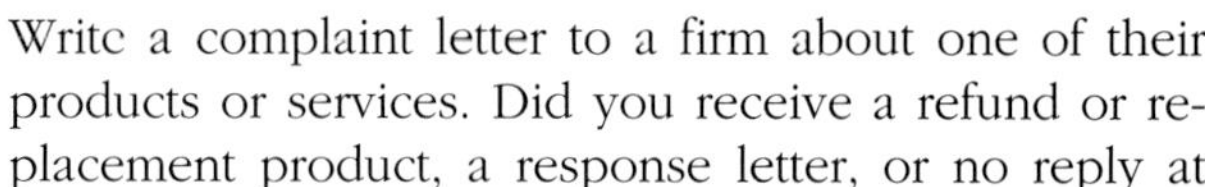

Write a complaint letter to a firm about one of their products or services. Did you receive a refund or replacement product, a response letter, or no reply at all? How does the type of response affect your attitude toward the company?

INTERNET EXERCISE

Support for this exercise can be found on the Web site for *Marketing for Hospitality and Tourism*, www.prenhall.com/kotler.

Go to three Web sites of hospitality or travel organizations. If you had a complaint, is there any way to give your complaint through these Web sites? Explain what you found.

REFERENCES

1. Christopher W. L. Hart, *Extraordinary Guarantees* (New York: American Management Association, 1993), pp. 164–165.
2. Ibid., pp. 97–98.
3. This section draws heavily from Christopher W. L. Hart, "Hampton Inns Guests Satisfied with Satisfaction Guarantee," *Marketing News* 25, no. 3 (February 4, 1991): 7.
4. Hart, *Extraordinary Guarantees*, p. 175.
5. Roger R. Callan and Jacqueline Moore, "Service Guarantee: A Strategy for Service Recovery," *Journal of Hospitality and Tourism Research* 22, no. 1 (1998) 61–69.
6. The McDonalds Corporation. Retrieved January 19, 2001 from the World Wide Web: *http://www.mcdonalds.com/corporate/press/financial/2001*.
7. Vincent S. C. Heung, M. Y. Wong, and Qu Hailin, "Airport-Restaurant Service Quality in Hong Kong," *Cornell Hotel & Restaurant Administration Quarterly* 41, no. 3 (June 2000): 95–96.
8. John Bowen and Stowe Shoemaker, "Relationship in the Luxury Hotel Segment: A Strategic Perspective," *Center for Hospitality Research* (Ithaca, NY: Cornell University, 1997). An overview of this research paper can be found in the February 1998 issue of the *Cornell Hotel and Restaurant Administration Quarterly*.

9. For an interesting discussion of alternative strategies for delivering customer value, see Michael Treacy and Fred Wiersema, "Customer Intimacy and Other Value Disciplines," *Harvard Business Review* (January/February 1993): 84–93.
10. Cheryl Ursin, "The WOW Factor," *Restaurants USA* (March 2001). pp. 27–31.
11. Thomas E. Caruso, "Got a Marketing Topic? Kotler Has an Opinion," *Marketing News,* June 8, 1992, p. 21.
12. Dan McGinn "Burger Time; Case Study" *MBA Jungle,* (May 2001): 42–44.
13. Frederick F. Reichheld and Keith Aspinall, "Building High-Loyalty Business Systems," *Journal of Retail Banking* (Winter 1993/1994): 21–29.
14. James L. Heskett, Earl W. Sasser Jr., and Leonard A. Schlesinger, *The Service Profit Chain* (New York: Free Press, 1997).
15. Leonard L. Berry and A. Parasuraman, *Marketing Services: Competing through Quality* (New York: Free Press, 1991), pp. 136–142.
16. Colleen Dejong, "Loyalty Marketing at a Glance; Hotel Programs," *Colloquy,* retrieved by World Wide Web on 10/24/2001, *http://www.colloquy.com/cont_matrix.asp?industry=Hotel.*
17. James H. Donnelly Jr., Leonard L. Berry, and Thomas W. Thompson, *Marketing Financial Services: A Strategic Vision* (Homewood, IL: Dow Jones–Irwin, 1985), p. 113.
18. Ruthanne Terrero, "Battleground for Customer Loyalty Lies in the In-Room Guest Experience," *Hotel Business*, September 21, 2000–October 6, 2000, p. 30.
19. Thomas E. Caruso, "Kotler: Future Marketers Will Focus on Customer Data Base to Compete Globally," *Marketing News,* June 8, 1992, p. 21.
20. Frederick F. Reichheld and W. Earl Sasser Jr., "Zero Defections: Quality Comes to Services," *Harvard Business Review*, 68 (September/October 1990): 105–111.
21. Ibid.
22. Philip Kotler, John T. Bowen, and James C. Makens, *Marketing for Hospitality and Tourism* (Upper Saddle River, NJ: Prentice Hall, 1996); "Hotel Values Profit from Service," *Hospitality* (February 2000): 32–34.
23. David Cravens, "Introduction to Special Issue," *Journal of the Academy of Marketing Science* 23, no. 4 (Fall 1995): 235.
24. Reichheld and Sasser, "Zero Defections."
25. "Hotel Values Profit from Service," pp. 32–34.
26. *Feelings Consultant Marketing Manual* (Bloomington, MN: Better Than Money Corporation, n.d.). The Technical Research Programs Institute does studies on customer complaints and the success of compliant resolution.
27. Linda M. Lash, *The Complete Guide to Customer Service* (New York: Wiley, 1989), pp. 68–69.
28. Janelle Barlow and Claus Moller, *A Complaint Is a Gift* (San Francisco, CA: Berrett-Koehler, 1996).
29. Majorie Coeyman "You Call This Service?" *Restaurant Business*, May 15, 1997,. pp. 93–104
30. Howard Schlossber, "U.S. Firms: Quality Is the Way to Satisfy," *Marketing News* 25, no. 3 (February 4, 1991): 1. Bruce Adams, "Customer Relationship Management Uncovers Revenue from Loyal Guests," *Hotelmotel.com,* May 21, 2001, p. 36
31. Charles Partlow, "How Ritz-Carlton Applies TQM," *Cornell Hotel and Restaurant Administration Quarterly* 34, no. 3 (August 1993): 16–24.
32. Philip Crosby, *Quality Is Free* (New York: Mentor, 1980).
33. J. M. Juran, *Juran on Quality by Design* (New York: Free Press, 1992), p. 9.
34. Stephen S. Hall, *Quality Assurance in the Hospitality Industry* (Milwaukee, WI: ASQC Quality Press, 1990), p. 23.
35. Robert Buzzel and Bradley T. Gale, *The PIMS Principles: Linking Strategy to Performance* (New York: Free Press, 1987), p. 120.
36. Christopher W. L. Hart, James L. Heskett, and W. Earl Sasser Jr., *Service Breakthroughs* (New York: Free Press, 1990); H. James Harrington, *Poor Quality Cost* (New York: ASQC Quality Press, 1987).
37. Robert A. Brymer and David V. Pavesic, "Job Satisfaction: What's Happening to the Young Managers," *Cornell Hotel and Restaurant Administration Quarterly* 30, no. 4 (February 1990): 90–96.
38. D. Keith Denton, *Quality Service* (Houston, TX: Gulf Publishing Company, 1989).
39. Ibid., p. 140.
40. Berry and Parasuraman, *Marketing Services*, pp. 78–79; Adams, "Customer Relationship," p. 36.
41. Bonnie J. Knutson, "Ten Laws of Customer Satisfaction," *Cornell Hotel and Restaurant Administration Quarterly* 29, no. 3 (November 1988): 16.
42. Jafar Jafari and William Way, "Multicultural Strategies in Tourism," *Cornell Hotel and Restaurant Administration Quarterly* 35, no. 6 (December 1994): 73–75.
43. Charles G. Partlow, "How Ritz-Carlton Applies TQM," *Cornell Hotel and Restaurant Administration Quarterly* 34, no. 4 (August 1993): 19.
44. Adams, "Customer Relationship."
45. Tamer T. Salaneh and John R. Walker, "The QA Payoff," *Cornell Hotel and Restaurant Administration Quarterly* 30, no. 4 (February 1990): 59.
46. See Christopher H. Lovelock, *Managing Services* (Upper Saddle River, NJ: Prentice Hall, 1992); Robert G. Murdick, Barry Render, and Roberta S. Russell, *Service Operations Management* (Needham Heights, MA: Allyn and Bacon, 1990).
47. Jonathan Dahl, "Tracking Travel," *Wall Street Journal,* September 27, 1994, p. B1.
48. Philip Kotler and Gary Armstrong, *Principles of Marketing,* 9th ed (Upper Saddle River, NJ: Prentice Hall, 2001), p. 453.
49. Carolyn U. Lambert, Joseph M. Lambert, and Thomas P. Cullen, "The Overbooking Question: A Simulation,"

Cornell Hotel and Restaurant Administration Quarterly 30, no. 2 (August 1989):15–20.

50. Mark Pestronk, "Finding Hotels Liable for Walking Guests," *Travel Weekly* 49, no. 37 (May 7, 1990): 371.
51. Dahl, "Tracking Travel."
52. Carolyn U. Lambert and Thomas P. Cullen, "Balancing Service and Costs through Queuing Analysis," *Cornell Hotel and Restaurant Administration Quarterly* 28, no. 2 (August 1987): 69–72.
53. David H. Maister, "The Psychology of Waiting Lines," in *Service Encounter*, ed. John A. Czepiel, Michael R. Solomon, and Carol F. Surprenant (Lexington, MA: D.C. Heath, 1985).

Appendix A: The Five-Gap Model of Service Quality

A widely used model of service quality is known as the five-gap model (Figure 11A-1). This model defines service quality as meeting customer expectations. In the words of those who developed the model, "Knowing what customers expect is the first and possibly the most critical step in delivering service quality. Stated simply, providing service that customers perceive as excellent requires that a firm know what customers expect." This model is closely linked to marketing because it is customer based. The model has five gaps.

Gap 1: Consumer Expectations versus Management Perception

Hospitality executives may fail to understand what consumers expect in a service and which features are needed to deliver high-quality service. When management does not understand what their customers want, a gap 1 exists. For example, a manager may develop a system to ensure that all guests wait no longer than 15 minutes to check in. However, if guests start getting upset after 10 minutes, this system will cause dissatisfaction. Talking to guests before developing the check-in system would enable the manager to learn that the critical time was 10 minutes, not 15 minutes. Marriott Hotels observed that guests were not using the complimentary bath crystals provided as a bathroom amenity. They discontinued the bath crystals in favor of cable television, a more important benefit to most guests than bath crystals. Originally, management felt that bath crystals would be considered a benefit. However, after observing their guests, it was found that guest satisfaction could be increased by offering a different service.

Many firms conduct initial studies to find out what their market wants, but later they become internally focused and oblivious to the fact that customers' needs have changed. If customer needs change but the product does not, the marketing mix becomes less attractive to the target market, and gap 1 has increased. Managers should walk around their operations, talk with customers, and encourage feedback. Management can also gain information on customers from marketing information systems.

Gap 2: Management Perception versus Service Quality Specifications

Gap 2 occurs when managers know what their customers want but are unable or unwilling to develop systems that will deliver it. Several reasons have been given for gap 2: (1) inadequate commitment to service quality,

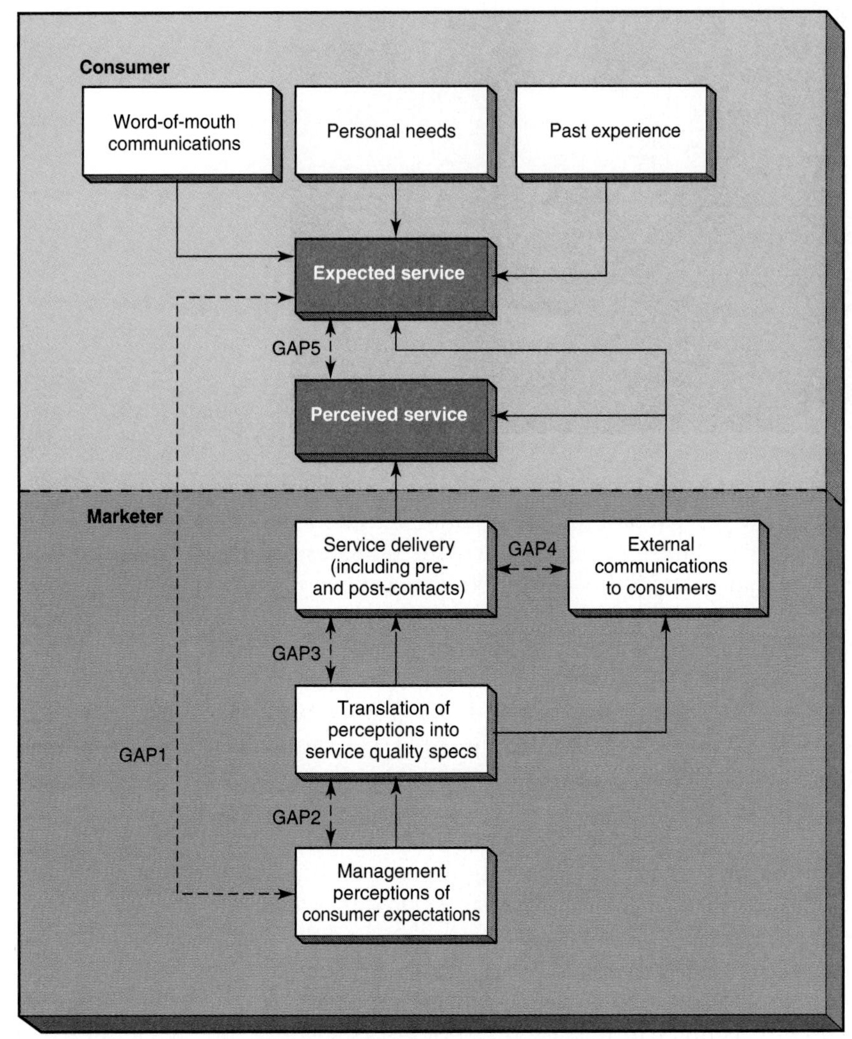

Figure 11A-1
Conceptual model of service quality—the gap analysis model. *Source:* A. Parasuraman, Valerie Zeithaml, and Leonard L. Berry, "A Conceptual Model of Service Quality and Its Implications for Future Research," *Journal of Marketing,* Fall 1985, p. 44. Reprinted with permission of the American Marketing Association.

(2) lack of perception of feasibility, (3) inadequate task standardization, and (4) absence of goal setting.

Some companies look for short-term profits and are unwilling to invest in people or equipment. This almost inevitably causes service quality problems. Hotel owners who are reluctant to provide enough operating capital can be a cause of gap 2 errors. For example, the hotel owner who budgets for just enough linen to get by may discover that the linen inventory quickly drops below critical levels as linen is stolen and destroyed. A visitor experienced this in Ft. Lauderdale, Florida. The guest returned from a walk on the beach to a freshly cleaned room, started to get ready to take a shower, and noticed that there were no towels in the room. The guest called housekeeping and explained that he had to take a shower to get ready for a business appointment and there were no towels in the room. Housekeeping apologized, saying they were short on towels. In about fifteen minutes, a housekeeper arrived with towels, causing the

Gap 1 is reduced when managers talk to customers. Courtesy of United Airlines.

guest to arrive late for the appointment. Incidents such as this detract from positive guest experience, create unnecessary tasks, and decrease employee morale. In this case, hotel management knew that the linen inventory was low, but the owner either did not want to invest in or did not have the money to supply the hotel properly.

Sometimes managers feel that improving an existing problem is not feasible. For example, most business guests want to check out after breakfast. They are usually in a hurry to get started with the day's business. Many hotel managers understand this but accept a ten- to twenty-minute wait as the best that they can do, as they are unwilling to hire extra employees to help during the rush period. Bill Marriott Jr. felt that the problem was important enough to develop a system to solve it and invented express checkouts. Guests receive their bills the evening before. If they are accurate, the guests simply dropped them off with their keys at the front desk. Today, most hotel chains use some type of express checkout system. Some hotels make use of technology and allow the guest to check the accuracy of bills on their television screens and check out using in-room television equipment. The express checkout system was developed by a person who viewed reducing checkout queues as a challenge rather than a problem that was an inherent part of the system. Bill Marriott eliminated this gap 2 error. Bill Marriott demonstrated that capital is not the only cure for a gap 2 problem. Innovative thinking can also eliminate gap 2 problems. Sometimes we need to look for unconventional solutions to the problem. Translating customer needs into service specifications is critical to service quality.

Finally, goals must be accepted by employees. Management must show its support through measurement of results, communication, and rewarding employees for superior service.

Gap 3: Service Quality Specifications versus Service Delivery

Gap 3 is referred to as the service-performance gap. Gap 3 occurs when management understands what needs to be delivered and appropriate specifications have been developed but employees are unable or unwilling to deliver the service. Gap 3 errors occur during moments of truth, when the employee and the customer interact. Service operations that use machines to deliver service are less likely to have gap 3 errors. Machines do not make human errors, and guests expect less from machines. For example, a person using a computerized check-in station in a hotel does not expect the machine to give her a cheerful greeting and be able to give directions to the coffee shop. Employees, however, are expected to act cheerfully and solve the guest's problems. When they do not, guests may perceive a problem with functional quality.

Gap 3 errors can be minimized through internal marketing programs. Management of the human resources functions (hiring, training, monitoring working conditions, and developing reward systems) is important in reducing gap 3 errors. Gap 3 errors are also the result of customer contact employees being overworked. This can occur when a business is understaffed or an employee is required to work a second shift for an employee that called in sick. Under these conditions employees will become tired and stressed. They lose their enthusiasm for the job and become less willing to solve customer problems. This lack of customer orientation leads to gap 3 errors.

Gap 4: Service Delivery versus External Communications

Gap 4 is created when the firm promises more in its external communications than it can deliver. Earlier in the book we mentioned the advertising campaign put on by the government of Bermuda, inviting travelers to enjoy the attractions of the island during its uncrowded low season. Visitors were disappointed when they discovered that many attractions were closed during the off season. Marketers must make sure that operations can deliver what they promise.

During the last week of ski season, skiers were surprised to find that only half the runs on one side of the mountain had been groomed. This was particularly annoying and even dangerous, because the half-grooming occurred on intermediate runs where less than expert skiers might suddenly encounter bad conditions. The runs had been perfectly groomed all season until that final week. Late-season arrivals undoubtedly felt they had been slighted.

The Regent of Fiji encountered a severe problem when a military takeover occurred and discouraged tourism. A consultant, Chuck Gee, dean of the School of Travel Industry Management at the University of Hawaii, was hired to advise during this crisis. Chuck's advice was: "Do nothing different. Do not reduce your staff, your lighting, your food quality, or your service." When asked why, Chuck's answer was that the Regent had positioned itself as a luxury resort and must continue to offer that level of service even if only one guest appeared. He further explained that the Regent knew that there were risks when it entered this market and must now be prepared to accept them and pay the price to continue as an upscale resort.

Lack of consistency can also cause gap 4 problems. Hotel policies were discussed during a marketing seminar. After the seminar a manager from La Quinta told of a problem with a guest when the cashier refused to cash a personal check. The check was over the limit that La Quinta had set for personal checks. However, the guest had cashed a check for the same amount during a previous stay at a La Quinta Inn. The first desk clerk had given the implicit message that it was okay to cash personal checks for that amount. The clerk may have known the guest, had enough cash, and felt the guest should receive a favor. This clerk did not realize that problems were being developed for the next La Quinta. Customers expect chains to have similar products and policies. Inconsistency results in gap 4 errors.

Gap 5: Expected Service versus Perceived Service

Gap 5 is a function of the others. As any of the other gaps increase in size, gap 5 also increases. It represents the difference between expected quality and perceived quality. The expected quality is what the guest expects to receive from the company. The perceived service is what the guest perceives he received from the company. If the guest receives less than he expected, the guest is dissatisfied.

The five-gap service model provides insights into the delivery of quality service. By studying this model, we can develop an understanding of the potential problem areas related to service quality. This insight will help to close any gaps that may exist in our operations.

Appendix B: Forecasting Market Demand

Defining the Market

Market demand measurement calls for a clear understanding of the market involved. The term market has acquired many meanings over the years. In its original meaning, a market was a physical place where buyers and sellers gathered to exchange goods and services. Medieval towns had market squares to which sellers brought their goods and buyers shopped for them. In today's cities, buying and selling occurs in what are called shopping areas rather than markets.

To an economist, the term market describes all the buyers and sellers who transact over some good or service. Thus the limited-service hotel market consists of all the consumers who use limited-service hotels and the companies who supply limited-service hotel rooms. The economist is interested in the structure, conduct, and performance of each market.

To a marketer, a market is the set of all actual and potential buyers of a product or service. A market is the set of buyers, and the industry is the set of sellers. The size of the market hinges on the number of buyers who might exist for a particular market offer. Potential buyers for something have three characteristics: interest, income, and access.

Consider the market for Carnival Cruises. To assess its market, Carnival must first estimate the number of customers who have a potential interest in going on a cruise. To do this, the company could conduct a random sampling of consumers and ask the following question: "Do you have an interest in taking a cruise?" If one person out of ten says yes, Carnival can assume that 10 percent of the total number of consumers are the potential market for cruises. The potential market is the set of consumers that professes some level of interest in a particular product or service.

Consumer interest alone is not enough to define the cruise market. Potential consumers must have enough income to afford the product. They must be able to answer yes to the following question: "Can you afford to purchase a cruise?" The higher the price, the fewer the number of people who can answer yes to this question. Thus market size depends on both interest and income.

Access barriers further reduce the cruise market size. If Carnival markets its cruises in remote areas not served by travel agents, the number of potential customers in these areas is limited. The available market is the set of consumers that has interest, income, and access to the product.

For some market offers, Carnival might have to restrict sales to certain groups. A particular state might not allow the signing of a contractual agreement by anyone under the age of twenty-one. The remaining adults make up the qualified available market—the set of consumers that has interest, income, access, and qualifications for the product.

Carnival now has the choice of going after the whole qualified available market or concentrating on select segments. Carnival's served market is the part of the qualified available market that it decides to pursue. For example, Carnival may decide to concentrate its marketing efforts on the east coast, the Chicago area, and the southwest. These areas become its served market. Carnival and its competitors will end up selling a certain number of cruises in their served market. The penetrated market is the set of consumers that has bought cruises.

Figure 11B-1 brings these market concepts together with some hypothetical numbers. The bar on the left of the figure shows the ratio of the potential market—all those who are interested—to the total market. Here the potential market is 10 percent. The bar on the right shows several possible

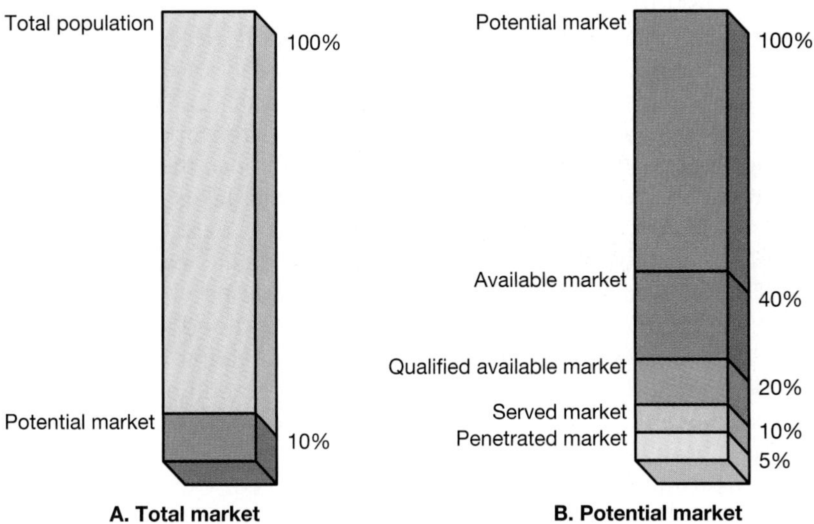

Figure 11B-1
Levels of marketing definition.

breakdowns of the potential market. The available market—those who have interest, income, and access—is 40 percent of the potential market. The qualified available market—those who can meet the legal requirements—is 50 percent of the total available market (or 20% of the potential market). Carnival concentrates its efforts on 50 percent of the qualified available market—the served market, which is 10 percent of the potential market. Finally, Carnival and its competitors already have penetrated 50 percent of the served market (or 5% of the potential market).

These market definitions are a useful tool for marketing planning. Carnival's management can take a number of actions if they are not satisfied with current sales. It can lobby to get the age for signing a legal contract lowered. It can expand its markets in North America or in other areas of the world. Carnival can lower its prices to expand the size of the potential market. It can try to attract more buyers from its served market through stronger promotion or distribution efforts to target current customers. Or it can try to expand the potential market by increasing advertising to convert noninterested consumers into interested consumers. This is what Carnival did when it created the "Fun Ships."

Market Areas for Restaurants

In the restaurant industry, it is common to describe market areas geographically and call them trade areas. Trade areas vary by type of restaurant and area description. For example, in rural areas it is common for people to make a 100-mile round trip to dine at a favorite restaurant. In contrast, 90 percent of the customers of a fast-food restaurant in a residential area of a major city live within three miles of the restaurant. People are not willing to spend a great deal of time getting a fast-food meal. But if they eat at a specialty restaurant such as a Hard Rock Café, they are willing to drive across town. Thus Hard Rock Café's trade area may encompass a fifteen-mile radius. A McDonald's in the same town may define its trade area as a three-mile radius.

John Melaniphy, a restaurant site location expert, describes the trade area of a restaurant as an area that provides 85 percent of the restaurant's business. Restaurants that serve out-of-town guests can examine customers' zip codes and find out where their guests are staying while they are visiting the city. He gives other factors that influence the trade area of a restaurant. Topography defines trade areas. Rivers, lakes, or mountains may set boundaries. Psychological barriers can also exist. For example, expressways, airports, and industrial parks may create barriers. Demographic differences in neighborhoods can also create psychological barriers. For example, residents of a lower-class neighborhood may feel more comfortable eating in their own neighborhood than eating in a restaurant in an upper-middle-class neighborhood, even though both restaurants are the same distance from their houses and have the same average check.

Competition has a big impact on the trade area. Sometimes competition from the same chain may define a trade area. For example, in a city that has eight McDonald's, an adjacent McDonald's may set the boundaries of the trade area for another.

Traffic flows and road patterns also help define trade areas. Accessibility is an important consideration: the better the access, the more extensive the trade area. People also become accustomed to traveling in certain directions and are more likely to travel four miles to a restaurant that they pass every day going to work than four miles in a direction that they travel infrequently. Thus a knowledge of normal traveling routes to major employment and shopping areas is useful in determining a trade area.

Measuring Current Market Demand

We now turn to some practical methods for estimating current market demand. Marketers will want to estimate three different aspects of current market demand: total market demand, area market demand, and actual sales and market shares.

Estimating Total Market Demand

The total market demand for a product or service is the total volume that would be bought by a defined consumer group in a defined geographic area in a defined time period in a defined marketing environment under a defined level and mix of industry marketing effort.

Total market demand is not a fixed number but a function of the stated conditions. One of these conditions, for example, is the level and mix of industry marketing effort. Another is the state of the environment. Part A of Figure 11B-2 shows the relationship between total market demand and these conditions. The horizontal axis shows different possible levels of industry marketing expenditure in a given period. The vertical axis shows the resulting demand level. The curve represents the estimated level of market demand for varying levels of industry marketing expenditure. Some base sales (called the market minimum) would take place without any marketing expenditures. Greater marketing expenditures would yield higher levels of demand, first at an increasing rate and then

Figure 11B-2
Market demand.

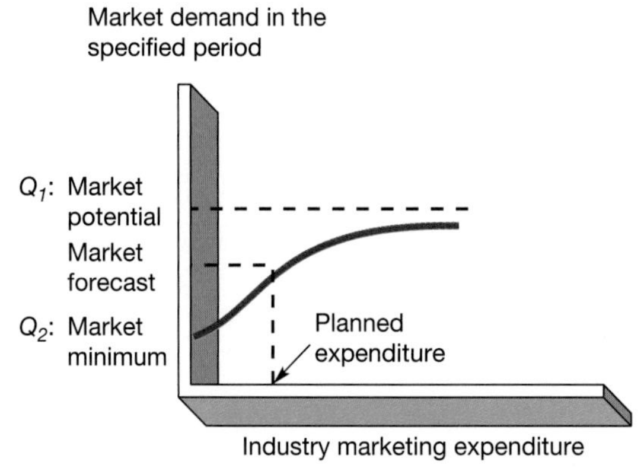

A. Market demand as a function of industry marketing expenditure (assumes a marketing environment of prosperity)

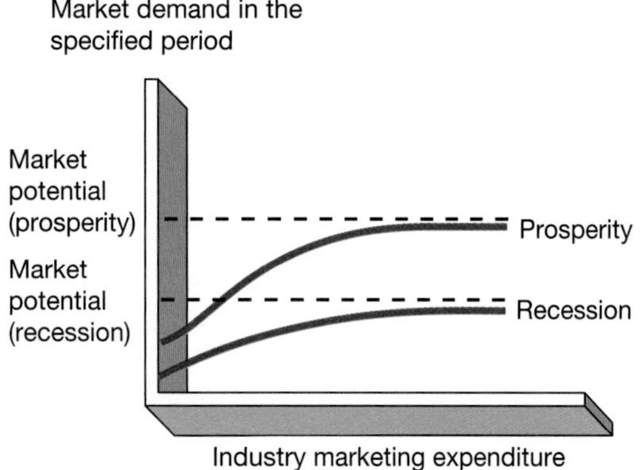

B. Market demand as a function of industry marketing expenditures (under prosperity vs. recession)

at a decreasing rate. Marketing expenditures above a certain level would not cause much more demand, suggesting an upper limit to market demand called the market potential. The industry market forecast shows the level of market demand corresponding to the planned level of industry marketing expenditure in the given environment.

The distance between the market minimum and the market potential shows the overall sensitivity of demand to marketing efforts. We can think of two extreme types of markets, the expandable and the nonexpandable. An expandable market, such as the market for air travel, is one whose size is affected by the level of industry marketing expenditures. In terms of Figure 11B-2, in an expandable market, the distance between Q_1 and Q_2 would be fairly large. A nonexpandable market, such as the market for opera, is one whose size is not much affected by the level of marketing expenditures; the distance between Q_1 and Q_2 would be fairly small. Organizations selling in a nonexpandable market can take primary demand—total demand for all brands of a given product or service—as a given. They concentrate their marketing resources on building selective demand—demand for their brand of the product or service.

Given a different marketing environment, we must estimate a new demand curve. Figure 11B-2 shows the relationship of market demand to the environment. A given level of marketing expenditure will always result in more demand during prosperity than it would during a recession. Marketers should carefully define the situation for which they are estimating market demand.

Estimating Area Market Demand

Companies face the problem of selecting the best sales territories and allocating their marketing budget optimally among these territories. Therefore, they need to estimate the market potential of different cities, states, and even national markets (see Marketing Highlight 11-1). Two major methods are available: the market-buildup method and the market-factor index method. The market-buildup method calls for identifying all the potential buyers in each market and estimating their potential purchases. The market-factor index method is used in the fast-food industry. A common method for calculating area market potential is to identify market factors that correlate with market potential and combine them into a weighted index.

Many companies compute additional area demand measures. Marketers now can refine state-by-state and city-by-city measures down to census tracts or zip code centers. Census tracts are small areas about the size of a neighborhood, and zip code centers (designed by the U.S. Postal Service) are larger areas, often the size of small towns. Information on population size, family income, and other characteristics is available for each type of unit. Marketers can use these data for estimating demand in neighborhoods or other smaller geographic units within large cities.

Estimating Actual Sales and Market Shares

Besides estimating total and area demand, a company will want to know the actual industry sales in its market. Thus it must identify its competitors and estimate their sales. The industry's trade association often will collect and publish total industry sales, although not listing individual company sales separately. In this way, each company can evaluate its performance against the industry as a whole. Suppose that the company's sales are increasing at a rate of 5 percent a year and industry sales are increasing at 10 percent. This company is actually losing its relative standing in the industry.

Forecasting Future Demand

Forecasting is the art of estimating future demand by anticipating what buyers are likely to do under a given set of conditions. For example, an association wants to book 100 rooms for three nights in a 250-room hotel next year. They will pay $95 per room per night. The current rate structure of the hotel is as follows: rack rate $150, corporate rate $125, and average rate $105. Should the manager take the 300 room nights at a low rate, or does the manager turn down this request for $28,500 of business? Without forecasting, it is difficult to answer this question. Forecasts help managers maximize their profits.

Most markets do not have a stable industry or company demand, so good forecasting becomes a key factor in company success. Poor forecasting can lead to overstaffing and excess inventories or understaffing and running out of products. The more unstable the demand, the more the company needs accurate forecasts and elaborate forecasting procedures.

Forecasting Methods

Many firms base their forecasts on past sales. They assume that the causes of past sales can be uncovered through statistical analysis and that analysts can use the causal relations to predict future sales. One popular method, time-series analysis, consists of breaking down the original sales into four components—trend, cycle, season, and erratic components—and then recombining these components to produce the sales forecast. Trend is the long-term, underlying pattern of growth or decline in sales resulting from basic changes in population, capital formation, and technology. It is found by fitting a straight line through past sales.

Cycle captures the medium-term wave movement of sales resulting from changes in general, economic, and competitive activity. The cyclical component can be useful for medium-range forecasting. Cyclical swings, however, are difficult to predict because they do not occur at regular intervals.

Season refers to a consistent pattern of weekly, monthly, or quarterly sales movements within the year. In the hospitality industry, we usually think of seasonal changes on a yearly basis, but weekly and hourly sales changes are important. The seasonal component can be related to weather factors, holidays, and trade customs. The seasonal pattern provides a norm for forecasting short-range sales. Yield management depends on forecasting demand by day, by flight or cruise, and by hour of the day. Historical sales patterns are carefully analyzed, such as examining sales for Tuesdays of the second week of September or total passengers and the mix of passengers on flight 482 each Wednesday afternoon at 3:30. Forecasting in the airline industry is further complicated by the presence of interconnecting stops. Large hospitality companies such as airlines, hotel chains, and car rental firms, such as Hertz, depend on sophisticated software to analyze huge volumes of data.

Finally, erratic events include fads, strikes, snowstorms, earthquakes, riots, fires, and other disturbances. These components, by definition, are unpredictable and should be removed from past data to reveal the more normal behavior of sales. Most of these events cannot be accurately forecasted, but a few, such as snowstorms and strikes, lend themselves to short-run forecasting. Hotel managers in Washington, DC, know that if a major snowstorm is predicted for the city, room demand will increase. Visitors will be unable to leave the city and will want to retain their rooms. Office workers may be unable to return home and will also want a room. Managers who have a knowledge of the past behavior of demand when erratic events occurred can factor this into their thinking in times of crisis management.

The first step in managing demand is understanding the factors that affect the demand of the firm's market segments. The payday of a major employer may drive area customer demand. For example, in north Dallas the Friday and Saturday nights after a payday at Texas Instruments are much busier than nonpayday weekends. There also may be seasonal variations. The Boulders, a resort in Arizona, charges more than $500 a room in season, yet closes in July and August because of a lack of demand for rooms at less than half this price. Holiday periods have a positive influence on demand at most resorts. Business travel drops off between mid-December and mid-January, during the summer period, and over weekends. Although there is fluctuation in demand, much of the fluctuation can be explained. Managers must understand the factors that drive demand and build it into their forecasts.

Suppose that a 250-room hotel had an occupancy of 76 percent, selling 69,350 room-nights during the year at an average rate of $80. During the last seven years, the number of room-nights sold and average rate have both increased by 5 percent. The hotel has undergone two expansions to keep up with the growth. This information suggests that next year the hotel will sell 72,818 room-nights (69,350 × 1.05) at an average rate of $84 (1.05 × $80). The manager first has to determine whether the hotel has the capacity to handle the increase. If the hotel sold out to business travelers from Tuesday to Thursday during February through May and September through October, it is unrealistic to expect that the growth will continue at a 5 percent rate because it will be constrained by capacity. The only opportunity to increase occupancy is during the low-demand periods.

Let us assume that a recession is expected next year. As a result, the number of room-nights is expected to drop by 10 percent, and the average rate is expected to decrease by 15 percent as competitors cut their rates to attract customers. If the manager did not factor in the recession and projected based solely on past information, the occupancy and average room rate would be greatly overstated. Taking the recession into consideration, the forecast will call for a lower occupancy at a greatly reduced room rate.

When a forecast calls for a decrease in sales, it is important to document the reasons for the decrease. This is especially true of regional recessions. A regional economy with a heavy dependence on one industry can suffer a regional recession when that industry declines, while the rest of the country enjoys prosperity. When the hotel management sends its forecast showing a decline in sales to the home office, it will be rejected unless it is well supported. In many cases when a director of sales has presented a marketing plan calling for a decrease in sales without supporting documents to defend the projected decrease, corporate management required the director of sales to increase the forecast. In this scenario, the hotel fails to meet the revised forecast, and the director of sales is fired for not meeting the sales goal. Managers must forecast accurately and provide information to support their forecasts.

Statistical Demand Analysis

Time-series analysis views past and future sales as a function of time rather than as a function of any real demand factors. But many factors affect the sales of any product. Statistical demand analysis is a set of statistical procedures used to discover the most important real factors affecting sales and their relative influence. The factors most commonly analyzed are prices, income, population, and promotion.

Statistical demand analysis consists of expressing sales (Q) as a dependent variable and trying to explain sales as a function of several independent demand variables $X_1, X_2, \ldots X_n$. That is,

$$Q = f(X_1, X_2, \ldots X_n)$$

Using a technique called multiple-regression analysis, various equation forms can be statistically fitted to the data in the search for the best predicting factors and equation. For example, a restaurant near Marquette University in Milwaukee, Wisconsin, found that its sales were explained by whether Marquette University was in session and the preceding week's sales:

$$Q = 2614.3 + 1610.7X_1 + 0.2605X_2.$$

where X_1 is a dummy variable* indicating whether Marquette was in session, with 1 given when it was in session and 0 used when it was not in session, and X_2 is last week's sales. For example, if Marquette had just finished a term and management wanted to predict sales for next week when last week's sales were \$6,000, forecast sales for next week would be

$$\begin{aligned} Q &= 2614.3 + 1610.7X_1 + 0.2605X_2 \\ &= 2614.3 + 1610.7(0) + 0.2605(6000) \\ &= 2614.3 + 0 + 1563 \\ &= \$4177.30 \end{aligned}$$

The manager could also expect a gradual decline in sales (since the preceding week's sales will be falling) as activity around the campus slows down. For example, if the restaurant achieved the forecasted sales

*The researcher used a dummy variable to give a value to nominal data; it is called a dummy variable because the value is created by the researcher.

of $4,177.30, the next week's projected sales would be $3,702.49. The decline is due to the drop in the previous week's sales from $6,000 to $4,176.30. Sales for the restaurant when the university is not in session will level off at $3,535 in the sixth week of the break.

Two precautions apply to the use of regression in forecasting. First, the equation above will not be sensitive to extraordinary events. For example, on parents' weekend the restaurant may generate very high sales. The equation does not include parents' weekend as a variable; therefore, it is unable to project sales accurately for this event. The sales for the week after parents' weekend will be overstated because the figure for the previous week will be extraordinarily high. Second, it is dangerous to forecast outside the range of the different variables used to build the forecast. For example, if a manager examines the relationship between advertising and room sales, the manager may find that room sales increase $5 for every dollar spent on advertising. If the hotel advertising expenditures had ranged from $75,000 to $150,000, we could not necessarily expect this relationship to hold up for advertising expenditures of $250,000, because this level of advertising has not been tested.

The precautions cited earlier illustrate two types of errors caused by the misuse of regression analysis. Statistical demand analysis can be very complex, and the marketer must take care in designing, conducting, and interrupting such analysis. Yet constantly improving computer technology has made statistical demand analysis an increasingly popular approach to forecasting.

Two other forecasting techniques used in the hospitality industry are moving average and exponential smoothing. A moving average is the average of a set number of previous periods (n); this average is used to predict sales for the next period. For example, if a restaurant had sales of $12,000, $12,500, $13,000, and $12,500 over the last four weeks, using a four-week moving average, the sales forecast for the next week would be $12,500.

$$\frac{\$12,000 + \$12,000 + \$13,000 + \$12,500}{4} = \$12,500$$

A limitation of moving averages is that the latest period used in the average has the same weight as the current period. Exponential smoothing is a simple but useful mathematical technique, which allows recent periods to be weighted.

The forecasting techniques presented in this chapter represent a few of the techniques used by managers. It is not within the scope of this book to provide a detailed explanation of all forecasting techniques. We simply want to illustrate that tools are available to assist managers with their forecasts.

Boston Market

12 Pricing Products: Pricing Considerations, Approaches, and Strategy

The real issue is value, not price.
Robert T. Lindgren

The idea seemed almost too good to be true: The founders of Boston Market, maybe the fastest-growing restaurant chain ever, developed a way to build a network of 1,200 restaurants in only a few years and yet still recorded a profit right from the get-go. Startup costs? They weren't a problem. Development costs? No sweat. In an industry where everything takes time, Boston Market seemed to offer instant gratification. When the company went public in 1993, Wall Street took a big bite of this ripe fruit. And it was sweet. As profits rose from $16 million in 1994 to $67 million in 1996, the stock soared and investors gorged.

But the fruit has begun to sour, according to Wall Street analysts and some investors. In the past years, Boston Market has gone from a wild success story to a cautionary tale of marketing mistakes, operational difficulties, and declining sales. Two of the major mistakes that lead to Boston Market's problems were over discounting their products and overpaying for real estate.[1] In the following section we discuss some of their discounting policies.

Boston Market makes its money at dinner, but in 1996 decided to pursue the lunch trade with its carver sandwiches of ham, turkey, and meatloaf. In 1997, a bigger sandwich, the Extreme Carver, was introduced for an additional 50 cents. The target market for this sandwich was the young male adult segment, the heaviest fast-food user.

A marketing program with TV commercials featuring ESPN sports anchor Keith Albermann was accompanied with a flood of coupons offering discounts of 20 percent to 25 percent. Tests showed that an amazing 95 percent of targeted

consumers remembered the ads. Store averages increased from 50 to 200 lunchtime sandwiches per day, for an average weekly gross sales increase of 3.4 percent. Unfortunately, this just wasn't enough. Big Macs were selling for 55 cents on a special promotion and Whoppers went for 99 cents, so Boston Market churned out those discount coupons. When the company adjusted sales for all the discounts, it discovered that weekly net sales had actually fallen by 0.8 percent.

"The prolonged marketing strategy of discounting has hurt sales because it hasn't driven up business enough to make up for some of the effect its having on dinner," said Daren Rugen for the company. Boston Market hadn't counted on customers coming into the stores in the evening for discounted sandwiches instead of ordering full-priced dinners. The company discovered that 50 percent of its sandwich sales were occurring in the evening. Instead of backing off on the discount program, Boston Market responded to the problem with further discounting. Following the mass layoff of personnel, Scott Beck said, "We are going back to our roots—dinner."[2]

Boston Market shows how important pricing decisions can be to a company. Boston Market's decision to discount its price through aggressive couponing had a major negative impact on the company. This policy hurt sales and profits. The new pricing strategy also positioned Boston Market closer to the fast-food sandwich restaurant chains, moving it away from its position as a home-meal replacement restaurant. Boston Market returned to its core business of providing home-meal replacements at a fair price; however, the damage had been done. The value of the company declined, and Boston Market restaurants were sold. On May 26, 2000, Boston Market Corporation, operating approximately 650 company-owned restaurants nationwide in twenty-eight states, became a wholly-owned subsidiary of the McDonald's Corporation.[3]

Chapter Objectives

After reading this chapter, you should be able to:

1. Outline the internal factors affecting pricing decisions, especially marketing objective, marketing-mix strategy, costs, and organizational considerations.
2. Identify and define the external factors affecting pricing decisions, including the effects of the market and demand, competition, and other environmental elements.
3. Contrast the differences in general pricing approaches, and be able to distinguish among cost-plus, target profit pricing, value-based pricing, and going-rate.
4. Identify the new product pricing strategies of market-skimming pricing and market-penetration pricing.
5. Understand how to apply pricing strategies for existing products, such as price bundling and price adjustment strategies.
6. Discuss the key issues related to price changes, including initiating price cuts and price increases, buyer and competitor reactions to price changes, and responding to price changes.

PRICE

Price is the only marketing mix element that produces revenue. All others represent cost. Some experts rate pricing and price competition as the number one problem facing marketing executives. Pricing is the least understood of the marketing variables, yet pricing is controllable in an unregulated market. Pricing changes are often a quick fix made without proper analysis. The most common mistakes include pricing that is too cost oriented, prices that are not revised to reflect market changes, pricing that does not take the rest of the marketing mix into account, and prices that are not varied enough for different product items and market segments. A pricing mistake can lead to a business failure, even when all other elements of the business are sound. Every manager should understand the basics of pricing.

Simply defined, **price** is the amount of money charged for a good or service. More broadly, price is the sum of the values consumers exchange for the benefits of having or using the product or service. Price goes by many names:

> You pay rent for your apartment, a rate when you stay overnight in a hotel, tuition for your education, and a fee to your physician or dentist. Airlines, railways, taxis, and bus companies charge you a fare. A hotel charges you a room rate. The bank charges interest for using their money. The price for driving your car on Florida's Sunshine State Parkway is a toll. The price of a front-desk clerk is a wage, while a bartender receives a wage and tips. A real estate agent who sells a restaurant charges a commission. Finally, income taxes are the price for the privilege of making money.[4]

It is important for marketers and managers to have an understanding of price. Charging too much chases away potential customers. Charging too little can leave a company without enough revenue to maintain the operation properly. Equipment wears out, carpets get stained, and painted surfaces need to be repainted. A firm that does not produce enough revenue to maintain the operation will eventually go out of business. In this chapter we examine factors that hospitality marketers must consider when setting prices, general pricing approaches, pricing strategies for new products, product mix pricing, initiating and responding to price changes, and adjusting prices to meet buyer and situational factors.

Factors to Consider When Setting Prices

Internal and external company factors affect a company's pricing decisions. Figure 12-1 illustrates these. Internal factors include the company's marketing objectives, marketing mix strategy, costs, and organizational considerations. External factors include the nature of the market, demand, competition, and other environmental elements.

Internal Factors Influencing Pricing Decisions

Marketing Objectives

Before establishing price, a company must select a product strategy. If the company has selected a target market and positioned itself carefully, its marketing-mix strategy, including price, will be more precise. For example, Four Seasons positions its hotels as luxury hotels and charges a room rate that is higher than most. Motel 6 and Formula One have positioned themselves as limited-service motels, providing rooms for budget-minded travelers. This market position requires charging a low price. Thus, strategic decisions on market positioning have a major influence on price.

The clearer a firm is about its objectives, the easier it is to set price. Examples of common objectives are survival, short-run profit maximization, market-share maximization, and product-quality leadership.

Survival. Companies troubled by too much capacity, heavy competition, or changing consumer wants set survival as their objective. In the short run, survival is more important than profit. Hotels often use this strategy when the economy slumps. A manufacturing firm can reduce production to match demand. During a recession a 300-room hotel still has 300 rooms to sell each night, although the demand has dropped to 140 a night. The hotel tries to ride out the slump in the best way possible by cutting rates and trying to create the best cash flow possible under the conditions. This strategy inevitably directly affects immediate competitors and sometimes the entire industry. Competitors in the hospitality industry

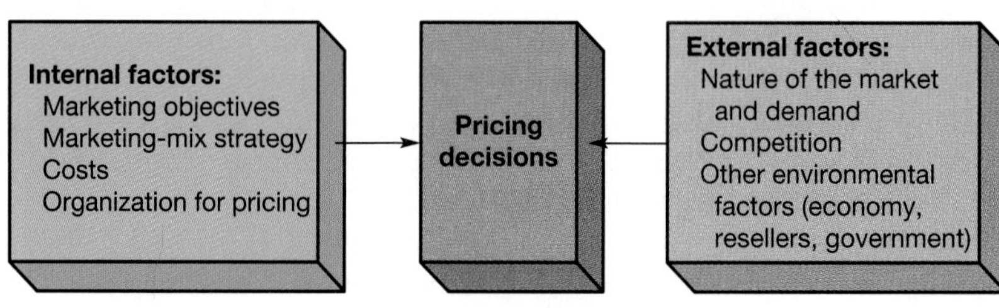

Figure 12-1
Factors affecting price decisions.

are highly cognizant of price changes and will usually respond if they feel threatened. Thus result is in soft markets: not only does occupancy fall, room rates also fall and profits fall.

Observers of the hospitality industry have sometimes suggested that competition using a survival pricing strategy should be monitored carefully but not necessarily emulated. If the hotel is one of two in a market such as a small town, the effect of price discounting could be considerable. On the other hand, if the hotel is in Orlando, Florida, it is one of many and represents a fraction of the total room supply. In this case competitors with a strong marketing program may want to use their marketing skills to gain customers rather than cut their price. Also, for a hotel with good marketing it can make sense to allow a competitor to lower prices and skim off the budget-conscious customers, leaving more profitable business for them, particularly if the hotel using a survival strategy has a small market share.

Current Profit Maximization. Many companies want to set a price that will maximize current profits. They estimate what demand and costs will be at different prices and choose the price that will produce the maximum current profit, cash flow, or return on investment, seeking current financial outcomes rather than long-run performance. For example, a company may purchase a distressed hotel at a low price. The objective becomes to turn the hotel around, show an operating profit, and then sell. If the hotel owners can achieve a successful turnaround, they may receive a good capital gain.

Some entrepreneurs develop a restaurant concept with the objective of selling the concept to a major chain. They realize that the concept's viability must be proved through a small chain that produces a high net profit. If they can do this, they may attract the attention of a major corporation. The pricing objective in this case is current profit maximization.

Market-Share Leadership. Other companies want to obtain a dominant market-share position. They believe that a company with the largest market share will eventually enjoy low costs and high long-run profit. Thus prices are set as low as possible. Marriott strives to be the market-share leader in its class. When it opens a new hotel, Marriott builds market share as quickly as possible. For example, Marriott opened its resort on Australia's Gold Coast with $99 rates; six months later the hotel charged almost twice this rate. Low opening rates created demand. As the demand increased, low-revenue business was replaced with higher. Such a strategy uses price and other elements of the marketing mix to create the awareness of better value than the competition.

Product-Quality Leadership. The Ritz-Carlton chain has a construction or acquisition cost per room that often exceeds $500,000. Besides a high capital investment per room, luxury chains have a high cost of labor per room. Their hotels require well-qualified staff and a high employee/guest ratio to provide luxury service. They must charge a high price for their luxury hotel rooms' product.

Groen, a manufacturer of food-service equipment, is known for its high-quality steam-jacketed kettles. Kitchen designers specify Groen equipment because of its known quality, enabling the company to demand a high price for its equipment. To maintain its quality, Groen must have a well-engineered product comprised of high-quality materials. It also must have the budget to ensure that it maintains its position as a quality leader.

"I know it's late, but I'd like some sushi. How far do I have to go?"
You needn't ever leave the comfort of your Four Seasons room to be transported by a talented chef. Room service menus abound with regional selections: from deep-dish pizza, to striped bass without unwanted calories, to homemade chicken soup at midnight. For the same breadth of choice in another unequalled setting, visit our restaurants downstairs. In this value-conscious era, the demands of business demand nothing less. For reservations, phone your travel counsellor or call us toll free.
FOUR SEASONS HOTELS
FOUR SEASONS • REGENT HOTELS AND RESORTS
Four Seasons • Regent. Defining the art of service at 40 hotels in 19 countries.

Four Seasons Hotels use non-price factors in their advertisements. They feature product attributes that will create value for their target market. Courtesy of Four Seasons–Regent Hotels and Resorts.

Quality leaders such as Ritz-Carlton and Groen charge more for their products, but they also have to reinvest in their operations continuously to maintain positions as quality leaders.

A bowl of chili and a beverage does not exceed \$10 in most restaurants, but the Red Sage Restaurant in Washington, DC, charges twice that amount for its southwestern cuisine. Patrons pay for more than just a bowl of chili. This two-story restaurant spent \$5 million to re-create the wide-open spaces of the west. More than 100 craftsmen and artists were employed to create stunning original designs, such as murals of horses and a cloud sculpture that flashes blue lightning.[5]

Other Objectives. A company also might use price to attain other, more specific objectives. A restaurant may set low prices to prevent competition from entering the market or set prices at the same level as its competition to stabilize the market. Fast-food restaurants may reduce prices temporarily to create excitement for a new product or draw more customers into a restaurant. Thus pricing may play an important role in helping to accomplish the company's objective at many levels.

The case of two upscale restaurants in New York, both owned by former major league baseball players, offers an example of contrasting pricing strategies.[6] Mickey Mantle's restaurant purposely established a high price for alcoholic beverages. "A beer here isn't cheap," said John Lowy, co-owner. "We charge more than other bars to keep out the kids. This is a high-exposure place. If something bad happened, it would get out real quick."

An opposite pricing strategy is employed at Rusty Staub's Restaurant. Rusty's pricing philosophy for wine is unique for the industry. He believes that "the better the wine, the less the markup." "We work on a thin margin," said Staub. "A lot of people in the industry say that you should charge at least three times the cost of the wine. But we're way under that. I want people to know we're one of the great-value restaurants."

12.2 Ritz Carlton
Rusty Staub's Restaurants

Which pricing philosophy is correct, Mantle's or Staub's? It all depends on the objectives an owner is attempting to meet. These objectives fit with the company's marketing strategy. There is never one pricing strategy that is right for all competitors in the hospitality industry.

Marketing Mix Strategy

Price is only one of many marketing mix tools that a company uses to achieve its marketing objectives. Price must be coordinated with product design, distribution, and promotion decisions to form a consistent and effective marketing program. Decisions made for other marketing mix variables may affect pricing decisions. For example, resorts that plan to distribute most of their rooms through wholesalers must build enough margins, into their room price, to allow them to offer a deep discount to the wholesaler. Owners usually refurbish their hotels every five to seven years to keep them in good condition. Prices must cover the costs of future renovations.

A firm's promotional mix also influences price. A restaurant catering to conventioneers receives less repeat business than a neighborhood restaurant and must advertise in city guides targeted to conventioneers. Managers of restaurants who do not consider promotional costs when setting prices will experience revenue/cost problems.

Companies often make pricing decisions first. Other marketing-mix decisions are based on the price a company chooses to charge. For example, Marriott saw an opportunity in the economy market and developed Fairfield Inns, using price to position the motel chain in the market. Fairfield Inns' target price defined the product's market, competition, design, and product features. Companies should consider all marketing-mix decisions together when developing a marketing program.

Costs

Costs set the floor for the price a company can charge for its product. A company wants to charge a price that covers its costs for producing, distributing, and promoting the product. Beyond covering these costs, the price has to be high enough to deliver a fair rate of return to investors. Therefore, a company's costs can be an important element in its pricing strategy. Many companies work to become the low-cost producers in their industries. McDonald's has developed systems for producing fast food efficiently. A new hamburger franchise would have a hard time competing with McDonald's on cost. Effective low-cost producers achieve cost savings through efficiency rather than cutting quality. Companies with lower costs can set lower prices that result in greater market share. Lower costs do not always mean lower prices. Some companies with low costs keep their prices the same as competitors, providing a higher return on investment.

Costs take two forms, fixed and variable. ***Fixed costs*** *(also known as overhead)* are costs that do not vary with production or sales level. Thus, whatever its output, a company must pay bills each month for rent, interest, and executive salaries. Fixed costs are not directly related to production level. Variable costs vary directly with the level of production. For example, a banquet produced by the Hyatt in San Francisco has many variable costs; each meal may include a salad, rolls and butter, the main course, a beverage, and a dessert. In addition to the food items, the hotel provides linen for each guest. These are called variable costs because their total varies with the number of units produced. Total costs are the sum of the fixed and variable costs for any given level of production. In the long run, management must charge a price that will at least cover total costs at a given level of sales.

12.3 Embassy Suites
Fairfield Inn
Hyatt

Managers sometimes forget that customers are not concerned with a business's operating costs; they seek value. The company must watch its costs carefully. If it costs the company more than competitors to produce and sell its product, the company must either charge a higher price or make less profit.

Many hospitality companies are developing sophisticated models and software to better understand costs and their relations to price. Embassy Suites recognizes this relationship and believes that the most valuable guest is not necessarily the one who pays the highest price for a suite. A contribution model developed by Embassy Suites now examines costs to acquire and service guests, such as room labor costs, advertising, special promotions, and associated costs.

Organizational Considerations

Management must decide who within the organization should set prices. Companies handle pricing in a variety of ways. In small companies, top management, rather than the marketing or sales department, often sets the prices. In large companies, pricing is typically handled by a corporate department or by regional or unit managers, under guidelines established by corporate management. A hotel develops a marketing plan that contains monthly average rates and occupancies for the coming year. Regional or corporate management approves the plan. The hotel's general manager and sales manager are then responsible for achieving these "averages." In times of high demand, they can achieve rates significantly above their projected average, whereas in periods of low demand, they will be below their objective. Management may have some freedom in the prices it charges for different groups, but at the end of the financial period, they are responsible for achieving their overall pricing and occupancy objectives.

Many corporations within the hospitality industry now have a revenue management department with responsibility for pricing and coordinating with other departments that influence price. Airlines, cruise lines, auto rental companies, and many hotel chains have developed revenue management departments. According to Brian Rice, the director of revenue planning and analysis for Royal Caribbean Cruise Line, the development of a revenue management department was an evolutionary process.

12.4 Royal Caribbean

> To practice effective revenue management we needed to make sure that our pricing structures were supportive of what we were doing in inventory management, and that sales were targeting the same market segments we needed to push. Now we have got to the point where we meet weekly with the sales group to set priorities, we also work with advertising, inventory management and reservations.[7]

The potential rewards are enormous from professional revenue management in a large hospitality company. According to Brian Rice, "If the average yield at Royal Caribbean goes up by $1 a day, it is worth $5.5 million and 100% of it goes to the bottom line." Brian conservatively estimated the monetary benefits of "baby-sitting" the revenue on a day-to-day basis at Royal Caribbean at over $20 million per day.[8]

Royal Caribbean Cruises has developed a revenue management department with the responsibility for price and coordinating with other departments that influence price. Courtesy of Royal Caribbean International.

External Factors Affecting Pricing Decisions

External factors that affect pricing decisions include the nature of the market and demand, competition, and other environmental elements.

Market and Demand

Although costs set the lower limits of prices, the market and demand set the upper limit. Both consumer and channel buyers such as tour wholesalers balance the product's price against the benefits it provides. Thus, before setting prices, a marketer must understand the relationship between price and demand for a product.

Rudy's was one of the finest restaurants in Houston. It prospered during Houston's boom in the 1970s and early 1980s. In 1982, oil prices plummeted, sinking Houston's oil-dependent economy into a recession. It remained in a depressed state for the rest of the decade. The demand for fine dining fell, and Rudy's suffered. Its lunches were just breaking even. Management considered a price increase as a way to push revenue above the break-even point. On the surface this may have seemed like a good idea: Just charge each customer $5 more, and the revenue would move above break-even. This tactic assumed that the market was price inelastic.

Business had dropped at Rudy's because people could no longer afford their prices. An increase in price would have further reduced the size of the market that could afford the restaurant's prices. Another restaurant in Houston adapted its pricing tactics to fit the recession. La Colombe d'Or offered a three-course meal for the spot price of a barrel of oil. When the morning price of oil was $12.62 a barrel, they charged $12.62 for a meal that cost $20 to $25 in comparable restaurants. The promotion gained the restaurant national and local publicity. The meal was a loss leader because most guests ordered wine with their meal. The restaurant frequently booked business luncheons, and the host of a business luncheon generally does not force guests to order the cheapest item on the menu. As a result, La Colombe d'Or sold many meals at regular prices and had healthy wine sales. Yet even with the loss leader the owner realized that other prices must offer value.

Cross Selling and Upselling

The owner of La Colombe d'Or utilized **cross selling,** one of the basics of effective revenue management. Cross-selling opportunities abound in the hospitality industry. A hotel can cross sell F&B, exercise room services, and executive support services such as a fax, and can even sell retail products ranging from hand-dipped chocolates to terrycloth bathrobes. A ski resort can cross sell ski lessons and dinner sleigh rides.

Upselling is also part of effective yield management. This occurs through training of sales and reservations employees to continuously offer a higher-priced product, rather than settling for the lowest price. One proponent of upselling believes that any hotel can increase its catering revenue by 15 percent through upselling.[9]

Hundreds of upselling opportunities exist. They must be recognized and programs implemented to ensure their success. The common practice of offering after-dinner coffee can be turned into an upselling opportunity by offering high-image upgraded presentations of coffee and tea rather than the standard pot of coffee. Gourmet coffee sales are expected to reach or exceed 30 percent of U.S. coffee sales.[10]

Price changes are easy to make and are often seen as a quick fix to a complex problem. Although it is easy to increase or decrease prices, it is hard to change a perception that your price is incorrect. Pricing decisions require a good understanding of the customer, market factors including the economic environment, and competition.

In this section we look at how the price demand relationship varies for different types of markets and how buyer perceptions of price affect pricing decisions. We also discuss methods for measuring the price demand relationship.

Pricing in Different Markets

The seller's pricing freedom varies with different types of markets. Economists recognize four types of markets: pure competition, pure monopoly, monopolistic competition, and oligopolistic competition. Under pure competition, the market consists of many buyers and sellers trading in a uniform commodity such as wheat, copper, or financial securities. A pure monopoly consists of one seller. The seller may be a government monopoly, such as the U.S. Postal Service, a private regulated monopoly, such as a power company, or a private nonregulated monopoly, such as DuPont when it introduced nylon.

12.5 United States Postal Service

Most hospitality firms operate in monopolistic competition or oligopolistic competition. Under monopolistic competition, the market consists of many buyers and sellers who trade over a range of prices rather than at a single market price. A range of prices occurs because sellers can differentiate their offers to the buyers. Either the physical product can be varied in quality, features, or style, or the accompanying service can be varied. Buyers see differences in sellers' products and will pay different prices. Sellers develop differentiated offers for different customer segments and, besides price, freely use branding, advertising, and personal selling to set their offers apart. Because there are many competitors, each firm is less affected by competitors' marketing strategies than in oligopolistic markets. For example, in a large city there are many sit-down service restaurants. Each restaurant is differentiated by price and nonprice factors.

Under oligopolistic competition the market consists of a few sellers who are highly sensitive to each other's pricing and marketing strategies. The sellers are few because it may be difficult to enter the market. Each seller is alert to competitors' strategies and moves. If a major airline cuts its fares by 10 percent, it will quickly attract additional customers. Other airlines will cut their fares in reaction to the competition. On the other hand, if an oligopolist raises its price, its competitors might not follow the lead. The oligopolist would then have to retract its price increase or risk losing its customers to competition.

Consumer Perceptions of Price and Value

In the end it is the consumer who decides whether a product's price is right. When setting prices, management must consider how consumers perceive price and the ways that these perceptions affect consumers' buying decisions. Like other marketing decisions, pricing decisions must be buyer oriented.

"We can't see the value of our product," explains Carlos Talosa, senior vice president of operations at Embassy Suites. "We can only set price. The market value is set by our customers and our ability to sell to it." According to Talosa, "Even in recessionary times, consumers aren't necessarily buying the cheapest options, but they are demanding value for their dollars and rightly so. If you aren't value-selling, then you are giving away precious assets."[11]

Pricing requires more than technical expertise. It requires creative judgments and awareness of buyers' motivations. Effective pricing opens doors. It requires a creative awareness of the target market, why they buy, and how they make their buying decisions. Recognition that buyers differ in these dimensions is as important for pricing as it is for effective promotion, distribution, or product policy.

When consumers buy a product, they exchange something of value (money) for something else of value (the benefits of having or using the product). Effective, buyer-oriented pricing involves understanding the value consumers place on the benefits they receive from the product. Such benefits include both actual and perceived benefits. When a consumer buys a meal at an upscale restaurant, it is easy to figure out the value of the meal's ingredients. But it is very difficult to measure the value that customers will give to this product. Some guests come for the service, and others put great value on the chef's ability. Still others may value the restaurant's prestige and atmosphere. If customers perceive that the price is greater than the product's value, they will not buy.

Marketers must try to look at the consumer's reasons for choosing a product and set price according to consumer perceptions of its value. Because consumers vary in the values that they assign to products, marketers often vary their pricing strategies for different segments. They offer different sets of product features at different prices. For example, a quarter-pound hamburger might cost $3 at McDonald's, $6 at a sit-down service restaurant such as Bennigan's, and $9 in an exclusive city club.

Buyer-oriented pricing means that the marketer cannot design a marketing program and then set the price. Good pricing begins with analyzing consumer needs and price perceptions. Managers must consider other marketing-mix variables before setting price. Most hotel and restaurant concepts are designed by identifying a need in the marketplace. The product concept usually contains a price range that the market is willing to pay. La Quinta Inns identified a market that did not value many amenities found in a full-service motel, the commercial traveler staying for one night. These guests did not use cocktail lounges, hotel restaurants, and banquet and meeting facilities. By eliminating these features, La Quinta saved money in both construction and operating costs. They passed these savings along to the customer as lower prices, offering the same sleeping room at a lower price than that of midscale hotels.

Consumers tend to look at the final price and then decide whether they received a good value. For example, two people dining in a restaurant receive their bill and see that it is $80. The diners then decide whether they were satisfied during the postpurchase evaluation. Rather than going over each item on the menu individually and judging its value, they judge the entire dining experience against the cost of that experience. If a restaurant offers a good value on food but a poor value on wine—charging $7 a glass for house wine, for instance—a couple who consume six glasses of wine may feel that the check total is too high when $42 for wine is added to the bill.

Melvyn Greene, a hotel marketing consultant, once interviewed guests immediately after they had paid their bills and were leaving the hotel. Only about one-fifth could remember the room rate they had just paid. They could, however, state whether they had received good value. Most of the guests had stayed for more than one day, made phone calls, and used the hotel's food and beverage outlets. The room rate was only one part of the charges on their total bill. They tended to accept the charges and sign their charge card.[12] The guests based their perception of value on the total dollar amount of the bill, the products they had received, and their satisfaction with those products.

Different market segments evaluate products differently. Managers must provide their target markets with product attributes that the target market will value and eliminate those features that do not create value. Then they have to price the product so that it will be perceived to be a good value by the desired target market. For some markets, this means modest accommodations at a low price; for other markets, this means excellent service at a high price. Perceived value is a function of brand image, product attributes, and price.

Analyzing the Price–Demand Relationship

Each price a company can charge will lead to a different level of demand. The demand curve illustrates the relationship between price charged and the resulting demand. It shows the number of units the market will buy in a given period at different prices that might be charged. In the normal case, demand and price are inversely related, that is, the higher the price, the lower the demand (Figure 12-2). Thus the company would sell less if it raised its price from P_1 to P_2. Consumers with limited budgets will usually buy less of something if its price is too high.

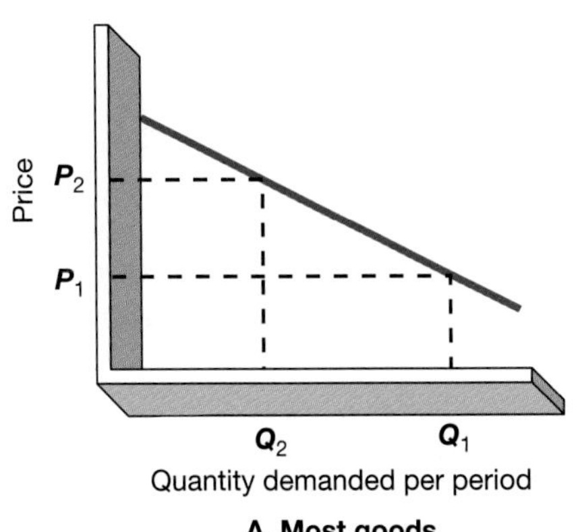

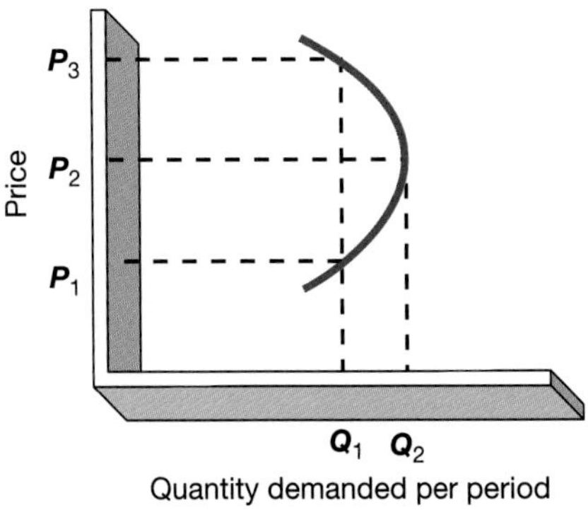

Figure 12-2
Two hypothetical demand schedules.

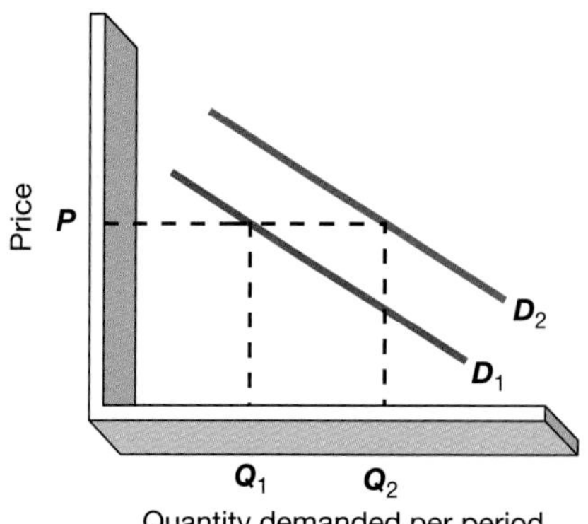

Figure 12-3
Effects of promotion and other nonprice variables on demand shown through shifts of the demand curve.

Most demand curves slope downward in either a straight or a curved line. But for prestige goods, the demand curve sometimes slopes upward. For example, a luxury hotel may find that by raising its price from P_1 to P_2, it will sell more rooms rather than fewer: Consumers do not perceive it as a luxury hotel at the lower price. However, if the hotel charges too high a price (P_3), the level of demand will be lower than at P_2.

Most company managers understand the basics of a demand curve, but few are able to measure their demand curves. The type of market determines the type of demand curve. In a monopoly, the demand curve shows the total market demand resulting from different prices. But if the company faces competition, its demand at different prices will depend on whether competitors' prices remain constant or change with the company's own prices. Here we will assume that competitors' prices remain constant. Later in the chapter we discuss what happens when competitors' prices change.

Estimating demand curves requires forecasting demand at different prices. For example, a study by Economic Intelligence Unit (EIU) estimated the demand curve for holiday travel in Europe. Their findings suggested that a 20 percent reduction in the price of visiting a holiday destination increases demand by 35 percent. A 10 percent reduction in price increases demand by 23 percent, whereas a 5 percent decrease results in a 15 percent increase in demand.[13] The EIU study used vacation destinations in the Mediterranean and assumed that other variables were constant.

Researchers can develop models which assume that other variables remain constant. For managers, things are not that simple. In normal business situations, other factors affect demand along with price. These factors include competition, the economy, advertising, and sales effort. If a resort cut its price and then advertised, it would be hard to tell what portion of the increased demand came from the price decrease and what portion came from the advertising. Price cannot be isolated from other factors.

Economists show the impact of nonprice factors on demand through shifts in the demand curve rather than movement along it. Suppose that the initial demand curve is D_1 (Figure 12-3). The seller is charging P and selling Q_1 units. Now suppose that the economy suddenly improves or

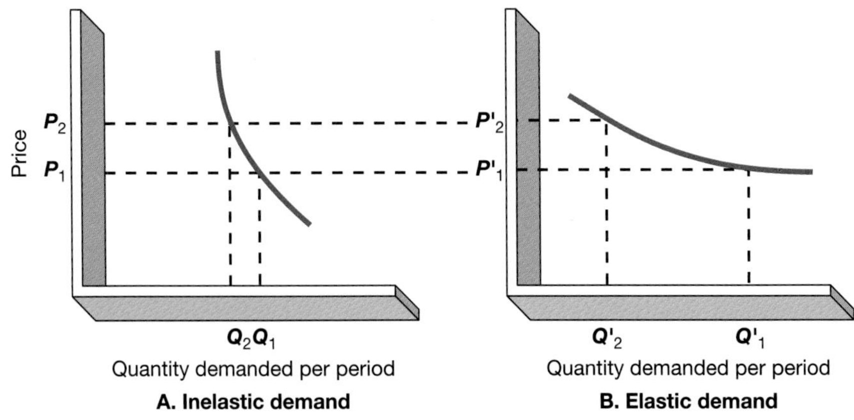

Figure 12-4
Inelastic and elastic demand.

the seller doubles its advertising budget. Higher demand is reflected through an upward shift of the demand curve from D_1 to D_2. Without changing the price, *P,* the demand has increased.

Price Elasticity of Demand

Marketers also need to understand the concept of price elasticity, how responsive demand will be to a change in price. Consider the two demand curves in Figure 12-4. In Figure 12-4A a price increase from P_1 to P_2 leads to a small drop in demand from Q_1 to Q_2. In Figure 12-4B, however, the same price increase leads to a large drop in demand from Q_1 to Q_2. If demand hardly varies with a small change in price, we say that the demand is inelastic. If demand changes greatly, we say the demand is elastic.

$$\frac{\text{\% change in quantity demanded}}{\text{price elasticity of demand}} = \text{\% change in price}$$

Suppose that demand falls by 10 percent when a seller raises its price by 2 percent. Price elasticity of demand is therefore –5 (the minus sign confirms the inverse relation between price and demand) and demand is elastic. If demand falls by 2 percent with a 2 percent increase in price, elasticity is 1. In this case the seller's total revenue stays the same: the seller sells fewer items but at a higher price that preserves the same total revenue. If demand falls by 1 percent when the price is increased by 2 percent, elasticity is 1-2 and demand is inelastic. The less elastic the demand, the more it pays for the seller to raise price.

What determines the price elasticity of demand? Buyers are less price sensitive when the product is unique or when it is high in quality, prestige, or exclusiveness. Chains try to differentiate their brand to create a perception of uniqueness. Consumers are also less price sensitive when substitute products are hard to find. After the closure of the Neil House in downtown Columbus, Ohio, Stouffer's Hotel became one of the few places in the central business district to hold a major banquet function. With supply down, they could charge more for their banquets. They maintained this advantage until new hotels were built and the market became competitive.

12.6 Stouffer's Hotel

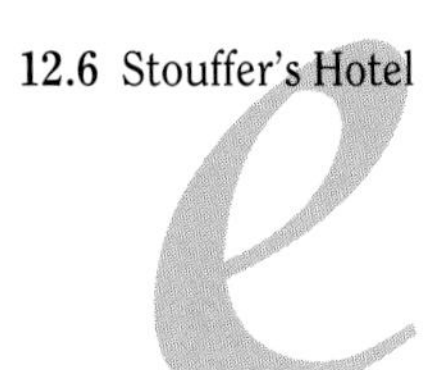

If demand is elastic rather than inelastic, sellers will generally consider lowering their prices. A lower price will produce more total revenue. This practice makes sense when the extra costs of producing and selling more products do not exceed the extra revenue.

Factors Affecting Price Sensitivity[14]

We will now look at some factors that affect price sensitivity. These include the unique value effect, the substitute awareness effect, the business expenditure effect, the end-benefit effect, the total expenditure effect, the shared cost effect, the sunk investment effect, and the price quality effect.

Unique Value Effect. In Houston the Pappas family has converted failed locations into successful restaurants, taking what had been dead restaurants and turning them into businesses with a one-hour wait on weeknights. The Pappas family did not have to use coupons or other price discounts to sell their food. They created a perception of value by giving large portions of food at a moderate price, which appealed to the upper lower class and the middle class. As Ralph Hitz said, "Give them value and you will create volume."

Creating the perception that your offering is different from those of your competitors avoids price competition. In this way the firm lets the customer know it is providing more benefits and offering a value that is superior to that of competitors, one that will either attract a higher price or more customers at the same price. The K&W chain of cafeterias in North Carolina offers a consistent and fairly predictable menu of basic items such as chicken breast, prime rib, and family style vegetables and desserts. Customers sometimes can be heard complaining about the lack of menu creativity, but they consistently return. K&W has discovered a price–value relationship that is recognized and appreciated by a broad spectrum of the people in North Carolina.

Substitute Awareness Effect. The existence of alternatives of which buyers are unaware cannot affect their purchase behavior. Hotel restaurants often charge more for meals based on the substitute awareness effect. The guest who arrives in the evening, being unfamiliar with the city, will usually have breakfast in the hotel. The guest knows that a better value probably exists elsewhere but is unfamiliar with other restaurants in the city. Although the breakfast in the hotel may cost twice as much as a meal in a nearby restaurant, the search costs, the time it would take to find the restaurant, and the travel time to it are greater than the dollar savings of the meal.

Restaurants that target the convention market or out-of-town guests use the substitute awareness effect to their advantage. These restaurants have large advertisements in the city's entertainment magazines that are distributed in the hotels. They are often not the choice of the local resident, who perceives them as overpriced, but they do attract hotel guests who are unaware of alternatives. There must be a continuous source of uninformed customers to use the substitute awareness effect as the rationale for charging premium prices.

When consumers discover products offering a better value, they switch to those products. Many hotel restaurants are empty in the evening. They are perceived as overpriced by the local market. Hotel guests have time during the day to find alternatives. These hotels often view food and beverage as a required amenity rather than an opportunity to compete for local business. A better philosophy is to use food and beverage as a means to attract customers.

Business Expenditure Effect. When someone else pays the bill, the customer is less price sensitive. An executive fully reimbursed for all travel expenses is unlikely to be attracted to a discount rate offer for a hotel room and a restaurant offering a $9.99 dinner special. This person would probably prefer to stay in an upscale hotel, have room-service breakfast, and eat lunch and dinner in a more expensive restaurant. When setting rates, management needs to know what the market is willing to pay. If a hotel can attract executives who have a generous travel allowance and are willing to pay high room rates, they are leaving money on the table by offering discounts.

Airlines will offer a second business class ticket free when one is purchased at full price. Hotels will offer bonus frequent flyer miles. Both of these promotions are taking advantage of the business expenditure effect. The airline knows that the business will pick up the full-fare ticket, and the business traveler will be able to take a companion along for free. The hotel knows that because the traveler's company will pay for the hotel room, cutting prices by a few dollars might not bring in extra business travelers, but giving the business traveler bonus frequent flyer miles that they can use for vacation trips will. The business expenditure effective has numerous applications in the hospitality and travel industry.

Many hotels use information about corporate per diem rates to determine rate structures and identify target markets that are willing to pay the price. For example, when the Mandarin Oriental chain entered the U.S. market with a hotel in San Francisco, a survey of potential corporate clients was conducted to learn their per diem rates. From this information, target markets were identified.

End-Benefit Effect. Customers are more price sensitive when the price of the product accounts for a large share of the total cost of the end benefit. For example, a Japanese couple paying $2,000 in air fare to travel to Australia will pay $150 a night for a luxury ocean-front hotel. The $150 is a small cost of the end benefit (their vacation). Many families driving to the Gold Coast from Sydney (a 500-mile trip) are looking for less expensive accommodations. These families are often on a limited budget and will prefer a less expensive motel a few blocks from the ocean.

When the Japanese couple goes to Dreamworld (a theme entertainment park), they will pay the $39 per person entrance fee without hesitation. The $78 admission fee is a small portion of the price of their vacation. However, the local family of four looking for weekend entertainment may view the $39 adult charge and $29 charge for children as high. In this case the $136 entry fee amounts to a large portion of their entertainment expenses for the month. To attract the local customer, Dreamworld offers yearly passes for just twice the single admission charge and second visit passes for $12, which allow the purchaser to enter any time during the next three months. Dreamworld knows that if it were to raise its prices by 20 percent, it would lose more local customers

12.7 Disney Dreamworld

than international travelers. Thus it is important for Dreamworld to know its customer mix. If 75 percent of Dreamworld's customers are local residents, Dreamworld must be cautious about its price increases. It is common for tourist attractions such as Dreamworld to provide special rates for local residents. For example, a water slide near Disney World in Orlando, Florida, offered a special rate to families who could produce a local driver's license.

Upscale hotels can use the end-benefit effect as a tool to convince potential customers to pay an additional amount for hotel rooms. A company holding a two-day sales meeting may spend $500 in air fare, pay $300 in salary per day, and spend $50 in materials and $50 in speakers' fees per participant. Thus, before room, food, and beverage costs, $1,200 is invested in each participant. A smart hotel salesperson may convince the meeting planner to upgrade by pointing out that the hotel costs are a small portion of the total costs. The sales presentation might be structured like this:

> And the difference between our luxury accommodations and the hotel accommodations you're considering is only $30 per night or $60 per participant, which is a small portion of your total cost per participant. Don't you think it's worth $60 to instill pride in your employees and show them that you care enough about them to put them in one of the best hotels in the city? Surely, the attitude difference this will create in the participants will play a significant role in the total success of the conference. Let's get the contracts drawn up for your sales meeting right now while we still have the space.

When working with price, the end-benefit price is an important concept to consider. The end-benefit price identifies price-sensitive markets and provides opportunities to overcome pricing objections when the product being sold is a small cost of the end benefit. To take full advantage of this effect, remember that many purchases have nonmonetary costs. For example, a mother planning the wedding of her daughter wants everything to be perfect and to avoid embarrassing moments. High emotional involvement often makes the buyer less price sensitive.

Total Expenditure Effect. The more someone spends on a product, the more sensitive he or she is to the product's price. For example, limited-service chains such as Hampton Inns, Red Roof Inns, and La Quinta have made a successful effort to appeal to salespersons. The travel expenses of a salesperson can be significant, especially for those who average two to three days a week away from home. A salesperson who saves just $20 a night can realize annual savings of more than $2,000. This savings adds to the profit of salespeople on straight commission. Companies that pay the expenses of their salespeople can save $2,000 times the number of salespeople that they employ. Thus a company with twelve salespeople can save $24,000.

The total expenditure effect is useful in selling lower-price products or products that offer cost savings to volume users. The hotel concepts mentioned earlier provide salespeople with the benefits that they seek in a hotel: clean comfortable rooms, security, free telephone calls, and a coffee shop nearby.

The total expenditure effect is a dominant decision-making force for thousands of travelers who are provided with a set figure per trip. Many truckers are given a predetermined amount of cash such as $500 for a trip. Expenditures over that level are not reimbursed. Not all motels desire the business of truckers, but those who do are highly cognizant of the fixed expenditure of their guests. They realize that ample parking for a sixteen- or eighteen-wheeler, a clean room with two beds, and a reasonable price will attract business.

Hotels that cater to upscale travelers frequently feature one king-size bed in a room because few people on unlimited or high-expense accounts wish to share a room. Quite the opposite is true of truckers or pipeline construction teams with fixed-expenditure travel budgets. A $40 room shared by two extends a fixed budget.

Aspen Skiing Company is an example of a company that takes the total expenditure effect into account when they make their pricing decision. They know that most of their customers are from out of state. They know these customers want well-maintained facilities and are willing to pay good money for them. Only 20 percent of their budget on a ski trip goes toward lift tickets (see Marketing Highlight 12-1).

Shared Cost Effect. Purchasers are less price sensitive when they are sharing the cost of the purchase with someone else, extending conferences with a weekend vacation component. Delegates to a conference that ends Friday may choose to spend the weekend at the resort or hotel if the hotel offers a special leisure package. This package is especially attractive because the airfare for the person attending the conference is usually tax deductible or paid by the company. The total cost of the vacation is reduced because the expenses were shared.

Sunk Investment Effect. Purchasers who have an investment in products that they are currently using are less likely to change for price reasons. For example, if IBM has held its last ten regional sales meetings at the Omni in Atlanta, the company will have invested much time working with the hotel's conference service staff. The staff will know exactly how IBM wants rooms set up, which menus the conference planners prefer, the arrival patterns of the guests, and so on. IBM will also have worked with the staff to avoid repetition of any mistakes made during previous conferences. IBM's meeting planners may have invested weeks of time working with Omni's staff. Because of this, they may be hesitant to change even if another hotel offers a lower price.

12.8 IBM

The sunk investment effect is one reason it can be difficult to get companies to change hotels. Once the company finds a hotel that performs well and meets its needs, price becomes less of an issue. On the other hand, a hotel that frequently turns over its convention service and sales staffs will require the corporate meeting planner to educate new staff members regularly. Here the meeting planner has no sunk investment; the planner will entertain other offers and make a decision based on price.

The concept of sunk investment combined with elasticity's of demand for various customer segments provides a powerful argument for maintaining high prices for corporate customers. Eric Orkin, a pioneer in pricing and yield management, argues that some hotel chains have erred

Marketing Highlight 12-1

Aspen Skiing Company Knows Out-of-State Visitors Are Less Price Sensitive

In the summer of 1997, Aspen Skiing Company announced a 5.3 percent price increase, raising the price of a day lift ticket to $59.[1] This placed Aspen as the most expensive U.S. ski area for the tenth consecutive year.

Maureen McDonald, spokeswoman for Aspen, said, "We are doing $8 million in mountain improvements. We really feel the experience is worth it. We have very uncrowded conditions, and we are going to stay that way." Many Aspen-bound skiers would not pay the full $59 price, as the majority of Aspen skiers are out-of-state destination skiers who purchase multiday discount packages. The price of a six-day lift ticket increased 2 percent, to $304, or $50.66 per day. The four-day ticket was $266, or $56.60 per day.

A special discount card for Coloradoans known as the Aspen Classic Pass could be purchased for $10 and would reduce lift-ticket prices to $19 for restricted dates. Discounts were not available for peak periods such as December 25 to 31.

Despite the availability of the Aspen Classic Pass, Colorado skiers accounted for only 7 percent of Aspen's customers in 1996, with 7,798 cards sold. Children's tickets for 1997 were priced at $9 early season and $19 to $29 for the rest of the ski season.

A ski industry consultant, Jerry Jones, said, "Aspen wants to be positioned as the highest-priced supplier of the ski experience" for image purposes but "Aspen is not a $59 product compared to Vail Resorts. Vail has more to offer and better overall skiing terrain."

Ski lift prices were $52 at Vail in 1996. Vail's CEO, Adam Aron, said that his company would not raise prices sky high. By 1997, Vail controlled multiple Colorado ski resorts within easy driving distance of one another: Vail, Breckenridge, Beaver Creek, and Keystone. This permitted Vail to offer a four-mountain lift ticket.

Jim Felton, spokesman for Vail, said, "The price of a lift ticket represents less than 20 percent of the cost of a destination ski vacation." Lodging, transportation, and food make up the majority of costs, and many of these are outside the direct control of a ski resort. Felton went on to say, "Pricing decisions this year are more complex than ever. We all have different competitive pressures and different market niches that must be considered."

[1]Penny Parker, "Aspen Still King of the Hill—for Price," *Denver Post,* July 9, 1997, pp. C1, C8.

in following the lead of car rental companies by offering large corporations special discounts at all hotels within their chain. Orkin contends that this practice provides the lowest rates to those most able to pay and that it inevitably leads to similar moves by competitors, thus removing any advantage. Adding to this negative strategy is the fact that it often spreads to midsize customers, thus decreasing revenue further.[15]

Price Quality Effect. Consumers tend to equate price with quality, especially when they lack any prior experience with the product. For example, a friend may recommend that you stay at the Grand Hotel on your trip to Houston. If you call to make the reservation and they offer you a $49 weekend rate, you may perceive this rate as too low for the class of hotel that you want and select another. The Grand Hotel may have met all your needs, but because of the low price, you assumed it would not.

A high price can also bring prestige to a product, because it limits availability. Restaurants where the average check is more than $100 per person for dinner would lose many of their present customers if they lowered their prices. In cases where price is perceived to relate to quality or where price creates prestige, a positive association between price and demand may exist with some market segments. For example, the Gosforth Park Hotel, an upscale hotel in Newcastle, England, found that occupancy increased as their rates increased.[16]

Competitors' Prices and Offers

Competitors' prices and their possible reactions to a company's own pricing moves are other external factors affecting pricing decisions. A meeting planner scheduling a meeting in Chicago will check the price and value of competitive hotels. Because of this, a hotel salesperson must learn the price, quality, and features of each competitor's offer. A hotel might do this in several ways: It can send out comparison shoppers to price and compare other competitors' products. It can review competitors' price lists and sample their products. The hotel can also ask buyers how they view the price and quality of each competitor's hotel or restaurant.

Once a company is aware of its competitors' prices and offers, it can use this information as a starting point for deciding its own pricing. For example, if a customer perceives that the Sheraton in Singapore is similar to the Hilton, the Sheraton must set its prices close to those of the Hilton or lose that customer. Additionally, the Sheraton would have to charge less than more luxurious hotels and more than those that are not as good. Sheraton uses price to position its offer relative to its competitors' offers.

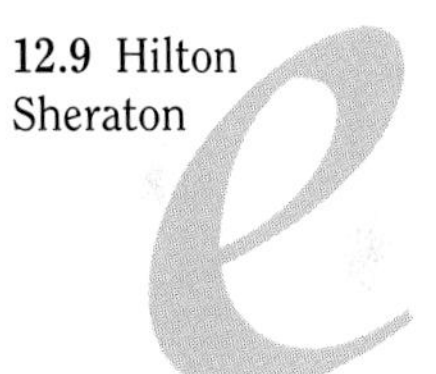
12.9 Hilton Sheraton

Other External Elements

When setting prices, the company must also consider other factors in the external environment. Economic factors such as inflation, boom or recession, and interest rates affect pricing decisions. For example, the recession of 2001–2002 forced many restaurants to reduce their prices. Most could not offer the same product at a lower price and survive. The restaurants created new menus with lower-cost items, items that could be sold at a lower price.

When reacting to environmental pressures created by the macroenvironment, a company must consider the impact its pricing policies will have on its microenvironment. For example, members of the distribution channel are often affected by price changes. In the fall of 1990, American Airlines offered its frequent flyers a $50 round-trip companion fare. United Airlines reacted by offering a $25 companion fare, followed by Northwest, which offered a buy-one-get-one-free fare. Travel agents found themselves reissuing hundreds of tickets, for no additional commissions, so that their clients could take advantage of these promotions. Some airline promotions resulted in travel agents rewriting tickets at a reduced fare, requiring that they do additional work, only to lose commissions. The travel agents grew irritated with the airlines over these promotions.[17]

All areas of the environment can affect pricing. Meeting new government regulations can cause costs to increase, or governments can streamline processes, reducing costs. If proenvironmental groups succeed in getting pesticides banned, food prices may increase. Marketers must know the laws concerning price and make sure that their pricing policies are legal (see Marketing Highlight 12-2). Marketers must also use environmental knowledge gained through marketing information systems in making pricing decisions.

General Pricing Approaches

The price the company charges will be somewhere between one that is too low to produce a profit and one that is too high to produce any demand. Product costs set a floor for the price; consumer perceptions of the product's value set the ceiling. The company must consider competitors' prices and other external and internal factors to find the best price between these two extremes.

Companies set prices by selecting a general pricing approach that includes one or more of these sets of factors. We look at the following approaches: the cost-based approach (cost-plus pricing, break-even analysis, and target profit pricing), the value-based approach (perceived-value pricing), and the competition-based approach (going rate).

Cost-Based Pricing

The simplest pricing method is cost-plus pricing, that is, adding a standard markup to the cost of the product. Food and beverage managers often use the cost-plus method to decide wine prices. For example, a bottle of wine that costs $14 may sell for $28, a 100 percent markup on cost. The gross profit is $14.

Cost as a percentage of selling price is another commonly used pricing technique in the restaurant industry. Some restaurant managers target a certain food cost and then price their menu items accordingly. For example, a manager wanting a 40 percent food cost will price the items two and a half times greater than their cost. The multiplicand is found by dividing the desired food cost percentage into 100. A manager desiring a 30 percent food cost would multiply the cost by 3.33. Managers using this type of pricing should realize that a restaurant is not 100 percent efficient. To make up for spoilage, shrinkage, and mistakes, managers will usually have to price 3 to 4 percentage points below their desired food cost. Thus a manager wanting a 40 percent food cost would need to price the menu at 36 percent to 37 percent. The adjustment figure varies depending on the volume and efficiency of the operation. In high-volume, limited-menu operations, it is lower.

For managers using this technique, it is advisable to use prime cost, the cost of labor and food, when determining menu prices. There is often a trade-off between labor and food costs; thus prime cost is a truer reflection of the cost of producing a menu item. For example, if a restaurant makes its own desserts, the cost of the ingredients is usually cheaper than that of buying a similar product from a bakery; however, there are no labor costs for the preparation of the purchased product. It is better to look at both labor and food costs to determine prices.

Does using standard markups to set prices make logical sense? Generally, no. Any pricing method that ignores current demand and competition is not likely to lead to the best price. Some restaurateurs use the same markup percentage despite the cost of the item. For example, using a 100 percent markup, a bottle of wine that costs $6 would sell for $12, and a bottle that costs $15 would sell for $30. In the first case, the gross profit is $6; in the second case it is $15. The costs of serving each bottle of wine are identical, except for the carrying costs. It would be smart to reduce the markup on the higher-priced bottles if doing so would sell more wine. Here it would make more sense to price the wine based on demand and optimum profitability instead of using a straight markup. If there is a demand for five bottles per night at $24, selling the wine at $24 that costs $15 will create more profit than two bottles at $30.

Most managers who use the cost as a percentage of selling price to price their menus use this technique to develop a target price. They adjust the individual prices for menu items based on factors such as what the market will bear, psychological pricing, and other techniques discussed in this chapter.

Markup pricing remains popular for many reasons. First, sellers are more certain about costs than about demand. Tying the price to cost simplifies pricing, and managers do not have to adjust as demand changes. Second, because many food and beverage operations tend to use this method, prices are similar, and price competition is minimized.

Break-Even Analysis and Target Profit Pricing

Another cost-oriented pricing approach is break-even pricing, in which the firm tries to determine the price at which it will break even. Some firms use a variation of break-even pricing called *target profit pricing*, which targets a certain return on investment.

Target profit pricing uses the concept of a break-even chart (Figure 12-5). For example, a buffet restaurant may want to make a profit of $200,000. Their break-even chart shows the total cost and total revenue at different levels of sales. Suppose that fixed costs are $300,000, and variable costs are $10 per meal. Variable costs are added to fixed costs to find total costs, which rise with volume. Total revenue starts at zero and rises with each unit sold. The slope of the total revenue reflects the price. If the restaurant sells 50,000 meals at a price of $20, for example, the company's revenue is $1 million.

At the $20 price, the company must sell at least 30,000 units to break even; that is, at this sales level, total revenues will equal total costs of $600,000. If the company wants a target profit of $200,000, it must sell at least 50,000 meals, or 137 meals a day. This level of sales will provide $1 million of revenue to cover costs of $800,000, plus $200,000 in target profits. On the other hand, if the company charges a higher price, say $25 per meal, it will need to sell only 33,334 meals, or 92 a day, to meet its target profit. The higher the price, the lower the company's break-even point. The selling price less the variable cost represents the gross profit or contribution that the sale makes toward offsetting fixed costs. The formula for the break-even (BE) point is

BE = fixed costs / contribution (selling price – variable cost)

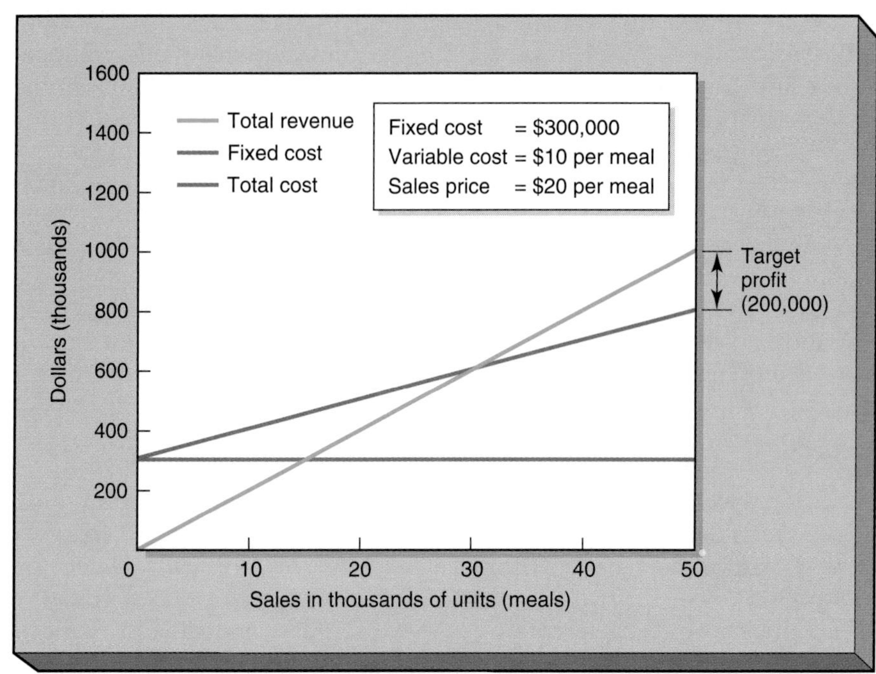

Figure 12-5
Break-even chart for determining target price.

In the previous example,

> BE = \$300,000 / \$10 (\$20 selling price – \$10 variable cost) = 30,000 meals

Hotels use the concept of contribution margin to set rates when demand drops. Hotels will set low rates, rationalizing that at least they are covering their variable costs. This can be effective if it creates additional demand. However, some hotels try to steal business during good times by cutting rates. Figure 12-6 is a spreadsheet that shows the increase in occupancy needed to make up for a reduction in rate. This chart illustrates the difficulty of recuperating from any substantial cut in prices in an inelastic market. At 70 percent occupancy, a hotel that lowers its rate from \$75 to \$60 (20%) will need to increase its occupancy to 95.5 percent to offset the decrease in price.[18]

Much depends on the relationship between price and demand. For example, suppose a company calculates that given its current fixed and variable costs, it must charge a price of \$30 for the product to earn its desired target profit. But marketing research shows that few consumers will pay more than \$25 for the product. In this case the company must trim its costs to lower the break-even point so that it can charge the lower price that consumers expect.

Value-Based Pricing

An increasing number of companies are basing their prices on the product's perceived value. **Value-based pricing** uses the buyers' perceptions of value, not the seller's cost, as the key to pricing. Value-based pricing means that the marketer cannot design a product and marketing program

The price of rate-cutting

Present occupancy	Reduction in present rate: 5%	10%	15%	20%	25%
	Occupancy required to make up for reduction				
76%	81.4%	87.7%	95.0%	103.6%	114.0%
74	79.3	85.4	92.5	100.9	111.0
72	77.1	83.1	90.0	98.2	108.0
70	75.0	80.8	87.5	95.5	105.0
68	72.9	78.5	85.0	92.7	102.0
66	70.7	76.2	82.5	90.0	99.0
64	68.6	73.8	80.0	87.3	96.0
62	66.4	71.5	77.5	84.5	93.0
60	64.3	69.2	75.0	81.8	90.0
58	62.1	66.9	72.5	79.1	87.0
56	60.0	64.6	70.0	76.4	84.0
54	57.9	62.3	67.5	73.6	81.0
52	55.7	60.0	65.0	70.9	78.0
50	53.6	57.7	62.5	68.2	75.0

(Based on cost of operating additional occupied rooms equal to 25% of present rate)

Figure 12-6
Price of rate-cutting. From *The Horwath Accountant*, 47, no. 7 (1967), p. 8.

and then set the price. Price is considered along with other marketing-mix variables before the marketing program is set. The company uses the nonprice variables in the marketing mix to build perceived value in the buyers' minds, setting price to match the perceived value.

Consider the various prices different restaurants charge for the same items. A consumer who wants a cup of coffee and a slice of apple pie may pay $2 at a drugstore counter, $3 at a family restaurant, $4 at a hotel coffee shop, $7 for hotel room service, and $8 at an elegant restaurant. Each succeeding restaurant can charge more because of the value added by each type of service.

Any company using perceived-value pricing must learn the value in the buyers' minds for different competitive offers. Sometimes researchers ask consumers how much they would pay for each benefit added to the offer. One method of identifying how much customers are willing to pay involves using a technique called trade-off analysis. Researchers ask buyers how much they would pay for a hotel room with and without certain amenities. This information provides an idea of which features add more value than they cost. If the seller charges more than the buyers' perceived value, its sales will suffer. Many companies overprice their products, resulting in poor sales. Other companies underprice. Underpriced products sell very well, but they produce less revenue than they would if the company raised its price to the perceived-value level.

Jack Welch, the former CEO of GE, stated, "The best way to hold your customers is to constantly figure out how to give them more for

Wendy's offers a number of products for under $1.00 to create a perception of value with their customers. Courtesy of Wendy's.

less."[19] More and more marketers have adopted value pricing strategies. They strive to offer just the right combination of quality and good service at a fair price. This can result in redesigning existing brands to provide more quality or offer the same amount of quality for a lower price. For example, Holiday Inn was developed for customers who just wanted a room without the restaurant facilities. They are able to offer express rooms at a lower price, creating value for this market.

Understanding the value a segment places on a product can help marketers allocate their supply among the different segments. A study of meeting planners provided evidence that meeting planners perceived a greater value in paying $200 for a room than $175. Apparently, planners, like many guests, associate quality with higher prices.[20]

The price of a hotel room may vary according to the type of customer. The hotel may have a rate for individual business guests, a group rate for groups of ten or more, and a convention rate for associations that want to hold large functions at the hotel. If a hotel has the objective of maintaining 60 percent occupancy at an average rate of $90, it will need to determine its mix of customers and the average rate per segment. For example, it might develop the following mix to achieve a $90 rate:

	Percent of Business	*Average Rate*
Business	30	$100
Corporate group	40	$90
Association	30	$80

To achieve its target rate of $90, the hotel would have to sell above the average rate in peak times to compensate for discounted prices during off-peak times. It is important to develop target rates and keep on track toward meeting these goals. If the hotel offers a group 100 rooms for three nights at a rate of $75, they will need to make up $4,500 [(100 rooms × 3 nights × $90 target rate) – (300 × $75 actual rate)] in revenue. They must either sell to other groups above the $90 target rate, sell more business rooms at the $100 rate, or increase the targeted occupancy rate and sell additional rooms.[21]

A successful guest price mix depends on careful study of the behavior profiles of major guest segments. For most hospitality companies, this begins with a separation of guests into leisure and business segments. Such segmentation of each category may then occur, providing greater information about these major guest categories. Undoubtedly, the most important distinguishing profile characteristics of these two major segments is their relative degree of price elasticity. In general, business travelers exhibit inelastic price behavior and leisure travelers an elastic price response.

Competition-Based Pricing

A strategy of **going-rate pricing** is the establishment of price based largely on those of competitors, with less attention paid to costs or demand. The firm might charge the same, more, or less than its major competitors. Some firms may charge a bit more or less, but they hold the amount of difference constant. For example, a limited-service hotel chain may charge $10 more than Motel 6 in markets where they compete. This form of pricing is quite popular. When elasticity is hard to measure, firms feel that the going price represents the collective wisdom of the industry concerning the price that will yield a fair return. They also feel that holding to the going price will avoid harmful price wars.

Pricing Strategies

New Product Pricing Strategies

Pricing strategies usually change as a product passes through its life cycle. The introductory stage is especially challenging. Several options exist for pricing new products: prestige pricing, market-skimming pricing, and market-penetration pricing.

Prestige Pricing

Hotels or restaurants seeking to position themselves as luxurious and elegant will enter the market with a high price that will support this position. Nightclubs may charge a cover charge to attract a certain type of clientele and create an image of exclusiveness. In each of these cases, lowering the price would reposition the business, resulting in a failure to attract the target market.

Market-Skimming Pricing

Price skimming is setting a high price when the market is price insensitive. Price skimming can make sense when lowering the price will create less revenue. For example, the owner of the only motel in a small town in

Louisiana can set high prices if there is more demand than rooms. Price skimming can be an effective short-term policy. However, one danger is that competition will notice the high prices that consumers are willing to pay and enter the market, creating more supply and eventually reducing prices. Price skimming is common in industries with high research and development costs, such as pharmaceutical companies and computer firms. It is seldom possible for an extended period of time in the hospitality industry due to the relative ease of entry by competitors.

Market-Penetration Pricing

Rather than setting a high initial price to skim off small but profitable market segments, other companies set a low initial price to penetrate the market quickly and deeply, attracting many buyers and winning a large market share. Theodore Zinck's, a cocktail lounge in downtown Dallas, opened with prices about 20 percent lower than the competition. Management had negotiated a low lease, giving Zinck's a competitive advantage. Competitors could not match Zinck's lower prices because of their higher overhead. The policy allowed Zinck's to attract many customers quickly.

Several conditions favor setting a low price: the market must be highly price sensitive so that a low price produces more market growth, there should be economies that reduce costs as sales volume increases, and the low price must help keep out competition.

Existing-Product Pricing Strategies

The foregoing strategies are used primarily when introducing a new product. However, they can also be useful with existing products. The strategies below are ones that can used with existing products.

Product-Bundle Pricing

Sellers who use product-bundle pricing combine several of their products and offer the bundle at a reduced price. For example, hotels sell specially priced weekend packages that include room, meals, and entertainment or offer commercial rates that include breakfast and a newspaper. Price bundling can promote the sales of products consumers might not otherwise buy, but the combined price must be low enough to convince them to buy the bundle. The items added to the core service must show more value to the customer than they cost to provide.

Product-bundle pricing is a strategy that has been well developed by cruise lines, tour wholesalers, and casinos. Cruise lines typically offer fly–cruise or fly–drive cruise packages in which the services of an auto rental company, airline, cruise line, and hotel are combined at a price well under the cost of purchasing each separately.

Price bundling has two major benefits to hospitality and travel organizations. First, customers have different maximum prices or reservation prices they will pay for a product. Thus, by packing products we can transfer the surplus reservation price on one component to another component of the package. For example, customer "A" may be willing to pay $60 for a hotel room near Disneyland and $120 for a three-day pass to

Disneyland. Customer "B" is willing to pay $80 for a hotel room and $95 for a three-day pass. If a hotel that wants to get $80 for its rooms is able to get discounted three-day passes to Disneyland and offer a package that includes a room for two for two nights and 2 three-day passes for $350, both customers will take advantage of the package. Even though the room price of $80 was above what the one customer wanted to pay, when the room and tickets are packaged together the components are below the reservation price. In this case the three-day pass was $25 below customer A's reservation price for the pass and the hotel price was $20 a night above what customer A wanted to pay. When they were packed together, the passes and the room were $10 less than customer A's reservation price for the package. Customers have different reservation prices; by bundling we can transfer surpluses from one component to another to expand the market.

12.10 Disneyland

A second benefit of price bundling is the price of the core product can be hidden to avoid price wars or the perception of having a low quality product. For example, a Las Vegas hotel that normally has an average rate above $100, may sell rooms to airlines for $45 to help fill the hotel. The airline will bundle the hotel with a round trip air ticket. The airline's package includes two nights in the hotel and airfare from Los Angeles for $249. This creates a much better perception for the hotel than if it ran an advertisement pushing $45 room rates. The $45 rates will give a message to some that the hotel is desperate for business, to others who do not know the hotel it will give a perception of a hotel of the $45 quality level and guests who had paid $109 for a room may ask for a refund. By selling the rooms to an airline and creating a bundled product, the hotel avoided the image problems that can come with low rates. Hotels can also create their own bundles. For example, The Royal Palms Hotel and Casitas in Phoenix offers a "Royal Romance Package." The package includes champagne, chocolate-covered strawberries, a rose-petal

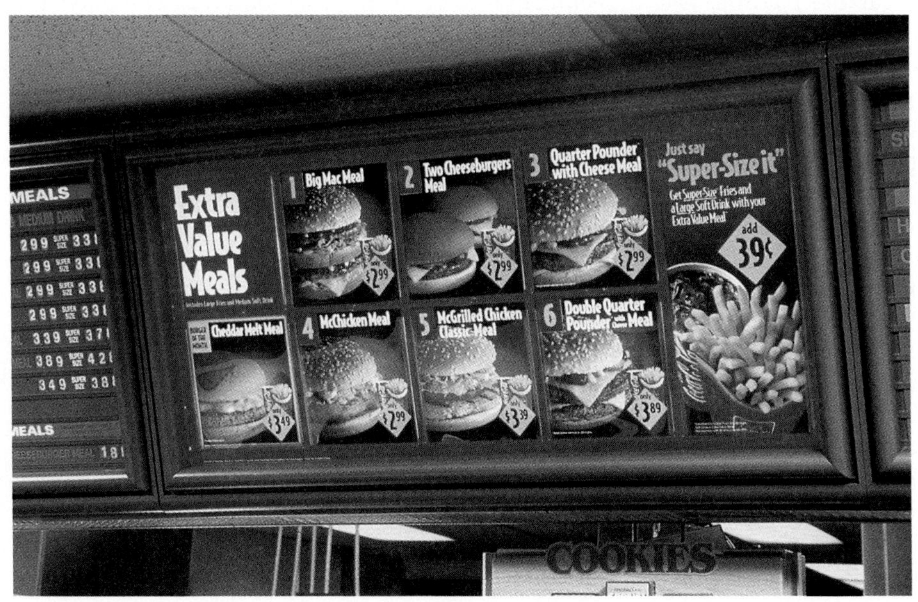

McDonald's bundles its sandwiches with a drink and french fries. This makes it easier and faster for guests to order and promotes the sales of french fries.

Marketing Highlight 12-2

Segmented Pricing: The Right Product to the Right Customer at the Right Time for the Right Price

Many companies would love to raise prices across the board—but fear losing business. When an opera company located in the nation's capital was considering increasing ticket prices after a difficult season, Ticket Services Manager Jimmy Legarreta decided there had to be a better way. He found one after carefully reviewing opera economics. Legarreta knew—and his computer system confirmed—that the company routinely turned away people for Friday and Saturday night performances, particularly for prime seats. Meanwhile, midweek tickets went begging.

Legarreta also knew that not all seats were equal, even in the sought-after orchestra section. So the ticket manager and his staff sat in every one of the opera house's 2,200 seats and gave each a value according to the view and the acoustics. With his revenue goal in mind, Legarreta played with ticket prices until he arrived at nine levels, up from five. In the end, the opera raised prices for its most coveted seats by as much as 50 percent but also dropped the prices of some 600 seats. The gamble paid off in a 9 percent revenue increase during the next season.

Legarreta didn't have a name for it, but he was practicing "segmented pricing," an approach that also has many other labels. Airlines, hotels, and restaurants call it **yield management** and practice it religiously. Robert Cross, a longtime consultant to the airlines, calls it "revenue management." In a book by that name, Cross argues that all companies should apply revenue-management concepts, which emphasize an aggressive micromarket approach to maximizing sales. "Revenue management," Cross writes, "assures that companies will sell the right product to the right consumer at the right time for the right price."

Segmented pricing and yield management aren't really new ideas. For instance, Marriott Corporation used seat-of-the-pants yield-management approaches long before it installed its current sophisticated system. Back when J. W "Bill" Marriott was a young man working at the family's first hotel, the Twin Bridges in Washington, DC, he sold rooms from a drive-up window. As Bill tells it, the hotel charged a flat rate for a single occupant, with an extra charge for each additional person staying in the room. When room availability got tight on some nights, Bill would lean out the drive-up window and assess the cars waiting in line. If some of the cars were filled with passengers, Bill would turn away vehicles with just a single passenger to sell his last rooms to those farther back in line who would be paying for multiple occupants. He might have accomplished the same result by charging a higher rate at peak times, regardless of the number of room occupants.

Cross's underlying premise: No two customers value a product or service exactly the same way. Furthermore, the perceived value of a product results from many variables that change over time. Some of Cross's clients use sophisticated yield-management simulation models and high-powered computer systems to predict sales at different price levels, but the technique doesn't have to be rocket science. If you understand your customers' motivation for buying and you keep careful sales records, it's possible to adjust prices to remedy supply-and-demand imbalances. Legarreta, for example, ended his midweek slump by making opera affordable for more people, yet he accurately predicted that the in-crowd would pay higher prices for the best weekend seats.

Probably the simplest form of segmented pricing is off-peak pricing, common in the entertainment and travel industries. Marc Epstein, owner of the Milk Street Café in Boston, discovered that technique more than ten years ago, when he noticed he had lines out the door at noon but a near-empty restaurant around his 3:00 P.M. closing time. After some experimentation, Epstein settled on a 20 percent discount for the hours just before noon and after

2:00 P.M.—and he's pleased with the results. "If we didn't offer this, our overall revenue would be less," he argues. Epstein did not feel he could simultaneously raise prices during the lunch rush; instead, he has expanded the corporate-catering side of his business, where he can charge more per sandwich because "the perceived value of a catered lunch is higher."

Many other companies could conceivably segment their prices to increase revenues and profits. Cross cites examples ranging from a one chair barbershop, to an accounting firm, to a health center. But there are risks. When you establish a range of prices, customers who pay the higher ones may feel cheated. "It can't be a secret that you're charging different prices for the same service," Cross advises. "Customers must know, so they can choose when to use a service. "

The moral of the story? You can never know too much about your customers and the different values they assign to your product or service. With that customer knowledge comes the power to make the best pricing decisions.

Sources: Portions adapted with permission from Susan Greco, "Are Your Prices Right?" *Inc.* (January 1997): 88–89. Copyright 1997 by Goldhirsh Group, Inc., 38 Commercial Wharf, Boston, MA 02110. Other information from Robert G. Cross, *Revenue Management: Hard-Core Tactics for Market Domination* (New York: Broadway Books, 1998); and William J. Quain, Michael Sansbury, and Dennis Quinn, "Revenue Enhancement, Part 3: Picking Low-Hanging Fruit—A Simple Approach to Yield Management," *Cornell Hotel and Restaurant Administration Quarterly* (April 1999): 76–83. Also see Plumrao Desiraju and Steven M. Shugan, "Strategic Service Pricing and Yield Management," *Journal of Marketing* (January 1999): 44–56.

Courtesy of Galveston Island Convention and Visitor's Bureau

turndown, dinner for two, and a room for two nights for $799. The rack rate is above $500, but rather than cut the rate to below $300, the resort bundled a number of different products that have value to a couple wanting to get way for a few days.[22]

Price-Adjustment Strategies

Companies usually adjust their basic prices to account for various customer differences and changing situations. We look at the following adjustment strategies: discount pricing and allowances, discriminatory pricing, and yield management.

Volume Discounts. Most hotels have special rates to attract customers who are likely to purchase a large quantity of hotel rooms, either for a single period or throughout the year. Hotels usually offer special prices or provide free goods for association and corporate meeting planners. As an example, suppose that a convention held by an industry association is attended by people who pay their own room charges. The association may prefer to receive a free room-night for every 20 room-nights booked, rather than a room rate that is $5 lower. They can use the free nights for their staff and invited speakers, reducing the association's total costs. Besides group rates, hotels offer corporate rates to companies that will guarantee their use of the hotel for an agreed-upon number of room-nights each year.

Discounts Based on Time of Purchase. A seasonal discount is a price reduction to buyers who purchase services out of season, when the demand is lower. Seasonal discounts allow the hotel to keep demand steady during the year. Hotels, motels, and airlines offer seasonal discounts during selling periods that are traditionally slower. Airlines often offer off-peak prices, based on the time of day or the day of the week that the passenger flies. International flights adjust the price according to seasonal demand. A flight from Auckland to Sydney may cost $699 round trip during the Christmas season, whereas in July the same flight may cost $329. Restaurants offer early bird specials to attract customers before their normal rush. Unfortunately, the various discount rates offered by a company sometimes clash to negate the desired positive effects. Restaurants commonly offer senior-citizen discounts but would also like to induce this market segment to visit the restaurant early in the evening before the rush begins. Senior citizens often feel no reason to accept the early bird special because they will qualify for a discount at peak hours.

Discriminatory Pricing. The term **discriminatory pricing** often invokes mental images of discrimination on the basis of race, religion, gender, or age. Sex-based price discrimination has historically served as a promotional tactic in nightclubs and bars that offer a ladies night or ladies-only coupon by which prices of admission or for drinks are heavily discounted. In California, a suit was filed against an establishment that offered ladies-only discounts. The court ruled against the owner of the establishment under the Civil Rights Act.[23] Discriminatory pricing refers to segmentation of the market and pricing differences based on price elasticity characteristics of these segments. Price discrimination as used in this chapter is legal and is viewed by many as highly beneficial to the consumer.

Companies often adjust basic prices to allow for differences in customers, products, and locations. In discriminatory pricing, the company sells a product or service at two or more prices, although the difference in price is not based on differences in cost.

Suppose, for example, that a steak dinner has a menu price of $20, and the demand is 100 dinners at this price. If the restaurant lowers the price to $14, demand increases to 200 dinners. If the variable costs for preparing and serving the dinner are $8, the gross profit in each case will be $1,200. However, if we assume that of the 200 persons willing to pay $14 for the steak, 100 were part of the group willing to pay $20, $600 of potential income is lost from these 100 customers.

Price discrimination works to maximize the amount that each customer pays. In the case illustrated, we would charge $20 to customers willing to pay $20. Those who are only willing to pay $14 would be charged $14. How do we do this? We can't ask the customer, "Would you like to pay $20 or would you like to pay $14?" Obviously, everyone would say $14. Instead, we give different prices to different segments, offering the highest price to those segments that are less price sensitive. For example, our standard price is $20 for the dinner. We offer an early bird special of $14 to diners arriving before 6:00 P.M. A person who works until five o'clock probably is unwilling to rush home and rush to the restaurant to take advantage of the discount. This customer prefers to relax at home after work and arrive at the restaurant at 8:00 P.M. However, retired persons who may be more price sensitive, but less time sensitive, would be attracted by this special. The restaurant could also choose to send a coupon in a direct-mail coupon package to prospective customers. The price-sensitive customers would keep the coupon and use it the next time that they went out to eat. Other people who receive the coupon would throw it away. These customers do not want to be bothered with filing the coupon and then looking for it when they want to go out to eat. To these customers the $6 savings is not worth the hassle of using the coupon. Price discrimination discriminates in favor of the price-sensitive customer.

The supersaver fares on airlines usually require an advance purchase and a stay-over on a Saturday night. The weekend stay eliminates most business travelers, whereas the advance purchase eliminates family emergencies and business trips made on short notice. Airlines know that business travelers and those traveling for emergencies are less price sensitive; that is, they exhibit inelastic price behavior. Airlines offer low fares with the leisure traveler in mind. The leisure traveler uses discretionary income to pay for travel and as a result is more price sensitive than the business traveler. A reduction in price often results in additional demand from the leisure segment.

Table 12-1 shows the prices available on a typical flight. Notice that coach seats range from $629 to $129 for a senior citizen who has purchased tickets in advance through a multiple-coupon book. The lower fares are aimed at the price-sensitive leisure traveler. Like the airlines, many hotels discriminate between the leisure and business segments. Hotels in central business districts that cater to business travelers suffer low occupancy on weekends. Many of these hotels have developed lower-priced weekend packages to entice the leisure traveler.

Table 12-1
Examples of Airfare Categories for a Flight from Detroit to Los Angeles

First class: 32 seats, 36 fares

Examples of first-class fares:
$944, normal first-class fare
$849, normal fare with 10% senior-citizen discount
$629, free upgrade from full coach fare for Worldperks Gold member
$305 or $239, free upgrade on 14-day advance purchase excursion fare for Worldperks Gold member; limited number of seats at each fare
Free, Worldperks frequent-flier award ticket

Coach class: 256 seats, 22 fares

Examples of coach fares:
$629, normal fare
$566, normal fare with 10% senior-citizen discount
$466 or $238, one-way military fare; limited number of seats at each fare
$309, bereavement fare
$239, excursion fare with 14-day advance purchase
$189, visit USA fare, good for foreign travelers
$179, excursion fare (sale currently in effect) with seven-day advance purchase
$129, senior-citizen travel based on coupon booklet

Special fares

Convention fares, usually 5% off lowest excursion fare or 40% off normal coach fares
Group fares, specially negotiated for group travel; generally close to lowest excursion fare
Bulk fares, special deals for tour operators
Tour fares, for travelers on a tour package, such as a cruise
Corporate fares, negotiated with certain corporations; can be from 10 to 35% off the full coach or first-class fare

Source: Reprinted with permission of *The Detroit News.*

Low variable costs combined with fluctuations in demand make price discrimination a useful tool for smoothing demand and bringing additional revenue and profits to most businesses. This form of pricing uses lower prices to attract additional customers, without lowering the price for everyone.

Major sectors of the hospitality industry, such as airlines, hotels, cruise lines, and railroads, are faced with enormous fixed costs. Companies in these sectors are faced with the need to fill seats or beds. Richard Hanks, vice president of revenue management for the Marriott Corporation, believes that "our greatest opportunity cost is an empty room." Marriott has designed a pricing system based on discriminatory pricing to fill rooms and maximize revenue opportunities. Marriott refers to the concept as fencing.[24] The purpose behind fencing is to keep price-inelastic customers from using rates designed for price-elastic segments.

Fencing at Marriott is accomplished by establishing restrictions that allow customers to self-select price discriminatory rates that are best for them. Such fences include advance reservations and nonrefundable advance purchases. These policies permit price-sensitive customers to enjoy lower rates and inelastic segments to pay full fare without restrictions.

Richard Hanks strongly defends this strategy:

> The fact of the matter is, if it weren't for incremental leisure guests, business guests would have to pay a higher price for their rooms in order for the hotel to meet financial obligations. I'd like to offer all our guests a $79 room, but in order to cover the costs of the hotel and ensure returns to our investors, we must differentiate. The bottom line is this: Either we accommodate both guests, one paying $79 and one paying $125, or we ask the business guests to pay $145. These are the choices.[25]

To price discriminate successfully, the following criteria must be met:[26]

1. Different groups of consumers must have different responses to price; that is, they must value the service differently.
2. The different segments must be identifiable and a mechanism must exist to price them differently.
3. There should be no opportunity for persons in one segment who have paid a lower price to sell their purchases to other segments.
4. The segment should be large enough to make the exercise worthwhile.
5. The cost of running the price discrimination strategy should not exceed the incremental revenues obtained. This is partly a function of criterion 4.
6. The customers should not become confused by the use of different prices.

Yield Management. One application of discriminatory pricing is yield management. A yield management system is used to maximize a hotel's yield or contribution margin. This is done by the rates that a hotel will charge and the number of rooms available for each rate based on projected occupancies for a given period. These systems help hotels achieve the maximum contribution margin based on the demand for hotel rooms. The concept behind yield management is to manage revenue and inventory effectively by pricing differences based on the elasticity of demand for selected customer segments.

An effective yield management system establishes fences to prohibit customers from one segment receiving prices intended for another. For example, business travelers on an expense account exhibit somewhat inelastic price behavior. Leisure travelers are commonly more price sensitive (price elastic). A typical fencing strategy for leisure travelers would be to require a Friday and Saturday night stay with a thirty-day advance reservation. This effectively fences out business travelers, who then pay higher rates to stay during a business week with little or no advance reservations.

Yield management involves the development and use of different rate classes based on the projected demand for the service. These rates are used to maximize yield. The formula for yield is

$$\frac{\text{room-nights sold}}{\text{room-nights available}} \times \frac{\text{actual average room rate}}{\text{room rate potential}} = \text{yield}$$

A hotel with sufficient history can project occupancy based on current booking patterns. If low occupancy is projected, the hotel will keep lower rate classes open to increase occupancy. The lower rates will typically use price discrimination techniques that favor the leisure traveler. Sheraton, for example, has twenty-one-day advance supersaver rates. The idea is to create extra demand with low rates attracting guests that the hotel would not have received otherwise. If the projected occupancy is high, the lower rates will be closed, and only the higher rate classes will be accepted. Today, several computerized systems are available that automatically project occupancy levels for a given date and suggest pricing levels for each day. It is common for a yield management system to increase revenues by at least 5 percent. Reservations for Hyatt's Regency Club concierge floors climbed 20 percent after Hyatt implemented yield management. One Hilton hotel increased its average transient rate by $7.50 with no reduction in occupancy the first month after installing a yield management system.[27]

Yield management systems must be based on sound marketing. They should be developed with the long-term value of the customer in mind. One early yield management system cut off reservations from travel agents when projected occupancy for a given date was high. This was done to eliminate travel agency commissions when the hotel could sell the rooms. This system saves money in the short term by saving travel agency commissions. However, in the long term the hotel could lose a significant portion of its travel agency business. Think of the person who wants to stay at the Regal Hotel in Orlando and fly to Orlando on Delta. The travel agent informs the client that the airline is confirmed, but no rooms are available at the Regal, so a reservation was made at the Gator Hotel. The client calls the Regal only to find that rooms are available. The client now thinks the travel agent is pushing the Gator Hotel and gets upset with the travel agent. The travel agent becomes upset with the Regal and refuses to book future business with them. The Regal gains short-run extra revenue but loses the travel agent's business in the long term. Yield management programs should focus on long-term profitability, not just the maximization of one day's revenue.

With some yield management systems, customers staying a longer period can be charged more than those staying only a few nights. Normally, one might expect a concession for longer stays. Sometimes the longer stay may take the guest into a period of high occupancy. These yield management systems average the occupancy over the guest's stay. For example, based on the occupancy levels in the following table, a guest checking in May 8 and checking out May 10 would be quoted a $65 rate as the lowest available rate. A guest checking in May 8 and checking out May 12 would be quoted $85 as the lowest available rate, because the hotel can sell rooms for May 10 and 11 at a minimum of $105 a night. Under this system the staff must be well trained to explain rate differences to the guest.

Projected Occupancy

May 8	60%	May 10	85%
May 9	60%	May 11	90%

Yield management systems can be useful in managing the number of rooms available for transient demand. Most hotels have a base of transient demand composed of individual guests who pay a high rate. Some of these transient guests are business persons who may stay in the hotel several times during the year. Groups make their reservations well in advance of the transients; thus a salesperson sometimes wants to take the sure business. When group business displaces transient business, the average rate drops, and some displaced transient guests may never return, deciding to stay at an alternative hotel. Yield management systems help eliminate the problem of displaced transient guests by projecting the number of transient rooms that will be used on any given date.

If used properly, yield management systems can provide extra revenue. A good yield management system benefits both the hospitality company and the guest. It opens low-rated rooms for the leisure traveler during times of low occupancy and saves rooms during periods of peak demand for the business traveler willing to pay full rates. The company gains, because yield management focuses on maximizing revenue, not cutting costs.

A yield management system requires the availability of good data. This has forced many hospitality companies to go back to the basics and develop sound information-retrieval systems for internal data, such as booking patterns, and to develop and use better forecasting methods. The end result is that without even using yield management, the company is in a far better position to make intelligent management decisions.

An effective yield management system depends on several variables.[28] These are the ability to segment markets, perishable inventory, ability to sell product in advance, fluctuating demand, low marginal sales costs, high marginal production costs (can easily add another room), booking pattern data, information on demand pattern by market segment, an overbooking policy, knowledge of effect of price changes, a good information system for internal and external data, and ability to fence customer segments.

Use of yield management within the hospitality industry is expanding to new sectors. The Dalmahoy Golf and Country Club Resort near Edinburgh, Scotland, implemented a yield management program for its golf-course operation. This tied the costs of an annual membership to the time and day that the purchaser used the golf course.[29]

12.11 Dalmahoy Golf and Country Club Resort

Regarding the ethics of yield management, many industry observers and consumer advocates have voiced concern. Steve Hall, executive director of the International Institute for Quality and Service in Tourism, has responded to these concerns.[30] "Revenue management is important, it is honorable, it is ethical, and it is fair."

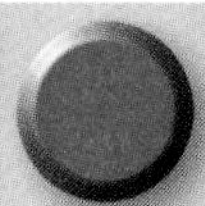

Marketing Highlight 12-3

Price Fixing

Federal legislation on price fixing states that sellers must set prices without talking to competitors. Otherwise, price collusion is suspected. Price fixing is illegal per se; that is, the government does not accept any excuses for price fixing. Even a simple conversation between competitors can have serious consequences.

During the 1980s, American Airlines and Braniff were immersed in a price war in the Texas market. Each carrier undercut the other until both were offering absurdly low fares, and each was losing money on many flights. In the heat of the battle, American's CEO, Robert Crandall, called the president of Braniff and said, "Raise your fares 20%. I'll raise mine the next morning." Fortunately for Crandall, the Braniff president warned him off, saying, "We can't talk about pricing!" As it turns out, the phone conversation had been recorded, and the U.S. Justice Department began action against Crandall and American for price fixing. The charges were eventually dropped. The courts ruled that because Braniff had rejected Crandall's proposal, no actual collusion had occurred, and that a proposal to fix prices was not an actual violation of the law.

This case and others like it have made most executives very reluctant to discuss prices in any way with competitors. Even during informal meetings, such as receptions during association meetings, managers should be advised not to discuss prices. In obtaining information on competitors' pricing, they rely only on openly published materials, such as trade association surveys and competitors' brochures.

Sources: For more on public policy and pricing, see Louis W. Stern and Thomas L. Eovaldi, *Legal Aspects of Marketing Strategy* (Upper Saddle River, NJ: Prentice Hall, 1984), Chapter 5; Thomas T. Nagle, *The Strategy and Tactics of Pricing* (Upper Saddle River, NJ: Prentice Hall, 1987), pp. 321–337; and Robert J. Posch, *The Complete Guide to Marketing and the Law* (Upper Saddle River, NJ: Prentice Hall, 1988), Chapter 28.

Although yield management may be ethical, it may not be viewed as fair by the guest. A study of perceived fairness of yield management demonstrated that "many common yield management practices used in the hotel industry were viewed as highly unacceptable by survey respondents."[31]

Unacceptable practices

1. Offering insufficient benefits in exchange for restrictions
2. Imposing too severe a restriction on discounts
3. Not informing customers of changes in requirements to receive price discounts

Acceptable practices

1. Availability of information concerning pricing options
2. A substantial discount offered for cancellation restrictions
3. Reasonable restrictions for a discounted rate
4. Different prices for products perceived by the customer as different

Last-Minute Pricing

The ongoing fear of "product spoilage" from unsold inventory creates a market for last-minute inventory selling. The use of revenue management helps considerably to reduce this problem, but many members of the hospitality industry such as small hotels do not use yield management systems.

Private companies known as consolidators or travel consolidators acquire excess inventory from diverse members of the hospitality industry, create consumer packages, and sell them at discounts to the public. Participating suppliers such as bed and breakfasts and guest ranches often sell their available inventory at discounts of 50 percent or more.

Airports in Germany contain booths in which travelers may purchase these discounted travel packages. The product assortment varies according to availability at various destinations, but bargain rate travel packages are available for flexible travelers.

The Colorado Hotel and Lodging Association provide last-minute reservations at below-market rates for its 540 members. Travelers make reservations without a service charge by calling 1-800-ENJOY-CO.

12.12 Colorado Hotel and Lodging Association

Although last-minute pricing provides an outlet for unsold inventory, it is not a substitute for effective marketing and a well-devised pricing strategy.

Psychological Pricing

Psychological pricing considers the psychology of prices, not simply the economics. Earlier in the chapter, we discussed the relationship between price and quality. Prestige can be created by selling products and services at a high price.

Another aspect of psychological pricing is reference prices; these are prices that buyers carry in their minds and refer to when they look at a given product. A buyer's reference price might be formed by noting current prices, remembering past prices, or assessing the buying situation. Popular products often have reference prices. For a given type of restaurant, most consumers have a preconceived idea about the price or price range of certain items, such as a cup of coffee, a strip steak, or a hamburger. For example, a pizza chain may advertise its medium pizza for a price that they know is $2 less than the competition to establish a reference price for pizza eaters. But their price for beverages and extra items will be the same as that of the competition. The reference item creates the perception of value; consequently, little would be gained by cutting the price of the other items.

Customers tend to simplify price information by ignoring end figures. For instance, there is greater perceived distance between $0.69 and $0.71 than there is between $0.67 and $0.69. Consumers also tend to round figures. One restaurant study found that consumers round prices ranging from $0.86 to $1.39 to a dollar, from $1.40 to $1.79 to a dollar and a half, and from $1.80 to $2.49 to two dollars. If this is the case, there may be little change in demand caused by a price increase of $0.30 from $1.45 to $1.75, but there may be a significant decrease in demand between $1.75 and $2.05. [32]

The length of the field is another consideration. The jump from \$0.99 to \$1 or the jump from \$9.99 to \$10 can be perceived as a significant increase, although it is only \$0.01. Taco Bell's value prices were all under \$1, and therefore only two digits. Some psychologists argue that each digit has symbolic and visual qualities that should be considered in pricing. For example, because the number 8 is round, it creates a soothing effect, whereas 7 is angular, creating a jarring effect.[33]

Promotional Pricing

When companies use promotional pricing, they temporarily price their products below list price and sometimes even below cost. Promotional pricing takes several forms. Fast-food restaurants will price a few products as loss leaders to attract customers to the store in the hope that they will buy other items at normal markups. Donut shops may offer coffee for 25 cents, knowing that a customer will usually buy at least one donut. A Jack-in-the-Box offers three hamburgers for a dollar, knowing that they will sell French fries and a soft drink with each order. During slow periods, hotels may offer a special promotional rate to increase business. Rather than just discount prices, well-managed hotels will create special events: a Valentine's weekend special including a room, champagne upon arrival, a dinner for two, and breakfast in the room; or a theater package including a room, tickets to a play, dinner for two, and breakfast for two. These promotions give the guest a reason to come; the bundle of products adds value for the customer. The promotion creates a positive image, whereas straight price discounting can create a negative image.

The gaming industry is particularly aware of the importance of product bundling and promotional pricing. Bruce Rowe, director of gaming information technology development at Promus Companies, the parent of Harrah's, stated, "We are in the adult entertainment business; our main product offering is gambling and there are many components that support it, such as hotels, entertainment facilities, and restaurants." Harrah's views hotel rooms as a means to entice and enable customers to gamble. "All patrons are welcome to stay in the hotel," said Rowe, "but to maximize revenue, casinos must ensure that rooms are readily available for the most profitable gaming customers."[34] Hotel pricing at Harrah's reflects the fact that the company's main product offering is gaming, and a hotel room is only a supporting product for gaming.

Value Pricing

The term *value pricing* is confusing. It could be argued that anytime a product/service is purchased, at any price, the buyer must have perceived value in that product. Value pricing has become synonymous with the term *every day low prices* (EDLP). It has been used as a marketing strategy by some members of the hospitality industry, such as Taco Bell and Southwest Airlines.

"Value pricing can be extremely risky. Properly conceived and executed, it can earn positive results." It can also be disastrous.[35] In its simplest form, value pricing means offering a price below competitors on a permanent basis. This is different from promotional pricing, in which price may be temporarily lowered during a special promotion.

Value pricing is risky if a company does not have the ability to cut costs significantly. It is usually most appropriate for companies able to increase long-run market share through low prices (Taco Bell) or niche players with a lower-cost operating basis who use price to differentiate their product (Southwest Airlines). A study of value pricing in retail stores showed that "retailers can be profitable charging low prices but only when they have low costs."[36]

Prior to initiating a strategy of value pricing, managers must ask themselves:

- What will happen if this starts a price war?
- Can our company significantly lower costs or increase productivity to compensate for lower prices?
- What is the price elasticity of our products?
- Can we gain significant market share or ensure a strong market niche position with this strategy?
- Can we reverse this strategy if it doesn't work, or will we create price levels that can't be sustained and can't easily be raised?

Price Sensitivity Measurement

Value pricing has sometimes failed because in reality it was simply low pricing and became a cost-based strategy without considering the consumer's perception of value.[37] A technique known as price sensitivity measurement (PSM) helps to establish a balance of price with product or service value based on consumer's perceptions of that value. Value pricing based on PSM is more likely to be successful than simply picking prices because they are low and undercut the competition.

PSM utilizes a target consumer survey with four questions from which the aggregate results are graphed to give an idea of consumer price sensitivity. The four questions are:

At what price on the scale do you consider

1. The product or service to be cheap?
2. The product or service to be expensive?
3. The product or service to be too expensive, so expensive that you will not consider buying it?
4. The product or service to be too cheap, so cheap that you would question the quality?

Taco Bell used PSM to establish prices in its successful value pricing strategy. Instead of using the conventional approach to pricing of first developing a new food item and then determining what the price should be, Taco Bell first determined what consumers were willing to pay for a specific type of item and then determined what the company needed to do to develop a product in that price range. If this price was too low to deliver a profit, it was dropped from further consideration.[38]

Other Pricing Considerations

Price Spread Effect

The restaurant industry has historically employed a rule of thumb that the highest-price entree should be no more than 2.5 times as expensive as the lowest-price entree. The rationale is that if the price span is too great, customers will purchase predominantly the low-price items, which probably carry the lowest margins. A study at Cornell University in the Terrace Restaurant tended to confirm that this rule of thumb is indeed correct.

Price Points

The concept of price points is well known and used throughout the retail industry. Some restaurant operators, particularly chain operations with sit-down menus, also employ the concept. Price points are important to the hospitality industry.

Retailers and restaurateurs cannot offer the customer all possible product offerings. A retailer cannot maintain sufficient inventory to offer shoes at prices varying by only \$1 between \$29.95 and \$32.95. Instead of offering selections at \$29.95, \$30.95, \$31.95, and \$32.95, a retailer will select one price point, such as \$32.95, and no others in that range. The idea behind this is to simplify inventory and to force consumers who wanted a pair of shoes at \$29.95 to pay \$32.95. It is felt that the consumer is actually willing to pay \$32.95 if that is the only price point available within a certain price range.

A restaurant operator must make similar price-point decisions. A steak house cannot offer \$1 price points between \$11.95 and \$21.95 for a steak. Instead, the manager must select cuts and price points that will satisfy customers and maximize revenue. There is no reason to offer an \$11.95 price-point cut if customers are willing to pay \$12.95.

12.13 J.C. Penney
Ponderosa Steak House

Price points vary by retailer and by restaurant. J.C. Penney and Ponderosa Steak Houses both have price points that they feel are psychologically best suited for their customers. Saks of Fifth Avenue and Ruth's Chris Steak House have different price points for their customers.

PRICE CHANGES

Initiating Price Changes

After developing their price structures and strategies, companies may face occasions when they want to cut or raise prices.

Initiating Price Cuts

Several situations may lead a company to cut prices. One is excess capacity. Unable to increase business through promotional efforts, product improvement, or other measures, a hotel may resort to price cutting. In the late 1970s, many companies dropped follow-the-leader pricing, that is, charging about the same price as their leading competitor and aggressively cut prices to boost sales. As the airline, hotel, rental car, and restaurant industries have learned in recent years, cutting prices in an industry loaded with excess capacity generally leads to price wars as competitors try to regain market share.

Companies may also cut prices in a drive to dominate the market or increase market share through lower costs. Either the company starts with lower costs than its competitors, or it cuts prices in the hope of gaining market share through larger volume. In January 1991, Burger King launched a promotion to cut the price of its Burger Buddies, two 1-ounce hamburgers, from 89 cents to 29 cents. The fast-food restaurant hoped that the price promotion would increase store traffic. They also made sure that they would not lose money on the promotion by requiring customers to buy French fries and a soft drink to get the Burger Buddies at the 29-cent price. Taco Bell started the pricing trend several years earlier when it slashed prices on its basic products to 59 cents. McDonald's entered the price war with 59-cent hamburgers, French fries, and soft drinks.

In mid-1991, Taco Bell sought to become the value leader in the fast-food industry by introducing a line of snack items for 39 cents. The new menu items were rolled out after test marketing in Los Angeles, Dallas/Fort Worth, Oklahoma City, and Youngstown, Ohio. The new items lowered check averages, but required the same amount of labor to make as the larger items. Taco Bell claimed that the products overcame these disadvantages by expanding their customer base.[39]

Initiating Price Increases

On the other hand, many companies have had to raise prices in recent years. They do this knowing that price increases may be resented by customers, dealers, and their own sales force. However, a successful price increase can greatly increase profits. For example, if the company's profit margin is 3 percent of sales, a 1 percent price increase will increase profits by 33 percent if sales volume is unaffected.

A major factor in price increases is cost inflation. Increased costs squeeze profit margins and lead companies to regular rounds of price increases. Companies often raise their prices by more than the cost increase in anticipation of further inflation. Companies do not want to make long-run price agreements with customers. They fear that cost inflation will reduce profit margins. For example, hotels prefer not to quote a firm price for conventions booked three years in advance. Another factor leading to price increases is excess demand. When a company cannot supply all its customers' needs, it can raise its prices, ration products to customers, or both. When a city hosts a major convention, hotels may charge rates that are twice the average room rate. They know that the demand for hotel rooms will be great, and they can take advantage of this demand.

In passing price increases on to customers, the company should avoid the image of *price gouger*. It is best to increase prices when customers perceive the price increase to be justified. Restaurants had an easier time implementing increased menu prices after the price of beef jumped, because their customers noticed this price increase in the supermarket. If food prices are going down while the other costs of operating a restaurant are going up, it is difficult to gain customer acceptance of the need for a price increase. Restaurant managers should try to time price increases so that they will be perceived as justified by customers, such as when increases in the price of food receive media attention, after an increase in the minimum wage, or when inflation is in the news. Price increases should be supported with a company communication program informing customers and employees why prices are being increased.

Buyer Reactions to Price Changes

Whether the price is raised or lowered, the action will affect buyers, competitors, distributors, and suppliers. Price changes may also interest the government. Customers do not always put a straightforward interpretation on price changes. They may perceive a price cut in several ways. For

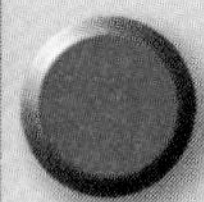

Marketing Highlight 12-4

The Internet Makes It Easy for Customers to Find Price Information

Hotels used to sell excess inventory to wholesalers. The wholesalers would then bundle the rooms with air, ground transportation, and other activities creating a package. The package would then be advertised and sold through travel agents. The persons that would buy the package were usually not the hotel's customers. Thus, the wholesaler created extra demand for the hotel, justifying selling the rooms at a lower rate to the wholesaler. The Internet has changed the relationship between the hotel and the wholesaler. Now some wholesalers contract for inventory and simply resell the inventory over the Internet, in direct competition with the hotel.

This competition should increase in the future as consumer advocates are teaching consumers to check Internet wholesalers. Jayne Clark, in an article in *USA Today*, writes that consumers should first check the hotel's Web site, then check the sites of two hotel discounters, then call the hotel's toll free number and ask for any discounts for which they might qualify such as the Automobile Association of America or hotel and airline loyalty programs, then go back and recheck the discount sites again. Following her process we came up with the results on the facing page for a weekday room booked two weeks out.

One problem with wholesaler undercutting hotels is the hotel is losing control of the rate structure. Clark states hotels rates are taking on a "rug bazaar" aspect where the customer expects to haggle, shop around, and get a reduced price. Some hotel companies are now moving to gain control of their rates. Marriott has been working on a single-rate concept. Scott Dahl, Lodgian management company, says his company is adopting a single-rate policy. "We don't want the consumer to think there is a better price anywhere else. I think the industry has done itself a disservice. Wherever guests look there is a better rate, so they're never convinced they're getting the best one."

Priceline.com is a wholesale outlet that works under a different model to help protect the hotels' images and avoids selling to the hotels' customers at a lower price. Priceline customers make a bid on what they are willing to pay for a hotel room of a certain class in a geographic area, for example, the French Quarter of News Orleans, or downtown News Orleans. Bidders may select one or more regions of a city, but they cannot specify a hotel. In fact the customer does not know the name of the hotel they are staying in until they receive the notification of a winning bid. Once the bid is accepted, changes or cancellations cannot be made. If the guest is a member of the hotel's loyalty program, the guest does not receive any points because they bought the room from Priceline, not the hotel. Thus the restrictions for the traveler are significant.

In the Priceline model, a hotel agrees to sell a block of rooms to Priceline at a certain price. Priceline then decides the markup it wants and accepts bids that meets this markup. For example, a hotel agrees to let

example, what would you think when you see a restaurant advertising a buy-one-meal-get-one-free special? If you know the restaurant and have a positive feeling, you might be attracted. Someone who doesn't know the restaurant may feel it is having trouble attracting customers or that there is something wrong with the food or service. Or you might wonder if portion size has been reduced or inferior-quality food was being served. Remember, buyers often associate price with quality when evaluating hospitality products that they have not directly experienced.

	WASHINGTON		LOS ANGELES	
	Holiday Inn Capitol	Double Tree Crystal City	Hyatt Regency	Sofitel Los Angeles
Hotel's Toll Free Number	$239.00	$209.00	$161.00	$359.00
Hotel Direct	$139.00	$209.00	$161.00	$179.00
Hotel's Web Site	$139.00	$188.10	$179.00	$169.00
Expedia.com (Online travel agency)	$139.00	$199.00	$ 94.00	$119.00
hoteldiscounts.com (Online discounter)	$179.95	$199.95	$189.95	$119.95

Contacts were made on March 6, 2002, for a room on April 11, 2002. *Note:* Low prices for a hotel room rate will vary across sources by time of inquiry and time of stay. This is an illustration of the variance in price, not that one source offers better prices than another source.

Priceline sell rooms on a particular night for $35; Priceline accepts a bid of $55 for the room. In addition, Priceline charges the successful bidder 20 percent for "taxes" and a $5.95 fee. Thus, priceline collects $71.95 from the customer, and pays the hotel $35 plus actual taxes of $2.62. If the customer had purchased the room from the hotel directly, they would have paid about $90, including taxes. Usually only the most price sensitive customers will purchase rooms through priceline.com because of these restrictions. A customer who wants to stay at a Hilton would not use Priceline. Thus, the Priceline model keeps the discounted hotel rate transparent to the customer.

Hotel companies must take control of their pricing; having a variety of prices is confusing to the customers and can damage the image of the hotel. As long as significant differences in prices exist, travel writers will explain to customers how to use the Internet to gain the best price. Hotel companies need to regain control of their prices and move to a single-rate plan.

Sources: Laura Bly, "Priceline Nets Lodging Discount," retrieved on October 12, 2001, from the World Wide Web, *http://www.proquest.umi.com/pqdweb?Did=000000074198256&Fmt=3&Deli=1&Mtd=1&Idx;* Jayne Clark, "Learn the Hotel Rate Game," *USA Today*, September 22, 2000, 5D; Arthur Frommer, "ON A BUDGET; Looking for Last-Minute Deals? Try the Internet," retrieved on October 12, 2001, from the World Wide Web, *http://www.proquest.umi.com/pqdweb?Did=000000056465625&Fmt=3&Deli=1&Mtd=1&Idx.*

Similarly, a price increase that would normally lower sales may have a positive meaning for buyers. A nightclub that increases its cover charge from $5 to $10 might be perceived as the "in place" to go.

Competitor Reactions to Price Changes

A firm considering a price change has to worry about competitors' reactions. Competitors are most likely to react when the number of firms involved is small, when the product is uniform, and when buyers are well informed.

One problem with trying to use price as a competitive advantage is that competitors can neutralize the price advantage by lowering their prices. In a competitive market where supply exceeds demand, this often sets off price wars in which the industry as a whole loses. In the United States, Burger King and McDonald's are locked in a fierce battle for market share. When one of these fast-food giants cuts its price, the other usually follows. Ninety-nine-cent Big Macs are matched by 99-cent Whoppers.

12.14 British Airways
Delta
TWA

In early 1991, British Airways cut its thirty-day advance purchase fares by 33 percent. Delta and Pan Am matched British Airways. TWA more than matched the British Airways offer by slashing its fares to London by 50 percent. British Airways lost the competitive advantage of lower fares when competitors quickly matched its price.[40]

Competitors may choose to retaliate in different markets. For example, when Southwest Airlines cut prices on its Houston to San Antonio flights, its competitors reacted by cutting prices on their Houston to Dallas flights. The Houston-to-Dallas flights were Southwest's bread and butter. By hitting here, the competition hurt Southwest more than they could have by matching prices on the Houston-to-San Antonio route. Competitors may also react to a price cut with nonprice tactics. When Continental Airlines offered a "chicken-feed" discount fare, the competition responded by not booking their connecting passengers on Continental's flights. Continental was forced to rescind its price cuts. Before cutting prices, it is essential to consider competitive reactions. As we mentioned at the beginning of the chapter, price is a very flexible element of the marketing mix. It can easily be matched by the competition. A firm that lowers its price and has it matched by competition loses both its competitive advantage and profit.[41]

Trade Ally Reactions to Price Changes

Earlier mention has been made of the reaction of travel agents to heavy discounting by airlines. This is an example of trade ally reactions.

The hospitality and travel industry represent such an interconnected and interdependent group of firms that pricing actions by major participants such as airlines, cruise lines, and ski resorts have a domino effect on others.

Shoeshine attendants sometimes complain that a dramatic cut in airfares is bad for business. Airports are jammed with people wearing sneakers, sandals, and other footwear that requires no polish. Business travelers are lost in the crowd and may not see the shoeshine stands due to the traffic.

Suppliers to firms that offer deep discounts may also be asked to offer special discounts or risk losing business. Independent firms such as limousine services and food vendors may be tempted to raise prices due to increased traffic.

Communities such as resorts and convention cities are greatly concerned by the pricing activities of airlines, ski resorts, and other principal players and may be expected to exert considerable pressure on managers concerning their pricing strategies. They want to keep prices low to encourage tourism. Besides pressure for low prices from some local governments, governments also view the hospitality industry as a source of income by local, state, and federal governments. Visitors to a region are seldom voters in that area and are therefore viewed as excellent tax revenue sources by elected officials. Room taxes, airport departure taxes, sales taxes, and other imaginative taxes directly add to the price of a hospitality product. In some heavily taxed areas, taxation and visitor tariffs may add 20 percent to the price.

This situation often requires strong political action by the hospitality industry and supportive groups such as local retailers. Hotels in New York State won a three-year battle to repeal a 5 percent tax on rooms. Hotels in New York City were particularly hard hit. Guests will still be forced to pay 14.25 percent plus a $2 surcharge on hotel rooms. Hoteliers argued that the tax was a major factor in driving convention and meeting business from the city.

Following the repeal of the 5 percent tax, Stephen Morello, president of the New York Convention and Visitors Bureau, stated, "Tomorrow we'll be calling the 44 conventions worth $52 million that said they couldn't come to New York City last year because of the tax."[42]

Responding to Price Changes

Here we reverse the question and ask how a firm should respond to a price change by a competitor. The firm needs to consider several issues. Why did the competitor change the price? Was it to gain more market share, to use excess capacity, to meet changing cost conditions, or to lead an industrywide program change? Does the competitor plan to make the price change temporary or permanent? What will happen to the company's market share and profits if it does not respond? Are other companies going to respond? What are the competitors' and other firms' responses likely to be to each possible reaction?

Besides these issues, the company must make a broader analysis. It must consider its own product's stage in the life cycle, its importance in the company's product mix, the intentions and resources of the competitor, and possible consumer reactions to price changes.

When Marriott's Fairfield Inns were just getting started, they offered a special $19.95 coupon, $16 less than their average daily rate. Their competitors decided not to match the rate because Fairfield had only thirty hotels at the time. Joan Ganje-Fischer, vice president of Super 8, said that if a major chain such as Super Eight, Econo Inns, or Days Inns offered the $19.95 special, it would catch the attention of the other organizations. A price war would be the likely result of such a cut by a major chain. But because Fairfield Inns consisted of only 30 units, major competitors were unwilling to reduce rates across their hundred-plus motel chains. Fairfield Inns used size to their advantage, recognizing that the larger chains would be unwilling to give up revenue from hundreds of hotels and thousands of rooms to match the price of a thirty-unit chain.[43]

12.15 Days Inns
Econo Inns
Super 8

At the end of a pilot strike against United Airlines, the company announced a refund of half the cost of any flight taken during a one-week period. United wanted to attract customers who were forced to use other airlines when it cut service during the strike. By limiting price reductions to one week, United avoided getting into a price battle. Competitors who were doing well because of United Airlines's plight chose not to discount fares and conceded United the lower fares for a week.[44]

These examples show how companies can avoid competitive reactions to price changes by planning those changes carefully.

KEY TERMS

Cost-plus pricing Adding a standard markup to the cost of the product.

Cross selling The company's other products that are sold to the guest.

Discriminatory pricing Refers to segmentation of the market and pricing differences based on price elasticity characteristics of the segments.

Fixed costs Costs that do not vary with production or sales level.

Going-rate pricing Setting price based largely on following competitors' prices rather than on company costs or demand.

Price The amount of money charged for a product or service, or the sum of the values consumers exchange for the benefits of having or using the product or service.

Pure monopoly The market consists of one seller; it could be government monopoly, a private regulated monopoly, or a private nonregulated monopoly.

Survival It is used when the economy slumps or a recession is going on. A manufacturing firm can reduce production to match demand, and a hotel can cut rates to create the best cash flow.

Upselling This occurs through training of sales and reservation employees to offer continuously a higher-priced product that will better meet the customer's needs, rather than settling for the lowest price.

Value-based pricing Uses the buyer's perceptions of value, not the seller's cost, as the key to pricing.

Yield management Yield management is a pricing method using price as a means of matching capacity with demand. The goal of yield management is to optimize the yield or contribution margin.

Chapter Review

I. Factors to Consider When Setting Price

1) Internal factors

a) Marketing objectives

i) Survival. It is used when the economy slumps or a recession is going on. A manufacturing firm can reduce production to match demand and a hotel can cut rates to create the best cash flow.

ii) Current profit maximization. Companies may choose the price that will produce the maximum current profit, cash flow, or return on investment, seeking financial outcomes rather than long-run performance.

iii) Market-share leadership. When companies believe that a company with the largest market share will eventually enjoy low costs and high long-run profit, they will set low opening rates and strive to be the market-share leader.

iv) Product-quality leadership. Hotels like the Ritz-Carlton chain charge a high price for their high-cost products to capture the luxury market.

v) Other objectives. Stabilize market, create excitement for new product, draw more attention.

b) Marketing-mix strategy. Price must be coordinated with product design, distribution, and promotion decision to form a consistent and effective marketing program.

c) Costs

i) Fixed costs. Costs that do not vary with production or sales level.

ii) Variable costs. Costs that vary directly with the level of production.

d) Organizational considerations. Management must decide who within the organization should set prices. In small companies, this will be top management; in large companies, pricing is typically handled by a corporate department or by a regional or unit manager under guidelines established by corporate management.

2) External factors

a) Nature of the market and demand

i) Cross selling. The company's other products are sold to the guest.

ii) Upselling. This occurs through training of sales and reservation employees to offer continuously a higher-priced product that will better meet the customer's needs, rather than settling for the lowest price.

b) Pricing in different markets. There are four types of markets:

i) Pure competition. The market consists of many buyers and sellers trading in a uniform commodity.

ii) Monopolistic competition. The market consists of many buyers and sellers who trade over a range of prices rather than a single market price.

iii) Oligopolistic competition. The market consists of a few sellers who are highly sensitive to each other's pricing and marketing strategies.

iv) Pure monopoly. The market consists of one seller; it could be a government monopoly, a private regulated monopoly, or a private nonregulated monopoly.

c) Consumer perception of price and value. It is the consumer who decides whether a product's price is right. The price must be buyer oriented. The price decision requires a creative awareness of the target market and recognition of the buyers' differences.

d) Analyzing the price demand relationship. Demand and price are inversely related; the higher the price, the lower the demand. Most demand curves slope downward in either a straight or a curved line. The prestige goods demand curve sometimes slopes upward.

e) Price elasticity of demand. If demand hardly varies with a small change in price, we say that the demand is inelastic; if demand changes greatly, we say that the demand is elastic. Buyers are less price sensitive when the product is unique or when it is high in quality, prestige, or exclusiveness. Consumers are also less price sensitive when substitute products are hard to find. If demand is elastic, sellers will generally consider lowering their prices to produce more total revenue. The following factors affect price sensitivity:

i) Unique value effect. Creating the perception that your offering is different from those of your competitors avoids price competition.

ii) Substitute awareness effect. Lack of the awareness of the existence of alternatives reduces price sensitivity.

iii) Business expenditure effect. When someone else pays the bill, the customer is less price sensitive.

iv) End-benefit effect. Consumers are more price sensitive when the price of the product accounts for a large share of the total cost of the end benefit.

v) Total expenditure effect. The more someone spends on a product, the more sensitive he or she is to the product's price.

vi) Shared cost effect. Purchasers are less price sensitive when they are sharing the cost of the purchase with someone else.

vii) Sunk investment effect. Purchasers who have an investment in products that they are currently using are less likely to change for price reasons.

viii) Price quality effect. Consumers tend to equate price with quality, especially when they lack any prior experience with the product.

f) Competitors' price and offers. When a company is aware of its competitors' price and offers, it can use this information as a starting point for deciding its own pricing.

g) Other environmental factors. Other factors include inflation, boom or recession, interest rates, government purchasing, birth of new technology.

II. General Pricing Approaches

1) Cost-based pricing. Cost-plus pricing: a standard markup is added to the cost of the product.

2) Break-even analysis and target profit pricing. Price is set to break even on the costs of making and marketing a product, or to make a desired profit.

3) Value-based pricing. Companies base their prices on the product's perceived value. Perceived-value pricing uses the buyers' perceptions of value, not the seller's cost, as the key to pricing.

4) Competition-based pricing. Competition-based price is based on the establishment of price largely against those of competitors, with less attention paid to costs or demand.

III. Pricing Strategies

1) Prestige pricing. Hotels or restaurants seeking to position themselves as luxurious and elegant will enter the market with a high price that will support this position.

2) Market-skimming pricing. Price skimming is setting a high price when the market is price insensitive. It is common in industries with high research and development costs, such as pharmaceutical companies and computer firms.

3) Marketing-penetration pricing. Companies set a low initial price to penetrate the market quickly and deeply, attracting many buyers and winning a large market share.

4) Product-bundle pricing. Sellers using product-bundle pricing combine several of their products and offer the bundle at a reduced price. Most used by cruise lines.

5) Volume discounts. Hotels have special rates to attract customers who are likely to purchase a large quantity of hotel rooms, either for a single period or throughout the year.

6) Discounts based on time of purchase. A seasonal discount is a price reduction to buyers who purchase services out of season when the demand is lower. Seasonal discounts allow the hotel to keep demand steady during the year.

7) Discriminatory pricing. This refers to segmentation of the market and pricing differences based on price elasticity characteristics of the segments. In discriminatory pricing, the company sells a product or service at two or more prices, although the difference in price is not based on differences in cost. It maximizes the amount that each customer pays.

a) Yield management. A yield management system is used to maximize a hotel's yield or contribution margin.

8) Last minute pricing. Although last-minute pricing provides an outlet for unsold inventory, it is not a substitute for effective marketing and a well-devised pricing strategy.

9) Psychological pricing. Psychological aspects such as prestige, reference prices, round figures, and ignoring end figures are used in pricing.

10) Promotional pricing. Hotels temporarily price their products below list price, and sometimes even below cost, for special occasions, such as introduction or festivities. Promotional pricing gives guests a reason to come and promotes a positive image for the hotel.

IV. Other pricing considerations

1) Price spread effect. The restaurant industry has historically employed a rule of thumb that the highest-price entrée should be no more than 2.5 times as expensive as the lowest-price entrée.

V. Price Changes

1) Initiating price cuts. Reasons for a company to cut price are excess capacity, unable to increase business through promotional efforts, product improvement, follow-the-leader pricing, and to dominate the market.

2) Initiating price increases. Reasons for a company to increase price are cost inflation or excess demand.

3) Buyer reactions to price changes. Competitors, distributors, suppliers, and other buyers will associate price with quality when evaluating hospitality products they have not experienced directly.

4) Competitor reactions to price changes. Competitors are most likely to react when the number of firms involved is small, when the product is uniform, and when buyers are well informed.

5) **Responding to price changes.** Issues to consider are reason, market share, excess capacity, meet changing cost conditions, lead an industrywide program change, temporary versus permanent.

Discussion Questions

1. One way of increasing revenue is through upselling. Give examples from the hospitality or travel industries of when upselling can result in a more satisfied guest.
2. You have just been hired as the dining room manager at a local hotel. The manager asks you to evaluate the menu prices to see if they need to be adjusted. How would you go about this task?
3. A number of factors affecting price sensitivity are discussed in this chapter. Provide some examples of the application of these factors in hospitality or travel businesses.
4. Many restaurants have unbundled their products to lower prices. For example, some restaurants that normally included a salad bar with all meals now offer a dinner price that includes the salad bar and a lower à la carte that does not. Why do you think these restaurants are unbundling their products? When is price bundling effective?
5. Give an example of an effective use of price discrimination. Support your reasons for thinking that it is a good example.
6. Does yield management create and maintain customers, or is it a short-term approach to increasing revenue?
7. Airlines and hotels give bonus frequent flyer miles, gifts, and free companion tickets to attract the business traveler. These promotions are often provided in lieu of a price cut. The traveler benefits personally, although their company does not get the benefit of lower rates. Is this ethical?

Experiential Exercise

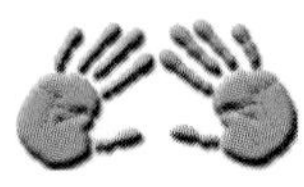

Do the following:

Conduct a price comparison of several hotels or restaurants in the same class. What price differences did you find? Do you feel the companies that had the higher prices could justify those higher prices by offering additional features or a higher quality product?

Internet Exercise

Support for these exercises can be found on the Web site for *Marketing for Hospitality and Tourism,* www.prenhall.com/kotler.

Choose a large hotel in a city of your choice. Do an Internet search to see how many different prices you can find for the same type of room. Write up your findings.

References

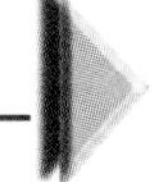

1. Margaret Webb Pressler, "Coming Home to Roost?" *Washington Post,* October 19, 1997, p. H1.
2. Rob Reuteman, "Boston Chicken President Beck Blames Self for Laying an Egg," *Rocky Mountain News, Business*, June 8, 1997, pp. 1G and 12G.
3. Boston Market Corporation, retrieved April 16, 2001, from the World Wide Web: *http://www.boston-market.com4_company*.
4. David J. Schwartz, *Marketing Today: A Basic Approach*, 3d ed. (New York: Harcourt Brace Jovanovich, 1981), pp. 270–273.
5. Janet Denefe, "Yearning for Learning," *F&B Magazine* 2, no. 1 (March/April 1994): 13.
6. Jack Smith, "Of Fame and Fundamentals," *F&B Magazine* 2, no. 1 (March/April 1994): 34–35.

7. "Royal Caribbean Breaks Through," *Scorecard: The Revenue Management Quarterly* (Third Quarter 1992): 3.
8. Ibid., p. 6.
9. Howard Feiertag, "Up Your Property's Profits by Upselling Catering," *Hotel and Motel Management* 206, no. 14 (August 19, 1991): 20.
10. Gail Bellamy, "Hot Stuff: Upselling Coffee and Tea," *Restaurant Hospitality* 75, no. 2 (February 1991): 120–124.
11. "Embassy's Suite Deal," *Scorecard: The Revenue Management Quarterly* (Second Quarter 1993): 3.
12. Melvyn Greene, *Marketing Hotels and Restaurants into the 90's* (New York: Van Nostrand Reinhold, 1987).
13. Anthony Edwards, "Changes in Real Air Fares and Their Impact on Travel," *EIU Travel and Tourism Analyst* 2 (1990): 76–85.
14. This sections draws on Thomas T. Nagle, *The Strategy and Tactics of Pricing* (Upper Saddle River, NJ: Prentice Hall, 1987).
15. Eric B. Orkin, "Strategies for Managing Transient Rates," *Cornell Hotel and Restaurant Administration Quarterly* 30 no. 4 (February 1990): 39.
16. Greene, *Marketing Hotels and Restaurants into the 90's*, p. 47.
17. Isae Wada, "Agents Irate over Airlines 2-for-1 Fares," *Travel Weekly* 29, no. 96 (November 29, 1990): 1.
18. The Horwath Accountant, 47, no. 7, 1967, p. 8.
19. Philip Kotler and Gary Armstrong, *Principles of Marketing* (Upper Saddle River, NJ: Prentice Hall, 2001), p. 387.
20. Leo M. Renaghan and Michael Z. Kay, "What Meeting Planners Want: The Conjoint-Analysis Approach," *Cornell Hotel and Restaurant Administration Quarterly 28*, no. 1 (May 1987): 73.
21. Greene, *Marketing Hotels and Restaurants into the 90's*, p. 42.
22. David Cogswell and Sara Perez Webber
23. John E. H. Sherry, "Sex-Based Price Discrimination: Does It Violate Civil Rights Laws?" *Cornell Hotel and Restaurant Administration Quarterly* 35, no. 2 (April 1994): 16–17.
24. Richard O. Hanks, Robert G. Cross, and Paul R. Noland, "Discounting in the Hotel Industry: A New Approach," *Cornell Hotel and Restaurant Administration Quarterly* 33, no. 1 (February 1992): 23.
25. "Rational Pricing at Marriott," *Scorecard: The Revenue Management Quarterly* (Third Quarter 1993): 4.
26. John E. G. Bateson, *Managing Services Marketing* (Fort Worth, TX: Dryden Press, 1992), p. 339.
27. Eric B. Orkin, "Boosting Your Bottom Line with Yield Management," *Cornell Hotel and Restaurant Administration Quarterly* 28, no. 4 (1988): 52–56.
28. Sheryl E. Kisner, "The Basics of Yield Management," *Cornell Hotel and Restaurant Administration Quarterly* 30, no. 3 (November 1989): 14–19.
29. William H. Kaven, and Myrtle Allardyce, "Dalmahoy's Strategy for Success," *Cornell Hotel and Restaurant Administration Quarterly* 35, no. 6 (December 1994): 87–88.
30. "The Ethics of Revenue Management," *Scorecard: The Revenue Management Quarterly* (Third Quarter 1993): 9; "Pricing Considerations in Menu Expansion and New Product Development," presented at the *National Restaurant Association's Marketing Research Group Meeting*, New Orleans, LA, September 21, 1981.
31. Sheryl E. Kimes, "Perceived Fairness of Yield Management," *Cornell Hotel and Restaurant Administration Quarterly* 35, no. 1 (February 1994): 29.
32. JoAnn Carmin and Gregory X. Norkus, "Pricing Strategies for Menus: Magic or Myth," *Cornell Hotel and Restaurant Administration Quarterly* 31, no. 3 (November 1990): 50.
33. "High Stakes at Harrah's," *Scorecard: The Revenue Management Quarterly* (First Quarter 1993): 3.
34. Ibid.
35. David K. Hayes and Lynn M. Huffman, "Value Pricing: How Long Can You Go?" *Cornell Hotel and Restaurant Administration Quarterly* (February 1995): 51–56.
36. Stephan J. Hock, Xavier Drege, and Mary E. Park, "EDLP, Hi–Low, and Margin Arithmetic," *Journal of Marketing* 58 (October 1994): 27.
37. Robert C. Lewis, and Stowe Shoemaker, "Price-Sensitivity Measurement," *Cornell Hotel and Restaurant Administration Quarterly* 38, no. 2 (April 1997): 48–55.
38. Ibid., p. 46.
39. Richard Martin, "Taco Bell Rolls Out a New 39-Cent Snack Menu," *Nation's Restaurant News* 25, no. 25 (June 24, 1991): 3; Richard Martin, "McDonald's Kicks Off Value Menu Blitz," *Nation's Restaurant News* 25, no. 1 (January 7, 1991): 3; Scott Hume, "Burger King Backs Low-Price Buddies," *Advertising Age* 61, no. 53 (December 24, 1990): 2.
40. Isae Wada, "TWA Slashes Transatlantic Fares by Half," *Travel Weekly* 50, no. 14 (February 18, 1991): 11.
41. Nagle, *The Strategy and Tactics of Pricing*, pp. 95–96.
42. "NYC: Tax Cut, CHRAQ News and Reviews," *Cornell Hotel and Restaurant Administration Quarterly* 35, no. 4 (August 1994): 6.
43. "Fairfield Cuts Rates to Gain Stronger Presence," *Hotel and Motel Management* (June 19, 1989): 11.
44. John A. Quelch and Melanie D. Spencer, "United Airlines: Price Promotion Policy," *Harvard Business Case 586-089* (Cambridge, MA: Harvard University Press, 1986).

BIG

13 Distribution Channels

Adversarial power relationships work only if you never have to see or work with the other party again.
Peter Drucker

In 1991, Little Caesar's negotiated a strategic alliance with Kmart, one of the largest discount chains in the United States. According to the agreement, Kmart would replace other in-store food service with 1,200 Little Caesar's over a five-year period. Kmart would gain a brand-name restaurant for shoppers instead of the generic cafeteria/food bar featured previously. Little Caesar's would gain additional distribution with the hope that once exposed to Little Caesar's in Kmart, the customer would also buy from traditional Little Caesar's stores. Kmart also agreed to contribute to Little Caesar's national advertising fund, thus providing improved media opportunities. The management of Little Caesar's was elated.

Some franchisees were not impressed. Initially, they were upset because the agreement included carry-out sales when they had thought it would be in-store consumption only. They felt that carry-out sales would be direct competition with their stores. In response, a group of disgruntled franchisees formed the Association of Little Caesar's Franchisees (ALCF), which claimed to represent seventy franchisees who operated more than 550 stores of the 4,000-unit chain. The ALCF claimed that some members had seen sales dip as much as 20 percent after a Little Caesar's opened in a nearby Kmart. The ALCF also complained that some Kmarts, which were located in the same mall as a Little Caesar's, were allowed to install a competitive Little Caesar's. A town of 5,000 people in North Carolina had two Little Caesar's franchises, a new one in the Kmart and the original franchisee. The ALCF also complained that the agreement stipulated that Kmart had to contribute to national advertising, but not to the local fund.

Some ALCF members felt that Kmart took away their customers while benefiting from the dollars they spent on local advertising. The ALCF was so bitter that they collected a monthly membership fee for a fund to bring legal action against Little Caesar's. Not all franchisees were upset. Many thought the association with Kmart was a good move and would expose Little Caesar's name to millions of Kmart shoppers.

In 1997, Kmart renewed its commitment with Little Caesar's, announcing that it would roll out 850 "cobranded" restaurants. The restaurants were to feature a Little Caesar's Pizza Station or Little Caesar's Express. Little Caesar's worked out its differences with its franchisees, and there was no negative reaction from its franchisees to this announcement. Little Caesar's has developed a new channel for its products, Kmart, while regaining the goodwill of its franchisees.

The Little Caesar's case shows that distribution systems are delicately balanced: What is good for one member of the channel may not be good for another, resulting in conflict and power struggles. Managers must give careful thought to the choice of distribution channels, as this can have long-term effects. Managers must also work to resolve conflicts within the distribution channel when they do occur.[1]

Chapter Objectives

After reading this chapter, you should be able to:

1. Describe the nature of distribution channels, and tell why marketing intermediaries are used.
2. Understand the different marketing intermediaries available to the hospitality industry and the benefits each of these intermediaries offers.
3. Know how to use the Internet as a distribution channel.
4. Discuss channel behavior and organization, explaining corporate, contractual, and vertical marketing systems, including franchising.
5. Illustrate the channel management decisions of selecting, motivating, and evaluating channel members.
6. Identify factors to consider when choosing a business location.

13.1 K-Mart
Little Caesar's Pizza

Nature and Importance of Distribution Systems

If we view properties as the heart of a hotel company, distribution systems can be viewed as the company's circulatory system.[2] Distribution systems provide a steady flow of customers. A well-managed distribution system can make the difference between a market-share leader and a company struggling for survival. Many hospitality companies are making greater use of the marketing channels available to them. For example, Ritz-Carlton receives a significant share of business from travel agents because of aggressive development of this channel. Marriott entered a marketing alliance with New Otani Hotels, giving Marriott exposure to Japanese travelers in North America. In return, New Otani gained Marriott's marketing expertise to help reach Americans traveling to Japan.[3] In today's competitive environment, it is not enough to count on a central reservation system and your own sales force. Companies must develop increasingly complex distribution networks.

13.2 Ontami Hotels
Ritz Carlton

Competition, a global marketplace, electronic distribution techniques, and a perishable product have increased the importance of distribution. Innovative ways of approaching new and existing markets are needed. Globalization has meant that many hotel companies must choose foreign partners to help them market or distribute their products. Sheraton built an alliance with the Welcome Group in India, which manages Sheraton Hotels on the Indian subcontinent. New electronic distribution methods have resulted in the growth of international reservation systems such as Utell. Finally, the importance of distribution has increased because hospitality products are perishable. RCI, a time-share exchange company, uses its large membership base to negotiate special hotel rates for its members. The agreement works well for both parties: hotels have a chance to sell rooms during a soft period, and RCI can offer its members a benefit.

Nature of Distribution Channels

A **distribution channel** is a set of independent organizations involved in the process of making a product or service available to the consumer or business user.[4] Development of a distribution system starts with the selection of channel members. Once members have been selected, the focus shifts to managing the channel. Distribution networks in the hospitality industry consist of contractual agreements and loosely organized alliances between independent organizations.[5] Marketing, distribution systems are traditionally used to move goods (tangible products) from the manufacturer to the consumer. In the hospitality and travel industries, distribution systems are used to move the customer to the product: the hotel, restaurant, cruise ship, or airplane.

We first look briefly at traditional distribution systems. These systems provide the framework for the development of hospitality distribution networks. The products used by hospitality and travel companies come through distribution channels; thus, it is important to understand their structure. Graduates of hospitality and tourism programs often work for companies that distribute products. Graduates with restaurant experience may find themselves working for a company that distributes food or beverages to restaurants. They may sell food-service equipment or table top items to restaurants and hotels. They may sell supplies to hotels. Some graduates have taken jobs as food brokers. The food **broker** works as an **agent** for the manufacturer, trying to create demand for a product. For example, if Mrs. Smith's pies develops a new no-bake pie for the food-service industry, brokers representing Mrs. Smith's pies would introduce the product to food-service managers they think will be interested in using it. The hospitality and travel industries use billions of dollars worth of products, all moved through distribution channels. These distribution channels create thousands of jobs.

Why Are Marketing Intermediaries Used?

Why does Shenago China sell its chinaware to restaurants through an intermediary? Although doing so means giving up control over pricing the products, Shenago does gain advantages from selling through an intermediary. The company does not have to maintain several display rooms and a large sales force in every major city. Instead, a restaurant supply company displays, promotes, and makes personal sales calls. The restaurant supply house sells hundreds of other items. Their large assortment makes them a convenient supplier to the restaurant industry. The sales potential from their product assortment allows them to make personal sales calls, send catalogs, and provide other support for the products that they represent. Selling through wholesalers and retailers usually is much more efficient than direct sales.

A restaurant manager can make one call to a restaurant supply house and order a French knife, a dozen plates, a case of candles, a dozen oyster forks, a case of wine glasses, and a case of cocktail napkins. Each of these items is produced by a different manufacturer, but they are all available through one phone call. To the purchaser, this means access to small quantities of products, because these become part of a large order. This reduces inventory requirements, number of deliveries, and

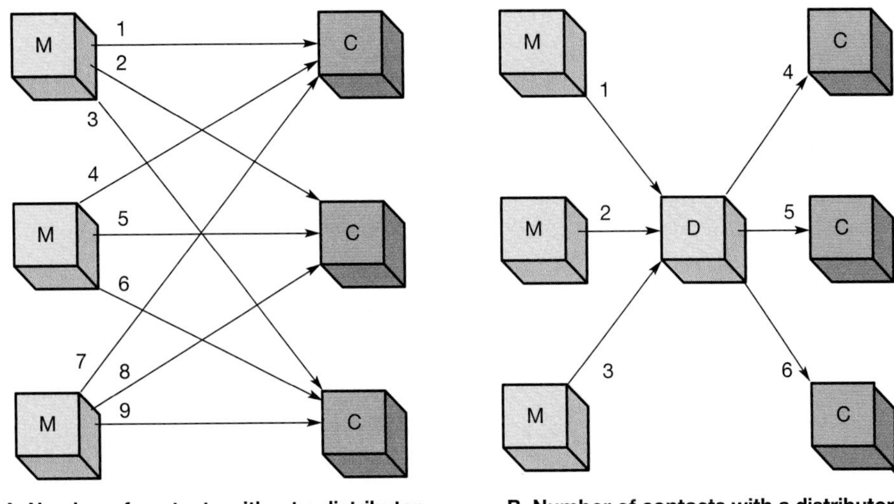

Figure 13-1
How a distributor reduces the number of channel transactions.

number of processed invoices. Figure 13-1 shows one way that intermediaries can provide economies. Without distribution systems, the restaurateur would have to call individual manufacturers, such as a knife manufacturer, a china company, and a paper company. Each of these manufacturers would receive thousands of calls from individual restaurants. This would create unnecessary work and shipping costs for both the manufacturer and the customer, as represented in Figure 13-1A. Figure 13-1B shows the efficiencies created by a distribution system. The restaurants or customers call one distributor and get all of their supplies. The manufacturers can reach many restaurants through one distributor.

Distribution Channel Functions

A distribution channel moves goods from producers to consumers. It overcomes the major time, place, and possession gaps that separate goods and services from those who would use them. Members of the marketing channel perform many key functions:

1. *Information:* gathering and distributing marketing research and intelligence information about the marketing environment
2. *Promotion:* developing and spreading persuasive communications about an offer
3. *Contact:* finding and communicating with prospective buyers
4. *Matching*: shaping and fitting the offer to the buyer's needs, including such activities as manufacturing, grading, assembling, and packaging
5. *Negotiation:* agreeing on price and other terms of the offer so that ownership or possession can be transferred
6. *Physical distribution:* transporting and storing goods

7. *Financing:* acquiring and using funds to cover the costs of channel work
8. *Risk taking:* assuming financial risks such as the inability to sell inventory at full margin

The first five functions help to complete transactions. The last three help to fulfill the completed transactions.

All these functions have three things in common: They use scarce resources; they can often be performed better through specialization; and they can be shifted among channel members. Shifting functions to the intermediary may keep producer costs and prices low, but intermediaries must add a charge to cover the cost of their work. To keep costs low, functions should be assigned to channel members who can perform them most efficiently. For example, many airlines encourage passengers to use travel agents. The travel agents answer the passenger's questions, issue the ticket, collect the payment, and when the passenger's plans change, they reissue the ticket. Travel agents are also conveniently located, and many will deliver a ticket to their clients the same day it is booked. It would not be economically feasible for an airline to set up a similar distribution system.

Number of Channel Levels

Distribution channels can be described by the number of **channel levels.** Each layer that performs some work in bringing the product and its ownership closer to the final buyer is a channel level. Because the producer and the final consumer both perform some work, they are part of every channel. We use the number of intermediary levels to show the length of a channel. Figure 13-2 shows several consumer distribution channels.

Channel 1, called a **direct marketing channel,** has no intermediary level. It consists of a manufacturer selling directly to consumers. For example, a restaurateur may buy produce directly from the grower at a farmer's market. Channel 2 contains one level. In consumer markets, this level is typically a **retailer.** The Fisherman's Pier restaurant in Geelong, near Melbourne, Australia, purchases its fish from a fisherman's co-op. The co-op markets the fish, allowing the fishers to specialize in fishing, not marketing.

13.3 Land o' Lakes
Sunkist

Many of the agricultural products purchased by the hospitality industry come from cooperatives. In the United States, Sunkist, Diamond Walnuts, and Land o' Lakes butter are all producer cooperatives. New Zealand Milk Products Company is also a cooperative and sells dried milk and cheese throughout Southeast Asia and Latin America.

Channel 3 contains two levels. In consumer markets, these are typically a **wholesaler** and a retailer. This type of channel is used by smaller manufacturers. Channel 4 contains three levels. The jobber buys from wholesalers and sells to smaller firms that are not served by larger wholesalers. From the producer's point of view, a greater number of intermediaries in the channel means less control and more complexity.

All the institutions in the channel are connected by several types of flows. These include the physical flow of products, the flow of ownership, payment flow, information flow, and promotion flow. These flows can make channels with only one or a few channels very complex.

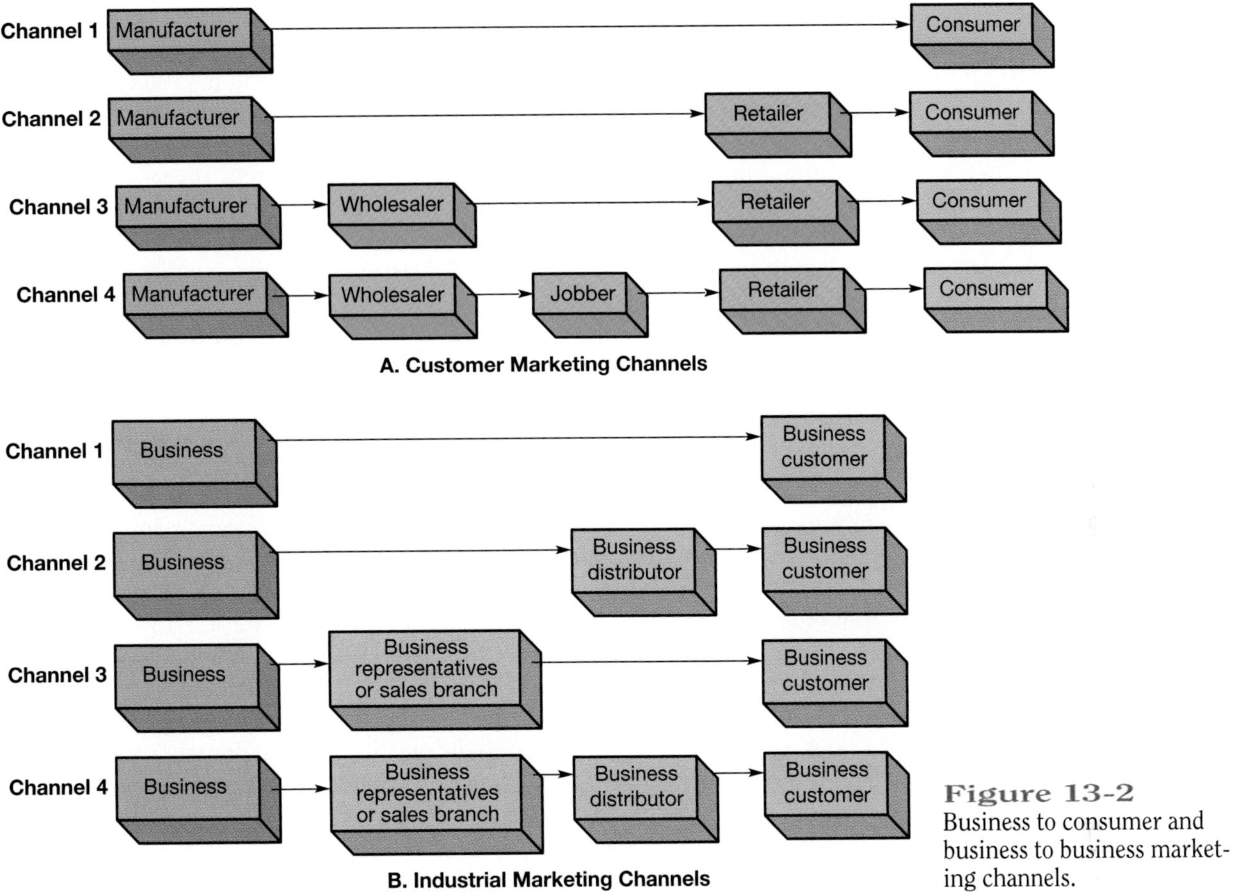

Figure 13-2
Business to consumer and business to business marketing channels.

Marketing Intermediaries

Many specialized channels are available to hospitality and travel organizations. We discuss the following components of a hospitality or travel distribution system: travel agents; tour wholesalers; specialists; hotel representatives; national, state, and local tourist agencies; consortia and reservation systems; global distribution systems; the Internet; and concierges. A manager must choose the intermediaries that will make up the distribution system and the number of levels that the distribution system will have.

Travel Agents

One way of reaching a geographically diverse marketplace is through travel agents. There are about than 31,000 travel agents in the United States.[6] The number of travel agents has been decreasing in recent years. This is due to the airlines driving their customers to the Internet and the decrease in commission paid to travel agents by the airlines. In 1994, airlines paid 10 percent commission to travel agents. Now most U.S. airlines pay 5 percent commission, with many having a $50 cap and some moving to a $20 cap on the amount of commission paid. This has lead some agencies to charge a $20 to $25 fee for issuing tickets. Non–United States typically pay 8 percent commission, with some having a $100 cap.[7] In addition to selling airline tickets, travel agents book about $11 billion in hotel sales, and nearly all cruise travel.[8] Hotels typically pay 10 percent commission to travel agents, and cruise lines can pay up to 15 percent. The combination of reduced commissions and growth of direct sales from hotels and airlines to the consumer has lead to a steady decrease of travel agents in the United States since 1995. However, sales have been increasing, leading to more sales per travel agency.

Hotels interested in travel agency business are listed in airline reservation systems and hotel guides. Hotels also send information packages to travel agents that include collateral material and hotel news, including updates about hotel packages, promotions, and special events. Travel agents are also invited to visit hotel property on familiarization tours (fam trips). Airlines assist with these trips by providing free airfare. It is important that fam trips be well organized.[9] Finally, promotional campaigns can be directed at travel agents through travel agent publications such as *Travel Weekly, Travel Trade,* and *Travel Agent.* The use of promotional campaigns targeted at travel agents is discussed in Chapter 15.

Hotels seeking travel agent business must make it easy for agents to make reservations. Providing toll-free reservation numbers is essential to servicing travel agents. Hotels that generate many bookings from travel agents have a separate number dedicated to business travel. Travel agents like to be paid quickly. Hotels that want travel agent business will process commissions rapidly. Hyatt guarantees payment within one week of the guest's departure.[10] Foreign chains are now paying commissions in the travel agent's local currency, eliminating the need for the agent to go through the costly process of converting a commission check. On a $50 commission foreign currency check, the travel agent stands to lose nearly the full amount because most banks charge a minimum of $30 to $40 per transaction for processing and converting checks drawn on a foreign bank.

Hospitality providers who serve travel agents must remember that agents entrust the hotel with their customers. In a travel agency market survey, travel agents rated reputation for honoring reservations as the most important factor in choosing a hotel.[11] Other important factors are listed in Table 13-1. Hotels must do everything possible to make a favorable impression on guests booked through travel agents to ensure future business from that agent. When business is obtained through an intermediary, the hospitality provider, such as a hotel or cruise line, has two customers, the guest and the intermediary. The majority of cruise lines will not sell directly to the ultimate consumer, but insist that bookings be made through travel agents or tour operators.

"Travel agents are changing the way they make hotel reservations. They are turning away from toll-free telephone numbers to booking hotel rooms directly through computer systems. Travel agents' computer systems, which were referred to as computer reservation systems (CRS) for years, are now called global distribution systems (GDS) because of their global reach."[12] These systems allow hotels to display information con-

Table 13-1
Factors Very Important to Agencies Selecting a Hotel*

Factor	Percentage
Reputation for honoring reservations	90%
Reputation for good guest service	83%
Ease of collecting commission	77%
Room rates	76%
Prior success with booking clients at a particular hotel	76%
Efficiency of hotel's reservations system	70%
Commission rate	64%
Special rates with a particular hotel	61%
Bookable through computerized reservations system	48%
Relationship with hotel sales representative	31%
Client requests for hotel offering frequent stay programs	26%

*Percentage of agencies.

Source: Travel Weekly 53, no. 65 (August 18, 1994): 118.

cerning their properties for use by travel agents when making reservations.

Companies are a major source of travel bookings. U.S. corporations spend over $150 billion on travel. Each dollar of that amount represents a cost that corporations would like to reduce. Consequently, companies make arrangements with travel agents and in some cases set up their own travel agency. Many organizations sign an exclusive agreement with one travel agency, and employees are required to book through this firm. The travel agency assumes responsibility for locating the least expensive travel alternatives for the company.

Tour Wholesalers

Tour wholesalers assemble travel packages usually targeted at the leisure market. These generally include transportation and accommodations, but may include meals, ground transportation, and entertainment. In developing a package, a tour wholesaler contracts with airlines and hotels for a specified number of seats and rooms, receiving a quantity discount. The wholesaler also arranges transportation between the hotel and the airport. Retail travel agents sell these packages. The tour wholesaler has to provide a commission for the travel agent and give consumers a package that is perceived to be a better value than what they could arrange on their own. Additionally, tour operators have to make a profit for themselves. The profit margin on each package is small. Generally, wholesalers must sell 85 percent of the packages available to break even.[13] This high break-even point leaves little room for error. As a result, it is not uncommon for a tour wholesaler to go broke. Thus it is important that hospitality providers check the history of the tour operator, receive a deposit, and get paid promptly. Additional security is provided by dealing with tour

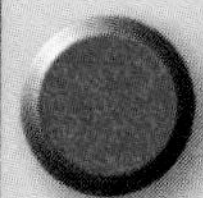

Marketing Highlight 13-1

Top Ten Ideas for Working with Travel Agents

- Pay commissions promptly. Be sympathetic to agents' need for prompt payment and take action on their behalf.
- Make a companywide commitment to the agent market, starting from the top.
- Educate your staff to the importance and the special needs of the agent market.
- Initiate a trading-places program for your hotel staff and travel agents to foster better understanding of each other's needs and responsibilities.
- Recognize and reward agents who book your hotel frequently.
- Through sales brochures, electronic listings, and hotel directory advertising, provide agents with detailed information on the facilities and services that your hotel offers. Include information on booking and commission procedures.
- Work with your local tourism organizations to initiate familiarization trips for travel agents.
- Be sure to qualify agents asking for a free or reduced-rate visit.
- Create educational opportunities for agents by sponsoring seminars on how to plan meetings or incentive packages.
- Provide information on special events, packages, and promotions as far in advance as possible so that agents will be able to sell them. If you offer last-minute "specials" to consumers, inform agents as well.

Source: Reprinted by permission of Elsevier Science, Inc., from "Hotels and Travel Agents, the New Partnership," by Christopher Schulz, *Cornell Hotel and Restaurant Administration Quarterly* 35, no. 2 (April 1994): 45, © 1994 Cornell University.

operators who are members of the U.S. Tour Operators Association (USTOA). USTOA requires its members to post a $100,000 indemnity bond for its consumer payments protection program. This ensures refund of tour deposits and payments in the event of financial failure of any of its members.[14]

With the increased number of international resorts, tour wholesalers are becoming a powerful member of the distribution channel. It is impossible for travel agents to know every resort. Instead, they rely on catalogs provided by tour wholesalers. If a couple wants to holiday on Saipan, they will be given the catalog of a tour operator covering Micronesia. The catalog will contain a selection of several luxury hotels, four-star hotels, three-star hotels, and tourist hotels. The wholesaler writes a description of each. The hotel may provide information, but the tour operator decides on the description of the hotel that goes in the brochure.

If a couple wants to stay at a luxury hotel, the brochure may include only three luxury hotels. Others are eliminated from consideration and will not be part of the couple's awareness set. The couple will choose a resort that seems to offer the best value based on the information provided by the tour wholesaler. Thus the tour wholesaler exerts a powerful force over resorts, especially remote international markets.

The Caribbean resort industry is particularly dependent on tour wholesalers, who provide over half the business. One effect of the power of tour wholesalers in this area is the existence of substantial discounts to them regardless of seasonal demand. This seriously affects the ability of Caribbean hotel managers to control pricing through tools such as yield management (see Chapter 12). It also affects cash flow. Caribbean wholesalers collect payment from customers three to six months before they arrive at a hotel, but most hotels had to wait sixty days after guest arrival for payment from wholesalers.

Airlines may also serve as tour operators. Almost all major airlines have vacation packages promoted through brochures and their Web sites. An airline such as Air New Zealand offers farm/ranch or bed and breakfast packages for the FIT (foreign independent traveler) market. Visitors to New Zealand can book auto rentals or camper rentals and reservations with these specialized lodging providers through the tour desk of Air New Zealand.

Specialists: Tour Brokers, Motivational Houses, and Junket Reps

Tour brokers sell motor coach tours, which are attractive to a variety of markets. Tours through New England to view the fall foliage, trips to college and sporting events, tours built around Mardi Gras, and regularly scheduled tours of the Washington, DC, area are examples of popular motor coach trips. Some motor coach tours are seasonal, some are based on one event, and others are year round. For hotels on their routes, motor coach tours can provide an important source of income.[15]

Motor coach tours are very important to museums and historic restorations such as Historic Colonial Williamsburg in Virginia. Hospitality providers such as historic restorations, hotels, and destination cities usually participate in a travel conference sponsored by the American Bus Association. Booth space is rented, and salespeople representing these providers scramble to make appointments with bus tour companies that serve their area.

13.4 American Bus Association

Motivational houses provide incentive travel offered to employees or distributors as a reward for their efforts. Companies often use incentive travel as a prize for employees who achieve sales goals or for the sales team achieving the highest sales. The incentive trip is usually to a resort area and includes first-class or luxury properties. For resorts or up-market properties in destination cities, such as New York, San Francisco, Chicago, or Boston, motivational houses represent an effective distribution channel. Ways of reaching tour brokers and incentive houses include trade magazines and trade associations, such as the National Tour Association and the Society of Incentive Travel Executives.[16]

Junket reps serve the casino industry as intermediaries for premium players. Junket reps maintain lists of gamblers who like to visit certain gaming areas, such as Reno, Las Vegas, or Atlantic City, and they work with one or a few casinos rather than the entire industry. They are paid a commission on the amount the casino earns from the players or in some cases on a per player basis. Members of a junket receive complimentary or low-cost hospitality services, including air transportation, ground transportation, hotel lodging, food and beverage, and entertainment. The amount of complimentary services received depends on the amount players gamble in the casino.

Hotel Representatives

Hotel representatives sell hotel rooms and hotel services in a given market area. It is often more effective for hotels to hire a hotel representative than to use their own salesperson. This is true when the market is a distant one and when cultural differences may make it hard for an outsider to penetrate the market. For example, a corporate hotel in Houston may find that it is more effective to hire a hotel representative in Mexico City than to send a sales manager there. Hotel sales representatives should represent noncompeting hotels. They receive a straight commission, a commission plus a salary, or a combination of both. It takes time for a hotel representative to learn a company's products and inform the market about them. The choice of a hotel representative should not be taken lightly. Frequent changes in hotel representatives are not cost-efficient or cost-effective.

National, State, and Local Tourist Agencies

National, state, and local tourist agencies are an excellent way to get information to the market and gain room bookings. National associations promote tourism within their own countries. Their impact can be important to hotel chains that have locations throughout the country. State agencies promote the state resources and attractions overseas, nationally, and in the state itself. State tourist agencies usually have tourist information centers strategically located throughout the state, often at entrance points. Regional associations can also help the independent and chain operators.

13.5 The Sydney Convention and Visitors Bureau

The Sydney Convention and Visitors Bureau (SCVB) has offices in London, Melbourne, and New York, in addition to its main office in

This photo is an example of one of the images supplied by the Sydney Convention and Visitors Bureau to promote Sydney. Courtesy of the Sydney Convention and Visitors Bureau.

Sydney. The staff in these offices work to bring meetings and conventions to Sydney by making them aware of the facilities and amenities the city has to offer. The SCVB also provides materials for organizations to help promote their meeting in Sydney. For example, they provide promotional videos of Sydney, postcards for teaser campaigns, slides for presentations, and brochure shells with images of Sydney that can be overprinted with the program, registration material, or other information. They also help the event planner match their needs with what the city has to offer, including venues for meeting, lodging accommodations, and ideas for unique activities. One suggestion is a private breakfast on Shark Island in the middle of Sydney Harbor, with the sunrise over the Opera House and the harbor bridge. Another is having an Australian bush theme party in a five-star hotel complete with live kangaroos, koalas, and sheep sheering. The SCVB, like other convention and visitors bureaus, serves as a channel to bring business to their city or region.[17]

Consortia and Reservation Systems

Reservation systems such as Loews Representation International, Steigenberger Reservation Service, and International Reservations and Information Consortium are expanding their services. Reservation systems provide a central reservation system for hotels. They usually provide the system for small chains or provide an overseas reservation service, allowing international guests to call a local number to contact the hotel.

In ski areas, the ski resort may operate the hotel's reservation system. The resort will book hotel reservations at independent hotels or motels for a commission such as 15 percent. Because the resort commonly has its own lodging, independent hotel and motel managers sometimes fear the power of this organization and may refuse to cooperate in joint promotional efforts, as they do not wish to share their database.

A consortium is a group of hospitality organizations that is allied for the mutual benefit of the members. Marketing is often the reason why consortia are formed. The consortium allows a property to be independent in ownership and management while gaining the advantages of group marketing. An example of a consortium is Leading Hotels of the World. The distinction between consortia and reservation services is becoming blurred as reservation services such as SRS, Utell, and Supranational are now expanding into marketing activities. It is a natural evolution for reservation systems to add additional services once they have a critical number of hotels as subscribers.

Four of the largest consortia, as measured by rooms represented, are Supranational, Logis de France, Leading Hotels of the World, Golden Tulip, and Utell. Logis de France is an association of more than 4,000 small one-, two-, and three-star hotels in France. Logis de France is a consortium, with hotels identifying themselves as members of the organization through signage on the hotel and road signs. Utell is the largest representation company with regional centers throughout the world. It represents more than 6,400, answers more than 22,000 reservation inquiries each day, and booked 9.6 million room-nights in 2000.[18] Utell has taken advantage of technology by linking up to all major global distribution systems. Utell also developed its own Web site and HotelBook.

13.6 TravelWeb

Additionally, it is linked to TravelWeb, Travelocity, and Expedia. One feature of its Web site is UtellVision, a system that allows reservation agents throughout the world to see pictures of a property on their computer terminals. This organization markets hotels to the incentive market, conference planners, tour operators, corporate meeting planners, travel agents, and wholesalers. The difference between a consortium and reservation company is that the consortium provides a more comprehensive range of marketing services and its members pay for these services with initial joining fees and annual fees. Reservation companies gain the majority of their revenue by charging for each reservation they book. As a representation company, Utell provides more marketing services than a reservation company but less than a consortium.[19]

Hotel chains have their own central reservation systems, but they still rely on external central reservations to provide access to customers. Pegasus purchased REZsoultions to become the largest central reservation system. On an average business day, Pegasus processes over 130,000 reservations for 38,000 hotels.[20]

Regions are also developing consortia to promote their area as a tourism attraction. For example, tourist attractions in the Bath area of the United Kingdom have formed the Association of Bath and District Leisure Enterprises (ABLE). This type of cooperative allows smaller hospitality organizations to develop and distribute promotional material. Travel agents have formed consortia to negotiate lower rates for hotel rooms, airlines, and other tourist products. One of the larger travel agent consortia is Woodside Management Systems. Consortia can also develop vertical marketing systems by negotiating special prices on supplies that members may use.[21]

Global Distribution Systems

Global distribution systems (GDSs) are computerized reservation systems that serve as a product catalog for travel agents and other distributors of hospitality products. These reservation systems were originally developed by the airlines to promote sales. The major GDSs are Amadeus, Galileo, Sabre, and Worldspan. Amadeus is the market leader in Western Europe and Latin America. There are over 155,000 travel agency terminals connected to Amadeus.[22] Galileo connects travel agents to 500 airlines, forty car rental companies, 47,000 hotels, 370 tour operators, and all the major cruise lines.[23] As GDSs expand their Internet capabilities, they are expanding into other hospitality products. For example, Worldspan now represents MyGolf-Time.com, enabling clients to book tee times on courses through Europe, North America, and South America. Through Worldspan's Internet site named Go!, lets Go! Agents can book airlines, hotels, rental cars, and shows and make restaurant reservations all from one site.[24] This creates a new model for travel agents, with reduced airline commissions, travel agents now have to make use of systems like Worldspan to book more of their client's travel products to survive. As this model evolves, restaurants, shows, golf courses, and other tourist products will be distributed by GDSs. Ninety-six percent of the travel agents in the United States are connected to at least one computer reservation system.[25]

13.7 Go! MyGolf-Time.com

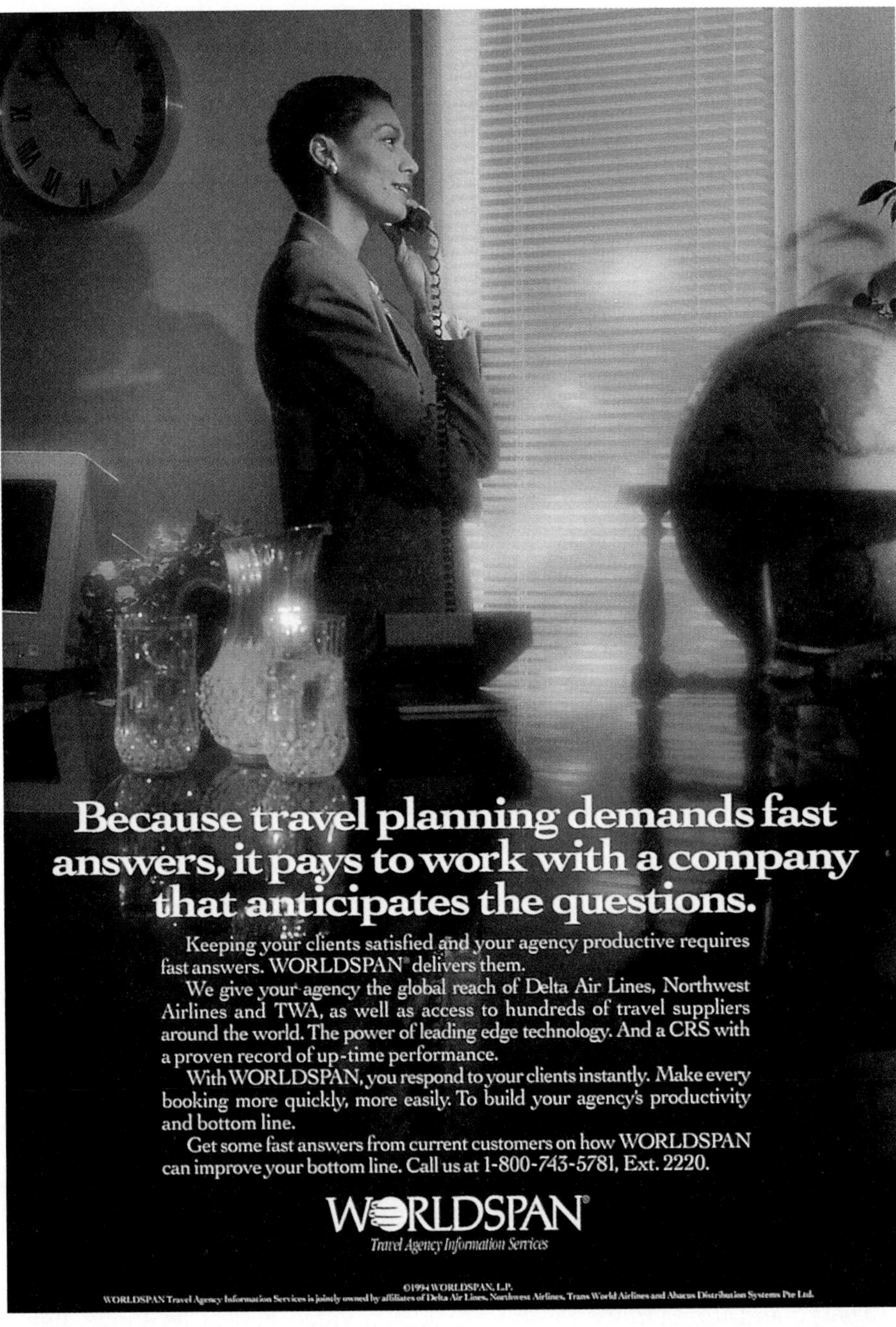

Global distribution systems such as Worldspan make travel products available to travel agents and corporate travel planners around the world. Courtesy of Worldspan.

Internet

In Chapter 5, we discussed how managers could use the Internet to gain marketing information. The Internet is quickly becoming an effective distribution channel. Bruce Rosenberg, the vice president of marketing and distribution for Hilton, states that Hilton's site accounts for thousands of reservations per month.[26] Today, over a billion dollars in travel products are booked on the Web, and major hotel chains such as Hilton and

Marriott book millions of dollars worth of rooms over the Web. In 1997, Michael Pusateri of Marriott estimated that $10 billion in travel products would be booked over the Internet by the year 2000; his estimate was off by $2.4 billion, as $12.4 billion was booked.[27] In 2003, this number is estimated to be $25.2 billion, about 10 percent of the total travel business market, allowing plenty of room for rapid growth in the coming years.[28] In fact, Charles Thackston, of Sabre, feels that by 2004, 20 percent of travel products will be purchased by on-line corporate and consumer customers.[29]

"All of us are interested in getting on the information superhighway because we know the channels of travel distribution are changing," said Nancy Vaughn, Best Western's director of corporate communications.[30] Mary Sweenson, managing director of worldwide communications for Best Western, said the Internet allows Best Western to reach the 72 percent of their customers who do not use a travel agent.[31] Total hotel sales over the Internet are now over $5 billion.[32] Marriott's Internet reservation system takes in over 10,000 reservations in one day. Southwest Airlines receives over a billion dollars in ticket sales through its site.[33]

Restaurant companies are also using the Internet as a distribution channel. Pizza Hut and Domino's have on-line ordering systems. TerraNet was developed in Boston for customers wanting home delivery of restaurant meals. The database allows the user to search by restaurant name or type of food. The Internet user then gets information on the menu, including color photos of the dishes. The customer can select either takeout or delivery. After they have made their selection, they get the amount owed, including any delivery charges.[34] Just as hotels sell reservations over the Internet, restaurants have developed sites that allow for their customers to reserve a table.

Some of the advantages of the Internet are that it never closes, it is open twenty-four hours a day, seven days a week, has worldwide coverage, and can transmit color pictures. The capability of transmitting color photographs to millions of people across the globe makes the Internet an exciting distribution channel. It allows companies to make their products tangible through the use of color photos and videos. The Grand Aleutian is a remote resort 800 miles southwest of Anchorage. It attracts fishermen and those who want to explore the Aleutian Islands. It only has 112 rooms, yet through an Internet site called Historic Inns of America, it can provide thousands of potential guests with color photos of its rooms and food and beverage facilities and allow them to make inquiries through e-mail. Similarly, the Rutledge Victorian Inn can show color pictures of its exterior and its rooms. Hyatt provides a video tour of the Park Hyatt Tokyo, and the Stardust Casino provides a video clip of its show "Enter the Night." These examples show how small, independent properties can use the Internet to gain access to travelers across the country and the world.

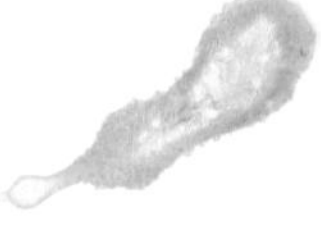

By using a menu, Web sites can provide a lot of information while enabling users to quickly access information of interest. Mandalay Bay Resort gives daily rates on their Internet site. The resort has a wide swing in rates based on their convention and meeting business. A customer driving up from Las Vegas uses this information to choose the less expensive days to come to the Mandalay Bay. Providing this information creates a win-win situation because these are also days when the resort needs business. The Hyatt's site provides information on each hotel, has an enrollment form for their Gold Passport, a list of discounted rooms, information on golf packages, and much more. Yet somebody wanting information on the Hyatts in the Chicago area could go right to the directory and find that information. Although many customers will decide to make a reservation while they are on the Internet, others use the Internet as a source of information, but like to talk to a live person to make their reservation. The reservation for this person is quicker because they already know what they want as the Internet site answered many of their questions.

Visitors to an Internet site have the ability to print hard copies of information provided on the site's pages. Hilton takes advantage of this by providing an interactive map for each of the hotels linked to its home page. The map can be zoomed in and out to provide as much detail as the prospective guest needs. Marriott, Taco Bell, and other restaurant and hotel companies have maps as part of their sites or have a link to MapQuest, an Internet-based mapping program. This makes it easier for tourists to find a hotel or a restaurant in an unfamiliar city. Some restaurants are providing coupons that can be printed. The Internet also allows interaction with the guest through e-mail and by phone and mail when the guest provides the appropriate information.

One of the major advantages of the Internet is it saves labor. The Internet is an excellent example of how service companies can get the customer to be their employee. When making reservations or purchasing products on-line, the customer is acting as a reservation agent. It would take a reservation center with over 100 full-time employees, a building to house them, and equipment to serve them to take in an equivalent number of reservations that Marriott takes in on its Internet site.

13.8 Expedia.com
Mandalay Bay Resorts
Marriott
Priceline.com

Travel agencies such as Travelocity and Expedia are capitalizing on the benefits of the Internet. Expedia is one of the top fifty Internet sites and has had over 7 million unique visitors in one month.[35] There are also a variety of wholesalers based on the Internet, such as travelscape, Hotwire!, and Priceline. Hotels commit a block of rooms and the rate for those rooms to the wholesaler. Internet wholesalers are typically used to sell rooms during distressed periods. As we mentioned in the pricing chapter, hotels have to be careful to maintain price integrity when using Internet wholesalers, as these rooms are sold on Internet sites that compete with the hotel's site. Priceline's system does not specify any particular hotel or airline; thus, someone with a brand preference cannot compare prices with specific hotels. Persons who purchase from a wholesaler pay the wholesaler, and the hotel bills the wholesaler to collect their money. Thus, if the hotel wants to capture guests for their database, they need to collect the guests' names and addresses when they register, as the wholesale companies sometimes use their address for all their customers. Hotels selling rooms through an Internet wholesaler should make their reservationists and desk staff aware that they are doing this and that there may be a delay from the time the guest books the hotel room and when the wholesaler transfers the information to the hotel. Guests that are new to Internet booking are often anxious and call the hotel to confirm the booking after making the reservation. The hotel may have no record, and the reservationist can spend valuable time trying to sort out the status of the reservation. By simply asking the guest how they made the reservation, the hotel employee can identify those who book with a wholesaler and inform them that the reservation has not been transferred yet, and advise them when to check back.

The Internet is rapidly becoming an important distribution channel with relatively low costs, allowing the independent operator to gain access to world markets. It allows the multiunit operator to give information about all locations, including color brochures and guided tours of the property. This information is valuable to the individual traveler, meeting planner, and the travel agent. Hospitality and travel companies are now producing separate sites to meet the information needs of these unique segments.

Concierges

Concierges, bell staff, and front-desk employees can be good sources of business for local hospitality products and travel, such as restaurants, tours, and fishing guides. Concierges can be a major source of business for a restaurant that has a unique menu, atmosphere, or simply excellent food and service. These attributes will be an attraction to travelers. Restaurants wishing to cultivate a relationship with concierges usually invite them for a complimentary meal, so that they can experience the restaurant firsthand. The restaurant's management will also volunteer the restaurant as a site for the local concierge association meetings if the restaurant has meeting space. The restaurant should also supply the hotel with menus they can show to guests asking about the restaurant. Finally, the restaurant will instruct the staff on how to handle calls from a concierge. For example, even though the concierge knows that there is no chance of getting a reservation at a popular restaurant on a Saturday night, they are still obliged to call because the guest has requested it and is standing at their side. Thus, when such requests do come, the person answering the phone at the restaurant should be courteous and understand the situation.

Channel Behavior and the Organization

Distribution channels are more than simple collections of firms tied together by various flows. They are complex behavioral systems in which people and companies interact to accomplish goals. Some channel systems consist of formal interactions among loosely organized firms. Others consist of formal interactions guided by strong organizational structures. Channel systems do not stand still. New types surface and new channel systems evolve. We now look at channel behavior and how members organize to do the work of the channel.

Channel Behavior

A distribution system consists of dissimilar firms that have banded together for their common good. Each channel member is dependent on the others, playing a role in the channel and specializing in performing one or more functions.

Ideally, because the success of individual channel members depends on general channel success, all channel firms should work together. They should understand and accept their roles, coordinate their goals and activities, and cooperate to attain overall channel goals. By cooperating they can more effectively understand and serve the target market.

But individual channel members rarely take such a broad view. They are usually more concerned with their own short-run goals and their dealings with the firms operating closest to them in the channel. Cooperating to achieve overall channel goals sometimes means giving up individual company goals. Although channel members are dependent on each another, they often act alone in their own short-run best interests. They frequently disagree on the roles each should play or who should do what for which rewards. Such disagreements over goals and roles generate **channel conflict.**

Horizontal conflict is conflict between firms at the same level of the channel. For example, some Pizza Inn franchisees may complain about other Pizza Inn franchisees cheating on ingredients and giving poor service, thereby hurting the overall Pizza Inn image.

Vertical conflict, which is more common, refers to conflicts between different levels of the same channel. At the beginning of this chapter, we mentioned the agreement between Little Caesar's and Kmart. For Little Caesar's, this agreement provided a great opportunity to increase sales and add 1,200 new outlets to its distribution system. However, to some Little Caesar's franchisees it meant an erosion of their sales.[36]

Some conflict in the channel takes the form of healthy competition. Without it, the channel could become passive and noninnovative. But sometimes conflict can damage the channel. For the channel as a whole to perform well, each channel member's role must be specified, and channel conflict must be managed. Cooperation, assignment of roles, and conflict management are attained through strong channel leadership. The channel will perform better if it contains a firm, agency, or mechanism that has the power to assign roles and manage conflict.

Today, the complexity of channels has made it more difficult to manage channel members and act in the best interest of all channel members. Some forms of conflict are the result of management not thinking about how marketing decisions will affect all of a firm's channel members. For example, Embassy Suites had to modify a promotion it developed with Hertz offering cash payments to Hertz customers who were renting cars and staying overnight. The promotion offered Hertz's customers with a confirmed hotel reservation a cash voucher if they would switch to an Embassy Suites Hotel. Embassy Suites saw an opportunity to reach hotel customers who were making an immediate purchase, and Hertz saw an opportunity to build business by offering its customers a cash bonus. It seemed like a good idea for both companies, but the American Society of Travel Agents protested the agreement. They felt that the hotel chain was unfairly taking commissions away from travel agents who had made the original reservations.[37] Both Embassy Suites and Hertz failed to recognize the negative impact that the promotion would have on one of their channel members, the travel agent.

In a large company, the formal organizational structure assigns roles and provides needed leadership. But in a distribution channel made up of in-

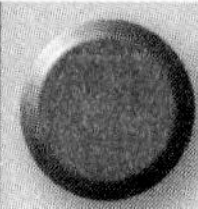

Marketing Highlight 13-2

The Hilton Model

Hilton Hotels has initiated a number of comprehensive programs designed to serve agents while bolstering agent recognition and appreciation. Their initiatives include the following:

- Centralized reservation systems. Hilton's toll-free Private Travel Agent Reservation Line assists agents with inquiries and reservations for Hilton Hotels nationwide. Staffed by forty reservationists trained exclusively for work with travel agents, the line offers around-the-clock information every day. Hilton's other central reservation services include automated services such as SABRE, Apollo/Galileo, Amadeus/SystemOne, Datas II, and Covia's Inside Availability; expanded rate categories; automatic rate updates; rate returns; contests; and other marketing messages.
- Centralized commission payment. Hilton gives agents consolidated payments for bookings at Hilton Hotels nationwide. Commission checks are issued biweekly for hotels enrolled in Hilton's central commission program, and all other commissions are paid within forty-eight hours of guest checkout. Check statements include commission amount, folio number, hotel name, number of nights, and guest name. Hilton identifies which rates are commissionable at the time of reservation.
- Hilton fam club. Recognizing the importance of agent familiarization trips, Hilton introduced its chainwide "fam" policy, which extends to agents a 50 percent savings off the minimum rack rate at each Hilton Hotel.
- Hilton Direct. The Hilton Direct toll-free customer service and meeting arrangement system offers agents information on availability and rates of hotel conference facilities within twenty-four hours of any inquiry.
- Travel agent help desk. The toll-free help line provides agents with research on commission payments, assistance with CRS bookings and format questions, and comprehensive assistance with Hilton's travel agent marketing and sales programs.
- Travel agent advisory board. Comprising nine travel industry professionals and five Hilton executives, the agent advisory board provides feedback for the company's travel agent programs and ensures that relations between travel agents and hotels continue to improve.

Source: Reprinted by permission of Elsevier Science, Inc., from "Hotels and Travel Agents, the New Partnership," by Christopher Schulz, *Cornell Hotel and Restaurant Administration Quarterly* 35, no. 3 (April 1994): 45, © 1994 by Cornell University.

dependent firms, leadership and power are not formally set. Traditionally, distribution channels have lacked the leadership needed to assign roles and manage conflict. In recent years, new types of channel organizations have appeared to provide stronger leadership and improved performance.[38]

Channel Organization

Historically, distribution channels have been loose collections of independent companies, each showing little concern for overall channel performance. These conventional distribution systems have lacked strong leadership and have been troubled by damaging conflict and poor performance.

Growth of Vertical Marketing Systems

One of the biggest recent channel developments has been the vertical marketing systems that have emerged to challenge conventional marketing systems. Figure 13-3 contrasts the two types of channel arrangements.

A conventional distribution channel consists of one or more independent producers, wholesalers, and retailers. Each is a separate business seeking to maximize its profits, even at the expense of profits for the system as a whole. No channel member has much control over the other members, and no formal means exist for assigning roles and resolving channel conflict. For example, most hotels pay a commission to travel agents. No formal contract is signed between the hotel and every agent. The hotel simply communicates its policy and can, if it wishes, make rooms unavailable to travel agents on a temporary basis.

By contrast, a **vertical marketing system (VMS)** consists of producers, wholesalers, and retailers acting as a unified system. One channel member either owns the others, has contracts with them, or wields so much power that they all cooperate.[39] The VMS can be dominated by the producer, wholesaler, or retailer. VMSs were originally developed to control channel behavior and manage channel conflict. Another major benefit is economies through size, bargaining power, and elimination of duplicated services. VMSs have become dominant in consumer marketing, serving as much as 64 percent of the total market.

We now look at the three major types of VMSs shown in Figure 13-3. Each type uses a different means for setting up leadership and power in the channel. In a **corporate VMS,** coordination and conflict management are attained through common ownership at different levels in the channel. In an administered VMS, leadership is assumed by one or a few dominant channel members. In a contractual VMS, they are attained through contractual agreements among channel members.

13.8 Red Lobster

A corporate VMS combines successive stages of production and distribution under single ownership. For example, Red Lobster has its own food-processing plants and distributes food products to its restaurants. Breweries in Great Britain own pubs, which serve only the beers of the owner brewery.

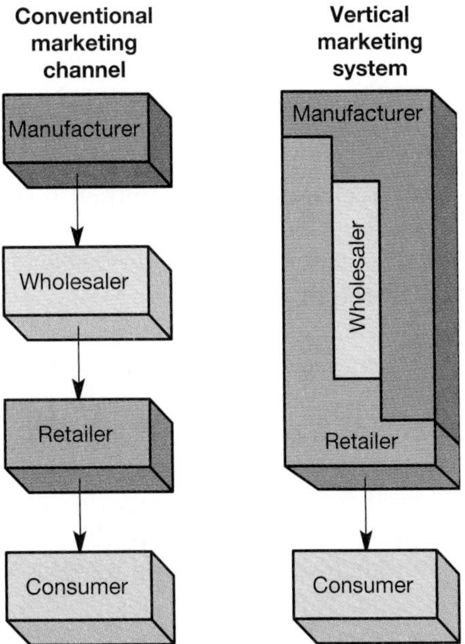

Figure 13-3
Major types of vertical marketing systems.

BEST TWO LETTERS ON YOUR KEYBOARD.

Your computer is more powerful than you think. Just type in BW and it can reach every Best Western in the world. This reservation access code allows you to make and confirm reservations, compare rates, check availability and obtain information about all our new programs and amenities.

You'll find we've introduced some new frequent traveler clubs. And that's just one of our many changes. We're also spending more than a billion dollars upgrading hotels worldwide. We've enacted tough new inspection standards at 3,400 locations in more than 50 countries.

And you can bring them all up on the screen with just the touch of a button. Well, two buttons.

YOUR BEST BET IS A BEST WESTERN.

For information or reservations, call our Travel Agent Help Desk at 1-800-334-7234.

Best Western is a type of contractual VMS. It provides its members with marketing services, such as this reservation access code allowing travel agents to make reservations from their computers. Courtesy of Best Western International, Inc., and Lord, Dentsu and Partners.

An **administered VMS** coordinates successive stages of production and distribution not through common ownership or contractual ties but through the size and power of the parties. For example, in the 1970s a popular beer brand gained an exclusive right to supply draft beer in a restaurant or bar through the power of its brand. The producer would not allow a bar serving its beer on tap to serve any others, claiming that other beers on the same line could reduce the quality of their product. They argued that other beer companies might use dirty tools to clean the lines and set the pressure improperly. They used their brand power to eliminate competition.

The world's airline industry has been affected by administered VMSs since the birth of the industry. Many nations continue to cling to a subsidized national carrier known as a flag carrier. These airlines often exert an inordinate amount of power over reservations systems, tour operators, and travel agencies within their respective nations.

The third type of VMS is contractual. A **contractual VMS** consists of independent firms at different levels of production and distribution who join through contracts to obtain economies or sales impact. A contract with a hotel representative would be an example of a contractual VMS. An important form of contractual VMS is franchising.

Franchising

"Franchising is a method of doing business by which a franchisee is granted the right to engage in offering, selling, or distributing goods or services under a marketing format which is designed by the franchisor. The franchisor permits the franchisee to use its trademark, name, and advertising."[40] Franchising has been the fastest-growing retailing form in recent years. The 700,000 or more franchise operations in the United States now account for about $850 billion of all retail sales.[41] Industry analyst Stephen Rushmore found that franchised hotels account for more than 65 percent of the existing U.S. hotel-room supply.[42] One of the reasons for the popularity of franchising is that it is the safest way to start a new business. Estimates of the success rate for different methods of starting a business are as follows:[43]

- *Starting a new business*: a 20 percent chance for survival
- *Buying an existing business:* a 70 percent chance for survival
- Buying *a franchise*: a 90 percent chance for survival

Franchises have been popular forms of distribution for both hotels and restaurants. Some popular hotel franchises include Choice Hotels, Holiday Inns, Days Inns, Sheraton Inns, and Hilton Inns. Restaurant franchises include McDonald's, Burger King, Kentucky Fried Chicken, Pizza Hut, and T.G.I. Friday's. Franchises have been responsible for shifting the restaurant business from individual operators to multiunits. Franchised restaurant companies had sales of $79 billion in 1991 and accounted for more than half of all restaurant sales. They achieved this through a network of 106,000 locations.[44]

13.9 Hilton Inns
Kentucky Fried Chicken
Pizza Hut
Sheraton Inns

For the right to use the name, methods of operation, and other benefits that come with a franchise, the franchisee pays an initial fee, a royalty, and a marketing fee to the **franchise organization.** In the case of hotels, a fee for use of the central reservation system is also charged. Radisson charges an initial fee that is a minimum of $50,000. The royalty is 4 percent of gross room revenue, the marketing fee is 1.75 percent of gross room revenue, and the reservation fee is 2 percent of gross room revenue.[45] Note that these percentages are gross percentages. The franchisor can verify gross receipts through tax reports.

The initial fee and the royalty depend on the brand equity of the franchise. For example, McDonald's is recognized as a fast-food restaurant around the world. People in London, Paris, Hong Kong, and New York recognize McDonald's. The stronger the market position is, the more valuable the brand name. Thus a McDonald's franchise offers more value than a Mr. Quick franchise. The advantages of the franchise to the franchisee (person or organization buying the franchise) are:

- Recognition of brand
- Less chance of a business failure
- National advertising, premade advertisements, and marketing plans
- Faster business growth
- Help with site selection
- Architectural plans
- Operational systems, software, and manual to support the systems
- National contracts with suppliers
- Product development
- Consulting
- Help with financing

The disadvantages of purchasing a franchise are:

- Fees and royalties are required.
- It limits the products sold and the recipes used.
- The franchisee is often required to be open a minimum number of hours and offer certain products.
- A poorly operated company can affect the reputation of the entire chain.
- The franchisor's performance affects the profitability of franchisees.
- Some franchisees may not benefit from national advertising as much as other franchisees—often a source of conflict.

One of the reasons that companies decide to franchise is that it allows for increased distribution of their products. The franchisee's money expands the business, while the franchisor collects an initial fee and royalties. Franchising is not effective for all companies. The company must be able to offer the operational systems, management support, and a good business concept. For new businesses it requires time and money to provide a good franchisee package. Smaller chains often franchise to people who are close to business. For example, franchising is used in smaller restaurant chains to help them retain managers. It is difficult for a small chain to compete with opportunities that a large chain offers its managers. Some small chains combat career opportunities the large chains offer by helping their best managers get their own store through franchising. This allows the chain to keep managers who might otherwise grow bored and unchallenged. The advantages of franchising for the franchisor are as follows:

- Receives a percentage of gross sales
- Expands brand
- Support for national advertising campaign
- Negotiating support for national contracts with suppliers

The disadvantages of a franchise for a franchisor are as follows:

- There are limits on other options of expanding distribution; for example, the ability to develop alliances may be limited if the alliances violate the territorial agreements of the franchisees.
- Franchisees must be monitored to ensure product consistency.
- There is limited ability to require franchisees to change operations; for example, Pizza Hut had a difficult time getting franchisees to add delivery when Domino's was developing the delivery market.
- Franchisees want and need to have an active roll in decision making.

A variation of the traditional form of franchising is subfranchising. In this form of franchising, the franchisor sells the right to distribute a franchise to a third party, and this agent then sells to the franchisees.[46] For example, a franchisor sells the right to distribute and manage franchises to a subfranchisor. The subfranchisor then receives payment from the franchises it has sold and passes a portion of these fees to the franchisor and retains the rest. The subfranchisor also provides management support for their franchisees. One researcher estimates that 31 percent of quick-service restaurants and 37 percent of family restaurants use subfranchise contracts.[47] This allows the franchisor to expand by taking advantage of an agent's management and marketing resources. Another example would be a company that would become a subfranchisor, selling franchises to its franchisees or business associates. For example, Uni-Marts, a gas and convenience store, is a subfranchisor for Blimpie Subs and Salads restaurants.[48]

Alliances

Alliances are another form of contractual agreement. **Alliances** are developed to allow two organizations to benefit from each other's strengths. In the beginning of the chapter, we mentioned the alliance between the Welcome Group and Sheraton Hotels. It would be difficult if not impossible for Sheraton to go into India by itself because of that nation's regulation of foreign-owned businesses. The Welcome Group offered Sheraton an Indian partner. Additionally, the Welcome Group had a good reputation in India and understood how to do business there. Sheraton offered the Welcome Group a name that was known to the international business traveler. Sheraton offered training and management support systems. Thus both partners benefited from the alliance.

Restaurants are expanding their locations through alliances with hotel chains. This provides the restaurant with a good location and access to the hotel's guests. The hotel gains the value of the brand name of the restaurant. For example, Trader Vic's, one of the first restaurants to align with hotels, has locations in several Hiltons, the Marriott Royal Garden Riverside (Bangkok), and the New Otani hotels in Tokyo and Singapore. Ruth's Chris Steakhouses has locations in hotels operated by Marriott, Holiday, and Westin. Good Eats, a casual, regional chain well known in Texas, has developed an alliance with Bristol Hotels.[49] The new resorts opening in Las Vegas are developing alliances with branded restaurants; names such as the Rainforest Café, California Pizza Kitchen, Benihana, Wolfgang Puck Café, Tony Roma's, and Gordon Biersch can be found in the resorts. Additionally, many resorts have food courts similar to those in the malls, featuring branded fast-food outlets. The use of branded restaurants is attracting the attention of hotel management and creating opportunities for restaurants to expand their distribution.

13.10 Benihana
California Pizza Kitchen
Gordon Biersch
Rainforest Café
Tony Roma's
Wolfgang Puck Café

Alliances by two or more noncompeting firms are a popular and effective way of expanding markets. For example, restaurants are developing alliances with convenience stores and hotel properties to distribute their products. 7-Eleven stores sell Dunkin Donuts in 2,000 of its stores. Embassy Suites has Red Lobster restaurants located in its hotels. Chain fast-food operations located in convenience stores allow the store to offer brand-name products, and the chain gains additional high-traffic distribution points. Many consumers perceive hotel restaurants to be overpriced and of poor quality. The introduction of well-known chain restaurants into hotels overcomes this problem.

Table 13-2
Hotel and Restaurant Franchise Costs

HOTEL FRANCHISES

CHAIN	HEADQUARTERS	TOTAL FRANCHISED PROPERTIES/ROOMS	ADDITIONAL PROPERTIES/ROOMS (BY YEAR END)	FEE STRUCTURE (U.S. DOLLARS)
Ramada	New Jersey	992/121,961	63/8,623	Initial: $350/room, $35,000 minimum Royalty: 4% gross rooms revenue Ad/marketing: combined with reservation fee (see reservation fee) Reservation: combined with ad fee, 4.5% gross rooms revenue
Days Inn of America	New Jersey	1,951/164,845	88/8,280	Initial: $350/room, $35,000 minimum Royalty: 6.5% gross rooms revenue Ad/marketing: included in royalty fee Reservation: 2.3% gross rooms revenue and initial entry charge to gain access (lesser of $100/room or $10,000)
Holiday Inn Worldwide	Atlanta	2,241/403,093	43/5,046	Initial: $30,000/room; $75,000 Crowne Plaza Royalty: 5% Ad/marketing: 2.5%, Crowne Plaza Express, 3% Reservations: 1%
Best Western International	Phoenix	4,082/309,661	300/25,500	Initial: $25,000 minimum/100 rooms Royalty: annual dues $3,676 for 100 rooms Reservation: 25 cents/room/day, first year, then fee based on prior year's room-nights booked Ad/marketing: annual dues $2949 for 100 rooms
Choice Hotels International Comfort	Silver Springs, MD	2,661/239,696 1,688/129,833	219/28,088 157/11,972	Initial: $300/room, $50,000 minimum, $50,000 for suites Royalty: 5.25% of gross rooms revenue Ad/marketing: 2.1% of gross rooms revenue, plus 28 cents/room/day (for all brands) Reservation: 1.75% gross rooms revenue, plus $1 per night confirmed through system (all brands)
Embassy Suites	Beverly Hills, CA	155/38,510	24/5,969	Initial: $500 per suite, $100,000 minimum Royalty: 4% gross suite revenue

				Ad/marketing: 4% gross suites revenue Reservation: 4% gross suites revenue
Fairfield Inns by Marriott	Washington, D.C.	500/53,200	17/1,500	Initial: $400/room new builds; $200/room conversion Royalty: 5.5% room sales Ad/marketing: 2.5% of room sales Reservation: 1% of room sales and $3.50/ reservation

Sources: FranchiseZone, retrieved from World Wide Web on 5/8/02, *http://www.entrepreneur.com; Franchise Digest,* retrieved from World Wide Web on 5/8/02, *http://www.lodgingnews.com/subs/fd/fd39.asp*

RESTAURANT FRANCHISES

FRANCHISE SYSTEM	FRANCHISE FEE	ROYALTY (%)	ADVERTISING ROYALTY (%)	TOTAL INVESTMENT[a] ($000S)	INVESTMENT/SALES RATIO (U.S. ONLY)
Applebee's Neighborhood Grill & Bar	30,000	5	4.2	400	0.23
Arby's	37,500	4	3.0	525–850	1.10
Burger King	50,000	4.5	4.0	1,000	0.94
Domino's Pizza	1,000–3,000	5.5	3.3	75–150	0.22
KFC	20,000	6	6	600–800	1.04
McDonalds	45,000	3.5	4.0	575	0.37
Pizza Hut	18,350	6	6	N/A	N/A
Subway Sandwiches & Salads	10,000	8.0	2.5	40	0.15
T.G.I. Friday's	75,000	4.0	4	2,000–2,500	0.63

Sources: Investor Relations, retrieved from World Wide Web on 5/8/02, *http://www.applebees.com;* Fact Sheet, retrieved from World Wide Web on 5/8/02, *http://www.triconglobal.com/investors/fact.htm; Domestic Franchising,* retrieved from World Wide Web on 5/8/02, *http://www.dominos.com; Franchise Opportunities,* retrieved from World Wide Web on 5/8/02, *http://www.burgerking.com/companyinfo/; Franchising,* retrieved from World Wide Web on 5/8/02, *http://www.arbys.com/arb03_b.html; Subway Capital Requirements,* retrieved from World Wide Web on 5/8/02, *http://www.subway.com*

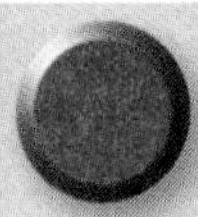

Marketing Highlight 13-3

Restaurant Franchising

These days, it's nearly impossible to stroll down a city block or drive on a suburban street without seeing a Wendy's, a McDonald's, a Pizza Hut, or a Starbucks. One of the best-known and most successful franchisers, McDonald's, now has 21,000 stores worldwide and racks up more than $30 billion in systemwide sales. Gaining fast is Subway Sandwiches and Salads, one of the fastest-growing franchises, with more than 13,000 shops in sixty-four countries.

How does a franchising system work? The individual franchises are a tightly knit group of enterprises whose systematic operations are planned, directed, and controlled by the operation's innovator, called a franchiser. The franchisee is required to pay for the right to be part of the system. Yet this initial fee is only a small part of the total amount that franchisees invest when they sign a franchising contract. Start-up costs include rental and lease of equipment and fixtures and sometimes a regular license fee. McDonald's franchisees may invest as much as $600,000 in initial start-up costs. The franchisee then pays McDonald's a service fee and a rental charge that equal 11.5 percent of the franchisee's sales volume. Subway's success is partly due to its low start-up cost of just $100,000, which is lower than 70 percent of other franchise system start-up costs. However, Subway franchisees pay an 8 percent royalty on gross sales, highest in the food franchise industry, plus a 3.5 percent advertising fee. The franchiser provides its franchisees with a marketing and operations system for doing business. McDonald's requires franchises to attend its "Hamburger University" in Oak Brook, Illinois, for three weeks to learn how to manage the business; franchisees must also adhere to certain procedures in buying materials.

In the best cases, franchising is mutually beneficial to both franchiser and franchisee. Franchisers can cover a new territory in little more than the time it takes the franchisee to sign a contract. They can achieve enormous purchasing power. Franchisers also benefit from the franchisees' familiarity with local communities and conditions and from the motivation and hard work of employees who are entrepreneurs rather than "hired hands." Similarly, franchisees benefit from buying into a proven business with a well-known and accepted brand name. And they receive ongoing support in areas ranging from marketing and advertising to site selection, staffing, and financing.

As a result of the franchise explosion in recent years, some fast-food franchisers are facing worrisome market saturation. One indication is the number of franchisee complaints filed with the Federal Trade Commission against parent companies, which has been growing by more than 50 percent annually

Airlines are developing alliances to access customers in other parts of the world and to provide their customers with new destination opportunities. For example, SAS developed an alliance with Continental Airlines to give it access to the U.S. market. Before the alliance, SAS served only a handful of U.S. cities. Since the alliance, Continental's U.S. flights can be used to feed into SAS's flights to Europe. Continental gained the SAS passengers flying into Newark and other U.S. gateways, who will now use Continental to reach their final destination in the United States.

The National Motor Coach Network, a marketing consortium of motor coach operators, has developed a partner program to bring charter business to preferred hotels. Now tour operators sometimes extend their trips to include an overnight stay. In the past, operators preferred a day trip to staying overnight in an unfamiliar hotel. A network representative

since 1990. The most common complaint is that franchisers "encroach" on existing franchisees' territory by bringing in another store. For example, McDonald's franchisees in California and other states recently complained when the company decided to open new company-owned stores in their areas. Franchisees may object to parent company marketing programs that may adversely affect their local operations. For instance, franchisees strongly resisted McDonald's "Campaign 55" promotion, in which the company reduced prices on Big Macs and Egg McMuffins to 55 cents in an effort to revive stagnant sales. Many franchises believed that the promotion might cheapen McDonald's image and unnecessarily reduce their profit margins. Another complaint is higher-than-advertised failure rates. Subway, in particular, has been criticized for misleading its franchisees by telling them that it has only a 2 percent failure rate when the reality is much different. In addition, some franchisees feel that they've been misled by exaggerated claims of support, only to feel abandoned after the contract is signed and money has been invested.

There will always be a conflict between the franchiser, who seek systemwide growth, and the franchisees, who want to earn a good living from their individual franchises. One new direction that may deliver both franchiser growth and franchisee earnings is expansion abroad. Fast-food franchises have become very popular throughout the world. For example, Domino's has entered Japan with master franchisee Ernest Higa, who owns 106 stores in Japan with combined sales of $140 million. Part of Higa's success can be attributed to adapting Domino's product to the Japanese market, where food presentation is everything. Higa carefully charted the placement of pizza toppings and made cutmark perforations in the boxes for perfectly uniform slices.

It appears franchise fever will not cool down soon. Experts estimate franchises capture 50 percent of all U.S. retail sales.

Sources: Norman D. Axelrad and Robert E. Weigand, "Franchising—A Marriage of System Members," in Sidney Levy, George Frerichs and Howard Gordon, eds., *Marketing Managers Handbook,* 3rd ed. (Chicago: Dartnell, 1994), pp. 919–934; Andrew E. Sewer, "McDonald's Conquers the World," *Fortune,* October 17, 1994, pp. 103–116; Roberta Maynard, "The Decision to Franchise," *Nation's Business,* January 1997, pp. 49–53; Cliff Edwards, "Campaign '55 Flop Shows Power of Franchisees," *Marketing News,* July 7, 1997, p. 9; Richard Behar, "Why Subway is the biggest Problem in Franchising," *Fortune,* March 16, 1998, pp. 126–134, and Patrick J. Kaufman and Sevgin Eroglu, "Standardization and Adaptation in Business Format Franchising," *Journal of Business Venturing,* January 1999, pp. 69–85.

visits all participating hotels before they are accepted. The alliance brings business to the hotels and provides motor coach operators with negotiated rates at hotels that meet their standards.[50]

Growth of Horizontal Marketing Systems

Another channel development is **horizontal marketing systems,** in which two or more companies at one level join to follow a new marketing opportunity.[51] By working together, companies can combine their capital, production capabilities, or marketing resources to accomplish more than one company can working alone. For example, Seaworld offers tickets at a discount to an automobile club, which promotes these discount tickets as one benefit for its members. In return, Seaworld gains access to several hundred thousand automobile club members. In another example, Sears and McDonald's joined forces to market the McKids line of "fun clothes for small fries." McDonald's franchisees and Sears stores worked together to develop local promotion programs. Such symbiotic marketing arrangements have increased in number in recent years, and the end is nowhere in sight.

American Express, the Coeur d'Alene resort, and K2 Skis worked together to offer a free pair of skis at check-in if the guest booked an American Express "Ski Week Holiday."

Growth of Multichannel Marketing Systems

In the past, many companies used a single channel to sell to a single market or market segment. Today, with the proliferation of customer segments and channel possibilities, more companies have adopted **multichannel marketing** distribution. Such multichannel marketing occurs when a single firm sets up two or more marketing channels to reach one or more customer segments.[52] For example, McDonald's sells through a network of independent franchisees but owns more than one-fourth of its outlets. Thus the wholly owned restaurants compete to some extent with those owned by McDonald's franchisees.

The multichannel marketer gains sales with each new channel but also risks offending existing channels. Existing channels can cry "unfair competition" and threaten to drop the marketer unless it limits competition or repays them in some way. For example, franchisees have brought lawsuits against franchisors that have developed competing operations in their market area.

Selecting Channel Members

Selecting channel members involves a number of factors, including customer needs, the company's ability to attract channel members, the economic feasibility of the channel member, and the control that might be given up to gain a channel member.

Customer Needs

Selecting channel members starts with determining the services that consumers in various target segments want. The Victoria House in Belize caters to customers from the United States. Its customers do not want to call Central America to reserve a room but need an easy way to communicate with the hotel. In response, the Victoria House aligned with a Houston travel agent with a toll-free number. The travel agent receives reservations directly from guests and from other travel agents throughout the United States, relaying the information to the Victoria House.

A large resort such as the Fiesta Americana in Puerto Vallarta, Mexico, might consider aligning with a wholesaler. The wholesaler would put together a package that includes airfare, rooms, and ground transportation and distribute it through travel agents in the United States. In doing so, the wholesaler provides a package that gives guests everything they need to go on a vacation in Puerto Vallarta, eliminating the worry of finding their way around a foreign country. To design an effective channel, the company must understand the services its customers require and then balance the needs of those customers against the feasibility and costs of meeting them.

Attracting Channel Members

Companies vary in their ability to attract qualified intermediaries. Well-known hotel companies that have a reputation for paying commissions promptly and honoring the reservations of travel agents will have no trouble gaining the support of travel agencies. A new hotel chain with only a few hotels will have difficulty getting most of the country's 32,000 travel agents to sell its chain. It would be wiser for the new chain to choose one travel agency chain or work in key cities that are likely to generate business.

When contracting with a hotel sales representative, the hotel company will want to investigate the number and type of other hotels that the firm represents. It will also want to investigate the size and quality of its workforce. Just as a company carefully chooses its employees, it should carefully choose channel members. These firms will represent the company and will be partially responsible for the company's image.

Evaluating Major Channel Alternatives

Economic Feasibility of the Channel Member

Each channel will produce different levels of sales and costs. The business that channel members bring must offset the cost of paying and supporting the channel member. These costs are measured two ways: directly and by opportunity costs. For example, some casinos use bus operators to bring customers to them. The bus operator is paid a fee for each bus, plus the riders get an incentive, such as a free roll of quarters from the casino. Some casinos found that the cost of bringing a bus customer to the casino was greater than the casino's win from the bus customer. Previous management felt good because the buses brought hundreds of customers to the casino. However, when the buses were evaluated from an economic standpoint, they were found to be unprofitable because they did not cover their direct costs. Another direct cost of working with intermediaries is the support they will need from the company. Intermediaries require brochures and other collateral material, training, familiarization trips, and regular communication. A company should limit the size of their distribution system to one that they are able to support.

When the MGM Grand hotel opened, it used tour operators to fill many of its rooms. This business brought a low room rate, but the room rate more than covered the variable cost of the room, creating an operating profit. As demand for the MGM Grand's rooms grew, the MGM could sell their rooms directly through travel agents and receive a higher room rate. At this point there was an opportunity cost associated with the tour operator, that is, the difference between the tour operator's rate and the higher rate that could be received through travel agents. An opportunity cost is created when we sell a product for a lower price than its market value. Opportunity costs are created when we discount products, only to find out that we could sell them for a higher price. In the example, the hotel decreased its allocation of rooms to tour operators and increased its allocation to travel agents to reduce the opportunity cost of selling rooms to tour operators.

A company must regularly evaluate the performance of its intermediaries. As business changes, the value of an intermediary may change, as was the case with MGM. The intermediary may not perform as expected. In this case the company must work with the intermediary to try to bring about the desired performance, or eliminate the intermediary if they become unprofitable.

Checking on intermediaries is a delicate business. Sometimes problems may be due to improper support from the supplier. Companies need to evaluate the support that they are giving their channel members and make the necessary adjustments. Underperforming intermediaries need to be counseled. They may need more training or motivation. If they do not shape up, it might be better to terminate them.

Control Criteria

An important consideration in the choice of channels is control. Using sales representatives offers less control than building your own sales force. Sales representatives may prefer to sell rooms in other hotels because it requires less effort. They may avoid smaller customers, preferring instead to call on larger companies who can use most of the hotels that they represent.

Control is also an important consideration in franchising and choosing multiple-channel members. One problem with franchising is that a company sacrifices some control to gain wider distribution. The company may have trouble getting franchisees to add new products or to participate in promotions. Some companies have problems getting their franchisees to meet quality control standards.

When a firm adds multiple channels, it must consider the rights of existing channel members. Often, existing channel members limit their activities with new channel members. For example, earlier in the chapter we talked about the promotion between Embassy Suites Hotel and Hertz. The promotion was modified because it went against the interests of another channel member, the travel agent.

Each channel involves a long-term commitment and loss of flexibility. A hotel firm using a sales representative in Mexico City may have to sign a five-year contract. During this five-year period, the hotel company may develop an alliance with an airline or hotel company based in Mexico. The sales representative in Mexico City may become unnecessary, but the company will be unable to end the relationship until the contract has ended. There is often a trade-off between the benefits created by developing a long-term alliance and the loss of flexibility that often comes with such alliances. Understanding the trade-offs and how the marketplace might change in the future can help a manager make decisions regarding the length of contractual agreements with channel members.

Responsibilities of Channel Members and Suppliers

The company and its intermediaries must agree on the terms and responsibilities of each channel member. For instance, hotels make it clear to travel agents which rates are commissionable and the amount of commission to be paid, and they often guarantee to pay the commission within a certain number of days. Wendy's provides franchisees with promotional support, a record-keeping system, training, and general management assistance. In turn, franchises must meet company standards for physical facilities, cooperate with new promotional programs, provide requested information, and buy specified food products. To avoid disputes, it is important that companies have an explicit arrangement in writing with their channel members.

After the selection of the channel members, a company must continuously motivate its members. Just as a firm must market to its employees, it must also market to its intermediaries. Most firms use positive incentives during times of slow demand. For example, during slow periods, hotel or rental car companies often increase the percentage of commission that they pay. Keeping channel members informed about the company's products is another way to motivate channel members. Hotels with sales representatives must keep them informed about changes in facilities and new products. A company must provide communication and support for its channel members.

Business Location

One of the most important aspects of distribution for hospitality organizations is location. For businesses whose customers come to them, the business must be conveniently located. Many retailers will say that the three secrets of successful retailing are "location, location, and location." There is no single formula for location. A good location for a Ritz-Carlton Hotel will be different from that of a Motel 6 or a Burger King. Restaurant sites tend to be evaluated on the ability of the local area to provide business. Hotel sites are evaluated on the attractiveness of their location to persons coming to that destination. In both cases, location depends on the firm's marketing strategy. Each firm will have its own set of location evaluation characteristics.

In general, there are four steps in choosing a location. The first is understanding the marketing strategy and target market of the company. La Quinta motels cater to the traveling salesperson and other midclass hotel guests arriving primarily by automobile. Locations are typically along freeways outside major metropolitan areas. They are close enough to the central business district to offer convenient access, yet far enough away to allow economic purchase of the site. Hyatt, on the other hand, caters to groups and the businessperson who often arrives by plane. Hyatt hotels are often located in the heart of the central business district. The location decision, like other marketing decisions, cannot be separated from the marketing strategy.

The second step of the selection is regional analysis, which involves the selection of geographic market areas.[53] A restaurant chain may plan to expand into a new metropolitan market. They may need to find a region that will support at least five new stores. A business hotel chain expanding into Southeast Asia may target key cities such as Singapore, Bangkok, Kuala Lumpur, and Jakarta. The chain wants to have a presence in major cities of the region so that business travelers can stay in the chain as they travel throughout the region.

A firm would want to make sure that a region has sufficient and stable demand to support the hotel(s) or restaurant(s). A growing area with a diverse economic base is attractive. Houston's hotels and restaurants suffered in the 1980s when oil prices plummeted because of the area's heavy dependence on one industry. During a ten-year period, many ho-

The Waldorf Astoria promotes its prime location. "At the heart of the world stands the Waldorf Astoria, the flagship of Hilton Hotels, a marvelous and soothing environment where the quality and service of yesterday still exist today. Approach on Park Avenue and stand for a moment outside. You're at the center of the center of it all, bounded by the theaters of Broadway, the country's most fashionable shopping district along Fifth Avenue, the United Nations, the commerce of the world." From a promotional brochure from the Waldorf Astoria, a Hilton Hotel. Courtesy of Hilton Hotels Corporation.

tels were taken over by lenders. Areas based on one industry are often attractive when that industry is in favor but are highly vulnerable when that industry suffers.

This is equally true when tourism and hospitality are the primary industries. Miami Beach experienced industry problems when some European tourists were assaulted or killed. The ski industry and ski resort towns depend on the whims of nature. Too little or too much snow can create major economic problems.

Once the firm has chosen a geographic region, the next step is to select an area within that region. If a restaurant chain wants to open five restaurants in a metropolitan area, it must choose sites at which to place its restaurants. The chain will look at the demographic and psychographic characteristics of the area. Competition and growth potential of the different areas will be evaluated. The result will be a choice of five areas within the region that seem most promising.

Finally, the firm will choose individual sites. A key consideration in site analysis is compatible businesses. A restaurant or hotel will look for potential demand generators. For a hotel these can be major office complexes, airports, or integrated retail, residential, and business complexes. A restaurant may look for residential communities, shopping centers, or motels without food and beverage facilities. Demand generators vary depending on the target markets of the business. It is important for firms to have a good profile of their customers when they look for customer sources within a given area.

In addition to demand generators, a firm will also look at competitors. If there is an adequate supply of similar restaurants or hotels, the site will usually be rejected. Hotels have entered saturated markets, just to gain a presence in that city. Competition is not always a negative factor. Restaurants often tend to be clustered, creating a restaurant row. This can be beneficial. Customers going to one restaurant are exposed to a selection of others.

Site evaluation includes accessibility. Is the site easily accessible by traffic going in different directions or do uncrossable medians create a barrier? Is the site visible to allow drivers to turn? Speed of traffic is also a factor. The slower the traffic is, the longer the visibility. Restaurant sites at intersections with a stoplight have the benefit of exposure to waiting drivers. The desirability of the surroundings is another consideration. Is the area attractive? If the site is in a shopping center, is the center well maintained? Other considerations for the site include drainage, sewage, utilities, and size.

Often, companies will develop a profile of preferred sites. For example, Carl's Jr. restaurant, a fast-food hamburger restaurant, developed this profile:[54]

- Free-standing location in a shopping center
- Free-standing corner location (with a signal light at the intersection)
- Inside lot with 125-foot minimum frontage
- Enclosed shopping mall
- Population of 12,000 or more in a one-mile radius (growth areas preferred)
- Easy access of traffic to location
- Heavy vehicular/pedestrian traffic
- An area where home values and family income levels are average or above
- Close to offices and other demand generators
- A parcel size of 30,000 to 50,000 square feet
- No less than two or three miles from other existing company locations

The choice of a site is often determined by a checklist, statistical analysis, or a combination of both. A checklist usually contains items such as those listed in the profile and specific building requirements. Items such as building codes, signage restrictions, availability of utilities, parking, and drainage are also included in a checklist. A common type of statistical analysis used in site selection is regression analysis. The dependent variable in the equation is sales, and the independent variables are factors that contribute to sales. Typical independent variables might include population within the market area, household income of the market, competitors, and attributes of the location.

Restaurants have been downsizing to allow access to smaller markets and new types of locations. For example, Captain D's fast-food seafood restaurant developed a 1,800 square-foot location that seats 33 to 42 dinners. It's original design called for 128 seats and the design required 3,250 square-feet. This makes the unit feasible in locations that do not have room for a full-size unit or cannot support the sales the larger unit would require. McDonald's was one of the first chains to develop smaller units that made it feasible for McDonald's to go into smaller towns and inside retail outlets. Chili's, a casual service restaurant, has developed a smaller version with a reduced menu called Chili's Too for airport and other non-traditional locations. The Cheesecake Factory, a popular sit-down service restaurant, developed its Cheesecake Factory Café as an outlet for its signature desserts.[55] As good locations become more difficult to find, restaurants are looking for nontraditional locations and building units that will fit these sites. They are then using the strength of their brand name as a competitive advantage. Location is a key attribute for a hotel or restaurant. The location must not only be favorable at the present time, but also must continue to be good throughout the life of the business.

13.11 Cheesecake Factory
Chili's

KEY TERMS

Administrative VMS A vertical marketing system that coordinates successive stages of production and distribution, not through common ownership or contractual ties, but through the size and power of one of the parties.

Agent A wholesaler who represents buyers or sellers on a more permanent basis, performs only a few functions, and does not take title to goods.

Alliances Alliances are developed to allow two organizations to benefit from each other's strengths.

Broker A wholesaler who does not take title to goods and whose function is to bring buyers and sellers together and assist in negotiations.

Channel conflict Disagreement among marketing channel members on goals and roles—who should do what and for what rewards.

Channel level A level of middleman that performs some work in bringing the product and its ownership closer to the final buyer.

Contractual VMS A vertical marketing system in which independent firms at different levels of production and distribution join together through contracts to obtain more economies or sales impact than they could achieve alone.

Corporate VMS A vertical marketing system that combines successive stages of production and distribution under single ownership. Channel leadership is established through common ownership.

Direct marketing channel A marketing channel that has no intermediary levels.

Franchise organization A contractual vertical marketing system in which a channel member called a franchiser links several stages in the production distribution process.

Horizontal conflict Conflict between firms at the same level.

Horizontal marketing systems (HMS) Two or more companies at one level join to follow new marketing opportunities. Companies can combine their capital, production capabilities, or marketing resources to accomplish more than one company working alone.

Multichannel marketing Multichannel distribution, as when a single firm sets up two or more marketing channels to reach one or more customer segments.

Retailer Business whose sales come primarily from retailing.

Vertical conflict Conflict between different levels of the same channel.

Vertical marketing system (VMS) A distribution channel structure in which producers, wholesalers, and retailers act as a unified system: either one channel member owns the others, or has contracts with them, or has so much power that they all cooperate.

Wholesaler Firms engaged primarily in wholesaling activity.

Chapter Review

I. Nature of Distribution Channels. A distribution channel is a set of independent organizations involved in the process of making a product or service available to the consumer or business user.

II. Reasons That Marketing Intermediaries Are Used. The use of intermediaries depends on their greater efficiency in marketing the goods available to target markets. Through their contacts, experience, specialization, and scale of operation, intermediaries normally offer more than a firm can on its own.

III. Distribution Channel Functions

1) **Information.** Gathering and distributing marketing research and intelligence information about the marketing environment.

2) **Promotion.** Developing and spreading persuasive communications about an offer.

3) **Contact.** Finding and communicating with prospective buyers.

4) **Matching.** Shaping and fitting the offer to the buyers' needs.

5) **Negotiation.** Agreeing on price and other terms of the offer so that ownership or possession can be transferred.

6) **Physical distribution.** Transporting and storing goods.

7) **Financing.** Acquiring and using funds to cover the cost of channel work.

8) **Risk taking.** Assuming financial risks, such as the inability to sell inventory at full margin.

IV. Number of Channel Levels. The number of channel levels can vary from direct marketing, through which the manufacturer sells directly to the consumer, to complex distribution systems involving four or more channel members.

V. Marketing Intermediaries. Marketing intermediaries available to the hospitality industry and travel industry include travel agents, tour operators, tour wholesalers, specialists, hotel sales representatives, incentive travel agents, government tourist associations, consortia and reservation systems, and electronic distribution systems.

VI. Internet. The Internet is an effective marketing tool for hospitality and travel companies. Companies can use pictures, both still and moving, to display their product. Customers can make reservations and pay for products directly from the Internet.

VII. Channel Behavior

1) **Channel conflict.** Although channel members depend on each other, they often act alone in their own short-run best interests. They frequently disagree on the roles each should play on who should do what for which rewards.

a) **Horizontal conflict.** Conflict between firms at the same level.

b) **Vertical conflict.** Conflict between different levels of the same channel.

VIII. Channel Organization. Distribution channels are shifting from loose collections of independent companies to unified systems.

1) **Conventional marketing system.** A conventional marketing system consists of one or more independent producers, wholesalers, and retailers. Each is a separate business seeking to maximize its own profits, even at the expense of profits for the system as a whole.

2) **Vertical marketing system.** A vertical marketing system consists of producers, wholesalers, and retailers acting as a unified system. VMSs were developed to control channel behavior and manage channel conflict and its economies through size, bargaining power, and elimination of duplicated services. There are three major types of VMSs: corporate, administered, and contractual.

a) **Corporate.** A corporate VMS combines successive stages of production and distribution under single ownership.

b) **Administered.** An administered VMS coordinates successive stages of production and distribution, not through common ownership or contractual ties, but through the size and power of the parties.

c) **Contractual.** A contractual VMS consists of independent firms at different levels of production and distribution who join through contracts to obtain economies or sales impact.

i) Franchising. Franchising is a method of doing business by which a franchisee is granted the right to engage in offering, selling, or distributing goods or services under a marketing format that is designed by the franchisor. The franchisor permits the franchisee to use its trademark, name, and advertising.

ii) Alliances. Alliances are developed to allow two organizations to benefit from each other's strengths.

3) Horizontal marketing system. Two or more companies at one level join to follow new marketing opportunities. Companies can combine their capital, production capabilities, or marketing resources to accomplish more than one company working alone.

4) Multichannel marketing system. A single firm sets up two or more marketing channels to reach one or more customer segments.

IX. **Channel Management Decisions**

1) Selecting channel members. When selecting channel members, the company's management will want to evaluate each potential channel member's growth and profit record, profitability, cooperativeness, and reputation.

2) Motivating channel members. A company must motivate its channel members continuously.

3) Evaluating channel members. A company must regularly evaluate the performance of its intermediaries and counsel underperforming intermediaries.

4) Responsibilities of channel members and suppliers. The company and its intermediaries must agree on the terms and responsibilities of each channel member. According to the services and clientele at hand the responsibilities are formulated after careful consideration.

X. **Business Location.** There are four steps in choosing a location:

1) Understanding the marketing strategy. Know the target market of the company.

2) Regional analysis. Select the geographic market areas.

3) Choosing the area within the region. Demographic and psychographic characteristics and competition are factors to consider.

4) Choosing the individual site. Compatible business, competitors, accessibility, drainage, sewage, utilities, and size are factors to consider.

Discussion Questions

1. Discuss how you think technology will change distribution channels in the hospitality and travel industries over the next five years.
2. Explain how international travel changed distribution channels in the hospitality and travel industries.
3. What are the major differences between a distribution channel for a business making tangible products and a firm producing hospitality and travel products?
4. Can a business have too many channel members? Explain your answer.
5. Explain the difference between a tour wholesaler and a travel agent.
6. Why is franchising such a fast-growing form of retail organization?
7. According to the International Franchising Association, between 30 and 50 percent of all new franchise applicants are people who formerly worked in large corporations and who lost their

jobs as a result of corporate downsizing. How do you think these midlevel, midcareer corporate executives will adapt to life as franchise owners? How will their previous corporate experience help them? How will it hurt them?

Experiential Exercises

Do one of the following:

1. Visit a restaurant that offers take-out service. What have they done to facilitate take out service? For example, do they have a special order and pickup area; do they have paper menus to take home; do they accept phone, fax or Internet orders; and do they have special packaging for take-out? Report on what you find and any suggestions that you might have.
2. Investigate franchises available in the hospitality or travel business. Select a franchise you feel would be a good business investment based on what the franchise offers and the fees the franchiser charges. Support your findings in a two- to three-page report.

Internet Exercise

Support for these exercises can be found on the Web site for *Marketing for Hospitality and Tourism*, www.prenhall.com/kotler.

Find a hospitality or travel company that allows customers to make reservations directly through their Web site. Who do you think will make reservations through this site and do you think the design of the site is effective? Explain your answer.

References

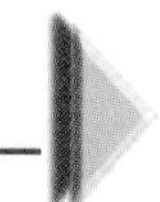

1. Milford Prewitt, "Little Caesar's Licensees Debate Kmart Deal," *Nation's Restaurant News* 25, no. 23 (June 10, 1991): 1, 3; Milford Prewitt, "Little Caesars, Kmart Deal Riles Franchisee Group," *Nation's Restaurant News* 26, no. 21 (May 25, 1992): 1, 40; Laura Liebeck, "Hall Hails Kmart Comeback, but Results Need Improvement," *Discount Store News,* June 2, 1997, pp. 11.
2. E. Raymond Corey, Frank V. Cespedes, and V. Kasturi Rangan, *Going to Market* (Boston: Harvard Business School Press, 1989), p. xxvii.
3. Amy Ricciardi, "Marriott, Otani Enter Marketing Pact," *Travel Weekly* 51, no. 12 (February 10, 1992): 3.
4. Louis W. Stern and Adel I. El-Ansary, *Marketing Channels*, 3d ed. (Upper Saddle River, NJ: Prentice Hall, 1988), p. 3.
5. Corey, Cespedes, and Rangan, *Going to Market.*
6. Tricia A. Holly, "ARC Figures Show Rise in Sales, but Drops in Pay and Locations," *Travel Agent*, February 21, 2000, p. 6
7. Jennifer Michels, "Worldspan Goes Farther," *Travel Agent*, November 20, 2000, p. 24; "Infobite," *Travel Agent*, February 21, 2000, p. 20.
8. Robert C. Lewis, *Marketing Leadership in Hospitality: Foundations and Practices*, 3d ed. (New York: John Wiley and Sons, Inc., 2000).
9. For more information on familiarization trips, see *How to Plan and Program Travel Agent Familiarization Tours* (Washington, DC: Hotel Sales and Marketing Association, undated).
10. James R. Abbey, *Hospitality Sales and Advertising* (East Lansing, MI: Educational Institute of the American Hotel and Motel Association, 1989).
11. Fran Golden, "Room for Growth," *Travel Weekly* 53, no. 65 (August 18, 1994): 118.
12. Rita Marie Emmer, Chuck Tauck, Scott Wilkinson, and Richard G. Moore, "Marketing Hotels Using Global Distribution Systems," *Cornell Hotel and Restaurant Administration Quarterly* 34, no. 6 (December 1993): 80.
13. Michael M. Coltman, *Tourism Marketing* (New York: Van Nostrand Reinhold, 1989).
14. Chuck Y. Gee, James C. Makens, and Dexter J. L. Choy, *The Travel Industry* (New York: Van Nostrand Reinhold, 1989).
15. For more information on tour brokers, see *HSMA/Group Tour Information Manual* (Washington, DC: Hotel Sales and Marketing Association, undated).

16. Coltman, *Tourism Marketing.*
17. Sydney Convention & Visitors Bureau, retrieved from the World Wide Web on November 28, 2001; *http://www.scvb.com.*
18. The Utell Solution, retrieved from the World Wide Web on January 12, 2001, *http://www.utell.com/brands/UI/corpinfo.htm.*
19. France Martin, "Consortia Extend Hotels' Regional, Global Reach," *Hotels* 25, no. 9 (July 1991): x; Chris Baum, "How Utell Reacts to the Market," *Hotel*, 25, no. 9 (September 1991): 73–74; James Carper, "The New Brand of SRS," *Steigenberger Hotels* 25, no. 10 (October 1991): 72–74.
20. "Pegasus Product and Service Overview," retrieved from the World Wide Web on November 29, 2001, *http://www.rez.com/products_services/overview.htm.*
21. See J. C. Holloway and R. V. Plant, *Marketing for Tourism* (London: Pitman, 1992), pp. 124–126.
22. Amadeus *About US* section, retrieved from the World Wide Web on November 29, 2001, *http://www.amadeus.com/en/50/50.jsp.*
23. Galileo, About Galileo Section, retrieved from the World Wide Web on November 29, 2001, *http://www.galileo.com/about/.*
24. Jennifer Michels, "Worldspan Goes Farther," *Travel Agent*, November 20, 2000, p. 24.
25. Ibid., p. 135; Alan Fredericks, "Agency Automation," *Travel Agency Survey 1992*, in *Travel Weekly* 51, no. 65 (August 13, 1992): 87–90.
26. "The H in Hilton Stands for Hi-tech," *Nation's Restaurant News,* November 3, 1997, p. C14.
27. Fran Golden, "Panel Expects Internet to Have Profound Effect on Marketing," *Travel Weekly,* March 31, 1997, p. 10.
28. Michels, "Worldspan Goes Farther."
29. Charles T. Thackston, *Presentation at the HSMAI Annual Meeting* (Scottsdale Arizona): June 6, 2001.
30. Ken Western, "Internet Inn: Best Western Marketing on Network," *Arizona Republic,* January 31, 1995, p. E1.
31. David Vis, "Best Western Is Latest Hotel Chain to Market Properties on Internet," *Travel Weekly* 54, no. 8 (January 30, 1995): 1, 53.
32. Ed Watkins, "The Internet as Distribution Weapon," *Lodging Hospitality,* March 1, 2000, pp. 30–32
33. Tess Romita, "Sky's the Limit for Airlines Online," *Business2.com,* January 23, 2001, p. 114.
34. Michelle Johnson, "Technically Speaking, Plugged In," *Boston Globe,* September 9, 1994, p. 87.
35. "Introduction to Expedia, Inc." (January 2001), Promotional brochure published by Expedia, Inc.
36. Gibson, R. (July 29, 1999) Little Caesars Pizza Isn't Slimming Down, It Wants Drive-Thru—Sudden Closure of 300 Outlets Fuels Some Speculation, but Is Move to Remodel," *Wall Street Journal*, on-line, retrieved April 21, 2000, from the World Wide Web: *http://proquest.umi.com/pqdweb?ts.*
37. Dinah A. Sprotzer, "Hotel Chain Shifts Policy on Coupons," *Travel Weekly* 51, no. 8 (January 27, 1992): 11.
38. See Irving Rein, Philip Kotler, and Martin Stroller, *High Visibility* (New York: Dodd, Mead, 1987).
39. Stern and El-Ansary, *Marketing Channels.*
40. Andy Kostecka, *Franchising in the Economy* (Washington, DC: U.S. Government Printing Office, 1987), p. 2.
41. M. Malley. "Proposed Law Offers No Real Help for Franchisees." *Hotel and Management*, 125 (5) p. 14, retrieved April 21, 2000, from the World Wide Web, *http://proquest.umi.com/pqdweb.*
42. Stephen Rushmore, "Hotel Franchising: How to Be a Successful Franchisee," *Real Estate Journal* (Summer 1997): p. 56; cited in James R. Brown and Chekitan S. Dev, "The Franchisor–Franchisee Relationship," *Cornell Hotel and Restaurant Administration Quarterly* (December 1997): 30–31.
43. Michael Levy and Barton A. Weitz, *Retailing Management* (Homewood, IL: Richard D. Irwin, 1995): pp. 29–35.
44. "Franchise Report," *Restaurant Business* 90, no. 5 (March 20, 1991): 106–117; "The Top One Hundred," *Restaurant Business* 90, no. 17 (November 20, 1991): 116–132.
45. David Fraboutta, " The Price of Franchising" *Hotel and Motel Management,* May 21, 2001, pp. 23–32
46. See Yae Sock Roh and William P. Andrew, "Sub-franchising," *Cornell Hotel and Restaurant Administration Quarterly* (December 1997): 39–45.
47. R. Bond, *Source Book of Franchise Opportunity* (Homewood, IL: Dow Jones–Irwin, 1993): pp. 216–301.
48. Roh and Andrew, *"Sub-franchising,"* p. 40.
49. Robert Strate and Clinton Rappole, "Strategic Alliances between Hotels and Restaurants," *Cornell Hotel and Restaurant Administration Quarterly* (June 1997): 50–61.
50. Bill Poling, "Motor Coach Network Launches Partner Program for Hotels," *Travel Weekly* 51, no. 83 (October 15, 1992): 7.
51. See Lee Adler, "Symbiotic Marketing," *Harvard Business Review* (November/December 1966): 59–71; P. Varadarajan and Daniel Rajaratnam, "Symbiotic Marketing Revisited," *Journal of Marketing* (January 1986): 7–17.
52. See Robert Weigand, "Fit Products and Channels to Your Markets," *Harvard Business Review* (January/February 1977): 95–105.
53. See Avijit Gosh, *Retail Management* (Fort Worth, TX: Dryden Press, 1990), pp. 216–249.
54. Donald E. Lindberg. *The Restaurant from Concept to Operation* (New York: Wiley, 1985), p. 35.
55. Paul Frumkin, "Have Concept, Will Travel: Chains Find Smaller Units Have Legs," *Nation's Restaurant News,* February 19, 2001, pp. 55–58.

D-MINUS
15:00
EXCITING BEGINNING

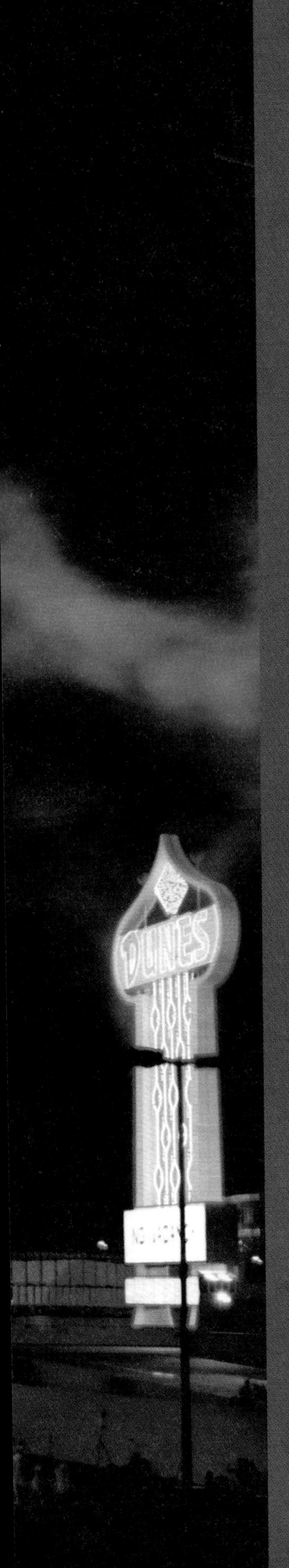

14

Promoting Products: Communication and Promotion Policy and Advertising

I don't know who you are. I don't know your company. I don't know your company's product. I don't know what your company stands for. I don't know your company's customers. I don't know your company's record. I don't know your company's reputation. Now— what was it you wanted to sell me?
McGraw–Hill Publications

On October 23, 1993, as many as 200,000 people watched a multi-million-dollar pyrotechnic show. Later that evening and the next morning, hundreds of millions of people would see glimpses of the same show on their television. The event was the implosion of the Dunes hotel, a publicity event to celebrate the opening of the Treasure Island Resort in Las Vegas. Mirage Resorts, the parent company of the Treasure Island, purchased the Dunes property for future expansion. Steve Wynn, CEO of Mirage Resorts, developed a plan to raze prematurely the ten-story sign and twenty-three-story north tower of the Dunes. The empty buildings were going to have to be razed at some point, so why not raze them as part of an opening celebration for the Treasure Island?

Today, building implosions are a common and cost-effective way of clearing land. Thus, if the Dunes implosion was to attract the media's attention, it would have to be extraordinary. Steve Wynn hired a pyrotechnics expert and developed a spectacular show. The show included six minutes of fireworks set from the building's roof. This was followed by explosions of fireballs, representing cannon shots from a replica of the HMS Britannia *at the Treasure Island. These cannon shots first hit the ten-story Dunes sign, bringing it to the ground. Then they hit the building, igniting 550 gallons of aviation fuel and sending flames shooting up the building. Finally, 365 pounds of dynamite were detonated, sending the building to the ground.*

Besides this event, the resort placed an ad that appeared simultaneously on all three major television networks. As viewers changed channels, they saw the same message, hinting of the opening of a wonderfully mysterious place. This unique placement of the ads created its own publicity. The resort also placed one-page ads featuring a skull and crossbones in key cities throughout the country. Steve Wynn purchased an hour of network time from NBC at a cost of $1.7 million to show The Adventure Begins. This was an infomercial in the form of a movie, which featured the implosion of the Dunes. The movie was shot at the Treasure Island and subtly takes viewers on a tour of the property. The purchase of the time ensured that his production would be aired on the desired date. Some cost was offset through the sale of commercials. Wynn timed the show for the end of January. The opening and the Christmas and New Year holidays would ensure good business until January. Wynn thus timed it to generate interest in the hotel during what could be a slack period. After NBC broadcast the movie, Mirage Resorts then featured The Adventure Begins as a choice on in-room television in the Mirage and Treasure Island.[1]

Most hotels and restaurants do not have $4 million to spend on opening promotions. However, the techniques applied by the Treasure Island apply to all operations. The opening promotion of the Mirage was well planned and creative. Maximum benefit was gained from every promotional dollar spent because of preplanning. The resort used several different media and integrated its publicity and advertising efforts. To be effective, promotional efforts must be well planned and well executed.

Chapter Objectives

After reading this chapter, you should be able to:

1. Outline the six steps in developing effective communications.
2. Define the ways of setting a total promotional budget: affordable, percentage-of-sales, competitive-parity, and objective and task methods.
3. Explain each promotional tool—advertising, personal selling, sales promotion, and public relations—and the factors in setting the promotion mix: type of product and market, push versus pull strategies, buyer readiness states, and product-life-cycle stage.
4. Describe the major decisions in advertising, including setting objectives and budget; creating the advertising message; selecting advertising media; and choosing media types, vehicles, and timing, and evaluating advertising.

14.1 Mirage Resorts

Modern marketing calls for more than developing a good product, pricing it attractively, and making it available to target customers. Companies must also communicate continuously with their present and potential customers. Every company is inevitably cast into the role of communicator and promoter.

What is communicated should not be left to chance. To communicate effectively, companies often hire advertising agencies to develop effective ads, sales-promotion specialists to design sales-incentive programs, and public relations firms to develop corporate images. Salespeople are trained to be friendly, helpful, and persuasive. For any company the question is not whether to communicate, but how much to spend and in what ways.

THE COMMUNICATION PROCESS

Today there is a new view of communications as an interactive dialogue between the company and its customers that takes place during the preselling, selling, consuming, and postconsuming stages. Companies must ask not only "How can we reach our customer?" but also "How can our customers reach us?"

Thanks to technological breakthroughs, people can now communicate through traditional media (newspapers, radio, telephone, television), as well as through newer media forms (computers, fax machines, cellular phones, and pagers). By decreasing communication costs, the new technologies have encouraged more companies to move from mass communications to more targeted communication and one-to-one dialogue.

The salesperson's manner and dress, the place's décor, the company's stationery—all communicate something to the buyers. Every brand contact delivers an impression that can strengthen or weaken a customer's view of the company. The whole marketing mix must be integrated to deliver a consistent message and strategic positioning.

A company's total marketing communications program, called its **promotion mix,** consists of a specific blend of advertising, sales promotion, public relations, and personal selling to achieve advertising and marketing objectives. The four major promotion tools are defined next:

Advertising: Any paid form of nonpersonal presentation and promotion of ideas, goods, or services by an identified sponsor.

Sales promotion: Short-term incentives to encourage the purchase or sales of a product or service.

Public relations: Building good relations with the company's various publics by obtaining favorable publicity, developing a good corporate image, and handling or heading off unfavorable rumors, stories, events.

Personal selling: Oral presentation in a conversation with one more prospective purchasers for the purpose of making sales.[2]

The starting point is an audit of all the potential interactions target customers may have with the company. For example, someone interested in planning a vacation would talk to others, see television ads, read articles, talk to a travel agent, and look for information on the Internet. The marketer needs to assess which experiences and impressions will have the most influence at each stage of the buying process. This understanding will help marketers allocate their communication dollars more efficiently.

There are six steps in developing effective communications. The marketing communicator must (1) identify the target audience, (2) determine the communication objectives, (3) design the message, (4) select the communication channels, (5) select the message source and (6) measure the communications' results process.

Identifying the Target Audience

A marketing communicator starts with a clear target audience in mind. The audience may be potential buyers or current users, those who make the buying decision or those who influence it. The audience may be individuals, groups, special publics, or the general public. The target audience will heavily affect the communicator's decision on what will be said, how it will be said, when it will be said, where it will be said, and who will say it. To create effective communication, a marketer must understand the target audience by creating a message that will be meaningful to them in a media they will understand. For example, a study of bed and breakfast owners found that other than word of mouth, they felt the two most important communication channels were brochures and guidebooks. When guests of bed and breakfasts were asked the channels they used most often, the two highest—other than word of mouth—were magazine and newspapers (one category) and signs.[3] Managers need to understand their target markets before they can communicate with them.

Determining the Communication Objective

Once a target audience has been defined, the marketing communicator must decide what response is sought. Of course, in most cases the final response is purchase. But purchase is the result of a long process of consumer decision making. The marketing communicator needs to know where the target audience stands in relation to the product and to what state it needs to be moved.

The Indian tribes of South Dakota wished to increase significantly tourist visitation to their reservations. Their objectives were:

- To provide guests for bed and breakfast operations.
- To increase the market for Indian products.
- To participate in other tourism-related incomes.
- To correct misconceptions about the American Indian. It was deemed important to show that the Lakota, Dakota, and Nakota people are living cultures.

This combination of economic and cultural education objectives led to the development of the Alliance of Tribal Tourism Advocates (ATTA) as a communication vehicle. Instead of depending on the South Dakota Department of Tourism or other organizations, Indians would promote themselves. "If you want to visit an Indian, the best person to talk with is a Native American," said Ronald L. Neiss, acting director of ATTA and a member of the Rosebud Sioux Tribal Council.[4]

The target audience may be in any of six buyer readiness states: awareness, knowledge, liking, preference, conviction, or purchase, which are shown in Figure 14-1.

Awareness

First, the communicator must be able to gauge the target audience's awareness of the product or organization. The audience may be totally unaware of it, know only its name, or know one or a few things about it. If most of the target audience is unaware, the communicator tries to build awareness, perhaps by building simple name recognition. This process can begin with simple messages repeating the name. Even then, building awareness takes time. Suppose that an independent restaurant named the Hungry Hunter opens in a northern suburb of Houston. There are 50,000 people within a three-mile radius of the restaurant. Initially, the restaurant will have little name recognition. The Hungry Hunter may set an objective of making 40 percent of the people living within three miles of the restaurant aware of its name.

Red Roof Inns utilize the color of their roofs and locations with good visibility (near freeways) to create awareness. Another Red Roof strategy is to develop several properties in an area simultaneously. This has a

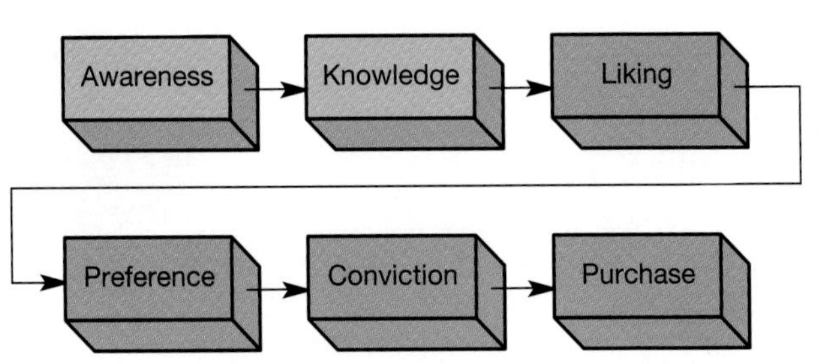

Figure 14-1
Buyer readiness states.

"mushroom" effect, as motorists suddenly see Red Roof Inns everywhere. People forget names of other people, places, and products. Thus, awareness communication is a never-ending responsibility. A product must have top-of-mind awareness.

Knowledge

14.2 Red Roof Inns
Ruth's Chris Steak House

The target audience might be aware of the company or product but know little else. The Hungry Hunter specializes in wild game, but the market may not be aware of this. The restaurant may decide to select product knowledge as its first communication objective.

The chain of Ruth's Chris Steak House restaurants uses a simple slogan and advertises on a quarter-page in airline in-flight magazines. The message is directed at frequent flyers that deserve a "sizzling reward." The advertisement features a color photo of a very thick steak, a list of restau-

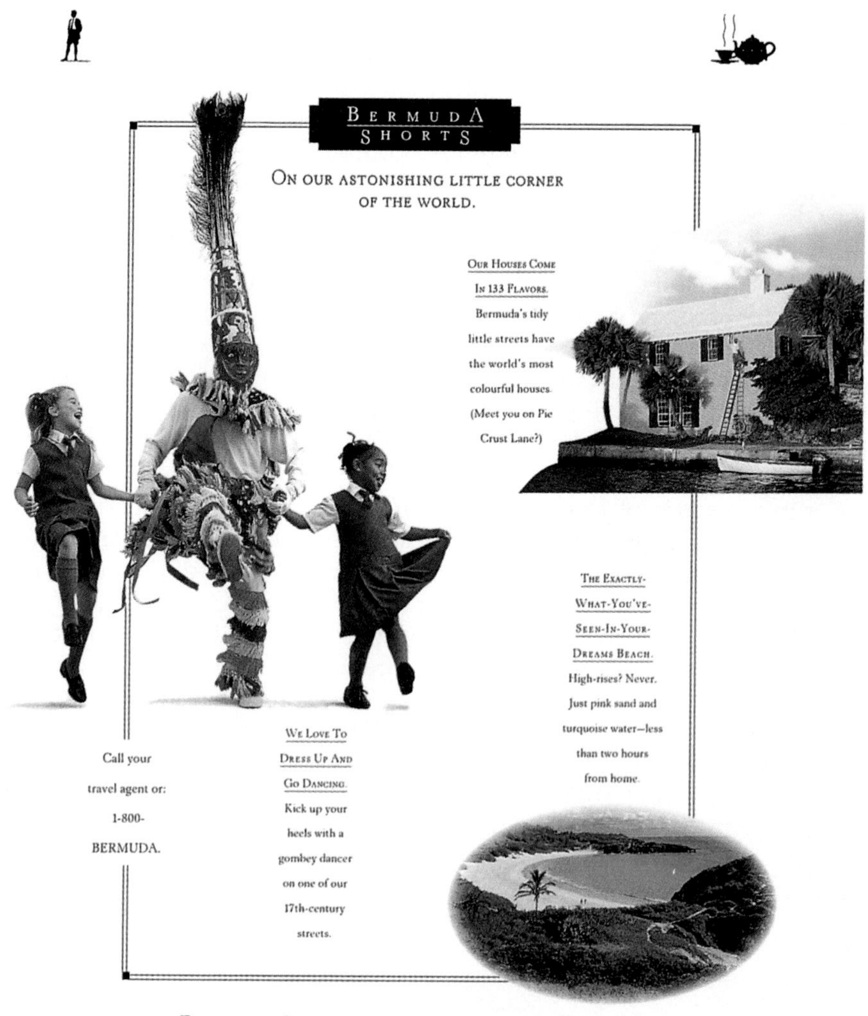

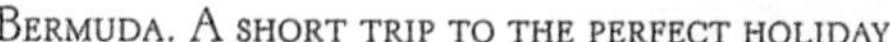

Bermuda uses the slogan "Bermuda. A Short Trip to the Perfect Holiday." Most consumer advertisements for Bermuda mention that Bermuda is less than two hours away. The Bermuda Department of Tourism knows that most people are aware of Bermuda, but many people do not know that it is only about two hours off the east coast of the United States. Courtesy of the Bermuda Department of Tourism and DDB Needham Worldwide, Inc.

rant addresses, and the slogan of Ruth's Chris Steak House, "Home of Serious Steaks." This simple message quickly gives the reader knowledge of restaurant location, size of the steak, and seriousness of the restaurant as a steak house.

Liking

If target audience members know the product, how do they feel about it? We can develop a range of preference such as a Likert scale covering degrees of liking, for example, "dislike very much," "dislike somewhat," "indifferent," "like somewhat," and "like very much." If the market is unfavorable toward the Hungry Hunter, the communicator must learn why and then develop a communication campaign to create favorable feelings. If unfavorable feelings are based on real problems, such as slow service, communication alone cannot do the job. The Hungry Hunter will have to fix its problems and then communicate its renewed quality.

Preference

A target audience might like the product but not prefer it to others. In this case the communicator must try to build consumer preference. The communicator will promote the product's quality, value, performance, and other features. The communicator can check on the campaign's success by measuring audience preferences after the campaign. If the Hungry Hunter finds that many area residents like the name and concept but choose other restaurants, it will have to identify those areas where its offerings are better than for competing restaurants. It must then promote its advantages to build preference among possible customers.

Conviction

A target audience might prefer the product but not develop a conviction about buying the product. Marketers have a responsibility to turn favorable attitudes into conviction, because conviction is closely linked with purchase. Communication from the Hungry Hunter will work toward making their target market believe they have offered the best steaks at a fair value in their market area.

Purchase

Finally, some members of the target audience might have conviction but not quite get around to making the purchase. They may wait for more information or plan to act later. The communicator must lead these consumers to take the final step. Actions might include offering the product at a low price, offering a premium, or letting consumers try it on a limited basis. The Hungry Hunter may provide a "Tuesday Night Special," offering prime rib or its seafood of the day for $14.95 instead of the usual price of $19.95.

14.3 Hungry Hunter

Design the Message

Having defined the desired audience response, the communicator turns to developing an effective message. Ideally, the message should get attention, hold interest, arouse desire, and obtain action (a framework known

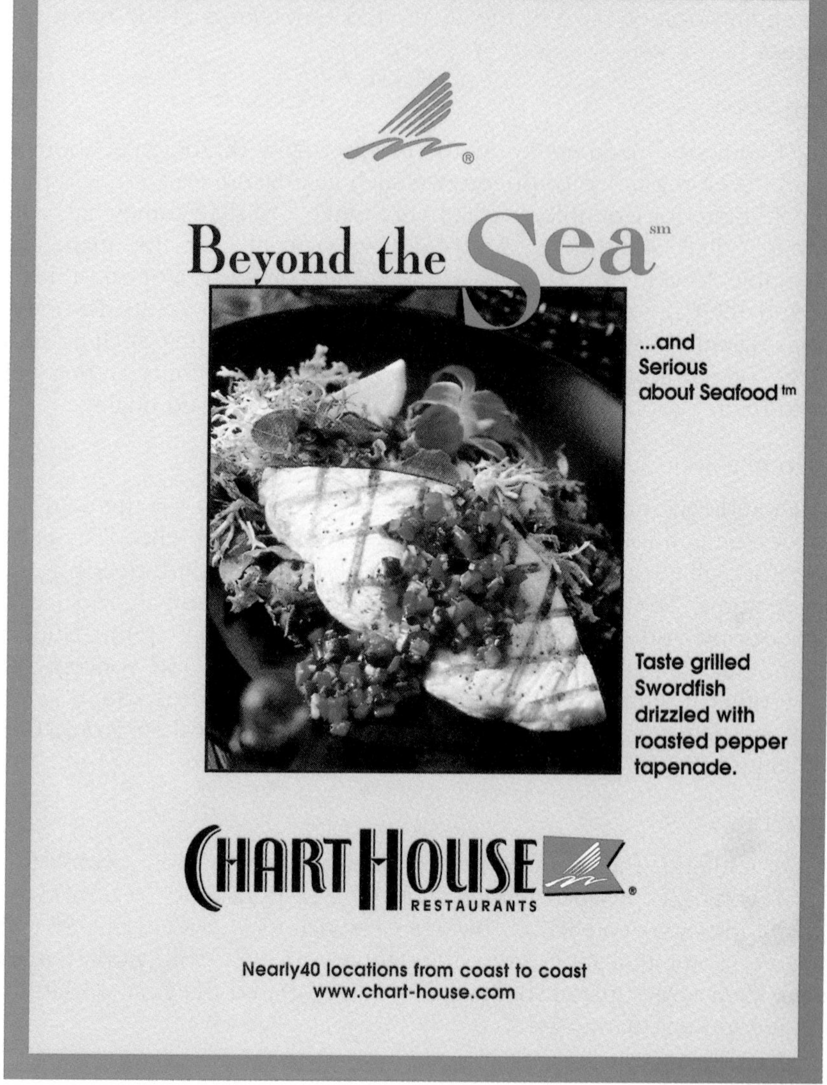

Chart House is an upscale restaurant long known for the stunning locations of their restaurants. Whether perched on a picturesque hillside, based at the foot of a majestic mountain, or nestled on a pier overlooking the ocean, the views are great. However, great food is what brings repeat business. Thus, Chart House developed the "Beyond the Sea" campaign to let their target market know that they were serious about food and to accentuate their new seafood-focused menu. The campaign featured ads in lifestyle publications such as Boston Magazine *and* Delta Sky. *The print ads were coordinated with outdoor and radio. Copyright Chart House Enterprises, Inc. Used with permission.*

as the AIDA model). In practice, few messages take the consumer all the way from awareness to purchase, but the AIDA framework does suggest the desirable qualities of a good message.

In putting the message together, the marketing communicator must solve three problems: what to say (message content), how to say it logically (message structure), and how to say it symbolically (message format).

Message Content

The communicator has to figure out an appeal or theme that will produce a desired response. There are three types of appeals: rational, emotional, and moral.

Rational appeals relate to audience self-interest. They show that the product will produce desired benefits. Occasionally, rational appeals are overlooked. This is the traditional problem of missing the forest because of the trees. The city of Denver received considerable negative feedback from large potential conventions because it did not have a 1,000-room convention hotel, yet development costs were too high to justify building such a structure.

The problem was solved when the existing 511-room Hyatt Regency and the 613-room Marriott Hotel, one block apart, joined forces to jointly market their properties as a 1,000-room hotel suitable for conventions. By marketing the two hotels as one, several customer benefits became apparent, such as elimination of duplicate planning meetings, a single bill combining charges at both hotels, free telephone calls between the two hotels, combined service staffs, and posting of events at both hotels.[5]

Emotional appeals attempt to provoke emotions that motivate purchase. These include fear, guilt, and shame appeals that entice people to do things that they should (brush their teeth, buy new tires) or stop doing things they shouldn't (smoke, drink too much, overeat).

Emotional appeals are widely used by resorts and hotels to stimulate cross purchases:

- Commercials on in-room television, posters, and desktop tents promote the health center and the need to reduce stress and work off "pounds gained from eating in the hotel."
- The "Think of the Spouse and Kids at Home" theme is widely used to promote a myriad of products available in the hotel, from hand-dipped chocolates to stuffed animals. This appeal is also used to convince the business guests to purchase a vacation for the family at one of the chain's resort properties.

Moral appeals are directed to the audience's sense of what is right and proper. They are often used to urge people to support such social causes as a cleaner environment, better race relations, equal rights, and aid to the needy.

Moral appeals clearly are used by a subsector of the lodging industry: the religious camp and retreat sector. Members of this sector range from a monastery with half a dozen guest rooms to summer camps for children and luxurious resort-style hotels, such as that developed by a minister near Charlotte, North Carolina.

Moral appeals usually dwell on the need for spiritual renewal in the right environment with fellow believers. These organizations communicate through religious leaders, previous guests, and advertisements in religious publications.

Message Structure

The communicator must also decide how to handle three message structure issues. The first is whether to draw a conclusion or leave it to the audience. Early research showed that drawing a conclusion was usually the most effective. More recent research, however, suggests that in many cases the advertiser is better off asking questions and letting buyers come to their own conclusions.

The second message structure issue is whether to present a one- or two-sided argument. Usually, a one-sided argument is more effective in sales presentations except when audiences are highly educated and negatively disposed.

The third message structure issue is whether to present the strongest arguments first or last. Presenting them first creates strong attention but may lead to an anticlimactic ending.[6]

Message Format

The communicator also needs a strong format for the message. In a print ad, the communicator has to decide on the headline, copy, illustration, and color. To attract attention, advertisers can use novelty and contrast, eye-catching pictures and headlines, distinctive formats, message size, position, and color, shape, and movement. If the message is to be carried over the radio, the communicator has to choose words, sounds, and voices. The "sound" of Tom Bodett promoting Motel 6 is different from that of an announcer promoting Hyatt.

If the message is to be carried on television or in person, all these elements, plus body language, must be planned. Presenters plan their facial expressions, gestures, dress, posture, and hairstyle. If the message is carried on the product or its package, the communicator has to watch texture, scent, color, size, and shape. For example, color plays a major communication role in food preferences. When consumers sampled four cups of coffee that had been placed next to brown, blue, red, and yellow containers (all the coffee was identical, but the consumers did not know this), 75 percent felt that the coffee next to the brown container tasted too strong, nearly 85 percent judged the coffee next to the red container to be the richest, nearly everyone felt that the coffee next to the blue container was mild, and the coffee next to the yellow container was seen as weak.

14.4 Angel's Diner
McDonalds

The restaurant chain Angel's Diner employs the use of its menus as a format to transmit more than product and price information. The back of each menu contains "15 Golden Rules" and a color picture of gift merchandise for sale in the diner. Guests are encouraged to take miniature menus home.

Message Source

Messages delivered by attractive sources achieve higher attention and recall. Advertisers often use celebrities as spokespeople, such as Michael Jordan for McDonald's. Celebrities are likely to be effective when they personify a key product attribute. But what is equally important is that the spokesperson have credibility.

The use of living personalities to serve as spokespeople for a company or product carries inherent problems:

- Celebrities are often difficult to work with and may refuse to participate in important media events or to pose under certain conditions.
- Living personalities are sometimes publicly embarrassed.

Qantas Airlines has been successful using a kangaroo and a koala bear as symbols. McDonald's has effectively used the imaginary Ronald McDonald, and Embassy Suites used Garfield. Animals and cartoon characters are dependable and unlikely to create negative publicity.

Selecting Communication Channels

The communicator must now select channels of communication. There are two broad types of communication channels: personal and nonpersonal.

Personal Communication Channels

In personal communication channels, two or more people communicate directly with each other. They might communicate face to face, person to audience, over the telephone, or even through the mail. Personal communication channels are effective because they allow for personal addressing and feedback.

Some personal communication channels are controlled directly by the communicator. For example, company salespeople contact buyers in the target market. But other personal communications about the product may reach buyers through channels not controlled directly by the company. These might include independent experts making statements to target buyers, such as consumer advocates and consumer buying guides, or they might be neighbors, friends, family members, and associates talking to target buyers. This last channel, known as word-of-mouth influence, has considerable effect in many product areas.

Personal influence carries great weight for products that are expensive, risky, or highly visible. Hospitality products are often viewed as being risky, because they cannot be tried out beforehand. Therefore, personal sources of information are often sought before someone purchases a travel package, selects a restaurant, or stays at a hotel.

Companies can take several steps to put personal communication channels to work. They can devote extra effort to selling their products to well-known people or companies, who may in turn influence others to buy. They can create opinion leaders—people whose opinions are sought by others—by supplying certain people with the product on attractive terms. Finally, the firm can work to manage word-of-mouth communication by finding out what consumers are saying to others, taking appropriate actions to satisfy consumers, correcting problems, and helping consumers to seek information about the firm and its products.[7]

A common form of personal communication used by hotels and cruise lines is to invite key guests, prospective customers, and members of the community to dine with the captain or general manager. A creative

The Peabody Hotel Group has used ducks successfully in its advertising campaigns. This ad associates the ducks with different organizations that have held their meetings at the Peabody Orlando. The Peabody uses the names of the organizations as a form of testimonial. Courtesy of Peabody Hotels and Turkel Schwartz & Partners.

and always successful version is to dine in the kitchen, where guests are greeted by the chef, given samples of dishes being prepared, and made to feel "right at home."

The Condado Plaza Hotel and Casino in San Juan, Puerto Rico, uses one of the oldest and most effective means of communications, a personal letter. A personal letter is sent by the president on high-quality paper in an executive-size envelope to prior hotel guests. As an added incentive for the guest to return, a coupon good for $100 in hotel services is enclosed. This time-proved method of communication remains effective in an age of fax, e-mail, and information superhighways.

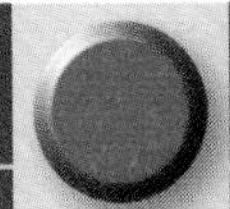

Marketing Highlight 14-1

Thank You—A Great Personal Communication

Two of the most powerful words in any language are thank you. That's why Jennifer Smith, sales manager for the West Airport Comfort Inn & Sleep Inn of Indianapolis, Indiana, decided to initiate a special thank you program for guests.

Jennifer's objectives were to increase corporate business and let guests know that the inn appreciated their patronage and wanted them to return. She felt that a handwritten note would be appreciated in this high-tech world of e-mail, Internet, and voice-mail communications.

Names and addresses were obtained from business cards left by guests in a fish bowl qualifying them for a monthly drawing. After the drawing is held, any one of the three desk clerks write thank you notes during slow times on the desk. Each desk clerk is provided personalized business cards, which are included with the handwritten note.

The Thank You Program was started in May 2000. Since then, Jennifer has spoken with many guests who were amazed that the inns took time to write a personal note to them. One client mentioned that he really liked having the business card sent from a front desk associate rather than a general manager or salesperson. Because the desk associates are usually the ones to make reservations, guests like having the name of someone to ask for when they call back for future reservations.

Jennifer said, "These thank you notes really help to build rapport between desk associates and guests even if the guest stayed just one time. I think the notes convey to our guests that our hotel staff cares for them as individuals and does not just see them in an impersonal way or simply another corporate traveler. I plan to continue this program indefinitely."

An adaptation of this technique was used by the new general manager of the Palace Hotel in Beijing, China, Peter L. J. Finamore. The manager was transferred from a sister property in Hong Kong and sent his new business card, along with a bright yellow and red greeting card that said, "Keep this card and see you at the Palace Hotel, Beijing." Members of hotel management meet thousands of guests, drop-by visitors, and others during the year. In many cases, particularly in Asia, cards are exchanged. The card collection should serve as a personal database for the manager, who can later use it to keep in touch with guests and prospective guests. Visitors to Beijing, particularly first-time visitors, would welcome the opportunity to become a guest in a hotel run by an "old friend."

Nonpersonal Communication Channels

Nonpersonal communication channels are media that carry messages without personal contact or feedback. They include media, atmospheres, and events. Major **media** consist of print media (newspapers, magazines, direct mail), broadcast media (radio and television), and display media (billboards, signs, posters). **Atmospheres** are designed environments that create or reinforce the buyer's leanings toward purchasing a product. The lobby of a five-star hotel contains a floral display, original works of art, and luxurious furnishings to reinforce the buyer's perception that the hotel is a five-star hotel. **Events** are occurrences staged to communicate messages to target audiences. Public relations departments arrange press conferences, grand openings, public tours, and other events to communicate with specific audiences.

The Scanticon Princeton (a conference center) used its lobby as a gallery for original artworks by members of the Princeton Artists Alliance. This resulted in excellent publicity, including a full-page story with pictures and the address of Scanticon Princeton in the Sunday edition of a major Philadelphia newspaper.

Nonpersonal communication affects buyers directly. In addition, using mass media often affects buyers indirectly by causing more personal communication. Mass communications affect attitudes and behavior through a two-step flow of communication. In this process, communications first flow from television, magazines, and other mass media to opinion leaders and then to the less active sections of the population. This two-step flow process means that the effect of mass media is not as direct, powerful, and automatic as once supposed. Rather, opinion leaders step between mass media and their audiences. Opinion leaders are more exposed to mass media and carry messages to people who are less exposed.

The two-step flow concept challenges the notion that people's buying is affected by a trickle down of opinions and information from higher social classes. Because people mostly interact with others in their own social class, they pick up fashions and other ideas from people like themselves who are opinion leaders. The two-step flow concept also suggests that mass communicators should aim their messages directly at opinion leaders, letting them carry the message to others.

14.5 Sheraton Convention Hotel

The restaurant in the Lakewood, Colorado, Sheraton Convention Hotel offered a strange and negative message to a potentially important market segment. A large sign at the restaurant's entrance said, "Breakfast Special \$3 for guest; \$5 for nonguest." When the receptionist was asked why the price difference existed, the answer was, "It's a marketing tactic to encourage guests to eat here."

The hotel is located on Union Avenue, a busy four-lane street in the center of office complexes. Denny's, the nearest sit-down breakfast restaurant, is located on the other side of the street. Guests are unlikely to drive or walk there, crossing four busy lanes of traffic, if the breakfast price in the hotel is reasonable; yet they might invite local business associates to meet them for breakfast in the hotel, only to face a potentially embarrassing situation. Serious thought must be given to any message that will be seen or heard by potential customers. It is very easy to offend customers seriously and may be increasingly difficult to create messages that are positive and effective.

Selecting the Message Source

The message's impact on the audience is also affected by how the audience views the sender. Messages delivered by highly credible sources are persuasive. For example, pharmaceutical companies want doctors to tell about their products. Memphis used prominent people to promote that city as a convention and meeting site. A video was produced in which convention planners, tour wholesalers, and association officials endorsed the city as an ideal convention location.

The use of a golf course by recognized golf pros and celebrities is a means of achieving positive communication with average golfers. Interestingly, in the case of downhill skiing it appears that use of a resort by celebrities such as Hollywood stars is more effective than use by members of the national ski team.

What factors make a source credible? The three factors most often found are expertise, trustworthiness, and likability. Expertise is the degree to which the communicator appears to have the authority needed to back the claim. Doctors, scientists, and professors rank high on expertise in their fields. Trustworthiness is related to how objective and honest the source appears to be. Friends, for example, are trusted more than salespeople. Likability is how attractive the source is to the audience. People like sources who are open, humorous, and natural. Not surprisingly, the most highly credible source is a person who scores high on all three factors: expertise, trustworthiness, and likability.

Measure the Communications' Results

After sending the message, the communicator must evaluate its effect on the target audience. This involves asking the target audience whether they remember the message, how many times they saw it, what points they recall, how they felt about the message, and their past and present attitudes toward the product and company. The communicator would also like to measure behavior resulting from the message: how many people bought a product, talked to others about it, or visited the store.

Holiday Inns developed a series of advertisements around a character named Mark. Mark was a thirty-seven-year-old slacker who lived with his parents. Mark would ask his parents for things offered by a Holiday Inn, and would receive a reply from his mother, "What! Does this look like a Holiday Inn?" For example, when his parents ask him for rent, he replies kids should stay free. His mom shouts back, "What! Does this look like a Holiday Inn?" These advertisements were humorous, but also got across the benefits of staying at a Holiday Inn. Holiday Inn was interested in creating more than humor, they wanted results. So they measured the brands recognition, recall, and REVPAR, before the campaign and after the campaign began. They found increases in all three of these metrics.[8]

Figure 14-2 shows an example of feedback measurement. Looking at hotel brand A, we find that 80 percent of the total market was aware of it, that 20 percent of those who were aware had tried it, but that only 20 percent of those who tried it were satisfied. These results suggest that although the communication program created awareness, the product failed to give consumers the satisfaction expected. The company should therefore try to improve the product while continuing the successful communication program. With hotel brand B, the situation was different: Only 40 percent of the total market was aware of it. Only 10 percent of those had tried it, and 80 percent of those who tried it were satisfied. In this case, the communication program needed to be stronger to take advantage of the brand's power to create satisfaction.

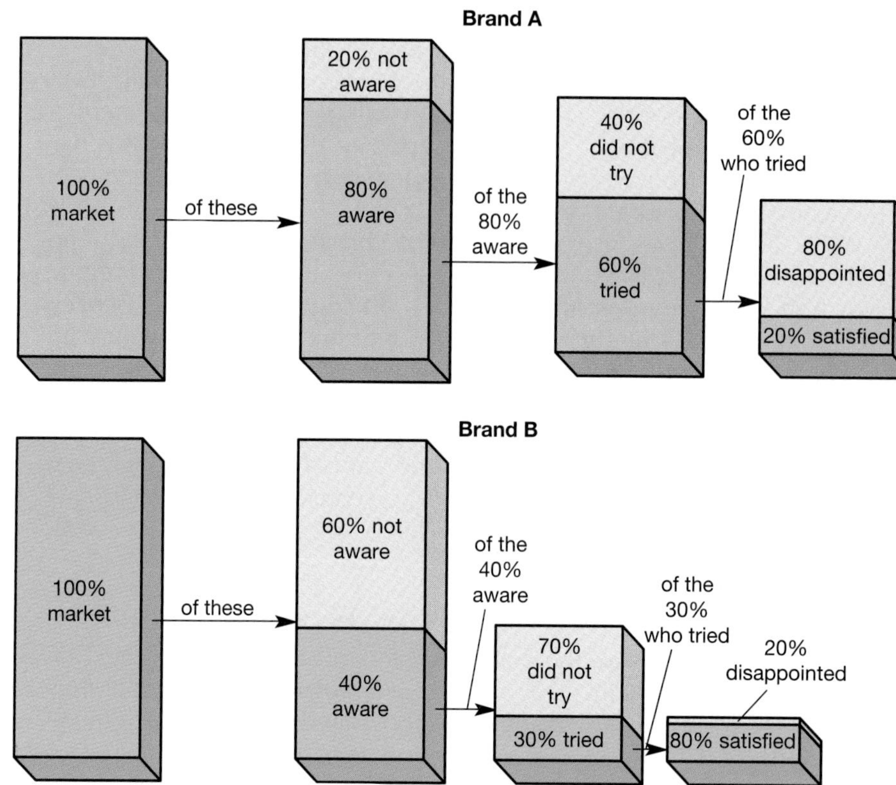

Figure 14-2
Feedback measurements for two brands.

Establishing the Total Marketing Communications Budget

One of the hardest marketing decisions facing companies is how much to spend on promotion. John Wanamaker, the department store magnate, once said, "I know that half of my advertising is wasted, but I don't know which half. I spent $2 million for advertising, and I don't know if that is half enough or twice too much."

Large budgets are not required for well-planned and well-executed communications. Pam Felix, owner of the California Tortilla restaurant in Bethesda, Maryland, states, "As an independent I do not have much of an ad budget." Felix uses humor as the basis of her promotions. She claims, "The goofier we are, the more money we make." Her main communication tool is a newsletter called *Taco Talk*. An example of one of her successful promotions was Jungle Noise Day. Everyone who came in and made a noise like Tarzan received free chips and salsa. There is a lack of parking in Besthesda, and as a result parking tickets are common. Felix gives anyone who comes in with a parking ticket a free taco to help relieve the pain of getting the ticket. She uses these wacky promotions to create a fun atmosphere and also as a way to give something back to her customers.[9]

How do companies determine their promotion budget? Four common methods are used to set the total budget for advertising: (1) the affordable method, (2) the percentage of sales method, (3) the competitive parity method, and (4) the objective and task method.[10]

Affordable Method

Many companies use the affordable method: They set a promotion budget at what they think the company can afford. One executive explained this method as follows: "Why it's simple. First, I go upstairs to the controller and ask how much they can afford to give this year. He says a million and a half. Later, the boss comes to me and asks how much should we spend and I say 'Oh, about a million and a half.'"[11]

Unfortunately, this method of setting budgets completely ignores the effect of promotion on sales volume. It leads to an uncertain annual promotion budget, which makes long-range marketing planning difficult. Although the affordable method can result in overspending on advertising, it more often results in underspending.

Percentage of Sales Method

Many companies use the percentage of sales method, setting their promotion budget at a certain percentage of current or forecasted sales, or they budget a percentage of the sales price. Some firms use this method because it is easy. For example, some restaurateurs know that the mean expenditures for promotion for restaurants is 4 percent; therefore, they set their promotion budget at 4 percent.

A number of advantages are claimed for the percentage of sales method. First, using this method means that promotion spending is likely to vary with what the company can "afford." It also helps management to think about the relationship between promotion spending, selling price, and profit per unit. Finally, it supposedly creates competitive stability because competing firms tend to spend about the same percentage of their sales on promotion.

However, despite these claimed advantages, the percentage of sales method has little justification. It wrongly views sales as the cause of promotion rather than as the result. The budget is based on availability of funds rather than on opportunities. It may prevent increased spending which is sometimes needed to turn around falling sales. Because the budget varies with year-to-year sales, long-range planning is difficult. Finally, the method does not provide a basis for choosing a specific percentage, except past actions or what competitors are doing.

Competitive Parity Method

Other companies use the competitive parity method, setting their promotion budgets to match competitors' outlays. They watch competitors' advertising or get industry promotion spending estimates from publications or trade associations and then set their budgets based on the industry average. For example, the advertising expenditures for the average hotel is 1 percent of sales, and the marketing budget is 5 percent. However, for limited service hotels the advertising expenditure is 2 percent of sales and the marketing budget.[12]

Two arguments are used to support this method. First, competitors' budgets represent the collective wisdom of the industry. Second, spending what competitors spend helps to prevent promotion wars. Unfortunately, neither argument is valid. There are no grounds for believing that competition has a better idea of what a company should be spending on promotion. Companies differ greatly, and each has its own special promotion needs. Furthermore, there is no evidence to indicate that budgets based on competitive parity prevent promotion wars.

Objective and Task Method

The most logical budget setting method is the objective and task method. Using this, marketers develop their promotion budgets by (1) defining specific objectives, (2) determining tasks that must be performed to achieve these objectives, and (3) estimating the costs of performing them. The sum of these costs is the proposed promotional budget.

The objective and task method forces management to spell out its assumptions about the relationship between dollars spent and promotional results. It is also the most difficult method to use, because it can be hard to determine which tasks will achieve specific objectives. Management must consider such questions even though they are difficult to answer. With the objective and task method, the company sets its promotion budget based on what it wants to accomplish.

Managing and Coordinating Integrated Marketing Communications

The company must now divide the total promotion budget among the major promotional tools: advertising, personal selling, sales promotion, and public relations. It must carefully blend the promotion tools into a coordinated promotion mix that will achieve its advertising and marketing objectives. Companies within the same industry differ greatly in how they design their promotion mixes. Thus a company can achieve a given sales level with varied mixes of advertising, personal selling, sales promotion, and public relations.

Companies are always looking for ways to improve promotion by replacing one promotion tool with another that will do the same job at less expense. Many companies have replaced a portion of their field sales activities with telephone sales and direct mail. Others have increased their sales promotion spending in relation to advertising to gain quicker sales.

Designing the promotion mix is even more complex when one tool must be used to promote another. Thus, when McDonald's decides to run a million-dollar sweepstakes in its fast-food outlets (a sales promotion), it has to run ads to inform the public. Many factors influence the marketer's choice of promotion tools.

Nature of Each Promotion Tool

Each promotion—advertising, personal selling, sales promotion, and public relations—has unique characteristics and costs. Marketers must understand these characteristics to select their tools correctly.

Advertising

Because of the many forms and uses of advertising, generalizing about its unique qualities as a part of the promotion mix is difficult. Yet several qualities can be noted. Advertising's public nature suggests that the advertised product is standard and legitimate. Because many people see ads for the product, buyers know that purchasing the product will be publicly understood and accepted. Advertising also allows the seller to repeat a message many times. Large-scale advertising by a seller says something positive about the seller's size, popularity, and success.

Advertising can be used to build a long-term image for a product (such as Four Seasons or McDonald's ads) and also stimulate quick sales (as when Embassy Suites in Phoenix advertises a promotion for the Fourth of July holiday). Advertising can reach masses of geographically dispersed buyers at a low cost per exposure.

Advertising also has shortcomings. Although it reaches many people quickly, advertising is impersonal and cannot be as persuasive as a company salesperson. Advertising is able to carry on only a one-way communication with the audience, and the audience does not feel that it has to pay attention or respond. In addition, advertising can be very costly. Although some forms, such as newspaper and radio advertising, can be done on small budgets, other forms, such as network TV advertising, require very large budgets.

A critical challenge faced by hotel marketers is creating an immediate awareness of brand name to ensure that their properties are included in the traveler's evoked set of lodging choices. The evoked set of brand preferences and the relative impact of advertising and prior stay were investigated in a study of frequent travelers. It was found that chains whose names were well established in a traveler's evoked set most often won the traveler's business. There was little influence on chain name recall of prior stay without ad exposure nor influence on ad exposure without prior stay. The combined effect of ad exposure and prior stay was an important influence on brand selection.[13]

Personal Selling

Personal selling is the most effective tool at certain stages of the buying process, particularly in building buyer preference, conviction, and purchase. Compared with advertising, personal selling has several unique qualities. It involves personal interaction between two or more people, allowing each to observe the other's needs and characteristics and make quick adjustments. Personal selling also lets all kinds of relationships spring up, ranging from a matter-of-fact selling relationship to a deep personal friendship. The effective salesperson keeps the customer's interests at heart to build a long-term relationship. Finally, with personal selling the buyer usually feels a greater need to listen and respond, even if the response is a polite "no thank you."

These unique qualities come at a cost. A sales force requires a longer-term company commitment than advertising; advertising can be turned on and off, but sales force size is harder to vary. Personal selling is the company's most expensive promotion tool, costing industrial companies an average of $225 per sales call.[14] American firms spend up to three times as much on personal selling as they do on advertising.

Sales Promotion

Sales promotion includes an assortment of tools, coupons, contests, cents-off deals, premiums, and others, and these tools have many unique qualities. They attract consumer attention and provide information that may

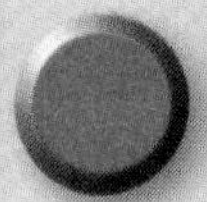

Marketing Highlight 14-2

Southwest Airlines

Founded twenty-seven years ago at Love Field in Dallas, Southwest Airlines sees itself as the "love" airline. The company even uses LUV as its New York Stock Exchange Symbol. Southwest showers most of this love on its passengers in the form of shockingly low prices for highly dependable, no-frills service. In 1992, Southwest received the Department of Transportation's first-ever Triple Crown Award for best on-time service, best baggage handling, and best customer service. Southwest rated first in customer satisfaction among the nation's nine major airlines. It repeated this feat in the years 1993 through 1996.

Customers have returned Southwest's love by making it the industry's most profitable airline. In an industry plagued by huge losses—$12.8 billion between 1990 and 1994 alone— Southwest has experienced twenty-five straight years of profits. In 1992, when the industry lost $3 billion, Southwest made $91 million. Over the past ten years, its revenues, have grown 388 percent and net earnings by 1,490 percent. Southwest has successfully beaten off determined challenges from several major competitors who have tried to copy the Southwest formula, including Continental Lite, Delta Express, and Shuttle by United. In 1998, Southwest was recognized by *Fortune* magazine as one of the nation's six most admired companies. All this from an airline only one-quarter the size of industry leader American Airlines.

Southwest's amazing success results from two factors: a superior marketing strategy and outstanding marketing communications. The marketing strategy is a simple one. Southwest knows its niche and stays with it. It has positioned itself firmly as the short haul, no-frills, low-price airline. Its average flight time is one hour; its average one-way just $75. In fact, its prices are so low that when it enters a new market, it actually increases total air traffic by attracting customers who might otherwise travel by car or bus. For example, when Southwest began its Louisville-Chicago flight at a one-way rate of $49 versus competitors' $250, total weekly air passenger traffic between the two cities increased from 8,000 to 26,000. To these practical benefits, Southwest adds one more key positioning ingredient—lots of good fun. With its happy-go-lucky CEO Herb Kelleher leading the charge, Southwest refuses to take itself seriously. For example, when an aviation company once confronted Southwest for using its slogan, "Just Plane Smart," Kelleher challenged the company's CEO to a public arm-wrestling match, with the slogan going to the winner. Kelleher was quickly pinned, but the CEO showdown became a national media event, winning Southwest lots of publicity. Southwest was later allowed to continue using the slogan.

In another instance, Northwest Airlines ran ads claiming that it ranked number one in customer satisfaction among the nation's eight largest airlines. Southwest, which at the time rated number one among the nine largest airlines, responded in classic Southwest fashion. Print ads boldly proclaimed, "After lengthy deliberation at the highest levels, and extensive consultation with our legal department, we have arrived at an official corporate response to Northwest Airlines' claim to be number one in customer satisfaction. Liar, liar. Pants on fire."

As the arm wrestling and "liar, liar" incidents suggest, Southwest has little trouble communicating with consumers in a very memorable way. But beyond these special cases, the airline dispenses a carefully coordinated flow of marketing communications, ranging from media advertising, special events, and public relations to direct marketing-personal selling.

Entering a new city presents the greatest communications challenge. For example, when Southwest entered Baltimore in 1993, East Coast consumers knew almost nothing about the airline. The Baltimore campaign began with public relations and community affairs events. Says the president of

Southwest's advertising agency, "We always start with the public relations side. . . . Then we integrate government relations, community affairs, service announcements, special events, and advertising and promotions. By time Southwest comes into the market, the airline already is part of the community."

Five weeks before the first flight, CEO Kelleher and Maryland's Governor William Schaefer held a news conference to announce Southwest's entry into Baltimore. The governor gave Kelleher a basket of products made in Maryland; Kelleher gave the governor a flotation device—a "lifesaver" from high airfares for the people of Baltimore. Southwest next dramatized its $49 fare between Baltimore and Cleveland by flying school children to Cleveland for a day to visit the Rain Forest at Cleveland Metroparks Zoo. This event garnered substantial media coverage in both Baltimore and Cleveland.

A week later, Southwest employees took to Baltimore's streets, standing on street corners and handing out flyers promoting Southwest's "Just Plane Smart" slogan. At about that time, Southwest sent direct mail to frequent short-haul travelers in the Baltimore area offering a special promotion to join its Rapid Rewards frequent-flier program. The public relations and community affairs efforts set the stage. Next, the company began running "Just Plane Smart" television and print commercials, and outdoor ads shouted, "Hello Baltimore, Good-bye High Fares." The integrated communications campaign was incredibly successful. In all, 90,000 Baltimore passengers purchased tickets before the start of service—a company record for advance bookings.

When the introductory fanfare had settled down, Southwest set up a Baltimore marketing office to continue working on local advertising, promotions, and community events. And now, of course, Baltimore travelers will be treated to the unique brand of more personal communication dispensed by Southwest's cheerful employees.

Southwest workers often go out of their way to amuse, surprise, or somehow entertain passengers. During delays at the gate, ticket agents will award prizes to the passenger with the largest hole in his or her sock. Flight attendants have known to hide in overhead luggage bins and then pop out when passengers start filing onboard. Veteran Southwest fliers looking for a few yuks, have learned to listen up to announcements over the intercom. A recent effort: "Good morning and gentlemen. Those of you who wish to smoke will please file out to our lounge on the wing, where you can enjoy our feature film, *Gone With the Wind.*" On that same flight, an attendant later made this announcement: "Please pass all cups to the center aisle so that we can wash them out and use them for the next group of passengers."

Southwest owes much of its success to its ability to deliver dependable, no-frills, low-cost service to its customers. But success also depends on Southwest's skill at blending all of its promotion tools—advertising, sales promotion, public relations, personal selling, and direct marketing—into an integrated marketing communications program that communicates the Southwest story.

Sources: Extract from Kennet Labich, "Is Herb Kelleher America's Best CEO?" *Fortune*, May 2, 1994, pp. 44–52. Other information from Charles Butler, "General Excellence: Southwest Airlines," *Sales & Marketing Management* (August 1993): 38; Jennifer Lawrence, "Integrated Mix Makes Expansion Fly," *Advertising Age*, November 8, 1993, pp. S10, S12; Jackie and Kevin Feidberg, "Is This Company Completely Nuts?" *Executive Excellence* (September 1996): 20; Wendy Zellner, "Southwest's Love Fest at Love Field," *Business Week,* April 28, 1997, p. 12E4; Thomas A. Stewart, "American's Most Admired Companies," *Fortune*, March 2, 1998. pp. 70–73; Stephanie Gruner, "Have Fun, Make Money," *INC.* (May 1998): 123; and Chad Kaydo, "Riding High," *Sales & Marketing Management* (July 1998): 64–69 Also see About Southwest Airlines at *www.southwest.com.*

lead the consumer to buy the product. Sales promotions offer strong incentives to purchase by providing inducements or contributions that give additional value to consumers, and they invite and reward quick response. Advertising says "buy our product." Sales promotion says "buy it now."

Companies use sales promotion tools to create a stronger and quicker response. Sales promotion can be used to dramatize product offers and to boost sagging sales. Its effects are usually short-lived, however, and are not effective in building long-run brand preference.

Public Relations

Public relations offers several advantages. One is believability. News stories, features, and events seem more real and believable to readers than do ads. Public relations can reach many prospects who avoid salespeople and advertisements. The message gets to the buyers as news rather than as a sales-directed communication. Like advertising, public relations can dramatize a company or product.

A relatively new addition to the promotion mix is the infomercial. This is a hybrid between advertising and public relations. Companies provide interesting stories on videotape for use on television during periods of light viewing, such as early morning. Infomercials provide enough information to keep the attention of viewers, combined with a "soft" approach to product or brand advertising.

Hospitality marketers tend to underuse public relations or use it only as an afterthought. Yet a well-thought-out public relations campaign used with other promotion mix elements can be very effective and economical.

Factors in Setting the Promotion Mix

Companies consider many factors when developing their promotion mix, including the following: type of product and market, push versus pull strategy, buyer readiness state, and product life-cycle stage.

Type of Product and Market

The importance of different promotion tools varies among consumers and commercial markets. When hospitality firms market to consumer markets, they spend more on advertising and sales promotion and often very little on personal selling. Hospitality firms targeting commercial organizations spend more on personal selling. In general, personal selling is used more heavily with expensive and risky goods and in markets with fewer and larger sellers. A meeting or convention is customized for the organization putting on the event. It takes a skilled salesperson to put together a package that will give clients what they want at an appropriate price that will provide good revenue for the company.

Push versus Pull Strategy

The promotional mix is heavily affected by whether a company chooses a push or pull strategy. The two strategies are contrasted in Figure 14-3. A push strategy involves "pushing" the product through distribution channels to final consumers. The manufacturer directs its marketing activities (primarily personal selling and trade promotion) at channel members to induce them to order and carry the product and to promote it to final consumers. For example, Dollar Rent-A-Car offered travel agents a 15 percent commission instead of 10 percent, to persuade them to order its brand for clients. Continental Plaza Hotels and Resorts developed a promotion that gave travel agents an extra $10 in addition to their normal commission for bookings. A push strategy provides an incentive for channel members to promote the product to their customers or push the product through the distribution channels.

14.6 Continental Plaza Hotels
Dollar Rent-A-Car

Using a pull strategy, a company directs its marketing activities (primarily advertising and consumer promotion) toward final consumers to induce them to buy the product. For example, Sheraton placed an ad for its Hawaiian properties in the Phoenix, Arizona, paper. Interested readers were instructed to call their travel planner or ITT Sheraton. If the strategy is effective, consumers will purchase the product from channel members, who will, in turn, order it from producers. Thus, under a pull strategy, consumer demand "pulls" the product through the channels.

Buyer Readiness State

Promotional tools vary in their effects at different stages of buyer readiness. Advertising, along with public relations, plays a major role in the awareness and knowledge stages, more important than that played by "cold calls" from salespeople. Customer liking, preferences, and conviction are more affected by personal selling, which is closely followed by advertising. Finally, closing the sale is accomplished primarily with sales calls and sales promotion. Only personal selling, given its high costs, should focus on the later stages of the customer buying process.

Figure 14-3
Push versus pull promotion strategy.

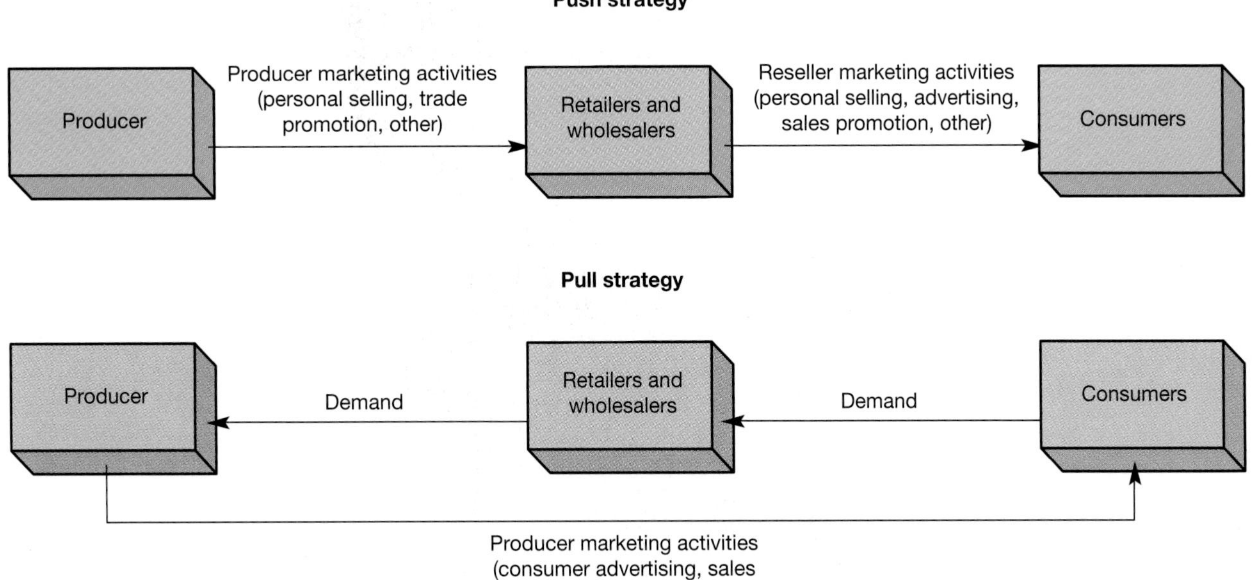

Product-Life-Cycle Stage

The effects of different promotion tools also vary with stages of the product life cycle. In the introduction stage, advertising and public relations are good for producing high awareness, and sales promotion is useful in product early trial. Personal selling must be used to get the trade to carry the product in the growth stage; advertising and public relations continue to be powerful, while promotion can be reduced because fewer incentives are needed. In the mature stage, sales promotion again becomes important relative to advertising. Buyers know the brands, and advertising is needed only to remind them of the product. In the decline stage, advertising is kept at a reminder level, public relations is dropped, and salespeople give the product only a little attention. Sales promotion, however, may continue to be strong.[15]

MANAGE THE INTEGRATED MARKETING COMMUNICATION PROCESS

Many companies still rely on one or two communication tools to achieve their communication aims. This practice persists in spite of the fragmenting of mass markets into a multitude of minimarkets, each requiring its own approach; the proliferation of new types of media; and the growing sophistication of consumers. The wide range of communication tools, messages, and audiences makes it imperative that companies move toward *integrated marketing communications* (IMC). As defined by the American Association of Advertising Agencies, IMC is "a concept of marketing communications planning that recognizes the added value of a comprehensive plan that evaluates the strategic roles of a variety of communications disciplines—for example, general advertising, direct response, sales promotion and public relations—and combines these disciplines to provide clarity, consistency, and maximum communications' impact through the seamless integration of discrete messages."

A study of top management and marketing executives in large consumer companies indicated that over 70 percent favored the concept of integrated marketing communications. Several large advertising agencies—Ogilvy & Mather, Young & Rubicam, Saatchi & Saatchi—acquired major agencies specializing in sales promotion, public relations, and direct marketing in order to provide one-stop shopping. But to their disappointment, most clients have not bought their integrated marketing communications package, preferring to put together the specialized agencies by themselves.

Why the resistance? Large companies employ several communication specialists to work with their brand managers. Each communication specialist knows little about the other communication tools. Furthermore, the specialists usually have favorite outside agencies and oppose turning their responsibilities over to one superagency. They argue that the company should choose the best specialist agency for each purpose, not second- and third-rate agencies just because they belong to a superagency. They believe that the ad agency will still put most of the advertiser's money into the advertising budget.

Nevertheless, integrated marketing communications does produce stronger message consistency and greater sales impact. It gives someone responsibility—where none existed before—to unify the company's brand images and messages as they come through thousands of company activities. IMC will improve the company's ability to reach the right customers with the right messages at the right time and in the right place.

Advocates of integrated marketing communications describe it as a way of looking at the whole marketing process instead of focusing only on individual parts.

We have looked at the steps in planning and sending communications to a target audience. But how does the company decide on the total promotion budget and its division among the major promotional tools to create a promotion mix?

ADVERTISING

The remainder of this chapter examines advertising in more detail: Subsequent chapters will deal with personal selling and sales promotion. We define **advertising** as any paid form of nonpersonal presentation and promotion of ideas, goods, or services by an identified sponsor. The hospitality and travel industries spend billions of dollars on advertising. In 2000, the top hospitality and travel advertisers were:[16]

1. McDonald's Corp.	$ 1,273,000,000
2. Tricon Global Restaurants	$865,000,000
3. Hilton Hotels Corp.	$335,000,000
4. Wendy's International	$296,000,000
5. Marriott International	$248,000,000
6. UAL Corp. (United Airlines)	$214,000,000
7. Darden Restaurants	$198,000,000
8. Six Continents PLC	$183,000,000
9. Royal Caribbean International	$181,000,000
10. AMR Corp. (American Airlines)	$167,000,000

This list provides evidence that the fast-food industry in the United States has reached the mature stage and fast-food companies are fighting for market share. McDonald's, Burger King, and Wendy's are stepping up their campaigns and try to take market share from each other. The pizza chains continue to discount their products through coupons. Marketing wars such as the burger wars and pizza wars are fought with advertising dollars. Marketing wars break out in mature markets where growth of the market is slow. To increase their sales, companies must try to steal market share from their competitors.

Advertising is a good way to inform and persuade, whether the purpose is to sell Hilton International Hotels around the world or to get residents of Kuala Lumpur, the capital of Malaysia, to stay at a nearby resort on the island of Langkawi. Organizations have different ways of managing their advertising. The owner or the general manager of an independent restaurant usually handles the restaurant's advertising. Most hotel chains give responsibility for local advertising to the individual hotels, while corporate management is responsible for national and international advertising. In some corporate offices, the director of marketing handles advertising. Other firms might have advertising departments to set the ad-

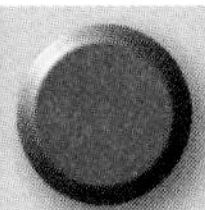

Marketing Highlight 14-3

How Does an Advertising Agency Work?

Madison Avenue is a familiar name to most Americans. It's a street in New York City where some major advertising agency headquarters are located. But most of the nation's 10,000 agencies are found outside New York, and almost every city has at least one agency, even if it's a one-person shop. Some ad agencies are huge. The largest U.S. agency, Young & Rubicam, has annual worldwide billings (the dollar amount of advertising placed for clients) of more than $6 billion. Dentsu, a Japanese agency, is the world's largest agency with billings of more than $10 billion.

Advertising agencies were started in the mid-to-late nineteenth century by salespeople and brokers who worked for the media and received a commission for selling advertising space to various companies. As time passed, salespeople began to help customers prepare their ads. Eventually, they formed agencies and grew closer to the advertisers than the media. Agencies offered more advertising and marketing services to their clients.

Even companies with strong advertising departments use advertising agencies. Agencies employ specialists who can often perform advertising tasks better than the company's own staff. Agencies also bring an outside point of view to solving the company's problems, along with the experience of working with different clients and situations. Agencies are partly paid from media discounts and often cost the firm very little. Since a client can drop its agency at any time, most agencies work hard to do a good job. Smaller clients are generally charged a fee because they often do not use much commissionable media.

Full-Service Ad Agencies. Advertising agencies usually have four departments: creative, which develops and produces ads; media, which selects media and places ads; research, which studies audience characteristics and wants; and business, which handles the agency's business activities. Each account is supervised by an account executive; staff members in each department are usually assigned to work on one or more accounts.

Agencies often attract new business through their reputation or size. Generally, however, a client invites a few agencies to make a presentation for its business and then selects one of them.

Ad agencies have traditionally been paid through commissions and some fees. Under this system, the agency receives 15% of the media cost as a rebate. Suppose that the agency buys $60,000 of magazine space for a client. The magazine bills the advertising agency for $51,000 ($60,000 less 15%), and the agency bills the client for $60,000, keeping the $9000 commission. If the client bought space directly from the magazine, it would pay $60,000, because commissions are only paid to recognized advertising agencies.

Both advertisers and agencies have become increasingly unhappy with the commission system. Larger advertisers complain that they pay more for the same services received by smaller ones simply because they place more advertising. Advertisers also believe that the commission system drives agencies away from low-cost media or noncommissionable media and short advertising campaigns. Agencies are unhappy because they perform extra services for an

vertising budget, work with an outside advertising agency, and handle direct-mail advertising and other advertising not done by the agency. Large companies commonly use an outside advertising agency, because it offers several advantages.

MAJOR DECISIONS IN ADVERTISING

Marketing management must make five important decisions in developing an advertising program. These decisions are listed in Figure 14-4 and discussed next.

account without receiving additional revenue. As a result, the trend is now toward paying either a straight fee or a combination commission and fee. Some large advertisers are tying agency compensation to the performance of the agency's advertising campaigns. Today, only about 35% of companies still pay their agencies on a commission-only basis.

Another trend is also hitting the advertising agency business. In recent years, as growth in advertising spending has slowed, many agencies have tried to keep growing by acquiring other agencies, thus creating huge agency-holding companies. One of the largest of these megagroups, Saatchi & Saatchi PLC, includes several large agencies: Saatchi & Saatchi Compton, Ted Bates Worldwide, DFS Dorland Worldwide, and others with combined billings exceeding $15 billion. Many agencies have also sought growth by diversifying into related marketing services. These new megagroup agencies offer a complete list of integrated marketing and promotion services under one roof, including advertising, sales promotion, public relations, direct marketing, and marketing research.

Specialized Ad Agencies. The hospitality and travel industries often use the services of specialized ad agencies. The specialty advertising agency offers a variety of merchandise, such as coffee mugs, dishes, luggage, and thousands of other items used in sales promotions and employee incentive programs. Some observers feel that this form of agency is primarily a broker of products.

The incentive agency is important to the hospitality and travel industries as a provider of guests. Again, many observers feel that it should not properly be classified as an ad agency.

The brochure ad agency once again is an enterprise that many feel is incorrectly called an ad agency. This company specializes in the production and delivery of travel-industry-related brochures. Brochure ad agencies acquire and maintain rack space in restaurants, truck stops, motel lobbies, museums, and other places frequented by highway travelers. Restaurants, motels, and tourist attractions who depend on transient highway customers often view the work of these agencies as highly valuable.

Special Location Agencies. In New Zealand and Australia, a highly unusual specialized ad agency has developed. Some people find the work of this agency to be intrusive. This company acquires the rights to the back of the entrance door in public rest rooms and places ads in this location.

Other specialized ad agencies have acquired advertising space that should be considered by members of the hospitality and travel industries. These include airport advertising, ball field advertising, transit advertising on public conveyance, and shelter advertising (ad space on bus stop shelters and benches). Given the wide diversity of members of the hospitality and travel industries, virtually every specialized medium probably has a useful role for some firm.

Source: See Walecia Konrad, "A Word from the Sponsor: Get Results or Else," *Business Week* (July 4, 1988), p. 66; "Saatchi Leads Top 11 Megagroups," *Advertising Age* (March 29, 1989); R. Craig Endicott, "Ad Age 500 Grows 9.7%," *Advertising Age* (March 26, 1990), pp. S1–S2.

Setting the Objectives

The first step in developing an advertising program is to set advertising objectives. Objectives should be based on information about the target market, positioning, and marketing mix. Marketing positioning and mix strategies define the role that advertising must perform in the total marketing program.

An advertising objective is a specific communication task to be accomplished with a specific target audience during a specific period of time. Advertising objectives can be classified by their aim: to *inform, persuade,* or *remind.* **Informative advertising** is used heavily when introducing a new product category and when the objective is to build primary demand. When an airline opens a new route, its management often runs full-page advertisements informing the market about the new service. Stouffer Hotels ran a two-page spread in *Business Travel News* introducing the new Stouffer Concourse Hotel in Atlanta. The ad targeted corporate meeting planners, giving them information on function space, conference rooms, and other features of the hotel. Junior's Deli, in the Westwood section of Los Angeles, uses direct-mail campaigns to create new customers. New residents in the neighborhood receive a gift certificate for a Deli Survival Kit, which contains a chunk of beef salami, two types of cheese, a loaf of fresh rye bread, and a home-baked dessert. The kit is absolutely free, with no purchase required, but the certificate must be redeemed at the restaurant. More than 1,000 new neighbors come in to claim their kits each year. Thus, the kit not only informs potential customers about the restaurant, but also results in visits to the restaurant by customers who sample its products.[17]

Persuasive advertising becomes more important as competition increases and a company's objective becomes building selective demand. Some persuasive advertising has become comparison advertising, which compares one brand directly or indirectly with one or more other brands. For example, Burger King used direct-comparison advertising against McDonald's. Table tents in Burger King show a picture of a hamburger. Inside the hamburger is a white circle depicting the size of a McDonald's hamburger compared with Burger King's hamburger. The copy read, "The only one who won't like our new burger is McDonald's. The new Burger King 2.8 oz flame-broiled hamburger has 75% more beef than McDonald's hamburger."

The use of direct-comparison advertising is a controversial subject. Many marketers believe that comparison ads are not appropriate as they obviously draw attention to the competitor rather than strictly to the company's product. An unwritten rule of using comparison ads is that the prestige brands and market-share leaders should never use this tactic be-

Figure 14-4
Major advertising decisions.

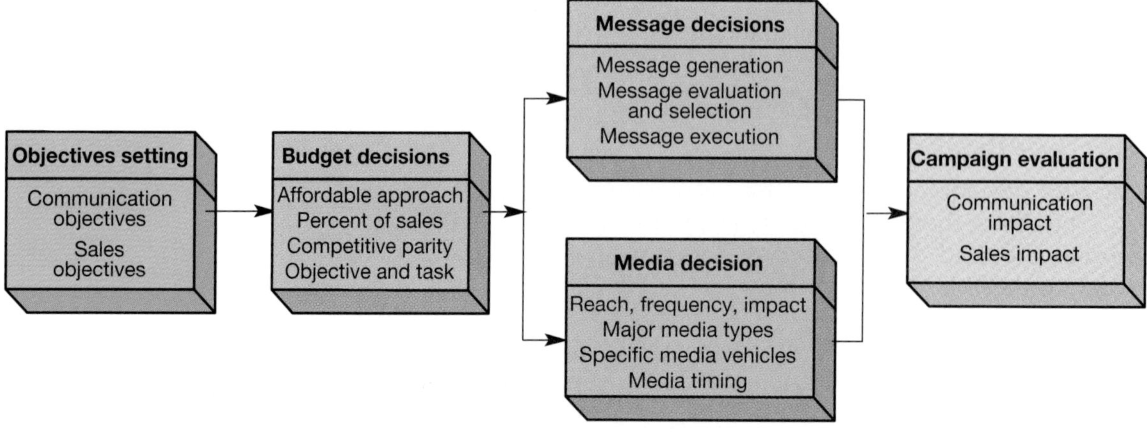

cause it draws attention to competitors and causes the customer to question the value of the market-share leader or prestige brand.

Reminder advertising is important for mature products, because it keeps consumers thinking about the product. Expensive McDonald's ads on television are designed to remind people about McDonald's, not to inform or persuade them. The Old Spaghetti Warehouse, a restaurant chain based in Dallas, sends customers a postcard thanking them for their patronage. The postcard features a message such as "Till We Meet Again" or "Can't Stop Thinking About You." A handwritten thank you from the manager appears on each card.[18] The personalized thank you card creates goodwill and reminds the customer about the restaurant.

Advertising is not a substitute for poor products. For an advertising campaign to create long-term sales, the product advertised must create satisfied customers. One mistake frequently made by the owners of new restaurants is advertising before the operation has gone through a shakedown period. Eager to get a return on their investment, the owners advertise before the restaurant's staff is properly trained and the restaurant's systems are tested under high-demand situations.

Because most people look forward to trying a new restaurant, advertising campaigns are usually effective, resulting in waits during peak periods. However, success can be short lived when restaurateurs deliver poor quality food, poor service, or poor value. Dissatisfied customers quickly spread negative word of mouth to potential customers, who are eager to find out about the new restaurant. Frequently, advertising a noncompetitive product will quicken the product's death through negative word. The owner of a restaurant in Houston who went through this experience and ultimately went out of business blamed his loss on fickle customers. In his words, "The restaurant used to have waits every night of the week. Now, the restaurant is empty. I can't believe how fickle customers are." The customers weren't fickle; in fact, they knew exactly what they wanted: good food and good service. These were things the restaurant did not offer when they first opened.

The president of a hospitality marketing, advertising, and public relations firm believes that the implementation of an effective advertising campaign is one of the fastest ways to jeopardize the performance of a mediocre property. You must first be sure that the property can live up to the promises your advertising makes. If your property or service is inconsistent with the claims made, the money you spend to generate additional business will probably do little more than increase the number of dissatisfied guests.[19]

Even highly satisfied customers need frequent reminders. Ski and scuba diving resorts share a common problem. Satisfied guests often fail to return because they wish to experience new slopes and new dive areas. Years may pass before the guest is ready to return. Reminder advertising can shorten that period of time.

Setting the Advertising Budget

After determining advertising objectives, a company can establish an advertising budget for each product. The role of advertising is to affect demand for a product. The company wants to spend the amount needed to

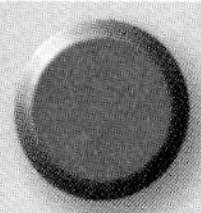

Marketing Highlight 14-4

Association Advertising

Hospitality firms often belong to an association such as a local chamber of commerce, hotel/motel association, or restaurant association. They may also belong to independent promotional associations such as the Australian Dine Out, Preferred Hotels, or Leading Hotels.

Sooner or later the manager of every hotel, restaurant, bed and breakfast, and other hospitality enterprise must decide whether to join an association and, if so, what degree of cooperation to provide. There is a wide diversity of opinion covering the possible benefits from advertising and promotion through an association such as the local visitors bureau. Some associations distribute free magazines or newspapers to visitors that are read and used. Others seem to provide ineffective support.

Remember that any funds given to associations come directly from the company's advertising budget. A decision to join and support an association must be based on an evaluation of possible gains for the company, not simply on an emotional plea to support the group.

The marketing power of hospitality chains offers a genuine threat to independents. An independent hotel, for instance, cannot hope to match the spending levels or brand-building thrust of chains.

Organizations such as Preferred Hotels exist to provide a group identity for independent hotel members. Organizations such as Preferred may also offer a frequent-flyer program, worldwide directory, promotional programs for intermediaries such as travel agents, and central reservations. For some member hotels, such as the Captain Cook Hotel in Alaska, the Preferred Hotels' central bookings accounts for 80% of transient bookings. Preferred Hotels annually spends over $1 million in advertising to promote member luxury hotels and another $3 million in cooperative advertising. Associations also exist for budget hotels, such as Friendship Inns. Friendship charges members a royalty per room, such as 49 cents per room, of which 30% goes toward advertising.

Source: Glenn Withiam, "Unchained Melody: How Independent Hotels Work in Harmony," *Cornell Hotel and Restaurant Administration Quarterly,* 28, n. 2 (August 1987): 78–79.

achieve the sales goal. Four commonly used methods for setting the promotional budget were discussed earlier in the chapter. These methods—the affordable method, the percentage of sales method, the competitive parity method, and the objective and task method—are also often used when determining the advertising budget. The advertising budget also has some specific factors that should be considered when setting a budget:

- **Stage in the product life cycle.** New products typically need large advertising budgets to build awareness and gain consumer trial. Mature brands usually require lower budgets as a ratio to sales. For example, a neighborhood casual restaurant may want to budget $2,000 a month for advertising in its first year of operation and $1,000 a month after its first year. By the end of the first year, it should have established a clientele. After this point it will need to maintain its existing customers and gain new customers (albeit at a lower rate than the first year). Its loyal customers should be spreading positive word of mouth by the end of the first year.
- **Competition and clutter.** In a market with many competitors and heavy advertising support, a brand must be advertised more frequently to be heard above the noise of the market.

- **Market share.** High-market-share brands usually require greater advertising expenditures as a percentage of sales than do low-share brands. Building a market or taking share from competitors requires larger advertising budgets than maintaining current share. For example, McDonald's spends about 18 percent of its sales on advertising.
- **Advertising frequency.** Larger advertising budgets are essential when many repetitions are needed to present the brand's message.
- **Product differentiation.** A brand that closely resembles others in its product class (pizza, limited-service hotels, air travel) requires heavy advertising to set it apart. When a product differs greatly from those of competitors, advertising can be used to communicate differences to consumers.

How much impact does advertising really have on consumer purchases and brand loyalty? One study found that advertising increased purchases by loyal users but was less effective in winning new buyers. The study found that advertising appears unlikely to have a cumulative effect that leads to loyalty. Features, displays, and especially price have a stronger impact on response than advertising.[20]

These findings were not well received by the advertising community, and several advertising professionals attacked the study's data and methodology. They claimed that the study measured primarily short-run sales effects and thus favored pricing and sales promotion activities that tend to have a more immediate impact. Most advertising, takes many months or even years to build strong brand positions and consumer loyalty. Long-run effects are difficult to measure. This debate underscores the fact that the measurement of sales results from advertising remains in its infancy.

Strategic versus Tactical Budgets

The last three areas deal with strategic issues, building brand awareness, and brand image. Another budget decision is deciding how much will be spent for strategic advertising and how much will be spent on tactical advertising. Tactical advertising deals with sales promotions and often includes price discounts. Thomson, the United Kingdom's largest tour operator, divides its £7,000,000 advertising budget equally between tactical and strategic advertising. It refers to its strategic advertising as advertising to build brand awareness for Thomson and holiday destinations. This advertising starts in the summer of 2002 for the 2003 holiday season. In early 2003, during the prime booking season the ads will become more tactical and focus on price.[21]

Overall Promotional Budget

Another factor in planning the advertising budget is the overall promotional budget. To gain synergy between the different elements of the promotional mix, money should be available for training employees about new promotions, in-house sales promotion materials, collateral material, and public relations.

Consistency

In his book *Guerrilla Advertising,* Jay Conrad Levinson states that the advertising budget should be viewed like rent, something that has to be paid each month.[22] When times are tough, there is often a tendency to cut the advertising budget. The rent, employees, utilities, and suppliers all have to be paid; the advertisements for the coming month are seen as discretionary. This view of advertising can lead to continued poor sales and the eventual decline of the business.

Opportunities to Stretch the Budget

Hospitality companies often have ways they can stretch their advertising dollars. Trade-outs are one of these ways. Trade-outs involve trading advertising for products the media company can use, such as rooms, food, or travel. A trade-out can be a good way of getting advertising without using cash. To be a good deal, the target market of the media gained through the trade must match the target market of the restaurant, hotel, or travel company. Second, the advertisements should be played when the market will be exposed to them. Another way of expanding the budget is through cooperative advertising, that is, two or more companies getting together to pay for an ad. For example, a credit card company may pay for a portion of an advertisement if it is mentioned in the ad, and cruise lines will provide cooperative advertising for their top agents. Travel agents can also use tagging, that is, placing their ad below a wholesaler's, resort's, or cruise line's advertisement, so that those reading the ad and interested in the product come to the travel agent's ad immediately after reading the main advertisement.

The Final Budget

The advertising budget is a subset of the marketing budget. It is dependent on the objectives of the marketing plan and the promotional plan. Setting an advertising budget becomes a complex process. It must consider the other uses of the marketing budget. It must balance the objectives of the advertising plan against the money available from the company. The method most effective for setting a budget is the objective and task method: determining what needs to be done and then developing a budget to accomplish the task, as long as the expense results in positive returns. However, often the budget is dictated by the corporate office. In this case the marketing manager has to defend his or her case for a higher budget or make do with a lower budget. If a lower budget is required, the budget must be reviewed and prioritized, with the lower-priority items being eliminated.

The final advertising budget will make effective use of the funds allocated to the budget. It will take into account funds needed for other areas of the promotional mix. Finally, it will provide funds for promotional campaigns throughout the year.

Message Decisions

The message decision is a third decision in the advertising management process. A large advertising budget does not guarantee a successful advertising campaign. Two advertisers can spend the same amount on advertising with dramatically different results. Studies have shown that creative advertising messages can be more important than the number of dollars spent. No matter how big the budget, advertising can succeed only if its message gains attention and communicates well.

Good advertising messages are especially important in today's costly and cluttered advertising environment. All this advertising clutter bothers some consumers and causes big problems for advertisers. Take, for instance, the situation facing network television advertisers. They typically pay $100,000 to $200,000 for thirty seconds of advertising time during a popular prime-time TV program and even more if it is an especially popular program or event such as the Super Bowl (over $1,900,000). In such cases, their ads are sandwiched in with a clutter of sixty other commercials, announcements, and network promotions per hour. Furthermore, advertising across all media segments, including network TV, has soared.[23]

Until recently, television viewers were an almost captive audience for advertisers. Viewers had only a few channels from which to choose. Those who found the energy to get up and change channels during unwelcome commercial breaks usually found only more of the same on other channels. With the growth in cable TV, VCRs, and remote-control units, today's viewers have many more options. They can avoid ads altogether by watching commercial-free cable channels. They can "zap" commercials by pushing the fast-forward button during taped programs, instantly turn off the sound during a commercial, or "zip" around the channels. Advertisers take such "zipping" and "zapping" seriously. One author claims that 60 percent of all TV viewers may regularly be tuning out commercials.[24]

Thus, just to gain and hold attention, today's advertising messages must be better planned and more imaginative, entertaining, and rewarding to consumers. Creative strategy will play an increasingly important role in advertising success. Developing a creative strategy requires three message steps: generation, evaluation and selection, and execution.

Message Generation

Hotels, resorts, bed and breakfasts, and cruise lines face an inherent barrier to effective communication with the customer. This is the intangibility of the product. A hotel's product is experienced only at or after the time of purchase. This characteristic of services in general poses genuine challenges for message creation. As the editor of the *Cornell Quarterly* pointed out, "An advertisement can depict a product—a food item, a desk, an exercise machine—but how does one illustrate a hotel stay?"[25]

Creative people have different ways of developing advertising messages. Many start by talking to consumers, dealers, experts, and competitors. Others imagine consumers using the product and determine the benefits that consumers seek. Although advertisers create many possible messages, only a few will be used.

Marketing managers bear a responsibility to review critically the message, the media, and the illustration and creative concepts recommended by the advertising agency. A fine line sometimes exists between responsible review and unwarranted intrusion into the professional work of advertising agencies. Marketing managers for client companies such as a hotel or excursion train are expected to know their products, customers, and employees better than any ad agency. In the final analysis, they must assume responsibility for messages that fail to motivate customers or that offend employees. On the brighter side, they can also shine in the glory of creative, well-received advertising.

Message Evaluation and Selection

The advertiser must evaluate possible appeals on the basis of three characteristics. First, messages should be meaningful, pointing out benefits that make the product more desirable or interesting to consumers. Second, appeals should be distinctive. They should tell how the product is better than competing brands. Finally, they must be believable. Making message appeals believable is difficult, because many consumers doubt the truth of advertising. One study found that, on average, consumers rate advertising messages as "somewhat unbelievable."

Storyboards like this one are used to convey television advertising messages before the ad is produced on film. Courtesy of Australia Tourist Commission.

(MUSIC UP)
ANNCR: (VO) Was it aeons of isolation from the rest of the world?
Or was it the way the wind blew?
Or the way the rain fell?
Was it the angle of the sun?
Or was it a bird blown off course
that found its way here
with a single seed that grew...
...and changed the course of history?

Somehow we just evolved differently.

Australia. Feel the wonder.

For your free 130-page travel planner, call 1-800-395-7000.

Message Execution

The impact of the message depends on what is said and how it is said—message execution. The advertiser has to put the message across in a way that wins the target market's attention and interest. Advertisers usually begin with a statement of the objective and approach of the desired ad.

The advertising agency's creative staff must find a style, tone, words, and format for executing the message. Any message can be presented in different execution styles, such as the following:

1. *Slice of life* shows one or more people using the product in a normal setting. Bennigan's developed a television ad showing friends enjoying an evening at Bennigan's.
2. *Lifestyle* shows how a product fits with a lifestyle. For example, an airline advertising its business class featured a businessperson sitting in an upholstered chair in the living room, having a drink, and enjoying the paper. The other side of the ad featured the same person in the same relaxed position with a drink and a paper in one of the airline's business-class seats.
3. *Fantasy* creates a wonder world around the product or its use. For instance, Cunard's *Sea Goddess* features a woman lying in a raft in the sea, with the luxury liner anchored in the background. A cocktail server in a tuxedo is walking through the ocean carrying a drink for the woman.

   The use of fantasy has also occurred in the development of resort hotels. Disney may have started the trend with hotels on the property of Disney World, but Hyatt Corporation, Westin Hotels and Resorts, and many others have adopted the concept. Such hotels are designed to surround the guests with a fantasy ambience, including costumed employees, entertainment, and dramatic physical structures such as waterfalls, a pyramid, or a miniature Amazon River. Fantasy hotels are expensive to build and maintain, with costs per room running $300,000 or more and 2,000 or more employees.

   The human psyche is receptive to fantasy. Archaeologists often have difficulty discerning whether cave paintings represent fantasy or sights really observed. Many children's books, cartoons, and top-selling novels are fantasy. It is not surprising that fantasy advertising is effective within an industry that appeals to one's desire to escape.
4. *Mood or image* builds a mood or image around the product, such as beauty, love, or serenity. No claim is made about the product except through suggestion. Bally's resort in Las Vegas developed an advertisement designed to change its image after its $37 million renovation. The headlines in the ad were: "To them a watch does more than tell time, A car is not merely transportation, And their resort is Bally's in Las Vegas."
5. *Musical* shows one or more people or cartoon characters singing a song about the product. Many cola ads have used this format. Delta Airlines used music effectively in its "We Love to Fly and It

Shows" campaign. Certain cultures seem particularly receptive to the use of theme songs and sing-along melodies in advertisements. Australians often use simple but catchy melodies in their advertisements. Brazilians often use adaptations of samba music, particularly music that was popular during carnival.

6. *Personality* symbol creates a character that represents the product. The character might be created by the company, such as McDonald's Ronald McDonald, or real, such as Tom Bodett of Motel 6.
7. *Technical expertise* shows the company's expertise with the product. Hotels often use this style in advertisements directed toward meeting and convention planners, emphasizing that they have the technical expertise to support the meeting planner. American Airlines make heavy and frequent use of expertise, particularly that of its pilots and mechanics.
8. *Scientific evidence* presents survey or scientific evidence that the brand is better or better liked than one or more other brands. During the month of May 1992, Northwest Airlines had the highest percentage of on-time arrivals, the lowest level of mishandled baggage, and the lowest level of customer complaints of the seven largest airlines, according to the Department of Transportation's (DOT) *Air Travel Consumer Report.* Northwest took advantage of this achievement by developing an advertisement using the DOT survey results. Northwest only included the top seven airlines, however. Southwest, the eighth largest airline, had actually beaten Northwest in all of these categories. Southwest developed a humorous ad to counteract Northwest's claim, stating that

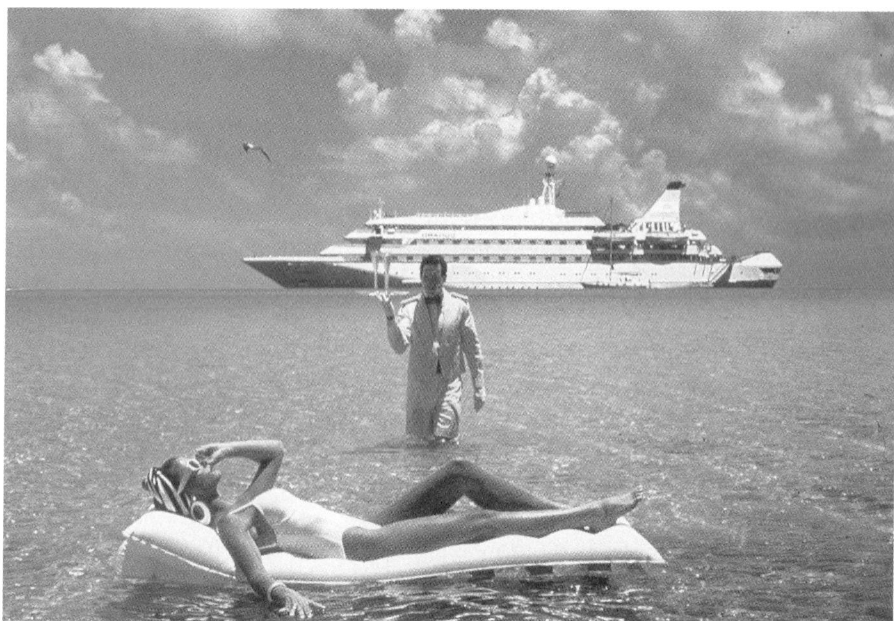

This ad used fantasy to carry out its message that the Sea Goddess *provides excellent service. Courtesy of Cunard Line.*

Advertising agencies will present mock-ups of ad concepts for the client to review. Marketing managers must critically review the message, the media, illustrations, and creative concepts recommended by the advertising agency. These are two mock-ups presented to Grand Heritage Hotels—both were rejected by Grand Heritage. Grand Heritage is a collection of elegant luxury hotels with historical significance located in North America and Europe, including the Pontchartrain in New Orleans; the Brazilian Court in Palm Beach, Florida; Thornbury Castle in Avon, England; and the Hotel Royal Monceau in Paris.

The purpose of this ad is to attract inquiries from potential clients interested in Grand Heritage managing their hotel. The ad has attractive graphics, but they detract from the message. Grand Heritage wants to convey to potential clients that their management team will perform and produce results. However, an ad conveying an image of business performance would create a more positive image than a circus performer.

This ad is very creative and draws an analogy between Grand Heritage's success in the hotel business and what would happen if it went into the farming business. The problem is that Grand Heritage's luxury image and a farmer standing in a field are incompatible.

their official corporate response was "Liar, liar. Pants on fire." And they used DOT results to back their claim.

9. *Testimonial evidence* features a highly believable or likable source endorsing the product. For example, sports personalities such as Michael Jordan and Tiger Woods, or other well-known figures, such as Bill Cosby.

The advertiser must also choose a tone for the ad. Hyatt always uses a positive tone, with ads that say something very positive about its own products. They avoid humor that might take attention away from the

14.7 Taco Bell

message. By contrast, Taco Bell ads have used humor, in the form of an odd, but cute, little talking Chihuahua. The hungry little dog has become famous for his Spanish language statement, "Yo Quiero Taco Bell," meaning *I want Taco Bell.* The little dog pushed Taco Bell's sales up 4.3 percent in 1997.[26]

Southwest countered Northwest's claim that they had won the "triple crown" with this advertisement. Courtesy of Southwest Airlines.

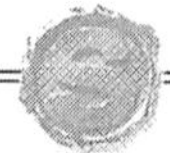

After lengthy deliberation
at the highest executive levels,
and extensive consultation
with our legal department,
we have arrived at
an official corporate response
to Northwest Airlines' claim
to be number one
in Customer Satisfaction.

"Liar, liar. Pants on fire."

Okay. We lost our temper for a moment. Northwest Airlines didn't really lie. And, its pants aren't actually on fire. Northwest simply excluded Southwest Airlines from its comparison.

Fact. According to the U.S. Department of Transportation's Consumer Report for May, the real leader in Customer Satisfaction is Southwest Airlines. That means we received the fewest complaints per 100,000 passengers among all Major airlines, including Northwest Airlines.

More facts. The Department of Transportation's Consumer Report also shows Southwest Airlines best in On-time Performance (highest percentage of systemwide domestic flights arriving within 15 minutes of schedule, excluding mechanical delays), best in Baggage Handling (fewest mishandled bags per 1,000 passengers), as well as best in Customer Satisfaction, from January through August 1992.

It's all there in black and white.

Fly the real No. 1. You'll know there's no substitute for satisfaction. Call Southwest Airlines or your travel agent for reservations.

SOUTHWEST AIRLINES℠

Just Plane Smart℠

1-800-I-FLY-SWA (1-800-435-9792)

Finally, format elements will make a difference in an ad's impact and cost. A small change in design can make a big difference in an ad's effect. The illustration is the first thing the reader notices. That illustration must be strong enough to draw attention. Then the headline must effectively entice the right people to read the copy. The copy, the main block of text in the ad, must be simple but strong and convincing. These three elements must effectively work together. Even then, a truly outstanding ad will be noted by less than 50 percent of the exposed audience. About 30 percent of the audience exposed to the ad will recall the main point of the headline. Approximately 25 percent will remember the advertiser's name, and fewer than 10 percent will have read most of the body copy. Less-than-outstanding ads will not achieve even these results.

Media Decisions

The fourth step is to choose the media to carry the message. The major steps in media selection are (1) deciding on reach, frequency, and impact; (2) choosing among major media types; (3) selecting specific media vehicles; and (4) deciding on media timing.

Deciding on Reach, Frequency, and Impact

To select media, the advertiser must decide what reach and frequency are needed to achieve advertising objectives. Reach is a measure of the percentage of people in the target market who are exposed to the ad campaign during a given period of time. For example, the advertiser might try to reach 70 percent of the target market during the first year. Frequency is a measure of how many times the average person in the target market is exposed to the message. For example, the advertiser might want an average exposure frequency of three. The advertiser must also decide on desired media impact, the qualitative value of message exposure through a given medium. For products that must be demonstrated, television messages using sight and sound are more effective. The same message in one magazine (*Newsweek*) may be more believable than in another (*National Enquirer*).

Suppose that the advertiser's product has the potential to appeal to a market of one million consumers. The goal is to reach 700,000 consumers (70% of one million). Because the average consumer will receive three exposures, 2.1 million exposures (700,000 × 3) must be bought. If the advertiser wants exposures of 1.5 impact (assuming that 1.0 impact is the average), a rated number of exposures of 3.15 million (2.1 million × 1.5) must be bought. If 1,000 exposures with this impact cost $10, the advertising budget must be $31,500 (3,150 × $10). In general, the more reach, frequency, and impact that the advertiser seeks, the larger the advertising budget will have to be.

Gross rating points (GRPs) show the gross coverage or duplicated coverage of an advertising campaign. GRPs are determined by multiplying reach times frequency. In the example above, an ad with a reach of 700,000 and frequency of three exposures would produce 210 gross rating points if the market was one million. Each gross rating point is equal to 1 percent of the market.

Waste is the part of the medium's audience not in the firm's target market.[27] An entrepreneur owning a single restaurant in Worthington, Ohio (north of Columbus), will find that only about 20 percent of those reading the *Columbus Dispatch* will be in that entrepreneur's market area. Thus he or she will probably advertise in other media. A travel agency may advertise in a newspaper targeted at seniors knowing that only 50 percent of the readers will spend more than $1,000 on travel annually. The travel agency factored this in when they purchased the media. Despite the waste, the medium still offered a good value. In choosing media, the circulation aimed at your target market is the important factor, not the total circulation.

Choosing among Major Media Types

The media planner has to know the reach, frequency, and impact of each major media type. The major advertising media are summarized in Table 14-1. The major media types, in order of advertising volume, are newspapers, television, direct mail, radio, magazine, and outdoor. Each medium has advantages and limitations. For example, McDonald's uses outdoor

Table 14-1

Profiles of Major Media Types

MEDIUM	ADVANTAGES	LIMITATIONS
Newspapers	Flexibility; timeliness; good local market coverage; broad acceptance; high believability	Short lift; poor reproduction quality; small pass-along audience
Television	Combines sight, sound, and motion; appealing to the senses; high attention; high reach	High absolute cost; high clutter; fleeting exposure; less audience selectivity
Direct mail	Audience selectivity; flexibility; no ad competition within the same medium; personalization	Relatively high cost; junk mail image
Radio	Mass use; high geographic and demographic selectivity; low cost	Audio presentation only; lower attention than television; nonstandardized rate structures; fleeting exposure
Magazines	High geographic and demographic selectivity; credibility and prestige; high-quality reproduction; long life; good pass-along readership	Long ad purchase lead time; some waste circulation; no guarantee of position
Outdoor	Flexibility; high repeat exposure; low cost; low competition	No audience selectivity; creative limitations
E-mail	Audience selectivity; personalization; low cost	Need to gain permission; message must be relevant or it will be viewed as junk mail

boards to provide directional signs designed to let drivers know where McDonald's restaurants were located and when to exit the highway. Outdoor boards also appeal to McDonald's because it allows them to convey a single national message along with a localized message on promotions, products, and prices. James Keller, vice president of marketing for Gannett, said the ability to customize boards to local marketing needs is one of the strengths of outdoor advertising.[28]

Media planners consider many factors when making their media choices, including the media habits of target consumers. Radio and television, for example, are the best media for reaching teenagers. The nature of the product also affects media choices. Resorts are best shown in color magazines. Fast-food ads targeted at young children are best on television. Different types of messages may require different media. A message announcing a Mother's Day buffet would be conveyed effectively on radio or in newspapers. A message that contains technical data, such as an ad explaining the details of a travel package, might be disseminated most effectively in magazines or through direct mail. Cost is also a major factor in media choice. Television is very expensive; newspaper advertising costs much less. The media planner looks at both the total cost of using a particular medium and at the cost per thousand exposures, that is, the cost of reaching 1,000 people.

Ideas about media impact and cost must be reexamined regularly. For many years, television and magazines dominated the media mixes of national advertisers, while other media were neglected. Recently, costs and clutter (competition from competing messages) have increased, and audiences have dropped. As a result, many marketers have adopted strategies targeted at narrower segments, and TV and magazine advertising revenues have leveled off or declined. Advertisers have increasingly turned to alternative media, ranging from cable TV to outdoor advertising. Given these and other media characteristics, the media planner must decide how much of each type of media to buy. Table 14-2 is a comparison of Marriott's and Wendy's media expeditures.

Selecting Specific Media Vehicles

The media planner must now choose the best specific media vehicles within each general media type. A comparison of the top television shows in the United States with younger (18–34) and older audiences (35–54) found there were no shows that appeared on the Top 10 List for both groups (Table 14-3). Each group had a unique set, thus advertising must know the favorite media of its target market. Magazine vehicles include *Newsweek, Travel and Leisure, The New Yorker,* and *Town and Country.* If advertising is placed in magazines, the media planner must look up circulation figures and the costs of different ad sizes, color options, ad positions, and frequencies for various specific magazines. The planner then evaluates each magazine on such factors as credibility, status, reproduction quality, editorial focus, and advertising submission deadlines. The media planner decides which vehicles give the best reach, frequency, and impact for the money.

Table 14-2
Comparison of Marriott's and Wendy's Use of Media[a]

MEDIUM	MARRIOTT	WENDY'S
Magazine	4,261,000	5,000
Sunday magazine	471,000	0
Newspaper	20,279,000	0
Outdoor	295,000	1,915,000
Network TV	0	41,954,000
Spot TV	10,094,000	39,518,000
Syndicated TV	0	8,424,000
Cable TV	2,955,000	2,386,000
Network radio	3,594,000	0
Spot radio	6,175,000	215,000
Total measured media	48,911,000	94,416,000
Total unmeasured media	90,800,000	29,700,000
Total media	139,711,000	124,1163,000

Source: "The Advertising Fact Book," *Advertising Age* (January 2, 1995).

[a]Terms used in the table: *Unmeasured media* is an estimate of direct mail, sales promotion, couponing, special events, and other promotional activities. *Network TV* is advertising on the major networks: ABC, CBS, NBC. *Spot TV* is TV purchased on a market-by-market basis. *Syndicated TV* includes satellite-distributed syndicated TV and Fox Broadcasting Company. *Cable TV* includes CNN, ESPN, Family Channel, MTV: Music Television, WTBS, USA Network, and other such channels.

Media planners also compute the cost per 1,000 persons reached by a vehicle. If a full-page, four-color advertisement in *Newsweek* costs $100,000 and *Newsweek's* readership is 3.3 million people, the cost of reaching each 1,000 persons is $28. The same advertisement in *Business Week* may cost only $57,000 but reach only 775,000 persons, at a cost per 1,000 of about $74. The media planner would favor magazines with the lower cost per 1,000 for reaching target consumers.

Table 14-3
Top Television Shows with Younger Audiences (18–34) and Older Audiences (35–54)

YOUNGER AUDIENCES (18–34)			OLDER AUDIENCES (35–54)		
SHOW	AUDIENCE (MILLIONS)	COST PER AD	SHOW	AUDIENCE (MILLIONS)	COST PER AD
Friends	16	$350,000	*ER*	17	$600,000
Survivor	15.2	$300,000	*60 Minutes*	10.3	$150,000

Sources: Top 20 US Television Series, retrieved from the World Wide Web on 5/11/02, *http://www.pazsaz.com/tvseasn.html; Television Advertising,* retrieved from the World Wide Web on 5/11/02, *http://www.televisionadvertising.com/faq.htm*

The media planner must also consider the costs of producing ads for different media. Whereas newspaper ads can cost very little to produce, flashy television ads may cost millions. The average cost of producing a single thirty-second television commercial is $180,000. Some ads with special effects can cost over $1 million for a thirty-second spot.[29]

The media planner must thus balance media cost measures against several media impact factors. First, costs should be balanced against the media vehicle's audience quality. For a corporate hotel advertisement, *Business Week* would have a high-exposure value; *People* would have a low-exposure value. Second, the media planner should consider audience attention. Readers of *Vogue,* for example, typically pay more attention to ads than do readers of *Newsweek*. Third, the planner assesses the vehicle's editorial quality; *Time* and the *Wall Street Journal* are more believable and prestigious than the *National Enquirer*.

14.8 National Enquirer
Wall Street Journal

Media planners are increasingly developing more sophisticated measures of effectiveness and using them in mathematical models to arrive at the best media mix. Many advertising agencies use computer programs to select the initial media and then make further media schedule improvements based on subjective factors not considered by the media section model.[30]

Deciding on Media Timing

The advertiser must also decide how to schedule advertising over the course of a year. For a hotel or resort, effective advertising requires knowledge of the origin of its guests and how far in advance they make their reservations. If guests living in Connecticut make their reservations in November to go to a Caribbean resort in January, it will not be effective for a resort to advertise in December after consumers have already made their vacation plans. Restaurants with a strong local demand may decide to vary their advertising to follow the seasonal pattern, to oppose the seasonal pattern, or to be the same all year. Most firms do some seasonal advertising.

Finally, the advertiser must choose the pattern of the ads. Continuity means scheduling ads evenly within a given period. Pulsing means scheduling ads unevenly over a given period. Thus fifty-two ads could either be scheduled at one per week during the year or pulsed in several bursts. Those who favor pulsing feel that the audience will learn the message more completely and that money can be saved. Once they have done a burst of ads, they remove themselves from the advertising market. A company could use a six-month burst of advertising, for example, to regain its past sales growth rate. This finding led Budweiser to adopt a pulsing strategy.[31]

Road Blocking. Advertisers can sometimes use a tactic known as road blocking to help ensure that an intended audience receives the advertising message. The tropical island resort, Great Keppel in Queensland, Australia, knew that its audience in Brisbane, Sydney, and Melbourne listened to certain FM rock stations. Great Keppel purchased drive-time radio spots for exactly the same time on all rock stations in the three markets. This prevented listeners from switching stations to avoid the advertisement.

Campaign Evaluation

Managers of advertising programs should regularly evaluate the communication and sales effects of advertising.

Measuring the Communication Effect

Measuring the communication effect reveals whether an ad is communicating well. Called copy testing, this process can be performed before or after an ad is printed or broadcast. There are three major methods of advertising pretesting. The first is direct rating, in which the advertiser exposes a consumer panel to alternative ads and asks them to rate the ads. Direct ratings show how well the ads attract attention and how they affect consumers. Although it is an imperfect measure of an ad's actual impact, a high rating indicates a potentially effective ad. In portfolio tests, consumers view or listen to a portfolio of advertisements, taking as much time as they need. The interviewer then asks the respondent to recall all the ads and their contents. The recall can be either aided or unaided by the interviewer. Recall level indicates the extent to which an ad stands out and how well its message is understood and remembered. Laboratory tests use equipment to measure consumers' physiological reactions to an ad: heartbeat, blood pressure, pupil dilation, and perspiration. The tests measure an ad's attention-getting power but reveal little about its impact on beliefs, attitudes, or intentions.

There are two popular methods of posttesting ads. Using recall tests, the advertiser asks people who have been exposed to magazines or television programs to recall everything they can about the advertisers and products that they saw. Recall scores indicate the ad's power to be noticed and retained. In recognition tests, the researcher asks readers of, for instance, a given issue of a magazine to point out what they have seen. Recognition scores can be used to assess the ad's impact in different market segments and to compare the company's ads with those of competitors.

Measuring the Sales Effect

What quantity of sales are caused by an ad that increases brand awareness by 20 percent and brand preference by 10 percent? The sales effect of advertising is often harder to measure than the communication effect. Sales are affected by many factors besides advertising, such as product features, price, and availability. One way to measure sales effect is to compare past sales with past advertising expenditures. Another is through experiments.

To spend a large advertising budget wisely, advertisers must define their advertising objectives, develop a sound budget, create a good message, make media decisions, and evaluate the results.

Advertising draws much public attention because of its power to affect lifestyles and opinions. Advertising faces increased regulation to ensure that it performs responsibly.

KEY TERMS

Advertising Any paid form of nonpersonal presentation and promotion of ideas, goods, or services by an identified sponsor.

Atmosphere Designed environments that create or reinforce a buyer's leanings toward consumption of a product.

Channel conflict Disagreement among marketing channel members on goals and roles—who should do what and for what rewards.

Events Occurrences staged to communicate messages to target audiences, such as news conferences or grand openings.

Informative advertising Advertising used to inform consumers about a new product or feature to build primarty demand.

Media Nonpersonal communications channels, including print media (newspaper, magazines, direct mail), broadcast media (radio, television), and display media (billboards, signs, posters).

Promotion mix The specific mix of advertising, personal selling, sales promotion, and public relations a company uses to pursue its advertising and marketing objectives.

Reminder advertising Advertising used to keep consumers thinking about a product.

Chapter Review

I. The Communication Process

1) Identify the target audience.

2) Determine the response sought. Six buyer readiness states: awareness, knowledge, liking, preference, conviction, and purchase.

3) Design a message.

a) AIDA model. The message should get attention, hold interest, arouse desire, and obtain action.

b) Three problems that the marketing communicator must solve:

i) Message content (what to say). There are three types of appeals:

a) Rational appeals: relate to audience self-interest. They show that the product will produce desired benefits.

b) Emotional appeals: attempt to provoke emotions that motivate purchase.

c) Moral appeal: directed to the audience's sense of what is right and proper.

ii) **Message structure (how to say it).**

a) Whether to draw a conclusion or leave it to the audience.

b) Whether to present a one- or two-sided argument.

c) Whether to present the strongest arguments first or last.

iii) **Message format (how to say it symbolically).**

a) Visual ad: using novelty and contrast, eye-catching pictures and headlines, distinctive formats, message size and position, color, shape, and movement.

b) Audio ad: using words, sounds, and voices.

c) Message source: using attractive sources to achieve higher attention and recall, such as using celebrities.

4) **Choose the media through which to send the message.**

a) **Personal communication channels:** used for products that are expensive and complex. It can create opinion leaders to influence others to buy.

b) **Nonpersonal communication channels:** include media (print, broadcast, and display media), atmospheres, and events.

5) **Measure the communications' results.** Evaluate the effects on the targeted audience.

II. Establishing the Total Marketing Communications Budget

1) **Four common methods for setting the total promotion budget**

a) **Affordable method.** A budget is set based on what management thinks they can afford.

b) **Percentage of sales method.** Companies set promotion budget at a certain percentage of current or forecasted sales or a percentage of the sales price.

c) **Competitive parity method.** Companies set their promotion budgets to match competitors.

d) **Objective and task method.** Companies develop their promotion budget by defining specific objectives, determining the tasks that must be performed to achieve these objectives, and estimating the costs of performing them.

2) **Managing and coordinating integrated marketing communications**

a) **Advertising** suggests that the advertised product is standard and legitimate; it is used to build a long-term image for a product and to stimulate quick sales. However, it is also considered impersonal, one-way communication.

b) **Personal selling** builds personal relationships, keeps the customers' interests at heart to build long-term relationships, and allows personal interactions with customers. It is also considered the most expensive promotion tool per contact.

c) **Sales promotion** includes an assortment of tools: coupons, contests, cents-off deals, premiums, and others. It attracts consumer attention and provides information. It creates a stronger and quicker response. It dramatizes product offers and boosts sagging sales. It is also considered short-lived.

d) **Public relations** has believability. It reaches prospective buyers and dramatizes a company or product.

3) **Factors in setting the promotion mix**

a) **Type of product and market.** The importance of different promotional tools varies among consumers and commercial markets.

b) **Push versus pull strategy**

i) **Push strategy.** The company directs its marketing activities at channel members to induce them to order, carry, and promote the product.

ii) **Pull strategy.** A company directs its marketing activities toward final consumers to induce them to buy the product.

c) **Buyer readiness state.** Promotional tools vary in their effects at different stages of buyer readiness.

d) **Product life-cycle stage.** The effects of different promotion tools also vary with stages of the product life cycle.

III. Major Decisions in Advertising

1) **Setting objectives.** Objectives should be based on information about the target market, positioning, and market mix. Advertising objectives can be classified by their aim: to inform, persuade, or remind.

a) **Informative advertising.** Used to introduce a new product category or when the objective is to build primary demand.

b) **Persuasive advertising.** Used as competition increases and a company's objective becomes building selective demand.

c) **Reminder advertising.** Used for mature products, because it keeps the consumers thinking about the product.

2) **Setting the advertising budget.** Factors to consider in setting a budget are the stage in the product life cycle, market share, competition and clutter, advertising frequency, and product differentiation.

3) **Creating the advertising message.** Advertising can only succeed if its message gains attention and communicates well.

a) **Message generation.** Marketing managers must help the advertising agency create a message that will be effective with their target markets.

b) **Message evaluation and selection.** Messages should be meaningful, distinctive, and believable.

c) **Message execution.** The impact of the message depends on what is said and how it is said.

4) **Media decisions**

a) **Deciding on reach, frequency, and impact**

b) **Choosing among major media types.** Choose among newspapers, television, direct mail, radio, magazines, and outdoor.

c) **Selecting specific media vehicles.** Costs should be balanced against the media vehicles: audience quality, ability to gain attention, and editorial quality.

d) **Deciding on media timing.** The advertiser must decide on how to schedule advertising over the course of a year based on seasonal fluctuation in demand, lead time in making reservations, and if they want to use continuity in their scheduling or if they want to use a pulsing format.

5) **Advertising evaluation.** There are three major methods of advertising pretesting and two popular methods of posttesting ads.

a) **Pretesting**

i) Direct rating. The advertiser exposes a consumer panel to alternative ads and asks them to rate the ads.
ii) Portfolio tests. The interviewer asks the respondent to recall all ads and their contests after letting them listen to a portfolio of advertisements.
iii) Laboratory tests. Use equipment to measure consumers' physiological reactions to an ad.

b) Posttesting
i) Recall tests. The advertiser asks people who have been exposed to magazines or television programs to recall everything that they can about the advertisers and products that they saw.
ii) Recognition tests. The researcher asks people exposed to media to point out the advertisements that they have seen.

c) Measuring the sales effect. The sales effect can be measured by comparing past sales with past advertising expenditures and through experiments.

Discussion Questions

1. Explain the difference between promotion and advertising.
2. Why do large hotels spend a major part of their promotional budget on personal selling?
3. Recently, a number of restaurants have shifted some of their promotional budget from advertising to public relations. What benefits does public relations offer that would make the restaurants spend more?
4. The percentage of sales method is one of the most common ways of setting a promotional budget. What are some advantages and disadvantages of this method?
5. Apply the four major tools in the marketing communication mix to a hospitality or travel company by showing how a company can use all these tools.
6. According to advertising expert Stuart Henderson Britt, good advertising objectives spell out the intended audience, the advertising message, the desired effects, and the criteria for determining whether the effects were achieved (for example, not just "increase awareness" but "increase awareness 20%"). Why should these components be part of the advertising objective? What are some effects that an advertiser wants a campaign to achieve?
7. What factors call for more frequency in an advertising media schedule? What factors call for more reach? How can you increase one without either sacrificing the other or increasing your advertising budget?

Experiential Exercises

Do one of the following:

1. Provide an example of a communication from a hospitality or travel company that does a good job of communicating with a specific market segment. The example can be any form of communication: for example, an advertisement, a sales promotion, or publicity.
2. Find an example of a promotion for a hospitality company that uses the push promotion strategy. Explain how the company is using the strategy.
3. Bring to class an example of a hospitality or travel company's advertising and an ad from one of its competitors. Which ad do you think is more effective? What is the most striking part of the ad? What do you like most about each ad? What changes would you suggest to make the company's advertisement better?

INTERNET EXERCISE

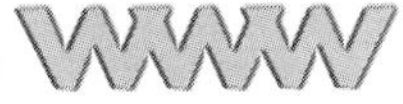

Support for these exercises can be found on the Web site for *Marketing for Hospitality and Tourism,* www.prenhall.com/kotler.

Find several advertisements for a hospitality or travel industry organization. Then visit their Web site. Is the communication provided on the Web site congruent with and support their print advertising and broadcast advertising? Explain your answers.

REFERENCES

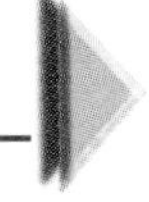

1. David Baines, "A Mogul and His Mirage Are a Reality Placing Their Bets," *Vancouver Sun,* March 3, 1994, p. A1; Scott Craven, "Dunes Hotel Brought Down in the Face of New Mega Resorts," *Phoenix Gazette,* October 28, 1993, p. B6; Jefferson Graham, "Vegas Casino Opens with a Blast," *USA Today,* October 27, 1993, p. D1; Jamie McKee, "New Resorts Spend Millions to Reach National Audience," *Las Vegas Business Press* 10, no. 37 (November 1, 1993): 1.
2. These definitions, except for sales promotion, are from *Marketing Definitions: A Glossary of Marketing Terms* (Chicago: American Marketing Association, 1960). Also, Peter D. Bennett, *Dictionary of Marketing Terms* (Chicago: American Marketing Association, 1988).
3. Marc Lubetkin, Bed-and-Breakfast, *The Cornell Hotel & Restaurant Administration Quarterly,* August 1999, Vol 40, No. 4, pp. 84–90.
4. Konnie Le May, "South Dakota Tribes Beating Tom-toms to Drum Up Increased Tourist Trade," *Star-Ledger,* May 8, 1994, Sec. 8, p. 6.
5. Steve Raabe, "2 Hotels Link Up for Sales," *Denver Post,* May 4, 1994, p. C1.
6. For more on message content and structure, see Leon G. Schiffman and Leslie Lazar Kanuk, *Consumer Behavior,* 4th ed. (Upper Saddle River, NJ: Prentice Hall, 1991), Chapter 10; Frank R. Kardes, "Spontaneous Inference Processes in Advertising: The Effects of Conclusion Omission and Involvement on Persuasion," *Journal of Consumer Research* (September 1988): 225–233.
7. K. Michael Haywood, "Managing Word of Mouth Communications," *Journal of Services Marketing* (Spring 1989): 55–67.
8. Mike Beirne, "Breaking out of the hotel rut," *Brandweek* (June 5, 2000), pp. 36–38.
9. Gregg Cebrzynski, "Goofy promotions, or how to generate word of mouth with wax lips," *Nation's Restaurant News,* Jan 17, 2000, Vol 34, No. 3, pp. 18–20.
10. For a more comprehensive discussion on setting promotion budgets, see Michael L. Rothschild, *Advertising* (Lexington, MA: D. C. Heath, 1987), Chapter 20.
11. Quoted in Daniel Seligman, "How Much for Advertising?" *Fortune* (December 1956): 123.
12. The Hospitality Research Group of PKF Consulting, as cited in *Hotel and Motel Management,* May 15, 2000, p. 44.
13. Michael S. Morgan, "Traveler's Choice: The Effects of Advertising and Prior Stay," *Cornell Hotel and Restaurant Administration Quarterly* 32, no. 4 (December 1991): 40–49.
14. "The Rise (and Fall) of Cost per Call," *Sales and Marketing Management* (April 1990): 26.
15. For more on advertising and the product life cycle, see John E. Swan and David R. Rink, "Fitting Market Strategy to Product Life Cycles," *Business Horizons* (January/February 1982): 60–67.
16. R. Craig Endicott, "100 Leading National Advertisers," *Advertising Age,* September 24, 2001, pp. s1–s4
17. Leslie Ann Hogg, *50 More Promotions That Work for Restaurants* (New York: Walter Mathews Associates, Inc., 1989), p. 11.
18. "Spaghetti Warehouse Says Thanks by Mail," *Nation's Restaurant News* 26, no. 13 (March 30, 1992); p. 14.
19. Peter C. Yesawich, "Execution and Measurement of Programs," *Cornell Hotel and Restaurant Administration Quarterly* 29, no. 4 (February 1989): 89.
20. Gerald J. Tellis, "Advertising Exposure, Loyalty, and Brand Purchase: A Two-Stage Model of Choice," *Journal of Marketing Research* (May 1988): 57–70.
21. Scheherazade Daneshkhu, "Media: A Trade in Dreams of Escape," *Financial Times,* February 10, 1997, p. 15.
22. Jay Conrad Levinson, *Guerrilla Advertising* (New York: Houghton Mifflin, 1994).
23. T. Case. (March 6, 2000), "Magazines in Prime Time," *Adweek* (on-line), retrieved April 21, 2000, from *http://proquest.umi.com/pqdweb?TS.*
24. Christine Dugas, "And Now, a Wittier Word from Our Sponsors," *Business Week,* March 24, 1986, p. 90; see also Felix Kessler, "In Search of Zap-Proof Commercials," *Fortune,* January 21, 1985, pp. 68–70; Dennis Kneale, "Zapping of TV Ads Appears Pervasive," *Wall Street Journal,* April 25, 1988, p. 29.
25. Withiam Glenn, "Hotel Advertising in the 80's: Surveying the Field," *Cornell Hotel and Restaurant Administration Quarterly* 27, no. 1 (May 1986): 33–34.

26. Philip Kotler, *Marketing Management,* (Upper Saddle River, NJ: Prentice Hall, 2000), p. 580.
27. Joel R. Evans and Barry Berman, *Principles of Marketing* (Upper Saddle River, NJ: Prentice Hall, 1995), p. 432.
28. Scott Hume and Alison Fahey, "McDonald's Readies Major Blast via Outdoor Boards," *Advertising Age,* March 30, 1992, p. 58.
29. Jane Meyers and Laurie Freeman, "Marketers Police TV Commercial Costs," *Advertising Age* (April 3, 1989), p. 51.
30. See Roland T. Rust, *Advertising Media Models: A Practical Guide* (Lexington, MA: Lexington Books, 1986).
31. Philip H. Dougherty, "Bud 'Pulses' the Market," *The New York Times* (February 18, 1975), p. 40.

15 Promoting Products: Public Relations and Sales Promotion

There are many misconceptions about public relations.
One of the most widespread is that it's easy.
Peter Celliers

The launch of Sputnik I in 1957 started a series of successes for the Soviet Union's space program. These achievements became propaganda vehicles promoting the achievements and advantages of communism. Kennedy used the "space gap" between the United States and the Soviet Union to his advantage, claiming that the Republicans had let the Soviet Union pass the United States. He campaigned under the banner of a New Frontier.

After Kennedy's election in 1960, the American space program had some success. In May and July 1961, America's self-image was boosted by the suborbital flights of Shepard and Grissom. However, the pride these flights provided was short lived. In July 1961, Gherman Titov flew a seventeen-orbit mission for the Soviets, making the suborbital flights look like child's play.

NASA was eager to build America's pride. It canceled a third suborbital flight and announced that John Glenn would be America's first person to orbit the world. Glenn was well known to most Americans. He had served as a pilot in World War II and the Korean War and made headlines in 1957 for setting a new cross-continent flying speed record. As a result of this achievement, he was invited to participate on two television host shows and was the most publicized of the seven U.S. astronauts.

NASA's publicity machine set the stage for the event. It was America's first attempt at an orbital flight with America's most publicized astronaut. NASA needed to create as much hype as possible to give Americans a sense they were still in the space race. As a result of this hype, over 100 million people were expected to watch the televised launch of Friendship 7.

Bud Grice, a Marriott sales manager, thought about all those people who were expected to watch the launch. What a great way to expose Americans to a growing Marriott corporation. Grice knew that Marriott could not afford television ads, but the idea of all those people watching the coverage of the launch intrigued him; if only Marriott could communicate with an audience of that size.

On February 20, 1962, 135 million Americans watched Glenn take off on his five-hour, three-orbit flight. Grice was one of them, and he was still thinking about the opportunities created by so many people watching a single event. Once the flight was off, cameras switched to the Glenn residence. There were scores of reporters at the residence and the area was a beehive of activity. The Glenns lived in the Washington, DC, suburb of Arlington, Virginia, not too far from Marriott's corporate headquarters. Grice saw his opportunity. He would have lunch delivered to Mrs. Glenn by Marriott's Hot Shoppes. He put buckets of fried chicken with large Marriott labels in a station wagon and had it delivered to the Glenn residence. The real test would be getting through the police barricades. This proved to be too easy a challenge as the driver simply said that he was delivering Mrs. Glenn's lunch. The Marriott vehicle pulled up in front of the residence, and the Marriott containers were soon seen by an estimated 100 million Americans still watching television.

In a conversation with President Kennedy after the flight, Glenn stated that he was looking forward to spending some time with his family and that he would like to stay at a Marriott hotel because they were so good to his wife. Marriott again had another public relations opportunity. They invited Glenn to stay in a complimentary Marriott suite and received additional publicity when the press followed Glenn into the Marriott.

This story illustrates several uses of public relations. First, we are shown how governments use events to promote their ideologies. Second, we see how public relations can be planned to take advantage of opportunities. In this case, Grice created an event, serving lunch to Mrs. Glenn, to gain exposure of the Marriott name to millions of viewers. Finally, through being aware of Glenn's desire to stay in a Marriott hotel, Marriott gained additional publicity from the event.[1]

Chapter Objectives

After reading this chapter, you should be able to:

1. Understand the different public relations activities: press relations, product publicity, corporate communications, lobbying, and counseling.
2. Understand the public relations process: research, establishing marketing objectives, defining the target audience, choosing the PR message and vehicles, and evaluating PR results.
3. Know how the different PR tools are used: publications, events, news, speeches, public service activities, and identity media.
4. Implement a crisis management program in a hospitality business.
5. Discuss the growth and purpose of sales promotion, setting objectives, and selecting consumer promotion tools.

15.1 NASA

e

Public Relations

"Public relations, perhaps the most misunderstood part of marketing communications, can be the most effective tool."[2] Definitions for public relations differ widely. We think that this definition by Hilton International best fits the hospitality industry: "The process by which we create a positive image and customer preference through third-party endorsement."[3]

Public relations (PR) is an important marketing tool that until recently was treated as a marketing stepchild. PR is moving into an explosive growth stage. Companies are realizing that mass marketing is no longer the answer to some of their communication needs. Advertising costs continue to rise, while audience reach continues to decline. Advertising clutter reduces the impact of each ad. Sales promotion costs have also increased as channel intermediaries demand lower prices and better commissions and deals. Personal selling can cost over $500 a call. In this environment, public relations, holds the promise of a cost-effective promotional tool. The creative use of news events, publications, social events, community relations, and other PR techniques offers companies a way to distinguish themselves and their products from their competitors.[4]

The public relations department of cruise lines, restaurant chains, airlines, and hotels is typically located at corporate headquarters. Often, its staff is so busy dealing with various publics—stockholders, employees, legislators, and community leaders—that PR support for product marketing objectives tends to be neglected. Many four- and five-star hotel chains have corrected this deficiency by hiring local public relations managers.

In the past it was common for the marketing function and PR function to be handled by two different departments within the firm. Today these two functions are increasingly integrated. There are several reasons for this integration. First, companies are calling for more market-oriented PR. They want

Marketing Highlight 15-1

Taco Bell Provided Example of Creative Publicity

On April Fools' Day (April 1, 1996), Taco Bell placed a full-page ad in seven major papers saying that it had purchased the Liberty Bell and would rename it the Taco Liberty Bell. Although this was a paid advertisement, it created a flood of publicity and newspapers and television news programs picked up the story. Some readers were upset over Taco Bell's treatment of a national shrine. Overall the ad was a clever publicity ploy, creating what Taco Bell said was $22 million worth of free publicity. The ad became a news event and was mentioned across the country by both print and broadcast media. The ad marked the launching of Taco Bell's "Nothing Ordinary About It" $200 million advertising campaign.

Courtesy of Taco Bell Corp.

One industry analyst said, "Taco Bell still understands a lot about the value of 'sizzle' in today's marketplace." The attention-grabbing ploy served not only to tout the new advertising campaign but also to reinforce Taco Bell's image as a hip, rebellious restaurant chain that is anything but staid. In this world of advertising clutter, where it is sometimes hard to tell the ads from the stories on the evening news and where itchy remote control fingers can make the distinction obsolete, it takes creativity to stand out. To borrow from Taco Bell's former ad campaign, sometimes you've got to break the rules. The advertisement represents an innovative use of advertising to gain publicity.

Sources: Louise Kramer and Richard Martin, "Taco Bell Commits $200M to Reverse Sales Declines," *Nation's Restaurant News* (April 15, 1996), pp. 1, 4; Rick Van Warner, "April Fools! Reaction to Taco Bell Prank Hits Nerves, Funny Bones," *Nation's Restaurant News* (April 15, 1996).

their PR departments to manage PR activities that contribute toward marketing the company and improving the bottom line. Second, companies are establishing marketing PR groups to support corporate/product promotion and image making directly. Thus marketing PR, like financial PR and community PR, serves a special constituency, the marketing department.

Major Activities of PR Departments

PR departments perform the five activities discussed below, not all of which feed into direct product support.

Press Relations

The aim of **press relations** is to place newsworthy information into the news media to attract attention to a person, product, or service. One reason for the growth of press relations in the hospitality industry is its credibility. Most types of publicity are viewed by the consumer as third-party information. A favorable write-up of a restaurant in the local newspaper by the food editor has more impact than an advertisement written by the restaurant's management.

Product Publicity

Product publicity involves various efforts to publicize specific products. New products; special events, such as food festivals; redesigned products, such as a newly renovated hotel; and products that are popular because of current trends, such as nonfat desserts, are all potential candidates for publicity. Table 15-1 provides an example of a timetable for a public relations campaign for the opening of a new hotel.

Corporate Communication

Corporate communication covers internal and external communications and promotes understanding of the organization. One important marketing aspect of corporate communication is communication directed toward employees, such as company newsletters. Companies also need to manage their communication with their stockholders to make sure the stockholders understand the company's goals and objectives.

Lobbying

Lobbying involves dealing with legislators and government officials to promote or defeat legislation and regulation. Large companies employ their own lobbyists, whereas smaller companies lobby through their local trade associations.

Counseling

Counseling involves advising management about public issues and company positions and image.[5] Counseling is important when there may be sensitive issues associated with the business. For example, water is a scarce commodity in Las Vegas. Major resorts with water displays, such as the Mirage, counsel their managers on the resort's water conservation efforts, such as recycling the hotel's wastewater to be used in the hotel's fountains.

PUBLICITY

Publicity is a direct function of public relations. Publicity is the task of securing editorial space, as opposed to paid space, in print and broadcast media to promote a product or a service. Publicity is a popular PR tool used in the five activities mentioned earlier. Some popular uses of publicity are described next.

15.2 Hard Rock Café
Mirage Resorts

One of the uses of publicity is to assist in the launch of new products. For example, when the Hard Rock Café announced that it was going into the hotel business with the development of the first Hard Rock Hotel, the media covered the event during the initial announcement and the groundbreaking ceremonies. Later, when the hotel opened, a concert staged at the hotel featuring Sheryl Crow was broadcast on MTV. This concert, the uniqueness of the hotel, and a concert the following day by the Eagles and Sheryl Crow ensured that the opening of the hotel received worldwide publicity.

Publicity is also used with special events. To be successful the press release developed to gain the publicity must be of interest to the target audience of the media the company is targeting. For example, a food editor will be interested in recipes and food history that will have value for her readers.

Table 15-1

Sample Timetable for Preopening Public Relations for a Hotel

This schedule begins six months before the hotel opening, at which time the announcement of construction plans and the groundbreaking ceremony will have been completed.

150 to 180 days before opening

1. Hold meeting to define objectives and to coordinate public relations effort with advertising; establish timetable in accordance with schedule completion date.
2. Prepare media kit.
3. Order photographs and renderings.
4. Begin preparation of mailings and develop media lists.
5. Contact all prospective beneficiaries of opening events.
6. Reserve dates for press conferences at off-site facilities.

120 to 150 days before opening

1. Send announcement with photograph or rendering to all media.
2. Send first progress bulletin to agents and media (as well as corporate clients, if desired).
3. Begin production of permanent brochure.
4. Make final plans for opening events, including commitment to beneficiaries.

90 to 120 days before opening

1. Launch publicity campaign to national media.
2. Send mailings to media.
3. Send second progress bulletin.
4. Arrange exclusive trade interviews and features in conjunction with ongoing trade campaign.
5. Begin trade announcement.

60 to 90 days before opening

1. Launch campaign to local media and other media with a short lead time; emphasize hotel's contribution to the community, announcement of donations and beneficiaries, and the like.
2. Send third and final progress bulletin with finished brochure.
3. Commence behind-the-scenes public tours.
4. Hold hard-hat luncheons for travel writers.
5. Set up model units for tours.

30 to 60 days before opening

1. Send preopening newsletter (to be continued on a quarterly basis).
2. Hold soft opening and ribbon-cutting ceremony.
3. Hold press opening.
4. Establish final plans for opening gala.

The month before opening

1. Begin broadside mailing to agents.
2. Hold opening festivities.
3. Conduct orientation press trips.

Source: Reprinted by permission of Elsevier Science, Inc., from "Public Relations for the Hotel Opening," by Jessica D. Zive, *Cornell Hotel and Restaurant Administration Quarterly*, 22, no. 1, p. 21. © 1981 by Cornell University.

A travel editor will be interested in unique aspects of the destination, not just the hotel's features. A business editor is interested in the financial success of the operation. A press release should be written for a target audience and have value for the media's audience. We will now look at some ways publicity can be used to enhance an organization's image.

Influence Specific Target Groups

Companies can use publicity to build a positive image with specific groups. For example, McDonald's sponsors special neighborhood events in Hispanic and black communities for good causes. The sponsorship of the events and the publicity generated from the sponsorship builds up a good company image.

Defend Products That Have Encountered Public Problems

After a series of hotel fires made national news, the Adam's Mark Hotel in Houston invited a television crew to come to the hotel and see the latest safety devices incorporated into the hotel. As a result, they received several minutes of coverage on the evening news, showing that the fire safety problem had been addressed.

Tourist destinations are particularly influenced by negative publicity. When disaster hits a region or city, tourists instantaneously learn of the problem and quickly find alternative destinations. In part, tourism recovery depends on the reintroduction of a tourism destination. The reintroduction must overcome the adverse publicity resulting from the natural disaster, and it may take several years to rebuild business to pre-disaster levels. The speed of recovery depends on:[6]

1. The extent of damage caused by the disaster
2. The efficiency with which tourism partners bring their facilities back on-line
3. An effective marketing message that clearly states that the destination is once again open (or still is) and ready for business

Build the Corporate Image in a Way That Projects Favorably on Its Products

Ramada, a brand of Cendant Corporation, is a sponsor of Childreach International. Steve Belmonte, president and CEO of Ramada, is the chairman of Childreach's Honorary Board and its television spokesman. The television coverage of Childreach is worth $8 million. This has created great exposure for the projects Ramada helped make possible and Ramada's CEO.

Belmonte states the benefits of this sponsorship are many. Awareness of Ramada has increased. It brings together the franchisees and franchiser who come together to work for Childreach. It unites the company. It also makes the employees feel good about the company. By focusing on one major charity, Ramada has gained national exposure and pulled the company together.[7]

Olive Garden restaurants developed a charity program that tied in their sponsorship of a team Rafanelli, entering the "Olive Garden Rafanelli V-10" in the American Le Mans races. The company worked with America's Second

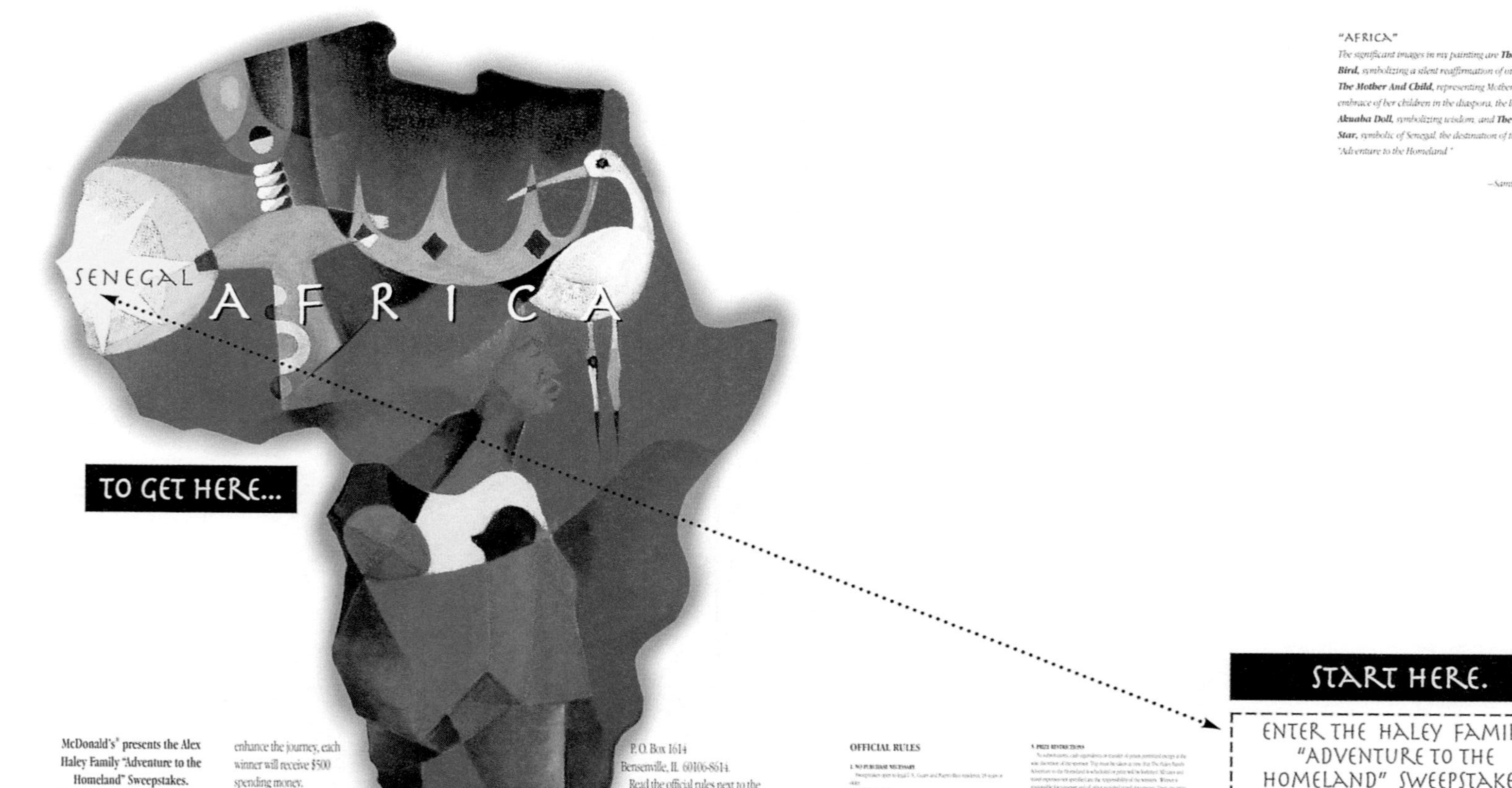

McDonald's sponsors a promotion targeted at African-Americans called "Adventures to the Homeland." Ten winners and their companions will travel to the west coast of Africa with William Haley, the son of Alex Haley, author of Roots. Courtesy of McDonald's Corporation. Original painting titled "Africa," by Samuel Akainyah.

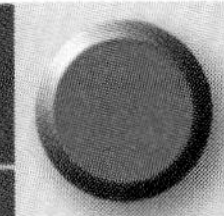

Marketing Highlight 15-2

Singapore Suntec Centre

An article about the Singapore International Convention and Exhibition Centre in *Meetings and Conventions* provides a good example of effective publicity. The Centre, nicknamed Suntec, received a feature article in a magazine that targets Suntec's customers. The article included key information about Suntec, such as that the Centre features a 129,000-square-foot convention hall, an exhibition hall of the same size that can be divided into four rooms, a 23,000-square-foot ballroom, a 600-seat auditorium, twenty-six meeting rooms, and the latest technology in audiovisual systems. The article then described the tourist attractions of Singapore and hotels within walking distance of the Suntec.

Timing. Evaluating this article from a PR standpoint, several aspects make it effective. First, the timing. The article was written about nine months before Suntec opened. The lead time for many of Suntec's customers will be over a year. Thus the article is timed to start bringing in inquiries for business shortly after the Centre opens. If the PR releases had waited until the Centre opened, business generated by the release would have been at least a year away. The advance publicity allows the Centre to make an announcement nine months before opening, and certainly the official opening of the Centre will allow for additional PR. Smaller businesses, such as restaurants, do not need a large lead time. Restaurant customers make purchase decisions with short lead times. Many restaurants will have a "soft opening." They will not seek publicity when they initially open, but will get their delivery system fine-tuned. They start their PR campaign with an "official grand opening" when they know that they are ready to provide excellent service to the customer. The timing of a press release is a key success factor.

Media and message. Media selection is important. In this case the medium was a magazine that has a readership consisting of professionals who make decisions on the sites for major meetings and conventions. It is important that PR be targeted; marketing publicity that is not aimed at an organization's target market has little value. The article included technical information about the Centre, information this professional audience will want. It is important to make sure that the message will be of interest to the audience. Most media make their money from selling advertising. Their advertising rates are based on their circulation or the size of their audience. To keep their circulation, they must print or broadcast messages that will be of interest to their audience. If they receive a press release that is interesting and relevant to their audience, they are likely to use the piece. A different publicity piece should be written for each audience.

Follow-up. The article included a phone number for the Centre, making it easy for a planner to contact the Centre.

Source: Loren G. Edelstein, "Suntec Centre: All the More Reason to Meet in Singapore '95," *Meetings and Conventions* 29, no. 12 (1994):121.

Harvest to help fill their food banks in its "Drive Against Hunger" program. The "Drive Against Hunger" was linked to race car "driving" by donating eight truckloads of food in the eight cities where the Le Mans races were held. By tying the two events together, Olive Garden was able to create synergy across the events in its public relations efforts. This example illustrates the benefits of planning and integrating marketing communications.[8]

Clearly, public relations can make a memorable impact on public awareness at a fraction of the cost of advertising. The company does not pay for the space or time obtained in the media. It pays for a staff to develop and circulate stories and manage certain events. If the company develops an interesting story, it could be picked up by all the news media and be worth millions of dollars in equivalent advertising. Furthermore, it would have more credibility than advertising. Some experts say that consumers are five times more likely to be influenced by editorial copy than by advertising.

The Public Relations Process

Effective public relations is the result of a process. This process must be integrated with the firm's marketing strategy. One common misconception about public relations and publicity is that quantity is more important than quality. Some PR firms measure success by the number of articles placed in media. As in other marketing efforts, public relations should be meaningful to the target market.

The PR process consists of the following steps: research, establishing the market objectives, defining the target audience, choosing the PR messages and vehicles, implementing the PR plan, and evaluating the results.

Research

Before a company can develop a public relations program, it must understand the company's mission, objectives, strategies, and culture. It should know the vehicles that will be effective in delivering messages to the target audience. Much of the information needed by a PR manager will be contained in a well-written marketing plan. Ideally, the PR manager should be involved in the formation of the marketing plan.

The firm's environmental scanning system is another important source of information for the PR manager. Analysis of this information should identify trends and give the firm insights into how they should react to these trends. For example, many hotel and restaurant companies are now showing what they are doing to save and protect the natural environment.

Establishing the Marketing Objectives

Once the PR manager has identified opportunities through product experiment and research, priorities can be established and objectives set. Marketing PR can contribute to the following objectives:

- *Build awareness.* PR can place stories in the media to bring attention to a product, service, person, organization, or idea.
- *Build credibility.* PR can add credibility by communicating the message in an editorial context.
- *Stimulate the sales force and channel intermediaries.* PR can help boost sales force and franchisee enthusiasm. Positive stories about a new menu item will make an impression on the customers, employees, and franchisees of a restaurant chain. The publicity Ritz-Carlton receives from winning the Baldrige Award provides their sales force with great ammunition when they make a sales call.
- *Hold down promotion costs.* PR costs less than direct mail and media advertising. The smaller the company's promotion budget is, the stronger the case for using PR to gain share of mind.

Specific objectives should be set for every PR campaign. The Wine Growers of California hired the public relations firm of Daniel J. Edelman, Inc., to develop a publicity campaign to convince Americans that wine

The Grand Geneva resort received four pages of space in this write-up on Wisconsin meetings and incentives. The magazine targets the resorts markets and thus is an example of well-placed PR. PR pieces such as this have more credibility than advertisements. Courtesy of Sprecher/Barrett/Bertalot and Company.

drinking is a pleasurable part of good living and to improve the image and market share of California wines. The following publicity objectives were established: (1) develop magazine stories about wine and place them in top magazines (*Time, House Beautiful*) and in newspapers (food columns, feature sections); (2) develop stories about wine's many health values and direct them to the medical profession; and (3) develop specific publicity for the young adult market, college market, governmental bodies, and various ethnic communities. These objectives were refined into specific goals so that final results could be evaluated.

The Homestead of Hot Springs, Virginia, conducts special weekends that serve as a part of that hotel's promotion mix. These weekends bring members of the media to the resort and give them an event to write about in addition to the resort's amenities. A spring wine and food festival serves as an excellent PR tool for invited guests, including meeting planners and journalists. A seven-course meal with twelve wines served in a formal setting serves as a dramatic event.[9]

The restaurant association in many cities sponsors a Taste of the Town. This event features food from the city's restaurants. The restaurants have a chance for exposure to many potential customers in one evening. The association usually charges an admission fee, which helps to ensure that those attending are interested in finding out about restaurant fare rather than obtaining a free dinner. The fee is then donated to a charity, providing additional publicity.

Defining the Target Audience

A relevant message delivered to a target audience by the appropriate vehicle is crucial to the success of any PR campaign. Effective PR practitioners carefully identify the publics that they wish to reach. They then study these publics and find media that can be used as vehicles to deliver their message.

They identify issues that will be important to the public and form the message so that it will seem natural and logical to the target audience.

Choosing the PR Message and Vehicles

The PR practitioner is now ready to identify or develop interesting stories about the product or service. If the number of stories is insufficient, the PR practitioner should propose newsworthy events that the company can sponsor. Here the challenge is to create news rather than find it. PR ideas include hosting major academic conventions, inviting celebrity speakers, and developing news conferences. Each event is an opportunity to develop a multitude of stories directed at different audiences.

Event creation is a particularly important skill in publicizing fund-raising drives for nonprofit organizations. Fund-raisers have developed a large repertoire of special events, including anniversary celebrations, art exhibitions, auctions, benefit evenings, bingo games, book sales, cake sales, contests, dances, dinners, fairs, fashion shows, parties in unusual places, phone-atones, rummage sales, tours, and walkathons. No sooner is one type of event created, such as a walkathon, than competitors spawn new versions, such as read-a-thons, bike-a-thons, and jog-a-thons. The Fairmont Hotel in New Orleans upgraded its bathroom amenities, resulting in a disposal problem for the cartons of shampoo it had used before the upgrade. The hotel created an essay contest, with the winner receiving the shampoo. The hotel timed the event to coincide with the Democratic National Convention, when the town would be filled with members of the media. In their press release the Fairmont claimed that the contest gave the Democrats a chance to "wash the Republicans out of their hair." This line and the timing of the event resulted in international coverage of the event.[10]

Trine Palace is an historical restoration of the original governor's mansion when North Carolina was a British colony. Located in New Bern, this attraction draws thousands of tourists annually. The month of December used to be a poor month for attendance with inclement weather and preparation for Christmas occupying the minds of potential visitors. Trine Palace developed a Christmas tour that included actors costumed as the original governor and wife, tables heaped with Christmas food (for display only), strolling bagpipe musicians, Christmas candles, holly, and a reception for guests following the tour at which punch and cookies are served. This relatively simple idea has become so successful that December is now among the top attendance months.

New York's Vista Hotel decided to offer a Cajun dinner, but needed a "hook" to make the event authentic and newsworthy. That hook was Paul Prudhomme, the colorful Cajun chef. The Vista arranged to host a publication party for Paul's Cajun cookbook at the hotel during the Cajun dinner. This type of creative thinking creates a great PR event from an otherwise interesting but not particularly newsworthy event.[11]

Implementing the Marketing PR Plan

Implementing publicity requires care. Consider the matter of placing information in media. Exciting information is easy to place. However, most press releases are less than great and might not get the attention of busy editors. A chief asset of publicists is their personal relationship with media editors. Public relations practitioners are often ex-journalists who know many media editors and what they want. PR people look at media editors as a market to satisfy, so that they will continue to use the company's press releases.

Publicity requires extra care when it involves staging special events, such as testimonial dinners, news conferences, and national contests. PR practitioners need a good head for detail and for coming up with quick solutions when things go wrong. Most hotel corporations have a crisis plan included as part of their PR plan. In this plan they state who can talk to the media and who should not. These plans usually state that staff should not speak to media, but instead direct inquiries to the director of public relations.

Evaluating PR Results

The contribution of PR is difficult to measure, because it is used along with other promotion tools. If it is used before other tools come into action, its contribution is easier to evaluate.

Exposures

The easiest measure of PR effectiveness is the number of exposures created in the media. Publicists supply the client with a clipping book showing all the media that carried news about the product and a summary statement, such as the following:

> Media coverage included 3,500 column inches of news and photographs in 350 publications with a combined circulation of 79.4 million; 2,500 minutes of air time on 290 radio stations and an estimated audience of 65 million; and 660 minutes of air time on 160 television stations with an estimated audience of 91 million. If this time and space had been purchased at advertising rates, it would have amounted to $1,047,000.[12]

This exposure measure is not very satisfying. There is no indication of how many people actually read, heard, or recalled the message and what they thought afterward. There is no information on the net audience reached, because publications overlap in readership. Because publicity's goal is reach, not frequency, it would be useful to know the number of unduplicated exposures. It is also important that publicity reach target markets. A common weakness of publicity is that the persons exposed to it are not part of the company's target market.

Awareness/Comprehension/Attitude Change

A better measure is the change in product awareness/comprehension/attitude resulting from the campaign (after allowing for the effect of other promotional tools). For example, how many people recall hearing the news item? How many told others about it (a measure of word of mouth)? How many changed their minds after hearing it? The Potato Board learned, for example, that the number of people who agreed with the statement "potatoes are rich in vitamins and minerals" went from 36 percent before the campaign to 67 percent after the campaign, a significant improvement in product comprehension.

Sales-and-Profit Contribution

Sales-and-profit impact is the most satisfactory measure, if obtainable. A well-planned public relations campaign is usually part of an integrated promotional campaign. This makes it very difficult to isolate the impact of the PR campaign.

Major Tools in Marketing PR

Publications

15.3 Disney
McDonald's

Companies rely extensively on communication materials to reach and influence their target markets. These include annual reports, brochures, cards, articles, audiovisual materials, and company newsletters and magazines. Brochures can play an important role in informing target customers about a product, how it works, and how it is to be assembled. McDonald's developed a series of brochures discussing the quality ingredients that it uses, the actions that it has taken to help protect the environment, and the nutritional content of its products. Thoughtful articles written by company executives can draw attention to the company and its products. Company newsletters and magazines can help build the company's image and convey important news to target markets. Audiovisual materials, such as films, slides-and-sound, and videocassettes and audiocassettes are coming into increasing use as promotion tools. The cost of audiovisual materials is usually greater than the cost of printed material, but so is the impact. Many resort destinations use videos to promote their properties. Disney World created a twenty-minute video aimed at families considering it as a vacation site. Wet-N-Wild developed a four-minute video aimed at travel agents, tour agents, and other members of the distribution channel.

McDonald's developed a creative and potentially trend-setting annual report for stockholders on videotape. This contained statements by members of top management as well as commercials. Publicly traded hospitality corporations with thousands of stockholders should consider the annual report and other stockholder communication as opportunities to promote the company's products and services, not simply as information required by law.

Events

Hospitality companies can draw attention to new products or other company activities by arranging special events, such as the Homestead wine and food festival mentioned earlier. Events include news conferences, seminars, outings, exhibits, contests and competitions, anniversaries, and sport and cultural sponsorships that will reach the target publics. Sponsoring a sports event, such as the Coors International Bicycle Class, gives these companies a chance to invite and host suppliers, journalists, distributors, and customers, as well as bring repeated attention to the company's name and products.

News

A major task of PR professionals is to find or create favorable news about the company, its products, and its people. News generation requires skill in developing a story concept, researching it, and writing a press release. But the PR person's skill must go beyond preparing news stories. Getting the media to accept press releases and attend press conferences calls for marketing and interpersonal skills. A good PR media director understands press needs for stories that are interesting and timely and for releases that are well written and attention getting. The media director needs to gain the favor of editors and reporters. As the press is cultivated, it is increasingly likely to provide better coverage to the company.

A proven technique for writing a good press release is to use the Hey-You-See-So approval. Imagine that a teenager saw a friend in front of the high school. The teenager might yell, "Hey (attention getter) Bill and Helen (you), look what I have, three tickets for Saturday's rock concert (see). Let's plan to go (so)." When this simple technique is followed in a press release, effectiveness is increased.

Another journalistic technique is to write a press release in an inverted pyramid form. Think of a pyramid standing on its point and remember that editors can and do shorten a press release to serve space requirements. A press release should be written so that the bulk of the information the company wishes to transmit is contained in the first paragraph. Each additional paragraph simply adds to the original and is less and less damaging to the story if clipped by an editor.

Speeches

Speeches are another tool for creating product and company publicity. Iaccoca's charismatic talks before large audiences helped Chrysler sell its cars. Increasingly, company executives must field questions from the media or give talks at trade associations or sales meetings. These appearances can build or hurt the company's image. Companies are choosing their spokespersons carefully and using speech writers and coaches to help improve the speaking ability of those selected.

The creation of a high-quality speech is costly for any company. A considerable amount of staff and executive time must be devoted to the project. It therefore makes sense to obtain maximum PR mileage from each speech. This is accomplished by printing copies of the speech or excerpts for distribution to the press, stockholders, employees, and other publics. A speech that is given but not distributed represents a wasted PR opportunity.

Public Service Activities

Companies can improve public goodwill by contributing money and time to good causes. A large company typically will ask executives to support community affairs where their offices and plants are located. In other instances, companies will offer to donate a certain amount of money to a specified cause from consumer purchases. Called cause-related marketing, it is used by a growing number of companies to build public goodwill.[13] Restaurant and hotel chains will donate so much of each sale to a charitable cause for a given amount of time. For example, a fast-food restaurant may donate five cents from every sandwich purchased on a certain day to the Muscular Dystrophy Association.

Identity Media

Normally, a company's PR material acquires separate looks, which creates confusion and misses an opportunity to create and reinforce corporate identity. In a society subject to overcommunication, companies must compete for attention. They should strive to create a visual identity that the public immediately recognizes. The visual identity is carried by the company's logos, stationery, brochures, signs, business forms, business cards, buildings, uniforms, dress codes, and rolling stock.

Public Relations Opportunities for the Hospitality Industry

Individual Properties

Public relations are by far the most important promotional tool available to entrepreneurs and individual properties such as a single restaurant, tourist attraction, bed and breakfast, tour operator, or hotel. Seldom can these enterprises afford costly advertising or other promotional programs. Successful PR programs by individual operators have demonstrated winning strategies that can be emulated by others.

Tom McCarthy states that employees should be trained to look for public relations opportunities. For example, a convention service manager developed a story about 200 chinchilla breeders who were meeting at the hotel, a bell person heard that a famous person would be a speaker at a dinner in the ballroom, and a room clerk found out that one of the hotel guests was 104 years old. All these stories resulted in positive exposure for the employees' hotels.[14]

Build PR Around the Owner/Operator

The owner/operator and the enterprise itself often become one and the same in the minds of customers. Obviously, this strategy holds dangers, such as the death of the owners, but benefits usually exceed risks. Michael Lefever, a professor at the University of Massachusetts, relates the success of a restaurant operator named Joe. The name of this restaurant—not surprisingly—was Joe's. Joe used to drive a Cadillac with two magnetic signs advertising his restaurant. Everyone in the community knew Joe and watched for his car as it rolled about town. Joe built his own personal image by wearing white cook's pants, a starched white shirt, and big comfortable black shoes that squeaked. Joe wore this uniform everywhere. If people failed to see Joe coming, they knew by the aroma of his big cigar that he was near. Joe knew the power of visibility and built a gigantic window so that passersby could look directly into the kitchen. He had a team of "trained chefs" who knew the value of show biz. They stirred, flipped, and flamed dishes to the delight of all. Joe knew the value of show biz, but most of all he realized the value of "Joe." Joe's most powerful PR asset was that he was always at the restaurant. He called this personal goodwill. Customers came to see Joe. In turn, he knew them by name and greeted each with a firm handshake. Joe was a pro at "selling Joe."[15]

The owner/operator of a fishing lodge in Costa Rica had been a circus trapeze artist before retiring to the jungles of Costa Rica. Each year, U.S. and Canadian TV and radio talk shows featured this entrepreneur and his fishing lodge. This owner/operator knew that the media is always hungry for a good human interest story.

Individuals successful at promoting themselves often use theatrical costumery such as Joe's squeaky shoes or General MacArthur's corncob pipe. Ken Hamblin, an African American columnist and talk show host, is never seen without a hat. Obesity, a wart on the nose, a bony appearance, a limp, a mustache, and dozens of other personal characteristics have been used successfully to build memorable personalities. As increasing numbers of men wear ponytails and earrings, the blue suit and white shirt IBM-type appearance may become a differentiating "costume."

Build PR around Location

Some restaurants and bed and breakfasts are almost impossible to find without a compass and topographical map. Normally, this would be viewed as the kiss of death for a hospitality firm. Hundreds of owners/operators of these enterprises have turned their lemon into lemonade. The isolation and obscurity of the enterprises is used as a PR tactic.

A restaurant in San Francisco lies directly under a freeway that collapsed during an earthquake. Sure enough, instead of discouraging patrons, interest increased as the restaurant was featured on national TV as the little restaurant that refused to succumb to an earthquake.

The Solitaire Lodge in New Zealand is located on a beautiful but isolated lake. The owner originally felt that U.S. fly fishing fans would find his lodge irresistible. This was not to be, as the owner sadly discovered that fly fishing fans desired rivers, not lakes. The owner then changed tactics and successfully promoted the lodge as a great getaway place and a wonderful location to observe Halley's comet free of nighttime light pollution. This unusual twist brought the lodge to the attention of major U.S. newspapers, which carried the story free of charge.

Build PR around a Product or Service

Wall Drug Store is a major tourist stop and tourist attraction for the state of South Dakota. Located in a town of less than 1,000 residents, Wall Drug daily attracts 15,000 or more visitors during tourist season. Wall Drug's reputation was built on free ice water. Before the days of air-conditioned cars, Mr. and Mrs. Ted Hustead, the owners, saw tourists passing by on their way to the Black Hills. These folks looked thirsty and indeed they were. Ted hand painted a few signs reading "Free Ice Water—Wall Drug" and placed them along the highway. Before Ted returned from planting these signs, tourists had already found their way to Wall Drug. They have never stopped coming. Today, word of mouth and PR have replaced many of the road signs, but Wall Drug remains the free ice-water stop.

The Raffles Hotel in Singapore has a colorful and long history, but most visitors know it as the birthplace of the Singapore Sling. Today the renovated bar serves thousands of Singapore Slings. Even the empty

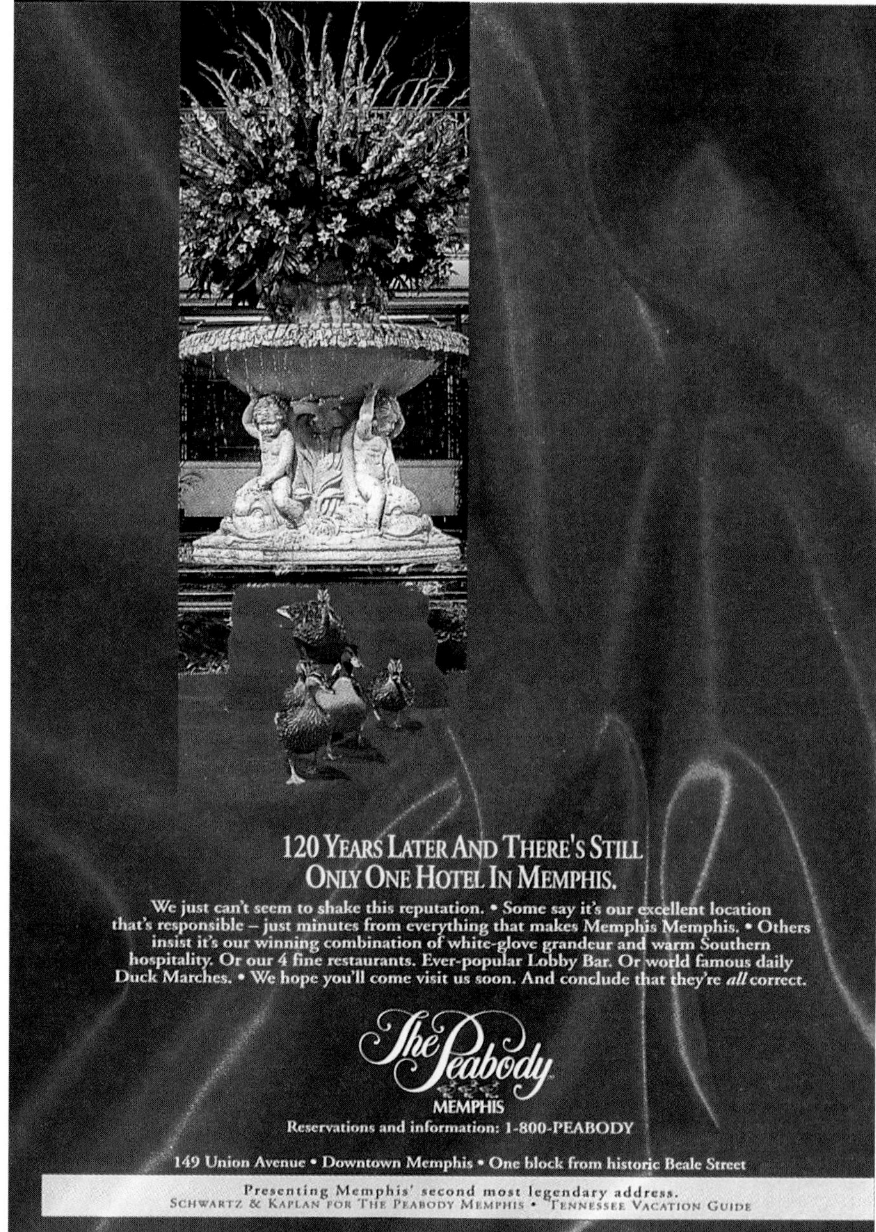

The story has it that an early owner of the historic Peabody Hotel in Memphis went on a hunting trip, had a little too much to drink, and let live ducks loose in the hotel's fountain. When the hotel was being renovated in the 1980s, the new owners played up this historical event into a brilliant PR campaign. The Peabody ducks have received millions of dollars worth of print and broadcast time. Today people from all over still come to see the ducks. Courtesy of Peabody Hotels and Turkel Schwartz & Partners.

15.4 Peabody Hotel
Ramada Inn of Antigua

glasses are sold and serve as a PR vehicle throughout the world. Hospitality enterprises throughout the world have built a solid and long-lasting image around a drink, a dessert, a special entree, fireplaces in the guest rooms, and even ducks. The Peabody Hotel of Memphis became well known for a flock of ducks that daily waddled from the rooftop via the elevator to a fountain in the lobby. When The Peabody opened their Orlando property, the Peabody ducks became one of the features of the property, creating publicity for the new hotel.

The Ramada Inn of Antigua, Guatemala, has a wood-burning fireplace in each guest room. On chilly evenings a staff member appears to light the fireplace in each occupied room.

Unique service also serves as a PR focal point. Usually, this means exceptionally fine service, but sometimes the reverse is true. Occasionally, a bar and grill or a restaurant gains a reputation for having the rudest and sometimes the ugliest wait staff anywhere in the country. A Dallas bar and grill popular with the lunchtime business crowd was notorious for its surly staff. Those familiar with the place loved to take unsuspecting newcomers to see how badly their companion could be insulted. Fans of the TV program *Cheers* will recall the disrespectful Carla and how she nevertheless maintained a peculiar charm.

Crisis Management

An important area of public relations is crisis management. Not all publicity is good. Hotels are open twenty-four hours a day, major airline companies have thousands of flights a day, and fast-food companies serve millions of customers each day. There are times when things go wrong; sometimes it is management's fault, and sometimes it is beyond management's control. Managers must realize that things do go wrong: guests fall asleep while smoking, people are poisoned by tainted or spoiled restaurant food, thieves rob guests, planes crash, earthquakes destroy buildings, and flooding occurs somewhere every spring. A crisis management program will reduce the negative effects of these events (Table 15-2).

The first step in crisis management is to take all precautions to prevent negative events from occurring. As a communications consultant, Eric Bergman states in crisis management we should concentrate more on the management and communication and less on the crisis.[16] Robert Irvine divides crises into two main categories, a sudden crisis and a smoldering crisis.[17] A sudden crisis is the one that comes without any warning. These can be natural disasters such as earthquakes and floods, workplace domestic violence, an outbreak of food poisoning, and fires. Smoldering crises can include sexual harassment by supervisors, safety violations that could result in fines or illegal actions, health code violations, and fire code violations.

The sudden crises need to be anticipated. Mitroff states that crisis management is a series of ongoing, interrelated assessments or audits of kinds of crises and forces that can pose a major problem to a company.[18] Companies and their management need to determine those crises that have a chance of occurring and develop plans in case they do occur. Hotels should have fire plans, and employees should know what to do in case of a fire. Hotels in areas where earthquakes are prevalent should have an earthquake plan. For example, Deborah Roker, public relations director for Sonsesta International Hotels, designed a crisis-communication program for each of the hotels in the eighteen-property chain. She conducts a half-day training session annually at each property, going over crisis management plans with department heads. Part of this training includes a session at which managers are asked challenging questions that may be asked by guests or the media.[19]

Smoldering crises can often be eliminated with good management. Smoldering crises give warning before they occur. It may be a drop in

FOR IMMEDIATE RELEASE

Contact: Barbara Wiener
US Franchise Systems, Inc.
(404) 235-7400

MICROTEL INN & SUITES SURVEY OFFERS INSIGHT INTO WHAT TRAVELERS WITH DISABILITIES WANT MOST FROM THEIR HOTEL

ATLANTA (August 18, 1997) – For the 20 million people with disabilities who travel every year, the path is seldom easy.

Now, the results of a survey taken by Microtel Inn & Suites and parent company Atlanta-based US Franchise Systems (USFS) via the internet offers new insight into understanding handicapped travelers' needs and the accommodations they are looking for. According to respondents, what travelers with disabilities want most from their hotels are accessible showers, large bathrooms and accurate information when calling ahead for reservations.

Microtel – all newly-constructed, interior corridor, limited service hotels with daily rates starting at $35 – has been changing the face of the hospitality industry as it plans for 1,000 new hotels in development by the year 2000.

Says Mike Leven, president and CEO of USFS, "We want to be the preferred hotel chain for travelers with disabilities. Because all Microtels are newly constructed, we are in the unique position to be on the ground floor both physically and psychologically to truly serve the needs of these travelers, and that's what we're working toward."

Following is what respondents want most from their hotel, in order of preference:

1. **Accessible showers**
2. **Large bathrooms**
3. **Accurate information when calling ahead, with knowledgeable reservationists**
4. **Helpful staff, sensitive to the needs of the disabled**

more.../

13 CORPORATE SQUARE SUITE 250 ATLANTA, GA 30329 404 321-4045 FAX 321-4482

This press release is well written and tells an interesting story. It was picked up by both consumer and trade publications. Courtesy of U.S. Franchise Systems, Inc.

5. Enough space in room for easy maneuverability
6. Suitable beds
7. Aesthetically pleasing guest rooms
8. Refrigerator in guest rooms
9. Accessible parking
10. Easy access to guest room controls

The survey attracted travelers of varying ages and income, the majority wheelchair users (73%), and the remaining sight or hearing impaired (5%) and "other" (22%). Mostly 35 years of age or older (75%), with an annual income of $35,000 or more (60%), most spend at least 10 nights away from home each year in hotels (vs. with friends or family) and typically with a companion or family member. The majority travel for leisure and make reservations by calling the hotel directly.

With the help of Travelac and its president Don England – the wheelchair-user consultant who advises Microtel on accessibility prototype plans for all its properties – Microtel developed the survey to be proactive, not only by striving to meet ADA (Americans with Disabilities Act) guidelines by making existing properties more accessible and to be consistent in all its hotels, but by practicing "attitude" accessibility to be more conscious, aware and friendly to travelers with disabilities as well.

For reservations or information about Microtels around the U.S., contact 1-888-771-7171 toll-free. To participate in the internet survey, or to offer suggestions regarding the survey or Microtel's accommodations for travelers with disabilities, go to **www.microtelinn.com**.

####

Based in Atlanta, Ga., US Franchise Systems, Inc. was formed in August 1995 by Michael A. Leven, a 37-year veteran of the lodging industry, and Neal K. Aronson, former principal of a New York investment firm, when the company purchased the franchise system rights to Microtel Inn, Microtel Inn & Suites and Microtel Suites. The company, traded on the Nasdaq National Market System also acquired the franchise rights to Hawthorn Suites, a limited service extended-stay product, in 1996, and plans for 200 properties by the year 2000. USFS is committed to growing, marketing and servicing unique franchise brands that will provide consumers and franchisees alike with a product that exceeds their expectations in quality, consistency and value.

M139/bw

Courtesy of U.S. Franchise Systems, Inc.

Table 16-2
Crisis Communication Dos and Don'ts

DO	
Do have a crisis plan that includes natural disasters, security breaches, safety issues, and strikes.	**Do** verify the identity of callers asking questions.
Do update your plan often.	**Do** increase security if necessary; make security highly visible to reassure guest.
Do train employees regularly and document training for legal purposes.	**Do** keep detailed notes of disclosed information.
Do attend to the injured immediately and call 911.	**Do** say when you are unable to answer a question and give a reason, such as, "I do not have that information yet."
Do cooperate fully with all government entities.	**Do** initiate information updates or hold a press conference.
Do have one spokesperson available at all times to discuss the crisis, usually the general manager.	**Do** advise a reporter if information has been reported inaccurately.
Do speak truthfully and authoritatively.	**Do** show concern for guest safety; stress your past safety record.
Do provide factual information to the media and be sensitive to their deadlines and job functions.	**Do** make forgiving and forgetting mandatory behavior after a labor strike.
Do keep guests informed.	**Do** create a positive follow-up campaign.
Do advise employees of their roles.	**Do** review your insurance policy, including business-interruption insurance.
Do show concern for employees affected by the crisis.	**Do** accept incoming calls from the front desk, switchboard, and reservation center concerning the crisis.
DON'T	
Don't wait for a crisis to design a plan.	**Don't** answer reporters by saying, "No comment."
Don't wait for a crisis to train employees.	**Don't** favor some reporters over others.
Don't treat the injured as liabilities.	**Don't** fail to respond to any questions or negative impressions.
Don't admit fault until an investigation occurs.	**Don't** allow switchboard, front desk, or any other employees to answer questions.
Don't offer to pay injured parties' medical bills.	**Don't** freeze up when being recorded for television.
Don't speak off the record to anyone.	**Don't** allow anyone to speak to media except the designated spokesperson.
Don't speak in hotel jargon.	**Don't** become defensive when asked questions.
Don't provide lurid descriptions.	**Don't** release names of victims.

Source: Julie Miller, "Crisis to Calm, Its the Crisis Communication Dos and Don'ts," *Hotel and Motel Management,* 211 (16), Aug 11, 1997, p. 18.

grades on a health report, an informal claim that a supervisor is practicing sexual harassment, grease dripping from exhaust ducts, or strangers walking the property. Good sanitation practices reduce the risk of serving poisoned food. Strict policies regarding sexual harassment create a climate where sexual harassment is not tolerated. Regular cleaning of kitchen ducts and employee training can eliminate grease fires in the kitchen. Hotels that train all their employees to look out for suspicious actions and report them to security can reduce the risk of crimes against guests. A well-managed property is the best form of crisis management.

The Internet is an area where major crises are being spawned. A damaging message about your organization (whether true or not) can be spread over the Internet to millions of people.[20] This has two important implications for management. First, the stakes of crisis management have been raised. It is very important to reduce the risk of a crisis occurring. Second, managers should monitor chat groups on the Internet to find out what they are saying about their organization. For example, a hotel in Miami should monitor the various chat groups for tourists to Miami.

When a crisis does occur, good communication with the press can reduce the impact of negative publicity. For example, a fire in a guest room resulting in no injuries could result in negative or positive publicity. If the hotel provides no information to the press, the headline might read "Regal Hotel Fire Forces Evacuation of 360 Guests." If the hotel contacts the press, the hotel has a chance to tell their story. In this case the hotel could state that there was a hotel fire. "The smoke alarm went off at 12:33 A.M., setting the hotel's fire plan into action. The fire department was called and employees conducted an orderly evacuation of the hotel as a precautionary measure. No one was injured and all guests were able to return to their rooms within thirty minutes. Ms. Roberta Dominquez, the general manager of the Regal, praised the quick action of the employees. She stated that as a result of the hotel's monthly fire drills all employees knew exactly what to do." The headline from this story might read: "Well-trained Employees Quickly Move Guests to Safety."

To have good crisis management, the company should appoint a spokesperson. Other employees should be instructed to refer media to this person. This ensures that the company is giving a consistent story based on facts. Second, this person should gather the facts and speak only from facts. Stephen Barth states that this person needs to make timely statements and keep the press updated.[21] If the press receives regular updates from the spokesperson, this will help to get them from trying to gain information from other employees. Barth also suggests that the spokesperson never use the term "no comment." He claims that this raises suspicion. Using the term "I don't know at this time" is a better response. If the hotel has a public relations agency, the agency should be contacted. In a major crisis, it is a good idea to seek the help of a public relations firm. Finally, the company should notify the press when a crisis does occur and keep the press updated. The media will learn about the event, so it is best that they find out from the company. Every company should have a crisis management plan and instruct employees in crisis management as part of their initial training. As Mitroff states, "It is no longer a question of if a major crisis will strike an organization, but only when."[22]

Sales Promotion

Sales promotion consists of short-term incentives to encourage the purchase or sales of a product or service. Sales promotion includes a variety of promotional tools designed to stimulate earlier or stronger market response. It includes consumer promotion (samples, coupons, rebates, price-off, premiums, contests, demonstrations), trade promotion-buying allowances (free goods, cooperative advertising, and push money), and sales force promotion (bonuses and contests). Often a well-planned sales promotion can result in publicity. The Omni San Antonio Hotel offered a Teacher's Appreciation Special in recognition of their contribution as educators. This sales promotion created goodwill among the teachers and the community and generated publicity for the hotel. It also generated room sales during a soft period.[23] Applebee's gives a free child's meal to students who make an A. This rewards students who get good grades and provides the school with a no-cost way of recognizing students who have done well. In addition to the public relations benefits, it also brings the child's parents and siblings to Applebee's when the free meal is redeemed. Thus, Applebee's generates profitable sales from the promotion.

15.5 Applebee's

Sales promotion tools are used by most organizations. Estimates of annual sales-promotion spending run as high as $100 billion. Spending has increased rapidly in recent years. Formerly, the ratio of advertising to sales promotion spending was about 60:40. Today, in many consumer packaged-goods companies, the picture is reversed, with sales promotion often accounting for 60 percent or 70 percent of all marketing expenditures. Sales promotions are most effective when they are used with advertising or personal selling. Consumer promotions must normally be advertised and can add excitement and pulling power to ads. Trade and sales force promotions support the firm's personal selling process. In using sales promotions, a company must *set objectives, select the right tools, develop the best program, pretest and implement it,* and *evaluate the results.* These steps are discussed next.

Setting Sales Promotion Objectives

Sales promotion objectives vary widely. Consumer promotions can increase short-term sales or they can be used to help build long-term market share. The objective may be to entice consumers to try a new product, lure consumers away from competitors, or hold and reward loyal customers. For the sales force, objectives include building stronger customer relations and obtaining new accounts.

Sales promotions should be consumer franchise building; that is, they should promote the product's positioning and include a sales message. Ideally, the objective is to build long-run consumer demand rather than to prompt temporary brand switching. If properly designed, every sales promotion tool has consumer franchise-building potential.

Selecting Sales Promotion Tools

Many tools can be used to accomplish sales promotion objectives. The promotion planner should consider the type of market, the sales promotion objectives, the competition, and the costs and effectiveness of each tool. The main consumer promotion tools are described next.

Consumer Promotion Tools

The main consumer promotion tools include samples, coupons, premiums, patronage rewards, point-of-purchase displays, contests, sweepstakes, and games.

Samples. Samples are offers of a trial amount of a product. Some samples are free. For others, the company charges a small amount to offset its cost. McDonald's offered a cup of coffee and an apple-bran muffin for $1. Normally, the coffee and the muffin were offered for 95 cents each. The promotion was designed to get customers to try the muffin. There are some people who do not eat bran muffins and by "charging" 5 cents for the muffin, McDonald's avoided giving the muffin away to customers who would never buy one in the future.

The Inn on the Park in Houston invited potential customers and influential community members to stay in the luxury hotel at no charge. The promotion accomplished two objectives: (1) salespeople were aided in selling corporate contracts, because many of their potential customers had experienced the hotel; and (2) positive word of mouth about the hotel was created. Sampling is the most effective but also the most expensive way to introduce a new product.

Sampling by the staff who are employed by a hospitality firm such as a hotel, restaurant, or ski resort can be a very useful educational and promotional device. Thorough knowledge of the product is particularly beneficial to up selling. It is difficult for anyone to recommend a premium-priced Bordeaux or California Merlot if they have no idea how the wine tastes. The sales and reservation staff of a hotel or resort can more convincingly sell a prospect on the idea of upgrading to a poolside cabaña or suite if they have a personal knowledge of the product.

How does the staff obtain personal knowledge of the product or services of a company? Several successful approaches have been used to accomplish staff product knowledge:

1. Provide continuous training programs. Invite suppliers such as vintners, cheese producers, and gourmet coffee distributors to provide samples and assist with product training.
2. Offer sales and performance incentives that include prizes on the property, such as a five-course meal, a month's use of the health club, or a weekend in the deluxe suite.
3. Create an employee's day in which the staff has full use of the facility. Country clubs often provide a special day in which employees and sometimes their families are treated to exclusive use of the pool, the golf course, the restaurant, and even the ballroom for an evening dance.
4. Share product information with employees through newsletters or product brochures. Often, product information brochures remain only in the offices of the purchasing department, the F&B manager, or some other executive office.
5. Talk continuously about the company's products and services in a positive and upbeat manner. People have a tendency to forget

the many positive attributes of the facilities and the services that surround us daily.

15.6 Aloha Airlines
Ski Limited

Preston L. Smith, the president and CEO of Ski Limited, regularly sends memos to company managers urging them to hit the slopes. Smith personally manages to ski over sixty times each season. "Everyone skis here. It's a way of sharing the customer's experience. It's also a way to achieve personal growth because skiing is exhilarating and exciting."[24]

Coupons. Coupons are certificates that offer buyers savings when they purchase specified products. More than 220 billion coupons are distributed in the United States each year, with a total face value of more than $55 billion. Coupons can be mailed, included with other products, or placed in ads. Coupons are most popular in the restaurant industry; however, hotel, rental car companies, tourist attractions, and cruise lines also use coupons. American Express cardholders received coupon packs featuring mid- and upscale restaurants. The prestige of American Express allows these restaurants to use coupons without detracting from their image.

Some restaurants have suffered from over-couponing. In the "pizza wars," the major chains fought for market share by distributing coupons at least once a week. Some pizza restaurants posted signs saying that they would honor competitors' coupons to neutralize the impact of competitor advertising. During the pizza wars, the price of pizza dropped to the discounted coupon price for most customers. These customers felt they were getting poor value if they purchased a pizza without a coupon. Over-couponing should be avoided, because it lowers the price so that the coupon no longer offers a competitive advantage.

Besides stimulating sales of a mature product, coupons are also effective in promoting early trial of a new product. For example, when a fast-food chain develops a new product, it often introduces the product in print advertisements featuring a coupon. The coupon provides an incentive and reduces the risk for customers trying the new product.

Joint promotions using coupons create goodwill for those who distribute the coupons and those who redeem them. For example, Aloha Airlines and Pizza Hut sponsored a joint promotion. Aloha Airlines gave passengers a coupon for a free pizza with the purchase of another of equal or greater value. They distributed the coupons on flights that had on-time arrivals.[25]

Many professional marketing consultants and observers of marketing and sales practices feel that too much promotion creates a commodity out of a differentiated product. It is argued that companies spend millions of dollars and years of effort to develop a distinct image and a high level of product differentiation in the minds of consumers, only to have it destroyed by promotions.

In far too many cases, promotions have created an impression that margins were unreasonably high to begin with or the company could not have made this offer. They have also led to coupon wars and other forms of price discounting, all the while detracting from the intrinsic value of the company's product or service.

Packages. Promotions often involve packages of a number of the company's products. Packages are particularly popular with hotels and resorts that have a number of products to offer. The Ritz Carlton in Tyson's Corners developed a Fine Art of Cuisine weekend. The weekend features gourmet meals matched with the appropriate wines. The hotel developed packages around the meals, tastings, and demonstrations. For $600 guests receive a room, tickets to the Grand Wine Tasting, and the Chef's brunch.[26] Packages can also be developed around local events. The Best Western Palm Beach, Florida, created a three-night package that includes a room for three nights, tickets to two baseball games (several teams had spring training near the hotel), a continental breakfast, and an evening cruise on a casino ship. The price of the package is $256.[27] Promotions such as these bring in business during a slow period and create a memorable experience for the guest.

Premiums. Premiums are goods offered either free or at low cost as an incentive to buy a product. For example, fast-food restaurants often offer a free promotional glass instead of their normal paper cup. A self-liquidating premium is a premium sold to consumers who request it. McDonald's in Australia offered Batman figures for 95 cents with the purchase of a burger.

Many restaurants, such as the Hard Rock Café, have discovered that promotional items such as caps, T-shirts, and sweatshirts can be sold at a good profit, thus creating another profit center for the company. Others offer a premium-priced drink or dessert that is served with a special glass or plate. Guests actually pay for the glass or plate in the price of the product, take the "gift" home with them, and are reminded of a pleasant restaurant experience each time it is later seen. Pat O'Brien's in the French Quarter of New Orleans serves a Hurricane in a commemorative glass. These glasses can be seen in homes throughout the world. The name recognition developed through its Hurricane glasses has helped to make Pat O'Brien's a major tourist attraction in the French Quarter.

Patronage Rewards. Patronage rewards are cash or other awards for regular use of a company's products or services. For example, most airlines offer frequent-flyer plans that award points for miles traveled. Most of the hotels chains have a frequent stay program and many restaurants have frequent diner programs. These program reward local customers, gather guest information, and ideally create a positive change in the consumer behavior of the member. This change could be more frequent purchases, larger purchases, or spreading positive word of mouth.

Hotels or restaurants can also create events to show their appreciation of loyal customers. For example, a casino invited 25,000 of its best customers to come to "Free Hug Friday." Five thousand players showed up to get a mug of Hershey's chocolate kisses and a hug from the company's executives. The players thought it was great and the casino brought 5,000 of their best players out in one night.[28]

Another type of patronage rewards are specials for repeat customers. The Elephant Walk restaurants in Massachusetts are constantly looking for fine wines. Often their finds are wines that have a limited availability. From their search for fine wines, they feature six wines each month. These are usually wines that do not have enough availability to put on their regular wine list. Customers are e-mailed information about the wines and can reserve a bottle for lunch or dinner. The restaurant sells these wines at normal retail levels, about half what a restaurant would normally charge for the wine. This promotion creates goodwill with their frequent customers and gives them another reason to dine at the restaurant. The unique promotion has also generated publicity for the restaurant.[29]

Point-of-Purchase Displays. Point-of-purchase (POP) promotions include displays and demonstrations that take place at the point of purchase or sale. For example, a representative of Richmond Estate Wines might offer a taste of their wines in the Robina Tavern package store.

The value of POP has long been recognized by the retailing industry and is making rapid inroads in restaurants, hotels, auto rental companies, and other hospitality industry firms. Hospitality firms have discovered that POP may be used (1) to disseminate information about the company's products or services, and (2) to sell additional products and services, thus adding to gross revenue.

Hotels use display racks in the lobby to promote other hotels in the chain and additional services, from valet parking to sleigh rides. Restaurants such as Perkins, the Village Inn, and Denny's use the space near the cash register to create eye-catching displays of bakery items and desserts to be taken home by the guests.

Several years ago, Farrell's Restaurants in Hawaii discovered a means to add over 10 percent to the bottom line without decreasing prices or adding new customers. Farrell's appealed heavily to families with preteenage children. Keeping the customer profile in mind, a decision was made to design a new passageway out of the restaurant before reaching the cash register. This passageway involved walking through thousands of gift, candy, and gum items selected for child irresistibility. This unique and colorful passageway served as a giant POP that added revenue directly to the bottom line.

Contests, Sweepstakes, and Games. Contests, sweepstakes, and games give consumers a chance to win something, such as cash or a trip. A contest calls for consumers to submit an entry—a jingle, guess, or suggestion—to be judged by a panel. A sweepstake calls for consumers to submit their names for a drawing. A game presents consumers with something every time they buy bingo numbers or missing letters that may or may not help them win a prize. A sales contest urges dealers or the sales force to increase their efforts, with prizes going to the top performers.

15.7 Sheraton

Before the Olympic games in Spain, Sheraton's in the Pacific Region ran a promotion offering two trips to the games in Barcelona as its gold prize, five regional holidays as its silver prize, and 10 two-night stays at the Sheraton closest to the winner for the bronze prize. The contest featured the slogan "Sleep at a Sheraton and Wake Up in Barcelona." Sheraton gave key clients a kit entitled "Inspired Excellence," which included a commemorative medallion and a luxurious brochure. Many of these kits were hand delivered by Sheraton salespeople. A separate contest was designed for travel agents, offering them an incentive to promote the contest to their customers. Additionally, point-of-purchase material was displayed at the front desks of Sheraton Hotels and television advertising supported the campaign. This campaign was primarily a sales promotion, but it used other areas of the promotional mix for support.

Rack brochures can be used for cross promotions, such as promoting hotels at tourist attractions and visitor centers. A less expensive form of the brochure is a rack card, which can be printed on one or two sides. Courtesy of Bill Bard Associates, Monticello, N.Y.

A modification of a contest is providing a commission for a charity that brings in business. For example, Godfather's Pizza will sponsor a school night. Godfather's will donate $1 per pizza to the school when the person ordering the pizza identifies themselves as being associated with the school. This creates both sales and goodwill for Godfather's.

Promotions can involve contests for employees along with guests. Len Lesko, the general manager of the Holiday Inn in Youngstown, Ohio, developed a contest to encourage customer service. Whenever an employee helps out another employee, they receive a "thank you" from the employee they helped. At the end of the week, the "thank yous" are put into a drawing for $50.[30]

Tom Feltenstein, a restaurant marketing consultant, suggests a program where loyal customers are sent a $20 gift certificate. They can use $10 toward the purchase of their meal and the other $10 they give to an employee who provides them with the best service. Thus, the employee tries to pick up as much money as possible by providing exceptional service.[31]

Developing the Sales Promotion Program

The third step in developing a sales promotion is to define the full sales promotion program. This step calls for marketers to make other decisions. First, they must decide on the size of the incentive. A certain minimum incentive is necessary if the promotion is to succeed. A larger incentive will produce more sales response. The marketer must also set conditions for participation. Incentives might be offered to everyone or only to select groups. Sweepstakes might not be offered in certain states, to families of company personnel, or to persons under a certain age.

The marketer must then decide how to promote and distribute the promotion program. A restaurateur can distribute coupons at the restaurant, by mail, or in an advertisement. Each distribution method involves a different level of reach and cost. The length of the promotion is also important. If the sales-promotion period is too short, prospects who would not buy during that time will be unable to take advantage of it. If the promotion runs too long, the deal will lose some of its "act now" force.

The question of how to distribute a promotional program has resulted in problems for companies. An example is a restaurant that decided to print 10,000 flyers announcing a promotion and have employees stick them under the windshield wiper of cars in a shopping center. The following results occurred: Employees threw most in the dumpster, several auto owners threatened to sue, claiming their wipers had been broken, the owner of the shopping center demanded someone clean up the mess, and, finally, an employee and a car owner engaged in a fistfight. The employee won the fistfight, but the company paid an out-of-court settlement to the auto owner with a broken nose.[32]

Restaurant promotions often consist of cards, flyers, coupons, and other devices featuring two-for-one specials, 20 percent off, free drinks, or other "hooks." Normally, these bear a date at which the promotion becomes ineffective. In theory, this should work well, but in actuality, customers often present coupons months or even years old and become enraged when they are told that the promotion is no longer in effect. A prospective new owner or buyer of any hospitality company should ask if there are outstanding promotions in the community. Many new owners have been shocked to witness a flood of promotional coupons that negatively affected cash flow.

Other problematic media used by hospitality companies include hot-air balloons bearing the company's logo that crashed on freeways or atop buildings, road signs that ended up in strange places such as the mayor's lawn, and sponsored bicycle races in which the restaurant rider crashed through a competitor's storefront. In today's "I'll sue you" environment, it is wise to discuss proposed promotions with an attorney and with the company's insurance agent prior to initiation.

Marketing managers need to set promotion dates, which will be used by production, sales, and distribution. Some unplanned promotions may also be needed, requiring cooperation on short notice.

Finally, the marketer has to decide on the sales-promotion budget. It can be developed in two ways. The marketer can choose the promotions and estimate total cost. However, the more common way is to use a percentage of the total budget for sales promotion. One study found three major problems in the way that companies budget for sales promotion. First, they do not consider cost-effectiveness. Second, instead of spending to achieve objectives, they simply extend the previous year's spending, take a percentage of expected sales, or use the "affordable approach." Finally, advertising and sales promotion budgets are too often prepared separately.[33]

Partnerships can stretch a budget. The Palm, a national upscale steakhouse, developed a promotion with a Chicago car dealer to promote its Chicago restaurant. The car dealer offered a $20 gift certificate for the Palm to all who test drove its luxury model cars. The cost of the certificate was split equally between the partners. The dealership gained an incentive to attract customers with a certificate that was steeply discounted, and the restaurant gained additional customers for $10 per table.[34] Partnerships can also be used to acquire prizes in sweepstakes. Companies will often discount or provide merchandise in exchange for advertising exposure.

Pretesting and Implementing the Plan

Whenever possible, sales promotion tools should be pretested to determine if they are appropriate and of the right incentive size. Consumer sales promotions can be pretested quickly and inexpensively, yet few promotions are ever tested ahead of time. Seventy percent of companies do not test sales promotions before initiating them. To test sales promotions, researchers can ask consumers to rate or rank different promotions. Promotions can also be tried on a limited basis in selected geographic test areas.

Companies should prepare implementation plans for each promotion, covering lead time and sell-off time. Lead time is the time necessary to prepare the program before launching it. Sell-off time begins with the launch and ends when the promotion ends.

Evaluating the Results

Even though result evaluation is important, many companies fail to evaluate their sales promotion programs. Others do so only superficially. Many evaluation methods are available, the most common of which is sales comparisons before, during, and after a promotion. Suppose that a company has a 6 percent market share before the promotion, which jumps to 10 percent during the promotion, falls to 5 percent immediately after, and rises to 7 percent later. The promotion appears to have attracted new customers and more purchases from current customers. After the promotion, sales fell as consumers used inventories or moved purchases forward. For example, a person planning on traveling to see relatives in New York in June may move the trip forward to April to take advantage of an airline promotion that expires April 30. The long-run rise to 7 percent means that the airline gained some new users, but if the brand's share returned to the prepromotion level, the promotion changed only the timing of demand rather than total demand.

The results of consumer research will demonstrate the kinds of people who responded to the promotion and their postpromotion buying behavior. Surveys can provide information on how many consumers recall the promotion, what they thought of it, how many accepted it, and how it affected their buying patterns. Sales promotions can also be evaluated through experiments that include variables such as incentive value, length, and distribution method.

Clearly, sales promotion plays an important role in the total promotion mix. To use it well, the marketer must define sales promotion objectives, select the best tools, design the sales promotion program, pretest, implement, and evaluate the results.

Local Store Marketing

Local store marketing, also called local area marketing or neighborhood marketing, is defined as a low-cost, hands-on effort to take advantage of all opportunities within the immediate trading area to promote and market a business.[35] Although all areas of the promotional mix are used, public relations is the heart of any local area marketing program. Local area marketing is used by both small and large companies; however, it is an area where small companies can compete just as effectively as large companies. Independently owned businesses, such as restaurants or travel agencies, have an advantage over large companies because the owners become permanent fixtures of the community, whereas the large companies tend to replace their store managers every two or three years. Research has shown that 75 percent of a restaurant's customers come from within a ten-minute drive. With fast-food restaurants, the radius shrinks to three to five minutes drive time.[36]

Examples of public relations activities included in local store marketing are providing tours of your facility. Primary schools look for places to take their students on field trips. A restaurant or hotel can be an exciting venue. A short tour, followed by a tasting and providing the students with a coupon (so that they can show their parents where they went), can be a good way to create business and goodwill. Many suburban areas have weekly papers; providing a weekly or monthly article on travel, food, or wine is a good way to gain exposure. If the articles are well written, the paper will appreciate the free articles, and the writer will gain exposure and credibility in the local market. Being a speaker at meetings of local social and service clubs is another way to gain exposure. During the holiday season, a business can become a depository for charities collecting toys for disadvantaged children. But don't accept this task passively. For example, if the local firefighters ask you to collect toys for their campaign, suggest that the campaign be started with a kick-off drive, including fire engines, sirens, and firemen in uniform in your parking lot on a Saturday. If they agree, call the local news station and get some television coverage.[37]

Cause-related promotions are another local area marketing tactic. These promotions bring business to the hotel or restaurant and help the community. Rock Bottom restaurants frequently creates promotions that are cause related. For example, one of the beers the brew pub creates is

Firechief Ale. The company developed a fiery line of appetizers and teamed them with its Firechief Ale to create a promotion that helped local firehouses. Dallas-based Canyon Café promotes a charitable cause at the grand opening of each of its restaurants. This has given the restaurant a reputation for being a responsible business and a good neighbor.[38]

El Torito restaurants, based in California, had a television campaign in 1999. The campaign was based almost exclusively in Los Angeles because the chain could not afford to advertise in multiple markets. As a result restaurants outside of Los Angeles gained little benefit from the ads. Joe Herrera, the restaurant's manager, decided to scrap the television ads and build a local store marketing campaign. Its ad dollars went into local papers and community marketing. Now El Torito has a presence in all its markets, and Herrera stated the managers were happy to have the marketing help.[39]

A good local area marketing campaign creates goodwill in the community and exposure for the restaurant which translates into increased business and customer loyalty. Successful local marketers do not give products or money away freely; they evaluate every opportunity and make sure that the effort will be worthwhile. By being creative, managers can ensure that their local marketing efforts will be noticed.

Key Terms

Contests, sweepstakes, and games Give consumers a chance to win something, such as cash or a trip.

Corporate communications This activity covers internal and external communications and promotes understanding of an organization.

Coupons Certificates that offer buyers savings when they purchase specified products.

Counseling Involves advising management about public issues and company positions and image.

Event creation A particularly important skill in publicizing fund-raising drives for nonprofit organizations.

Lobbying Dealing with legislators and government officials to promote or defeat legislation and regulation.

Patronage rewards Cash or other awards for regular use of a company's products or services.

Point-of-purchase (POP) promotions Include displays and demonstrations that take place at the time of sale.

Premiums Goods offered either free or at low cost as an incentive to buy a product.

Press relations To place newsworthy information into the news media to attract attention.

Press release Information released to the media about certain new products or services.

Product publicity Various efforts to publicize specific products.

Public relations The process by which we create a positive image and customer preference through third-party endorsement.

Sales promotion Consists of short-term incentives to encourage the purchase or sale of a product or service.

Samples Offers of a trial amount of a product.

Chapter Review

I. Definition of Public Relations. The process by which we create a positive image and customer preference through third-party endorsement.

II. Five Public Relations Activities

1) **Press relations.** The aim of press relations is to place newsworthy information into the news media to attract attention to a person, product, or service.
2) **Product publicity.** Product publicity involves efforts to publicize specific products.
3) **Corporate communication.** This activity covers internal and external communications and promotes understanding of the organization.
4) **Lobbying.** Lobbying involves dealing with legislators and government officials to promote or defeat legislation and regulation.
5) **Counseling.** Counseling involves advising management about public issues and company positions and image.

III. Marketing Public Relations. Publicity is the task of securing editorial space; marketing PR goes beyond simple publicity. Marketing PR can contribute to the following tasks:

1) Assist in the launch of new products
2) Assist in repositioning a mature product
3) Build up interest in a product category
4) Influence specific target groups
5) Defend products that have encountered public problems

IV. The Public Relations Process

1) **Researching to understand the firm's mission, culture, and target of the communication**
2) **Establishing marketing objectives**
   - **a)** Build awareness
   - **b)** Build credibility
   - **c)** Stimulate the sales force and channel intermediaries
   - **d)** Hold down promotion costs

3) **Defining the target audience**
4) **Choosing the PR message and vehicles, such as event creation**
5) **Implementing the marketing PR plan**
6) **Evaluating PR results**
   a) Exposures
   b) Awareness/comprehension/attitude change
   c) Sales-and-profit contribution

V. Overview of the Major Tools in Public Relations

1) Publications. Companies can reach and influence their target market via annual reports, brochures, cards, articles, audiovisual materials, and company newsletters and magazines.

2) Events. Companies can draw attention to new products or other company activities by arranging special events.

3) News. PR professionals cultivate the press to increase better coverage to the company.

4) Speeches. Speeches create product and company publicity. The possibility is accomplished by printing copies of the speech or excerpts for distribution to the press, stockholders, employees, and other publics.

5) Public service activities. Companies can improve public goodwill by contributing money and time to good causes, such as supporting community affairs.

6) Identity media. Companies can create a visual identity that the public immediately recognizes, such as with company's logos, stationery, signs, business forms, business cards, buildings, uniforms, dress code, and rolling stock.

VI. Public Relations Opportunities for Individual Properties

1) Build PR around the owner/operator.

2) Build PR around the location. For instance, the isolation and obscurity of an enterprise can be used as a PR tactic.

3) Build PR around a product or service.

VII. Crisis Management

1) Take all precautions to prevent negative events from occurring.

2) When a crisis does occur:
   a) Appoint a spokesperson. This ensures that the company is giving a consistent story based on facts.
   b) Contact the firm's public relations agency if it has one.
   c) The company should notify the press when a crisis does.

VIII. Sales Promotion

1) Setting sales promotion objectives. Sales promotion objectives vary widely and can include increasing short-term sales, increasing long-term sales, getting consumers to try a new product, luring customers away from competitors, or creating loyal customers.

2) Selecting sales promotion tools. Many tools can be used to accomplish sales promotion objectives. The promotion planner should consider the type of market, the sales promotion objectives, the competition, and the costs and effectiveness of each tool. Common sales-promotion tools include samples, coupons, premiums, patronage rewards, point-of-purchase (POP), contests, sweepstakes, and games.

3) Developing the sales promotion program. The following steps are involved in developing a sales-promotion program:

a) Decide on the size of the incentive.
b) Set the conditions for participation.
c) Decide how to promote and distribute the promotion program.
d) Set promotion dates.
e) Decide on the sales promotion budget.

4) Evaluating the results. The company should evaluate the results against the objectives of the program.

Discussion Questions

1. What is meant by the term public? Can a company have more than one public?
2. Why might it make sense for a hotel chain to shift some of its advertising dollars to public relations?
3. Give some examples of how a hospitality organization might be able to gain publicity.
4. Is publicity free?
5. Compare and contrast publicity with advertising. What are the benefits and drawbacks of each?
6. Bring to class a sample of a hospitality or travel company's sales promotion. What is this sales promotion's objective? Do you think that it will accomplish its objective? What do yo think is the most interesting or intriguing part about the sales promotion? Should it be continued? Why or why not? What are some of the negatives associated with this sales promotion, and with sales promotions in general?

Experiential Exercise

Do the following:

Find a good example of publicity in a print medium. Copy the article and explain why you think the publicity is effective.

Internet Exercise

Support for these exercises can be found on the Web site for *Marketing for Hospitality and Tourism,* www.prenhall.com/kotler.

Find two Web sites of hospitality or travel organizations that offer public relations support. This could be corporate announcements, a "press room section," or a gallery of photos that one can download for publicity for publicity purposes. Report on the sites you found and the support they offered for persons wanting to write a story about the organization.

References

1. Dale Carter, *The Final Frontier: The Rise and Fall of the American Rocket State* (London: Verso, 1988); C. Dewitt Coffman, *Marketing for a Full House* (Ithaca, NY: School of Hotel Administration, Cornell University, 1975); Jon Trux, *The Space Race, from Sputnik to Shuttle: The Story of the Battle for the Heavens* (London: New English Library, 1985).

2. Jessica Miller, "Marketing Communications," *Cornell Hotel and Restaurant Administration Quarterly* 34, no. 5 (October 1993): 49.
3. Ibid.
4. Philip Kotler, "Public Relations versus Marketing: Dividing the Conceptual Domain and Operational Turf," (paper presented at the Public Relations Colloquium 1989, San Diego, CA: January 24, 1989).
5. Adapted from Scott M. Cutlip, Allen H. Center, and Glen M. Brown, *Effective Public Relations*, 6th ed. (Upper Saddle River, NJ: Prentice Hall, 1985), pp. 7–17.
6. Joe Durocher, "Recovery Marketing: What to Do after a Natural Disaster," *Cornell Hotel and Restaurant Administration Quarterly* 35, no. 2 (April 1994): 66.
7. Stephen White, "The Great Payback: Lodging Nurtures Its Identity and Social Obligations through Philanthropy," *Hotel & Motel Management*, September 17, 2001, p. 64.
8. "Olive Garden's Drive against Hunger Raises More than $1M," *Nation's Restaurant News,* June 25, 2001, p. 30.
9. Karen Weiner Escalera, "How to Get News Out of Nothing," *Lodging* (March 1992): 25–26.
10. Miller, "Marketing Communications," p. 49.
11. Arthur M. Merims, "Marketing's Stepchild: Product Publicity," *Harvard Business Review* (November/December 1972): 111–112; see also Katharine D. Paine, "There Is a Method for Measuring PR," *Marketing News,* November 7, 1987, p. 5.
12. Arthur M. Merims, "Marketing's Stepchild: Product Publicity," *Harvard Business Review* (November–December 1972): 111–112. For more on evaluating public relations effectiveness, see Katharine D. Paine, "There Is a Method for Measuring PR," *Marketing News*, November 6, 1987, p. 5; and Eric Stoltz and Jack Torobin, "Public Relations by the Numbers," *American Demographics* (January 1991): 42–46.
13. For further reading on cause-related marketing, see P. Rajan Varadarajan and Anil Menon, "Cause-Related Marketing: A Co-alignment of Marketing Strategy and Corporate Philanthropy," *Journal of Marketing* (July 1988): 58–74.
14. Tom McCarthy, "Add Publicity in the Mix," *Lodging Hospitality* (October 1999): 17.
15. Michael M. Lefever, "Restaurant Advertising: Coupons, Clauses and Cadillacs," *Cornell Hotel and Restaurant Administration Quarterly* 29, no. 4 (February 1989): 94.
16. Eric Bergman, "Crisis? What Crisis?" *Communications World* 11, no. 4 (April 1994): 19–23.
17. Robert B. Irvine, "What's a Crisis Anyway?" *Communications World*, 14, no. 7 (July 15, 1997), pp. 36–41.
18. Ian I. Mitroff, "Crisis Management and Environmentalism: A natural Fit," *California Management Review* 36, no. 2 (winter 1994): 101–114.
19. Julie Miller, "Crisis to Calm," *Hotel and Motel Management,* August 11, 1997, p. 261.
20. Louise Kramer, "Food for Thought: Playing Sound Bites," *Nation's Restaurant News* 29, no. 43 (October 30, 1995): 54.
21. Irvine, "What's a Crisis Anyway?"
22. Mitroff, *California Management Review*, p. 114.
23. "The Omni San Antonio Hotel," *San Antonio Business Journal*, July 20, 2001, p. 36
24. David H. Freedman, "An Unusual Way to Run a Ski Business," *Forbes*, (December 7, 1992), p. 28.
25. "Ad Watch," *Nations Restaurant News* 26, no. 19 (May 11, 1999): 12.
26. Jennifer Coleman, "The Fine Art of Fine Dining," *Travel Agent,* September 18, 2000, p. 96.
27. David Cogswell and Sara Perez Webber, "Spring Flings," *Travel Agent*, February 21, 2000, p. 108.
28. Tricia Campbell, "Cozying up to Customers, " *Sales & Marketing Management* (December 1999): 15.
29. Mary Ewing-Mulligan and Ed McCarthy, "Wine Lists Used Creatively Are Vintage Opportunity to Attract New Customers," *Nation's Restaurant News*, July 23, 2001, pp. 43–46.
30. Bridget Falbo, "Wow Customers with Service to Build Positive PR," *Hotel & Motel Management*, May 4, 1998, p. 45.
31. Tom Feltenstein, "Slay the Neighborhood Goliath," *Restaurant Hospitality* (October 1999): 38.
32. Michael M. Zefener, "Restaurant Advertising, Coupon Claims and Cadillacs," *Cornell Hotel and Restaurant Administration Quarterly* 29 no. 4 (February 1989): 98.
33. Roger A. Strang, "Sales Promotion Fast Growth, Faulty Management," *Harvard Business Review* (July/August 1976): 98.
34. Steve Weiss, "Promotions Trend: Get Yourself a Partner," *Restaurants and Institutions* 103 no. 26 (November 1, 1993): 78–93.
35. *National Restaurant Association, Promoting the Neighborhood Restaurant: A Local Store Marketing Manual* (Chicago: National Restaurant Association, 1988).
36. Tom Feltenstein, "Wily Underdogs with Fewer Resources Still Have Bite in Competitive Foodservice Industry," *Nation's Restaurant News*, May 7, 2001, p. 40.
37. Tom Feltenstein, *Restaurant Profits through Advertising and Promotion* (New York: Van Nostrand Reinhold, 1983).
38. Theresa Howard, "Chartible Promos Can Be Profitable Market Strategy," *Nation's Restaurant News,* June 9, 1997, p. 18.
39. Scott Hume, "Taking It to the Streets," *Restaurants and Institutions*, October 15, 1999, pp. 101–108.

NOKIA

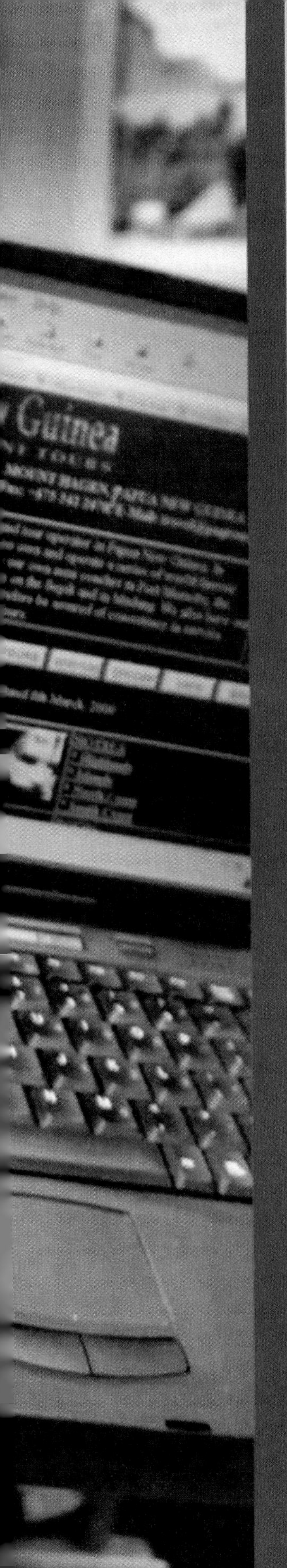

16 Electronic Marketing: Internet Marketing, Database Marketing, and Direct Marketing

Computers in the future may weigh no more than 1.5 tons.
Popular Mechanics, 1949

Wiley Eiya, tribal chief of the Huli tribe in Papua New Guinea (PNG), is on-line as he presents his Web site on a laptop screen at the International Tourism Fair in Berlin. For countries such as PNG, which have a low tourism budget, the Internet allows access to tourists around the world. Even though the government has not made a major effort to promote tourism in PNG, individual tour operators can have a presence on the Internet. This presence can include pictures of the spectacular scenery and the people of the highlands. The Internet allows smaller travel organizations to have international coverage for a low cost. Tourists all over the world are discovering remote destinations through the Internet.

Papua New Guinea is a remote island off the northern coast of Australia. It has a population of a little over 5 million, with most of its people living in rural villages. With over 860 distinct tribal languages, PNG is home to over one-fourth of the world's languages. The land was settled 10,000 years ago, with its early residents credited as being the first farmers on earth. Europeans did not come to the country until the 1930s and the tribes of the highlands had little contact with the outside world until the mid-twentieth century.

Travel writers Lipscomp, McKinnon, and Murray say this about PNG, "Few places in the world can match its famed waterways, fascinating village culture, abundant wildlife, smoking volcanoes, rainforest trekking and offshore diving experiences." The discovery of the highland tribes created an attraction for anthropologists and tourists interested in tribal culture. Its rich culture is only one of PNG's many tourist attractions. PNG is rapidly becoming known for

diving that rivals the diving at the Great Barrier Reef. Another activity is white-water rafting in the mountain streams. Coastal and river cruising offers tourists the comfort of modern ships, while they enjoy the rustic beauty of the country. It has many unique species of birds and mammals. Although the potential for tourism in PNG is great, the government continues to focus on other industries. Thus, the tourism potential is largely untapped. The numbers of tourists coming to the country has been around 20,000 in recent years. Even though the Internet provides PNG with a great opportunity to build its tourism, the growth of tourism still has to be managed. A country such as Papua New Guinea must make sure it has the infrastructure to support increased tourism, as well as policies in place to create sustainable tourism activities that do not destroy its culture and natural beauty. Thus the Internet can be a two-edged sword. It can bring more tourists, but the destination must still be able to support the tourists when they arrive.[1]

Chapter Objectives

After reading this chapter, you should be able to:

1. Describe the relationship between Internet marketing, database marketing, and direct marketing.
2. Evaluate a company's Web site and comment on its marketing potential.
3. Describe how to set up an effective database.
4. Discuss the growth of e-mail marketing.
5. Understand how databases can be used to develop direct marketing campaigns.

Electronic marketing is rapidly transforming the way hospitality and travel organizations conduct business. Electronic marketing is normally associated with Internet marketing. In this chapter we are expanding the focus to include database marketing and **direct marketing.** In practice, these areas are integrated. Internet marketing captures data which feeds into the firm's database; the database is used to generate profiles and lists, which enable the firm to have effective direct marketing campaigns; and two of the media for direct marketing are the Internet using e-mails and CD-ROMs with hyperlinks to the Internet. We start the chapter by looking at Internet marketing. Table 16-1 shows how marketing will change with the use of the Internet.

Internet Marketing

Underlying electronic business are two phenomena: *digitalization* and *connectivity*. Digitalization consists of converting text, data, sound, and image into a stream of bits that can be dispatched at incredible speeds from one location to another. Connectivity involves building networks and expresses the fact that much of the world's business is carried over networks connecting people and companies. These networks are called **intranets** when they connect people within a company; **extranets** when they connect a company with its suppliers and customers; and the **Internet** when they connect users to an amazingly large "information superhighway."

Over 500 million people have access to the Internet; in 1996 there were less than 50 million users. This tenfold increase in less than eight years shows why the Internet has become such an important marketing tool. About 40 percent of those using the Internet speak English; however, that percentage is expected to drop to less than 30 percent by 2005, as China moves into a strong second position. There are about 220 million Internet users in the United States, with almost half of Americans having access to

Table 16-1
How Electronic Marketing Will Change Marketing

MARKETING ACTIVITY	TRADITIONAL MARKETING	CYBERMARKETING
Advertising	Prepare print, video, or voice copy and use standard media vehicles such as television, radio, newspapers, and magazines. Usually only very limited information can be presented.	Design extensive information and put it on the company's Web page; CD brochures linked to your site; distribution of public relations information over the Internet.
Customer service	Provide service five days a week, eight hours a day in the store or over the phone in response to customer calls; provide on-site visits.	Provide seven-day, twenty-four-hour service response; send phone, fax, or e-mail solutions; allow customers to coproduce their customer service; access to frequent guest diner and flyer information over the Internet.
Selling	Phoning or visiting prospects and customers and demonstrating product physically or by projective equipment.	Videoconferencing with prospect; showing the product on the computer screen; enabling customers to purchase their own hospitality and travel products.
Marketing research	Use of individual interviews, focus groups, and mailed or phones surveys.	Use of newsgroups for conversation and interviewing, e-mail questionnaires; access to focus groups over the Internet.

the Internet at home. [2] Sixteen and one-half million of these Internet users booked over $10 billion worth of travel in 2000, making it the largest category of all on-line purchases.[3] The success of companies with the Internet is mixed. Professor Leong found that although most hotels in Singapore received less than 10 percent of their reservations over the Internet, some hotels were receiving 20 or 30 percent of their reservations.[4] The Internet represents an untapped opportunity for many companies. It is not only useful as a sales outlet, but it also provides a medium for communication between a company and its customers. Why do people purchase on-line? According to Henry Harteveldt of Forrester Research, on-line purchases are made for the following reasons:

- **Convenience:** On-line purchases can be made from any place at any time.

- **Information:** Customers can gain information about travel and travel destinations.
- **Price:** Consumers feel they get a better price; this is reinforced by airline phone reservations services that refer the customer to the Internet for lower prices. Price comparison is also easy.[5]

Some of the uses of a Web site include product sales, product awareness, assist the product's or brand's overall promotional campaign, allow customers to contact the company, provide public relations support, capture information from potential customers visiting the site, and provide information that will enable customers to enhance their use of the product. Charles Hofacker categorizes these activities into selling, communication, and providing content.[6]

Selling

Hotel, cruise, and airline companies are using the Internet to distribute their products directly to the customer. On-line travel agencies as well as discounters sell a variety of travel products through the Internet. One of the advantages of the Internet as a sales channel is that the customer does the work. The availability of technology to the typical customer has enhanced the opportunities for self-service. For example, a good Web site allows airline customers to choose their flight, select their seats, and make arrangements for special meals. A passenger that wants to explore all options and take twenty minutes to book a reservation can do this on the Internet; thus, the airline does not have the expense of an employee personally going through all the options with the passenger, making the Internet is an effective and efficient way of taking reservations. Internet technology can enhance customer satisfaction as it allows customers to access services when and where they want without the complications of interpersonal exchanges.[7]

One important aspect of an Internet site is to enable customers to contact the company and talk with an employee. American Airlines has found that in addition to a telephone number, a Web chat option is useful for clients using their home phone line. If they have a question, they can contact a representative without going off line.[8] LowAirfare.com features working with a live agent on its site. Agents can assistant several on-line customers at on time. While one customer is reviewing his or her options, the agent works with someone else. By providing personalized service through text chat, LowAirfare is able to keep 92 percent of those who begin a transaction. This is a much higher average than most travel online agents.[9]

16.1 LowAirfare.com
Dunkin' Donuts
Red Lobster

The Internet is also a good way to get rid of excess capacity. For example, Continental Airlines sends messages to its frequent travelers referring them to the Web site for specials. They can distribute low fares over the Internet, rather than advertise them publicly and set off a potential price war with a competitor. Airlines give the option of listing flights from lowest price to highest price. Thus, price-sensitive travelers can choose the flights where the airlines need customers. Cruise lines and hotel chains also list "specials," hoping to attract price-sensitive customers to fill up their ships and cruises.

Restaurants use their sites to sell merchandise such as gift cards and to take reservations. Dunkin' Donuts is known as much for its great coffee as it is for its donuts on the east coast of the United States. In the past Dunkin' Donuts could only distribute their coffee through their stores. Now they have an Internet site that allows them to sell their coffee to customers who have moved from the East Coast and find themselves without a Dunkin' Donuts near them. Their site features coffee "subscriptions," allowing customers to receive two pounds of coffee delivered to their door on a monthly basis.

Red Lobster sells both live lobsters and complete lobster bakes on its Web site. Morton's Steak House makes its custom-crafted wood-handled steak knives available. Even individual restaurants and smaller chains can sell merchandise over the Internet. For example, Cheeseburger in Paradise on Maui sells clothing.

Communication

One of the important uses of the Internet is communication. It can provide color views of the destinations and its related activities. The activities may be listed on a menu; thus, someone wanting water sports, hiking, art museums, or historical tours can click on the appropriate menu item and get the information needed. Information is presented in a way that will make potential customers want to come to the destination. A destination marketing organization (DMO) must work to see that the official site is well situated in the main search engines, so that it comes up when someone searches for information on the destination. If the DMO does not do a good job at managing its presence on search engines, a site not portraying the desired image of the destination may be the top one in the search engine. The task of managing the placement of a site near the top of the search engine lists is becoming more difficult as more and more engines are selling placements. Thus, one must pay to be at the top. Marketing Highlight 16-1 looks at some of the issues of designing a Web site for a tourism destination, as well as managing the destination's Web presence.

Web sites for hotels have the chance to communicate information to a number of different segments. The home page, can provide information targeted to reach a number of different audiences. For example, a food and beverage director of a hotel can develop a special site for banquets and catering. In addition to being linked to the home page, these specialized sites can be submitted to search engines.[10] Thus, someone looking for a place to hold a banquet can come to the hotel's banquet site directly. Remember that all a company's potential markets may not think of them as a provider of the service they desire. It is up to the company to communicate directly with the markets they wish to serve. Focus groups are a good way to evaluate the content and accessibility of sites designed for different clientele. Someone using an Internet site should be able to access the page with the information they need in three clicks or less.

16.2 Hyatt

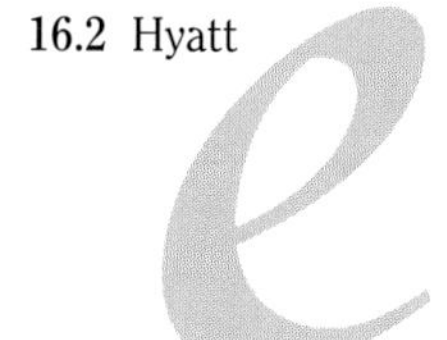

Hyatt hotels home page provides an example of a home page that is well indexed. From the home page, the user can go to a specific type of Hyatt (i.e., Park Hyatt), make a reservation, check on special offers, or order a gift certificate. For professional users there is a Press Room, a section for Travel Professionals, and a Meeting Planning Index. Each section provides information that will be relevant to the user.

Providing visual information on the Internet is certainly more cost-effective than printing and mailing out brochures. Many hotels offer visual tours and some chains, such as Courtyard, offer visual tours of the different types of hotels they have such as classic, downtown, and vacation hotels. Those hotels with a focus on meetings may use one of the meeting software packages such as MeetingMatrix, Optimum Settings, or Room Viewer, allowing the meeting planner to diagram the rooms with their desired set-up and e-mail it to the hotel and facilitating communication between the meeting planner and the convention service manager at the hotel.

The Internet allows companies to have a global reach. Someone from England traveling to Malaga, Spain, can find out about tourist attractions, places to stay, and places to dine. The English traveler does not have to know Spanish, as smart hospitality and travel companies will

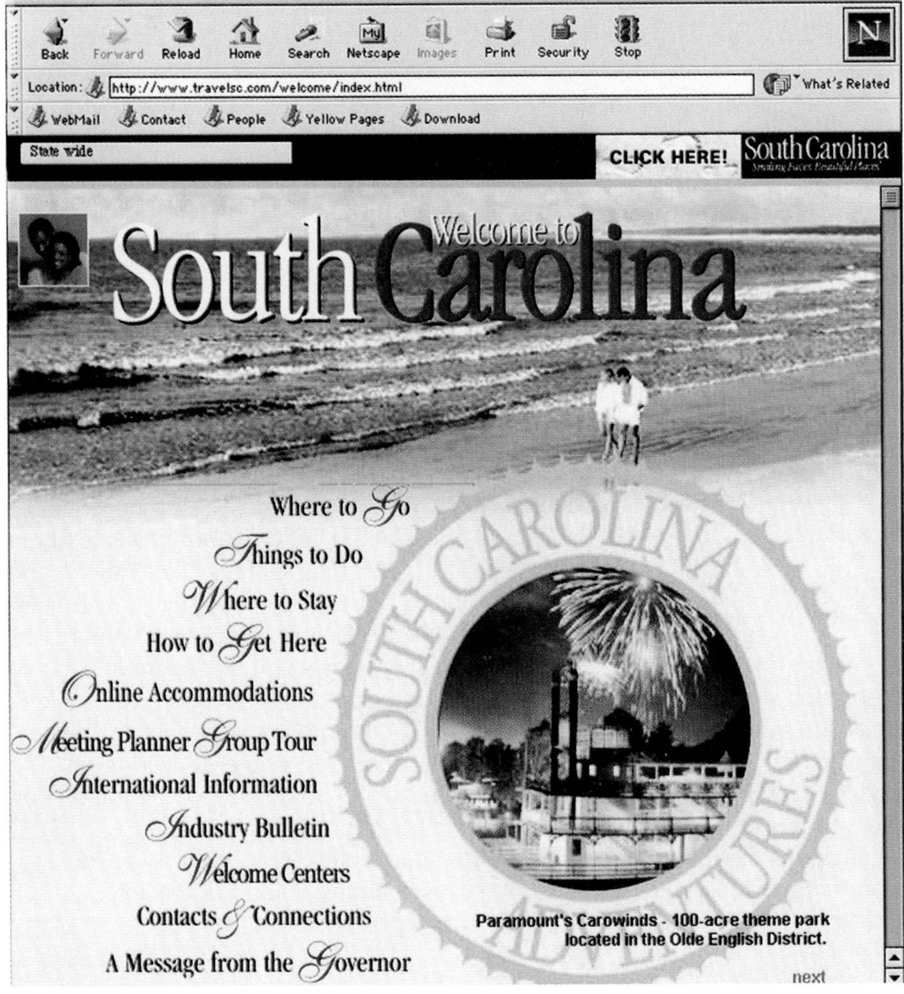

South Carolina realizes the importance of having a good Internet presence. AP Photo.

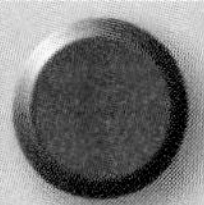

Marketing Highlight 16-1

Using the Web to Market Tourism Destinations

When a person buys a computer, they often buy an assortment of goods made by different companies. For example, the manufacturers of the computer, printer, and software are often different. Similarly a traveler will use air travel, a rental car, a hotel room, and purchase meals. Different companies provide these services. The goal of the traveler is to have an enjoyable experience. A properly designed Web site can facilitate the travelers' planning, helping to ensure they make the right choices and have an enjoyable experience. It can also serve as the distribution point for all the services they will need as they plan their vacation.

Tourism destinations emerge as umbrella brands, and they will need to be promoted in the global marketplace as one entity for each target market they try to attract. The emerging globalization and concentration of supply increase the level of competition and require new Internet marketing strategies for destinations. Hence, destination marketing organizations (DMOs) increasingly have to identify niche markets and develop their interactivity with tourists.

The distribution/allocation strategy of tourism products should follow a customer-oriented approach. A vertical marketing system should be in place, bringing together a set of products related with each destination available for selection. This implies that each tourist destination must have a major portal Web site acting as a gateway to the destination rather than relying solely on a fragmented number of individual Web sites put on-line by the trade. Indeed, customers require one-stop shopping.

The tourism destination portal site ought to be developed by the DMOs in partnership with the major market participants, through a contractual or corporate approach. This would have links from and to the Web sites of the other organizations that have business related to the destination. Partnerships are important because by building relationships with other companies the DMOs get access to their consumers while helping those companies expand their product offerings. Moreover, the development of Web sites by main travel intermediary players is also important as these may let the browser/visitor have access to destination information provided by the DMOs' sites and to compare the services offered by competing destinations in order to make his/her travel decision.

A portal site for marketing tourism destinations should provide information on four core areas:

1. How to get there (e.g., air travel)
2. Getting around (e.g., car rental)
3. Places to stay (e.g., hotel accommodation)
4. Things to do (e.g., places to see, dining, shopping, shows and events)

All the items should come with availability and reservation facilities. These may be provided through links to other sites such as the Hotel Reservation Network, Internet Travel Network, or the WorldRes Company. The latter is essentially a business-to-business site, in that it primarily serves other Internet companies. WorldRes provides a list of available rooms and prices at its 8,600 partner hotels to about 900 Web sites, including portals like Yahoo! and America Online, but predominantly travel sites. When a consumer visits one of those sites and makes a reservation, the transaction is reported back to WorldRes and, in turn, to the hotel that was booked. WorldRes takes a commission of between 3 percent and 10 percent of the cost of the booked room. The referring site gets up to 30 percent of the transaction fee paid by the hotel to WorldRes.

The investment bank Bear, Stearns Co. Inc. estimates hotel reservations made via the Internet will generate over $3 billion in revenues in 2002. In a recent market research study conducted by the NPD Group, 28 percent of visitors to hotel sites were found to actually book a reservation, and 84 percent of those were satisfied by the experience. Moreover, whereas it costs about 10 cents per dollar in revenue to book a reservation over the phone, a reservation booked online costs only 2 cents per dollar in revenue.

There are a number of criteria a DMO must take into account when designing its Web site. The Home Page is the destination's "storefront" on the Worldwide Web marketplace. It provides an index to the set of pages that describe the DMO and the tourism destination. The Web site should be organized into several main sections (e.g., *Content/Information*), including:

- *About the DMO*—this section may include a vision or a mission statement.
- *Tourism Products/Services*—using video-clips, audio, photos, and text to describe the benefits to the visitors of the destination's services. The Web is a great tool for market segmentation. Hence, the home page of the DMO's Web site should be utilized to immediately direct visitors to the most appropriate areas of information. An option of sending a CD-ROM through mail for less sophisticated users should be also considered. For example, a CD-ROM virtual tour of Las Vegas was created for the Las Vegas Convention & Visitors Authority (LVCVA) in conjunction with various corporate sponsors. The CD-ROM contains a vast multimedia directory featuring video clips produced by Vegas-area resorts and the LVCVA, stimulating high-resolution graphics, hot links to LVCVA member Web sites, valuable merchant discount coupons, and extensive Las Vegas destination information.
- *FAQ*—providing a list of frequently asked questions.
- *On-line Ordering*—a site must provide, or at least have links to, booking and reservation facilities. In the former situation, shopping cart software has to be available so that people can put multiple items in their cart from any number of product pages.
- *Interactive Request Form, Guest Book, or Survey*—the DMO needs to connect with its visitors. This may be accomplished by enticing potential tourists to sign the destination's Guest Book, and/or to fill out a survey. Thus the DMO captures valuable consumer information for database development and later e-mail marketing actions. Getting users to sign up on an e-mailing list is a great way to stay in touch with current and potential clients.
- *What's New*—this section is where the DMO can put updates or new copies of a newsletter.
- *Giveaways*—a site may add further value to the visitor by giving away other free products and services such as postcards, wallpaper, and screen savers.

The home page also needs graphics to look inviting. The best combination is a single, sparkling *graphic* combined with text making the overall look of the DMO's "storefront" graphically balanced, pleasing, and informative. The *background texture and/or color* used throughout the site should never overwhelm the text, but subtly complement it. The *page title* that is displayed at the top line of the Web browser is very important because it often shows up in search engines. The title should be descriptive, using keywords that people might use to find the DMO page. A small graphic at the top of each page as well as texture and colored backgrounds help to unify the Web pages.

Source: Paulo Rita, ISCTE-University of Lisbon, Portugal; *paulo.rita@iscte.pt.*

translate their information on their sites into the languages spoken by their target markets.

The Internet is an excellent medium to communicate what products are offered and the benefits of those products. However, information that is communicated should be accurate. Showing seven-year-old photos that were taken after a hotel's last renovation will not create trust with the buyer if they do not accurately represent the present condition of the hotel. Discussion with meeting planners has revealed they do not trust information received over the Internet. They view it much the same way as they view information received in an advertisement. They know the seller created it, and they are skeptical. However, once they find out through use of the product that the Internet is an accurate portrayal, then they view the Internet site as providing accurate information. When this happens they make greater use of the information and services the site provides. The Internet also provides the opportunity for interactive communication between the customer and the business. Basic principles of electronic marketing are explained in Table 16-2.

Providing Content

Professor Patti Shock states that it important to give customers a reason to come back to your site.[11] Some content that will bring customers back to the Web site include Internet specials, promotions, coupons, contests (post winner information), surveys (post results), news, links, giveaways (people love anything free), recipes, food tips, and games. A restaurant can create a "Site of the Day" award for interesting food-related sites, then archive previous winners so new visitors can view them. Restaurants can link the local movie theater listings or other events where people may go before or after they eat. The site can also invite visitors to subscribe to a weekly/monthly e-mail newsletter, in which the restaurant can announce any of the promotions being utilized. When visitors register, the company can obtain valuable demographic information and get their permission to communicate with them.

16.3 Hard Rock Café

Hard Rock Café developed its Web site to link together its different global products: Hard Rock Cafés, Hard Rock Hotels and Casinos, and Hard Rock concert venues. According to Toby Corey, president of USWeb, "The goal of the Web site was to foster a greater level of interaction with customers, offer high-profile opportunities to reach out to new customers and above all, provide an online experience every bit as enjoyable as the cafes, hotels and performance spaces themselves." Hard Rock partnered with USWeb, now part of CKS Interactive Advertising Agency, to develop the site for them. Hard Rock's site goes beyond providing information about its product. It provides content that will be useful to its target audience.[12] This content includes sweepstakes, photo galleries, free downloads of music, and daily rock industry news. Hard Rock has produced a site with content that will bring users.

Payard Patisserie & Bistro in New York provides recipes as well as photographs of plate presentations on their site. Amerigo, a chain of Italian restaurants in the southeastern United States, provides an "ask the chef" feature that archives questions and answers.[13] Hotels can include in-

Table 16-2
Three Basic Principles of Electronic Marketing

1. *Build and actively manage a customer database.* In this era of scarce customers, companies need to capture the names of and as much useful information as possible about potentially valuable prospects and customers. A rich customer database can provide the company with a strong competitive advantage. The company can search and rate different groups and individuals for their probability of responding to a given offer or highly tailored offers. A database permits a company's targeting to be superefficient.

2. *Develop a clear concept on how the company should take advantage of the Internet.* A company can develop a presence on the Internet in at least seven ways. The company can use the Internet to do research, provide information, run discussion forums, provide training, carry on on-line buying and selling (i.e., e-commerce), provide on-line auctioning or exchanging, and even deliver "bits" to customers.

The company's Web page must be appealing, relevant, and current if it is to attract repeat visits. Companies should consider using state-of-the-art graphics, sound, and video. They should add weekly news or features ("coming next week: Chef Lambert's summer barbecue recipes"). The site can be developed to provide valuable help, such as links to a map showing the location of the hotel or restaurant. Virtual Vineyard provides product expertise and a personal connoisseur to recommend choice wines, Holiday Inn books rooms over the Internet, and Chili's tells where its restaurants are located.

The company must view its Web page critically and ask a number of questions: Why would someone want to surf to our site? If I view the site using the equipment my customers use, does the site load quickly or is a customer likely to leave while they are waiting for graphics to load? What is interesting about our page? Why would someone want to return to our page? Why would someone want to advertise on our page?

3. *Be easily accessible and quick in responding to customer calls.* Customers have high and rising expectations about how quickly and adequately they should receive answers to questions and complaints sent in by phone or e-mail. Make sure the Internet user can communicate directly with the company on-line. People like to be able to communicate with other people. One advantage of the Internet is that we can communicate automatically. The computer can be programmed to book reservations, select and confirm seat assignments on airlines, and send confirmations of reservations, changes in flight plans and other information to the customer or perspective customer. However, when the user has a question that the computer cannot answer or they have a problem they would like to discuss, they should be given a phone number to call and an automatic e-mail option. Too many sites have the goal of having 100 percent electronic communication, and they do not include telephone contact information. When designing a Web site, one must not forget the customer and the importance of communicating with the customer in the method they desire. Often the preferred method for some communication is not electronic.

formation and links to destination attractions, weather information, suggestions for meeting planners, holiday and party recipes, and theme suggestions. One goal of an Internet site is to foster relationship marketing by creating a community of frequent users.

Web cameras have proven to be a popular source of content. Cheeseburger in Paradise has a loyal following among frequent visitors to Maui. Tourists to Maui make an appointment with their friends on the mainland to look at Cheeseburger's Web site at a particular time when they will appear in front of the camera waving to their friends at home.

Boston's upscale Tremont 647 has a camera in the kitchen, allowing visitors to their site to observe the food preparation. Chris Shaw of Mary's in San Diego has their "Marycam," which shows shots of people in the bar and dining room. "Sam's Cam" at Sam's Café in Tiburon, across the bay from San Francisco, shows the sunny vistas from his patio. San Francisco is often covered with a blanket of mist. Brian Wilson, the restaurant owner, says the view of the sunshine attracts people to the restaurant.[14] Caution should be used by the managers who wish to show guests in their facilities on the Web. They should check with a lawyer to understand the legal implications.

Web Site Development

A company's Web site must project its brand image. People coming to the company's site may not know anything about the company. They may have simply found the site on a search engine. Thus, the site should convey what the company is and what the company has to offer.[15] It should be easy to navigate. Users are not going to wait for graphics to load; if they take too long, they will exit. It is important to access your Web site the way that most customers will access it. If most of your customers are individual consumers, access the site from a modem. Some sites offer a choice of formats, a simple version for low-tech users and a version with enhanced graphics for those who have the technology. The site should also be organized so the users can quickly get to the information they need. Table 16-3 is a summary of the advice of Internet marketing experts regarding the design of a Web site.

Business-to-Business E-commerce

Business-to-business e-commerce accounts for the majority of Internet commerce. This is in part due to the size of business-to-business transactions and the efficiencies the Internet offers businesses. In the hospitality industry, the Internet is being used to create marketplaces where companies wanting supplies can be matched up with sellers of those supplies. The marketplaces match multiple purchasers with multiple sellers. These electronic hubs go by the name of vortexes, butterfly markets, or net market makers. In the absence of these hubs, each buyer and seller would have to first identify each other and then contact each other. This process would have to be repeated each time a transaction took place. With the electronic hub, the searching and contacting is done automatically.[16] The buyer receives the benefit of receiving offers from multiple companies, and the seller has the advantage of being linked with multiple buyers.

In addition to the marketplaces, the Internet facilitates one-to-one relationships between a buyer and a seller. Food supply companies and office supply companies use the Internet to receive orders from customers. As the Internet matures, its importance to the hospitality and travel industries will increase. The Internet has also had a significant effect on how database marketing is conducted.

Developing a Marketing Database System

To implement successful integrated direct marketing, companies must invest in a marketing database system. A marketing database is an organized collection of data about individual customers, prospects, or

Table 16-3

Tips for Managing and Developing a Web Site

- Remember people coming to your site may not know anything about the company. The site should convey the company's identity and what it offers.
- Make sure users can easily navigate through the site and can get back to the home page from every page.
- Remember your clients are coming to you for travel services. Keep graphics simple and enable your clients to move quickly through the site.
- Make sure you have a "contact us" page on your Web site. When you are contacted respond quickly, within six hours is desired, over twenty-four hours is too long. Make sure you give clients alternative ways to contact you such as toll-free phone numbers.
- Collect information and e-mail address through a "contact us" area. Ask permission to send information on specials.
- Make sure users can purchase your products over the Web. One hotel offers information on availability and pricing, but makes you call the hotel to make the reservation. To make matters worse they did not have the hotel's phone number on their site. Use automatic response mechanisms when appropriate, such as confirmations of reservations.
- Hillary Bressler states that a challenge faced by hotels is that sales leads don't trickle down from their **corporate Web sites.** A "microsite" or page linked to the corporate site to provide information about your hotel can solve this problem.
- Keep on top of the search engines to make sure your site comes up in the top listings. If you do not have the internal resources to do this, hire outside expertise.
- Keep up with new trends of communication such as wireless phones, PDAs, and other devices.

Sources: Hillary Bressler, "10 Tips to Make Your Webmarketing Click," *HSMAI Marketing Review* (Summer 2001): 30–31; Charles Hofacker, *Internet Marketing,* Austin, TX: Digital Springs, 1999; and Brad Alan Kleindl, *Strategic Electronic Marketing: Managing E-Business* (Cincinnati, OH: Southwestern College Publishing, 2001).

suspects that is accessible and actionable for such marketing purposes as lead generation, lead qualification, sale of a product or service, or maintenance of customer relationships.

Building a database involves investing in central and remote computer hardware, data-processing software, information enhancement programs, communication links, personnel to capture data, user training, design of analytical programs, and so on. The system should be user friendly and available to various departments. For example, in a hotel, reservations, sales, reception, food and beverage, accounting, and the general manager would all need access to the database. Building a database takes time and involves much cost, but when it runs properly, the selling company will achieve substantially higher marketing productivity.

Aruba, a Caribbean Island off the coast of South America, recently developed a database to track an increased inquirer conversion rate from 12 percent to 26 percent. The program, called Hug-and-Hold Inquirer Conversion and Repeat System, promotes the island with a three-issue cycle of the *Aruba Holiday Traveler.* Its advertisement aimed at tourists contains a toll-free 800 number. Callers to this number receive an information packet. In the past, 12 percent of those who called ended up

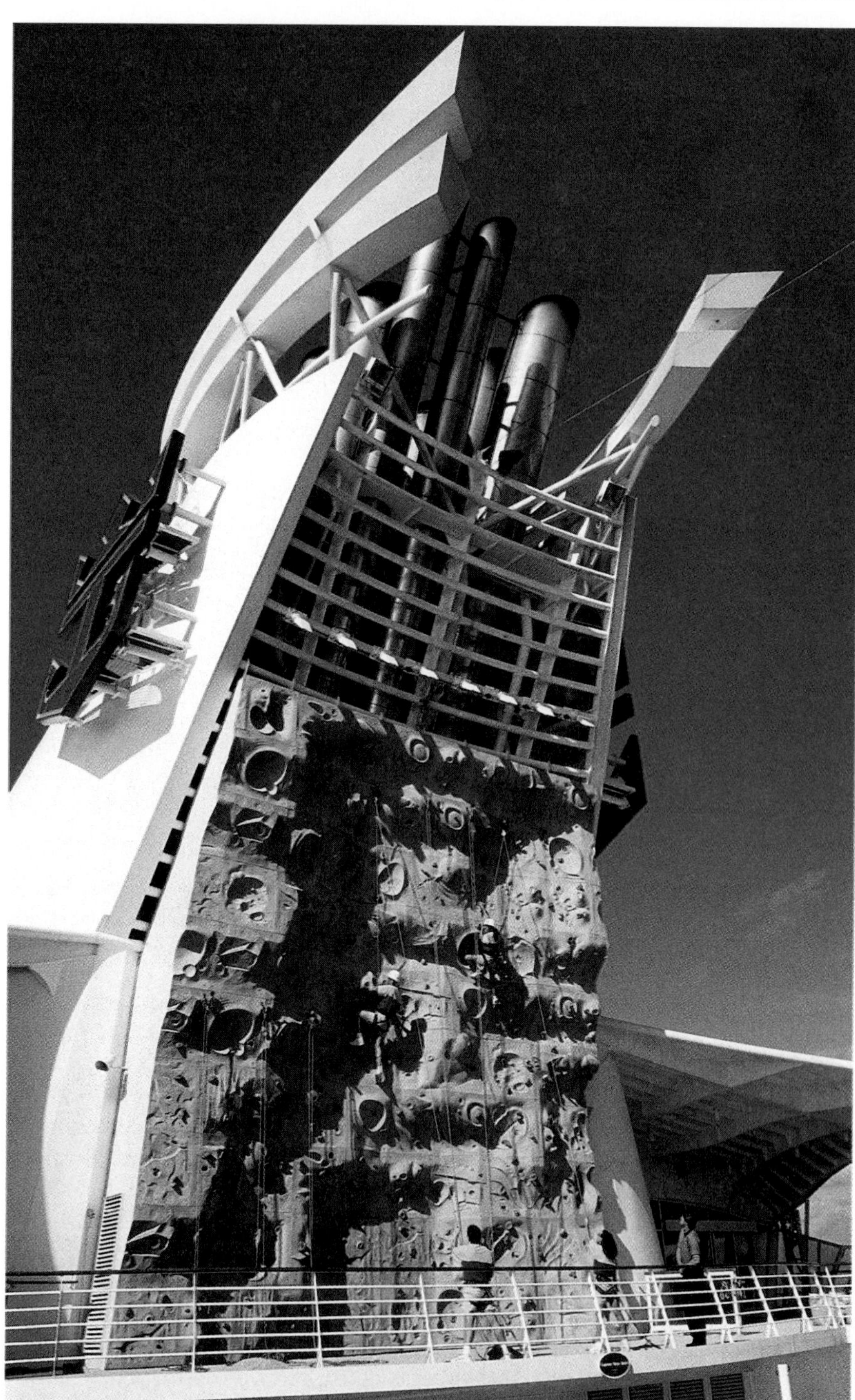

Royal Caribbean Cruise Lines keeps a customer database. By analyzing customer information, Royal Caribbean found its guests desired physical activities. Its new ships have rock-climbing walls, basketball courts, roller-blade tracks, and ice rinks. Courtesy of Royal Caribbean International.

going to Aruba. Aruba matches the Zip codes of the inquirer to a census track of income information. If the respondent is likely to earn an above-average income based on the information, the high-quality magazine *Aruba Holiday Traveler* is sent. The names of the people who receive the magazine are compared with the names of airport arrivals. The conversion rate of the inquirers who receive the magazine is 26 percent. The advertising in the magazine covers the cost of publishing and mailing.[17]

16.4 Aruba Holiday Traveler

One of the problems with database management in the hospitality industry is that a company may have a number of databases that do not talk to each other and/or they were not relational. A hotel could have a sales department database, a reservations database, an accounting database, and a front desk database. Often one or more of these databases was not integrated with the others. When this is the case, managers are not able to gain the advantage of having the information that the combined databases will provide. Today, new systems use the concept of a data warehouse. The data warehouse stores the information the company receives in a central repository of customer data.[18]

The early reservations systems were traditionally developed around individual customer files. This method was fast and efficient; however, it was impossible to relate the individual customers in order to find segmentation information. Today, companies use relational databases that allow a manager to look at relationships in the data. For example, if a resort hotel was projecting a low occupancy for the weekend after next, managers could query the database, asking for all guests who came to the resort on a weekend and lived within 250 miles. This would produce a list of guests who enjoyed the resort on weekends and could drive to the resort, thus they would not have to worry about higher last-minute air-fares. A restaurant could query the database for all persons who spent over $50 on a bottle of wine, if they wanted to develop a potential list for a special event pairing wine and food. The development of relational data warehouses has created a powerful marketing tool.

Once the data are housed in a warehouse they can be mined. Data mining is the exploration and analysis of a database by automatic or semi-automatic means to discover patterns or rules.[19] It is the process of automating information discovery.[20] Data mining is used to predict which customers are most likely to respond to an offer, to segment a market, and to identify a company's most loyal customers. Data mining software uses a variety of methods, including regression analyses and neural networks to find the best solution. One of the major benefits of data mining is that it is not limited to the relationships that the marketing manager may think exists, it explores all relationships with a variety of techniques. Data mining has increased the effectiveness and efficiency of direct marketing in the hospitality and travel industries.

Managers need to make sure the data in the databases are clean. This means there are no errors in the data. Errors are usually as a result of data entry. It is important that everyone using the database understand the importance of accurate data. For example, a guest whose last name is Smith and is entered into the database as Smyth will now have two files. The resort will not know her real value, because it is divided between the two files. If the resort sends direct mail, she could receive two pieces, one

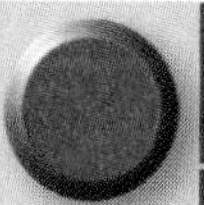

Marketing Highlight 16-2

Using Your Database for Customer Research: Defining the Power of Your Loyal Customers

Saunders Hotel Group (SHG) is nationally recognized for its expertise as owners and operators of landmark hotels in Boston, Connecticut, and Florida. The key to SHG's success is five decades of direct, hands-on experience in all areas of hospitality management. Additionally, SHG approaches new projects on an individual basis, customizing solutions in accordance with each hotel's unique situation.

From its very first foray into hotel ownership in 1936, Boston's Broadway Hotel, to its most recent, The Boston Park Plaza Hotel & Towers, SHG has taken calculated risks and won. But SHG cannot be accused of living in the past. Its tradition of industry "firsts" continues in both practical and emotional arenas. From the pioneering outsourcing of restaurant operations, Café Budapest, Legal Sea Food, and Anago, to launching of the industry's most comprehensive ecological program, SHG has remained at the forefront of innovation. As an innovator, SHG recently installed a state-of-the-art database marketing system, DM1.

The Lenox Upgrades Its Database Software to Increase Customer Loyalty. SHG worked with Group 1 Software to create a data warehouse solution to store its customer information. The system was installed at SHG's boutique hotel in Boston, The Lenox. The information stored in the system allows The Lenox to better serve its existing customers and market more effectively to new customers. Like The Lenox, more companies are recognizing the importance of retaining current customers.

The Lenox Researches the Needs of Its Customers. The management at The Lenox realized the importance retaining loyal customers. One of the first uses of their database was to find out how they could better serve their existing customers. This two-step process involved focus groups and survey research.

To ensure the members of the focus groups were important customers, SHG used its database to select customers that would be invited to the focus groups. This allowed them to specify which characteristics the focus group participants would possess. A problem with focus groups can arise when the members are recruited from a research supplier's list. These are often people who enjoy participating in focus groups, but do not have the desired characteristics. Using your database to recruit focus group members gives you control over who is participating in the focus group. This is important because it costs $50–$100 to recruit focus group participants, and incentives can add a similar amount. Thus, for each participant $150 is invested. You want to make sure the participants are representative of the segment you are interested in. Using your own list will accomplish this, if your data are accurate.

The following are examples of some types of information the focus groups produced. When asked to think about times they had received outstanding service at a hotel, one participant stated, "While planning a last-minute trip, I found the town's hotel rooms were booked, but somehow the hotel found me a room. Actions like this increase my loyalty to the hotel." Several members of the focus group indicated they are more particular when traveling for pleasure than when they are traveling for business purposes. As one customer put it, "Especially if I were here on a pleasure trip with my wife. That whole thought of being here for pleasure means that it has to be really nice. We are here for a "big smile" and to really enjoy this experience. With business, I can put up with an aggravation or two. Pleasure, I won't stand for a single one. Because that destroys this moment that I am trying to create with the person I'm with."

Business travelers have frequently mentioned they want a hassle-free stay. The moderator asked members of the focus group what a hassle-free stay is. One focus group participant responded, "You just want it hassle-free, where you go into the room and everything works. You don't have to spend time with the staff getting the basic things you need." Another participant commented, "In a hotel where the experience is hassle-free, the staff has the attitude that 'my job is your pleasure.'"

Focus group members were asked what would increase their loyalty. One responded that he stayed at Intercontinental Hotel in Bali and there were fresh flowers in the room. Another commented that small gifts given by management, once in a while, to let him know his business was appreciated increased his loyalty to a hotel. One customer stated that he was traveling with his wife, celebrating his birthday. The hotel gave him a dinner in their upscale dining room and presented him with a birthday cake at the end of the meal. He said that was an incredible experience for both he and his wife, particularly as he did not tell anyone at the hotel it was his birthday.

The focus groups at The Lenox allowed management to have in-depth conversations with their customers. The outcome of the focus groups was a better understanding of some of the hotel's features that are important to the customers and of the customers' service expectations. This information helped develop specific questions for a survey instrument. One of the limitations of a focus group is it only represents the views of a small number of people. A survey going to a larger group will either confirm or disconfirm that the opinions of the focus group are shared by a large segment of customers.

The Lenox Used Its Database to Generate Mailing Lists for Customer Surveys. Another one of the uses of a database is to select customers for satisfaction studies. Again, using your own database allows you to select the characteristics of who receives the survey. Satisfaction studies give the company a good understanding of how it is performing and what can be done to improve customer loyalty. These studies should be done from once every quarter to once every year. The Lenox mailed out 1,900 surveys, resulting in 550 completed surveys. From the survey data, The Lenox was able to determine what the most important attributes were for business pleasure travelers; who their competition was, as defined by their customers; and which chains their customers preferred for business travel and pleasure travel. Knowing who your competition is and how you are positioned against the competition is vital information for any company. Too often management chooses who their competition is, forgetting it is the customer who really determines the competition.

Summary of What The Lenox Learned. In today's competitive environment, it is important to have detailed information on your customers. Surveys are a good way of gaining this information. Using a customer database allows managers to select the characteristic of specific segments they are interested in, and allows management of the list so the same customers are not always being surveyed.

SHG partnering with Group 1's marketing research division provides an example of how companies can develop relationships with external suppliers to provide professional assistance on an as-needed basis. In this case, Group 1 provided the focus group moderator, developed the questionnaire, analyzed the data, and provided SHG with a report interpreting the results of the study. SHG gained the advantages of a full-service marketing department, without having the yearly overhead. Companies are realizing the benefits of having relationships with specialists.

Through its customer survey, The Lenox was able to learn who their competitors are, as defined by their customers. They could see the importance of different attributes to leisure and business travelers. They established benchmark scores to serve as service targets for the next period. Management learned specific actions that could be done to increase customer loyalty. They knew the importance and cost of these actions, allowing them to effectively use their assets. They also gained information that could be shared with supervisors and staff as they implemented different service improvement programs.

Note: The authors wish to thank Shiang-Lih Chen McCain, PhD, for her help in developing this marketing highlight.

under both names. This shows her that the resort does not really know her because they think she is two separate people. To be effective duplicate files have to be combined, and addresses must be accurate. A clean database starts with accurate entry. There are also software packages that can identify potential duplicate files and check addresses.

Sometimes employees will use fields in the database for their own personal notes. Training the employees in the use and importance of the database will correct this problem. For example, a desk clerk typed under the guest's name in the address file, "This guy is a jerk." He wanted to alert the other employees that the guest had the potential of creating problems. What the clerk did not realize is the address was used for direct mail. You can imagine the response the guest had when he received a letter from the hotel addressed to him with "This guy is a jerk" under his name. Employee training is a critical part of an effective database system.

Companies cannot always get all the information they need on their customers. For example, information that will give some information on a person's lifestyle is often difficult to collect directly from customers. To help management understand their best customer groups, they can enhance the data in their database by purchasing information on their customers. Acxiom, R. L. Polk, National Demographics, Database America, Infobase, and Donnelley Marketing are some of the companies that gather publicly available information on people. Database marketers can submit a list of their customers to one of these companies who will match these customers with files in their database and add the desired information. This information can include the number of children living at home, type of housing, and type of car. For database marketers one of the uses of data enhancement is to predict who is likely to want the services offered. The marketer will try to develop a more complete profile of best customers and then purchase mailing lists with the same profile. Determining the information that will be the most useful for enhancement is achieved by testing different models. When investigating how to enhance files, one usually takes a sample from the database and then tests the enhanced data. The response from direct marketing efforts will determine if the enhanced profiles provided a higher response rate than the unenhanced profile.

Using a Database to Create a Competitive Advantage

If you were a customer, why would you want to be on your database? By answering this question, you find out whether your database has a strategic focus or is mainly used for tactical purposes.[21] Most marketers use their database tactically. For example, one of the most frequent uses of database marketing is to use it with direct marketing. Direct marketing campaigns often target recent customers, inviting them to return or offering incentives, as well as encouraging loyal customers to come during soft periods. There is nothing wrong with this use of database marketing; in fact it often produces worthwhile results. However, if this is the only use of database marketing, much of the power of database marketing will be untapped.

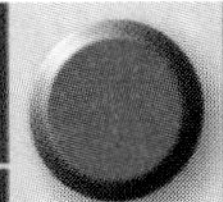

Marketing Highlight 16-3

Gazelle Systems Brings Database Marketing to Restaurants

Charlotte Bogardus, a former marketing executive for Starbucks Coffee Company, noticed that the hospitality industry was not utilizing databases to manage customer relationships. After working as a marketing consultant to Bruegger's Bagel Bakeries, Applebee's Neighborhood Restaurants, Saunders Hotel Systems, and other food service operations, she decided to start a company that would enable the food service industry to effectively use customer data. She started Gazelle Systems, which offers data collection, data warehousing, and knowledge management tools specifically designed to fit the needs of the food service industry.

One of the products is Restaurant Data Exchange (RDX), produced in a partnership with Information Resources. Information Resources is one of the leading providers of scanner based business solutions to the beverage industry. Charlotte Bogardus states, "Other industries, like the supermarket industry, have been quicker to unearth the information critical to boosting profits effectively. Defining and analyzing key performance metrics is critical to restaurant survival. We've developed a technology that captures timely POS [point-of-sale] data detail via the Web while protecting the privacy of each chain's essential customer information. We're excited to help participating members hone in on the knowledge they need to reach out to customers."

RDX allows chains to compare metrics across restaurants in the chain as well as metrics for individual units. The peer-to-peer comparisons include rating to other restaurants in the chain, the chain as a whole, and other restaurants with similar concepts and guest-check category. Some of the specific metrics available include the churn rate and revenue per available seat.

The churn rate compares the number of customers lost with those gained. As we mentioned in Chapter 11, restaurants will lose customers. Some customers move out of the area, and people make mistakes. Thus, it is inevitable that a company loses customers. However, well-managed restaurants can reduce the number of customers lost. Bogardus says that casual restaurants will normally loose 13–18 percent of its customers per year. A rate above 20 percent is an indication there are problems with the restaurant. The "churn rate" chart shows both the number of customers gained and the number lost.

Revenue per available seat (REVPSH) is similar to REVPAR in hotels. One of the most common restaurant metrics is average check. However, like average rate in a hotel, average check means little unless we have information about demand. One way of measuring demand in a restaurant is turnover, or how many times a seat is filled per time period. For example a 200-seat restaurant that serves 500 people per day has a turnover of 2.5 (500/200). If the restaurant has a check average of \$20, the REVPSH will be \$50 (2.5 × \$20). REVPSH can help managers try to increase their overall revenue by looking at both demand and check average.

Gazelle Systems also uses reverse appending, a process where credit card records can be matched with addresses, demographics, and psychographic information. About 60 percent of the customers can be identified through reverse appending. To protect the customer's privacy, no purchases other than those at the restaurant are given. This information is used to develop customer profiles and high-yield marketing programs. The profiles of the diners can also be matched with profiles of complimentary programs. For example, in one restaurant customers' profiles were similar to the profile of a premium brand of Scotch. The maker of the Scotch and the restaurant teamed up for a joint promotion. The restaurant gained promotional dollars from the manufacturer, the customers benefited from receiving benefits of the promotion, and the premium-brand Scotch company gained access to the restaurant's customers.

Louise's Trattoria is a chain of Italian restaurants located mostly in California. Gazelle defined their customers as "often female, interested in a healthy lifestyle, fine wines, foreign travel, and likely to try new things on the menu." Based on the profile provided by Gazelle, they remodeled their restaurants to have a more contemporary look. They also dropped half of their current menu items and added more eclectic items. One of the items they added, barbecued chicken on chopped salad, became one of their best sellers. Through the churn report, they were able to notice that two of their restaurants had almost all repeat customers; the restaurants were not attracting new customers. They developed marketing campaigns to initiate trial by new customers.

Many businesses outside of the hospitality industry have realized the importance of having and using customer information. Gazelle Systems has specialized in applying database marketing to the hospitality industry.

Let us return to the original question: Why would a customer want to be on your database? Vail Associates, operators of skiing facilities, are an example of what can happen when you provide answers to this question. They knew their customers wanted a hassle-free experience, and they wanted to maximize their time on the slopes. Vail Associates set about implementing a database system that would give their customers the experience they desired. If you rented skis at Vail Associates in the past, they have your information on file. Renting skis a second time then becomes a hassle-free experience. It didn't use to be that way. Everyone was asked for their boot size, what type of skis they wanted, and a number of other questions. Guests often spent a good deal of time waiting in line, instead of skiing. Now, if you are staying in one of Vail Associates's lodges, they will deliver the skis to the lodge, so they are ready when the guests arrive. The guests avoid the lines and the questions! Their upscale dining rooms are usually booked on weekends; if a lodging customer usually dines in one of these restaurants, the reservationist is prompted to ask if they would like to make a restaurant reservation when they book their room to avoid disappointment later.

These are just a few of the ways Vail Associates uses its database system to provide a better experience for its customers. Harvard Business School has produced a video entitled "Expanding Value: Building Loyalty" that which describes Vail Associates's database marketing in detail. By using its database strategically, Vail Associates has created a competitive advantage. It is providing its customers with a better product, one that offers more benefits than the competitors' products. [22]

Several other examples of strategic databases are provided by Ritz Carlton and Brennan's restaurant. Ritz Carlton's database receives input from the front-line employees. They update the database based on information received from guests during the normal course of their work activities. For example, if a room service waiter finds out that a guest likes a certain type of mineral water, the mineral water is placed in the guest's refrigerator. The database is also used for service recovery. If a guest has

Marketing Highlight 16-4

Manhattan East Suite Hotels Gives Customers What They Want before They Ask

"We've always given our customers what they want. Now we know what they want before they ask." This is how Priscilla Hurley, director of advertising for Manhattan East Suite Hotels, describes their new database, Marketing and Guest Information Center (MAGIC).

Manhattan East Suite Hotels is a collection of ten family-owned hotels in Manhattan, ranging in size from 80 to 522 rooms. Robert Tully, chief marketing officer for Manhattan East Suite Hotels, states, "In 1997 we merged our reservation systems into one reservation center for the company. The benefits were significant, however this took guest information away from the individual properties. The management of Manhattan East set out to develop a new database system to overcome this shortcoming." Tully states the new database had to perform three functions. First, repeat guests of Manhattan East had to be able to be recognized at all of the company's ten properties. Second, the information in the database had allowed Manhattan East to customize the stay for the guest. Finally, the database had to be clean. The hotel company did not want to have multiple records for the same guest.

The hotel selected relational database software developed by Group 1. The cost of the project including software, labor, and new hardware and consulting fees was over $500,000. The new database was fully integrated into their existing systems, giving each property full guest history information. The system cleansed the data and also was able to correct erroneous addresses and reimport them back into the system. Files from guests who had stayed at one of the hotels during the last two years were cleansed and entered into the database. By the end of the first year, 80 percent of Manhattan East's guests were being entered into the system, and 60 percent of these had individual preferences noted in their file.

In order to get the employees to realize the importance of entering accurate information, Manhattan East developed an incentive program for its employees, encouraging them to enter accurate data. Prizes included a car and trips to Walt Disney World.

The investment in the database system quickly began to pay off. Guest loyalty increased, through the ability to recognize repeat guests at all of the hotels. Customer satisfaction increased, and service ratings also increased. The system also allowed Manhattan East to use direct mail effectively. One promotion generated over $200,000 in incremental business, and a second promotion added an additional $50,000.

One of the promotions gave past guests a choice of free parking, a full breakfast for two, 1,000 airline miles, or $20 off of their room rate. The author received a 2.6 percent response rate. After the promotion Hurly began to analyze the results to see who participated in the program and what they requested.

Glenda Maldonado, front office manager at the Eastgate Tower, says, "A simple thank you for remembering is what it is all about." With MAGIC the hotel now can remember if a guest likes a certain newspaper, a specific type of pillow, or their room cleaned at a certain time of the day. This remembering creates loyalty, and loyalty creates increased profits.

Manhattan Suites provides a good example of the planning and implementation of a database by a hotel company. The hotel first decided what it wanted to achieve from a database. They then planned a system that would provide what they wanted. They trained their employees on the use of the system and the importance of data input. Finally, they used the information in the database to better serve their guests.

Sources: Joan Marsan, "Magical Marketing," *Hotels*, (October 1999), reprint; Robert C. Tully, "Risks and Rewards of Business Intelligence," *DM Review* (November 2000), reprint.

encountered a problem, all departments in the hotel are notified, and everyone works to regain the guest's confidence and loyalty. Brennan's in Houston developed a database that included the customer's favorite table, captain, and wine. This information is used to provide the guest with a great experience. These companies, like Vail Associates, have used their database to create a competitive advantage. Companies who use a database to provide the guest with a better experience are gaining a major benefit from their database. They are creating a competitive advantage based on the knowledge of their customers. They know why a customer would like to be part of their database. They know what the customer likes and dislikes and which messages will be relevant. One of the uses of a database is to develop contact lists for direct marketing. No direct marketing campaign can be successful if the list is poor. Thus, lists are a critical component of a successful direct marketing campaign.[23] In conclusion, companies need to provide benefits to customers for being in their database.

Direct Marketing

Jim Mastrangelo, director of sales, Ramada, states, "I've always been a strong believer in direct-mail advertising. Direct-mail advertising plays a very important part in the success of a hotel's marketing program. It's an excellent balance to outside sales calls and telephone solicitation. It presents your product to a client without the expense of a personal sales call. In addition, you're able to solicit many more clients than you could solicit individually through direct mail."[24]

The term **direct marketing** has taken on new meanings over the years. Originally, it was simply a form of marketing in which products or services moved from the producer to consumer without an intermediate channel of distribution. In this sense, companies that use salespeople are using direct marketing. As the telephone and other media came into heavy use to promote offers directly to customers, direct marketing was redefined by the Direct Marketing Association (DMA): Direct marketing is an interactive system of marketing that uses one or more advertising media to affect a measurable response and/or transaction at any location. In this definition, the emphasis is on marketing undertaken to obtain a measurable response, typically an order from a customer. Because of the nature of the transaction, it can also be called direct-order marketing.

Today, many users of direct marketing visualize it as playing a broader role, which can be called direct-relationship marketing.[25] These direct marketers use direct-response advertising media to make a sale and learn about a customer whose name and profile are entered in a **customer database,** which is used to build a continuing and enriching relationship. The emphasis is on building preferred customer relationships. Airlines, hotels, and others are building strong customer relationships through award programs and are using their customer database to match their offers more carefully to individual customers. They are approaching a stage where offers are sent only to those customers and prospects most able, willing, and ready to buy the product. To the extent that they succeed, higher response rates to promotions will be gained. Marriott Hotels, Resorts & Suites now claims to have the largest hotel database in the world, due to the Honored Guests Incentive program.[26]

The following examples illustrate ways in which the hospitality and travel industries are using direct marketing. Continental Airlines sent its OnePass members a coupon for a $198 child's round-trip ticket between any two cities that Continental serves in the contiguous United States. American Express offered its members in Houston a discount coupon to Birraporetti's restaurant. The San Diego Convention and Visitors Bureau placed an advertisement in *Travel Weekly,* offering a free "Travel Planner's Guide" to interested travel agents and meeting planners.

Ski Limited, which operates the Killington and Mt. Snow resorts in Vermont and Bear Mountain resort in California, has a database that tracks 2.5 million skiers and adds 250,000 skiers a year. The information includes home addresses, level of skiing ability, and past skiing expenditures. Ski Limited uses this information to determine where skiers come from, when they ski, and what level of services they desire at a resort. This allows the company to promote events aimed at certain segments, such as an amateur race for New York City skiers. In one promotion, 90,000 midweek lift ticket discount cards were mailed to skiers who lived at least three car-hours away and normally came to the resort only on weekends. This promotion had a great deal to do with changing ski days so that 50 percent of the company's revenues now come from midweek customers.[27]

Reasons for Growth of Direct Marketing

There are several reasons for the growth of direct marketing. Direct marketing allows **precision targeting.** A manager promoting a dinner featuring a variety of wines can send a mailing to customers who have purchased a bottle of wine in the restaurant costing more than $50 during the last six months. In a properly targeted and executed direct-marketing program, response rates of 10 percent to 20 percent are achievable. Thus it is possible to get from 50 to 100 sales from a list of 500 qualified names. Normally, one might expect this kind of response after contacting 2,000 potential customers.

Personalization is another advantage of direct marketing. Personalization can be expressed in several ways, for example, by personalizing the offer to fit the needs of the target market. This could be as simple as recognizing an interest that a restaurant's customers have in fine wines. Hotels can also develop unique offers directed at individuals, such as offering a special weekend package in celebration of a client's wedding anniversary. McDonald's, Burger King, and other fast-food restaurants develop birthday clubs and send reminder notices to the child's parents before the birthday, offering their restaurant as a location for the child's birthday party. In the last two examples, timing, another advantage of direct mail, helped to personalize the message. The manager can send the message before a person's birthday or anniversary or when a particular company will be planning its next sales meeting. The message will reach the client at the right moment.

16.5 McDonald's
Burger King

Direct marketing permits **privacy** because the direct marketer's offer and strategy are not visible to competitors. Continental Airline's $198 children's offer is not as likely to be matched by the competition, because it was not announced publicly. By using direct marketing in this way, Continental can sell inventory at a discount without starting a price war. Offers made by airlines to their frequent flyers often call for immediate action. In another instance, Continental offered up to $75 off tickets purchased within two weeks. Direct marketing is an excellent way to create immediate results. In periods of low demand, companies can target known customers to produce quick results.

The time-share resort Eagles Nest located in southwest Florida was a newly opened property coming into the summer or trough season. The management of Eagles Nest wanted to introduce the property to residents within 300 miles and fill rooms in the slack period. A New York list broker provided fifteen lists of upscale residents within the 300-mile limit. It was decided to conduct a test market on no more than 20 percent of the total list. Following the test market, a rollout of the remaining 80 percent would be undertaken. A direct mailing was designed that included a letter describing Eagles Nest and offering a great introductory price and a second envelope. This envelope was closed with a seal that said, "Don't open this till you read the letter."

This creative use of reverse psychology apparently worked in much the same way as telling a small child to stay out of the cookie jar. Inside the sealed envelope were six certificates. Five were redeemable for discounts or gift offerings, such as a free drink. The sixth was a return postage-paid reservation card. The results of this campaign amazed everyone. Eagles Nest received sufficient reservations from the test market that a rollout was unnecessary. Despite the fact that many fine Florida resorts offer summer specials, Eagles Nest filled up.[28]

Members of the casino industry such as Bally's of Atlantic City use direct marketing for premium player promotion and for the intermediaries known as junket reps who bring premium players to a casino. Casinos can and do direct special promotions to related junket reps that consistently provide profitable customers for the casino.

Another benefit of direct marketing is measurability. In Chapter 14 we quoted John Wanamaker: "I know half of my advertising is wasted, but I don't know which half." Direct marketing can be measured. If John Wanamaker had used direct marketing, he would have known if he was wasting his money or making a good investment. A manager can track the response to a particular direct-marketing campaign and usually determine the revenue that it produced.

Direct-marketing efforts may be measured in three ways: (1) the number of inquiries generated, (2) the ratio of conversions realized from inquiries generated, and (3) communication impact.[29]

Direct-marketing tools are expanding today with the emergence of fax machines and e-mail. Computer-driven communication offers considerable promise as an advertising and sales vehicle. Many companies now communicate directly to key customers through e-mail.

Telemarketing

One form of direct marketing that combines aspects of advertising, marketing research, and personal sales is telemarketing. Telemarketing employs the use of the telephone to reach customers or prospective customers. Skilled telemarketers employ careful time scheduling and tracking systems for calls that require callbacks. They also use role-playing to practice how they will react to various questions and objections that they are likely to encounter.

Experienced telemarketers carefully study times that are best to call. They study response rates, such as uncompleted calls and cooperative call responses. It is suggested the optimum times for conducting business-to-business telemarketing are after 10:00 A.M. and between 2:00 and 5:00 P.M. except for Monday mornings and Friday afternoons, which are undesirable calling times.[30]

E-mail

Two electronic forms of direct marketing media are e-mail and CDs. E-mail received a boost in popularity among direct marketers after the terrorist attacks of September 11, 2001, and the subsequent anthrax scare with regular mail. The spending on e-mail is expected to increase from $1 billion in 2001 to $9.4 billion in 2006. One of the problems with e-mail is the low cost of sending e-mails, which results in users receiving a lot of unwanted e-mails. The average e-mail user receives about 700 unsolicited messages a year, and this figure is expected to increase to 1,400 by 2006.[31] The result is that more and more e-mail goes unopened, and gaining permission to send someone an e-mail is becoming more important.

Judd Goldfeder, president of the customer connection, claims 50 percent of e-mails sent to restaurant customers by his clients are opened. This is because these e-mails provide the customer with useful information, they are sent to customers who feel they have an affiliation to the restaurant, and there is an opt-out option for people who do not want to receive future e-mails.[32] Janet Logan, an e-mail marketing expert, has these suggestions for effective e-mail marketing. Make the e-mail event-driven and related to events that will be of interest to the person receiving the e-mail.[33] For example, a person who has expressed interest in a Caribbean cruise will receive an e-mail on a Caribbean cruise promotion or a guest who likes jazz receives information on a jazz brunch. She also suggested integrating e-mail with Web marketing, as when an inquiry about a skiing vacation in the Alps on the Web can trigger a request to send the inquirer information ski packages. E-mails can include Web links, allowing the receiver to go directly to a Web site to receive more information. Travel wholesalers often send travel agents messages about promotions with a link to their Web site. This reduces the size of the e-mail, and allows the agent to get the detailed information they will need to sell the travel package. E-mail marketing can be both low cost and effective. John Martin provides this checklist to make sure e-mails are effective:

- The greeting should be personalized and other persons being sent the same message should not be listed.
- The name of the company sending the message is identified. When an outside supplier is sending the e-mail, their name may be listed. In this case it is important that the organization sponsoring the e-mail has its name listed before the supplier.

- The subject needs to be relevant to the reader.
- E-mails need to be short. The best e-mails use no more than sixty-five characters per line. Some browsers will break lines longer than this, creating a formatting problem.
- Text message is the preferred format because some browsers cannot accept enhanced HTML messages.[34]

CDs

CDs, both full-size and miniature CDs about the size of a business card, are replacing color brochures as a marketing communication. One of the advantages of using a CD is that it is small, making it inexpensive to mail and easy to take home from a trade show. Another advantage is the CD can have links to the company's Web site, directing prospective customers to parts of the site that will be useful for them. Using a full-size CD allows music to be incorporated into the promotional piece. The Broadmoor Hotel and Princess Cruises are two companies that use this type of CD. Princess features two videos on their CD, promoting their Alaska cruises. The first video shows the incredible sights a passenger will

Red Lobster uses a miniature CD housed in an attractive folder to recruit employees. Courtesy of Red Lobster.

see on an Alaskan cruise. The second video features the benefits of a Princess cruise. The songs on the CD have an Alaskan theme.

Companies are also using this technology to market to internal customers. Pappas Restaurants of Houston and Red Lobster restaurants are examples of companies that use CDs to recruit employees. Red Lobster's CD contains a video as well as four informational sections entitled About Red Lobster, Management Opportunities, What's in It for Me, and Contact Us. The Contact Us section provides the option of e-mailing, faxing, or mailing your resume to Red Lobster. The e-mail option provides a link to Red Lobster's e-mail address, and the page also includes a link to its Web site. Electronic forms of direct marketing, such as CDs and e-mail, should increase in popularity as technology available to Internet users and costs of printing increases.

Direct Marketing Builds Relationships

Direct marketing is an important tool in customer relationship management (CRM) programs. CRM is a name commonly given to loyalty programs or relationship-marketing programs that make use of technology. Today, airlines, hotels, travel agents, restaurants, and rental car companies operate in very competitive markets. The major way to grow market share is to steal it from the competition. Direct marketing allows companies to develop a strong relationship with their customers, which helps prevent them from switching to competitors. Hotel frequency programs offer their members special rates, upgrades based on availability, special amenities, their own floors, and often their own lounge with complimentary beverages. Airlines develop special offers for their frequent flyers. The general manager of a hotel often invites regular guests to an evening cocktail party. Managers recognize that spending money developing loyalty among current customers can be more effective than spending money trying to develop new guests. Studies have shown that it costs four to seven times as much to bring in a new customer as it does to maintain an existing one.

Latour Management of Wichita operates four restaurants in Wichita, Kansas. They sent 16,000 postcards to area residences, using a mailing list that profiled current customers in terms of postal code and income. The card offered a free dinner at one of Latour's restaurants if the recipient dined at the other three. The card featured names of each restaurant and a space for a signature by each restaurant certifying that the diner had purchased a meal. When the diner had three signatures, a free meal was available at the fourth restaurant. Diners had to turn in their cards to receive the free meal. Thus Latour could update its database using the address label on the card.

Another benefit of the promotion was that it exposed customers of one restaurant to others in the chain. During the first ten days of the campaign, the restaurants signed 500 cards accounting for 1,000 meals.[35]

Mauna Kea resort villas of Hawaii had a very real need to develop relationship marketing with prospective customers. After all, they were selling vacation villas for over $1 million each. Obviously, advertisements in most media would be inappropriate or too expensive. Mauna Kea developed a three-stage direct-mail program aimed at frequent visitors. During stage 1, a high-quality Japanese lounge jacket and a letter were sent free of charge to each prospect. In stage 2 a beautiful conch shell and another letter were sent. Stage 3 occurred when the guests arrived at Mauna Kea and reached their rooms. A third letter was placed conspicuously next to a free bottle of champagne. The result was a 40 percent lead generation response.[36]

Development of Integrated Direct Marketing

Most direct marketers rely on a single advertising vehicle and a one-shot effort to reach and sell a prospect. A one-time mailing offering a weekend package at a hotel is an example of a single-vehicle, single-stage campaign. A single-vehicle, multiple-stage campaign would involve sending successive mailings to a prospect to trigger purchases. For example, restaurants may send four notices to a household to entice the household to try the restaurant. As described previously, Mauna Kea resort villas used a three-stage campaign.

A more powerful approach is to execute a multiple-vehicle, multiple-stage campaign. This technique is known as integrated direct marketing (IDM).[37] Consider the following sequence:

Paid ad with a response channel → Direct mail mechanism → Outbound telemarketing → Face-to-face sales call

The paid ad creates product awareness and stimulates inquiries. The company then sends direct mail to those who inquire. Within forty-eight to seventy-two hours following mail receipt, the company phones, seeking an order. Some prospects will place an order; others might request a face-to-face sales call. Even if the prospect is not ready to buy, there is ongoing communication. This use of response compression, whereby multiple media are deployed within a tightly defined time frame, increases impact and awareness of the message. The underlying idea is to deploy select media with precise timing to generate greater incremental sales while offsetting incremental costs. A direct-mail piece alone may generate only a 2 percent response, but it is possible to generate responses of 12 percent or more using integrated direct marketing.[38]

The Delta Chelsea Inn of Toronto initiated an $80 million renovation program, the largest Canadian hotel building project in eighteen years. Management wished to reposition the Chelsea as offering "value on a grand scale." An integrated marketing program was selected to meet this objective using direct sales, media advertising to the general public and the trade, public relations programs, trade shows, and internal promotion. As a result, the Chelsea was able to maintain its market-share position in occupancy and narrow the gap between itself and major competitors.[39]

Sprecher/Barrett/Bertalot and Company developed an integrated direct marketing campaign for Cleveland. The response mechanism is an 800 number that potential visitors can call to get a free "Cleveland Card." The card offers discounts at major hotels and tourist attractions in the Cleveland area. The promotion was advertised in Detroit, Pittsburgh, and Cleveland. The advertising media consisted of a combination of television and regional newspapers. During the first quarter of 1995, Cleveland received 70,000 visitor information requests, more than the total for all of 1994.[40]

Key Terms

Corporate Web site Web sites that seek to build customer goodwill and to supplement other sales channels rather than to sell the company's products directly.

Customer database An organized collection of comprehensive data about individual customers or prospects, including geographic, demographic, psychographic, and behavioral data.

Data warehouse A central repository of an organization's customer information.

Direct-mail marketing Direct marketing through single mailings that include letters, ads, samples, foldouts, and other "salespeople with wings" sent to prospects on mailing lists.

Direct marketing Direct communications with carefully targeted individual consumers to obtain an immediate response and cultivate lasting customer relationships.

Electronic commerce (e-commerce) The general term for a buying and selling process that is supported by electronic means.

Extranet A computer network connecting a supplier and its customers.

Integrated direct marketing Direct-marketing campaigns that use multiple vehicles and multiple stages to improve response rates and profits.

Internet The vast and burgeoning global web of computer networks with no central management or ownership.

Intranet A computer network connecting people with an organization.

Marketing Web site Web sites designed to engage consumers in an interaction that will move them closer to a purchase or other marketing outcome.

Chapter Review

I. **Internet Marketing.** The Internet represents an untapped opportunity for many companies. It is not only useful as a sales outlet, but it also provides a medium for communication between a company and its customers.

1) **Sales.** One of the advantages of the Internet as a sales channel is the customer does the work.

2) **Communication.** Web sites have the chance to communicate information to a number of different segments. The home page can provide information targeted to reach a number of different audiences.

3) **Providing content.** It is important to give customers a reason to come back to your site by providing useful content.

4) **Web site development.** The site should also be organized so the users can quickly get to the information they need and project an image that supports the product or brand. See Table 16-2.

II. Developing a Marketing Database System. A marketing database is an organized collection of data about individual customers, prospects, or suspects that is accessible and actionable for such marketing purposes as lead generation, lead qualification, sale of a product or service, or maintenance of customer relationships.

1) **Why would a customer want to be on your database?** If you were a customer, why would you want to be on your database? By answering this question, you find out whether your database has a strategic focus or is mainly used for tactical purposes.

III. Direct Marketing. Direct marketing is an interactive system of marketing that uses one or more advertising media to affect a measurable response and/or transaction at any location.

1) **Reasons for the growth of direct marketing**

a) **Precision marketing.**

b) **Personalization.** Personalizing offers to fit the target market, and timing offers to fit the needs of the consumer, such as offers associated with a birthday.

c) **Privacy.** The offer is not visible to competitors.

d) **Immediate results.**

e) **Measurability.**

2) **Telemarketing.** Telemarketing is a form of direct marketing that combines aspects of advertising, marketing research, and personal sales.

3) **E-mail.** E-mail marketing can be both low cost and effective.

4) **CDs.** CDs, both full-size and miniature CDs about the size of a business card, are replacing color brochures as a marketing communication.

5) **Relationship marketing.** Direct marketing can be used to develop a relationship with customers. It costs four to seven times as much to create a customer as it does to maintain a customer.

6) **Integrated direct marketing.** Integrated direct marketing is a more powerful approach to direct marketing through a multiple-vehicle, multiple-stage campaign.

Discussion Questions

1. Discuss ways an Internet site can collect and use information from its visitors. For reference purposes you may frame the question so you are referring to the site of a hotel, restaurant, club, or a destination marketing organization.
2. Explain what a data warehouse is and why it is a popular data management tool.
3. Find an example of a good direct marketing campaign. Why do you feel it was effective?
4. Explain how Internet marketing, database marketing, and direct marketing are related.

Experiential Exercise

Do the following:

Sign up for a frequency club for hospitality or travel organization. (If you cannot find one you can go to the book's Internet site and sign up on-line.) What information did they request from you? Did the information seem useful? Is there information they should have asked for that they did not? Did they ask you if it was okay if they sent you information? See if you receive any response back from the company after signing up.

Internet Exercise

Support for these exercises can be found on the Web site for *Marketing for Hospitality and Tourism*, www.prenhall.com/kotler.

Go to two Internet sites for the same type of hospitality or tourism organization. For example, go to two restaurants, two destination marketing organizations, and so forth. Based on the information provided in this chapter, critique the Web sites.

References

1. Adrina Lipscomb, Rowan McKinnon, and Jon Murray, Papua New Guinea, Hawthorn, Victoria, Lonely Planet, 1998. Papua New Guinea, Introduction, Destinations, retrieved on December 21, 2001, from *http://www.lonelyplanet.com/destinations/autralasia/papua_new_guinea/index.htm,* Papua New Guinea Tourism, Tourism overview, retrieved on December 19, 2001, from *http://www.geocities.com/skyfdn/PNGtourismfacts.html.,* Papua New Guinea Tourism Resources, Introduction, retrieved from *http://www.geocities.com/skyfdn/;* Cruising in Papua New Guinea, Our tourism products, retrieved on December 19, 2001 from *http://www.paradiselive.org.pg/cruises.html.,* Cultural Excursions, retrieved on December 21, 2001, from *http://www.west.net/~exotic/excursions.htm,* Papua New Guinea Travel Guide, Pacific Islands travel, accommodations information, retrieved on December 21, 2001, from *http://www.pi-travel.co.nz/papua_new_guinea /scenic/p_content_scenic.html.*
2. Global Internet Statistics, Global Reach, Sources, and References, retrieved on December 19, 2001, from *http://www.glreach.com/blobstats/index/php3;* Eric Newburger, "Home Computer and Internet Use in the United States: August 2000," *U.S. Census Bureau* (September 2001).
3. Michael Pastore, "Growth Rates Slowing for Online Travel," retrieved on December 19, 2001, from *http://cyberatlas.internet.com.*
4. Choon-Chaing Leong, "Marketing Practices and Internet Marketing: A Study of Hotels in Singapore," *Journal of Vacation Marketing* 7, no. 2 (November 2000).
5. Kathleen Cassedy, "Know Your Online Customer," *HSMAI Marketing Review* (spring 2001):18–22.
6. Charles Hofacker, *Internet Marketing.* Austin, TX: Digital Springs, 1999.
7. Mary Jo Bitner, Stephen W. Brown, and M. L. Meuter, "Technology Infusion in Service Encounters," *Journal of Academy of Marketing Science* 28 (winter 2000): 138–149.
8. John Courtmanche, "Destination: Conversation," *1 to 1* (January/February 2001): 22+.
9. Ibid.
10. Patti J. Shock, "Resources on the World Wide Web," *Journal of Restaurant & Foodservice Marketing* 3, no. 1 (1998).
11. Patti J. Shock, "Understanding How the Web Works," *Journal of Restaurant & Foodservice Marketing* 3, no. 2 (1999).
12. Joel Reedy, *Electronic Marketing: Integrating Electronic Resources into the Marketing Process* (New York: Dryden Press, 2000).
13. Shock, "Resources on the World Wide Web."
14. Robert Klara, "Site Seeing," *Restaurant Business*, January 1, 2001, pp. 34–36
15. Hofacker, *Internet Marketing.*

16. Mohanbir Sawhney and Steven Kaplan, "Let's Get Vertical," in *Internet Marketing: Readings and Online Resources*, ed. Paul Richardson (New York: McGraw-Hill Irwin, 2001), pp. 263–271.
17. Jennifer J. Bono, "Marketing Database Heats Up Tourism for Sunny Aruba," *Direct Marketing* (October 1995): 18–21.
18. Martin Baier, Kurtis M. Ruf, Goutam Chakraborty, *Contemporary Database Management* (Evanston, IL: Racom, 2002).
19. Michael J. A. Berry and Gordon Linoff, *Data Mining Techniques* (New York: John Wiley and Sons, 1997).
20. Robert Groth, *Data Mining,* (Upper Saddle River, NJ, Prentice Hall, 1999).
21. See Rob Jackson and Paul Wang, *Strategic Database Marketing* (Chicago: NTC Publishing Group, 1994).
22. *Making Loyalty the Mission*, Harvard Business School Video, 1995.
23. Edward L. Nash, *Direct Marketing* (New York: McGraw-Hill, 1986).
24. James R. Abbey, *Hospitality Sales and Advertising* (East Lansing, MI: Educational Institute, 1989), p. 322.
25. The terms *direct-order marketing* and *direct-relationship marketing* were suggested as subsets of direct marketing by Stan Rapp and Tom Collins in *The Great Marketing Turnaround* (Upper Saddle River, NJ: Prentice Hall, 1990).
26. Clare Sambrook, "The World's Biggest Hotel Database," *Marketing* (March 4, 1993), p. 19.
27. David H. Freedman, "An Unusual Way to Run a Ski Business," *Forbes*, December 7, 1992, p. 28.
28. "Eagles Nest," *The Pete and Pierre Show, Consumer Campaigns*, Hake Communications, Inc., 224 Seventh Street, Garden City, NY 11530.
29. Peter C. Yesawich, "Execution and Measurement of Programs," *Cornell Hotel and Restaurant Administration Quarterly,* 29, no. 4 (February 1989): 89.
30. Robert A. Meyer, "Understanding Telemarketing for Hotels," *Cornell Hotel and Restaurant Administration Quarterly* 28, no. 2 (August 1987): 25.
31. Christine Larson, "Where We Go from Here," *Adweek,* November 12, 2001, pp. IQ1–IQ3.
32. Tracking Customer Habits, *Nation's Restaurant News*, May 21, 2001, pp. T6+.
33. Jant Logan, "Dialog marketing elevates e-mail effectiveness," *Customer Inter@Ction Solutions,* accessed December 30, 2001, *http://prquest.umi.com/pdqweb?Did=000000091700542.*
34. John Martin, "How to Use E-Mail Marketing to Increase Occupancy," *HSMAI Marketing Review* (summer 2001): 27–29.
35. Robin Lee Allen, "It's in the Mail: Latour's New Campaign, That Is," *Nation's Restaurant News* 26, no. 17 (April 27, 1992): 12.
36. "Mauna Kea," *The Pete and Pierre Show, Consumer Campaigns*, Hake Communications, Inc., 224 Seventh Street, Garden City, NY 11530.
37. See Ernan Roman, *Integrated Direct Marketing* (New York: McGraw-Hill, 1989), p. 108.
38. Ibid.
39. Nancy H. Arab, "Integrated Marketing Repositions Toronto Hotel: Occupancy Soars," *Public Relations Journal* 47, no. 3 (March 1991): 22–23.
40. "Cleveland Launches City's First Tourism Marketing Campaign," *USAE,* January 24, 1995, p. 201.

17 Professional Sales

Good listeners generally make more sales than good talkers.
B. C. Holwick

Many of the world's top salespeople don't carry the word "sales" in their title but daily serve as superior sales role models. Ruth Fertel exemplifies this best. Ruth Fertel founded Ruth's Chris Steak House, billed as "The Nation's Largest Upscale Restaurant Company," with 33 company and 44 franchised restaurants selling over 18,000 steaks per day and grossing over $320 million annually.[1] Let's examine briefly some of the success characteristics behind Ruth.

Optimism and a willingness to overcome adversity. *Ruth earned a degree in chemistry with a minor in physics at Louisiana State University, graduating at age nineteen. She taught briefly at McNeese Junior College in Lake Charles, Louisiana, but left to marry and raise a family.*

Fourteen years later Ruth, by then divorced, reentered the workforce as a lab technician at Tulane Medical School. Four years there convinced her that she couldn't earn enough to send her two sons to college, so she decided to go into business for herself. That was in 1965. One day, while scanning the classified section of the local newspaper, Ruth found an ad for a steak house for sale. "I can do that!" she thought to herself, although she had no prior experience and limited funds.

In short order, against the advice of her lawyer, her banker, and her best friend, Ruth mortgaged her home to buy the small restaurant, then called Chris Steak House. "To show you how naive I was at the time," recalls Ruth, "I was ready to borrow only the $18,000 required to buy the restaurant, but the bank suggested I take an additional $4,000 to buy food and supplies!"

Ruth compensated for her lack of experience with plain hard work. It paid off, and the people came. In the first six months, she cleared more than double her previous annual salary. Her restaurant soon became popular with the city's media personalities, political leaders, sport figures, and business people. The name "Ruth's Chris" became identified with quality and fine steaks.

Treating others correctly. *To what does Ruth attribute her success? "It's as simple as following the Golden Rule," says Ruth. "I treat my customers and my associates as I would want to be treated."*

Knowing your customers. *Despite the growth of Ruth's Chris, Ruth Fertel is determined not to lose touch with her clientele. Under her direction, the company distributes 50,000 copies of "Steak House Gang News," a glossy sixteen-page newsletter to customers. The company has also gathered 10,000 names of customers who want free issues by mail on a quarterly basis. Customer profiles will be among the magazine's features.*[2]

Confidence. *"I've always had a lot of confidence in my ability to do anything I set my mind to," said Fertel. "I'm not a restaurateur, I'm a business person who owned a restaurant. I just had confidence and never once thought I couldn't do it or would fail."*[3]

Honesty. *"A verbal contract with Ruth is as good as any contract," said her broker.*

Emphasis on quality. *"Get a good product, serve it with a smile at the right price, and take the profits to the bank," said Ruth. Ruth insists that her beef never be frozen to retain its tenderness and flavor. She demands that individual steaks be cut at each restaurant, broiled to diner's tastes, and served sizzling. Portions tend to be huge, twelve to eighteen ounces, because Ruth believes that larger cuts of meat hold onto their juices better during cooking. "If there's any secret to my business, it's in the quality," says Fertel.*[4]

The word failure doesn't exist. *Ruth will not allow any of her restaurants to close, despite economic difficulties. The Houston franchise threatened to shut down following a bad financial year. Fertel herself stepped in and bought the restaurant. She and her team have since turned it around.*

Concern for others. *Fertel made a public announcement in November 2000 that she had smoking-induced lung cancer. The reason for her announcement was that she wanted to sell young people on the idea that they should not smoke. Commenting on her situation she said, "I'm realistic, but I am tough. I love what I do and retiring was never in my plans anyway. So I guess I'll go out with my boots on."*[5]

Chapter Objectives

After reading this chapter, you should be able to:

1. Explain the role and nature of personal selling and the role of the sales force.
2. Describe the basics of managing the sales force, and tell how to set sales force strategy, how to pick a structure—territorial, product, customer, or complex—and how to ensure that sales force size is appropriate.
3. Identify the key issues in recruiting, selecting, training, and compensating salespeople.
4. Discuss supervising salespeople, including directing, motivation, and evaluating performance.
5. Apply the principles of personal selling process, and outline the steps in the selling process—qualifying, preapproach and approach, presentation and demonstration, handling objections, closing, and follow-up.

17.1 Ruth's Chris Steak House

Management of Professional Sales

Success or failure within the hospitality industry ultimately rests on the ability to sell. A roadside motel at an intersection of major highways or a popular restaurant with waiting lines is sometimes viewed as being above the need "to sell." No member of the hospitality industry can accept this as a long-run viewpoint.

Discourteous front-desk clerks and cashiers who would impress Grumpy of the Seven Dwarfs are part of one's sales force. These and all others who face the public can drive away or attract business. In the best cases, they can upsell through suggestive selling, thus increasing the check size by effectively suggesting desserts, special drinks, and even a gift certificate for a friend. Higher-margin suites can be sold instead of the lowest-price room.

Successful owners and managers know that they must sell continuously. County commissioners, tax evaluation officials, planning boards, the press, bankers, and the local visitor center must all be sold on one's hospitality business. Those in the backroom who check credit card reports, care for audiovisual equipment, serve as secretaries, and maintain the physical plant are also part of the sales team.

Libraries could be filled with tales of lost sales or needlessly fractured guest relationships because of a curt response or an unsavory attitude on the part of support staff who mistakenly believe that sales is not their responsibility.

Everyone must sell, but a few individuals have the specific responsibility for ensuring that payrolls can be met, invoices can be paid, and a fair return on investment can be achieved. These are the professional salespeople.

The term sales representative covers a broad range of positions in our economy, where the differences are often greater than the similarities. The following classification of sales positions has application in the hospitality industry:[6]

1. **Deliverer:** positions in which the salesperson's job is predominantly to deliver the product (e.g., restaurant supplies, hotel linens).
2. **Order taker:** positions in which the salesperson is predominantly an inside order taker (e.g., reservations or fast-food person) or outside order taker (e.g., the restaurant supply person calling on a chef).
3. **Missionary:** positions in which the salesperson is not expected or permitted to take an order but is called on only to build goodwill or to educate the actual or potential user. Airline and cruise line salespeople who call on travel agencies, work at trade shows, and conduct other public relations types of work are, in effect, missionary salespeople.
4. **Technician:** positions in which the major emphasis is placed on technical knowledge (e.g., the yield management salesperson who is primarily a consultant to client companies such as hotels or airlines).
5. **Demand creator:** positions that demand the creative sale of tangible products or of intangibles (e.g., most of the hospitality industry).

The positions range from the least to the most creative types of selling. The first jobs call for servicing accounts and taking new orders, whereas the latter require seeking prospects and influencing them to buy.

In this chapter we focus on six major areas:

1. Nature of hospitality sales
2. Sales force objectives
3. Sales force structure and size
4. Organizing the sales department
5. Recruiting and training a professional sales force
6. Managing the sales force

Nature of Hospitality Sales

Sales personnel serve as the company's personal link to customers. The sales representative *is* the company to many customers and in turn brings back much-needed customer intelligence. Personal selling is the most expensive contact and communication tool used by the company.

Cost estimates for making a personal sales call vary depending on the industry and the company, but one conclusion remains constant. However measured, the cost is high! According to *Business Week*, "There are 8 million people in the U.S. workforce who are directly involved in sales, and it now costs $250 and up to send any one of them on a call."[7] A nonhospitality company, E. I. DuPont de Nemours and Company, Inc., estimates a cost-per-field sales call of $500[8] and up, and an even higher estimate of $700 per visit is given by a researcher who included the salesperson's salary, cost of travel, technical support people, and cost of presentations.[9]

Add to this the fact that sales orders are seldom written on the first call and often require five or more calls, particularly for larger orders. The cost of obtaining a new client thus becomes enormously high, as depicted in Table 17-1. Despite the high cost, personal selling is often the most effective tool available to a hospitality company. Sales representatives perform one or more of the following tasks for their companies:

- **Prospecting.** Sales representatives find and cultivate new customers.
- **Targeting.** Sales representatives decide how to allocate their scarce time among prospects and customers.
- **Communicating.** Sales representatives communicate information about the company's products and services.
- **Selling.** Sales representatives know the art of salesmanship: approaching, presenting, answering objections, and closing sales.
- **Servicing.** Sales representatives provide various services to the customers—consulting on their problems, rendering technical assistance, arranging financing, and expediting delivery.
- **Information gathering.** Sales representatives conduct market research and intelligence work and fill-in call reports.
- **Allocating.** Sales representatives decide which customers to allocate scarce products to during product shortages.

The sales representative's mix of tasks varies with the state of the economy. During product shortages, such as a temporary shortage of hotel rooms during a major convention, sales representatives find themselves with nothing to sell. Some companies jump to the conclusion that

Table 17-1

Cost of Obtaining a New Client

NUMBER OF CALLS NEEDED TO CLOSE A SALE	TOTAL COST TO OBTAIN A NEW CLIENT AT VARIOUS ESTIMATES OF COST OF SALES CALL		
	AT $250	AT $500	AT $700
1	$ 250	$ 500	$ 700
2	500	1000	1400
3	750	1500	2100
4	1000	2000	2800
5	1250	2500	3500[a]
6	1500	3000	4200
7	1750	3500	4900
8	2000	4000	5600
9	2250	4500	6300
10	2500	5000	7000

[a]Five sales calls seems to be an estimate commonly given to obtain a new client.

fewer sales representatives are then needed. But this thinking overlooks the salesperson's other roles—allocating the product, counseling unhappy customers, and selling the company's other products that are not in short supply. It also ignores the long-run nature of hospitality sales.

Many conventions and conferences are planned years in advance, and hospitality salespeople must often work with meeting and convention planners two to four years in advance of the actual event. Resorts in the United States have concentrated much of their selling efforts on meetings and conferences, which now represent 35 percent of their customers.[10] This was not achieved by viewing professional sales as a short-run tactic. A senior analyst with Tourism Canada has demonstrated that Canadian resort salespeople are effective in reaching foreign markets. Guests in Canadian resorts are 60 percent Canadian and 40 percent foreign. By comparison, U.S. resorts have a mix of 91 percent American and 9 percent foreign.[11] Again, penetrating foreign markets is not accomplished in the short run.

As companies move toward a stronger market orientation, their sales forces need to become more market focused and customer oriented. The traditional view is that salespeople should worry about volume and sell, sell, sell, and that the marketing department should worry about marketing strategy and profitability. The newer view is that salespeople should know how to produce customer satisfaction and company profit. They should know how to analyze sales data, measure market potential, gather market intelligence, develop marketing strategies and plans, and become proficient at the use of sales tactics.

17.2 Days Inn
Super 8 Motel
Travelodge of Australia

Days Inns of America recognizes that the general manager (GM) is responsible for a property's sales efforts. "It is immensely important that the GM be equipped with the necessary sales and marketing tools," said John Russell, Days Inns' president.[12] Chains such as Days Inns, Super 8 Motel, and Travelodge of Australia must view the GM as the head of sales. Larger hotels and resorts, such as Sheraton, Hilton, Shangri-la, and Four Seasons, employ professional sales managers. In these cases, the GM is considerably less involved with details of the sales function.

Sales representatives need analytical skills. This becomes especially critical at the higher levels of sales management. Marketers believe that a sales force will be more effective in the long run if members understand marketing as well as selling. The newer concept is basic to the successful use of yield management in the hospitality industry.

This has become very clear as database marketing has gained importance within the hospitality industry. Group sales have been particularly affected. After viewing the importance of marketing information to sales, a hospitality industry writer with *Hotel and Motel Management* magazine concluded the following:[13]

- Closing sales has more to do with professionalism than anything else.
- Understanding the identity of real prospects increases sales productivity.
- Sales force members can save hours of time by having information about prospect group clients.

- It is critical to know what groups have a history of booking rooms in your type of hotel.

Sales Force Objectives

Hospitality companies typically establish objectives for the sales force. Sales objectives are essential for two reasons:

1. Objectives ensure that corporate goals are met. Goals may include revenue, market share, improving corporate image, and many others.
2. Objectives assist sales-force members to plan and execute their personal sales programs. Objectives also help to ensure that a salesperson's time and company support resources such as personal computers are efficiently utilized.

Sales force objectives must be custom designed annually for each company. Individual sales objectives are established to support corporate goals and marketing and sales objectives. Annual marketing and sales objectives are normally broken into quarterly and monthly objectives. Sales force members break them down further into personal objectives by day and week.

It is the responsibility of the sales manager to establish and assign objectives to individual salespeople. These are often developed after consultation with the salesperson. An experienced salesperson is in the best position to understand what is happening in the marketplace and to assist the sales manager in formulating realistic objectives.

Occasionally, annual objectives must be changed before year end. This is generally due to a dramatic occurrence, such as the outbreak of war, a natural disaster such as an earthquake, a dramatic change in the economy such as a massive currency devaluation, or new ownership of the hotel.

Although sales objectives are custom designed, there are general objectives commonly employed by members of the hospitality industry.

Sales Volume

Occupancy, passenger miles, and total covers are common measures of sales volume within the hospitality industry. They all mean the same thing: Bring in as many customers as possible. An emphasis on volume alone inevitably leads to price discounting, attracting undesirable market segments, cost cutting, and employee unhappiness.

Sales Volume by Selected Segments

Exclusive resorts, charter flight service, and upper-end cruises tend to operate with the philosophy that if one establishes volume objectives but restricts prospecting to highly selective segments, price and profits will take care of themselves. Although appropriate for a few niche players, this thinking cannot be applied to the majority of the hospitality industry. Nevertheless, the concept of establishing sales objectives by specific market segment is feasible and basic to effective sales. Sales strategies must be analyzed and reviewed continuously in view of quantitative sales results.

Canadian resort operators targeted the meeting and convention market, with the result that this segment made up 25 percent of their customer mix, compared with 35 percent for U.S. resorts. This led to questions of whether the differences were the result of the sales techniques employed in the two nations.[14]

Sales Volume and Price/Margin Mix

17.3 British World Airways
Hertz
Sheraton Hotels

Establish sales volume objectives by product lines to ensure a desired gross profit. This system is the basis for yield management. Salespeople often criticize the system as restrictive and unrealistic. The fact is, it works. British World Airways, Hertz, Sheraton Hotels, and Royal Caribbean Cruises are representative of the firms who use this system. Whether a yield management system is in place, establishing objectives by volume and by price/margin segments leads to improved revenue.

Upselling and Second-Chance Selling

Excellent profit opportunities exist for hospitality companies, particularly hotels and resorts, to upgrade price and profit margins by selling higher-priced products such as suites through upselling. A related concept is second-chance selling, in which the sales department contacts a client who has already booked an event such as a two-day meeting. Opportunities exist to sell additional services such as airport limousine pickup and delivery or to upgrade rooms or food and beverage from chicken to prime rib.

Second-chance selling encourages cooperation and teamwork between departments, such as catering, food and beverage, and sales. Hospitality researchers who have studied second-chance selling concluded, "Hoteliers (who do not employ second-chance selling) may be overlooking an opportunity to increase revenues substantially with little additional cost. By establishing specific values for business that has already been booked, hotel managers can encourage salespeople to increase the productivity of existing resources. If salespeople have clearly established goals and objectives for a second chance to increase their rewards, they may work harder to achieve goals."[15]

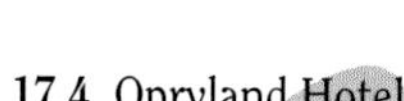
17.4 Opryland Hotel

Opryland Hotel discovered by accident the value of second-chance selling. A new member of the sales force rose to prominence by winning all sales contests. The sales manager discovered that because this person lacked a sales client base, common sense dictated another approach. This led the salesperson to recontact clients who had already signed contracts. It also clearly demonstrated the economic value of second-chance selling.

Market Share or Market Penetration

Airlines, cruise lines, major fast-food chains, and rental car companies are highly concerned with market share and market penetration. These concepts have considerably less meaning to many restaurants, hotels, resorts, and other members of the hospitality industry.

The management of most hotels is concerned primarily with measures such as occupancy, average room rate, yield, and customer mix. The corporate marketing department of a chain is, however, likely to be

Entertainment venues like Gameworks use a sales staff to sell their venues to organizations for parties. This type of venue is a popular spot for corporate parties and team building exercises. Courtesy of Gameworks.

concerned about market share, particularly if it is a dominant chain in a market such as Hawaii. Hilton, Sheraton, Aston Hotels and Resorts, and Outrigger Hotels actively compete for market share in that market.

There is evidence that hotel management companies are increasingly held accountable for clearly defined performance standards. Among these is the level of market penetration. This is a clear departure from the past, when contracts between owners and hotel management companies contained vague references to standards of performance.[16]

As a result, it is very possible that the sales department of hotels and resorts will increasingly be required to measure market potential and will be held accountable for a predetermined level of market penetration. Independent measures of market penetration such as STAR will undoubtedly assume increased importance in the measurement of hotel sales. STAR is a joint project of Smith Travel Research and PricewaterhouseCoopers. It provides information on average rate, occupancy, and REVPAR for Asia/Pacific, the Americas, Europe, the Middle East, and Africa.

Product-Specific Objectives

Occasionally a sales force will be charged with the specific responsibility to improve sales volume for specific product lines. This objective may be associated with upselling and second-chance selling but may also be part of the regular sales duties of the sales force. A sales force may be asked to sell more suites, higher-margin coffee breaks, holiday packages, honeymoon packages, or other product lines.

Excellent opportunities for enhanced revenues exist within many hotels and resorts from nonroom sales. Recreation club memberships, including children's programs, are sometimes sold to local residents. A

17.5 The Boca Raton Resort

properly designed club membership can generate substantial income from membership fees, dues, and food and beverage revenues. The Boca Raton Resort initiated a Premier Club Membership program that produced membership sales in excess of $40 million the first three years.[17]

If management places extreme attention on specific products, there is always a possibility that other product line members will be ignored. A common approach to encourage the sale of specific products is to set objectives for them and to reward performance with bonuses or other incentives.

Sales Force Structure and Size

The diverse nature of the hospitality industry means that different sales force structures and sizes have evolved. The structure of a sales force within the airline industry is different from that of a hotel or cruise line. In general, most restaurants do not use a sales force but depend on other parts of the marketing mix, such as advertising and sales promotion.

The hotel/resort industry traditionally uses a functional, hierarchical structure. Within this structure, hotel departments are organized around particular functions, such as housekeeping or sales. Department managers, including the sales manager, report to a general manager. In smaller hotels such as roadside motels, the GM usually serves as sales manager because the organization is not large enough to support functional departments. Within large hotels and resorts, the sales department may have directors of specialized sales such as a convention and meetings sales director or a corporate accounts sales director. These are organized on a functional basis.

The structure of a hotel sales department depends on the culture of the organization, size of the property, nature of the market, and type of hotel. A casino hotel might contain the same number of rooms as a ski resort hotel yet have a somewhat different organizational structure. Some casino hotels have sales directors who are responsible for working with junket reps and premium players. A resort hotel might have a sales director responsible for working with travel agents and tour wholesalers, or with nationwide ski clubs.

The sales force structures commonly used in the hospitality industry today are described next.

Territorial-Structured Sales Force

In the simplest sales organization, each sales representative is assigned an exclusive territory in which to represent the company's full line. This sales structure has a number of advantages. First, it results in a clear definition of the salesperson's responsibilities. As the only salesperson working the territory, he or she bears the credit or blame for area sales to the extent that personal selling effort makes a difference. Second, territorial responsibility increases the sales representative's incentive to cultivate local business and personal ties. These ties contribute to the sales representative's selling effectiveness and personal life. Third, travel expenses are relatively small, as each sales representative travels within a small geographic area.

A territorial sales organization is often supported by many levels of sales management positions. Each higher-level sales manager takes on increasing marketing and administration work in relation to the time available for selling. In fact, sales managers are paid for their management skills rather than their selling skills. The new sales trainee, in looking ahead, can expect to become a sales representative, then a district manager, and then a regional manager, and, depending on his or her ability and motivation, may move to still higher levels of sales or general management.

In designing territories, the company seeks certain territorial characteristics. Territories are easy to administer, their sales potential is easy to estimate, they reduce total travel time, and they provide a sufficient and equitable workload and sales potential for each sales representative. These characteristics are achieved through deciding on territory size and shape.

Salespersons in restaurant and hotel supply companies are often assigned to a territory. Hotels with international markets often assign their international salespeople to a territory such as Europe or a specific country such as France.

Territory Size

Territories can be designed to provide either equal sales potential or equal workload. Each principle offers advantages at the cost of some dilemmas. Territories of equal potential provide each sales representative with the same income opportunities and provide the company with a means to evaluate performance. Persistent differences in sales yield by territory are assumed to reflect differences in ability or effort of individual sales representatives. Customer density varies by territory, and territories with equal potential can vary widely in size. The potential for selling cruises in Chicago is larger than in several Rocky Mountain states. A sales representative assigned to Chicago can cover the same sales potential with much less effort than the sales representative who sells in the Rocky Mountain West. The sales representative assigned to the larger and sparser territory is going to end up with either fewer sales and less income for equal effort or equal sales through extraordinary effort. One solution is to pay the Rocky Mountain sales representatives more compensation for the extra effort. But this reduces profits on sales in these territories. Another solution is to acknowledge that territories differ in attractiveness and assign the better or more senior sales representatives to the better territories.

Alternatively, territories might be designed to equalize the sales workload. Each sales representative could then cover his or her territory adequately. This principle results in some variation in territory sales potential. This does not concern a sales force on straight salary, but when sales representatives are compensated partly on commission, territories will vary in their attractiveness even though workloads are equal.

Territory Shape

Territories are formed by combining smaller units, such as counties or states, until they add up to a territory of a given sales potential or workload. Territorial design must take into account the location of natural barriers, the compatibility of adjacent areas, the adequacy of transportation, and so on. Many companies prefer a certain territory shape because the shape can influence the cost and ease of coverage and the sales representatives' job satisfaction.

The territorial structure sales force is most commonly used by airlines, cruise lines, and rental car companies, and at the corporate level by hotel chains. It is not frequently used by individual hotel/resort properties, who instead seem to organize their sales departments by function or type of customer.

Market-Segment-Structured Sales Force

Companies often specialize their sales forces along market segment lines. Separate sales forces can be set up by different industries for the convention/meeting segment, the incentive travel market, and other major segments. This is the most common type of structure within the hotel industry. For example, associations have different needs than corporations, thus one salesperson may be assigned to the association market while another is assigned to the corporate market. In larger properties associations may be divided between state and national associations.

The obvious advantage of market specialization is that each sales force can become knowledgeable about specific market segments. The major disadvantage of a market-segment-structured sales force arises when the various members of a segment are scattered throughout the country or the world. This vastly increases the travel costs.

Market-Channel-Structured Sales Force

The importance of marketing intermediaries, such as wholesalers, tour operators, travel agencies, and junket reps, to the hospitality industry has created sales force structures to serve marketing channels. Travel agencies account for over 95 percent of all cruise line sales.[18] A cruise line naturally structures its sales force on a marketing intermediary basis. Commercial airlines receive 90 percent of their bookings through travel agencies, auto rental firms receive 50 percent, and hotels about 25 percent.[19]

Some hotels, such as those near historical sites, receive substantial bookings through motor coach tour brokers. The location, size, and type of hospitality company greatly affect the relative importance of travel intermediaries. This in turn affects whether a company designs its sales force structure by travel intermediary.

17.6 Aston Hotels and Resorts of Hawaii

Aston Hotels and Resorts of Hawaii manages thirty properties with 4,500 rooms. These are sold primarily through travel agents and wholesalers who supply 85 percent to 90 percent of Aston's business. "I differentiate between my customers who are the travel agents and the consumers who are the people who actually stay in the units," said Andre S. Tatibouet, CEO of Aston Hotels and Resorts.[20]

Customer-Structured Sales Force

A customer-structured sales force recognizes that specific customers exist who are critical to the success of the organization. The sales force is usually organized to serve these accounts through a key or national account structure.

When a company sells to many small accounts, it uses a territory-based sales force. However, large accounts (called key accounts, major accounts, or national accounts) are often singled out for special attention and handling. If the account is a large company with many divisions operating in many parts of the country and subject to many buying influences (such as General Motors or Mitsubishi), it is likely to be handled as a national account and assigned to a specific individual or sales team. If the company has several such accounts, it is likely to organize a national account management (NAM) division.

National account management is growing for a number of reasons. As buyer concentration increases through mergers and acquisitions, fewer buyers account for a larger share of a company's sales. Another factor is that many buyers are centralizing their purchases instead of leaving them to the local units. This gives buyers more bargaining power. Still another factor is that as products become more complex, more groups in the buyer's organization become involved in the purchase process, and the typical salesperson might not have the skill, authority, or coverage to be effective in selling to the large buyer.

Sheraton Hotels noted that business travelers were not shifting from one hotel chain to another as much as in the past. In response, Sheraton developed a reservations system that allowed the establishment of national accounts. When an account number is given, the correct rate for any Sheraton Hotel worldwide is known.

In organizing a national account program, a company faces a number of issues, including how to select national accounts; how to manage them; how to develop, manage, and evaluate a national account manager; how to organize a structure for national accounts; and where to locate NAM in the organization.

Andre Tatibouet of Aston Hotels and Resorts would surely argue that although his structure does not compensate the guest, it is nevertheless customer-directed because it places emphasis on his primary client, the travel agent. Undoubtedly, this is true and reflects the fact that all sales structures must be custom made for the individual hotel. A single sales structure cannot possibly be employed with equal success for all properties within a diverse chain such as Sheraton or Holiday Inn.

Combination-Structured Sales Force

Some hotels and resorts have a sales force that is structured by product, market segment, market channel, and customer. This is often a reaction to internal and market forces rather than the result of strategic thinking.

A large hotel might have a catering/banquet sales force (product), a convention/meeting sales force (market segment), a tour wholesale sales force (marketing intermediary), and a national accounts sales force (customer). Proponents of such a sales force feel that it encourages the sales force to reach all or most available customers. They also contend that it is impossible for a single salesperson to understand and effectively sell all the hotel's products to all available customer segments through all marketing channels. Sales specialists can become familiar with major customers, understand trends that affect them, and plan appropriate sales strategies and tactics.

Opponents of this system feel that in many cases this sales force structure indicates that the hotel is trying to be all things to all people in the absence of long-run goals and strategies. They contend that such a structure is difficult to manage and can be confusing to the sales force and the customer, as the same customer may be classified in different areas and thus be handled by more than one salesperson.

Regardless of which structure is used by a hotel or resort, there is a particular market segment that is neglected by many North American hoteliers: local markets. Many local markets offer potential, particularly for food and beverage and function room sales. Although a resort such as the Greenbriar in a rural area of West Virginia might not have a large local market, this is scarcely the case for most hotels. The Japanese seem to be particularly adept at penetrating this market, because 40 percent to 50 percent of Japanese hotel sales are accounted for by parties and other events from local companies.[21] A sales manager must be aware of the local market and develop a sales force structure appropriate for penetrating this market.

17.7 Dalmahoy Golf and Country Club Resort

Seven months after opening, the Dalmahoy Golf and Country Club Resort near Edinburgh, Scotland, recognized the need for a strong sales effort in the local market and for a combination-structured sales force. Dalmahoy was experiencing low occupancy and less than desirable membership growth. Many factors were involved, such as the Gulf War, a poor economy, and almost no awareness by Edinburgh area golfers. As a member of the U.K.-based Country Club Hotel Group, Dalmahoy had the assistance of this company's national sales force. The management of Dalmahoy knew that a strong property-level sales effort was also needed and employed two salespersons to serve the local market, plus a travel-trade manager to work with intermediaries to attract overseas business. The result was a 70 percent occupancy in 1994 compared with 64.5 percent for hotels in the United Kingdom. This compared with average occupancy of only 32 percent for the first seven months before the combination-structured sales force was put in place.[22]

Sales Force Size

Once the company clarifies its sales force strategy and structure, it is ready to consider sales force size. Sales representatives are one of the company's most expensive assets.

After determining the type and number of desired customers, a workload approach can be used to establish sales force size. This method consists of the following steps:

1. Customers are grouped into size classes according to their annual sales volume.
2. The desirable call frequencies (number of sales calls on an account per year) are established for each class.
3. The number of accounts in each size class is multiplied by the corresponding call frequency to arrive at the total workload for the country in sales calls per year.
4. The average number of calls a sales representative can make per year is determined.

5. The number of sales representatives needed is determined by dividing the total annual calls required by the average calls made by a sales representative.

Suppose that the company estimates that there are 1,000 A accounts and 2,000 B accounts required in the nation, and that A accounts require thirty-six calls a year while B accounts require twelve calls a year. This means that the company needs a sales force that can make 60,000 sales calls a year. Suppose that the average sales representative can make 1,000 calls a year. The company would need sixty full-time sales representatives.

The size of a sales force is determined by changes in the market, competition, and corporate strategies and policies. The sales process will also directly affect decisions concerning sales force size. The following describes several of the factors that influence the size of a hotel's sales force:

- **Corporate/chain sales support.** Several major hotel chains have employed a corporate sales force to reach the meeting/ convention/ conference market. The concept behind this sales force is that individual hotel properties may not be in a position to search out and track this important market and that a sales force representing the chain can recommend and sell all appropriate hotels within the chain, not simply a single property. In recent years, some chains have begun to question the value of this sales force and may drop this area of sales support. If this occurs, individual properties may find it necessary to employ one or more additional sales force members to ensure coverage of this important segment.
- **Use of sales reps.** Sales reps have traditionally been used by hotels and resorts to serve distant markets, particularly foreign countries. With the emergence of NAFTA and the growing importance of many foreign markets, several companies are rethinking the use of reps and may substitute salaried sales staff in these markets.
- **Team selling.** Team selling has proved to be an effective and powerful tactic to reach and retain key customers. Its opportunities and limitations are only beginning to be realized in the hospitality industry. It is uncertain how this may affect the size of a sales force.
- **Electronic sales.** Hospitality companies such as Club Med are currently using the Internet. Many observers feel this tool will dramatically change the sales process.
- **Travel intermediary dependency.** Hospitality industry members historically viewed travel intermediaries with mixed emotions. Some hotels may have allowed wholesalers to assume too great a degree of sales power. A study of Caribbean hotels found that "wholesalers play a valuable role in the Caribbean resort hotel industry by helping hotels market and sell their rooms. But in recent years, wholesalers' power has increased, causing operational and financial problems for some Caribbean resort-hotel operators."[23] In some cases it may be advisable to increase the size

of the sales force and aggressively seek ways to lessen wholesaler dependence.

The appropriate size of a hospitality company's sales force cannot be established solely by formula or by comparison to that of competitors. It must be remembered that a sales force is only one tool to accomplish objectives and goals.

The size of a sales force may need to increase to support new marketing strategies. The sales manager then has the responsibility to "sell" top management, because a budgetary increase will almost certainly be necessary. Similarly, a professional sales manager must be aware of changing trends and new technology such as database marketing and electronic marketing. Rather than tenaciously supporting a larger-than-necessary sales force, the sales manager must be prepared to downsize and substitute technology when appropriate.

Organizing the Sales Department

As discussed previously, hospitality companies traditionally design departments along functional lines. It is common to find hotels with several marketing-related departments, such as a sales department, a guest relations department, and an advertising and public relations department, but not a "marketing" department. In recent years, some hotels have given the title "sales and marketing" to the previously named sales department, but with limited training in marketing for the sales manager.

A sales manager may bear both marketing and sales responsibilities, although it is likely that the department will always emphasize sales. Today's sales managers may have two types of salespeople within their departments: an inside sales force and a field sales force. The term inside sales can be misleading because many field salespeople spend a great deal of their time inside the hotel calling clients and prospects, meeting with them, making arrangements with other departments, answering mail, and performing many other duties, such as completing sales reports.

Inside Sales Force

Inside salespeople include three types. There are technical-support persons, who provide technical information and answers to customers' questions. There are sales assistants, who provide clerical backup for the field salespersons. They call ahead and confirm appointments, carry out credit checks, follow up on deliveries, and answer customers' questions when they cannot reach the outside sales rep. There are also telemarketers, who use the phone to find new leads, qualify them, and sell to them. Telemarketers can call up to fifty customers per day compared with the four or five that an outside salesperson can contact. They can be effective in the following ways: cross-selling the company's other products; upgrading orders; introducing new company products; opening new accounts and reactivating former accounts; giving more attention to neglected accounts; and following up and qualifying direct-mail leads.

Telemarketing has found a role in the hospitality industry. Renaissance Cruises has developed and uses a telemarketing sales force to reach individual guest prospects. This is in direct contrast to the majority of the cruise line industry, which relies on a field sales force to call on travel agents rather than on the prospect agent.

Telemarketing has found disfavor among many recipients of these calls. Within the hospitality industry, meeting planners are besieged by hotel sales reps who have done no research concerning the planner. Instead, they commonly begin a conversation with the question, "Do you plan meetings?" Busy meeting planners find this disruptive and frustrating, particularly if frequently called by the same hotel but different sales reps.[24]

Due to the high turnover among hotel salespeople and lack of an updated prospect database, a meeting planner may be called two to three times within a year by a hotel's sales reps asking the same questions. Like all sales calls, telemarketing can be much more productive if the salesperson has basic information concerning the prospect. Telemarketing failed in one hotel company because members of the sales force were required to perform this function one day a week. The hotel's salespeople felt forced into an unpleasant task. The supervisor resigned, management gave up, and the sales force rejoiced.[25]

Another dramatic breakthrough in improving sales force productivity is provided by new technological equipment: desktop and laptop computers, videocassette recorders, videodisks, automatic dialers, electronic mail, fax machines, and teleconferencing. The salesperson has truly gone electronic. This development has been called sales automation. Not only is sales and inventory information transferred much faster, but also specific computer-based decision support systems have been created for sales managers and sales representatives.

Reservations Department

The reservations department is a very important inside sales area for many hospitality companies because reservationists may speak with 80 percent of a company's customers. This department is sometimes not viewed as part of the sales team. It is sometimes a separate department, and, unfortunately, the reservations and sales departments within a hotel may have little communication. In worst-case scenarios, they may actually find themselves at odds. This is not the case at Hyatt Hotels, where reservations are under sales/marketing.

A study of reservations departments at Hyatt Corporation, American Airlines, and Carnival Cruise Lines revealed that much can be done to improve the effectiveness of this critical inside sales force.[26] The results of this study showed that reservations training was critical. The training program prescribed was remarkably similar to that for any sales position. Hyatt focuses on technical aspects, including how to sell. Hyatt's philosophy is that the skills necessary to be an effective salesperson can be taught.

Reservationist candidates at American Airlines are interviewed and hired for their sales ability. Days Inns has a program to hire the elderly and the physically challenged and through training turn them into reservation salespeople. Training your reservationists to be good company representatives and teaching them how to sell will pay back big dividends in the long run.[27]

Electronics and Telephone Sales

A related area of growing importance to hotel sales managers is the management of sales from electronic and telephone distribution systems, such as the 800-number reservation system of a chain or an independent group such as Preferred Hotels. The importance of sales provided by such distribution systems is likely to grow, particularly as the number of personal computer owners and users increases and when airlines fully implement in-flight electronic interactive systems for passengers.

17.8 Windsor Hospitality Group

The Windsor Hospitality Group of Woodland Hills, California, advocates taking full advantage of electronic distribution channels. Woodland formed strategic alliances with several distributors of global reservation services and regularly screens these services to see how sales for individual properties are doing.[28]

Some hotel chains, such as Omni Hotels, have signed exclusive agreements with a single reservation service to manage worldwide reservations. Omni appointed Intel International to handle worldwide reservations for its forty-three properties in the United States, Mexico, Singapore, and Hong Kong. "With such a spread of destinations, it was important for us to select a reservation facility that could provide international marketing support," said James Schulten, owner and senior vice president of sales and marketing for Omni.[29] He went on to say that Omni is integrating the sales and marketing function on a worldwide basis and therefore had to have a system that facilitated rather than complicated the sales/marketing process.

The need for an integrated and seamless reservation system has been felt by many hotel chains. A customer reservation system (CRS) is increasingly required to offer travel agents direct links to a hotel company's entire inventory so that agents can be assured that booking rates won't change when their clients arrive at the hotel. Radisson Hotels, in cooperation with Apollo, developed seamless reservation availability, giving agents the ability to enter Radisson's reservations system, view the entire inventory, and make a reservation electronically.[30]

Many hotel chains and hotel sales managers have realized that they must be equally adept at managing technology as they are at managing people.

Field Sales Force

Today, sales managers face an increasingly complex marketplace, which has created the need to review the organizational design of the field sales force continuously. We next discuss different types of field sales forces as currently used by hospitality companies.

Commissioned Reps

Hotels and resorts commonly use commissioned sales representatives in distant markets where the market potential does not justify employing a salaried salesperson. A Los Angeles hotel may contract with commissioned sales reps in New York or Miami to reach companies and associations that are known to the local sales reps. Commissioned sales reps normally represent several different properties or chains but attempt not to represent competing clients. This is sometimes difficult in the case of chains, which have competing properties in the same location.

Foreign markets are commonly served by a commissioned sales rep. Unfortunately, the relationship between sales rep and hotel is not always satisfactory. This is often because sales reps are hired without conducting a careful analysis of the reps. Because there is no reason to use a nonperforming or otherwise unsatisfactory sales rep, it is important to follow a few simple rules when working with commissioned sales reps.

1. *Select markets with care.* Distant markets should be selected to match corporate goals and marketing/sales objectives, not simply to have someone represent the company in a location.
2. *Personally visit the market.* Meet with prospective sales reps, examine their offices, check out references, note their personal appearance, ask for a list of current clients, ask for a credit report, and clear the rep through the police and the Better Business Bureau or the equivalent. In general, it is important to be as careful or even more careful in hiring a sales rep to cover distant markets as in hiring a salaried sales force member. The U.S. Travel and Tourism Administration, which is part of the Department of Commerce, maintains offices in several overseas markets. People in these offices are often familiar with local sales reps and may be very helpful. It must be understood that in some developing nations a commissioned sales rep is considered to be a member of the client company's workforce and dependent on that company for a livelihood. Local courts often decide in favor of the rep and may award the rep large financial settlements in cases such as dismissal for failure to meet performance standards.
3. *Include the sales rep as part of the hotel's sales force.* This requires using adaptation of management tools discussed later in the chapter. It is important to visit the offices of distant sales reps occasionally. This requires an adequate budget for travel and may entail considerable effort to convince the GM that such an expenditure of time and money is worthwhile.

Salaried Sales Force

Most hospitality industry sales force members are paid a salary plus benefits. Additional compensation is sometimes available through commissions, bonus, profit sharing, or other financial remuneration. In some nations, a sales force, by law, is paid an additional month's salary at Christmas or New Year and may qualify for benefits unknown to North American companies, such as a month of paid vacation each year.

Traditionally, hospitality companies have employed members of the sales force to perform the sales function primarily in an individualized manner. This system continues to be the backbone of a hospitality sales force, but newer forms of organizing a field sales force are gaining acceptance.

Team Sales

Team sales has become a necessity in many industries. The hospitality industry is no exception. The concept of a sales team is two or more persons working in concert toward a common sales objective. These persons

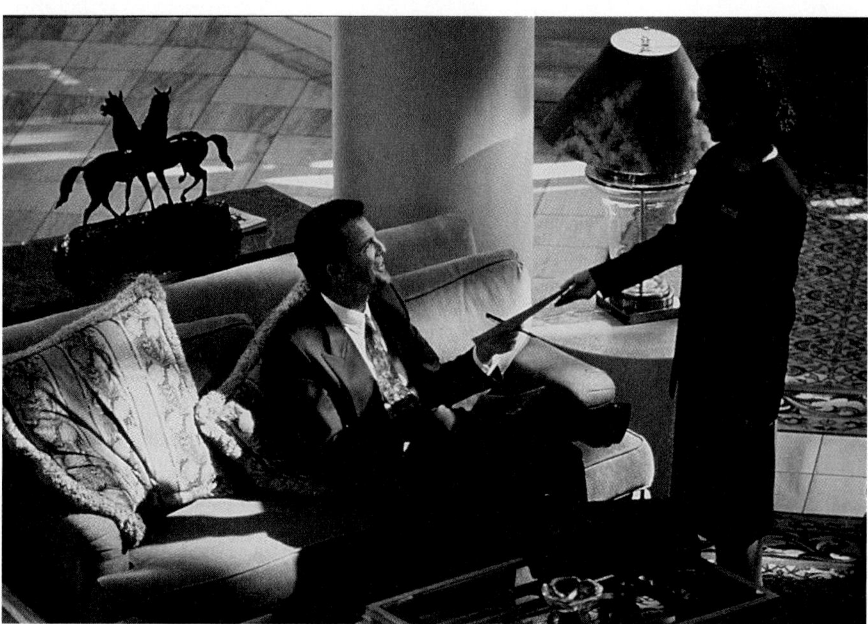

Today more employees are getting involved in the sales effort through the concept of sales teams. Courtesy of Hilton Hotels Corporation.

are not necessarily from the same company. The purpose for a team sales approach is to accomplish objectives through the synergism of two or more people that would be impossible or unduly costly through individual sales efforts.

In addition to traditional objectives, such as to increase occupancy in a hotel, other nonquantifiable objectives are sometimes established for teams. These generally deal with enhancing image and goodwill or using the team as a human resource training pool. People from various disciplines and departments are sometimes brought together to improve morale, teach teamwork, and cross-educate.

Teams within the hospitality industry have traditionally been used for specific tasks, which include but are not limited to the following:

- Sales blitz
- Travel mission
- Charity promotions
- Community improvement programs

Although teams are used for many purposes, the primary purpose for team sales should be to improve sales and the competitive position of a hotel, airline, cruise line, or other hospitality company. Teams are best used when the needs of the customer or prospect are complex and require the input of specialists. An example might be a large conference that requires the expertise and cooperation of an airline, a golf resort, and a ground transportation company.

Today the concept of team sales is moving beyond once-in-awhile use, such as during a sales blitz, to the allied concepts of relationship marketing and strategic alliances.

Relationship Marketing and Strategic Alliances

The goal of personal selling has traditionally been viewed as a specific contract with a customer. But in many cases the company is not seeking simply a one-time sale. It has targeted a major customer account that it would like to win and serve for a long period of time. The company would like to demonstrate to the account that it has the capabilities to serve the account's needs in a superior way, particularly if a committed relationship can be formed. The type of selling to establish a long-term collaborative relationship is more complex than a short run, one-time sales approach. Obtaining long-run commitment involves many more agreements than simply closing the sale.[31]

More companies today are moving their emphasis from transaction marketing to relationship marketing. The days of the lone salesperson working his or her territory and being guided only by a sales quota and a compensation plan are numbered. Today's customers are large and often global. They prefer suppliers who can sell and deliver a coordinated set of products and services to many locations, who can quickly solve problems that arise in their different locations, and who can work closely with customer teams to improve products and processes.

Companies recognize that sales teamwork will increasingly be the key to winning and maintaining accounts. Yet they recognize that asking their people for teamwork doesn't produce it. They need to revise their compensation system to give credit for work on shared accounts, they must set up better goals and measures for their sales forces, and they must emphasize the importance of teamwork in their training programs, while honoring the importance of individual initiative.

Relationship marketing is based on the premise that important accounts need focused and continuous attention. Salespeople working with customers under relationship marketing must do more than call when they think customers might be ready to place orders. They should monitor key accounts, know their problems, be ready to serve them in a number of ways, and strive to become part of the client's team.

When a relationship management program is implemented properly, the organization will begin to focus as much on managing its customers as on managing its products. At the same time, companies should realize that although there is a strong and warranted move toward relationship marketing, it is not effective in all situations. Ultimately, hospitality companies must judge which segments and which specific customers will respond profitably to relationship marketing.

The Boca Raton Resort and Club provides an example of the benefits that can accrue from relationship marketing. In 1994, the Cosmetic, Toiletry, and Fragrance Association met at this resort for the twenty-fourth consecutive time. "To keep a national association like CTFA coming back amidst a sea of competitors, our resort cannot merely serve as a site for their conference," explained David Feder, the Boca's senior vice president of sales and marketing. "We look to ourselves as much more than that: We can actually help associations fulfill their goals and shape their futures."[32]

Strategic alliances are a highly developed form of relationship marketing that are common between vendor and buyer or between noncompeting vendors and a common buyer. "Alliances are relationships between independent parties that agree to cooperate but still retain separate identities."[33] A strategic alliance may involve sharing a combination of any of the following: confidences, database, market knowledge, planning, resources, risks, security, and technology. Three types of strategic alliances have been characterized for the hotel industry:

1. **One-night stands.** These are short-term opportunistic relations, such as cross-advertising between a hotel and a restaurant or the selling agreement between Radisson Hotels and Britain's Edwardian Hotels.
2. **Affairs.** Medium-term tactical relationships account for alliances in this grouping. Hotels may participate with airlines in frequent-flyer programs.
3. **I dos.** This is equivalent to marriage. Parties in these arrangements expect long-term commitment. In some cases, equity investment is essential, such as the alliance between U.S. Air and British Airways.

Examples of strategic alliances within the hospitality industry include the following:

- An agreement between Carlson Hospitality Group, a division of Carlson Company, Inc., and Hospitality Franchise Systems (HFS), whereby HFS will operate existing food and beverage systems on a franchise or lease basis in Carlson's hotel properties. This agreement includes cooperative buying in which hotel companies can purchase supplies, services, and equipment at reduced prices.[34]
- An agreement was made between Hostmark International (Denver) and the Management Group (Chicago) to form a partnership to manage hotels. This alliance enables the two companies to approach major financial institutions as a national company rather than as two regional companies.[35]

Strategic alliances have become a necessity due to a variety of factors: globalization, complicated customer needs, large customers with multilocations, the need for technology, highly interdependent vendor/buyer relationships, intensified competition, and low profitability within the hospitality industry.

Strategic alliances directly affect the nature of the professional sales function within hospitality companies. The need for professional sales is dramatically enhanced. Salespeople must be better educated and able to understand sophisticated buyer needs and conduct complex negotiations.

Large customers may require services such as assistance with planning, extended financing, equity participation, and the use of technology, such as EDI (electronic data interchange). In turn, these needs affect the policies and procedures of suppliers. A buyer who demands that all invoices be sent and settled through EDI may create a need for new investment in hardware and software on the part of the suppliers.

Salespeople must be able to understand increasingly sophisticated buyer needs and communicate them to management. In many cases the real test of a salesperson's skills comes in the ability of that person to convince his or her own management of the need to change policies and procedures.

The remainder of this chapter is concerned with the process of sales management. The topics selected for discussion are basic to sales managers of virtually all hospitality companies. Although these concepts have application to the management of an inside sales force, a commission sales force, and team selling, they were developed primarily for the management of a traditional sales force composed of individual salaried salespeople. The majority of the remaining examples in this chapter refer to this traditional form of sales force.

Recruiting and Training a Professional Sales Force

Importance of Careful Selection

At the heart of a successful sales force operation is the selection of effective sales representatives. The performance difference between an average and a top sales representative can be considerable. One survey revealed that the top 27 percent of the sales force brought in over 52 percent of the sales. Beyond the differences in sales productivity are the great wastes in hiring the wrong person. When a salesperson quits, the costs of finding and training a new salesperson plus the cost of lost sales can be substantial. And a sales force with many new people is generally less productive.[36]

What Makes a Good Sales Representative?

Selecting sales representatives would be simple if we knew what traits to look for. Most customers say they want sales representatives to be honest, reliable, knowledgeable, and helpful. The company should look for these traits when selecting candidates.

Another approach is to look for traits common to the most successful salespeople in the company. A study of superachievers found that supersales performers exhibit the following traits: risk taking, powerful sense of mission, problem-solving bent, care for the customer, and careful planning.[37] One of the shortest lists of traits concluded that the effective salesperson has two basic qualities: empathy, the ability to feel as the customer does; and ego drive, a strong personal need to make the sale.[38]

Establishing a Profile of Desired Characteristics: Matching the Corporate Culture

The management of each hospitality company has a responsibility to determine a desired sales force profile. This is not solely the responsibility of a sales manager. The general manager, vice president marketing/sales, and others should help to determine the preferred characteristics for a sales force. Desired characteristics such as honesty, personal integrity, self-esteem, confidence, inner motivation, and desire to excel must be enunciated clearly by management.

The person who should first exemplify these is the sales manager. Management selects this person and then empowers him or her with primary responsibility for recruiting, training, motivating, and controlling the sales force.

The rhetoric of most hospitality companies regarding a desired sales force is much the same, but actually putting words into action varies. This is partially attributable to the fact that managers sometimes overlook the importance of their unique corporate culture and simply adopt a generic profile description. All hotels are not alike, nor are all cruise lines, nor are the members of any hospitality company.

The corporate culture within some organizations is formal and authoritarian. In others, a spirit of spontaneity and fun is encouraged. Substantial differences exist among hospitality firms. Both the employer and the salesperson need to fully recognize that success cannot be realized if the two parties are incompatible. A salesperson might be very successful with InterContinental or Four Seasons Hotels, but unable to adapt to the culture of Ramada or Novotel Hotels.

17.9 Novotel Hotel
Ritz-Carlton

The Ritz-Carlton Hotel Corporation embraces a corporate philosophy that both the guests it serves and its employees are cultured individuals who should be treated with respect and should be referred to as ladies and gentlemen. This message is transmitted in advertisements for openings, such as an advertisement in the *South China Morning Post* that read as follows: "The Ritz-Carlton Hong Kong, situated in the heart of Central, with 216 guest rooms, offering the finest tradition in hospitality, is now offering committed, energetic, and enthusiastic Ladies and Gentlemen opportunities to fill the following positions. . . ."[39]

In service encounters, customers perform roles and employees perform roles. Satisfaction of both parties is likely when the customer and service provider engage in behaviors that are consistent with each other's role expectation. Ritz realizes that its customers expect to be treated professionally and with a degree of formality. Thus, they communicate to their employees that they are ladies and gentlemen to prepare them for the role of providing professional service to their customers who are also ladies and gentlemen.[40]

Matching Career Acquisitions with Corporate Objectives

The aspirations of a salesperson must first be clearly understood by that person and then clearly communicated to the potential employer. The hospitality industry does not generally offer sales positions that allow a person to become wealthy from commissions or bonuses. Salespeople seeking great wealth are well advised to seek careers in commercial real estate or securities. Despite this, the hospitality industry does offer many advantages to a salesperson.

- The industry is fun. Unlike selling funeral plots or cancer insurance, the product is by nature fun and even exciting.
- Clients are generally personable and willing to listen, unlike industries in which the client has little time to talk and exhibits an aggressive knock-you-over attitude.
- Fellow salespeople and other colleagues are generally people oriented, gregarious, and enjoyable.

- Opportunities for travel exist, particularly in sales of airlines, cruise lines, travel agencies, and travel wholesalers.
- Opportunities for movement within the hospitality industry exist. Considerable career movement occurs within the industry. Salespeople move among the various industry members, such as from a hotel or resort to a cruise line or rental car firm.
- Management opportunities exist. Career growth to positions of sales manager are quite feasible. Career growth to vice presidency of sales or marketing is also possible.

It should be recognized that career promotion to general manager within hotels and resorts from sales historically has not often occurred, but is beginning to occur more frequently. These positions generally call for individuals with broader experience and training, including food and beverage, front desk, and other operational areas.

Neither the salesperson nor the company benefit by disguising true career objectives or the actual corporate culture. Experienced and astute sales managers seem to develop a sixth sense for determining whether a candidate's personality and background truly match the sales position. Once a salesperson is selected and hired, they have to be trained.

Sales Force Training

Sales training is vital to success, yet unfortunately remains a weak link within the hospitality industry. This is particularly problematic for recent graduates with little or no workplace experience. Fortunately, the situation is improving, as several hospitality companies now have training programs.

Sales training is not a one-time process, but is instead a career-long endeavor. Continuous training is part of the written philosophy of Singapore Airlines. This company believes that all employees must be trained and retrained continuously, including the basics.

Types of Training Required

Members of a sales force require three types of training:

1. **Product/service training.** Technology creates continuous change within the hospitality industry. Reservation systems, equipment such as airplanes or cruise ships, and entire operational systems change. Service delivery systems, menus, branch locations, and a myriad of other changes require regular and frequent training.
2. **Policies, procedures, and planning training.** As organizations increase in size and complexity, the need for formalized systems and procedures increases. Salespeople are often criticized by other departments for their failure to follow established procedures or conform to policies. Training is essential to ensure that all policies and procedures are understood.

   Effective salespeople continuously wink at some policies and procedures. This is generally done in an effort to satisfy customer needs and close the sale quickly. Unfortunately, a chronic failure to do things the "company way" inevitably leads to problems.

Hospitality salespeople receive much criticism for their lack of attention to detail in the barrage of paperwork that they must complete. Failure to complete paperwork correctly, on time, and in detail leads to costly errors, customer dissatisfaction, and ill will among other departments.

Today the sales force of many companies is becoming automated. Sales force members are expected to use computers throughout their career. This trend is likely to continue and will require continuous training of the sales force.

3. **Sales techniques training.** An age-old debate centers on the wisdom of attempting to teach techniques of selling. One camp firmly believes that salespeople are determined by genetics, personality, and motivation, not by training. The other side generally agrees that only a small percentage of individuals make effective salespeople but also contends that their effectiveness can be enhanced by learning sales basics such as the following:

- Prospecting
- Obtaining the initial sales call (setting the appointment)
- Conducting the sales dialogue
  —Becoming acquainted
  —Asking questions and probing for prospect's needs
  —Listening to what prospect says and doesn't say
  —Presenting benefits of product/service features to match prospect's needs
  —Overcoming objections
  —Further probing if necessary to determine needs
  —Closing the sale
- Follow-up
  —To continue sales dialogue if prospect did not buy
  —To say thank you for the order
  —To assure client that this was the correct thing to do
  —To look for opportunities to upsell or cross sell
  —To ask for leads and testimonials
  —To ask for another appointment or ask for another sale when client is again ready to purchase

Although sales training is most effective when customized, there are general factors that contribute to the success or failure of a salesperson. These should be considered when developing a sales training program.

Six factors have been determined to contribute to sales failure. Each is relevant to salespeople within the hospitality industry.[41]

1. Poor listening skills[42]
2. Failure to concentrate on top priorities
3. Lack of sufficient effort

4. Inability to determine customer needs
5. Lack of planning for sales presentations
6. Inadequate product/service knowledge

Sales training is the primary but not the sole responsibility of the sales manager. It has been suggested that hotel sales managers should spend 50 percent of their time selling, 30 percent supervising and training staff, and the remaining 20 percent with paperwork, meetings, and reviewing marketing plans.[43] Given the importance of an effective and professional sales force, others must assume some level of training responsibility.

Upper management, particularly the general manager and vice president of sales/marketing, has a critical role. The authority and respect afforded upper management enables these persons to establish and maintain a desired attitude in regard to policies, procedures, and planning. Members of upper management often assist in training by presenting an overview of the company and its history, culture, and norms. This sends a clear message to the sales force and helps to establish an effective learning attitude.

Sales managers often invite people from other departments, such as the chef or reservations manager, to attend sales meetings for the purpose of discussing product improvements. It is also important for salespeople to experience the company's service. Salespeople for a cruise line cannot effectively sell the excitement of sailing if they have never left dry land.

The hospitality industry has historically offered free or low-cost "fam trips" (familiarization trips) to travel agents and wholesalers. This may be considered as training of sales intermediaries. Other benefits, such as free flight privileges and expense accounts to entertain guests in the company's lounge and restaurants, also enhance product knowledge. These perks are often viewed with suspicion by employees and managers from other departments. It is essential that they be used judiciously. Sales managers have a responsibility to see that these necessary perks are not abused by members of their sales force.

Training Materials and Outside Training Assistance

Formal training may sometimes be necessary in which technical details must be memorized. The use of interactive video for this kind of training has proved effective. Some fast-food chains now use such systems to help train operational employees.

Videos, manuals, and books have a role, provided that they are carefully selected and viewed as additional learning tools rather than the sole means for training. These must be carefully selected. Many sales managers err in purchasing an expensive training system of tapes, videos, and programmed learning from an outside vendor. Later these may be found to be too generic in content.

Organizations such as the Hotel/Motel Educational Association, the National Restaurant Association, universities such as Cornell University, and training institutes such as polytechnics offer materials specifically designed for the hospitality industry.

Universities are now forging strategic relationships with companies and trade associations to train management and staff on an ongoing basis. A group of hospitality authors and researchers believes that "the main training partnership in the next century will be manifested by a closer alignment between the university, Hotel/Restaurant Management programs, and business partners. This alignment will plug into organizational needs, meaning fewer off-the-shelf programs."[44]

Preparatory training is enhanced by skills learned in the workplace. Ultimately, all training is perfected on the job. Some managers continue to believe that effective training consists solely of learning from one's trials and errors while selling. What is overlooked is that this is costly. For many, this sink-or-swim system is extremely threatening and creates unnecessary turnover and morale problems.

As the new salesperson learns through experience, it is critical for the sales manager to monitor progress and offer encouragement and suggestions for improving areas of weakness. Effective sales managers are effective teachers. Individuals who do not enjoy teaching or coaching may find that their own management careers are limited.

All teachers dread a moment of truth. That is the time in which grades must be given. Granting an A is pleasurable and easy, but placing an F on someone's record requires soul searching. The same is true for a sales manager, who must eventually come to the conclusion that no amount of training will create a professional salesperson of certain people.

Once this decision has been reached after serious study and thought, the sales manager has no alternative other than to release the salesperson promptly. Those who rescind this decision in the face of emotion-laden pleas for a second chance only postpone the inevitable.

Managing the Sales Force

Volumes of books and articles have been written about managing a professional sales force. The research and study dedicated to this subject clearly indicate that successful sales management is not the result of following a formula.

Successful sales managers cannot be described by a narrow profile. Successful sales managers come in all sizes, shapes, colors, and backgrounds. Perhaps, if a universal truth exists, it is that long-run successful sales managers exhibit a strong affinity for their subordinates, are willing to continuously learn, and must be reasonably bright. Even these conclusions sometimes seem to be disputed by observing some sales managers who meet objectives and please upper management yet seem weak in virtually every skill and talent normally accorded to successful sales managers.

The fact is that market conditions often have an inordinate influence over a sales manager's failure or success. An economic climate in which guests are begging for hotel rooms versus three years of deep economic recession with a surplus of hotel rooms can produce very different results. Despite their skills or lack thereof, sales managers may look weak or triumphant.

Hospitality sales management is neither a precise science nor a formula-based work procedure. Nevertheless, there are functions or processes that have historically been associated with the management of a professional sales force. These should never be confused with the formula-based system of some selling areas, such as that employed by door-to-door vendors or telephone solicitors. Successful long-run hospitality sales requires a far more professional outlook and approach.

Selecting Sales Strategies

Sales successes within the hospitality industry are not the result of a hit-and-run sales mentality. Success depends on the development of excellent long-run relationships with clients or accounts. The 80/20 rule prevails within the hospitality industry. A bed and breakfast, a highway motel, or a discount airline may find no relevance, but major hotels and major airlines know well the phenomenon. This concept says that a majority of a firm's business comes from a minority of its customers. These are commonly referred to as key, national, or major accounts. Certain corporate clients and travel intermediaries, such as travel agents, generally serve as key accounts. These companies provide large numbers of customers.

Based on the concept of key customers, there are six general sales strategies that must be recognized by members of the hospitality industry.

1. *Prevent erosion of key accounts.* It does little good to attract new customers if key customers are lost. Companies operating on this kind of treadmill inevitably have higher than average sales force turnover and experience employee morale problems. Determine reasons why key customers leave and initiate corrective steps. Initiate and carefully manage programs that treat key customers as royalty. A single sales/service person may be assigned to work with only a handful of key accounts. Unless these accounts are provided highly personal service, the risk of loss to a competitor is great.

   The CEO of a large hotel chain reportedly once told franchisees that they should view their properties as buckets with holes in the bottom. From these holes escape large numbers of customers. The message was that franchises must place even greater efforts into sales to attract new customers. Some who attended this meeting reported that the message had a depressing affect on the audience, who viewed themselves on a treadmill that regularly increased in speed. This was undoubtedly not the desired effect of the analogy. Instead, the message should have been that each of us has holes in our respective buckets, but it is our responsibility to close or lessen the size of these holes so that we retain more of our customers.
2. *Grow key accounts.* Key accounts usually offer more sales potential than is currently realized. Key accounts may split their businesses between several provider companies. A hotel property or a hotel chain seldom obtains all or even a majority of a company's business. There is increasing evidence that companies are willing to reduce the number of hotel providers, and to give more of their business to a few hotels, if these companies meet their requirements for service and price.

Sometimes the sales force of a hotel becomes enamored with what appears to be a sales opportunity gold mine. Unfortunately, when this happens, traditional customers and traditional marketing channels that have consistently produced for the hotel are momentarily forgotten. This is the old and familiar phenomenon of "the grass is always greener on the other side of the fence."

In the summer of 1994, the sales department of many U.S. hotels thought they had discovered a "sure fire" client that would fill their hotel rooms. Organizers of soccer's World Cup (soccer) convinced hotels to reserve large quantities of rooms for thousands of anticipated fans. Some luxury hotels blocked off up to 1,000 room-nights a week only to find that demand did not materialize, thus requiring them to release 50 percent to 80 percent of the reserved rooms.

Hyatt International Sales Vice President Craig Parsons later described previous demand predictions as ludicrous. "We lost a lot of rooms that will not be resold because they have been out of the inventory too long," said Parsons. "It's the busy summer season and we did not need to have these rooms out of inventory because we could have sold them anyway."[45]

In addition to negating probable sales, Hyatt may have also infuriated good customers who were unable to book reservations and probably selected another hotel. It is possible that some of the guests may be difficult to recapture, particularly if they liked the competitor's hotel.

3. *Grow selected marginal accounts.* Selected marginal accounts can become key accounts if given sufficient time and a consistent level of service. They are currently marginal accounts for a variety of reasons, such as the following:
   - Experimenting or sampling your product or service. If they like it, they might provide substantially more business.
   - Have received poor service in the past and therefore use your services only when necessary.
   - Account manager changes have resulted in splitting the business between various hospitality firms.
   - Comfortable with your service but competitors have acquired the bulk of their business through better follow-up.
4. *Eliminate selected marginal accounts.* Unfortunately, some accounts result in net losses for a hospitality company. These negative yield customers should be identified and eliminated whenever possible. It may be difficult to eliminate these customers due to an inability to identify them when the order or reservation is placed. A professional sales force has the responsibility to remove these customers from their list of prospects or active accounts, and refrain from future sales calls or sales promotions directed to them.
5. *Retain selected marginal accounts but provide lower-cost sales support.* Many accounts represent infrequent purchases or low-

yield business. These accounts cannot bear the cost of personalized sales calls or expensive promotions. A common method of dealing with these accounts is to assign them to an inside sales force. These salespeople don't make field calls, but instead interact with customers through telephone, telemarketing, catalogs, direct mail, and fax machines.

6. *Obtain new business from selected prospects.* The process of obtaining new accounts is costly and time consuming. Experienced salespeople know that it often requires five or more sales calls to obtain the business of a prospect. The cost of making a single sales call may be several hundred dollars when all costs are considered, such as travel expenses, salary, and benefits to the salesperson. The high cost of obtaining a new customer dictates that this person must have the potential to contribute significantly to profits. It is inefficient and nonproductive to pursue sales prospects who have little or no likelihood of ever providing significant returns to the company.

Sales Force Tactics: Principles of Personal Selling

We turn now to the purpose of a sales force—to sell. Personal selling is an ancient art. Effective salespersons have more than instinct. They are trained in tactics to achieve sales success. Selling today is a profession that involves mastering and applying a set of principles.

Today's companies spend hundreds of millions of dollars each year to train their salespeople in the art of selling. All the sales training approaches try to convert a salesperson from being a passive order taker to an active order getter. Order takers operate on the following assumptions: customers know their needs, they resent attempts at influence, and they prefer courteous and self-effacing salespersons.

In training salespeople to be order getting, there are two basic approaches: a sales-oriented approach and a customer-oriented approach. The first trains the salesperson in high-pressure selling techniques, such as those used in selling encyclopedias or automobiles. The techniques include exaggerating the product's merits, criticizing competitive products, using a slick presentation, selling yourself, and offering some price concession to get the order on the spot. This form of selling assumes that customers are not likely to buy except under pressure, that they are influenced by a slick presentation and ingratiating manners, and that they will not be sorry after signing the order, or if they are, it doesn't matter.

The other approach trains salespeople in customer problem solving. The salesperson learns how to listen and question in order to identify customer needs and come up with good product solutions. Presentation skills are made secondary to customer-need analysis skills. The approach assumes that customers have latent needs that constitute company opportunities, that they appreciate constructive suggestions, and that they will be loyal to sales representatives who have their long-term interests at heart. The problem solver is a much more congruent concept for the salesperson under the marketing concept than the hard seller or order taker.

We examine briefly eight major aspects of personal selling: prospecting and qualifying, preapproach, approach, presentation and demonstration, negotiation, overcoming objections, closing, and follow-up/maintenance.

Prospecting and Qualifying

The first step in the selling process is to identify prospects. Although the company will try to supply leads, sales representatives need skill in developing their own. Leads can be developed in the following ways:

- Through call-ins
- Having a booth at appropriate travel or trade shows
- Participating in international travel missions
- Asking current customers for the names of prospects
- Cultivating other referral sources, such as suppliers, dealers, noncompeting sales representatives, bankers, and trade association executives
- Through leads generated by the chain
- Joining organizations to which prospects belong
- Engaging in speaking and writing activities that will draw attention
- Examining data sources (newspapers, directories) in search of names
- Using the telephone and mail to find leads
- Dropping in unannounced on various offices (cold canvassing)
- Conducting a sales blitz

Howard Feiertag reminds managers not to overlook leads from internal sources. For example, working with accounts payable a manager can find suppliers that may be sources of business. The reservations department should be trained to prospect guests representing companies to find out if more business exists from those companies. Front desk staff should prospect guests representing new companies. Prospecting internally and externally should be done on a daily basis. Once prospects have been identified, they need to be qualified.[46]

Sales representatives need skill in screening out poor leads. Prospects can be qualified by examining their financial ability, volume of business, special requirements, location, and likelihood of continuous business. The salesperson might phone or write to prospects before deciding whether to visit them. Leads can be categorized as hot leads, warm leads, and cool leads.

Preapproach

The salesperson needs to learn as much as possible about the prospect company (what it needs, who is involved in the purchase decision) and its buyers (their personal characteristics and buying styles). The salesperson should set call objectives, which might be to qualify the prospect or gather information, or to make an immediate sale. Another task is to decide on the best approach, which might be a personal visit, a phone call, or a letter. The best timing should be thought out because many prospects are busy at certain times. Finally, the salesperson should plan an overall sales strategy for the account.

Approach

The salesperson should know how to greet the buyer to get the relationship off to a good start. This involves the salesperson's appearance, the opening lines, and the follow-up remarks. The opening line should be positive, for example, "Mr. Smith, I am Alice Jones from the ABC Hotel Company. My company and I appreciate your willingness to see me. I will do my best to make this visit profitable and worthwhile for you and your company." This might be followed by key questions and active listening to understand the buyer and his or her needs.

Presentation and Demonstration

The salesperson now tells the product "story" to the buyer, following the AIDA formula of gaining attention, holding interest, arousing desire, and obtaining action. The salesperson emphasizes customer benefits throughout, bringing in product features as evidence of these benefits. A benefit is any advantage, such as lower cost, less work, or more profit for the buyer. A feature is a product characteristic, such as weight or size. A common selling mistake is to dwell on product features (a product orientation) instead of customer benefits (a market orientation).

Companies have developed three different styles of sales presentation. The oldest is the canned approach, which is memorized sales talk covering the main points. It is based on stimulus/response thinking; that is, the buyer is passive and can be moved to purchase by the use of the right stimulus words, pictures, terms, and actions. Canned presentations are used primarily in door-to-door and telephone selling. The formulated approach is also based on stimulus/response thinking, but identifies early the buyer's needs and buying style and then uses a formulated approach to this type of buyer. The salesperson initially draws the buyer into the discussion in a way that reveals the buyer's needs and attitudes. Then the salesperson moves into a formulated presentation that shows how the product will satisfy the buyer's needs. It is not canned but follows a general plan.

The need/satisfaction approach starts with a search for the customer's real needs by encouraging the customer to do most of the talking. This approach calls for good listening and problem-solving skills. The salesperson takes on the role of a knowledgeable business consultant hoping to help the customer save money or make more money.

Sales presentations can be improved with demonstration aids such as booklets, flipcharts, slides, movies, and audiocassettes and videocassettes. During the demonstration, the salesperson can draw on five influence strategies:[47]

1. **Legitimacy.** The salesperson emphasizes the reputation and experience of his or her company.
2. **Expertise.** The salesperson shows deep knowledge of the buyer's situation and company's products, doing this without being overly "smart."

Advertising helps to create awareness; the approach is easier if the prospect thinks favorably of your company. Courtesy of Opryland Hotel.

3. **Referent power.** The salesperson builds on any shared characteristics, interests, and acquaintances.
4. **Ingratiation.** The salesperson provides personal favors (a free lunch, promotional gratuities) to strengthen affiliation and reciprocity feelings.
5. **Impression.** The salesperson manages to convey favorable personal impressions.

Negotiation

Much of business-to-business selling involves negotiating skills. The two parties need to reach agreement on the price and other terms of sale. Salespersons need to win the order without making deep concessions that will hurt profitability.

Although price is the most frequently negotiated issue, other issues include quality of goods and service offered, purchase volume, and responsibility for financing, risk taking, and promotion. The number of negotiation issues is virtually unlimited.

Unfortunately, far too many hotel salespeople rely almost exclusively on price as their negotiating tool. Even worse, they often begin negotiating from an already discounted price rather than from rack rates. Negotiations should always begin with rack rates, and price concessions should be given only when absolutely essential. Numerous bargaining tools exist, such as upgrades, complimentary tickets for the ski lift or golf courses, first-class coffee breaks instead of coffee and soft drinks, airport pickup, and use of hotel services such as the fitness center. A hotel sales force might package these amenities into bundles of services and give them names such as the President's Package, the Connoisseur's Package, and the Executive Package.

Sales force members should be taught to negotiate using services or bundled services as the primary negotiating tool rather than price. The possible difference in service package negotiations versus price negotiation is shown in Table 17-2. It is easy to see that the hotel benefits by offering a package of services rather than a price discount at all levels other than a 10 percent discount. Sales force members must understand the economic value of these kinds of trade-offs before they enter into the negotiation process.

Bargaining, or **negotiation,** which we use interchangeably, has the following features:[48]

- At least two parties are involved.
- The parties have a conflict of interest with respect to one or more issues.

Table 17-2
Hotel Negotiation Cost Comparison: Offering a Service Package versus Price

	50 GUESTS AT 3 NIGHTS EACH	
	COST/GUEST	TOTAL COST
President's Package		
Airport pickup and delivery limousine service	$15	$ 750
Bottle of champagne in room	$20	$1000
Technician to take care of AV during the meeting	2½ days at $50/hour × 20 hours	$1000
		$2750
PRICE DISCOUNTS	TOTAL REVENUE POTENTIAL	
Rack rate ($150/night; 50 guests at 3 nights each)	$22,500	
	REVENUE LOST	
10%	$ 2,250	
20%	4,500	
30%	6,750	
40%	9,000	
50%	$11,250	

- The parties are at least temporarily joined together in a special kind of voluntary relationship.
- Activity in the relationship concerns the division or exchange of one or more specific resources and/or the resolution of one or more intangible issues among the parties or among those they represent.
- The activity usually involves the presentation of demands or proposals by one party and evaluation of these by the other, followed by concessions and counterproposals.

Marketers who find themselves in bargaining situations need certain traits and skills to be effective. The most important traits are preparation and planning skill, knowledge of subject matter being negotiated, ability to think clearly and rapidly under pressure and uncertainty, ability to express thoughts verbally, listening skill, judgment and general intelligence, integrity, ability to persuade others, and patience. These will help the marketer in knowing when and how to negotiate.[49]

When to Negotiate. Consider the following circumstances in which negotiation in the hospitality industry is an appropriate procedure for concluding a sale:[50]

1. When many factors bear not only on price, but also on quality and service
2. When business risks cannot be accurately predetermined

Negotiation is appropriate whenever a zone of agreement exists.[51] A zone of agreement exists when there are simultaneously overlapping acceptable outcomes for the parties.

Formulating a Bargaining Strategy. Bargaining involves preparing a strategic plan before bargaining begins and making good tactical decisions during the bargaining sessions. A bargaining strategy can be defined as a commitment to an overall approach that has a good chance of achieving the negotiator's objectives. For example, some negotiators pursue a hard strategy with opponents, whereas others maintain that a soft strategy yields more favorable results.

The sales force of a hotel or resort is in a position to use negotiating skills nearly every day of their professional lives. Their negotiation process can be enhanced by understanding the negotiating strengths and weaknesses of the client, as shown in Table 17-3.

Bargaining Tactics during Negotiations. Negotiators use a variety of tactics when bargaining. Bargaining tactics can be defined as maneuvers to be made at specific points in the bargaining process. Threats, bluffs, last-chance offers, hard initial offers, and other tactics occur in bargaining.

Fisher and Ury have offered advice that is consistent with their strategy of principles negotiation. Their first piece of tactical advice concerns what should be done if the other party is more powerful. By identifying your alternatives if a settlement is not reached, it sets a standard against which any offer can be measured. It protects you from being pressured into accepting unfavorable terms from a more powerful opponent.[52]

Another tactic comes into play when the opposing party insists on arguing his or her position instead of his or her interests and attacks your

Table 17-3
Examples of Hotel Customer's Negotiating Strengths and Weaknesses

STRENGTHS	WEAKNESSES
1. Provide many guests.	1. Provide few guests.
2. Come in low or shoulder seasons.	2. Come in prime season.
3. Stay low-occupancy nights.	3. Stay high-occupancy nights.
4. Bring quality guests.	4. Bring undesirable guests.
5. Provide cross-purchase potential.	5. Provide little or no cross-sale potential.
6. Purchase upscale rooms.	6. Purchase lowest-priced rooms.

proposals or person. Although the tendency is to push back hard when pushed, the better tactic is to deflect the attack from the person and direct it against the problem. Look at the interests that motivated the opposing party's position and invent options that can satisfy both parties' interests. Invite the opposing party's criticism and advice ("If you were in my position, what would you do?").

Another set of bargaining tactics is responses to opposition tactics that are intended to deceive, distort, or otherwise influence the bargaining to their own advantage. What tactic should be used when the other side uses a threat, or a take-it-or-leave-it tactic, or seats the other party on the side of the table with the sun in his eyes? A negotiator should recognize the tactic, raise the issue explicitly, and question the tactic's legitimacy and desirability—in other words, negotiate over it. Negotiating the use of the tactic follows the same principled negotiation procedure: Question the tactic, ask why the tactic is being used, or suggest alternative courses of action to pursue. If this fails, resort to your best alternative to a negotiated agreement (BATNA) and terminate the negotiation until the other side ceases to employ these tactics. Meeting these tactics by defending principles is more productive than counterattacking with tricky tactics.

Overcoming Objections

Customers almost always pose objections during the presentation or when asked for the order. Their resistance can be psychological or logical. Psychological resistance includes resistance to interference, preference for established hotel or airline, apathy, reluctance to giving up something, unpleasant associations about the other person, predetermined ideas, dislike of making decisions, and neurotic attitude toward money. Logical resistance might consist of objections to the price or certain product or company characteristics. To handle these objections, the salesperson maintains a positive approach, asks the buyer to clarify the objection, denies the validity of the objection, or turns the objection into a reason for buying. The salesperson needs training in the broader skills of negotiation, of which handling objections is a part.

Closing

Now the salesperson attempts to close the sale. Some salespeople do not get to this stage or do not do it well. They lack confidence or feel uncomfortable about asking for the order or do not recognize the right psychological moment to close the sale. Salespersons need to know how to recognize closing signals from the buyer, including physical actions, statements or comments, and questions. Salespersons can use one of several closing techniques. They can ask for the order, recapitulate the points of agreement, offer to help the secretary write up the order, ask whether the buyers want A or B, get the buyer to make minor choices such as on color or size, or indicate what the buyer will lose if the order is not placed now. The salesperson might offer the buyer specific inducements to close, such as a special price.

A basic problem mentioned over and over by hotel sales managers is that some members of the sales force do not ask for the order. They may follow all the other steps to perfection but for some reason seem incapable of asking for the order.

Follow-up/Maintenance

This last step is necessary if the salesperson wants to ensure customer satisfaction and repeat business. Immediately after closing, the salesperson should complete any necessary details on delivery time, purchase terms, and other matters. Follow-up or foul-up is a slogan of most successful salespeople. The salesperson should develop an account maintenance plan to make sure that the customer is not forgotten or lost.

Motivating a Professional Sales Force

Some sales representatives will put forth their best effort without any special coaching from management. To them, selling is the most fascinating job in the world. They are ambitious and self-starters. But the majority of sales representatives require encouragement and special incentives to work at their best level. This is especially true of field selling, for the following reasons:

- **Nature of the job.** The selling job is one of frequent frustration. Sales representatives usually work alone, their hours are irregular, and they are often away from home. They confront aggressive, competing sales representatives; they have an inferior status relative to the buyer; they often do not have the authority to do what is necessary to win an account; they lose large orders that they have worked hard to obtain.
- **Human nature.** Most people operate below capacity in the absence of special incentives, such as financial gain or social recognition.
- **Personal problems.** Sales representatives are occasionally preoccupied with personal problems, such as sickness in the family, marital discord, or debt.

A basic model of motivating sales representatives follows:[53]

motivation ⟶ effort ⟶ performance ⟶ rewards ⟶ satisfaction

The model implies the following:

1. Sales managers must be able to convince salespeople that they can sell more by working harder or by being trained to work smarter.
2. Sales managers must be able to convince salespeople that the rewards for better performance are worth the extra effort.

Sales Force Compensation

To attract and retain sales representatives, the company has to develop an attractive compensation package. Sales representatives would like income regularity, extra reward for an above-average performance, and fair payment for experience and longevity. On the other hand, management would like to achieve control, economy, and simplicity. Management objectives, such as economy, will conflict with sales representatives' objectives, such as financial security.

Management must determine the level and components of an effective compensation plan. The level of compensation must bear some relation to the going market price for the type of sales job and required abilities. If the market price for salespeople is well defined, the individual firm has little choice but to pay the going rate. The market price for salespeople, however, is seldom well defined. For one thing, sales compensation plans differ in the importance of fixed and variable salary elements, fringe benefits, and expense allowances. Data on the average take-home pay of competitors' sales representatives can be misleading because of significant variations in the average seniority and ability levels of the competitors' sales forces. Published data on industry sales force compensation levels are infrequent and generally lack sufficient detail.

The company must next determine the components of compensation: a fixed amount, a variable amount, expenses, and fringe benefits. The fixed amount, which might be salary or a drawing account, is intended to satisfy the sales representatives' need for income stability. The variable amount, which might be commissions, bonus, or profit sharing, is intended to stimulate and reward greater effort. Expense allowances enable the sales representatives to meet the expenses involved in travel, lodging, dining, and entertainment; fringe benefits, such as paid vacation, sickness or accident benefits, pensions, and life insurance, are intended to provide security and job satisfaction. Fixed and variable compensations give rise to three basic types of sales force compensation plans: straight salary, straight commissions, and combination salary and commission.

Many companies in the hospitality industry suffer from high sales force turnover. A variety of reasons has been given to explain this situation, such as burnout. A survey of college graduates preparing to enter the hospitality industry ranked salary as number 10 among variables relating to what they wanted in a job.[54] A different study of young managers who left hospitality careers demonstrated that money was indeed important. Pay-related issues were the second most common reason for leaving, following long hours and inconvenient scheduling as the primary reason. One respondent wrote, "I had poor pay, high stress, low praise and recognition, and worked 75 to 80 hours a week, all for the chance to be a GM in 10 or 15 years with the same job characteristics."[55]

The importance of monetary rewards to a hospitality sales force must not be minimized. These people are expected to maintain a large fashionable wardrobe, to work long hours, experience stress, and often give up family experiences for the sake of their career. Under these circumstances, monetary reward becomes very important.

Hospitality managers should evaluate high sales force turnover from the standpoint of multicosts, such as constant recruiting and training, plus intangible opportunity costs. The cost of finding ways to elevate monetary compensation for valuable sales force members may then seem less unattractive.

Supplementary Motivators

Companies use additional motivators to stimulate sales force effort. Periodic sales meetings provide a social occasion, a break from routine, a chance to meet and talk with "company brass," and a chance to air feelings and to identify with a larger group. Sales meetings are an important communication and motivational tool.[56] They can also be used for training in subjects such as how to make effective presentations.[57] Thus the sales meeting can and should assume increased importance to the sales force.

Companies also sponsor sales contests to spur the sales force to a special selling effort above what would normally be expected. The contest should present a reasonable opportunity for enough salespeople to win. If only a few salespersons can win or almost everyone can win, it will fail to spur additional effort. The sales contest period should not be announced in advance or else some salespersons will defer some sales to the beginning of the period; also, some may pad their sales during the period with customer promises to buy that do not materialize after the contest period ends.

Sales managers of hotels and resorts sometimes offer vacations at sister properties for winners of a sales contest. When the winners visit a sister property, they are introduced to the sales department and often learn new techniques. In turn, this information is transmitted to others when the winners return and give a report in the next sales meeting.

Evaluation and Control of a Professional Sales Force

We have been describing the feed-forward aspects of the sales supervision, how management communicates what the sales representatives should be doing and motivates them to do it. Good feed-forward requires good feedback, and good feedback means getting regular information from sales representatives to evaluate their performance.

Sales Quotas

Many companies set sales quotas prescribing what their sales representatives should sell during the year and by product. Compensation is often tied to the degree of quota fulfillment. Sales quotas are developed from the annual marketing plan. The company first prepares a sales forecast. This forecast becomes the basis for planning production, workforce size, and financial requirements. Then management establishes sales quotas for its regions and territories, which typically add up to more than the sales forecast. Sales quotas are often set higher than the sales forecast in order to stretch sales managers and salespeople to perform at their best level.

Each area sales manager divides the area's quota among the area's sales representatives. There are three schools of thought on quota setting. The high-quota school sets quotas that are higher than what most sales representatives will achieve but that are attainable. Its adherents believe that high quotas spur extra effort. The modest-quota school sets quotas that a majority of the sales force can achieve. Its adherents feel that the sales force will accept the quotas as fair, attain them, and gain confidence. The variable-quota school thinks that individual differences among sales representatives warrant high quotas for some and modest quotas for others.

Developing Norms for Salespeople

New sales representatives should be given more than a territory, a compensation package, and training—they need supervision. Supervision is the fate of everyone who works for someone else. It is the expression of the employers' natural and continuous interest in the activities of their agents. Through supervision, employers hope to direct and motivate the sales force to do a better job.

Companies vary in how closely they direct their sales representatives. Sales representatives who are paid mostly on commission generally receive less supervision. Those who are salaried and must cover definite accounts are likely to receive substantial supervision.

The number of calls that an average salesperson makes during a day has been decreasing. The downward trend is due to the increased use of technology, such as phone, e-mail, and fax machines; the increased reliance on automatic ordering systems, and the drop-in cold calls owing to better market research information for pinpointing prospects. It is also due to difficulties in reaching prospects due to traffic congestion, busy prospect schedules, and other complexities of contemporary business.

Companies often decide on how many calls to make a year on particular-sized accounts. Most companies classify customers into A, B, and C accounts, reflecting the sales volume, profit potential, and growth potential of the account. A accounts might receive nine calls a year; B, six calls; and C, three calls. The call norms depend on competitive call norms and expected account profitability.

Regardless of how a sales force is structured, individual salespeople must classify their customer base. A salesperson responsible for channel intermediaries, such as tour operators and travel agents, quickly learns that not all are capable of producing the same sales volume/profit. This is equally true for a salesperson who has responsibility for the conference/meeting segment and to some degree even for the person responsible for national accounts.

Omni International Hotels emphasizes account planning with its sales force. The management of Dunfey Hotels Corporation, which became Omni International, believed that it is critical to understand the marketplace and to classify accounts as to their potential for Omni (Dunfey). President Jon Canas told a Harvard professor in a taped interview that not all prospects may be contacted in a particular year because they do not qualify as the best target customers. However, it is important to know the second- and third-tier prospects so that they can be contacted if a slowdown occurs within the top targeted groups.[58] Canas believed that this system was appropriate for all members of the hotel/resort industry.

Companies often specify how much time their sales force should spend prospecting for new accounts. Companies set up prospecting standards for a number of reasons. If left alone, many sales representatives will spend most of their time with current customers. Current customers are better-known quantities. Sales representatives can depend on them for some business, whereas a prospect might never deliver any business. Unless sales representatives are rewarded for opening new accounts, they might avoid new account development.

Using Sales Time Efficiently

Sales representatives need to know how to use their time efficiently. One tool is the annual call schedule, showing which customers and prospects to call on in which months and which activities to carry out.

Another tool is time-and-duty analysis. The sales representative spends time in the following ways:

- **Travel.** In some jobs, travel time amounts to over 50 percent of total time.
- **Food and breaks.** Some portion of the sales force's workday is spent in eating and taking breaks.
- **Waiting.** Waiting consists of time spent in the outer office of the buyer. This is dead time unless the sales representative uses it to plan or to fill out reports.
- **Selling.** Selling is the time spent with the buyer in person or on the phone. It breaks down into social talk and selling talk.
- **Administration.** This consists of the time spent in report writing and billing, attending sales meetings, and talking to others in the company about production, delivery, billing, sales performance, and other matters.

Actual face-to-face selling time can amount to as little as 25 percent of total working time.[59] If it could be raised from 25 percent to 30 percent, this would be a 20 percent improvement. Companies are constantly seeking ways to improve sales force productivity. Their methods take the form of training sales representatives in the use of "phone power," simplifying record-keeping forms, and using the computer to develop call and routing plans and to supply customer and competitive information.

Managing Trade Shows

Trade shows are commonly used as a means of generating sales leads, keeping in touch with commercial customers, and writing business. Members of the hospitality industry participate in many trade shows, ranging from local/regional ones to international travel missions sponsored by visitor destinations, travel associations, and government departments or ministries of tourism.

Unfortunately, the cost/return effectiveness of trade shows is often placed in peril or disregarded through lack of effective planning and control. The conclusions of a study of hospitality trade show exhibitors were that "it is likely that the true marketing potential of trade shows is not being realized. Commitments to more effective planning would enhance the productivity of trade shows for most companies."[60]

Six steps were suggested to improve trade show effectiveness:

1. Construct a mailing list of prospects using in-house information of the list of expected visitors from the trade show management company.
2. Identify potential leads and communicate with them before the show.
3. Promote the show with incentives that reflect the company's theme, products, and services.
4. Send letters to prospective buyers inviting them to make a personal contact at the show or at an alternative location.
5. Keep good records of visitor contacts made during the show.
6. Follow up with qualified prospects after the show.

Sales force control and training are also needed to ensure success. The following are items a sales manager should implement before a trade show:

1. Review trade show objectives with the sales force prior to the show.
2. Designate a trade show captain responsible for managing sales activities.
3. Designate times when certain salespersons are expected to work the booth.
4. Prohibit smoking, drinking, eating, and bunching together in the trade booth.
5. Show sales force members how to deal with complaining/difficult visitors, greet customers/prospects, particularly key ones, develop prospects, identify nonprospects, and process and use leads, business cards, competitive data, and customer/prospect information acquired at the show.

Other Control Techniques

Management obtains information about its sales representatives in several ways. One important source is sales reports. Additional information comes through personal observation, customers' letters and complaints, customer surveys, and conversations with other sales representatives.

Sales reports are divided between activity plans and write-ups of activity results. The best example of the former is the salesperson's work plan, which sales representatives submit a week or month in advance.

The plan describes intended calls and routing. This report leads the sales force to plan and schedule their activities, informs management of their whereabouts, and provides a basis for comparing their plans and accomplishments. Sales representatives can be evaluated on their ability to "plan their work and work their plan."

Many hospitality companies require their sales representatives to develop an annual territory marketing plan in which they outline their program for developing new accounts and increasing business from existing accounts. This type of report casts sales representatives into the role of market managers and profit centers. Sales representatives write up their completed activities on call reports. Call reports inform sales management of the salesperson's activities, indicate the status of specific customer accounts, and provide useful information for subsequent calls. Sales representatives also submit expense reports, new business reports, lost business reports, and reports on local business and economic conditions.

These reports provide raw data from which sales managers can extract key indicators of sales performance. The key indicators are (1) average number of sales calls per salesperson per day, (2) average sales call time per contact, (3) average revenue per sales call, (4) average cost per sales call, (5) entertainment cost per sales call, (6) percentage of orders per 100 sales calls, (7) number of new customers per period, (8) number of lost customers per period, and (9) sales force cost as a percentage of total sales. These indicators answer several useful questions. Are sales representatives making too few calls per day? Are they spending too much time per call? Are they spending too much on entertainment? Are they closing enough orders per 100 calls? Are they producing enough new customers and holding on to the old customers?

Formal Evaluation of Performance. The sales force's reports along with other observations supply the raw materials for evaluating members of the sales force. Formal evaluation procedures lead to at least three benefits. First, management has to communicate their standards for judging sales performance. Second, management needs to gather comprehensive information about each salesperson. Third, sales representatives know that they will have to sit down one morning with the sales manager and explain their performance or failure to achieve certain goals.

Salesperson-to-Salesperson Comparisons. One type of evaluation is to compare and rank the sales performance of a company's sales representatives. Such comparisons, however, can be misleading. Relative sales performance is meaningful only if there are no variations in territory market potential, workload, competition, company promotional effort, and so on. Furthermore, current sales are not the only success indicator. Management should also be interested in how much each sales representative contributes to current net profits.

Customer Satisfaction Evaluation. A salesperson might be very effective in producing sales but not rate high with customers. An increasing number of companies are measuring customer satisfaction not only with their product and customer-support service but with their salespeople. The customers' opinion of the salesperson, product, and service can be measured by mail questionnaires or telephone calls. Company salespeople who score high on satisfying their customers can be given special recognition, awards, or bonuses.

Qualitative Evaluation of Sales Representatives

Evaluations can also assess the salesperson's knowledge of the company, products, customers, competitors, territory, and responsibilities. Personality characteristics can be rated, such as general manner, appearance, speech, and temperament. The sales manager can also review any problems in motivation or compliance. The sales manager can check that the sales representative knows and observes company policies. Each company must develop its own evaluation procedure. Whatever procedure is chosen, it must be fair to the salesperson and the company. If members of a sales force feel that they are being judged against incorrect norms, they will quickly become dissatisfied and may leave the company.

Hospitality sales is a profession and must be treated as such. It is very much to the advantage of any hospitality company to develop a professional, loyal, and contented sales force. Measurement of a salesperson's value and contribution must not be left to the last minute or to inappropriate standards and measures. No aspects of sales management is more important than developing and using the correct appraisal system for members of a professional sales force.

Key Terms

Allocating Sales representatives decide on which customers to allocate scarce products to.

Communicating Sales representatives communicate information about the company's products and services.

Information gathering Sales representatives conduct market research and intelligence work and fill in a call report.

Prospecting The process of searching for new accounts.

Selling Sales representatives know the art of salesmanship: approaching, presenting, answering objections, and closing sales.

Servicing Sales representatives provide various services to the customers: consulting on their problems, rendering technical assistance, arranging financing, and expediting delivery.

Targeting Sales representatives decide how to allocate their scarce time among prospects and customers.

Chapter Review

I. **Sales Positions in the Hospitality Industry**

1) **Deliverer.** The salesperson's job is predominantly to deliver the product.

2) **Order taker.** The salesperson is predominantly an inside order taker.

3) **Missionary.** The salesperson is not expected or permitted to take an order but is called only to build goodwill or to educate the actual or potential user.

4) **Technician.** The major emphasis is placed on technical knowledge.

5) **Demand creator.** This position demands the creative sales of tangible products or of intangibles.

II. Sales-Force Objectives

1) **Setting objectives**

a) **Prospecting.** Sales representatives find and cultivate new customers.

b) **Targeting.** Sales representatives decide how to allocate their scarce time among prospects and customers.

c) **Communicating.** Sales representatives communicate information about the company's products and services.

d) **Selling.** Sales representatives know the art of salesmanship: approaching, presenting, answering objections, and closing sales.

e) **Servicing.** Sales representatives provide various services to the customers: consulting on their problems, rendering technical assistance, arranging financing, and expediting delivery.

f) **Information gathering.** Sales representatives conduct market research and intelligence work and fill in a call report.

g) **Allocating.** Sales representatives decide on which customers to allocate scarce products to.

2) **Upselling and second-chance selling.** Excellent profit opportunities exist for hospitality companies, particularly hotels and resorts, to upgrade price and profit margins by selling higher-priced products such as suites through upselling. A related concept is second-chance selling.

3) **Market share or market penetration.** These are two important objectives.

4) **Product-specific objectives.** Occasionally, a sales force will be charged with the specific responsibility to improve sales volume for specific product lines.

III. Sales-Force Structure

1) **Territorial-structured sales force.** Each sales representative is assigned an exclusive territory in which to represent the company's full line.

a) **Territorial size.** Territories are designed to provide either equal sales potential or equal workload.

b) **Territorial shape.** Territories are formed by combining smaller units until they add up to a territory of a given sales potential or workload.

2) **Product-structured sales force.** Company structures its sales force along product lines due to the importance of sales representatives knowing their products.

3) **Market-structured sales force.** Company structures its sales force based on market segments.

4) **Customer-structured sales force.** A sales force is organized by market segment such as the association market and the corporate market or by specific key customers.

5) **Combination-structured sales force.** A large hotel might have a catering/banquet sales force (product), a convention/meeting sales force (market segment), a tour wholesales sales force (marketing intermediary), and a national accounts sales force (customer).

6) **Determining sales force size**

a) Customers are grouped into size classes according to their annual sales volume.

b) The desired call frequencies are established for each class.

c) The number of accounts in each size class is multiplied by the corresponding call frequency to arrive at the total workload for the country in sales call per year.

d) The average number of calls a sales representative can make per year is determined.

e) The number of sales representatives needed is determined by dividing the total annual calls required by the average annual calls made by a sales representative.

IV. Organizing the Sales Department

1) **Inside sales force.** The inside sales force includes technical-support persons, sales assistants, and telemarketers.

2) **Field sales force.** The field sales force includes commissioned reps, salaried reps, and sales teams.

V. Relationship Marketing. The art of creating a closer working relationship and interdependence between the people in two organizations.

1) **Strategic alliances.** Alliances are relationships between independent parties that agree to cooperate but still retain separate identities.

2) **Reasons strategic alliances are necessary.** Globalization, complicated customer needs, large customers with multilocations, the need for technology, highly interdependent vendor/buyer relationship, intensified competition, and low profitability within the hospitality industry.

VI. Recruiting and Selecting Sales Representatives. The effective salesperson has two basic qualities: empathy, the ability to feel as the customer does; ego drive, a strong personal need to make the sales.

1) **When to recruit.** There are three methods: recruit and train salespeople in a batch process; recruit only as needed for replacement and growth; always recruit.

2) **Training.** There are three types of training: product/service training; policies, procedures, and planning training; sales techniques training.

3) **Directing sales representatives.** Responsibilities are developing norms for customer calls; developing norms for prospect calls; using sales time effectively (travel, food and break, waiting, selling, administration).

VII. Managing the Sales Force

1) **Selecting sales strategies.** The following are six general sales strategies:

a) Prevent erosion of key accounts.

b) Grow key accounts.

c) Grow selected marginal accounts.

d) Eliminate selected marginal accounts.

e) Retain selected marginal accounts, but provide lower-cost sales support.

f) Obtain new business from selected prospects.

2) Principles of personal selling. These are prospecting and qualifying, preapproach, approach, presentation and demonstration, negotiation, overcoming objections, closing, and follow-up/maintenance.

a) Basic model: Motivation, effort, performance, rewards, satisfaction.

b) Sales quotas and supplementary motivator.

3) Evaluating sales representatives. There are several means of formal evaluation of performance: sales-to-salesperson comparisons; current-to-past sales comparisons; customer satisfaction evaluation; qualitative evaluation of sales representatives.

VIII. The Sales Process. Prospecting and qualifying, preapproach, approach, presentation and demonstration, overcoming objections, closing, and follow-up and maintenance.

IX. Motivating a Professional Sales Staff. The majority of sales representatives require encouragement and special incentives to work at their best level.

1) Sales force compensation. There are three basic types of sales-force compensation plans: straight salary, straight commission, and combination salary and commission.

2) Evaluation and control of a professional sales force. Sales quotas, sales norms, and time management tools such as call schedules are common ways of controlling a sales force.

Discussion Questions

1. Why should companies be concerned about key or national accounts?
2. What are the most common methods of structuring a sales force?
3. Discuss the importance of establishing sales objectives and the various kinds of sales force objectives common to the hospitality industry.
4. Many people feel that they do not have the ability to be successful salespeople. What role does training play in helping someone to develop selling ability?
5. Discuss the process of negotiation and how it can be used effectively by sales force members.
6. Good salespeople are familiar with their competitors' products as well as their own. What would you do if your company expected you to sell a product that you thought was inferior to the competition's? Why?
7. It has been said that there are two parts to every sale—the part performed by the salesperson and the part performed for the salesperson by his or her organization. What should the company provide for the salesperson to help increase total sales? How does the sales manager's job differ from the sales rep's job?
8. A district sales manager voiced the following complaint at a sales meeting: "The average salesperson costs our company $40,000 in compensation and expenses. Why can't we buy a few less $40,000 full-page ads in *Time* magazine and use the money to hire more people? Surely one individual working for a year can sell more products than a one-page ad in one issue of *Time*." Evaluate this argument.

Experiential Exercise

Do the following:

Conduct an interview with a salesperson for a hospitality or tourism organization. Ask the salesperson about the job. Find out what a typical day is like, and what they like and dislike about the job. Ask how they feel technology will affect the sales department in the future. You may of course ask other questions that are of interest to you. Write up your finding in a report.

Internet Exercise

Support for these exercises can be found on the Web site for *Marketing for Hospitality and Tourism*, www.prenhall.com/kotler.

Find a hotel Web site that has a section for meeting planners. Do these sites appear to be taking the place of a salesperson or offering assistance to the sales department? Include the names of the sites you visited in your response.

References

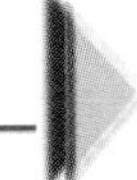

1. Bill Primavera, *Introducing the First Lady of American Restaurants* (Yorktown Heights, NY: Primavera Public Relations, Inc., 1995).
2. Jeffrey A. Tannenbaum, "Franchises Takes Complaints against Pearle to FTC," A New Newsletter, *Wall Street Journal,* February 16, 1994, pp. B2–3.
3. Robin Lee Allen, "Ruth Fertel: Tireless Entrepreneur," *Nation's Restaurant News,* September 21, 1992, p. 81.
4. John De Mers, "Rare Ruth," *USAir Magazine* (February 1990): 78.
5. Meredith Petran, "The Fourth Annual Restaurant Business High Performance Restaurant Leadership Awards: The Stars Come Out," *Restaurant Business,* March 1, 2001, pp. 22–34.
6. Adapted from Robert N. McMurry, "The Mystique of Super-Salesmanship," *Harvard Business Review* (March/April 1961): 114; see also William C. Moncrief III, "Selling Activity and Sales Position Taxonomies for Industrial Salesforces," *Journal of Marketing Research* (August 1986): 261–270.
7. John W. Veritz, "Taking a Laptop on a Call," *Business Week,* October 25, 1993, p. 124.
8. Everett Martin, "Its Jerry Hale on the Line," *Sales and Marketing Management* 145, no. 15 (December 1993): 74.
9. Susan Hancock, "How to Generate Leads for High Ticket Items," *Potentials in Marketing* 27, no. 5 (1994): 52.
10. Donna J. Owens, "To Offset Their Seasonality, Canada's Resorts Should Stretch Their Seasons by Appealing to Multiple Market Segments," *Cornell Hotel and Restaurant Administration Quarterly* 35, no. 5 (October 1994): 29.
11. Ibid., p. 30.
12. Lisa C. Weiss, "Days Inns of America: To Give 1400 General Managers One Year Membership to Hospitality Sales and Marketing Associations International," *Business Travel News,* November 8, 1993, p. 10.
13. Howard Feiertag, "Database Marketing Proves Helpful in Group Sales," *Hotel and Motel Management,* March 8, 1993, p. 14.
14. Owens, "To Offset Their Seasonality."
15. William J. Quain and Stephen M. LeBruto, "Second-Chance Selling," *Cornell Hotel and Restaurant Administration Quarterly* 35, no. 5 (October 1994): 81.
16. Peter Rainsford, "Selecting and Monitoring Hotel Management Companies," *Cornell Hotel and Restaurant Administration Quarterly* 35, no. 2 (April 1994): 34.
17. Michael P. Sim and Burritt M. Chase, "Enhancing Resort Profitability with Membership Programs," *Cornell Hotel and Restaurant Administration Quarterly* 34, no. 8 (August 1993): 59–62.
18. *The Cruise Industry: An Overview* (New York: Cruise Lines Association, July 1994), p. 31.
19. Christopher Schulz, "Hotel and Travel Agents: The New Partnership," *Cornell Hotel and Restaurant Administration Quarterly* 35, no. 2 (April 1994): 45.
20. Al Glanzberg and Glenn Withiam, "Andre Tatibouet: Maximizing Asset Value," *Cornell Hotel and Restaurant Administration Quarterly* 35, no. 2 (April 1994): 26.
21. Taketosh Yamazaki, "Tokyo Hotel Construction Push Roger On," *Tokyo Business Today* 59, no. 3 (March 1991): 50–51.
22. William A. Kaven and Myrtle Allardyce, "Dalmahoy's Strategy for Success," *Cornell Hotel and Restaurant*

Administration Quarterly 35, no. 6 (December 1994): 86–89.

23. Sheryl E. Kimes and Douglas C. Lord, "Wholesalers and Caribbean Resort Hotels," *Cornell Hotel and Restaurant Administration Quarterly* 35, no. 5 (October 1994): 75.
24. Phillip R. Mogle, "Planner under Siege," *Successful Meetings* (September 1990): 76.
25. Robert A. Meyer, "Understanding Telemarketing for Hotels," *Cornell Hotel and Restaurant Administration Quarterly* 28, no. 2 (August 1987): 26.
26. Barbara Jean Ross, "Training: Key to Effective Reservations," *Cornell Hotel and Restaurant Administration Quarterly* 31, no. 3 (November 1990): 71–79.
27. Ibid., p. 79.
28. Timothy Troy, "Windsor Winning with Tried and True Formula," *Hotel and Motel Management* 208 (November 22, 1993): 4.
29. "Intel to Handle Reservations for Omni," *Business Travel News,* November 22, 1993, p. 15.
30. Gina O'Brien, "Where the Action Is," *Travel Agent,* November 22, 1993, p. 26.
31. See Neil Rackham, *SPIN Selling* (New York: McGraw-Hill, 1988); Frank V. Cespedes, Stephen X. Doyle, and Robert J. Freedman, "Teamwork for Today's Selling," *Harvard Business Review* (March/April 1989): 44–54, 58.
32. "Resorts Makeup Means Sweet Smell of Success for Long-Term Client," *Cornell Hotel and Restaurant Administration Quarterly* 35, no. 3 (June 1994): 9.
33. S. Dev Chekitan and Saul Klein, "Strategic Alliances in the Hotel Industry," *Cornell Hotel and Restaurant Administration Quarterly* 34, no. 1 (February 1993): 43.
34. Bill Gillette, "HFS Carlson Strikes Strategic Alliance," *Hotel and Motel Marketing* 208, no. 2 (February 1, 1993): 1, 26.
35. Bill Gillette, "Hostmark Making Its Mark," *Hotel and Motel Management* 207, no. 1 (January 13, 1992): 3, 34.
36. George H. Lucas Jr., A. Parasuraman, Robert A. Davis, and Ben M. Enis, "An Empirical Study of Salesforce Turnover," *Journal of Marketing* (July 1987): 34–59.
37. See Charles Garfield, *Peak Performers: The New Heroes of American Business* (New York: Avon Books, 1986); "What Makes a Supersalesperson?" *Sales and Marketing Management* (August 23, 1984): 86; "What Makes a Top Performer?" *Sales and Marketing Management* (May 1989); Timothy J. Trow, "The Secret of a Good Hire: Profiling," *Sales and Marketing Management* (May 1990): 44–55.
38. David Moyer and Herbert A. Greenberg, "What Makes a Good Salesman," *Harvard Business Review* (July/August 1964): 119–125.
39. "Classified Post," *South China Morning Post* 49, no. 193 (July 14, 1993): 3.
40. K. Douglas Hoffman and John E. G. Bateson, *Essentials of Services Marketing* (Fort Worth, TX: Dryden Press, 1997), pp. 92–93.
41. Thomas N. Ingram, Charles H. J. Schuepher, and Don Hutson, "Why Salespeople Fail," *Industrial Marketing Management* 21, no. 3 (August 1992): 225–230.
42. Judi Brownell, "Listening: The Toughest Management Skills," *Cornell Hotel and Restaurant Administration Quarterly* 27, no. 4 (February 1987): 64–71.
43. Howard Feiertag, "Sales Directors Build Productivity and Profitability," *Hotel and Motel Management* 207, no. 19 (November 2, 1992): 14.
44. Florence Berger, Mark D. Fulford, and Michelle Krazmien, "Human Resource Management in the 21st Century: Predicting Partnerships for Profit," *Hospitality Research Journal* 17, no. 1 (1993): 90–91.
45. "U.S. Hoteliers Fail to Net Enough World Cup Trade," *Travel Trade Gazette*, U.K. and Ireland (June 1, 1994): 32.
46. Howard Feiertag, "Different People Should Perform Sales and Marketing Jobs," *Hotel and Motel Management,* February 4, 2002, p. 24.
47. Neil Rackman, *SPIN Selling*.
48. Jeffrey Z. Rubin and Bert R. Brown, *The Social Psychology of Bargaining and Negotiation* (San Diego, CA: Academic Press, 1975), p. 18.
49. For additional reading, see Howard Raiffa, *The Art and Science of Negotiation* (Cambridge, MA: Harvard University Press, 1982); Samuel B. Bacharach and Edward J. Lawler, *Bargaining Power, Tactics, and Outcome* (San Francisco, CA: Jossey-Bass, 1981); Herb Cohen, *You Can Negotiate Anything* (New York: Bantam Books, 1980); Gerald I. Nierenberg, *The Art of Negotiating* (New York: Pocket Books, 1984).
50. Lamar Lee and Donald W. Dobler, *Purchasing and Materials Management* (New York: McGraw-Hill, 1977), pp. 146–147.
51. This discussion of zone of agreement is fully developed in Raiffa, *Art and Science of Negotiation*.
52. Roger Fisher and William Ury, *Getting to Yes: Negotiating Agreement without Giving In* (Boston: Houghton Mifflin, 1981).
53. See Gilber A. Churchill Jr., Neil A. Ford, and Orville C. Walker Jr., *Sales Force Management: Planning, Implementation, and Control* (Homewood, IL: Richard D. Irwin, 1985).
54. See Ken W. McCleary and Pamela A. Weaver, "The Job Offer: What Today's Graduates Want," *Cornell Hotel and Restaurant Administration Quarterly* 28, no. 4 (February 1988): 28–31.
55. David V. Pavesic and Robert A. Brymer, "Job Satisfaction: What's Happening to Young Managers," *Cornell Hotel and Restaurant Administration Quarterly* 30, no. 4 (February 1990): 90–96.
56. Richard Cavalier, *Sales Meetings That Work* (Homewood, IL: Dow Jones-Irwin, 1983).

57. See Joyce I. Nies and Richard F. Tas, "How to Add Visual Impact to Your Presentations," *Cornell Hotel and Restaurant Administration Quarterly* 32, no. 1 (May 1991): 46–51.

58. Dunfey Hotels Corporation: *An Interview with Jon Canas*, president, video, case number 9-883-502 (Boston Harvard Business School, 1996).

59. "Are Salespeople Gaining More Selling Time?" *Sales and Marketing Management* (July 1986): 29.

60. Ali A. Poorani, "Trade-Show Management: Budgeting and Planning for a Successful Event," *Cornell Hotel & Restaurant Administration Quarterly* (August, 1996): 77–84.

18 Destination Marketing

Marketing should focus on market creation, not market sharing.
Regis McKenna

To be wise, a man should read ten thousand books
and travel ten thousand miles.
Li Bai, Chinese poet, Tang Dynasty

The Greater Milwaukee Convention and Visitors Bureau (GMCVB) wanted to produce a brochure with twenty reasons to visit Milwaukee, targeted at travel writers. Mary Denis, the bureau's tourism director, stated, "Originally, we envisioned some type of four-color brochure."[1] The audience for the brochure was later expanded to include the group market: meeting planners, association executives, and tour operators.

The advertising and public relations firm of Sprecher/Barrett/Bertalot and Company was given the task of creating the promotional piece. As it developed, John Sprecher was worried because the promotional piece did not have a theme. The day before the campaign was to be presented to the GMCVB, Sprecher was driving to a golf tournament sponsored by the GMCVB. He popped a CD of the BoDeans, a nationally known musical group from Milwaukee, into the car's CD player. While he was listening to the CD, he came up with the idea of packaging the promotion as a CD of Milwaukee's own BoDeans. Sprecher had previously talked to the group about doing a television commercial for Milwaukee. Although the television commercial was never produced, he remembered that the group was eager to help their hometown. He called the group's manager and asked if they would be willing to help on this promotion. The BoDeans and their record company, Slash Records, responded by donating a never-before-released single to the GMCVB.

The result was "20 Spins on Milwaukee." The front cover of the CD unfolded into a brochure that had twenty different spins on things to do in Milwaukee. The following are examples of the spins:

- ***Now You Can Spell Us Milwaukee.*** *A little bit of San Antonio comes to Milwaukee in the romantic, glimmering, new $10 million Riverbank. Meandering along the peaceful Milwaukee River through the very heart of downtown, Riverbank leads you to shops, dining, entertainment, and fun.*
- ***Open 365 Days a Year.*** *Milwaukee is a city that plays, weather or not. Come summer, along comes Summerfest, the world's greatest music festival, attracting over one million partiers to the city's beautiful lakefront. And in winter? Well, nothing's cooler than Milwaukee's Winterfest, a citywide, ten-day frolic of snow sculpting, ice skating, and warm camaraderie.*
- ***Would You Like Water with That?*** *In Chicago, it's Rush Street. But in Milwaukee, the rush is on to downtown's Water Street, a magnificent mile of pubs, eateries, sports bars, live music, and good times. Just one block from the Milwaukee River and Riverbank, Water Street rocks and rollicks every night with wall-to-wall friendliness.*

Bill Hanbury, president and CEO of GMCVB, described the CD as an excellent way to promote Milwaukee. "Milwaukee is experiencing a renaissance and we've finally found the perfect vehicle to convey the exciting things that are happening."[2] Dawn Poker, director of sales for the GMCVB, said that one unanticipated benefit of the promotion was that it repositioned Milwaukee from a sleepy midwestern town to a vibrant city. The innovativeness of the CD as a promotion had a halo effect—people now think of Milwaukee as an innovative city.

Tourist destinations are products. They need to be positioned and promoted just as other products do. John Sprecher feels that agencies and convention and tourist bureaus are often too familiar with a city that they are trying to promote. He advises that they step back and gain a fresh perspective on the destination that they are about to promote by taking a tour of the city, a tour that would be given to a visiting travel writer or meeting planner.

Chapter Objectives

After reading this chapter, you should be able to:

1. Discuss the benefits of tourism.
2. Explain tourism strategies and different options for creating and investing in tourism attractions.
3. Understand how to segment and identify visitor segments.
4. Explain how central tourist agencies are organized.

18.1 The Greater Milwaukee Convention and Visitors Bureau

The word **tourism** has many definitions. We use the British Tourist Authority's definition of tourism: "a stay of one or more nights away from home for holidays, visits to friends or relatives, business conferences or any other purpose except such things as boarding education or semi permanent employment."[3] This book uses the words tourism and travel interchangeably.

The Globalization of the Tourist Industry

The world had become a global community opening places unimaginable decades earlier: the wonders of Antarctica, the secrets of the Himalayas, the rain forests of the Amazon, the beauty of Tahiti, the Great Wall of China, the dramatic Victoria Falls, the origin of the Nile, and the wilds of Scottish islands. Travel has become a global business whose expanding market now leaves no place untouched.

According to the World Tourism Organization (WTO) of the United Nations, more than 625 million tourists traveled internationally in 1998, spending over $444 billion (excluding transportation). Tourism accounts for 8 percent of total world exports, more than 31 percent of international trade in services, and more than 100 million jobs worldwide. It employs more people than any single industrial sector and has infrastructure (lodging, transportation, and restaurants) investment conservatively estimated to exceed $3 trillion.[4]

18.2 World Tourism Association

Travel now affects every continent, country, and city. The economy is influenced either by people traveling elsewhere (import spending in other places) or travel service exports (expenditures by nonresidents in that place). Visitor destinations must decide how much travel service business they want to capture, because travel is today's fastest-growing business and is expected to become the world's largest industry in the next century. Yet, as an industry, it is subject to cycles, fashions, and intense competition.

The trade balance in tourism from developed countries has been declining since 1980, while developing countries have seen their surplus steadily increase. A challenge for countries developing tourism is to maintain the culture and natural beauty of the country, while providing the infrastructure for tourism.[5]

Tourist destinations do not need spectacular attractions such as an Eiffel Tower, Grand Canyon, or Leaning Tower to participate in today's tourism. The modest city of Ruili in Yunnan, southwest China, has only 60,000 residents but is vying for the title of "Top Tourist City," a distinction awarded by the China National Tourism Administration. Ruili spent 10 million Yuan to improve roads and actively promotes a water-sprinkling festival, its local jewelry manufacturing, local farms, and tropical scenes. The result was 800,000 foreign visitors each year from Thailand, India, Pakistan, and Myanmar, as well as 850,000 domestic tourists.[6]

As regions such as Eastern Europe and countries such as China develop, they will become generators of tourists, as well as destinations of tourists. China, for example, has seen the growth of outbound travel by private citizens grow from 880,000 travelers in 1991 to 2,410,000 in 1996. By 1997, Chinese citizens who traveled overseas spent over $10 billion and represented less than a percent of the country's population. This spending by the Chinese was enough to place them in the number 10 spot of tourism spenders, up from number 40 in 1990. Thus, the growth potential of the outbound Chinese travel market is tremendous. Two main drivers of China's outbound tourists are economic development and the Chinese culture. In China a person who is well traveled is considered to be "a wise man."[7]

Importance of Tourism to a Destination's Economy

The Tourism Destination

Tourists travel to destinations. **Destinations** are places with some form of actual or perceived boundary, such as the physical boundary of an island, political boundaries, or even market-created boundaries such as those of a travel wholesaler who defines a South Pacific tour solely as Australia and New Zealand. Central America consists of seven nations, but few, if any, national tourist offices or tour planners view it that way. A commonly packaged tour of Central America includes only two or three nations, such as Costa Rica, Guatemala, and Panama. Others are excluded for reasons of political instability or deficient **infrastructure.**

Although Australia and New Zealand are often packaged together for the North American visitor, Australia has worked hard for many years to make it a single destination rather than share the limited vacation time of Americans and Canadians. In turn, destinations within Australia, such as the state of Western Australia or cities such as Perth or Adelaide, feel that they must develop a distinct destination reputation to avoid being left out or used only as overnight stopovers.

The desire to become a recognized destination presents a difficult marketing challenge. Within eastern North Carolina, the town of New Bern has several interesting visitor attractions and events. The remainder of the county offers considerably less, yet visitor promotion funds are collected from a countywide hotel bed tax. Political pressure has forced tourism officials to promote Craven County as a destination rather than the town of New Bern. The promotion of a relatively unfamiliar town poses sufficient problems, but the promotion of a county greatly intensifies the challenge.

Macrodestinations such as the United States contain thousands of microdestinations, including regions, states, cities, towns, and even visitor destinations within a town. It is not unusual to find tourists who view their Hawaiian destination as the Kahala Hilton or the Hilton Hawaiian Village in Honolulu and may rarely, if ever, venture outside the perimeter of these destination resorts. Thousands of visitors fly to Orlando and proceed directly to Disney World, where most or all of their vacation is spent. These tourists do not view Florida or Orlando as their destinations, but, rather, Disney World.

Benefits of Tourism

Tourism's most visible benefit is direct employment in hotels, restaurants, retail establishments, and transportation. A second but less visible benefit consists of support industries and professions (such as yield management consultants, university tourism professors, and others), many of which pay considerably more than the visible employment opportunities such as restaurant personnel. The third benefit of tourism is the **multiplier effect** as tourist expenditures are recycled through the local economy. Governments use economic impact models to estimate overall employment gains in goods and services consumption resulting from tourism multipliers. Tourism's fourth benefit is state and local revenues derived from taxes on tourism.

Tourism helps shift the tax burden to nonresidents. For example, tourism accounts for more than half of Bermuda's foreign exchange and

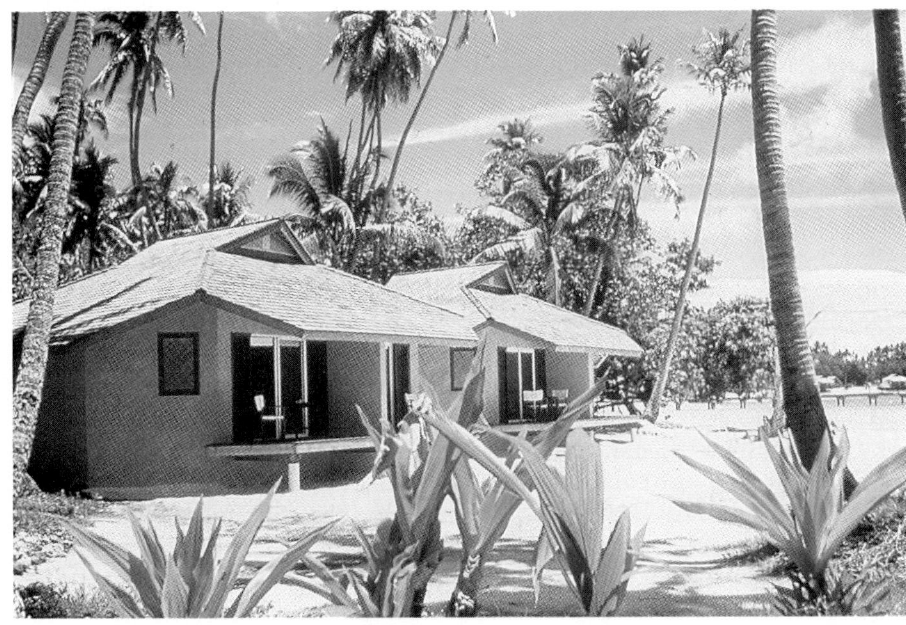

Islands in the South Pacific, such as Bora Bora, count on tourism to bring in much-needed foreign currency. Courtesy of Club Med.

tax revenues. Bermuda's $20 per head embarkation fee is one of the highest in the world, as are its import taxes on durables from cars to refrigerators. It is one of the few developed countries without an income tax. New York's cumulative bed tax on hotel rooms raises more than $300 million in annual revenues. Dallas, Los Angeles, and Houston all have bed taxes in excess of 12 percent. Hawaii derives nearly 40 percent of its total state and county taxes from tourism. Taxation of travelers has become a popular, often a hidden, tax, and includes taxes on airline ticket taxes, hotel taxes, and other user fees.[8]

Critics of such taxation contend that these schemes are taxation without representation and eventually lead to careless government spending or spending that has little relevance to promoting tourism and enhancing the travel experience. Hospitality and travel managers must make sure that bed taxes and other tourist-related taxes go back into promoting tourism and developing the infrastructure to support tourism.

Tourism also yields a fifth benefit: It stimulates exports of place-made products. Estimates of visitor spending on gifts, clothing, and souvenirs are in the range of 15 percent to 20 percent of total expenditures. The degree to which these products are made or assembled in a destination affects the economic impact on the local economy.

Destinations, however, may not welcome tourists uniformly. Due to location, climate, limited resources, size, and cultural heritage, some places have few economic choices other than to participate in tourism. Some engage in tourism with mixed emotions and, at times, ambivalence. For instance, Bali is concerned that tourism is destroying its culture as farmland becomes resorts and new jobs unravel family values. "Bali and tourism is not a marriage of love," observed a Bali tourism official, clearly focusing on the dilemma of cultural breakdown and an economy booming from the receipts of 500,000 tourists a year.[9]

Some people and businesses benefit from tourism; others may not. Even though a destination's economy may be better off from tourism, residents sometimes feel that losses in quality of life, convenience, and cultural and social values are not worth the economic benefits.

Management of the Tourist Destination

Destinations that fail to maintain the necessary infrastructure or build inappropriate infrastructure run significant risks. Italy's Adriatic Sea coast has been devastated by the adverse publicity associated with the growth of brown algae that made bathing nearly impossible. Growing pollution levels at the Grand Canyon and overcrowding in Yosemite Valley may significantly diminish the attractiveness of these great national parks. Some of East Africa's renowned game parks are being turned into dust bowls by tourists ferried around in four-wheel-drive vehicles.

A destination's attractiveness can be diminished by violence, political instability, natural catastrophe, adverse environmental factors, and overcrowding. Greece's national treasure, the formerly white marble Parthenon in Athens, stands as a pollution-stained symbol of environmental neglect. Thailand's beautiful beach resorts and temples have been severely damaged by pollution and poor sanitation. The Indian government's plans to create a "Visit India Year" were undermined not only by sectarian and caste violence, but also plane crashes. Western countries, including the United States and Japan, declared India to be an unsafe destination.

"Destination marketing is an integral part of developing and retaining a particular location's popularity. Too often, however, tourism planners focus only on destination developments without paying attention to retaining and preserving the attributes that attracted travelers to the destination in the first place."[10]

Several locations have been identified as suffering from a lack of destination maintenance. These include Pattaya, Thailand; Bali, Indonesia; and Huatulco, Mexico. Many North American destinations are also experiencing visitor overuse or destruction, including the Sedona, Arizona, area. A professional observer of this area noted that destructive visitor behavior could destroy the base on which Sedona's tourism is built.[11]

A theory offered by futurist August St. John argues that a resort destination will experience a life cycle similar to the product life cycle and eventually go into decline, or the destruction stage, as St. John calls it.[12] Tourism managers must manage their products and make sure that during the growth stage the foundation is built for an infrastructure that will support future tourism demands. In some cases, sustaining tourism in the mature stage may mean limiting the amount of tourists to a number that the infrastructure can handle. Tourist development must balance the temptation to maximize tourist dollars with preservation of the natural tourist attractions and the quality of life for local residents. This is often a difficult task (see Marketing Highlight 18-1). Those tourist destinations that do not manage their product may have a short life. Those tourist destinations that build solid infrastructures can look for increased business by expanding from a seasonal product to a multiseasonal product or by expanding the geographic base of their product. For example, Aspen, Colorado, expanded from winter skiing to summer recreation, education, and culture. Quebec promotes summer-fall tourism and its winter carnival and skiing. West Virginia is popular in the summer-fall seasons, but also aggressively promotes the spring and winter seasons.

Stratford, Canada's Shakespeare Festival, began as a small regional event and became a North American event for the United States and Canada. Most musical and cultural festivals in Europe followed the same pattern, such as Salzburg, Edinburgh, and Spoleto. Europe's Festival of Arts provides a selection among fifty musical festivals from Norway to Spain, with several dozen dance competitions, major summer art exhibits, and theater from London's West End to Berlin's Festival Weeks. The entire European continent, including Eastern Europe, has exploded in summer-place competition for tourists.

Sustainable Tourism

"Tourism planners need to take into account the capacity of a location's environment to support all [of the area's residents, not just tourists]. Without such planning, a destination can be damaged to the point that travelers will stay away."[13] From a marketing standpoint, sustainable tourism

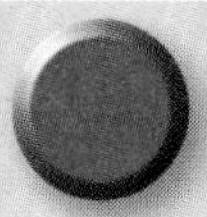

Marketing Highlight 18-1

Stop the Brutal Marketing

Bumper stickers in the resort town of Steamboat Springs, Colorado, publicly proclaim dissatisfaction with tourism promotion. "Stop the Brutal Marketing of Steamboat" may be seen on local autos and pickup trucks. Many are driven by employees of the visitor industry. A restaurant hostess, a beer truck driver, an art gallery assistant manager, and a convenience store clerk represent Steamboat's protesting citizens whose livelihood is derived directly from visitors.

Throughout the Rocky Mountain states, citizens are in revolt against the tourist industry. Colorado residents may vote that public funds should no longer be earmarked for tourism promotion. Advertising and promotion of Steamboat are supported by roughly $600,000 of tax-generated revenue. These funds and the marketing staff and programs that they support are clearly at risk. One of the authors of this text, a resident of Steamboat Springs, puts it this way:

> Greedy tourism developers brought us a bitter lemon but tell us it is a sweet plum. What is so sweet about $6.00-per-hour waiter and bed-making jobs in a community where a home is unaffordable, our streets are crowded with vehicles, and the term *professional career opportunity* often means being a night manager in a roadside motel, renamed a "resort hotel"?

Summit County, Colorado, one and a half hours away, is home to resorts such as Breckenridge. It is also a parking lot for a large and ever-growing complex of factory outlet stores at the base of some of the most majestic scenery in the nation. That's what many in Steamboat fear. Residents of Steamboat Springs and other resort communities point to visitor surveys in which respondents state that they are searching for a refreshing mountain experience. When asked what this means, visitors reply that they want to see clear streams, fresh air, uncluttered mountain views, and mountain meadows filled with Hereford cows, not houseware stores. Once constructed, those houseware, clothing, and luggage outlets produce much more revenue than is possible from Herefords. Consequently, their numbers grow as the Herefords decline.

Opponents of tourism promotion point to the growth of specialty manufacturing in Colorado cities such as Durango. Steamboat Springs is home to TIC, a national construction company with sales of nearly $500 million per year. Many feel that the funds currently used to promote tourism could better be utilized to encourage and develop new enterprises that might one day become other TICs.

An expanding tourism base inevitably places a heavy burden on infrastructure, available land, and air quality. Opponents worry that dependency on an expanded visitor industry places a community at risk of economic cycles similar to those of cities, which previously depended on steel, rubber, or chemicals. Quality versus quantity is a phrase often heard in the Rocky Mountains. "We're not opposed to the visitor industry, but we see no need for uncontrolled mass tourism," say the opponents. Why must the visitor industry set objectives of ever-increasing numbers of tourists, hotel occupancy, automobiles, or mountain bike riders? Are we really better off with crowded streets and sidewalks, or was the previous balance between ranching, mining, and tourism a better model? Couldn't the industry improve the quality of its existing product, charge higher rates, and attract a higher-class visitor, or must we forever measure success by head count?"

How can the visitor industry sustain itself if industry workers cannot find affordable lodging in the town and must drive an hour or more over an icy mountain pass? Why should visitors continue to select this destination if they must stand in line and receive uncaring, depersonalized service by disenfranchised employees?

Hospitality industry executives and tourism marketers, however, disagree. "We are witnessing the pack mentality of suicidal lemmings. Tourism promotion brought this community year-round employment and annual increases in sales tax receipts accompanied by help wanted signs."

can mean giving up current revenues from tourism by limiting capacity to ensure that there will be demand for tourism in the future.

Sustainable tourism is a concept of tourism management that anticipates and prevents problems that occur when carrying capacity is exceeded. This depends on an *environmental impact assessment* (EIA). An EIA typically follows these steps:

1. Inventory the social, political, physical, and economic environment.
2. Project trends.
3. Set goals and objectives.
4. Examine alternatives to reach goals.
5. Select preferred alternatives.
6. Develop implementation strategy.
7. Implement.
8. Evaluate.

Industry and Community Cooperation. Many communities that directly depend on tourism fail to coordinate important sectors of the economy. Estes Park, Colorado, offers an example of such a community. Retirees and other residents are upset by tourism traffic. Residents want a rustic mountain getaway with modern conveniences, which are provided through tourism-based revenue. "A lodging-driven Chamber of Commerce results in an unconcerned attitude by retailers and restaurants that do not see themselves as part of the underpinning of the tourism industry, even though data point in the other direction."[14]

Communities with these divisions must expect to face continuous discord among important constituencies. Successful long-run tourism destinations require cooperation in planning among constituencies.

Tourism Strategies and Investments

Tourist competition is fierce amid a growing and constantly changing tourist market. In addition to strong tourist destinations, declining places upgrade and make new investments, and new places appear. Leavenworth, Washington, an old logging and mining town, experienced revival when it transformed itself into a Bavarian village. Winterset, Iowa, John Wayne's birthplace, is now visited by tourists. Seymour, Wisconsin, lays claim to being home of the first hamburger, hosting August Hamburger Days. Seymour organizers once cooked the world's largest hamburger, weighing 5,520 pounds.

Countless examples exist of places rediscovering their past, capitalizing on the birthplace of a famous person, an event, a battle, or other "hidden gems." Places rely on various monikers for identification: Sheboygan, Wisconsin, as City of Cheese, Choirs, Children, and Churches; Crystal City, Texas, as the Spinach Capital of the World; Lexington, Kentucky, as the Athens of the West; New Haven, Connecticut, as the City of Elms. Many places still bear nicknames of their economic heritage: Hartford, Connecticut, as Insurance City; Holyoke, Massachusetts, as Paper City; Westfield, New York, as Buggy Whip City; and Paterson, New Jersey, as Silk City. These destinations are not likely to become international tourist destinations, but they can be effective tourist products in the regional tourism market.

In Shandong Province of China, the city of Qufu was the hometown of Confucius, the ancient philosopher and educator. The local tourism department features the Confucian culture as a way of differentiating the city. In keeping with the principles of Confucius, the local tourism department and the police cooperate in a program to reprimand tour operators and others who engage in unethical business practices. This program includes a tourist complaint center and a training program in ethics for local hotel employees.[15]

With the current U.S. trend toward shorter but more frequent vacations, many places within 200 miles or so of major metropolitan areas have found new opportunities to access the tourist market. Local tourism and convention bureaus tout the theme "Stay Close to Home." The Louisiana Office of Tourism spent $6 million to market a summer travel bargain program to a 500-mile market.

18.3 Darling Harbour
Louisiana Office of Tourism

Cities are also creating tourist attractions. Darling Harbour in Sydney has developed as a major tourist attraction. It is the location of the Sydney Convention and Exhibition Centre and is the home to numerous restaurants, retail stores, and attractions including Sydney Aquarium, Australian National Maritime Museum, and an Imax theater. The district is also within walking distant of the Star Casino and Sydney's Chinatown. It is easily accessible by monorail, water taxi, or train. By clustering a number of activities into one district, Darling Harbour gives tourists another reason to visit Sydney or stay an extra day to take in the attractions. In addition to attracting tourists, developments like Darling Harbour also provide benefits for local residents, providing the locals with a benefit of tourism.

Investment in Tourist Attractions

To attract tourists, destinations must respond to the travel basics of cost, convenience, and timeliness. Like other consumers, tourists weigh costs against the benefits of specific destinations and investment of time, effort, and resources against a reasonable return in education, experience, fun,

Darling Harbour is an example of a well-planned tourist center. Courtesy of The Sydney Convention and Visitors Bureau.

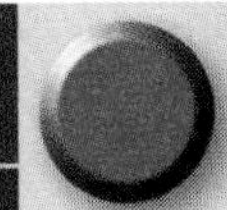

Marketing Highlight 18-2

Gambling on Central City

During the Colorado golf rush of the nineteenth century, the twin cities of Central City and Blackhawk, Colorado, were boomtowns with great wealth and instant millionaires. Then it all ended, and the two became decaying ghost towns for nearly 100 years, with a handful of residents, old mining bars, and a few tourist shops.

Boom times returned in 1991 when the Colorado state legislature permitted casino gambling in the two towns located less than an hour west of Denver in the Rocky Mountains. A majority of the 300 citizens of Central City as well as the 100 in Blackhawk approved gambling, and casinos soon were functioning in both towns.

At first, casinos proved to be an incredible source of riches for Central City. Millions of dollars were spent by casino operators to renovate historical old buildings and to improve the town's infrastructure, including new water and sewage facilities. The Historic Preservation Fund received over $2.5 million from gaming revenues to use for a variety of projects, including the renovation of Victorian-style homes owned by the residents. In 1996, every resident received about $7,500 to be used for home and ground improvements.

A sure sign that the honeymoon between residents and casinos had ended occurred when the powerful Central City Historic Preservation Committee blocked permits for new casino construction in anything other than existing buildings. This meant that casinos would forever be small operations and find difficulty competing with those in Blackhawk. Parking also became a severe problem, as buildings could not be torn down for parking and the mountain terrain offered few sites.

Meanwhile, the sister town of Blackhawk had other ideas and attitudes toward casinos. One observer offered the analogy of a brand new McDonald's competing against an old worn-out hamburger stand a mile away through traffic and without adequate parking. Blackhawk is procasino, encourages expansion of buildings and parking, and is the first town on a narrow winding road. Central City lies one mile farther up the road, with casinos that seem to lack the excitement of those in Blackhawk.

By 1996, Central City had witnessed the closing of twenty-one casinos and had only six remaining retail shops. The city had issued $19 million in municipal bonds. Some people felt that if casino revenue continued to decline, Central City might be unable to meet bond obligations. In 1997, the city government's budget was $350,000 with eight city employees, down from an $8 million budget in 1991 with 100 city employees.

Many casino operators believed that it was possible and perhaps inevitable for casino gambling to cease in Central City. Casino gambling in Colorado is supported by repeat frequent gamblers who represent about 90 percent of revenues. Many of these hard-core gamblers switched allegiances to casinos in Blackhawk, leaving Central City to low-spending tourists.

Anticasino attitudes by local residents seemed to be killing the goose with the golden egg. "It isn't that they don't know what's happening, it's that they don't care and many would even welcome the destruction of casino gambling in Central City," said an observer. "After all, many lived here and liked it when the place was a near ghost town and they don't welcome the new gambling-induced tourism. The casino industry rebuilt the infrastructure and improved the city. Now that improvements have been made, many residents feel that casinos are no longer needed and life would be better without them."

relaxation, and memories. Convenience takes on various meanings in travel decisions: time involved in travel from airport to lodging, language barriers, cleanliness and sanitary concerns, access to interests (beaches, attractions, amenities), and special needs (elderly, disabled, children, dietary, medical care, fax and communication, auto rental). Timeliness embraces factors that introduce risk to travel such as civil disturbances, political instability, currency fluctuations, safety, and sanitary conditions.

Places are increasingly developing events as a vital component in attracting tourists. Small or rural places typically initiate an event such as a festival to establish their identity. Urban newspapers and suburban weeklies often publish a list of events, festivals, and celebrations occurring within a day's driving distance. State and local tourism offices do the same, making sure that travel agents, restaurants, hotels, airports, and train and bus stations have event-based calendars for posting. Nearly every European country now has a 900 number that you can call in the United States to get a listing of forthcoming events. Major U.S. cities have summer programs of scheduled events, and some, such as Milwaukee, have well-established year-round events. Milwaukee's June-September lakefront festivals (Festa Italiana, German Fest, Afro Fest, Polish Fest, and others) attract tourists regionally and nationally.

Tourism investment ranges from relatively low-cost market entry for festivals or events, to multimillion-dollar infrastructure costs of stadiums, transit systems, airports, and convention centers. Regardless of the cost, urban renewal planners seek to build tourism into the heart of their city's revitalization. Boston's Quincy Market, New York's Lincoln Center, and San Francisco's Fisherman's Wharf are examples. The ability to concentrate attractions, facilities, and services in a convenient, accessible location is essential to create a strong destination pull.

In centrally planned economies (Eastern Europe and developing countries), governments control, plan, and direct tourist development. Tourism is necessary to earn hard currencies for trade and development and serves national purposes. Tourist expansion is highly dependent on public investments, which have proved to be woefully inadequate without private investment and market mechanisms to respond to changing consumer needs and wants. These nations now promote private investment through joint ventures, foreign ownership, and time sharing for individual investors. The Mexican Riviera (Puerto Vallarta, Cancun, Ixtapa) is an example of public-private combinations of successful tourism investments, where state investment in infrastructure works with private investment in tourist amenities, from hotels, restaurants, and golf courses to shopping areas.

Destination tourism in the United States builds increasingly on public-private partnerships or joint development in planning, financing, and implementation. Public authority is required to clear, develop, and write down land costs and to make infrastructure investments. The destination must often subsidize or provide tax incentives for private investment in hotels, convention centers, transit, and parking. Restoration is often carried out by nonprofit development corporations from the National Historic Trust to the U.S. Park Service, with private investment promoted through various tax incentives. From airlines to hotels, the tourist industry provides dedicated tax revenues from fuel, leases, bed taxes, and sales taxes to support a long-term bonus for capital construction of tourist-related infrastructure and other public improvements. Such steps made it possible for New York City to add the South Street Seaport Museum, Javits Convention Center, and Ellis Island Immigration Museum to its tourist attraction portfolio.

Destinations must make more than financial or hospitality investments to attract tourists. Places find that they must expand public services, specifically public safety, traffic and crowd control, emergency health, sanitation, and street cleaning. They must also promote tourism internally to their own citizens and business retailers, travel agencies, restaurants, financial institutions, public and private transit, lodging, police, and public servants. They must invest in recruiting, training, licensing, and monitoring tourist-related businesses and employees. Singapore's cab drivers are known for their professional training and service, which include English language exams, safety programs, and location skills. Some places invest little in that area, even though airport cabs and public transit may be the first encounter points that visitors have with a place and can be critical to tourist satisfaction.

Dubai is a good example of a city that has developed a good infrastructure along with tourist attractions. The airport at Dubai is world class and offers excellent duty-free shopping. The highway system is well designed and maintained, making it easy to get from the airport to the resorts. The hotels realize the importance of service and customer satisfaction. Once at the hotel, the guest can select from a variety of activities,

The Burj Al Arab and Jumeriah Beach Hotel. Courtesy of Jumeriah International.

including water sports, tennis, golf, or sightseeing tours. The resorts spend a great deal of effort training their employees who come from all over the world. The employee base also means that guests from almost any country will be able to find an employee speaking their language. Dubai set out on a strategy of using tourism to broaden its economic base and developed a plan to implement that strategy.

Two of the resorts in Dubai are the Burj Al Arab and the Jumeriah Beach Hotel. The Burj Al Arab is not only the world's tallest hotel, but also one of the most luxurious. All of its 202 rooms are two-story suites. Guests staying at the Burj Al Arab have a choice of airport transportation: a Rolls-Royce limousine or a helicopter. Each floor features a private reception, and there is a personal butler for each suite. The Jumeriah Beach Hotel has 600 rooms and eighteen restaurants and features a reef a little over a mile off shore for scuba divers. The hotel also features extensive meeting and conference facilities to attract international meetings.

Segmenting and Monitoring the Tourist Market

The decision to spend one's disposable income on travel versus new furniture, a boat, or other purchase alternatives involves important psychological determinants. Table 18-1 lists some of the major psychological determinants of demand for tourism. These determinants can be used as segmentation variables. Demographics and lifestyles are also important segmentation variables.

The growing percentage of retired Americans has vastly expanded the tourism business. An increasing percentage of two-career couples has resulted in a trend toward shorter, more frequent vacations. Longer vacations (ten or more nights) have been declining for years, while shorter vacations (three nights, including weekends) have become increasingly popular. Hotels and airlines have accommodated these trends with low-cost weekend excursion packages. Business travel now includes mixed business and leisure. To capture the trend toward shorter vacations within driving distance of home, new local and regional tourist attractions have been growing, as have family oriented resorts.

Foreign visitor travel has become an increasingly important segment of the North American travel industry. Since the decline of the U.S. and Canadian dollars, foreign tourism has grown each year. British Isles visitors seek out New York and Florida, while continental visitors have a strong fascination for the U.S. West, particularly California. Hawaii's tourist market consists of 66 percent from the mainland and 20 percent from Japan. Hawaii targets Japan because of its high GNP and spending, and because 50 percent of all Japanese visitors to the U.S. mainland spend part of their trip in Hawaii. The Japanese repeat market outspends U.S. mainland visitors by a 4:1 margin, $586 per day versus $119 per day.

Accommodating changing lifestyles and needs is a dynamic challenge for the tourism industry in light of demographic trends and income shifts. The high-living baby boomers of yesterday are today's older baby boomers. Where baby boomers once opted for status destinations and elaborate accommodations, older baby boomers now opt for all-inclusive resorts and package tours that promise comfort, consistency, and cost-effectiveness. Indeed, some see today's travelers returning to the 1950s-

Table 18-1
Psychological Determinants of Demand

Prestige. A level of prestige has always been attached to travelers, particularly long-distance travelers. Marco Polo gained historical fame through travel, as did the heroes of Greek and Roman mythology, such as Ulysses. Travel to Aspen, the Riviera, Switzerland, and many other destinations provides the traveler with a level of prestige, if only in the mind of the traveler.

Escape. The desire to escape momentarily from the day-to-day rhythm of one's life is a basic human need. Travel marketers have long recognized this need, as reflected by glamorous advertisements in which the word *escape* is often mentioned.

Sexual opportunity. This has both a positive and an ugly side. Travel has long been viewed as a means to meet attractive people. This has been part of the heritage of transatlantic ocean travel, the Orient Express, and riverboat travel. Unfortunately, the existence of sex tours to certain Oriental nations and the preponderance of houses of prostitution in some destination areas provide examples of a darker side.

Education. Travel in and of itself has historically been viewed as broadening. Many deeper psychological reasons for travel are masked by the rationale that educational benefits outweigh the cost, risks, and stress.

Social interaction. The opportunity to meet and interact with people previously unknown is a powerful motivator. Destination resorts and cruise lines commonly appeal to this need.

Family bonding. Family reunions have become an important market segment for many in the travel industry. In an era of intense pressure on the family, such as two careers, there is a strong need to refocus priorities and bond as a family. Unfortunately, the types of vacations selected by families do not always lead to bonding. If adults participate all day in activities such as diving, skiing, or golf, young children may be relegated to organized kids' programs and experience little bonding with parents.

Relaxation. Observers of human and animal conduct sometimes state that the human being is either alone or among a limited number of species that continue to play into adulthood. Destination resorts and cruise ships best exemplify need fulfillment for play. It is small wonder that cruise line travel has become a "destination" in direct competition with land-bound places.

Self-discovery. For many, travel offers the opportunity to "find oneself." Witness the action of many people following a dramatic event in their lives, such as a divorce or the death of a family member. Throughout recorded history, people have sought self-discovery by "visiting the mountain," "finding solace in the desert," and "losing oneself." Many cultures, including so-called "primitive" ones, have encouraged or even forced their youth to travel alone to find self-discovery. Youth hotels throughout the world serve a group of travelers, many of whom are seeking self-discovery. Temporary employment opportunities at resorts are often filled by those taking time off to learn more about who they are and wish to be. The concept of "holistic vacations" has been developed for people seeking self-discovery.

Source: Peter Hawes, "Holistic Vacations," *Hemisphere* (March 1995), pp. 85–87; A. J. Crompton "Motivations for Pleasure Vacations," *Annals of Tourism Research* 6 (1974): 408–424; A. Mathieson and G. Wall, *Tourism: Economics, Physical and Social Impacts* (Harlow, Essex, England: Longman, 1982).

style vacation that their parents enjoyed. These "new traditionalists" look for bargains, up-front costs, flexibility, and convenience.

Tourism planners must consider how many tourists are desired, which segments to attract, and how to balance tourism with other industries. Choices will be constrained by the destinations' climate, natural topography, resources, history, culture, and facilities. Like other enterprises, tourist marketers must know the actual and potential customers and their needs and wants, determine which target markets to serve, and decide on appropriate products, services, and programs.

Not every tourist is interested in a particular destination. A destination would waste its money trying to attract everyone who travels. Instead of a shotgun approach, destinations must take a rifle approach and sharply define target markets.

Identifying Target Markets

A destination can identify its natural target markets in two ways. One is to collect information about its current visitors. Where do they come from? Why do they come? What are their demographic characteristics? How satisfied are they? How many are repeat visitors? How much do they spend? By examining these and other questions, planners can determine which visitors should be targeted.

The second approach is to audit the destination's attractions and select segments that might logically have an interest in them. We cannot assume that current visitors reflect all the potentially interested groups. For example, if Kenya promoted only safaris, it would miss groups interested in native culture, flora, or bird species.

Tourist segments are attracted by different features. The local tourist board or council could benefit by asking questions keyed to segmentation variables. These variables, including attractions sought, market areas or locations, customer characteristics, and/or benefits sought, can help to define the best segments to target.

After a place identifies its natural target markets, tourism planners should conduct research to determine where these tourists are found. Which countries contain a large number of citizens who have the means and motivation to enjoy the particular place? For example, Aruba attracts mainly sun-and-fun tourists. The United States, Canada, and certain European countries are good sources. Eastern Europeans are ruled out because they lack the purchasing power. Australians are ruled out because they have their own nearby sun-and-fun destinations, even though "Aussies" are frequent travelers. This analysis can uncover many or few natural target markets. If many are identified, the relative potential profit from each should be evaluated. The potential profit of a target tourist segment is the difference between the amount that the tourist segment is likely to spend and the cost of attracting and serving this segment. The promotional cost depends on the budget. The serving cost depends on the infrastructure requirements. Ultimately, potential tourist segments should be ranked and selected in order of their profitability.

If the analysis identifies too few natural tourist segments, investments may be needed in infrastructure and visitor attractions. Visitor industry investments consist of infrastructure improvements (hotels, transportation, and the like) and attractions that can potentially attract new types of tourists. The payoff from these investments may come only some years later, but this lag is often necessary if the destination is to become an active participant in an increasingly competitive marketplace.

The Irish Tourist Board recently observed that many young European tourists visited the Emerald Isle to enjoy its natural, unspoiled beauty as backpackers and campers, but spent little. A serious question for Ireland was whether its tourism scorecard should be based on the number of tourists attracted (the prevailing standard) or their spending level. A consensus emerged that Ireland should try to attract a relatively small market of high-income tourists who stay longer, spend more, and are culturally and environmentally compatible.

Toward this end, the Irish Tourist Board now touts not only Ireland's mountains, water, and ancient buildings, but also its literary giants, such as Oscar Wilde, George Bernard Shaw, and James Joyce. The board wants to attract high-income, culture-seeking tourists to Dublin, where the sparkling Irish speech and wit can be experienced. The Irish are also ready to improve Dublin's hotel and restaurant facilities as an act of investment marketing.

18.4 Irish Tourist Board

Whatever tourist segment a destination seeks, it needs to be very specific. A ski area attracts skiers. Natural reefs attract snorklers and divers. Arts and crafts attract the art crowd, and gambling attracts gaming tourists. Yet even with such givens, potential visitors must be segmented by additional characteristics. Sun Valley, Aspen, Vail, and Alta appeal to upper-income and professional skiers, and Keystone, Winter Park, Cooper Mountain, and Telluride attract the family market. Tahoe and Squaw Valley draw the skiing and gaming markets. Monte Carlo appeals to an international gaming segment, while Deauville, France, promotes a more regional gaming market near Paris.

This advertisement targets families living in cities in south and central Florida. Courtesy of Yesawich, Pepperdine & Brown, Inc.

In Our Part Of Florida, The Choices Are All Yours. Naturally.

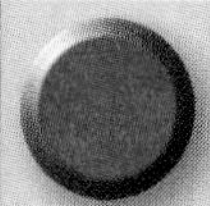

Marketing Highlight 18-3

Maryland Office of Tourism Development Case Study

The Challenge. The goal of the Maryland Office of Tourism Development, simply stated, is to generate tax revenues for the state through tourism-related points of sale such as hotels, restaurants, and attractions. Trahan, Burden & Charles's (TBC) challenge was to help the state get more than their fair share of the tourism dollars being spent in the Mid-Atlantic region.

The Path to Learning and Success. TBC recommended that the state undertake a fairly robust audience segmentation study to help determine its most lucrative target audiences, then targeting these clusters to optimize media expenditures. Among the findings of the Target Audience Segmentation Study, Maryland's best visitors were found to be (1) young families who lived within 400 miles of the state and who had children in the upper elementary and middle school grades; (2) professionals visiting Maryland for business, married, with children in the above age group; and (3) retiring couples with time on their hands and disposable income.

Once the priority target audience segments were identified, we investigated creative messaging options that would prove compelling enough for prospects to pick up the phone or go on-line to order a Maryland Visitor Kit and Vacation Planning Guide.

Like so many other states, Maryland had previously used travel industry-cliché advertising, that is, advertising featuring a montage of sun, fun, mountains, swimming, skiing, boating and nightlife. Our goal was to find a way to stand out from the crowd, while remaining ever mindful of the state legislature's monitoring of the Office of Tourism Development's efforts on a cost/call basis. Me-too advertising would not cut it given that the Maryland tourism budget is one-half to one-third of its neighboring states.

Following qualitative learning exercises, we found that the priority target audience segments were tired of the "montage" presentations the industry had been throwing at them and, in fact, were tired of taking "montage" vacations. They wanted something "more real." Something different. They wanted more than the national brand name restaurants; more than a quick visit to a museum; more than shopping at the same stores they had at home. While they wanted to sun themselves on beaches and take in professional sports, they also craved for experiences that were truly educational yet interesting. And they wanted these new experiences to be authentic.

TBC found that if the Maryland Office of Tourism Development featured these types of travel opportunities in its advertising, the priority targets would call and plan a trip to our state. They would spend money in Maryland, generating higher tourism-related state tax revenues.

TBC developed a comprehensive and synergistic print, television, and on-line advertising campaign to meet objectives and respond to research findings.

Tactics—Creative

Television. The television spot was designed as a sixty-second commercial, with the front thirty seconds focusing on Antietam National Battlefield, one of the Maryland Office of Tourism Development's key product development initiatives. The second thirty seconds focused on Maryland's many hidden treasures and served as a call-to-action for viewers, prompting them to call for their vacation guide and free coupon book.

TBC took a unique, cost-advantaged approach to producing the TV campaign. As the state's dollars needed mostly to be allocated to purchasing media, the agency's in-house production company, Charles Street Films, worked hard to minimize out-of-pocket production costs. TBC was able to obtain existing film footage and use stock footage at no charge to create the second thirty seconds of the spot while at the same time reducing the expense to the state and ultimately driving down the cost-per-lead of the campaign. The end result was a dynamic commercial at one-sixth the price of the national production average.

Print. The print campaign focused on the many authentic treasures that Maryland has to offer and targeted multiple audiences, including consumers, travel agents, group tour leaders, and meeting planners. Specific attention was paid to the five distinct geographic regions of the state, reflecting the diversity from Western Maryland to the Eastern Shore.

Print ads for the campaign employed a similar cost-saving strategy as was used for TV. TBC hired a local photographer to photograph Maryland for one flat fee, thus eliminating photography usage costs.

On-line. The interactive advertising campaign drafted behind the offline creative messaging and used nontraditional formats to capture the ever-elusive attention on the Web. TBC purchased units called Superstitials and Eyeblasters instead of banners because of the additional creative dimension offered. This format flexibility allowed for a better opportunity to communicate the Maryland tourism story, rather than relying on nuance or innuendo. For this reason, respondents to the Office of Tourism Development's on-line creative were more valuable than just "clicks"—they had a genuine interest in the proposition because they were more informed about the program prior to responding.

Public Relations. Additionally, TBC's Public Relations Department worked closely with the Maryland Office of Tourism Development to concept and produce a "Tourism Counts" Summit in collaboration with Maryland Speaker of the House Casper R. Taylor, Jr.'s office. The program invited national experts to speak on the subject. The summit won the 2001 Odyssey Award from the Travel Industry for excellence and exceptional achievement in tourism awareness.

Tactics—Media

TBC media thoroughly analyzed the target audience's media usage habits and recommended media that most efficiently delivered our messaging to the priority targets. In the past, the state had purchased regional spot and cable television in neighboring states such as Pennsylvania, New York, and Virginia. However, buying media regionally only allowed them to air four to six weeks throughout the year.

TBC Media recommended utilizing national cable television and buying the advertising as direct response. A comparison of the cost of national cable DRTV indicated that it was seventeen times more efficient than buying markets on a regional basis. DRTV would allow the state to track what network was delivering quality inquiries and provided the ability to quickly adjust the buy. National cable also allowed for the pinpointing of those networks that would best reach the most profitable visitor segments.

Because of the cost efficiencies of national DRTV cable, the state was able to air two strong flights, one in the spring and another in the fall. The length of each flight was eight weeks, extending the total on-air messaging to sixteen weeks.

Results. On every level, the campaign was a smash:

- The total campaign's cost-per-lead dropped 23 percent from $18 to $13.
- The television cost-per-lead dropped 30 percent.
- The print cost-per-lead dropped 19 percent.
- The on-line campaign delivered 1,300 percent more travel kit orders than the previous on-line campaign, while the cost-per-lead dropped 95 percent.
- The on-line campaign was also able to boast a 75 percent conversion rate, meaning that three out of four respondents to the on-line advertising ordered a travel kit.

Finally, the commercial and print executions were highlighted in many newspapers and magazines and have been finalists for several respected industry awards.

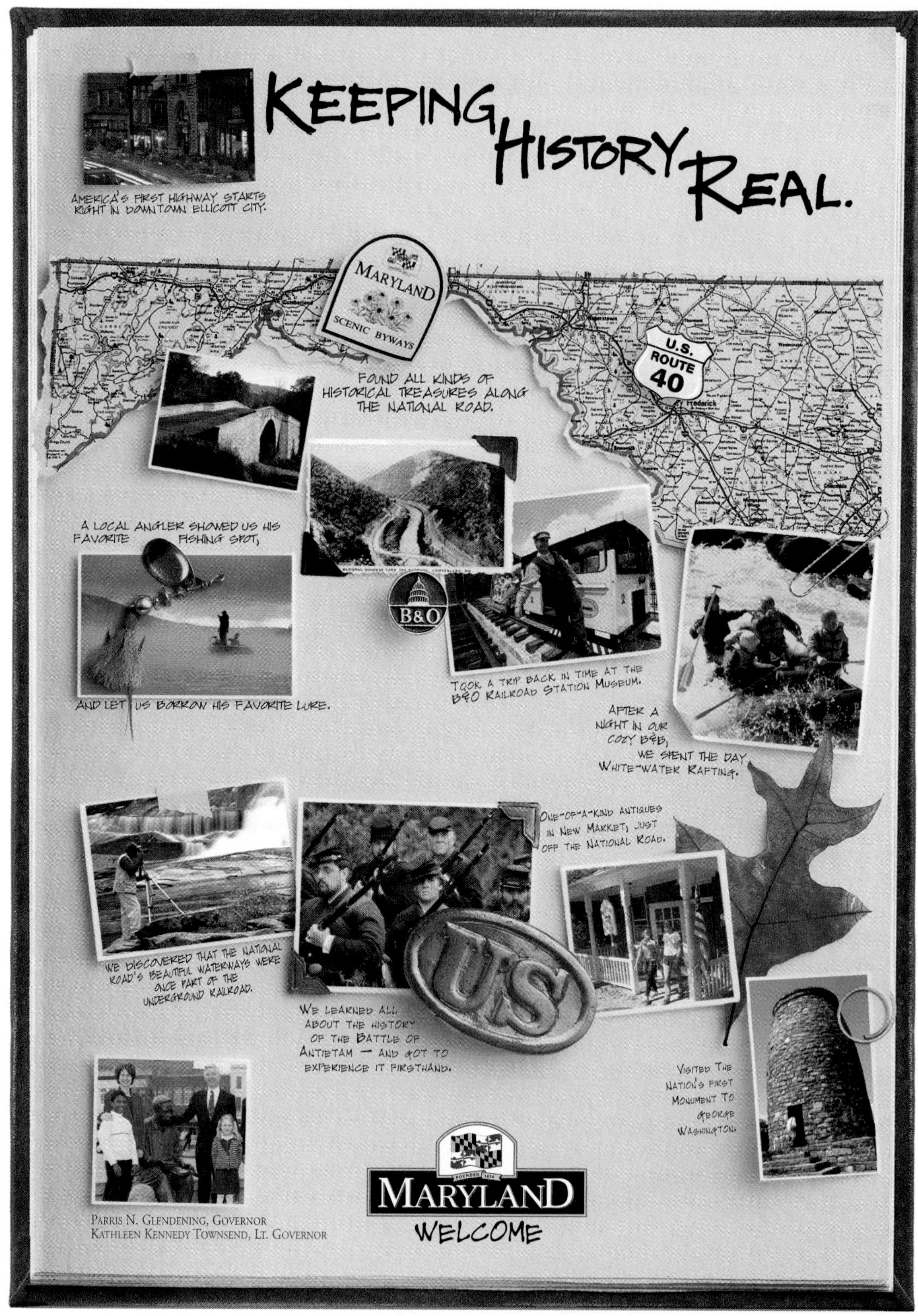

Compliments of Teahan, Burden and Charles Advertising and Public Relations.

Classification of Visitor Segments

Several classifications have been used to describe different visitor destination segments. The most commonly used classifications are based on whether the tourist travels with a group or independently. The common terms are group inclusive tour (GIT) and independent traveler (IT). National tourism offices, international airlines, and others involved in international travel frequently use these designations.

Here are some classifications describing tourists by their degree of institutionalization and their impact on the destinations:[16]

- **Organized mass tourists.** This corresponds to the GIT. These people have little or no influence over their travel experience other than to purchase one package or another. They commonly travel in a group, view the destination through the windows of a tour bus, and remain in preselected hotels. Shopping in the local market often provides their only contact with the native population.
- **Individual mass tourists.** These people are similar to the previous category but have somewhat more control over their itinerary. For instance, they may rent an auto to visit attractions.
- **Explorers.** These people fall in the IT classification. They plan their own itineraries and make their own reservations, although they may use a travel agent. They tend to be very sociable people who enjoy interacting with people at the destination.
- **Drifters.** These people, the backpacker group, will seldom, if ever, be found in a traditional hotel. They may stay at youth hostels with friends or camp out. They tend to mix with lower-socioeconomic native groups and are commonly found riding third-class rail or bus. Most tend to be young.

Another well-known tourist classification system is *Plog's categorization*[17] (Figure 18-1). These designations are similar to the groups mentioned previously, but range from psychocentric to allocentric. Plog observed that destinations are first discovered by **allocentrics** (backpackers or explorers). As the natives discover the economic benefits of tourism, services and infrastructure are developed. When this occurs, allocentrics are turned off and find another unspoiled destination. The nature of visitors now changes, with each new group somewhat less adventurous than the preceding group, perhaps older, and certainly more demanding of creature comforts and service. Finally, a destination becomes so familiar that the least adventurous group of **psychocentrics** finds it acceptable.

Monitoring the Tourist Markets

Tourist markets are dynamic, and a marketing information system is part of any well-run tourist organization. Destinations need to closely monitor the relative popularity of their various attractions by determining the number and type of tourists attracted to each. The popularity of the Metropolitan Museum of Art, Big Ben, or the Colosseum can suddenly or gradually

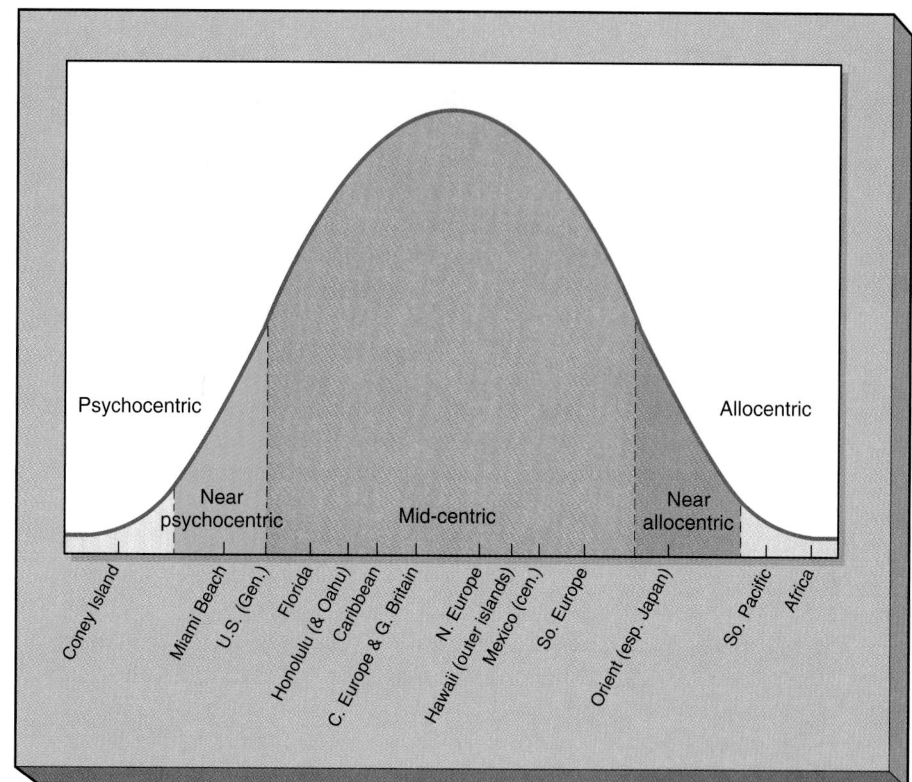

Figure 18-1
Plog's categorization of destinations. The height of the curve indicates the number of travelers in each category. Reprinted by permission of Elsevier Science, Inc., "Why Destinations Rise and Fall in Popularity," by Stanley C. Plog, *Cornell Hotel and Restaurant Administration Quarterly,* 14, no. 4, p. 58, © 1974 by Cornell University.

change. Marketing information systems help to identify and predict environmental trends that are responsible for these changes. Information should be collected on the changes in the wants of existing markets, emerging markets, and potential target markets. For example, in the mid-1990s the Japanese yen appreciated relative to Western currencies. Australia, a popular destination for the Japanese, now became even more of a value because of the increased purchasing power of the Japanese tourist. The state of Queensland increased its marketing efforts toward the Japanese to take advantage of the favorable currency exchange.

18.5 Las Vegas Convention and Visitors Authority

The Las Vegas Convention and Visitors Authority (LVCVA) conducts an annual tourist profile. Information for this profile is collected through customer surveys on an ongoing basis. Survey results indicate that the majority of visitors spend less than four hours a day gambling. The visitors are coming for entertainment and the nongaming amenities of the mega resorts. This information has helped to attract a number of new restaurants, such as Spago, Wolfgang Puck's, Café Coyote, Planet Hollywood, and the Dive. Las Vegas is quickly developing a reputation as a restaurant town. This further enhances its image as a diverse destination rather than just a gaming venue.

One job of a tourist organization is to increase the accessibility of a destination. The LVCVA uses information from its survey to identify emerging markets that can support direct airline flights. Armed with current travel patterns and projected travel patterns based on their surveys, the LVCVA makes presentations to airlines, trying to convince them to start new routes, which will be profitable for the airlines and provide another region of the country with direct air service to Las Vegas. The accessibility of Las Vegas by frequently scheduled and relatively inexpensive airfare is in part responsible for it being one of the top convention centers in the United States. This did not happen by accident; it happened as a result of efforts by the LVCVA.

The Wales Tourist Bureau used market research to identify a target market for the Swansea Marina. Using research, it identified persons in the West Midlands of England who had a similar socioeconomic profile to their existing users. These potential customers were reached through well-targeted advertising campaigns. The small size of the potential market for the Swansea Marina means that mass communication media would not be cost-effective. Rather than waste advertising dollars covering a broad market, information from the Wales Tourist Bureau was used to target the market effectively for the marina.[18]

Tourist organizations need information to stay competitive. Tourist products must change to meet the needs of the changing market. Emerging markets must be identified and served. New markets that can be served by the existing tourist product must be identified. Tourist organizations trying to accomplish these tasks without good information are at a disadvantage.

Communicating with the Tourist Market

Competition for Visitors Involves Image Making

Place images are heavily influenced by pictorial creations of the destination in movies or television, by music, and in some cases by popular entertainers and celebrities. Ireland exploits the John Wayne–Maureen O'Hara film *Quiet Man* as a successful image of the Irish, and Austria still relies on *The Sound of Music* image of its country's beauty and people. Burned to the ground by General William Sherman's army during the Civil War, Atlanta has revived its *Gone with the Wind* image by its selection as the site for the 1996 Olympics. The Olympics was billed as the city's second renaissance, the other being in 1864 after its wartime destruction. Australia's booming tourist business used actor Paul Hogan of the hit film *Crocodile Dundee* to dramatize the country's humor, adventure, and ruggedness. Australia also used Olivia Newton-John and Mel Gibson in ad campaigns, and Manchester, England featured the Beatles. Wales used Richard Burton, and Chicago touts Michael Jordan.

Television also affects destination attractiveness. The pub site for the television hit *Cheers* became an overnight tourist bonanza in Boston, while the Public Broadcasting System's serialization of English dramas opened Britain to American audiences. Late in 1990, the PBS eleven-hour series *The Civil War* also sparked record sales of Civil War reading material and memorabilia. The benefit for Virginia, where more than 60 percent of the war was fought over four years, was a record-breaking surge in tourism.

Changing an image, however, is more difficult. Las Vegas, for example, was once seen as a vice capital known for sex and gambling.

Gambling still accounts for a sizable 60 percent of the local economy, but consider these facts: Las Vegas is (1) a tourist mecca for sports, entertainment, recreation, and performing arts; (2) a major meetings and convention destination; and (3) a high-tech regional service center. Greater Las Vegas has become the fastest-growing region in the country. The choices Las Vegas makes in selecting a mix of communication messages and channels will largely determine its emerging identity.

State media investment on attracting tourists has grown rapidly in recent years. States such as Texas and Alaska have more than quadrupled their tourism media budgets. Nations and states invade and advertise in each other's markets. For instance, Illinois targets New York, California, Texas, and Japan. It produces multilingual travel guides, videotapes, and radio segments.

Destinations have formed partnerships with travel, recreational, and communication businesses on joint marketing efforts. They advertise in national magazines and travel publications and do vertical marketing with business-travel promotions to link the growing business-leisure segment of the traveling public, and they target travel agencies. Many states have located welcome centers along major interstate highways that include unstaffed two-way video systems to answer questions from a central location or otherwise assist travelers. States also target their own residents with brochures, maps, and a calendar of events.

Finally, effective destination imaging requires congruence between advertising and the place. Glossy photographs of sunsets, beaches, buildings, and events need to have some relationship to what tourists actually experience; otherwise, destinations run the risk of losing tourist goodwill and generating bad word of mouth. Travel agents are extremely responsive to feedback from customers.

Developing Packages of Attractions and Amenities

An effective way of communicating with potential travelers is by offering packages. Tourist organizations, cities, and states must develop a package of attractions and amenities in the hope of becoming a chosen destination. Travelers make comparisons about the relative advantages and disadvantages of competing destinations. Destinations must provide easy access to attractions by bus, boats, carriages, and planes. They need to distribute brochures, audiotapes, and videotapes to travel agents and individual prospects. City bus companies might prepare half-day, full-day, and evening tours to highlight the place's major attractions. Concentrating attractions, services, and facilities in a small area creates excitement, adventure, and crowds.

Destinations constantly discover hidden assets that have vast tourist potential. Illinois, for example, has more public and semipublic golf courses per population than any other state except Florida. It now promotes golf tours. One successful buyer has been Japanese tourist agencies, who have packaged a golf and Chicago shopping tour. Pennsylvania has reclaimed old coal mining areas with championship golf courses, expanding its recreational facilities to promote tourism.

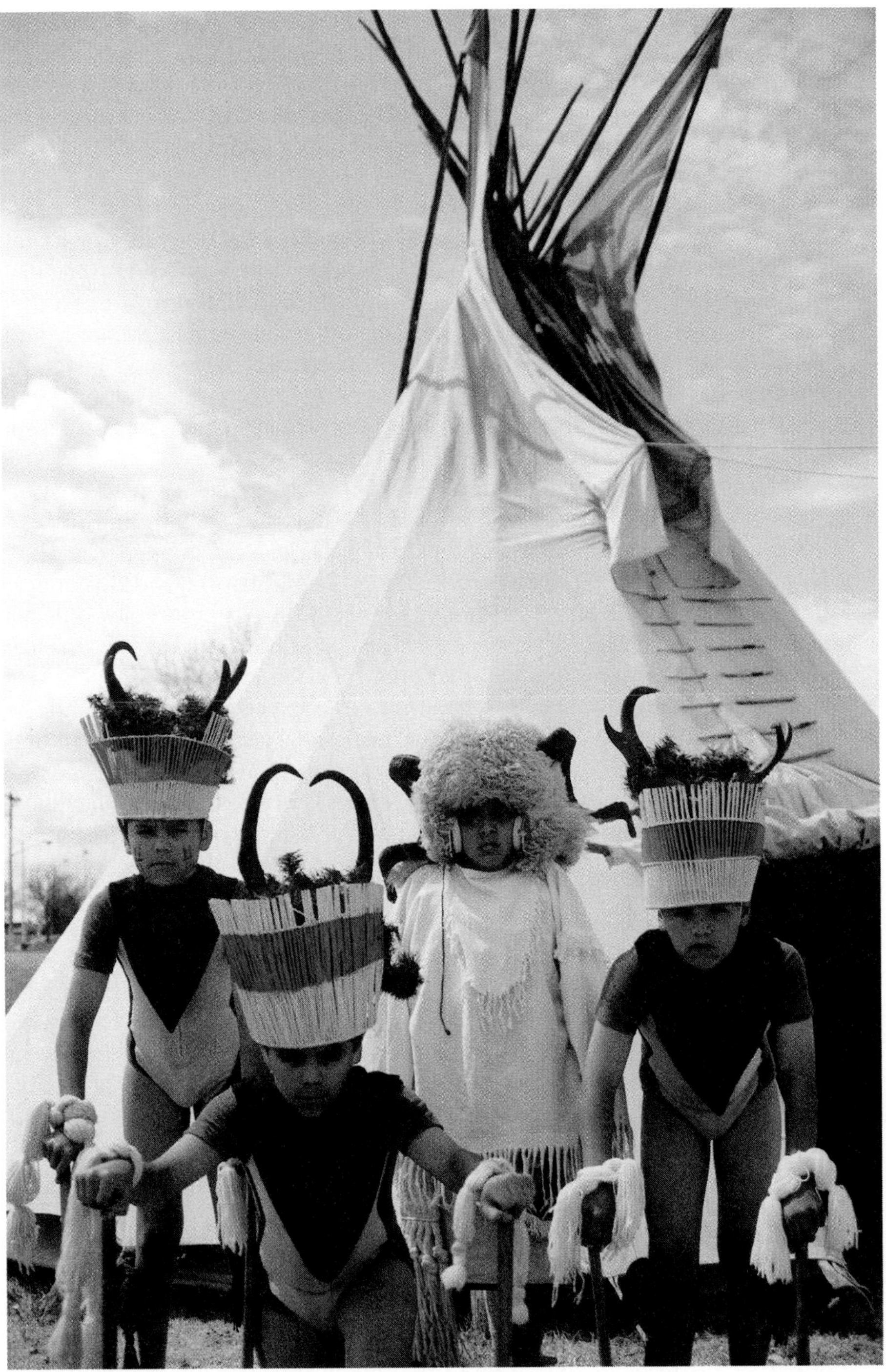

The Koshare Indian Dancers help preserve the cultural traditions of the region and help create a cultural tourism attraction.

The Koshare Indian Museum of La Junta, Colorado, is an example of a cultural tourist attraction. The museum houses one of the largest collections of North American art and artifacts in the world and a library on Native American history. The Native American dances are preserved by teaching them to the young men of the community who perform throughout the nation as the Koshare Indian Dancers.

A destination may promote one, a few, or many of its attractions. Chicago's marketing theme "Chicago's Got It" featured pictures of its famous architecture, lakefront, symphony, world's tallest building, financial exchanges, and Wrigley Field (home of the Chicago Cubs) to suggest that the city had everything: business, culture, entertainment, recreation, and sports. In contrast, San Francisco played off its well-developed image as seductive and mysterious: a photo of a foggy, softly lit Golden Gate Bridge with the copy, "In the Beginning, God Created Heaven and Earth. San Francisco Took a Little Longer."

Attractions alone do not attract visitors. Most places seek to deepen the travel experience by providing greater value and making the experience more significant and rewarding. Such appeals are couched in history, culture, and people. New York City is a case in point. About one in four of the city's visitors is a foreign tourist. Consequently, city officials must make New York "foreign friendly" by creating tours that emphasize nationality interests, designing brochures in a variety of languages, and providing hassle-free currency exchanges. To provide that value-added dimension and friendship, these tour packages try to deepen cultural bonds and ties between the United States and the foreign visitors.

Competition among destinations extends to restaurants, facilities, sports, cultural amenities, and entertainment. Which place has the most four-star hotels, best culinary fare, most museums and theaters, best wine and drink, best chefs, or best native, cultural, or ethnic flair? Campaigns are carried out in specialty publications. Testimonials and rankings are found in travel brochures, advertising, and travel guides.

Despite the best offers of a destination to portray a positive image through public relations and advertising, image building is affected by reports of disturbing societal problems, including human rights abuse. In 1996, the nation of Myanmar (Burma) established a goal of attracting 500,000 tourists. Compared with neighboring Thailand with 6 million tourists, this goal seemed low.[19]

Charges of human rights abuse from Western governments directly affected tourism development and growth. The government of Myanmar viewed its people as "contributing labor" to the development of the tourism-related infrastructure. International human rights observers viewed this development as forced labor. The United Kingdom–based Tourism Concern reported that the Myanmar State Law Order Restoration Council (SLORC) is "implementing projects earmarked for tourism through the use of forced labor and the displacement of people."[20] Tourism Concern reported that chained prison gangs and conscripted families had been used to build roads and prepare tourism sites. According to the reports, army members went from house to house taking people for forced labor.

18.6 Myanmar State Law Order Restoration Council

The SLORC denied these reports and stated that people were contributing their voluntary labor happily.[21] Whatever the truth, reports of human rights abuse, crime, disease, and other societal problems have a negative effect on tourism and may persist long after the problem is corrected.

ORGANIZING AND MANAGING TOURISM MARKETING

Making a destination tourist friendly is the task of a central tourist agency, which may be public, quasi-public, nonprofit, or private. These agencies are referred to as **national tourist organizations (NTOs)** (see Marketing Highlight 18-4). Outside the United States, this agency is often run by the central government, state, or province, together with local government officials. The European Travel Commission, a twenty-four-nation group bent on luring U.S. visitors to Europe, coordinates promotional activity in the United States. Some cities divide responsibilities for promoting tourist

BARBADOS
Your vacation is part of our heritage.

Since 1627, when English settlers first set foot on Barbados, this island, the most socially and politically stable country in the western world, has perfected the art of hospitality.

Barbados offers more cultural pursuits per square mile than any other Caribbean island. You can step back to the days when sugar was king and see the great plantation houses. Or relax amid the floral serenity of our botanical gardens with their rare collections of tropical plants. Or visit one of the only three remaining Jacobean houses this side of the Atlantic.

Or, if our beaches beckon too strongly, you can always immerse yourself in the entire history of Barbados, all under one roof. At the Barbados museum.

Make your next vacation the best it can be. Call your travel agent. Or, for information and brochures, call: USA 1-800-221-9831. Canada 1-800-268-9122.

Codrington College, theological seat of learning in the parish of St. John.

There are two main religions in Barbados. The other is Anglican.

Chattel houses are architecturally unique to Barbados and among the earliest dwellings.

Morgan Lewis sugar mill, the only surviving sugar windmill in the Caribbean.

This ad is sponsored by the Barbados Tourism Authority to promote tourism to the island nation. The toll-free 800 number makes it easier for the prospective traveler to receive information. Courtesy of D'Arcy Masius Benton and Bowles Canada, Inc., and the Barbados Tourism Authority.

and hospitality business; the former is largely public supported, and the latter is supported by the travel tourist business. In smaller communities, tourist travel activities generally fall under a local chamber of commerce and private support. Local chambers of commerce have become aggressive promoters of bed and breakfast lodgings in private homes.

Event Marketing

Events that attract a desired market and harmoniously fit with a community's culture can provide beneficial results, particularly if the event regularly reoccurs over a period of years. Events that occur only once or that require substantial capital investment for a community may not offer sufficient economic returns. A common reply by event promoters is that the public relations value of the event outweighs cost considerations. This claim must be carefully and objectively analyzed before acceptance. Events must also be examined for the possible effect they may have on the cultural/societal impact upon the host community. Events such as motorcycle rallies, spring vacations for college students, or events sponsored by controversial organizations are among those that have created anxiety and concern within host communities. "Destinations must choose their events to fit the needs of the locality, since each event draws its own type of crowd."[22] Gnoth and Anwar provide the following event planning framework.

A Decision Framework: Event Planning*

- What strategic factors relate to this event? To answer this question, one should take into account the following:
  - Mission, goals, and objectives of the event-tourism program
  - Philosophy, orientation, and attitude of the event's managers
  - Environmental scanning (e.g., noting similar events elsewhere)
  - Event-management structure
  - Appraisal of the internal organization in terms of strengths and weaknesses
  - Time frame for attaining targets
- What is the profile of visitors? The profile should include the following factors:
  - Who the visitors are
  - Where they come from
  - The benefits they seek in attending the event
- What is the expenditure profile? This question focuses on the following factors:
  - Expenditure per day
  - Item purchase

*Reprinted by permission of Elsevier Science, Inc., Juergen Gnoth and Syed Aziz Anwar, "New Zealand Bets on Event Tourism," *Cornell Hotel and Restaurant Administration Quarterly* 41, no. 4 (August 2000): 82–83, © 2000 Cornell University.

  - Foreign-exchange earnings
  - Incremental foreign-exchange earnings
  - Regional foreign-exchange distribution
  - Expenditures by local visitors
  - Expenditures by visitors from elsewhere in the country
  - Expenditures by visitors from overseas
  - Total expenditures from all sources
- What are the economic and social costs and benefits of the event? This question addresses financial, social, and physical factors, including the following:
  - Revenue estimates
  - Operating-expenditure estimates
  - Infrastructure-cost estimates
  - Cash-flow analysis
  - Sensitivity analysis to gauge the elasticity of demand to price changes
  - Employment estimates
  - Social-cost estimates
- What is the event's profile? This profile comprises the following issues:
  - Event history
  - Event proposal
  - Event sponsor
  - Event-rights holder
  - Governing body
  - Event critical path
  - Nature of event support required
  - Media coverage

Influencing Site Selection

Successful destinations realize that tourism and commercial marketing are integral factors in destination marketing. Professional groups from areas such as medicine and law regularly plan seminars and meetings at ski or golf resorts where business and pleasure mix. The American Hotel and Motel Association estimates that 25 percent of hotel revenue is generated by conventions and expositions and 10 percent more from meetings.

Tourist organizations differ significantly in their budget, revenue sources, and marketing programs. In general, chambers of commerce are critical for tourist boosterism by cooperating with the tourist travel industry in developing products and directing bookings, marketing, and total place promotion. They are tourist industry advocates, negotiators, and key connection makers with public officials and agencies. In nearly all cases, these agencies believe that they are underfunded relative to their tasks.

It is important for all tourism businesses and agencies to work together to promote the destination and to ensure that visitors' expectations

Marketing Highlight 18-4

National Tourism Organizations: How They Work

Countries and states usually have government or quasi-government agencies that market destination tourism. On the national level, these are referred to as national tourism organizations (NTOs). An NTO has two marketing tasks: (1) the NTO can formulate and develop the tourist product or products of the destination, and (2) it can promote them in appropriate markets. It can base its approach to development and promotion on market research and thus achieve a close match between the products and the markets. In doing this, the tourist organization is acting on behalf of the whole destination and is complementary to the development and promotion activities of individual tourist providers.

The NTO is responsible for the following functions:

- **Flow of research data.** The NTO coordinates tourism research for the area. Information on origin of visitors, length of stay, type of accommodation used, and expenditures on different tourism products are collected and disseminated to members of the organization. This information helps the NTO to evaluate trends and develop marketing strategy. It also provides valuable information to hospitality and travel businesses.
- **Representation in markets.** The NTO often has offices in major markets. These promote the country within the market. The promotion comes in the form of advertising with response mechanisms, such as advertisements in travel magazines featuring a toll-free number to call for additional information. Respondents receive a tour manual. The offices answer questions from prospective visitors and facilitate the development of distribution linkages. They also serve as important sources of information about trends in the market.
- **Organization of workshops and trade shows.** The NTO facilitates the interaction of tourism with members of the distribution channels, such as travel agents and wholesalers. In addition to developing workshops, the NTO purchases space at major travel shows and invites travel industry members to participate in the booth, either by displaying material or having a physical presence. This saves the member the cost of purchasing an individual booth.
- **Familiarization trips.** The NTO develops familiarization trips for key members of the distribution channel and travel writers.
- **Participation in joint marketing schemes.** Some NTOs provide cooperative advertising support to help members promote to selected markets. The British Tourist Authority, for example, helps to support British Airways advertising in the United States. It is hoped that these advertisements will develop additional tourists for Britain, thus helping the British hospitality and travel industry.
- **Support for new or small businesses.** NTOs may provide support for new products and small businesses that are important to the overall tourism of the area. For example, rural tourism, regional festivals, and bed and breakfast accommodations are often promoted by NTOs.
- **Consumer assistance and protection.** NTOs assist the consumer by providing product information. For example, in some countries there are classification schemes for lodging accommodations. These are designed to educate travelers concerning types of available lodging. Sometimes NTOs influence the design of lodging brochures and menus appropriate for a particular market segment.
- **General education.** NTOs conduct conferences and courses to educate travel industry providers from their nation to understand the needs of foreign markets.

Like other organizations, NTOs must develop a mission statement, goals, and a strategy. The following guidelines were developed to assist in formulating a mission statement:

1. The past experiences in the region with regard to tourism must be considered, including the salient characteristics and history of the region, the regional tourism organization(s), and the tourism business units.

2. The regional tourism organization must be prepared to adapt the region's mission in response to the characteristics of the regional tourism environment. For example, there is increasing concern for the protection of the ecological environment. This should be incorporated into a regional mission statement.
3. The region's tourism resources make certain missions possible and others not. Northern Canada, for example, is unlikely to become the surfing mecca of North America.
4. The preferences of the region's major tourism publics, such as regional tourism organizations, tourism business units, local governments, and community organizations, must be considered. A successful mission statement will attempt to incorporate the priorities and expectations of the major publics in the region.
5. The mission must be based on the region's distinctive competencies. A concerted effort must be made to concentrate on the region's strengths. If, for example, a region's major tourism resource is its cultural heritage, this should receive primary emphasis in the mission statement.

Goals provide direction to the organization. The following are typical tourism goals:

- **Economic:** to optimize the contribution of tourism and recreation to economic prosperity, full employment, and regional economic development.
- **Consumer:** to make the opportunity for and the benefits of travel and recreation universally acceptable to residents and visitors and to contribute to the personal growth and education of the population and encourage their appreciation of the geography, history, and ethnic diversity of the region.
- **Environmental and natural resources:** to protect and preserve the historic and cultural foundations of the region as a living part of community life and development and to ensure future generations an opportunity to enjoy the rich heritage of the region, as well as to ensure the compatibility of tourism, recreational, and activity policies with other regional and national interests in energy development and conservation, environmental protection, and judicious use of natural resources.
- **Government operations:** to harmonize to the maximum extent possible all government-related activities supporting tourism and recreation; to support the needs of the general public and the public and private sectors of industries involved with tourism and recreation; and to take a leadership role with all those concerned with tourism, recreation, and cultural heritage conservation.

The underlying objective of regional strategy formulation is to translate current conditions in the region into desired situations. For example, a region with the goal of increasing the economic benefits of tourism to a specific subregion may select a strategy to increase visitation to that area. A region that is highly dependent on one specific geographic market for its demand may adopt a strategy of diversification.

Destinations marketers who are able to influence site selection of groups such as associations can expect enviable visitors' income for the community. To have a chance of being selected as a meeting site, a destination must be included in the initial decision process. Careful study and research is needed of those responsible for site selection. Research of targeted associations and understanding who the real decision makers are within the providence of the site selection committee.

Sources: Chris Ryan, *Recreational Tourism: A Social Science Perspective* (New York: Routledge, 1991), pp. 5–34; A. J. Burkhart and S. Medlik, *Tourism: Past, Present, and Future* (London: Heinemann, 1981), p. 256; T. C. Victor Middleton, *Marketing in Travel and Tourism* (Oxford, England: Butterworth-Heinemann, 1994); Ernie Heath and Geoffrey Wall, *Marketing Tourism Destination* (New York: Wiley, 1992), p. 65; R. C. Mills and A. M. Morrison, *The Tourism System: An Introductory Text* (Upper Saddle River, NJ: Prentice Hall, 1985), p. 248; S. Crystal, "What Is the Meeting Industry Worth?" *Meeting News* 17, no. 7 (1993): 1, 11.

are met. State tourist organizations should work with national organizations and local organizations. Hotels and airlines help with fam trips sponsored by tourist organizations. Local business provides managers who make sales calls on behalf of the destination at regional, national, and international conferences. Promoting a destination is a team effort.

Key Terms

Allocentrics Persons with a need for new experiences, such as backpackers and explorers.

Destinations Places with some form of actual or perceived boundary, such as the physical boundary of an island, political boundaries, or even market-created boundaries.

Infrastructure The system according to which a company, organization, or other body is organized at the most basic level.

Macrodestinations Destinations such as the United States that contain thousands of microdestinations, including regions, states, cities, towns, and visitor destinations within a town.

Multiplier effect Tourist expenditures that are recycled through the local economy, being spent and respent.

National tourist organizations A national government or quasi-government agency that markets destination tourism.

Psychocentrics Persons who do not desire change when they travel. They like nonthreatening places and to stay in familiar surroundings.

Tourism A stay of one or more nights away from home for holidays, visits to friends or relatives, business conferences, or any other purpose, except such things as boarding, education, or semipermanent employment.

Chapter Review

I. Globalization of the Tourist Industry

1) Over a half-billion tourists. According to the World Tourism Organization (WTO) of the United Nations, more than 625 million tourists traveled internationally in 1998, spending over $444 billion (excluding transportation).

2) Tourism employs more people than any single industrial sector. Tourism accounts for 8 percent of total world exports, more than 31 percent of international trade in services, and more than 100 million jobs worldwide.

II. Importance of Tourism to a Destination's Economy

1) **Tourism destination**

   a) Destinations are places with some form of actual or perceived boundary.

   b) Macrodestinations such as the United States contain thousands of microdestinations, including regions, states, cities, towns, and visitor destinations within a town.

2) **Benefits of tourism**

   a) Employment.

   b) Support industries and professions.

   c) Multiplier effect. Tourism expenditures are recycled through the economy.

   d) Source of state and local taxes.

   e) Stimulates exports of place-made products.

3) **Management of the tourism destination**

   a) Destinations must maintain the infrastructure. Destinations that fail to maintain the necessary infrastructure or build inappropriate infrastructure run significant risks.

   b) Sustainable tourism. A destination's attractiveness can be diminished by violence, political instability, natural catastrophe, adverse environmental factors, and overcrowding.

   c) The preservation of natural attractions must be managed. Tourist development must balance the temptation to maximize tourist dollars with preservation of the natural tourist attractions and the quality of life for local residents.

III. Tourism Strategies and Investments

1) **Tourism competition is strong**

   a) New and upgraded destinations are constantly appearing.

   b) Destinations are rediscovering their past, looking for a tourism hook.

   c) Stay close to home. Local tourism and convention bureaus are trying to get the locals to visit their own region.

2) **Investment in tourist attractions**

   a) Destinations must respond to the travel basics of cost, convenience, and timeliness.

   b) Events are being developed as a way of attracting tourists.

   c) Urban renewal is being designed with the tourist in mind.

   d) A combination of public and private investment is being used to develop major tourism developments.

IV. Segmenting and Monitoring the Tourist Market. Tourism planners must consider how many tourists are desired, which segments to attract, and how to balance tourism with other industries.

1) **Identifying target markets**

   a) Collect information about its current visitors.

   b) Audit the destination's attractions and select segments that might logically have an interest in them.

2) **Classification of visitor segments**

   a) Group inclusive tour (GIT)

   b) Independent traveler (IT; formerly FIT)

3) Monitoring the tourist markets. Tourist markets are dynamic and a marketing information system is part of any well-run tourist organization.

V. Communicating with the Tourist Market

1) Competition for visitors requires image making.

2) Developing packages of attractions and amenities is an effective way of communicating with potential travelers.

a) Attractions alone do not attract visitors. Most places seek to deepen the travel experience by providing greater value and making the experience more significant and rewarding.

b) Competition among destinations extends to restaurants, facilities, sports, cultural amenities, and entertainment.

VI. Organizing and Managing Tourism Marketing. Making a destination tourist friendly is the task of a central tourist agency, which may be public, quasi-public, nonprofit, or private. These agencies are referred to as national tourist organizations (NTOs).

VII. Influencing Site Selection. Destination marketers who are able to influence site selection of groups such as associations can expect enviable visitors' income for the community.

Discussion Questions

1. How does a tourism destination determine what to promote and to whom it should be promoted?
2. What benefits does tourism bring to your area?
3. Choose one of the psychological determinants of demand listed in Table 18-1 and describe a tourism product that is based on the determinant you have chosen.
4. Choose what you believe to be a good tourism promotion for a city, region, state, or country and explain why you think it is a good promotion. In your critique, discuss the media used, target audience, and benefits the destination offers.

Experiential Exercise

Do the following:

Choose an event (festival, concert, play, etc.) in your area that draws tourists. Look into how the event is promoted and the benefits its brings to the community. Is this event effectively promoted? If yes, why? If no, how could it be improved?

Internet Exercise

Support for these exercises can be found on the Web site for *Marketing for Hospitality and Tourism*, www.prenhall.com/kotler.

Find two different sites of tourism promotion organizations. Evaluate how effective you feel these web sites are in promoting the destination. Explain your answer.

REFERENCES

1. "Milwaukee CVB Goes on the Record with New Promotion," *USAE* 14, no. 5 (January 31, 1995): 1.
2. Ibid.
3. Chris Ryan, "The Determinants of Demand for Tourism," in *Recreational Tourism: A Social Science Perspective* (London: Routledge, 1991), p. 5.
4. *Tourism Highlights 1999* (Madrid: World Tourism Organization, 1998), pp. 2–17.
5. Ibid.
6. "Ruili Strives to Become a Top Tourist City," *Travel China* 9, no. 13 (May 10, 1997); 9: *Tourism Highlights 1999,* pp. 2–17.
7. Changfeng Chen, "Rising Chinese Overseas Travel Market and Potential for the United States," in *Advances in Hospitality and Tourism Research*, ed. K. S. Chon and Connie C. B. Mok (Houston, TX: Conrad N. Hilton College, 1998), pp. 468–478.
8. Jonathan Dahl, "It Seems That Nothing Is Certain Except Taxes and More Taxes," *Wall Street Journal,* March 4, 1991, p. B1.
9. Susan Carey, "Tourist Spots Developing 'Green' Images," *Wall Street Journal,* May 10, 1991, p. A7.
10. Jim Bergstorm, Lawrence Yu, and Edgar Medweth, "Destination Maintenance: Why Sedona Needs Schnebly Hill," *Cornell Hotel and Restaurant Administration Quarterly* 35, no. 4 (August 1994): 32.
11. Ibid., pp. 33, 37.
12. Andrew Nemethy, "Resorts Go Up and Down," *Snow County* (November 1990): 31–32.
13. Edward Manning and T. D. Dougherty, "Sustainable Tourism," *Cornell Hotel and Restaurant Administration Quarterly* 36, no. 2 (April 1995): 29.
14. Susan Gregory and Kathy Koithan-Louderback, "Marketing a Resort Community," *Cornell Hotel and Restaurant Quarterly* 38, no. 6 (December 1977): 54.
15. "Qufu Stresses Confucian Culture and Tourism Market Order," *Travel China* 9, no. 13 (May 10, 1997): 9.
16. E. Cohen, "Towards a Sociology of International Tourism," *Social Research*, 39, no. 1 (1972): 164–182.
17. Stanley C. Plog, "Why Destinations Rise and Fall in Popularity," *Cornell Hotel and Restaurant Quarterly* 14, no. 4 (February 1984): 55–59.
18. Richard Prentice, "Market Targeting," in *Tourism Marketing and Management Handbook,* ed. Stephen F. Witt and Luiz Moutinho (Upper Saddle River, NJ: Prentice Hall, 1989), pp. 247–252.
19. J. S. Perry Hobson and Roberta Leung, "Hotel Development in Myanmar," *Cornell Hotel and Restaurant Administration Quarterly* 38, no. 1 (February 1997): 60–71.
20. F. Doherty, "Come Ye Back to Mandalay," *Tourism in Focus* 15 (spring 1995): 8.
21. "Bring Bicycle and Sleeping Bag," *Economist,* November 11, 1995, p. 34.
22. Juergen Gnoth and Syed Aziz Anwar, "New Zealand Bets on Event Tourism," *Cornell Hotel and Restaurant Administration Quarterly* 41, no. 4 (August 2000): 80.

19 Next Year's Marketing Plan

If you don't have a competitive advantage, don't compete.
Jack Welch

At Preferred Hotels & Resorts, we believe that the product preferences of affluent customers are as diverse as the consumers themselves.
Peter Cass

Hospitality companies know that planning and research go hand-in-glove. This is particularly true of companies such as Preferred Hotels & Resorts Worldwide who serve the affluent guest, as described by Peter Cass, president and CEO.

The rationale is that the experience of the truly discerning traveler is shaped by the "little things," beyond guaranteeing merely a clean, comfortable room and a desirable package of amenities. In-depth guest input will also be utilized to shape the criteria that go into defining the on-property guest experience. Through a proprietary customer satisfaction program currently under development, Preferred will refine still further fine points of detail that create a truly memorable and complete "luxury experience."

For example, at the Rittenhouse Hotel in Philadelphia, frequent guests are greeted nightly with an expensive pearl on their pillow instead of the usual chocolate. At Halekulani in Honolulu, which was recently named the number one hotel in the world by Gourmet magazine, guests are escorted to their room for swift, private check-in, and receive a welcoming box of chocolates made by their in-house chocolatrie soon afterward.

Although "comment cards" and guest preference sheets remain commonplace at many luxury hotels, no other worldwide lodging brand has built into its core mission the complete and total fulfillment of the guests' individual tastes, requirements, and predilections.

We have found that complete attention to detail—a total commitment to guest satisfaction that saves a guest time, energy, and efforts, provides

completely personalized and individualized service, and creates the experience of "intellectual surprise" for its consumers—is what drives our repeat business among the affluent.

To better understand their affluent consumer, Preferred Hotels & Resorts launched a market research effort that "drills down" to the deepest level of guest preference and expectation. Using a prospect identification and lifestyle data-collection system, detailed and segmented data are gathered not only about the preferences of luxury travelers but also about unperceived "micromarkets" that make up the luxury travel segment.

At the individual property level, the expectation is that property managers will soon be able to learn not only what kind of room guests prefer when they travel on business, but also what their favorite leisure activities are, what kind of wine they like to drink—even their favorite reading material. At the macrolevel, Preferred plans to target programs, promotions, and partnerships tailored to the micromarket segments that make up their customer bases. Examples are West Coast lawyers who golf or company CEOs who travel with children. Data collected from "drilling down" into the guest experience will enable Preferred to provide the ultimate in guest service. Unique data will also be provided that will become invaluable for partners who seek unique channels and distribution mechanisms in marketing to the affluent.

Initial Applications of the Research: "Experiential" Associations and New Marketing Programs

Although affluent guests value individuality and attention to detail, Preferred has begun to identify certain distinct attributes or expectations that define the affluent as a group. More than anything else, affluents tend to flock together around common symbols, expectations, and experiences. In a word, they associate themselves into groups. Membership in the group, in turn, comes to define participation in the affluent experience.

Association is built into the concept of the affluent experience so that Preferred's creation of programs that target the affluent can be understood as a universal affinity program for the discerning consumer. It is the ultimate "affinity program for the affluent."

Preferred has taken the affinity concept a step further by identifying an interlinked series of value and quality associations that respond to the affluent's desire for unique, memorable experiences and superior service, and by using that information to provide experiences that cater directly and uniquely to that desire.

Seabourn/Windstar

An example of the research in action is a partnership between Preferred and Seabourn/Windstar Cruises. The linkage is the proclivity of guests who stay at exclusive Preferred hotel properties to also take expensive cruises on these two cruise lines, among the world's finest. The customer reward is the ability to translate stays at Preferred hotels into free nights on these cruises. This allows Preferred and Seabourn/Windstar Cruises to share guest histories and databases that reveal a guest's preferences and thus guarantee the ability to service the guest "to the tee" with the expectation of creating return business.

Golf the Preferred Way

Another example of the application of the lifestyle marketing approach is "Preferred Golf," a partnership with Wide World of Golf, a worldwide marketer of upscale golf services. Preferred Golf provides Preferred guests with access to the world's finest golf courses by means of staying at a Preferred hotel or resort.

Engaging New Partners: Travel Agents and the Lifestyle Client Building Program

Lifestyle marketing programs that target the affluent have applications that extend far beyond merely "selling room nights."

For example, through programs such as Wide World of Golf and the cruise redemption program, Preferred properties and travel agents can work together to sell complete "experiential packages" for the affluent traveler. Travel agents enter Preferred's luxury marketing "loop" as partners and build relationships with discerning travelers. This goes well beyond the usual booking of air travel and hotels on the basis of price and availability. Client building is achieved through educational seminars, training programs, and special package promotions. Agents are encouraged to position themselves as key components of Preferred's affluent marketing channel.[1]

Chapter Objectives

After reading this chapter, you should be able to:

1. Know why it is important to have a marketing plan and be able to explain the purpose of a marketing plan.
2. Prepare a marketing plan following the process described in this chapter.

19.1 La Samanna Resort

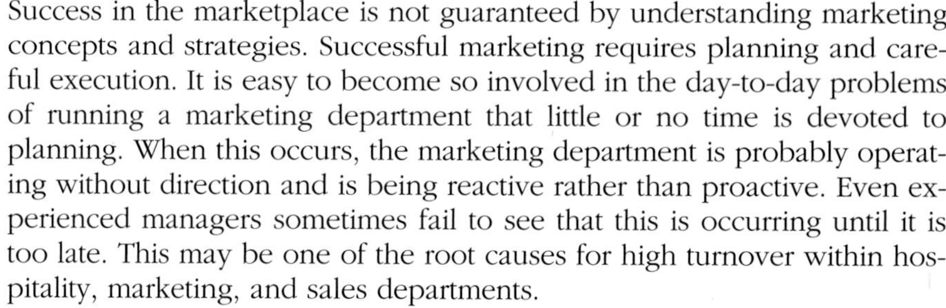

Success in the marketplace is not guaranteed by understanding marketing concepts and strategies. Successful marketing requires planning and careful execution. It is easy to become so involved in the day-to-day problems of running a marketing department that little or no time is devoted to planning. When this occurs, the marketing department is probably operating without direction and is being reactive rather than proactive. Even experienced managers sometimes fail to see that this is occurring until it is too late. This may be one of the root causes for high turnover within hospitality, marketing, and sales departments.

Purpose of a Marketing Plan

A marketing plan serves several purposes within any hospitality company:

- Provides a road map for all marketing activities of the firm for the next year
- Ensures that marketing activities are in agreement with the corporate strategic plan
- Forces marketing managers to review and think through objectively all steps in the marketing process
- Assists in the budgeting process to match resources with marketing objectives
- Creates a process to monitor actual against expected results

The development of a marketing plan is a rigorous process and cannot be accomplished in a few hours. Instead, it is best to set aside one or more days to develop next year's plan. Many marketing managers find it best to leave the office along with their staff and all necessary data while writing the plan. Constant interruptions that occur in the office are detrimental to the planning process.

To be effective, a new marketing plan must be written each year. Marketing plans written for periods longer than a year are generally not effective. At the same time, the annual marketing plan must be written against a longer-term strategic marketing plan that states what the company hopes to achieve, say, three to five years down the road.

Many managers believe that the process of writing a plan is invaluable because it forces those writing it to question, think, and strategize. A plan should be developed with the input and assistance of key members of the marketing department. The discussion and thought process required to produce a plan is stimulating and very helpful in team building. It is also an excellent training device for younger staff members who wish to be managers.

A marketing plan should contain the following sections:

I. Executive summary
II. Corporate connection
III. Environmental analysis and forecasting
IV. Segmentation and targeting
V. Next year's objectives and quotas
VI. Action plans: strategies and tactics
VII. Resources needed to support strategies and meet objectives
VIII. Marketing control
IX. Presenting and selling the plan
X. Preparing for the future

We examine the role played by each section of the marketing plan.

Section I: Executive Summary

The executive summary and a few charts or graphs from the body of the plan may be the only parts ever read by top management. Consequently, it is of great importance to write this section carefully, with top management in mind.

A few tips may assist in writing the executive summary:

- Write it for top executives.
- Limit the number of pages to between two and four.
- Use short sentences and short paragraphs. Avoid using words that are unlikely to be understood.
- Organize the summary as follows: describe next year's objectives in quantitative terms; briefly describe marketing strategies to meet goals and objectives, including a description of target markets; describe expected results by quarter; identify the dollar costs necessary, as well as key resources needed.
- Read and reread the executive summary several times. Never write it once and then place it in the plan. Modify and change the summary until it flows well, is easily read, and conveys the central message of the marketing plan.

SECTION II: CORPORATE CONNECTION

Relationship to Other Plans

A marketing plan is not a stand-alone tool. Instead, it must support other plans, such as the firm's strategic plan. Whenever possible, the marketing manager should participate in or provide input to the development of a strategic plan. If this is not practical, it remains imperative to understand the contents of the strategic plan prior to development of next year's marketing plan.

A marketing plan supports the company's strategic plan in several ways. Next year's marketing strategies and tactics must support strategic decisions such as the following:

- Corporate goals with respect to profit, growth, and so on
- Desired market share
- Positioning of the company or of its product lines
- Vertical or horizontal integration
- Strategic alliances
- Product line breadth and depth

Marketing-Related Plans

In large organizations, marketing-related plans are sometimes developed by people who do not report to marketing. This is usually the result of (1) originally establishing these departments independent of marketing, (2) political maneuvering in which a nonmarketing executive desired control of these areas, and (3) the failure of top management to understand the need to unify marketing-related activities.

Marketing-related areas in which plans may be written independently of marketing include the following:

- Sales
- Advertising and promotion
- Public relations and publicity
- Marketing research
- Pricing
- Customer service

If these plans are developed independently of a marketing plan with no consideration as to how they tie together, the result is often chaotic, counterproductive, and a source for continuous infighting among marketing-related areas.

When the organizational design of a company fails to place major marketing activities under the marketing umbrella, the task of writing and implementing a marketing plan is made more complex. Under these conditions, it behooves the marketing manager to invite the managers of other marketing-related areas to participate in the marketing plan development process. This action should then be reciprocated.

The activities of marketing and many other departments within a company are closely intertwined. Operations and finance are two areas that affect and in turn are affected by marketing. If guest experiences are diminished because of problem areas in operations, marketing will be adversely affected. Similarly, if financial projections are unrealistic for certain months or for various product lines, marketing will be called to task.

It is unrealistic to expect perfect harmony between marketing and other departments. It is by no means unrealistic to suggest that relations can usually be greatly improved and that a critical place to begin is by interchanging data, suggestions, and other assistance when department plans are being developed.

Corporate Direction

A good marketing plan begins with the fact that the only purpose of marketing is to support the enterprise. It is good politics and good sense to begin next year's plan by recognizing and restating these corporate elements. Let top management know that these helped to guide the development of next year's plan:

- Mission statement
- Corporate philosophy
- Corporate goals

Hospitality companies are highly sensitive to changes in their social, political, and economic environments. A manufacturer of food or toiletries may not immediately feel the impact of these changes, but airlines, hotels, auto rental firms, and cruise lines witness an instant reaction.

SECTION III: ENVIRONMENTAL ANALYSIS AND FORECASTING

The day the Gulf War was declared, hospitality firms felt the impact. Pleasure travel instantly evaporated as fear of possible terrorism gripped Americans. Unfortunately, some companies responded without clearly thinking. Several hotel chains quickly offered substantial discounts to guests. This did nothing to increase demand, but instead simply gave discounts to people who had to travel for business and would have paid a higher rate. A marketing plan is not a political or economic treatise, and hospitality marketers are not expected to be experts in these fields. They are expected to be aware of major environmental factors likely to affect the industry and the company, to consider their possible impact on marketing, and to respond quickly and intelligently to new events and trends.

Major Environmental Factors

Hospitality organizations need to anticipate the influence of these broad environmental factors on their business.

Social. Consider the possible impact of major social factors, such as crime, AIDS, and changing demographics. These factors will vary in their intensity and their geographic incidence. Social factors relevant to Los Angeles, or Sydney, Australia, may have little relevance to Rapid City, South Dakota.

Social conditions sometimes change rapidly to the benefit of alert marketers. The hotel market within India had long been considered as uninteresting by many hotel chains. In the 1990s, India's social and economic structure suddenly became conducive to midpriced hotel development.

In the mid-1990s, India had only 2,000 international standard midpriced hotel rooms in a nation of 900 million people, compared with 3.5 million midpriced rooms in the United States. The sudden emergence of a potentially gigantic market attracted many chains, including Holiday Inn Worldwide, Choice Hotels, Carlson Hospitality Group (Radisson), Southern Pacific Hotels (Australia), and Oberoi Group of Hotels (India).

A U.S. hotel executive observed, "It's much easier to do a hotel here than in China. We have more entrepreneurial freedom and business security."

Political. Legislation affecting taxation, pension benefits, and casino gambling are only a few examples of political decisions likely to affect marketing directly. International politics is increasingly important to corporate hospitality marketing plans. The opening of Vietnam to investors and tourists after years of being off limits provides risk as well as potential rewards for the hospitality industry.[2]

Economic. Changes in economic variables such as employment, income, savings, and interest rates should be recognized. The hospitality industry, especially the lodging and cruising sectors, are highly sensitive to business-cycle movements.

An assessment of major environmental factors should assist planners to modify strategies and possibly consider new market segments. It may also prevent rash changes in tactics, such as the pricing example during the Gulf War.

Competitive Analysis

It is common practice for hospitality companies to conduct a competitive analysis. In some cases, this analysis deals primarily with the observable physical properties of a competitor. For example:

OUR HOTEL	THEIR HOTEL
500 Rooms	600 Rooms
1 Ballroom	2 Ballrooms
Executive center	No executive center

An analysis solely of physical differences usually misses major competitive advantages or disadvantages. It is doubtful that most guests know or care about the room count of competitive hotels. They do recognize differences in service level, cleanliness, staff knowledge, and the responsiveness of the sales departments. A competitive analysis must extend beyond inventory comparisons. True competitive advantages are factors that are recognized by guests and influence their purchase decisions. A creative and alert marketing manager will recognize competitive variables that are truly of importance to the customers and are controllable. Such a manager will develop strategies and tactics to improve areas of weakness and enhance already strong points.

Based strictly on a comparison of physical attributes, many hospitality firms should not exist. Bed and breakfast establishments are usually old homes without a swimming pool and may have shared bathrooms;

yet they fill a competitive niche. Hertz and Avis may compete head-to-head, offering clean, late-model cars, but Rent-a-Wreck auto rental company successfully offers automobiles that many people would be ashamed to be seen driving.

The single best way to conduct a competitive analysis is to involve members of the marketing sales department, such as the sales force. These people often have difficulty discussing environmental variables such as interest rates, but they can talk knowledgeably for hours about the competition and guest preferences.

Market Trends

Market trends are a reflection of environmental and competitive variables. Market trend information for the hospitality industry is often available from outside organizations free of charge. Common sources include chambers of commerce, visitors bureaus, universities, government agencies, banks, trade associations, and commercial organizations such as CPA firms or consultants who publish information for publicity purposes.

Useful market trend information for writing a hospitality marketing plan includes the following:

- **Visitor trends:** origination areas, stopover sites, visitor demographics, spending habits, length of stay, and so on.
- **Competitive trends:** numbers, location, type of products offered (e.g., all-suite hotels), occupancy levels, average rates, and so on.
- **Related industry trends:** interdependence of the members of the hospitality industry upon airline flights, convention center bookings, new airport construction, and new highways. It is important to study trends for supporting or related industries.

Caterers of in-flight meals were dramatically affected by the trend among U.S. airlines to eliminate or reduce onboard meal service. Companies such as Dobbs International Services, who provided full-course meals, had to find new markets and new products. Caterair International Corporation diversified into the repair of airplane audio headsets, and Sky Chefs explored the private-label business and food preparation for prisons, schools, and hospitals. Randall C. Boyd, senior vice president marketing and customer service for Sky Chefs, said, "We are good sandwich makers, salad makers, and pasta makers. Whether a prisoner or a college student is eating our sandwich, we don't care."[3]

19.2 Sky Chefs

Select only those trends that are useful in developing the plan. It is of no value to fill a plan with pages of information that have little or no direct relevancy.

Market Potential

Estimates of market potential often seem to be ignored by those who write hospitality marketing plans. Marketing managers in hotels sometimes feel that the concept has no application to them. "We view all travelers as potential guests" is a frequently heard comment. Others reply that the concept is theoretical for the hospitality industry and applies primarily to consumer packaged goods.

These opinions are incorrect! Although it is true that measurement of true market potential is impossible, estimates can and should be made. The hospitality industry is notorious for ignoring or misinterpreting market potential estimates, thus leading to overbuilding, overcapacity, price cutting, and frantic advertising and promotion in an attempt to fill rooms or fill seats.

Market potential should be viewed as the total available demand for a hospitality product within a particular geographic market at a given price. It is important not to mix different hospitality products into an estimate of market potential.

It is common to hear individuals speak of the market for hotel rooms in a region as a number of room-nights. For purposes of writing a marketing plan, such figures are interesting but do not indicate market potential for your products. Most markets consist of a mix of hotel properties, ranging from luxury to budget, with specialty lodging such as all-suites, condominium hotels, bed and breakfasts, and others.

Each type of property faces its own peculiar market potential, except for times when a special event fills every bed in town. Estimates of market potential normally begin by examining the market for all hotels but should then shift to specific markets for your hotel and directly competitive properties. To be precise, market potential estimates should be shown as demand estimates at various price points; however, this is generally unnecessary for most marketing plans. The average marketing manager for a property such as a hotel finds it impossible to make good quantitative estimates of market potential in room-nights or dollars. These people lack marketing research support, and most were not trained in quantitative analysis. Therefore, market potential estimates are often expressed in "guesstimates," such as the market seems to be growing or declining by about 5 percent a year.

Warning! Even though precise estimates may be beyond the abilities of many hospitality marketing managers, it is essential to go through the thought process of examining market potential. Never assume that market potential is static or that it is unimportant to marketing success.

By engaging in the process of trying to guesstimate or estimate market potential, those who develop marketing plans will become aware of potentially important market conditions and can then adjust marketing strategies appropriately. Remember, the process of developing a marketing plan is not a precise discipline such as engineering or chemistry. The exercise of writing a plan is usually as important to marketing success as the plan itself.

Marketing Research

The need for marketing intelligence is ongoing. Much of the information acquired by marketing research in a current calendar or fiscal year will serve as the basis for developing next year's marketing plan. Marketing research needs vary considerably by type and size of the hospitality company. Companies such as Hertz or Hilton Hotels have corporate marketing research departments. An individual hotel property or car rental location may have need for additional marketing information. In these cases, the individual property or location is generally responsible for acquiring these data.

Marketing research needs can usually be divided into macromarket and micromarket information. Macromarket information includes but is not restricted to:

- Industry trends
- Social-economic-political trends
- Competitive information
- Industrywide customer data

Micromarket information includes but is not restricted to:

- Guest information
- Product/service information
- New product analysis and testing
- Intermediary buyer data
- Pricing studies
- Key account information
- Advertising/promotion effectiveness

One of the promising areas of marketing research has been called yield marketing by executives from two advertising agencies serving the hospitality industry. These advertising executives envision a linking of customer responses with a hotel's advertising and promotional efforts. This will be accomplished by linking sales, marketing, and reservations systems with property management systems through the use of small but powerful computers. This would enable a hotel to make accurate, quick measurements of the effectiveness and efficiency of past marketing investments, and will permit them to make better estimates of the value of future investments.[4]

It is imperative that marketing managers keep abreast of developments such as this and provide an appropriate marketing research budget to include advancing technology. Marketing research too often is reactionary rather than proactive. Studies are conducted when a problem occurs or when competitors unexpectedly offer new products.

An example of a possible need for advertising research was offered by an advertisement by Hotel Sofitel in the June 9, 1994, *Wall Street Journal*. This ad showed two smiling Caucasian men with one extending papers to another in front of the concierge desk. The ad's headline read, "They didn't name a type of service after the French for nothing." The copy went on to say, "At Sofitel, our 'French service' is more a way of life than a particular action. The little things that make all the difference. So when you stay with us, you're taken care of. Your requests, even those that may seem beyond what you'd expect to be fulfilled, will be honored by our concierge."

Although this particular advertisement addresses the issue of customer service in a positive way, one has to wonder how it might have been received by American readers.

- *French service.* Do Americans view French service as good, or do they view it as haughty and uncaring? Comments by American

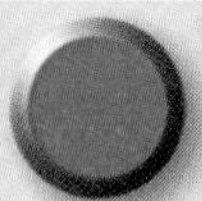

Marketing Highlight 19-1

Lee Witherow was assigned as the general manager of the Embassy Suites/Dallas Park Central property in Dallas, Texas. His charge was to convert this former Park Suites Hotel to the Embassy Suites flag. The hotel was performing under the market in penetration, average daily rate (ADR), and occupancy. When Witherow was assigned to this property, Embassy Suites' president Clyde Culp called the property "our company's biggest challenge and one of our most difficult hotels."

Upon arrival in Dallas, Witherow discovered a hotel that relied on two major clients for more than 42 percent of the property's occupancy; therein lay much of the hotel's ADR problems. As a result, Witherow developed a plan to replace a substantial amount of the current business with fewer rate-sensitive clients. Over the next two and one-half years, the hotel's occupancy grew by approximately 9 percent, and the ADR increased by approximately $19. The net result was an increase in revenue in excess of $2 million.

Witherow attributes much of the success experienced in Dallas to two factors: (1) Embassy Suites' 100 percent satisfaction guarantee, which states, "If you are not happy, we don't expect you to pay"; and (2) working with a hand-picked staff to ensure that each guest was happy 100 percent of the time.

With respect to the hotel's sales and marketing effort, the team took a two-pronged approach: they worked to build occupancy, at the same time replacing lower-paying customers with business that would help achieve the ADR goals.

To ensure that the sales and marketing teams realized the importance of their jobs, during the first year Witherow often spent 15 to 20 hours per week making calls with the team. This approach not only helped the team, but also helped Witherow to get to know his clients through relationship marketing.

At Embassy Suites, standard operating procedure requires the general manager to have his or her office in the lobby of the hotel. This not only provided Witherow with the opportunity to build relationships with his customers, but also provided his staff with direct access to the general manager. Simply put, happy employees make for happy and 100 percent satisfied guests.

Also adding to the success of the property, each month the Dallas hotel held an all-employee luncheon. During the meal, employees received awards and recognition, including a quarterly bonus based on the hotel's performance. Equally important, employees were informed of the hotel's financial performance, guest service ratings, and future goals. During this meeting, each department was informed of the role it would play in attaining these goals and what standards the department's employees would be measured against.

Witherow's assignment in Vicksburg was simple: achieve superior market penetration, raise customer service scores, and restore operating margins. Once again Lee found himself engaged in the development of a commonsense marketing plan to guide the company in a highly competitive market.

visitors to France often lead one to think of French service as poor. French food is widely admired by Americans, but is French service?

- *Two males.* What is the market target profile for Sofitel Hotels in the United States? Is it predominately middle-age white males as seemed to be depicted in the ad, or does it include women and non-Caucasians as well?

Sofitel's ad agency or ad department should conduct research using focus groups or some other methodology prior to running the ad. If so, the results should be positive.

Advertising research is often the responsibility of the ad agency, but in some cases it may be the responsibility of the property or corporate advertising or marketing. Adequate budget provisions must be made to include research of this nature.

Marketing, advertising, and sales managers need a continuous flow of reliable information. This occurs only when planned. A description of marketing research that is essential for the coming year must be part of the marketing plan.

Section IV: Segmentation and Targeting

Segmentation Analysis

The heart of any marketing plan is careful analysis of available market segments and the selection of appropriate target markets. Not all market segments are appropriate for a hospitality company. The selection of segments is the result of (1) understanding what the company is and what it wishes to be, and (2) studying available segments and determining if they fit the capabilities and desires of the company to obtain and secure them.

A common mistake within the hospitality industry is the selection of inappropriate segments. Marketing managers commonly err by allowing or encouraging the acquisition of low-yield segments in an effort to maintain occupancy. At the opposite extreme, companies sometimes feel they are serving "low-class" customers and attempt to attract quite different segments. If this is done in the absence of genuine product/service changes, the chances for success are slim to nonexistent.

In the case of a hotel, "A marketing plan tells you who is using your hotel, who might be using your hotel and where you can look to expand your business."[5] The Los Angeles Biltmore Hotel, which opened in 1923, had been the center of Los Angeles society for many years, but the property began to deteriorate in the 1960s. In 1984, the property was sold, and the new owners faced the task of restoring life to the hotel. One of the first discoveries by the new owners was that the Biltmore's marketing plan was confused. Some people believed that the hotel catered only to groups and tours, whereas others felt the hotel did not want their business and catered only to commercial and transient guests. The guest mix was found to be 28 percent commercial, 40 percent groups, and 32 percent leisure. The new management decided that a more appropriate mix was 40 percent commercial, 50 percent groups, and 10 percent leisure. With this directive in mind, the hotel was able to establish a new marketing plan that included repositioning the hotel, changing food and beverage operations, and changing prices.[6]

When developing a marketing plan, marketers must look to both internal and external data sources for information concerning market segments.

ANALYSIS OF INTERNAL DATA	ANALYSIS OF EXTERNAL DATA
Guest registrations	Published industry information
Credit card receipts	Marketing research
Customer surveys	Guesstimates after talking with competitors, vendors, and others in the industry
Business card analysis (generally placed in a box to qualify for a drawing, such as a free lunch)	

Targeting

No area of the marketing plan surpasses the selection of target markets in importance. If inappropriate markets are selected, marketing resources will be wasted. A high level of expenditures for advertising or sales promotion cannot compensate for misdirected marketing effort.

Target markets are selected from the list of available segments. These include segments currently served by the company and newly recognized markets. The selection of target markets is a primary responsibility of marketing management. This requires careful consideration of the variables already discussed in the development of the marketing plan. Far too many marketing managers in the hospitality industry simply select last year's target markets. Although it is normally true that the majority of target markets will remain the same, new ones appear and the order of importance can change between years.

Many Asian and Australian hotel managers have discovered that their key segments in terms of spending and room-nights are no longer American or European guests. Guests from Asian nations have surpassed in importance those from Western nations.

An influx of international guests caught many U.S. hotel managers by surprise. Many were unprepared for the special needs of foreign visitors, such as special cuisine and limited English language capabilities.

Choosing target markets and developing a marketing mix for those markets is an important part of any marketing plan. This ad targets meeting planners. Courtesy of Yesawich, Pepperdine and Brown, Inc.

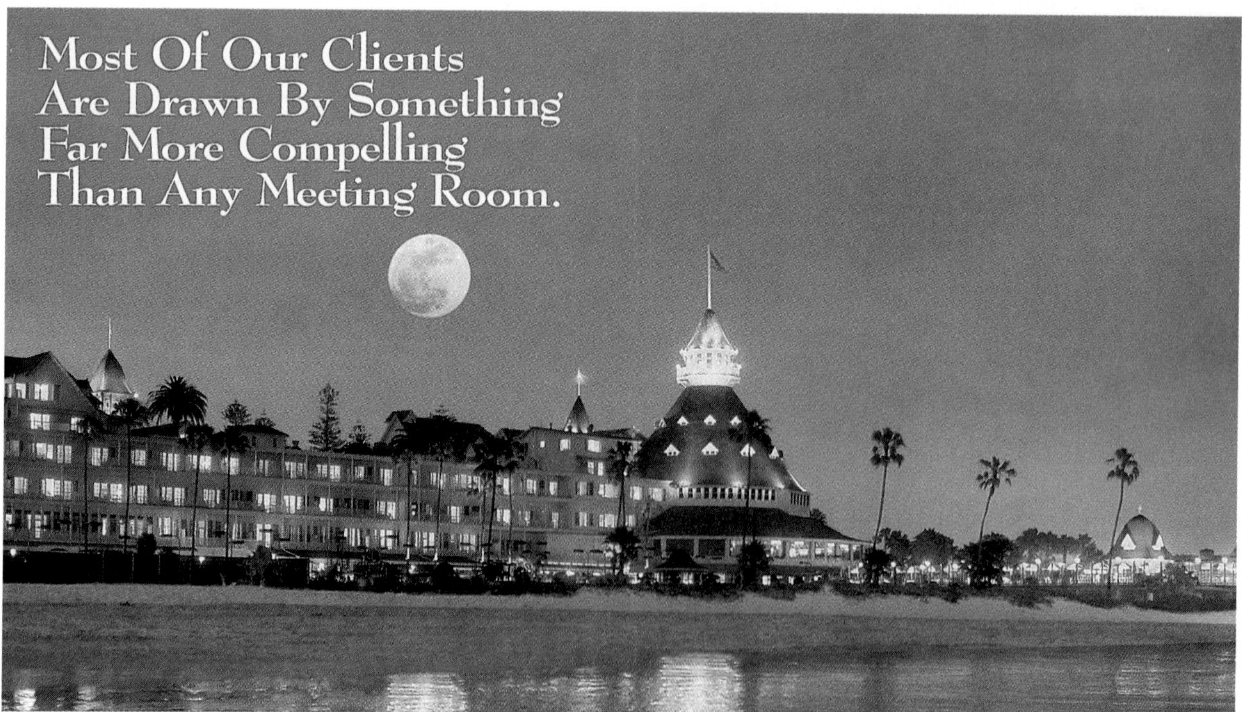

Most Of Our Clients
Are Drawn By Something
Far More Compelling
Than Any Meeting Room.

When you're planning a meeting in San Diego, an oceanfront view can be quite an attraction. Especially when combined with the world-renowned charm, service and amenities of the Hotel del Coronado. Here you'll find:
• 62,000 square feet of meeting space (much of which looks out onto the Pacific)
• A Grand Ballroom capable of accommodating 1,100 banquet-style
• Professional meeting coordinators on-site 24 hours a day
• 691 elegant guest rooms and suites
• Bayside golf, tennis, heated pools, health spa and nautical sports.
Do call us soon. We'll help you plan a meeting with more going for it than flexible floor plans.

World-Renowned
Hotel Del Coronado
A National Historic Landmark
Celebrating A Lifelong Romance With The Pacific
1500 Orange Avenue, Coronado, CA 92118
1-800-75-THE DEL • Fax: 619-522-8239

Women travelers no longer represent a fringe market for hospitality marketers. They represent a solid and growing percentage of travelers, with projections that they will constitute 50 percent of the market by the year 2002.[7]

A study of gender-based lodging preferences showed that "there were several significant differences between male and female business travelers in their hotel selection and use criteria."[8] For instance, women considered security, room service, and low price to be more important, whereas men were more concerned about the availability of a fax machine and suite rooms with separate bed and office spaces.

Marketing planners need to stay abreast of such preferences, relay them to other departments within the hotel, and utilize this information in the selection of market segments.

Section V: Next Year's Objectives and Quotas

Objectives

The establishment of objectives provides direction for the rest of the marketing plan. The purpose of marketing strategies and tactics is to support objectives. The marketing budget must be sufficient to ensure adequate resources to achieve objectives and to meet timetables that describe the time period in which expected sales results will occur.

Occasionally, there is confusion as to what constitutes an objective. Statements such as "To be the best in our industry" or "To provide excellent guest service" are accepted as objectives. This is always an error because these types of statements are slogans or mottos. They are not objectives! Objectives are:

- Quantitative (expressed in monetary terms [dollars, pesos] or unit measurements such as room-nights, passenger-miles, number of cars to rent, or occupancy)
- Time specific (one year, six months)
- Profit/margin specific (such as an average margin of 22%)

The process of establishing objectives is not an easy task and should not be accomplished by simply adding a random percentage to last year's objectives.

Objectives should be established after carefully considering the areas already discussed.

- Corporate goals
- Corporate resources
- Environmental factors
- Competition
- Market trends
- Market potential
- Available market segments and possible target markets

To ensure profitability and remain competitive in today's marketplace, it has become necessary to establish several subobjectives. For instance, a 1,000-room hotel will undoubtedly have two broad objectives: average occupancy and average room rate. By themselves, these

Table 19-1
Examples of Objectives Common to the Hotel Industry

OBJECTIVES:	AVERAGE OCCUPANCY	AVERAGE ROOM RATE
Subobjectives:	Occupancy per period of time Seasonal: prime, shoulder, trough Monthly Weekly Daily Weekend Midweek	Average rate per period of time and by type of room
	TYPES OF SLEEPING ROOMS	BY TIME
	Suites Pool side Regular room	Seasonal Monthly Weekly Daily Weekend
	Occupancy by type of sleeping room: Suites Pool side Cabaña Cottage Regular sleeping rooms Occupancy per type of function room: Ballroom Seminar room Executive conference room	*Note:* Yield objectives are used by many members of the hospitality industry, such as hotels, rental cars, cruise lines, airlines, and passenger rail.

OBJECTIVES:	ANNUAL SALES BY:	ANNUAL SALES BY: UNITS	DOLLARS
	Time period		
	Seasonal		
	Monthly		
	Weekly		
	Daily		
	Weekend		
	Department		
	Group sales		
	Incentive sales		
	Sales territory		
	Eastern U.S.		
	Western U.S.		
	Salesperson		
	Joe		
	Sally		
	June		
	Fred		

objectives do not serve as sufficient guides for developing marketing strategies. A set of subobjectives is needed, as shown in Table 19-1.

Other subobjectives may also be established by the marketing department. Again, these should support corporate goals and next year's primary objectives. They should never stand alone as objectives, unrelated to the primary function of the marketing department.

Each marketing support area needs to be guided by a set of subobjectives. This includes areas such as advertising, promotion, public relations, marketing research, and, of course, sales.

Establishing measurable quantitative objectives for these areas is not an easy task, but, increasingly, top management is requiring that such be done. Advertising and promotion are areas in which measurement of results is particularly difficult. Management would like to know what the dollar return was for advertising or how much market share or occupancy increased as a result of advertising/promotion. With few exceptions, such as direct advertising, current measurement techniques do not permit accurate measurements of this type. Consequently, measurable objectives for advertising such as share of mind and awareness level, are commonly used.

Quotas

No word creates more fear within the sales/marketing department than quotas. Yet, without quotas, the probability of accomplishing objectives is slim at best. To be effective, quotas must be:

- Based on next year's objectives.
- Individualized.
- Realistic and obtainable.
- Broken down to small units, such as each salesperson's quota per week.
- Understandable and measurable: for example, quota = $10,000 sales for product line x in week 5. An example of a quota that is not understandable or measurable is "to obtain 10% increase of market share early in the year."

Communicating the Plan

A sophisticated and brilliantly developed plan is of no use if it is not understood, believed, or used. "A marketing plan should not be just a call to action or a benchmark by which to judge the efficiency and effectiveness of decisions. The plan should also serve as a method for communicating marketing strategy to those people whose duty it is to implement or authorize the company's marketing strategies."[9] Several groups may serve as an audience for a marketing plan.

Top Management

This group must be convinced that the plan will accomplish the stated goals and objectives. Top management demonstrates acceptance or denial by their level of monetary support.

Marketing managers should strive for more than budgeting support. If top management "buys in" and demonstrates visible support, morale within the marketing department will increase, and other departments will be willing to lend support. To the contrary, the company grapevine quickly knows if marketing is only weakly supported by top management. Support from others will be weak at best if there is a perception that management is not solidly behind marketing.

Board of Directors or Group of Investors

Occasionally, a board of directors or an investor's group may ask to be apprised of next year's marketing plan. This group generally does not seek details but instead wants to know:

- Does the plan support corporate goals?
- What are the dollars and unit objectives?
- What are the major strategies to achieve these objectives?
- What is the cost?
- When can we expect to see results?

Subordinates

Members of the marketing and sales departments must understand and support the marketing plan. It is important to develop a group mentality that the marketing plan for next year is a realistic and important road map. Unfortunately, far too many people in hospitality companies believe that the development of a marketing plan is a waste of time because no one will ever pay it any heed.

Vendors

It is important to transmit some aspects of the marketing plan to selected vendors. This is particularly true as strategic alliances develop. Vendors such as advertising agencies, marketing research firms, computer software providers, public relations firms, consultants, and others need to know and understand the marketing plan. It may be advisable to include these people in the plan's development.

Other Departments

Other departments, such as housekeeping, front desk, customer service, and maintenance, will be affected by next year's plan. They have a right to know key elements of the plan.

It is common for marketing managers to be asked to briefly outline the marketing plan and answer questions in a monthly manager's meeting. If a forum such as this does not exist, marketing managers should initiate a review of next year's marketing plan with other department heads after obtaining clearance from the general manager or president.

Section VI: Action Plans: Strategies and Tactics

Marketing strategies are designed as the vehicle to achieve marketing objectives. In turn, marketing tactics are tools that support strategies. Far too often, strategies and tactics have little relationship to objectives. This is always an error and is commonly the result of the following:

- Desire to maintain status quo. Strategies and tactics do not change because they are perceived to be working even though solid proof of their effectiveness seldom exists.
- Lazy, incompetent, or unsure management. These people do not wish to risk their positions through new strategies and tactics.
- Failure to engage in marketing planning or to view the processes as being serious and meaningful to decision making.
- Undue heavy influence of outside vendors, such as advertising agencies, which do not wish to change direction or try new media.
- Failure to understand the relationship between objectives, strategies, and tactics.
- Myopic thinking that things are going well and one does not fix something that is not broken. Unfortunately, in the fast-paced, competitive hospitality industry, by the time the product is demonstrably broken, it is beyond repair.

Marketing strategies and tactics employ advertising and promotion, sales and distribution, pricing and product. Each must be custom designed to meet the specific needs of a company. It is unwise to follow ratios or industry averages concerning expenditures for advertising, new product development, or other strategy areas. Many managers have made the mistake of believing that if they expend at the same ratio as other firms in the industry, they are following a responsible direction. Nothing could be further from the truth.

Strategies and tactics must always be custom made to fit the needs and culture of a company and to allow it to meet or exceed objectives. A study was conducted of marketing strategies and tactics employed by restaurants. It was found that many restaurants employ weak strategies, including following the leader, rather than developing individualized, unique strategies and tactics. The authors concluded, "Firms that seem to exhibit no strategy cannot expect to enjoy long-run successful performance. They may enjoy excellent returns for a number of years, but at some point their lack of strategy will cause the business to fail. When they begin to experience the consequences of this lack of strategic direction, it may well be too late to mount an effective alternative, especially if they operate a larger number of units."[10]

Sales Strategies

The sales force must develop and use sales strategies to support objectives. Examples of sales strategies follow:

1. Prevent erosion of key accounts.
2. Grow key accounts.
3. Grow selected marginal accounts.
4. Eliminate selected marginal accounts.
5. Retain selected marginal accounts but provide lower-cost sales support.
6. Obtain new business from selected prospects.

A description of sales strategies should start with these six general strategies and indicate how the sales department is going to implement each one. The general strategy is supported by specific sales tactics, such as the following:

Outside the Company

- Sales blitz of all or targeted accounts and projects
- Telephone, direct mail, and personal sales calls to selected decision makers and decision influencers
- Trade booths at selected travel shows
- Sales calls and working with travel intermediaries: tour wholesalers, travel agencies, incentive houses, international sales reps, others
- Luncheon for key customers, prospects, or decision influencers
- Travel missions and other tactics

Inside the Company

- Training of sales staff
- Involvement and support of nonsales personnel
- Motivational and control programs
- Involvement and support of management

The selection of appropriate channels of distribution is basic to the development of successful sales strategies. Hospitality companies must be ever alert to changing distribution channels and the need for change.

19.2 Vashon Island Bed & Breakfast Association

Traditionally, the bed and breakfast (B&B) lodging sector has depended on a direct sales and reservation system between the guest and the B&B operator. Glenn and Sally Priest of Vashon Island, off the coast of Seattle, have demonstrated that a new distribution system is possible for B&Bs. Glenn is president of the Vashon Island Bed & Breakfast Association and also owner of the Sweetbriar B&B. Having previously served as sales manager for a computer software and services company, Glenn put his knowledge to work by developing an 800-number reservations service for the association and an electronic guest database.[11] Telecommuting has arrived in an industry sector previously viewed as somewhat old-fashioned.

Advertising and Promotion Strategies

Advertising and promotion strategies should be established by people within the company responsible for these strategies, such as the director of advertising, the sales manager, or the marketing manager. It is critical for this person to work with supporting groups such as an advertising agency, sales promotion firm, specialty advertising agencies, and consultants directly involved in the establishment and performance of advertising and promotion strategies.

It is inadvisable to give outside firms sole authority for deriving and implementing these strategies. History has shown that when this occurs the supporting group, such as an advertising agency, may produce brilliant copy and illustrations placed in well-respected media, only to find that the company fails totally to meet objectives. The reason is that outside groups may not view objectives the same way as the client. Many advertising agencies have won distinguished honors for ads that did little or nothing to increase sales or market share for the client. Outside professionals correctly view their client as the company or the company's management, not the end consumer. Unfortunately, this view leads to pleasing the managers who hired them rather than achieving corporate or marketing objectives. Theoretically, corporate and marketing objectives and those of the manager should be synchronized. In fact, there is often a wide gap between the two. In some cases, outside professionals disdain client corporate or marketing objectives and view these as a detriment or obstacle to the creative process. The ideal is for corporate managers responsible for advertising/promotion to work as a team with selected outside professionals to derive strategies and tactics that satisfy objectives in a timely and cost-effective manner.

When this is accomplished, the team will develop an advertising/promotion mix of vehicles that includes tactics selected to achieve objectives, not simply to provide commissions, make life easy for the

The Broadmoor's marketing plan included advertising to communicate the renovations and additions to the resort. Courtesy of Yesawich, Pepperdine and Brown, Inc.

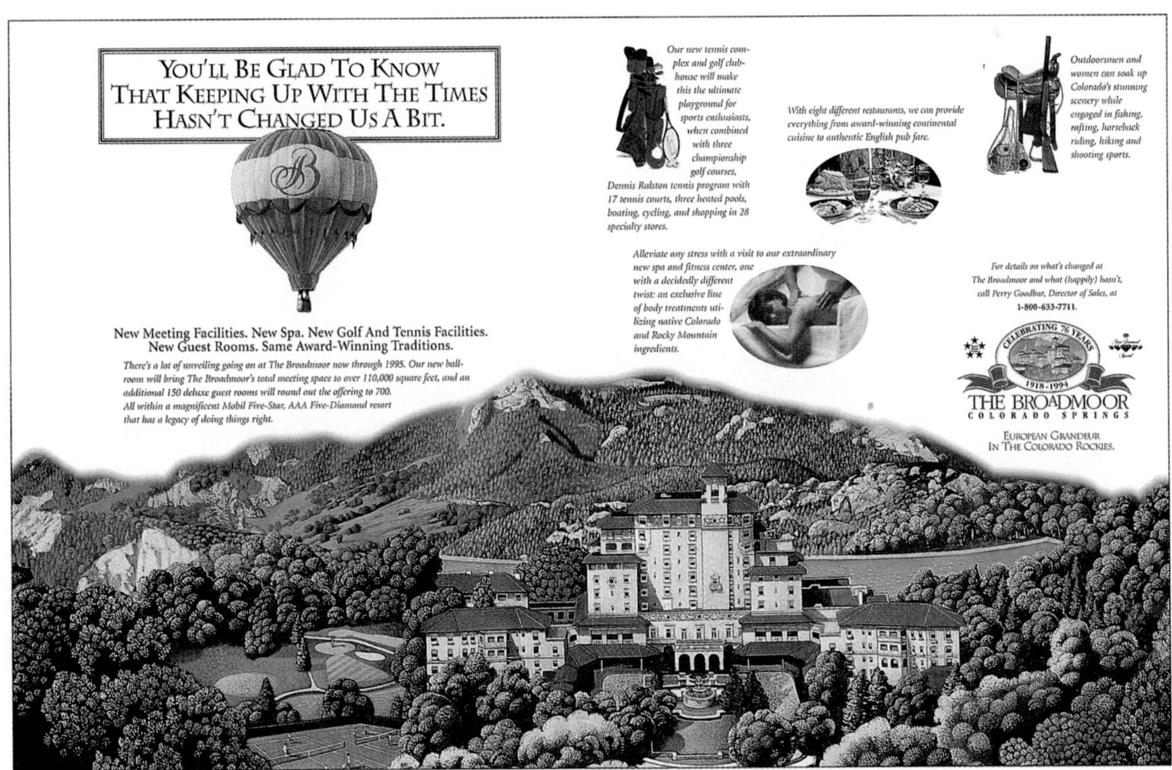

professionals, or produce a bland program that probably won't be criticized by management, but may accomplish little.

Those responsible for advertising/promotion strategies have the following responsibilities:

- Select a blend or mix of media that may include commissionable mass media, direct mail, trade shows, billboards, specialty advertising, and much more.
- Select or approve the message. This includes graphics, color, size, copy, and other format decisions.
- Design a media schedule showing when each medium, including noncommissionable media, will be employed.
- Design a schedule of events, such as public relations events.
- Carefully transmit this information to management.
- Supervise the development and implementation of advertising/promotion programs, with particular care given to timetables and budget constraints.
- Assume responsibility for the outcome. Increasingly, top management is requiring those in charge of advertising/promotion to prove effectiveness and to stand behind results.

Unfortunately, despite decades of marketing teaching and thousands of articles on the subject, many managers in the hospitality industry continue to equate marketing with advertising. They fail to realize that advertising is simply one part of marketing. The authors of the restaurant strategy study referred to earlier concluded: "Many firms [restaurants] have attempted to hold market share by increasing advertising expenditures. Advertising alone will not ensure success."[12]

Another area of the advertising/promotion mix that needs consideration in a marketing plan is cooperative advertising/promotion. This requires teamwork and a place in the budget. For example, in the case of a resort, cooperative opportunities exist between:

- Resort and resort community (e.g., all resorts, restaurants, and attractions at Myrtle Beach)
- Resort and tourism promotion groups (e.g., State Tourism Department or local chamber of commerce)
- Resort and suppliers (e.g., Citrus Board or Columbia Coffee)
- Resort and transportation companies (e.g., airlines, motor coach, cruise lines)
- Resort and sister hotels or resorts

19.3 Club Med

An example of cooperative advertising/promotion opportunities is offered by hotels in Mexico. After an examination of the brochures of ten hotel chains in Mexico, it was found that most made minimal or no reference to other Mexican hotels operated by the chain. Club Med made good use of this marketing tool. Club Med not only had a Mexican brochure for all their properties, but also even had a special supplemental brochure for Club Med properties near prestigious archaeological sites.[13]

Pricing Strategy

Many hospitality plans devote little attention to pricing. Such plans commonly list rack rates and indicate that there will be differences in shoulder and trough seasons, but say little else about pricing. This is an error and one of the primary reasons that many hospitality companies have removed pricing responsibility from marketing and assigned it to other departments, such as revenue management or yield management.

Pricing remains a function of marketing. If marketing managers do not maintain control of this area, they must interface with internal pricing departments. Marketing and sales departments will continuously be in conflict with pricing if pricing strategies are not understood and considered in marketing and sales plans.

For instance, sales has responsibility for working with intermediaries such as tour wholesalers and key customers. Both these customers will ask for price discounts. Commitments for large blocks of rooms, airlines seats, autos, or ship berths will inevitably create problems with revenue or yield management departments. Marketing and sales plans cannot be effective if they are developed without sales forecasts and revenue projections by major market segments. If forecasts and revenue projections are made without the input of the revenue or yield management departments, conflict will occur.

Review again the objectives and subobjectives presented in Table 19-1. These call for average room rate objectives for each product class by season of the year. Using the concepts and practices of yield management, pricing objectives may be considerably enhanced to include weekly objectives and objectives by subsegments. Marriott Hotels uses a strategy known as rational pricing. This calls for *fencing,* placing restrictions on customer segments selected due to their perceived level of price elasticity. Fencing restrictions will immediately affect marketing and sales plans. Marketing managers are also advised to work with the reservations department during the planning process. Reservations often have considerable latitude to adjust prices and may account for a significant percentage of sales.

Pricing objectives and strategies affect every facet of marketing and sales. Sales promotions and advertising must support pricing decisions. The selection of appropriate target markets and the emphasis to be given each again depends on pricing.

Marketing and sales managers who view themselves at war with pricing managers are probably doomed to eventual failure. Top management in many hospitality companies has begun to realize that a 10 percent upward adjustment in rates can produce favorable profit results in excess of cost cutting or traditional marketing and sales strategies to increase the number of guests.

Pricing strategies are of great importance to chain restaurants and need to be reviewed constantly. As an example, food service quality is the predominant influence on guest ratings for family, steak house, and casual dining restaurants. Family price appeal enhances a guest's rating for a family restaurant chain, but not necessarily for a steak house or casual dining.[14]

A marketer who has gained experience in a family restaurant chain might make erroneous pricing decisions when hired by a steak house or casual dining chain. Despite the fact that restaurant chains may seem alike, different pricing strategies may need to be developed for each.

Product Strategies

Marketing has an important role to play in the improvement of existing products and the development of new ones. In some hospitality firms, marketing is expected to be heavily involved in the process; in others, marketing assumes only an advisory role; and sadly, in others, marketing is excluded from the process.

Hospitality products are changing rapidly. Las Vegas has been transformed from an adults-only playground to a destination resort for families, in competition with Disney. Observers of the resort industry have concluded that "the traditional resort may no longer exist, or it may be just the core of a far more varied travel experience."[15]

19.4 Alexis Park Resort
Opryland Hotel

Marketing professionals can exert considerable input and strategic direction when planning basic product changes as dramatic as those occurring within the resort industry. Marketing can also help greatly to enhance revenue from product changes as additions to the current product line. Hundreds or thousands of new product opportunities exist in most hospitality companies. The Alexis Park Resort in Las Vegas invented "Cocktail Cruises," which is essentially a motorized cart driven by an employee who offers poolside guests drinks without moving.[16] The Opryland Hotel in Nashville uses a similar concept to sell hotel logo souvenir merchandise. "Whenever there is more to be sold than your customers are buying, profit potential is not being realized. Revenue boosting opportunities abound for the creative operator who is willing to offer facilities, services, and events that will attract customers and to train customer-contact employees to stimulate add-on sales and sales upgrades."[17]

The process of making product line changes requires the input and advice of many individuals and departments. Marketing may identify a need, such as the "neighborhood bakery" concept, for use in fast-food chains, but this new product concept directly affects production, finance, and human resources. When McDonald's, Burger King, and Wendy's experimented with fresh biscuits or croissants, they discovered that these products prepared from scratch or frozen dough required additional working space, equipment, and employee training.[18]

Section VII: Resources Needed to Support Strategies and Meet Objectives

Marketing plans must be written with available resources, or those likely to become available, in mind. A common error in writing a marketing plan is to develop strategies that are probably highly workable but for which there is insufficient support. Another error is to assume that top management will not provide additional support regardless of the brilliance of the plan. Marketing plans can and must be sold to top management. A balance between mythical "pie-in-the-sky" plans and total acquiescence to perceived inflexibility of management is needed in any solid marketing plan.

Personnel

Generally, the most costly and difficult resource needed to ensure success with marketing/sales strategies is personnel. Management commonly views the addition of personnel as unnecessary, impractical, or unwise given current budgetary restrictions.

Obviously, there are times when the addition of salespeople, secretaries, analysts, and others is absolutely essential. Be prepared to justify this request, and remember that many people, particularly salespeople, are not instantly productive. Training and recruiting costs must be considered with this resource request, as well as the time required by members of management to interview and work with these people.

The influence of the corporate culture cannot be overlooked in this process. Imagine a company such as the Ritz-Carlton with the philosophy "We are ladies and gentlemen serving ladies and gentlemen." Fulfillment of this pledge with appropriate new personnel is demanding and may be time consuming.[19]

Ski resorts in Colorado initiated a drug-testing program for all new hires, including seasonal personnel. This policy generated extra time and expense because many potential employees failed this test and could not be considered for employment.

A marketing plan may need to specify the type of person required for a position if this is not described elsewhere, such as in company policies and procedures. Some hospitality companies operate under the philosophy that "we are always hiring excellent people." Marketing managers must plan personnel needs ahead for seasonal cost differences, such as a month with heavy trade show expenses or several weeks when brochures will be mailed to key customers and prospects. Budgets should reflect careful planning of resource use, such as temporary help on a week-by-week basis. A carefully constructed budget is simply a reflection of a well-thought-out marketing plan.

Equipment and Space

The acquisition of equipment such as PCs, fax machines, car phones, and audiovisual equipment may be viewed as necessary or helpful to achieve marketing objectives. Space may also be a problem, particularly if new personnel are hired. Requests for additional space, such as a regional office or a storage area, are sometimes incorporated into the marketing plan.

Other Monetary Support

Monetary support not accounted for by salary, wages, and benefits must be considered carefully and included. This includes travel expenses, motivational costs, such as a trip to Las Vegas, and other monetary needs.

Research, Consulting, and Training

Hospitality companies often have need for outside professionals to assist with marketing research, such as focus groups; training, such as sales training; or consulting to provide objective outside appraisals and advice.

Miscellaneous Costs

This area should not be a source of slush funds. Many expenses, such as subscriptions to professional books and journals, may be included here.

Budgets

In larger organizations, corporate policies and procedures may direct marketing managers as to categories of expenses and items that may be included. Marketing managers of smaller companies may need to develop their own list and to use it each year as a guide to ensure that all essential resources are included.

Budgets should be established to reflect projected costs on a weekly, monthly, quarterly, and annual basis. This is not simply to make life easier for the finance/accounting area personnel next year.

Section VIII: Marketing Control

This discussion of marketing control presupposes that the sales plan is part of the marketing plan. This is not always the case; some hospitality organizations separate the two functions.

The essentials for writing a sales plan follow the same general procedure as those described for a marketing plan. A sales plan will not have need for all aspects of a marketing plan such as advertising or marketing research as these may be furnished by support departments. A sales plan will pay particular attention to the sales force and its objectives and to strategies to ensure that sales quotas are met and possibly exceeded.

Sales Objectives

Sales objectives must be established for each sales area, division, region, salesperson, and time period. The broad sales objectives discussed previously serve as the basis for establishing individual objectives. The sum of all sales objectives or quotas for members of the sales force must equal or exceed annual objectives.

One method of establishing annual sales objectives for the company is to begin with sales planning among members of the sales force. Each member should be expected to develop a list of all sales accounts currently served by that person, plus prospects for the coming year. From this, an estimate of potential sales by account and prospect will provide a means of forecasting next year's sales.

Management, beginning with the sales manager and ending with the general manager or other member of top management, then has the responsibility for critically examining these forecasts. Management seldom accepts the forecasts of the sales force without amending them, usually upward. This is known as bottom-up, top-down planning.

Management will amend sales force forecasts for the following reasons:

1. Sales force members often wish to protect themselves and give lower sales estimates than are actually possible.
2. The company has certain sales objectives that it expects based on the needs of the company.

3. Management may have access to marketing research information not available to the sales force.
4. Management may have a history of dealing with the sales force and realizes that forecasts are generally too high or too low by x percent.
5. Management may be willing to provide the marketing/sales department with additional resources that are unknown to members of the sales force.

A typical hotel sales forecast for a salesperson is shown in Table 19-2. Sales managers have the responsibility to work closely with their salespeople to ensure that sales forecasts are accurate. They must then provide a composite sales forecast for their department and present it to management.

Sales Forecast and Quotas

Eventually, all members of the sales force must be presented with sales quotas. Annual sales quotas should then be broken down into monthly and quarterly sales. Many sales managers and experienced salespeople break monthly quotas into weekly figures.

Sales managers have the responsibility for working with their salespeople to ensure that quotas are met or surpassed. It is important to evaluate sales results continually and develop corrective tactics if it appears that actual sales will not meet forecasts or quotas. Sales managers and salespeople who wait several months before evaluating actual sales against forecasts usually find it is too late to take corrective action.

Expenditures against Budget

It is also important for marketing/sales managers to monitor actual expenditures continually against budgeted figures. This, too, must be done on a regular basis.

Periodic Evaluation of All Marketing Objectives

The role of marketing and sales managers is sometimes compared to that of an adult baby-sitter. A frequent comment made by people in these positions is that they spend a great deal of time simply making sure that people under their direction perform tasks in a timely fashion. There is much truth in this comment because a critical role of marketing/sales managers is to ensure that all objectives are met or exceeded on time.

Managers responsible for functions such as advertising, promotions, and marketing research have a responsibility to ensure that all tasks are performed on time. If a summer rates brochure is printed three weeks after the due date, chances are very good that the sales force may miss the opportunity to send or deliver this advertising medium to prospects and key accounts during the time that they make travel decisions. In turn, the sales force may fail to make summer sales quotas. All marketing/sales tasks are important. If this is not true, the task and the position should be eliminated.

Table 19-2
Example of a Sales Forecast for a Hotel Salesperson

	SALES CURRENT YEAR			SALES PROJECTED NEXT YEAR		
SALESPERSON: JANET CHIN	ROOM NIGHTS	REVENUE	AVG. RATE	ROOM NIGHTS	REVENUE	AVG. RATE
Major commercial accounts (key accounts)						
1.						
2.						
3.						
4.						
Other commercial accounts						
1.						
2.						
3.						
4.						
Major intermediary accounts						
1.						
2.						
3.						
4.						
Other intermediary accounts						
1.						
2.						
3.						
4.						
Airline accounts						
1.						
2.						
3.						
4.						
Other accounts						
1.						
2.						
3.						
4.						
Prospects for next year						
1.						
2.						
3.						
4.						
Total accounts/prospects	Total current year			Totals projected next year		

Marketing Activity Timetable

One method commonly used by marketing/sales managers to ensure that tasks are completed on time is the use of a marketing activity timetable. This simple device lists major activities, the dates they must be completed, the person responsible, and a space for checking whether the task has been accomplished.

Readjustments to Marketing Plan

Human beings are incapable of devising a perfect marketing plan. Market conditions change, disasters occur, and many other reasons create a need to refine marketing plans. Generally, refinements should be made in the area of tactics, budgets, and timing of events rather than in major objectives or strategies. Changes in tactics normally do not require top management approval and are viewed as the normal responsibility of marketing/sales managers.

Section IX: Presenting and Selling the Plan

Changes in major objectives such as annual sales volume and in major strategies always require approval by top management. Marketing/sales managers are advised to refrain from considering changes in major objectives and strategies. Top management will almost certainly view the necessity for change as a reflection of poor management by marketing/sales managers unless the cause was a disaster, such as a major fire in a hotel.

Never assume that a marketing plan is so logical that it will sell itself. A marketing plan must be sold to many people. These include the following:

- *Members of marketing/sales department.* Many people within the marketing/sales areas do not believe in planning. They view the process of developing, writing, defending, and using a written plan to be a waste of time. Comments are frequently heard, such as "If management would just let us do our job and quit all this planning, the company would do better." This common sentiment may exist due to poor experience with prior planning, fear of the process, or genuine ignorance about the benefits. Marketing/sales managers need the support of subordinates in the planning process. It is best to sell the benefits of the process rather than to force acquiescence.
- *Vendors/ad agencies and others.* Outside organizations, such as advertising and marketing research agencies, need to be involved in the planning process. They must be made aware that their participation in the marketing planning process is an expected part of their responsibilities as team members.
- *Top management.* Top management must approve the annual marketing plan. It is seldom sufficient to write a lengthy plan, send it through company mail to top management, and expect an enthusiastic endorsement. Marketing/sales managers must sell the plan to members of management through meetings, such as a friendly luncheon and formalized presentations. Key members of the staff may be expected to participate in formal presentations. These appearances should always be treated with the same

careful planning and professionalism that would be expected if a sales presentation were made to a key prospect for $2 million worth of business. Use professional presentation materials when appropriate, such as 35mm slides, computerized presentations, overheads, and bound copies of the annual plan. Prepare selected charts, graphs, and tables that are easy to understand and quickly reinforce key points.

Section X: Preparing for the Future

The process of marketing planning is a continuum. The task is never ending. Marketing/sales managers must always be planning. In reality, the development of next year's marketing plan begins the day this year's plan is approved.

Data Collection and Analysis

Marketing plan development depends on the availability of reliable information. This task can always be improved. The process of data collection and analysis from internal and external sources continues each day. Marketing/sales managers must always be alert for methods to improve the process.

Marketing Planning as a Tool for Growth

A good marketing plan will assist your company and department to prosper and grow. What is not so obvious to many is that a good plan will also enable people to prosper and grow. This occurs in several ways:

- The participatory planning process allows people to understand the management process.
- People learn to become team players during the process.
- People learn to establish objectives and set timetables to ensure that they are met.
- The process of establishing realistic strategies and tactics to meet objectives is learned.
- People who approach the planning process with a receptive mind and employ the marketing plan will usually find it enhances their professional career.

19.5 Omni International Hotels

Many hospitality companies, such as Omni International Hotels, have developed a planning culture in which there is a respect for marketing planning as a positive process. This is a reflection of a corporate culture and top management support. Changes in top management sometimes mean that support for marketing planning will decrease or in some instances planning will be discouraged. A strong corporate culture that emphasizes and encourages planning within all levels of the company will be rewarded. Sometimes management becomes discouraged by the process, particularly when market conditions worsen as a new competitor threatens market share. It is at times like this that a corporate culture of planning provides stability and assurance of purpose and direction.

An example of the need for planning in poor economic times, rather than resorting to reactive "just-do-something" tactics, is offered by the

California Country Club (CCC) of Los Angeles. This club, like many others in southern California, had a waiting list of potential members until 1993. By March of that year, the waiting list had changed to one of people wanting to leave the club.

Instead of panicking and grasping for an immediate marketing cure-all, the management of CCC pursued a process of market planning, starting with an analysis of the market and competitors. The planning process allowed CCC to recognize marketing opportunities, such as pricing strategies, including the elimination of golf-only fees. The need for a customer-directed policy of "just say yes" was also discovered and implemented. These and other changes represented a complete turnover from previous policies and procedures, thus allowing the club to increase market share and revenue.[20]

A study of the process used by hotels to develop marketing plans has shown that "the most important features in the development of a marketing plan appear to be management participation and commitment at all levels, sufficient time for development, specific training in developing a marketing plan, and tying incentives to the achievement of goals and objectives."[21]

In good times or bad, consistency in marketing planning pays good dividends for any hospitality company and its employees.[22]

KEY TERMS

Competitive analysis An analysis of the primary strengths and weaknesses, objectives, strategies, and other information relative to competitors

Environmental factors Social, political, and economic factors that affect a firm and its marketing program.

Executive summary A short summary of the marketing plan to quickly inform top executives.

Market potential The total estimated dollars or unit value of a defined market for a defined product, including competitive products.

Market trends External trends of many types that are likely to affect the marketing in which a corporation operates.

Marketing objectives Quantitative and time specific accomplishment measurements as to what is expected of a marketing program.

Quotas Quantitative and time-specific accomplishment measurements established for members of a sales force.

Segmentation analysis The process of examining various submarkets and selecting those most appropriate for a company.

Timetable Specific dates to accomplish strategies and tactics.

Chapter Review

I. Purpose of a Marketing Plan

1) Serves as a road map for all marketing activities of the firm for the next year.

2) Ensures that marketing activities are in agreement with the corporate strategic plan.

3) Forces marketing managers to review and think through objectively all steps in the marketing process.

4) Assists in the budgeting process to match resources with marketing objectives.

II. Tips for Writing the Executive Summary

1) Write it for top executives.

2) Limit the number of pages to between two and four.

3) Use short sentences and short paragraphs.

4) Organize the summary as follows: describe next year's objectives in quantitative terms; briefly describe marketing strategies to meet goals and objectives; identify the dollar costs necessary as well as key resources needed.

5) Read and reread before final submit.

III. Corporate Connection

1) Relationships to other plans

- **a)** Corporate goals: profit, growth, and others
- **b)** Desired market share
- **c)** Positioning of the enterprise or of product lines
- **d)** Vertical or horizontal integration
- **e)** Strategic alliances
- **f)** Product-line breadth and depth

2) Marketing-related plans also include:

- **a)** Sales
- **b)** Advertising and promotion
- **c)** Marketing research
- **d)** Pricing
- **e)** Customer service

3) Corporate direction

- **a)** Mission statement
- **b)** Corporate philosophy
- **c)** Corporate goals

IV. Environmental Analysis

1) Analysis of major environmental factors

2) Competitive analysis

- **a)** List the major existing competitors confronting your firm next year.
- **b)** List new competitors.
- **c)** Describe the major competitive strengths and weaknesses of each competitor.

3) Marketing trends. Monitor visitor trends, competitive trends, related industry trends.

4) **Market potential**

a) Market potential should be viewed as the total available demand for a firm's product within a particular geographic market at a given price. It is important not to mix different products into an estimate of market potential.

b) Provide an estimate or guesstimate of market potential for each major product line in monetary terms such as dollars and in units such as room-nights or passengers.

5) **Marketing research**

a) Macromarket information: industry trends, social-economic-political trends, competitive information, industrywide customer data.

b) Micromarket information: guest information, product/service information, new product analysis and testing, intermediary buyer data, pricing studies, key account information, and advertising/promotion effectiveness.

6) **Desired action**

a) List and describe the types of macromarketing and micromarketing information needed on a continuing basis.

b) List and describe types of marketing research needed on a one-time basis next year.

V. Segmentation and Targeting. The selection of segments is the result of:

1) Understanding who the company is and what it wishes to be.

2) Studying available segments and determining if they fit the capabilities and desires of the company to obtain and secure them.

VI. Action: Segmentation and Targeting

1) List and describe each market segment available for next year in as much demographic and psychographic detail as is available and practical for use in developing marketing strategies and tactics.

2) Rank these segments in order of descending importance as target markets.

3) Continue this process for different product lines that require individualized marketing support such as conference and ballroom facilities.

VII. Next Year's Objectives and Quotas

1) **Objectives**

a) Quantitative objectives: expressed in monetary terms, expressed in unit measurements, time specific and profit/margin specific.

b) Other objectives: corporate goals, corporate resources, environmental factors, competitions, market trends, market potential, and available market segments and possible target markets.

c) Actions

i) List primary marketing/sales objectives for next year.

ii) List subobjective for next year.

iii) Break down objective by quarter, month, and week.

iv) List other specific subobjectives by marketing support area, such as advertising/promotion objectives.

2) **Quotas**

a) Based on next year's objectives

b) Individualized

c) Realistic and obtainable
d) Broken down to small units, such as each salesperson's quota per week
e) Understandable/measurable

3) Action quotas. Break down and list quotas for sales departments, sales territories, all sales intermediaries, each sales intermediary, and each salesperson.

VIII. Action Plans: Strategies and Tactics

1) Sales strategies

a) Prevent erosion of key accounts.
b) Grow key accounts.
c) Grow selected marginal accounts.
d) Eliminate selected marginal accounts.
e) Retain selected marginal accounts, but provide lower-cost sales support.
f) Obtain new business from selected prospects.

2) Actions: sales

a) List the six major sales strategies and indicate how these will be accomplished in the coming year.
b) List and describe all tactics that support major sales strategies.

3) Advertising/promotion strategies

a) Select a blend or mix of media.
b) Select or approve the message.
c) Design a media schedule showing when each medium, including noncommissionable media, will be employed.
d) Design a schedule of events.
e) Carefully transmit this information to management.
f) Supervise the development and implementation of advertising/promotion programs, with particular care given to timetables and budget constraints.
g) Assure responsibility for the outcome.

4) Action: advertising/promotion

a) Develop advertising/promotion strategies to meet marketing/sales objectives.
b) Develop an advertising/promotion mix of appropriate media.
c) Develop messages appropriate for the selected media to reach designed objectives.
d) Develop a media and event schedule.

5) Pricing strategy

a) Carefully review pricing objective with departments responsible for pricing, planning, and implementation.
b) Refine pricing objectives to reflect sales and revenue forecasts.
c) Describe pricing strategies to be used throughout the year.
d) Make certain that price, sales, and promotion/advertising objectives are synchronized and working in support of corporate objectives.

6) Product strategies

a) Describe the involvement of the marketing department in major strategic product development.

b) Describe the role of marketing in new-product acquisition or product development.
c) Describe ongoing or planned product development programs for which marketing has responsibility.

IX. Resources Needed to Support Strategies and Meet Objectives

1) Study and then list the need for new marketing/sales personnel, including temporary help during the next year.
2) Study and list the type and amount of equipment and space that will be needed to support marketing/sales.
3) Study and list the amount of monetary support needed next year.
4) Study and list the amount and type of other costs necessary next year.
5) Study and list the amount of outside research, consulting, and training assistance needed.
6) Prepare a marketing budget for approval by top management.

X. Marketing Control

1) Sales force members often wish to protect themselves and give lower sales estimates than are actually possible.
2) The company has certain sales objectives it expects based on the needs of the company.
3) Management may have access to marketing research information not viewed by the sales force.
4) Management may have a history of dealing with the sales force and realizes that forecasts are generally too high or too low by x percent.
5) Management may be willing to provide the marketing/sales department with additional resources.

XI. Presenting and Selling the Plan

1) Members of marketing/sales departments
2) Vendor/ad agencies and others
3) Top management

XII. Preparing for the Future

1) The participatory planning process allows people to understand the management process.
2) People learn to become team players during the process.
3) People learn to establish objectives and set timetables to ensure that they are met.
4) People learn the process of establishing realistic strategies and tactics to meet objectives.
5) People who approach the planning process with a receptive mind and employ the marketing plan will usually find that it enhances their professional career.

Discussion Questions

1. What is the purpose of a marketing plan?
2. What is the relevancy of environmental factors to an annual marketing plan?
3. Why is the determination of market potential so important?

4. How should market segments and targets be described in a marketing plan?

5. Should marketing objectives be described in quantitative terms? Why or why not?

6. What is the relationship, if any, between marketing strategies and marketing objectives?

7. Is marketing control really necessary in a marketing plan or is it an optional managerial exercise?

EXPERIENTIAL EXERCISE

Do the following:

Meet with a director of sales of a hotel, a general manager of a hotel, or the director of a tourism marketing organization and ask them to go over their marketing plan with you. Have them explain the process they use to develop a marketing plan.

INTERNET EXERCISE

Support for these exercises can be found on the Web site for *Marketing for Hospitality and Tourism*, www.prenhall.com/kotler.

Choose a hospitality or tourism organization in your area. On the Internet find information that would be useful to you if you were developing a marketing plan for the organization.

REFERENCES

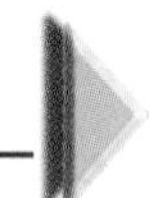

1. Condensed with permission from Peter Cass, "Luxury Lifestyle Marketing: New Frontier," *Hospitality Business Review* 2, no. 3 (Fall 1999): 27–30.
2. Perry J. S. Hobson, Henry C. S. Vincent, and Kye-Sung Chon, "Vietnam's Tourism Industry: Can It Be Kept Afloat?" *Cornell Hotel and Restaurant Administration Quarterly* 35, no. 5 (October 1994): 42–49.
3. Richard Gibson, "Flight Caterers Widen Horizons beyond Airlines," *Wall Street Journal,* January 16, 1995, pp. B1, B8.
4. Peter Warren and Neil W. Ostergren, "Marketing Your Hotel, Challenger of the 90's," *Cornell Hotel and Restaurant Administration Quarterly* 31, no. 1 (May 1990): 58.
5. Carl K. Link, "Developing a Market Plan: Lessons from the Inn at Plum Creek," *Cornell Hotel and Restaurant Administration Quarterly* 34, no. 5 (October 1993): 35.
6. L. K. Prevette and Joseph Giudice, "Anatomy of a Turnaround: The Los Angeles Biltmore," *Cornell Hotel and Restaurant Administration Quarterly* 30, no. 3 (November 1989): 32.
7. L. Taylor, "Women on the Move," Government Executive, 32, 72–74. Retrieved April 21, 2000, from the World Wide Web, *http://www.proquest.umi.com/pqdweb?TS.*
8. Ken W. McCleary and Pamela A. Weaver, "Gender-Based Differences in Business Travelers' Lodging Preferences," *Cornell Hotel and Restaurant Administration Quarterly* 35, no. 2 (April 1994): 51.
9. Francis Buttle, "The Marketing-Strategy Worksheet: A Practical Tool," *Cornell Hotel and Restaurant Administration Quarterly* 33, no. 3 (June 1992): 57.
10. Joseph J. West and Michael D. Olsen, "Grand Strategy: Making Your Restaurant a Winner," *Cornell Hotel and Restaurant Administration Quarterly* 31, no. 2 (August 1990): 77.
11. Jeffrey Young, "Vashon Statement," *Forbes* 153 (February 28, 1994): 110–111.
12. West and Olsen, "Grand Strategy."
13. Hanam Ayala, "Mexican Resorts: A Blueprint with an Expiration Date," *Cornell Hotel and Restaurant Administration Quarterly* 34, no. 3 (June 1993): 40.
14. Michael S. Morgan, "Benefit Dimensions of a Midscale Restaurant Chain," *Cornell Hotel and Restaurant Administration Quarterly* 34, no. 2 (April 1993): 44–45.
15. William P. Whelihan III and Chan Kye-Sung, "Resort Marketing Trends of the 1990's" *Cornell Hotel and Restaurant Administration Quarterly* 32, no. 2 (August 1991): 59.
16. Carl K. Link, "Internal Merchandising: Creating Revenue Opportunities," *Cornell Hotel and Restaurant Administration Quarterly* 30, no. 3 (November 1989): 56.
17. Ibid., p. 57.

18. Regina Robichald and Mahmood A. Khan, "Responding to Market Changes: The Fast Food Experience," *Cornell Hotel and Restaurant Administration Quarterly* 29, no. 3 (November 1988): 47.

19. William E. Kent, "Putting Up the Ritz: Using Culture to Open a Hotel," *Cornell Hotel and Restaurant Administration Quarterly* 31, no. 3 (November 1990): 16–24.

20. Jeffrey L. Pellissier, "Remarketing: One Club's Response to a Changing Market," *Cornell Hotel and Restaurant Administration Quarterly* 34, no. 4 (August 1993): 53–58.

21. S. Dev Chekitan, "Marketing Practices at Hotel Chains," *Cornell Hotel and Restaurant Administration Quarterly* 31, no. 3 (November 1990): 54–63.

22. For more on developing a marketing plan, see James C. Makens, *The Marketing Plan Workbook* (Upper Saddle River, NJ: Prentice Hall, 1985); James C. Makens, *Hotel Sales and Marketing Planbook* (Pfafftown, NC: Marion-Clarence Publishing House, 1990).

Case Studies

Guide to the Cases

Chapter	*Case*
1	1. The Sleep Well Motel
2	2. Cafeteria I.C.E.
3	3. Hardee's: Marketing in a Different Business Environment
3	4. The Excelsior Hotel
3	5. The Honolulu Armed Services YMCA
3, 4	6. Burger King: Selling Whoppers in Japan
4	7. The Auckland War Memorial Museum
5	8. Enterprise Rent-A-Car: Measuring Service Quality
5, 9	9. The Hunt Room: Change the Concept or Just the Decor?
5, 18	10. The Australian Tourist Commission
5, 18	11. Tanglewood Park: Vantage Golf Tournament
6	12. Gomez Executive Bus Service
6	13. Hawaiian Sights
7, 16	14. Design of Web Sites in the Tourism Industry
8	15. Coconut Plantation Resort
9, 10	16. Outback Steakhouse: Breaking the Rules, Creating New Rules
9, 15	17. The Grand Canyon Railway
11	18. New Zealand Heritage Park
11	19. Pricing Almost Destroys and Then Saves Local Restaurant
12	20. US Airways: The Airline Price Wars
12, 15	21. Winter at Zion Lodge
13	22. World View Travel, Inc.
14	23. McDonald's: Where to Go from Here?
14	24. Tropicana Fishing Lodge
14	25. Burger King: Searching for the Right Message
15, 8	26. Solitaire Lodge of New Zealand
15	27. The Ritz-Carlton, Millenia Singapore
16	28. The Teller House Uses Database Marketing
17	29. International Travel Agency
19	30. Superior Hotels
18	31. Motel 6

Case 1 The Sleep Well Motel

In April 1980, Will Shelton was evaluating information received from the owner of a motel that was for sale in Fort Morgan, Colorado. Will had answered an ad in the *Wall Street Journal* under the heading "Business for Sale." To Will's surprise, he received a call directly from Hank Bennington, the owner of the Sleep Well Motel of Fort Morgan, Colorado.

During the conversation, Mr. Bennington described his motel and his reason for wanting to sell. He also described the many advantages of living in Colorado and promised to send Will more information on his company. The next day an overnight package of information arrived at Will's home.

Background on Will Shelton

At forty-four years of age, Will felt that he had climbed the corporate ladder about as high as he was likely to go. He also had doubts about remaining in a large corporation the rest of his working life. The present position Will held was director of marketing research for a large electronics corporation located in Houston, Texas. Despite the title, Will felt his position was not satisfying. "Marketing research in an industrial company just isn't very exciting or personally rewarding; in fact, it's downright dull." This statement pretty well summarized Will's feelings. Although Will had been trained as an engineer, he discovered that engineering wasn't his primary interest and began to move into marketing. When the position of marketing research director opened in his company, Will applied and was elated when he learned he had received the position. In reviewing this move, Will stated that he believed the fact he had recently completed an MBA during part-time studies had helped him to obtain the position.

Will had recently gone through a divorce and his former wife had been awarded custody of the two boys. Because the laws in Texas called for a division of shared property and child support, Will had suffered a financial setback but was not faced with large ongoing payments to his former wife other than for child support. Despite his recent financial problems, Will felt he could raise sufficient money to purchase the motel with a bank mortgage.

In his earlier years, Will had studied and worked in New Mexico. He had learned to ski and also enjoyed hunting and fishing in that state. Will felt the people in that part of the United States were somehow more genuine and that life was better in many ways than his present life in Houston. As a result, when he read about a motel for sale in Colorado, Will had an automatic interest.

Background on the Sleep Well Motel

As Will began to pull his thoughts together, he reviewed what he had already learned about the Sleep Well Motel. This information had been gained through the telephone conversation with Mr. Bennington plus sales literature and a brief historical sketch that had been included with data sent by Mr. Bennington.

The motel had eighty rooms and had been affiliated with a chain several years ago but was no longer associated with this company. The property was located off U.S. Highway 76, which carried traffic between

Denver and Nebraska. Mr. Bennington did not have data concerning the profile characteristics of his customers but told Will that his customers were commercial travelers such as repair crews, independent sales reps, middle-aged retired couples, and young budget-minded travelers. The motel did not have an attached restaurant, but there was a café about two blocks away. There was also a laundromat nearby that was frequently used by his guests. The property was seventeen years old and was described as clean and comfortable but in need of "cosmetics" and new carpeting. Mr. Bennington said he had a dependable night clerk but served as the manager/front-desk clerk himself during the day. He said that dependable maid service was a problem for all the motels in the area, and his was no exception.

Reason for Selling

In the telephone conversation, Mr. Bennington stated he had recently lost his wife in a tragic car accident. Since that time he had been unable to concentrate on the business and now wanted to return to his home state of Illinois to be near his son's family. In addition, Mr. Bennington said he wanted to be perfectly candid. He said that after the car accident he failed to keep as close a watch on the business as he should have. Mr. Bennington admitted that he felt ill at ease in the field of marketing and felt the company would need strong direction in that area. He went on to say that Will should be a "natural" to manage this type of business.

After skimming the material, Will became increasingly enthused about the possibility of owning and managing this motel. He knew there were many additional questions he would need to ask in his next phone conversation. At the moment, the most exciting part was the possibility of living in Colorado and being his own boss. Will knew he would have to develop a list of penetrating questions to ask Mr. Bennington and also knew he needed to study the financial sheets in detail. That could come later. For the moment, Will was picturing himself on the slopes of Colorado's beautiful mountains gracefully skimming down the snow.

This case was written by Professor Cathy H. C. Hsu, Hong Kong Polytechnic University. Reproduced with permission.

Discussion Questions

1. Discuss the pros and cons of Will Shelton owning and operating the Sleep Well Motel.
2. Do you believe that Will's marketing/marketing research background will be of great assistance to him in running this motel?
3. Why do you suppose Mr. Bennington said that Will's marketing background would be a real benefit?
4. What kinds of marketing/sales tactics are best suited for a motel such as the Sleep Well Motel?

Case 2 Cafeteria I.C.E.

The cafeteria for employees of I.C.E. (the national electric company of Costa Rica—Instituto Costarricense de Electricidad) was experiencing difficulties, and top management felt compelled to see what corrective actions could be taken. Responsibility for correcting the problems had been assigned to Antonio F. Caas Mora, assistant manager for telecommunications.

The problems were two types. First, no one was satisfied with the time required for lunch. The time often extended beyond the allocated half an hour, resulting in loss of productivity. The second, related problem was how to change the lunchtime eating habits of the employees. The majority of employees used the main serving line, where they purchased a heavy traditional Latin meal. This required a considerable amount of time and also made the employees sleepy after eating. As a result, afternoon productivity among office personnel declined.

Background on I.C.E. and the Cafeteria

I.C.E. was the largest electric utility and the only telephone company in the nation of Costa Rica. It was owned and operated by the government of Costa Rica. Although I.C.E. had field office locations throughout Costa Rica, the central administrative offices were located in the city of San José in a modern fifteen-story building. A total of 4,486 persons were employed by I.C.E., and 1,453 of these worked in the central office building. This group used the cafeteria facilities.

The cafeteria had been in operation for five years. It was under the management of an employee cooperative. This cooperative was managed by an elected board of directors consisting of employees of I.C.E. The board of directors of the cooperative hired a full-time manager who had direct responsibility for the cafeteria operation.

Description of Employees

Employees who worked in the I.C.E. building and used the cafeteria were primarily white-collar personnel. A minority of blue-collar employees such as maintenance personnel used the cafeteria. Employees who worked in the I.C.E. building consisted primarily of administrators, staff specialists, engineers, clerical personnel, secretaries, and receptionists.

The Menu and Eating Habits

The cafeteria consisted of two serving lines; the main serving line was the most popular with the employees and was the one with the long waiting lines. This line served what was known as the *casado,* a typical Latin meal. The menu changed each day. A typical meal consisted of a meat dish such as a small steak, sausage, or liver. This was accompanied with rice, beans, and a vegetable such as corn or more commonly with potatoes.

The meals served in the main serving line reflected the cultural habits of Costa Ricans with traditional food. The noontime meal historically had been eaten with the family and required two or three hours, including family conversation and sometimes a short nap. This custom was the basis for closing stores during midday. It was still the custom in many parts of Latin America for all types of businesses to close until 2:00 or 3:00 P.M. The traditional long lunch hour meant that employees would arrive for work early in the morning, take a long lunch break, return for work, and stay late in the evening until 6:00 or 6:30 P.M. The management of I.C.E. had decided to break with this tradition to allow as smooth a workday as possible without the interruption of a long lunch break. The I.C.E. system closely paralleled that found in the United States.

There was evidence of change in eating habits in San José. Several U.S.-style restaurants had entered the market and did a brisk business at lunch with hamburgers, pizza, and other quick foods. McDonald's, Hardee's, and Pizza Hut were popular noontime restaurants, especially with younger people. After witnessing the success of restaurants such as McDonald's, the board of directors of the cooperative decided to open a sandwich line in the cafeteria. This was separate from the main serving line. It consisted of a long counter. Plastic food trays were placed on the counter and filled with stacks of unwrapped cold sandwiches such as cheese or ham and cheese. Other trays contained slices of fruit such as papaya or watermelon and cake. Coffee, milk, and carbonated beverages were available from dispensers located on the counter.

Two cash registers were located at the end of the main serving line, and one at the end of the sandwich line. Information was not recorded concerning the number of employees who used each line nor the average expenditure per person in the sandwich line. However, it was felt that the average lunch expenditure per employee would probably be about two-thirds of the per person expenditure in the main serving line.

Working Hours and Office Rules

The office hours at I.C.E. extended from 7:30 A.M. to 3:30 P.M., with half an hour for lunch. Employees were expected to arrive on time. This meant that some employees had to rise as early as 5:30 A.M., and few could rise later than 6:30 A.M.

Coffee breaks were not officially permitted, and there were no vending machines in the building. The policy of no coffee breaks had been instituted because many employees spilled coffee or other liquids on reports. It was also felt that a coffee break was unnecessary since half an hour was given for lunch. Workers would occasionally bring a cake or cookies from home and share them with employees in their work area even though this was officially frowned upon.

A system had been devised to prevent all employees from crowding into the cafeteria at one time. The doors of the cafeteria were locked until 11:00 A.M., at which time employees began to arrive on a set schedule by floors. The line closed promptly at 1:30 P.M.

Survey Results

Before attempting to make changes to correct the situation in the cafeteria, management felt it would be wise to conduct a survey among the employees. This was done through the use of a written questionnaire which was given to all persons using the cafeteria on a selected day. The results of this questionnaire follow.

Opinions Concerning Selected Factors (%)

	OPINION				
FACTOR	VERY GOOD	GOOD	AVERAGE	BAD	NO OPINION
Quality	0.63	16.46	44.78	23.42	14.71
Variety	4.59	35.28	28.96	18.67	12.50
Cleanliness	1.74	18.67	36.55	29.75	13.24
Courtesy	5.38	27.37	39.24	25.16	2.85
Convenience	8.07	30.70	34.65	23.26	3.32
Quality of cooking	8.39	35.28	33.70	18.83	3.80
Quantity	3.16	28.48	39.72	20.41	8.23

Opinions Concerning Type of Food Served (%)

	OPINION				
FACTOR	VERY GOOD	GOOD	AVERAGE	BAD	NO OPINION
Chicken w/rice	8.86	43.04	29.59	7.59	10.92
Shrimp w/rice	1.11	12.34	33.23	31.64	21.68
Meatballs	2.37	12.97	31.33	31.65	21.68
Sea bass	10.28	37.18	25.63	8.86	18.04
Breaded steak	4.11	22.47	34.02	18.04	21.36
Flank steak in sauce	3.64	24.68	30.85	15.82	25.06
Tongue in sauce	5.54	26.58	26.42	17.41	24.05
Chicken in sauce	3.32	23.10	29.43	16.30	27.85
Fried chicken	2.37	23.89	30.70	12.97	30.06
Pork chop	3.32	19.15	29.43	21.99	26.11
Spaghetti w/meat	1.90	13.77	29.11	33.07	22.15
Spaghetti w/tuna	2.37	10.92	26.42	34.18	26.11
Chickpeas w/tripe	3.64	17.56	28.80	28.01	21.99
Chop suey	1.90	14.40	24.05	38.76	20.89

Opinions Concerning Diet and Type of Meal (%)

	YES	NO	NO OPINION
Do you believe the diet is well balanced?	17.88	75.63	6.49
Do you feel that the special plate of the day should be eliminated?	27.69	66.61	5.70
Do you believe the casado should be eliminated?	26.42	68.04	5.54
Do you believe a lighter meal should be served?	36.23	14.40	49.37

Light Meal Preferences (%)

	YES	NO
Hot dogs	44.46	55.54
Hamburgers	30.85	69.15
Chicken	42.41	57.54
Pastry	36.55	63.45
Fruit	18.99	81.01
Sandwiches	49.53	50.47
Desserts	31.80	68.20
Soup	18.35	81.65
Salads	23.10	76.90
Fruit salads	33.86	66.14
Other	10.28	89.72

[a]If a light meal was served. This was answered by all respondents.

Answers Concerning Eating Habits (%)

	YES	NO	NO ANSWER
Do you follow a special diet?	14.72	76.58	8.70
Do you usually bring your lunch?	10.76	81.33	7.91

Average Time Taken to Eat Lunch (%)

20–30 minutes	18.83
30–45 minutes	61.87
45–60 minutes	12.50
Over 60 minutes	0.79
No answer	6.01

Observations Concerning Seating in Cafeteria

A series of observations were made in the cafeteria on typical days. The cafeteria held fifty-eight tables with four chairs each, for a total of 232 places. The utilization of this space on the days observed is shown in the tables that follow.

Use of Available Seating Capacity

TIME	AVAILABLE SEATS	PERSONS IN WAITING LINE	THEORETICAL SURPLUS OR SHORTAGE OF SEATS
Wednesday, August 16			
11:45	45	80	−35
12:25	16	90	−74
12:30	48	90	−74
1:05	68	40	+28
1:20	88	27	+61
Thursday, August 17			
11:15	44	16	+28
11:42	68	38	+30
11:56	39	43	−4
12:00	44	55	−11
12:10	80	53	+27
12:15	56	37	+19
12:30	56	52	−4
12:40	56	47	+9
12:55	26	46	−20
1:15	56	3	+53

Tables Occupied by One or Two People

	TABLES OCCUPIED BY ONE	TABLES OCCUPIED BY TWO	TOTAL
Wednesday, August 16			
11:42	12	22	34
11:56	6	26	32
12:00	6	38	44
12:10	3	30	33
12:15	15	18	33
12:30	6	26	32
12:55	15	20	35
1:15	6	14	20

Rate of Flow through Serving Line

Main line. After two days of observation, it was found that the average time required for a person to pass through the main serving line from the moment a person picked up a tray until leaving the cash register was slightly in excess of three minutes, with a range of two to four minutes. There was never a break in this line from the moment the cafeteria opened at 11:00 until it closed at 1:30. The line moved steadily, yet a waiting line would form between 12:00 and 12:45, which at times extended well into the hallway in front of the elevator and caused waiting times of twenty minutes before reaching the actual food line.

Sandwich line. The amount of time required per person to pass through the sandwich line ranged from .5 to 4 minutes. The average time for persons who used the sandwich line but did not use a sandwich grill to cook cold sandwiches was 2.10 minutes. The amount of time required in this line when someone used the sandwich grill located beyond the cash register ranged between 3 and 8 minutes, with an average time of 4.5 minutes. At times as many as eight or ten persons would be waiting to use the sandwich grill.

Discussion Questions

1. Can the use of marketing concepts/strategies be of use in solving the problem with Cafeteria I.C.E.?
2. What effect can an individual organization such as I.C.E. have on changing ingrained cultural habits such as those of noontime dining?
3. What would you suggest be done to increase patronage of the sandwich and fruit line?

Case 3 Hardee's: Marketing in a Different Business Environment

Downtown Seoul

"There should be more fast-food restaurants," exclaimed Moon Yong, a twenty-one-year-old college student, as she downed another French fry and sipped a Coke with a friend at Hardee's in Seoul, one of only two Hardee's in all of South Korea. Moon Yong and her female friends like fast-food restaurants, especially American ones. Korean kids find it fashionable to hang out in fast-food restaurants. "We'll stay here all afternoon," Moon Yong proclaimed.

In fact, American fast-food companies that have ventured into Korea target young people. Fast-food restaurants are especially appealing to young girls, who make up 70 percent of all customers. The girls like the French fries and beverages, and they sit in the restaurants for hours. As a result, South Korean fast-food restaurants are bigger than their American counterparts—about 300 seats versus 150 seats for U.S. restaurants.

Furthermore, despite the sometimes strong anti-American sentiment in Korea, Korean young people are drawn to the slice of Americana that the restaurants represent. Young Lee, president of Del Taco Korea Co., points out that "they like American and European music. So they want their food the same way. It is in this area that America is the leader, not electric parts or TVs." As a result, Mr. Lee and other fast-food executives in Korea make only a few subtle changes in the American menus to account for local tastes. In other countries, firms often make substantial changes.

Doing Business in South Korea

South Korea may seem to be the promised land for American fast-food chains. Faced with the saturated and highly competitive U.S. market, one would think that the chains would be flocking to South Korea. However, McDonald's has only four stores in the country—one store for every 10.8

million Koreans, as compared with fifty-one stores in Hong Kong (one per every 112,000 residents). Similarly, Wendy's has only thirteen outlets in South Korea, and Burger King has only twelve.

Why have U.S. fast-food restaurants been so slow to enter South Korea? In late 1991, the *Wall Street Journal* published a ranking of 129 countries based on the risk of doing business in each. The rankings combined each country's rankings on the basis of political risk, financial risk, and economic risk into an overall composite risk score. South Korea fell into the low-risk category with a composite score of 73.5 out of a possible 100. It ranked twenty-seventh on the list, just behind Portugal and ahead of Botswana. The low-risk category, which covered scores from 70 to 84.5, also included the United States, which ranked ninth with a composite score of 83.5. South Korea's political risk score was 63 out of 100, and it had scores of 47 out of a possible 50 of financial risk and 36.5 out of 50 on economic risk.

Even though South Korea's overall score suggested a low level of risk, analysts point out that it is a tough market. Land prices are especially high. A high-traffic site in Seoul, the capital city, can cost $7 million to buy or require a $1 million deposit to rent. The land for a factory may cost more than the factory. Raw material costs are the highest in Asia. Manufacturing wages have gone up 18 percent per year since 1986. Governmental restrictions, such as high tariffs and limits on certain imports, such as cheese and beef, frustrate food chains. Gaining government approval for investment takes time and can be very difficult. Companies also find it difficult to bring additional capital funds into the country. Korean firms, fearing new competition, resist entry and investment by foreign firms. Foreign firms also suspect that the Korean government doesn't really want foreign investment, especially if it will adversely affect domestic producers.

All these factors have resulted in a low level of foreign investment in South Korea. The Korea Development Institute, a government-funded think tank, indicates that the ratio of foreign investment to gross national products is 14.6:1 in Singapore and 1.61:1 in Taiwan but only 0.36:1 in South Korea.

Enter Hardee's

If entering the market in South Korea is so tough, why do Hardee's, McDonald's, and other firms even bother to try? For one thing, these firms see the flip side of rapidly rising Korean wage rates—disposable income has grown 141 percent since 1986, making Korea the largest consumer market in Asia after Japan. The average urban household in South Korea has an annual income of $12,400. Ten percent of the population has college degrees, and the number of two-income families is on the rise. These factors create demand for convenience foods and higher-quality products. Overall, however, the Korean consumer market lags behind that of other Asian countries, having about the same level of economic development. For example, Korea lacks modern convenience stores and large supermarkets that offer wide variety to consumers. Still, Hardee's believes that it has found a way around all of these stumbling blocks. Hardee's selected Kim Chang-Hwan, a wealthy local businessman, as its Korean franchisee. Mr. Kim's older brother manages a chain of retail stores that has many outlets near student hangouts. The Kims are converting several shoestores into Hardee's restaurants. In an "in-your-face" move, the Korean franchise opened its first Hardee's downtown Seoul just a few yards down the street from a popular McDonald's. King Nam Young, the franchisee's general manager, admits that Hardee's executives were concerned about the strategy, but so far his store's sales have equaled McDonald's.

McDonald's entered the country in 1986 by forming a 50:50 joint venture with a Korean accountant and entrepreneur, Ahn Hyo Young, and had planned to open fourteen stores by the early 1990s. However, the first store didn't open until 1988 and expansion has been very slow, resulting in part from the illness and death of Mr. Ahn. McDonald's indicates that it is now uncertain about where to find a new local partner. McDonald's employees also claim that the local franchise did not have enough capital when it started and that McDonald's had balked at the high cost of real estate.

Coors Tries Its Hand

Coors Brewing Company has announced that it too is moving into the South Korean market. Although it is not unusual for American brewers to do business in foreign markets, they have typically expanded through contract brewing, licensing agreements, or direct exports. However, Coors announced that it will enter into a joint venture with Jinro Ltd., a Korean distiller, to build its first offshore brewery. Thus it will become the first U.S. brewer to own part of a foreign-based brewery. The joint venture hoped to gain a 5 percent to 6 percent share of the Korean market by 1994.

Analysts suggest that U.S. brewers are showing more interest in foreign markets because of the slow growth in the U.S. market. A Coors spokesperson notes that to gain more business in the United States, you have to take it from someone else. In Korea, he notes, the beer market is growing 15 percent a year, and a company has a chance to earn some of that growth itself. American brewers are well positioned to expand. One industry executive states, "There is a movement toward lightness in all beverages (around the world) and American beers have always been very light compared to European beers."

Prior the Korean agreement, Coors had only licensed its beer in Canada and Japan and exported it to three other countries. Coors is entering South Korea despite Miller Brewing's recent departure. Miller pulled out of Korea because of high tariffs and the rising value of Korea's currency, the yuan. Coors won't have an easy time of it, even if its agreement works. The Korean government has licensed only two other brewers. These two national breweries produce several Korean beers and market Carlsberg beer under license. Also, one is licensed to sell one of Coors's toughest competitors—Budweiser. Like Coors, Ralston Purina has also decided to go against conventional wisdom. It has constructed a $10 million plant in Korea to produce its Chex breakfast cereal. But unlike Coors and the fast-food companies, Purina has some advantages. First, it will enter a market containing no strong local producer. Second, Purina is not a newcomer to the Korean market—it has been operating in Korea for twenty-five years. Purina began in Korea by producing feed for cows, hogs, poultry, and fish and later moved into cat and dog food. Purina has paid careful attention to the Korean market's development. It has found that the consumption of breakfast cereal closely follows the consumption of milk throughout the world. When it noted rising income levels and milk consumption in Korea, it decided that the time was right to dive into cereals.

Making It Easier

Despite the efforts of the fast-food companies, Coors, and Purina, the Korean government is still concerned about the low level of foreign investment. As a result, the government is slowly changing the rules. It now grants automatic approval for projects valued at less than $20 million, up from the $5 million limit. Moreover, foreign companies can now establish wholly owned subsidiaries. The government may also make it easier for foreign companies to bring in additional capital, and it is granting tax breaks to high-tech electronics companies and may offer cheap land to high-tech companies that locate in Korean industrial parks.

However, the government has been slow to offer similar benefits to processed foods or packaged-goods companies, and it has been reluctant to allow foreigners to build modern warehouses and distribution networks—facilities needed by consumer-product companies. Furthermore, the government often holds up products at customs and sponsors anti-consumption campaigns to turn public opinion against imported goods.

As a result of the positive changes and despite the problems, more foreign companies are establishing import offices and sales and distribution channels in Korea. Some businesspeople believe that if a company can find its way through the maze of Korean political, economical, and cultural barriers, it can reap substantial rewards.

Back in Downtown Korea

Meanwhile, Moon Yong and her friend have finished their Cokes and fries at Hardee's and decide to walk down the street to McDonald's to see what's happening there. They throw away their trash, wave to some friends, and leave the restaurant. The Hardee's manager watches them leave and wonders whether the fascination for things American will continue or whether Korean political, economic, and cultural forces will blunt efforts to open the Korean market. What can he do to keep Moon Yong and others like her coming back to Hardee's?

Sources: Adapted from Damon Darling, "South Koreans Crave American Fast Food," *Wall Street Journal,* February 22, 1991, p. B1; Monua Janah, "Rating Risk in the Hot Countries," *Wall Street Journal,* September 20, 1991, p. R4; Damon Darling, "U.S. Firms Take Chances in South Korea," *Wall Street Journal,* June 15, 1992, p. B1. Used with permission.

Discussion Questions

1. Based on information in the case, what kinds of trade restrictions does Hardee's face in working in Korea's trade system?
2. What aspects of Korea's economic, political-legal, and cultural environments are important for Hardee's to understand?
3. Why have Hardee's and the other companies in the case decided to enter foreign markets, and why have they selected Korea? Do you agree with their decisions?
4. What methods might Hardee's have used to enter the Korean market, and why did it select the method used?
5. What decisions has Hardee's made about its marketing program in Korea? What recommendations would you make about this program?

Case 4 The Excelsior Hotel

A most significant competitive threat was about to affect the four-star Excelsior Hotel. A new luxury hotel was under construction directly across the street. The staff was concerned that there might not be enough business to support two upscale hotels in the same market.

Hotel History

The 305-room Excelsior had operated in the city for ten years. During these years, it had served as the only upscale hotel in the city. It had an excellent location downtown between a 600-space parking deck and the Convention Center. The hotel featured an indoor swimming pool, a Jacuzzi, two restaurants, a cocktail lounge, and several unique amenities. Many of the rooms had balconies overlooking the garden level dining area and Greenhouse Café. Each floor was accessed by three glass-enclosed elevators. Other major attributes of the hotel were the ice skating rink located under the hotel and tunnel connecting the hotel with the Convention Center.

The Excelsior was managed by a management group but was owned by the Concept Corp., a real estate and investment company. An interview with the general manager of the Excelsior revealed the following:

- What are your goals for the hotel? "Locally, for the next year, we would just like to be competitive productwise. Our long-term goal is to be one of the leading hotels in our state."
- How do you perceive the increasing competitive pressure? "It has been tremendous. The increase in hotel rooms over the last five years within our competitive market has been unbelievable. The Stouffer will open up on July 1, and a new Sheraton will open up later this year. Radissons are going up left and right. A lot of smaller hotel chains are putting up budget hotels. Right now I would say we are overbuilt until the city gets its convention center expanded so that we can attract larger groups. There is not enough corporate business to go around to supply all of us with a decent occupancy."
- What actions does the Excelsior plan to take within the increasingly competitive environment? "To be competitive, you have to have the product. Once again that's our first step. We want to bring our overall product of service back up to a competitive level, meaning that we have to renovate and make some other adjustments decor-wise—new

rooms, new furniture, and some other things. Those are tangible things."

- Describe the relationship between the management and the hotel owners. "We are a management company. We don't own a nickel here. Our ownership is another company. They have a little different philosophy on how to make money and to provide quality service to the guests. They don't have the same idea regarding bottom-line profits and quality rendered to the guests. Obviously, you have to realize the relation between profit and quality service to the guest. If you put in "turn-down" service, it is costing you money. If you give your employees benefits, it costs you money. Anything you do other than supplying them with one towel and a clean room costs you money. It means that the profit level between what we feel is obtainable provided that we give the guests great service and what our ownership thinks we should make as a hotel is different. They feel we should make a lot more money."

The general manager was perplexed as to what direction the hotel should take. The building is in need of renovation to maintain its attractiveness and "image." There is pressure from the owners to offer less and make more, which is inconsistent with long-standing image. The biggest threat, though, is coming from the increased competition for the lucrative group business from newer hotels and convention centers. However, the city was beginning to enter a "renaissance" period with the planned expansion of the Convention Center, the completion of the Super Block area, and a push for retail stores and businesses to relocate downtown.

Discussion Questions

1. Why should a conflict exist between the philosophies of the hotel Excelsior's management group and its owner, the Concept Corp.?
2. What steps in addition to renovation should the Excelsior be taking to prepare for increased competition?

Case 5 The Honolulu Armed Services YMCA

The board of management of the Armed Services YMCA of Honolulu, Hawaii, was considering the possibility of converting the top two floors of the building into a commercial hotel. The location of the building within the downtown business area near the state capital seemed perfect to satisfy the lodging needs of budget-minded business travelers plus the military and their dependents, known as the temporary living allowance (TLA) market. Costs involved in operating the building as a YMCA were increasing rapidly, but revenue was not keeping pace. The concept of converting only the top two floors to moderate-priced hotel rooms was to allow the YMCA to continue to operate the traditional areas such as the gym while the conversion process was ongoing. If the rooms on the top two floors proved to be popular, the remaining floors could gradually be converted until the entire building became a moderate-priced hotel.

Description of the Building

Built in 1927, the architectural design of the building was neocolonial, incorporating the mode of Mediterranean culture. It stood five stories high and embodied several outdoor patios or lanais within its structure. Zoning restrictions and the construction of the building prevented the consideration of adding additional stories. The building was built in the form of a rectangular horseshoe and contained approximately 83,000 square feet. It had been solidly constructed of reinforced concrete and showed a few cracks but no major structural problems.

The wooden windowsills and frame suffered from dry rot and termites. It was felt that the tile roof might need to be replaced or repaired substantially in the next few years. The original plumbing remained throughout the building. Part of the wiring had been modernized, but a large portion of the original wiring still remained. Hot water was provided by large boilers which continued to function but required frequent maintenance. A parking lot in the foreground that could accommodate approximately seventy cars separated the YMCA building from Hotel Street. A privately owned taxi company had leased a portion of this parking lot for its own use. This cluttering aspect coupled with the trees in front of the building created a visibility problem for the premises.

The front section of the first floor facing Hotel Street consisted of a lobby, the front desk, a coffee shop and kitchen, a barbershop, and four office lease spaces. The front desk was a traditional YMCA-type semi-enclosed area. It was situated near the elevator and allowed the desk clerk good visibility of most of the activity in the ground-floor lobby area. The lobby was an open tiled area; it did not contain any traditional lobby furniture. Adjacent to it was a small area that contained beverage-dispensing machines.

Upon entering the lobby from the outside, the coffee shop was located to the left. It offered a traditional breakfast and lunch menu, and customer traffic was slow. Approximately half the seating area had been sectioned off by means of a rope with a closed sign attached to discourage patrons from sitting in the back area. The coffee shop offered counter and booth service and was patronized primarily by YMCA residents and by some nearby office workers who occasionally dropped in for coffee. The kitchen area was old and in need of remodeling.

The barbershop was a conventional men's barbershop and was distinguishable by a small, traditional, red-and-white-striped barber pole. About 90 percent of the customers were walk-ins. Several areas on the first floor had been converted to office space and leased out to tenants. This included the public men's room on the first floor next to the barbershop. The back section of the first floor included facilities traditionally associated with a "Y": a large gymnasium (4,816 square feet), two saunas, an exercise room, a swimming pool, men's and women's locker rooms, and shower areas. The entire second floor had been converted into offices, including space for the YMCA offices or to office space. The second floor also contained the original ceramiclike flooring and was quite impressive. The remaining area on the second floor served as airspace above the first-floor gymnasium with a running track around the edge.

The third floor consisted of two wings and a front section facing Hotel Street. The front section was utilized as a day-care center and living quarters for welfare mothers and was deliberately partitioned to prevent passage by male residents. The east wing included a recreational room with pinball machines, a TV viewing area, a lounge, program room, and laundry facilities, along with office space for the resident manager, executive director, and staff. The west wing was devoted to thirty-two individual rooms for residents with a communal shower and toilet area.

The fourth and fifth floors also consisted of two wings connected by the front section. This rectangular horseshoe arrangement was typical of buildings built in that era. The center portion of the building above the ground-floor swimming pool was open air. The entire space on the fourth and fifth floors was devoted to individual rooms with a communal shower–toilet area in each wing. Altogether, the building contained 244 individual units for residents: 32 on the third floor, 93 on the fourth, and 119 on the fifth. These were approximately 8 by 10 feet in dimension (or 75 square feet) and did not offer air conditioning, running water, or toilet facilities. During the summer months, the top floors were rather uncomfortable. Rental rates were $48 a week or $204 per month.

Approximately 99 percent of all persons utilizing the Physical Fitness Center, including the swimming pool and gym, were civilians. Only 30 percent of the YMCA residents were members of the military. The remaining resident mix consisted of a variety of transients, including young, low-budget backpacker tourists; older seasonal tourists whose primary source of income was social security; single men who were seeking employment in Hawaii; and others who exhibited drug- or alcohol-related problems. A few residents remained for months at a time, but most remained for less than two weeks.

The mix of tenants and residents in the building necessitated the employment of a full-time security officer and the use of surveillance TV cameras at critical spots within the building, such as doors leading to the female quarters. Unfortunately, the problems faced by many of the residents had led to several suicides or attempted suicides in the past years, including cases where residents leaped from their rooms.

Description of the Armed Services YMCA Organization

The Armed Services YMCA, a nonprofit organization, served as a department of the National Board of YMCAs throughout the United States. Its central mission was viewed as providing temporary lodging, recreation, and education for members of the U.S. military and their dependents. Special attention was directed to the military of junior ranks; nevertheless, all ranks were welcome. In total there were twenty-three branches of the Armed Services YMCA throughout the United States, with headquarters in New York City. There were also two branches in the Canal Zone and one branch located in Scotland.

The Honolulu Armed Services YMCA was the only branch established in Hawaii. There were three other YMCAs in Honolulu, but none of these belonged to the Armed Services Department nor did they share the same stated objectives. Although the primary mission of the Armed Services "Y" was to meet the needs of the military, in recent years it had taken on a broader responsibility of serving the community at large, as long as those activities did not interfere with the central mission of serving the military.

Discussion Questions

1. What do you think of the concept of converting the top two floors of the YMCA to a budget hotel and then gradually converting the rest?
2. Discuss the client mix that evolved in the YMCA and what effect this will have on any plans for hotel conversion.
3. Discuss possible strategic options for the YMCA.
4. Will conversion of the current building assist the Honolulu Armed Services YMCA to meet its mission?

Case 6 Burger King: Selling Whoppers in Japan

"International is where it's at," said Ron Paul, a Technomic consultant. "The fast-food burger category is going to find its better growth opportunity overseas. We're close to saturation in the United States. That's why McDonald's has been so aggressive in overseas markets."

That's also why Burger King has to be so aggressive in Japan. McDonald's entered the Japanese market twenty-five years ago and now has 2,000 outlets there generating $2.5 billion in sales—that's *half* of the entire fast-food burger market in Japan. In addition McDonald's generates 47 percent of its corporate profits from its 7,000 units overseas; whereas Burger King generates only 19 percent of company sales from its 1,600 units overseas. Worldwide, Burger King ranks fourth behind McDonald's, KFC, and Pizza Hut. With U.S. markets saturated, and the mad cow disease scare slowing sales in Europe, Burger King must find new areas to expand.

In Japan, Burger King will face stiff competition. Not only is McDonald's well entrenched there, KFC also has 1,040 stores in Japan, making it number two in the Japanese fast-food market. Between them, Big Mac and KFC create a formidable barrier to the entry of other firms. These big players have taken most of the good locations, leaving only marginal sites for would-be competitors. Just ask the folks at Wendy's, which made a major push in Japan in the 1980s, but after sixteen years has only sixty-seven outlets. Wendy's is having trouble finding deep-pocket players who want to open fast-food restaurants. Even local officials of Daiei, Inc., which licenses Wendy's in Japan, concede that the entry attempt has been a failure.

Burger King tried to enter the Japanese market once before. It began selling franchises there twenty years ago; franchisees paid an initial franchise fee plus royalties to the Parent Corporation. However, the royalties were too high and the operation failed. As if all that weren't enough, the number two burger place in Japan is a *local* competitor, Mos Burger, which has 25 percent of the market.

In addition to Burger King's previous failure, near saturation of the Japanese market, and stiff foreign and local competition, the company faces another problem in Japan. Burger wars have plagued the entire fast-food industry and almost eliminated profits—even for McDonald's. Burger King figures that pockets are less full than usual. However, as a result of the burger wars, Japanese consumers are accustomed to getting "cheap burgers," and Burger King's Whoppers tend to cost more.

Burger King realizes that this time it must find an innovative way to enter the market. It must attract attention and obtain good locations in a market that is tending toward saturation. This will not be an easy task. Land is very limited in Japan and costs much more than land in the United States, so finding good sites will be difficult. In addition, Burger King will have to convince Japanese consumers to pay more for a burger. Japanese customers tend to be careful purchasers and to look for good value for their yen.

The solution? Joint ventures. Burger King joined with Japan Tobacco, Inc., to form Burger King Japan. Because Japan Tobacco is two-thirds owned by the Japanese Ministry of Finance, it brings deep pockets with it. Its first move was to buy out Morinaga Love Hamburger chain and immediately convert the thirty-six Morinaga Love restaurants to Burger Kings. Now, other struggling burger chains have expressed an interest in being acquired by Burger King Japan. Even big retailers like Ito-Yokado are inquiring about the possibility of opening Burger King restaurants in their shopping centers as an alternative to McDonald's.

In addition, the Japanese government has relaxed restrictions on how gasoline is sold, and Burger King hopes to place stores in gas-and-burger outlets. Such an arrangement has advantages for both parties. Gas companies get a new competitive weapon with which to attract customers, and Burger King avoids the high cost of developing stand-alone sites. Furthermore, Burger King already operates gas and burger stations in New Zealand and Australia, so it has experience with this kind of operation, and Burger King is talking to Shell Sekiyu K.K., a unit of Royal Dutch/Shell Group.

Although some observers think that Burger King's lack of name recognition in Japan is a disadvantage, Burger King thinks it can capitalize on this void to create an upscale image. It believes that a high-class image will help to set it apart from McDonald's.

To appeal to affluent Japanese teenagers, nearly all Burger King restaurants will have a "retro look" of 1950s and 1960s pop culture. In some stores, Hollywood will set the tone with Marilyn Monroe, Marlon Brando, and James Dean staring at diners from the walls. Other store decors will center around rock'-n'-roll, with original albums by stars such as Elvis Presley lining the walls. All stores will have jukeboxes, checkered tile floors, and 1950s-style red dining seats. "I just love these chairs," says Shinoba Fukushima of the red dining seats at a Tokyo outlet. Sales for Burger King have jumped 40 percent to 50 percent with the pop theme.

For parents, the appeal may be somewhat different. Whereas McDonald's sells teriyaki burgers and fried rice in Japan, Burger King wants to focus on its traditional burgers. "There're not enough vegetables at most other places," says approving mother Midori Morisaka, who brought her five-year-old son to a Tokyo Burger King. So, the Whopper with its healthy serving of tomatoes and lettuce has strong appeal for her.

For Japanese consumers in general, Yuji Kagohashi, president of Burger King Japan, wants to bring Burger King's big competitive advantage— flame broiling—out into the open. "Japanese restaurants often put the kitchen's flames up front to lure in customers," he reasons, "and we can do the same. Why does Burger King hide its biggest weapon against McDonald's in the back of the restaurant?"

Putting the flames up front may be a good idea for Burger King for another reason—lack of promotional funds. With so many outlets to open, Burger King lacks funds to engage in the heavy promotional campaigns that McDonald's and KFC usually launch. Instead, it relies on promotional events such as grand openings, which generate publicity, and through circulars handed out in the local market.

Is the competition concerned? Not really—not at this time. "McDonald's is the king of burgers," says Shinji Minakata, managing director of Dairy Queen, a firm that has cut its product line back to coffee and ice cream because of inability to sell burgers in Japan. "McDonald's has ushered us into the age of eighty-yen hamburgers," says Sumeo Yokokawa, a manager at Kentucky Fried Chicken, Japan. "A burger is a burger for most people now; flame-broiling and extra vegetables are at best an incremental difference most customers don't really care about. "

McDonald's isn't cowed. The industry leader is moving ahead with plans to have 10,000 outlets in Japan by the year 2006. Even if Burger King opens 200 a year for the next decade, it will still remain far behind McDonald's in number of locations, and that can really make a difference. Remember Midori Morisaka? There's no Burger King in suburban Chiba where her family lives. To get a Whopper, she and her son had to make a long trip downtown. The question is, how many customers will build a preference for a burger that is so hard to get to? "We don't see them as a threat at all," adds Jun Fujita, assistant manager of a McDonald's in Tokyo's Setagaya neighborhood, where a Burger King will open in March. "Who's ever heard of Burger King?"

Sources: Alina Matas, "Burger King Corp. Plans 200 Stores for Japan," *Miami Herald,* July 16, 1996, p. 7; Jack Russell, "Burger King vs. Giants in Japan," *Advertising Age,* August 1, 1996, p. 34; Norihiko Shironzu, "Whoppers Face Entrenched Foes in Japan: Big Macs," *Wall Street Journal,* February 4, 1997, pp. B1, B6; Edith Hill Updike, "Burger King Wants to Build a Kingdom in Asia," *Business Week,* November 25, 1996, p. 52.

Discussion Questions

1. What aspects of Japan's economic, political/legal, and cultural environments are important for Burger King to understand?
2. Why have Burger King and other companies in the case decided to enter foreign markets? Why have they chosen Japan? Do you agree with their decisions?
3. Contrast Burger King's entry strategy twenty years ago with its present entry strategy. What are the differences? Is the new entry strategy likely to be more successful? If so, why?
4. Evaluate Burger King's proposed marketing strategy and program for Japan. Which elements of its marketing program do you think will be successful? Which ones are likely to be less successful?

Case 7 The Auckland War Memorial Museum

The director of the Auckland War Memorial Museum, Stuart Parks, was a worried man. He faced the problem of declining visitor attendance and realized that the basic challenge was to reestablish the museum as one of Auckland's visitor center points.

Visitor Decline

Annual museum attendance was 900,000 visitors, a 50 percent reduction from the 1978 peak of 1.8 million people. Declining visitor numbers reflected trends in other Western countries due to increasing competitive pressure from alternative leisure facilities. Double-digit inflation and an aging building had caused operating costs to double. Expenditures on infrastructure, such as improved security systems and replacement of antiquated lifts, constantly whittled away at the museum's capital base.

Forces Resisting Change

The museum council members were known to be conservative. The director considered them hidebound by tradition. The museum's role as a war memorial, and cultural sensitivities within New Zealand, placed severe restraints on the types of displays that had been developed. Lack of current market research and professional management skills meant that museum staff had a limited understanding why visitors attended the museum—and perhaps even more important, what else the museum needed to do to attract more visitors.

High on the Hill

The museum stands on high ground in the Auckland Domain. Visitors often remarked at the magnificent views the museum offered of Waitemata Harbour. Since the 1920s, the museum's classical lines had been the centerpiece of the central city's skyline. Volcanic upheavals in years past created a natural amphitheater. This, together with the well-tended botanical gardens that surrounded the building for several acres, combined to enhance the elegance and visual impact of the museum. The museum was an easy thirty-minute walk from downtown Auckland. Several major tourist hotels were located within a one-kilometer radius.

Gloom and Doom

High ceilings, imposing pillars, and lackluster decor resulted in a subdued atmosphere. Chatty tourists became solemn as their voices reverberated through the museum halls. The director was aware that visitors' imagination could be enhanced by new imaginative exhibits. Many of the existing displays seemed lifeless, and the director sensed that this could be contributing to falling attendance. Most displays were permanent. The director believed that new innovative displays with more popular appeal were needed.

Display Highlights

1. Maori Court contained a world-famous display of Maori art and culture. Features include a carved house and the last surviving war canoe.

2. Hall of Pacific Art portrayed the rich cultural heritage of the Pacific Islands.
3. New Zealand's unique fauna and natural history were featured.
4. The war memorial section contained static displays of New Zealand's military involvement. Dusty models of tanks and aircraft hint of battles fought and valor on the battlefield.
5. Various cultures were contrasted by an extensive decorative art collection.
6. New Zealand's colonial past was reproduced in replica of a nineteenth-century street scene.
7. A maritime collection highlighted the traditional relation between the land, its people, and the oceans surrounding New Zealand's windswept shores.

The Market

With a cosmopolitan population of 750,000, Auckland attracted tourists from other parts of New Zealand, as well as from overseas. As New Zealand's major gateway, the city attracted many international visitors.

Coach Tours

Numerous local tour bus operators included the museum among Auckland's places of interest. Foreign tourists often used this service. Museum staff involvement was minimal; tourists were left to find their own way around, often relying on the help of the bus driver.

Educational Role

School groups began visiting the museum in the 1930s. In 1984, 60,000 children visited the museum as part of classroom studies.

Current Promotional Methods

The museum produced a number of informative brochures. These were made available to tourists at focal points such as hotels, motels, and tourist information centers. Free information booklets had been published by such organizations as the Government Tourist Bureau. These had wide circulation, especially among incoming tourists. Local media often ran articles on exhibitions of special interest.

Competition

The museum council attributed the decline in visitor numbers to increased competition from alternative leisure facilities. The foresight of Auckland's early settlers had provided the city with a wide range of cultural attractions. The city is endowed with the museum, the art gallery, historic places, parks, and reserves. Waitemata Harbour provides perfect conditions for water sports and boat cruises. Families picnic at picturesque beaches along the harbor drive. Downtown Auckland retail shopping is varied and exciting, especially for New Zealand out-of-towners visiting the city. Cinemas and restaurants abound, reflecting the city's cosmopolitan reputation. Auckland caters to the energetic. An extensive range of sporting facilities is available, including many fine golf courses.

Source: This case was written by C. T. Courtney, Master of Commerce student at the University of Auckland, under the supervision of Dr. James C. Makens.

Note: The facts presented in this case are not intended to reflect current conditions. This case was amended from an earlier version written by Dr. James C. Makens. It is intended for instructional purposes only.

Discussion Questions

1. What role, if any, should the hospitality industry play in helping museums to attract more visitors?
2. Hospitality industry executives sometimes serve on the boards of museums. What marketing suggestions should a board member make to the museum?
3. What other nonprofit cultural enterprises serve travelers? Discuss ways that the hospitality industry can be of assistance to all of them.

Case 8 Enterprise Rent-A-Car: Measuring Service Quality

Kevin Kirkman wheeled his shiny blue BMW coupe into his driveway, put the gear shift in the park position, set the parking brake, and got out to check his mailbox as he did every day when he got home. As he flipped through the deluge of catalogs and credit card offers, he noticed a letter from Enterprise Rent-A-Car.

The Wreck

He wondered why Enterprise would be writing him. Then he remembered. Earlier that month, he'd been involved in a wreck. As he was driving to work one rainy morning, another car had been unable to stop on the slick pavement and had plowed into his car as he waited at a stoplight. Thankfully, neither Kevin nor the other driver had been hurt, but both cars had been considerably damaged. In fact, Kevin had not been able to drive his car.

Kevin had used his cellular phone to call the police; and while he waited for the officers to come, he had called his auto insurance agent. The agent had assured Kevin that his policy included coverage to pay for a rental car while his car was repaired. He had told Kevin to have the car towed to a nearby auto repair shop and had given him the telephone number for the Enterprise Rent-A-Car office that served his area. The agent had noted that his company recommended using Enterprise for replacement rentals and that Kevin's policy would cover up to $17 per day of the rental fee.

Once Kevin had checked his car in at the body shop and made the necessary arrangements, he had telephoned the Enterprise office. Within ten minutes, an Enterprise employee had driven to the repair shop to pick him up. They had returned to the Enterprise office where Kevin had completed the paperwork to rent a Chevy Lumina. He had driven the rental car for twelve days before the repair shop had completed work on his car.

"Don't know why Enterprise would be writing me now," Kevin thought. "The insurance company paid the $17 per day, and I paid the extra because the Lumina cost a little more than that. Wonder what the problem could be?"

Tracking Customer Satisfaction

Kevin tossed the mail on the passenger's seat and drove up the driveway. Once inside his house, he opened the Enterprise letter to find that it was a survey to determine how satisfied he was with his rental experience. The survey came with a cover letter that thanked him for using Enterprise and asked him to complete the survey so that the company could continue to improve its service. The survey itself was just one page with thirteen questions (see Exhibit 1).

Enterprise executives believe that the company has become the largest rental car company in the United States (in terms of revenue, number of cars in service, and number of rental locations), because of its laserlike focus on customer satisfaction, and because of its concentration on serving the home-city replacement market. Enterprise aims to serve customers like Kevin, who are involved in wrecks and suddenly find themselves without a car. While the more well-known companies such as Hertz and Avis battled for business in the cutthroat airport market, Enterprise quietly built its business by cultivating insurance agents and body-shop managers as referral agents, so that when one of their clients or customers needed a replacement vehicle, the agents would recommend Enterprise. Although such replacement rentals account for about 80 percent of Enterprise's business, the company also serves the discretionary market (leisure/vacation rentals) and the business market (renting cars to businesses for their short-term needs).

Throughout its history, Enterprise has followed the advice of its founder, Jack Taylor. Taylor believed that if the company took care of its customers first and its employees second, profits would follow. So the company tracks customer satisfaction carefully.

About one in twenty customers will receive a letter as Kevin did. The letters are mailed to customers selected at random about seven days following completion of a rental. On average, about 30 percent of the surveyed customers will return the completed survey in the enclosed postage-paid envelope. They mail the surveys to an outside service firm, which compiles the results and provides the company with monthly reports that employees in the branches can use to review their performance.

Continuous Improvement

Enterprise has been using the survey form for several years. However, its managers wonder what they could do to improve the survey. Should the survey ask more questions? What could the company do to improve the response rate? Is the mail questionnaire the best way to collect customer satisfaction data? Are there any sampling issues or response biases in its system?

Please mark the box that best reflects your response to each question.

	Completely Satisfied	Somewhat Satisfied	Neither Satisfied Nor Dissatisfied	Somewhat Dissatisfied	Completely Dissatisfied
1. Overall, how satisfied were you with your recent car rental from Enterprise on January 1, 2000?	☐	☐	☐	☐	☐

2. What, if anything, could Enterprise have done better? (*Please be specific*) ______________________________

3a. Did you experience any problems during the rental process? Yes ☐ No ☐

3b. If you mentioned any problems to Enterprise, did they resolve them to your satisfaction? Yes ☐ No ☐ Did not mention ☐

	Excellent	Good	Fair	Poor	N/A
4. If you personally called Enterprise to reserve a vehicle, how would you rate the telephone reservation process?	☐	☐	☐	☐	☐

	Both at start and end of rental	Just at start of rental	Just at end of rental	Neither time
5. Did you go to the Enterprise office	☐	☐	☐	☐
6. Did an Enterprise employee give you a ride to help with your transportation needs	☐	☐	☐	☐

7. After you arrived at the Enterprise office, how long did it take you to:	Less than 5 minutes	5–10 minutes	11–15 minutes	16–20 minutes	21–30 minutes	More than 30 minutes	N/A
♦ pick up your rental car?	☐	☐	☐	☐	☐	☐	☐
♦ return your rental car?	☐	☐	☐	☐	☐	☐	☐

8. How would you rate the ...	Excellent	Good	Fair	Poor	N/A
♦ timeliness with which you were either picked up at the start of the rental or dropped off afterwards?	☐	☐	☐	☐	☐
♦ timeliness with which the rental car was either brought to your location and left with you or picked up from your location afterwards?	☐	☐	☐	☐	☐
♦ Enterprise employee who handled your paperwork ...					
at the START of the rental?	☐	☐	☐	☐	☐
at the END of the rental?	☐	☐	☐	☐	☐
♦ mechanical condition of the car?	☐	☐	☐	☐	☐
♦ cleanliness of the car interior/exterior?	☐	☐	☐	☐	☐

	Yes	No	N/A
9. If you asked for a specific type or size of vehicle, was Enterprise able to meet your needs?	☐	☐	☐

	Car repairs due to accident	All other car repairs/ maintenance	Car was stolen	Business	Leisure/ vacation	Some other reason
10. For what reason did you rent this car?	☐	☐	☐	☐	☐	☐

	Definitely will call	Probably will call	Might or might not call	Probably will not call	Definitely will not call
11. The next time you need to pick up a rental car in the city or area in which you live, how likely are you to call Enterprise?	☐	☐	☐	☐	☐

	Once—this was first time	2 times	3–5 times	6–10 times	11 or more times
12. Approximately how many times in total have you rented from Enterprise (including this rental)?	☐	☐	☐	☐	☐

	0 times	1 time	2 times	3–5 times	6–10 times	11 or more times
13. Considering <u>all rental companies</u>, approximately how many times <u>within the past year</u> have you rented a car in the city or area in which you live (including this rental)?	☐	☐	☐	☐	☐	☐

Exhibit 1

Kevin glanced through his living room window at his BMW sitting in the driveway. "That's amazing," he thought, "you could never tell it had been in a wreck. The repair shop did a great job, and I'm satisfied with Enterprise also. Guess I should complete this survey to let the company know."

Discussion Questions

1. Analyze Enterprise's Service Quality Survey (Exhibit 1). What information is it trying to gather?
2. What are its research objectives?
3. What decisions has Enterprise made with regard to primary data collection: research approach, contact method, sampling plan, and research instruments.

Case 9 The Hunt Room: Change the Concept or Just the Decor?

The Rolling Hills Country Club is an established club in a major eastern city. Jimmy Johnson, the general manager of the Club, had just convened the regular weekly meeting of the executive committee. The first item on the agenda was The Hunt Room.

Hans Krueger, the food and beverage manager, claims that sales have been declining for the last five years. He states the overall concept of the room is excellent. There have been some minor upgrades (replacing the chairs and the carpet), but no major renovation has taken place since 1980. He feels it is time for a major renovation. He claims that the food, service, and pricing are fine, but the atmosphere has grown tired. He claims that the comment cards returned by the guests have been highly favorable. Mr. Krueger has submitted plans for a $250,000 renovation package. His package calls for an updating of the same concept.

Alice Whitaker, the catering manager, claims the concept is no longer viable. She states usage of the restaurant has dropped. She says the people who use the Hunt Room may still enjoy it, but a very small percentage of the members use the room. Jimmy Johnson is concerned that if the changes to the room are major he may lose the room's current customers and not be able to replace them with members drawn to the new concept. He is tending to side with Hans, viewing minor changes to the concept as a safe alterative.

The club has three restaurants: The Venetian Room, The Hunt Room, and The Terrace Room. The Venetian Room is the main dining room. It is a light open room that overlooks the golf course. Its menu is eclectic and includes a selection of European, American, and Asian cuisine. The average check in the Venetian room is $22 for lunch and $36 for dinner. The Hunt Room is the casual dining room. It has rich wood paneling, red leather chairs, and features paintings of hunting scenes on the walls. The Hunt Room's menu features beef, quail, and several seafood items. The average check is $32 for dinner. The Hunt Room closed for lunch in 1990, due to declining lunch sales. The Terrace Room is an informal room with the same menu for lunch and dinner. The menu is similar to one that might be found in a family oriented restaurant. It is on the ground floor and features a patio that is popular with members using the swimming the pool, who want more than the snack bar offers. The average check is $8 for breakfast, $10 for lunch, and $12 for dinner. Dinner business is very slow, except for the summer. In fact, Johnson is thinking of closing this room for dinner.

Referring to the Hunt Room, Alice Whitaker claims the club's members no longer want a heavy beef menu. She has also observed what she feels is a trend; members are seeking new dining experiences. They want excitement in the menus and would enjoy a room with a casual atmosphere. Additionally she claims that the restaurant prices have gradually crept up, and the restaurant is no longer considered casual dining. Those guests that want a casual meal usually end up in the Terrace Room or in a local restaurant. Ms. Whitaker feels the local restaurants offer better value for money.

Mr. Krueger responded by stating that the restaurant offers a much better value than it did when it opened. He claims that beef prices have risen by 140 percent since 1990, but he has absorbed some of these increases and menu prices have only increased by 100 percent. He further stated that he was not in competition with every restaurant in town—the club has prestige and members come here because it is their club. Krueger claims the club gives good value compared with the fine dining restaurants in town.

Jimmy Johnson did not want the discussion to escalate into an argument. He therefore tabled the discussion on the Hunt Room until more information could be obtained. He was also proceeding very carefully. He has only been at the club for two years. He has been able to maintain the status quo of the club but has not made any significant changes. The club's membership wait list has continued its downward trend. The club had an average wait of fours years in 1995, today the wait is eighteen months. Food and beverage sales have remained flat over the last three years, despite an average menu increase of 4 percent per annum. Jimmy feels he has "stabilized the club," but he has not been able to show increases in sales. He feels the turnaround has come, but also knows some board members are growing impatient. Thus, he feels a mistake with the new concept for the Hunt Room could cost him his job. He also knows many of the older board members enjoy the Hunt Room.

Another problem with the club is that the membership is aging. Most of the young members are sons or daughters of members. The club does not seem to attract members under forty. This makes it hard for Johnson to make changes as many of the older members do not want change, and the younger members who came to the club with their parents have grown used to it. They seem to like the club the way it is, yet they do not use the food and beverage facilities. Most of the younger members use the golf course and drop their children off at the pool. For the most part, their food and beverage sales are limited to the snack bars at the golf course and swimming pool.

Johnson ponders his options: do nothing, or try to keep things from declining. He knows preventing further declines is a significant accomplishment. However, he feels the board is looking for increases. If he makes a mistake with the Hunt Room, he will quickly lose his job. If he does nothing, he may be able to hang on for several more years but if he does not turn sales around eventually he will lose his job. *Note:* This is based on a real case; however, the names have been changed.

Discussion Questions

1. If you were the general manager, what process would you go through to determine a new concept for the Hunt Room?
2. What information would you seek? Where would you find this information?
3. What makes restaurant concepts grow out of favor? How often should a room be reconcepted?
4. Should club restaurants compete with local restaurants?
5. Brainstorm to come up with possible concepts for the Hunt Room. You should include decor and menu ideas.

Case 10 The Australian Tourist Commission

The Australian Tourist Commission (ATC) was planning a marketing research study within the United States. The plan had originated in the home office in Melbourne and was sent to regional offices for comment before soliciting bids. These regional offices were located in London, Frankfurt, New York, Los Angeles, Tokyo, and Auckland. Visitor traffic to Australia from the United States had grown at a slower rate than other major market areas. It was apparent that marketing strategies were needed to increase the number of American visitors to Australia. Before developing a new marketing plan, it was felt that a study should be conducted within the United States to identify target markets.

Research Objectives

Objectives had been identified for the study:

1. To identify and quantify groups in the U.S. population with the highest potential for holidaying in Australia.
2. To investigate in detail the factors that determine holiday destination choice among the high-potential groups.
3. To provide information indicating the types of holiday products taking into account time and cost factors, which would satisfy the holiday needs of the high-potential groups.
4. To investigate the awareness of and preferences for alternative destinations.
5. To provide information to guide publicity agencies as to the type of creative approaches that will appeal to and motivate the high-potential groups.
6. To provide a guide to media patterns that will enable efficient communication to the high-potential groups.
7. To identify the best distribution modes for holiday products aimed at the high-potential groups (e.g., airlines, travel agents, bank travel departments).
8. To investigate the role of the travel trade and its importance in determining holiday destination choice.
9. To determine past and intended future holiday behavior among the high-potential groups and to describe them in socioeconomic terms. Detailed information must be collected on the destinations visited on past trips and the sequence of these visits.

In addition to the objectives, the ATC felt that the study should be designed with the following purposes in mind:

- To enable the development of a comprehensive understanding of the destination selection process—essential if Australia is to be marketed more successfully in the United States.
- To enable the design of products of greatest appeal to the high-potential groups, in terms of cost, length of holiday, preferred standard of accommodation, and domestic transportation.
- To enable Australia to be promoted in a way that will capitalize on its perceived strengths, overcome its perceived weaknesses, and compete more effectively with the strengths and weaknesses of competing long-haul destinations.
- To provide an adequate measurement of the extent of awareness of and interest in various Australian features (e.g., the Barrier Reef, the outback, Sydney Harbor).
- To provide a detailed knowledge of the holiday planning process, including the time involved and the sources of information used.
- To enable more efficient communication and distribution of available products to the high-potential groups.

Proposed Methodology

It was the opinion of the ATC that the study should be divided into two stages. The first would be of a "qualitative" nature for the purpose of developing personality and attitudinal questions which would then be used in the second quantitative phase. The general opinion was that face-to-face interviews of thirty to thirty-five minutes each would be needed for both parts of the study. The use of telephone interviews was considered but rejected because it was feared that they could not provide the depth of answers needed, particularly as "trade-off" questions were being asked.

Due to the high cost of field research in the United States, it seemed imperative to minimize the sample size. Consequently, a total of 1,000 face-to-face interviews during the primary research were considered to be sufficient to provide good precision for estimates from the total sample and from the various subgroups.

The ATC felt that respondents should be selected on the basis of four criteria: (1) past travel experience, (2) future travel intentions, (3) travel desire, and (4) interest in Australia. Those who should be interviewed would include people who had never traveled and had no intention or desire to travel. The term travel was defined as long-haul international travel for pleasure purposes, excluding Mexico, Canada, and the Caribbean. In addition, people with immediate family living in Australia were to be excluded.

In the interests of efficiency, it was felt that the sample should over-represent key markets. Hence a screening process was to be used in the interviews. The screening questions were to be administered in sequential fashion, with the first criterion being "past travel experience." The sample structure emphasized those with extensive travel experience, as research indicated that this was a prime market for Australia. The recommended structure was:

- *Past travelers:* traveled in the last five years to a long-haul destination for pleasure, with or without a stated intention to travel.
  $N = 600$ broken down as:
  (a) At least 200 "experienced travelers"
  (b) At least 200 with "stated travel intention"
  (c) At least 200 with "interest in Australia"
- *Potential travelers:* stated intention to travel in the next three years, to a long-haul destination for pleasure, without past travel experience.
  $N = 300$ broken down as:
  (a) At least 100 whose primary intended destination is not U.K./Europe
  (b) At least 200 with "interest in Australia"
- Non/latent travelers:
  $N = 100$ comprising persons with no past travel experience and no stated intention to travel, but who:
  (a) Have an expressed desire to travel (to a long-haul destination for pleasure purposes)
  (b) Express an interest in visiting Australia

Although a random sampling technique was desired, the sample was to be heavily biased toward upper-income groups and not representative of the general mix of the U.S. population. Further sampling restrictions that were felt to be necessary included the following:

1. No interviews from persons who lived in rural areas or small urban centers.
2. Undersampling from the East Coast, with the exception of New York.
3. Undersampling from the southern states, with the exception of Florida.
4. Oversampling from California, Hawaii, New York, Texas, and Florida. The reason for this was an observation of incidence patterns based on data generated from past international visitor surveys by the ATC.
5. Use of a form of multistage sampling in which cities would be the primary unit. For reasons of cost, no more than twenty cities should be selected. This selection of cities should not be "purposive"; however, it should be a random selection of cities within the constraints specified below.

Responses

100	New York
50	Florida
50	Texas
150	California
100	Hawaii

50	New England
150	Eastern North Central
50	Western North Central
100	Other South Atlantic
50	Other Western South Central and Eastern South Central
100	Mountain
50	Pacific
1,000	

One of the reasons for the suggested sampling procedure was that the ATC had data on a large sample from the United States known as Travel Pulse plus data from an earlier ATC study known as the International Visitors Survey. It was felt that the new study should provide data that would be cross-comparable with the results from the previous studies.

U.S. Arrivals in Australia by Purpose of Visit (%)

Holiday	43
Visiting relatives	15
Business	23
Other	19
Total	100

Age of International Visitors to Australia (%)

0–4	8.3
15–24	14.5
25–34	20.4
35–49	23.5
50–64	22.3
65+	11.0

Occupations of International Visitors to Australia (%)

Professional (excluding teachers)	13.1
Teachers	3.5
Administrative workers	15.9
Clerical and sales workers	9.8
Service workers (including armed services)	3.9
Other	11.1
Inadequately described	5.8
Total (working persons)	63.1
Children (0–14 years)	8.3
Students (15 years and over)	4.8
Home duties	14.8
Independent means, pensioners, etc.	9.0
Total (nonworking persons)	36.9
Total	100.0

Seasonality of Foreign Arrivals to Australia Ranked by Number of Monthly Arrivals

	OCEANIA	AFRICA	AMERICAS	ASIA	EUROPE
January	7	6	5	5	3
February	6	4	3	4	12
March	4	2	4	3	10
April	3	8	7	8	4
May	9	9	11	11	5
June	11	12	12	12	9
July	2	7	10	7	6
August	12	11	8	10	2
September	5	10	9	9	8
October	10	5	6	6	7
November	8	1	1	1	11
December	1	3	2	2	1

Top Ten Origin Countries of Visitors to Australia (%)

New Zealand	28.9
U.K. and Ireland	14.6
United States	13.5
Japan	5.5
Papua New Guinea	4.4
Canada	3.2
Germany	2.7
Netherlands	1.9
Malaysia	1.8
Hong Kong	1.8

Regional Travel Patterns within the United States (Holiday Visitors per 100,000 Population)

Region/State	Visitors	Region/State	Visitors
East South Central	3.77	Mid Atlantic	10.56
Kentucky	3.9	New York	13.3
Tennessee	4.6	New Jersey	10.5
Alabama	3.6	Pennsylvania	6.4
Mississippi	2.4	East North Central	10.57
West South Central	9.06	Ohio	10.7
Arkansas	7.4	Indiana	8.6
Louisiana	3.4	Illinois	13.3
Oklahoma	12.6	Michigan	9.7
Texas	10.4	Wisconsin	7.3
Mountain	29.13	West North Central	14.67
Montana	28.4	Minnesota	18.3
Idaho	25.1	Iowa	14.6
Wyoming	10.8	Missouri	14.5
Colorado	28.1	North Dakota	8.7
New Mexico	22.8	South Dakota	13.4
Arizona	26.2	Nebraska	10.9
Utah	18.6	Kansas	13.5
Nevada	54.8	South Atlantic	11.12
Pacific	43.91	Delaware	6.6
Washington	33.0	Maryland	10.0
Oregon	29.9	District of Columbia	52.0
California	42.5	Virginia	7.3
Alaska	88.7	West Virginia	3.1
Hawaii	148.5	North Carolina	4.2
New England	9.06	South Carolina	4.8
Maine	5.4	Georgia	5.5
New Hampshire	2.4	Florida	23.7
Vermont	8.1		
Massachusetts	9.7		
Rhode Island	5.7		
Connecticut	11.8		

Discussion Questions

1. What is your opinion of the research objectives and purposes for the study?
2. What is your opinion of the proposed methodology?
3. Why do you suppose that travel to Australia from the United States was lower than desired? In answering this question, consider the cost of travel, time required, and other factors.
4. In your opinion, will information from the survey permit the ATC to address the issues raised in Question 3?

Case 11 Tanglewood Park: Vantage Golf Tournament

The Vantage championship golf tournament is in trouble with the county commissioners of Forsyth County, North Carolina. "As much as we value the Vantage tournament, when we look at the expenditure of county dollars going out and the fact that the intake of dollars from the tournament doesn't directly benefit the county, we have to have some limits," said Pete Brunstetter, chairman of the Forsyth County Commissioners.

Tanglewood Park has a budget of $4.8 million per year and golf is the primary moneymaker for the park, but over the past four years, Tanglewood has steadily lost money on its golf greens. In 1994, golfers paid about $1 million to play on the championship course where the Vantage is held. However, the amount of maintenance needed to keep this course in top shape and the loss of revenue when the course is shut down for repairs have created an economic problem. The general public who pays county taxes has been restricted from the greens to ensure that the course will be in shape for the Vantage tournament. Revenue from the championship course was expected to be $428,000 less in 1997 than in 1994. "We're trying to protect our investment," said Rich Schmidt, finance officer for the park.

The dilemma is that golfers who are viewed as "big-buck spenders" want to play where the pros play, said Francie Bray, director of marketing for the park. How much does the county get from these players and the thousands of visitors who attend the three-day tournament? Nobody knows! Officials with the County Tourism and Development Authority don't know and neither do officials of the Vantage tournament. They know that 30,000 people attend the tournament, but most are from Forsyth and surrounding counties.

So its doubtful that these people add much revenue to the county. They don't stay in hotels or make extra trips to the restaurant as a result of the tournament. Many observers feel that the only real spenders are the 500 people directly associated with the Vantage. That includes golfers, caddies, guests, and the media, said Richard Habegger, tournament director.

John Wise, general manager of the Adam's Mark Hotel in nearby Winston-Salem, said he expects some of the 615 rooms to be filled with tournament guests, but when asked how much the tournament helped, he said, "That's tough to say. If we didn't have the Vantage, we'd attract business from other events." An official from the Ramada Inn said that the 147 rooms for the tournament period were booked, but some had been sold to people attending weddings.

Despite a budget of $3 million by R. J. Reynolds to sponsor the Vantage, the company started the 1996 tournament with a $250,000 deficit. Tournament officials have noticed a slump in ticket sales and cut expenditures by airing the event on the Golf Channel rather than ESPN, which broadcast the event for ten years.

Pete Brunstetter said he wasn't certain of the future for the tournament but said that the county couldn't help to subsidize it. The lack of reliable statistics concerning the economic advantages of the tournament to the county and to the local visitor industry undoubtedly hurt. Elected officials responsible for the careful expenditure of tax money and professional managers of a county public park must support their decisions. The absence of reliable data make it nearly impossible to mount a defense the public will accept.

Source: Susan E. White, "Forsyth Isn't Reaping Enough from Golf Tourney, Many Say," *Winston-Salem Journal* September 7, 1997, pp. B1, B6.

Discussion Question For Chapter 5

1. The county commissioners need information to make a decision on the golf tournament. Using the marketing research process, develop a research plan that will provide the commissioners with the information they need.

For Chapter 18

1. Explain why it is important to develop information on the economic contribution of social events, both before and after the event.
2. What benefits will this tournament bring to the community?

Case 12 Gomez Executive Bus Service

After three months of operation, it was apparent that something needed to be done to increase the use of Gomez Executive Bus Service. The bus service was established to provide a new type of service between the two principal cities of Honduras (Tegucigalpa and San Pedro Sula). This service consisted of two nonstop trips each way. The trip was completed in three and one-half hours. Buses left from the Hotel Maya in Tegucigalpa and the Hotel Sula in San Pedro Sula. Trips began at 6:00 A.M. and 6:00 P.M. from both cities and arrived in the other at 9:30 A.M. and 9:30 P.M.

The Hotels Maya and Sula were considered to be the best hotels in each of the respective cities. They catered to business travelers, foreign tourists, and convention trade. Many of the guests lived in the United States, Europe, and Japan.

The buses were made by Mercedes-Benz and were considered to be the most comfortable and luxurious available anywhere with room for thirty-six passengers and a bar in the rear. A pair of uniformed and attractive young hostesses accompanied the passengers. During the trip, passengers were served their choice of free alcoholic beverages, soft drinks, coffee, tea, and sandwiches. Because the bus left from the best hotels in town, there was no reason for passengers ever to be exposed to long waiting periods in crowded bus terminals or to wait in long lines to purchase tickets. They could instead purchase tickets at a counter in the hotel lobby. Tickets were sold on a commission basis by a company that also sold sightseeing excursion trips. In the Hotel Maya, the service was advertised by the use of a hand-drawn sign about the size of ordinary notebook paper. The sign read:

BUS

EJECUTIVO

GOMEZ

SALE A SAN PEDRO SULA

6:00 A.M.

6:00 P.M.

Despite the fact that each bus had a capacity for thirty-six passengers, an average of only seven or eight were taking each trip. This was less than the number required for breakeven, which had been estimated at twelve.

Tegucigalpa, the capital of Honduras, had a population of approximately 300,000. San Pedro Sula, with 160,000 people, was known as the industrial center of Honduras. The highway between the two cities was in good condition. The countryside consisted of beautiful mountains and a few valleys.

Advertising

Prior to the beginning of the service and shortly thereafter, a series of newspaper advertisements was used in the two cities. These were later discontinued and television advertisements were used but were not scheduled for any particular program. The theme of the ads was directed to people who drove their cars between the two cities. Although a grand opening was never held, a total of fifty free tickets were sent to members of the press. It was not known if any of these tickets had been used, but as far as anyone could see, there had been no free publicity in any of the media. A free ticket was also sent to the Minister of Tourism, but no reply was received. A total of 400 letters were also sent to companies within San Pedro Sula and Tegucigalpa.

The typical customer who had been using the executive bus service came from the Honduran upper classes. There seemed to have been quite a bit of repeat business. The primary problem, according to Sr. Gomez, owner and manager, was a lack of advertising and publicity.

None of the passengers were tourists. It was felt that very few tourists came to Honduras simply to wander about as they do in Mexico and Europe. Most seemed to have a planned itinerary and prepurchased tickets for airline travel. The aid of an ad agency in helping to plan strategy had been dismissed because it was felt that no agency existed in Honduras that was sufficiently knowledgeable about marketing to assist in this project.

Pricing and Competition

To obtain permission for a new bus service from the Honduran government, Gomez was required to charge twice the regular fare charged by existing bus lines on this route. Four companies offered regular bus service between the two cities. These were San Juan, El Sol, Colombo, and Gomez. Each had its own bus terminal and ticket office.

- *El Sol.* The company El Sol offered bus service every two hours between the two cities. This service was generally considered good but not luxury class. Buses were not air conditioned nor was there service on board. There were also stops at small towns along the way. This company owned a small hotel in Tegucigalpa and would deliver and pick up customers directly from this hotel.
- *Colombo.* The service on this bus was nonstop and was considered to be very good, but buses were not air conditioned nor was there on-board service. Colombo owned a middle-class hotel in Tegucigalpa and picked up and delivered customers from this hotel.
- *San Juan.* This company offered service with stops between the two cities and ran every two hours. Service was generally considered average.

Airline Service

Commercial airline travel between the two cities was provided by SAHSA airlines. This airline was 40 percent owned by the ex-president of Honduras. The cost of single-class round-trip travel on SAHSA was five times the price of travel by the Gomez Executive Bus Service. The flight normally took twenty-five minutes, but Sr. Gomez felt that it was really a two-hour trip counting waiting time and trips to and from the airport. Flights were sometimes overbooked and canceled due to mechanical or weather problems.

It was also believed that a certain number of people were afraid to fly due to the difficult airport at Tegucigalpa. This airport had a short runway which literally ended on the edge of a mountain. There was no train service between the two cities, so the only other competitive means of travel was private auto. The distance between the two cities was 265 kilometers.

Although statistics were not available, it appeared that most of the customers of the Gomez Executive Bus Service paid for the ticket with their own funds. By contrast, it was felt that a great number of those who flew SAHSA did so with tickets purchased by their employers. It appeared as though SAHSA had chosen to ignore them, as the new bus service was not considered a threat by the management of SAHSA. Sr. Gomez believed that SAHSA was wrong and that he just needed time and the right marketing formula to experience success.

Discussion Questions

1. Why do you believe the Gomez Executive Bus Service has not yet reached the breakeven point?
2. Why do you believe that two competitive bus companies were vertically integrated with hotels?
3. What marketing strategies and tactics should Sr. Gomez use at this point?

Case 13 Hawaiian Sights

After nine months in operation, Hawaiian Sights was struggling to solicit support from tour operators. Despite earlier comments from many that this type of tour was needed and should sell without any problems, sales success had been elusive.

As a walking tour, Hawaiian Sights covered the least explored areas of "Olde Honolulu" ordinarily bypassed by tour buses: (1) the Civic and Historical Center, (2) downtown Honolulu, and (3) Chinatown. The tour allowed tourists to mingle and make friends with Hawaii's "real" people—away from Waikiki—and was viewed as an oral, historical excursion.

Tours began with an escort/guide meeting clients at a predetermined location in Waikiki. The group would board the city bus and disembark (twenty minutes later) in front of the state capital building. The narration continued for the next four hours. The group spent one hour for lunch and shopping on Fort Street Mall and returned to Waikiki on the city bus. The idea for Hawaiian Sights occurred to Evelyn Wako when she noticed that conventional city tours ignored the most important part of Hawaii, its people. The majority of tourists rode through Honolulu, viewing the city through bus windows. Evelyn felt that if tourists really wanted to learn about Hawaii, they had to get off those buses. Evelyn knew that walking tours were successful in Europe, so why not Hawaii?

The concept of a tour that forced customers to take the city bus and to walk was so different that operators of travel desks and travel agencies gave Hawaiian Sights little encouragement or cooperation. They also said that the original commission structure of 20 percent on a $20 (retail price) item did not produce enough revenue to interest them. Lunch was not included, but clients could eat at any of the restaurants or food concessions around the Fort Street Mall area. Tourists were encouraged to eat with the "natives" on benches in the tree-shaded mall. They could get to meet Hawaiians, observe life in Hawaii, feed the birds, or just be alone to shop in stores which were less expensive than those in Waikiki.

During each tour the escorts would board city buses with their groups at the Historical Center. Prior to boarding, the group was given a short briefing as to what would transpire. They were informed that more than 70 percent of Hawaii's population was "non-Caucasian." The tourists observed how the bus would change from a touristy one into a local bus the farther it moved away from Waikiki.

The unusual nature of Hawaiian Sights enabled it to be included in the tour brochures of several tour operators and two airlines. With sales lower than expected, Evelyn was searching for ways to advertise her tours. She felt that one way might be to distribute brochures to tourists on the street. She was thinking of hiring girls dressed in grass skirts to act as salesgirls. This was sure to bring some negative reaction from certain segments of the Hawaiian population. Evelyn knew that the hotel travel desks remained a key sales tool. Operators of one desk were negative from the beginning. They felt that their clientele were too upscale to ride the city bus.

Tourists who had taken the Hawaiian Sights walking tour rated it far superior to conventional bus tours. Hawaiian Sights offered a "satisfaction guaranteed or money back" guarantee, and so far no customer had expressed dissatisfaction. Despite this, Evelyn had not yet found a way to attract sufficient numbers of tourists to make the new business profitable.

Discussion Questions

1. Do you believe that Hawaiian Sights would appeal to most tourists who visit Hawaii? If not, why not?
2. What is the probable profile of the market segment for Hawaiian Sights?
3. What promotional techniques could Evelyn use to sell this tour to tourists? To the tour operators? To the clerks at the travel desks?
4. Why do you think the travel desks and travel operators have been unenthusiastic concerning Hawaiian Sights?
5. What do you think of Evelyn's idea to hire girls and dress them in hula skirts to distribute brochures on the sidewalks of Waikiki to passing tourists?

Case 14 Design of Web Sites in the Tourism Industry

Public Organizations

The Las Vegas Convention and Visitors Authority (LVCA) is the official destination marketing organization of Las Vegas. Its official Web site, *www.lasvegas24hours.com*, went on-line on August 1997. The site includes information about conventions, lodging, and attractions in Las Vegas. Initially, the purpose was solely one of providing an on-line brochure containing over 500 pages of information. No e-mail facilities were embedded in the site. In order to respond to a number of requests, these were included at a later stage.

The Web site has been running separately/independently from the overall marketing strategy of LVCA. In other words, it is not integrated within the Marketing Strategy and Communication Plan. LVCA's goal in promoting Las Vegas as a tourist destination is to further develop its brand image as the entertainment capital of the world. Thus, this goes beyond gaming, by including other attributes such as dining, shopping, shows, and so on. With the redesign of the Web site currently underway, it is also an intention to finally articulate it with advertising actions.

The LVCA collects the e-mail address from its Web site visitors. It also conducts short on-line surveys from time to time on visitors' satisfaction with the Web site. It has built databases for its three targeted segments: meeting planners, travel agents, and leisure consumers. The Web site currently experiences over 7,000 daily users. LVCA hasn't developed any demographic profiles for its Web site users. Actually, this is a major concern which is to be put into practice along with the redesign of the site.

LVCA collaborates offline with organizations from other regions, promoting the southwest of the United States as a triangle of complimentary attractions: Las Vegas, Grand Canyon, and the Southwest Pacific Coast (San Diego, CA). It cooperates on-line with other organizations within the region through related links with major hotels, tourism agencies, and the Nevada Commission on Tourism (*www.travelnevada.com*). LVCA is also part of a community of seventeen partners supporting the Web site *www.lasvegas.com* ("One City, One Site"), a profit site operated by the Donrey Media Group which also owns the *Las Vegas Review-Journal*.

Las Vegas major competitive destinations may be grouped into three categories:

- Leisure—Orlando, San Francisco, Los Angeles, New Orleans
- Conventions—Chicago, Atlanta, Orlando, New York
- Gaming—Atlantic City and (to some extent) Mississippi

Three entities are involved in the design of the Web site: the LVCA, a Web vendor (which has been changed), and an advertising agency. Most of the data maintenance of the Web site is done in-house by the Web manager. The Web site is updated on a weekly basis, and the site is now being subjected to a major revision by the first time (once in every two years).

The most important features of a Web site for destination marketing are considered to be user-friendliness and usefulness, that is, providing a good balance between graphics and functionality. The LVCA's revised

Web site will strengthen these characteristics, and will be more interactive.

The LVCA's site has some unique features, such as:

- Keyword Search and Calendar Search that are used by 75 percent of the visitors
- Hotel and Motel Search that is used by 60 percent of the visitors
- Weather page, which is also frequently used

The site has also Ipix photos.

The Nevada Commission on Tourism (NCOT) is the state agency dedicated to promoting tourism in the Silver State. Its mission is to offer a composite view of the state, to emphasize the promotion of rural areas, underlining Northern Nevada. The official Web site of the NCOT is *www.travelnevada.com*, which has been on-line for four years. The purpose is to make available to the traveler an on-line visitor center, providing more information and assisting him/her on planning a trip to Nevada. It aims to attract visitors to travel beyond Las Vegas or Reno, enticing them to extend their stay and go to other places.

The Web site has proven to help increase the number of inquiries about the state and to stimulate the growth in requests for the Visitors' Guide Booklet. Moreover, the site helped save some money on telemarketing (toll free 1-800 number), but not on print.

A research program for data collection is running which consists of sampling inquirers (telephone survey) in order to assess conversion ratios. Furthermore, the site has provided ongoing on-line surveys for its users. The NCOT collaborates offline with other organizations in the region as a member of the Western States Policy Tourism Council, which gathers eleven western states of the United States.

The major competitive destinations for Nevada are

- For the pleasure/leisure market—California (Anaheim-Disneyland), Florida (Orlando-Walt Disney World), Hawaii.
- For the gaming market—New Jersey (Atlantic City), Mississippi, other emerging states, including those expanding Indian gaming.
- For the conventions market—New York, Illinois (Chicago), Georgia (Atlanta), Florida (Orlando, Miami).

Both NCOT and an Advertising Agency have been involved in the design of the Web site. Its maintenance, updating, enhancement, and redesign is conducted through the ad agency. The site is redesigned once a year. This takes place when a new annual Nevada Visitors Guide/Booklet is published. Moreover, the site is updated every two months, namely, its Calendar of Events, which coincides with the publication of the *Nevada Magazine*. In addition, there is a new overall theme every month which is also addressed by the lieutenant counselor.

The most important feature of a Web site for destination marketing is to have content-rich, updated, and very complete information. NCOT's site provides information on Nevada broken into six territories. It has a comprehensive hotel/motel listing, as well as calendar of events in the state.

Private Companies

The main purpose of conducting Internet/on-line activity is to provide information on the different properties/resorts, as well as their services and prices, in order to entice users to make reservations and come to the resorts.

The major players in Las Vegas are the Mirage Resorts Group (Bellagio, Mirage, Treasure Island, Golden Nugget), Mandalay Bay Group (Mandalay Bay, Luxor, Excalibur), Park Place (Paris Las Vegas, Flamingo Hilton, Las Vegas Hilton, Circus Circus), MGM (MGM Grand, New York New York), Boyd Gaming Corporation (Stardust, Sam's Town, Fremont), and Harrah's.

Whereas the Las Vegas Convention and Visitors Authority's promotion gives more weight to conventions, the main resort groups emphasize the gaming/casino activity more.

It is generally agreed that the LVCVA should be in the centerpiece of offering a Web site portal for Las Vegas as a tourist destination. However, in reality two other sites have been in that position—*www.vegas.com* and *www.lasvegas.com*. The former is part of a large regional media group that includes the *Las Vegas Sun* newspaper, *Showbiz Weekly, Las Vegas Life, Las Vegas Weekly,* and *Las Vegas Golfer*. The latter is operated by the Donrey Media Group which also owns a major Las Vegas newspaper, the *Las Vegas Review Journal*. This site is run with the support of seventeen partners, primarily government agencies, including the LVCVA. Interestingly, *www.vegas.com* is given preference and considered more popular than *www.lasvegas.com* as a portal site to Las Vegas.

The design of the Web sites are usually outsourced. A number of senior executives are also involved. The maintenance and information updating is mostly done in-house.

The most important features of a Web site are considered as being:

- To be visually/graphically attractive
- To provide correct and up-to-date information
- To be interactive
- To enable chat lines and stimulate consumer comments
- To provide availability and booking on-line
- To develop the right promotion on-line to entice the transient guest by providing attractive offers, interactive tools (e.g., weather information, driving directions, what to do), and using banners for brand-image building
- To offer a toll-free number
- To capture data for conducting direct email campaigns. Retail databases are built with names and addresses of customers and prospects who visit the sites and inquire about further information.

Dotcoms

The portal sites for Las Vegas are clearly *www.vegas.com,* and *www.lasvegas.com*. They usually receive over 300,000 visitors with more than 4 million page views a month. However, they are facing increasing competition from other sites such as *www.lasvegascitysearch.com, www.cimedia.com* (a Cox Communications interactive media city guide), *www.virtualcities.com,* and Microsoft's SideWalk *(http://sidewalk.com)*. Actually, according to a recent research from Media Metrix (1999), a leader in Internet audience and digital media measurement, MSN Sidewalk has surpassed all competing on-line city guides in terms of consumer reach, achieving a reach of 7.3 percent, compared with other local guides such as Digital Cities, with a reach of 6.3 percent, and City Search, with a reach of 5.5 percent.

The dotcom sites are normally designed and maintained in-house. Major information updating takes place once a week (e.g., entertainment), whereas a lot of news is updated on a daily basis (e.g., classified ads, travelscape info).

The most important features of a Web site for destination marketing are seen as providing quality content/information current and complete on the destination (e.g., resorts, restaurants, show listings, dining weather), ease of navigation/usability, and booking facilities (hotels, flights). It is expected that in the near future the latter will be extended to also accommodate e-commerce on shows, restaurants, and sightseeing tours. Frequently Asked Questions and Bulletin Boards are also considered important characteristics.

Search Engine Positioning

Due to the clutter of sites available on the World Wide Web, DMOs ought to position themselves as the portals of their destinations. A sample search on the Yahoo! directory as well as on the other major search engines (AltaVista, HotBot/Lycos, Excite, Infoseek, WebCrawler, Northern Light) by typing the name "Las Vegas" as a key word resulted in the following numbers. The Yahoo! directory found 969 Web sites on Las Vegas. In number of Web pages, the Northern Light search engine found 1,313,971 pages on Las Vegas.

In terms of search engine positioning, *www.lasvegas.com* is by far the best positioned. It consistently appears on the top twenty Web sites on Las Vegas: AltaVista (1), Excite (3), Hotbot/Lycos (5), Infoseek (9), WebCrawler (14), and Northern Light (19). *www.vegas.com* comes ahead of *www.lasvegas.com* on Hotbot/Lycos (3) and Northern Light (17) but it does not show up on Excite, WebCrawler and AltaVista. *www.Lasvegas 24hours.com,* the official Web site of the LVCVA, is only visible in Altavista (11) and Infoseek (26).

Hyperlinks

Using the Alta Vista search engine, the actual number of Web sites hyperlinked with each of the main dotcoms were found as follows: (1) *www.vegas.com* (8,570); (2) *www.lasvegas.com* (1,938); (3) *www.lvol .com* (1,212); and (4) *www.lasvegas24hours.com* (1,017). Curiously, some hotel resorts have even more links, such as the MGM Grand (1,235). Other national dotcom companies have most of the highest number of links: City Search (8,232), Virtual Cities (4,899), Cimedia (2,438), and MSN Sidewalk (2,319).

Source: This case is courtesy of Paulo Rita, *paulo.rita@iscte.pt,* ISCTE–University of Lisbon, Portugal.

Discussion Questions

1. What types of organizational buyers will use the Internet for information? What type of information will they need?
2. What can a destination marketing organization do to make sure these potential planners will find the information they need?
3. Should a destination marketing organization try to have the dominant site for the destination they market or should they leave this up to private providers of hospitality and tourism services?

Case 15 Coconut Plantation Resort

The management of Blackfield Hawaii Corporation was faced with a decision concerning the most appropriate type of restaurant for its resort development. The new restaurant must complement the existing resort. Additionally, it should not replicate similar types in the immediate resort area. The new restaurant was planned as a freestanding 150- to 200-seat unit between beachfront hotels, condominium units, and the main highway. There was a divergence of opinion concerning what type of restaurant it should be. Suggestions that had been offered to Bob Cooper, vice president for corporate development, included a moderately priced family restaurant with all three meals, a deluxe tablecloth restaurant, a fast-food restaurant, a lunch and dinner steak and chops restaurant, and a specialty restaurant such as an Italian restaurant.

Description of Coconut Plantation Resort

Coconut Plantation Resort was located on the eastern coast of the island of Kauai, off Highway 56, less than two miles from the largest town, Kapaa, and approximately eight miles from Lihue. The Blackfield Hawaii Corporation, a land development company, specialized in developing commercial and residential properties. The company did not wish to become involved in the operational end of the business but preferred to develop properties for others to lease and operate.

The resort complex covered ninety acres of prime resort land with beach frontage. Hotels had been built on fifty acres. These included:

Holiday Inn	311 units
Kauai Beach Boy	243 units
Islander Inn	200 units

The remaining land was designated for condominiums, a shopping center known as the Market Place, two additional hotels, and the independent freestanding restaurant under question.

The condominiums and hotels were planned to have the following numbers of units:

- Hotels

Travelodge	350–400
Hawaiian Pacific Resort	297

- Condominiums
  Condominium Development 1,180
  (50% one-bedroom; 50% two-bedroom)
  Condominium Development 2 160
  (100% one-bedroom)

The Market Place shopping center had been fully completed and was in operation. It offered a variety of retail stores featuring Polynesian fashions, jewelry, scrimshaw (carved ivory), art goods, a twin-screen movie theater, various food outlets, and many other shops that appealed to tourists.

Restaurants within Coconut Plantation Resort

Several restaurants existed within Coconut Plantation Resort. These were located within the hotels and within or adjacent to the Market Place. Each of the three existing hotels had a restaurant, and each of the two new hotels would also contain restaurants. Restaurants located in or near the Market Place appeared to be well established and included:

- Fast foods
  Ice cream parlour
  Mexican outlet
  Chinese outlet
  Hamburger outlet
- Other
  Steaks, fish, chops
  Buzz's Steakhouse
  The Spindrifter
  J.J.'s Boiler Room

With the exception of the fast-food establishments and J.J.'s Boiler Room, all of the hotel restaurants and independent restaurants served three meals a day. Demand for breakfast had apparently reached market saturation. Buzz's Steakhouse was phasing out its breakfast service, and others, such as Holiday Inn and Spindrifter, had stretched their breakfast menu to span a brunch period. The Holiday Inn had recently initiated a special noontime buffet for Japanese tour groups.

All the restaurants operated on a limited-menu concept and featured steaks, chops, limited seafood, and a few other specialty items. There appeared to be little genuine diversification or originality in food service among the table service restaurants in Coconut Plantation Resort. All of the operations except the Kauai Beach Boy were chain based, where limited menus were a key to standardization and efficiency.

Description of Kauai

As the northernmost island in the chain of Hawaiian Islands, the island of Kauai is situated about twenty air minutes from Honolulu. Known as the "Garden Island" due to its lush foliage and beautiful tropical setting, the island offered an almost ideal climate, with average temperatures near the coast of 71°F in February and March and 79°F in August and September. Rainfall varied widely depending on location, but the summit of Waialeale was the wettest spot in the United States, with a recorded rainfall of 486 inches a year. Twenty miles away, Kekaha on the southern coast had an average rainfall of 20 inches per year. The normal annual rainfall in Lihue was about 40 inches per year. Most of this occurred between October and April, with January as the wettest month.

The island of Kauai constituted a county with a total resident population of about 35,000. The largest towns on Kauai were Kapaa, with approximately 3,600 residents, and Lihue, with about 3,100. The ethnic makeup of the resident population was Japanese, 27.5 percent; Filipino, 19.1 percent; Caucasian, 20.0 percent; Hawaiian and part Hawaiian, 18.4 percent; Chinese, 0.3 percent; mixed, 13.2 percent; and other, 1.1 percent.

Tourism on Kauai

Kauai was usually considered as the last island to be visited by tourists. Tour groups commonly arranged for it to be last, due to its unique beauty and Polynesian atmosphere. The island was also a popular weekend or short-holiday vacation site for residents of Honolulu. A mix of group (GIT) and nongroup travelers visited Kauai, but a majority (55%) were represented by independent travelers (ITs). These persons did not travel in a large group with a set itinerary and a prepurchased package of services.

Each of the resort hotels had at least one table service restaurant. These served three meals a day. The variety and quality of food and service tended to resemble those of the hotels in Coconut Plantation Resort. A Polynesian decor was common throughout these resorts. Although it was not unusual to find a different specialty dish associated with each restaurant, in general the menus were quite similar.

The nearest resort to Coconut Plantation Resort was the 416-room Coco Palms Resort, which was located less than two miles south. The Coco Palms was built in a grove of 100-year-old coconut palms on the grounds where Kauai's ancient kings held court. The decor of the Coco Palms was Polynesian, with thatched-roof cottages, flaming torches, drums, canoes, and other decor typical of the South Pacific. A restaurant known as Coconut Palace was located at the Coco Palms. This restaurant was frequently mentioned by travel writers, who referred to it as an "Award-Winning Restaurant." It featured Polynesian specialties such as *kupa hei maka* (green papaya soup).

Purchasing Habits of Condominium Users

The possible effect of condominium occupants on a new restaurant was felt to be a factor for consideration. A study had been conducted by the School of Travel Industry Management of the University of Hawaii and demonstrated that occupants of condominiums spent less in restaurants than was spent by occupants of hotels. It also showed that the amount spent in restaurants by this group declined as the length of stay increased. The restaurant eating habits of condominium occupants was restricted primarily to the main meal of the day.

Discussion Questions

1. What additional information, if any, is needed before selecting the type of restaurant to build?
2. What are the probable market targets for this restaurant?
3. What marketing strategy should be employed prior to opening?

Case 16 Outback Steakhouse: Breaking the Rules, Creating New Rules

Most people will include restaurants on their list of the toughest businesses in which to be successful. Thousands of restaurants compete for customers, ranging from giant chains to mom-and-pop, hole-in-the-wall eateries. Moreover, restaurant owners have tried everything. Catchy new ideas often spawn too-rapid growth or encourage imitators who steal customers.

Restaurant owners have learned from all the successes and failures, however, and certain rules for success have emerged. Find a good location, operate as many hours as possible to spread fixed costs, and keep food costs as low as possible. Control personnel costs. Design a highly centralized structure that leaves nothing to chance. Following these rules, so the conventional wisdom goes, increases chances for success.

Given this wisdom, it is surprising that *Inc.* magazine recently chose Outback Steakhouse's developers as the "Entrepreneurs of the Year." Outback seems to violate all the established rules. In fact, the chain uses the phrase "No Rules. Just Right." in its advertising. One might characterize its strategy, however, as "New Rules. Just Right."

Modest Ambitions

When Chris Sullivan and Robert Basham began to toy with the idea of starting a restaurant, they knew the industry's conventional wisdom well. Over a sixteen-year period, they had learned the business by working with the Steak & Ale chain, guiding Bennigan's growth from 32 to 140 units, and opening 17 Chili's restaurants. In 1987, they had modest ambitions when they used their own resources to open five restaurants in the Tampa area. They believed that these units, if successful, would support their lifestyles, leaving plenty of time for golf and boating.

Sullivan and Basham's research identified an opportunity in the steak house business. Despite consumers' widely publicized decisions to eat less red meat, both upscale steak houses and budget-priced chains such as Golden Corral were doing well. Consumers still liked to splurge by eating good steaks, and they wanted to eat those steaks in casual restaurants, not at home. Sullivan and Basham saw an opening for a midrange steak house with a causal atmosphere that targeted adults aged twenty-five to fifty-four. The two founders realized, however, that they needed to beef up their management team. They knew restaurant operations and how to cut real estate deals, but they needed a "food guy." They found him in Tim Gannon, a friend who had been successful in the New Orleans restaurant business. Gannon brought with him a collection of great recipes that he could teach young chefs to prepare quickly.

Finally, they needed a name. The movie *Crocodile Dundee II* was popular at the time, and Australia had a mystique that implied a friendly, casual approach to life. The team settled on Outback because consumers could remember the name easily, and it suggested a rugged, outdoorsy quality that would give the chain a point of differentiation.

Strategic Decisions

Having settled on the team, target market, concept, and name, the founders were ready to complete their strategy. First, they considered location. One major factor dictated location: Outback would offer only dinner—no breakfast, no lunch. This meant that Outback did not need to build in the high-rent center-city areas needed to attract the business lunch crowd. Instead, Outback searched for sites in suburban locations where people were at night. Because Outback was a destination, it could occupy a B location in an A market.

The dinner-only decision also meant that employees had to work only one shift a day. Managers could come in at 3:00 P.M. and leave by midnight. Many other restaurants experienced rapid turnover of managers because of six- to seven-day weeks and sweatshop hours. Outback prohibited its managers from working more than five days a week. The founders wanted the managers to have fuller personal lives and not to destroy their marriages.

Waiters, waitresses, and bartenders also liked the plan because they depended on tips, and they typically earned little tip money at lunch. Outback servers handled only three tables at a time, so they could provide excellent service. With tables that turned over in about an hour and an average $16 per person "ticket" including the bar tab, a server could earn up to $30 an hour in tips and $125 a night.

Serving only dinner meant that cooks focused on that meal. Tim Gannon observed that "when you're preparing food all day long, it diminishes the quality. When you have to prepare for only one shift, you can be flawless." Outback's limited menu also meant that it could focus on food quality. For example, the chain bought meat from only one supplier, and it demanded that the supplier purchase meat only from a selected area in Nebraska and Colorado. Gannon believed that these two areas produced the best steers. The chain used chicken that had never been frozen. It knew where to get the best onions, potatoes, and lettuce. Each restaurant had its own salad dressings, bread, and other items made from scratch. This emphasis on food quality produced higher-than-average food costs of 39 percent versus 36 percent or less from most restaurants. However, Outback provided generous portions and maintained its philosophy of moderately priced entrees.

The managers designed the typical Outback to occupy about 6,000 square feet, with the roomy kitchen accounting for more than half the space. The restaurants had only 220 seats. If they had more, the managers reasoned, food requests could swamp the kitchen and negatively affect service. Outback's logistics meant that a server could deliver a properly cooked steak twelve minutes after the steak order reached the kitchen, just as other waitstaff picked up the salad plates.

Outback designed a restaurant management system that would make managers act like owners and enable decentralized control. Each restaurant's manager invested $25,000 and signed a five-year contract. The manager earned a base salary plus 10 percent of the unit's cash flow, defined as earnings before taxes, interest, and depreciation/amortization. A unit serving 3,800 customers per week, reaping annual sales of $3.8 million, and generating a cash flow of $905,000, would yield a manager a salary and bonus package of over $135,000 per year, well above the industry average. Thus Outback's management turnover was only 5.4 percent versus 30 percent to 40 percent for the industry.

Being owners also meant that managers were picky about whom they hired. Instead of hiring experienced cooks and waitstaff they had to train to be friendly, they focused on hiring seventy-five to eighty friendly people they could train. There was no corporate-level human resources department. Corporate headquarters had only fifty-five people to oversee the 210 steak houses—the only management layer between manager and founders, versus an industry average of four to five layers.

Outback promoted its restaurants with extensive advertising on college campuses and at professional football, basketball, hockey, and golf events. The ads featured supermodel Rachel Hunter.

Paying Off

Conventional or not, Outback's strategy has paid off. In a recent survey, *Restaurants and Institutions* magazine gave Outback top honors for food quality and service. Outback also posted the strongest sales and unit growth rates for the casual steakhouse sector. The number two player, Lone Star Steakhouse, has only 104 units and average unit sales of $2.6 million, even though it offered both lunch and dinner. The strategy has also paid off for investors, who have seen the stock price jump from $3.50 per share at the initial public offering in 1991 to $39 in 2002. By the end of 2001, Outback had over 600 units and sales of almost $2 billion—not bad for three guys with modest ambitions.

Sources: Adapted from Jay Finegan, "Unconventional Wisdom," *Inc.* (December 1994): 44–54 (Copyright 1994 by Goldhirsh Group, Inc. Used with permission.); *www.outback.com,* accessed 6/3/02.

Discussion Questions

For Chapter 9

1. How did the design of the Outback Steakhouse help to ensure its success? Think about the atmospherics, the menu and food product, and the delivery process.

For Chapter 10

2. The Outback Steakhouse was designed with the internal, as well as the external customer in mind. Explain some of the design features that were related to the internal market (employees).

Case 17 The Grand Canyon Railway

One interesting feature of the southwestern United States is the area known as the "Four Corners," the only place in the United States where four states meet at one point. Within the 130,000 square miles of the Colorado Plateau in this region lie many wonders of nature. The plateau contains eight national parks, twenty national monuments, as well as numerous other nationally designated areas and huge tracts of national forests. This wealth of natural features and the cultures of the various Native American tribes in the region have made the area an important destination for tourists, especially those interested in natural history and culture.

The "crown jewel" for this region is generally considered to be the Grand Canyon, one of the seven natural wonders of the world. This wonder of nature is 190 miles long, one mile deep, and between 4 and 18 miles wide. The Grand Canyon covers 1,900 square miles of the Colorado Plateau and is home to 1,000 species of plants, 250 species of birds, and 70 species of animals. A number of Native American tribes are found in the region of the Grand Canyon, including the Hualapai, Hopi, Navajo, and Havasupai (who live on the floor of a side canyon).

The principal attraction to visitors is the sheer size and beauty of the canyon itself. The walls of the Grand Canyon are made up of many layers of rock, with widely varying textures, colors, and hues. This panorama of nature changes by the season, weather, and time of day. Generally, the morning and late afternoon offer the most striking views for visitors to the canyon. The South Rim in Grand Canyon National Park (Grand Canyon NP) is open year-round, whereas the North Rim (also in the park) is closed in winter. In the summer months, Grand Canyon NP becomes quite crowded with visitors and motor vehicles. Consideration is being given by the National Park Service to ban vehicles from the park and move visitors around the park by shuffle buses.

Williams, Arizona, serves as one important "jumping off" point for visitors traveling to Grand Canyon NP, with the South Rim of the canyon only fifty-nine miles north of the town. Williams is closely identified with travel to the canyon and has even registered the trademark "The Gateway to the Grand Canyon," which no others may use. At an elevation of 6,800 feet, Williams, by itself, has many attractions in the town and surrounding area such as lakes for swimming and fishing, horseback riding, and a downtown listed on the National Register of Historic Places. The surrounding Kaibab National Forest in the vicinity of Williams offers opportunities for camping, fishing, and hiking for both visitors and residents alike.

The town has for many years been an important transportation hub for both rail and highway. Williams is closely identified with Route 66, also known as the "Mother Road," that connected Chicago, Illinois and Santa Monica, California, long before the interstate highway system was developed. Williams has the last stretch of the original Route 66 bypassed by the interstate system (in this case, I-40). Even before highways became highly developed, Williams has served as a railroad terminal (since 1882) for the forerunners of the Atchison, Topeka, & the Santa Fe Railroad (Santa Fe); the latter continues to serve the town today with freight-only service.

The most popular way for visitors to get from either Williams or Flagstaff (thirty-two miles to the east) to Grand Canyon NP is by motor vehicle, although the pending restrictions on vehicles might be expected to change this somewhat. An attractive alternative for some visitors is to travel between Williams and the Grand Canyon by rail. The Grand Canyon Railway (GCRy) offers this option with one round-trip per day. This rail service, which operates purely as a tourist railroad, began operations in September 1989 and has provided daily service since that day (except for December 24 and 25).

Historically, rail service on this line began much earlier, but passenger service was abandoned in the 1960s due to economic pressures from the automobile. Freight service from the Santa Fe was abandoned in 1974, with no work performed on the track between Williams and the Grand Canyon until 1989. The work to get the GCRy running was monumental, because all engines and passenger cars had to be acquired and completely rebuilt. In addition, the depot at Williams and the adjoining Fray Marcos Hotel were in need of substantial refurbishing. In the depot, operating offices, ticket offices, a waiting room, and souvenir shop are found. All of this work was accomplished in a span of seven months to be ready for the September 1989 opening.

Today, the GCRy provides an interesting and nostalgic way for visitors to travel to the canyon. During the summer months, daily round-trip rail service is provided by steam locomotive, and in the winter diesel locomotives are used due to the severity of weather conditions. For all service, passengers travel in railcars that date from 1923 and are reconditioned to approximate that time period. Departure from Williams is at 9:30 A.M. and arrival at Grand Canyon NP is at 11:45 A.M., in the center of the park's historic district at the 1910 Grand Canyon Depot. The train departs from the Grand Canyon at 3:15 P.M. and arrives back in Williams at 5:30 P.M. No smoking is allowed on the train in any of the railcars.

Reservations can be made by calling a toll-free number, 1-800-THE TRAIN. Information about the train ride, but not reservations, is available on the railroad's website, *www.thetrain.com*. Different classes of service are offered to travelers, depending on the fare paid and the car in which a passenger rides. The basic coach service is priced at $49.50 per adult and $19.50 per child. Snacks are available for purchase; Diet Coke and Coke are complimentary in this class, with the latter served in GCRy keepsake bottles. Club Class, which includes the availability of alcoholic beverages and complimentary coffee and pastries in the morning, is priced at an additional $14.50.

The Coconino Main Class provides recliner chairs, a full continental breakfast, appetizers and champagne in the afternoon, and the availability of alcoholic beverages for an additional $49.50 per person. Coconino Dome Class represents a further upgrade. The service level is the same as Coconino Main Class, but passengers ride in an upper level enclosed dome, which provides unsurpassed views of the surrounding landscape. The highest class of service, Chief Class, is provided in a railcar with an open-air rear platform; complimentary continental breakfast, coffee, tea, and juice are provided in the morning and champagne and appetizers in the afternoon. This class of service is priced at an additional $64.50 per person.

For all classes, the entrance fee to Grand Canyon NP is an additional charge. Other services are also available from the GCRy for additional charges. Continental breakfast is served in the terminal for $5.95 per person until the train departs. Narrated motorcoach tours of the South Rim of the Grand Canyon are available from the Fred Harvey Transportation Company (the concessionaire for Grand Canyon NP) of varying lengths, some of which include lunch. Packages are available which may include one or two nights at the Fray Marcos Hotel in Williams and one night at a hotel in Grand Canyon NP. During the ride from/to Williams many natural and man-made venues can be seen. There is formal narration for some of these venues and a printed guide is available for purchase, which describes these sights and provides a history of the GCRy. Interestingly, only a very limited view of the Grand Canyon is available from the train just as it arrives at and departs from the park. In Coach Class, each railcar has an attendant who serves beverages (Coke and Diet Coke), goes around with snacks for sale, and engages in conversations with the passengers. During the summer, many of these attendants are college students on break from their studies.

The Grand Canyon Railway uses costumed performers in a number of different ways to simulate an earlier time period. Before the train departs from Williams, performers stage an "Old West" gunfight, just as was found some 100 years ago. Performers also move among the railcars, often singing songs of the "Old West," during the trip to the Grand Canyon. Passengers are encouraged to sing along with the performers. All of the performers are costumed in the type of dress found at the "turn-of-the-century."

On the return trip, the activities are slightly different. A group of performers stage a train robbery, just as was found during earlier times in the southwestern United States. Passengers are included in portions of the action, but none are actually robbed. Eventually, the sheriff captures the train robbers and takes them away to be put in jail. Passengers, especially younger children, enjoy this activity, which makes the trip back to Williams seem much shorter than it actually is. The other activity that some engage in is to take a nap, because many are tired due to their activities at the high altitude and in the low humidity of the Colorado Plateau.

A recent survey conducted by the GCRy found that many passengers rate their train trip experience as excellent. Perhaps just as important, these passengers say that they would recommend the GCRy trip to friends. Additionally, the most satisfied passengers were likely to return again. Passenger satisfaction derives from the varied experiences received during the round-trip ride and the Grand Canyon itself, with the latter experience not under control of the GCRy but rather the National Park Service.

This case was prepared by Dr. Fredrick M. Collison and is intended for classroom use. The situations portrayed here do not imply either effective or ineffective management on the part of the Grand Canyon Railway. The case was written based on published materials of the railroad, the National Park Service, the *Williams-Grand Canyon News,* and the author's personal experience.

Discussion Questions

1. What are the components of the product offered by the GCRy and received by the passengers?
2. How appropriate are the components of the product that you mentioned in Question one?
3. In what ways does the GCRy contribute to the marketing to travelers of Williams, Grand Canyon NP, and the surrounding Colorado Plateau?
4. Would you take this train ride? Why or why not?

Case 18 New Zealand Heritage Park

Heritage Park in Auckland, New Zealand, was designed as New Zealand's first and only tourist theme park. It was modeled to international standards but was not intended to become another Disneyland-style operation. The park's purpose was to present a 100 percent New Zealand content in as lively and dynamic a way as possible and to encourage visitors to participate, not merely observe. The operation hoped to establish itself quickly as a major tourist attraction and also to plan an important role in encouraging visitors to venture out and see the real New Zealand for themselves.

Conceptualization

New Zealand Heritage Park (NZHP) was the idea of Terry Beckett, who formulated the concept with the realization of New Zealand's tourist potential and the lack of entertainment facilities to accommodate them. The planning phase for the NZHP involved input from two groups of internationally renowned theme park consultants. The first, Economic Research Association (ERA), was based in San Francisco and had performed over 130 studies for Disneyland and worked on projects for Universal Studios and Knotts Berry Farm.

The Product

The attractions within the park represented the three main themes around which the park revolved:

1. *Natureworld.* This included displays of native plants and animals. Native birds were housed in a large free-flight aviary which allowed visitors to walk through. There were trout pools that could be viewed from above and below the surface, swamplands, and two islands in the man-made lake, which included a children's playground.
2. *Agriworld.* This featured various aspects of New Zealand's farming, horticulture, and forestry and included deer and a number of farm animals, some of which formed part of the park's farm show. There was also a period sawmill, a giant kauri log, and gum digging and goldpanning displays.
3. *Cultureworld.* This was designed to display aspects of the nation's Maori culture, including their heritage, history, and legends. Included in this area were carving and weaving displays and an audiovisual show. There was also a professional Maori concert party performing songs and dances.

The park also offered a restaurant, serving New Zealand food and wines, various snack bars, a souvenir shop selling native products such as Maori carvings, and a miniature golf course. The participatory nature of the park was emphasized in such activities as gold panning, wood carving, and weaving, which visitors were encouraged to try.

Pricing

The park opened initially with admission prices of $7 per adult and $3.50 per child, with those under five years old free. There was also a fee for admission to the Maori concert party, set at $3 and $1.50 for adults and children, respectively. Research revealed that this price was perceived as being too high (mainly by residents of Auckland, who were the major patrons of the park at the time). There was a downward revision to $6 for adults with all children free. The admission fee to the concert was dropped. However, the admission price was still perceived as being too expensive, and a further adjustment resulted in a $5 adult and a $2.50 child's admission. Beckett felt the price was extremely reasonable considering the fact that the park was a four-hour experience and many other tourist attractions in the Auckland area enjoying patronage for only one-fourth of that time were charging comparable rates.

Promotion

Promotion of NZHP was aimed at two major groups: New Zealanders, either out-of-towners or residents within the Auckland area, and overseas tourists. Advertising to the former group was a relatively simple matter with a number of newspaper advertisements. One series was designed to increase awareness of the park and the other to advertise special features and events. This group was not intended to be the park's major market segment.

Promotion to overseas tourists was different. NZHP prepared a trade pack, including a personalized letter of introduction from Beckett, a selection of brochures and pamphlets providing information on park features, the summer and winter program of activities, restaurant menus, and park charges. There was also a schedule of commission arrangements for travel agents. This pack was distributed to selected travel agents in the defined overseas target markets of the United States, Japan, and Australia.

Overseas missions were organized to the various New Zealand tourist and publicity departments in conjunction with the inbound tour operators' council. Beckett saw these missions as fulfilling three objectives: the promotion of New Zealand as a tourist destination, the promotion of Auckland as a tourist stopover, and the promotion of NZHP as a tourist attraction. One such venture was the inclusion of six Cultureworld employees in an August tourist and publicity department Asian mission to Kuala Lumpur, Singapore, Bangkok, and Jakarta. Other promotions for NZHP included the production of a video about the park for distribution to all New Zealand overseas tourist offices and for show on inbound cruise ships before docking in Auckland. There was additional advertising in the Air New Zealand and JAL in-flight magazines.

Promotion was also aimed at tourists in Auckland. Beckett scored what he considered to be a major coup in being allowed to deposit pamphlets in the guest rooms of Auckland's premier hotel, the Regent. A joint promotional campaign was launched in conjunction with three other tourist attractions: Victoria Park Market, Kelly Tarleton's Walk-Through Sea Aquarium, and Harbour Cruises on Board the Pride of Auckland. Each attraction actively promoted the others, and a concession ticket to all four was introduced with a free bus link. The latter project provided immediate success in boosting attendance. The relative effects of other promotional efforts had yet to be felt because there was up to 12 months' lead time before material had fully filtered through the overseas distribution.

Markets

In the first eight months of operation, the largest market was New Zealanders. However, Beckett expected this situation to alter with the dissemination of promotional material overseas. He believed that Australians would become the largest per capita market, followed by Americans and then the Japanese, although he stated that the U.S. market would provide the greatest returns in terms of per capita expenditure.

Research for the months of July and August revealed the following approximate visitor percentages:

Auckland residents	50
Other New Zealand residents	5
Schools and special-interest groups	10
Overseas tourists	35

Of the overseas tourists, Australians represented approximately 51 percent, Americans 19 percent, and Japanese 10 percent of the total. The remaining 20 percent were from other sources.

Source: This case was written by Kim Ng and Lawrence Hughes, Master of Commerce students at the University of Auckland under the direction of Dr. James C. Makens.

Discussion Questions

1. In your opinion, has New Zealand Heritage Park selected the right market targets?
2. Why do you suppose attendance has been slow from overseas visitors?
3. What additional promotional strategies/tactics should the park use to attract overseas visitors?
4. What is your opinion of the pricing employed by the park?

Case 19 Pricing Almost Destroys and Then Saves a Local Restaurant

"As I pulled into the gravel parking lot I knew immediately that the Mexicatessan was a warm, friendly Mexican restaurant. There was nothing new here and I don't mean that in a negative way. Nothing looked new but it all looked comfortable, well worn with the passage of time. The front entrance is laden with business cards stapled over the last 30 years. A World War II photo of the owner adorns one wall and Mexican motifs line the walls and ceiling right next to the window air conditioners. Somehow this all looked familiar, although I knew I had never been to the Mexicatessan before."

This is how Sally Bernstein, the restaurant reviewer for the *Houston Post,* described the Mexicatessan in an article celebrating the restaurant's thirtieth birthday. Mr. and Mrs. Herrera established the Mexicatessan in 1957. The restaurant, located in a lower-middle-class neighborhood, attracts both locals and Houston's rich and famous. In the early 1980s, the restaurant's profitability started to drop. Herrera worked long, hard hours producing a high-quality product that his customers enjoyed, but he received very little reward for his time and investment. He had a good product, a good location, and a strong following. The problem was pricing. The prices at the Mexicatessan were far below those of the competition. Herrera wanted to offer good value, and he felt that he had to keep his prices below the chains. He used price to gain a competitive advantage against the chain's expensive buildings and their large regional advertising budgets.

Instead of attracting and maintaining loyal customers, the Mexicatessan's low prices almost destroyed the business. The prices were not high enough to produce sufficient cash flow to keep the restaurant in good repair. Herrera was unable to receive financial reward for his efforts. After several years of struggling, the owner commissioned a research project to see how he could increase his cash flow. The research suggested that his prices were 50 percent less than those of the competition, even though his customers thought the food quality was better. Herrera decided to increase his prices so that they were only 10 percent less than the competition. He felt this price difference and his food quality would offset the competitive advantages of the chains. He set out to achieve his strategy through a series of planned price increases. Because achieving his target would mean price increases of 70 percent or more on some items, the first price increase was about 25 percent, with subsequent price increases gradually moving him to his desired pricing levels. Over a three-year period from 1982 to 1985, the menu prices increased by 40 percent to 70 percent. This was a bold move at a time when Houston was in the middle of a decade-long recession.

After the price increases, the Mexicatessan's revenues increased at a higher percentage than the price increases, indicating that there was little resistance to the price increases. Herrera's customers still thought they were getting good value. The price increases allowed him to put a new roof on the building, hire additional staff, decorate the restaurant's interior, and receive a good return on his investment. This case study demonstrates the importance of price. Operations that charge too little often do not have money to maintain the business, although they have many customers and appear prosperous.

Herrera was lucky. It is easier to move up the price of a product that is underpriced than it is to lower the price of an overpriced product. Companies that overcharge create a negative attitude among those who have tried their products. Even when prices are lowered, customer attitudes may remain unchanged. Pricing must be a carefully planned management process.

Discussion Questions

1. Why was Mr. Herrera reluctant to raise his prices? How did these low prices almost destroy the business?
2. Using this case as an example, explain how the concepts of demand, price, and profits are interrelated.

Case 20 US Airways: The Airline Price Wars

Suppose you wanted to fly from Seattle to San Jose, California. The fare in June 1995 would have been $22; in 1997, it would have been $59. The fare from Detroit to Minneapolis—which is roughly the same distance—would have been $126. Obviously, airlines don't set their fares based on distance. So, why do these fares vary so greatly?

One reason is the contrast between operations of discount airlines such as Southwest (the Seattle-to-San Jose route) and a major airline such as Northwest Airlines (Detroit to Minneapolis). Southwest Airlines (known as the Love Line because its original home was Love Field in Dallas, Texas) is a no-frills airline. It offers no food services, complimentary drinks, extensive baggage handling, or other amenities. It flies a limited number of direct, usually short, routes, carefully selecting its routes based on the popularity of the flights. If lots of passengers normally take a certain route, then Southwest might choose to operate only on that route. Also, Southwest frequently flies into alternative airports rather than the most popular airport. The Seattle-to-San Jose route is a good example of a Southwest route. There are many passengers flying from Seattle to the San Francisco Bay area of California. So, Southwest cuts fares on that route to lure passengers, and cuts costs by flying into a nearby alternative airport—in this case, San Jose.

When Southwest began operations at Seattle, competing airlines routinely charged fares to San Francisco ranging from $89 to $119. Southwest entered with prices between $39 and $59. One of the local airlines reduced its prices to $25, and Southwest responded with $22. How did this price-war tactic work? Not so well. After instituting the $22 fare, a 137-seat Southwest Boeing pulled away from the gate in Seattle with only nineteen passengers on board. The revenue from the flight was $418, compared with a cost of $6,567.04—not exactly a recipe for success. Things were so bad that the flight attendant jokingly asked passengers to shift to one side of the plane so that when they taxied past the competition, it would look like the plane was full. Even if the airplane had been full, revenues would not have covered half the cost of the flight.

If fare wars result in such losses, why do airlines engage in them? The primary cause is relatively flat air traffic growth. Although the number of flyers grew rapidly after World War II, the rate of growth slowed greatly in the 1980s and 1990s. In 1991, the number of airline seats sold actually declined. Facing lower traffic, airlines cut routes and parked surplus aircraft in the Southwestern deserts. Cut-rate companies then leased these surplus planes at low rates and went into business. So, reductions by the major airlines actually provided the inexpensive planes that fueled competition. As competition increased in a flat market, fares had to decline, with the result that many major and discount lines were forced into bankruptcy, including Eastern, TWA, Braniff, and Mark Air.

This explains the situation in Detroit, where you would probably have been flying Northwest Airlines, not a discount airline. Because Northwest carries 74 percent of Detroit's outbound passengers, it has a lock on the Detroit to Minneapolis route. With little competition, it can charge higher prices. In fact, Northwest is the nation's highest-priced airline.

"Any passenger who pays more than 30 cents a mile is probably being overcharged," asserts Tim Hannegan, assistant director for aviation competition for the General Accounting Office, watchdog for the U.S. Congress on federal programs. Using data from 1996, *Consumer Reports* evaluated mileage and fares. Northwest's average cost for flights up to 300 miles was 68 cents per mile. Examples of other Northwest fares and mileage are Detroit to Traverse City, \$154 or 74 cents a mile; Detroit to Kalamazoo, \$228 or 90 cents a mile; and Detroit to Grand Rapids, \$135 or \$1.12 per mile. According to the *Consumer Reports* study, US Airways was the second most expensive airline at 58 cents a mile, and Southwest was the least expensive at 17 cents a mile. Northwest called the study's data flawed, saying that the study ignored fixed costs for flights on routes with few passengers, which raises its overall costs. To get the kind of lock on an airport and routes that Northwest has in Detroit requires airlines to service all routes, not just the most popular ones.

Not only is Northwest expensive, travelers also give it low ratings on factors such as on-time arrivals, ease of airport check-in, and convenience of scheduling. A survey of business travelers on nine major carriers, conducted by J. D. Powers and Associates, found Northwest below average in customer satisfaction for flights under 500 miles and only average for longer flights. The best-rated airlines were Continental, TWA, United, American, and Southwest. All this suggests that competition among airlines results in lower fares and better service.

Airlines don't compete only on price. They also offer special promotions. For example, Southwest has launched a mileage war in which it gives fliers in the Rapid Rewards Program double mileage credits on flights between twenty selected Western cities. That means that a flier might qualify for a free flight by flying Southwest only four times in one year. Other airlines have used tie-in offers. For example, in a recent promotion, anyone purchasing an Aurora Limited Production Numbered Gold Roller Ball pen in a specified time period received 500 bonus Delta SkyMiles. Purchasers of an Aurora Sole Three-Piece Pen set received 1,000 bonus miles. Sometimes multiple airlines will participate in a promotion. Customers who purchased a 35mm Samsung camera received a thirty-two-page Travel Saver booklet offering discounts on travel, including a certificate for \$500 in airfare discounts good for several airlines.

With all this competition, how can an airline get a "lock" on an airport? Usually, the airline uses the airport as a hub. When it first negotiated with the airport. The airline may have contracted to provide service on a large number of routes and to use most of the available gates. In return, the airport was assured of a steady stream of revenue from the airline and avoided the need to negotiate with a large number of airlines. Over time, however, passenger traffic grows, and many airports expand so that they have more gates than are needed by the main airline. This creates a situation in which discounters and other airlines might enter the market. However, the major airline still has competitive weapons that it can use to defend its market.

The most obvious weapons are price, size, and lots of cash. Consider the situation that existed in Charlotte, North Carolina. Charlotte, with 1.2 million inhabitants, is the second largest city in the Southeast, but its Douglas International airport had no discount airlines. The Atlanta-to-Charlotte route was heavily traveled and expensive. Douglas International even had twenty-one available gates out of the total of sixty-four. This seemed to be a ripe situation for a discount airline such as ValuJet. Yet ValuJet chose at first to ignore the Charlotte market, instead starting service on routes producing much less business than would have been realized between Charlotte and Atlanta.

Why did ValuJet avoid Charlotte? The most formidable obstacle in Charlotte was US Airways Group, which had 94 percent of all flights into and out Charlotte. If a discounter enters the market, US Airways will cut fares to defend its market. A fare war actually would be more costly to US Airways than to ValuJet, because US Airways has much higher costs than ValuJet. However, US Airways had the cash to survive a long fare war—ValuJet did not.

But fares and costs are not the whole story. US Airways also had connections to many other cities to which passengers wanted to travel. So, although US Airways cost more, it was also more convenient for flyers. Notes Ray Martin, sales manager for Southern Bag Corporation, "You can get back home quickly and easily." That is very important to the business travelers, who make up only 48 percent of air travelers but who account for 66 percent of airline revenues. Without access to connecting flights, a discounter would have trouble cracking the Charlotte market unless it also established flights to Atlanta, Washington, New York, and other popular destinations.

Another factor is the willingness of communities to offer incentives to airlines. "We're starting to see a lot of support from communities that know we have other choices," says David Ulmer, vice president of planning for ValuJet. For example, in Newport News, Virginia, a city-operated economic development group paid ValuJet $1.9 million. In Jackson, Mississippi, the Chamber of Commerce provided free advertising for the airline. With so many cities anxious for their services, discounters can pick and choose where they want to go. There is no need to enter a sustained battle with a major airline such as USAirways in Charlotte.

Eventually, however, the easy pickings ran out, and ValuJet chose to enter the Charlotte market anyway. To do so, it had to offer fares that were 68 percent below those of USAirways and Delta—its major competitors. Moreover, neither the airport nor the city used financial incentives to lure ValuJet—they didn't want to upset their contracts with USAirways. Of course, USAirways responded with lower prices so that, eventually, lower fares will prevail on the more popular routes, but it may mean higher fares on less popular routes.

Sources: Rick Brooks, "Flying to Charlotte Is Easy—but It Isn't Cheap," *Wall Street Journal,* June 14, 1995, p. S1; Jim Frederick, "The Chaos Theory of Airline Pricing," *Working Woman* (March 1997): 30–33; Sean Griffin, "Southwest Airlines Cuts Fares for Flights between Western Cities," *News Tribune,* May 7, 1997, p. 507B; Greg Jaffe, "ValuJet Air Plans Service to Charlotte," *Wall Street Journal,* January 24, 1996, p. S1; Stacy Perman, "What Cheap Seats?" *Time,* July 14, 1997, p. 63; Joan M. Steinauer, "A Case for Incentives," *Incentive,* July 1997, p. 19; Gerry Volgenau, "Northwest Airlines under Fire for Prices on Flights," *Detroit Free Press,* June 18, 1997, p. 6.

Discussion Questions

1. What internal and external factors affect pricing decisions in the airline industry?
2. What marketing objectives have the various airlines selected?
3. Which airline industry costs are fixed and which are variable? What implications does this cost structure hold for airline operations?
4. What is the nature of demand and competition in the airline industry? Does demand differ between the business and leisure segments?
5. What pricing and other marketing recommendations would you make to USAirways to help it protect its markets?

Case 21 Winter at Zion Lodge

Zion National Park (ZNP) is located in southwestern Utah at the edge of the Colorado Plateau, within an area that also contains Bryce Canyon, Capitol Reef, and Canyonlands National Parks, as well as Glen Canyon National Recreation Area. To the south of ZNP in Arizona lies Lake Mead National Recreation Area and Grand Canyon National Park, with the North Rim two and one-half hours away and the South Rim five hours away.

ZNP was originally established as Mukuntuweap National Monument in 1909, incorporated into Zion National Monument in 1918, and became a national park in 1919. The Kolob Canyons section of the park, which is accessed by a separate entrance to ZNP, was added in 1939. ZNP covers approximately 230 square miles and consists of towering cliffs and canyons of multihued rock formations. The elevation varies from about 3,700 feet at the floor of the canyon to over 8,700 feet.

The main access to the park is provided by I-15 from the west, an interstate highway that connects Los Angeles (8 1/4 hours, 430 miles away), Las Vegas (3 hours, 155 miles), and Salt Lake City (5 3/4 hours, 310 miles). I-15 also continues northward to the U.S.-Canadian border in Montana. Access from the east of ZNP is via Utah Route 9 and the Zion-Mt. Carmel Highway, which connects the park with Bryce Canyon and Grand Canyon (North Rim) National Parks.

Park Description

The ZNP area was originally inhabited by Ancestral Puebloans (formerly called the Anasazi) from as long as 2,000 years ago. In recent times, the Paiute Indians dwelled in the canyon area, followed more recently by Mormon settlers who occupied the canyon beginning in the mid-1800s. Traces remain throughout the park of all three groups of inhabitants, although the park is being allowed to revert to its natural state. ZNP was established to protect the unique flora, fauna, and geology of this region of the Colorado Plateau.

Within ZNP are found some 75 species of mammals, 270 species of birds, and 800 species of plants, a few of which are found nowhere else in the world. Visitors can see sedimentary rock formations that tower up to 4,000 feet above the floor of the canyon. The walls often consist of multihued layers that flow along the cliff faces. In the Kolob Canyons section of ZNP is found the largest natural stone arch in the world. Winter can bring an additional accent to the rock formations when snowfall provides a white blanket to some of the park's geological features. Additional information can be found at the park's Web site, *www.nps.gov/zion*. Information about the surrounding area, including lodging, dining, and shopping in the nearby towns of Springdale, Mt. Carmel in Junction, and Kanab can be found at *www.zionpark.com*.

Lodge Facilities

Zion Lodge lies on the main road through the southern portion of ZNP, approximately three miles north of the Visitor Center. Amfac Parks and Resorts operates Zion Lodge, since becoming the concessionaire in 1968 with the purchase of the Fred Harvey Company. Fred Harvey and his firm were instrumental in the development of numerous restaurants and hotels in the U.S. southwest, especially at some of the better known national parks. The name, however, lives on in Amfac's retail division, the Fred Harvey Trading Company. As part of its contract with the National Park Service, Amfac uses 10 percent of its revenue for property improvements.

The lodge consists of a number of individual buildings. The main lodge building contains the visitor reception area, dining room, gift shop, snack bar (open during the peak season), and administrative offices. The reception area is staffed twenty-four hours per day and contains a large open area with comfortable seating. This main lodge has been undergoing renovation and restoration to retain the European character of the original building that was destroyed by fire and immediately rebuilt in 1966.

Accommodations at Zion Lodge consist of three types of rooms. Two large, two-story motel-style buildings contain eighty-one guestrooms. Standard motel rooms contain one or two queen beds and can accommodate up to five adults. Motel suites consist of a king size bed with a queen sleeper sofa in an adjoining sitting room. All motel rooms include a private bathroom with amenities such as a hairdryer and basic toiletries. Rollaway beds are available for any of the motel rooms. All the motel rooms are handicap accessible, as is the main lodge and dining room.

Forty cabin-style accommodations, which were recently renovated, are available in separate buildings of either two or four units each, all with a private porch. Each cabin unit is furnished with two double beds, private bath, walk-in vanity and closet area, and bath amenities as found in the motel units. The most striking features of the cabins are vaulted ceilings and a sitting area with a gas log fireplace that lights with the flip of a switch, a most welcome amenity on a cold winter night.

Reservations for the lodge can be made through Amfac's central reservation system, either via telephone or its Web site (*www.amfac.com*). Amfac also manages other park-type lodging, including those at Grand Canyon, Bryce Canyon, Yellowstone, Everglades, and Death Valley National Parks, and a number of other facilities throughout the United States. All reservations must be guaranteed for one night via a credit card such as American Express, Discover, JCB, MasterCard, or Visa. Amfac does not guarantee the room rate, which is subject to approval by the National Park Service.

The basic room rates for the 2002–2003 winter season are found in the table below. The rates for the holiday periods 12/23/02 through 01/03/03 and 02/11/03 through 02/16/03 are $10 higher for each room category. Additional persons in a room beyond two are charged $5 per person, with up to three additional occupants in a motel room and up to two additional occupants in a cabin unit. Children sixteen and under are not charged the additional per person rate, but are subject to the maximum occupancy limits. A package rate is available at $79 per night for a motel room and $89 per night for a cabin unit that includes dinner for two (entree with soup or salad, nonalcoholic beverage, and dessert), not including tax or gratuity. Rates during following peak season are $90 per night for a motel room and $100 per night for a cabin unit, both double occupancy.

The gift shop is located on the first floor of the main lodge building, just off the lobby and reception area. The shop offers a wide range of merchandise for sale, including clothing items such as T-shirts, sweatshirts, hats, caps, and gloves, most bearing the ZNP logo or name. Souvenirs include various food items such as tea, hot chocolate, candy, and the like, all bearing the Fred Harvey Trading Company name. The shop also offers authentic handmade items of the Native American cultures of the region, including silver and turquoise jewelry and Kachina dolls.

TYPE OF ACCOMMODATION	1 OR 2 ADULTS	3 ADULTS	4 ADULTS	5 ADULTS
Motel Room	$107	$117	$127	$137
Western Cabin	$116	$126	$136	N/A
Motel Suite	$135	$145	$155	N/A

Notes: 1. Rates are applicable for 12/01/02–12/22/02, 01/04/03–02/07/03, and 02/17/03–03/17/03.

2. Rates do not include Utah tax.
3. Children sixteen and under stay at no extra charge, but are included in the count of number of room occupants.
4. Base rates for the holiday periods 12/23/02–01/03/03 and 02/11/03–02/16/03 are $10 greater than those shown above.

Sources: Zion Lodge, *Rates & Policies.* Retrieved 6/3/02 from *www.zionlodge.com/accommodations/011B_rates_policies.htm.*

Items are carefully labeled to indicate which are truly authentic reproductions made by crafts people of the area.

Dining

The dining room is located on the second floor of the main building, with access by either stairs or an elevator. The room is finished in natural wood, with large picture windows providing panoramic views of one of the canyon walls. Historic pictures of Zion Lodge and ZNP are found on the perimeter walls of the dining room. The dining room serves three meals per day, with some variation in hours between the summer and winter seasons.

Hearty breakfasts are served beginning at 7:00 A.M. during the winter. Entree items include French toast, omelets, eggs with bacon, sausage, or ham. All these items include home-fried potatoes. Many side items such as fruit juice, fresh fruit, hot or cold cereal, and beverages such as coffee or tea are also available. The price for breakfast entrees ranges from approximately $2.95 to $6.95. Lunch is served beginning at 11:00 A.M. during the winter season. Soup, hamburgers, other sandwiches, and salads make up the main items available at lunch, which can at times be busy as tour buses may stop at the lodge for a lunch break. Prices for lunch vary between $1.95 and $8.95.

Dinner is served from 5:30 until 8:00 P.M. during the winter, with reservations required (the only meal with this requirement). A number of specialties are offered, including broiled yellowfin tuna (ahi), N.Y. strip steak, or St. Louis–style baby back ribs. One signature entree of the lodge's restaurant is Utah red mountain trout. Side dishes include pasta, French fries, and a baked sweet potato with accompanying cinnamon-flavored butter. On the lighter side, one can even choose a buffalo burger with accompanying side.

Entrees at dinner are priced from $7.95 to $15.95, exclusive of beverage and dessert. As part of the winter package for two, soup or salad, entree, beverage, and dessert are included, not including tax and gratuity. Desserts include a hot fudge sundae, mud pie, and cake.

This case was prepared by Dr. Frederick M. Collison and is intended for classroom use. The situations portrayed here do not imply either effective or ineffective management on the part of the National Park Service (NPS) or Amfac Parks and Resorts (Amfac). The case was written based on published materials of the NPS and Amfac, Web sites of these organizations, and the author's personal experience. Used with permission.

Case Assignment: Develop Promotional Plan

Option 1. As a major class project develop a promotional plan for the Zion Lodge. Use the Internet and other sources of information to develop the plan.

Option 2. Develop a promotional idea for Zion Lodge.

Case 22 World View Travel, Inc.

The president and the general manager of World View Travel were discussing the possible need for new strategies to meet increased competition and to take advantage of a market they both regarded as unsaturated.

History of the Company

World View Travel was located in a southwestern U.S. city of 150,000 population and was owned by Rene Townsend and her husband, Bob. Although Bob was a full partner, he continued to work full time in his career as a pathologist and did not participate in active management of the company. Rene served as president and shared management responsibilities with Sylvia Franklin, the general manager.

After ten years of operation, World View had become the largest travel agency in town. Prior to establishing World View, Rene had worked two years for a competitive travel agency. At that time only two travel agencies existed in town, with eight or nine employees each. The growth of World View had been fairly constant and some in the industry regarded it as extraordinary. In the first year of operation, World View recorded over $1 million in billings. Growth occurred each subsequent year, despite the existence of two recessions in the 10 years.

City Location

The southwestern city in which World View was located consisted of approximately 150,000 residents with approximately 30 percent classified as minority. The largest part of the minority population were Mexican Americans. Blacks represented approximately one-fourth of the minority group.

The city was heavily represented by a middle class, and although there were lower-income areas, there were surprisingly few areas that could be regarded as slums. This was due to a combination of a good industrial base, good public administration, and a civic pride among the residents. There were four major employers in the area and many smaller ones. The city was corporate headquarters for a company listed on the New York Stock Exchange and one listed on the American Exchange. These were involved in electronics and pharmaceuticals.

The predominant industries in the city were banking-finance, insurance, pharmaceuticals, and electronics. The city also boasted a large medical complex which attracted many patients from outside the area and two universities. The city was located on a major interstate highway and was served by three major airlines and two commuter airlines. Two national hotel chains operated downtown properties, and several chains operated motels along the interstate highway.

Competition

Eleven travel agencies existed in the city. One of these was an in-house agency for the largest employer in town. Consequently, very little direct business was generated by this company for any of the ten independent agencies. All the agencies offered a mixture of services and were not particularly distinguishable in terms of product offering or market segments served. The largest increase in numbers of travel agencies had occurred three or four years earlier, and there currently seemed to be relative stability in the industry. There were no rumors of new firms opening in town or major expansion by competitors.

Description of World View Travel

After establishing World View Travel, Rene personally called on companies in the area and asked for their travel business. This approach proved to be so successful that after only three years of operation, her agency was as large as that of any competitor. Most of the calls were made to people who Rene or her husband knew through prior business or social settings. Rene admitted to having a distaste for "cold calls" to organizations and firms unknown to her and preferred to call persons with whom a prior contact of some kind had been established. In several cases these were referrals by friends or satisfied clients. Time after time she was told by the prospect that this was the first time the owner or manager of a travel agency had ever asked for their business.

Location

The location of World View was not conducive to walk-in. World View leased space in a new office building located on a side street in a light industrial park. The street was not a thoroughfare and dead ended in a cul-de-sac. A sign in front identified World View Travel but was not large or particularly distinct from the signs of neighboring businesses.

Client Mix

The mix of billings for World View was approximately 56 percent commercial and 44 percent group and individual. Of the commercial accounts, six clients had billings of $500,000 or more. These were the larger companies in town. World View did most of the travel business for the second-largest employer in town. However, Rene said that this business was not evenly distributed among all departments within the company. She was certain there were two or three major departments within the client company that did not deal with World View.

The rest of the commercial business came from a mixture of small- and medium-size companies. Rene emphasized that she had purposely tried to have a large mix of commercial clients. She stated that it was likely that on a time-per-client basis, the sales productivity and earnings were less for small clients than for large ones and felt that from a standpoint of the bottom line, her agency would probably be better off with fewer of the smaller commercial clients and more of the larger ones. For instance, "We probably could get every bit of the business of the second-largest employer in town. However, that frightens us since we would then have too many of our eggs in one basket. At this point, we feel we're better off with a larger number of corporate clients, even if some are relatively unproductive."

Revenue comparisons between international and domestic billings revealed that revenue from all international billings contributed 15 percent while domestic contributed 85 percent. Nearly all the services performed by World View could be considered as outbound. A small percentage consisted of making local reservations for corporate clients and helping with inbound groups such as sales meetings and seminars in which corporate clients brought visitors to the local area.

In reviewing the current customer and product mix, Rene commented that she felt commercial business would be significantly more important in the future. The failure of other agencies to gain reputations as strong corporate service firms meant that World View could strengthen its relationship with the area's major employers, resulting in more travel billings. Rene also expressed interest in moving toward the meeting and convention planning business on both an inbound and an outbound basis. She believed that corporate clients were receptive to professional outside assistance in this area and that in the future professional fees could be charged for this service. If a decision was made to expand in this area, changes or additions to the number of sales personnel would be needed.

Advertising and Promotion

Advertising was not regarded as an activity that deserved a heavy budget appropriation. Rene confined advertising to the Yellow Pages. Advertisements were purchased in high school annuals and theater programs, but these were regarded as contributions in terms of their effect on sales. A limited number of baggage tags and flight bags were purchased which had the name World View, but these were limited in quantity and given only to selected clients. Rene felt that the best advertising was word-of-mouth referrals based on professional service for clients.

A special corporate relations program existed which seemed to have been very successful. This consisted of the following factors:

1. A free $100,000 automatic free flight insurance policy for corporate clients who flew on tickets issued by World View.
2. A corporate-rate hotel program. A handbook of nearly 350 pages was given to all corporate clients. This contained names of hotels and the best corporate rates available to them.
3. An emergency 800 number that could be used in case of a travel problem anywhere in the United States.
4. A special training program for executive secretaries to acquaint them with the basics of business travel. This seminar was conducted at the offices of World View and had been popular with executive secretaries.
5. A regular newsletter that was sent to clients.
6. The addition of a special staff person to recheck all fares to ensure the lowest cost to the client.
7. A computer-generated statistical capability to assist major clients in analyzing their travel expenditures and trends.

The Future

The past ten years had been rewarding ones for World View. Rene and Bob were confident that their travel agency was as well equipped to meet future opportunities and challenges as any in town. Rene spoke very encouragingly of the future. She felt that the most difficult years were behind and that the future offered excellent opportunities for growth. Rene summarized her feelings by saying, "World View Travel may look quite different ten or even five years from now, but we intend to remain the leading travel agency in this area. In fact, there is no reason we have to confine our plans to this area. We proved we were capable of success in this market and there is no reason we can't think in broader terms. We have the organization, the know-how, and the desire to grow; its just a matter of setting our objectives, deciding on a strategy, and getting on with the task."

Discussion Questions

1. How would you describe World View Travel? What kind of agency is it?
2. What kind of an image do you feel this agency has?
3. What do you consider to be the primary strengths and weaknesses of this agency?
4. What are the primary target markets for World View in the next year? The next five years?
5. Which of the four marketing "Ps" (product/package, price, place, promotion) have contributed directly to the success of World View?
6. Which of the following general strategies should World View employ: sell out, retrench, do nothing/status quo, or planned growth?
7. If you believe World View Travel should adopt a marketing plan for continued growth, which strategy or strategies should the agency employ?

Use the chart below to answer question 7.

	YES	NO
A. Product		
1. Product line extension (use same product mix but go after new market segments)?		
Why?		
2. Product offering expansion?		
Examples:		
New product		
Examples:		
Will we need to find new market segments?		
If so, what are they?		
B. Place		
1. A centralized strategy?		
Why?		
2. A decentralized strategy?		
Why?		
C. Promotion		
Paid advertising:		
To reinforce corporate image?		
To sell products?		
If yes, what kinds?		

Case 23 McDonald's: Where to Go from Here?

Who doesn't remember "You deserve a break today" or "Two all beef patties, special sauce, lettuce, cheese..."? Although we haven't heard these slogans in a long while, they nudge our memories and cause a host of thoughts and feelings to flood our consciousness. They might evoke memories of scenes from specific ads—shots of juicy burgers and crispy French fries, or of McDonald's birthday parties when we were young, or of dinner out with our folks. These slogans did what they were supposed to do. They got our attention, caused us to think positively about the product, and left us with warm, fuzzy feelings about the brand. In doing so, they may have caused us to think, "We haven't been to McDonald's for a while—let's go there for lunch."

But can you recall any recent McDonald's ad campaigns or slogans? Probably not, and that's a problem for McDonald's. If you can remember ads, do they give you a warm, fuzzy feeling? Again, probably not. Lately McDonald's advertising hasn't been particularly memorable and sales—particularly breakfast sales— have been in a slump for several years.

To attack this sales slump, in 1997 McDonald's instituted Campaign '55. In this campaign, some items, such as the Egg McMuffin, the Big Mac, and other sandwiches were put on sale for '55 cents. In order to get the advertised item at 55 cents, however, customers had to buy French fries and a large drink at regular prices. This confused many consumers who had not realized that they had to purchase the other items. In addition, it meant that they usually ended up spending about $3, more than they had intended. To many consumers, the special prices were not all that special.

To inform consumers about Campaign '55, Leo Burnett created ads using the tag line "My McDonald's." The content of these ads changed from month to month to promote the changing specials—for example, Quarter Pounders instead of Big Macs were featured. Originally, the ad agency had planned to use price comparisons. However, comparisons were difficult because consumers couldn't really get advertised products for 55 cents without spending more money on other items.

Why was the 55-cent price chosen? In a word, nostalgia. McDonald's was founded in 1955. The consumer was supposed to think about the McDonald's that they had known over the years and develop a warm glow that would be reinforced by getting burgers at unbelievably low prices. Unfortunately, because it was confusing to consumers, the campaign didn't work as intended. Instead of feeling good about an inexpensive burger, many consumers fell baited by a "false promise of a 55-cent burger." Once they'd had a negative experience with the 55-cent special, they reacted negatively to future advertising for a "new" 55-cent deal. Instead of increasing as expected, sales initially slumped as Campaign '55 went into effect. Only months later did sales increase, and then only by about one percent.

Contrast the Campaign '55 experience with McDonald's Teenie Beanie Babies and Monopoly promotions earlier in the year. Both of these were highly successful—especially the Beanie Babies. Stores initially had trouble keeping up with the demand for Beanie Babies, and sales soared by 15.4 percent in the first month. By comparison, for the Campaign '55 special, some stores initially experienced sales decreases of as much as 6 percent.

Why did some promotions work so well and the other not at all? One answer can be found in the nature of the promotions. The Beanie Babies and Monopoly promotions were clear-cut (if you already knew how to play Monopoly!); they created little consumer confusion. They involved free merchandise rather than reduced prices, and the Beanie Babies promotion was aimed at children.

Who really likes McDonald's? The fast-food giant's major market is children and young adults. Children can't respond to a nostalgia campaign featuring prices based on McDonald's founding. Most of our warm feelings about McDonald's were created when we were young, not when we were older. Campaign '55 was aimed at adults, what some analyst's view as a lesser McDonald's market. However, McDonald's seems to have had trouble getting that message. In 1996, it introduced the Arch Deluxe in an effort to appeal to adults. The Arch Deluxe was supposed to be a more "sophisticated" adult sandwich—one that children would not want. Ads created by Leo Burnett showed children wrinkling up their nose at the Arch Deluxe. This not-so-subtly communicated the message that the Arch Deluxe was for adults. But if adults got the message, it didn't make them flock to McDonald's.

Changing lifestyles, changing consumer preferences, the absence of distinctive products, and the relatively bland taste of most of its products appear to be bigger problems for McDonald's than the current sales slump. The traditional fast-food market has been young families who want to feed their children inexpensively. But lately, the population has aged and couples are having children at a later age, which means they have higher earnings and may be less price sensitive. These smart shoppers are looking for more than just a burger at a low price.

Over the years, McDonald's has not changed its image greatly. Although the company has modernized its restaurants, it still uses the same basic design with the golden arches. The menu board is now so crowded that customers sometimes find it difficult to locate the items they seek. "McDonald's is not an advertising problem; it's much more a strategy problem," says marketing consultant Jack Trout. "You're looking at a decade of floundering and trying to be everything for everybody. There's been no focus." Trout is referring to the company's many changes in advertising themes and shifts in campaigns between adults and children.

In an attempt to refocus, McDonald's recently put its main advertising account up for grabs, and DDB Needham won the account that had formerly belonged to the Leo Burnett agency. DDB Needham landed the account with the slogan "Did someone say McDonald's"? Switching ad agencies may refocus Mcdonald's advertising on celebrating the experience of eating there. This is important in the restaurant industry. "There's no question we can move a lot of customers through our doors when we lower the price," said Brad Ball, a senior vice president at McDonald's. "But customer after customer says price is not the number 1 driver. McDonald's happens to be in the restaurant business, but the experience you have with the food goes way beyond what it is you're eating."

A copywriter at DDB Needham penned the famous "Two all beef patties..." slogan years ago. So a return to Needham should usher in a new era of advertising for McDonald's. The ad firm has been asked to "reconfirm and redefine the brand positioning of McDonald's, what it is and what it should be" says Mr. Ball. To do this, DDB Needham will have to work with Leo Burnett, which retains control over marketing to children, including the Ronald McDonald ads. Thus, the two firms will have to work together to redefine McDonald's.

In 1996, McDonald's gave Fallon McElligott, a Minneapolis advertising agency, the opportunity to update its image. That agency created a series of ads aimed at the adult market. One ad featured Ronald McDonald in a bar chatting up women—with beer visible in the background. For obvious reasons, this ad never made it to the television screen. Thus, the answer is not as simple as pitching McDonald's to adults in "an adult way."

DDB Needham will have a difficult task in redefining McDonald's in the "Did someone say McDonald's?" campaign. It will have lots of money to spend—the majority of the $500 million that McDonald's anticipates spending. But to be successful, the agency will have to decide what to say, whom to say it to, and how to say it, questions that have eluded answers for a decade.

Sources: Sally Goll Beatty and Richard Gibson, "In Latest Flip Flop, McDonald's Orders Up New Agency," *Wall Street Journal,* July 30, 1997, pp. B1, B2; Richard Gibson, "McDonald's Franchisees Approve Cuts in Some Sandwich Prices to 55 Cents," *Wall Street Journal,* March 3, 1997, p. B4; Richard Gibson, "McDonald's 'Campaign '55' Promotion to Be Clarified and Advertised More," *Wall Street Journal,* May 20, 1997, p. B1; Richard Gibson, "McDonald's Aims to End Confusion about Promotion," *Wall Street Journal,* May 23, 1997, p. B1.

Discussion Questions

1. What were the objectives of the various McDonald's campaigns discussed in the case of "You deserve a break today," "Two all beef patties...," Campaign '55, Beanie Babies, and Monopoly?
2. How could McDonald's have pretested the Campaign '55 advertising?
3. What suggestions do you have for McDonald's new advertising campaign? Try creating some different types of advertisements using the "Did someone say McDonald's?" slogan.
4. What recommendations would you make regarding future sales promotions for McDonald's?

Case 24 Tropicana Fishing Lodge

How does a fishing lodge fit into our operations as a major producer of bananas? This was the question that faced the Costa Rican division of an international banana company.

Location and Description of Tropicana

Tropicana was a fishing lodge located on the Caribbean coast of Costa Rica. It was situated on the banks of the River Pastura. It could be reached by light plane, as there was a paved landing strip on the nearby properties of Del Monte. It could also be reached by means of a mountain highway from San José. This road was 98 percent paved and required approximately three to three and one-half hours of travel. Fog could be a problem on this road and could impede travel. A small dock had been built to accommodate loading and unloading the boats. A series of steps, including rather steep steel ones with a rope handhold, led to the grassy bank above.

Immediately behind the lodge was a banana plantation. A cement sidewalk separated the plantation from the lodge and homes. The grounds surrounding the lodge were well kept and quite attractive. The beauty was not dramatic or awe inspiring, but was instead peaceful and relaxing. Jungle growth could be seen on the opposite bank of the river, and monkeys could be heard howling in the forest.

The lodge was built in the fashion of a jungle building—it was not constructed on the ground but on wooden stilts. This allowed ventilation and helped to prevent rotting. It also helped to discourage insects and small animals from entering. The lodge was small but would accommodate twenty-two guests. Guest rooms were contained in a separate cabin that formed an "L" to the main lodge. The rooms were clean and well maintained. Each room had a bathroom with a shower and other bathroom fixtures. Beds were of the single bed or bunk-bed style. There was no air conditioning in the rooms, but the evening breeze was pleasant. A light blanket was sometimes necessary.

Recreational Facilities

Fishing for tarpon and snook was the primary entertainment offered by Tropicana. This occurred in the intercoastal canal which ran from Limón to the Nicaraguan border. It was also done in lagoons and the mouths of rivers. The river in front of Tropicana offered little opportunity for fishing; it was necessary to go downstream thirty to forty minutes by boat to reach fishing sites.

Three principal areas were noted for tarpon and snook. One was in a lagoon forty minutes downstream and to the south of Tropicana. Another was downstream and north of Tropicana near the village of Parismi-nas. This was forty-five minutes to one hour away and was near a competitor's lodge. The third was much farther north, in the area of Toruguero. This was roughly one and one-half hours away.

The scenery in the intercoastal canal and along the jungle rivers was beautiful. One could see a variety of birdlife, including many rare species. Monkeys could be heard and sometimes seen in the trees. Both Walt Disney and Jacques Costeau had made movies featuring the region. Crocodiles were difficult to see. Deer, marguary, jaguar, and many small animals also lived there but were rarely seen. Botanists and other nature lovers could find hours of enjoyment in the variety of trees, flowers, orchids, and other plant life, including a perfume tree that filled the air with a beautiful aroma in the evening.

There was little or no opportunity to exploit commercial hunting in the area. The area was not known for ducks or geese, and the deer were quite small. In addition, much of the area was gradually being turned into national parks, and wildlife would be protected. Swimming or water skiing in the lagoons and intercoastal waterway would be dangerous due to submerged logs. There was also the possibility of sharks. The Caribbean coast represented miles of uninhabited dark sand beach. It had palm trees and was attractive but was not developed. Moreover, it was very difficult to reach the beach from Tropicana. The surf at the mouth of the river was too strong to permit entry into the sea with the flat-bottom boats and motors. Thus the boats could not be used for ocean fishing.

Any large-scale building projects such as a large lodge, modern tennis courts, or a golf course would require land. This would almost certainly have to come from land that was profitably planted in bananas.

Fishing Season

Although Tropicana remained open all year, guests were advised that fishing was impossible from November 1 to January 15. This was the time of year when the heaviest rains occurred. The longest periods of dry weather were from the latter part of January through most of May and then again from August through October. The single best month for snook fishing occurred in late August until November 1. A schedule of the best fishing months versus the traditional months of high occupancy at Tropicana follows. This schedule presented certain difficulties in promoting Tropicana as a year-round lodge. During the months May through August, Tropicana had to compete with vacation areas in the United States. September and October represented excellent months for fishing but relatively weak ones for occupancy due to the fact that school was open in the United States. In addition, these were fall months in the United States, with nice weather conditions there. November and December were winter months in the United States and could be promoted as vacation months, but fishing was impossible during that time. Increased promotion would be necessary to reduce the dependency on three to five months of natural draw. November, December, and half of January would remain poor months due to weather and fishing conditions. Thus Tropicana would face, at a maximum, nine favorable months.

MONTH	FISHING CONDITIONS	FIVE HIGHEST MONTHS OF OCCUPANCY AT TROPICANA (APPROXIMATELY 80% OF TOTAL OCCUPANCY)
January	Good	
February	Excellent	1
March	Fair	2
April	Fair	3
May	Excellent	
June	Excellent	
July	Good	
August	Good	
September	Excellent	4
October	Excellent	5
November	Bad	
December	Bad	

Value of Lodge

It was difficult to estimate the market value of the lodge, but Eric estimated that it would probably be valued somewhere between $150,000 and $250,000 (U.S.). A difficulty in appraising the lodge was that its success was tied directly to the banana company, which owned and operated the source of electrical power for the lodge. A buyer might find this factor of concern. However, a generator and an independent well would not be difficult to acquire.

Competitors

- *Azul Grande*. The fishing lodge of Azul Grande was the primary competitor and could accommodate twenty-four guests. This lodge was located in the fishing village of Parisminas and could be reached only by private airplane or boat. It was not as attractive as Tropicana. It was surrounded by poor fishing shacks, and was older in appearance than Tropicana. However, it was clean and well maintained. A monkey in the front yard greeted all visitors. Clients for this lodge were almost exclusively from the United States. The owners advertised in select outdoor magazines. The owner also appeared on TV talk shows when he was in the United States. Bookings in the United States were handled through an exclusive agent in Chicago who worked on a commission basis.
- *Isla Del Sol*. This fishing lodge was located at the mouth of the San Juan River, which forms a border for Nicaragua and Costa Rica. The manager/owner was a Mr. Laurie from Detroit. This lodge was experiencing difficulty in breaking even and was open six months or less each year.
- *Casa Fantastica*. This fishing lodge was also located at the mouth of the San Juan River and was open six months or less each year. There was no information concerning the success of this lodge, but it was apparent that the management was fairly aggressive, as witnessed by advertisements from the outdoor magazine *The Salt Water Sportsman*.

Rates

Rates for competitive fishing lodges on the Caribbean coast ranged from $2,000 to $3,500 per person per week. Tropicana and other lodges did not encourage guests to come for periods of less than five days. This was due to the cost of transportation. It also provided a guest with more opportunities to catch fish. Guests who stayed for shorter periods of time sometimes arrived when fishing was poor and returned to spread stories of poor fishing. All lodges provided competitive services, although Tropicana provided even more individualized attention to guests and was willing to spend more time and money to transport guests to good fishing sites.

Promotion and Client Profile: Las Perla

Promotion for Tropicana was handled primarily through ads in the English print newspapers in San José. Word-of-mouth advertising seemed to be the primary means by which people heard of the lodge. A review of the guest book indicated that the majority of guests had been from the United States; the second largest group were Costa Ricans.

Discussion Questions

1. What promotional strategies/tactics would you suggest for Tropicana?
2. Discuss the differences in management and marketing between a commercial fishing or hunting lodge and a commercial hotel.
3. Could the marketing of diverse hunting/fishing lodges be conducted effectively by an independent group responsible for multiple properties?

Case 25 Burger King: Searching for the Right Message

Advertising's Ups and Downs

Burger King has shown how powerful and yet ineffective advertising can be. In 1974, with its market share hovering about 4 percent, Burger King introduced the "Have It Your Way" advertising campaign. The ad focused on Burger King's strategy of making burgers according to customer requests instead of serving already prepared, standardized burgers. Many people still consider this campaign to be Burger King's best ever. In the early 1980s, however, Burger King began to flip from one advertising campaign to another, trying to keep its sales growing. In 1982, it introduced "Battle of the Burgers" campaign, featuring the slogan "Aren't You Hungry for Burger King Now?" The "Broiling vs. Frying" campaign followed in 1983, driving home the point that Burger King flame-broiled its burgers instead of frying them. "The Big Switch" theme guided advertising until 1985. All of these centered on Burger King's advantages over McDonald's, and they helped increase market share from 7.6 percent in 1983 to 8.3 percent in 1985. Then, disaster struck. With its market share peaking at 8.7 percent, Burger King unveiled its now infamous "Search for Herb" ad campaign. The campaign centered on Herb, an eccentric nerd who was supposedly the only person never to have tasted a Burger King Whopper. Consumers were supposed to search for Herb and earn a chance to win valuable prizes. The campaign flopped. Sales inched up only 1 percent, far short of executives' 10 percent projections. The campaign led consumers to focus on Herb rather than the Whopper, and Burger King found itself in the uncomfortable position of associating its image with a "nerdy" personality.

Following Herb, Burger King's market share began a steady decline. Burger King tried to reverse its slide with its "This Is a Burger King Town" theme in 1986–1987, and followed it with a "Best Food for Fast Times" message. In 1988, the chain tried the "We Do It Like You'd Do It" campaign, which again focused on flame broiling. However, because of confusing situations, bad humor, and bad acting, the campaign never succeeded in increasing sales. In 1989, Burger King launched its "Sometimes You Gotta Break the Rules" campaign. Burger King wanted this slogan to convey the idea that it was "breaking the rules" of the burger industry by flame broiling, not frying its burgers, and by making the burgers to meet individual customer requests. Another disappointing campaign was "BK Tee Vee," featuring MTV personality Dan Cortese, rapid editing, and a voice-over that shrieked, "I love this place." Ads targeted teenage males, but the majority of Burger King's customers—parents and people on the go—found the commercials to be loud and irritating.

Thus, since the mid-1980s, Burger King has had trouble persuading consumers that they should prefer its restaurants to those of McDonald's and other competitors. With its long string of lackluster, quick-changing advertising campaigns, Burger King has failed to establish a solid image that would differentiate it from competitors. If anything, the ads only confused consumers as to what advantages Burger King offered.

By 1993, Burger King held a 6.1 percent market share, barely ahead of Hardee's 4.4 percent and Wendy's 4.1 percent. It lagged far behind McDonald's, which dominates the industry with a 15.6 percent market share. Moreover, Burger King's sales were growing more slowly than those of its rivals. So for the fourth time in five years, Burger King's managers decided to put its advertising account up for review, seeking a new agency and a new ad campaign.

Not the Only Problems

Failed advertising campaigns are only the most visible of Burger King's problems. Its marketing stumbles involve other, deeper issues. Since the 1980s, Burger King has wrestled with internal problems. Management has lacked focus and direction and has struggled with marketing-mix decisions. Franchisees, who often felt that headquarters had no well-thought-out strategy, became confused and angered. To make matters worse, in-store operations were less than spectacular—service in many Burger King restaurants was slow, and food preparation was inconsistent. Many stores needed remodeling.

Burger King lost its focus on its core product—flame-broiled burgers made the way the customer wanted them. It introduced a variety of unrelated products, ranging from pizza and tacos to ice-cream bars. A failure to concentrate on its leading product, the Whopper, confused customers. Many customers also believed that Burger King served lower-quality food.

In the age of the price-conscious consumer, McDonald's and Wendy's listed and responded with lower-priced combo meals. Burger King's higher prices and its refusal to provide discounts contributed to its below-average sales growth.

Burger King's promotion problems also involved more than just its television commercials. Many in-store promotions failed. And the dinner-basket program—combo meals along with table service—showed that Burger King was not listening to its customers. Fast-food patrons really wanted low prices and quick but high-quality food, not a higher-priced, sit-down meal. In addition to chewing up a number of advertising agencies, the company also tossed out some marketing managers.

Back to the Basics

With the help of CEO Jim Adamson, a former marketer from Revco Drug Stores who came to Burger King in July 1991, Burger King has begun a turnaround. Adamson came to Burger King as president of company-owned outlets. In 1993, he moved up to become the eighth Burger King CEO since 1980. Adamson took a hands-on approach that pleased franchisees. He listened and responded to franchisee problems and recommendations. For example, Burger King initiated Operation Phoenix, a program to improve sales, service, and quality by offering franchisees help with menus, pricing, and local advertising. Management finally locked into a strategy of concentrating on Burger King's core product—flame-broiled, bigger burgers. In 1998, the company started pruning items from the menu. It also launched a new pricing structure featuring \$0.99, \$1.99, and \$2.99 value meals that allow it to compete on price with McDonald's.

In addition to resolving its internal problems, Burger King is also attending to its major external problem—lack of effective advertising. It has hired a new advertising agency, Ammirati and Puris/Lintas, to communicate a new "Back to the Basics" positioning. Ammirati's Helayne Spivak describes Burger King's image as "The Voice of the People," as opposed to McDonald's image as the "Voice of a Corporation," and Wendy's image as the "Voice of Dave." Burger King is a company that listens to its customers. To communicate this message, the advertising agency will use about \$180 million of Burger King's total \$250 million promotion budget. Burger King has been spending \$180 million on television and radio, with about 40 percent going for national advertising and 60 percent to local. Ammirati and Puris/Lintas must now create an advertising campaign that will successfully communicate Burger King's competitive advantages and pull more customers into its 5,700 restaurants.

Discussion Questions

1. What are the objectives of Burger King's advertising?
2. Why did Burger King's corporate strategy and past advertising fail to achieve these objectives?
3. What suggestions do you have for Burger King's new advertising campaign?
4. What recommendations would you make regarding future sales promotions for Burger King?

Case 26 Solitaire Lodge of New Zealand

Halley's Comet

Halley's comet is a hard act to follow! Finding another "event" around which to build the next promotional push in the lucrative U.S. market was the question facing Reg Turner, the hardworking, ebullient owner of Solitaire Lodge. Forward bookings represented full utilization of the capacity of the six-suite lodge through the next three months, but there were few sales after that.

Recognizing that Halley's comet could best be observed from a smog-free environment in the southern hemisphere, Reg promoted Solitaire Lodge as the place to be. This captured the imagination of travel writers in the United States and Canada, who gave Reg exceptional publicity in publications such as the *Los Angeles Times*. Reg knew that the Halley's comet special promotion had caught the imagination of North American clients. It was clear that clients would respond to special promotional events.

Location and Description of Solitaire

The lodge stood on a majestic headland overlooking the quiet beauty of Lake Tarawera, fifteen kilometers from Rotorua, New Zealand. Rotorua itself was a major tourist attraction for both New Zealand and overseas tourists and enjoyed daily scheduled air services which linked the city with both Auckland and Christchurch International Airports. Access to Lake Tarawera was a tar-sealed road that wound past the Blue and Green Lakes, themselves a local tourist attraction. After passing the Buried Village, yet another tourist attraction, the road meandered through seven kilometers of bush-lined scenery before reaching Lake Tarawera.

The lake was at times tranquil and serene and at times mysterious and foreboding. Tourists arriving at the lake for the first time often commented on the awesome presence of Mt. Tarawera, which stood high and often mist-shrouded at the far end of the lake. The lodge was situated on the headland at the end of the road. A cobble-stoned drive led through stands of deciduous blossom trees and New Zealand native bush to the imposing wrought-iron gates of Solitaire Lodge. Visitors were able to drive to the door of the old cottage, situated at the center of the building complex. This served as the dining and communal lounge facilities of the lodge.

Luxury and Seclusion

Fanning out on both the left and right wings of the cottage stood suites, with three on each wing. Each was completely self-contained and enjoyed a floor-to-ceiling view of the lake. The first reaction of many arriving guests was wonderment at the beauty and seclusion of the location. The interior of the suites was finished in New Zealand native timber, which created an atmosphere of rustic charm. Furnishings were luxurious and comfortable. Separate and private bathroom facilities were attached to each suite. Adjacent to the buildings was a small geodesic dome containing hot spa pool facilities for the use of guests.

Stepping outside, guests were able to wander down a well-maintained path which led to the lakeside some 100 meters distant. Guests enjoyed the panoramic views of the lake from several elevated vantage points along the way. A boathouse and jetty stood in a clearing at the bottom of the path. Viewed from the lake, the lodge presented a striking profile. The hexagonal shape of the structure complemented the natural angles of the headland itself, and many visitors commented on the complete harmony of building and location.

History

Reg Turner visited Lake Tarawera soon after arriving in New Zealand from the West Indies. English born and educated, Reg had learned to fly during an eight-year stint with the Royal Air Force. Reg arrived in New Zealand with $3,000 in his pocket and a dream that one day he would own and operate a fishing lodge. A chance visit to Lake Tarawera fired his ambition. Advised by a real estate agent of the availability of a suitable cottage and land, Reg accepted the challenge, raised the money, and acquired the location that was to become Solitaire Lodge.

Reg hosted a wealthy American couple visiting New Zealand on the cruise ship *Queen Elizabeth* who saw a brochure for the lodge. At the end of their visit, the couple told Reg that he was "too cheap" and gave him a $500 donation toward the lodge building fund. At that moment, Reg made the decision to seek funding to build a lodge and determined that his target would be wealthy Americans.

When Solitaire Lodge opened for business, the product was oriented around fishing for rainbow trout. The fishing season, which allowed fishing during the period November 1 to June 30, was coupled with the services of Reg Turner as guide. Promotional activity focused on the quality of the fishing and the professional services of Turner. Brochures advertising the fishing were distributed around other tourist accommodations in the area. Reg saw the market as foreign tourists already in the Rotorua area and New Zealanders looking for a short holiday break. No direct competition was seen to exist. Huka Lodge, an up-market location 50 miles distant, was seen as a "role model" for the future Solitaire Lodge to try to emulate.

The business of Solitaire Lodge continued to grow erratically. Turner paid his first promotional visit to the United States to attend a major conclave of trout fishermen. His purpose was to promote fly fishing in New Zealand to the fly fishing market of the United States. The visit proved unsuccessful. Turner learned that fly fishermen wanted to dry-fly fish in rivers and streams. Turner also came to realize that the U.S. perception of a fishing lodge was different from his own. U.S. fishermen sought spartan adequacy only, not luxury.

Redefining the Product

Turner realized that his product needed to be redefined for marketing efforts in the United States to succeed. He likened his lodge to the U.S. concept of "country Inns"—privately owned guest houses in rural locations offering "get away from it all" facilities. Turner traveled throughout the United States visiting former clients, their friends, and selected travel agents in Los Angeles and New York. His promotional message was "Come and visit a country inn of New Zealand." Business continued to grow steadily through word of mouth. Turner also noticed an increasing number responding to advertising signs placed at roadsides between Rotorua and Lake Tarawera.

Promotional Boost

Solitaire Lodge received a promotional boost when selected as the subject of a travel article by Air New Zealand's *Jetaway* magazine. Reg saw an opportunity to use this PR type of promotion and began to make himself known to travel writers in both New Zealand and the United States.

The Fly-Drive, Free-Wheeling Market

Within New Zealand, promotional efforts focused on attracting the growing fly-drive free-wheeling (FDFW) market, which contributed 200 bookings during the year. Reg saw a chance in the market and ceased his efforts at promoting through travel agents, recognizing the importance of brochures in rental car agencies and the ubiquitous road signs.

Solitaire Lodge gained a promotional boost when visited by the prestigious Hideaway magazine. The resulting article praised Solitaire to its exclusive readership as a country retreat of the highest standard. Turner immediately raised prices and noticed an upsurge both in bookings from the states and in ITs attracted by the brochures and road signs.

The product had become clearly positioned as a luxury lakeside retreat and enjoyed significant repeat business. Turner noticed an upswing in three-day bookings for small business conferences. The expanded lounge facilities were expected to enhance Solitaire's competitive advantage in the New Zealand domestic "mini" convention market.

Turner continued to use PR opportunities such as radio talk-back shows and interviews with travel writers to build the image of the lodge and of himself as a larger-than-life sportsman, outdoors man, hunter, and raconteur. The highly successful Halley's comet promotion had fired his ambition anew and raised the challenge of developing a successor promotion. The room rate, meantime, had again been raised.

Discussion Questions

1. What lesson can be learned from the repositioning strategy employed by Reg Turner?
2. What do you believe was primarily responsible for the success of Solitaire Lodge—the advertising, public relations, repositioning, or some other factor?
3. What do you believe Reg Turner needs to do to continue attracting guests?

Case 27 The Ritz-Carlton, Millenia Singapore

Walter Junger, the executive assistant manager in charge of food and beverage for the Ritz-Carlton, Millenia Singapore Hotel, envisioned an opportunity to create an exciting event for Singapore, the first annual New World of Food and Wine Festival. As a native of Austria, Walter was familiar with the tradition of food and wine festivals, which were relatively unknown in Singapore.

The management of the Ritz-Carlton, Millenia Singapore, also believed the idea had merit and backed the concept with an adequate budget, personnel, and managerial support. The event had multiple purposes:

1. To develop a scholarship fund for promising Singapore students to pursue a food and beverage career.
2. To create favorable publicity for the hotel.
3. To provide a forum for the presentation of the Ritz-Carlton, Millenia Singapore Lifetime Achievement Award for Food and Beverage Excellence to a person who had dedicated his or her life to the art of culinary refinement or wine appreciation.
4. To provide an enjoyable evening for invited guests.
5. To advance the knowledge and appreciation of wine and fine food.
6. To enhance relations with selected wineries and distributors.

7. To showcase the cutting-edge developments over the last ten years, especially in the "new world" (such as "Fusion Cuisine").

The festival was planned and organized as a four-day epicurean extravaganza featuring chefs and winery representatives form North America, South America, South Africa, Australia, and China. During these four days, the festival featured exciting and innovative gastronomic creations and wine tasting of premium wines on a grand scale for the first time in Singapore. This festival was on the cutting edge of food and beverage trends, highlighting the achievements of nontraditional food and beverage sources over the last decade.

Just as Singapore is a multicultural crossroad, this festival served as a meeting point for the best new offerings from the New World of Food and Wine. The opening cocktail reception was a superb culinary experience showcasing the talents of the Ritz-Carlton, Millenia Singapore culinary team. Against a tropical poolside setting, the team led by executive chef Peter Schoch presented innovative creations from restaurants of the Ritz-Carlton, Millenia Singapore. The culinary delights that evening included oysters from Australia, the United States, and South Africa; and a selection of caviar, black pepper scallops, and Hoisin lobster on hot garlic pesto; bourbon-marinated lamb loin on roasted pablano pepper sauce; and a flambé station accompanied by a homemade ice-cream selection. All these were accompanied with Green Point sparkling and still wines from the House of Moet et Chandon, Australia. Live music further enhanced the ambiance.

Guests were able to meet and talk with participating chefs and winery representatives. These included Jeff Cook of Robert Mondavi Winery; Wayne Donaldson from Green Point Winery; Stefano and Franca Manfredi of Bel Mondo Restaurant, Sydney; chef Ramiro Rodriguez Pardo of Argentina; the Arizu family, owners of Luigi Bosca Vineyards of Mendoza, Argentina; and several others. In addition to the opening cocktail reception, the festival was divided into thirteen sections of wine tasting and dining, with prices ranging from $50 (Singapore) to $180.

Walter Junger served as chairman of the festival and received excellent cooperation from a cross-functional team that included the director of public relations, events/promotion manager, executive chef, director of banquets, beverage manager, room service manager, Greenhouse Restaurant manager, director of catering, Snappers Restaurant manager, and reservations supervisor. The level of planning and team work by this group resulted in a highly successful festival. Almost all the events during the festival were sold out, and some even had waiting lists.

The highlight of the festival was the presentation of the Ritz-Carlton, Millenia Singapore Lifetime Achievement Award for Food and Beverage Excellence, worth $7,000, to one of the participating chefs, winemakers, and winery representatives. Judges for this prestigious award were Fred Ferretti of *Gourmet* magazine, United States; C. P. Tiong of *Wine Review,* Singapore; Andre Blanc of Ecolab, Asia; and Walter Junger, executive assistant manager of the Ritz-Carlton, Millenia Singapore. After two grueling days of interviews with each nominee, the decision was unanimous: chef Ramiro Pardo was selected the winner. Chef Pardo had been cooking for people from all over the world for forty years. His restaurant Catalinas was awarded the top prize as "The Best Latin American Restaurant" by the Association of Latin American Gastronomic Journalists.

During the gala dinner, an auction of rare wines was conducted to raise funds for the Ritz-Carlton, Millenia Singapore Food and Beverage Scholarship Fund. The scholarship benefited a promising Singaporean who excelled in his or her profession. The auction was well supported by guests and eventually raised over $18,000. The gala dinner ended on a high note: The Ritz-Carlton, Millenia Singapore was presented a Five-Star Diamond Award for Food and Beverage Excellence by the American Academy of Hospitality Sciences.

Discussion Questions

1. Was the New World of Food and Wine Festival a good public relations event? Explain and support your answer.
2. If you were the public relations director for the Ritz Millenia, in what types of media would you try to get publicity? Explain how your message would vary across the various types of media.
3. How does this event create goodwill with the target market of Ritz-Carlton?

Case 28 The Teller House Uses Database Marketing

Effective database marketing combined with key customer programs are the ingredients for success at the Teller House Casino of Central City, Colorado. How else could you effectively market the last casino on a twisting mountain road lined with casinos in the gambling towns of Blackhawk and Central City? With limited parking and limited casino space, the Teller House faces heavy competitive pressure. The general manager, Roger Shuttleworth, described the overall problems as location and restrictions on all casinos in Central City that do not permit expansion beyond the constraints of existing historical buildings in which they are housed.

The twin cities of Blackhawk and Central City initiated casino gambling in 1991, but by 1997 Blackhawk was rated as the number one casino city in Colorado, whereas Central City had dropped to third place. Twenty-five casinos had ceased operation in Central City and more seemed likely to close, whereas those in Blackhawk grew larger and more attractive to casino gambling customers.

Like other casinos, the Teller House depended on high spending and frequent gamblers. The Teller House had tried table games, but a $5 maximum bet law in Colorado made them unprofitable. Slot machines and video poker games now represent the only casino offerings.

During the gold rush days of the nineteenth century, the Teller House had served as a hotel, bar, and restaurant and remained well known for the "Face on the Barroom Floor." In 1997, the main floor of the Teller House served as a casino, bar, and restaurant. The second floor, furnished in Victorian style, was marketed for use in weddings, receptions, and anniversaries. Lodging facilities were no longer available at the Teller House.

As a well-known historical site, the Teller House enjoyed a reputation well beyond Colorado. Unfortunately, hard-core gamblers showed little interest in history, and history buffs showed little interest in gambling. The perception among dedicated slot players was that crowded casinos with lots of action must be good payout casinos as opposed to smaller, quieter ones such as the Teller House.

Roger knew that the Teller House must retain and build its group of key customers. A sophisticated database marketing program was managed by Kim Estrames, who collected player data electronically by means of a plastic Teller House Casino Club Card from players who inserted the card into a box attached to the slot or poker machine. Players were encouraged to join the club and use the card to accumulate points which could be redeemed for cash or gifts and also allowed them to participate in club activities. Use of the card permitted the Teller House to accumulate usage data about each player and cross tabulate it against demographic data, including address, zip code, date of birth, and length of club membership. Usage information included type of game preferred, average amount bet per visit, total amount bet since becoming a member, total win/loss, last date of play, and total membership points earned.

Kim said that this information was invaluable in designing promotional programs for key customers but had proven to be of limited use in attracting new players. "The fact that a frequent player lives in a certain zip code or is a certain age does not mean that neighbors of the same age will also be avid slot players," said Kim. She added that the database had proven effective in developing programs aimed at combating key player defection, as these people could be identified easily. Unlike some casinos, the Teller House did not rely as heavily on media aimed at a general market or on enticement coupons. Instead, the Teller House preferred to develop programs for known heavy gamblers. One of Kim's responsibilities was to measure the impact of each promotional program. As an example, this information revealed that newsletters were a more effective medium than tabloid-type publications sent to known gamblers.

Everyone at the Teller House, from management to the floor personnel, understands that success depends on continuously pleasing those hard-core gamblers and enticing them to return. Theme programs such as a cruise theme found employees dressed in tropical attire and offering tropical drinks to patrons.

Slot machine tournaments were designed for key players to build enthusiasm and differentiate the Teller House. Players were ranked by the Teller House based on their amount of play. A VIP club was designed for "A"-level players, who were occasionally given premiums such as a 99 percent silver commemorative Teller House Coin. New programs offering player excitement were continuously developed by the marketing/sales department. Ideas were welcome from any employee.

Discussion Questions

1. Explain how creating and using a database creates a competitive advantage?
2. How did the Teller House use their database to create customer loyalty?
3. Was the database marketing at the Teller House part of an integrated marketing program? Explain your answer.

Case 29 International Travel Agency

The president of International Travel Agency was concerned about the performance of the sales force. It was felt that members of the sales force did not really utilize their sales opportunities, but instead thought only about selling a ticket to a customer from point A to point B. The sales force did not seem to have an interest in maximizing sales and profits by aggressively selling the entire product mix.

In total, the agency had a sales force of eight. Three members of the sales force were referred to as executive sales consultants. These people called on commercial accounts and were expected to spend more of their time outside the office. The remaining five persons were referred to as travel counselors and worked entirely within the agency.

None of the travel counselors who worked within the agency were assigned a quota. The executive sales consultants, who worked outside the office, were assigned a sales quota. Failure to meet a quota would be discussed with the salesperson, but no other action was usually taken unless this failure continued for several months. If serious and persistent deficiencies existed, the salesperson could be subject to discharge.

The agency provided nine to twelve familiarization (fam) trips for members of the sales force each year. This meant that each salesperson could experience at least one trip per year, as they were assigned on a rotating basis. These trips did not reduce time from the salesperson's guaranteed number of days of annual vacation. The purpose of a fam trip was to acquaint travel agents with destination areas and the services of airlines, hotels, restaurants, and so on.

The president felt that the agency could maximize profits by selling more travel services to clients and that the sales force was concerned only about selling tickets. An analysis of the product mix of International Travel revealed that approximately 85 percent was accounted for by airline tickets. The remaining 15 percent consisted of allied travel services, including hotels, rental cars, and entertainment. Of these, the majority consisted of hotel reservations. Less than one percent was accounted for by the sale of traveler's checks. One of the members of management offered the analogy of a businessman entering a clothing store. If a customer purchases a suit, the salesclerk asks if the customer might need a new shirt or tie to go with the suit. Travel agents are no different. They write a ticket from Chicago to Hong Kong or London for a client and never bother to ask if the client needs hotel accommodations, rental cars, travelers checks, or other services that an agency handles.

The president of International Travel had tried to encourage the sales force to sell other services but felt that they seemed uninterested in taking the time and effort required. The president believed that maximizing sales of the complete product mix would lead to maximum profits and that something must be done to encourage cross-selling.

Discussion Questions

1. What can be done to encourage the sales force to engage in more cross-selling?
2. Does the current fam trip program serve as a motivational tool for the sales force?
3. Discuss what is needed in terms of sales incentives and sales controls to achieve the objectives of International Travel Agency.

Case 30 Superior Hotels

Jan Trible, president of Superior Hotels, was concerned with the future expansion of the company. Superior Hotels had built a strong reputation in the management of time-share resorts in Florida. The company had recently acquired a consulting contract for a ski resort in the Rocky Mountains, which would mark its entrance into a new area of resort management. Now there was serious discussion concerning the advisability of entering the commercial hotel segment of the hotel industry within cities of 100,000 to 200,000 in population.

Management of Time-Share Resorts

The management style of Superior Hotels was exemplified in the management of the company's time-share resorts. Superior managed five time-share resorts, with a total of 240 units. The company maintained a policy of not accepting management contracts for time-share projects that were in trouble. The company philosophy maintained that most of these had been ill planned and probably had little likelihood of long-range success. Jan personally believed that a major shakeup in the time-share industry was coming and that many existing projects would fail.

The Superior Hotel policy was to begin working with the developers of a time-share resort at the beginning of the project. It was felt that developers have a short-run viewpoint, but a management company must think of the long run. The policy was to become involved in the entire planning process of the project, including blueprints and interior decorations. If a developer refused to cooperate, Superior would remove itself from future management. Management believed that a time-share project differed considerably from a conventional hotel or resort development.

1. A time-share project has hundreds or thousands of owners. A conventional hotel or resort has one or a few.
2. Time-share projects receive high-intensity use, with 95 percent occupancy being normal. Furniture, carpeting, and other furnishings can wear out in one-third the time. Therefore, rules of thumb developed for hotels would often not apply in time-share.

3. The guest assumes a proprietary interest in time share. Guests are extremely critical because they view the units as theirs and complain about things that a hotel guest would accept.
4. A great deal of hype goes into the sales of a time-share unit, and guests arrive with extreme expectations. Superior has to bring reality into the dreams that the sales department create.
5. The long-run success of a time-share unit depends on attracting the same guests each year for as long as twenty years or more. If guests became dissatisfied and enough guests decided to drop their ownership, resales can be very difficult and the entire project can be in jeopardy.

Several management practices had been developed by Superior to deal with these complexities.

Owner Feedback

Owner comment sheets were distributed to each owner/guest during each visit. Jan took pride in the fact that she read each one personally. These sheets covered a variety of areas, from general appearance of the unit to any evidence of insects and rodents. If the comments were particularly bad, a member of management, including Jan, would personally contact the owner and report on the steps that had been taken to correct the problem.

Feedback was also received in "owner coffees." These weekly meetings with owners included attendance by one or more members of management. These could include the resort owner, the head of housekeeping, the director of internal management, and others. A quarterly newsletter was published by Superior and sent to all owners. In addition to information of a general nature such as changes in air fares to the resort, the newsletter was personalized to the extent that it reminded all owners of their vacation week.

Recreation Management

Superior Hotels believed that even the most beautiful and best-maintained resort could eventually become boring. To ensure that guests would find something new each year, a recreation program was established with a full-time professional in charge. Programs were designed for all ages. These employed some of the successful concepts of Club Med.

Supervised programs for children allowed parents a freedom they could not enjoy at most resorts. Hot dog parties, beach parties, tennis competition, seashell classes, and many other programs offered a variety of recreational and educational pursuits. Each recreational program was monitored as to attendance and guest satisfaction and weak ones were eliminated. A dominant feature of all the programs was the opportunity for interaction among guests. Jan believed that a guest at the average resort could spend a week and never develop new friendships. Hopefully, the recreation programs encouraged friendships to develop.

Housekeeping and Maintenance

The turnover of a majority of the guests one day and the mass arrival of an equal number the next provided special housekeeping and maintenance problems for time-share projects. A full-time maintenance crew was employed, and a large inventory of replacement furnishings was carried. If a TV set or electric range had a problem, it was replaced immediately rather than sending a repairman. With only one vacation week, Jan felt that a guest did not want to share it with a repairman. Housekeeping was performed for the time-share resorts under contract with an independent housekeeping company. Housekeeping managers were responsible for examining each room personally and ensuring that corrections immediately followed discovery of a problem.

The Superior Hotel Image and Philosophy

"All Superior properties must be first class; there is no room in this corporation for mundane or second-class properties." This statement by Jan summed up the company's philosophy. The philosophy concerning quality had led management to change its policy concerning the new properties it would manage. The company recently initiated a policy of holding an equity position in all future properties. This decision was made for two reasons. First, an ownership position would allow Superior to have a stronger voice in the development and management of properties and would help to ensure quality. Second, Superior Hotels had no interest in "bringing up" properties to a desired quality and performance level only to find that the managers had decided not to renew the management contract.

Corporate Objectives

The management and ownership of Superior Hotels desired for the company to be recognized as a strong national resort and commercial hotel management company within ten years. It was felt that resort properties offered limited growth opportunities because the most desirable locations had been developed by others.

The best strategy for the next five years seemed to lie in the development of first-class commercial properties within sun-belt cities of 100,000 to 200,000 people. It was felt that the development of three new properties per year in this market was realistic. Sun-belt cities were felt to offer the best potential for growth because of the scarcity of 150- to 200-room high-quality hotels. These second-tier cities remained important industrial and agricultural centers and did not usually offer truly first-class hotel accommodations. In many cases a respected medical complex had been developed in these cities, and it was felt that this factor alone would serve as a magnet for visitors.

Discussion Questions

1. What are the core competencies of Superior Hotels? Management of resorts? Management of time-share resorts? Management of ski resorts? Management of commercial hotels? Other?
2. Do you believe that Superior Hotels should be entering diverse markets such as ski resorts and commercial hotels?
3. Do you believe that Superior Hotels can effectively market and manage a wide diversity of properties?
4. What would you advise Jan Trible to do?

Case 31 Motel 6

"Hi, Tom Bodett for Motel 6 here. I'm sitting in room 201 in Yuba City, California, and it's wild. We're watching color TV, I'm talkin' on the phone, and my family's thumbing through the Yellow Pages. I'm tellin' you, we're having a ball." This is an excerpt from one of the most successful radio campaigns for a hospitality company—Motel 6's campaign featuring Tom Bodett. The following is one of the spots from the series:

> Hi, Tom Bodett for Motel 6 with a plan for anyone whose kids are on their own now. Take a drive, see some of the country, and visit a few relatives. Like your sister Helen and her husband Bob. They're wonderful folks always happy to pull the hide-a-bed out for you, but somehow the smell of mothballs just isn't conducive to gettin' a good night's sleep. And since Bob gets up at 5:30, well that means you do, too. So here's the plan. Check into Motel 6. 'Cause for around twenty-two bucks, the lowest prices of any national chain, you'll get a clean, comfortable room, and Helen and Bob'll think you're mighty considerate. Well you are, but maybe more important, you can sleep late and not have to wonder if the towels in their bathroom are just for decoration. My rule of thumb is, if they match the tank and seat cover, you better leave 'em alone. Just call 505-891-6161 for reservations. I'm Tom Bodett for Motel 6. Give my best to Helen and Bob, and we'll leave the light on for you.

For twenty-four years, Motel 6 never had an advertising campaign. Price and word of mouth brought in guests. This strategy worked well against independents and small regional chains. Eventually, other low-priced chains emerged, and price was no longer a point of differentiation for Motel 6. Occupancy of the hotel dropped from 81 percent in 1981 to 69.5 percent in 1985. In 1985, Kohlberg, Kravis, Roberts and Company (KKR) purchased Motel 6. KKR hired Joe McCarthy to run Motel 6, and McCarthy hired Hugh Thrasher to head up marketing. In February 1986, McCarthy awarded their advertising contract to the Richards Group in Dallas.

The advertising agency spent almost one year conducting research. They held scores of focus groups to find out who stays at a Motel 6, what they like, and what they dislike. The 6 in Motel 6 stands for $6 a day, the original price of a Motel 6 room in 1962. To provide a room for $6, the original hotels were built inexpensively, with few conveniences. In 1985, when KKR took over, Motel 6 did not offer rooms with telephones, and it cost $1.49 to have the television turned on. In the early hotels, television sets were coin operated, and guests paid by the hour. In 1986, the price of a room was $17.95 systemwide, regardless of location. Guests paid cash in advance, because Motel 6 didn't take credit cards. There was a charge for children sharing the same room with their parents. Families paid a rate determined by a complicated formula. Guests had to write to the hotel for a reservation, because there was no central reservation system. The advertising agency found that all these factors were guest irritants.

Information obtained from the research was used to redesign the company's marketing mix. Phones were added, and free local phone service was offered. There was no service charge for hook-up to long-distance calls. The order for 50,000 phones by Motel 6 was AT&T's largest phone order by a public company. The addition of phones made Motel 6 more attractive to salespeople and added a sense of security for the leisure traveler, both for themselves and in knowing that families could reach them. The charge for television was dropped, and the room charge for children staying in the same room was also dropped. The price of a room was changed from a standard price across all geographic markets to one that reflected local market conditions. When management felt they had developed a product that was right for the market, Motel 6 started its radio advertising campaign in November 1986. In October 1986, Motel 6 had consumer awareness of less than 10 percent. By the end of the year, radio spots had lifted awareness to more than 50 percent. Revenues went from $256 million in 1986 to more than $425 million in 1989. Occupancy jumped from 66.7 percent to 72.7 percent in 1987, ending a six-year decline marked by an occupancy drop of almost 15 points.

Sources: Carol Hall, "King of the Road," *Marketing and Media Decision* 24, no. 3 (March 1989): 80–86; Marke W. Cunningham and Chekitan Dev, "Strategic Marketing: A Lodging 'End Run,'" *Cornell Hotel and Restaurant Administration Quarterly* 24, no. 3 (August 1992): 36–43.

Discussion Questions

1. Explain how a marketing campaign like the one mentioned in this case study could come from a marketing plan?
2. What stages (sections) of the marketing planning process would create awareness for the product changes that were needed for Motel 6 to be competitive?
3. The actual plan for carrying out the advertising program would be in what section of the marketing plan?
4. To upgrade a major chain requires large sums of money. Should Motel 6 have started to advertise when they were halfway through the project to start to recap some of their expenses? Why or why not?

Glossary

Administrative VMS A vertical marketing system that coordinates successive stages of production and distribution, not through common ownership or contractual ties, but through the size and power of one of the parties.

Advertising Any paid form of nonpersonal presentation and promotion of ideas, goods, or services by an identified sponsor.

Agent A wholesaler who represents buyers or sellers on a more permanent basis, performs only a few functions, and does not take title to goods.

Alliances Alliances are developed to allow two organizations to benefit from each other's strengths.

Allocating Sales representatives decide on which customers to allocate scarce products to.

Allocentrics Persons with a need for new experiences, such as backpackers and explorers.

Ansoff product–market expansion grid A matrix developed by cell, plotting new products and existing products with new products and existing products. The grid provides strategic insights into growth opportunities.

Aspirational group A group to which a person wishes to belong.

Atmosphere Designed environments that create or reinforce a buyer's leanings toward consumption of a product.

Attitude A person's enduring favorable or unfavorable cognitive evaluations, emotional feelings, and action tendencies toward some object or idea.

Augmented products Additional consumer services and benefits built around the core and actual products.

Aural The dimension of atmosphere relating to volume and pitch.

Backward integration A growth strategy by which companies acquire businesses supplying them with products or services, for example, a restaurant chain purchasing a bakery.

Behavioral segmentation Dividing a market into groups based on consumers' knowledge, attitude, use, or response to a product.

Belief A descriptive thought that a person holds about something.

Benefit segmentation Dividing the market into groups according to the different benefits that consumers seek from the product.

Brand image The set of beliefs consumers hold about a particular brand.

Broker A wholesaler who does not take title to goods and whose function is to bring buyers and sellers together and assist in negotiations.

Buying center All those individuals and groups who participate in the purchasing and decision-making process and who share common goals and the risks arising from the decisions.

Cast members A term used for employees. It implies that employees are part of a team that is performing for their guests.

Causal research Marketing research to test hypotheses about cause-and-effect relationships.

Channel conflict Disagreement among marketing channel members on goals and roles—who should do what and for what rewards.

Channel level A level of middleman that performs some work in bringing the product and its ownership closer to the final buyer.

Cognitive dissonance Buyer discomfort caused by postpurchase conflict.

Communicating Sales representatives communicate information about the company's products and services.

Competencies scope The range of technological and other core competencies that the company will master and leverage.

Competitive advantage An advantage over competitors gained by offering consumers greater value either through lower prices or by providing more benefits that justify higher prices.

Competitive analysis An analysis of the primary strengths and weaknesses, objectives, strategies, and other information relative to competitors.

Competitors' strategies When competitors use segmentation, undifferentiated marketing can be suicidal. Conversely, when competitors use undifferentiated marketing, a firm can gain an advantage by using differentiated or concentrated marketing.

Concentric diversification strategy A growth strategy whereby a company seeks new products that have technological or marketing synergies with existing product lines.

Confused positioning Leaving buyers with a confused image of a company.

Conglomerate diversification strategy A product growth strategy in which a company seeks new businesses that have no relationship to the company's current product line or markets.

Consumption phase Takes place when the customer consumes the service.

Contests, sweepstakes, and games Give consumers a chance to win something, such as cash or a trip.

Contractual VMS A vertical marketing system in which independent firms at different levels of production and distribution join together through contracts to obtain more economies or sales impact than they could achieve alone.

Convention A specialty market requiring extensive meeting facilities. It is usually the annual meeting of an association and includes general sessions, committee meetings, and special-interest sessions.

Core product Answers the question of what the buyer is really buying. Every product is a package of problem-solving services.

Corporate communications This activity covers internal and external communications and promotes understanding of an organization.

Corporate meeting A meeting held by a corporation for its employees.

Corporate mission statement A guide to provide all the publics of a company with a shared sense of purpose, direction, and opportunity, allowing all to work independently, yet collectively, toward the organization's goals.

Corporate VMS A vertical marketing system that combines successive stages of production and distribution under single ownership. Channel leadership is established through common ownership.

Corporate Web site Web sites that seek to build customer goodwill and to supplement other sales channels rather than to sell the company's products directly.

Cost-plus pricing Adding a standard markup to the cost of the product.

Counseling Involves advising management about public issues and company positions and image.

Coupons Certificates that offer buyers savings when they purchase specified products.

Create and maintain customers The purpose of a business.

Cross selling The company's other products that are sold to the guest.

Cross training Training employees to do two or more jobs within the organization.

Culture The set of basic values, perceptions, wants, and behaviors learned by a member of society from family and other important institutions.

Customer centered Companies that deliver superior value to their target customers.

Customer database An organized collection of comprehensive data about individual customers or prospects, including geographic, demographic, psychographic, and behavioral data.

Customer-delivered value The difference between total customer value and total customer cost.

Customization A product designed to meet the specific needs of customers.

Customized marketing Marketing in which the company adapts its offers to the needs of specific customers or buying organizations.

Data warehouse A central repository of an organization's customer information.

Decline The period when sales fall off quickly and profits drop.

Degree of product homogeneity Undifferentiated marketing is more suited for homogeneous products. Products that can vary in design, such as restaurants and hotels, are more suited to differentiation or concentration.

Demands Human wants that are backed by buying power.

Demographic segmentation Dividing the market into groups based on demographic variables such as age, gender, family size, family life cycle, income, occupation, education, religion, race, and nationality.

Demography The study of human populations in terms of size, density, location, age, sex, race, occupation, and other statistics.

Derived demand Organizational demand that ultimately comes from (derives from) the demand for consumer goods.

Descriptive research Marketing research to better describe marketing problems, situations, or markets, such as the market potential for a product or the demographics and attitudes of consumers.

Destinations Places with some form of actual or perceived boundary, such as the physical boundary of an island, political boundaries, or even market-created boundaries.

Detachment phase When the customer is through using the product and departs.

Direct marketing Direct communications with carefully targeted individual consumers to obtain an immediate response and cultivate lasting customer relationships.

Direct marketing channel A marketing channel that has no intermediary levels.

Direct-mail marketing Direct marketing through single mailings that include letters, ads, samples, foldouts, and other "salespeople with wings" sent to prospects on mailing lists.

Discriminatory pricing Refers to segmentation of the market and pricing differences based on price elasticity characteristics of the segments.

Drop The action taken towards a product that may cause harm or customer dissatisfaction.

Echo boomers (baby boomlet generation) Born between 1977 and 1994, these children of the baby boomers now number 72 million, dwarfing the GenXers and almost equal in size to the baby boomer segment.

Economic environment The economic environment consists of factors that affect consumer purchasing power and spending patterns. Markets require both power and people. Purchasing power depends on current income, price, saving, and credit; marketers must be aware of major trends in income and changing consumer spending patterns.

Electronic commerce (e-commerce) The general term for a buying and selling process that is supported by electronic means.

Empowerment When a firm empowers employees, it moves the authority and responsibility to make decisions to the line employees from the supervisor.

Environmental factors Social, political, and economic factors that affect a firm and its marketing program.

Environmental management perspective A management perspective in which a firm takes aggressive actions to affect the publics and forces in its marketing environment rather than simply watching and reacting to it.

Event creation A particularly important skill in publicizing fund-raising drives for nonprofit organizations.

Events Occurrences staged to communicate messages to target audiences, such as news conferences or grand openings.

Exchange The act of obtaining a desired object from someone by offering something in return.

Executive summary A short summary of the marketing plan to quickly inform top executives.

Existing competitor Companies can position themselves against current competitors.

Expected service The service that the customer feels he will receive from a service provider.

Experimental research The gathering of primary data by selecting matched groups of subjects, giving them different treatments, controlling related factors, and checking for differences in group responses.

Exploratory research Marketing research to gather preliminary information that will help to better define problems and suggest hypotheses.

Extranet A computer network connecting a supplier and its customers.

Facilitating products Those services or goods that must be present for the guest to use the core product.

Family life cycle The stages through which families might pass as they mature.

Financial intermediaries Banks, credit companies, insurance companies, and other businesses that help finance transactions or insure against the risks associated with the buying and selling of goods.

Fixed costs Costs that do not vary with production or sales level.

Forward integration A growth strategy by which companies acquire businesses that are closer to the ultimate consumer, such as a hotel acquiring a chain of travel agents.

Franchise organization A contractual vertical marketing system in which a channel member called a franchiser links several stages in the production distribution process.

Freedom from deficiencies A type of service quality that focuses on conformance to specifications.

Functional quality The quality of the process of delivering a service.

Gender segmentation Dividing a market on the basis of gender.

General need description The stage in the industrial buying process in which a company describes the general characteristics and quantity of a needed item.

Generation X A generation of 45 million people born between 1965 and 1976; named Generation X because they lie in the shadow of the boomers and lack obvious distinguishing characteristics; others names include "baby busters," "shadow generation," or "yiffies"—young, individualistic, freedom-minded few.

Geographic scope The range of regions, countries, or country groups where the corporation will operate.

Geographic segmentation Dividing a market into different geographic units such as nations, states, regions, counties, cities, or neighborhoods.

Going-rate pricing Setting price based largely on following competitors' prices rather than on company costs or demand.

Growth The product life-cycle stage when a new product's sales start climbing quickly.

Growth–share matrix A model developed by the Boston Consulting Group to assist managers to plan business portfolios.

Horizontal conflict Conflict between firms at the same level.

Horizontal diversification strategy A product growth strategy whereby a company looks for new products that could appeal to current customers, which are technologically unrelated to its current line.

Horizontal integration A growth strategy by which companies acquire competitors.

Horizontal marketing systems (HMS) Two or more companies at one level join to follow new marketing opportunities. Companies can combine their capital, production capabilities, or marketing resources to accomplish more than one company working alone.

Hospitality industry Made up of those businesses that do one or more of the following: provide accommodation, prepared food and beverage service, and/or entertainment for the traveler.

Human need A state of felt deprivation in a person.

Human want The form that a human need takes when shaped by culture and individual personality.

Incentive travel A reward participants receive for achieving or exceeding a goal.

Income segmentation Dividing a market into different income groups.

Industry scope The range of industries that a company will operate in.

Information gathering Sales representatives conduct market research and intelligence work and fill in a call report.

Informative advertising Advertising used to inform consumers about a new product or feature to build primarty demand.

Infrastructure The system according to which a company, organization, or other body is organized at the most basic level.

Integrated direct marketing Direct-marketing campaigns that use multiple vehicles and multiple stages to improve response rates and profits.

Interactive marketing Marketing by a service firm that recognizes that perceived service quality depends heavily on the quality of buyer–seller interaction.

Internal marketing Marketing by a service firm to train effectively and motivate its customer-contact employees and all the supporting service people to work as a team to provide customer satisfaction.

Internal records information The product life-cycle stage when a new product is first distributed and made available for purchase.

Internet The vast and burgeoning global web of computer networks with no central management or ownership.

Intranet A computer network connecting people with an organization.

Introduction The product life-cycle stage when a new product is first distributed and made available for purchase.

Joining The product life-cycle stage when the customer makes the initial inquiry contact.

Learning Changes in a person's behavior arising from experience.

Lifestyle A person's pattern of living as expressed in his or her activities, interests, and opinions.

Lobbying Dealing with legislators and government officials to promote or defeat legislation and regulation.

Macrodestinations Destinations such as the United States that contain thousands of microdestinations, including regions, states, cities, towns, and visitor destinations within a town.

Macroenvironment The larger societal forces that affect the microenvironment: competitive, demographic, economic, natural, technological, political, and cultural forces.

Manufacturing concept (production concept) Holds that customers will favor products that are available and highly affordable, and therefore management should focus on production and distribution efficiency.

Market The set of actual and potential buyers of a product.

Market homogeneity If buyers have the same tastes, buy a product in the same amounts, and react the same way to marketing efforts, undifferentiated marketing is appropriate.

Market positioning Formulating competitive positioning for a product and a detailed marketing mix.

Market potential The total estimated dollars or unit value of a defined market for a defined product, including competitive products.

Market segmentation Dividing a market into direct groups of buyers who might require separate products or marketing mixes.

Market targeting Evaluating each market segment's attractiveness and selecting one or more segments to enter.

Market trends External trends of many types that are likely to affect the marketing in which a corporation operates.

Marketing A social and managerial process by which people and groups obtain what they need and want through creating and exchanging products and value with others.

Marketing concept The marketing management philosophy that holds that achieving organizational goals depends on determining the needs and wants of target markets and delivering desired satisfactions more effectively and efficiently than competitors.

Marketing environment The actors and forces outside marketing that affect marketing management's ability to develop and maintain successful transactions with its target customers.

Marketing information system (MIS) A structure of people, equipment, and procedures to gather, sort, analyze, evaluate, and distribute needed, timely, and accurate information to marketing decision makers.

Marketing intelligence Everyday information about developments in the marketing environment that help managers to prepare and adjust marketing plans.

Marketing intermediaries Firms that help the company to promote, sell, and distribute its goods to final buyers; they include middlemen, physical distribution firms, marketing-service agencies, and financial intermediaries.

Marketing management The analysis, planning, implementation, and control of programs designed to create, build, and maintain beneficial exchanges with target buyers for the purpose of achieving organizational objectives.

Marketing manager A person who is involved in marketing analysis, planning, implementation, and control activities.

Marketing mix Elements include product, price, promotion, and distribution. Sometimes distribution is called place and the marketing situation facing a company.

Marketing objectives Quantitative and time specific accomplishment measurements as to what is expected of a marketing program.

Marketing opportunity An area of need in which a company can perform profitably.

Marketing research The systematic design, collection, analysis, and reporting of data and findings relevant to a specific marketing situation facing a company.

Marketing services agencies Marketing research firms, advertising agencies, media firms, marketing consulting firms, and other service providers that help a company to target and promote its products to the right markets.

Marketing Web site Web sites designed to engage consumers in an interaction that will move them closer to a purchase or other marketing outcome.

Market-oriented strategic planning The managerial process of developing and maintaining a viable fit between the organization's objectives, skills, and resources and its changing market opportunities.

Market-segment scope The type of market or customers a company will serve.

Maturity The stage in a product life cycle when sales growth slows or levels off.

Media Nonpersonal communications channels, including print media (newspaper, magazines, direct mail), broadcast media (radio, television), and display media (billboards, signs, posters).

Membership groups Groups that have a direct influence on a person's behavior and to which a person belongs.

Microenvironment The forces close to a company that affect its ability to serve its customers: the company, market channel firms, customer markets, competitors, and the public.

Micromarketing A form of target marketing in which companies tailor their marketing programs to the needs and wants of narrowly defined geographic, demographic, psychographic, or benefit segments.

Moment of truth Occurs when an employee and a customer have contact.

Motive (or drive) A need that is sufficiently pressing to direct a person to seek satisfaction of that need.

Multichannel marketing Multichannel distribution, as when a single firm sets up two or more marketing channels to reach one or more customer segments.

Multiplier effect Tourist expenditures that are recycled through the local economy, being spent and respent.

National tourist organizations A national government or quasi-government agency that markets destination tourism.

Observational research The gathering of primary data by observing relevant people, actions, and situations.

Olfactory The dimension of atmosphere relating to scent and freshness.

Opinion leaders People within a reference group who, because of special skills, knowledge, personality, or other characteristics, exert influence on others.

Order-routine specification The stage of the industrial buying process in which a buyer writes the final order with the chosen supplier(s), listing the technical specifications, quantity needed, expected time of delivery, return policies, warranties, and so on.

Organization image The way a person or group views an organization.

Organizational buying process The decision-making process by which formal organizations establish the need for purchased products and services and identify, evaluate, and choose among alternative brands and suppliers.

Organizational culture The pattern of shared values and beliefs that gives members of an organization meaning and provides them with the rules for behavior in that organization.

Overpositioning Giving buyers a too-narrow picture of the company.

Patronage rewards Cash or other awards for regular use of a company's products or services.

Performance review The stage of an industrial buying process in which a buyer rates its satisfaction with suppliers, deciding whether to continue, modify, or drop the relationship.

Personality A person's distinguishing psychological characteristics that lead to relatively consistent and lasting responses to his or her environment.

Phase-out The ideal method of removing an unpopular or unprofitable product; it enables a product to be removed in an orderly fashion.

Physical evidence Tangible clues such as promotional material, employees of the firm, and the physical environment of the firm. Physical evidence is used by a service firm to make its product more tangible to customers.

Point-of-encounter Any point at which an employee encounters the customer.

Point-of-purchase (POP) promotions Include displays and demonstrations that take place at the time of sale.

Political environment Laws, government agencies, and pressure groups that influence and limit the activities of various organizations and individuals in society.

Premiums Goods offered either free or at low cost as an incentive to buy a product.

Press relations To place newsworthy information into the news media to attract attention.

Press release Information released to the media about certain new products or services.

Price The amount of money charged for a product or service, or the sum of the values consumers exchange for the benefits of having or using the product or service.

Primary data Information collected for the specific purpose at hand.

Problem recognition The stage of the industrial buying process in which someone in a company recognizes a problem or need that can be met by acquiring a good or a service.

Product Anything that can be offered to a market for attention, acquisition, use, or consumption that might satisfy a want or need. It includes physical objects, services, persons, places, organizations, and ideas.

Product concept The idea that consumers will favor products that offer the most quality, performance, and features, and therefore the organization should devote its energy to making continuous product improvements.

Product development Developing the product concept into a physical product to assure that the product idea can be turned into a workable product.

Product features Product features that enhance customer satisfaction is one type of service quality.

Product publicity Various efforts to publicize specific products.

Product specification The stage of an industrial buying process in which the buying organization decides on and specifies the best technical product characteristics for a needed item.

Products and applications scope The range of products and applications in which the company will participate.

Promotion mix The specific mix of advertising, personal selling, sales promotion, and public relations a company uses to pursue its advertising and marketing objectives.

Prospecting The process of searching for new accounts.

Psychocentrics Persons who do not desire change when they travel. They like nonthreatening places and to stay in familiar surroundings.

Psychographic segmentation Dividing a market into different groups based on social class, lifestyle, or personality characteristics.

Public relations The process by which we create a positive image and customer preference through third-party endorsement.

Pure monopoly The market consists of one seller; it could be government monopoly, a private regulated monopoly, or a private nonregulated monopoly.

Quality The totality of features and characteristics of a product that bear on its ability to meet customer needs (American Society for Quality Control).

Quotas Quantitative and time-specific accomplishment measurements established for members of a sales force.

Reference groups Groups that have a direct (face to face) or indirect influence on a person's attitude or behavior.

Relationship marketing Relationship marketing involves creating, maintaining, and enhancing strong relationships with customers and other stakeholders.

Reminder advertising Advertising used to keep consumers thinking about a product.

Retailer Business whose sales come primarily from retailing.

Role The activities that a person is expected to perform according to the persons around him or her.

Run-out Removing a product after existing stock has been depleted; used when sales for an item are low and costs exceed revenues, such as the case of a restaurant serving a crabmeat cocktail with sales of only one or two items per week.

Sales promotion Consists of short-term incentives to encourage the purchase or sale of a product or service.

Sample (1) A segment of a population selected for marketing research to represent the population as a whole; (2) Offer of a trial amount of a product to consumers.

Secondary data Information that already exists somewhere, having been collected for another purpose.

Segmentation analysis The process of examining various submarkets and selecting those most appropriate for a company.

Self-concept Self-image, the complex mental pictures people have of themselves.

Selling Sales representatives know the art of salesmanship: approaching, presenting, answering objections, and closing sales.

Selling concept The idea that consumers will not buy enough of an organization's products unless the organization undertakes a large selling and promotion effort.

Service culture A system of values and beliefs in an organization that reinforces the idea that providing the customer with quality service is the principal concern of the business.

Service inseparability A major characteristic of services; they are produced and consumed at the same time and cannot be separated from their providers, whether the providers are people or machines.

Service intangibility A major characteristic of services; they cannot be seen, tasted, felt, heard, or smelled before they are bought.

Service perishability A major characteristic of services; they cannot be stored for later use.

Service variability A major characteristic of services; their quality may vary greatly, depending on who provides them and when, where, and how they are provided.

Service-profit chain A model that shows the relationships between employee satisfaction, customer satisfaction, customer retention, value creation, and profitability.

Servicing Sales representatives provide various services to the customers: consulting on their problems, rendering technical assistance, arranging financing, and expediting delivery.

SMERF SMERF stands for social, military, educational, religious, and fraternal organizations. This group of specialty markets has a common price-sensitive thread.

Social classes Relatively permanent and ordered divisions in a society whose members share similar values, interests, and behaviors.

Societal (ethical) quality Delivering products that will not cause harm to a customer or society as a whole. It is a type of quality that often goes unobserved by the guest.

Societal marketing concept The idea that an organization should determine the needs, wants, and interests of target markets and deliver the desired satisfactions more effectively and efficiently than competitors in a way that maintains or improves the consumer's and society's well being.

Specific product attributes Price and product features can be used to position a product.

Standardization Creating a standard of quality for customers within the product and maintaining it.

Strategic alliances Relationships between independent parties that agree to cooperate but still retain separate identities.

Strategic business units (SBUs) A single business or collection of related businesses that can be planned separately from the rest of the company.

Supplier search The stage of the industrial buying process in which a buyer tries to find the best vendor.

Supplier selection The stage of the industrial buying process in which a buyer receives proposals and selects a supplier or suppliers.

Suppliers Firms and individuals that provide the resources needed by a company and its competitors to produce goods and services.

Supporting products Extra products offered to add value to the core product and to help to differentiate it from the competition.

Survey research The gathering of primary data by asking people questions about their knowledge, attitudes, preferences, and buying behavior.

Survival It is used when the economy slumps or a recession is going on. A manufacturing firm can reduce production to match demand, and a hotel can cut rates to create the best cash flow.

Tactile The dimension of atmosphere relating to softness, smoothness, and temperature.

Targeting Sales representatives decide how to allocate their scarce time among prospects and customers.

Technical quality The quality of the core product that a guest receives in a transaction. It is the quality of the guest room in a hotel, the meal in a restaurant, and the car from a rental agency.

Timetable Specific dates to accomplish strategies and tactics.

Tourism A stay of one or more nights away from home for holidays, visits to friends or relatives, business conferences, or any other purpose, except such things as boarding, education, or semipermanent employment.

Trade dress Hospitality companies total visual image and overall appearance.

Transaction Consists of a trade of values between two parties; marketing's unit of measurement.

Underpositioning Failing ever to position the company at all.

Upselling This occurs through training of sales and reservation employees to offer continuously a higher-priced product that will better meet the customer's needs, rather than settling for the lowest price.

Value-based pricing Uses the buyer's perceptions of value, not the seller's cost, as the key to pricing.

Vertical conflict Conflict between different levels of the same channel.

Vertical marketing system (VMS) A distribution channel structure in which producers, wholesalers, and retailers act as a unified system: either one channel member owns the others, or has contracts with them, or has so much power that they all cooperate.

Vertical scope The number of channel levels (from raw materials to final product and distribution) in which the company will engage.

Visual The dimension of atmosphere relating to color, brightness, size, and shape.

Wholesaler Firms engaged primarily in wholesaling activity.

Yield management Yield management is a pricing method using price as a means of matching capacity with demand. The goal of yield management is to optimize the yield or contribution margin.

Index